H.M. the King and Aust. Nurses

Lent by Aust. War Museum

TASMANIA'S WAR RECORD
1914-1918

EDITED BY
L. BROINOWSKI

WITH AN INTRODUCTION BY
Major-General SIR J. GELLIBRAND, K.C.B., D.S.O.

The Naval & Military Press Ltd

Published by

The Naval & Military Press Ltd
Unit 5 Riverside, Brambleside
Bellbrook Industrial Estate
Uckfield, East Sussex
TN22 1QQ England

Tel: +44 (0)1825 749494

www.naval-military-press.com
www.nmarchive.com

In reprinting in facsimile from the original, any imperfections are inevitably reproduced and the quality may fall short of modern type and cartographic standards.

PREFACE

TOWARDS the end of 1919, when most of the soldiers had returned, the suggestion was made that a record be prepared for publication of the work of Tasmania and Tasmanians in the war. The proposal was put before the Premier (Sir Walter Lee), who received it heartily, and after consultation with his Cabinet, agreed that the Government should guarantee the publication and provide a small amount of money for necessary clerical assistance.

After consultation with a number of senior officers of Tasmanian units, an executive committee was formed consisting of Major-General Sir John Gellibrand, K.C.B., D.S.O., Lieutenant-Colonel D. P. Young, President of the Tasmanian Branch of the Returned Sailors and Soldiers' Imperial League of Australia, and Mr. L. Broinowski. To the last-named was assigned the task of directing the compilation of material and editing the book. Except for actual clerical work, almost entirely in the compilation of the muster-roll, no payments were made for the services of any of those who in one way or another had to do with the making of the book.

This has no pretention to being a military history; it aims at giving to the people of this generation and of generatons yet to come an idea of what Tasmanian soldiers did and endured and of the less glorious but very useful work done by thousands of men and women who remained at home. For that reason, the narrative, so far as the military side is concerned, resolves itself, in the main, into the stories of isolated actions of Tasmanian units with such a sketch of the times and events between the fighting as may preserve some continuity of narrative.

There are certain omissions, which are regrettable but unavoidable. Tasmanian nurses who did splendid work were merged in the Australian Army Medical Corps, and it has been impossible to obtain any account of their doings. A number of Tasmanians were incorporated in the Australian Flying Corps, but not as a Tasmanian unit, and the same thing applies to Engineers. Efforts were made to get an account of their doings, but these were not successful, and it was a choice between omitting them altogether or of giving an account of organisation and work which would have in it nothing distinctively Tasmanian. That was the case also in regard to the Navy. Tasmanians served with courage and distinction both in the British and in the Australian Navy, but there was no part of their work which could be cut off from the rest and recorded as being distinctively Tasmanian.

The Muster Roll has been compiled with care from the records, and by advertisement a request was made for the names of Tasmanians who enlisted out of the State in any branch of the British or Australian Naval or Military Forces. If errors be discovered in the Roll, they must be ascribed to causes beyond the control of the executive committee which is responsible for the book.

Acknowledgment is due to the large number of men who so readily took up the unaccustomed work of historical narrative, and without whose assistance the book would have been impossible. The chapter on the Australian Army Medical Corps was provided by Lieutenant-Colonel W. E. L. Crowther, D.S.O. The account of the 3rd Light Horse Regiment is taken from a narrative written and published by Lieutenant-Colonel Bell, C.M.G., D.S.O., who kindly allowed it to be used, and Lieutenant C. A. Bennetto, M.C., was good enough to read the proofs. The material for the Artillery record came from Major Allan Crisp, D.S.O., and from Mr. V. R. Taffin and Sergeant T. Briggs. For the 12th Battalion, use was made of the Battalion History, which Lieutenant-Colonel C. H. Elliott, C.M.G., D.S.O., allowed to be taken in its entirety. The story of the 15th Battalion was furnished by Lieutenant-Colonel R. E. Snowden, Captains Good and Brettingham-Moore, M.C., and Lieutenant B. C. Newland. The narrative of the doings of the 26th Battalion comes from Captains G. Bond, M.C., Gray, and Hinman, M.C.; the 40th from Captain F. Green, M.C.; the 47th from Lieutenant H. G. Smith, M.C, D.C.M.; and the 52nd from Lieutenant-Colonel Lane; and the Army Service Corps by Lieutenant-Colonel D. P. Young, A.S.C. The account of experiences of prisoners in Germany was supplied by Lieutenant A. H. Collier, the material relating to military organisation in the State was prepared by Captain Webster, who also arranged for the compilation of the Muster Roll. The account of the work of the Repatriation Department was prepared by Lieutenant-Colonel Humphreys, Deputy Commissioner for Tasmania.

Acknowledgment must be made also of the excellent spirit in which the publishers, Messrs. J. Walch and Sons Ltd., took up and forwarded the proposal, and in particular of the most valuable assistance of Mr. Geoffrey Walch, whose personal efforts and enthusiasm were invaluable in overcoming many difficulties.

CONTENTS

CHAPTER I.
ORGANISING FOR BATTLE

WAR DECLARED.—Hostilities begun.—Forming an army.—The first embarkation.—To Egypt.—Claremont Camp.—Reinforcements.—State War Council.—A Call to Arms.—Conscription Referendum.—The Recruiting Committee.—A Tasmanian Battalion. Page 1

CHAPTER II.
EGYPT AND GALLIPOLI.

12th BATTALION.—Arrival in Egypt.—Mena Camp.—Preparing for Gallipoli.—The Landing.—The First Days.—A Sad Reunion.—Digging in.—Hard Times.—Tasmania Post.—Advancing New Trenches.—A Severe Test.—Relieved.—Lone Pine.—Back to Lemnos.

15th BATTALION.—Formation and Departure.—A Dark Landing.—Shrapnel Gully.—The "Death Trap."—Pope's Hill.—Quinn's Post.—Fighting Against Odds.—A Respite.—Fatigue Duties.—An Attack in Force.—Heavy Casualties.—A Rest at Lemnos.—Back to the Line.—The Evacuation.

3rd LIGHT HORSE.—Off to Gallipoli.—Under Fire.—Courtney's Post.—Poor Rations.—Pope's Hill.—Signalling Equipment.—Heavy Casualties.—Quinn's Post.—Improved Conditions.—A Rest Camp.—Back to Egypt.

9th BATTERY.—A Good Start.—On the Peninsula.—A Good Position.—Effective Shooting.—The Last Shot.

26th BATTALION.—Formation and Training.—Dangerous Duties.—The Toll of Sickness.

ARMY SERVICE CORPS Page 10

CHAPTER III.
FRANCE AND BELGIUM I.
(12TH AND 15TH BATTALIONS.)

12th BATTALION.—Billets and Reserves.—The Firing Line.—The Somme Offensive.—Pozieres.—The Ypres Salient.—Back to the Somme.—Mud.—A Forward Move.—Louverval.—A Slight Rest.—Through the Hindenburg Line.—A Four Months' Spell.—Polygon Wood.—Out of the Line.—Wet Quarters.—An Era of Sport.—Messines.—Passchendale Ridges.—The German Rush.—Mont de Merris.—Scattered Fighting.—General Plumer's Commendation.—The Great Advance.—The Final Battles.—Demobilised.

15th BATTALION.—Re-forming in Egypt.—In France.—On the Somme.—The First Battle Pozieres.—Trench Warfare.—Back to the Somme.—A Bitter Winter.—Guedecourt.—Lagnicourt.—Bullecourt.—A Shattered Battalion.—Gapaard.—Lesquatre Rois Cabinet.—Desultory Warfare.—The Battle of Ypres.—A Rest that Failed.—A Defensive Line.—Post-Internationale.—The Attack at Hamel.—Cerisy Gailly.—Breaking the Line.—The End of Hostilities.—Christmas in Belgium. Page 42

CHAPTER IV.
FRANCE AND BELGIUM—II.
(26TH AND 40TH BATTALIONS.)

26TH BATTALION.—Armentieres.—Messines.—The Somme.—A Futile Attack.—A Distinguished Success.—Moving About.—The Battle of Flers.—Lagnicourt.—Bullecourt.—Polygon Wood.—Passchaendale Ridge.—Back to the Somme.—A Brilliant Coup.—The Great Advance.—Mont St. Quentin.—The Last Fight.

40TH BATTALION.—Arrival in France.—Trench Warfare near Armentieres.—Ploegsteert.—The Battle of Messines.—Preparation for 3rd Battle of Ypres.—Attacks at Ypres on the 4th and 12th October, 1917.—Back to Messines.—The German Offensive.—Line near Molancourt.—Villers Brettonneux and Hamel.—The Battle of Amiens.—Attack at Proyart.—Capture of Bray by the 40th Battalion.—Advance Along the Somme.—The Attack on the Hindenburg Line
Page 87

CHAPTER V.
FRANCE AND BELGIUM—III.
(47TH AND 52ND BATTALIONS.—ARTILLERY.)

47TH BATTALION.—Birth in Egypt.—Welcome to the Prince.—A Desert March.—Pozieres.—The Ypres Salient.—A Bitter Winter.—Bullecourt.—Messines Ridge.—Passchendaele.—The Somme Again.—Disbanded.

52ND BATTALION.—Organisation in Egypt.—The Waving of Hands.—In the Front Line.—Mouquet Farm.—In Flanders.—The Flers Sector.

ARTILLERY.—9th Battery.—17th Battery.
Page 114

CHAPTER VI.
EGYPT AND PALESTINE.
(3RD LIGHT HORSE.)

Western Egypt.—Upper Egypt.—A Bombing Raid.—Fighting Near Katia.—Battle of Romani.—Patrol Work.—Maghdaba.—Rafa.—Palestine.—Sad Trials.—Hard Going.—A Short Rest.—Beersheba—A Successful Attack.—Bald Hill.—A Wet Xmas.—Jericho.—Across the Jordan.—A Rearguard Action.—A Dull Routine. "Vale," "View," and "Vaux" Posts.—Final Operations.—After the Armistice.—Back to Egypt.—The Return Home.
Page 138

CHAPTER VII.
THE AUSTRALIAN ARMY MEDICAL CORPS.

MEDICAL ORGANISATION.—The War Zone.—Field Ambulance.—Clearing Stations.—Heroic Stretcher Bearers.—Lines of Communication.—Base.

TASMANIAN SECTIONS.—The Bearers.—Winter in France.—The Difficulties of Salvage.—Regimental Medical Officers.—3rd. Field Ambulance.—No. 1 Australian Casualty Clearing Station.—Anzac Cove.—France and Belgium.—7th Field Ambulance C. Section.—The Nurses.
Page 169

CHAPTER VIII.
PRISONERS IN GERMANY.

Behind the German Front.—Miserable Experiences.—Life in the Camps.—The Notorious Neimeyers.—Attempts to Escape.—The Holyminden Tunnel.—Hospital Experiences.—Huddled Together in Huts.—Christmas on the Baltic.—Life at Wistenburg.—The Armistice Period. Page 180

CHAPTER IX.
THE CIVILIAN EFFORT.

THE RED CROSS.—The First Efforts.—Work Circles.—A Wonder of Organisation.—Shipments of Goods.—Care of the Wounded.—The V.A.D.'s.—The Hostels.—Information Bureau.—The Men's Part.

BATTALION FUNDS.—The A.I.F. Lounge.—Tobacco Fund.—Mayor's Patriotic Fund.—Disabled Soldiers' Fund.

THE O.A.S. FUND.—"Diggers'" Appreciation.—Comforts for the Trenches.—The Tasmanian Fund.—Other Comforts Funds.—Public Support.—The Northern Branch.

BELGIAN RELIEF.—The Tasmanian Contribution.—Clothing for Children.

SERBIAN RELIEF.—French Red Cross.

Y.M.C.A. FIELD SERVICE.—Work in Tasmania.—Camp Life.—Finding the Money.

THE AGENT-GENERAL.

REPATRIATION. Page 185

DISTRICT ENLISTMENTS - - - - - Page 209

TASMANIA'S MUSTER ROLL - - „ 217

TASMANIANS ENLISTED IN OTHER STATES - - - 369

LIST OF ILLUSTRATIONS

"H.M. the King and Australian Nurses" - Frontispiece

	Facing page
"Claremont Camp"	1
"H.M.A.S. Sydney"	4
"Tasmania Post"	14
"A Gallipoli Trench"	32
"Transport in the Mud"	40
"Infantry on the March"	56
"Fortified Shell Holes" (taken from the Air)	72
"Duckwalk in Winter"	86
"Attacking Infantry"	116
"Artillery in Action"	132
"Light Horse in Palestine"	160
"At the Casualty Clearing Station"	168
"Regimental Aid Post"	172

INTRODUCTION
BY
MAJOR-GENERAL SIR JOHN GELLIBRAND, K.C.B., D.S.O.

To those who took an active part in the Great War, and to those who devoted themselves to the essential war work at home, a record, however limited in scope, appeals as a lasting memorial of the past, a bitter-sweet reminder of present obligations, and a standard of comparison in national work and devotion for all time to come.

In the theatre of war the horizon of the individual is limited to an extraordinary degree, except in the case of a chosen few. The soldier's world is restricted to a few yards of the front line and a few miles in depth back to a rest area; the home worker's sphere of personal effort is hardly greater in extent. Hence it comes that personal knowledge is reduced to a scale that few are willing to admit, and that mis-information or complete ignorance as to the part played by others is almost universal.

A war record does not aim at complaining or criticising the value of the work done, but is rather an attempt to detail the facts in such a manner as to enable those interested to gain a fair impression of what was done and suffered by the women and men concerned.

In the Great War sailor and soldier alike were destined to become minute component atoms in gigantic organisations; each, it is true, with an appointed place and duties, but to all except their immediate superiors they were in reality "bayonets" for action purposes or "mouths" from the ration point of view. For all that, both our officers and men undoubtedly succeeded in maintaining their self-reliant individualism without falling short of their duty as component atoms. To this characteristic quality we owe the proud record that our men were able to preserve the high standard of the early days of their service afloat, in the field, and in the air, and thereby proving that modern war is not a matter of machines nor is organised blind obedience the one essential for victory.

In studying a record of war work, it is desirable above all things to gain an insight into the collective mind and spirit of the organisation concerned, whether in the field or in the home sphere, for it is on these that the merit of the work depends as a rule. The fierce joy of battle at dawn is replaced by the stern determination to hang on, and that in turn gives way to the bitter hope of early relief. There is the feeling of physical fitness and well being after the longed for rest and replacement of casualties, which by degrees is changed during the course of operations into a weariness of mind and body that almost welcomes a wound or other reason for digging in. To engage in an action where the troops are nearing the limits of physical endurance, when the casualty lists have reduced their comrades to a handful, is in itself a tribute to the mutual confidence between the men and their leaders; to continue the action under such conditions until the order to halt is received from higher authority is the supreme merit of a true soldier.

As regards the purely military aspects of service in the Australian forces, there is one that deserves remark above all others. Not only were our troops placed from the beginning to the end under leaders who knew what they wanted, who continued to learn right up to the victorious end, and who satisfied themselves personally that their subordinates were up to their work, but the leaders themselves were well aware that added to the pressure from above there was a no less imperative demand from below—to prove fitness in all things for command and to exercise it continuously without loss of standard. It would be indeed hard to describe the effect or assign a true value to this double pressure as it affected the work of our troops, but of the two there is little doubt that the pressure exerted from the ranks was of the utmost importance. One of the most curious reasons assigned by the Prussians for their ultimate failure was the non-observance of the old Hohenzollern custom for their King to look on the faces of his dead on the battlefield. As witness to the fact that their deaths were not due to his fault or neglect. Australian leaders were well able to carry out this soldier's duty with aboding sorrow in his heart, yet proud to know that the silent figures bore no witness against them.

As in so many other matters, the conditions of work under the peaceful surroundings of home life have much in common with service in the field The long hours of extra work and time taken from the workers' own employment, given under the stimulus of hope for a safe return of the loved one, are as freely given when the worker is suffering from the agonies of uncertainty or the proud sorrow of lifelong loss.

It is not out of place in considering the war record of the State to look from the past to the present and then to the future in an attempt to trace the influence of the work on the community and on the individual. So far as the former is concerned, there is no aspect of national life that is not deeply affected by the tragic years of war and reconstruction. We have lost many whose lives promised to play a full and honourable part in carrying out the high ideals of our national motto. Many who survived have returned broken in health and prematurely aged, and unfit to take their due share in the work of the community. Others may have fallen into the error of mistaking cause and effect, and return without having realised the significance of what they took part in. These three factors carry a weight which cannot be minimised, and their effect on our life as a community must be felt for many a long day. Our consolation and reward will come when the loyal spirit of co-operation, the disregard of petty motives, the unselfish devotion to a common cause, that characterised the work done throughout the war, became typical of our national life in peace.

It is no small national asset that our sailors and soldiers have brought back to their native land, to set against the terrible debit of loss and sorrow caused by the war. To have travelled in foreign lands is in itself an education, both as regards the things that ought to be done and those that should not be done. To witness the daily life, the strength and weakness of the national spirit of other nations, their outlook on life and their hopes and fears for the future, are alike calculated to make the wanderer glad to return and anxious to place home life on a still higher plane. To many the most important factor of gain is the national welding together of the various groups of the community regardless of creed, occupation or birthplace, due to the universal devotion to a common cause and a whole-hearted belief in all that is implied by "Australia will be there." To put the matter bluntly: Many a man enlisted from a State, but all who came back felt they returned to Australia. Politically, our men may still adhere to this or that party, yet underlying that adherence is a feeling of a higher allegiance—no matter how indefinite in form—to an ideal Australia, white, straight, and pleasant for all the citizens, but resolved and ready to take a man's part to prevent the peace of the world being disturbed again.

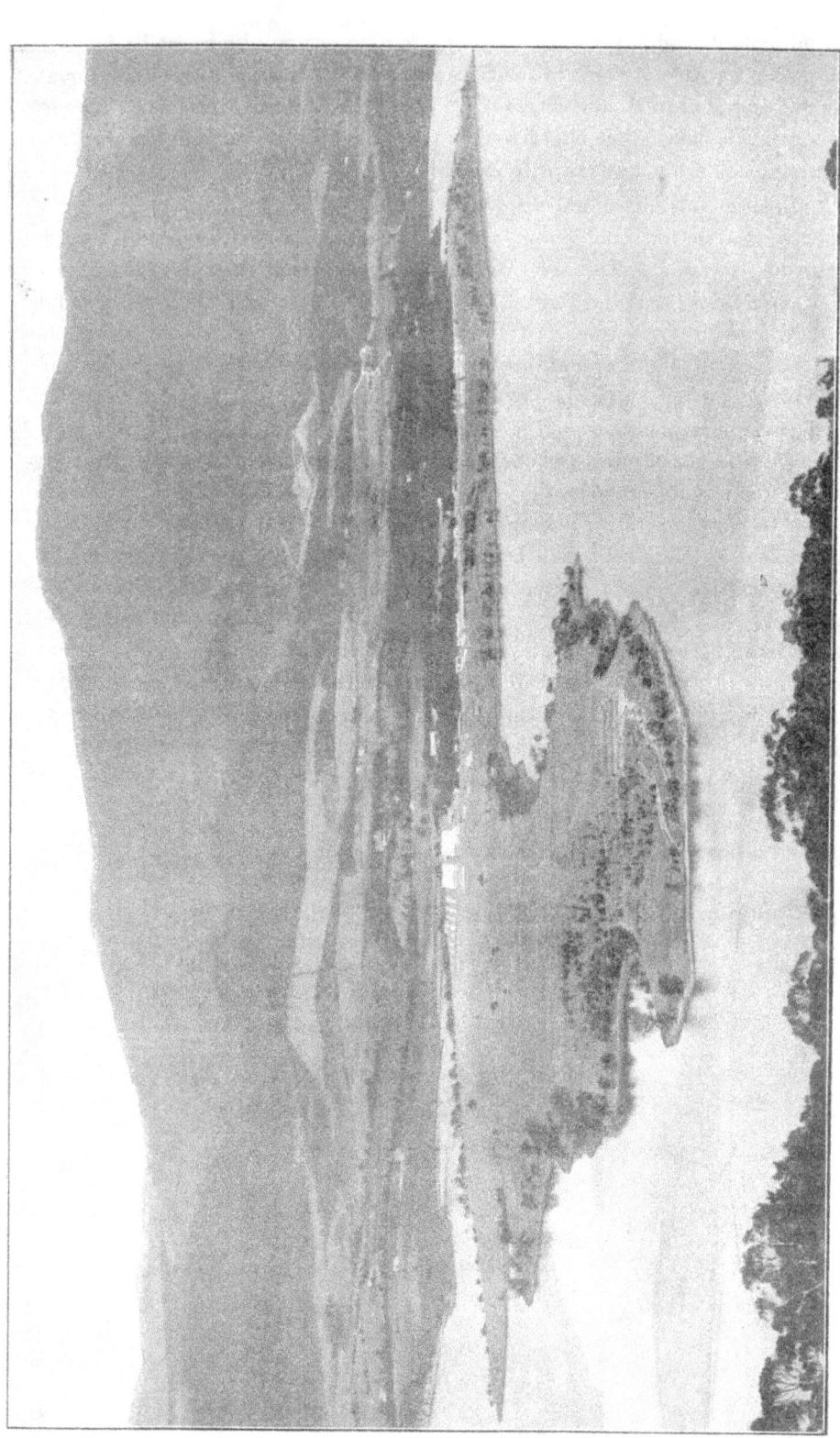

Claremont Camp

J. W. Brattie, Photo.

CHAPTER I.

ORGANISING FOR BATTLE

WAR DECLARED.—Hostilities begun.—Forming an army.—The first embarkation.—To Egypt.—Claremont Camp.—Reinforcements.—State War Council.—A Call to Arms.—Conscription Referendum.—The Recruiting Committee.—A Tasmanian Battalion.

The memory of the days between the assassination of the Arch-Duke Ferdinand at Serajevo and the actual outbreak of war is perhaps more vivid now in the minds of those who went through them than the actual impression was at the time. Events succeeded one another with such rapidity that while people were still wondering whether there was to be a war, war was upon us. The news of the assassination of the Grand Duke, even though he was heir-apparent to the Throne of Austria-Hungary, was received in this far-away place with no more thrill than would be occasioned by any other sensational murder. Then came a quick exchange of negotiations and diplomatic messages; then war between Germany and Austria on the one side and France and Russia on the other; and then, while people were discussing the question of whether Great Britain was under an obligation, moral or honourable, to enter the war, Great Britain was already in it.

In Tasmania, as in other parts of the Empire, there was enthusiasm—some of it futile, some of it a little foolish. We took up the cry raised in England of "Business as usual." We sang patriotic songs on all possible occasions; but in the main the enthusiasm was a serious one, and the obligations which we had assumed, although still imperfectly understood, weighed heavily upon the community.

The first official intimation in Tasmania that the British Empire was likely to be involved in a European War was received at 9.30 p.m. on the 2nd of August, 1914, when orders were issued to the Artillery to be in readiness for action from 9 a.m. on the 3rd of August.

By 11.45 a.m. on the 4th of August notices were served on Wireless Experimenters in Tasmania directing them to dismantle all radio telegraph aerials and gear at their addresses.

At 10.30 p.m. the same day the Commissioner of Police undertook to watch any movements on the part of the crew of the German ship *Oberhaussen*, lying at Port Huon.

At 2 p.m. on the 5th of August, His Excellency the State Governor notified the District Commandant that war had broken out with Germany. This message was followed at 2.10 p.m. by a telegram from the Defence Department, Melbourne, and arrangements were immediately made to adopt war measures.

The first overt act of war performed in Tasmania was on the 5th of August, when steps were taken to seize the German ship *Oberhaussen*, which was loading timber at Port Huon. At 4.30 p.m. the District Naval Officer requested assistance of troops to support a Naval party that he had despatched an hour earlier to seize the *Oberhaussen*. A detachment of the 93rd Infantry, under the command of Lieutenant E. I. Linnell, was immediately detailed for this duty. On arrival of this detachment at Port Huon it was found that the Naval party had taken possession of the *Oberhaussen* without opposition. The services of the detachment were, therefore, not required.

The District Naval Officer, Captain Dunne, who had called out the Naval Reserves on the previous day, detailed an armed party of 11 men, under Sub-Lieut. R. Young, to proceed in two motor cars to Port Huon to take possession of the *Oberhausen*. This party started a 3 p.m., but were delayed about half way by a tree which had fallen across the road. Fortunately the Huon motor 'bus eventually arrived from the other end, and was promptly commandeered to transport the party to the Huon. On arrival at 7.30 p.m., the German captain was found ashore in the act of getting his clearance papers, and apparently in ignorance that war had been declared. Possession was promptly taken, and the ship was brought up to Hobart, and anchored off Rosny Point by noon on the 6th, under a naval guard.

In the meantime naval arrangements had been made for the examination of all vessels approaching the harbour and for the speedy transmission of the information gained. At first the *Cartela* only was employed, but later on the *Warrentina* was added to the service. This service, both at sea and on land, was maintained throughout the whole period of the war by means of relief crews and detachments.

At this date the State Commandant, Colonel W. J. Clark, assisted by a staff of seven officers, had mobilised the troops required for garrisons and guards, and had carried out all the administrative work in connection therewith.

On the 8th of August cable censorship commenced, under Major G. E. Harrap, V.D., at Launceston, and Lieutenant G. Roberts at Hobart. On the afternoon of the same day steps were taken by the Defence authorities, in co-operation with the Civil Police, for the arrest and detention of all German Army and Navy Officers and Reservists in Tasmania as prisoners of war, and arrangements were made to keep the subjects of Austria-Hungary under surveillance in anticipation of war being declared against that nation.

On the 10th of August the Defence Department called for volunteers over 19 years of age to form an Expeditionary Force of all arms for Europe. Applications were to be restricted to men now serving and to those who had already received training. This call to arms was followed by a telegram from General Bridges, then Inspector-General, notifying that Tasmania would require to furnish one Squadron of Light Horse, one Field Artillery Battery, half a Battalion of Infantry, as well as portion of Ammunition Column, details of Engineers, and Divisional troops.

As recorded elsewhere, the nation's urgent need of volunteers was universally advertised, and officers were at once appointed to register and tabulate applications for enlistment. But even before this step, such great enthusiasm was manifested by the manhood of Tasmania that on the same day the Commandant was able to report by wire the gratifying total of 570 registrations. For days past, the Anglesea Barracks had been invaded by the eager ones anxious to take up the Mother Country's quarrel, not questioning her justification in entering the fray, and in addition, Headquarters were inundated with numerous written applications and inquiries concerning enlistment.

On the 13th of August a Training Camp, under the command of Major R. P. Smith, A.F.A., was established at Pontville, and training was immediately proceeded with. Then recruiting was begun in earnest. Immediately instructions to enrol volunteers were received, officers were appointed specially for this work, and Area Officers throughout the State were instructed to take local action. Commanding Officers of Militia Units also were invited to assist in obtaining volunteers. Preliminary arrangements for establishing camps and training staffs were forthwith undertaken, and these steps produced the desired result. Such a ready response was forthcoming that Tasmania soon obtained her quota of the First Expeditionary Force.

On the 1st of September, instructions were received to the effect that all suitable volunteers for foreign service were to be attested and put into training at the Expeditionary Force Camps. These were required for reinforcements and new units. Following these instructions, approval was received for the enrolment of volunteers to be performed by the Mayors and Wardens of Municipalities outside metropolitan areas. The assistance of these gentlemen was therefore invoked. The response to this request was typical of the deeply loyal and patriotic feeling in the State, and all, without exception, promised their whole-hearted support and sympathy. At the same time the District Headquarters staff and enrolling officers were working at top speed, and every facility and encouragement were given to intending volunteers. Despite the high physical standard required, and the rigorous medical examination to be passed, men were readily enough forthcoming, so that just one month after it was considered that the desired numbers had practically been obtained. The Commandant, therefore, conveyed to the Wardens the thanks and appreciation of the Defence Department for the valuable assistance they had rendered.

The Tasmanian portion of the Expeditionary Force embarked at Hobart on the 20th October, 1914:—

Name of Transport.	Unit.	Officers.	Other ranks.
A.2. GEELONG—	Headquarters and 4 Companies 12th Battalion (Colonel L. F. Clarke, D.S.O.)	20	516
A.2. GEELONG—	9th Field Battery (Major W. L. H. Burgess)	4	117
A.2 GEELONG—	No. 2 Section 3rd Field Artillery Ammunition Column	1	80
A.2. GEELONG—	Divisional Ammunition Column, Details (Lieutenant A. A. Evans)	1	37
A.2. GEELONG—	Engineers, 3rd Field Coy (No. 4 Section)	1	43
A.2. GEELONG—	3rd Field Ambulance (C Section)	2	27
A.2. GEELONG—	Nurses	2	—
A.2. GEELONG—	"C" Squadron, 3rd Light Horse (Captain E. St. L. Lewis)	5	118
A.13 KATUNA—	12th Battalion, details	—	11
A.13. KATUNA—	9th Field Battery, details	1	23
A.13. KATUNA—	No. 2 Section 3rd Field Artillery, Ammunition Column	1	22
A.13. KATUNA—	Divisional Ammunition Column Details	—	12
A.13. KATUNA—	"C" Squadron, 3rd Light Horse, Details	1	30
Total		39	996

The Tasmanian section of the 4th Australian Army Service Corps, consisting of Lieutenant C. G. Farmer and 26 others, had embarked on the Geelong at Melbourne, having previously been sent to the mainland to train with the South and Western Australian portions of the unit.

In addition to the above, the following officers were selected for staff duties for the Expeditionary Force, and proceeded from Tasmania for the purpose of taking up their respective duties:—

Major W. E. Cass, G.S.O.
Captain D. P. Young, A.A.S.C.
Captain J. Gellibrand, Headquarters A.I.F.
Captain R. M. Millar, Pay Corps.
Lieutenant L. S. Whitfield, S.O.V.S.

A few days prior to embarkation a number of warships arrived, and also transports carrying a certain number of South Australian troops, who went into camp at Pontville, and with the Tasmanian Infantry were formed into the 12th Battalion, under the command of Colonel L. F. Clark. Two transports also arrived with New Zealand troops on their way to the Front, and these were landed, and carried out a route march through the city and out towards Risdon.

The newspapers were not permitted to make any reference to the presence either of the warships or of the transports, or as to the date of departure of Tasmanian troops, and, in pursuance of this same policy, the Tasmanian troops were taken quietly to the wharves without giving the citizens an opportunity of seeing them or giving them a send-off. Yielding, however, to a strongly expressed public sentiment a few days before embarkation the troops were allowed to march through the city through dense lines of cheering people giving them an enthusiastic God-speed.

The two transports, the *Geelong* and the *Katuna*, which carried the Tasmanian detachment, were joined on to the New Zealand transports, and later, in King George's Sound, joined the main body of the fleet of 28 ships carrying troops from all States. The escort consisted of British, Australian, and Japanese warships. One of the escorting ships was the *Sydney*, and it was on this voyage that she was detailed to meet and destroy the German raider *Emden*, which had done so much mischief.

During the voyage training as far as possible in the limited space available was carried out, consisting chiefly of instruction in musketry, loading and unloading being practiced with dummy cartridges. Lectures were given daily by officers on scouting, outposts and other subjects dealing as they did with infantry tactics, trench warfare, reconnoitring, and indication of targets, also co-operation between Artillery and Infantry, all of these subjects being equally important to the Light Horsemen as to the other arm of the service. The voyage, though long (seven weeks), was never monotonous, owing to all ranks being fully occupied with training and ship's routine, all ranks being keen to become efficient and fit for the great work in front of them. The health of the troops throughout was excellent. Unquestionably the harder task fell to the officers and men who were on the *Katuna* with the horses, this party having 161 horses to attend to. The care of horses on board ship entails a lot of hard work and no little anxiety. When the weather is rough horses get down, a number of men suffer with seasickness, and thus more work is thrown on fewer men. Again, when going through the tropics the atmosphere between decks has to be experienced to be realised. The horses lost numbered eight only, which, considering the length of the voyage, and the varying weather, is a low percentage. The horses on the whole landed in Egypt in excellent condition, due mainly to the fact that they were exercised every day during the trip. The *Katuna* arrived at Alexandria on 8th December, 1914, and the *Geelong* on the 9th.

As soon as Tasmania's quota of the First Expeditionary Force embarked from Hobart, arrangements were made to remove the Camp from Pontville to Claremont, as the former place was unsuitable, owing to the inadequate

H.M.A.S. 'Sydney'

Lent by Aust. War Museum

water supply and other disadvantages. From a health point of view it is doubtful whether a better site than Claremont could be obtained anywhere. At first the troops were quartered in tents, but as time went on and these became the worse for wear, huts were substituted. With the exception of the First Force and a few other details, the whole of the troops who embarked from Tasmania were trained and equipped in this Camp. A large number of gifts were provided from all parts of Tasmania for the comfort and convenience of troops in the Camp.

The undermentioned officers, in turn, performed the duties of Camp Commandant:—Major R. P. Smith, Captain F. Harbottle, Captain K. Ogilvy, Captain H. C. Davis.

About the middle of November, 1914, when it was decided to enrol still further reinforcements for the Australian Imperial Force, the assistance of the Wardens throughout Tasmania was again solicited. They were requested to make the same arrangements for the medical examination and the despatch to camp of volunteers as they did before, except that this time the men were to be sent to Claremont instead of to Brighton Junction. So recruiting went on, though more slowly. But the general public were not unmindful of the seriousness of the situation; it was that they were unaware of the immediate need for reinforcements. It was not till after the famous landing on Gallipoli had become known that the public fully comprehended the fact that reinforcements must be regularly maintained and despatched in order to augment the fast depleting ranks of the A.I.F. The most eager of our eligible manhood having already gone forward, it was left to the more cautious men to discover what their duty to their country was, and they, in ever increasing numbers, soon realised where their duty lay. For men of all classes and walks of life, married men and single, men with ties and without, irrespective of creed, position, and political views, came forward at the Nation's call. Throughout the War it was a notable fact that on every occasion when British troops suffered in the nature of a reverse, and particularly when Australian troops suffered severe casualties, a stimulus was automatically given to recruiting in Tasmania.

It was not till the end of 1915 that a systematic organisation was employed to secure recruits. Up to this time the good results obtained (viz., 6281 enlistments) were mainly due to the inestimable help furnished by the press and by the appeals made by our public men from the platforms. Then, in order primarily to control and organise recruiting, and secondly, to deal with the question of employment of returned soldiers, it was decided by the Federal Cabinet to form in each State a War Council which should work in concert with the Federal Parliamentary War Committee.

The State War Council of Tasmania was formed in October, 1915, under the direction of the Federal Government, for the purpose of stimulating and organising recruiting in the State, and the repatriation of our returned soldiers. The Council was composed of leading publicists, professional men, members of the Staff of the the 6th Military District, and representatives of Commerce and Labour. The first Chairman was the then Premier (Hon. John Earle), who was succeeded by the Hon. W. H. Lee in April, 1916, the latter gentleman continuing in the position until the Council was dissolved in April, 1918, on the establishment of the present Repatriation Department.

The activities of the Council at first were mainly centred in recruiting. Committees were appointed in every Municipality throughout the State, whose business it was to co-operate with a staff of Recruiting Sergeants, in interviewing all men in the State supposed to be fit for military service, and forwarding to the Council the result of their enquiries. This information was recorded and tabulated, and formed a very valuable basis for all subsequent recruiting effort in the State. The work of these Committees, which was often of a most delicate nature, for a long time entailed continuous service, and they deserve much credit for the efficient way in which it was carried out. The paid staff engaged totalled nearly forty at one time, and the result of the examinations was as follows, viz.:—

    Men examined 7,445
    Passed as fit for active service 4,151
    Passed as fit for home service 624
    Deferred 260
    Total entered camp 3,230

In October, 1916, the work of recruiting was taken over by the Defence Department.

The control of patriotic fund collections was vested in the Council in September, 1916, and arrangements made for the issue of permits to collect and the prevention of overlapping.

In all, 624 applications for permission to collect were reviewed, of which 585 were granted and 39 refused.

The War Council was also responsible for the administration in Tasmania of the Australian Soldiers' Repatriation Fund, for the relief and assistance of returned soldiers. Altogether, 361 applications for assistance from this Fund were received, which were dealt with as follows, viz:—

    91 granted by way of loan £6,115   0   0
    113 granted by way of gift £2,275   0   0
    11 taken over by the Closer Settlement Board.
    61 refused, and the balance withdrawn or informal.

The question of Land Settlement, the medical treatment of returned men and securing employment for them, came also within the scope of the Council's activities, and in every phase of repatriation valuable information was collected and the trail blazed, so that the work of those who came after was thereby considerably lightened.

This is a very condensed account of the work of this body, and would not be complete without some acknowledgment of the vast amount of time given to it cheerfully and in an honorary capacity by some of the busiest men in the State, many of whom were also filling other important public offices during a time of great stress. Much of the success of the Council was due to the organising ability of the Hon. Secretary (Mr. F. Lindsay Gunn). Recognition of this has been evidenced by his appointment as Chairman of the State Board of Repatriation.

In January, 1916, a "Call to Arms" appeal was made. For this, organisation became necessary, and as the result of a request from the Prime Minister, each of the fifty-one Local Government areas "Committees of Five" were formed, to each of which recruiting sergeants were attached. Captain K. A. Ogilvy, Reserve of Officers, was appointed Recruiting Supervisor.

These "Committees of Five" organised means of obtaining recruits, and followed up and interviewed all those who answered "Yes," or "Yes, later" on the War Census Card, and also those giving unsatisfactory reasons for refusing to enlist; with the result that whilst February produced 433 recruits, 977 fit men enlisted in March of the same year. From then onwards a steady decline set in.

In August, 1916, it was announced that the British Army Council required 16,500 men per month from Australia, and that double the number was required for the month of September. Tasmania's share of this number for September was 1,400 men and thereafter 400 men per month. Recruiting literature and posters of all kinds were distributed, and the scheme culminated by a special appeal, when meetings were held in all centres, and addresses delivered by popular speakers; but the total enlistments for this month were only 301, an increase of 34 over the previous month. Of the grand total of the replies received from the "Call to Arms," 10.1 per cent. entered camp before 30th September, 1916. On 29th September, 1916, the War Service Proclamation was issued, and recruiting passed out of the hands of the War Council. The total number of recruits obtained by the State War Council was 3,230, of which number 918 enlisted from 1st July to 30th September, 1916.

On 29th September, 1916, a Proclamation was issued by the Governor-General calling up on the 2nd October all single men between the ages of 21 and 35, and of these, those medically fit and who did not claim exemption were placed in a training camp at Western Junction. When it became known that a Military Service Referendum—which was to decide whether conscription should or should not come into force—was to be taken, and as the opinion prevailed that the referendum would be carried, 408 of those reporting under the Proclamation volunteered for service with the A.I.F., whilst another 372 who were liable under Proclamation entered the A.I.F. Camp without reporting to the Military Registrars, making a total of 780 between 2nd October and 23rd November. During the period covered by the War Service Regulations (29th September to 23rd November, 1916), the voluntary enlistments amounted to approximately 1,460, including the 780 men liable under the Proclamation, of which October produced 1,030. As it became apparent that a negative vote would be recorded the number of enlistments fell rapidly, until in December only 97 men were enlisted, probably accounted for in no small degree by the Christmas holidays. After the withdrawal of the Proclamation, Captain Ogilvy was appointed Director of Recruiting. The Recruiting Sergeants who had carried on during the period of the Proclamation and applied themselves to the task of enlisting volunteers who did not come within its scope, continued under his direction. After a few weeks, however, instructions were received to discharge all Recruiting Sergeants pending the issue of a new recruiting scheme, but during the interval recruiting was carried on by the Military Registrars and Assistant Registrars retained after the withdrawal of the Proclamation. Recruiting during this period was very much disorganised, and very poor results were obtained.

On the 1st of December, 1916, instructions were received from Headquarters that a new recruiting scheme had been approved, and that a Director-General of Recruiting for the Commonwealth had been appointed. Shortly afterwards a State Recruiting Committee was formed.

At the first meeting of the Committee, held on 22nd December, 1916, Captain K. A. Ogilvy was appointed Organising Secretary, and five Recruiting Officers with Organisers appointed to the five Federal electorates. Under the State Recruiting Committee local Recruiting Committees numbering 76 and consisting of prominent residents of the districts who were interested in the Nation's welfare and who were, by reason of over age or incapacity, unfit for active service, were formed in the various parts of the State. The number of recruiting depots in Tasmania was 56, consisting of 50 municipal offices, the Recruiting Office in each Federal electorate (5) and the Claremont Camp. Enlistments, however, were not confined to these depots, as men were enlisted wherever they came forward, provided the necessary means were at hand. Five Recruiting Officers and thirteen Organisers were employed by the State Recruiting Committee. Recruiting was continued under this scheme; from 1st January to 30th June, 1917, the State Recruiting Committee enlisted 1,016, or an average of 39 per week. From various causes only 856 reported at camp, and during that period 299, or 35 per cent., were discharged from camp for various reasons, such as being medically unfit, under age, enlisting without the consent of parents, etc.

The cost of finally accepted men was over £6 per head, exclusive of cost of rail fare. The total number of recruits enlisted in the Military District of Tasmania from the beginning of the War until 30th June, 1917, cannot be accurately ascertained. A large number of men, after being enlisted, became non-effective for various reasons, such as death, desertion, discharged from camp, and failure to report at camp. Up to 30th June, 1917, out of the number enlisted in this State, 11,967 were effective. These effectives were made up as follows:—

Married men	2,426	20.27 per cent.
Single men	9,541	79.73 per cent.
	11,967	100.0 per cent.

TOTAL TASMANIAN ENLISTMENTS.

Units.	To date.	Officers.	Other ranks.	Totals.
Flying Corps	8/ 5/18	20	86	106
3rd Light Horse Regiment	26/ 4/18	6	584	590
3rd F.A. Brigade	26/ 4/18	5	1,119	1,124
6th F.A. Brigade	30/ 6/17	4	153	157
Field Artillery Reinforcements Siege Brigade	30/12/16	2	37	39
Heavy Artillery				
3rd Fd. Co. Engineers (and 6th do.)	30/10/17	1	330	331
12th Infantry Battalion	21/ 2/18	65	3,665	3,730
15th Infantry Battalion	17/11/15	17	771	778
26th Infantry Battalion	19/10/15	20	1,124	1,144
40th Infantry Battalion	13/10/17	47	2,292	2,339
4th M. Gun Co.	8/ 9/17	1	304	305
Divisional Am. Column	30/ 6/17	6	43	49
Tunnelling Companies	7/12/17	—	249	249
No. 4 A.S. Corps	2/ 3/18	2	99	101
1st Aus. Clearing Hospital		5	117	122
1st and 2nd A.G. Hospital	7/ 5/17	—	130	130
7th Field Ambulance	1/ 5/15	3	86	89
Hospital Depot, Egypt		—	30	30
Convalescent Hospital, England		—	27	27
Dental Corps	12/ 8/18	5	8	13
Nurses	23/ 4/19	79	—	79
Chaplains	15/ 1/19	15	—	15
Remount Unit	20/ 7/18	1	116	117
Railway Unit	5/10/18	—	55	55
Cycling Company	28/ 4/16	1	33	34
Trench Mortar Battery	7/ 5/17	—	72	72
Miscellaneous Details	15/ 1/19	6	143	149
General Service Reinforcements	12/10/18	8	530	538
Mining Company	31/ 1/18	2	129	131
Officers and O.R. allotted to Miscellaneous Units in other Districts	2/ 3/18	41	15	56
		362	12,302	—12,664

The 40th Battalion was Tasmania's contribution to the 3rd Australian Division, which was formed in Australia early in 1916, while the 4th and 5th Divisions were being formed in Egypt. At first it was understood that Tasmania was to find a complete Battalion, but later it was announced that the Island State would provide two Companies, a Machine Gun Section, and Battalion Headquarters, while the Geelong District (Victoria) was to find the remaining two Companies, and Lieutenant-Colonel J. E. C. Lord was to command the Battalion.

In Tasmania this was a disappointment, and it was felt that it would be an encouragement to recruiting if the State were called upon to provide a complete Battalion, and so representations were made by the District Commandant and Parliamentary representatives that Tasmania could find 1000 men, and would gladly do so for the honour of the State. In reply to this, the Minister of Defence (Senator Pearce) made the following statement to the mainland press:—

"The number of men enrolled in Tasmania was so small that it was found impossible to form a Battalion. All that it has been possible to form is a Headquarters Staff, a Machine Gun Section, and two Companies of Infantry. The remaining Companies have to be supplied by Victoria. . . . . I am loath to point out that for what has happened the manhood of Tasmania is to blame." (Mercury, 17/3/16).

That statement was made on the 18th March, and it seems as if our Parliamentary representatives must have fallen on the Minister of Defence and forced him to modify his views on the manhood of Tasmania, for on the 21st March notification was received that the 40th Battalion would be a Tasmanian unit. This was announced at once, and by the 1st April not only was the establishment of the Battalion complete, but the first reinforcement had also been raised. After completing the prescribed three months' training in Tasmania, on the 1st July the Battalion embarked from Hobart on H.M.A.T. *Berrima,* and arrived in England on the 23rd August, where it encamped at Lark Hill with the remainder of the Division for training purposes.

On the 22nd November the Battalion left Southampton for France, and disembarked at Le Havre on the following day.

CHAPTER II.

EGYPT AND GALLIPOLI.

12th BATTALION.—Arrival in Egypt.—Mena Camp.—Preparing for Gallipoli.—The Landing.—The First Days.—A Sad Reunion.—Digging in.—Hard Times.--Tasmania Post.—Advancing New Trenches.—A Severe Test.—Relieved.—Lone Pine.—Back to Lemnos.

15th BATTALION.—Formation and Departure.—A Dark Landing.—Shrapnel Gully.—The "Death Trap."—Pope's Hill.—Quinn's Post.—Fighting Against Odds.—A Respite.—Fatigue Duties.—An Attack in Force.—Heavy Casualties.—A Rest at Lemnos.—Back to the Line.—The Evacuation.

3rd LIGHT HORSE.—Off to Gallipoli.—Under Fire.—Courtney's Post.—Poor Rations.—Pope's Hill.—Signalling Equipment.—Heavy Casualties.—Quinn's Post.—Improved Conditions.—A Rest Camp.—Back to Egypt.

9th BATTERY.—A Good Start.—On the Peninsula.—A Good Position.—Effective Shooting.—The Last Shot.

26th BATTALION.—Formation and Training.—Dangerous Duties.—The Toll of Sickness.

ARMY SERVICE CORPS

The transports carrying the First Australian Expeditionary Force arrived without accident at Alexandria, and here for the first time the men learnt what was to be their immediate destination. Prior to this, within Tasmania and among the men who were going, there was much doubt as to the exact use that was to be made of them. A theory which found acceptance among a good many was that, being only partially trained men, they would be put to garrison duty to relieve the regular British troops and enable them to strengthen the front lines. Even when they reached Egypt and that fact was made known, people still had much doubt. Many considered that the fact of their being landed in Egypt was evidence that there was no present intention of using them for fighting purposes, and it is quite possible that the British War Office itself had at the time no very clear notion as to what use was to be made of the men who in its eyes ranked only as amateurs. It must be remembered that these were the days before the Kitchener Army surprised the world, and when it was still believed that only those who had had years of training could make up an effective fighting force.

From Alexandria the troops comprising the First Australian Division were taken by train to Cairo, and thence to their camp at Mena, where they were distributed into their various Brigades. The journey is thus described in the Regimental history of the 12th Battalion:—

"We disembarked at Alexandria and entrained for Cairo (120 miles away), a most enchanting trip to all ranks, the large majority of whom had never previously been out of Australia. The natives, men, women, and children, the donkeys, camels and oxen, palms and tropical vegetation, the muddy Nile with the numberless canals and small water-courses and quaint irrigation machinery, comprising water-wheels, spiral screws, buckets on long poles balanced by a stone at one end, etc., the primitive wooden ploughs, all were sources of wonder and delight.

After detraining, we all boarded trams and had the first of many rides along the tree-bordered embankment to Mena House, 'neath the shade of the famous Pyramids of Cheops. Half a mile away, in a long, sandy valley up which ran a road called 'Infantry road,' we pitched the tents that were to be our home during our second period of training. The 1st and 2nd Brigades were on the south side of the road, and on the north was the 3rd, which now came under the immediate command of its Brigadier, Colonel E. G. Sinclair-MacLagan."

Here a rigorous course of training was instituted under conditions which were very trying, which tested to the full the endurance of the men. They had a march daily of some two miles to their training ground, going in full marching order, carrying heavy packs, under a burning sun and with penetrating sand blowing on to them, causing much chafing and discomfort. For the first two months they were given very little time for recreation, and leave was a rarity. After that time, however, it was found that more recreation was needed, and a weekly holiday was instituted. Dining huts and cinema halls were erected at the camps, giving some certain amount of comfort which had previously been considered unnecessary.

At the end of February preparations were made for the Gallipoli campaign—although all that the men knew was that they were to prepare themselves for a journey, and that some kind of adventure was in front of them. The only Tasmanian unit which then came into the scheme was the 12th Battalion. The Light Horse, it was known, could not be used as a mounted force on Gallipoli, and the Artillery also were left behind, but arrived in time to take part in the landing. The 15th Battalion also landed on the evening of Anzac Day. Later on, the Light Horse also came into action on Gallipoli, but for the time being they had the irritating knowledge that their comrades were on their way to some real fighting, while they had to remain with such patience as they could manage in the dull routine of camp.

We may now follow the fortunes of the 12th Battalion in its Gallipoli adventure. This Battalion was made up of more than half Tasmanians and the rest South Australians and West Australians, and was under the command of Colonel L. F. Clarke, with Lieutenant-Colonel S. Hawley second in command—both being Tasmanians.

The Battalion was the first complete unit to march out from Mena on this famous adventure. Going to Alexandria by train, the troops embarked on transports and were taken to the little island of Lemnos, where they remained for seven weeks, still unknowing what was their eventual destination. Here training was continued, but it was not confined to the ordinary routine. The nature of some parts of the training made it clear to the men who took part in it that they were destined for some difficult and dangerous work. They were practised in assaults up steep hill sides, and also made several practice landings from the transport.

The orders for the landing provided that the 9th, 10th, and 11th Battalions should land simultaneously, each supported by a Company of the 12th, which was then to serve as a rallying point on which the other 3 Companies should concentrate, while the 3rd Brigade Headquarters should land with the 4th Company. What actually happened, of course, with troops who had not then learned as they did later, the value and necessity of keeping a reserve in hand, was that every boat load, as soon as they reached the beach, went straight up the hill at the enemy.

On 19th April, in comformity with the above-mentioned orders, "B"

"C" and "D" Companies transhipped to the *Ionian, Malda* and *Suffolk* respectively. "A" Company remained on the *Devantia*. On the 22nd the Destroyer *Ribble* came alongside the *Devantia,* and all hands practiced climbing down rope-ladders on to her deck and learned where each man was to be stationed. There were 6 ship's boats attached to the destroyer, each carrying about 25 men. Two trips (or tows) for each boat were necessary to land "A" Company, Battalion H.Q., and the Machine Gun Section. The second "tow" embarked first and went below and the first tow remained on the deck opposite the boat they were to occupy. One of the crew of the *Ribble* steered and men were told off to row the boats back from the beach to the *Ribble* after landing the first "tow."

At 2 p.m. on 24th, we weighed anchor and by 3 p.m. had cleared the harbour of Mudros. It was a wonderful sight to see the long line of battleships (headed by the giant Queen Elizabeth), cruisers, destroyers and transports steaming "line ahead" and stretching into the far distance.

Late that night we dropped anchor near the Island of Imbras, and just before midnight the *Ribble* came alongside once more. The sea was so calm that the *Devantia's* gangway was let down and we walked aboard in comfort instead of having to climb down a rope ladder on to a tossing destroyer below.

About 1 a.m. on the morning of the never-to-be-forgotten 25th April we became conscious that other destroyers on our right and left were also speeding across the glassy waters. The majority of the 3rd Brigade were in destroyers, which were to steam to within about a quarter of a mile of land, when the troops would row ashore. Those who were on cruisers embarked on the ships' boats about a mile from shore and were towed in by steam pinnaces.

The 12th Battalion was disposed on destroyers as follows:—H.Q. and "A" Coy., *Ribble;* "B" Coy. (5 and 8 platoons) *Scourge;* (6 and 7 platoons) *Foxhound;* C. Coy. (9 and 10 platoons) *Colore;* (12 and 13 platoons) *Beagle;* "D" Coy. (13 and 14 platoons) *Chelmer;* (15 and 16 platoons) *Usk.*

As we steamed on a light was seen ahead, but we could not tell if it was on shore or a screened guiding light of our Navy. We approached the land in darkness, no sound being heard from ship or shore, and we were beginning to wonder if we would land unopposed after all, when a rifle shot was heard, followed almost at once by others, and soon a regular fusilade broke out all along the cliffs overlooking our landing place. Many of the first "tows" got ashore without a single casualty, others had quite a number. The boats of the second "tows", which came ashore after dawn had broken, were not so fortunate, and suffered severely, one or two boats having their entire loads mown down by machine gun fire.

No one gave a thought to the orders for the Battalion to assemble on the beach as a Brigade reserve. There were the enemy on the hill top firing at our comrades in the boats, and every man went straight ahead. Brigade Headquarters suffered severely, Lt.-Col. Hawley, 2nd in command, was hit while standing in his boat, holding it with an oar to prevent it running back from the beach as the men jumped out, and did not actually land. Captain J. Northcolt, our Adjutant, was wounded shortly after reaching the beach, and our C.O., Colonel Clarke, was killed, and Major Elliott, senior Coy. Commander, wounded just as they reached the top of the hill (afterwards named Walker's Ridge) within two hours of landing.

When the Brigade assembled three days later the command devolved on Major E. Hilmer Smith, O.C. "B" Coy.

"Recording the doings of the 12th Battalion for the first day on Gallipoli, resolves itself into personal reminiscences of small bodies of troops. The nature of the country prevented any combined movement, and the Battalion, after landing, advanced inland in small parties, led by officers, for about three miles. About 9 a.m. the main Turkish force attacked, and gradually we were forced back from the ground we had gained, until, by night fall, we were holding the ridge on the eastern slopes of Shrapnel Gully.

During the night of 25th, 26th April orders were received from Captain Ross, Staff-Captain 3rd Brigade, to assemble on the Beach, as the 3rd Brigade had orders to re-form. Word was passed along the line for the men of the 12th Battalion to assemble on the Beach, and by 12 noon on the 26th April 50 men had reported; scouts continued to bring in others, and by 2 p.m. about 100 had joined up. As a new arrival came in sight he was greeted with cheers from his comrades. Many were the hand-shakings and embraces witnessed, and many humorous and pathetic sights were seen during this, our first reunion after going into action.

"At 12 noon, on the 26th, orders were received to return immediately to the firing line at the head of Shrapnel Gully, as the Turks were attacking in force. The party, in command of Major E. Hilmer Smith, with Lieutenants Margetts, Foster, Burt, and Houghton, set off, reaching the firing line about 2.30 p.m., where they were immediately absorbed in the battle. The Turks repeatedly charged, but were repelled. It was here that Private (now Captain) Tostevin, of the M.G. Section, first distinguished himself. Shortly after our arrival, the last man of a machine gun installed in this position was killed, and no other gunners could be found. The word for gunners was passed along the line, and Tostevin, with blood streaming from his face, came running up, and, at great personal risk, rushed to the position and brought the gun into action again. About this time the casualties were very heavy. All that night and the next day fighting continued without cessation.

About dawn on the 28th April, an order was passed along the line signed by General MacLagan (G.O.C. 3rd Brigade) for all men of the 3rd Brigade to assemble once again on the beach. The second reunion of the 12th Battalion was commenced by 8 a.m. A small party of ten collected under a ledge in Shrapnel Gully and proceeded to the beach, picking up others on the way. On arrival, they were met by Captain Ross, and directed to a section of the beach to await orders. Old comrades continued to join up during the day, worn out with three days' fighting. They dropped on the beach as they stood—hungry, clothes in tatters, many without boots—and slept till daylight next day. The officers reporting at this time were Major Smith, Lieutenants Margetts, Burt, Houghton and Vowels, with W.O. Kennedy. The 29th was spent reorganising; small batches of men continued to report to Battalion Headquarters during the day. By 4 p.m. about 200 had assembled. The other units of the Brigade had also re-assembled during the day, and shortly before dark we formed up as a Brigade, and marched towards the right flank, bivouacing on the slopes of McLaren Ridge in holes scratched in the ground with our entrenching tools—the only ones available. Heavy rain fell during the night, and the holes became pools of water.

On the morning of the 30th the first roll-call was made, but out of a full Battalion muster at the landing only seven officers and 196 others answered their names. The rest of the day was spent in reorganising. Major Smith was appointed to command. The Battalion was organised into three companies under Captains Kayser and Burt and Lieutenant Vowels. While the Battalion was reorganising bullets were dropped around, and a rumour started that snipers were active on the slopes of the opposite hill. A sniper drive was organised. A line of men, about ten paces apart, was formed, and, with fixed bayonets, they scrambled up the hill, searching every holly bush with bayonet thrusts. In the large clumps of bushes one man would crawl in under the bushes while another stood on guard. It looked more like a rabbit hunt in burrows than anything else, but the result was nil. Our first salvage work was done on this day. Parties were sent out collecting rifles, packs, overcoats, etc., and mounds of each article were made.

The night of the 30th April—1st May was spent on outpost duty, and early next morning issues were made preparatory to going into the line again. During the night about 50 more stragglers joined up. At 9 a.m. we moved in single file along over the ridge, and up a very rough gully to the north of Shrapnel Green, taking about four hours to travel one and a half miles. Our rendezvous was immediately behind what was afterwards known as "Boulder's Dump." We relieved the 8th Battalion in the line that afternoon (1st May). The relief was completed by 6 p.m., and the next two days and nights were spent in repelling the Turks and digging in. This was where the Battalion first earned its reputation as a "Digging Battalion." In 48 hours the trenches were made habitable and formed a good solid defensive line. The work was continued in shifts till the job was finished."

The 12th Battalion has the distinction of being the first unit which took up the business of making entrenchments on a systematic and thorough scale. The trenches were very well arranged, and the men worked with furious zeal, backed by the driving power of their officers.

After four days out of the trenches for the purpose of reorganising and refitting, the 12th Battalion took up a new trench position, where it remained without relief for 13 consecutive weeks. During this time the men endured many privations, owing to food and water difficulties, and the absence of proper cooking utensils. Some relief was obtained by the despatch of a party to the beach to retrieve from their old transport some means of cooking, and the water difficulty was solved by Private Casanova, a West Australian member of the Battalion, who, by the use of the divining rod, of which he was an expert, discovered a well of fine and cool drinking water, which lasted six weeks.

The defensive works which the Battalion had constructed were soon to be put to a severe test. On the 20th May a heavy bombardment began from the Turkish batteries, the prelude, as it afterwards appeared, to a determined attack, which had the intention of driving the Australians out of Gallipoli into the sea. The plan of construction of these trenches stood the test, with the result that while the Battalions on the right and left suffered very severely, the Tasmanians only had 12 casualties. The strength of the Battalion at this time had been reduced to 300, and the supply of ammunition was quite inadequate for any large operations, and, inconceivable as it may now sound, the Battalion machine guns had not been replaced.

When, therefore, on the night of the 20th, the Turks made their onslaught across what afterwards became known as "Tasmania Post," the Tasmanians had to meet them with a rifle only, and even then with strict and necessary orders to reserve their fire—not because this was the best tactics, but because there was a danger, if the attack was a determined one, of ammunition running out. When the Turks reached to within 250 yards of the trench, the order was given for "rapid fire, aim low." Up to this time the men had restrained themselves under conditions which, especially for troops new to discipline, were exceptionally trying, but now they made up for it and gave what appeared the overwhelming attacking party, a very hot time. Notwithstanding all that the defenders could do, the Turks actually reached the trench, but could not capture it. Our men fought with the utmost determination, and through the whole of that night of strenuous fighting no weakness was shown.

When the dawn came the Turkish attack was finished, and our men were

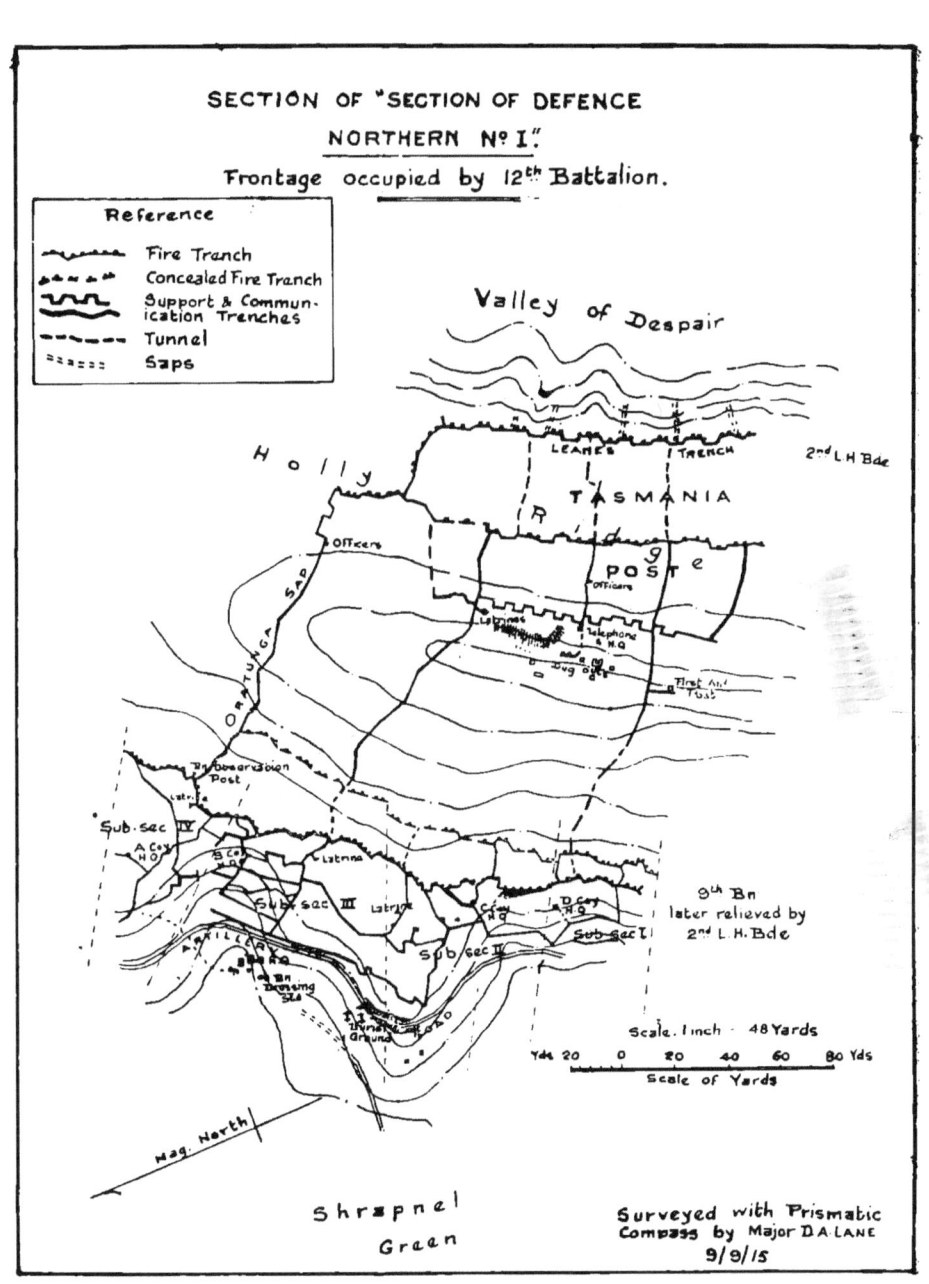

Tasmania Post

able to see what a price the enemy had paid for its attempt. In the short sector immediately in front of the Tasmanian line over 500 dead Turks were counted, and the remainder had retired after their first unpleasant taste of fighting against Tasmanians. The end came none too soon, for our men were utterly exhausted, and the supply of ammunition had almost entirely run out.

The intense summer heat made it absolutely necessary for both sides to dispose immediately of the hundreds of dead who lay in No Man's Land, and on 22nd May a temporary armistice of 12 hours was agreed upon, and joint action was taken by the Australians and Turks to bury the dead. The conditions under which this work was carried out was so horrifying that any that might still have had any illusions about the glory of war lost them once and for all. On both sides the terms of the armistice were honorably and loyally observed.

For some weeks after this a slow forward movement was carried on by means of tunnels driven down the hill and up the opposite ridge, eventually forming the redoubt which became known as "Tasmania Post." These operations were rendered necessary by the arrival of reinforcements and the consequent insufficiency of accommodation behind the trenches. The work was carried on continuously for the whole 24 hours of each day by a system of relief parties, and continued for eleven weeks without cessation.

The utility of this system of trenches connected by tunnels was shown when a demonstration was needed to keep the Turks on the watch and prevent them detaching reinforcements to oppose a British advance from Helles. An ingenious ruse was adopted to give the Turks the idea that the Battalion was several times stronger than it was in reality. Men were stationed at intervals in the main trenches, and, on a given signal, jumped over the top and dashed down the hill into the valley, where they entered the lower trenches and then returned by the underground tunnels to their original positions. They repeated this manoeuvre over and over again, and the Turks imagined from this that a large force was concentrating in the lower trenches below "Tasmania Post," and started and kept up a furious but futile bombardment on that position, while the Tasmanians were safe in the upper trenches.

The Tasmanian trench system attracted a great deal of attention from our own side, and was recognised as being the most effective and best devised on Gallipoli. They were frequently visited by General Birdwood, and on one occasion by the Commander-in-Chief, General Sir Ian Hamilton, who expressed appreciation of their excellence.

One of the most trying tasks for the men during all this period was the carrying of sufficient water 1½ miles from the beach in old petrol tins, under cover of darkness and up very rugged hills. It was exhausting work, but had to be done, and the men endured with what cheerfulness they could manage.

The living conditions were, at this time, to say the least, difficult, and with the outbreak of dysentery and the consequent deterioration in physical power, the spirit of the Battalion underwent a severe test. Through the months of June, July, and August the plague of flies, the awful stench, the hard food and lack of water and scarcity of sleep tried all ranks to the utmost, but through it all one could always hear a tune being hummed, or a joke being cracked by some comrade.

About the end of July the Turks established themselves in a trench which threatened "Tasmania Post." They were able to carry on their operations in comparative safety owing to the thick scrub of holly bushes, which prevented the Tasmanians from getting a correct idea of their position and of the work which they were carrying out. Fortunately, a considerable number of these bushes had been cut off by rifle bullets, and the materials were there, provided a day and a wind favourable to the operations were found, for a big bush fire. The time had come. Balls of tow soaked in kerosene were skilfully thrown, and the obstruction was rapidly cleared. It was then possible to take measures to counteract the danger, and to get into a position from which the Turkish trenches might be captured. This entailed very severe work of tunnelling, so as to make connections close to the trench. The men worked hard, and had nearly completed their task when the order came that the trench must be captured at once, but, much to the disgust and discontent of those who had done all the preliminary work, the attack was put in the hands of the 11th Battalion, and the 12th went into reserve, after thirteen weeks in the trenches. The attack was successful, but at heavy cost to the 11th, and it became necessary for the 12th Battalion to hold the position while the others reorganised. Early in August Major Hilmer Smith was evacuated sick, and Major J. L. Whitham assumed command, his first duty being the preparations for the attack on Lone Pine.

The part played by the 12th Battalion in the Lone Pine attack is not commonly recognised. The Battalion was detailed as part of Divisional Reserve, and the sole reference in the Commander-in-Chief's despatches to the work done by it during the action is contained in the bare statement:— "Part of the 12th Battalion, the Reserve of the 3rd Brigade, had therefore to be thrown into the melee."

For some days previous to 6th August many troops had been landing over-night, including some Units of Kitchener's New Army. The valleys in rear of our positions were filled with these Troops, and it became evident that "there was something doing." On 5th August Company Commanders were assembled, and details of attack on Lone Pine, which was to be made next day by the First Brigade, were gone into. Company Commanders during the afternoon reconnoitred the trenches and positions which they would be required to occupy in event of the Divisional Reserve being required. These trenches were at that time occupied by Battalions of the 2nd Brigade. Arrangements were completed for leaving the area occupied by us, as it was thought possible that the results of the action would bring about a general advance All gear and material that it would not be possible to take forward was stacked in Company or Battalion dumps. A spirit of eager anticipation simply manning trenches. That night an extra rum issue was made to all ranks.

Early on 6th August reinforcements for the Battalion arrived, and their welcome was a warm one, both by friend and foe. Lieut. T. Haslam was in command of these reinforcements, and was appointed to "D" Company. The Battalion at the time was very weak as regards strength of Officers.

During the morning of 6th August orders were issued for all ranks to sew on to their tunics arm bands of white calico 6in. wide, one on each sleeve, and a patch 6in. square behind the right shoulder. These were to serve as distinguishing marks, and any person not wearing these marks was to be treated as an enemy. Company Commanders were therefore very careful to ensure that all men under their command complied with this order.

Before midday final arrangements had been completed, and everyone took to his possie and awaited developments.

At 4.30 p.m. our artillery commenced a heavy bombardment of the Turkish trenches, paying particular attention to Lone Pine and other points to be attacked. In the valley below the 12th Battalion position was a Howitzer Battery of the Lowland Division, and for over an hour the Infantrymen from their more or less secure retreats watched the Gunners going down under the Turkish counter-battery fire. Major G. B. Carter, Medical Officer to the

12th Battalion, calmly walked down to the battery position and applied first aid to the wounded, regardless of the terrible shrapnel fire that was drenching the Battery.

At 5.30 p.m. three Battalions of the First Brigade assaulted Lone Pine with the bayonet. The position was a remarkably strong one. The trenches were provided with overhead cover and protected by wire. The ground to be traversed by the assaulting troops was a slight decline varying from 60 to 120 yards wide. This was swept by a perfect hail of rifle, machine-gun, and shrapnel fire. The wire had been greatly destroyed by the artillery fire, but the overhead cover had been smashed in only a few places. After a short but bloody struggle the position was captured.

The actual attack and capture of a position is not always the most difficult and costly part of an operation. Counter-attacks by the enemy are sure to be made, and holding a position against these counter-attacks is often the hardest and most trying work of all. It was so in the case of Lone Pine.

At 6 p.m. the 12th Battalion received orders to move to their allotted positions in close support in Gun Lane. Platoons fell in and rolls were called in record time, Companies moving independently to their positions. Whilst passing along Artillery Road, they came under a perfect hail of shrapnel, meant principally for our batteries at the Pimple. The area covered by this fire was passed at the double, and the Battalion assembled in Gun Lane. Here they lay, whilst the Turkish shells constantly fell on the parados of the Road, but fortunately not one struck actually in the Road. This fire was drawn by the batteries at the Pimple, which was only a short distance from where the Battalion was lying. It is noteworthy that the casualties suffered by the Battalion whilst waiting for three hours in Gun Lane were remarkably light, in view of the intensity of the hostile fire. Lieut. Ogilvy, of "A" Company, was unfortunately amongst those killed.

About 9 p.m. "A" Company was ordered to reinforce the troops in Lone Pine, and was followed immediately by "D" Company. These Companies filed through tunnels to an underground firing line, which formed their jumping off point.

The area over which they had to advance was the same over which the troops had charged to the attack about 3½ hours previously, and their dead and dying encumbered the ground in all directions. In some places they lay in groups where machine guns had covered them. It was a veritable field of carnage, with dying and badly wounded men groaning for water or writhing in their death agonies. Hostile machine guns still played across this ground, and shrapnel enfiladed it. However, Lone Pine was reached with little loss.

The trenches in the captured position presented an awful appearance. Dead literally carpeted the ground, and in some cases blocked the trenches. Tunnels and communication trenches were crowded with wounded and dying to such an extent that communication became extremely difficult. It was almost impossible for a Platoon Commander to maintain control of his Platoon, and in the inevitable confusion command was exercised by Officers over men of various Units in their vicinity. The Turkish batteries during this period maintained a steady fire on the position.

It is difficult to follow the operations of the two Companies of the Battalion without taking the part played by each separately. The first problem for the Company Commanders to solve was to collect their men, who arrived at various places in the support trenches (originally Turkish firing line). This was accomplished, and "A" Company, commanded by Captain L. Mullen, was collected in the left of Lone Pine, and early next day occupied a portion of the firing line and successfully resisted the repeated counter-attacks made by the Turks during the 7th and night of 7th-8th August. "D" Company, commanded by Major D. A. Lane, was collected in the support trenches in the right of Lone Pine, and spent the night of 6th-7th August and morning of 7th in clearing the trenches and communications to the firing line of dead.

During the morning of the 7th the enemy succeeded in regaining a portion of the Lone Pine trenches on the right, held by the 2nd Battalion, and about 2 p.m. "D" Company was ordered to reinforce the Battalion.. Communication between O.C. "A" and "D" Companies with Battalion H.Q. was difficult, and orders were issued to them by G.O.C. First Brigade direct.

As already mentioned, the Turkish firing line had become our support line, and as the enemy had prepared elaborate overhead cover, the passage to the firing line resembled passing through a tortuous tunnel. The Turkish dead lay in heaps, and there was no alternative but to walk along a line of bodies. The Company passed along the firing line till contact was gained with the enemy where they had effected a lodgment during the morning. The trenches here were extremely narrow and not well traversed. Our own and Turkish dead lay anywhere and everywhere, and in some instances our own wounded were still lying at the bottom of the trench. All that afternoon a terrific bomb battle was maintained, the bombs being the old jam-tin type lit by a fusee or match. Soon after nightfall the Turks made a vigorous attempt to recapture their lost trenches, and a hard and bloody fight set in. In this the two Companies of the 12th Battalion were hotly engaged the night through. The men were in poor physical condition, due chiefly to the ravages of dysentry, but they stuck to their positions, and by dawn the Turkish counter-attack was beaten back.

During the 8th "A" and "D" Companies of the 12th were withdrawn, and later "B" Company, under command of Lieut. H. Massey, was sent into the Pine. This Company met with some stiff fighting, and unfortunately lost Lieut. Woodhouse, who was reported missing after the action.

"C" Company of the 12th were utilised during the action of Lone Pine in stretcher-bearing; thus the whole Battalion took part in the action. Two Officers were killed, and both Major Lane and Captain Rafferty were wounded, but remained on duty.

On being withdrawn from Lone Pine, the Battalion returned to its bivouac in Clarke Valley, and, after a couple of days rest, relieved the 11th Battalion in "Tasmania Post," which they garrisoned continuously till 10th September, when they in turn were relieved by the 4th Light Horse.

All hands were now promised a month's rest, and at the end of August the 1st and 2nd Brigades were sent back to Lemnos, where an outbreak of diphtheria kept them quarantined till the end of October. No further offensives were undertaken, and on the 3rd Brigade sector at any rate, no extension of the trench system was made, though minor improvements continually kept fatigue parties busy.

From 10th September to 22nd October the 12th Battalion remained in reserve, two companies relieving alternately the 10th and 11th Battalion's front line Companies every four days. On the 19th September Major C. H. Elliott returned from England and took over the command from Major Whitham. On 22nd October the Brigade sector was reorganised, the 12th Battalion being given a separate sector, instead of providing relief for the 10th and 11th Battalions, whose front was now considerably reduced. On Saturday, 6th November, we received word that Patrobas had won the Melbourne Cup on the 2nd idem. Several sweeps had been run on the event.

On 14th the 2nd Battalion relieved "A" Coy. in the line. The 3rd Brigade were due to return this night, the 9th and 11th Battalions leaving by the same boats for Lemnos, but it blew too hard for them to land. They got away on 16th, and the 10th and 12th were to leave next night. but though the 10th Battalion got away on 21st, it was the 25th before the 12th embarked, so that

7 complete months were spent here on the Peninsula. Captain I. S. Margetts was the only officer who was there the whole time, and very few of the men held the same record of service.

On reaching Lemnos, we marched into a camp at Sarpe, and experienced bitterly cold and windy weather for the first week. Training was carried out in the mornings and sports in the afternoons.

On 8th December Major J. Gellibrand was promoted Lieut.-Colonel and appointed to command the 12th Battalion, taking over from Major Elliott.

On 12th December, two Battalions of the 2nd Brigade returned to Lemnos and we got the first "dinkum oil" that the Peninsula was to be evacuated. This event was successfully carried out on the night 19th-20th December. On the 24th the Xmas "billies" were issued. These were the first of our annual Xmas boxes, sent by the Australian Comforts Funds and greatly they were appreciated and looked forward to by all ranks.

The 15th Battalion was composed (Queensland organisation) of two Companies of Tasmanians and six of Queenslanders, one Company of Tasmanians being under the command of Major Snowden, the other under Captain H. C. Davies. The Tasmanian Companies were formed in October, 1914, and went into camp at Claremont, being the first troops to train there. In November, 1914, the Battalion concentrated in Victoria, and went into camp at Broadmeadows, together with the 13th, 14th, and 16th Battalions, the Brigade being under the command of Colonel Monash. On December 22nd the 15th Battalion embarked on the Transport *Ceramic* for Egypt, arriving there early in February, 1915.

The whole of the 4th Brigade went into camp at Aerodrome Camp, some nine miles from Cairo, and after undergoing further training there, proceeded to Alexandria early in April to embark on the Transport *Australind* for Lemnos Island. On arrival at Lemnos a special course of training had to be gone through, including quick disembarkation into boats.

On the night of the 24th April, 1915, the Transport *Australind,* in common with the remainder of the transports at Lemnos, proceeded to sea with the object of going to Gallipoli, half of the 15th Battalion only being on the *Australind*. This half included the Tasmanians in the battalion. The transport had two pontoons on board, and as these were to assist the Imperial troops to land at Cape Helles, the *Australind* proceeded to the entrance to the Dardanelles, whilst the rest of the Australian convoy proceeded to Anzac. The troops on the *Australind* were, therefore, the only Australians to witness the landing at Cape Helles, which was effected by the British and French troops at daybreak on the 25th of April. From the transport, the *River Clyde* could be plainly seen as she was run on shore, a mile away, while a little in rear of the *Australind* the *Queen Elizabeth,* with her immense 15in. guns, opened fire at the Turkish position at a range of about seven or eight miles.

After discharging the pontoons the *Australind,* at 11 a.m. on the morning of the landing, proceeded along the coast to Anzac Cove, where, some hours previously, the first Australian troops had landed. Owing to the heavy shell fire close to the beach, no troops were landed in the afternoon, but as soon as darkness set in preparations were made to effect the landing of all troops on transports. At 6.30 p.m. on the 25th of April, the troops from the *Australind* left the transport for the shore, some two miles distant, on a destroyer. After proceeding to within a few hundred yards of the shore, under fire the whole time, the destroyer stopped, and the troops were transferred to smaller boats, and by this means taken to the shore, where they arrived at about 8 p.m. As each party arrived on shore it was directed or led to certain positions in the general line that had been decided on. As a result of this, the members of the battalion were scattered all along the firing line, only about 500 men being left under the command of the battalion commander. Most of the Tasmanians remained together, and after marching for some time were directed to "dig in." This they did on quick time as the bullets and shrapnel were flying very thick. When day broke the firing got heavier, but the trenches had been well constructed, and the casualties were not heavy. After holding the position for 12 hours orders were received to advance to a position about 500 yards in front. This position was occupied at the double, and the battalion dug in. The losses during the forward move were not heavy.

With the assistance of the Indian Mounted Battery, the Turks were held in check, and no attack was made on this part of the line during the time it was held by the 15th Battalion, but during this time they were subjected to heavy shrapnel fire, causing a number of casualties. The position they held was at the head of what was afterwards known as "Shrapnel Gully."

The battalion headquarters remained in this position until the 28th of April, when they proceeded to the beach, for the purpose of re-organisation. On arriving there, the fit of the remainder of the battalion met them with a cheer and inquiries regarding the doings of each company, and met with the reply that, although the losses had been heavy, the men were in good spirits, and eager to avenge their lost comrades. The battalion remained on the beach until the morning of the 29th, and members were thus able to enjoy their first undisturbed sleep since the landing.

On the afternoon of the 29th, the battalion was moving up Monash Gully, preparatory to taking over the Pope's Hill position, which was done on the morning of the 30th.

The position occupied by the Tasmanian Company was known as the "Death Trap," on account of its exposed position, and the shallowness of the trenches; the ground being of a rocky nature, a great deal of hard digging had to be done to secure a couple of feet of cover. Owing to the fact that the Turks had a machine gun laid on to the position, the digging could only be done at night time, and even then could not be done without loss.

The line occupied was about 400 yards from the Turkish trenches. On the Sunday after the landing orders were issued that a combined attack of the 4th Brigade was to be made on the enemy in front of "Pope's Hill," and at 7.30, after a heavy artillery bombardment, the Tasmanian portion of the Brigade moved forward to the attack. The Turks were evidently prepared for the attacking party, who were met with concentrated machine gun fire from all the guns in the vicinity, and although by this time darkness had set in, heavy losses were suffered. However, the attack was pushed home, and the position captured, but when morning broke it was found that there were not sufficient men to occupy the ground captured. The R.M.L.I. were, therefore, ordered to occupy the position on the left of the Tasmanians, but owing to heavy fire they could not advance far enough to be of any use in protecting the left flank, with the result that the Tasmanian right flank was in touch with the 13th Battalion, but the left flank was exposed. The Turks, taking advantage of this, pushed their troops in, but were unable to recapture the trenches, although they fought stubbornly all day. On the night of the 4th May, after being without sleep for two nights, the members of the 15th Battalion were ordered to retire. The retirement was effected without loss. The losses during the two days had been exceptionally heavy, and owing to the exposed position water and food could not be brought forward except at great risk.

After retiring, one day's rest was allowed, and orders were received for the 15th Battalion to take over Quinn's Post, named after Captain (afterwards Major) Quinn, of the 15th, whose company had held it from the day of the landing. Quinn's Post was admittedly the worst position on Gallipoli to hold. The line of trenches occupied by the Australians was in some parts only 15 yards from the Turkish trenches, while at the most distant part not more than 50 yards separated the trenches. Owing to the nature of the ground, only one line of trenches could be constructed, as the position was like a saucer with the trenches on the rim.

A small knoll, not unlike a cup, was situated in the centre, but it was too small to allow of a trench being dug on it. Scarcely a night passed on Quinn's without a raid being made by one side or the other.

In front of Quinn's only the best of the Turkish troops were stationed. On one occasion a dozen dark forms could be seen advancing from the Turkish lines; immediately fire was opened by the Tasmanians, and although it was too dark to see the object plainly, good shooting was done. One Turk after another dropped, until only one remained, and from the way he stumbled it was evident that he was hit, but still he came on until he was on top of the Tassies' parapet. Then he stopped, turned round, and dropped. It was afterwards found that he had six bullet wounds, but owing to his splendid build and courage, he kept on until he reached the trenches.

The losses on Quinn's, as a result of bombs, were very heavy, but this was to be expected when one remembers the closeness of the trenches. Luckily this closeness saved the troops from shell fire, and it was only on two occasions that shells fell in the trenches, but unfortunately on these occasions heavy losses were sustained.

Very little rest was enjoyed by the Tassies, as they occupied the trenches nearest to the Turks. Even when allowed away from the position for rest, a peaceful night could not be anticipated, as attacks were being made nightly, and those stationed in reserve had to be ready to proceed to the posts immediately if the position looked serious.

This state of things continued until the 9th of May, when orders were received that an attack was to be made by the 15th Battalion on the Turkish position in front of Quinn's. At 10.30 on the night of the 9th the attacking parties jumped over, and although under heavy fire, quickly gained the Turkish trenches without suffering very heavily. They were sent out as a reconnaissance in force for the purpose of obtaining information, but after the trenches were gained they were instructed to try and hold the trenches, but owing to the Turks holding the position on the right, left, and centre, this could not be done; therefore, at 9 a.m. the following morning orders were given to retire. The retirement was made in good order, but the losses were heavy.

After this attack the Turks kept quieter, and although bombs were constantly being thrown into the trenches, the night raids stopped. This state of things continued until the 19th May, when information was received by Battalion H.Q. that an aeroplane reported a very large body of Turks advancing from a town some 20 miles away. It was thought, as a result of this information, that an attack would take place that night or the following morning. Orders were, therefore, issued to be prepared for it. It was anticipated that the attack would probably take place at five o'clock on the morning of the 20th, and at 5.30 the Turks were seen in the indistinct light advancing on our trenches. The attack was evidently not confined to our sector, as heavy firing could be heard all along the line. The fighting continued until 7 a.m., when the Turks had to retire, their losses being very heavy, while our losses were small. An hour later another attack was made, and as on this occasion, the light was good, they were picked up at longer range. The attack was confined to Courtney's Post (on the right of Quinn's),

Quinn's Post, and Pope's Hill (on the left of Quinn's). After an hour's hard fighting the Turks again retired with heavy losses.

At eleven o'clock the same morning the Turks made their final attack for the day, all available troops being concentrated on Quinn's Post. The orders to the 15th Battalion were to hold the post at all cost. Then commenced one of the hardest fights the Tassies had been in to date. Line after line the Turkish troops came forward, only to be shot down by the defenders of Quinn's, ably assisted by the troops on their right and left, who, not being engaged in front, assisted the 15th by their fire from the flanks. With only 500 men in the trenches at Quinn's, and 10,000 attacking, it seemed impossible for the position to be held, but the orders were "stick to the post," and stick to it they did. Had it not been for the support given by the artillery and the troops on either side, it is doubtful whether the attack could have been resisted. The enemy were so close at one time that the shell fired at them from the Australian and British artillery raised the dust from the parapet on Quinn's Post. Eventually the Turks were forced to retire, leaving over 5000 dead in front of Quinn's alone. Two days later they asked for an armistice to bury their dead. The Australian losses were very small. The armistice was granted. To all the troops, especially those on Quinn's Post, that day was like a glimpse of heaven after a month in hell. A month of shell fire, bombs, and rifle fire, men walking with bent backs to prevent their heads appearing above the trench, mines exploding when least expected, and then on the call of the bugle all firing ceased on both sides. Soon afterwards heads began to appear above the trenches, and the stretcher parties began to appear.

A dividing line was laid half-way between the Australian and Turkish trenches, over which neither side was allowed to pass. Very soon the "Aussies" could not resist the opportunity of going out for a stretch, and they could be seen with their toes on the line trying to carry on a conversation with the Turks a few feet away. It was quite a common sight to see an "Aussie" cutting a button from a Turk's coat, while the Turk was doing the same to him. It is hard to imagine that men who had been trying to kill one another the day before should do this, but such is human nature in war; the personal element does not enter. At 4.30 p.m., with a "Good-bye, Turk; I pot you in ten minutes," the Aussies went back to their trenches, and ten minutes later on the sound of the bugle, every gun and rifle on Gallipoli seemed to go off at once, and to continue to go off as quickly as possible for an hour afterwards.

The heavy firing was kept up that night, and well into the following day, after which the battalion settled down to general warfare again.

The day after the armistice it was found that the Turks were mining to get under our trenches, as a result of which volunteers were called for men to take on mining, and as the Tasmanian Company of the battalion had a large proportion of miners, it was selected to supply the necessary men to dig tunnels to intercept the Turks.

This work was so well carried out that, although the Tassies exploded a number of charges and did a great deal of damage to the Turkish trenches, no Turkish mine was exploded up to the time the battalion went into "rest," on the 30th May. Quinn's Post was taken over from the 15th on the night of the 30th May, and the battalion went into "rest" about 300 yards in rear. At 4 a.m. the following morning a great explosion was heard, and the order was given to "stand to"; five minutes later word was received that the Turks had blown up a section of Quinn's, and had occupied the trenches.

Orders were at once given to advance on the post at the double, and as the advance could only be made in single file, it took some time for the last men of the battalion to reach the position by the time day had begun to break, and the position was well observed.

Two companies of Tasmanians were ordered to take the trenches, and after half an hour's hard fighting this was done after inflicting heavy losses on the enemy. The losses of the Australians in numbers were comparatively small, but, unfortunately, Major Quinn (after whom the post was named) was killed. He was one of the first to occupy the position on the day of the landing, and had been on it practically continuously up to the day of his death.

After the Turks had been driven out of the front line, the trenches were occupied by the 15th Battalion, reinforced by the 16th, and although, apparently, all the Turks had been driven out, men were still being hit with rifle bullets, and it was thought that our own men were under the impression that portion of the trenches were still held by the Turks, but on investigation it was found that a section of trenches known as the "Bomb-proof" (a covered trench connected with the front line, but 20 yards in rear) was still occupied by the Turks. Orders were given to the Tasmanian Company to occupy the entrance to this trench, and as a result the Turks had no means of escape. After holding out for an hour they surrendered, and on their coming out it was found that they totalled 19, each armed with a rifle, plenty of bullets, and a bag of bombs.

The Turks were so delighted at escaping alive from the trap, that one of them endeavoured to kiss the first officer he met, much to this officer's surprise; so much so that he thought the Turk was going to fight, and prepared to shoot him with his revolver.

During the day the Turks several times tried to take the trenches, but were each time beaten off with heavy losses. The following day the 15th Battallion were allowed to leave the trenches on Quinn's and proceed to "Rest Gully," about 200 yards from the beach, for a rest. With the exception of two days, this was the first rest the battalion had had since the day of the landing, over five weeks previously. For a week they were allowed to take things easily, and during this time an assembly of the brigade was called, and the members were addressed by General Godby, who complimented, in the highest terms, the members of the 15th and 16th Battalions for their excellent work on Pope's Hill, and particularly on Quinn's. For this work decorations were awarded to the commanding officer of each battalion.

During the "rest week" the Tassies enjoyed their first good wash since the 25th April, and although shell fire on the beach was very heavy, it did not prevent them indulging in a daily swim.

After the week's rest, orders were given to dig communication trenches towards the outpost on the left flank, and the battalion continued on its work until about a week before their big attack on 8th August.

From the day of the landing until the 1st June, the 15th were under fire practically the whole time, and as a result their losses were, it is understood, heavier than any other battalion for that period. The Tasmanian Company was in every engagement, and to give an idea of the fierceness of the fighting, it might be stated that only one of the original six Tasmanian officers remained unwounded after the 14th day, and only three of the 30 battalion officers who landed on the first day remained unwounded for the same period.

Quinn's Post was the most difficult position held during the occupation of Gallipoli, although Pope's Hill was very hard to hold owing to the difficulty of getting supplies. When first held by the 15th, the only means of reaching the trenches was by means of a very steep hill about 200 yards high. Portion of this could only be covered by the use of a rope.

The men killed on Pope's Hill were buried in a valley at the foot of the hill. Those killed on Quinn's, in a position set aside, only ten yards in rear of the firing line.

After the strenuous fighting in which the Battalion had been engaged during these last two months it was, with the rest of the Brigade, placed in reserve being the bivouac in the vicinity of Walker's Ridge until July. The work in reserve was even more arduous than that in the trenches, and consisted mostly of providing parties for taking supplies and preparing sheltering positions for the troops, which it was rumored were soon to be landed to take part in the big fight predicted for the early part of next month.

The monotony of this work was extremely wearying, and the increasingly hot weather, during which only small quantities of water of very poor quality were available, made living conditions very unpleasant. Dysentery and diarrhoea became rife, and the healthy state of the men began to decline. In spite of this, they worked cheerfully, and were gradually brought up in numbers by reinforcements, and by the return of men who had been convalescing in Egypt.

One of the things that made life bearable was the possibility of obtaining a swim in the beautiful waters of the Mediterranean, and this was enjoyed to the utmost by all ranks. The sporting instinct of the bathers was kept alive by the fact that this recreation was being taken under fire, although this in no way deterred them, and in spite of the victims that Beachy Bill and the ever-vigilant machine-gunners of the Turks claimed.

As the heat increased, it brought us the tenacious Gallipoli fly, which practically prevented sleep in the daytime, and simply attacked the food supplies in swarms. Every night, from the trenches to the beach, Anzac stood to arms for several hours, as this was the time of the festival of Ramadan, when the Turk, after his devotional exercises, became fanatical, and very likely to attack.

Some extremely good work was done by the 15th in unloading heavy material from barges at the beach. On one occasion, when the beach master despaired of removing some material which needed taking from a barge, into which it had been neatly dropped by a crane from one of the ships, a Launceston boy, who had had previous experience in his civil life in this kind of work, stepped forward, and requested to be allowed to take a hand according to his own ideas. There was no crane available on the shell-swept beaches of Anzac, a fact which had been quite overlooked apparently by the people who loaded the barge, and as all other attempts had failed, he was given the opportunity. A gang was placed at his disposal, and with the most primitive tackle he succeeded, much to the admiration of the beach staff, in removing all the material from the barges to the beach in time to enable them to be towed out clear of range of gun fire before daylight. The carrying out of the fatigues in an equally satisfactory way made the Tasmanians very popular with the beach staff; General Leslie, who was looking after this portion of the work for the Corps, often said that had it not been for the way in which the men worked during this period of our stay on Gallipoli, it would have been impossible to adequately maintain the troops with all the requirements of food, ammunition and water for so many men.

About the end of July rumours spread among the troops of new landing to be made at Anzac, and some very fine work was done in providing sheltering terraces for the occupation of the extra troops to give the necessary punch out from Anzac.

A good deal of sapping was also done under the very eye of the Turks to get better communication of the left flank, which was to be the objective of the Brigade to which the 15th Battalion was attached. A Brigade of

Indian troops who were to assist in the August fight was bivouaced beside us. They had seen some of the fighting powers of the Australians at Cape Helles, and were strong in their admiration of the skill of our boys with the bayonet. As preparations went on, things began to liven up from the Turks' point of view, and we were subject to daily shelling from their guns, and had bombing visits from their aeroplanes, which were naturally anxious to find out all they could of our new dispositions. The last few days before the 5th August were occupied in the issue of extra rations and iron rations, the sharpening of bayonets, and the disposing of those wonderful cooking vessels, which had been constructed from every kind of tin imaginable, and the breaking down and clearing away of the bivouacs which had sheltered the men during their period out of the lines, which was so incorrectly termed a rest.

The whole scheme for the attack to join up with the new landing, to take place a few miles north of Anzac, was very closely considered by officers of all ranks, and explained in every detail to the men. This was most essential, as the movement was to be carried out at night, and in thick country, where there was very little room for manoeuvre. As soon as it was dark, on the night of August 6th, the troops moved out, battalion by battalion, in single file, along saps leading to the left flank. This flank of Anzac had been held from the day of the landing by the New Zealand Division. and a start was made this night by the New Zealanders clearing a way on the extreme left for the other troops to move out in rear of them. And so all the time the Brigade, having got to the limit of the saps, was moving along the open beach. Heavy fighting was going on in the valleys and on the hills just above them. Torpedo boats lying close into shore kept their searchlights and guns playing on to the heights above, and in this way occupied the attention of the enemy while the delicate manoeuvre of extending the line to the left was being carried out. The men had instructions to avoid using the rifle as much as possible, and, where necessary to clean up the position by the use of the bayonet. It was a good test of battle discipline that these men were subjected to moving along the dark in unknown country, with casualties occurring among them all the time, and no opportunity for the moment of hitting back, but they stood up to it well, and touch was never lost, nor wrong direction taken, throughout a night march, made on a scale equal to that famous achievement at Tel-el-Kebir. The task which was allotted the 4th Brigade was to move towards the Abdel Rahman Bair, which was the objective, by way of the Aghyle Dere, which was a steep and rugged gully thickly overgrown with prickly scrub. At the entrance to the valley we picked up our guide. a New Zealand officer, who during the preceding month had spent many days behind the Turkish lines in making a very clever reconnaisance, which was of great value to those taking part in the march and subsequent fighting. With this assistance and that of Turkish spies, the difficult task of moving up this valley was continued, and it was not long before the Battalion came in contact with the enemy, who was in strength, and occupying a position which was difficult to define, and awkward to attack, on account of its protection from observation.

The labor which had been expended during the previous few days in the sharpening of bayonets now bore fruit, and the stubborn opposition offered by the Turks was swept aside, not, however, before a good many casualties on our side had taken place.

Heavy fighting went on throughout the night, and gradually the enemy were driven from position after position, and the Battalion advanced over rough, broken country, every yard of the advance being obstinately disputed. On our right flank our sister Battalion, the 16th, and the Ghurkas were making a fine clearance in similar country, the latter using their kookeries with deadly effect, and the type of country was admirably suited for their fighting qualities. It can well be imagined that in such country control was difficult to maintain, and officers and non-commissioned officers had to take exceptional personal risks in collecting their commands and keeping them in hand, so as to give the assault a vigorous push, and to keep the enemy on the retreat. The valour and fighting discipline of our troops can be well appreciated by anyone who has found himself moving in unknown bush country in pitch darkness, even when there was no one opposing the advance, and when daylight dawned, and we had an opportunity of looking back over the country which had been covered by the Division during the night, we really wondered how we had been able to dislodge the enemy from the position they had been holding, and to move in any kind of formation over the stony ridges and densely overgrown valleys, which, in themselves, seemed sufficient obstacles, from a military point of view, to hold up troops in the attack.

The next morning found the enemy driven from all his positions, but our men were very fatigued, on account of the continued rapid advance over country suitable to the enemy and the heavy fighting in which they had been engaged. The position to be occupied by us, however, was reached, and the line completed, with the 13th British Division on our left and in touch with the Indian Brigade on our right, and in this position the Battalion dug in. This digging in under fire was done in remarkably quick time, during which a good many casualties occurred, but it was an excellent performance, considering the exhausted condition of the men, many of them suffering from dysentry, so much hard work, and indifferent food, which they had been living on during the very trying hot weather of July. This completing of the line, however, was only the first move towards driving the Turks back from the Abdel Rahman Bair, but it acted as a cover, under which the landing of the new forces of British Territorials was made at Suvla Bay, and, looking down from the heights, we were overjoyed to find below us a fleet of transports pouring out reinforcements, which we fully anticipated would enable the desired object to be achieved.

Very little rest was obtained during the day, and at night the next phase of the battle was taken. The Abdel Rahman Bair was at that time the key to the position on the Peninsular, the capture of which would have meant getting possession of the famous 971 Hill, and cutting the Turkish defence of the Peninsular in two, thus preventing supplies and reinforcements being sent to the Helles enemy army. It would also have meant our artillery being able to place the heavy guns which had been landed for the purpose, so that the forts protecting the Straits would have been shelled from their rear, and the dash which the Navy had proposed through these Sraits to be carried out.

For the 4th Brigade another night attack had been planned, and the 15th Battalion led the Brigade. By nightfall the Turks had withdrawn a short distance, and this night's advance had the advantage of the thick undergrowth, giving concealment from observation for a time, but our patrol soon got in touch with him, and waiting till he got our troops in a nicely-cleared field, he opened a heavy machine gun and rifle fire from our front and left flank. A deployment was immediately ordered, and was well carried out, considering the long time it was since anything but trench warfare had been used by our men, and also that we had a large number of reinforcements, who were taking part in their first fight. So far, fighting at close quarters continued, but eventually the enemy made a heavy counter attack on our left flank, and the Brigade was drawn back, covered by a cleverly carried out rearguard action by our Brigade machine gun section.

The Battalion suffered most heavily during the two night engagements losing 103 killed, 262 wounded, and 95 missing. Fighting continued for some days, and sections of the unit took part in it, and casualties continued. Trench warfare in this section of the line was resumed, and a part was taken over by the 15th. As far as could be seen at the time, the great results anticipated from the new landing at Suvla Bay had not been achieved, and the fact that it had not had better results, after the heavy losses we had incurred, had a most depressing effect on all ranks.

After the heavy fighting which had been their lot since the landing, they had risen nobly to the effort they had been called to make in this August fighting, but the reaction had a serious effect upon them, and the numbers on sick parade became larger each day. They were all very glad, therefore, when on the 13th September orders were given that they were to be taken off for a real rest at Lemnos Island; and a good idea of the wastage that had taken place may be obtained from the record of the strength of the Battalion, which on embarkation showed that it consised of 11 officers and 136 men.

The rest at Lemnos was much appreciated by the men after the strain of being months in a position, every portion of which was within range of rifle fire. Very little work was done, just sufficient physical drill and marching being ordered to maintain fitness, and the strength of the unit was built up from time to time by the arrival of fresh reinforcements, until it was at about half that laid down for a fighting battalion.

Mudros was a very different kind of place to what we had known of it during the few days of concentration before the landing. Then the fields looked beautiful, with growing crops and pretty wild flowers, and fields of red poppies, and occasional picturesque old villages snuggled away in spots protected from weather and the enemies that the inhabitants of past years were threatened with. Now the war influence was being shown; crops and cultivation of various kinds had given place to huge camps, hospitals, and storehouses filled with the advance base supplies of a large army. The harbour was crowded with shipping of every kind, warships ranging from submarines to battleships, and merchantmen from stern punt liner. The Greeks too had changed, and had learned the art of profiteering, and the men often wondered why the authorities did not take a hand and deal severely with those who exceeded the price laid down, and mulcted the men for articles that they very badly needed. However, the spell did the troops a lot of good, and when at the end of October they got orders to up camp and re-embark for Anzac, they were in really good spirits.

The 4th Brigade took up a position between the New Zealanders and the British troops, near the head of the Sharlik Dere, the 15th Battalion being placed in Hay Valley. Things were nice and quiet in this part of the line, and the trenches were a good distance apart; snipers and machine guns were, of course, busy, but our rifle shots were able to cope with the former, now that we had a percentage of telescopic-sighted rifles issued, and the lot of the enemy machine gunners was made uncomfortable by a small three-pounder Hotchkiss gun which had been obtained from the navy, and was worked almost in the front line by crews supplied by the various battalions, under that very gallant officer, Major Black, of the 16th Battalion, whose record until his death on the field was almost identical with the Tasmanian V.C. of the Brigade, Colonel Murray.

During the latter part of November the weather began to get very bad, and heavy falls of snow, though at first a novelty to the Queenslanders of the Battalion, made things extremely uncomfortable for troops not clothed and equipped to meet such conditions.

On the 24th of November a ruse of complete silence along the whole line was commenced; orders came that for 48 hours all guns, rifles, etc., were to refrain from firing, and that during day time all men were to be completely hidden from view, the idea being to make the Turks believe that the evacuation, which had been talked of in the press about this time, and had even been mentioned in the House of Commons, had really begun. The effect obtained was very weird and uncanny, and it is no wonder that the enemy showed those sure signs of being jumpy that are best understood by men who have been facing them in trenches for months, and have become accustomed to quickly perceive any change of morale among those on the opposite side of the trench. The Turks could be seen moving openly about and exposing themselves in the trenches, plainly unable to understand whether we had really gone away, or were about to attack. Apparently H.Q. considered the ruse a success, as it was ordered to be continued for another 24 hours. In the meantime, however, the enemy was seen to be massing in the trenches in the vicinity of what was known as the Farm, and all the available artillery and ships' guns were concentrated in a heavy bombardment of this position, which must have inflicted heavy casualties in the crowded front line trenches; it at any rate had the effect of further preparing the way for the final evacuation, which was decided upon by Lord Kitchener immediately he had the opportunity of viewing the situation from the front line trenches at a spot where the opposing trenches came closely together. About this time it was realised that it would be advisable, wherever possible, to provide good overhead covered places for the troops as a protection against the weather, and also against the heavy artillery, which it was anticipated the Bulgars would make available for the Turks, now that the former had joined the Central Powers.

The position occupied by the 15th was very suitable for this type of work, and as there were a large number of miners in the ranks, a wonderful system of underground barracks was constructed, with kitchens, storerooms, and large chambers, with about fifty feet of earth between them and the surface, entered by tunnels, and connected up in such a way as to avoid the possibility of confusion if the troops wanted to leave them in a hurry. During a bombardment the bulk of the men could be sheltered in these works, and, as soon as it was over, were available for immediate fighting when required. The men were also very snug and comfortable in the cold, wet weather, which was now being experienced. Large food and ammunition dumps were also built up close to the lines, as the tracks became extremely difficult to negotiate for the mule trains, and preparations of a general nature was carried out to meet the needs of an army, situated as this one was, for a winter campaign.

No sooner were these arrangements completed than rumors came of the removing of the bodies of troops from the Peninsula; it was given out that no attacks could be made, owing to the difficult nature of the ground under winter conditions, and that, under the circumstances, the opportunity would be taken of sending various units to Lemnos or Egypt, and giving them a chance to rest and re-fit preparatory to active operations in the spring, and that only sufficient troops were to be left to garrison Anzac. When, however, the ordnance stores on the beach were opened up, and the opportunity given to the men to practically take what they required, and when someone made the discovery that a large portion of some of the food dumps were only dummies, the truth gradually dawned on all ranks that it really was intended to remove us, and give up the ground that had been so dearly won. The secret was well kept, and the enemy, puzzled with the "silence ruse" earlier in the month, and various mechanical devices fixed up for the firing of fixed rifles and the exploding of bombs at given intervals, made no attempt to attack.

In some parts of the line the scouting patrols even reported that the Turks were busy wiring in front of their lines, in preparation to meet an attack, and strong, elaborate preparations had been made for many casualties. The only one, so far as the Brigade was concerned, was a broken limb, the result of hurrying down one of the rough mountain sides to the water's edge. The fine fighting discipline of the Australians was shown once again, and the opportunity given of proving the worth of individual initiative. There was no hurry or confusion, and the final evacuation of this portion of the Peninsula was carried out under the very nose of the enemy, in a manner which added fresh laurels to those already won by the fighting men of the Antipodes.

After the 12th Battalion and the 9th Battery had left Egypt, the 3rd Light Horse Regiment, of which "C" Squadron was Tasmanian, continued active training. Then came news of the landing on Gallipoli, and of the part played in it by Tasmanian troops. Immediately afterwards the Regiment learned, to its infinite pleasure, that its period of inactivity had ended. On April 27 the officers were called together by Brigadier-General Chauvel, who told them that reinforcements were urgently needed at Gallipoli, and that the Higher Command was intending to call for volunteers from the Light Horse Regiments to supply these reinforcements, but that he and Brigadier-General Russell, of the New Zealand Mounted Brigade, had conferred and offered to take the two Brigades dismounted in their entirety in order to preserve the entity of the Brigades. Subsequently this offer was accepted by the authorities. The time at the disposal of the Regiment prior to their embarkation was short, and as the Regiment was at that time considerably over strength with the Reinforcements, they were able to pick and choose the fittest and most suitable men. The remainder of the Regiment were formed into a detail camp under the command of Major C. Mills for the purpose of looking after the horses and to supply reinforcements to the Regiment later on.

On 9th May the Regiment left camp at Heliopolis to entrain at Palais-de-Koubleh en route for Alexandria, where they arrived and were disentrained upon the wharf, where they were issued with fresh clothing and embarked upon the *Grantully Castle* about midday. The vessel steamed out with 446 other ranks and 26 officers of the 3rd Regiment on board. Upon the transport also was the whole of the New Zealand Mounted Brigade, including Brigade Headquarters, about 2,400 all told. The transport of the Regiment, including vehicles and horses, were not embarked upon the *Grantully Castle* but proceeded with the Brigade transport *Kingstonian*. The voyage passed without incident, and though the men were somewhat crowded, the accommodation and rations were very good throughout, and the men made as comfortable as the circumstances would permit.

The *Grantully Castle* arrived at Cape Helles about daybreak on 12th May, where she anchored for a few hours, and all ranks eagerly watched the flashes of the guns and listened to their roar. In the afternoon the transport again got under way, and arrived off the beach at Anzac in the dusk of the evening. Disembarkation was immediately commenced, the New Zealand Brigade being first to make the landing, followed by the 3rd L.H. Regiment. The method of disembarkation was by means of destroyers, which conveyed the troops close into shore, from whence they were transferred into barges in order to effect the landing. Several trips were necessary before the operation was completed, and during the landing the troops, many of them for the first time, came under actual rifle fire, the bullets playing all round the vessel, but fortunately no casualties occurred. When the *Kingstonian* arrived it was found that it was absolutely impossible to land the wheeled transport, and Captain Lewis was relieved of his command and rejoined the Regiment, whilst the vehicles and horses were sent back to Alexandria with a detachment under the charge of Transport Sergeant E. G. Lowe. Disembarkation of the Regiment was completed, and they were then assembled in units beneath the shelter of the hills that fringed the coast. After a short delay orders were given to advance across McLagan's Ridge into Shrapnel Valley, and with frequent halts, under hot fire the whole way, they continued their way until they reached the area between Courtney's Post on the left and Johnson's Gully on the right, where the Regiment was halted and bivouacked for the night in the valley. Early the following morning the different units were allotted bivouac areas. Headquarters occupied a natural ravine just to the right of Courtney's Post; behind them were placed "A" Squadron, with "B" Squadron in the rear, and "C" (Tasmanian) Squadron the furthest behind, just off Johnson's Gully. These positions were immediately occupied, with instructions to dig in, but whilst these operations were in progress an attack was made upon Quinn's Post, and this area came under intense shrapnel, rifle and machine-gun fire, resulting in many casualties, and the troops were then removed to a place of safety, and the future preparation of bivouacs took place mainly at night. During the day the Regiment was employed on fatigue duties, building barricades along the road, and digging saps and connecting trenches to circumvent the snipers, besides the usual Regimental fatigues, which were very arduous, as all rations and stores had to be carried up from the beach, which was distant about 1½ miles. During these fatigues the troops were much exposed to snipers, and casualties were frequent.

On 14th May "B" Squadron were detached and sent up to reinforce the 15th and 16th Battalions, who were holding Quinn's Post, and had suffered severe casualties in the attack the day before. They remained there for 48 hours, suffering severe casualties, and subsequently rejoined the Regiment in the valley.

On the night of 16th May one gun team, under Sergeant-Major McCaw, was detached from the Regiment and went into the trenches on Steel's Post with the 1st Infantry Brigade. The gun was posted on a trench platform, the parapet being strengthened in front with sand bags, but no overhead cover was provided. Sergeant-Major M'Caw and Driver Hampshire were wounded, and evacuated during the night. On the afternoon of the 18th, the enemy heavily shelled with 9.2's, and during the night they made several determined attacks in mass formation, some succeeding in reaching our trenches. Our machine gun fired continuously until shortly before daybreak. when the position was smashed up, and it was necessary to move to Courtney's Post, joining the 14th Battalion, where the gun continued to fire until the attack ceased. Trooper Roy Watson was killed whilst firing the gun. Altogether about 20,000 rounds of ammunition were put through the gun during this operation. Shelling continued throughout the 20th. The gun position was located on the 21st, and every morning at daylight the enemy concentrated a heavy fire on it with light artillery, which necessitated the removal of the gun every morning for a few minutes until the bombardment ceased. Owing to the importance of this point and the nature of the country it was necessary to keep the gun in the position selected. The section was divided into three, the first shift putting in 24 hours in the trenches, the second being in reserve and the third on fatigue. Owing to the activity of the enemy at night, little rest was obtainable. The Engineers drove a blind trench to within a few feet of the opposing trenches, in which an additional gun was placed, and on the nights of May 30th to June 1st the guns demonstrated. On the morning of June 1st the gun was again placed in the blind trench, and, in conjunction with the gun on the platform in the main trench, gave covering fire with good results to the 10th Light Horse Regiment, who attacked from Quinn's. The gun in the blind trench was located and the trench smashed up by shell fire. The gun was damaged, and had to be abandoned till nightfall, when it was recovered. Thirteen thousand rounds were expended during these operations by both guns. A few days later the New Zealand Infantry took over Courtney's Post, and the section rejoined the 1st L.H. Brigade on Pope's Hill.

New and alternative positions were made on the left of Pope's Hill, and five positions were occupied by the three sections of the Brigade. By this time the different guns had suffered severely, and all of them had several holes through the jacket, which somewhat deteriorated their efficiency. It was impossible at this time to get them replaced, and they had to continue in action.

On 17th May Lieut.-Colonel F. M. Rowell was detached from the Regiment to command Pope's Post, and Major D. Fulton assumed command. About this time volunteers were called for from men who had had previous mining experience. A considerable number of men answered the call and were detached and formed into a special unit, being bivouacked at the bottom of Monash Gully. Corporal Mason, of "B" Squadron, specially distinguished himself at this branch of work, for which he was awarded the D.C.M.

The following day, about daybreak, the enemy shelled the Regiment with 9.2 shells from the direction of Maidos. The position occupied by "A" and "B" Squadron came under the most intense fire, especially the former, who were temporarily driven out of their dug-outs. Many of these shells failed to explode, and an examination of the duds showed that they were dated back to the last Franco-Prussian war of 1870. They did very little damage, and their effect was very local, only one man being killed; he was caught in the open by a shell which exploded within a few feet of him. The bombardment proved the preliminary to an attack in force by the enemy on all positions, which started the following night.

On the following morning, when the attack was still at its height, the Regiment moved up into the trenches at Pope's Hill to relieve the 1st Light Horse Regiment, who had gone straight there on landing; a few details only were left behind to guard the stores and equipment. During the week the Regiment had occupied these positions on the hill below Courtney's Post; they had had a very strenuous time, preparing dug-outs and doing fatigue work along the valley, which at the time hardly presented any cover at all from the numerous Turkish snipers in the surrounding hills. The consequence was that casualties were numerous; indeed, in this Regiment they were more numerous during this week than in any other week of the campaign on Gallipoli. The whole Brigade was handicapped by the fact that their Field Ambulance had not been landed with them, and that satisfactory arrangements had not yet been made for evacuating with the Ambulance already there. This entailed a great deal of extra work upon the Stretcher-bearers, who had to carry the wounded the whole way to the beach to the Casualty Clearing Hospital there. The work of these Stretcher-bearers was beyond praise; they worked fearlessly in the open, collecting the wounded, and afterwards evacuated them along a valley which was more or less constantly under rifle and machine gun fire, and frequently shelled by shrapnel;

more especially was this the case on the 19th, while the general Turkish attack was in progress, as they evacuated not only our own casualties, but a considerable number of other units who were suffering severely, taxing the accommodation of the Medical Aid Posts to their limit. This standard of excellence was kept up during the whole period on the Peninsula, and there was no class of men who did better work.

Rations at first consisted mostly of tinned beef, biscuits, jam, bacon, and cheese. The beef varied much in quality. The jam, generally speaking, was very poor; the bacon very salt and fat, and the cheese, especially in the hot weather, unfit for consumption owing to continued exposure. Water was very scarce indeed at first; practically the whole amount was carried in barges from Lemnos and stored in tanks at the junction of Shrapnel and Monash Gullies, where the men drew their rations individually. The ration was very small and hardly sufficed for drinking and cooking. Fortunately, the sea was close at hand, by which means the men were able to keep themselves comparatively clean, although swimming was a somewhat dangerous pastime, the swimmers being frequently exposed to snipers and high explosive and shrapnel artillery fire. Great difficulty was experienced in drawing rations and supplies owing to the exposed position of the Supply Depot, and numbers of men were killed and wounded daily by snipers, and occasionally by shell fire. No provision was made at this depot for the protection of perishable supplies, and on the few occasions when fresh meat did arrive the men had the mortification of seeing it condemned owing to the fact that the flies, who soon appeared in millions, had rendered it entirely unfit for consumption. Sanitary accommodation was very difficult to arrange; the ground available was limited, and frequently positions exposed to enemy fire had to be utilised. There was an entire absence of any material to make suitable latrines, and this led to a great increase in the breeding of the flies and communication of disease from one to another by this means. Issues of clothing were plentiful, except that the issue of winter clothes was delayed too long, but there was absolutely no provision to store and salve the return clothing, leading to a great wastage of this material.

When the Regiment arrived on Pope's Hill they at once took over from the 1st Light Horse Regiment and went into the trenches, during which operation Major E. St. Lewis was severely wounded through the chest, and evacuated. "C" Squadron occupied the left sector, "A" Squadron the centre, and "B" Squadron the right sector, and remained in these positions for one week. The day shift lasted from 4 a.m. to 4 p.m., and the night shift for the other 12 hours. The shift off duty occupied the support trenches. Post Headquarters were situated just behind the firing line, in the centre of the position, and Regimental Headquarters behind the junction of the left and centre sectors; Regimental Details bivouacking in dug-outs on the side of the hill still further back.

Communications were maintained by the Regimental Signallers from Post Headquarters, wires radiated to the various sectors, and a duplicate line ran back to Brigade Headquarters. Lateral lines connected the different posts, and where the lines followed along a sap liable to shell fire these ran in a notch cut along the surface of the sap, but there was no extensive burying of lines; earth circuits were used, and the great shortage of telephone material brought many improvisations into use, especially in the manufacture of switchboards. At Pope's Post Headquarters an exchange was used composed of a portion of a shell box, into which rough brass bars were used, with cartridges for plugs. Bell telephones never intended for military use, which had been hurried from Alexandria, were commonly installed for lateral connection. Obsolete types of army telephones such as "D" 2 were brought to light, and again pressed into service. Visual equipment was held ready

A Gallipoli Trench

for emergency or to be used in a possible advance, but never actually came into action. Hurried instructions were given in the use of the telephone, but messages had to be spoken, as the Signallers were not sufficiently expert at this time to use the Morse Code, and conditions were totally adverse to extensive training of any kind. The supernumerary Signallers had already been absorbed before leaving Egypt, and on Gallipoli the number of the Signallers per Squadron had to be increased to four in order to ensure a continuous service; also additional telephone stations were usually required in the trenches, and these facts, combined with the loss of men evacuated sick or wounded, made it necessary to requisition reinforcements from the Squadron. Two Signallers trained at Broadmeadows, Victoria, arrived in each draft of reinforcements, and somewhat lessened the tension. At no time was it found that the establishment laid down provided sufficient men to cope with the great development of the Field Telephone as an instrument of modern warfare.

Although the attack on the Turks upon Pope's Hill was repulsed on the 19th, firing by them was continued the whole day and night, and the Regiment was kept fully occupied in the trenches.

On May 21 the enemy raised the Red Crescent from their position opposite Courtney's Post and asked permission to bury their dead, and under cover of the White Flag several Turks left their position, but retired on being fired on. Two combatant officers and one medical officer entered our position on Pope's Hill, where they surrendered and were sent to Brigade Headquarters. The enemy attacked immediately the White Flag was lowered, and kept up a heavy fire all night, but no actual assault was made on this position. Major D. Fulton, the Acting C.O. of the Regiment, was wounded in the chest and shoulder and evacuated, Major Barrett taking his place. The following day firing lessened to a great extent, and the troops in the trenches had an easier time, but the remainder of the Regiment was kept busy in improving trenches and fire positions, large fatigue parties working day and night for this purpose. Casualties were not very heavy, and mainly occurred as the result of sniping on the hill behind the trenches or in the trenches themselves from enfilade fire. To combat this picked shots from this and other Regiments were chosen and posts selected, connected by telephone to Post Headquarters, where these picked men sniped against the enemy snipers, and in a very short time proved their superiority in this branch of warfare, rendering the trenches and the valley itself much more safe. These men were practically detached from the Regiment, and relieving one another from time to time, devoted their whole attention to this one object.

On May 24 the Armistice that had been asked for was granted, and at 7 a.m. White Flags were raised on all posts and all firing ceased. Parties from both the enemy and from our own troops left the trenches and proceeded to gather the wounded and bury the dead. This work continued until 4 p.m. on the same day, when the parties returned to their trenches and hostilities recommenced.

On the morning of the 25th our Regiment on Pope's Hill witnessed the sinking of H.M.S. Triumph, having a good view of the whole proceedings, even the actual striking of the torpedo being viewed, the time elapsing between the impact of the torpedo and her final disappearance being exactly 20 minutes.

On the 26th the Regiment went out of the trenches into general reserve behind Section Headquarters in what was known as Headquarters Gully. Heavy fatigues were again the order of the day, and in case of alarm the inner defences were manned. The area allotted to the Regiment was too small to accommodate them all, and "A" Squadron, under Major Priestley, was bivouacked some distance down the valley, but on 3rd June this Squadron was sent to reinforce the 2nd Light Horse Regiment, who were now occupying the trenches on Pope's Hill, and who were considerably under strength owing to severe casualties received while making a sortie from Quinn's Post on the 15th. On June 4 an attack was made by the enemy on Quinn's Post, and the 3rd Regiment manned the reserve trenches, where they suffered casualties. In the evening they moved their quarters and went into bivouac at the foot of Pope's Hill as local reserve. Construction of the road up to the top end of Monash Gully was commenced, a task that led to the occurrence of many casualties.

On 30th June the Regiment again returned to Pope's Hill, the Turks having attacked the left sector of the post the previous night and been repulsed. From this time onwards the Regiment occupied alternately the trenches in Pope's Hill for one week, and were in reserve in the gully below Pope's Hill for the next fortnight. Parties were now detailed for the purpose of training in bomb-throwing, a training ground being allotted close to the beach. Sickness by this time had become very prevalent, which, combined with the numbers being evacuated, considerably reduced the Regimental strength, and on going into Pope's Hill the Regiment had to be reinforced with one and a half Squadrons of 2nd Light Horse Regiment, and from this time onwards no single Regiment was of sufficient strength to hold the post unaided, but on every occasion was reinforced, the reinforcements holding the right sector of the position. About this time rumours were rife of a big attack to be made on all the Turkish positions, which was confirmed by the orders received by the Regiment. Numerous fatigues were requisitioned to supply reserves of ammunition and sand bags, which had to be carried from the beach, a distance of nearly two miles. The troops occupied night out-posts every night. The additional work entailed considerable hardships owing to the depletion of the Regiment from sickness. Web equipment was issued, also colour patches to be worn on the back as a distinguishing mark for the information of our Artillery in case of advance. On August 6 the operation order was received for the forthcoming attack. "A" Squadron and two troops of "B" Squadron came down from Pope's Hill, where they had been reinforcing the 1st Light Horse Regiment, and the attack on the Turkish position commenced at 5.30 p.m. by the Australian Division on the right of the line by an advance on Lone Pine, which was in full view of the troops from Pope's Hill, and anxiously watched by them. The 1st Light Horse Regiment held Pope's Hill, and the 2nd Light Horse Regiment Quinn's Post. The 3rd Regiment were detailed as Brigade Reserve. Lieut. Barnett and 112 men arrived from Heliopolis to reinforce the Regiment, the strength of which was now 14 officers and 358 other ranks. These were the first reinforcements received by the Regiment since arriving on Gallipoli. The next morning the Regiment marched out of Pope's Reserve Gully and took up their respective reserve positions, "A" and "B" Squadrons occupying the flat ground at the bottom of the gully between Pope's and Quinn's, whilst "C" Squadron went up to Quinn's Post, where they waited in the rear to act as reserve to this post. The actual attack started shortly after 4.30 a.m. On Quinn's the first attacking wave failed to get past the parados, the troops being mowed down by machine gun fire, very few regaining the trench, and the position was so hopeless that the C.O. obtained permission to retain the second wave in the trenches at Pope's. The 1st Regiment, led by the C.O. of the post (Major Glasgow), were more successful, and entered the third line of the enemy's trenches, which they held for two hours, and then came under very heavy bombing and enfilade fire from Quinn's, owing to the non-success of the attack there, which compelled them to retire with very heavy casualties.

On August 9 the Regiment took over Quinn's Post, the 2nd L.H. Regiment occupying Pope's Hill, and the 1st. L.H. Regiment, who were much below strength, owing to their heavy casualties in the attack, going into reserve in the gully below. The Regiment occupied this post until October 6, during which period the conditions were very trying. There were practically no reserves behind them, and in consequence all leave to the beach was stopped, and the men were unable to take advantage of the sea bathing, and became very dirty and verminous. Rations were comparatively plentiful, but of very poor quality, and the sick rate became appalling. The troops were practically continuously on duty, and hardly ever left the trenches. A detachment of the Leinster Fusiliers were sent to reinforce the Regiment, but they were so decimated by dysentery, or other sickness, that they were of very little practical use. Fortunately, the enemy was not very active, and hostilities consisted mainly of reciprocal bombing between the enemy's trenches and our own, which on our part at least resulted in no casualties, except those incurred from our own bombs, either as the result of faulty manufacture, and incorrectly marked fuses, or from accidents occurring through the bombs striking the wire netting defences and falling back into the trenches. Occasionally, also, we came under shrapnel fire, which resulted in a few casualties. The troops behaved very well under these trying circumstances, and though many were sick and fit for hospital gamely refused evacuation as long as they were able to stand and hold a rifle.

On October 3 a detachment of 30 men, under Capt. G. J. Bell, D.S.O., left for a new bivouac area in Sazli Beit Dere, and next day a further detachment of 100 men was sent to join Capt. Bell, and two days later the remainder of the Regiment were relieved by two companies of 17th Battalion of the 5th Infantry Brigade and the M.G. Section of the 12th L.H. Regiment, and subsequently marched round to their new bivouac area, carrying their equipment and stores with them. One gun of the M.G. Section had, late in August, been sent back to the second line of defence in Monash Gully, where it was used for the training of the new men, and was also valuable in giving covering fire to convoys to and from the beach and dumps in Monash Gully; this gun now rejoined the Regiment, and the whole section moved round to the left with the other troops.

On October 7 official news was received that Lieut.-Col. F. M. Rowell, C.O. of the Regiment, had died from acute peritonitis on board the hospital ship *Gloucester Castle* en route for Alexandria, and was buried at sea. This officer became sick in the beginning of August, just prior to the big attack which took place on the 7th, and was so anxious to participate in this that it was only with great difficulty, after several days' sickness, he was persuaded to leave his post and be evacuated. To the Regiment already depleted and in a bad state of health the news came as a staggering blow, for during his period of command he had obtained the respect and affection of all ranks for his soldierly qualities, and the Regiment was confidently looking forward to his early advancement and probable command of the Brigade.

Once settled down in the new post the Regiment at once became busy in making a new bivouac area, in strengthening, improving, and extending the defences, by the deepening of the trenches already there, and the making of new trenches and saps for connection between the different posts. C Squadron were camped on terraces in the gully below Destroyer Hill, and B Squadron in dug-outs on the right side of Camel's Hump, where they linked up with the 1st L.H. Regiment on their right. The M.G. Section prepared a 33ft. tunnel through the bottom slope of Destroyer Hill, with a good gun position; and night firing directors were arranged on the gun platform. A similar position was in process of construction through Camel's Hump, on the opposite side of the gully, but this entailed long and arduous labor, and was still incomplete at the date of evacuation. During the nights they occupied gun positions between Destroyer Hill and Camel's Hump.

At this period for the first time on the Peninsula the Regiment got into touch with its Field Ambulance, which proved a great boon in the matter of supplies of medical stores and in the evacuation of sick and wounded.

Rations now became very much improved; issues of meal, milk, rice, and sometimes bread or flour, were added to the diet scale, and fresh meat was comparatively a frequent issue. Medical comforts were obtainable in fair quantity and variety, and a sick kitchen was established where men debilitated or suffering from gastro-intestinal complaints could receive proper feedings. The water ration, though still limited, became more regular, and a storage tank was provided where it could be chlorinated previous to use. Arrangements were made whereby parties could proceed to Imbros for the purpose of purchasing extra rations from the store ships there, this being the first opportunity the troops had of supplementing their rations by personal purchase; the stores available, however, were very scanty, and it was seldom that a quantity could be secured by any one unit.

By this time the Regiment was properly settled down in its new position; fatigue parties still continued to improve and extend the defences, and patrols were sent out nightly between our front line and the Turkish position, about 800 yards distant; corresponding enemy patrols were frequently encountered and shots exchanged. During the day the troops were exposed to continual sniping and intermittent shell fire. The sniping was most dangerous at the entrance to the Dere, where there was a mule camp, and this position also was the most frequently shelled; a few casualties occurred from this source. C Squadron's terraces were subject to indirect fire from the enemy, and several casualties resulted from falling bullets in this area.

The Regiment had now been six months on the Peninsula without a rest, and it had been resolved to send the whole Brigade in turns over to Lemnos to go into a rest camp there, and on 10th November the first party, consisting of a third of each unit of the Brigade, left for Lemnos. The Regimental party consisted of three officers and 63 other ranks. It was intended that this party should remain for one month, and then return and be replaced by a second party, but owing to the unforeseen circumstances of the evacuation they remained there until the troops had left the Peninsula, when they returned by separate boat to Egypt. Whilst there this portion of the Regiment resumed its training, special attention being paid to the lessons learnt during the war, especially bomb-throwing. Recreations of different kinds were also organised, which, combined with the rest and good feeding, rapidly restored the men to condition.

On December 12 confidential instructions were received for the Regiment to prepare for embarkation for Imbros on 13th and 14th instants, and in the evening, under strict march discipline, they proceeded to the rendezvous, where they embarked upon the *H.M.T. Abbassieh* at midnight, and arrived at Mudros Bay on the 14th. The following day they transferred to *H.M.A.T. Karoo*, and sailed, arriving at Alexandria on the 19th, where they left the following morning, and proceeded to Aerodrome Camp at Heliopolis. The portions of the Regiment who were at this time at Lemnos embarked on *H.M.A.T. Caledonian* on the 23rd, arriving at Alexandria on the 26th, from whence they entrained the following morning for Heliopolis, where the Regiment was rejoined.

During the first few weeks the health of the troops on Gallipoli was good, and the casualties considerably outnumbered the evacuations from sickness, but it was a very short time before lack of proper sanitary arrangements, and the hard conditions under which the men were living, caused a great increase in the incidence of disease, which steadily rose until it culminated in the period during which the Regiment occupied Quinn's Post, at which time there was scarcely a sound man in the Regiment. Evacuations at this time were very high, and this high rate continued later on, when we moved round to the left, though the greater majority of the sickness was probably during the period mentioned. In the few weeks prior to the evacuation the sick rate was again declining, as the men began to feel the benefit of the better rations and the comparative rest that they enjoyed there.

It was about the middle of August, 1914, that the recruits were enlisted for the formation of a battery of artillery, afterwards to be known as the 9th Battery, Field Artillery, Australian Imperial Forces, for services abroad. The command of this Battery was entrusted to Major W. L. H. Burgess, of the New Zealand Staff Corps, then on exchange duty from New Zealand. After some two months' training, the Battery was embarked on the troopship *Geelong*, and sailed on the 20th October, 1914, for an unknown destination. This ship called at Albany, when it was taken in convoy with other transports, and made its way via Colombo and Aden to the Red Sea, and it was there we learnt that our destination was to be Egypt. Early in December we landed in Egypt, and were encamped at a place called Mena, at the foot of the ancient Pyramids, the tombs of the Pharoahs, where we remained training hard until March of 1915. There the First Australian Division was concentrated and trained, and it was there that the 9th Battery first made its name, where, by putting up a record of coming into action and opening fire in 35 seconds, it gained the title of "The Galloping 9th."

In March, 1915, orders were received for embarkation, and early in April found this Battery, with other troops, on board a transport in Mudros Bay, the port of Lemnos Island, where we stayed until the evening of the 24th April. That evening we sailed for an unknown destination, knowing that on the following morning we would be under fire, and within the next 24 hours, probably in the heat of action. The sensation was new to most, and everyone was looking forward eagerly to receiving their baptism of fire. We were aroused at dawn on the morning of that memorable 25th of April, 1915, by the thunder of guns, and we found that our Infantry had landed on the precipitous and inhospitable coast of Gallipoli—a spot afterwards famous for the gallantry there displayed, and known as "Anzac Cove"— and through the drifting morning mist we could faintly discern the burst of shrapnel and the flashes of the rifles. As the mist cleared, we saw our Infantry established on the ridge, fighing desperately, and we were destined to watch them struggle for existence for four days without being able to render any support. On the fifth day orders came for us to disembark, but without our guns. This was done with enthusiasm, yet bitter was the disappointment of all at not being able to take our guns with us, and we were shortly to get our first taste of shell fire. Officers and men were embarked in large flat-bottomed boats, specially designed for the purpose, and were towed ashore by a naval pinnace. During that trip the enemy opened fire on us with high bursting shrapnel. This proved to be more terrifying than effective. Most of us no doubt were afraid of being hit, but what each feared most was that others should think he was afraid. Immediately the boats touched the shore the men sprang ashore, and we were immediately ordered to the right flank of the position. On arrival there, we found we were to relieve the 7th Battery, which had been in action for some days. The relief took place in daylight, and we began to look about. The guns had been dug in, and emplacements made for them in the foremost infantry line, without a single strand of barbed wire to protect their front from the enemy, and 200 yards in front of us was the Turks' position, from which our guns were plainly visible, and from which sniping was being carried out with appalling results to the unwary. This day was spent in close observation of the enemy's position, and fire was directed to registering likely points at which the enemy might assemble for a night attack, which was feared before the following dawn. This attack was made, and the Battery created considerable havoc amongst the enemy, and dispersed them with very heavy casualties, and prevented the attack from being pushed home. Four days later the Battery was relieved in turn by the 7th Battery, and our personnel were bivouacked on the side of a steep hill known as Victoria Gully. The day after this relief was carried out, Major Burgess was severely wounded, along with the Brigade Commander, and the officer in charge of the 7th Battery was killed. The command of the 9th Battery then became temporarily vested in Lieutenant J. R. Ellis. Some days afterwards, the guns of the 9th Battery were brought ashore, and were emplaced on the forward edge of a precipitous cliff known as Razorback Ridge. This position was well chosen, for it commanded an extensive view of the whole of the enemy's left flank, and commanded the approaches to our extreme right flank. It was an open position, from which direct laying could be employed; yet it was a position of extreme difficulty for the enemy to range on to, as time was afterwards to prove, for these guns remained in action in this identical position, in full view of the enemy, until the evacuation in December, during which time they expended more ammunition than any other eight-pound battery on the Anzac position.

One of the principal tasks allotted to the Tasmanian Artillery was to neutralise the Turkish batteries, which were emplaced in a grove of trees known as the Olive Grove, approximately 4000 yards to the south of our position. Here was located amongst others that gun known as "Beachy Bill," which used, at most inopportune and inconvenient times, to rake the beach and our supply depots. Although the Tasmanian Battery had not the show of power to carry out successfully a destructive shot against the Olive Grove batteries, they were responsible for, and always succeeded in effectively neutralising the fire of these batteries at any given moment; in fact, so efficient was the Battery in this respect, that on one occasion when "Beachy Bill" spoke at night, his second shell had scarcely arrived before salvo after salvo from the 9th Battery forced the enemy's artillery to desist.

On the 15th of May, 1915, the enemy prepared and launched a very powerful attack against our position. The 9th Battery opened fire on the particular task allotted to it, namely, the approaches to our right flank, and by their effective and well-directed fire inflicted heavy casualties upon the enemy, and were largely instrumental in preventing them from reaching our position.

Early in August of the same year we carried out offensive operations against an important Turkish position known as the Lone Pine. Here the Battery again distinguished itself, and in spite of the heavy fire that was continually directed against it, maintained all its guns in action, and afforded the maximum support possible to our gallant Infantry. It was for his services in this engagement that Major W. L. H. Burgess was afterwards to receive the Distinguished Service Order, and several of his men the Military Medal. The close of the Lone Pine operations marked the termination of our advance, and during that time onwards the role of this Battery was confined to harassing the enemy's approaches, and engaging in movement behind its lines.

Thus passed the intolerable summer with its heat, dust and flies, and winter set in with its hard frosts and heavy snow storms, which the Battery endured in its exposed position until the 18th of December, when the position was evacuated. Until the last moment this Battery kept its guns in action, withdrawing them as ordered, and, under orders from higher authority, left one gun on the position, with a crew to work it, until the evacuation was complete, when the gun was totally destroyed by the crew before leaving, and its crew embarked from the shores of Gallipoli on the last ship to leave that barren coast, leaving behind them many of their number, but carrying away with them honor and glory, and a name, the memory of which all Tasmanians should be proud.

The part played in the Gallipoli Campaign by the 26th Battalion was less conspicuous than that of some of the other Tasmanian, or partly Tasmanian, units, because it did not arrive until late. Nevertheless, it did good service—and paid for it.

The Tasmanian portion of the Battalion, "C" and "D" Companies, was formed about the end of April, 1915. "A" and "B" Companies were recruited and formed in Queensland, which State supplied, also, the Commanding Officer of the Battalion, Lieut.-Col. Ferguson. Lieut.-Col. Gould, of Tasmania, was second in command.

The Tasmanian portion, two full companies, each of 228 men, in one lot of reinforcements, numbering 44, received three weeks' training at Claremont Camp, and on May 22nd "C" and "D" Companies left Hobart for Brisbane, where the whole Battalion was assembled, and had five weeks' training. Here Lieut.-Colonel Gould died of illness, and Major H. Foster became second in command, Major D. M. Davis being sent from Tasmania to take his place as Commanding Officer of "D" Company.

On June 28th, the Battalion embarked, at Brisbane, on the *Aeneas*, for Egypt. It landed at Suez on August 2nd, and on the next day entered Polygon Camp, at Heliopolis. Here intensive training was carried on for a month, and on September 3rd the Battalion left Alexandria for Gallipoli.

The Battalion landed on Gallipoli on the night of September 12th, and three days later encamped at Taylor's Hollow, where it endured a baptism of fire. This happened next day on the road towards Chalak Dare. As a result, "C" Company had three men wounded, and "D" Company one killed and two wounded.

For several weeks the work of the Battalion was of dull utility, with risks from the enemy's fire, but no chance of a blow in return. Handling stores on the beach and carrying them, the making of roads, and wharf building, were the chief occupations, but always with additions to the list of casualties. For the last six weeks the Battalion held an important line at Russell's Top, where fighting with the Turks was continuously carried on at some loss.

It was while holding the line here that the Battalion had its first experience of tunnel fighting, which, owing to the proximity of the opposing lines, was carried on on an extensive scale. At one place the Turkish front trench was not more than ten feet away, and the tunnelling under the ground and bombing above the ground necessitated continuous and strict vigilance by night and day.

During Lord Kitchener's visit to Gallipoli, when it is assumed that the final decision to evacuate was taken, he came up to the Battalion's position at Russell Top, from which a commanding view could be obtained of almost the whole of the British line and from which the tremendous superiority of the Turkish position could be clearly gauged.

But, as with the rest of the troops, dysentery and other forms of sickness were the greatest trials the men had to endure. Amongst the victims to the dysentry scourge was Major Foster, whose health was so seriously impaired that he was unable to rejoin the Battalion. How cruelly this told on them can be gathered from the medical records of the casualties suffered on the Peninsula, which were 25 killed, 97 wounded, and 595 evacuated sick.

On the night of December 12th, the Battalion left the Peninsula, and went to Lemnos, where it had three weeks of rest and recuperating. After that the Battalion went back to Egypt, and, in camp at Tel-el-Kebir, had two weeks' training.

Early in February it was transported to Ferry Post, on the Suez Canal, where for some time it had the hard work of making fortifications and doing outpost duty. The next move was to Moascar, where the Battalion remained until the middle of March, when it embarked for France.

After being trained as a Divisional Train, the Australian Army Service Corps found, on arrival in Egypt, that the work of transport and supply in connection with the encampments at Mena and Maadi was to be carried out as in times of peace, accurate accounts having to be kept of all supplies. Most of the necessary forms had to be improvised, but, thanks to previous Militia Training of officers and a large percentage of N.C.O.'s, the work was carried on satisfactorily to troops and finance officials alike. On a much larger scale than ever obtained in Australia, supply depots were formed and the difficulty of preserving meat and other perishable goods was successfully overcome.

Stores to hold approximately 18,000 lbs of meat and the same quantity of bread daily, were erected by men of the A.A.S.C., large marquees were obtained from the Ordnance Department for grocery stores, and the regular work of supply was inaugurated and subsequently carried out. Contracts for the first lot of supplies were made by the British Head-Quarters Staff in Egypt, but after that the responsibility rested entirely with the A.A.S.C.

The overseas daily ration scale of bread and meat was not so generous as that allowed in Australia, where 1¾ lbs. bread and 1½ lbs. meat was issued. The Egyptian allowance being 1 lb. of each commodity. Suplemented with a daily ration allowance of sixpence per head, which was spent regimentally, the troops were, on the whole, well provided for.

Allotted to the A.A.S.C. were motor cars given to the A.I.F. by patriotic citizens who in many cases enlisted in order to drive them. These cars greatly facilitated the work of the unit as there was often difficulty in obtaining sufficient of the staff of life, and a hurried visit by a supply officer to Cairo for bread and other requisites was often necessary. It was not altogether surprising the daily baking of bread should have been belated as it is said that the ovens in use were those built by Napoleon during his occupation of the land of Pharoah.

Pending the arrival of the A.A.S.C.'s own Transport, native carts with mules were utilised, and proved very poor substitutes for our own horses and waggons.

Notwithstanding the many days required for getting horses trained for their arduous work after the long sea voyage, the animals in time adapted themselves to their duties and proved a credit to their Australian breeding. Men accustomed to feed their horses on good oats, chaff, and bran, were soon expert in the matter of new and hitherto unknown provender but always were dissatisfied with the class of "feed." Short-cut straw, called "tibbin" supplemented with crushed barley, maize, and an inferior bran, were the chief items in the new diet, and in season, a species of lucerne, known as "berseene" was found to be very beneficial to the horses. A host of Egyptians

Lent by Aust. War Museum

Transport in the Mud

were engaged in the work of crushing barley, and the ancient practice of grinding it between the upper and nether millstones was the means employed.

The G.S. waggons, manufactured in Aussie, were faithfully constructed and have been known to stand the strain of a load requiring 16 horses to pull it through desert sand. The Artificiers in the Unit were hard worked, but succeeded in keeping the numerous harness sets in splendid working order.

Some days prior to the embarkation for Lemnos, the A.A.S.C. were engaged loading transports. These supplies were taken ashore at the Dardanelles pending the establishment of a regular service distribution there. For the first week or two the rations consisted of tinned beef and biscuits; and the conveying of cases from the beach to the trenches was no easy task. On occasions, owing to absence of proper direction and consequent casualties, an issue had to be sent out from the beach depot as many as five times before reaching its destination. Later, when the troops had properly dug in, supply depots were established, and rations became more varied and plentiful, though firewood was always a scarcity and cooking in consequence problematical. Firewood, considered in Egypt a limited commodity, was on the Peninsula a much more sought after article. Supplies brought from the line- of communication were altogether inadequate. Many and varied were the expedients resorted to in trying to meet the cooks' requirements, but the supply never equalled the demand. Water had to be pumped ashore from large tank vessels towed to the beach from depots on lines of communication. This job of work devolved on the A.A.S.C., and the casualties sustained in carrying it out were fairly heavy.

Necessary supplies of all kinds were landed nightly from barges towed across from Imbros, where they had been loaded from supply ships. Owing to the darkness the work of landing and checking the goods was fraught with considerable difficulty, and this was augmented by the activities of the Turkish gun known as "Beachy Bill."

Quite a considerable store of medical comforts had been established in the depot on the beach, but not much benefit was derived by the troops as a couple of H.E. shells from Anafarta completely demolished the stacks, to the grief of many who had hopes of finding some means of getting their share of the luxuries.

In August, 1915, the large beach depots were handed over to the Imperial Army Service Corps personnel, and smaller depots established at various points in connection with the Suvla Bay and Lone Pine operations. The Australian Army Service Corps saw to the stocking of these depots, and issued supplies therefrom to the Australian Imperial Force and certain Imperial units until the evacuation.

CHAPTER III.

FRANCE AND BELGIUM I.

(12TH AND 15TH BATTALIONS.)

12th BATTALION.—Billets and Reserves.—The Firing Line.—The Somme Offensive.—Pozieres.—The Ypres Salient.—Back to the Somme.—Mud.—A Forward Move.—Louverval.—A Slight Rest.—Through the Hindenburg Line.—A Four Months' Spell.—Polygon Wood.—Out of the Line.—Wet Quarters.—An Era of Sport.—Messines.—Passchendale Ridges.—The German Rush.—Mont de Merris.—Scattered Fighting.—General Plumer's Commendation.—The Great Advance.—The Final Battles.—Demobilised.

15th BATTALION.—Re-forming in Egypt.—In France.—On the Somme.—The First Battle Pozieres.—Trench Warfare.—Back to the Somme.—A Bitter Winter.—Guedecourt.—Lagnicourt.—Bullecourt.—A Shattered Battalion.—Gapaard.—Lesquatre Rois Cabinet.—Desultory Warfare.—The Battle of Ypres.—A Rest that Failed.—A Defensive Line.—Post-Internationale.—The Attack at Hamel.—Cerisy Gailly.—Breaking the Line.—The End of Hostilities.—Christmas in Belgium.

The conclusion of the Gallipoli campaign had left the Tasmanian troops free for service elsewhere. After varying periods of refitting and reorganisation and some training in Lemnos and Egypt, they were, in different sections, taken across to France, where a new era in their history began.

The 12th Battalion embarked at Alexandria on the 29th March, 1916, and reached Marseilles seven days later, and on the afternoon of the same day entrained for Godeswaersvelde (God's Fair Field), reaching there in the early morning of the 8th of that month.

Here the Battalion had its first experience of billeting near the village of Strazeele, and was glad of shelter in barns and lofts rather than tents, as the first fortnight was intensely cold and wet. To give the men confidence in their gas masks, all were made to walk through a trench full of gas the next day.

On the 20th of April the Battalion route-marched to Sailly-Sur-la-Lys, where the Third Brigade took up the role of Reserve Brigade to the 1st Division, who were now in the line near Fleurbaix. The march was the first on the French pave roads (paved with nine-inch stone blocks). The weather was very wet, and after three months on the hot sands of Egypt the new conditions had a disastrous effect on the boots of the men. Training was carried on for three weeks, and though the village was well within range of the enemy's guns they had a quiet, uneventful time, excepting for occasional gas alarms. Difficulty was experienced in getting the men to take cover from aircraft, as all were anxious to see the 'planes, then quite a novelty to most of them.

On the 18th of May the 3rd Brigade moved into the line, the 9th and 11th Battalions being in the trenches, and the 10th and 12th in close support. Large working parties were sent forward each night burying telephone cables, etc. On the 7th June the 12th Battalion relieved the 11th, and took over the left sector in the line—all four companies having three platoons in the trenches and one in support. Subsequently it became the normal rule to have two companies in the line and two in support.

The 1st Division had relieved the "Bantam" Division (men under 5 feet 4 inches), and they had an immense amount of work to do in heightening all the parapets, which were also considerably thickened.

Considerable activity prevailed on the part of the trench mortars, and there were frequent duels between our Stokes and Medium ("Pudding") mortars and the German Minenwerfer. The Australians began to make use of their Lewis machine guns, of which they had two, though by the middle of 1918 they had 32 per battalion.

The 12th was relieved on the 29th of June by its sister Battalion, the 52nd, the relief taking place a company at a time on four successive nights, and the 12th returned to Sailly-Sur Lys.

On the 1st of July the British offensive on the Somme commenced. On the 2nd the Battalion billeted at Outtersteene. It is interesting to note that between the date they left there and the 31st December—a period of 25 weeks—the Battalion made 55 moves. On the 11th, after a five-mile march from billets, they entrained at Godeswaersvelde, and detrained at Doullens on the same day. It was a very hot day, and the Battalion found it had to march another 14 miles to its new billets at Halloy. This was probably the most trying march the Battalion ever did, yet, although a few men with sore feet fell back during the march, they all reached their billets within an hour of the Battalion's arrival at Halloy in the late evening.

The period, 12th to 20th July, was occupied in marching in five stages to the Somme battlefield in front of Albert, and the Battalion bivouacked in the old German front line trenches in Sausage Valley, near La Boiselle.

We remained here on 21st and 22nd, while officers reconnoitred the ground in front, and on the evening of the latter day we moved into the fierce struggle of the great British offensive.

The story of Pozieres is soon told—it is contained in the one word, "grit." It was our first experience under heavy shell fire, the artillery on Gallipoli being negligable, and the Fleurbaix sector a very quiet one.

The site of the village of Pozieres on the top of the ridge on the main road from Albert to Baupaume, made it of extreme urgency to the Germans to endeavour to hold the position, and long and grim was the battle for superiority.

On the night of the 22nd the Battalion moved up Black Watch Alley, a communication trench named after the famous Scottish Regiment, and in conjunction with the 11th Battalion made good two objectives in the form of a series of trenches protecting the village, and dug in on its outskirts. On the 23rd we passed through Pozieres, the 12th Battalion occupying the northeast corner.

On the 24th heavy fighting took place in the old German support lines on our right, and several counter-attacks were made on our front, but not pushed home.

On the 25th our trenches were bombarded out of existence, it being quite impossible to trace their outline in the mass of shell-holes covering the whole area. The great majority of our 365 casualties for the period of four days in the line were suffered in this bombardment.

The enemy had a great advantage, in that he was able to bring fire from our front and also from Thiepval on our left flank (almost left rear, so great was the salient). Although the Battalion later experienced many "hurricane" bombardments of much greater intensity, it never had to endure anything approaching that of the 25th July, when we were subjected to an almost ceaseless bombardment with heavy guns for 14 hours, from 4 a.m. to 6 p.m. Yet even through all this, the few heroes surviving at 7 p.m., when arrangements were being made for the relief (only two officers and about 40 men remained of the three front line companies) were successful in beating off several attempted counter-attacks.

It was a very small and very subdued Battalion that marched back in three days' stages to excellent billets at Berteaucourt, where we remained 12 days. Here a number of reinforcements were drafted in, nine N.C.O.'s were promoted to commissioned rank, and the Battalion reorganised.

On 9th August we started to move back towards the firing line, and at our first halt Captain W. W. S. Johnston joined the Battalion as R.M.O.

A few days' training and another four days' marching saw us bivouacked on 18th August in trenches at Tara Hill, just in front of Albert.

On the evening of the 19th we relieved the 4th Battalion in the front line, now about 1200 yards beyond Pozieres. Battalion Headquarters and the Regimental Aid Post were in old German dug-outs near a cemetery on the outskirts of Pozieres, a heavily shelled area, from which a level stretch of ground ran forward about 800 yards towards the enemy, and then there was a deep narrow gully, on the other side of which ran our front line trenches. A sap called "Ration Trench" ran forward across the level, perhaps receiving its name from the liberal supply of "iron rations" received from the enemy. The 9th Battalion on our left also used this communication trench, and a lot of casualties were suffered there. From the end of the trench overlooking the gully one could see the ruins of the famous "Mouquet Farm," which from its underground cellars and tunnels provided ample cover to the defending troops, made it a veritable thorn in the flesh of the British.

On the night of 20th-21st August we were shelled heavily at periods through the whole night.

On the 21st we received orders to advance our line, and at 6 p.m. the Battalion went "over the top" once more. Although a number of casualties were suffered, resistance was quickly overcome, and finding a small bank, the companies were soon dug in securely. Corporal H. E. Lord and a patrol of A company pushed through our own protective barrage and bombed the dug-outs in "Mouquet Farm" itself, though it was some weeks later before this strong point was finally taken and consolidated by the Canadians. On the right, where the old German support line was within the sector covered by the advance, a large number of casualties were inflicted on the enemy, Private F. Manser being largely responsible for the capture of a machine gun and the slaughter of its crew.

In this engagement the 10th Battalion on our right lost 120 men by shell fire in the front line between 5.30 and 6 p.m., and could not re-organise in time to participate in the attack. Fortunately, we were able to form a defensive flank to protect our new position.

All through the 22nd we were heavily shelled, and in the evening were relieved by the 24th Battalion, who were evidently seen moving forward, as such a heavy barrage was put down that the relief had to be delayed for some time.

After the R.M.O. of the incoming Battalion had taken over, Captain Johnston went forward through the barrage to the front line to render first aid to Lieutenant Leo Butler and other wounded men, for which action he was awarded the M.C.

On relief, we bivouacked again on the "Brickfields," near Albert, where General Birdwood came and talked to the boys about the recent fighting. The Battalion's casualties for the four days in the line were 230.

After a three days' march we entrained once more at Doullens on 26th August, and arrived at Proven (in Belgium) by 4.30, marching to billets in Poperinghe by 7 p.m.

After two days here and four days in "Ontario Camp," we moved to "Scottish lines," where a fortnight's training was carried out and a N.C.O.'s school started.

They next moved into reserve at Chateau Belge, then into close support in "Railway Dug-outs" half a mile forward of Ypres, and finally went into the line at Hill 60. This well-known spot is merely a bank built up out of the spoil from the Ypres-Commes Canal, on which their right flank rested, and was of such importance as being the crest of a rise which gave command of the communications for miles in both directions.

A great amount of fierce fighting had taken place here with a deal of mining, and the whole ground was a mass of mine craters and shell holes. The 3rd Brigade started rivetting the trenches with sand bags, when a heavy fall of rain caused almost the whole of a week's work to slip away and become useless, and the work was re-started with the aid of "A" frames. "A" frames are made of wood, with arms about six feet long, which are stood on their heads in the trenches, corrugated iron or wire-netting hurdles being stretched from one frame to the next along the side of a trench, the frame preventing them from closing in, and a duck-board track is laid along the cross pieces.

On the 15th of October the Battalion route-marched through most interesting country to Nordasques, about 20 miles from Calais. There they held the first ballot on the question of Conscription in Australia.

After a week's rest they received orders to return to the Somme, their first camp being on a hill top at Fricourt Farm. Heavy rain had fallen, and the whole place was a sea of mud. After miserable six days the Battalion moved to the outskirts of Bernafay Wood, a distance of about three miles, which took them nearly the whole day, owing to the congestion on the roads, progress being finally made by breaking down into single file. In this camp there was practically no shelter for the men, though tarpaulins were obtained later on. The initiative of the "diggers," however, was equal to the occasion, and many remarkable expedients were adopted to make a little hole in the side of a bank partly waterproof. To add zest to their enjoyment two six-inch guns were placed just on the edge of the Battalion's billeting area, and every time they were fired every light would go out.

While the Battalion waited here, the general offensive was being pushed on, despite the almost insuperable difficulties of getting transport across the miles of country torn by four months' fighting and now rendered a quagmire by the heavy rains. An endeavour was being made to push the Huns back to the high ground on which Bapaume stands, so that we could be sure of dry trenches for the winter. It was not to be, however, and the last push, on 5th November, rendered futile by the incessant rain and the interminable mud, saw us held in the bottom of a long valley, with the enemy on the heights of Bapaume, watching our lines of communication for miles back.

The Battalion's next tour of duty in the line was one of the worst ever experienced. It was still raining on the night of the 7th November, when they moved into "Switch Trench," a wide shallow ditch full of slimy mud and without a particle of cover. On the 8th the rain ceased, and the weather turned bitterly cold; the Battalion Headquarters moved into "Pilgrim's Way," with the companies in trenches in front of Guedecourt. The ground was so shell torn and rain-soaked that the sides of the trenches continually slid into the bottom, and it was difficult to obtain shelter or cover in them.

This was the Australians' first experience of a French winter, and the Corps had rather a bad record for the number of evacuations from "trench feet," though the 12th did not lose many, with the exception of D Company, which had a particularly wet sector and had to send 27 out of the line. After the Battalion had received instructions in the precautions to be taken to prevent trench feet, their evacuations almost ceased, and the Corps had one of the best records for the B.E.F., which fact is a tribute to the discipline of the men and to the Australian Comforts Fund for the socks forwarded.

The Battalion's next period out of the line was spent in a little village about four miles north of Amiens, to which town leave was given to a proportion of the men each day. The billets were poor and the weather cold, and everyone was more or less miserable.

On the 5th of December the Battalion went back into the line in front of Flers, to the left of Guedecourt. Captain C. N. Richardson was appointed the Battalion's first "Works Officer," his duties being to supervise the detailing of all fatigue parties and to secure continuity of policy. This later became a most important position in every Infantry Battalion, as it was of great assistance to a Battalion Commander in his administration.

The Battalion did not go into billets during its next period out of the line (13th to 30th December), but stayed in the war zone, out of range of all but the Huns' high velocity guns. Here they made their first acquaintance with the "Nissen" Hut, constructed like a baker's oven, of corrugated iron, being about 15 feet wide and 8 feet high in the centre, and normally about 40 feet long, though they could be built longer by using extra material, which was all a standard size.

The Battalion was chiefly employed in laying a telephone cable, which was buried 6 feet deep so as to escape being broken by shell fire. We had to work on Christmas Day, but left off early, and all hands had a really good dinner, the parcels from the Australian Comforts Fund being distributed in the afternoon.

On 30th December we relieved the 11th Battalion in the line in front of Flers, two companies being in the front line and two in reserve. A slight depression marked the inner flanks of the companies, and it had been found too wet to dig a trench here, so runners had an exciting time dodging enemy snipers when urgent messages had to be sent to the left company by daylight. The front line was duck-boarded, but the whole of the surrounding ground was in such a wet crumbling state that it was almost impossible to dig a "possie" in which to obtain rest. The communication trench forward was not duck-boarded, and the traffic soon churned the mud at the bottom to the consistency of soft glue, so that nearly all traffic had to go over the top.

On 8th January we were relieved by the 52nd, our sister battalion of the 4th Division, and on the 9th moved back to billets at Dernaucourt, where next day the battalion was bathed at Vivier Mill, and training commenced. At this time a number of partly trained reinforcements were drafted in to complette their training with the battalion, with which they were to serve.

On 14th we moved our billets to Bresle, just north of the Amiens-Albert road.

The end of January found us in a Nissen hut camp in Bazentin Wood, in which only the stumps of the trees remained. These provided an excellent addition to the small coal issue, and very welcome the wood was, as the cold continued intense. A good fire would be kept in a hut till 10.30 p.m., and yet by 7 a.m. next morning tins of milk and eggs would be frozen solid, and even the loaves of bread would be found to contain icicles in their very centre.

The weather being too cold for drill, and the fatigues not being very heavy, partly on account of the frozen state of the ground, great attention was paid to the tidiness of the huts, and every day the competition was very keen as to which should have its arms, clothing and kits arranged in the neatest and most orderly manner.

On the 11th February we relieved the 4th Battalion in the line at Eaucourt l'Abbaye, near the famous Butte de Warlancourt, on the right of the main Albert-Bapaume road. Two companies were in the line, and the greater part of the other two were billetted in the cellars of the old abbey.

No Man's Land was here found to be very narrow, even the enemy's Verey light flares falling in our front line. On 16th February a heavy "pineapple" (light trench mortar) barrage was put down on our forward posts, inflicting a number of casualties, including Major J. A. W. Kayser, who was killed a few days after getting his majority and before he learned of his promotion.

The frozen ground prevented any improvement in the line, which was here only some three feet deep, while our barbed wire entanglements (?) consisted of a single strand, which at any rate served to prevent men wandering into the Hun lines.

On the 19th we were relieved by the 10th Battalion, but remained in close support in trenches near the front line. On the 21st Captain Johnston, our R.M.O., resumed duty with the battalion.

At this time the 9th Battalion was out of the line, training for an attack on a small Hun salient which enfiladed part of our line. On the 23rd they came back into the line, and on the 24th a patrol they sent out found that the German front line had been evacuated. This proved to be the commencement of the Hun retirement to the shelter of the famous Hindenburg line, of which up to that time we had reports from the Flying Corps only. There is probably little doubt that to the 3rd Brigade is due the credit of making the first advance after the stagnation of the winter in the trenches.

At 1 p.m. on 25th February the 10th Battalion carried by assault the enemy support line which we had named "Wheat trench." The policy of the enemy in their retirement was to withdraw their main forces, leaving a few picked men with machine guns to hold up our advance as long as possible. As soon as the 10th Battalion had made good their objective, they were relieved by the 12th, who suffered a good many casualties in moving over the open ground just captured, the three officers of "D" Company, Captain Burt, Lieutenants Laing and Marriott being among the wounded.

On 26th a minor operation by a patrol under Lieutenant Hart cleared Malt trench.

At daybreak on the 27th the battalion went over the top, and cleared Le Barque and Ligny, two little villages, separated by a wood about 200 yards in width.

The composition of the attack was "A" Company, under Captain Newland, on the left, then a platoon from "B" Company next, half of "C" and a similar number from "D," who formed the right flank. The attackers kicked off from Wheat trench and proceeded along the Blue Cut road, and when Malt trench (about 300 yards off) was reached, the battalion formed into line and lay on both flanks of the road directly in front of the wood and facing the villages, "A" Company and "B" Company platoon on the left and "C" and "D" on the right. Here we rested, and awaited the signal to advance ahead. The signal—a pistol shot—was given just before dawn broke, and then we pushed ahead quietly, but swiftly. Owing to the open country on the left "A" Company found it necessary to advance along the outside of the wood in single file for about 200 yards, and then push through the underbush and continue the advance in line, the other companies meantime advancing in their original formation. Owing to the undergrowth, the attack was almost upon the enemy posts before being detected—the enemy immediately opened up a solid rifle and machine gun fire.

Sergeant Whittle and Lieutenant Butler were the first to open up with bombs. Meantime the centre and extreme left were busy dislodging the opposition. Owing to the swift and determined attack by our men, the resistance by the enemy was of short duration, and in a few minutes' time the battalion had occupied the trench running round the front of the villages. "C" and "D" on the right in front of Ligny, and "A" and "B" on the left in front of Le Barque and resting on the Warlencourt road. Owing to no connection here, a machine gun and bayonet post was established about 200 yards ahead to prevent surprise.

The total number of our casualties was not very large. Amongst the wounded Captain Newland and Lieutenant Bensley were hit during the attack, and shortly after Captain Webber was wounded whilst proceeding through Le Barque. Beyond intermittent shelling into the town during the day, we were not worried over much.

During the morning Captain Houghton came up from supports and took over as senior officer in the front line; later in the day he was successful in establishing outposts in front of our right flank and towards Thilley. Late that night we were relieved by the 4th Battalion, and then proceeded back to billets at Bazentin.

On 1st March we moved back to Dernaucourt, where a syllabus for a fortnight's training was drawn up. Here we first practised the attack under an artillery barrage on two, three or four objectives. Lieutenant Kelly, who had just returned from a School of Instruction, taught us the "model platoon" oganisation, wherein every man had a special task, being a rifleman, Lewis gunner, bomber, rifle grenadier, or "mopper-up." The duty of the last named was to go over with the last line of the attackers, when the objective was an enemy trench, and on no account to go past the trench when it was captured, but to make an exhaustive search for any deep dug-outs, and account (by capture or otherwise) for any enemy lurking therein. The necessity of these men had been learned in the Somme offensive, when repeatedly the first of a series of enemy trenches had been taken without opposition and passed over by our troops, who later were shot in the back by the Huns, who emerged from deep dug-outs where they had been sheltering from our artillery fire.

The men were very keen on the new drill, and worked hard. The winter, with its long spell in the forward area, and the "stalemate" of trench warfare again under the worst possible conditions, had reduced the morale of the men to a low ebb. Now, however, that the enemy had commenced to retire, and conscious of the leading part they felt they had played in starting that retirement, all ranks were in the highest spirits.

Casualties in the recent fighting (including three company commanders) had left the battalion very short of officers. Major Rafferty being on leave and Captain Houghton evacuated sick, left Colonel Elliott and Captain Jorgenson the only senior officers with the unit, yet despite the fact that three companies were commanded by subalterns and all were under establishment, the discipline of the battalion was seldom better than during this month.

On 15th March we moved to Baizieux, where Divisional Headquarters were located, and another two weeks were spent with musketry and field training, night outposts, and brigade and a divisional scheme being carried out. During this time the British line was being pushed forward, keepng a constant pressure on the retiring Hun, and on 17th March the 5th Division had the honour of capturing Bapaume.

On 4th April we moved to Mametz on our way back to the line. This was one of the few wet route marches the battalion had to endure, a heavy snowstorm all the morning making everyone most uncomfortable.

On 5th April we had a long march on duck-boards through the late battle area, passing to the right of Bapaume on to the clean, unbroken country tor which we had longed for the past four months, finally halting for the night at Fremicourt.

On the afternoon of Good Friday (6th April) the Battalion went into the line in front of the little village of Louverval. There was, of course, no system of trenches, but each platoon dug its own little "strong post."

We were now within less than a mile of the "Hindenburg Line," and the Battalion got orders to take the village of Boursies, the last on the Bapaume-Cambrai road before reaching the line.

The attack was to be made in three distinct phases, and after 24 hours' postponement A. B and C Companies went over the top at 3 a.m. on Easter Sunday. Owing to the brilliant leadership of Captain Newland, A Company on the right drove the enemy from a strong point at a windmill near the main road and made good the outskirts of the village. B Company in the centre, under Lieutenant Dadson, did good work with the bayonet in a sunken road, while C Company, in an open valley on the left, were held up by severe M.G. fire, and only partly made good their objective.

About 10 p.m that day the enemy made a severe counter-attack, but after a slight initial success were driven back with heavy casualties, and the Battalion was pushed forward and a lot of new ground consolidated by morning.

On Easter Monday, soon after daybreak, Lieutenant R. D. Newitt cleared some trenches on the south side of the main road, inflicting a number of casualties on the enemy, and a bomb team went right through the village of Boursies, reporting it unoccupied.

About dusk the enemy was seen to be retiring, and during the night the Battalion, supported by a company of the 11th Battalion, again moved forward, and dug in without opposition in front of Boursies.

This was one of the most successful engagements that the 12th Battalion took part in, and was almost the only one where it did not work in conjunction with other Battalions, except for keeping touch on the flanks.

On Easter Tuesday (10th) the 11th Battalion commenced to relieve the 12th, and by noon of the 11th April the Battalion was back in billets at Morchies.

After a few days' spell we relieved the 9th Battalion on the night of the 14th April in front of the village of Lagnicourt. The strength of the Battalion was now only 600, and we had a front of 3600 yards to hold, six yards per man, so that when sentry groups, platoon strong posts, and company reserves were supplied, it may be imagined there were fairly wide gaps in the line.

On the morning of the 15th the enemy made a determined effort to stop the victorious advance of the British troops. Some 12 regiments were rushed up from Cambrai, and about an hour before daybreak launched a heavy attack on a four battalion frontage held by the Anzac Corps. The enemy had orders to hold the village of Lagnicourt for 24 hours, to enable them to remove some batteries of artillery they had hoped to capture.

They struck with greatest strength up a little valley leading to the village, which had been taken over by our D Company from D Company of 9th Battalion some five hours earlier. It happened that this company was the weakest in the Battalion, and had the widest front to hold, and although the men fought with the bitterest determination, they were overwhelmed by weight of numbers, no less than 65 out of 110 being casualties.

A Company, under Captain Newland, B Company, under Captain Holyman, and C Company, under Captain Appleby, although hard pressed and almost surrounded, held their ground, and when daylight broke finally drove the attackers back to the shelter of the Hindenburg Line. Battalion Headquarters were about 600 yards in the rear of Lagnicourt in a deep sunken road, and here a gallant fight was put up by the Headquarters Details, stopping the breach in the line till the 9th Battalion was able to come up from the Brigade reserve line.

By 10 a.m. the line was completely restored, the artillery making some very pretty shooting as the fugitives poured through the gaps in the thick belts of wire by which the Hindenburg Line was protected. Soon after this Lieutenant-Colonel Elliott was wounded while going round the front line to see that all was in order.

April 15.—Major H. James assumed command of the Battalion, and at once completed the tour of inspection of the front line, and was satisfied that we had not only re-established ourselves in our old position, but that we had inflicted extremely heavy casualties on the enemy. This was particularly apparent on both sides of the sunken road, where A Company made their wonderful stand. We not only killed a large number of the enemy, but 155 prisoners and one machine gun passed through Battalion Headquarters on to Brigade. During the evening Battalion Headquarters moved up into the support line in order to be in closer touch with the depleted companies.

April 16.—A very quiet night and day followed the attack, and in the afternoon advance parties from the 7th and 8th Battalions arrived preparatory to relief. The weather was particularly objectionable for a relief—it rained heavily all the afternoon and well into the night, and in consequence the darkness was intense and the mud indescribable. The 7th Battalion availed themselves of the guides supplied by us, and effected a good relief of our two left companies, but the 8th Battalion preferred to act independently, and, in consequence, got badly lost—partly due to the intensely dark night. At midnight we sent out scouts to find them, and the relief was finally completed at 2.15 a.m.

April 17-21.—The Battalion moved back once again to the ruined village of Fremicourt, where the men were allowed to thoroughly rest themselves and smarten up generally. On the 21st two platoons of C Company, under Lieutenant R. D. Radford, were sent to Morchies to act as an escort to the heavy batteries situated in and around the village. In the event of an attack or a break through the line, it was their duty to form a defensive flank, or to delay the enemy sufficiently long to enable the batteries to withdraw. The weather was particularly fine during this week in Fremicourt—spring having come in almost a day. The Corps Commander visited the Battalion and conversed with the men almost every other day, and they were in high spirits in anticipation of the long spell the Corps was to get in a few days, as soon as the 2nd Division made a big attack in conjunction with the 3rd Army.

April 24.—It was rather a surprise, therefore, that orders were received on the 24th April for the Battalion to relieve the 6th Border Regiment in the Beugny-Ytres line—this being the Corps line of defence. The Battalion was relieved in Fremicourt by the Northumberland Fusiliers, and we in turn relieved the Border Regiment; "relief complete" was reported at noon. The accommodation in this line was fairly good. Some platoons were accommodated in deep dug-outs, others were in improvised shelters in the trench and in banks, and one company was billeted in the out-buildings of Delsaux Farm. They were all able to utilise their field cookers and thus get regular and hot meals.

April 25.—On the 25th April the half company of C Company, detached for duty at Morchies, were relieved by the 8th Northumberland Fusiliers, and reported back to the Battalion.

April 26-May 2.—The fine weather continued during the whole of our tour of duty in the Beugny-Ytres line, which was extremely fortunate, as after-events proved, for the men were able to thoroughly rest themselves. During the next five or six days a very heavy bombardment was carried on in the sector immediately to our north, and aerial reconnaissance was very keen.

May 3.—At 3 a.m. on 3rd May, the 3rd Army, with 62nd British Division and 2nd Australian Division, on the extreme right attacked, and —so far as the right flank was concerned—strong opposition and fierce fighting was encountered in the vicinity of Bullecourt. At 3 p.m. orders were received from Brigade for the Battalion to "stand to" and to be prepared to move at any moment. At 11 p.m. we moved, and occupied abut 1,000 yards of the Beugny-Ytres line, between Beugnatre and Vaulx, being to the north of the sector vacated.

May 4.—At 4 a.m. we were again warned to move with instructions to relieve the remnants of the 26th and 28th Battalions in the Noreuil-Longatte road. The Battalion moved off in small parties from 7 a.m. onwards, and, being under observation, were subjected to a considerable amount of shelling en route. The relief was finally completed by noon without casualties. The Noreuil-Longatte road is situated on high ground, and is only slightly sunken. Moreover, it is very little more than 2,000 yards from Bullecourt village itself. All communication to the forward area was done across country, consequently this road was a seething mass of 12th Battalion men, making themselves temporary homes in the "front line" side of the bank of the road, ration and ammunition carrying parties, stretcher bearers and walking wounded, therefore we were subjected to heavy shelling throughout the day. During the afternoon advance parties from the Companies and the Adjutant from Headquarters went forward to reconnoitre the forward area and make arrangements for the relief of the 2nd Battalion in the line during the evening.

This was effected without any hitch or casualty during the early part of the night, and A, B and C were in the line and D Company in support with Headquarters in a sunken road about 800 yards behind the line.

On taking over the line, it was discovered that we had penetrated the Hindenburg Line and were holding his first system of trenches, known as O.G. 1 and O.G. 2. Our right post, however, rested on the Reincourt road, and the unit on our right formed a protective flank, as the line fell back in this direction to Lagnicourt.

The 2nd Division, in making the attack, pierced the Hindenburg Line, and in spite of fierce counter-attacks and intense shelling, retained their hold. The 1st Brigade, on relieving them, had exploited the success by systematically bombing their way to the right, and had thus won 500 to 600 yards of trench from the enemy. This was how the matter stood when the 12th Battalion took over. On 5th May we continued these tactics, and crossed the Reincourt road, and by bombing our way along A Company were able to capture about 100 yards of trench, ably led by Lieutenant E. R. Heurtley-Reed.

Concentrated shelling during the afternoon, however, forced us to evacuate this part of the trench, which the enemy re-occupied.

May 6.—During early morning on the 6th May the enemy concentrated his forces on our front, and launched a violent counter-attack, using flammenwarfer. The strength of this attack forced our line back, and the enemy occupied O.G. 2 and parts of O.G. 1, but a wonderful rally was made by Captains J. A. Foster and J. E. Newland, and within three hours we had driven the enemy out and were again occupying O.G. 1 and 2. During the attack the Company signallers of A Company, with a power buzzer unit complete and some wounded men, were down a dug-out, and remained there during the whole attack, and were afterwards relieved by their own men again.

In the meantime D Company and Headquarters had suffered heavy casualties in the sunken road in the rear. This was under direct observation and enfilade fire from Inchy and Pronville, and was heavily bombarded all day. D Company was used exclusively as a carrying company, and did good work in keeping up a somewhat meagre supply of bombs and ammunition to the front line. After our re-occupation of the line, it was necessary to send D Company up to strengthen, and the carrying was done by all and sundry details at Headquarters.

During the night the Battalion was relieved in the line by the 10th Battalion. It is almost questionable whether the relief was advantageous, as the companies were withdrawn to the sunken road at Headquarters, where the accommodation was totally inadequate. The nerve strain was certainly relieved, but the shelling in this road was even more intense than in the front line itself, and our casualties were consequently heavy. Hot meals were brought up from the cookers at Noreuil, and the men rested—or, at least, did not fight—for it can hardly be called rest under conditions such as these.

May 7.—On 7th May, much to our surprise and disgust, the Battalion was again ordered into the line, and, owing to the weak strength, the Commanding Officer, Major H. James, reorganised it into a company, each company forming a platoon. He himself took the company into the line, and the Adjutant took one of the platoons. Two other officers, just arrived from schools of instruction and consequently fresh, were sent up from the transport lines, and each took a platoon; enabling the other officers, who were tired out, to remain in the sunken road.

Captain A. S. Vowles acted as C.O. by receiving instructions from Brigade Headquarters and transmitting them to Major James in the line. Lieutenant I. N. Holyman assisted him as Adjutant.

May 8.—During the night and the following day the shelling was intense at intervals, but no attacks or bomb fighting transpired in the Battalion sector.

Rain fell in the early morning and made the white clay trenches very uncomfortable and repulsive, and efforts were at once made to bury and dispose of the German dead which were apparent everywhere.

The Battalion was relieved during the latter part of the night by the 53rd Battalion, but just prior to midnight the shelling became so terrific it was feared an attack was impending. The S.O.S. was fired and the magnitude of the bombardment was trebled. This lasted the best part of an hour and a half, when it gradually quietened without any attack eventuating.

May 9.—Relief was completed at 3 a.m., when the Battalion moved out to bivouac near Vaulx, where a steaming hot stew was awaiting them. About 9 a.m. we again moved, and marched in easy stages via Beugnatre and

Favreuil to a camp in the vicinity of Biefvillers. The Quartermaster had tents erected and blankets waiting for the men, who were soon asleep.

The Battalion left camp at 7 a.m. on 10th May and marched to Bapaume. This town had been so badly destroyed by the Huns as they retired that an undamaged house could not be found, nevertheless quite comfortable billets were found for the men. Quite a number of men were quartered in the Hospital, whose roof was in quite good order, although the lack of windows made it rather draughty.

Great interest was taken in the ruins of the Cathedral, a hole in the floor of which disclosed a vault with a large number of human skulls, but no other bones. Diggers could be heard all over the town making discordant noises on the pipes taken from the organ.

There was a high rampart on one side of Bapaume, and the 3rd Brigade Headquarters was located in an old German dug-out in the side of this. Standing on the top of the rampart and looking back over the valley in which we had spent those four cold wet winter months, and noting how open to observation our lines of communication were, made us wonder how we had got through as well as we did.

A fortnight was spent in training, during which rumours were rife as to a long rest that was hoped for.

On 22nd May the Battalion moved by a long two days' march to Ribemont, a pleasant little village on the River Ancre. This was the commencement of what proved to be a four months' spell out of the line, as owing to the abnormal wet weather about the 31st July, when the attack on the Passchendale ridges commenced, the 1st Australian Division was kept standing by till 20th September.

The first week was chiefly occupied in cleaning up uniforms and equipment in the mornings and with sports in the afternoons. On 28th May a Brigade sports meeting was held, but as all hands were out of form no records were broken. Lieutenant Geo. Vaughan, 12th Battalion, won the 120 yards and 440 yards championships.

A small rifle range was formed in an adjacent quarry, and all hands were put through a musketry course. On 4th June a company competition in drill, bayonet fighting, and bombing was won by B Company. On 12th-13th June a Divisional sports meeting was held in a large natural amphitheatre on the edge of Henencourt Wood. Foot races, tug-of-war, and horse and transport events were the order of the day, causing intense interest to the crowds of onlookers. A number of diggers in fancy costumes caused roars of laughter between the events.

On 24th June the Battalion moved to Beaussart, a small village with poor billets, not very far from Beaumont Hamel. It was close to the old front line of June, 1916, and of course had not been cultivated, neither was it very shell-torn, so formed an excellent training ground. Here we carried out field training in anticipation of open warfare in the event of a "break through" in the forthcoming offensive, commencing with Battalion outposts by day and night, progressing to Brigade attacks, and culminating with a Divisional repetition of an attack at dawn on the village of Serre, as originally carried out on 1st July, 1916.

This fortnight was a fairly easy one for the men of the Battalion, but rather strenuous for the officers, who had to reconnoitre the ground in advance, and carried out several schemes without troops. Rain interfered with the training on several occasions.

On 6th July the Battalion returned to its billets at Ribemont.

On Sunday, 8th July, General Birdwood unveiled a memorial to all members of the 1st Australian Division who fell at Pozieres. Nearly all the senior officers of the Division and a large proportion of those of other Divisions and from the Australian Corps Headquarters were present, and a Guard of Honour was selected representative of all units of the Division.

On 12th July the Division was reviewed on the main Amiens-Albert road by His Majesty King George V.

On 16th July the Battalion moved to Bronfay Farm, near Bray-sur-Somme. This was in the sector held by the French prior to the offensive of July, 1916, and the camp comprised of long wooden sheds, the sides of which were sloped out near the ground, making a recess for the stowing away of equipment. In a large barn the Y.M.C.A. had installed a cinema, and here we experienced for the first time the pleasures of an evening "at the pictures," though later this became quite the usual thing when out of the line.

We remained here till 24th July, practising open warfare, attacks on villages, and did some field firing at disappearing targets.

The next move was a short one, to another camp a little nearer Albert, where we stayed till 27th July, on which day we had breakfast at 3 a.m., marched out at 6 a.m., entrained at 8.30, journeyed north once more, detrained near Hazebrouck at 5.30 p.m., and marched to billets at Longue Croix, where we arrived at 8.30 p.m.

On Sunday, 2nd August, Battalion Commanders received a call to 3rd Brigade Headquarters at 8 p.m. to find that orders had been received for a move to an area near St. Omer early next morning. At one time an order of this nature would have caused consternation, but on this occasion word was passed round at tattoo that the Battalion would move at reveille, and somehow everything was ready in time.

We travelled by motor lorries, and after an hour's route march arrived at Nielles-les-Blequin, a very pretty village nestling at the bottom of a valley with steep, thickly-wooded sides.

The Battalion was to have stayed here for a three days' musketry course, but the morning after our arrival it commenced to rain, and continued without ceasing to about 3 p.m. on 4th August. This rain had the effect of hanging up the British offensive on the Ypres front commencing on 31st July.

The Battalion returned to Longue Croix on 6th August, and on the 9th marched to Steent-Je, a tiny village about a mile from Bailleul, where we stayed till 13th September, practically "marking time" till it was our turn for the line in the "fight for the ridges." The time was employed in keeping the men physically fit with route marches, football and company and battalion sports, as well as training them.

On 28th August two composite Battalions from the 3rd Brigade marched past General Sir Herbert Plumer.

On 31st August Battalion C.O.'s attended a conference at Brigade Headquarters relative to the forthcoming attack on Polygon wood, and for the next three weeks all hands were busy preparing for the battle. A landscape model map had been prepared showing all the details of the country in miniature, and all hands were shown this, the various objectives being explained, attention drawn to "pill-boxes" and other enemy strong points. On 13th and 14th September the Brigade marched to "Scottish Lines." On 16th we moved to Miomac Camp, near Reninghelst, and on the 18th moved to bivouacs at Chateau Belge, near Ypres.

On 19th September we moved to Half-way House, a set of underground dug-outs close behind the front line. Shortly after midnight of 19th-20th September we moved off again, and though we had but a short distance to go, it proved a terribly arduous task. Rain had been falling for several hours, ceasing about 10 p.m., and the whole country was a sea of mud.

Although the head of the column moved very slowly, with frequent halts, companies in the rear found it impossible to keep touch, and only part of two companies reached the "jumping off" tapes that had been put down by the Intelligence Section by compass bearing earlier in the evening. A strenuous hour's work by Headquarters staff got all finally in place half an hour before "zero" hour, during which a further trial was to await us. The 11th Battalion was in front, close to the enemy front line, ready to seize the first objective, the 12th had the second objective, and the 9th and 10th Battalions in the rear were to pass through the others to take the third objective.

The enemy seemed to have become aware of the impending attack, and a heavy barrage was opened on the assembled troops. Fortunately, the soft ground caused the shells to burst almost straight up into the air, so that few casualties were inflicted except from direct hits, but the lines in the rear crowded forward in the hope of getting out of the line of fire, and for a while it looked as if disaster was pending. Fortunately five o'clock arrived, and with a deafening crash and rattle our barrage opened, and the whole Brigade streamed forward en masse in the glimmering dawn.

As the tale of Pozieres is told in the word "grit," so the tale of Polygon Wood is told in the word "dash." The attack was made under cover of a tremendous barrage, and the orders were to follow this closely, and so well were these carried out despite a few casualties from an occasional short-falling shell, that all enemy resistance was overcome before he could get his machine guns into action.

From the line of attack of the 12th Battalion one could see the barrage for about two miles on our left flanks, and a wonderful sight it was to see the dense line of bursts of smoke and dust creeping slowly forward.

As the enemy had excellent opportunities for counter-attacks with troops concealed in dug-outs and pill-boxes in the woods and behind adjacent ridges, the barrages halted long enough beyond each objective to give the troops detailed to take same, an opportunity to start consolidating the positions, so as to have a line of defence ready in case of the repulse of the troops taking the second and third objectives.

The signal that the protective period had elapsed and that the barrage was about to move forward again was given by firing a round of smoke shells from the guns, and a most striking and effective signal it proved to be.

The task of the 11th Battalion at the first objective was easily accomplished with the aid of the whole Brigade, and we soon moved on, leaving them hard at work digging in and organising carrying parties to send forward stores and ammunition for the other three Battalions.

It was a remarkable sight to see the men moving forward in this attack, most of them sauntering along with their rifles slung over their shoulders. Their apparent indifference, however, was only assumed, for they kept well up to the barrage so that the shrapnel was in many instances bursting in the air above their heads. Several instances occurred of men pushing beyond our barrage in their eagerness to put out of action the pill-boxes and other strong posts.

Lieutenant Geo. Vaughan won the Military Cross for a particularly dashing attack on a pill-box and surrounding trenches.

The objective of the 12th Battalion was about 80 yards short of the edge of Polygon Wood, and all hands set to work with such a will that in about three hours a complete trench was dug along the Battalion frontage to a depth of about four feet. We were fortunate in finding the ground here dry and sandy, and a great contrast to the sticky morass through which the advance had been made.

Just at dusk the S.O.S. signal went up on our left, and our barrage came down all along the line, but no counter-attack developed on our front, and at dawn on the 21st, in accordance with the pre-arranged plan, the barrage was again put down, and was reported to have smashed an enemy counter-attack that was just about to develop. A fairly quiet day followed, and that night the 3rd Brigade was relieved by the 1st Brigade, and moved back to Half-way House, arriving there about daylight on the 22nd. We rested that day, and in the evening moved back to a camp at Dickebush.

On the afternoon of 23rd September we embussed on motor lorries and moved back to Steenvoorde, where we stayed in good billets till the 30th. Most of the time was spent quietly, with Battalion drill and specialist training in the mornings and sports in the afternoons.

All hands were jubilant at the success of the long-talked-of attack on Polygon Wood, and at the short tour of duty in the line, with very slight casualties. "Shock troops will do us," was the diggers' verdict.

On 30th September the motor lorries carried us once more towards the sound of the guns, and we bivouacked that evening in an open field near Chateau Cigard. Just at dusk a Hun 'plane came over and dropped 16 bombs in quick succession near our field. Fortunately nearly all fell in an adjacent field, but the last three fell among some trees bordering the one occupied by the Battalion, and a dozen casualties were suffered.

On the evening of 1st October we relieved the 48th Battalion in support on Westhoek Ridge, one of the several that had been captured in the recent fighting, but some distance behind the front line. We were heavily shelled at intervals during the 2nd, and a lot of gas shells were also fired at us. Late that night we were relieved by the 4th Battalion, and moved back to bivouac near Chateau Belge, where we rested all the 3rd, returning to the line the same evening.

At 6 a.m. on 4th October the 3rd general attack by the British was most successfully launched, but on this occasion the 3rd Brigade was in reserve, and received many hard knocks on the lines of communication carrying forward supplies and ammunition, without gaining much glory. One most regrettable incident of this kind occurred on the morning of 5th October, when a party were waiting in a trench for the days' rations to arrive, when a large shell, landing in the midst of them, killed no less than 16 and badly wounded three.

On the night of the 5th we relieved the 4th Battalion in the front line, now on the forward slope of the main ridge, though further to the left towards Passchendale, the crest had still to be won. This relief was one of the worst we had experienced. The advance had been so rapid and the lines of communication so bad that they had been unable to get forward sufficient duck-boards to make a passable track, and continuous rain that had been falling made a quagmire of the shell-torn country through which we floundered, often up to our knees, and uncertain if we were moving in the right direction or not.

On the night of the 7th we were ordered to capture a prisoner in order to identify the troops opposed to us, and Lieutenant A. L. S. Davey, with a small party, ran a most successful raid on a small wood called Celtic Copse, capturing a machine gun and ten prisoners, and winning the M.C.

On the night of the 8th we were relieved by the 10th Battalion, but remained in close support. It rained and blew hard all night, not a very promising beginning for the fourth phase of the general attack, which was made at 5.30 on the 9th.

October 9.—No advance was to be made on our front, and after a most satisfactory daylight relief by the 29th Battalion, we moved back in small parties to a Nissen hut camp near Chateau Belge, where the quarter-master

Infantry on the March

Lent by Aust. War Museum

had blankets, packs and a hot meal ready waiting for the men. We left this camp next morning at 10 a.m., and marched along the wet, slushy roads by companies, navigating the closely congested traffic, and finally billeted in Scottish Lines Camp on the Poperinghe-Ouderdom road.

There is very little to relate concerning our 14-day rest in this camp. The weather was particularly inclement and training grounds inconvenient, therefore we merely resorted to close order drill and general smartening up, with plenty of recreational training to keep the men in good spirits. The enemy was very consistent in his night bombing, and hardly a night passed without bombs being dropped within a radius of 2,000 yards, and in one instance, just after dawn, in 9th Battalion transport lines, adjoining our camp. It is also interesting to note that the original 12th Battalion Band instruments were received from the A.I.F. Kit Store, and a band started for the first time in France.

October 24.—The Battalion moved out during the morning of the 24th, and embussed on the Busseboom-Ouderdom road, proceeding direct to Ypres, where we were comfortably billeted in the old battered Belgian Infantry Barracks, and remained there for a week, carrying out **brigade** fatigues and working parties.

October 30.—At 9 a.m. on 30th October the Battalion left Ypres in small parties by way of the Lille Gate and Menin road, and relieved the 8th Battalion on Westhoek and Anzac Ridges. Although we only rested here during the middle hours of the day to partake of a hot meal and to refresh ourselves before moving up to the line, we were shelled fairly heavily—as everyone was in this area—and suffered casualties. We moved again at 4 p.m., and relieved the 5th Battalion in the line on the forward slope of the ridge in front of Zonnebeke, relief being complete at the early hour of 6.45 p.m. A Company was in the line on the right, B Company on the left, D Company in support on the rear slope of the ridge, and C Company in reserve, at the rear of Battalion Headquarters, in the Soda Water Factory in Zonnebeke. The ground in front was in an atrocious condition, it being almost impossible to dig trenches of any kind. B Company, in Daisy Wood, in many cases built barricades of brushwood and took shelter behind them. Fortunately for us, under these conditions, the enemy was a fair distance from us, and separated on a large frontage by a morass or swamp, which was impassable. The front line companies were not troubled very much by the enemy, but C Company in Zonnebeke were shelled very heavily and consistently by guns of a fairly large calibre, which were evidently searching for artillery; and he also extensively used gas shells in the rear of the Battalion area, and Headquarters and C Company suffered casualties in consequence. In spite of the disadvantageous conditions, we maintained a hostile attitude towards the enemy, and patrolled vigourously during the night with strong fighting patrols where possible to do so. On the night of the 3rd-4th November Lieutenant Walduck took out a patrol and gained contact with the enemy on the Waterdamhoek road, and inflicted casualties on him before returning to our lines.

November 5.—The 4th Battalion relieved us by 6.45 p.m. on the night of the 5th November, and we proceeded without incident and during a lull in the bombardment to our old billets in the Infantry Barracks at Ypres, where we stayed till the 9th inst. Proceeded then to Vancouver Camp, in the Halifax area—a hutted area and probably comfortable under decent climatic conditions, but very cramped for even our depleted unit, and muddy in the extreme.

The Battalion left here on the 11th inst., and embussed for the Renescure area, being billeted at a village called Campagne-lez-Wardrecques, where we stayed for two days. The Battalion then put up a fairly good record in marching by leaving this village at 7.30 a.m. and proceeding via Blendecques—Wizernes—Clety to Campagne-lez-Boulonnais, a distance of 20 miles, without a single man falling out. We stayed here until the 18th inst., allowing the men to thoroughly rest themselves, and then marched on another 12 to 14 miles to the Hubersent area, where we were to spend our month's rest. The billets here were very meagre, the peasants unsociable, and the area very scattered. Headquarters and A Company were at Hubersent, B Company a full mile away in one direction at Fasurne, C Company a mile and a half in another direction at Rolet, and D Company at Bout de Haut. As a training area it was particularly good, plenty of fallow ground and paddocks being available for company and battalion manoeuvres. Miniature 20 yards company rifle ranges were at once inaugurated, and specialist training carried on for the first week or ten days by bombers, riflemen, Lewis gunners, rifle grenadiers, signallers, and intelligence platoon, interspersed with battalion route marches.

Training was then extended, and battalion manoeuvres were practised, including advance guards, outpost schemes, and trench to trench attacks. The country was well adapted for this work, and allowed of comprehensive operation orders to be framed and effectively carried out.

Battalion competitions were instituted in company and battalion drill and specialist's work, the Battalion winning the Brigade competition for drill. Football was very popular among the men during the cold weather, and—thanks to the Australian Comforts Fund and Brigade Y.M.C.A.—plenty of footballs were available for all companies, and great rivalry existed between them, and also extended to neighbouring units, especially the 10th Battalion and 3rd Field Ambulance. A leave lorry was also made available every day, and about 30 men went into Boulogne for the whole day.

The Battalion remained in this area until December 13th, when they entrained at Samer, and moved into a hut camp in the Kemel area and in rear of the Messines-Wytschaete Ridge. After remaining here a day or so, they again moved into bivouac, as a support Battalion, at Wulverghem, and provided large working and carrying parties every night for the 10th Battalion in the line.

December 24.—On Christmas Eve the Battalion relieved the 10th Battalion in the line immediately in front of Messines, and on the extreme right of the Divisional sector, being flanked by the 2nd Division and separated from them by the River Douve.

The country here was exceptionally flat, and a good communication trench led from the rear, past Battalion Headquarters, almost to the front line, although there was an overland duck-board track which was invariably used by the carrying parties at night.

The defences in rear of the front line were poor, and offered practically no accommodation, and considering the period which had elapsed since the ridge had been captured, reflected little credit on the troops who had occupied this sector. The country was in very good condition, and torn very little by shell-fire considering the important battle which had been fought over it, and formed a striking contrast to the ultimate line taken up after the Somme battle, which the Australians had to hold during the preceding winter.

During this tour in the line, snow was thick on the ground, and remained so until we were relieved on the first night of the year by the 10th Battalion. This necessitated a very careful camouflage of all new works carried on in the support lines and front line, as well as the dumps in rear.

Special snow suits were also provided for the patrols, who went out every night and easily maintained a superiority in No Man's Land.

On December 28th the Battalion suffered a great loss in the deaths of Captain W. A. Connell, Lieutenants J. A. Campbell and P. T. Miller, all of whom were killed in B Company Headquarters by a small pineapple bomb.

January 2.—We moved back again to Wulverghem, and acted again as a support battalion, Headquarters, A and C Companies being in the camp there. B Company at Bristol Farm, and D Company in close support at Bethlehem Farm. Each night large working and carrying parties were sent forward to carry R.E. material into the front line and to continue the defence works in support and reserve trenches.

Before going into the line again the thaw commenced, and roads were in a deplorable condition. Trenches were almost uninhabitable, and owing to the sides fretting, the riveting frames were almost useless.

On 9th January we again relieved the 10th Battalion in the same sector, and the state of the tenches after inspection was almost worse than anticipated. Duck-boards at the bottom of the trench—ostensibly to keep the men's feet dry—had sunk in four inches or five inches of mud, and were lost to sight. The looseness of the soil in these parts, and, in consequence, the excellent quality of the mud, easily compensated for the lack of shell holes commented upon previously. The weather thus seriously hampered the progress of the work.

During the whole of the 15th January and during the night, it rained incessantly, and thus the River Douve flooded, being over 100 yards wide in parts—and made the trenches uninhabitable, many being waist deep in water. The Germans were in a no better plight, for all that day, they—as well as our fellows—were forced to expose themselves and to dry their clothes in the sun. One of the cookers, situated at Stinking Farm, on the banks of the Douve, was washed away, with many hot food containers and gum boots. The former was recovered when the floods subsided, but many of the latter —never. It was during such periods as these that the constant supply of socks supplied by our Comforts Fund and other similar institutions proved invaluable. We had a drying room at Stinking Farm, and a pair of dry socks was sent up into the line every night for every man with the rations, and the wet ones returned at dawn and dried again during the day.

The 8th Battalion relieved us on the 16th January, and we once again pulled back to our old camp at Wulverghem, this time occupying the role of forward Battalion of the support Brigade.

During the day men were sent out working on the roads and decauville railways, and C Company went "en masse" to Liffey House dug-outs to work for the Divisional Signalling Company under very uncomfortable and cheerless conditions.

January 23rd.—On this day we once again trekked back to our familiar sector, relieving the 8th Battalion.

A particularly quiet tour ensued, in fact, it was almost uncanny in its quietness. For three days the enemy was not heard to fire a single gun and not a machine gun, although our 18-pounders harassed his tracks and our Vickers and Lewis guns kept up a continuous fire at night.

On 25th January General Birdwood visited the Battalion, going right through the support lines and then on to the other Battalions of the 3rd Brigade on our left.

This tour of the line was completed without incident at 9.25 p.m. on 31st January, when we were relieved by the 30th Battalion, 5th Division, and moved back to a very fine camp at Neuve Eglise, known as Shankill Huts.

A very pleasant month was spent here. Lieutenant-Colonel Elliott was temporarily in command of the 3rd Brigade, and Major H. A. MacPherson acted as C.O. 12th, and when he went on leave Major J. A. Foster assumed the command.

The weather was generally fine, though cold. In the mornings training was carried on and in the afternoons football and other sports kept the men fit and busy. The 3rd Brigade Concert Party, "The Boomerangs," gave performances nightly to crowded houses in a large hall in Neuve Eglise.

Several very interesting lectures on the early stages of the War, and on the battles of Verdun, Ypres, etc., illustrated by large diagrams, were given by Captain Blis, lecturer to the 2nd Army, and were followed very closely by appreciative crowds of the diggers.

A Divisional football competition (Australian rules) was held during the month, the 10th Battalion winning from the 12th in the Brigade preliminary, though they in their turn were defeated by the 8th (Victorian) Battalion in the final.

The Battalion was more successful in a rifle shooting competitoin, held at this time, scoring a very fine win indeed. The Army Rifle Association (England) presented medals for a platoon competition in each division of the B.E.F., one Lewis gun team of three and 17 riflemen, under their officer, to fire at disappearing targets from three different ranges.

Competitions were first held between the 16 platoons of each Battalion, then between the winning Battalion platoon of each Brigade, and the three winning Brigade platoons competed on an independent range for the Divisional championship. No 2 platoon, A Company, 12th Battalion, commanded by Lieutenant A. W. Clemes, scored an easy win in each competition, the closest being in that between the platoons of its own Battalion, and were keenly disappointed that they could not try their skill against the winning platoons of the other four Divisions for the championship of the Australian Corps.

On 19th February a Battalion sports meeting was held, and in the evening partook of a belated Christmas dinner, the Australian Comforts Fund parcels being also distributed. Great was the excitement and pleasure of every man as he unfastened the ribbon and opened his cardboard box from "home."

On 27th February we were pleased to welcome back to the Battalion our "Doc.," Major Johnston, wounded at Polygon Wood.

About this time the 40th Battalion moved to a camp about a mile from ours, and many visits were paid to old friends from Tassie. On the 28th we had the pleasure of beating our countrymen in a friendly game of football.

On 2nd March we embussed once more, and moved back towards the line again, a piercing wind making it one of the coldest days of the winter. On this occasion we were in the sector between that recently occupied and the one occupied on our first visit to the Ypres sector in October, 1916, that is to say, our left flank now rested on Hill 60, which had been our right flank formerly. The battles of June-October, 1917, however, had now given us the high ground of the Messines-Passchendale ridges, and our reserve line was now approximately where our front line had previously been.

Our first quarters were in Crater dug-outs, a long set of catacombs in a spoil bank on the side of the Ypres-Comines Canal. Here we stayed till the 10th, sending working parties forward each night, and then relieved the 10th Battalion in the line in front of White Chateau. Just as the relief was complete, Captain Harry Webber, who had risen from private to be one of the senior company commanders, was killed by a shell which burst in his dug-out.

On 13th March about 60 of the enemy made a raid on one of our posts, which was repulsed with heavy loss, and six unwounded and five wounded

Huns were taken prisoners. The local commander sent in the following report:—"To Adjutant,—Fritz had a go, but came a thud. Can I have two platoons to repair support line? Our casualties are fairly slight. About six more wounded squids are on our wire yet."

At this time a lot of gas was being used, and on the early morning of the 17th the enemy subjected our back areas to a heavy bombardment of gas shells for about two hours. Although other units suffered casualties, none of the 12th were evacuated gassed.

All hands were hard at work strengthening our trenches and defensive works generally, as we had been warned that a big German offensive was expected. On 22nd March we received word that the blow had fallen the previous day in the south, from the Scarpe to the Oise.

The Brigade expected to be relieved on the 24th, but on this day the 10th Battalion had to come into the line again, as the 2nd Brigade, which was to have taken our place, relieved the whole of the 2nd Division on our left, so that, that unit would be free to join the 3rd, 4th, and 5th Australian Divisions already on their way south to help stop the push for Amiens.

The 12th Battalion moved back to Crater Dug-outs, where it was relieved on 3rd March by units which had been engaged in the German attack.

On the 4th motor lorries conveyed the Brigade to Caestre, where we entrained on the 5th (after billeting the night at Borre), detraining at Amiens at 7 a.m. the next morning. We were billeted at Coisy and Flesselles till 12th April, and had just got orders to send officers forward to reconnoitre the line where the other four Australian Divisions were busily engaged stemming back the oncoming hordes of the enemy, when we received orders to return to the north, where the enemy on 9th April had made the second phase of his attack, pushing through our lightly held lines near Armentieres.

On the evening of the 12th we bivouacked near the citadel overlooking Amiens, and a grand, though awe-inspiring, view we had. As soon as it got dark flights of enemy aircraft came over, dropping bombs on the town, causing fires in many cases. They seemed to make a special target of the railway station, where we were to entrain later in the night, and in fact the 2nd Brigade had 80 casualties there that evening.

At 1.30 a.m. on the 13th we moved off, and by 2 a.m. were waiting in the streets outside the station. At 4.30 we entrained, but owing to the civilian signal and points—men having taken shelter from another raid, we did not move till 7.15, when we shunted to another line. After waiting here till 8.45 we drew out to a cutting on the outskirts of Amiens, where we were left till 10.45, when we started off finally.

About 11.30 p.m. we reached Hondegham, detrained at midnight, and marched via Hazebrouck to Borre. What a difference 10 days had made in this little village—on the 4th everything so quiet and peaceful and on the 14th the whole place deserted and many houses shattered.

During the last 48 hours the 1st and 2nd Brigades had marched forward North of the Forest of Nieppe till they met the oncoming Hun, where they had forced him to halt and dig in. The 3rd Brigade, coming up later, was kept in reserve, and dug a line of strong posts in front of the villages of Borre and Pradells to hold the ridge running from Hazebrouck to Strazelle. The sudden break through of the Germans had caused a large belt of rich pastoral country to be evacuated by the inhabitants. Fresh milk, poultry, and roast pork in consequence formed a welcome addition to our menu for quite a while. The majority of Battalions kept a regimental cow for some time, but we nevertheless did a lot of work to save the cattle of our Allies, on one day no less than 95 beasts being handed over to the representative of the **French Mission.**

In addition to the 1st Australian and other British Divisions that were sent to stop the rush for Hazebrouck a number of French troops were rushed to the spot, and on 19th April the 12th Battalion relieved a French regiment opposite Meteren.

At Battalion Headquarters the services of an interpreter rendered the relief an easy matter. The French commander was most particular to explain the whole of his sector, drawing a number of plans to clear up points not clear on our maps, but some of the junior commanders had to find out about their front by personal reconnaisance. One company commander reported relief complete in the following terms:—"Adjutant, 12th Battalion. Absolutely tickled to death; he can't speak English, I can't speak French, so there you are. I know as much now as when I started. Everything O.K."

For a couple of days we were busy digging in and strengthening the position, a lot of sniping being done by the opposing forces, when we got orders that the village of Meteren, which was on high ground giving a good view of the surrounding country, was to be attacked. Again the plan of making the attack in more than one phase was adopted, and on the night of 22nd/23rd April the 12th Battalion on the right and 11th Battalion on the left pushed their flanks forward with a view to encircling the village. The attack by our "B" Company was most successful, a number of prisoners and machine guns being captured.

The next evening we were relieved by the 9th and 10th Battalions, who were not so successful in completing the attack, the enemy being warned by their previous evening's experience. "A" Company 12th Battalion, which had been in reserve during our attack, lost Lieutenant Heurtley-Reed and a number of men in attempting to "mop up" the village after it should have been surrounded by the other Battalions.

After a few days in support where our billets were intermittently shelled the days being spent in trench digging, the 3rd Brigade on the 28th moved into reserve, the 12th Battalion being billeted in a hut camp at Borre railway siding, formerly occupied by a railway unit.

We remained here six days, sending working parties forward to the line at night. Only one shell fell in the camp, and that most unfortunately burst right on one of the huts, killing 11 and wounding 14 of the occupants.

On 4th May we returned to the line, relieving the 8th Battalion in front of Strazeele Station, about a mile to the right (south) of our previous sector, and spent four wet days there. It was a comparatively quiet time, except for a raid on one of our posts, on the 8th inst., which was repulsed without loss on our side. Lieutenant E. W. D. Laing, while standing on the parapet directing a working party, was killed by a shell early on 8th May.

On relief by the 10th Battalion we moved into support near Pradelles, Battalion Headquarters being in a large cellar of the village brewery, and was made very comfortable with furniture salvaged from the ruins of the local Chateau.

On the 13th May we moved into reserve, bivouacing at La Creule, near Hazebrouck. Here training was commenced again, special attention being given to Lewis gunners, and the Battalion was given a hot bath in baths erected near by.

On 18th May we moved back to the Sercus area, about four miles behind Hazebrouck. For eight days we carried out specialist training and Battalion drill in the mornings, and recreational training and sports in the afternoons, the Brigade concert party giving open air performances in the evenings.

On 22nd May the Brigade was inspected by, and marched past the Divisional Commander, General Sir H. B. Walker.

On the 27th we relieved the 3rd Battalion in front of Strazeele station, having moved half the Battalion frontage to the right of the sector previously occupied. The policy of daylight raiding was continued with unvaried success, the enemy being given no respite by the daring initiative of the "diggers."

The culminating point was reached at 1 a.m. on 3rd June, when the Brigade brilliantly captured the Mont de Merris, a small hill overlooking a large portion of our lines in this sector.

The attack was made with a trench mortar barrage, which opened in the midst of an enemy relief, inflicting heavy casualties. Two hundred and thirty prisoners and a large number of machine guns and trench mortars were captured. The bulk of the attack fell to the lot of the 11th Battalion, only our "D" Company being engaged.

On 4th June we were relieved by the 6th Battalion and moved to La Kreule. On the 6th, and 4th Battalion C.O.'s and the G.O.C. 3rd Brigade were summoned to Divisional Headquarters, where they were congratulated by General Sir Herbert Plumer, 2nd Army Commander, on the success of the attack on Mont de Merris.

On 7th June we moved back to Sercus once more, where our week's training was marked by an outbreak of "Spanish Influenza" then prevalent on the Continent. About 80 men were evacuated from the Battalion in a few days.

On 12th June a Brigade sports meeting was held, the 10th Battalion beating the 12th by a couple of points for the General's Cup. Captain W. R. Jorgenson won the 100 yards championship, and the 12th, the tug-o'-war.

On 16th the Battalion moved into support near Pradelles, and was employed strengthening Strazeele defences.

On 25th June we relieved the 9th Battalion in the front line on the Strazeele front, astride the Bailleul-Hazebrouck railway. "B" and "D" Companies were in line, the latter being on the left, and "A" and "C" Companies in support. Battalion Headquarters was situated in a farmhouse on the railway, about 1000 yards in the rear of the line.

The enemy at this particular period was very nervy, and any slight artillery activity on either flank would bring down an S.O.S. barrage on his whole divisional front. The battalion experienced this on the night 2nd-3rd July, when the 8th Battalion raided the enemy—two battalion frontages to our left—and extremely heavy retaliatory fire was put down on our entire front, but by sheer luck we suffered no casualties at all. At this time we had some American officers and N.C.O.'s attached to the unit for experience, and this was the first time they had heard or seen shell fire to any extent, and according to the report they submitted to their company, they were much impressed, both at the intensity of the fire, the flare signals used by the Germans, and most of all the coolness of our men through it all.

Just before dark, on the evening of the 4th July, the enemy put down a violent barrage on the front line, particularly on Mont de Merris, which the 10th Battalion occupied, and the left of our sector, where "D" Company were entrenched. This soon extended over the whole of the Strazeele defences and along the main road to Pradelles. Communication was soon lost to our left front line and support companies, but we kept touch with our right companies, and, fortunately, by a direct line with 10th Battalion Headquarters on our left. It afterwards transpired that the enemy attempted a twilight raid on our "D" Company and the 10th Battalion on the left, but was completely repulsed without obtaining identification of any kind. The whole incident—although intense—only lasted about three-quarters of an hour, after which we passed an abnormally quiet night.

On the evening of the 5th July we were relieved by the 1st Battalion without incident, and moved back to a camp at Weke Meulin, about a mile out of Hazebrouck.

The training in this camp was restricted to a large extent owing to the activity of enemy aircraft, so that platoon lectures and instruction were generally given in the shadow and shelter of the hedges around the fields. One company a day—together with Lewis Gunners—fired on the 100 yards rifle range. The Battalion also had to supply working parties under the supervision of Engineer and Pioneer Battalion officers, who worked on the Divisional and Corps lines of defence around Borre and Hazebrouck.

Another move was made on the 13th July by daylight, when we relieved the 8th Battalion in a reserve position in rear of Rouge Croix. Although the trenches and accommodation were better than is generally provided in reserve positions of this kind (sundry mattresses, chairs, etc., from neighbouring farm houses), no one felt really comfortable, owing to the fact that a 12 inch gun was situated in our midst, and would belch forth when least expected, and bring retaliatory fire upon the sector.

We were not exactly sorry, therefore, when we received orders to move forward on the evening of the 15th July to a position in the support line. "B" and "C" Companies occupied positions in the Court Croix Switch and "A" and "B" Companies in the Rouge Croix Switch. Battalion H.Q. was situated over a mile in the rear, at Mango Farm which made administrative work particularly difficult, for, as an example, it took Headquarters officers 4½ hours to make a tour of inspection of two companies only, by which time it was almost daylight.

Nothing of much importance happened, until the night 21st-22nd July, when we relieved the 9th Battalion in the line on the Moolenacker sector. "A" and "B" Companies were in the line, "B" Company in support and "C" Company in reserve. "D" Company on the left was subjected to a considerable amount of shelling from light field guns, in fact, the Company headquarters eventually became untenable and was blown in on the night of the 23rd July.

The British Division on our left (on the opposite side of the stream or ditch known as Meteren Becque) was raided on the night 25th-26th July and without advising us of their plan of action, evacuated their front line posts and retired to the support line. This left our flank in the air, therefore "D" Company, using their initiative, sent out a fighting patrol with a Lewis gun and surprised a party of Germans in their new position and finished up by capturing a machine gun and killing its crew. On meeting the opposition, the raiding party apparently withdrew and we were able to tell our neighbours that things were again normal, and they once again occupied their old line.

An inter-company relief took place on the 26th-27th. "B" and "C" Companies moving into the line-(the latter on the left) "A" Company in support and "D" Company in reserve.

Instructions were received from Brigade H.Q. that it was essential to discover the identity of the unit on our front, and in consequence a fighting patrol was sent out from "B" Company on the right under Corporal Hammersley. The patrol very soon came into contact with the enemy, who put up a stiff resistance. The N.C.O. soon discovered that a party of the enemy had moved out and were endeavouring to cut off his retreat, and he at once brought his Lewis gun to bear on the isolated post and ordered his men to retire whilst he covered their retreat. During this plucky action he was himself wounded and it is gratifying to know that his bravery was in some measure compensated by the award of a bar to his Military Medal. The object of the patrol was also attained, for one member brought in a shoulder-strap of one of the Germans they had killed—the 13th R.I.R.

The 10th Battalion attacked on our right on the night of the 29th July on a well-devised plan, and captured the village of Merris with 180 prisoners and 36 machine guns, only suffering 39 casualties themselves. We co-operated in a small way on their left flank, merely to divert his attention, and were fortunate in capturing 3 prisoners, who were hiding in a ditch in a very demoralised state of mind.

On the night 30th-31st, we were relieved by the 7th Battalion, relief being complete at 1.40 a.m., and moved back to a camp at L'Hoffand, about half a mile out of Hazebrouck.

The next night we were warned to embark for the Heuringhem area, but before we did so, the enemy planes came over and dropped two bombs within 100 yards of the camp. We were relieved just before midnight by the Lancashire Fusiliers and embussed at 3 a.m. on 2/8/18, arrived at Heuringhem about 6 a.m. From here the Battalion marched to a somewhat scattered area around the villages of Coubronne and Le Rons.

On Sunday, 4th August, the fourth anniversary of the outbreak of the war, representatives of each unit of the 2nd Army attended a church parade at Terdeghem. After the conclusion of the service and the subsequent march past, General Sir Herbert Plumer, commanding the 2nd Army, called together Major-General Glasgow, the 3 Brigade Commanders, and the 3 senior Staff Officers of the 1st Australian Division, and paid a very high compliment to the work of that unit while serving with the 15th Corps.

"The Division had been in the line for 110 days without relief, and had carried out such a vigorous offensive during that time as to necessitate no less than 9 divisional reliefs by the enemy on the opposing front. Heavy casualties had been inflicted on several occasions and 1000 prisoners less 16, captured. The various offensives had been skilfully planned and vigorously executed. The initiative dash and determination with which the general patrol work, and especially the daylight raiding, were carried out, were without parallel in the records of the Second Army. He wished them every good fortune when they rejoined the Australian Corps in the 4th Army."

We remained here during showery weather until August 6th, when the Battalion marched through Heuringhen and Blendecques and entrained at Arques, after being served with hot cocoa in the station yard by the Australian Comforts Fund. The troop train left about 5.30 p.m. but "D" Company remained behind to load the remainder of the Brigade and left at 9 p.m. We detrained at Hangest at 3 a.m. in darkness and proceeded along an unknown road in the cold dawn, and eventually arrived—very tired—at our billets in the village of L'Etoile. The men breakfasted and—some of them—slept during the day, for we had orders to embuss again that night at 7.30 p.m., and finally left at 9 p.m. A protracted journey eventually brought us to the outskirts of Rainneville at midnight. Our guides were not present, however, to meet us, and after an effort to locate our bivouac ground at a map-reading near Poulainville (new country and a foggy night) we piled arms at the side of the road and made an effort to sleep whilst waiting for dawn to break.

At dawn we found our guides, or they found us, and proceeded to our bivouac site, and breakfasted and rested. But our respite was of short duration and the men were too excited. The bombardment had been intense during the early hours but had now ceased, which rightly indicated that an advance had been made. The sky was thick with our planes, going and coming, some on reconnaissance work, some on contact work, and others on bombing raids.

During the morning columns of hundreds and thousands of prisoners were seen being escorted to the P.O.W. cages. The men were in high spirits.

We left again at 2.45 p.m., and had a long march (and the afternoon was hot) through Pont Novelles and Corbie finally arriving at Vaire about 11 p.m., when the Battalion bivouaced in a field near the church, tired out. Although we had marched twenty miles, the latter part was interesting, as it was new ground, and the many ambulances and medical relay posts, situated in what was only this morning our support line, indicated the extent of our advance. The observation balloons were being moved forward almost as fast as we were marching, and the men, being in good fettle, jokingly said that they were our objective, which we had failed to reach at nightfall.

August 9th.—Reveille was not sounded—but passed round—at 5 a.m. with instructions to be ready to move at 7 a.m., but it was 10 a.m. before we actually got moving. We marched off in column of platoons at 50yds. distance and proceeded via Hamel and Warfusse to an assembly point south west of Bayonvillers.

It was very apparent to everyone that, with the exception of Hamel, the front line trenches and support areas occupied by the remainder of the corps during the spring and summer, had not been subjected to nearly the same amount of shelling that the First Division had experienced in the Hazebrouck area, and the knowledge came somewhat as a surprise.

The cookers came up to this assembly point and we had our mid-day meal, and moved again at 6 p.m., in artillery formation to a point south west of Harbonnieres. Here the men piled arms and prepared to settle themselves for the night, but as usual their rest was of short duration, for at 9.30 p.m. we again had instructions to move further up to the line. The Battalion then accomplished a truly remarkable feat, which had been carried out many times on the parade ground and then generally in the day time, but now for the first time in reality. The whole Battalion moved in its present formation (lines of half platoons on a two-company frontage) on a pitch dark night, across 1,000 to 2,000 yards of unknown country, and successfully crossed two thick belts of barbed wire and a sunken road without at any time loosing touch or direction. The whole movement was carried out with hardly a sound. This brought us to a position south east of Harbonnieres and Battalion Headquarters was in the village itself.

August 10th.—Orders were received during the early morning for the Brigade to attack, and in consequence we moved off at 7.15 a.m. in the same formation as on the previous night. The 10th and 11th Battalions were attacking at 8 a.m. under a barrage, and our job was to support the 11th Battalion. We maintained this formation until we were within 1,000 yards of the enemy when we came under heavy machine gun fire. Company Commanders quickly deployed their companies and obtained the best available cover in shell holes, disused trenches, etc. It was at this juncture that Colonel Elliott was wounded, just as he was taking cover behind some heaps of dirt, and Major McPherson at once assumed command. We suffered intermittent shelling throughout the day, but lost but few men by it, although Lieutenant M. Blacklow was badly wounded by one shell, and afterwards succumbed at the Dressing Station near by.

August 11th.—At 2 a.m. the Commanding Officer was called to Brigade Headquarters and received orders for an attack at 4 a.m. (It is interesting to note the short notice given for an important attack such as this proved to be.) On his return, Company Commanders were called and other officers roused the men, and word was sent back to the Quartermaster to send a meal and water up "at the toote." The plan of action was explained and the meal disposed of, and the Battalion was ready to move at 3.30 a.m. We barely reached the jumping off tape (an imaginary one) by 4 a.m. when the barrage opened up and the companies advanced in perfect order. It was a thick, foggy morning, and the tanks, which were to assist in the attack, proved themselves to be quite useless, as they had no means to ascertain their direction in the fog, and floundered around in big circles. During the attack the 11th Battalion was on our left, and the 10th Battalion and 2nd Brigade on the right. Our line of attack took us through Crepe Wood, which the enemy saturated with gas, making it very difficult for our men to proceed, as the undergrowth was very thick. By 7 a.m. we had enveloped the large village of Lihons, which was our objective and pushed reconnoitring patrols out in front to get in touch with the enemy. Lieutenant G. T. Gandy went with one patrol and took a Lewis gun with him. He estimated that he penetrated 1,000 yards to 1,500 yards in the misty light, and finally sighted a team of horses dragging a gun out of its position. He opened fire and a horse was seen to fall and the gun crew dispersed.

On settling down in our new line we ascertained our exact position and discovered that there was a very large gap between our left flank and the 11th Battalion. Before we had time to rectify this the enemy sent a fairly large party through, which troubled us very much by firing into our rear, and the support Company (C Company) under Captain Jorgensen, was sent forward to deal with the intruders. After a little bother they were ejected, and quite a number of isolated parties and individual Fritzes were found hiding in Crepe Wood, and dealt with. Throughout the day the front line, Battalion Headquarters and surrounding woods were heavily shelled with 5.9 guns, those of small calibre being shifted back into new positions.

The 2nd Battalion relieved us that night at 2 a.m., and we moved back to the same position we were in before moving to the attack. We spent a somewhat quiet day and enjoyed a couple of good meals, but orders were received for two of our companies to relieve two companies of the 11th Battalion in the front line, which was situated in the old French trenches in use prior to the July, 1916, offensive, in front of Vermandovillers. This was effected by "A" and "C" Companies during the evening.

August 13th.—Heavy "counter-preparation" barrages were fired by our artillery at dawn, and shortly afterwards. (This was done to break up any counter attacks which might be forming.) The men had rather a good time in the line, for it was quite comfortable there, little shelling, and they had found an old canteen of Fritze's, but most of the contents had gone, either taken away by him before retiring or "loaned" by some enterprising diggers, who had got in first. However, there were some very nice mineral waters, something like soda water, which proved acceptable. "C" Company was relieved by a company of the 23rd Battalion and moved back to supports.

The next day "A" Company was relieved by the 11th Battalion, and the whole Battalion was relieved on the day following (August 15th) by the 16th Battalion, and marched back to the old brick field near Guillemont, being bombed on the way, but suffering no casualties.

We left the next morning at 8.30 a.m. and moved back to Vaire, and the Battalion bivouaced on the banks of the Somme. We stayed here for five days and during that time the weather was beautifully hot, in fact the diggers were swimming in the river practically all day long. On the 18th August, Major D. G. Shaw, from the 10th Battalion, joined us and was appointed to command temporarily.

Orders were again received from Brigade Headquarters on 21st August for another move, and we took up a position as reserve Brigade south of Morcourt. The Battalion was bivouaced in a wood, and about 30 yards from

Headquarters a gun, captured from the Germans only a few days previous, was firing back all the ammunition the Germans had left, as fast as it could.

August 23rd.—At 2 a.m., in the bright moonlight, the Battalion moved off in single file, looking like a great serpent, as it wended its way along the gullies in order to keep in the dead ground. The assembly point was St. Germaine Wood and the companies were just in position when the barrage opened at 4.45 a.m. In spite of the good natural cover provided by some chalk quarries "B" and "D" Companies suffered a number of casualties from howitzer shell fire.

The Battalion was not called upon until 2 p.m., when it passed to the left of Provart and through the 1st Brigade line and made a wonderful advance of over 2,000 yards, covering very difficult and exposed country and capturing the village of Chuignolles. The last position from which the enemy was dislodged was at the top of some very steep cliffs, resembling some of those at Anzac more than anything else, and it is certianly difficult to understand how the enemy allowed himself to be ousted from this almost impregable position by a handful of tired troops, who had to cross 800 to 1,000 yards of open country, swept by machine gun fire before scaling the cliffs. It was during this advance that Major J. A. Foster was killed by a sniper, when indicating to his men the direction they were to take on coming out of Marly Wood.

August 24th.—The enemy was much quieter during the day and "A" Company was enabled to push out 200 yards east of Carenne Wood without opposition, and thus obtain a better field of fire.

The next day the units on our flanks advanced and we were instructed to conform with the movement at 4 p.m. The barrage given to us was very weak, however, and "A" and "B" Companies (under Lieutenants G. Vaughan and E. Terry respectively) suffered heavily from machine gun fire. The attack evolved itself into a fierce bombing fight up the old disused communication trenches, and as we forced the Germans back, so we used his own bombs that he had left behind to throw at him. It was during this heavy fighting that Lieutenant Terry was killed. "C" Company, on the left of Carenne Wood (under Lieutenant G. T. Gandy) was having an equally strenuous time in keeping touch with the 11th Battalion, for the ground at this point was a high plateau and as flat as a billiard table, so, of course, it was "goodbye" if you showed your head above the trench. But in spite of this we established an advanced post in Olympic Wood and thus threatened the enemy's rear and forced him to retire during the night.

On the morning of the 26th August the 11th Battalion advanced and took up a position in front of our line, and we automatically became the support Battalion and were ultimately relieved by a unit of the 6th Brigade during the afternoon, when we moved back to a bivouac in St. Germaine Wood. Major McPherson again commanded us, as Major Shaw was slightly wounded in the arm during the stunt.

The next day we left at 8.30 a.m. and marched through Mericourt and Chipilly and bivouaced in a gully south of Cerisy.

Owing to the heavy casualties the Battalion had sustained during the last fortnight it was found necessary to re-organise into three Companies of three platoons each, and consequently A, B, C, and D Companies now became X, Y, and Z Companies.

After a fortnight's spell in this gully the Battalion moved in motor busses to trenches on Mt. St. Quentin, just outside Peronne, and afterwards moved into huts in a wood near Tincourt. While in this camp they were utilised at night to dig a defence line, stretching across the Divisional front in advance of the village.

On September 18th the Battalion moved up to the front line immediately in front of Jeancourt, and in conjunction with the other units of the Brigade, attacked at 6 a.m. penetrating 2,000 to 3,000 yards into the enemy's territory. The 12th Battalion made the initial attack and carried the line over the first ridge and down the forward slopes in advance of Grand Priel Wood. It was during this attack that Captain S. R. Houghton distinguished himself and his company by capturing more prisoners than the strength of the company which he attacked. This, in conjunction with other brave and valuable work gained him the D.S.O.

The 10th Battalion then passed through our line of posts and pushed the enemy back to a position not less than 600 yards from the famous Bellicourt Tunnel in the Hindenburg line. During the fighting the Battalion captured two 7.7 guns two Trench Howitzers and 38 machine guns.

For two days we had a rather quiet time, as the enemy did not shell very much. On the night of the 21st September we relieved the 10th Battalion in the line, Y Company being in the line on the right, Z Company on the left and X Company in support.

At midnight on the night 23rd/24th September we were relieved by an American Unit, and left the line—as it afterwards transpired—for the last time. On relief we again moved back to the camp in Tincourt Wood. The next morning the third batch of 1914 men were sent back to Australia for six month's leave, all of them in the highest of spirits, in the expectation of spending Christmas at home in "Aussie."

On 26th September the Battalion entrained at Tincourt and proceeded to Longpre—the transport left the preceding day and travelled by road. We detrained at 7 p.m., and after a long and tedious march along unknown roads in the dark, we arrived at our billets in the village of Ergnies at 11 p.m. We were rather unfortunate in being allotted this village, as it was entirely surrounded by trees, and in consequence received very little sun to dry the roads. which were atrociously muddy.

After a couple of days rest and clean up, the Companies started on a steady syllabus of training. Parade ground work, route marches, musketry, Lewis gunnery and recreational training receiving most of our time.

On 7th October we were moved to the adjacent village of Surcamps, where two companies were in Nissen Huts and the other company in the stables of the chateau. Major McPherson having returned to Australia on 1914 leave prior to the Battalion leaving Ergnies, the unit was now commanded by Major E. W. Tulloch (11th Battalion.)

The Division Commander reviewed the Brigade on 11th October, and a very fine sight was presented with the Brigade in line.

On 20th October we were again moved back to Ergnies, and Padre Hayden did wonderful work in endeavoring to improve the men's conditions of living, and providing them with an improved reading and writing room (which was a tumble-down shed rented from a Frenchman.)

The Battalion remained here till 6th November, when we entrained for Tincourt, under orders for another tour of duty in the line, but on the 11th of the month we received the welcome news that the Armistice between the Allies and Germany had been signd.

Our next stay of any considerable time was at Sars Potteries, where we remained about six weeks in wet and cold weather, and finally moved to excellent billets among very friendly people at Chatelet, a suburb of Charleroi, from which we were demobilised.

15TH BATTALION.

The New Year of 1916 found the 15th Battalion greatly under strength bivouacked in the deep sand bordering the railway line near the station of Ismailia, not far from the shores of Lake Iimsah. There were not sufficient tents to shelter everybody, so many of the men made "possies" for themselves with a couple of oil-sheets and a few old sticks, and it was surprising how cosy some of these abodes were, as many of the nights were quite cold. At first, as one might have expected, after the evacuation, with so many men suddenly dumped down to be fed far from a base, with but a single line of railway, things were very scanty in the way of victuals. However, for the first week or so the Battalion was resting, and all parades were abandoned. Gradually, however, the men were acclimatised to camp life once more, with its parades and drills and bugle calls after the more easy discipline in the trenches. Ismailia, however, was only a temporary camp while the sites were being chosen and the tents erected in the new situation at Moascar. While the preparations were going on for moving out the men were given light field exercises in the desert intermingled with many a good game of football played on a particularly hard patch of the desert's surface.

When all was ready we moved over into our new quarters.

We found ourselves camped alongside our old friends the New Zealanders, with whom, of course, the 4th Australian Brigade, of which the 15th Battalion was a part, went to form the 2nd A.N.Z.A.C. Division. Training of a general kind, especially night marching and fighting, was strenuously carried out. About this time there was considerable concentration on the part of the enemy with the object of actually invading Egypt and taking advantage of a good deal of unrest that was being experienced there. The Canal was being strongly held well on the enemy side of it, but the Division to which the 15th Battalion was attached was held as a mobile reserve with the role of delivering a strong night counter attack when the time came for such a movement. This type of tactics made the manoeuvres of a very interesting nature. The reason for the 4th Australian Brigade being attached to the New Zealand Division in 1915 was that the latter contained too many mounted troops and not sufficient infantry to bring them correctly under the British Army establishments, but during the time we had been on the Peninsula this difference had been made good by the Government sending out the New Zealand Rifle Brigade, and as there was reorganisation going on among the Australian Units and were no longer wanted to make up the strength of the New Zealanders, instructions were issued that we should leave them and join the huge Australian camp at Tel-el-Kebir.

We were sad at leaving our old comrades with whom we had fought since the day of the landing, and for whom we had a great admiration, their technical branches were well trained and their infantry of a very fine type; the best of good fellowship had existed between us and the fighting qualities mutually appreciated.

It was here that we received the news that we were to be posted from our old friends the New Zealanders and were to be split up into two separate Battalions, and to remain the 15th, and the other to win fame later as the 47th Battalion.

All ranks hated the idea of the chance of their being separated from the unit with which they had been serving in the line, and those of the 4th Brigade who had to go on to the 12th Brigade felt very sore; the 4th had been composed of four good fighting battalions and our Brigadier-General, Sir John Monash, who was immensely popular with the men, had proved himself a skilful leader and competent and just administrator. The splitting of the battalion into two units was done in a thoroughly impartial way, always with an eye on the military effect, and those chosen to go bowed to the inevitable with the true Australain sporting spirit.

After the two new divisions, the Fourth and Fifth, had been formed, the 4th Brigade (13th, 14th, 15th, and 16th Battalions) formed part of the 4th Division, but were allowed the privilege of retaining their original colours, similar in shape to those of the 1st Division, while the remainder of the 4th Division colours were round circle.

There was yet another move in store for us before the Battalion was divided, and this was to the old battle-ground of Tel-el-Kebir, which was the largest Australian camp ever seen in Egypt. It was here that Lieut.-Colonel Snowden, with Lieut. Terry as Adjutant, and Lieuts. Wilson and Lane from Tasmania were transferred to the new unit, the 47th Battalion. The Tasmanians then left with the 15th Battalion were Captain Corrigan and Lieut. Brettingham Moore. At Tel-el-Kebir the Battalion, under its old Commander, Lieut.-Colonel Cannan, once more came up to strength.

In the early days in April word was received to march overland to Serapeum on the canal, and this the 4th Division accomplished in three days over the burning sands with very little water, only meeting their transport at the pre-arranged halting places for the night. This march was one of the severest tests the men were ever put to in Egypt, and as a test for endurance it certainly showed their mettle.

The first day's marching took us to Mahsanah, a distance of 14 miles, where we rested for the night. The next day's march carried us to Moasca, a distance of 17½ miles. This distance was practically all across desert, and with the exception of about three miles of heavy sand, the walking was very good. The day was very hot, but luckily not sultry, and now and then a cool breeze would come along, lasting a few minutes. Altogether 132 men of the brigade fell out during this day's march; of these 118 were able to rejoin their units before sunset. The third day's marching, from Moasca to Serapeum, was exceptionally trying owing to atmospheric conditions, a warm southerly wind, with high temperature, prevailed, and in addition the road lay through a defile, the dust being heavy, and the men pestered by flies and mosquitoes. The men did marvellously well until after midday, and until then strict march discipline was maintained. Each hour a spell was given for ten minutes, but a few spells were cut short to try and escape the hordes of flies and insects that collected as soon as the men were stationary. After midday the marching was almost unbearable, and altogether a total of 460 men of the brigade fell out on this day's march, and of this number 413 rejoined their units during the night, most of the remainder eventually arriving at hospitals.

From Serapeum, which was Divisional Headquarers, the 15th Battalion was split up into companies, each holding one of the little forts scattered along the canal bank. It fell to the lot of the Tasmanian "D" Company to garrison the little fort of Deversoir at the head of the Great Bitter Lakes, and for the month which the company held the post, most of us carried away pleasant memories of the cool waters of the canal and deep shade of the pine trees which lined the further bank and to which the men would swim when off duty. Here many a hearty greeting was shouted as the great illuminated hospital ships would glide past in the night bearing many a sick and wounded comrade back to "Aussie."

At last we got word to prepare for transhipment to France, and late one evening the whole Battalion steamed out of Serapeum on our way to Alexandria, where we were to embark on the *Transylvania* for Marseilles, where we arrived in the middle of June and immediately took train for Northern

France. Three days of new sights and sounds and smells, and late one evening we descended from our train at Bailleul and heard at last the thunder of the German guns and saw the flashes as our own replied to them. Now began our slow progress from billet to billet on our way to take our turn in the line. Le Maison Blanche and Jesus Farm will always be names to be remembered as the first ones we heard in France. From the latter billet "D" Company supplied "wiring" and trench digging parties to the front line, and it was on one of these that we sustained our first casualty on the sacred soil of France. Later we were moved to the support lines in the Bois Grenier sector near Armentieres, and held them with the 13th Battalion, while the 14th and 16th Battalions held the front line trenches.

The ensuing is an account related by a member of the unit, who enjoyed and suffered the pleasant and bad times through which the Battalion passed, covering a period extending from its arrival in France till its relief of the 6th and 12th Battalions in the front line trenches to the left of Gueudecourt in November, 1916.

"The battalion, upon arrival in France, entrained at Marseilles for Ballieul, and for nearly four days and nights they were railed through the beautiful French countryside, as thousands of other Australian troops had been before them, past the smiling fields and happy and prosperous looking little villages, down the magnificent valley of the Rhone with its fertile tree covered banks, providing sites for stately chateaux under towering cliffs crowned with the old grey walls of ancient fortresses and through broad and bushy valleys, on the further slopes of which could be seen the grey slate roofs of picturesque hillside villages and towns. The railway line throughout was fringed with gaily coloured poppies, daisies and wild flowers, and after the arid hungry sand of Egypt it was a dream country, "a thing of beauty, and a joy for ever" well worth fighting for. The troops were crowded round the doors and windows of the trucks from sun up until the beauties of each fresh scene were lost in the shades of evening, and it was with this vivid and eloquent impression of some of the wonders of the country which each man felt that he had come to fight for, that the battalion detrained."

The 15th Battalion had just finished preparing for a raid after careful schooling of picked men in the specially prepared grounds behind the line, which grounds are made to an exact replica of the opposing German trench, when orders were received to march down and take our places in the great offensive which had just begun on the Somme. From Bailleul we took train to Candas, and then marched to Nours, where we were billeted for several days. Thence through many villages—Idmas, Rubempre, Herissart—we passed, staying a day here and a day or two there, till we came to Warloy, about six miles from Albert. Here we waited expectantly to go up into the line, but some delay held us back, and we saw with envy a Battalion of the 1st Division marching back to billets, each man bearing some trophy, such as a German "juchelhauben" from off the head of one of the Kaiser's Prussian Guard, which had been badly cut up by our fellows in the capture of Pozieres village. We heard later that the delay was caused by the 2nd Australian Division having been held up by the uncut wire and failing to take the whole of their objective. They were given another chance, as an Australian Division had never failed before, and three days later carried the position with great dash in spite of weariness and heavy losses. At last we got the word to move forward, and late one evening moved up and bivouacked on a ridge above Albert. When day broke we got a good panoramic view of some of the battlefields, and could see our shells bursting in the German trenches. An hour later we were on the march again, and only just in time, for as our last platoon moved off the ridge down came a

Fortified Shell Holes (taken from the Air)

Lent by Aust. War Museum

heavy curtain of German shrapnel, our position evidently having been spotted by an enemy observer.

We passed through Albert under the famous leaning statue, which seemed to hold out its arms in benediction over us, and passed into the wilderness of the battle area beyond. Here we halted for a while and stragglers grinned as they hobbled past and wished us luck, and said it was "Hot up there." Just as dusk was falling we entered the area of the enemy's barrage, and following the guide supplied by the unit we were to relieve, went forward into the maze of old German trenches in a roundabout route to Pozieres village, or at least the pile of ruins which bore that name. At the foot of Pozieres Ridge the Battalion ran into a particularly heavy barrage, and had to wait some time till it decreased in intensity. "D" Company was in the rear of the column, and one platoon was detached to bring water into the line over the shrapnel-swept zone beyond the village. The men of the unit we relieved were like men in a dream from the terrible shelling and the length of time they had been in the line.

The Tasmanians held the post of honor on the left of the line, the furthest point in the salient, with their left flank guarded by a Battalion of Royal Fusiliers, which later were relieved by the 7th Suffolks. For six days the Battalion held this ground, which was littered with dead, both in and around the trenches, and if a man were shot, his body could not be thrown over the parapet without drawing down a burst of shellfire, so keen were the enemy's observers. Their snipers were also busy, and many a duel was fought between riflemen on opposing sides.

At last, on the 8th August, 1916, we were given orders to prepare to assault the opposing trenches at 9.23 in the evening. Each Company Commander was summoned to Headquarters and given the minutest details of the attack, which he in turn passed on to his platoon commanders, and through them to the N.C.Os. and men. Also all watches were synchronised, as the bombardment of the enemy trenches was to be of a very intense character, and to last for only two minutes. To a Company of Suffolks was allotted the task of taking the short sector of trench which had faced the Tasmanians for the last six days at a distance of only 50 yards, with no wire entanglements between. Our men were moved further down the trench, and had to assault blind trenches at a distance of nearly 200 yards, with our left flank skirting a strong German trench running at right angles to the main line of attack. The enemy were very uneasy this night, and some minutes before our attack developed began sending up red and green flares asking for artillery support. Our barrage fell just before theirs came down, and then things happened as in a nightmare. Everything was enveloped in a pall of smoke from our own smoke shells, and through this the glare of the enemy's bursting shells showed red as blood. Our men moved steadily forward, but were met with a hurricane of fire from three sides, the machine guns playing the most deadly havoc in our ranks. Very few reached the German positions, some 15 in all, and many of them wounded. These, however, cleared the trench and took 32 prisoners and two machine guns, besides much ammunition and Red Cross material. The fighting in the trench was hand to hand and very severe, but in spite of odds our men showed marked superiority, and completely broke the German morale. This handful of men, under Captain Brettingham-Moore, maintained their exposed position all night, and broke up an incipient counter attack with the help of an enemy machine gun.

The Suffolks having failed to take their objective after heavy losses, Colonel Cannan ordered the position to be evacuated, which was done at dawn along the sunken road which leads from Pozieres to Bapaume.

All day the heavy guns pounded the German flanking positions, and so heavy was the fire that many Germans left their trenches and surrendered rather than face death from the shell fire. On the evening of the 9th August the 16th Battalion, with the remnants of the 15th, occupied the position which had been evacuated that morning, and which the enemy had never re-occupied, believing it still to be held by our men. Two days later the Battalion was relieved, and so ended the first Battle of Pozieres. The position now held was on the ridge overlooking the crumbling ruins of Mouquet Farm.

The casualties in the Battalion during this tour were 15 officers and 415 other ranks.

We returned to Albert on August 14th, resting again at the brickfield. On August 16th we marched to Warloy. At about this time Brigadier-General Brand took command of the brigade and Major McSharry of the 15th Battalion, Brigadier-General Monash having gone to England to take command of the Third Division, and Colonel Cannan a brigade of that division.

On August 17th we marched to Lavigoyene, and on August 18th to Halloy, and on the 23rd to Vadencourt Woods, arriving back at Albert on August 26th. We marched forward via Albert, 1st Avenue, Kay Trench, and Tom's Cut, and relieved the 24th Battalion A.I.F., at 3.45 a.m. on August 27th. We were relieved during the night by the 13th Battalion, and moved to Crater Trench reserve, and then back to Brickfields at Albert on the evening of the 28th. The battalion's casualties during this tour were 100 all ranks. Artillery fire was continuous and very heavy. We then marched to Warloy on the 29th, and to Rembempre on September 3rd, to Bonnieville on September 4th, to Gezincourt on the 6th, and entrained at Doullens on September 8th, reaching Poperinghe on the same day. We then marched to Reninghelst, where we stayed until September 17th. Here officers and men proceeded to the forward area each day, in order to become acquainted with the routes to be followed by the battalion when their turn came for the trenches.

On the afternoon of September 17th the battalion moved via La Cleyte and Dickebusch to Voormezeele, and relieved the 102nd Canadian Battalion. Things were quiet during the relief, and we had no casualties. Two companies held the front line and one in support, with the other in reserve. Communication and front line trenches were found to be in a very weak condition, and the work to improve them was pushed on. Generally the enemy's shelling was fairly light and well distributed, and his machine guns and snipers very lively at night, although they were kept well in hand by our men during the day. The weather was very wet, but the improvement work was steadily pushed on. Through the agency of strong patrols our men held charge of No Man's Land, and on the morning (about 5.30 o'clock) of September 20th, one of the patrols captured an enemy officer and man.

On the morning of September 25th a strong patrol of our bombers, under an officer, attempted to penetrate the enemy trench on our front assisted by artillery fire on both flanks. They managed to penetrate the first line of enemy wire, but found another just underneath the parapet. This line was overgrown with grass and weeds, and had not been touched by artillery fire since being erected. Our men could not get through and returned to our line without informing the enemy of what their intentions were.

The enemy trench mortars were very active on the 26th, causing some casualties and a fair amount of damage to the defences. We were relieved on October 8th by the 51st Battalion A.I.F., and marched back to Ontario Camp at Reninghelst. All men received a bath and change of clothing here, and an unusual amount of gas helmet drill was performed, and representatives from the battalion made a thorough reconnaissance of the new area shortly to be occupied by the battalion. The G.O.C. Division inspected the brigade on October 11, and presented honours to those who had been awarded them for the past operations on the Somme. On October 12th General Plumer reviewed the brigade.

The battalion moved out during the afternoon of October 13th, and by 8 p.m. had completed the relief of the 4th Battalion A.I.F. in the front line at Zillebeke. Life here seemed very quiet after the battalion's experience on the Somme. A considerable number of reinforcements arrived, and were very welcome. Fairly quiet throughout the day, things generally livened up towards the evening, chiefly owing to trench mortar duels, our casualties totalling about 30. Two companies held the line, with two in support. The ground in this area did not allow of digging owing to water, therefore our defences consisted chiefly of breastworks. Mining was carried on extensively by both sides, and portions of trench known to be mined were lightly manned. On October 19th the battalion was relieved by the 8th London Regiment during the night, and marched about ten miles to huts at Reninghelst. The next day was occupied in bathing and removing mud from clothing and equipment. On October 29th we marched to Godewaersvelde, about twelve miles further back on the French side of the border. Here we carried on with training during the morning and sports during the afternoon. The weather was cold, but straw was plentiful in the billets.

On October 26th the battalion marched to Castre, and entrained ror Pont Remy, about four miles from Abbeville, on the well known Somme River, where they arrived at 7 a.m. on the 27th. Usual training was carried on with until November 1st, when we marched to L'Etoyle and rested during the night. Next day's march carried up to Picquigny, where we stayed until November 25th. The usual routine was morning parades, afternoon football. On November 5th the battalion boarded motor lorries, and passing through Amiens halted on the Amiens-Albert road, about two miles from Albert. The greater part of the battalion was employed loading and unloading ammunition near Meaulte. The stay here was very uneventful, and on November 15th the battalion marched to Pommer's Redoubt, which resembled a sea of mud. Men were camped in tents and huts, made of a mixture of old blankets, bags, etc. The battalion was employed in road-making and working at railhead. This was known as the most severe winter experienced in France for many years, and as the men had poor accommodation and only one blanket each, they felt it very much. On November 22nd the battalion moved to Bazentin-le-Grande, where they were made more comfortable in Nissen huts, and were still occupied at road repairing in the vicinity of Delville Wood. They were unlucky in having to remain in this area until after Christmas, although the rest of the division moved back nearer Amiens. On Christmas Day each man received a small bottle of beer and some cake or pudding. Owing to the state of the country the men had to spend their spare time indoors and make their own amusements, which they generally managed to do. New Year's Day passed much the same as Christmas, only stout was substituted for beer. Our casualties in this area from shell-fire totalled about 40. Trench feet was a very difficult proposition to combat, and although everything possible was done, a number of men had to be evacuated.

On January 15th, 1917, the battalion moved back to Mametz Wood. Here we received a badly needed bath and change of clothing, and had a fairly easy time until starting for the trenches. On January 23rd C and D Companies moved up to the support line behind Guedecourt Wood. They moved into the front line next night, while A Company stayed in support and B Company in the reserve. We relieved the 45th Battalion. The position here was very open, and allowed no movements during day time. Communication trenches were absent, and front line trenches very shallow. While our heavy artillery was ranging on the German position in front on the 26th, a few shells fell short, causing some casualties, including Captain Nicholls, killed.

On the night of February 1st and 2nd the battalion attacked the enemy position on our front. The attack was entrusted to A and B Companies, B Company to make a demonstration on the left and D Company supplied carrying parties and parties to dig communication trenches between the old and new positions. The attack commenced at 7 p.m. A Company on the left gained its objective very quickly, but C Company found itself unable to get through the enemy's wire, so that they had to enter the trench further to the left and bomb their way down, which they did. Both companies had received losses, which weakened their strength considerably. About 50 prisoners, apart from a number of killed and wounded, were taken. The enemy placed a heavy barrage on our new and old positions, and greatly hampered the supplying of ammunition. At about 4 a.m. our scouts reported the enemy to be massing in his communication trenches in large strength. Machine guns and rifle fire could not be used against them, and the artillery did not respond sufficiently to materially affect the enemy in his counter-attack, which was launched at 4.30 a.m. The fighting was severe for about 15 minutes, but eventually the remains of A and C Companies were overwhelmed, and had to retire to their old position, leaving behind a few prisoners, chiefly wounded, and a few A.M.C. attending them. The remainder of the day was very quiet, and chiefly engaged evacuating wounded.

On the night of February 4th another attack on a much larger scale was made on the Guedecourt position. The whole of the 13th Battalion attacked, supported by the 14th Battalion. The attack succeeded, and after repelling three counter-attacks the position was held. Captain Murray, 13th Battalion, was awarded the V.C. for work during this attack.

On February 7th the battalion marched to Becourt, about three miles from Albert. During the past fortnight the weather had been bitterly cold, and the ground frozen, but it now began to thaw, becoming wet and muddy again. This was our first sight of civilians for over three months. The usual training was carried on here, during which an unfortunate accident took place at rifle grenade practice, Sergeant Gilbert being killed and Lieutenant Moore and several others wounded. On February 23rd the battalion marched further back via Meaulte and Dernancourt to Ribermont, where it was billeted. Headquarters were established in the upper portion of a school, which carried on as usual down below. Training was carried out here on a more extensive scale than had been possible for some months, the whole division very often taking part. As the training was all open warfare practice, we were looking forward to something in that line in the near future.

On March 22nd the battalion moved forward to Fricourt Farm, leaving there again on the 26th for Bazentin-le-Petite, resting there the night. Two twelve-inch guns were to be seen here captured from the Russians by the Germans, and from them by the British during the Somme push. Marching again on the 27th, we passed through Le Sars, and passed the renowned Butte de Warlencourt, arriving at Grevillers, near Bapaume, at 5 p.m., staying the night, and moved again next day to Favreuil, about two miles beyond Bapaume. Some very inviting-looking German dugouts, nicely fitted with beds, stoves, easy chairs, etc., were here but as several such places had been blown up lately by delayed mines, the men were warned not to inhabit them.

On April the 1st the battalion moved from the village and dug a defensive position about a mile forward. On the evening of April 3rd we moved to the front, and occupied an outpost line in front of Lagnicourt. During the night of the 4th the line was pushed forward about 600 yards, Headquarters being established on the forward edge of Lagnicourt village. The line was pushed forward about another 600 yards on the night of the 5th. We suffered very slight casualties. One of B Company outposts was blown out by artillery fire on the 6th, and we were relieved on that night and retired to the position in front of Favreuil. Resting here two days, we moved again from the front on the night of April 9th for the first attack undertaken on Bullecourt.

The weather was wet and cold, with heavy snowstorms, and the men carried full marching order, the intention of the army commander being that, as soon as the Hindenburg Line was broken, the cavalry waiting a few miles behind between Vaux and Favreuil would then push through, and the fighting would develop into open warfare. A similar attack was being made north, in front of Arras. The battalion reached the 14th Battalion position, which was to be the starting point at about 1 a.m. The 14th and 15th Battalions were to attack on the same frontage, headquarters being established on the old railway line directly in front of Noreuil. The "jumping-off" line, a sunken road about 60 yards in front of headquarters, was packed with men of the 14th and 15th Battalions. At the time the attack was to commence no order was received to do so, and just at dawn word came that the attack was to be postponed owing to the tanks being unable to get into position in time. As they were being relied on to destroy the enemy's wire, consisting of two separate bands about 40 yards thick, it was impossible to attack without them.

Lieutenant-Colonel McSharry was now faced with the problem of retiring in full view of the enemy with the 700 men. The men started off in pairs for the Favreuil position, and those who avoided Noreuil village retired safely, a few casualties occurring in the village. After resting during the day, the battalion moved again to the attack, this time in fighting instead of marching order. Most of the men were now feeling the effects of the marching, loss of sleep, and exposure, and were anxious for the attack to start and get it over. At 3.30 a.m. on April 11th the attack commenced. No artillery was used for the attack, which was as silent as possible considering the presence of tanks. The enemy had had a day's warning, of which he had taken advantage by reinforcing his artillery and infantry. The tanks, with the exception of one, either caught fire or were put out of action before reaching the German wire, which our men found in perfect order. Even so, they managed to penetrate it and take possession of the trenches behind, after having their ranks sadly depleted. The attack on Bullecourt village itself had failed, so that the enemy still had the commanding position, and attempts to move between our old and new positions with supplies were unsuccessful. The new position was a very intricate mass of trenches lightly manned with men, who, after repelling several masses of the enemy, found themselves short of bombs, which were really the only useful ammunition, so the position looked as serious as it was. Between the first and second line trenches the enemy had underground tunnels connecting the two lines ten feet below the surface, and the fire trenches were ten feet wide and eight feet deep, with three fire steps and numerous deep dugouts. A German counter-attack took place at 10 a.m. Our men were helpless, with two choices—to remain until they were killed or captured, or run the gauntlet of a shower of lead from their old positions. The majority chose the latter, but those who got back were very few, although a fair number who were wounded were collected during the afternoon. All the men who could be got together were employed bringing in wounded, who lay in the snow in No Man's Land while it was yet daylight. The Germans gave us a fair deal while this work was going on, in some cases assisting. That day's survivors of the battalion will always remember the little Doc., Captain O'Regan, and his staff, attending the wounded. Of the troops of the battalion who actually took part in this attack only four officers and 52 men returned unwounded.

The remains of the battalion, consisting of four officers and about 120 men, returned to Favreuil position, and entrained at Bapaume on the evening of the 12th, and disentrained at Albert on April the 13th, and marched to Mametz, staying there until April 19th, when we moved to Ribermont. Reinforcements began to arrive, and the battalion was gradually restored to its normal strength. Several N.C.O.'s were granted commissioned rank to replace fallen officers. General Birdwood attended brigade church parade, and spoke to the battalion, after which there was a march past. On May 13th the battalion, with the exception of A Company, entrained for Bailleul, in Belgium. A Company followed on the 14th. On disentraining we marched to Doulieu, about three miles from Estairs, and were billeted in farm houses. The country here did not offer facilities for practice manoeuvres, as the country was all intensely cultivated. Close order drill and a lot of route marching was the general routine. On August 2nd General Godley visited the brigade, and expressed himself as pleased with the training being carried out, and with the appearance of the brigade during the march past. On nearly all the marches the men were able to bathe in the canal.

The battalion moved from Doulieu billets on May 31st, and marched to a bivouac ground west of and near Neuve Eglisse. Specialists, such as Lewis gunners, signallers, scouts and bombers were hard at work practising while here, and one officer and some scouts from each company proceeded to the front line each day to become familiar with the different routes, landmarks, etc. On July 7th the battalion moved forward to the vicinity of La Plusdouvre Farm. The 4th Brigade was held in support to the 2nd Army, which had captured the Messines-Wytschaete Ridge. On June 8th the battalion returned to the bivouac position near Neuve Eglisse, and resting there for the night moved forward again on the 9th to the relief of the Second Otago Regiment and First Canterbury Rifles, New Zealand Forces, in support near Gooseberry Farm, in front of Messines Ridge. On the night of June 10th we relieved the 46th Battalion, A.I.F., in the front line facing Steignast Farm, and began to consolidate the new trenches. Parties of our men moved forward during the night to try and occupy Gapaard Farm, but were held up by heavy enemy fire coming from machine guns mounted in trees, so a strong post was formed near the farm. The front line and support trenches were heavily shelled during the night. On the night of June 12th the battalion completed the capture of Gapaard Farm, and captured Lesquatre Rois Cabinet, around which six strong posts were formed. At 3 a.m. on June 13th the battalion was relieved by the 11th Cheshire Regiment, and moved back to Hill 63. Two companies were camped in underground galleries and the remainder in tents. The battalion was congratulated by the Army Commander for the capture of Gapaard and Lesquatre Rois Cabinet. About half of the battalion was employed on fatigue work. On June 17th the battalion moved back a few miles to bivouac ground to Neuve Eglisse. The first match of the brigade cricket competition was played here on the

21st and the 15th Battalion's sports were held on the 24th of June. A number of officers and men were reconnoitring the forward area routes each day. On June 26th H.R.H. the Duke of Connaught inspected the 2nd Anzac Corps at Bailleul. Representatives from each unit were sent to the parade. Little drill was done here, most of the men being employed on working parties.

On 28th of June the battalion moved to the Hill 63 position, and on the 29th relieved portion of the 2nd New Zealand Brigade in the front line near La Truile Farm. The relief was complete by 11.30 p.m. The weather was very wet and the new trenches nearly half full of water. The men were working very hard while here, besides having the duty of defending the position, they had to make the front and support lines defensible by widening, deepening and wiring them. The enemy was active in all branches, especially the air force and artillery, while ours seemed rather quiet. On July 3rd "A" and "B" Companies, which were in support and reserve, relieved "C" and "D" Companies in the front line. The weather improved considerably, also conditions in the trenches. Our artillery seemed now to be doing strenuous counter-battery work. The Battalion Headquarters and Ultimo Avenue, "C" Trench, were concentrated on by the enemy with 4.2 and .77 cm. guns. We were relieved by the 14th Battalion on the morning of July 8th. Shelling was heavy, but there were no casualties, and the Battalion moved back to supports; "A" Company to dugouts and breastworks in Bunhill Row, "B" Company in tunnel at Prowse Point, "C" Company to dugouts in Ontario Avenue while "D" Company was scattered in different trenches, with Battalion Headquarters at St. Ives Post Office. At 9 a.m. on July 10th the enemy shelled Bunhill Row so heavily that "A" Company had to move away to Ontario Avenue trench. On July 13th about noon our relief by the 52nd Battalion was completed and we marched back to De Seule Camp on the Bailleul-Armentieres Road.

We stayed here until the 19th; the mornings were occupied with parades, the afternoons in sport, chiefly cricket.

We moved on July 19th to Oultersteene, about 10 miles back, and were billeted. Work here was chiefly route marching and close order drill during the next fortnight, after which the Battalion prepared to move up to the forward area again. On August 3rd the Battalion moved into reserve at the foot of Messines Ridge. While here the Battalion headquarters position was obliterated by artillery fire, and headquarters staff moved forward to the slope of Messines Ridge, where they shared cover with the 13th Battalion, who were in support. Major Sampson was slightly wounded here. The companies were employed on forward fatigue work, which was very heavy and constant, owing to the large amount of defensive works that were being constructed. On August 14th the Battalion moved ino the front line at Steignast and Gaapard Farms, and relieved the 14th Battalion. Heavy rains had commenced a few days previously, and as this area had been very much cut up during the Messines offensive, the conditions in the partly constructed trenches were very uncomfortable.

Air forces of both sides were very active at that time. Major Mundell, second in command, being temporarily in command, was killed by machine-gun fire on the night of August 19th while visiting the outposts. The Major had risen from the ranks of the Battalion and was well liked by all ranks. The 13th Battalion relieved us during the night of August 20th, and we marched back to Neuve Eglisse, where about 30 per cent. of the houses were still capable of providing shelter, and a few civilians still lived here, despite the fact that every night found the village being bombed and long range shells were not unusual during the day. We stayed here six days and then moved forward to support line in front of Messines Ridge, relieving the 16th Battalion. The troops were employed on fatigue work. The stay here was very short, and we were relieved by the 16th Manchester Regiment during the evening of August 28th and marched back to Dranoutre, bathed and cleaned up and marched on to Lamotte Wood on August 30th, some men in billets and some in tents.

On September 1st we moved by motor lorry to Lesbourg, about 25 miles away, and marched on a few miles to Predefin, where we were billeted. Nearly three weeks were spent here practising for the coming operations in front of Ypres. General Plumer, Second Army Commander, was a spectator and critic at one of the manoeuvres here. On September 19th we boarded motor lorries, and passing through Fruges, Aire, and St. Omer, arrived at Wallon-Capell, in Belgium. We left again on the 21st and marched to Steenvoorde, about ten miles away. On the 23rd motor lorries carried us via Reninghelst and Poperinghe to Vlamertinghe and we camped in the open about two miles from Ypres. Next day we moved to the ramparts of Ypres. On the evening of the 25th the Battalion moved forward to Gordon House and rested till 1 a.m. on the 26th, when it moved forward to take up its position for the attack to take place at dawn.

The Brigade had two objectives, the first being about 700 yards distant and named the Red Line, being entrusted to the 16th Battalion, and the second objective named the Blue Line, about 1200 yards distant, to be carried by the 14th Battalion on the left and 15th Battalion on the right. Our creeping barrage dropped down at 5.50 a.m., and was certainly the heaviest the Brigade had ever been supported by. During the attack the enemy artillery seemed to be used chiefly on back area and counter-battery work and little affected the attacking troops. The Red Line was reached without many casualties to our men. Here the attackers waited for twenty minutes, while our artillery concentrated on the Blue Line. The 14th and 15th Battalions then pushed forward to the Blue Line, which was reached with losses to the 15th Battalion of nine officers and about 150 men. The Battalion's captures amounted to about 200 prisoners and eight machine-guns, and a large number of killed and wounded. Two heavy counter-attacks were launched by the enemy at 2 p.m. and 7 p.m., but beyond sending up the S.O.S. signal, there was little left for the infantry to do, as the enemy seemed unable to move against our artillery and machine-gun fire, and those who did reach our trenches were soon disposed of. In these two counter-attacks we captured a few prisoners.

On the 27th the enemy again attacked, but with damage only to himself. During the afternoon of the 28th the enemy concentrated his artillery on the forward area, causing some casualties, but his infantry did not attack. The 45th Battalion relieved us this night at about 11 p.m., and we returned to Ypres. Here the cooks awaited us with hot tea and stew. We marched back to Halifax camp on the 29th, rested the night, and moved per motor lorries to Steenvoorde the next day. We stayed here and carried on with training until October 10th, when we again moved forward. Starting at 8 a.m. with full marching order for Halifax Camp, 14 miles distant, which we reached without a man falling out.

We moved on to Ypres on the 12th and into reserves at Kit and Kat on the 13th, then into support at Zonnebeke on the 14th. We had fairly large casualties here, a number of them owing to gas, and altogether had a very uncomfortable time in this place, where there was once a village. We moved into the front line on the night of the 16th, and relieved 14th Battalion. We experienced a fairly lively time here, and were relieved by 13th Battalion on 19th, and moved back to about four miles to dugouts capable of holding several hundred men. They were good protection, but very wet and unhealthy. We moved forward about a mile on the 21st, and relieved the 14th Battalion, and were employed on fatigue work until relieved by the 8th Battalion on the 23rd. We then marched back to Ypres, moving again next day by motor lorries to Reninghelst and camped in tents.

After spending three days here bathing and cleaning up, the Battalion marched to railway sidings at Oulterdom on October 27th and entrained, our destination being Crepy. Part of the journey was done by train, the remainder by motor lorry, and we reached Crepy at 3 a.m. on October 28th, remaining here until November 15th. During this time reorganisation had been completed and we were being converted into parade-ground soldiers. News came here that the division would proceed back to the Gamaches area for their long deferred rest. The 15th Battalion commenced its march on November 17th and reached its destination, Friville-Escarbotin on November 24th. During the march a halt was called at the site of the old wind-mill from which King Edward III. viewed the Battle of Cressy. On arrival at Friville, all prepared to make themselves comfortable, as our stay here was to extend over six or eight weeks. The civilians here were very kind, and helped towards the comfort of the men whenever possible. That, together with comfortable quarters, promised a pleasant rest.

On December 4th news reached us that the British attack on Cambrai, although successful in the beginning, had turned into a reverse after the heavy enemy counter-attack, and the 4th Australian Division, of which we were a part, prepared to move to that front. The promised two months' spell turned out to be one week, and 6 p.m. on December 5th found the Battalion entrained for Peronne, which was reached on the morning of the 6th. Having disentrained, the Battalion moved forward to Moislains and were accommodated in huts. Here we stayed until the 18th, being prepared to move at one hour's notice, being at the disposal of either the 7th or 9th Army Corps. As events turned out we were not needed, and time was chiefly occupied with Brigade or Divisional manoeuvres. On December 19th the Battalion moved forward to Templeux la Fosse and camped in tents on the edge of the village. Here we had two Brigade exercises per week, the remainder of the time spent in constructing a reserve line about three miles further forward, which later on was found useful in the big German Push of 1918. Inter-Battalion football matches supplied the amusement on Saturday afternoons, and the Brigade Pierrots' performances were well patronised during the evening. Here the Battalion celebrated its fourth Christmas away from Australia. The men received one and a half bottles of English beer and a few cigarettes. Eatables of any kind were difficult to procure, but a representative from the Battalions was sent to Amiens and managed to buy some vegetables and other food. The cooks put their best foot forward, and the Christmas dinner, if not dainty, was wholesome and plentiful. One of the Battalion machine-gunners celebrated New Year's Day by shooting down a German aeroplane; the passengers were not injured and managed to burn the 'plane before being captured. During this period the country was snow covered and bitterly cold. About January 10th the Battalion left Templeux-La-Fosse and entrained at Peronne for Bailleul, moving by stages to the forward area, which was reached on about January 17th.

The Battalion took over the line from Belgian Wood group of outposts to Chateau Road Group fronting the village of Wervicque. Every one was doubly alert here owing to the fact that the coming German offensive was expected to open on this front. The front line trenches were situated on a ridge overlooking a flat which during this weather was a swamp and through

F

which our outpost line ran about 250 yards beyond the front line. At 2 a.m. on the morning of the 24th two parties of the enemy raided two of our outposts, but were repulsed. With the help of a heavy barrage of trench mortars he again raided at 2.30 a.m. on the 25th, but was repulsed, leaving two prisoners in our hands. Owing to information received from a prisoner, the whole division "stood to" from 3 a.m. until 6 p.m. on the 28th of February. At 3 a.m. our artillery placed a barrage along the enemy's front for 30 minutes, and again at 5.45 a.m. for ten minutes, but no attack was made by the enemy, and the day passed quietly. We were relieved by the 9th Battalion during the night of March 1st. Just when the relief was about complete the enemy put down a heavy barrage, and the Battalion was held in case it was needed. But the attack took place against the right Battalion, the 13th, who were also in the middle of their relief by the 10th Battalion. The Battalion marched back to crater dugouts on the canal, being relieved at noon next day by the 12th Battalion. We moved back per motor lorries to Neuve Eglisse where we camped in Nissen huts and stayed until March 25th. Here we had a few casualties from long range guns. The Battalions' sports were held on March 24th, but were not as successful as they might have been, owing to the transport and advance parties having moved south, and several events were postponed. While here the Battalions' issue of Christmas parcels arrived.

Reveille sounded at 3 a.m. on March 25th, and the Battalion moved out at 4.30 a.m. We marched about five miles and boarded motor lorries, which carried us via Steenwerck, Merville, Lillers, and St. Pol, to Bavincourt, about 12 miles south of Arras. News was received here that Paris had been shelled. Practically every town of any importance that was within range was being shelled at that time, and Bailleul, Hazebrouck, and St. Pol were being evacuated by the civilians.

At midday on the 26th an urgent order came for the 4th Brigade to move forward, and the Brigade was on the march 15 minutes after receipt of the order. The roads were crowded with English troops and transports, and a few civilians retiring from the front. About three hours' marching brought the Battalion to Beinvillers au Bois, and we commenced digging a defensive line on the ridge in front of the village. Later on, orders came for the Brigade to establish itself in front of Hebuterne, on the line, which before the Somme offensive was the old British front line. The Battalion moved forward at dusk, and was consolidating in its new positions by 11 p.m. A few of the enemy with machine-guns had penetrated the village, and these were captured. The other two Brigades of the Division, the 12th and 13th, had moved further south to the Amiens front, while the 1st, 2nd, and 5th Divisions were still up north. The first night was very quiet, the enemy artillery being silent, and no artillery at all behind our Brigade to make a noise.

On the morning of the 27th the enemy artillery opened up, and the weight of it left us wondering how it was moved forward so quickly. His infantry attacked at 5 p.m., but was repulsed with heavy loss to himself. The Brigade had a battery of field guns supporting it on the 28th, and from this on our artillery increased in numbers and weight very quickly. We experienced heavy artillery fire from 9 a.m. until 7 p.m. on the 28th, and another attack by infantry, who massed in full view of our men, with the result that none of the enemy reached our lines, but portion of the attack moved to our right on the New Zealand front. The men had never during their stay in France had such good targets. From this on the enemy concentrated his artillery chiefly on the village. On the morning of April 5th both the Germans and the British decided to attack, the Germans on a wide front, and the British on Rosignol Wood. The German artillery opened at 5 a.m. and the British at 5.30 a.m. The attack on Rosignol Wood by the 11th Brigade of English troops supported by artillery and eight tanks failed, and the Germans were repulsed all along the front and suffered heavy losses. During this day prisoners were captured representing three enemy divisions, making a total of 15 enemy divisions identified on the 4th Brigade front during our stay in this part. The four Battalions of the Brigade were all in the front line without any support or reserve units. Wet weather set in on April 1st, which made it worse for the men, who by now were being worn out and on fairly short rations. On April 9th we were relieved by the 10th Royal Fusiliers Regiment, relief was complete by midnight, and we moved back to the shelter at Rosignol Farm.

Resting here two days, we then moved forward to Sailly-au-Bois and into supports on the 13th. Our artillery was active and appeared much heavier than the enemy's. On the 20th we relieved the 16th Battalion in the front line and were in turn relieved by the New Zealand Rifle Brigade during the night of April 24th. We boarded motor lorries at 4 a.m. on the 25th and reached Rainville at 10 a.m., marched to Allainville, where we camped. On the 27th we moved to Pont Noyelles and then to a ridge behind Villers Brettoneaux, and on the 28th into support to the 14th Battalion. On May 4th we relieved the 14th Battalion on the left of Villers Brettoneaux, staying here until May 9th, during which time the weather was wet. Artillery and air forces of both sides were very active. We were relieved by the 14th Battalion during the night of the 9th and marched to Blangy-Tronville, the companies digging in about a mile from the village. From there we moved to Bois-de-Abbe in support to the 14th Battalion, which we relieved in the front line on May 18th. The position here was the extreme right of the British front, the troops joining us being French, one of the outposts containing a few of our men and some Frenchmen, being called the Post-Internationale. The 41st Battalion relieved us on May 20th and we moved back to reserve for one night, then on to La Motte, and to Freschencourt on the 22nd. The village was heavily bombed during the night, two officers being killed and a few men wounded. The Brigade attended church parade at Querrieu on the 26th, and was afterwards inspected by General Birdwood.

On May 31st the Battalion moved forward and relieved the 55th Battalion in the front line at Hamelet. The line was held by two companies, with one in support and one in reserve, and was quiet during the day, but livened up considerably during the night and early morning. Arrangements were made here to bring one platoon at a time from the front to have a bathe in the river near Corbie. Our casualties here were fairly light, and we were relieved on June 26th and marched back to the vicinity of Daours. About 200 American troops with their officers joined us here to train with the Battalion, which they were to accompany in the attack on July 4th. This move was to enable them to gain experience before entering the line as a complete unit on their own. Parade hours here were taken up chiefly with bombing, rifle grenade, bayonet practice, Lewis gun, and signalling training, and having the plans of the forthcoming attack thoroughly understood by all ranks. The Prime Minister, Mr. Hughes, visited the Brigade here and made a speech to the men. The Battalion moved forward on the night of the third of July to take up its position for the attack on the 4th.

July 4th, being "Independence Day," was a fitting day for the Americans who accompanied the Battalion to celebrate their first "brush" with the enemy. The attack took place at the familiar hour of "dawn," and was very successful. There was some very subborn fighting, shortly after the attack commenced, at Pear Trench, which was a "strong post," and little damaged by our artillery. After a short delay the companies overcame this resistance, and pushed forward, the position being finally "mopped up" by headquarters. On reaching their objective beyond Hamel, supplies of ammunition were brought up by aeroplanes, and dropped at selected spots. This was the first time that idea had been put into practice. Altogether our 'planes were exceptionally prominent during the attack, and did a considerable amount of bombing. The Battalion's first V.C. was won here by a Queenslander, of "A" Company. The Battalion had a fair number of casualties, especially among officers. The Battalion spent three days in their new position, which they consolidated, and repelled several heavy counter attacks. They then returned to the left of Villers-Brettoneaux, where they rested one night. M. Clemenceau, Premier of France, inspected the men of the Brigade who took part in the attack. The next day we marched back to Querrieu, and bivouacked, remaining there until July 30. During this period the usual routine was carried out. The Brigade held their sports at Querrieu, and Division held a race meeting at Allainville. Both were successful, but the races were marred by an unfortunate accident during a race, resulting in two of the divisional officers being killed. General Monash was present at a Brigade church parade at Querrieu, after which he presented medals and ribands to men and officers who had won them previously. The enemy bombing 'planes were very active at this time, but did no harm to the 15th Battalion. On July 31st the Battalion moved out from Querrieu, and relieved the 2nd Trench Regiment of Zouaves in the front line beyond Cachy village, to the right of Villers Brettoneaux. "B" and "C" Companies occupied the front line "A" and "D" Companies remaining in support at Cachy village, the nucleus being stationed at Rivery, near Amiens. All branches were very quiet during our stay here, just the usual trench routine, every day the same. On August 4th we were relieved by a Canadian Battalion, and moved to Canal Banks, near Vaire-sous-Corbie. On the morning of August 6th the enemy shelled us heavily from 4 a.m. till about 7 a.m., during which the C.O., Lieut.-Colonel M'Sharry, C.M.G., D.S.O., M.C. (Queensland), and Lieutenant Hines (Tasmania) were killed, and Captain Heffer, Adjutant, severely wounded. Major Sampson (Tasmania) now took command of the Battalion, and general preparations were made for the attack to take place on August 8th. The 15th Battalion was placed for the attack on the left flank of the second wave, which had to pass through the 3rd Division, A.I.F., one hour after the first objective had been taken. The 15th Battalion task was to capture the village of Cerisy Gailly. "A" Company attacked the centre of the village, with "B" Company on left, and "D" Company on right flank, "C" Company being in support. "A" and "D" Companies were aided by a tank which preceded them in the attack. The attack was most successful, and a large number of prisoners and machine guns were captured. Considering the depth of the advance, our casualties were very light. The Battalion was relieved at about 1 a.m. on August 9th by the 1st Battalion, A.I.F., and moved over to support the 13th and 16th Battalions, taking up a position in a sunken road, and deep embankment, to the right of the village of Morcourt. We were again relieved during the evening of the 10th August, and moved back to Sailly-le-Sec, where we had a few days' spell, and straightened up for the next move. On August 13th we moved out from Sailly-le-Sec, and bivouacked in sunken road near Harbonnierres. We stayed here a few days, and on August 16th moved forward to the relief of the 2nd Battalion, A.I.F., in front line at Lihons. "A" and "B" Companies took over the front with "C" and "D" Companies in support. ration carrying, etc. The front line here ran through the old original French front line of 1914. The Battalion gained considerable ground by silent penetration, and our area was continually shelled and heavily bombed by enemy 'planes. During the night of August 25th we were relieved by the 59th French Infantry Regiment. During the relief we experienced an exceptionally heavy gas bombardment, and suffered the heaviest casualties from gas during our experiences. The Battalion was transported per motor lorries to Allainville, where they billeted. The majority of the casualties from the gas were evacuated from here. From August 8th the Battalion was practically commanded by Tasmanians—Major B. Sampson, D.S.O., commanding the Battalion; Captain Domeny, M.C., of "A" Company; Captain Goss, M.C., "B" Company; Lieutenant Gonninon, M.C., "C" Company; Lieutenant Smith, "D" Company. The Battalion rested here some few days, and re-organised. The next move was per motor lorries to within a mile of Peronne, rested there three nights, and then marched forward about ten miles beyond Peronne, where they stayed about a week, moving forward again on September 15th to the front line near Jeancourt, and took part in the attack on September 18th. Dummy tanks were an unusual feature of this attack, and were carried forward by mules and men.

The battalion advanced as far as Villaret, capturing a large number of prisoners and some guns, our casualties being very light in comparison to the enemy's. The battalion held its new line, which was opposite the advance posts of the Hindenburg Line, for a week, during which time it advanced considerably by peaceful penetration. It was then relieved by American troops, and returned to Tincourt on September 26th, and stayed the night, entraining next day for Hangest, and then marched to Cruoy, where it was billeted. The usual training was carried out here and reinforcements received.

The news of the Armistice was received here, followed by the news that the 4th Division would be one of the A.I.F. units to represent Australia with the army of occupation, and it was to prepare for the march to the Rhine. Shortly after this the Battalion entrained at Sailly-sur-Somme, passed through Amiens, Villers Brett, Rosiers, and detrained, rested a few days, and travelled about 30 miles per light railway, where it again rested, and made final preparations for the march. All men who were not expected to be physically fit enough to complete the march were not to accompany their unit.

After some days' marching had been completed, news was received that the Australians would not be represented in the army of occupation by any infantry troops. This was a great disappointment to the Australian infantry, who thought that they had earned their right to be represented. Arrangements were then made for the infantry to occupy certain villages in Belgium, and the units continued their march to their respective areas. The 4th Division occupied a line of villages from Phillipeville to Dinant, the 15th Battalion being quartered at Phillipeville. The accommodation was very good, being chiefly army and police barracks. The majority of the billets were later on fitted with electric light at the men's own expense, and at the end of the first week everybody was fairly comfortable. Two halls were available for dancing, and at least two per week were held. Parades were fairly easy, and consisted chiefly of route marches. The chief sport was rugby football.

The battalion's fifth Christmas away from home was celebrated here. The battalion had no regimental funds, so money for extras for Christmas and New Year was subscribed in the unit, and the old custom of the officers acting as "mess orderlies" and serving out the men's Xmas dinner was observed. Classes were formed where possible, and men who wished to, attended, to prepare themselves for civilian life. Some men went to a school at corps headquarters with the same object. About twice per week a draft of men would leave the unit for England on their way to Australia until, about March, the strength of the units became so small that it was decided to combine the four battalions in the brigade and make one unit of them, occupying one village.

By the end of May, 1919, practically the whole of the battalion was in England or Australia. A number of men took advantage of the non-military employment system, whereby they were allowed to receive instruction in certain trades with English firms, still receiving their army pay, and if receiving no pay from their employers an additional 6/ per day sustenance allowance. Practically all the officers and men of the Battalion who had been captured during the war had been returned to England by June, 1919, and England was the scene of many happy re-unions during that month.

Duckwalk in Winter

Lent by Inst. War Museum

CHAPTER IV.

FRANCE AND BELGIUM—II.

(26TH AND 40TH BATTALIONS.)

26TH BATTALION.—Armentieres.—Messines.—The Somme.—A Futile Attack.—A Distinguished Success.—Moving About.—The Battle of Flers.—Lagnicourt.—Bullecourt.—Polygon Wood.—Passchaendale Ridge.—Back to the Somme.—A Brilliant Coup.—The Great Advance.—Mont St. Quentin.—The Last Fight.

40TH BATTALION.—Arrival in France.—Trench Warfare near Armentieres.—Ploegsteert.—The Battle of Messines.—Preparation for 3rd Battle of Ypres.—Attacks at Ypres on the 4th and 12th October, 1917.—Back to Messines.—The German Offensive.—Line near Molancourt.—Villers Brettonneux and Hamel.—The Battle of Amiens.—Attack at Proyart.—Capture of Bray by the 40th Battalion.—Advance Along the Somme.—The Attack on the Hindenburg Line.

On the 16th March, 1916, the 26th Battalion, which had been re-organised and equipped, and had had a period of training in Egypt after the Gallipoli Campaign, embarked for France on the *Northrand*, being one of the two first Australian Battalions to land in that country. They disembarked at Marseilles and were immediately entrained, and after three days' journey encamped at Morbeck and had their first experience of billets, most of the men being billeted in scattered barns and lofts, where they underwent further training for two weeks. The Battalion then entered into active operations and took up part of the Bois Grenier line in front of Armentieres, where they remained until the middle of June.

Here the first trench raid by the Australians was carried out by the 26th and 28th Battalions. It was a small affair, but several Germans were killed and a fair number taken prisoners. The only casualties suffered by the Battalion were Lieutenant Murdoch, who was in charge of the trench mortar party, and was killed by shellfire immediately after the raid, and two of the raiding party wounded. The insufficient supply of reinforcements from Tasmania after Armentieres had a particular effect on this Battalion. Those who were forthcoming were drafted mostly to the 12th and 15th Battalions, and consequently the 26th lost more and more its Tasmanian character and developed into more of a Queensland unit.

Shortly afterwards, the Battalion was transferred to Messines, and here had its first unpleasant experience of gas. This was a new thing, for which all were fairly well prepared, but notwithstanding this there were a number of casualties. This part of the line was held for a fortnight, up to the 11th July.

During this time the Battalion had to endure heavy attacks, and particularly suffered from minnenwerfer fire. The men believed that they were to have a chance of getting something back, the Battalion being under orders to attack at Messines, but unfortunately there was a great explosion of munitions at Audruicq, which made this impossible, and the arrangements were cancelled. Immediately afterwards the Brigade was transferred from this area to the Somme. Upon arrival there the Battalion was quartered at Fiesseles and Vignacourt near, Amiens, for some five days, and afterwards for a week at Warloy, a few miles from Albert, and on the 25th July was moved up to Brickfield and then to Tara Hill preparatory to attacking Pozieres Ridge.

On the night of the 27th July orders were received for all senior and specialist officers to proceed up to Pozierés, which had just previously been captured by the 1st Division, to reconnoitre the country over which the attack was to be made. This reconnaissance was carried out in daylight and with extreme difficulty owing to the fact that the enemy was still heavily bombarding the remains of Pozieres village, and consequently the knowledge gained of this country was scanty.

On the evening of the 28th the Battalion moved through Contalmaison and Pozieres, and, in conjunction with the 25th and 28th Battalions, took up their position in advance of the front line, then held by the 6th Brigade.

The attack was timed to commence at 10 minutes after midnight, but this was apparently anticipated by the enemy, who opened up a tremendous bombardment on the line where the attacking forces were assembled preparatory to moving forward. The ground to be crossed before reaching the first German trench was approximately 500 yards, and owing to the practically continuous bombardment by both British and German guns, was very difficult to move over, and the advance had to be made in the teeth of concentrated artillery, trench mortar and machine gun fire and the German Very lights, rockets, etc., made it practically as light as day. The attacking troops reached the German wire, but found it practically untouched by the previous bombardment, and therefore impassable. This, together with the enormous casualties suffered and the approach of daylight, necessitated a retirement. The remains of the Battalion withdrew to Sausage Gully, and later to Tara Hill, to be reinforced and reorganised.

On the 4th August the Battalion, with the 27th and 28th Battalions, renewed the attack for the same objectives. Jumping off trenches in advance of the front line had been prepared in the interval, and as the enemy wire had been effectually destroyed by bombardment the attack was in this case completely successful, and a new line was taken up on the forward slopes of the ridge overlooking Martinpuich, Courcellette, and the country towards Bapaume.

Captain W. F. Hinman, who belonged to the Battalion, carried on the work of reconnoitring the ground over which the attack was to be made, and for his successful work, which was of material assistance, was awarded the Military Cross.

The two Tasmanian Companies which took part in this battle were under Captains Geo. Bond and W. H Gray, and the former was awarded the Military Cross, he having had command of one Tasmanian Company in both battles.

Some idea of the severity of the operations may be gained from the fact that in these two battles for the ridge the 7th Brigade suffered 2300 casualties.

It was immediately after this that while holding the captured line the Battalion, or such small portion of it as was left, distinguished itself very particularly. A heavy German counter-attack was made in a determined effort to recover the ground which they had lost, and it was mainly owing to the courage and determination of the 26th Battalion that this was repulsed.

It was now necessary to withdraw the Battalion from the line, owing to the number of casualties which it had suffered and the exhausting nature of the fighting. It was given a period for rest and re-construction to bring it up to effective strength. During this period of training, on the 10th of August the Battalion was reviewed at Warloy by His Majesty the King.

The position was a serious one; the Army was short of men, and none could be spared for any extended period of rest, and the Battalion was therefore ordered to return to the line at Pozieres.

The first work to be undertaken was to dig the jumping-off trench behind Mouquet Farm. A severe German shell fire made this very difficult, but it was carried out successfully, although it resulted in considerable loss to the Battalion, the casualties about this time including the Commanding Officer, Colonel Ferguson.

The Battalion was then taken out of the line and moved back again to the North, and eventually was billeted at Steinworde, where some weeks were spent in reorganisation. Although considerable time was spent in training the Battalion enjoyed a much needed rest.

Colonel O'Donnel was temporarily in command in place of Colonel Ferguson, who had been wounded, with Major D. M. Davis second in command. The Battalion was transferred to the front line, where it took over a sector in the Ypres salient, and remained there about a month. The next move was from the Ypres sector back to the Somme, and here it took part in the attack on the German trench system in front of Flers from the 5th to the 14th November.

On the 3rd November the Battalion moved from Dernancourt and encamped in dugouts and destroyed trenches in the vicinity of High and Delville Woods. Under the original scheme for this attack the 26th Battalion was allotted a position in close support to the rest of the 7th Brigade, who were to attack on the 5th November, and on the night of the 4th the Battalion moved up into its allotted position. However, owing to the failure of one of the Battalions to reach the assembly position, one Tasmanian Company together with a few other details, was called in at the last minute to take this Battalion's place, and was hurried up in daylight, and reached the assembly place just in time for the attack at 9 o'clock on the 5th November. The men were fatigued, as they had been marching all night in the rain and the mud, which in the trenches was waist high. The Germans held a very strong position in the system of trenches well known as the Maze, and which had proved impregnable against all attacks up to that time and afterwards. The attack was apparently anticipated by the enemy, and as soon as the men got out of the trench they were met by a curtain of machine gun fire, which proved disastrous to the attacking forces, who only gained a few yards of ground, and were compelled to dig in. Heavy casualties were suffered, but the Battalion had to hold the position until the following night, and were subjected to a furious bombardment and a raid just shortly before being relieved. The Battalion then retired to huts in Mametz Wood, preparatory to going back for reorganisation. However, this did not eventuate, and the Battalion was recalled to the line a week later to take part in renewing the attack on the same position.

This attack, which took place on the morning of the 14th November, under even more aggravated conditions, was again a failure. The Battalion held the line for a few days before the attack, and suffered heavy casualties and endured extreme hardships owing to the rain and mud. As an example of the difficulties produced by the mud it might be added that stretcher bearer teams during these attacks were composed of 16 men per stretcher instead of four.

Some idea of the casualties may be gained from the fact that only two of the original Tasmanian officers were left with the Battalion after this attack, viz., Captains Bond and Gray; and Captain Hinman on Brigade Headquarters.

After the inaction and monotony of holding the line near Guedecourt through one of the severest winters experienced during the war, the news of the German retirement from the Somme battlefield came as a welcome relief.

The Battalion, which at the time was back in the reserve area spending the periodical four days rest, soon received orders to proceed up to take its turn in the front line, which, owing to the enemy retirement had now ceased to be a well-defined and known trench system. The duty assigned was to clear the enemy from a trench system known as Malt Trench, some distance north of the ruins of Le Sars.

On the night of the 2nd March, 1917, the Battalion reached the assembly position preparatory to advancing against the enemy, who had previously been reported to be holding their position lightly. On arrival, however, it was found that the enemy were strongly entrenched behind extensive barbed wire entanglements, which were undamaged. As the attacks had been planned without any support from artillery, the Battalion Commander decided to defer the attack until the necessary artillery support could be obtained. After events proved this to have been a wise decision, as, when a few nights later the Battalion did attack, after the entanglements had been wrecked by shell fire, a strong resistance was offered by the German rearguard, who were heavily supported by machine guns. The enemy were, however, driven from their position to another line on the Bapaume Ridge, which then became their last stronghold before Bapaume. It was in this action that Captain Cherry, who was afterwards awarded the Victoria Cross in the attack on Lagnicourt, gained the Military Cross.

After holding the new position for 24 hours the Battalion was withdrawn again to the reserve area to refit and prepare for the next attack.

Meanwhile the German retirement had passed beyond Bapaume, and on March 20th the Battalion moved forward through Bapaume to take up a sector of the line in front of Vaulx-Vraucourt, some five or six miles northeast of Bapaume. Here the country was open and untouched by the shell fire, which had turned the area of the Somme battlefield into a ruinous waste, devoid of all grass and vegetation. The line was held by a series of outposts, which were connected by patrols, while the enemy position lay round the village of Lagnicourt, some 1500 yards ahead.

To the 26th Battalion was allotted the task of driving the enemy from Lagnicourt, and by the 26th March the preparations were complete. In the early morning the attacking companies, who were supported by the 27th Battalion on the left flank, moved off, and soon afterwards had passed right through the village, leaving small mopping-up parties to round up the Germans who were left. By dawn the line was established some few hundred yards beyond Lagnicourt, and posts were hurriedly dug to prepare for the counter attack which it was considered certain the enemy would make to recover the possession of the village, which was one of the advanced posts of the famous Hindenburg line.

The enemy were soon visible massing in front of Queant, and during the day three strong counter-attacks were repulsed by the Battalion, which, though forced back a couple of hundred yards, still maintained a position well in front of the village. It was during these attacks that Captain Cherry was killed, after rendering such distinguished service that he was awarded a posthumous Victoria Cross.

The line so held was finally, on the evening of the 26th March, handed over to the 5th Brigade, and the Battalion retired by stages to re-form behind Bapaume. The casualties in this action were naturally considerable, as the Germans both strenuously defended, and afterwards made determined efforts to regain the village.

After the battle of Lagnicourt the Battalion moved back to dug-outs and trenches in advance of Favreuil, and after a few days' rest returned to Bapaume and camped in tents in a position just outside the town. Here a considerable number of reinforcements arrived and the Battalion was brought fairly well up to strength. This period of rest and training proved to be practically the best the Battalion had ever experienced. The ground between Bapaume and Flers was full of old shell holes, trenches, and wire entanglements, and live ammunition and bombs, both German and our own, were found everywhere in abundance. In consequence of these advantages produced by the fighting during the Somme battle of 1916, and owing to the fact that an excellent field firing range had been prepared, this area left little to be desired from a training point of view. The Battalion was also again put through practise in night operations, which had very rarely been carried out since leaving Egypt.

After a moderate period of very useful training the Battalion moved up into support in the corps line of defence in the rear of Vaux. Then in a short time to close support along the sunken roads on the general line of Vaux-Longat and Vaux-Morchies.

On the 1st of May the Battalion took over the brigade front, occupying what was known as railway embankment, and from this line the attack known as Bullecourt was launched on the 2nd of May, under the command of General Gellibrand.

The Battalion, though not being one of the front line units, was used to support the attack on the right flank. This meant continuous work as trench clearing parties and carrying parties, jobs which were equally difficult and probably equally unhealthy as being in the actual front line owing to the fact that the Germans put down an incessant barrage on the lines of communication.

The casualties as might have been expected were very heavy, and the following evening the Battalion moved back to Favreuil, in front of Bapaume. After a day here the Battalion returned to the front line and was occupied in constructing trenches. Soon afterwards the Battalion in company with the rest of the Division was moved out to rest at first near Albert and afterwards around Bapaume. This proved to be the longest and most beneficial rest the Battalion ever had during its period in France.

Although a good amount of training was carried out, this interspersed with sports meetings, horse racing, and football matches, proved a welcome recreation after the monotony of the front line work in the early part of the year, and the sharp fighting during the German retreat to the Hindenburg Line.

At the end of August the Australian Corps was moved up to the North and the Battalion found its billets around Renescure, and indulged in a very short period of training preparatory to its taking part in the great attacks of Polygon Wood and Passchaendale.

About the 12th September the Battalion commenced to move up from the back areas towards the front line by easy stages, and eventually found shelter in the open country behind Ypres. In this area units were nightly subjected to heavy bombing from the German planes, which at this time were very active owing to their knowledge that an attack was forthcoming in front of Ypres.

On the 20th September the Battalion in company with the rest of the 1st and 2nd Divisions went over the top with a final objective to the left of Polygon Wood. The attack was almost unique as far as the Battalion's experience had gone in that although it was conducted over a fairly wide front and a large number of troops were engaged everything went according to time table, and the various objectives outlined preparatory to the attack were taken with almost mathematical precision. After the taking of the objectives the Battalion was relieved and moved back into the area just behind Ypres.

Meanwhile the attack had been carried forward a further stage on the 26th September, and on the 4th October the Battalion again took part in an attack which was launched towards Passchaendale Ridge. The success of this was marred by the fact that heavy rains had fallen since the end of September and the ground which had been almost blown to pieces by the heavy shell fire was turned into a veritable morass.

The losses here were so considerable that during the next few days' fighting the Battalion was amalgamated with the 28th Battalion, both being placed under the command of Colonel Travers, our own Battalion Commander, and the line was eventually carried forward to a cross-roads at the top of Broodseinde Ridge. Eventually the Battalion, considerably depleted in strength and wearied by the terrific fighting which had taken place over the Flanders mud at its worst, returned by motor buses to Steenvoorde in November. The respite however was brief, and after the Battalion had been partially reinforced, it moved forward again into line under Major J. A. Robinson.

The policy at this time was to maintain an active defence and by strong fighting patrols to test the German lines and if possible to ascertain the location and strength of the units opposed to us. This was carried out extensively with success, and in addition a series of defensive positions was constructed by the unit. Special commendation of this work was made by both Brigade and Divisional Commanders. This really completed the fighting in this area as far as the Battalion was concerned, and we were then removed to the line between Messines and Ploegstaert. The position here was on the low-lying ground immediately in front of the Warneton Tower and overlooked by the German positions on the forward slope of the Messines Ridge. This sector was fairly quiet, with the exception of trench mortars which were used by the enemy very extensively. Although the front was quiet the conditions of occupation were very severe. It was now mid-winter and the ground was generally covered with snow and frozen hard, while owing to the fact that the Germans had such superiority in overlooking our positions it was impossible for the men to make themselves as comfortable as would have been done in a better position. The trenches very often were full of mud and water, and during their period in the front line the men simply had to grin and bear it. However, good, keen work was done here, in spite of these drawbacks, and by the use of strong and active fighting patrols we gained in a very short time complete control of "No Man's Land." By this we were enabled to greatly improve our defences, and were able to set out strong barb-wire entanglements. Christmas Eve saw the Battalion on its way out of the front line, after being relieved by the 28th Battalion. This meant seven days out of the line, and then back again to the same position.

After about a month in this area the Division was given a spell and the Battalion moved to Neuve-Eglise, from thence to Locre, and then entrained for a training area near Boulogne. In this area the Battalion had a good spell for about a month. Training was not very severe, and a good system of sports meetings was evolved. At the end of the month the Battalion again entrained for the front, and after detraining at Steenweerk marched to a hutted camp at Canteen Corner.

The Unit was employed here in the construction of defensive positions in advance of Plugsteert. Towards the end of March the great Hun offensive commenced in the "Somme" area, and the whole Australian Corps was rushed down South before the end of March to assist in the attempt to stop the advancing Germans who then had captured Albert and were within a few miles of Amiens. The Unit detrained at Amiens and after one night in billets at Corbie proceeded to take up a position in the line, relieving the 4th Division which had stopped the German advance between Buire and Dernancourt.

The position taken over here consisted of a few potholes on the ridge overlooking the Albert railway, and work was immediately commenced on the construction of a line and the general defence of the position. This was accomplished in a short time and the position made fairly secure. A bold attitude was taken up towards the enemy, and with the help of the 2nd Divisional Artillery it was soon impossible for the enemy to show a head above ground. The Battalion had two or three turns in the line here and rested between whiles just in advance of Franvilliers.

Just before the attack on Vill-sur-Ancre the Battalion was employed in laying underground cable and during the attack acted as Brigade reserve. The next move was to the reserve area between Villiers Bretonneux and after a few days moved up to the support area and camped on the railway embankment near some French guns, one of which blew up one day, causing us about a dozen casualties.

Again we moved to Ville-sur-Ancre and occupied the line there. From thence back again to the Villiers Bretonneux area and relieved the front line Battalion, our front crossing the railway. After ten fairly good days in the line we were relieved and went into close support just in advance of Bois L'Abbaye.

Whilst the Battalion was out of the line the 28th Battalion made a daylight attack and captured a line almost in front of Monument Wood.

At this stage our Commanding Officer, Lieut.-Colonel Travers, D.S.O. and Bar, left the Unit for Australia. While under his command the Unit had made wonderful progress, and had achieved many successes, partly owing to his great organising abilities.

We then took over from the 28th Battalion after ten days in support (which as a matter of fact was spent in nightly visits to the line in parties of no less than 150 strong laying cables and preparing for attacks to come). We continued the policy of offensive defence, and "B" Company, which included quite a number of Tasmanians under Lieut. A. Green, scored a great success in a daylight attack on the 14th July in taking two more trenches and capturing some 10 or more of the enemy. Although small in nature this attack was very severe, and was carried out by a mere handful of men, and in fact was one of these affairs which did so much to keep up the morale of our own troops and to weaken the already dwindling morale of the enemy.

Although every effort was made by the enemy to regain the position captured the advantage gained by our men was held. As a direct result of this further attacks were immediately prepared, and although our line was now in advance of the French, with whom we held what was known as the "International Post" (the Battalion being on the extreme right of the British line) it was decided that we should attack a position some 1000 yards in advance and capture what was known as the "Mound." This was apparently the dumping ground of all the earth excavated from the cutting when the railway line was originally built. It was of considerable height and had a length of four to five hundred yards, and afforded excellent observation over the surrounding country, which was flat for miles.

The attack was launched at dusk on the 16th July, and was for the main part entrusted to "D" Company, which then consisted chiefly of Tasmanians under the command of Captain Murphy. "C" Company, another Tasmanian Company, was divided in two, one half going over as close support to "D" Company, the other half as close support to "A" Company. "B" Company remained in its then advanced position almost at right angles to the French.

The spirit displayed by the troops in this attack was marvellous, both in the offensive and the defensive, and showed that the past few weeks spent in gaining control of "No Man's Land" by small patrol fighting had raised the morale to the highest pitch.

The troops of "D" Company were out hidden in grass from the previous night as movement was impossible in daylight and no food other than that in their possession over night was to be had. The ground over which they had to attack resembled a billiard table with not a scrap of protection to be had anywhere. The position was taken and held against strong counter attacks launched by large bodies of the enemy who made many and desperate efforts to regain the position. But once having gained it there was no thought of retirement.

Lieut. Green's Company immediately prior to the attack secured two strong posts, which had they been allowed to remain in the enemy's possession would undoubtedly have had disastrous results. In taking these two posts three machine guns and 10 prisoners were captured, while a large number of the enemy were killed. "D" Company took many prisoners, machine guns, trench mortars, and also a complete set of instruments from an observation post on "The Mound."

It was during this attack that Lieut. A. C. Borella won his V.C., thus making the 2nd to the credit of the Battalion.

While viewing the success of the Unit the Divisional Commander, Major-General Rosenthall, who had ascended the "Mound" to see the result achieved, was severely wounded in the arm. As was to be expected our casualties were fairly numerous, but the advantages gained were certainly commensurate with the loss.

Now very much reduced in strength we were relieved by the 6th Brigade, and returned to the original support trenches to recuperate. Here a considerable number of reinforcements joined the Battalion and its strength was brought up to about 800 and preparations were commenced for our part in the opening of the great offensive which was to commence on the 8th August.

The Canadians took over the right of the line and we joined them with our right flank on the railway embankment.

With a section of tanks to assist we were given the first phase of the attack to carry out which meant an advance of 2½ miles to a line in advance of La Bastille Mill. The 28th Battalion were on our left and the 25th Battalion supporting.

The night of the 8th August was exceptionally dark, and in view of the enormous number of troops engaged great care was necessary to ensure quietness so as to create if possible the element of surprise. Aeroplanes were used to cover the noise of the approaching tanks. Just prior to zero hour the Germans opened up a half-hour of very heavy shell fire on and around the jumping off position. This however ceased, and gave us sufficient time to make a splendid advance, when our artillery opened fire as a declaration that the great attack had commenced.

The morning broke with a thick fog which without doubt assisted the attack. Fighting however was fierce from the outset, but whatever resistance was met was dealt with emphatically and wiped out of existence. We reached our objective in good time just in advance of our flank units, and although our numbers were considerably lessened the same dauntless spirit prevailed. All sorts of tactics had been adopted to overcome the machine guns met with, and every post or position by the dead around it proved how well and truly the men had put their training to the test, played their part, and gained their end.

The captures by the Battalion will help to show some of the obstacles that had to be overcome:—Prisoners, 160; enemy dead (noticed by cursory observation), 160; guns taken, one 5.9 battery, four 4.5 Howitzers, eleven 77 mm. field guns, while there were also dozens of machine guns and trench mortars.

As the mist cleared away revealing the scene the 4th Division moved through us, and at the same time our "Travelling Kitchens" arrived up on to our position and dished out to all on their positions as much hot food as they wanted. This was an accomplishment never before equalled during the Battalion's experience in France, and certainly could not have been more appreciated. We remained where we had halted over night and on the following morning moved forward about 11 a.m. in extended order to Harbonniers. On the march we learnt that we were to be used in a very close support in a further attack moving only a few hundred yards in rear of the front line troops.

The attack commenced at 2 p.m. Three tanks were employed on our sector, but owing to the absence of any support from artillery they were very quickly put out of action. The commencement was very lively, and one could see the German gunners load up and fire at point blank range. However, as the advance was rapid, they soon left their guns, and we eventually pulled up in advance of Vaux-Villiers.

At this point there appeared to be a gap between the 1st and 2nd Divisional positions and as the actual position could not at the time be ascertained we were ordered to attack with the 28th Battalion on our left and to push forward, and if possible to act with the 1st Division, who were also moving forward that day.

The attack took place on the morning of the 11th of August, and was successfully carried out in every detail, and though we were not in actual touch with the 1st Division we were able to locate their posts and know that all was clear between them and us.

The Battalion had by this time suffered very heavy casualties and was relieved the same night, moving back to a line of trenches in front of Harbonniers.

Here we remained for a few days to return to the lines if necessary. However the Division was relieved, and we movd back by bus to Bussy to reorganise and recuperate. The Battalion was again strengthened by reinforcements and in a fortnight we moved up to the front line. On the next day we commenced to attack from the rear of Dompiere at 8 a.m., and had attached to us one section of the Royal Artillery.

By this time the result of our repeated onslaughts and successes was becoming plain, and the enemy was now not showing a great amount of fight. We advanced in open order for a considerable distance with little opposition.

On approaching the high ground near the River Somme immediately in front of Peronne we were subjected to intense machine gun fire from posts which were left on our side of the canal to hold up the advance. Practically all the bridges except one had been blown up after their artillery had withdrawn to the opposite side of the canal.

On reaching the top of the ridge we again came under heavy direct fire, and after strenuous work we reached the canal banks just about 12 noon, capturing and killing only a moderate number of the enemy. Their artillery then blew up the one remaining bridge, and canal and river were both impassable, thus forcing us to occupy the railway running almost along the bank of the canal. On the opposite side of the river near Mont St. Quentin the attack by the 5th Brigade had commenced, and we were relieved by the 4th Division, the next evening moving back to Dompiere, the point from which our attack had commenced.

Next morning we were ordered forward again to cross the river and move up in support of the 5th and 6th Brigades who had reported the capture of Mont St. Quentin. The capture however was not quite complete as the enemy were still holding a portion of the town on top of the hill, and being under direct observation we came in for very heavy shell fire right up to Clery. We were ordered to shelter under the cover of huge embankments along the river side, where we remained for the night while the 5th and 6th Brigades renewed their attacks. The following night we moved up closer into support and had hardly got settled down when word came that we were to continue the attack at 6.30 a.m. the following morning. Up to this time no opportunity had been given us to reconnoitre the new line and no certain information as to its exact location could be given. A hurried reconnaissance was carried out, and officers and N.C.O.'s were given a line to assemble on. The attack was most difficult, as we had to conform to the movements of an English Division on our left, the 5th Australian Division on our right, and each apparently had been given different times at which to attack.

At last the attack was launched and was a particularly hard fight from start to finish. Although the enemy's artillery concentration was frightful we gained our objective and were able to hold on. The casualties here were enormous, practically two Companies being wiped out, while the other two Companies also suffered severe losses.

Two of our Companies advancing over the low level ground approaching Peronne were subjected to severe machine gun and artillery fire, and it became almost impossible to move. The enemy could clearly be seen behind their machine guns firing at point blank range. Just how the position was taken and held was little short of marvellous.

After 48 hours of the worst gruelling the Battalion had yet experienced we were relieved.

During this attack a very large proportion of the Tasmanians of the

Battalion were killed, amongst them being Captain A. O. Woods, M.C. We then moved by easy stages to a reserve area and we camped along the canal bank, which proved to be an ideal spot for swimming and boating. After fourteen days in rest we again commenced our move forward, and by forced marches passed through Peronne and were in reserve when the attack on the Hindenburg Line between St. Quentin and Canberai was launched.

After the first phase of the attack by Australian and American troops we moved up through Tincourt and at once resumed what eventually turned out to be our last and most successful fight.

We advanced to Bullecourt and captured trenches in the first of the Hindenburg series, and the following morning attacked and captured the Buravoir line on the 4th October, 1918. Our casualties were again exceptionally heavy as our task was the final objective of the Brigade and we were to go as far as possible, all the time of course subjected to heavy machine gun and shell fire.

On this occasion the whole of the Battalion headquarters were one by one made casualties.

After being relieved by American troops we were sent back to rest behind Amiens, and were still in this position when the Armistice was declared. We then moved to Belgium with the 4th Army at Charleroi and remained in this area until demobilisation was completed.

40TH BATTALION.

The 40th Battalion arrived in France on the morning of the 24th November, 1916, disembarking at Le Havre, and after spending a few days in billets near Bailleul, on the 2nd December marched to, and occupied, the city of Armentieres, as reserve battalion of the 10th Brigade, which Brigade had now taken over the trenches immediately south of the River Lys, and immediately east of Armentieres.

On the 9th December the Battalion relieved the 38th Battalion in the trenches immediately south of the Lys. This was the first tour of duty in the front line. Winter conditions prevailed, the trenches being very wet and in a bad state of repair, but the sector was comparatively quiet, the few casualties during the first few days coming mostly from enemy sniping.

After occupying this front line position until the 16th December, the Battalion was relieved and became Support Battalion of the Brigade, occupying buildings in the shattered suburb of Armentieres known as Houplines, and on the 20th December again took over the same trenches as before. This meant Xmas Day in the front line. For three or four days prior to Xmas day the enemy waved white flags from his trenches, evidently with the idea of establishing an unofficial respite for festivities, but he received no encouragement from our side of No-Man's-Land, and on Xmas night the 37th Battalion successfully raided the enemy from the 40th Battalion sector.

On the 28th December the Battalion was relieved and again went into reserve in Armentieres, and on the 3rd January, 1917, again took over the same front line trenches. That same evening shortly after dark the enemy attempted a raid on the 40th Battalion trenches. After nearly an hour's preliminary bombardment a party of the enemy, numbering about eighty, appeared in front of Hobbs' Farm and got within a few yards of our parapet, but were driven off by the garrison by means of rifles, bombs, and a Lewis gun. The enemy left some dead in No-Man's-Land, while our casualties from the bombardment numbered 8 killed and 23 wounded. This was the first time the Battalion had met with an enemy raid, and on several subsequent occasions the results were similar. It is a fact of which the 40th Battalion is justly proud that the enemy were never over their parapet.

On the 9th January the Battalion again went into support in Houplines, and while here a party of four officers and 60 other ranks attempted to raid the enemy trenches at a point about 600 yards south of the River Lys. The raid was unsuccessful, as the enemy, warned of the raid by our wire-cutting programme with trench mortars, had filled his front line trench with wire, and our party were unable to enter. They returned, having sustained 10 casualties.

On the 14th January the Battalion again took over the same front line trenches as before, and on the 19th January were relieved by part of the 9th Brigade. The 10th Brigade now became Reserve Brigade of the Division, and were stationed in Armentieres until the 26th January, when the 40th Battalion took over part of the Bois Grenier sector from a British unit. This sector was about a mile south of the one previously occupied.

On the 28th January a raiding party of eight officers and 220 other ranks of the 10th Brigade raided the enemy trenches at Pont Ballot on the Houplines Sector. This party was made up of two officers and about 50 other ranks of each Battalion in the Brigade, and each Battalion party operated separately. The 39th and 40th Battalion parties had to enter the enemy trenches at a certain point, while the 38th and 37th parties had to effect an entrance on the left and right respectively of this point. The parties of the 37th and 38th Battalions failed to get through the enemy wire, but the 39th and 40th parties got through and penetrated the enemy position to a depth of 200 yards, inflicting casualties on the enemy. Owing to the failure of the flank Battalions to join up with the 39th and 40th in the enemy trenches the main object of the raid, namely, to round up a number of prisoners, was not attained.

On the night of the 31st January, after an hour's heavy preparatory bombardment, a large party of the enemy made another attempt to raid the 40th Battalion trenches near the Lille Road. The ground was white with snow, and the enemy, being dressed in white garments, got close to our parapet without being seen. He was driven off by the determined action of one post containing a few men, and the attempt was a failure. Our casualties during the bombardment were heavy, numbering over sixty, as the ground was frozen hard, which made the shrapnel effect of the enemy's high explosives very severe.

From the 6th to the 8th February the Battalion was in support at Chapelle D'Armentieres, and on the night of the 8th took over the Battalion sector on the right of the one previously occupied. Here the Battalion attempted another raid and was unsuccessful. The raid was attempted without artillery assistance, but our party, consisting of three officers and 50 other ranks, found the enemy well prepared, with the gap in his wire mended and a strong garrison behind it, who opened fire as soon as our party reached the wire. We were unable to get through the entanglements, and withdrew with eight casualties.

On the 20th February the Battalion went back into support at Chapelle d'Armentieres, and on the 25th again took over the left Battalion sector at Bois Grenier. On the 2nd March the Battalion was relieved and moved back to Armentieres, and a few days later the 10th Brigade became Reserve Brigade of the Division, and marched back to Tatinghem, near St. Omer, for training, after 14 weeks of continuous trench warfare.

The Battalion remained at Tatinghem in hard training until the 5th April, when it entrained back to Steenwerck, and on the 8th April relieved the 34th Battalion in the Houplines Sector. With the spring, the artillery activity on both sides had increased, and the trenches east of Armentieres could no longer be called quiet.

Shortly after dark on the 12th April, after a long and heavy bombardment, the enemy attempted another raid on the 40th Battalion at Hobbs' Farm. The enemy party was caught by two Lewis guns when about 20 yards from our parapet, and retired in disorder, leaving dead in front of our trenches. It was discovered later from a prisoner that this raiding party was part of a specially trained raiding force which had been recently brought on to our front. Three nights later the enemy again put down a heavy bombardment on our trenches, and when a raid appeared certain to happen he switched his bombardment across the River Lys on to the trenches held by a British unit on our left, and successfully raided them, capturing several prisoners.

On the 16th April the Battalion was relieved at Houplines, and after remaining in support in Armentieres until the 27th April, crossed the River Lys into Belgium, and occupied a support position in the defences of Ploegsteert Wood, which was just behind the front line at St. Yves.

On the 6th May the Battalion moved forward and relieved the 39th Battalion in the front line trenches immediately south of the River Douve, in the sector known as St. Yves. While here preliminary orders were received that the 3rd Australian Division would take part in the forthcoming attack on the Messines-Wytchaete Ridge. On the 7th May the enemy attempted to raid the sector, but the attempt never really developed, as it was broken by the prompt and accurate fire from our artillery.

On the 15th May the Battalion moved out of the line and went back to Romarin, engaged continuously in carrying ammunition, making artillery positions, digging assembly trenches, and other necessary work preparatory to an attack. Casualties here were continuous, as the enemy's artillery was very active, and communications, batteries, and ammunition dumps were being constantly shelled.

On the morning of the 31st May, with the object of procuring information from enemy prisoners, the 40th Battalion sent a raiding party of three officers and forty other ranks to the enemy trenches immediately south of the River Douve. Through a delay in getting across No-Man's-Land the party did not reach the enemy trenches till daylight was just breaking, and a bomb fight resulted on the enemy parapet, in which both sides suffered severely. Our party withdrew when it was too light to remain longer, without being able to secure a prisoner. Our casualties numbered two killed and 18 wounded.

On the night of the 4th June the 40th Battalion position at Romarin was heavily shelled by gas-shell for several hours, which compelled the Battalion to move to another area until after daylight, when the breeze purified the atmosphere. This was the first heavy gassing undergone by the Battalion, and casualties numbered 36, but it was perhaps useful training for the approach march two nights later.

The attack on the Messines-Wytchaete Ridge was carried out on the 7th June, 1917, with nine divisions. The 3rd Australian Division was on the extreme right flank of the attack on the right of the New Zealand Division, whose objective included the town of Messines. The Division attacked with the 10th Brigade on the left and the 9th Brigade on the right, with the 11th Brigade in reserve. The 10th Brigade attacked with the 39th Battalion south of the River Douve, and the 40th Battalion north of that stream, while the 38th Battalion leap-frogged through the 40th

Battalion, and the 37th Battalion through the 39th Battalion, "D" Company of the 40th Battalion was detached and came under the orders of the 37th Battalion, who were advancing to the farthest objective (known as the "Green Line").

The distance of the 40th Battalion objective beyond the enemy front line averaged 400 yards. It included an intricate trench system immediately north of the River Douve, and to the Battalion was also entrusted the task of throwing light bridges across the Douve, which flowed across No-Man's-Land in front of the 10th Brigade. These bridges were necessary to enable the part of the 40th Battalion south of the stream to get across, and were also necessary for the 38th Battalion, who were leap-frogging through the 40th Battalion at a later stage. The assembly trenches of the 40th Battalion were astride the Douve.

At 11 p.m. on the night of the 6th June the Battalion left Romarin in order to get into position for the attack. Before going far we ran into heavy gas shelling. The enemy, knowing that an attack was pending, was saturating the country round Ploegsteert with gas in order to prevent any concentration for the attack. Gas masks had to be worn, and not only was the march difficult under these conditions, but casualties from gas and high explosive were heavy. The Battalion ultimately reached its assembly trenches after sustaining over 90 casualties during the approach march.

At 3.10 a.m. the attack began, simultaneously with the explosion of several mines under the enemy trenches, and a heavy artillery bombardment. The 40th Battalion moved forward behind the artillery barrage, threw their bridges across the stream, and attacked the enemy position. No solid resistance was met with; over 100 prisoners were captured, many casualties were inflicted on the enemy, and the Battalion objective was gained by 3.30 a.m. Shortly afterwards the 38th Battalion passed through the 40th, on their way to the next objective. During the whole of the day the Battalion position was heavily shelled by the enemy, and our casualties were numerous and continuous.

At 10.15 a.m. "D" Company of the 40th Battalion moved forward towards the last objective with the 37th Battalion. This Company had a hard fight against heavy machine gun fire, and brilliant work was carried out in reaching the objective. Their casualties were heavy, and included three officers out of four. The objective was gained and a line consolidated on the right of the 37th Battalion, between that Battalion and the Douve.

At 7.30 p.m. the enemy counter-attack developed on our front, but it melted away under the fire of our artillery. The next day "D" Company returned to the 40th Battalion position on the first objective, where the Battalion remained until 8.30 a.m. on the morning of the 9th June, when they were relieved by the 42nd Battalion and moved back to Nieppe for re-organisation and rest.

The casualties during the battle were:—

	Officers.	Other Ranks.
Killed in action	—	41
Died of wounds	—	5
Wounded	6	297
Total	6	343

The Battalion remained at Nieppe till the 11th June, and then moved to Wulverghem, working there until the 18th, when the whole Brigade bivouacked near Kemmel Hill, and a Brigade syllabus of training was begun. On the 20th July the Battalion moved forward and occupied support trenches in the newly-captured trenches on the Messines Ridge, immediately north of Messines, where 14 days were spent. This was one of the most unpleasant times that the Battalion ever passed. Enemy shelling was constant, and it rained incessantly until the trenches became streams of water.

On the 4th August the Battalion was relieved by the 13th Battalion and moved back to a camp near Dranoutre, and on the 14th August moved back by train and road to the village of Becourt, near the town of Desvres. The whole Division had moved to this area, and training and reorganisation was commenced. After several weeks of training, on the 22nd September the Division was inspected by the Commander-in-Chief (Sir Douglas Haig), a sure indication that the Division would be "over the top" very shortly. Within 24 hours afterwards orders were received that the Division would move forward to Ypres to take part in the third Battle of Ypres, which had already commenced. On the 25th September the 40th Battalion left Becourt, and after three days on the road reached Winnezeele. Here the Battalion received preliminary orders for the attack, and on the 1st October moved forward to Vlamertinghe, approximately eight miles from where the attack was to commence on the 4th October.

On the 4th October the 3rd Australian Division took part in the third battle of Ypres. The Division attacked with the 10th Brigade on the left and the 11th Brigade on the right. The 10th Brigade attacked with the 37th Battalion, taking the first objective, the 38th Battalion the second objective, the 39th Battalion the third objective, and the 40th Battalion the last objective.

The Battalion left Vlamertinghe on the evening of the 3rd October, and marched through and beyond Ypres, reaching the assembly position at 4 a.m., where the Brigade occupied shell holes and waited for Zero hour, which had been fixed at 6 a.m. At 5.30 a.m. our assembly position was heavily shelled, causing numerous casualties. It was afterwards found that the reason for this bombardment was that the enemy intended to attack at 6.10 a.m., and that his assaulting troops were actually in position in front of us. When our barrage came down at 6 a.m. it fell on the enemy in his assembly position, and when we went forward behind this barrage, most of the enemy who were left surrendered.

The first three objectives were taken after fairly solid fighting, and then the 40th Battalion leap-frogged through the 39th Battalion, and made for the last objective on the Broodseinde Ridge. Along the top of the ridge was a line of concrete forts, known as "pill-boxes," with a strong trench system heavily wired, and from this position heavy machine-gun fire was coming. Our casualties from this were very heavy, and probably the stiffest fight the Battalion ever had resulted. From shell-hole to shell-hole the Battalion crept forward under a tornado of machine-gun fire, men falling every yard, and when about 200 yards from the ridge, the position looked critical, in view of our casualties and the enemy's strong resistance. But the left company saved the situation. Taking advantage of some "dead" ground on the extreme left of our advance, they worked forward on to the ridge, from where they enfiladed the enemy position with Lewis guns, while the other three companies, under cover of this fire, rushed and captured the position with a determined assault. Approximately 300 prisoners, with 17 machine guns, were captured there by the Battalion.

As soon as the objective was gained, a defensive line was consolidated, which was subjected to intermittent shelling for the remainder of the day. During the next 36 hours several local counter attacks were made by the enemy on the army front, but it was not until about 5 p.m. on the 5th October that a counter attack was attempted on the 40th Battalion, and the New Zealanders on the left. After a heavy bombardment of our position and communications, two columns of the enemy appeared about 1000 yards away on our left front. It was estimated that there were about 500 men in each column. Our artillery and machine guns caught the enemy as he deployed into close waves, inflicting heavy casualties and scattering the enemy in confusion.

Before midnight on the 5th October the Battalion was relieved by a unit of the 66th British Division, and marched back to Vlamertinghe. Our casualties during the operation were—

	Officers.	Other ranks.	Total.
Killed	1	49	50
Wounded	6	198	204
	7	247	254

On the 9th October a further attack was made. From the ground won by the 3rd Australian Division on the 4th October the attack was carried forward by the 66th British Division. The whole attack failed, chiefly owing to the indescribable mud conditions, which made movement of men slow, and movement of artillery impossible.

On the 12th October the attack was renewed, the 3rd Australian Division continuing the attack from the ground won on the 4th October, as the 66th Division had failed to advance the line in their attack on the 9th October. From the 4th October till the 12th October heavy rain had fallen almost continuously, and the Ypres battlefield was a sodden waste of mud.

The 3rd Australian Division attacked with the 9th Brigade on the right and the 10th Brigade on the left. Of the 10th Brigade, the 37th Battalion were to take the first objective, the 40th Battalion the second objective, and the 38th Battalion were to advance through and beyond Passchendaele. The 39th Battalion was in reserve. The atack was timed to open at 5.25 a.m. At 4.30 a.m. our assembly positions were heavily shelled, as the enemy had received warning of the attack from a British soldier who had deserted early in the evening to the enemy.

At 5.25 a.m. the Brigade pushed forward under heavy artillery and machine-gun fire. After going about 100 yards, the 37th Battalion was held up, and 38th and 40th Battalions telescoped into the 37th Battalion, causing a good deal of confusion, and the three Battalions pushed on together, hoping to be able to re-organise when the first objective was reached. Our casualties were severe and progress was slow through the mud. Part of the 40th Battalion captured the enemy position in Augustus Wood, taking about 40 prisoners there and killing a number of the enemy; but the ground generally was impassable. Numbers of our men were stuck in the mud and unable to get out; some had to be packed up with timber and dragged out the following day. On our left the New Zealanders were unable to advance through the mud and uncut wire, and we were subjected to enfilade fire from the left flank in consequence. Our Lewis guns and rifles were choked with mud, and we were unable to return the enemy fire. Casualties were increasing so rapidly that disaster seemed inevitable.

At 7 a.m. the first objective was reached by the remnants of the Brigade, numbering about 200 of the three Battalions. Our left flank was in the air. We were being fired on from the front, left flank, and rear, and were almost entirely without artillery support. Under these circumstances it was decided to remain on the first objective until the New Zealanders were able to come up on our flank.

During the morning the enemy made an attempt to cut off the Brigade by getting round our left flank. This made the position so serious that at 1.45 p.m. the Brigade had to withdraw some distance to protect the flank. The 9th Brigade also withdrew to conform to this movement. No further attempt to advance was made. What was left of the 40th Battalion spent the next day in digging out and carrying back the wounded. Even if reinforced, a further advance would have been impossible through the morass. Passchendaele was only 2000 yards away, and though after the 12th October several further attacks were made by the Canadians, the village was not captured until the 6th November, after three weeks of constant fighting.

The casualties of the Battalion during the 12th and 13th October were—

	Officers.	Other ranks.	Total
Killed	2	77	79
Wounded	5	163	168
Prisoners	—	1	1
	7	241	248

On the 15th October the Battalion moved back through the remains of Ypres, and then embussed to Becourt, part of the Divisional Training Area. On arrival there the strength of the Battalion was barely 200, but reinforcements and drafts from hospital began to arrive, and the time was occupied with reorganising, re-equipping, and training.

On the 10th November the Battalion left Becourt and moved back by stages towards the line, taking over a reserve position at Romarin as Reserve Battalion, the 10th Brigade having taken over the front line position immediately south of the River Douve.

On the 21st November the Battalion took over the left of the Brigade sector known as the Warneton Sector. The enemy artillery activity was considerable, the enemy apparently expecting further offensive operations on that part of the front on the appearance of the Australian Corps. Two days later marked the completion of the first year in France of the 40th Battalion, and the following casualty statistics were compiled:—

	Officers.	Other ranks.	Total.
Killed	9	233	242
Wounded	25	1067	1092
Prisoners	—	1	1
Total	34	1301	1335

On the 29th November the Battalion moved back into support in dugouts on the side of Hill 63, and was there chiefly engaged in improving the front line trench.

On the night of the 30thNovember-1stDecember a most successful raid raid was carried out by a party of four officers and 72 other ranks of the 40th Battalion. The enemy trenches raided were immediately north of the railway line from La Basse Ville to Warneton. At 5.15 p.m. on the 30th November a party of the 39th Battalion raided this point, killing a number of the enemy and bringing back several prisoners. About 20 casualties were sustained by the 39th Battalion party. At 1.15 a.m. during the same night the 40th Battalion party crossed No-Man's-Land and entered the enemy trenches at the same point. They found a new garrison moving in to relieve the one which had been badly mauled during the earlier raid, and also found a large working party repairing the broken trenches. The enemy was completely disorganised and taken by surprise. All resistance was overcome rapidly, dugouts and trenches were quickly cleared, and our party did great execution before withdrawing. Our casualties were one missing and one wounded. Two of the enemy were brought back for identification purposes, while it was estimated that quite 100 were killed or wounded.

On the 6th December the Battalion again went into the front line south of the River Douve, remaining there until the 15th, when we were relieved by the 26th Battalion and moved back to Neuve Eglise as part of the Division in Reserve. Here Christmas week was spent during intense cold.

On the 27th January the 40th Battalion moved to Hill 63, remaining there in support until the 4th February, when we relieved the 38th Battalion in the Warneton Sector, carrying on ordinary trench routine until the 12th February, when we returned to Hill 63 and remained there working on rear defences until the 16th February. We then returned to the front line. During this tour in the line the chief incident was the successful action of one of our fighting patrols in smashing an enemy raiding party as it crossed No-Man's-Land on the way to raid one of our posts.

On the 25th February the Battalion was relieved by the 34th Battalion, and moved back to Romarin as part of the Reserve Brigade engaged on improving the Corps defence line. We remained there until the 4th March, when we were relieved by the 20th Battalion and entrained for Lumbres, from where we marched to the village of Seninghem. The whole Division was now in reserve, and remained so until the opening of the German Offensive on the 21st March.

While at Seninghem a competition was commenced in the 3rd Australian Division to decide the best platoon in the Division. Similar competitions were being carried out in every Division in the British and Overseas Forces, but before the completion of the competition in the 3rd Division the German offensive opened, and the question of the best Platoon in the Division was held over until the more pressing matter had been dealt with. The competition was eventually decided on the Somme, and resulted in a win for a platoon of the 40th Battalion.

On the opening of the German offensive on the 21st March the Battalion was at once warned to be ready to proceed back to the fighting line, and on the 23rd March started for Flanders, where another attack was expected, but while on the way the whole Division was stopped and ordered to the Somme. After remaining for two days at Campagne the Battalion entrained at St. Omer on the afternoon of the 26th March, and detrained at Mondicourt at 4 a.m. on the following morning, with information that the line was broken, the enemy was only a few miles away, and we might expect to be in action shortly after daylight. However, orders were awaited, and at 1 p.m. we moved off, and after marching several miles were picked up by motor busses and taken to Franvillers, where Divisional Headquarters had been established. From there we at once marched to Heilly, coming under enemy artillery fire during the march, and shortly after dark bivouacked in the open near Heilly as Reserve Battalion of the 10th Brigade, with the 37th and 38th Battalions in front on the high ground from the junction of the Mericourt-L'Abbe-Sailly-le-Sec Road with the Bray-Corbie Road—to a point on the River Ancre about 1000 yards east of Mericourt-L'Abbe.

Next day, the 28th March, information was received that the main body of the enemy was advancing towards Morlancourt, and the 40th Battalion was ordered to advance at 4 p.m. through the Brigade defence line, and prevent the enemy seizing the high ground between that line and the village of Morlancourt. This ground was already held by the enemy advance guard.

Owing to transport difficulties during the hurried move to the Somme the Brigade had neither trench mortars nor machine guns available, nor was there any artillery behind us to render assistance. At 4 p.m. the 40th Battalion advanced through the line held by the 37th and 38th Battalions under heavy enemy artillery and machine gun fire, and in spite of this resistance continued to advance, driving the advanced parties before them. After advancing several hundred yards the enemy main body was seen advancing in column about 2500 yards away, as he came over the hill south of Morlancourt. The Battalion continued on, but the enemy hesitated, deployed, advanced in artillery formation for a short distance, and then went to ground, presumably to dig in, while his machine guns were pushed out in front and the fire became hotter than ever. After an advance of 1200 yards beyond the line held by the rest of the Brigade no further advance was possible under the heavy fire. A copse alive with machine guns could not be passed without artillery or trench mortars, and the Battalion went to ground and dug in. After dark the 39th Battalion moved up to our left flank, and a Battalion of the 11th Brigade did the same on our right flank. The casualties in the Battalion during the day numbered over 160. Next morning machine guns were brought forward to our position, and the divisional artillery began to move in behind us.

On the 29th March our position was shelled constantly during the day. That night the copse previously mentioned was captured, and our right flank was advanced about 600 yards.

Next morning, about 11.30 a.m., the enemy attack developed on a fairly large scale. Dense waves of the enemy advanced diagonally across our front towards the 11th Brigade line, but our artillery, machine guns, and Lewis guns smashed the attack in a decisive manner, and the enemy waves melted away before reaching the Australian line.

Before daylight on the 31st March we were relieved by part of the 11th Brigade, and moved back about 2500 yards to Ribemont as reserve Battalion. The casualties of the Battalion during the 28th, 29th, and 30th March were:—

	Officers.	Other ranks.	Total.
Killed	2	44	46
Wounded	10	169	179
Prisoner	—	1	1
Total	12	214	226

On the evening of the 3rd April the Battalion took over the right half of the Brigade front line, with the left flank on the north corner of Marrett Wood. The next day an attack was beaten off by the 39th Battalion on our left, and on the north side of the Ancre the 4th Division met the full force of the attack, and after a hard day's fighting with varying success, kept the enemy back. During this attack our position in Marrett Wood was heavily shelled, causing 23 casualties in the 40th Battalion.

On the night of the 6th April the Battalion was relieved by the 37th Battalion, and went back into support trenches east of Mericourt L'Abbe until the 9th April, when we took over the left of the 10th Brigade sector, about 500 yards east of the villages of Treux and Buire, remaining there until the 12th April, when we moved back into reserve at Ribemont.

On the 16th April the Battalion took over the sector astride the Ancre.

While here a successful encounter by one of our fighting patrols secured a prisoner. On the 22nd April we were relieved and moved back into the reserve position at Ribemont, where we were heavily shelled during the next two days. On the night of the 26th April the Battalion again went into the front line astride the River Ancre. While here a raid was carried out by two officers and 34 other ranks of the 40th Battalion on an enemy post about 500 yards north of Ville-sur-Ancre. This raid was completely successful. Our party sustained no casualties and disposed of about 20 of the enemy in the post, bringing back one prisoner. Two nights later two of the enemy were captured by one of our patrols.

On the 1st May the Battalion was again relieved by the 38th Battalion and moved back to Ribemont until the 5th May, when we took over the same front line sector as before. On the 8th May it was reported by Brigade observers that there were indications that the enemy were withdrawing from Ville-sur-Ancre. Consequently orders were received from Brigade that a party of one officer and 30 other ranks of the 40th Battalion and a similar party of the 39th Battalion were to push forward that night and occupy the village. As was expected, the information was incorrect, and both parties were held up on the outskirts of the village by heavy machine gun fire. They withdrew with casualties. A few days later Ville-sur-Ancre was captured by the 6th Brigade after a hard fight, and 600 prisoners were taken from the village and the defences round it.

On the 9th May the 40th Battalion was relieved by the 24th Battalion, and moved back to Frechencourt, the whole Division now being in reserve. Here sports and training were commenced and continued till the 22nd May, when we moved south to Blangy-Tronville, and were there employed chiefly in burying cable in the vicinity of L'Abbe Wood, until the 4th June, when we moved forward and occupied Villers-Bretonneux and support trenches to the west of that town.

At Villers-Bretonneux the Battalion was placed in support positions in and west of the town. On account of its great strategical importance, the town was strongly fortified by a system of "keeps" at cross-streets, from which Lewis guns controlled all the streets and the approaches to the town. Villers-Bretonneux was heavily and consistently shelled by the enemy every night.

On the evening of the 11th June the 40th Battalion relieved the 38th Battalion in the front line east of the town, this line being astride the main road from Amiens to St. Quentin. The front line consisted of posts among high crops of wheat.

On the night of the 13th June a party of the 40th Battalion was detailed to find an enemy post and obtain a prisoner. A post was located behind an old aeroplane hangar, about 100 yards in advance of our line, and under cover of a shower of rifle grenades a party of one officer and eight men rushed it. The party found that the post consisted of a trench behind the hangar, in which tunnelled dugouts had been constructed. They threw bombs into the trench and jumped in after they had exploded. They found the dugouts full of frightened Germans, among whom they threw more bombs, but as soon as the enemy realised the small strength of our party, they began to make a fight of it, and as they appeared to number over 60, our party, who had no more bombs, withdrew with one killed and four wounded out of a total of nine. The enemy casualties must have been heavy from the bombs in the crowded dugouts. Next day the post was destroyed by artillery and trench motars.

On the 18th June the Battalion was relieved, and moved back to its former position in and west of Villers-Bretonneux. After remaining here for four days we went back into a reserve position near Blangy Tronville, where all available personnel were engaged in burying cable between Villers-Bretonneux and Aubigny.

On the 26th June we moved to Querrieu, where training and sports were begun, and remained in that area till the 11th July, when we returned to the line and relieved the 50th Battalion in the trenches, about 1000 yards east of Hamel. We remained there until the 2nd August, and then had two days in support, afterwards going back into the front line with the remainder of the 10th Brigade to hold the Divisional front during the opening stages of the battle of Amiens, which opened on the 8th August, and which Ludendorff describes as "a black day for Germany."

In the opening stages of the battle of Amiens the 10th Brigade, including the 40th Battalion, played no part beyond holding the front line while the attacking troops moved forward, and soon after the battle opened we became part of the Corps reserve. Zero hour was at 4.20 a.m., and four hours later the 40th Battalion moved behind the attacking troops to Accroche Wood, and rested till evening, when we advanced another two and a half miles to Reginald Wood, remaining there until the 10th August, when the 10th Brigade was ordered into the battle.

On the evening of the 10th August the enemy was holding the line of Germaine Wood-Proyart-La Flaque, and the plan laid down for the Brigade was to advance by night with tanks up the Amiens-St. Quentin road, through the enemy outpost line, to a point 1200 yards east of La Flaque, and then to turn due north towards the Somme, thus getting behind the enemy position, and cutting him off.

The attack was unsuccessful by reason of the fact that tanks have great difficulty in keeping direction by night, and consequently these tanks were compelled to move up the road with the infantry, with the result that the noise of their coming was like that of many traction engines, which duly warned the enemy of the attack.

When nearing the German outpost line enemy aeroplanes came and dropped flares over the road, and, by the light of these flares, bombed the column, causing many casualties and a good deal of confusion. The advance was continued, and in addition to the enemy bombing, artillery and machine guns opened on to the road. By the time we reached a point 400 yards east of La Flaque, all the tanks were out of action from enemy fire, and the casualties in the leading Battalion (37th) were very heavy. The Brigade here took cover while the situation was reported, and instructions were then received for the 37th and 39th Battalions to withdraw while the 38th and 40th Battalions dug in on a suitable line from which Proyart might be attacked at a later stage. This was done, and the following day the 40th Battalion remained there under constant enemy artillery fire.

On the morning of the 12th August the 40th Battalion, with the 37th Battalion on the left, was ordered to move forward slowly and work the enemy out of his position in front, which was strongly defended with machine guns. The objective of the Battalion was the valley south of the Proyart-Chuignes road, and to get to this objective we had to advance 1300 yards over open ground, under direct observation and machine-gun fire. The plan adopted to carry this out without suffering heavy casualties was for patrols to work forward till they reached a position from which the enemy guns could be attacked, and the attacks would then be made by platoons moving up behind the patrols in a series of bounds.

This plan was completely successful, and yard by yard, under heavy fire, the Battalion dribbled forward in small parties, dislodging the enemy from one post after another, until the position was won. One incident in the advance is worthy of mention, and gives some indication of the resistance encountered. To give covering fire to his Company, Sergeant P. C. Statton, of the 40th Battalion, with a small party of men, had two Lewis guns firing on enemy machines from behind an embankment on the Proyart-Chuignes road. From here Sergeant Statton could see that the 37th Battalion had reached the railway line east of Proyart, but was held up by several machine guns firing from posts about 150 yards in front of that Battalion. Statton, with three men, therefore took advantage of the embankment to get to a point about 80 yards to the left of these guns. Armed only with his revolver, he rushed across the open ground at the machine-gun posts, the men in which were still firing on the 37th Battalion, and did not see him coming. He shot two men on the first gun, and the remainder were killed by the three men with him. He then rushed the next, and killed the crew, with the exception of one man, for whom he had no shot left. This man attacked Statton with his bayonet, who wrenched the rifle from the enemy's hand, and killed him with his own bayonet. He then made for the next two guns, but the crews of these left their guns and fled, only to be picked off by our Lewis gunners waiting behind the embankment.

Sergeant Statton and his party were all this time under fire from the enemy in front, and one man of the party was killed and one badly wounded. Statton and the remaining man then crawled back to safety. For his bravery on this occasion Sergeant Statton was afterwards awarded the Victoria Cross.

The objective gained by the 40th Battalion was consolidated, and before daylight on the following morning we were relieved by a British unit, and moved back to bivouac at Reginald Wood.

The next few days were spent resting at Reginald Wood, and on the evening of the 21st August we crossed the Somme, and moved to Sailly Laurette. On the 23rd August the Battalion received orders that we would attack the town of Bray that night.

The 23rd August marked the opening of what is known as the battle of Bapaume, during which, in ten days' fighting, the enemy was driven from one side of the old Somme battlefields to the other, and the line of the Somme was turned. The first 24 hours of the battle consisted of a series of assaults at selected points along the front, and one of these points was Bray.

The Battalion left Sailly-Laurette at 8 p.m., and arrived at the assembly point, about 300 yards west of Bray, at 12.45 a.m. The attack was planned for 1 a.m. The enemy outpost line was about 100 yards west of the town.

The ultimate objective of the Battalion was to capture the town and consolidate a line 500 yards to the east of it, and the plan of attack laid down was for a company to advance quickly through the northern outskirts of the town, and another company through the southern edge, and both companies to dig in on the objective. A third company was detailed to clear Bray of the enemy, and the remaining company was held in reserve, and part of it used for getting ammunition forward.

At 1 a.m. our barrage opened and the Battalion moved forward behind it, over-running the enemy outpost line, and capturing prisoners and machine guns there. The Company taking the northern edge of the town met with the bulk of the enemy resistance, in the shape of heavy shelling with high explosive and gas. This company moved on in the darkness, dislodging the enemy from his posts, and capturing several machine guns. The other company on the right met with less trouble till after Bray was behind them, when several machine guns were captured. On reaching the objective both of these companies exploited their success by sending patrols forward, who captured more guns and prisoners. The company whose duty it was to clear the town had several sharp encounters with the enemy in the streets, but the majority of the enemy garrison had taken refuge in cellars, from which they were taken without much difficulty.

As soon as daylight came, great numbers of the enemy were seen in front of our new line, making back towards Suzanne. Shortly afterwards enemy aeroplanes came over, and for the remainder of the day the town and the ground west of it was heavily shelled by the enemy.

Our casualties during the operation numbered less than 50, and we captured nearly 200 prisoners and machine guns. The attack was a difficult one on account of the fact that it was carried out during the hours of darkness, but the unexpectedness and dash of it took the enemy completely by surprise. Publicity was given in the official communiques that the capture of Bray was a Tasmanian affair, and the Battalion received a congratulatory cable a few days later from the Governor, Premier, and leader of the Opposition of the State.

August 24 was spent in consolidating the position gained and making ready for a further advance, as orders were soon received that the 10th Brigade would continue the advance on the following morning (August 25), to capture the triangular piece of ground with Bray, Suzanne, and Cappy as the points. This meant a maximum advance of 3000 yards.

The 40th Battalion was to be on the right of the Brigade front, with the task of advancing astride the Bray-Cappy road to Cappy. It was not expected that heavy resistance would be met with, as the enemy was not likely to risk a large force in that bend of the Somme.

At 2.45 a.m. the Battalion moved forward. Several machine-gun posts were captured, but no serious opposition was encountered, except by the left company, which was held up by a nest of machine guns directly in front. The situation was relieved by the company on their right sending a party across which bombed its way down the trench in which the enemy were, capturing four machine guns and 22 prisoners. The objective, which was reached at 4 a.m., was gained with 22 casualties, while we captured 29 of the enemy with eight machine guns.

The Battalion remained near Cappy until the 28th August, when we moved to Vaux Wood, in support of the 38th Battalion, who were about to attack Curlu. On arrival at the support position half of the Battalion was detached as a flank guard for the Brigade. The advance continued slowly during the 29th August, and on the following the 40th Battalion took part in two minor operations of some consequence.

The first of these operations was the capture of the village of Clery by B Company of the Battalion. The western outskirts of Clery were not strongly held by the enemy, but on the eastern edge he had established a strong line of resistance. On entering the village the company met with heavy machine gun and rifle fire, and accordingly took cover while the scouts crawled forward among the ruins to locate the source of it. They passed right through the village and found the enemy strong posts, consisting of a trench, with a garrison and machine guns, on the eastern side of Clery, near the road which crosses the Somme at that point. This was reported to artillery, which bombarded the position, while our men moved forward towards it. They got to within a hundred yards of the position with few casualties, and then, under cover of the fire of their Lewis guns, rushed it. After a short and sharp fight the enemy surrendered with three machine guns and 59 prisoners, which was more than the total strength of the company that captured them. As soon as the position was gained the enemy counter-attacked with about 80 men, but this party was dispersed by Lewis gun fire. A few of our scouts then moved forward, and by very resourceful methods captured no less than three enemy machine guns and crews, as a result of which our line was advanced about 200 yards east of Clery.

Meanwhile D Company of the 40th Battalion had been ordered to attack Clery Copse, on the top of the ridge N.E. of Clery. It was believed that heavy resistance would be met with here, as the enemy was seen to be concentrating in the rear of the copse, and this supposition proved to be correct. D Company made its way along a shallow trench towards the copse under heavy fire from both flanks and the front. Casualties were heavy, and included one officer killed and one badly wounded out of the three officers in the company. They at last reached the top of the ridge on which the copse stands, and made their way along another trench towards it. But the casualties continued, and it could now be seen that our men were almost surrounded, as the enemy was closing in on both sides. Under cover of our Lewis gun fire, which kept the enemy back, the company was withdrawn, carrying the wounded, and as the last of the company (excepting two men who were captured) withdrew down the hill, the enemy was seen to rush the trench where a few moments before the whole company had been. It was afterwards ascertained from the enemy that he had met a counter attack at Clery Copse, and though we failed to get the copse that day, there is no doubt that our attack upset his plans by meeting this counter attack before it developed.

Our casualties had been so continuous during the last few days that at this stage two companies of the Battalion were merged into one, and all companies were reduced from four platoons to two, as the fighting strength of each company did not exceed 60 men.

The following day (August 31st) was one of the most momentous of the year, and began with the attack by the 2nd Australian Division on Mt. St. Quentin, with the 3rd Division on their left. The latter attacked with the 10th Brigade on the right and the 9th Brigade on the left. The 10th Brigade attacked with the 38th Battalion on the right, supported by the 37th Battalion.

The attack opened at 5 a.m. Clery Copse was taken by the 38th Battalion in the first objective, and soon after passing it, the 40th Battalion moved up and filled a wide gap which appeared between the 38th and 39th Battalions. The 40th Battalion made for and captured Berlin Wood, taking there 45 prisoners, and just beyond the wood two trench mortars, with a crew of 12 men, were also taken. The Battalion then pressed on and occupied a trench 800 yards west of the Mt. St. Quentin-Bouchesvesnes road. Just beyond the road the enemy could be seen in great numbers, and the Commanding Officer of the 40th Battalion decided to push forward two companies and attempt to dislodge the enemy from the road before his counter attack developed. These two companies moved up separate trenches towards the enemy. The right company (with a total strength of 31) got to within 50 yards of the road, when he saw a German just ahead in the trench. He fired, and the German dropped. At the sound of the shot a row of German heads appeared above the bank by the roadside, and some of the owners of the heads paid the penalty for not being on the lookout, as one of our Lewis guns swept the top of the bank. The enemy on the road behind the bank at once started to throw bombs at our party, but the latter got out of the trench and rushed the road. A sharp bomb and bayonet fight took place on the road, and although outnumbered, our party captured this point, killing about 30 of the enemy and sending back as prisoners 33 of the Prussian Guard.

Immediately beyond the road were great numbers of the enemy, apparently concentrating in the valley, and as both his flanks were in the air, the Company Commander withdrew and established a line immediately west of the road.

Meanwhile the other company on the left had a less successful experience. They reached the road by means of a trench, and there a bomb fight with the enemy took place, which resulted in the enemy being driven from the road at that point, but our company was so reduced by casualties from the bombs that the Company Commander withdrew the remainder of his men and joined up with the company on his right.

The enemy concentration in the valley was at once reported, and the artillery bombarded the enemy position for several hours, until after dark, with the result that no enemy counter attack took place.

That night was fairly quiet, and at 4 a.m. next morning the 10th Brigade moved back as the 11th Brigade went forward to continue the attack. Our casualties during the battle of Bapaume, from August 24th to August 31st, numbered one officer and 29 other ranks killed, and six officers and 123 other ranks wounded.

The 1st September found the Battalion resting at Hem, and on the 5th we moved forward to Berlin Wood, which we had captured a few days before, and spent the night there in bivouac. We remained there until the evening of the 8th September, when, after dark, we moved through our outpost line east of Roisel, through light enemy shelling, and took up a position in the old German trenches on the line between Haut Wood and Hesbecourt. The enemy was now retreating towards the Hindenburg Line, and the next night our patrols went forward, but each patrol met with the enemy in force, as he was preventing any penetration of his position by means of patrols, and delaying our advance to the Hindenburg Line as long as possible.

On the night of the 10th September we were relieved by the 4th Battalion, and moved back several miles to bivouac at Red Wood, just south of Driencourt.

The 29th September was the day fixed for the attack on the Hindenburg Line by British, Australian and American troops. On the left of the attack the plan laid down was for the 27th and 30th American Divisions to capture the St. Quentin Canal Line and the Nauroy Line beyond it, and for the 3rd and 5th Australian Divisions to pass through the Americans and take the last part of the Hindenburg Line, known as the Beaurevoir Line and the ridges beyond it. The 3rd Australian Division was to attack through the 27th American Division on their right. Of the 3rd Australian Division, the 10th Brigade was on the left of the attack immediately south of Vendhuille, and the 11th Brigade on the right. The 10th Brigade was disposed with the 38th Battalion on the right, the 39th in the centre, and the 40th on the left.

Elaborate preparations had been made for exploiting the expected success, and although the attack was ultimately successful and the Hindenburg Line was broken, the 3rd Australian Division would have been unable to advance through that line but for the fact that the 5th Australian Division and the 46th British Division broke through the enemy position first and turned the position. In other words, on the front of the 3rd Division the opening attack was a tragic failure for reasons which are given.

The failure lay with the Americans. They had taken over the line a few days before the attack, and their troops had been pushed back about 1000 yards by the enemy in a minor attack on the 27th September. This attack failed, and it was believed that numbers of Americans were still out in front in isolated posts, unable to get back. The only safe course then would have been for the Americans to clear up that lost ground some time before the hour planned for the big attack, but they chose the fatal course of starting from their disorganised position, without a barrage, an hour before zero hour, trusting to be able to capture the lost ground and to be ready to continue the attack proper from the line where the barrage started at zero hour.

The result was that their disorganisation increased, and by the time they got to the proper "jumping-off" line the barrage was far away in front, the enemy resistance had increased, and they could get no further, and when the 3rd Australian Division arrived in due course, expecting to find the Americans out in front beyond the canal, they had to meet an enemy counter-attack and save the American Division from complete disaster.

The 40th Battalion left their bivouac, near Ronssay, at 7 a.m., and moved towards Bony, soon coming under heavy artillery fire. Before going far it was realised that the American attack was not proceeding according to plan, and on coming to the top of the ridge, about 1200 yards west of where the American attack should have commenced, we came under enemy machine gun fire, and great numbers of Americans were seen coming back in disorder. The whole Brigade continued to push on, and the 40th Battalion reached the valley about 800 yards west of Gillemont Farm by about 9 a.m. Here an unforseen situation was apparent. The Americans had not advanced beyond their "jumping-off" line, and the enemy were attacking them in force. The Americans in front of the 40th Battalion were holding the trenches which passed through the ruins of Gillemont Farm, and the commanding officer began to move the battalion forward under heavy artillery and machine gun fire, to the assistance of the Americans. By the time our leading platoons reached the American trenches the enemy had also reached them, and the Americans seemed incapable of resistance. Parties of the 40th Battalion quickly took in the situation, and attacked the enemy with bomb and bayonet, driving them out of the American position. The task of organising this position for defence and putting the leaderless Americans with our troops was carried out.

The enemy had retired from the American trenches to a system of trenches about 150 yards away, and our scouts crawled forward and reported that the enemy was holding this position strongly, and had also concentrated in great numbers in rear of it. Some of our Lewis gunners then moved forward and fired on the enemy concentration, while the enemy retaliated with machine guns, and his artillery made all movement in the rear of our position impossible.

The situation was reported to Brigade, and we were ordered to remain in our position awaiting orders for the resumption of the attack. The battalion remained in this position all that day, and at daylight next morning when our scouts pushed forward they found that the enemy had withdrawn several hundred yards to the vicinity of Bony. This withdrawal had come about by reason of the fact that the 5th Australian Division had broken the Hindenburg Line at Bellicourt on our right, and further to the south the 46th British Division had crossed the canal at Bellenglise.

Early on the morning of the 1st October orders were received that the Brigade would advance to the St. Quentin Canal Tunnel. The advance was at once begun in artillery formation, but the enemy had withdrawn beyond the tunnel towards Le Catelet, and his resistance was limited to artillery fire on our parties as they moved forward. The tunnel was reached with few casualties, and a halt was called here while the 2nd Australian Division moved up to pass through us and make the attack on the Beaurevoir Line.

The 40th Battalion remained in support on the Canal Tunnel until the evening of the 2nd October, when we withdrew to Ronssoy. Our casualties during the operations numbered 15 killed and 80 wounded.

This was the last operation against the enemy in which the 40th Battalion took part. We moved back to reserve in preparation for a further advance, but with the breaking of the Hindenburg Line the enemy's military position became almost impossible, and the last hope of the German High Command of staving off complete disaster was broken. On the 4th October Germany requested the President of the United States to take in hand the restoration of peace on the basis of his "Fourteen Points," and before the 3rd Division was again called upon to take the offensive the Armistice was signed.

CHAPTER V.

FRANCE AND BELGIUM—III.

(47TH AND 52ND BATTALIONS.—ARTILLERY.)

47TH BATTALION.—Birth in Egypt.—Welcome to the Prince.—A Desert March.—Pozieres.—The Ypres Salient.—A Bitter Winter.—Bullecourt.—Messines Ridge.—Passchendaele.—The Somme Again.—Disbanded.
52ND BATTALION.—Organisation in Egypt.—The Waving of Hands.—In the Front Line.—Mouquet Farm.—In Flanders.—The Flers Sector.
ARTILLERY.—9th Battery.—17th Battery.

After the withdrawal from Gallipoli it was found possible, as the Australian forces were not then engaged in active operations, to create another two divisions, and accordingly the 4th and 5th Australian Division were formed at Tel-el-Kebir, and the 47th Battalion, which was one of the four battalions of the 12th Brigade of the new 4th Division, came into being at this historic place on March 3, 1916. The nucleus of the unit originated from the 15th Battalion—a Battalion which had seen much hard fighting in the early days on the Peninsula, and had made for itself a great name, so that it can be seen that the 47th Battalion had at its inception officers and men who had faced the ordeal and emerged with credit. And so the unit was fledged to and maintained the fine example set by its sister Battalion. Three Companies were Queenslanders and one Company Tasmanians, and a more happy, keen, and determined body of men would have been hard to collect together, with its first Commanding Officer and Adjutant, Tasmanians in the persons of Lieut.-Col. R. Eccles Snowden, and Lieutenant E. Terry, both of whom had seen service with the 15th Battalion until the formation of the 4th Division and Company Commanders were: "A" Coy., Major Fulton; "B" Coy., Capt. McLaughlin; "C" Coy., Capt. D. V. Hannay; "D" Coy., Capt. A. E. Morgan. With the influx of reinforcements some men who had just arrived from Australia, and others returned casualties, it soon began to assume the form of a battalion, and training was strenuously pushed on with, on lines to prepare for the Western Front, for it was a recognised fact, barring an attack from the Turks, that this would be its ultimate front. Singularly enough it was here on its training ground that General Wolseley had attained a glorious victory over the Egyptians, led by Arabi Pasha. The equipping of the unit was another large item, which alike the organisation, training, and other matters connected with the formation of the unit, was proceeded with apace and smoothly.

On about the 30th of March, 1916, the Battalion, along with other units of the 4th Division, was inspected by H.R.H. the Prince of Wales, who was accompanied by General Sir W. R. Birdwood, and other Staff Officers of the A.I.F., of which the following is an account related by a member of the Battalion who witnessed this memorable sight: "A red-letter day in the history of the Battalion was the great occasion when it, in common with the rest of the 4th Division, was introduced to the Prince of Wales, who, while the Battalion was still in the chrysalis stage, came to Egypt to serve on General Sir John Maxwell's staff. It was at Tel-el-Kebir, the scene in 1882 of a great British victory over Arabi Pasha's forces, that the Australian Army was camped, and after many weeks of severe training the news that the Prince was to visit the camp was hailed with delight by all, and when it was found that there was to be no formal parade, but that the troops would be expected simply to line up and give him a welcome, the men of every platoon or section throughout the division vowed that their reception would be given with a zest worthy of an officer of such consideration—and it was. On that burning hot morning of the Prince's visit, when the heat waves were eddying up into the scorched air from the desert, and the shimmering, dusty white road through the camp was almost deserted; when the Gyppos, engaged in preparing the foundation for the tram line across the desert, had even forgotten to chant at their work, thousands of diggers, the large majority divested of every garment save their shorts, boots, and helmets, lined each side of the main road through the camp. Some in search of vantage points mounted the crazy structures wherein were housed the exorbitantly priced tinned fruits, chocolate, biscuits, and tobacco of the Dago canteens, the while almost apoplectic Greeks, Jews, Gyppos, and weird mixtures of the same nationalities, besought them to descend lest the worst should happen. Then some keen eye of the expectant crowd picked up a cavalcade shrouded in a cloud of dust, advancing down a minor road towards the back of the camp. There was a hurried turning of heads, and then, with a roar, the crowd was off in a mad stampede for the other road. They burst upon it, and overflowed upon either side just as the Prince's party was entering the rows of tents. That was the Prince's introduction to the 4th Division, and what he thought of that heaving, almost naked mob of wild-looking, breathless savages, bursting with a roar and yelling indescribable upon his route through the camp, it would be hard to imagine. Everyone went quite mad, and coo-eed and yelped, cheered and shouted like fiends from the pit, and all for the sake of a boy, pink-cheeked and blushing with surprise, embarrassment, and probably anxiety, lest these wild Antipodeans should utterly overwhelm his staff and himself. He was riding a spirited animal, and with one slim hand continually at the salute found some difficulty in controlling it, for by this time it was snorting and gambolling in a very passable imitation of the antics of the diggers, so much so that a staff captain rode out ahead of the Prince and asked the troops to quieten their exuberance a little, and to leave a wider road for the Prince. This was done, and he continued his way through the Australian lines, accompanied by a roar of cheering, and leaving behind him the impression of youth, and general speculation amongst the sunburnt, roughened, and husky diggers as to how long his present fresh English complexion—almost that of a girl—would last under the fierce attentions of the desert sun."

Every digger who was with the 47th at Railhead across the canal on the desert side of Serapeum will remember the Anzac Day sports in 1916. All the Brigades, which were not actually holding the trenches out in the desert, were given a holiday, and 47th men jostled hundreds from other units on that day in the attempt to secure a seat in the narrow gauge supply train which at that time extended no further than some eight or nine kilometres beyond the canal. Tens of thousands of men assembled on the banks of the canal, and again they saw the Prince. The canal was filled with men from the desert enjoying the luxury of a swim, and the banks were brown with thousands of others, sunning themselves, or playing and frolicking about, and all as naked as the day they were born. There an incident characteristic of the Australian soldier occurred. A huge crowd of diggers assembled on one bank and loudly cheered the Prince as he passed down the canal, but in the general pandemonium he did not notice them. Thereupon some started the count, and they counted him out. An officer drew his attention to the disgruntled crowd of Anzacs, and he waved his hand and saluted, whereupon the whole mob stood up and very solemnly counted him in again. These, however, are some of the lighter incidents in connection with the life of the Battalion, and very soon they were to be shipped for France to undergo the first trials of blood and fire with which they were to become all too familiar before the end of the long endurance test of the Somme battle.

On an afternoon at the beginning of April, 1916, farewell was said to Tel-el-Kebir, and the great march across the Desert from that place to Serapeum commenced.

This task, which had been the subject of most methodical preparation from all staffs, was a test of endurance which, one would venture to say, much more seasoned troops might not have come through so splendidly, but on the other hand here were Australians facing a task determined to see it through, it only needed to see the decisive and all-confident countenances of those troops as they set upon their journey on that March afternoon and one would have predicted the result—a glorious triumph—carried out by troops who had already, by their gallant fighting on Gallipoli, stamped the word "fame" upon their name.

Officers and men had already preceded the unit to arrange the disposition of the new camp site, and along with them also by train the Transport of the Battalion.

Throughout the march the order was full marching order; at ordinary times one would sink his feet an appreciable depth in the sand, but this weight added helped to sink still further in; then that was alright, the sinking in, but came the getting out for your next steps; it needed men whose hearts were in the right place to see it through.

And so this march went on for three days, with nothing else but the huge sameness as far as the eye could see, mile upon mile of sand; yet through it all cheerfulness was supreme; men would have their little jokes, and then of an evening would gather and sing their favourite melodies or one would tell of "the" best girl back in Australia, and so this characteristic followed them right through the war; particularly noticeable was this on mail days, when the Regimental Postman would be besieged, all anxious for the letters from home, then the pleasure of reading them and the huge beam of happiness and the beating heart of joy, but the yearning for the time to come when all would again see and, yes, see, their best girls in Australia. But when on the third day the Battalion left Moascar on its final stage, all were agreed upon arrival at Serapeum, with this enormous test of fitness completed, that it was quite nice again to settle down to camp life, which was pitched at Railhead, Serapeum, and training proceeded with

The Battalion here formed part of the Garrison of the Canal Defences, and manned the outpost system at Habeita and Gabul Habeita, but the attack which was daily expected did not develop on the particular part of the front which the Battalion held. This outpost system was a series of strong posts at intervals of, in some cases, miles, but not out of touch with each other; they were selected in places that commanded a great range of fire, stoutly backed up with "A" frames and rivetted, still after a heavy sandstorm very little remained of what was once a defensive position; then they would have

Attacking Infantry

Lent by Aust. War Museum

to be again prepared. It was while at this place that the first Anniversary of the glorious landing on the Peninsula took place in the form of a Church Service in the forenoon and an Aquatic Carnival on the Canal in the afternoon, which was attended with much gusto. All time, when not manning the outpost system, was devoted to training, more particularly open manoeuvre work. The general health and conduct of the Battalion was excellent.

Now, about the middle of May, after a night march and a practice attack on the Suez Canal in the early morning, camp was pitched on the banks of the canal at Serapeum itself, and, as in all camps in Egypt, there was the following of Jews, Arabs, Greeks, and others. These fellows would do anything for a piastre in addition to cutting your hair, or a shave.

On the 1st of June, after three months' strenuous work, the Battalion, along with the rest of the units comprising the 4th Division, was considered to be capable of taking the field, with the 1st and 2nd Australian Divisions, who had gone through the same routine which the Battalion had just completed, and sailed previously for France. It set out for the Port of Alexandria, and embarked on the 2nd of June, sailing the same day for the Port of Marseilles, where, on arrival, disembarkation was proceeded with immediately, and the unit entrained for Bailleul, which place was reached after a 62 hours' train journey. The run through was an immense experience for all, and the whole-hearted way in which the whole of the populace of the French towns through which the Battalion passed, received all, certainly gave one a splendid first impression of the French.

Stops were made at numerous stations en route, where, at different ones, French Red Cross workers had prepared tea, and distributed other appreciables; at stations where a stop was made long enough, it was common to see numbers of the chaps going for a stroll along the roads with French girls, who could not speak a word of English, while the digger on the other hand perhaps knew "Wee" and "Bon"; still along they went, both talking away, neither knowing what each other were talking of. Then there were heaps of flowers, and all anxious to give you some, while at the stations at which a halt was not made, the crowds gathered and let forth a cry of *Vive les Australiennes*. The French had made a magnificent stand, along with our other Allies, for nearly two years against the German hordes, and in consequence had lost heavily, so that it can be imagined how genuine was their delight to see Australians and other British troops pouring into their country to help with them smash the Boche. By those in authority all detail of the Big Push to commence on the 1st July was well known.

On arrival at Bailleul, the Battalion detrained, and proceeded to billets at Outersteene a village situated about a mile from Merris both of which places figured prominently in the latter stages of the War, for it was here the German advance of 1918 (in the north) was checked.

The first pay day on French soil provided never-to-be-forgotten sights. The men in their careless fashion got through far more than enough of cheap French champagne—bottled lightning at five francs a time—and in one billet at least later on in the evening there was such a Bacchantic festival as that quiet spot had probably never seen before or has since. One man was diving into the horse pond with all his clothes on, and within half an hour these fiery well-fed soldiers from the Antipodes, with a group of marvelling and frightened peasants as an audience, were engaging in half a dozen free fights in the paddock, while one respectable old cow, a matron of many offspring, was dashing frenziedly round the field with the remains of a cardigan jacket, blue, woollen military pattern, decorating its fine spread of horns.

The work of preparation was still carried on, and it was the general concensus of opinion by all, that billet life although many of them little better than stables, was much more agreeable than life under canvas; and the change of climate, from the heat of Egypt to the clear air of France, another appreciative factor. Here it was that Field Marshal Sir Douglas Haig inspected the Battalion and commented upon it in a most favourable manner.

This unit was one whose striking power was now complete, fully equipped, and trained in the art of warfare. A move was made from this village on an afternoon in the beginning of July, for the first tour of duty in the trenches. The first stage of the journey was accomplished on the same afternoon, and billets occupied at Boote till the following afternoon, when the final stage was made, and the Battalion, for the first time since its inception, manned the front line trenches, immediately in front of Fleur Baix, relieving a unit of the 1st Australian Division, Battalion Headquarters being established in the town of the aforementioned place. It was a remarkably quiet sector, and an ideal one for the Battalion's initiation to the line, although the enemy's snipers were fairly accurate, and casualties principally accrued from that source. The line was held lightly, and patrolling carried out strenuously. At this place the first casualty in the unit occurred, a Queensland man being killed. From this position a move was made back to billets occupied previous to making a move to the line, the Battalion remaining in them for a few days, then entraining at Bailleul, it went south to the Somme.

Detraining at Doullens, it set out on a march of over ten miles for Berteaucourt-les-Dames, arriving the same afternoon. Billets were found at this village to be of a decidedly more agreeable nature than the last occupied in Flanders. Training was pushed ahead, particular regard being paid to wood fighting. Health and discipline remained good, the unit being remarkably free of crime. After some days here, orders were received for another move, the Battalion marching to Herissart, and going into billets for the night, whence, on the following morning, it marched to Vardencourt Wood, where they occupied huts for a few days. The Battalion now became part of the Fourth Army. About the beginning of August a move was made to just outside Albert, which was once a large and prosperous town, but at this time was well on its way to ruin, owing to being under enemy fire for the past two years. Here the Battalion bivouacked for the night, moving to Tara Hill the following day. The following is an account given by a member of the battalion of this march to the south:—"There was to be bloodletting in earnest soon, and after a period of hopes and fears, and one or two bitter disappointments when the battalion got nearly, but not quite, into the line, they were marched off down south, always singing, happy and gay and carefree, bivouacking in the woods under the stars, eating, drinking, drilling, and frolicking, under a bright spring sun after the day's march, until the increase of traffic, the thickening encampments, and the numbers of motor ambulances carrying the slightly wounded, generally cheerfully smoking and looking pleased with themselves and with life, back to rest camps, betokened their approach to the big push—the great July drive against the Somme defences. The final stage of the journey, their equipment complete to the last detail, brought them within sight of the hanging statue of the Virgin and Child on the tower of Albert Church."

The Albert Cathedral, the Church of Notre Dame de Bebrieres, with the famous gilt Virgin hanging head downwards from the Campanile, once a treasured beauty of the town, was now shattered and shell torn, for Kultur in its effort for world domination pays no respect to church or discriminates between structure of any kind.

This Cathedral, with its dome, at the top, of which stood the Virgin Mary holding Our Lord as a child in her arms, was a landmark for many miles round, and the Hun, who had held the elevated and commanding positions around the town since both sides had settled down to trench warfare, had shelled this dome so that now, instead of it being upright, it was the reverse and just holding by some iron bands.

It had been said by the French that within three months of this statue falling war would end; still there it hung in its almost reverse position till it was finally dislodged by enemy shell-fire during his big drive of 1918.

In close proximity to this place was the immense mine crater of La Boiselle, calculated to be 100 feet deep and 100 feet wide, by far the largest mine crater on record. Here our engineers had tunnelled for many months preceding the Big Push, and powerful explosives had been placed in position, so that, with the commencement of the offensive, and by the firing of this mine many hundreds of tons of earth had been thrown into the air, and the loss of lives to the enemy must have been considerable.

The activities of all arms of our forces were really remarkable. Throughout the whole day our 'planes could be seen in twos and threes, and whole flights actively patrolling the newly-won positions and going further back on bombing raids. Then captive balloons, better known as "Sausages," were everywhere to be seen, whilst against our numbers one could see perhaps a couple of enemy balloons, all these factors making it particularly hard for movement to take place over their side, for, should movement occur, our artillery would be brought to bear on it immediately, and artillery was there. For in the long depression running up towards Contalmaison (called "Sausage Valley"), it was there wheel to wheel almost; especially noticeable was this when a barrage was put down, for then it seemed as though the whole sky was ablaze and the sound of the continual drum-fire was deafening. It was said, given a still night, the rumble could be heard in England.

Then after this aerial activity and a certain amount of necessary movement by day, as soon as the dusk of evening drew on, gun teams were everywhere to be seen hustling ammunition up to the guns, which were simply pouring out "iron rations" for the Hun. Then waggons loaded with rations, or limbers with pickets, barbed wire, sandbags, and tools, and all the other hundred and one things used in war, and so this went on through the whole night, and then with the breaking of dawn, up went the balloons again. Whilst in this area a promising Tasmanian, Corporal W. G. Andrewatha, received wounds which caused his death. A soldier respected by his comrades, he would have certainly risen much higher in the army.

And now, after two days here, came another move which brought the Battalion to the Sunken Road, in front of Contalmaison, where it occupied a defensive system of trenches, and supplied working parties to units of its own brigade manning the front line. Casualties here occurred more heavily. On the morning of August the 6th the front line system in front of Pozieres, familiarly known to members of the unit as O. G. 2, was reconnoitred by the Commanding Officer and Officers of the Battalion preparatory to moving up and occupying it in relief of the 48th Battalion, a move which was carried out the same afternoon, via Sunken Road and Tramway Trench, "C" and "D" Companies holding the front line, "A" and "B" Companies in support, Battalion Headquarters being established near Pozieres Church, nothing of which remained whereby it could be recognised, the whole country being literally shell swept. Pozieres is commented upon by General Birdwood as for consistent shell fire, it would be impossible to get worse, and so he said, "Could you withstand the shelling of Pozieres, you can certainly go through anything which is likely to be." Major Fulton, an officer of much promise, was killed during the first day, and losses were very heavy, as can be readily understood when one comes to think all the Battalion had to do was to sit and let the Hun rain shells upon it, and in a system of trenches which had been previously held by him, and taken a few days before in the Big Push.

The condition of these trenches was owing chiefly to our own artillery, which had played havoc with them, which speaks volumes for the batteries, and now far from being a trench system, it was in conformity with the country all round, and might be said to be a system of shell-holes with dead Germans everywhere.

Splendid was the work done by stretcher-bearers, as owing to the communication trenches being smashed in with the Hun fire, the wounded had to be carried out in the open country. This was done day in, day out, by those who were lucky enough to escape, and by reinforcements. These brave fellows were sometimes by a direct hit blown in the air, casualty and all.

The prisoners taken by the British and French during this push, which commenced on July 1st and which the Australians entered into on Sunday, July 23rd, with the attack upon Pozieres ran into five figures, they representing the *elite* of the German Army, and the ground won was extensive, many villages being taken.

The enemy had constructed elaborate dug-outs and trenches, some of these dug-outs very many feet below the earth, had numbers of rooms fitted up with electric light, carpets on the floor and pictures hung round the wall, bedsteads, chairs, tables, in fact one might say all the necessaries of a home, but the Hun took care that they came from French homes.

The Company Commanders before Pozieres were as follows:—"A" Coy., Major Fulton; "B" Coy., Captain McLaughlin; "C" Coy., Captain D. V. Hannay; "D" Coy., Captain J. H. Wilson.

Amongst others killed during this operation were the following Tasmanians:—Sergeant Cubit, Corporals Diprose, Cann, and Winters, all men with an Army future before them.

Special mention might also be made of the work of the Battalion M.O., Captain Jones, and *Padre*, Captain-Chaplain Devine, who were both unceasing in their efforts to alleviate the sufferings of the troops.

The following account is given by a member of the battalion of this tour of duty at Pozieres:—"Those who still survive who were on fatigue duties, while troops from England, Scotland, Wales and Australia were hurling themselves against the defences of Pozieres village, are not likely to forget it. A slow and cautious advance up Sausage Gully, and then, when fairly in among the guns, down came a thick barrage and it was as though hell had broken loose. The flashes of thousands of guns placed almost wheel to wheel, showed nothing but long lines of steel helmeted men in single file going steadily forward, plunging mules, cursing drivers, and perspiring gunners. Those fatigue parties came back sadly depleted in numbers, and then it was their turn for Pozieres and the ridge behind it. The division had to hold what had been so gallantly won by the 1st and 2nd Divisions, and hold it, of course, they did. Through incessant and continuous artillery fire of terrific intensity, squatting in shallow trenches and no trenches at all, carrying rations, water and ammunition, patrolling, praying, cursing, dying, the battalion, with its sister units, held on until the enemy gave up the attempt to shake them out of the newly-won trenches and their reliefs came. The next morning the sole remaining officer of "D" Company (Tasmanians), a second lieutenant, ordered a roll call, and it was a dishevelled drawn and dirty crowd that answered the summons. One by one the platoons were checked, 27 men out of 40 odd in one, 17 for another, 12 for yet another, until the officer in charge of the last—number 16 platoon, which had gone into action with one officer, two sergeants, two corporals, two lance-corporals and over 40 men—was called for. A lank and blood-bespattered lance-corporal stepped out and gave his platoon strength at seven men. The first D.C.M. to be won by the battalion was awarded to the sergeant, who, for the greater part of the time at Pozieres was in charge of this No. 16 platoon, Sergeant H. Smith, who was afterwards to win his commission and an M.C."

After a couple of days, the Battalion was relieved, and marched back to Tara Hill, thence to Berteaucourt-les-Dames, via Contay, and training was carried on for a fortnight.

It now marched to man the trenches at Moquet Farm, which was held for some few days; another system similar to Pozieres, and situate about midway between Pozieres and Thiepval. Conditions were very unpleasant, owing to the heavy rain and shell-torn country; to put it mildly, it was "a sea of mud." Pozieres was one of the worst towellings-up which the battalion ever received, although Messines and Passchendale were as bad, and it was finally almost completely wiped out at Dernancourt while helping to check the last German thrust against Amiens. Mouquet Farm was far from one of the most pleasant places in the world. At this time the armies still stuck to the old trench systems, and the approach to the front line before Mouquet Farm, which the Prussian Guard held in strength, was up trenches everywhere a foot deep in thick mud, in which dead bodies were lying buried in the slime, which, in places, took one up to one's waist in water. Gunfire was heavy, and casualties were frequent, but the men of all units stuck it out, and upon their relief by the Canadians, about Sept. 10th, were entrained for the Ypres salient, which the Canadian troops had just left. It encamped at Princess Patricia Lines, near La Clytte, whence the depleted ranks were filled up and every opportunity given the troops for bathing, till a move was made to the line in relief of the Canadians in the Ypres Salient.

It was at this stage that the first change of Commanding Officer took place. Colonel R. E. Snowden, who had commanded the Battalion successfully through hard fighting since its inception, being replaced by Major Flintoft, who had up to this time acted as second in command. Colonel Snowden left amid the general regrets of all ranks alike. The line was held lightly and by patrols, Battalion Headquarters being established at the Brassiere, for some time, inter-company reliefs took place till a move was made back to Ridge Wood as Battalion in support, while it held the trenches the battalion tickled the Boche up with diligent sniping, while the artillery sent over several stormy barrages, which blew parapets, earthworks, machine gun nests and incidentally not a few Boche, high into the air.

Here it was that the battalion lost Sergeant W. Vaughan, a man beloved by all ranks, who was on the eve of getting his commission. Sergeant Vaughan was killed while on trench patrol, and when the news reached his platoon's section of the trench there was hardly a man of all that hard bitten crew who was able to speak. He was carried back by his comrades and buried the next day in a little cemetery in Ridge Wood. During this tour Lieut. Ferguson (Queensland) was also among the killed. He was in charge of a wiring party when the enemy located it, and, turning machine-guns on them, he received wounds which caused his death. Although he had only been associated with the Battalion a short period, during that time he had, by his genial ways, made himself liked by all, and had certainly given proof of much promise.

The Battalion from here proceeded to Murrumbidgee Camp, and from the latter place of billets near Mont de Cats. The first bitter days of the approaching winter—that awful winter of 1916-17, which will be for ever remembered by those who suffered its cruel attentions—were now making themselves felt, and after their easy time in the salient the battalion knew that they were "for it" again. Rumour was no lying jade this time, and November saw them once more trekking south. The battalion entrained at Godewaersvelde, and again proceeded to the Somme sector, once more forming part of the Fourth Army, billeting at Le Toile. Only a brief space elapsed at this village ere the Battalion route-marched to Vignacourt. Remaining for the night, a move was made next morning to Flesselles, a few days being spent here, and it embussed for Dernancourt. The Battalion at the beginning of November moved into the line via Mametz, Bernafay, and Delville Woods, occupying a sector of the line to the left of Gueudecourt, in relief of the 6th and 12th Battalions, A.I.F. relief was completed about midnight, supporting companies being in Cheese Road, and Battalion Headquarters in Bull's Road in front of Flers. The line here was in a somewhat elevated position, with Le Transloy to the right and Ligny-Thilloy some distance away on the left front, with the tall chimney in Bapaume a distance away on the left front. Company Commanders at this stage: "A" Coy., Captain F. R. North; "B" Coy., Captain McLaughlin; "C" Coy., Captain J. W. Miller; "D" Coy., Captains A. E. Morgan and D. V. Hannay.

Conditions were found to be very trying, snow falling heavily, and the whole country in a very sodden condition. It was mud in excelsis, and the battalion grovelled in it, lived in it, slept in it, and above all cursed it, until after holding the line for about ten days, a move was made to a defensive system known as Switch Trench, the Battalion supplying working and carrying parties, and being Battalion in support. From here it went to Townsville Camp, near Bernafay Wood, detachments acting as working parties to forward battalions. The next move came back to Flesselles, towards the latter part of November, where the Battalion remained in training. Christmas, 1916, was spent in this village, and on the 2nd January, 1917, the unit route-marched to La Housaye, thence, via Dernancourt and the route previously taken, to occupy the sector held as on the previous tour of the front line system, near Guedecourt, the only material change being that the Hun had retired from a position held by him and known as Fritz's Folly, which the Battalion now occupied as a Company Headquarters. The enemy was not found to be very troublesome, being apparently prepared to sit tight, and, incidentally, supply all light required. Numbered among the casualties here was Lieut. W. Drew, M.M., an officer who, by his ability and genial ways, had won for himself a place high in the hearts of officers and men of the unit; he would have certainly risen high in the army. Here the second change of command took place. Colonel Flintoft, after a successful command, being replaced by Col. Eric Lewis. Colonel Flintoft proceeded to Training Battalion in England. After tour of holding the line policy, the Battalion moved to camp at Mametz Wood, thence to billets at Bazieux, via Becourt South Camp.

At this spot the Battalion became detached, and took up the role of a labour battalion, entraining at Mericourt, and detraining at Abbeville, it moved to billets at Le Titre and Auxi Le Chateau, Battalion Headquarters being at Argenvillers, along with one Company. Its work here was to dismantle huts and fill in the defensive system of trenches which had become useless owing to the Boche retirement of 1917. In conjunction with this work, all time available was fully used in training, and much useful work done in the latter. Quite a number of reinforcements here joined up, and the Battalion was again up to fighting strength in officers and men.

With the work completed, orders were received to entrain at Abbeville, which move was made about April 4th, detraining taking place at Albert, and marching to huts at Orvilliers, where on the following day a march was made to Biefvilliers, via Le Sars, Butt-o-Warlencourt, and Baupaume. Orders were received and preparations made for an attack, movement taking place on the afternoon of April 10th to Vaux Vraucourt, thence to positions in the Noreuil-Longatte Road. At 4.30 a.m. on the 11th April, in conjunction with other units of the 12th and 4th Brigades, an attack, supported by tanks, was launched on the Hindenburg Line on a sector to the right of Bullecourt, Tommies co-operating on the left. The attack was successful, numerous prisoners taken, and heavy casualties inflicted on the enemy. This was the famous Hindenburg Line, which was said by officers high in the German Army to be impregnable, a fine network of trenches, with many lines of barbed wire entanglements, at which, on the first attempt by Australian troops, was penetrated to some depth, and it so happened that this Battalion took part in the first attack. Casualties were fairly numerous, the enemy using largely gas shelling.

This attack appeared to be more an experiment for the tanks, for without any artillery preparation the attack developed, tanks going forward rolling down the barbed wire, through which the troops passed, and charging, dislodged the enemy from his strongholds.

To be one of the crew of a tank is far from one of the pleasantest positions in the army, although, strange to say, not the least sought after; out of some eleven tanks taking part in this operation two or three returned.

As can be quite easily imagined, these huge weapons of warfare offer a splendid target to enemy artillery, and they receive more than their issue from the heavies.

The country to the front of Bullecourt is of a very level nature, and here throughout the whole afternoon could be seen his reinforcements moving forward, but the counter-attack which followed met with little or no success.

During this counter-attack splendid work was done by Lieut. R. Armitage; he had with his platoon won a position in the attack, which the Hun now tried to wrest back; this gallant officer, with his men, although practically surrounded by the enemy, fought fiercely to retain the position; he held out till his death, bombing to the last.

Snow fell heavily as evening drew on, and the whole landscape presented one huge stretch of whiteness.

Relief was effected on the afternoon of April 11th, by a unit of the 13th Brigade, and the Battalion moved back to Baupaume, entraining at this place, along with other units of the brigade, late in the afternoon of 12th April, surrounded with the "luxuries of travelling," for in cattle trucks were crowded forty and fifty men to travel the whole night through with standing room only—many of these trucks had no covers, this was the best available—and detraining the following morning at Albert, from whence a move was made to huts near Fricourt. Here the Battalion was inspected by General Birdwood, who congratulated it upon the attack upon the Hindenburg Line.

After a few days it marched to Lavieville, and again in billets. A fighting force has very little rest, especially in days of warfare, as this Great War was. Here the third and final change of Commanding Officer took place.

Col. Eric Lewis, who had done useful and good work as Commanding Officer, being succeeded by Lieutenant-Colonel A. P. Imlay, who had been second in command since January 17th. Divisional competitions were held, and the Battalion emerged with more than one victory. A Divisional parade was held, and presentation of medals and ribbons made by General Birdwood, in which members of the Battalion participated.

The Battalion was kept hard at work training, and much night work was carried on, such as night marches, attacks on positions, etc., and musketry received particular attention.

The unit now route-marched to Midlands Huts, above Albert, entraining at Aveluy, and detraining at Bailleul, proceeded to billet near Steenweerck, becoming attached to the Second Army, under command of General Sir Herbert Plumer. Every opportunity was taken of reconnaisance by Officers and N.C.Os. of the front line and approaches to Messines. Indeed, the training was very thorough, all down to Section Commanders being supplied with a small map of the whole position, and by means of conferences, lectures, and rehearsals, the whole detail of the attack became common knowledge to all ranks.

Then the Engineers had constructed a plan in miniature of the position, which was viewed by the troops as often as possible; all these preliminaries was very fine, and every individual became perfectly clear as to his own particular task, and gained a thorough grasp of the whole business.

The Battalion moved to Bulford Camp, near Wulverghem, via Canteen Corner, and on the morning of June 6th moved forward in fighting order to take part in the attack on the final objective on Messines Ridge. All troops wore a distinguishing mark, which was two pink bands, one on either arm.

Tanks co-operated in the attack, the four assisting this unit being known as "Our Emma," "Lucifer," "Rumble Belly" and "Creeping Jenny."

The general plan of the sector of the portion of the attack allotted to this Battalion was as follows:—

The mines were to be fired just previous to daybreak; New Zealanders were then to go over and take the village of Messines and certain trenches, after which the Hun was to be subjected to a further heavy bombardment of ten hours; during this time this unit (along with other units taking part in the second phase of the attack) was to move from Bulford Camp, which move was made at the appointed time, on to tape lines in front of the New Zealanders.

Two Battalions of the 12th Brigade were to make the attack, viz., 45th Battalion on the left, 47th on the right, our objective being Owl support trench, which was about 800 yards in front of the N.Z. position, 3rd Australian Division on right, with an English division on the left.

At the appointed time this unit attacked and captured the final objective. The enemy troops opposite us were the 40th Division, composed of the 100th, 134th and 181st Saxon Regiments, belonging to the 19th Royal Saxon Army Corps.

Casualties were, considering the immensity of the attack, fairly light. Here again, when the attack might have been pushed further, instead of this consolidating and holding on to the line, and especially a system that the Hun had been driven from, casualties became heavy, and when the Battalion moved out, after about three days in the line, to billets at Le Creche, many of its most promising officers and men were among the killed. The officers suffered heavily, for out of the twenty-one officers of the unit taking part eight were killed and seven wounded, and, roughly, about half the battalion casualties. Included among these, three out of the four company commanders were killed—Captains J. W. Miller and L. Davy and Lieutenant D. Salmon, also Lieutenants C. D. Scott, G. Goode and Dixon. Here a halt was made for, roughly, 14 days, and then came a move to hutments at Romarin Camp. The health of the Battalion maintained the usual high standard, and morale excellent.

Now, orders came to reconnoitre positions on Hill 63, and the same afternoon the Battalion marched to dugouts at the above-mentioned place. This spot, in close proximity to the Catacombs, Hyde Park Corner, and Red Lodge, had, until the attack on Messines Ridge, been a quiet part, but now presented a sight which would give one the impression that there had been a battle waged round about. From here could be seen away to the right the town of Lille, with its big chimneys. The Boche submitted this part to an occasional fairly heavy gas shelling. Working parties were the order of the day. It was while at this part that the Divisional Commander, Major-General Holmes, C.M.G., D.S.O., was killed. He, in company with Mr. Holman, Premier of New South Wales, was proceeding to Messines Ridge, when an enemy shell cauesd his death. Major-General Holmes had seen lengthy and distinguished service, and by his death it was felt a great soldier had been lost. He was replaced by Major-General Sinclair M'Lagan.

After this forward tour the unit, about the beginning of August, 1917, route-marched to billets and canvas at Doulieu, via Romarin and Steenwerck, and, as on all these short respites from the line, training was carried on to its fullest extent. Many reinforcements and casuals joined up. Now, marching forward via Wulverghem and Neuve Eglise, the Battalion went in to hold the line in front of Wytschatte Ridge, with Battalion Headquarters at Derry House, an old Hun pill-box, in relief of an English Regiment, the King's Royal Rifles. After holding the line, it was moved back, and acted as Battalion in support till relief was effected, and the unit moved to hutments at Aldershot Camp (Wulverghem). The Battalion, after a few days here, route-marched to Caudescue, near the Nieppe Forest, arriving at midday. The unit moved the following morning for Staple, a village not far distant from Cassell (Second Army Headquarters). The Battalion occupied billets scattered round the area, and after being here for a few days embussed and moved into billets at Fruges. Hard training was here carried out, and the discipline of the Battalion was a very gratifying factor to those in command. Here, as on every available opportunity, Battalion sports were held, also a boxing tournament and concerts, which are much appreciated on the lighter side of war. Embussing at Fruges, there came a forward move, with a few days' halt at Steenvorde; the unit went into Zonnebeke, via Ypres. After a few days in the line, during which the casualties were light, the Battalion was relieved, and moved to Halifax Camp, in the vicinity of Reninghelst. Embussing here, it again moved back to Steenvorde, and preparations for an attack at Passchendale were made. The Battalion went forward to Gordon Area, outside Ypres, thence, via Hell-fire Corner and Birr Cross Roads, to a position, and on the night of the 11th of October moved forward in fighting order to the attack on Passchendale Ridge, all companies taking part.

Company commanders at this stage were "A Coy. Captain Young, "B" Coy. Captain Gibson, "C" Coy. Captain E. O. Williams, M.C., "D" Coy. Captain A. M. Anderson.

On the 12th October, at 4.30 a.m., the barrage went down, and at Zero Hour the Battalion attacked, and took all objecives, New Zealanders on right, Third Division on left. Numerous prisoners were taken. Here the Boche held some splendid defensive positions, which were taken at the point of the bayonet. The enemy's shelling at this part was accurate, three shells falling in the vicinity of Battalion Headquarters, resulting in over 30 casualties, the greatest number of which were killed. Also numbered among the casualties were Lieutenants J. D. A. Collier and A. C. H. Gibbs, both of whom were badly wounded and taken prisoner. During the afternoon of 12th October, the Hun counter-attacked on our left (Third Division Sector.) The Battalion still held on, but owing to their left flank being left in the air. it was found advisable to conform with the movement on the left, and so the Battalion fell back a little. The whole while the Hun was shelling heavily, and during this attack the Commanding Officer, Lieut.-Col. A. P. Imlay, received nasty wounds in both legs. He, in company with Lieut.-Col. (now Brigadier-General) R. L. Leane, was directing operations, when a heavy from the enemy caused both to become casualties, their wounds being of a similar nature. The unit now came under the command of Captain J. Brack, and remained so till relief was effected, on the night of the 14th October, by a unit of the 4th Brigade. Rain fell heavily during the 12th, and the country was nothing more than a huge bog. The unit moved out to the Canal Dugouts, close to Ypres. General Birdwood made a tour of inspection of the Battalion, and congratulated them on the attack.

After remaining here a couple of days the Battalion embussed, and moved again to Halifax Camp, where, after remaining for two days, it entrained at Vramatinghe, detraining at Wizernes, and embussing at the same place, it moved to billets at Delette, near St. Omer. The unit came temporarily under the command of Lieut.-Col. A. V. Deeble. Training was pushed ahead, and after some few days the Battalion set out on a route march to the coast, doing the journey in stages, the first halt being made at Coupleveille, thence Estree le Crecy, Canchy, and other villages, to Berthencourt-sur-Mer, near Le Treport, where the Battalion went into billets, some of the best occupied in France, for, as was thought, a lengthy rest, combined with training, to prepare for the spring offensive. The march down had occupied eight days, and the whole of the arrangements throughout the journey were perfect, and the men in great spirits, in anticipation of the much-talked-of rest. (For the Division had long been promised a spell from the line.) The wastage on the march was practically at a minimum. Here Captain Simmons, who had been commanding "D" Company, took over command temporarily, being ably backed up by Captain N. F. Bremner as Adjutant, Lieutenant-Col. A. V. Deeble taking over command of the 48th Battalion (another unit of the brigade).

But owing to General Byng's Push at Cambrai, the rest proved to be an illusion. The Battalion, along with other units of the Division, was sent up in support, entraining at Eu, and detraining at Peronne, it moved to huts at Haut-Allaines, just outside of Peronne, where Christmas of 1917 was spent. It was very cold, snow being thick upon the ground. Major D. V. Hannay, who had been attending the Senior Officers' School at Aldershot, now reported back, and assumed command temporarily. Remaining here till the middle of January, then entraining at Peronne, the Battalion moved north. Detraining at Bailleul, it marched amid a heavy fall of snow, via Fletre, to Godewaersvelde, the following morning entraining at the last-mentioned place, and going forward to hutments at Ridgewood. From here by narrow-guage rail to a forward point, detraining, it moved into the line at Hollebeke, and after about a week in this part of the line, a move came to Parret Camp, near Vormozelle, where the Christmas celebrations, which had been postponed till the unit moved into more congenial quarters, were held, the men being provided with a splendid repast. While at this place, the Commanding Officer Lieut.-Col. A. P. Imlay. who had been wounded at Passchendale, reported back, and again took over command of the Battalion. Now the Battalion moved in to hold the line on the right side of the Canal at Hollebeke, and from here marched into billets at Meteren, close to Bailleul, and remained there in training till the Hun commenced his great push on the Somme, and on the morning of March 25th, it embussed and went south, along with other units of the A.I.F. to stop the Hun advance.

Arriving at Arras, the Battalion moved via Basseux and Bailleulval to Berles-au-Bois in support of a Scottish Regiment. At midday on the 26th March word was received that the Hun had taken Hebuterne and was still advancing with armed cars, and the Battalion immediately moved out in fighting order and took up a position in front of the village, but the attack never materialised. Then orders were received for the Battalion to move out to Hannescamps, via Monchy-au-Bois, in anticipation of attacking Hebuterne. Then this move was cancelled, and came the order for the Battalion to march to Senlis, near Albert, a distance of roughly 25 kilometres, and leaving Berles-au-Bois at 9.30 p.m. on 26th March, and marching all night, it arrived at 6 a.m. on the 27th. The inhabitants had just previously left the village, it now being under enemy shell fire. A halt was not to be made here long, for at 10 a.m. on the 27th orders were received for the Battalion to move forward through Hennencourt, where it got into artillery formation, then line, and came in contact with the enemy roughly about on the railway line, running the Amiens side of Dernancourt. Here the line was established. He attacked on the morning of the 28th. We took numerous prisoners and inflicted heavy casualties, and likewise on the 29th.

This was a fairly severe test on the men, having had little or no rest since leaving Meteren.

Throughout this night march every precaution was taken, such as advance screen, flank and rear guards, and strict orders as regards night marching—for without doubt the correct disposition of the enemy line was not exactly known; therefore, the necessity for readiness to attack.

On the morning of April 5th, the Hun, after a heavy artillery barrage, lasting four hours, attacked our line in force, and we withdrew in conformity with other units some 150 yards back. Reinforcements were brought up, and at 4.30 p.m. the same afternoon we attacked and drove the Hun out and established our line as it stood previous to his attacking. It was during the enemy attack on March 28th that Sergeant S. R. McDougall won his V.C., and eight days later for performing deeds almost as daring won the M.M. His work at all times with the Battalion was of a high standard, but throughout the whole of the Dernancourt operations his work was of a brilliant nature. He was absolutely fearless, and his contempt of danger was amazing. Although many were the brave deeds performed during the war, it is doubtful if any can compare with the wonderful doings of this soldier, and he must hold a place high in the ranks of the Army of Heroes. On the night of April 6th the Battalion was relieved by a unit of the 2nd Division A.I.F., and moved to Baizieu, from where on the following day it marched to La Housaye, thence to Cardonette and Flechencourt, and then moved out on the afternoon of April 24th to support the counter-attack to be made on Villiers Brettoneux by the 13th and 15th Brigades A.I.F.

It halted at Daours, and two days later moved to the line in front of Villers Brettoneux, Battalion Headquarters being in the chateau on the Villers Brettoneux-Amiens main road, close to the former place. Here after some time in the line, the Battalion moved back to Blangy Tronville to again move back to practically the same position in the front line system.

From here the unit moved to the Hospice St. Victor, at "Rivery," Amiens, and on May 25th, 1918, at this place was disbanded through lack of reinforcements, the officers and men comprising it being drafted to other units of the Brigade. Thus came to an end a Battalion which had had an illustrious history, having been through the whole of the fighting on the Western Front since the commencement of the Big Push in 1916. Of the C.O., Lieutenant-Colonel A. P. Imlay, D.S.O. and Bar, one cannot say too much, a man possessed of great capabilities and knowing full well when and how to use them. He had commanded the Battalion with credit, and the same might be said of the Adjutant, Captain N. F. Bremner, D.S.O., a soldier of much ability. The nucleus of the unit comprised men who had been through Anzac, and the Battalion also went through Egypt, Somme 1916-17-18, Fleur Baix, Pozieres, Mouquet Farm, Flanders 1916-17-18, Ypres, Flers, Gueudecourt, Bullecourt, Messines, Zonnebeke, Passchendale, Dernancourt, and Villers Brettoneux.

52ND BATTALION.

During February of 1916 orders were received to the effect that units in the 1st Division were to be equally divided to form nucleus of a new Division, namely, the 4th Division. Company commanders of the 12th Battalion were instructed by their commanding officer, Lieutenant-Colonel J. Gellibrand to equally divide their companies throughout, giving a just distribution of officers and N.C.O.'s to each. This very fair distribution subsequently proved of the greatest value to that portion of the Battalion which went to form the 52nd Battalion of the 4th Division.

On the 1st March, 1916, the 52nd portion of the 12th Battalion, under command of Major D. A. Lane, marched out of Serapeum for Tel-el-Kebir. The officers detailed to the 52nd from the 12th were—Major D. A. Lane, Captains H. A. M'Pherson and C. H. Perkins, Lieutenants H. M. Massey, Fraser, W. Kennedy, C. Blakeney, Von Bibra, W. H. Christophers, C. H. Stubbings, and Weston.

Major Baker was appointed to command the 52nd, but did not assume command, being in hospital, from where he returned to Australia. On 5th March Lieutenant-Colonel M. P. Beevor, of 10th Battalion, took over command of the 52nd.

On 3rd March the Battalion was reinforced by 480 other ranks from the Zeitoun training camp.

Training and organisation were quickly in full swing, but the heavy demand made on the new Infantry Battalions to supply Divisional units, Artillery and Pioneer Battalions, with personnel, interfered both with training and organisation. In spite of these disadvantages, training progressed rapidly, and much zeal was put into the work by all ranks.

Towards the end of March the 4th Division was ordered to the Suez Canal, and was to proceed there by a series of route marches. On 31st March the 52nd Battalion marched out of Tel-el-Kebir at 6 a.m., arriving at their first stage, Masamah, at 11.25. The following day Moascar was reached, and during the afternoon of the 2nd April the Battalion arrived at Serapeum, and occupied the camp vacated by the 12th Battalion. During the whole three days' march the Battalion did not have a man fall out through inability to continue the march.

At Serapeum training was vigorously pushed ahead, and the Battalion was reinforced by drafts from the training depots.

On 16th May the Battalion marched out of Serapeum to relieve the 46th Battalion in front line trenches at Habeita. After an exhausting march on the 17th, the temperature being up to 120 degrees in the shade, Habeita was reached and trenches taken over.

The frontage held by the Battalion was extensive, and consisted of a series of posts, each self-maintained, but in a position to support, or be supported by posts on either flank.

On 27th May the Battalion moved back to rail head, the 53rd Division taking over front line from the 4th Division A.I.F. During the next few days training was carried on, and equipment completed.

On 4th June, 1916, the Brigade marched from rail head en route for France. On the 6th the Battalion left Alexandria for Marseilles, arriving there on the night of the 11th, and next day entrained for Hazebrouck. The reception given the Australian troops at Marseilles was as enthusiastic as it was spontaneous. From every window or garden wall flags or handkerchiefs were waved, and large numbers of the inhabitants followed the Battalions through the streets. The journey through France appeared to be through a country of waving hands. As the troop train went by everyone within sight stopped to wave. At the stations people cheered and waved, and the girls crowded along for souvenirs. When passing through a village people stopped in the streets to wave, while others crowded to doors and windows, and waved, or threw kisses. Old men and women working in the fields invariably stopped work to wave. Even although half a mile away, they waved. The ploughman pulled up in the furrow to give a wave of the hand, and then bent to work again. In one instance a damsel was milking the cow, she desisted from abstracting the milk to give a few moments to waving. In another case, on passing a house close to the line, an old lady could be observed at her supper. She waved from where she sat. Three days' continuous welcome of this description did not pass without leaving some impression on the troops.

The Battalion detrained at Castre, near Hazebrouck, on 15th June, and moved into billets at Fletre. This was their first experience of billeting.

On 19th June a move was made nearer to the front line, and billets in the vicinity of Sailly were occupied, and on 23rd the 52nd Battalion relieved its twin sister, the 12th Battalion, in the front line, which they garrisoned till 11th July, when they were relieved by a unit of the 15th Brigade. On being relieved, the Battalion returned to its old billets at Fletre. On the 13th they were again on the move, and marched to Bailleul, where they entrained for Candas, arriving at the latter town early next day, and going into billets at Halloy-les-Pemois. The stay here was a long one, and the Battalion was exercised in route marching, company training, and battalion training. Great attention was paid to the fitting of boots and feet inspections. On the 28th July the 3rd Brigade passed through the 52nd's billets, and great was the enthusiasm as the 12th Battalion marched by. Next day the Battalion performed a long and hot march to Herissart, and three days later moved into billets at Harponville.

On 5th August a night march was made via Warloy and Senlis to Albert, bivouacing on the Brickfields. Here the battalion was engaged in providing working parties, making roads, and carrying ammunition and food to units in the front line, the 13th Brigade being divisional reserve. On the 13th, the 52nd Battalion moved up to La Boiselle, being detailed as reserve battalion to the Brigade, which had now taken over a sector of the front line from the 4th Brigade. The following night, the 13th Battalion, the 50th Battalion, and 51st Battalions attacked Ferme du Mouquet, but failed to hold such of their objectives as were secured. On the 16th the Brigade was relieved by units of the 1st Division, and went into bivouac at the Brickfields.

During these operations the 52nd Battalion had about 80 casualties, of whom not more than 10 were killed or died of wounds. Captain A. E. Hunt, officer commanding D Company, was severely wounded, losing his left eye.

On the 16th the 3rd Brigade bivouaced alongside the 13th Brigade at the Brickfields, and again old comrades met. Next day the 52nd marched to Warloy, and thence on the 19th to La Vicogne, and on the 20th to Bonneville. During the stay at this village refitting and training was the order of the day.

On 26th August, the Battalion marched to Herisart, and thence by two marches again found themselves, on the 29th, bivouaced on the Brickfields at Albert. The weather was wet and the ground extremely muddy.

Preparations were now pushed forward for another attack on Mouquet Farm, a name already ominous, as heavy fighting had been going on for the past fortnight in the vicinity of this farm. On 31st the Battalion moved to La Boiselle, a village in name only, as at this time jumbled masses of brick and timber alone marked the site of a once quiet village. Next day orders were received for the attack, which was to take place at 5.10 p.m. on the 3rd September. Preliminary reconnaissances were carried out by the Battalion intelligence officer (Lieutenant A. M. Maxwell) and an officer from each company.

At about 3.30 p.m. on 2nd September, Battalion headquarters were in position in rail trench, near Kay's Dump, and within half an hour the commanding officer (Lieutenant-Colonel M. I. Beevor) was wounded, and command of the Battalion devolved on Major D. A. Lane.

During the night of 2nd-3rd September all companies of the 52nd Battalion filed into position in assembly trenches, the movement being complete at 2.51 a.m. on 3rd September. The first wave of each company was in front trench, and remaining waves in assembly trenches. It now but remained to wait for zero time, 5.10 a.m., when the first barrage would fall. The troops were cheery, and excitement was high.

All night the artillery maintained a slow barrage on the enemy's front line, and communication trenches. At 5.10 a.m. the artillery fire resolved itself suddenly into a continual crash, and the bursting shells on the Bosche front line presented a magnificent, though dreadful, spectacle. At 5.14 a.m. the 52nd dashed forward with much spirit, and in some instances a short, fierce, and bloody hand-to-hand combat ensued, bayonets and rifle butts coming into free play.

Each company seized its objective, and C Company evidently pushed on, and came under our own barrage. The company commander, Captain Ekyn-Smythe, drew them back into shell craters and holes, but, unfortunately, was about this time mortally wounded. He fell, and the company again pushed forward, and as an organised unit ceased to exist. During the morning every officer of the Battalion who "hopped over" was either killed or wounded, with the exception of Lieutenant D. S. Maxwell. This officer now commanded A Company, and stragglers from the other companies of the Battalion, and proceeded to consolidate the trenches won from the enemy. The determination of Lieutenant Maxwell and his handful of men, and their valiant resistance of enemy counter attacks throughout the 3rd and 4th September were the means of holding the ground won at such fearful cost, and preventing the left flank of the 49th Battalion from being turned.

During the night of 4th-5th September what remained of the 52nd Battalion were relieved by the 13th and 16th Canadians, and assembled at La Boiselle, during the morning moving into Albert.

The casualties of the Battalion in this battle were extremely heavy, the first roll-call showed 240 killed or missing, and over 200 wounded. Of the officers who actually went over the parapet, only three returned, and two of these were wounded. Captain Littler, O.C. A Company, and Captain M'Namara, his second-in-command, were among the killed, and also Captain Massey, O.C. B Company, and Lieutenant Wadsley. Altogether nine officers were killed.

On 6th September, the Battalion marched to Warloy, entraining at Authievle, near Doullens, on 8th, for Belgium, where they remained in billets for twelve days at Steenvoorde. After a further rest at Chippawa camp, near Reningshelst, the Battalion took over a section of the St. Eloi sector from a unit of the 16th Australian Infantry Brigade.

On 14th September, Major Lane was promoted to Lieutenant-Colonel, and appointed to command the Battalion.

Whilst occupying the St. Eloi sector, the enemy exploded a mine in front of the unit on the 52nd Battalion's left flank, and some sharp fighting took place, in which the 52nd supported their neighbors with rifle and Lewis gun fire, and were instrumental in preventing the enemy from occupying the crater.

The 11th Queen's Battalion relieved the 52nd Battalion in the St. Eloi sector on the 23rd October, and on the 27th the Battalion was back in the 4th army area, being billeted at Bruigny-L'Abbe. On the 13th November, after continuous route marching, the Battalion bivouaced in the famous Delville Wood, being held in brigade reserve to battalions in the line.

On 26th November, the 52nd Battalion relieved the 49th Battalion in the Flers sector, of the front line trenches. The weather was so bitterly cold that companies in the front line had of necessity to be relieved every 48 hours. The greatest precautions were taken to avoid casualties from trench feet, and from this complaint the 52nd came off very lightly.

The Battalion moved into close support on the 2nd December, being relieved by the 51st, and on the 5th were relieved from duty in the line by the 10th Battalion.

On the 6th December Buire again sheltered the Battalion, but before Christmas more comfortable billets were occupied at Vignacourt.

For Christmas Day festivities each officer of the Battalion subscribed a day's pay towards comforts for the men. Five cases of beer, extra meat and vegetables, were obtained, and all ranks indulged in what is vulgarly termed a "blow out." Unfortunately the Christmas parcels from home did not arrive till some days later.

The 6th January saw the Battalion again on the move, and on the 8th they were again in close support in the Flers sector, taking over the front line from the 50th Battalion on the 17th. Enemy shelling was very active and continuous. The ground at this time was deep in snow, making patrolling difficult. The cold at this period was very severe, and the experiment of issuing sandbags lightly stuffed with straw, into which the men on duty could thrust their feet, was tried, and proved remarkably successful.

On the 28th the 52nd was relieved by the 49th Battalion, and moved back to Bendigo camp. Here for a couple of weeks the men were employed in fatigue duties and in constructing a dug-board track from near Bazentine to Flers. On the 16th February they made use of this track in relieving the 49th Battalion at Flers, and hence the 52nd again found itself in close support of the front line, where they remained till the 23rd. On being relieved on that day by the 6th Battalion, the 52nd withdrew to Launceston camp, and on the 25th were back at Buire. Here training was carried out, and equipping and reorganisation of companies and headquarters details was completed.

On the 21st March, 1917, Lieutenant-Colonel H. Pope assumed command of the Battalion, Lieutenant-Colonel Lane being detailed for a spell of duty in England. On this day the Battalion marched out from Buire, and a few days later was engaged at Lavignicourt. Just prior to this action, Captain G. B. Bailey, the regimental medical officer, was killed. His loss was deeply regretted by all ranks.

From this time onward the 52nd Battalion ceased to be for all practical purposes in any way a Tasmanian unit, and its subsequent history, except for scattered details, does not properly belong to a Tasmanian record.

9TH BATTERY.

After the conclusion of the Gallipoli campaign, some two and a half months were spent in Egypt reorganising the forces and training for open warfare. This training was carried out at a place called Tel-El-Kebir, where many years before the British troops so gloriously distinguished themselves, and it was on these ancient battle fields that the training was carried out.

Towards the middle of March units were moved to the coast, and embarkation was commenced, and with those units which embarked was the 9th Battery, then under the command of Major R. S. Gee. After an uneventful voyage of about four days, the Battery was disembarked at Marseilles, arriving there on the 30th of March, 1916, and was immediately sent into an encampment at a place called Fournier, within the town boundaries. Here a week was spent in exercising the horses and enjoying the sights of the Rivereia. Then was commenced the long and tedious railway journey northwards. This journey occupied some three and a half days, but ordinarily should be done in less than 18 hours, but so heavy were the calls upon the French railway services, and so great was the traffic, that the delays incidental to them and consequent upon watering the horses at frequent intervals, rendered the journey far longer than would otherwise have been the case. This was the early spring, and the country in the south of France and in the Rhone Valley was exceedingly beautiful and picturesque; but of this we soon tired, for we were eager for the work which was ahead of us. Eventually we arrived at Havre, at approximately 3 a.m., and to our surprise and astonishment found on the station there a "Bouffet," run by English ladies, who were Red Cross Workers, and they supplied us with excellent coffee, sandwiches, and cake, which was most acceptable after the long and weary journey. The best part of a week was spent at Havre, when, except for the horses, we obtained from the Ordinance Stores the complete equipment for a battery, and so efficient was the staff in the Ordinance Stores there that a whole brigade was completely equipped in three days.

We were not allowed to remain here long, for as soon as the equipment was obtained we received orders to entrain, and after 22 hours' travelling we disentrained at a picturesque village in the north-east of France, close to the Belgian border, known as Godewaresvelde. The weather was such as is usually encountered in the early spring, and we got our first days of French mud, which contrasted very strongly with what we had been accustomed to in Egypt. After a brief stay here, we received orders which culminated in our taking over a battery position on the outskirts of the village of Fleurviaux, where we were destined to spend a pleasant six weeks or two months. This was our first taste of war on the Western Front, and, fortunately for

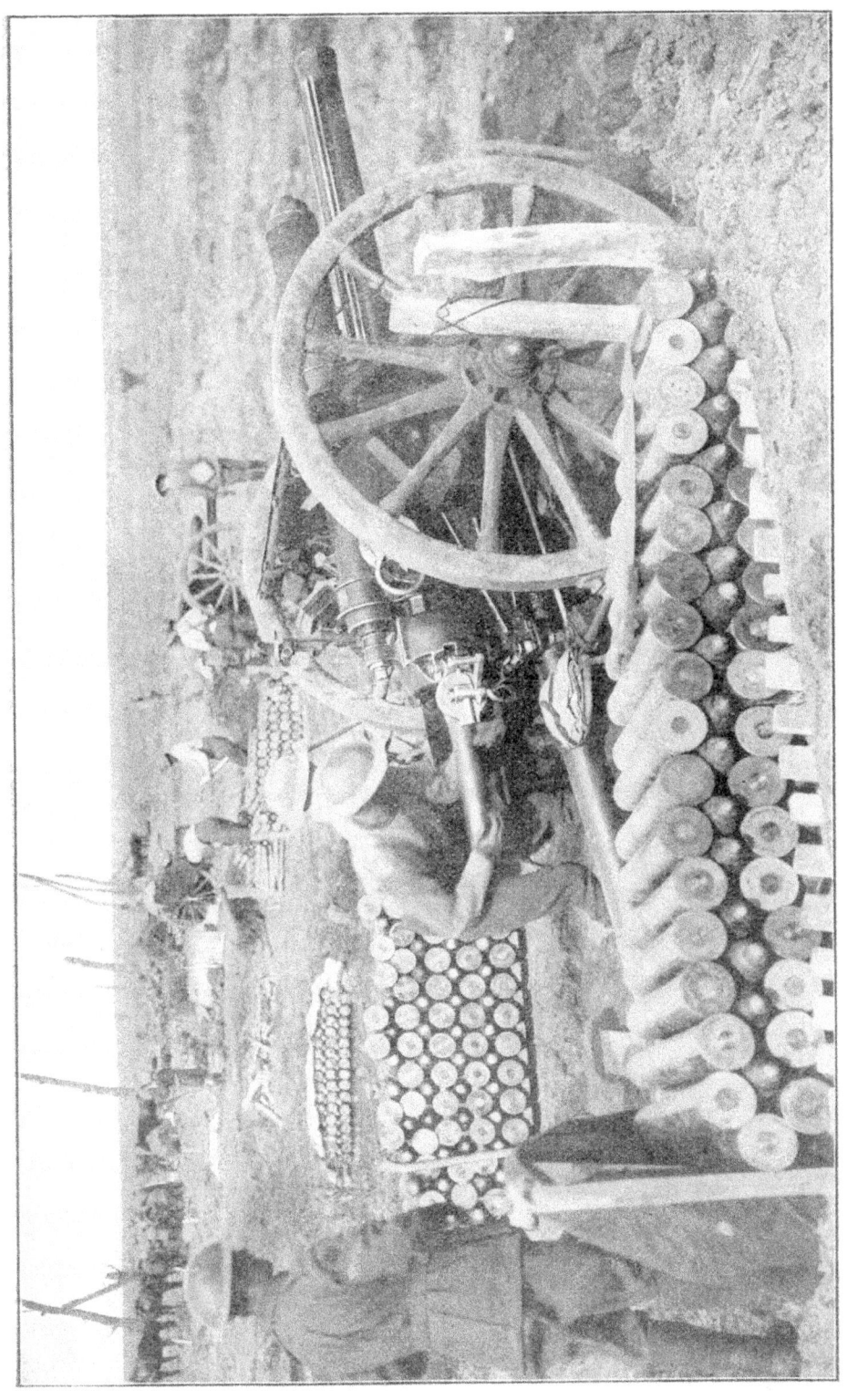

Lent by Aust. War Museum

Artillery in Action

us, the authorities had seen fit to put us into a quiet sector of the line which we afterwards christened the nursery, and it was here that we learnt the rudimentary principles of the role of artillery in trench warfare.

At first we did very little, but as we became more efficient our work increased, until finally we were supporting raids on the enemy's trenches every night, and when the battery was withdrawn from that sector it was one of the liveliest sectors on the Western Front.

June of that year found the battery in the department of the Somme, where it was destined to play its part in supporting those advances which made the Australians famous, and resulted in the capture of Pozieres. This was a strenuous time, and the battery was continuously in action for 22 days without respite. Eventually it was withdrawn, being relieved by an Indian battery, and was allowed to spend a quiet week in billets before moving to another part of the line.

That move soon came, and we next found ourselves occupying positions in that notorious cemetery or charnel house, known as Ypres Salient. Fortunately, however, our stay there was destined to be of short duration, and in six weeks we were withdrawn, to be moved back to the mud and slush of the department of the Somme. We had just left a place of mud and slime but, bad as that was, it could not compare with what we were to go through on the way to our positions near the battered village of Fleures, and there, on a forward slope, in an almost "open" position, we were exposed to the full force of the enemy's artillery. Weeks passed, but no relief came. Eventually, orders came for a move; that move, however, turned out to be worse than to remain still. The mud was frightful; horses sunk in it to their bellies, men to their waists; in places guns went completely out of sight, and the move, although only about half a mile, took several days to accomplish.

On arrival at our new position, we found practically no shelter or protection from either the weather or the enemy's fire, and this was early December, with a winter set in in deadly earnest. The pluck and grit of all ranks when they saw what lay in front of them, and the manful and masterful way in which they overcame almost insuperable difficulties, could not fail to stir the pride and admiration of those who knew them. Before a week was over, the guns had been emplaced in efficiently constructed gun-pits, and the men were housed in dugouts, which, at the same time, were considered most comfortable, but which people at home would regret to see a dog consigned to, and six weeks were spent in this position, and the men were by no means idle. An expenditure of 600 rounds per day was the normal output of each battery, and in addition to that, constant endeavours were made to drain and render the battery position habitable. Frequently a dug-out would be bailed out at night, and in the morning a foot of water would be covering the floor. Then came the hard frosts, and the battery had to survive, and did survive, the rigours of the severest winter that France has yet known. In January they were withdrawn from the line for a brief period, to return a few days later to a position a few hundred yards further to the south, and there they remained through the latter part of January and February until the enemy commenced to withdraw, and our advance started. This was our first taste of moving warfare. Some three miles had to be covered over shell-torn country, which, at first glance, seemed to be almost impassable, but yet the persistency, dogged determination and endurance, typical characteristics of the Australian troops, surmounted all these difficulties, and we soon found ourselves in the open country well behind the enemy's vacated position.

Then followed the attacks at Doignes and Hermes, where the battery, controlled by a forward observing officer, rendered excellent support to our infantry, and wrought considerable havoc amongst the ranks of the retreating enemy. By this time, spring was approaching, and the battery was emplaced in a position about 2,000 yards to the westward of the Canal Du Nord, whence it was withdrawn to a rest area to refit. Hardly, however, had we reached the billet area when orders were received to entrain, and we were again sent northwards to a sector of the line a few miles to the northward of that sector which we first occupied in France, and we soon found ourselves emplaced in a position a few hundred yards to the west of Ploegsteert Wood, where even the most casual observer could not fail to discern the huge preparations which were in progress for some gigantic offensive.

This offensive began, and the battery played its part in supporting the infantry in the battle of Messines. The position occupied by the battery was in an open field, under a screen of camouflage, made of coloured rags, interlaced with wire netting supported by poles, which extended in a long line across the field, and which was supposed to conceal, but rather marked, the position of some five or six batteries; and here with practically no cover or shelter for the detachment, the battery maintained almost a constant fire for three weeks on the enemy's positions, and it was in this position that many of its number became casualties through the well-directed fire of the hostile batteries. When zero hour arrived on the day of attack, and all the batteries thundered anew to form a protective barrage for the infantry, it seemed as if a great weight was lifted from the shoulders of all concerned, for then the enemy's artillery ceased its efforts to silence or neutralise our batteries, and confined its attention either to stopping our infantry or to looking after their own safety, and getting their guns away. That afternoon the battery moved forward to a change of position, and after three or four days in their new position it was withdrawn from the line. But no rest was yet for them, and it was moved northwards to the coast of Belgium, where big preparations were being made for another offensive, and we took up, and occupied a position on the outskirts of the town of Nieuport, where several weeks were spent in carrying out destructive shoots on the enemy's breast-works, and being subjected to exceptionally heavy artillery fire. We were not destined to remain here long. The offensive, which was apparently contemplated, never eventuated, and we were destined for further work elsewhere, and the end of August saw us again moving eastward through Ypres to take up a position about 400 yards to the westward of Sanctuary Wood, where we were to support the gallant attacks of our infantry on Polygon Wood, and the series of offensive actions incidental thereto. From this period onward for the next couple of months the battery was to go through the most trying ordeal of the whole war. There were several changes of position over almost impossible country, torn with shell-holes and strewn with the unburied carcases of many gallant animals, who had literally "died in harness," and it was during these next two months that the enemy's counter-battery work was at its fiercest, and the casualties were heavy. Yet no one grumbled, and the battery continued under the most adverse and trying conditions effectively and efficiently to give the infantry that support which they so urgently needed.

In the middle of December the battery was relieved, and it sorely needed relief. Its strength had been depleted to almost half its original number; horses were scarcely sufficient to man the vehicles, and both men and horses were almost completely worn out. But we were to receive our reward, and for ten weeks we were allowed to remain in rest billets, and this saw us through the worst part of the winter 1917-1918.

In November, 1917, we occupied our next position a few miles to the east of Mount Kemmel, which except for frequent bombardments by gas shells, was a particularly quiet sector of the line. It was while we were on this sector that we received the news of the Huns' successes in the department of the Somme, and of the retirement of the Allied troops, and suddenly we received orders to move southward in support; this we eagerly did. The rest and the quiet winter months had put fresh vigour into all ranks, and they were eagerly looking forward to the lively work which was expected to follow. We were not kept waiting long, for we were soon occupying positions covering Amiens, and there assisted our infantry in stemming the German advance, and we were engaged constantly in that sector until August, 1918, when we received orders to prepare to occupy a new position about 1,000 yards west of the Hamel. This was occupied on the evening of the 7th of August, and on the 8th of August we were supporting the infantry in that attack which was so eminently successful, from which the Huns never recovered, and which was the turning point in the war.

Then about 10 o'clock in the morning of the 8th of August we moved forward to give support to the infantry, and from that time forward became engaged in moving and open warfare, which was the last phase of warfare in which the battery was employed. By a series of short and rapid advances, the battery kept in touch with the infantry, rendering them the maximum support it could afford, until the Hindenburg Line was reached, when it took up a position on the outskirts of the village of Bony, through which ran the famous Hindenburg Line. This was the last position occupied by the battery, and on the 6th of October, 1918, the battery, with worn-out personnel, horses and equipment, was withdrawn from the line, to which they never returned. During the process of their re-fitting and re-organising, the Armistice was signed, and the personnel by drafts was returned to Australia.

17TH BATTERY.

The 17th Battery was formed at Claremont in September, 1915, and after training there embarked per *Mokia* for Melbourne on October 7th.

We formed a Battery of the 6th A.F.A. Brigade at Keilor Road Camp, North Essendon, where we trained until the 22nd November, 1915, when we embarked for overseas per s.s. *Persic*, Transport A34.

We proceeded direct to Suez, where disembarkation took place on 23rd December, and afterwards entrained for Zeitoun, camping at Aerodrome Camp, Heliopolis.

After practically six days' leave, and after inspection by Brigadier-General Johnston (who took command of 2nd Div. Artillery), the Battery was moved to Maadi Camp for further training and allotting horses. The Battery moved from here after 18 days to Ferry Post on the Suez Canal. Whilst here the Battery went through a course of shooting and field manoeuvres. After a few weeks' training the guns and equipment were handed over to the 3rd Brigade, N.Z.F.A., and the personnel and horses moved to Moascar Camp en route for France. Whilst here everything was got in readiness for the sea voyage.

We left on 16th March, 1916, for Alexandria, embarked and sailed per s.s. *Eboe*, Transport G.0601, on the 17th, arriving at Marseilles on the morning of the 23rd, entrained the same day for Le Havre, where the unit arrived on the 26th, and camped at Sanvic. We left here on 31st March for the firing-line. After taking in ammunition at Aire, the Battery moved to waggon lines at Erquingham and took up a position at Dead Man's Farm near Bois Grenier to the right of Armentieres.

After several weeks' action here a move was made to Ploegsteert, and after three days' action another move was made to the Somme, where a position was taken up in Sausage Gully to the right of La Boiselle.

After a month's solid action we moved out on rest to St. Leger, where we met the 9th Battery, who were also resting. From here another move was made into action at Mash Gully behind Ovillers and to the left of La Boiselle. Whilst here we met the 52nd Battalion just before their Mouquet Farm action.

After leaving this position a move was made northwards to Ypres for a fortnight's action, when the Battery came out for a long rest at Steenvoorde, where sports, etc., were carried out.

Another move was made to the south, a position being taken up at Flers, where the Battery suffered its first death on 2nd November, 1916, one killed and three died of wounds. The Battery transferred its position from Flers to Gun Valley, which was in front of Delville Wood, where two more of the Battery were killed. To get to gun positions it was necessary to wade through mud and slush waist deep. In February, 1917, the Battery moved out to rest and carry out shooting practice for aeroplane observation at Franvilliers.

We moved from here to Buire, where the Battery was joined by the left section of the 59th Battery, the whole forming a six-gun Battery. At Buire the weather was intensely cold, and very severe frosts were experienced. Towards the middle of March, 1917, the Battery moved to Mametz Wood, the waggon lines being at Hobart Camp and the guns to the right of Delville Wood. Another move was made after a fortnight's action at Bellevue Farm, Albert, for one day, and was recalled to action at Ervilliers, and was kept rather busy in this vicinity, and later moved to Velu Wood, where, although under shell-fire, we were able to play the 9th Battery several games of football.

Our next move was to Steenwerck in support to the 40th Battalion, the Battery going into action behind Messines. At the beginning of July, 1917, the Battery moved to Ghyvelde, about 10 miles from Dunkerque, being about five days' road journey. Here a number of the men were allowed leave when possible, the guns being in position at Nieuport, about a mile from the coast, this being about 12 miles from waggon lines. The horses and men were able to do a good deal of bathing while in this neighbourhood. This was the first position in which the Battery felt the effects of mustard gas.

After a month's stay another move was made, this time to Dickebusch, the battery being in action at that famous and dreaded place, Ypres. After being in action for one month we moved to Neuve Eglise, the battery being in action at Messines. Xmas, 1917, was spent at this place. Everyone contributed something towards a Xmas treat, and the Q.M. was despatched to Hazelbrook and St. Omer, where plentiful supplies were bought, and everyone had a very jolly time, despite the intense cold. This time a great number of the men had leave to Paris.

The battery left Messines for Strzeele at the beginning of April, 1918. Entraining for the Somme the morning the Germans broke through on the New Zealanders, the battery going into action at Healey, which at one time was well out of shell fire, and the boys often spent a pleasant hour here when camped at Albert. The only fresh water here was in Healey itself, so that it was necessary for the waggon lines to move back to Freshincourt. Although Healey was only about 2000 yards from the enemy, the boys had a great time, as the civilians in their hurried departure left everything as it stood, including a plentiful supply of wines and other comforts. As the enemy were driven back the battery moved up to Ribenmont. Moved again over in front of Corbie, where everything was put in readiness for the great stunt beginning on the 8th of August.

This was indeed something to be remembered, as we got a good start and followed the infantry closely, a stop being made for the night at Bayonvilliers. Moving on each day over beautiful country, it was indeed glorious to see the splendid roads that the enemy had been using, but which were at last in our possession. From now on to the last position the battery occupied in front of Buciynz was one continual move. Although horses and men suffered severely from gas and want of sleep everybody was enjoying it, as the end was in sight. The battery ceased firing about the 25th October, 1918, the personnel then being under half strength; horse strength was also reduced to half. The battery suffered about 250 casualties whilst in France.

From now on things were very easy, everybody doing their utmost to get home. All the battery reached home about October, 1919. The first reunion was held in Launceston on August, 1919, and the second on 7th August, 1920, at Hobart.

More men gained commissions from the ranks than from any other Australian battery. Practically every kind of decoration was won by members of the battery (with the exception of the V.C.).

CHAPTER VI.

EGYPT AND PALESTINE.

(3RD LIGHT HORSE.)

Western Egypt.—Upper Egypt.—A Bombing Raid.—Fighting Near Katia.—Battle of Romani.—Patrol Work.—Maghdaba.—Rafa.—Palestine.—Sad Trials.—Hard Going.—A Short Rest.—Beersheba— A Successful Attack.—Bald Hill.—A Wet Xmas.—Jericho.—Across the Jordan.—A Rearguard Action.—A Dull Routine. "Valle," "View," and "Vaux" Posts.—Final Operations.—After the Armistice.—Back to Egypt.—The Return Home.

After the return from Gallipoli, the 3rd Light Horse Regiment went into camp at Egypt for rest and re-organisation. At this time the monthly reinforcements which had been arriving regularly were all present in the Detail Camp, and from these the Regiment was made up to strength, the fittest men being chosen, and upon the Regiment moving out for Western Egypt those much debilitated from the Gallipoli campaign were left behind to recruit their health. Major Mills took charge of C Squadron, and Major Laurie replaced him as O.C. Details Camp, while Capt. Bell and Capt. Lewis were appointed to the command of A and B Squadrons respectively, shortly afterwards receiving the rank of Major.

On December 28th, 1915, only two days after the whole of the Regiment had returned from Gallipoli, orders were received to set out on a journey to Wadi Naturun, and the next day it left Heliopolis and proceeded mounted across the desert in the direction of Wardan, where it reported to the G.O.C. 53rd Division. On the way across the transport horses found great difficulty in moving through the heavy sand. On New Year's Day the Regiment again moved out, and marched to Bir Hooker, which they reached on January 3. At Bir Hooker they joined up with the advance post of the 53rd Division, to which they became attached, under the command of Brigadier-General Taylor, the G.O.C. 153rd Brigade, the whole force operating in this area being under the command of Brigadier-General Dallas, consisting of 53rd. Division, one Squadron Egyptian Cavalry, 150 of the Bicaneer Camel Corps, and 1st L.H. Brigade, his Headquarters being at Wardan.

The Regiment remained at Bir Hooker for a fortnight, during which time it was engaged in patrolling the Wadi. Rations and water were sent up by the light railway which ran from Khatatba to the Salt and Soda Works situated at Bir Hooker, and beyond this had to be transported by camels, consequently it was necessary to detail parties for the purpose of trying to secure a local supply of water by digging wells. C Squadron was sent forward and bivouacked at Lake Beida, where they discovered a good working supply, and Headquarters moved out to the L.H. Wells. Reconnaissance was carried out daily to Lake Garr and the head of the Wadi. On 17/1/16 a mounted patrol was reported 8 miles out in a north-westerly direction from the Papps but touch could not be gained. The telephone wire from Bir Hooker was interrupted every night by the Arabs, and occasionally cut.

On 19/1/16 a detachment of the 1st L.H. Field Ambulance, consisting of Capt. McLean and 14 other ranks, arrived at Beida and established a hospital. They were accompanied by the Dental Officer, Lieut. Cunningham, and the men were for the first time enabled to secure proper dental attention. By February 12 wells at Lake Gan had been developed and a good supply of water obtained, and the remainder of the Regiment with the detachment of Field Ambulance moved and camped alongside of the lake, where their duties were to reconnoitre the surrounding country on both sides of Lake Garr. Daily training was resumed, mainly in the form of Regimental and musketry drill, for which the country was specially adapted. The M.G. Section accompanied the Regiment, and though no actual gun positions were occupied, emergency positions were prepared and training again carried out. The Signallers maintained connection with the Infantry Brigade Headquarters at Bir Hooker, a distance of 12 miles; 9 miles of this was a ground line, and was frequently interfered with by the Bedouins, and until their Chief was instructed in the seriousness of the offence this kept the linemen busy. In spite of the distance and the leaky high resistance, a satisfactory service was maintained.

The rations and forage issue at this time was very irregular and poor, and frequent complaints through the C.O. did not take effect for some time, though latterly the conditions improved somewhat, partly by an increase in the rations themselves, but more especially by the establishment of a Regimental Canteen.

On March 3 a telephone message was received from local Headquarters at Bir Hooker to make preparations to return to Khatatba. The Regiment moved out from El Garr, and reached Khatatba, where they received a message that the Regiment was to entrain for Upper Egypt.

On March 9 the Regiment left Khatatba in three trains, accompanied by the horses and 1st Line Transport, and after a long train journey reached their destination (Girga).

B Squadron, under the command of Major G. J. Bell, D.S.O., marched mounted and took up a position at Beit Khalif, situated about 10 miles south-east of Girga, in the desert. C Squadron remained in reserve at Girga with Regimental Headquarters.

At Beit Khalif the duty of the Squadron was to patrol the neighboring desert, day observation posts were maintained, and night out-posts. On the right they were in comparatively close touch with A Squadron at Quara. Periodical patrols on camels were sent on reconnaissance into the neighboring hills, and the passes that led from them into the desert beyond, the patrol lasting three days in a country where all water had to be taken with them. A Squadron did similar patrols towards Beit and Kharga. C Squadron provided a guard on the station and policed the town of Girga and the country close by, and also provided escorts to the ration parties proceeding to Quara and Beit Khalif.

At this time new Australian Divisions were being formed, and there was a great demand for volunteers to enlist in the Artillery, and as the Regiment was then considerably over strength several of the Sergeants, and about 100 other ranks, took advantage of the opportunity to make the exchange. The weather became very disagreeable; besides being very hot, almost daily Khamseens were blowing, filling the air with dust from the horse lines and surrounding country. The horses were watered and bathed in the Nile or canals adjoining different camping grounds, and the men not infrequently went in with them, subsequently acquiring bilharziosis as the result.

On May 5 the Regiment, less A Squadron, which had entrained on 4th inst., left Girga and proceeded to Kantara by train, bivouacking for the night near the fresh water canal, where they were rejoined by A Squadron.

On the morning of the 18th the Regiment marched out mounted from Kantara, with the rest of the Brigade with the exception of the 1st L.H. Regiment, who had preceded them to the scene of operations at Romani, and arrived at Hill 70, where the Brigade camped. The Regiment remained here until the 26th, their duties being patrol and general reconnaissance work of the neighboring country, maintaining touch with the troops at Duedar. On the 26th the Regiment marched out from Hill 70 and proceeded across the desert to Romani; the limbers accompanied it, but found great difficulty in negotiating the steep sand hills, composed of loose, shifting sand. The baggage was transported by camels. On arrival at Romani the Regiment took over the camp lately occupied by the Imperial Yeomanry, and later by the 2nd. L.H. Brigade. Owing to the confusion caused by the surprise attack at Katia and Oghratina on Easter Monday, and the subsequent heavy work, this camp had been neglected, and was in a very bad sanitary state. Representations were made to the higher authorities to have fresh ground allotted, but owing to military exigencies it was impossible to do so at the time. At this time also there was a great scarcity of sanitary equipment, but following a visit of inspection by the A.D.M.S. of the area this state of things was remedied.

On May 30 the Regiment moved with the Brigade (less 1st. Regiment) to Hod-El-Debabis to act as reserves to the New Zealand Mounted Rifle Brigade, who were operating at Bir Salmana. This occasion, however, did not arise, and the Regiment returned to camp, which was reached at midnight. The following morning at 6.30 the camp was visited by a Turkish aeroplane, which dropped 10 bombs, killing five men and wounding one officer and 20 other ranks, also killing 36 horses, wounding nine others, and stampeding a large number of our own and the other Regiments. As a result of this stampede, many horses were either lost, or had subsequently to be evacuated, whilst not a few perished directly from exhaustion, the total figures for the bomb raid being 47 horses killed and died from wounds, 10 men killed or died of wounds, one officer and 16 other ranks wounded. On the following day the Regiment moved camp to a position about 1000 yards east, where an opportunity was given to adopt a more effective formation against air raids and also to improve the sanitary conditions.

On June 2 C Squadron, under Major C. Mills, moved out to Hod-El-Sagia, about 10 miles south-east, for the purpose of making wells to supply sufficient water for the Brigade. Water was struck at about 5ft., and proved to be good stock water. They returned the following day, bringing in four Arabs who were suspected of being used by the Turks to supply information concerning our troops. At this time daily patrols were sent to Katia, and outposts were detailed each night. On the 4th B Squadron, under Major G. J. Bell, D.S.O., brought back from Katia a party of 20 Bedouins with their flocks who were met with in the neighborhood of Bir-El-Hamisab.

During the ensuing month the Regiment was engaged in various reconnaissances and patrol work.

On July 19 the enemy were reported by air reconnaissance to be in force at Bayud at the strength of 2000 men and 3000 camels, at Jamiel 1500 to 2000 men and 1000 camels, at Bir-El-Abd 3000 men and 2000 camels. On the 20th the enemy were reported to be closing in towards Romani, and the 2nd A.L.H. Brigade got in touch and captured a few Turks between Oghratina and Hod-El-Sagia. The 2nd. Regiment got in touch with the enemy at about 200 yards west of Oghratina, had one man severely wounded, and captured one Turk. The 3rd L.H. Regiment remained in reserve at Katia during the day, supplied the rearguard, and covered withdrawal of the 1st and 2nd Regiments. On this day 2000 Turks were reported entrenched at Oghratina.

On the 23rd the Brigade moved out from Romani to get in touch with the enemy, reaching Katia. The 1st. Regiment formed the advance guard, and they engaged an enemy patrol 1 mile west of Oghratina. Two guns of the Ayrshire Royal Horse Artillery occupied the high ground east of Hod-Umm-Ugba to shell the enemy's camp at Oghratina and Hod-El-Negiliat. B Squadron, under Major G. J. Bell, D.S.O., marched to the position north-west of Negiliat to carry out a reconnaissance under cover of fire from these guns, and reported the enemy to be entrenched at Hod-El-Negiliat. A and C Squardons moved forward to a position east of Hod-Ugba to cover the retirement of the 1st L.H. Regiment, and were rejoined by B Squadron at 7.45 p.m. when they withdrew, acting as rearguard to the Brigade, and arrived at Romani at midnight. Lieuts. J. T. Bigg and L. J. Cowell, with 3 men, each remained out all night at Ogratina and Hod-El-Sagia respectively, to keep in touch with the enemy and report his movements during the night.

On the 25th the Brigade moved out at 2 a.m. to relieve the 2nd A.L.H. Brigade, the 3rd. Regiment supplying the advance guard. Katia was reached, and "all clear" reported. Major Bell, D.S.O., with B Squadron, reconnoitred towards Oghratina and El-Rahab. They gained touch with the enemy at 6 a.m. east of Hod-Umm-Ugba, and had one man slightly wounded. Major L. A. Lewis, with A Squadron, got in touch with the enemy at Hod-El-Mazahmi and Hod-El-Dhakar, but sustained no casualties. Major C. Mills, with C. Squadron, patrolled through Hod-El-Amoia and Hod-Ayish, which were both unoccupied by the enemy, to Hod-El-Sagia, which was held by the Turks, and took 3 prisoners. The enemy were particularly active all day. For some days the routine of patrols and reconnaissances continued.

Owing to the enemy having occupied Katia on the night of 2nd-3rd August, the 1st Brigade held a line from No. 1 Infantry Post just south of Kat-Tib-Gannett to Hod-El-Anna. The 3rd Regiment took up a line on the 3rd, holding from No. 1 post exclusive to Mount Meredith inclusive. A Squadron held the right sector, being in touch with the 2nd Regiment on their right; B Squadron the left sector, coupling up with the Infantry on the left; C Squadron being held in reserve behind the centre of our position. Listening posts, in charge of N.C.O.'s, were thrown out in front of each Squadron to report the earliest enemy movement.

At 11.40 p.m. the listening post reported that the scouts of the advancing Turks had made their appearance, and at this time the first shots were exchanged. At 12.20 a.m. the enemy's Infantry Lines appeared, and they made a bayonet charge on the Cossack Post Line, situated at the base of Mount Meredith, and at this time the reserve Squadron was sent up to support the firing line. The advancing Turks came under heavy fire from our picquet line, which held them up for a considerable period. We were now reinforced by one Squadron of the 1st L.H. Regiment, which was placed to the south of Mount Meredith. The 2nd Regiment, on our right, was forced back by superior numbers from Hod-Abu-Adi, and was reinforced by the other two Squadrons of the 1st. Regiment. Our Regiment held the ground just above this Hod till 4 o'clock, but the Turks were now swarming up Mount Meredith from the south-west, and dominated this position. They poured heavy rifle, machine gun, and shrapnel fire into our force at daylight, and were able to enfilade our right flank, owing to the compulsory retirement of the 1st and 2nd Regiments, and at 5.30 A and C Squadrons were compelled to fall back, partly owing to pressure of the enemy and partly to difficulty in obtaining ammunition. They withdrew on to Wellington Ridge, where they were reinforced by the 2nd Brigade and a Company of King's Own Scottish Borderers. Here the Regiment re-formed, less B Squadron. B Squadron, on the left, was able to hold its position, but having lost communication with the rest of the Regiment, reported directly to Divisional Headquarters, and was ordered by General Chauvel to withdraw and act as Divisional Troops. The re-formed portion of the Regiment joined up with the 2nd Regiment, but lost touch with the 1st Regiment and Brigade Headquarters. They then moved to the right flank, which was all the time being turned, and towards Hod-El-Dyuk were joined by the 6th Regiment, and came under the command of Colonel Royston, commanding the 2nd Brigade. They then extended to the right, and occupied all the high ground covering the railway, and ultimately succeeded in stopping the enemy's turning movement. The N.Z. M.R. Brigade, the 3rd. L.H. Brigade, and 5th Mounted Brigade came from the direction of Duedar, and attacked from the south-west, squeezing the enemy from this direction, and capturing 600 prisoners. The whole line then swung round to our left, and advanced to Mount Meredith and Hod-El-Anna, where they halted and held an outpost line for the night. During this attack enemy air craft were very active, and dropped numerous bombs, more especially at rail head, whilst supplies and ammunition were being drawn, and inflicted heavy casualties on our transport.

At 4.30 a.m. on the 5th a general advance was ordered, the Regiment acting as Brigade reserve. The enemy were now retiring on Katia, and the line advanced to Bir-Sagid without opposition, passing over the area defended by the 3rd Regiment on the day previously. The number of enemy dead lying in this position supplied ample evidence of the effectiveness of our fire on that occasion, and the numbers of prisoners and abandoned stores passing through our line to the rear gave further indication of the disorganised state in which the enemy were at this time.

A general advance by five Brigades was ordered upon Katia, which was quickly reached, but on coming into action we were met by heavy machine gun and shell fire. The 3rd Regiment was in the centre, and was unable to cross the swamp between it and the enemy. The flank attacks failed, and the Brigades were withdrawn, and arrived at Romani at 1 a.m. the following morning.

During these operations the Regiment was absent from camp for 59 hours; the majority of the horses were without water for the whole period. The men themselves were in a very little better state, as the one water bottle they carried into action was soon exhausted, and no further supplies arrived. Rations reached them in small quantities and at a very belated hour. The weather was extremely hot, constant night posts of different kinds were a necessity, and very little rest and sleep were obtainable; so naturally, when the attack was finally repulsed, both men and horses were thoroughly exhausted. The casualties for the two days were 14 killed, 36 wounded, and 4 missing, and 95 horses killed and missing. On the 6th and 7th the Regiment rested.

On the 8th two-thirds of the Brigade moved out, made up as follows:— Each Regiment supplied 2 Squadrons, totalling 236 in strength; only the fittest horses were selected, the rest of the Brigade remaining in camp under the command of Lieut.-Col. D. Fulton. Major Lewis, with A Squadron and part of C Squadron, was attached to 1st. L.H. Regiment; Major Bell, with B Squadron and portion of C Squadron, to 2nd L.H. Regiment. This arrangement was necessitated by the depletion of the Brigade by the loss of men and casualties from wounds and sickness. The Brigade moved to Katia, where they halted for two hours, watered the horses, and fed up. A and B Squadrons moved via Oghratina to Hod-El-Khirba, and from there north-east to the vicinity of Hod-Abu-Shilla, and then back towards Hod-El-Hisha, where the advance guard got into touch with the enemy at 6 o'clock the following morning. The Brigade then moved forward, and took up a position on a ridge about two miles north-west of Bir-El-Abd, A and B Squadrons occupying the extreme left of the position, with A Squadron on the flank. During the advance the troops came under shell fire from two enemy 9.2 guns, situated in the vicinity of Bir-El-Abd. From this position an attempt was made to advance at 11.30, which failed owing to the concentration of enemy machine gun fire on the advanced troops. At 1.30 the enemy made an advance on the left of our position, at the same time bombarding this position with high explosives and shrapnel, inflicting several casualties. A short time previously the enemy had located our Artillery, and inflicted heavy casualties among their gun teams, which necessitated some considerable delay in salving the guns, and our troops had to remain in an exposed position during the operation of the withdrawal of the guns, but when this was completed they retired to Oghratina. From there they moved to Hod-El-Negiliat, where they stayed till the morning of the 15th, arriving back at Romani on that date.

During these operations and at Romani Regimental communication was carried out by the Signallers. On arrival abundant work presented itself for the Signal personnel. Kat-Tib-Gannett overlooked the front for miles, and being situated close to the camp was always occupied by several helio stations, which were connected to B.H.Q. by telephone, consequently it was never difficult for signal stations to keep touch with Headquarters. At night the outposts close to the camp were kept in touch by telephone. Eight electric lamps were issued, and the Begbi lamps were withdrawn. During the actual attack by the Turks on Romani the absence of any provision for laying cables was severely felt, and sole reliance had to be placed upon visual signalling to keep touch between Regimental Headquarters and the Squadrons, which proved a very difficult matter.

On arrival at Romani the Regiment was given a well-earned rest, which was very much needed, as prior to the actual attack it had been kept busy by constant daily reconnaissances, involving for the most part travelling by night, and during the actual engagement they had a very strenuous time.

On August 8 Major Bell, in charge of two troops from each of the 1st, 2nd., and 3rd. Regiments left camp, and scouted country bounded by Hill 110, Oghratina, Hod-Umm-Ugba, and Katia for Turkish stores. Nothing of importance was discovered, and the party returned. From this time till the 15th ordinary camp duties were carried out, including supplying of patrols every third day to Hill 110, and Katia, Hod-Umm-Ugba, Bir-El-Theila, Hod-Abu-Darum, and Bayieh.

From September 15 till October 2 the Regiment was actively engaged in patrol and reconnaissance work. The Regiment remained at Duedar until October 2nd, when they were relieved by the 5th L.H. Regiment, and proceeded through Hill 70 to Kantara, independent of the Brigade, which remained at Hill 70.

During the Romani campaign the troops suffered considerably from sickness of various kinds, septic sores becoming very prevalent and troublesome, and leading to great disability. The rations on the whole were of good quality and quantity, though there was a comparative shortage of fresh vegetables. The Regimental Canteen continued in operation during the earlier days, but finally was abandoned when the A.I.F. Canteens made their appearance there, for the first time in the history of the Regiment. The visit to Kantara was in the nature of a rest after the strenuous operations during the Turkish attack, and for the purpose of re-equipping. Whilst here arrangements were made to send parties in turn to Sidi-Bishr, at Alexandria, for a change of scene to recruit. A third of the Regiment went at a time, special trains being provided and a week being allotted to each party. Major C. Mills, Major Lewis, and Capt. Bennett reported to the School of Instruction at Zeitoun for three weeks' course of training. The attendance at these schools now became a feature of the Regimental Training, and from time to time parties of both officers, N.C.O.'s, and men were detailed to attend a class where the latest developments in modern warfare were expounded. Special classes were arranged to teach cooking, which were availed of by all the Regimental Cooks. Major G. J. Bell was transferred to the 4th. Camel Regiment as S.I.C.

On November 2 the Brigade left Kantara, and marched to Hod-El-Geila, where they went into camp. The Regiment remained here, doing ordinary camp duties, until the 24th. On the 24th the Brigade, less 1st Regiment, moved out, and marched on independently by Regiments to Arnussi. While here day Observation Posts were posted daily, and an outpost line held during the night; patrols to Hill 225, El-Abasi, and Gererat were also sent out.

On December 20 the Regiment left Gererat with the Brigade, and arrived at El-Arish on the 21st, which, contrary to expectation, was found clear of enemy. El-Arish had been occupied by the Turks for some time, and was an advance base for their operations on the Sinai Peninsula. An abundance of fresh water was found, which was a pleasant change to horses and men, after the brackish water they had been used to.

On the 22nd the Regiment left camp, less 1 troop detailed to act as camel escort, and concentrated with the Brigade in Wadi-El-Arish until rations arrived, and on 23rd proceeded to the Divisional rendezvous, a point 2 miles North-West of El-Maghdaba. The Regiment moved off with the Brigade from the rendezvous, and advanced across an open flat on the South of telegraph line, which ran from El-Arish to Maghdaba. The Regiment moved at the trot on the flank of the Brigade, and contined in this position under fire of the enemy's Artillery. One troop was sent out at the gallop to act as ground scouts, and found impassable ground in the front, when sections left was ordered, and the Regiment followed in rear of the Brigade until the bad ground was passed, and then resumed its position on the right of the line. The Brigade came under heavy machine gun fire from the enemy's trenches, and orders were received to move to the right, into the bed of the Wadi, which was done over very broken ground. The Regiment was then ordered to move down the Wadi dismounted.

The Turks were strongly entrenched to the number of about 1500, and held a line of redoubts across the Wadi-El-Arish. The advance was continued very slowly, owing to the difficult nature of the ground, and consequent delay in bringing forward the machine guns. It was also difficult to locate the cross fire from the enemy's trenches, but when these were located word was sent back of the definite positions of the enemy redoubts; these were then shelled, and a more rapid advance was made to the fork of the Wadi. At this point A Squadron were on the right, and in a position to bring cross fire on No. 1 Redoubt. Two more machine guns joined up, and when all the machine guns were in a position to provide covering fire, an advance across the fork of the Wadi was made. B and C Squadrons were half-way across and the I.C.C. were covering their advance with machine guns. A white flag was hoisted at this time, but our troops continued to fire; bayonets were then fixed, and No. 1 Redoubt was assaulted and taken without further opposition, but the redoubt itself was still under fire from the enemy in the neighboring positions, though their fire did more damage to their own prisoners than to our troops. The trenches in No. 1 Redoubt were at once occupied by the machine guns, and fire brought to bear upon No. 2 Redoubt, B and C Squadrons continuing the advance towards No. 2 Redoubt, reinforced on the left by two Companies of the Imperial Camel Corps. A Squadron, on the south of the Wadi, gained considerable ground, and the force attacking No. 2 Redoubt advanced in short rushes and took it with the bayonet, A Squadron and 1 troop of the 2nd Regiment joining up at this time. The whole Regiment, with the Imperial Camel Corps, manned this redoubt and opened fire upon No. 3 Redoubt, which was being strongly attacked by the 2nd L.H. Regiment. A and C Squadrons received orders to join up with this force, which they did, and assisted in the assault under the leadership of Major Markwell, of 2nd Regiment, and the redoubt was taken. B Squadron received orders to proceed north along the Wadi-El-Arish and attack the water supply, which was taken without opposition, after which they rejoined the Regiment in time to participate in the capture of No. 3 Redoubt. There was no further determined resistance, and the wounded were gathered into groups and small fires lit to aid the Field Ambulance in their collection. This was necessitated, owing to the scattered nature of the attack, and the fact that dusk was already falling. The Regiment re-formed at the fork of the Wadi, where the horses had been collected, and moved back to the wells at about 8 p.m. An officer and 4 men were sent as guides to the Ambulance waggons to collect all wounded, and when this was completed, they moved back to the divisional rendezvous, and thence back to El-Arish with the Brigade, where they arrived at 7 o'clock on 24th. This Regiment captured 50 officers and 234 other ranks and much booty, including the Battalion records. The remainder of the stores and equipment were collected the following day by other units. At about 9 o'clock two enemy aircraft flew over, and dropped 12 bombs on the beach at El-Arish, but did no damage.

On the morning of January 8 the Regiment received instructions to proceed with the Division to Rafa. The Regiment received orders to advance to the attack on the left of the 1st. Regiment, and support them in the assault on the enemy's trenches. Prior to making this attack a personal reconnaissance was made by all officers, and the Regiment then formed up in Squadron lines of troop column in the following order:—A Squadron under Major Lewis on the left, B Squadron under Major Brooks in centre, and C Squadron under Major Mills on the right. The Regiment moved in this formation at a smart trot to within 2000 yards of the enemy's entrenched position, where they dismounted behind a low bank, and formed up in lines of ½ Squadron Column, with a distance of 120 yards between the lines. The horses were sent back and we attacked them with bombs and machine gun fire, but caused practically no casualties. The Squadron leaders were then called up, each allotted a section, and the objective was explained.

An advance was then made to a low ridge within 800 yards of the enemy trenches, down a gradual slope, with no cover, in full view of the enemy, and early in the advance the enemy opened up with rifle and machine gun fire, but though the fire was heavy it was scattered and the range faulty. No check was made, and few casualties resulted. On reaching the position the 2nd line immediately joined the first, and the machine guns and Lewis guns, which had been covering the advance, came up. The enemy's fire was very heavy, and it was some time before superiority of fire on our part was gained. One signaller during these operations was killed and 2 wounded. This was the first time telephone connection had been used in the open battlefield, and it proved entirely satisfactory. Some trenches partly completed by the enemy were found on this ridge, and though only 12 inches deep, were the only cover available, and though they could not accommodate men, were made use of for Machine Gun and Lewis Gun positions. The enemy's positions were considerably higher than our own, and consequently they commanded a great field of view and fire between their trenches and the Regimental position, the ground between them being perfectly level and devoid of cover. It was consequently impossible to advance, and so heavy fire was kept continuously on the enemy's position to afford cover to the right flank, who were steadily pressing forward over a more favourable line of advance. At 1 p.m. the Regiment was reinforced by the 10th Regiment. Ammunition was brought up and quickly distributed, and orders were received to advance. This was done by short rushes, with a few men at a time, the movement starting from the centre, and continuing until sufficient men were in position to afford covering fire for the flanks, by which means they advanced to within 400 yards of the enemy's position. Here the Regiment came under heavy enfilade fire, A Squadron on the left receiving the heaviest casualties, owing to the fact that there was no one on this left flank to support them. It was found necessary to dig in, but the ground being hard, and the only implement available a bayonet, it was some time before any protection was afforded. The Regiment remained in this position, during which time two Squadron Leaders were wounded (Majors Mills and Lewis, the latter seriously), and the Regiment generally suffered heavy casualties. Great praise is due to the Regimental Stretcher Bearers for the fearless manner in which they carried out their duties under the heavy fire. Though the shell fire was heavy, it was inaccurate and caused comparatively few casualties.

Permission was granted for the Regiment to withdraw to the original position, which was done. Orders were then received to work to the right, and support the 2nd Regiment, one Squadron was left behind and the other 2 Squadrons moved to the right, but before a proper junction could be made the redoubt at Hill 225 fell and another frontal advance was ordered, and the ground made good up to the trenches. The wounded were collected, and a party detailed to bury the dead and mark the graves. The Regiment's casualties were 10 killed and 49 wounded. The Regiment then moved for El-Arish, which was reached at midday, where the cooks, who had been left behind, had a meal ready for the men.

During the period of the Maghdaba and Rafa actions there were nine complete nights during which the Regiment was either fighting or advancing, which, in addition to the strenuous work during the actual fights, led to great exhaustion amongst the troops by the time the whole operations were completed. From this time until April 16 the Regiment had a fairly easy time, doing outpost and patrol duty at different stations. Special lectures were given on the defensive measures to be taken against gas, with practical demonstrations with the Gas Helmets, which were now issued to the Regiment for the first time. Major G. J. Bell rejoined the Regiment as Second in Command.

On April 16, 1917, the Regiment moved out from Khan Yunis, and arrived at Shellal next day, and the Squadrons then proceeded to take up their respective positions. C Squadron shortly afterwards came under long range fire from the enemy, who retired as they advanced. On the 19th instructions were received to move out and occupy a line to point 340, near Kirbet-Erk, on the Wadi-El-Sharia, and to entrench and hold it for the night.

On moving out to take up this line, we encountered about 1000 enemy cavalry, half of which were moving south of Wadi-Imlieh, and the other half between that Wadi and Wadi-El-Sharia. The whole of this force was advancing rapidly in a westerly direction, towards the 2nd L.H. Regiment, with the obvious intention of turning the right flank. In order to check this movement the C.O. 3rd Regiment rushed C Squadron, under Major Bennett, out between the Wadi-Imlieh and the Wadi-El-Sharia, and followed this movement by placing B Squadron, under Major Brooks, astride the Wadi-El-Sharia. C Squadron darted quickly forward, under cover of the broken ground, and brought heavy Hotchkiss and rifle fire to bear on the enemy's centre, completely surprising them, and causing the Northern half of the force to move off in a Northerly direction, and the other half to the South-West, splitting the force in two, and completely breaking up the attack. A Squadron, under Major A. Dick, was then sent out south of the Wadi, to engage the Southern portion of the enemy force. Owing to the broken nature of the ground, the greater portion of the advance had to be dismounted. B Squadron, astride the Wadi, connected on the right of C Squadron, and on the left with 2 troops of 2nd Regiment suitable positions were taken up, and heavy Hotchkiss Gun and rifle fire opened on the enemy, who were about 2000 yards away, who then dismounted and advanced within 1300 yards of our own troops. The enemy retired to their original positions, after leaving snipers and Machine Guns in the heavy crop to cover their retirement. The Regiment held these positions until they received orders to rejoin the Brigade at Khirbet-Erk, covering the retirements of 2nd L.H. Regiment.

During the next month the Regiment was kept busy with patrol and reconnaissances under distressing weather conditions.

On May 22, 1917, the Regiment moved with the Brigade with the object of raiding and destroying the Turkish Railway Line between Auja and Beersheba. B Squadron supplied the right flank guard. Essani was reached at 6 p.m on the 23rd. After a short halt it proceeded to a point about three miles South-East of Khalasa. B Squadron had a slight engagement with enemy snipers, and surrounded and held large bodies of Bedouins, pending completion of the operation. Meanwhile 1st and 2nd Regiments advanced upon the railway, and afforded protection to the demolition party, consisting of Engineers, reinforced by Regimental parties selected for their knowledge and experienced in the use of explosives. These parties then destroyed several miles of the railway track. The Regiment then returned to camp, acting as rearguard to the forces.

On June 10, Lieut.-Col. Fulton formally handed over command of the Regiment to Major G. J. Bell (who was then S.I.C.) at a Regimental parade, Lieut.-Col. Fulton proceeded to Cairo the same day to take up the appointment of Commandant of Australian Headquarters. Upon Major Bell assuming command of the Regiment, Major J. J. Brooks was appointed S.I.C. Major Bell was promoted Lieut.-Col. on the 14th. At this period the Anzac Mounted Division was in support to the front line, and were camped at Abasan el Kebir, about 8 miles N.N.E. of Rafa. In spite of all precautions the dust was a great source of discomfort to the troops. All ranks lived here in bivouacs erected over dug outs as a defensive measure against aerial attacks, the enemy at this time having superiority of the air and being very aggressive. While in this camp our time was occupied in firing practices on the range, Hotchkiss Gun Training, grazing of horses, and cleaning of saddlery and equipment. An occasional trip was made to the beach, where a day's swimming was much enjoyed by all. On completion of the period in support the Division moved to Marakeb, situated on the coast about 6 miles North-West of Abasan, and were then in reserve for a similar period. From this camp weekly parties of 1 officer and 10 men proceeded to Egypt on 7 days' leave, and men who were run down and in need of rest proceeded to Desert Corps Rest Camp, Port Said. Everything possible was done here to amuse the men. Sports Meetings, Concerts, Boxing Tournaments, etc., were arranged, and this period was very much looked forward to, the absence of dust being especially appreciated. A certain amount of training was carried out. At the expiration of the allotted period in reserve the Division moved to Shauth, 12 miles East of Rafa, and about 4 miles West of Wadi Guzze. This was also a very dirty and dusty camp; it was a standing camp for troops in the front line, and the constant heavy traffic had very much cut up the surface of the whole area. Here, as also in the support areas at Fukhari and Abasan el Kebir, scorpions, centipedes, and other venomous spiders were very prevalent, and men were frequently bitten by them. At this period a very large number of the Regiment suffered from Septic Sores; these sores break out on the hands, legs, and face, and were apparently similar to what is known in Australia as "Barcoo Rot" and in the South African Campaign as Veldt Sores. They were particularly hard to cure, and entailed a great deal of work on the Medical Staff, it being a common occurrence to have a hundred men under treatment at a time. A hospital was established on the beach at Marakeb, where the worst of these cases were sent, and the dieting and sea bathing obtainable there usually had the desired effect. The work that we were called upon to do here was mainly reconnaissance of the enemy's position and patrols and outpost duty.

The Turks were holding a line from the sea covering Gaza and running South-West on the high ground West of the Main Road to Beersheba, embracing Birket el Sana and Abu Hareira, then due South, crossing the Wadi Imlieih at Bir Ifteis, then S.S.W. through Hill 730 and 770 South to 810 and 820 S.E., across to Um Farrath and Hill 1070, around Ras Hablein to Ras Gannam, thence to Hills 1180 and 1280, thus practically surrounding Beersheba, their Southern main point, and which was the sector of the enemy's line which more especially concerned us, and to which we paid particular attention.

There was keen rivalry displayed between Units engaged on patrols and reconnaissances as to who could get the closest to the enemy's lines, and those left in camp would spend the day in speculating how far out our patrols were, as the enemy's fire could easily be heard from Camp. It was remarkable the apparent lack of enterprise shown by the enemy in not endeavoring to ambush our patrols. They always appeared to be quite satisfied to keep us as far away from them as possible by opening up fire at long range, and making no effort to surprise us.

At 1 a.m. on July 4 the Regiment moved out with the Brigade to take part in a reconnaissance in strength of the enemy's lines covering their main road to Beersheba from Point 410 on the Wadi Imleih running in a S.E. direction along the Wadi across Wadi Hanafish East to Hills 770, 810, and 820 to astride the Rafa-Beersheba road. B Squadron acted as left flank guard to the Brigade and moved into position to Hills 510, to 550. A Squadron moved forward with a Machine Gun Section to a line Hill 630 to Wadi Hanafish. The enemy was occupying Hill 630, but one Troop moving rapidly forward in extended order, he withdrew, after firing a few shots. A party of about 20 enemy with two Machine Guns held a small stone building on the West bank of the Wadi Hanafish, but Lieut. Kelly with his troop working round to their left flank came into action against them, and they withdrew. These two Squadrons remained in position all day, and they were intermittently shelled by the enemy, but the soft nature of the ground localising the effect of the shells no casualties were suffered. C Squadron remained in reserve. At 5 p.m. two enemy cavalry squadrons moved out to attack the 2nd Regiment, who were on our right, but coming under fire, quickly changed direction towards Hill 630. A Squadron withheld their fire till the enemy were in close range, and then opened up with Machine Gun and Hotchkiss causing many casualties among the enemy, who immediately galloped off. Orders to withdraw were received and acted upon at 6.30 p.m. under heavy shell fire from the enemy, but no casualties occurred. Then came a 10 mile ride back to camp. These stunts were frequent while the unit was in the front line, and were very hard on both men and horses, as they meant two nights with practically no sleep and a hard day's work in a very hot sun, with, in the men's case, only one bottle of water to drink, the horses usually having to go without water till returning to camp. Tired as the men were on return to camp, their horses were always their first thought, and no one turned in himself till his horse had been properly cared for. Cooks were usually left in camp, and had a meal ready for the men on their return.

On the 6th July, 1917, the Regiment took over Ghabi Works (three redoubts known as "X," "Y," and "Z"), one squadron garrisoning each redoubt. These redoubts, which were situated about 4½ miles S.W. of Shauth, were for the protection of our right flank against an enveloping attack by enemy cavalry. While here our horses had to proceed daily to the Wadi Ghuzze for water. This meant a trip of 12 miles, the practice being to go down in the morning and water, graze till about 2 p.m., water again, and return. All drinking and washing water had to be carted from the same place, and this meant a lot of work for transport horses and drivers, it being a very heavy and dusty road.

On 8th July, the Regiment (less one Troop occupying each redoubt), with two M.G. Sections, left Ghabi at 3.45 a.m. to take part in a reconnaissance being made by Anzac Mounted Division, who were to make good a line running from Point 510 Abu Shawish Road East to Point 630 El Girheir South-East to 730, 770, 810, 820, Taweil el Habari to 720 Abu Yahia and S.W.W. toward Um Auja and Rashid Bek. The Regiment was responsible for clearing of Rashid Bek and Um Auja. The remainder of the Brigade being in reserve at Khasif. The Regiment was formed into two Squadrons under Major A. Dick and Major W. J. Bennett respectively, the whole being in command of Major J. J. Brooks, D.S.O. (S.I.C. of the Regiment). Major Dick's Squadron supplied the advance guard and right flank guard, and Major Bennett the rearguard and left flank guard. Bir el Esani was reached at 6.45 a.m., where we watered; Rashid Bek was reached at 8.15 a.m., and Major Dick's Squadron, with one section M.G. Squadron, was sent to Um Auja, which was occupied at 8.30 a.m. The remainder of the Regiment remained at Rashid Bek. Observation posts were established and touch gained by helios with N.Z.M.R. Brigade on our left and with the Anzac Mounted Divisional Headquarters. Our observation posts sighted 15 enemy mounted men in the vicinity of Rashid Bek, but they withdrew as we advanced. A few shells were fired at Major Dick's Squadron at Um Auja, but did not cause any casualties. Orders for withdrawal were received at 5.50 p.m., and the Regiment returned to camp (watering at Esani en route), arriving at 10.50 p.m. During the day the new C.I.C., General Sir Edmund Allenby, K.C.B., inspected the Ghabi defences, Lieut.-Col. Bell, D.S.O., escorting him through the works.

On 14th July Ghabi Works were handed over to the Auckland Mounted Rifles Regiment, and this Regiment marched to Shauth. At 10.30 p.m. the same day the Regiment (less one Squadron) moved out on an ambush scheme with the object of endeavoring to capture enemy patrols in the neighborhood of Um Auja. Esani was reached at 1.30 a.m., and one Squadron under Major Bennett proceeded to Um Auja. Two troops of this Squadron were posted 1000 yards N.E. of Rashid Bek, and two troops at a point near Point 860, south of Um Auja. These troops were in position at 3.15 a.m. and remained in hiding. The other Squadron took up a position at Tel Itweil, one troop being sent before daylight to a position just south of Point 750. At dawn an enemy observation post could be seen on Point 780, Abu

Chalyun, by the troops at Um Ajua. At 6.30 a.m. an enemy patrol, 26 strong, was sighted coming along the track north of Um Ajua; its scouts turned south and moved to a point about 1500 yards north-west of Point 780; here three dismounted men (presumably Bedouins) were seen to meet the scouts, and one scout moved slowly forward, and evidently sighting us galloped back to the patrol, who hastily returned in a northerly direction towards Khebaina. One of our troops unsuccessfully attempted to cut them off. Another enemy patrol was sighted at 6.30 a.m. east of the road near Point 780, Abu Chalyun. This patrol also withdrew upon seeing the other galloping away. The scheme having failed, the Regiment withdrew and returned to camp, arriving at 1 p.m. On the 18th July the Regiment moved off at 9.30 p.m. with the 2nd Regiment, and marched to Abu Rigal. Regimental Headquarters, with one Squadron, remained at Point 750, one Squadron moved to Khalassa, and the other to Point 820. All were in position by 3 a.m., and remained hidden until 7 a.m., when the Squadron at Khalassa moved out, and crossing the Wady Imalaga moved to the junction of the Abu-Shawish-Khalassa-Beersheba roads, then turned north, keeping their right flank about half a mile east of the Abu Shawish road till meeting the 2nd L.H. Regiment operating from the north near Wadi Esani. The Squadron from Point 820 moved north, with their right flank in touch with the other Squadron and their left on the Wadi Imalga until the 2nd L.H. Regiment was met near Rashid Bek. Several small enemy posts were observed, but they all retired in the direction of Beersheba as we advanced. Three enemy mounted men watering at holes on Abu Shawish road were fired on, one horse being killed and the rider captured. The Regiment then concentrated at Goz Lakheilat, and established observation posts. Orders to withdraw were received at 7 p.m., and camp was reached at 1.45 a.m. At 2.15 a.m. (just half an hour after our return to camp) orders were received to draw rations and be formed ready to move off again at 3.30 a.m., the reason for this being that a force of Turkish Cavalry had been reported as advancing toward Goz el Basal. Some of the men had already turned in, and in fact were asleep, but they were roused up, rations were hastily drawn, and the Regiment was ready at the appointed hour. The Brigade proceeded to Goz el Basal, remaining there till 12 p.m., but the anticipated attack did not materialise, and we returned to camp, arriving at 3 p.m. On the 22nd Major A. Dick with five troops took over an outpost line extending from about 2000 yards east of Fara to El Dammath. At 1.30 a.m. on 23rd July, in consequence of the report having been received that Beersheba had been evacuated, the Brigade was again ordered out, and moved off at 4 a.m., proceeded to El Buggar, watering at Gamli en route. The report having been found to be incorrect, we returned to camp, arriving at 3 p.m., with the exception of one Squadron, which took over the day outpost line and withdrew at dark.

The regiment remained at Shauth till 18th August doing the same kind of work as that just described, and, at the end of this time, owing to insufficient sleep and hard work combined, with such discomforts as insufficient water and continual dust, both men and horses were sorely in need of the rest on the beach. During the period in the front line about 100 men were evacuated sick, the principal causes being debility and septic sores.

The period of rest was occupied in the usual way, the first aim being to get men and horses fit and well, and at the same time more efficient in the art of warfare. The usual training was carried out in bombing, Hotchkiss gunnery, and gas. The Desert Corps commander inspected the regiment on 11th September, and expressed himself pleased with the appearance of men, horses, and equipment. On the 18th September we moved out again into the supports area, and camped at Kilo 9 (near Fukhari). There the period was put in in the usual way—firing practices on the range, training in preparing to meet cavalry, regiment in attack, etc., etc. An alarm forming up area, for the Brigade was allotted and the turn out practised. At about this period, owing to the advent of some new fighting planes on this front, we were holding our own with the enemy in the air, and we often had the pleasure of witnessing a duel which ended victoriously for us.

On 3rd October we moved with the remainder of the Brigade to a new camp site on the beach at Rafa. About this time it became apparent to all ranks that we were preparing to launch an offensive at an early date; dumps were being established near the front line, and there was a general appearance of bustle everywhere. While here special attention was paid to intercommunication with aeroplanes, lectures on the subject being given and schemes carried out. On the 24th October, the regiment moved to Fukhari. A dump of all surplus gear had been formed at Rafa, and each man carried only the absolute minimum amount of clothing and necessaries. We remained at Fukhari for one day, and on the 26th we again moved off, and by a series of night marches arrived at Asluj on the night of the 29th.

At 6.30 p.m. on the 30th the Anzac Mounted Division left Asluj, and marched N.E., the object being to envelope and attack Beersheba from the east and north-east in co-operation with other brigades attacking from the south. Point 1390, situated north-east of Beersheba, was reached, and from here the regiment was sent forward, the objective being Tel el Saba, which was seen to be strongly held by the enemy with several machine guns, which were placed in stone huts and sangars, and were thus well protected from our fire from all quarters. Two squadrons advanced mounted till within about 1200 yards of their objective, when, coming under heavy fire, they dismounted and advanced on foot, the horses being placed under cover in the Wadi. The Auckland Mounted Rifles co-operating on our right, the attack was pushed home under covering fire from our artillery, which did excellent work in dislodging machine guns. We advanced in short rushes down each bank of the Wadi, both of which, being very flat, were swept by machine gun and rifle fire; a good many casualties were sustained here, and most commendable bravery and utter disregard of danger was shown by the stretcher-bearers in dressing and attending to the wounded on these exposed positions. L./Cpl. A. C. Rodgers, medical detail, and Tpr. T. R. Hogarth, the latter being posthumously awarded the M.M., were killed. The enemy surrendered upon the final assault being made. Our casualties were one officer and ten other ranks killed, and 18 other ranks wounded. Upon Tel el Saba being captured the horses were brought up the Wadi, and evidently were observed by the enemy, who concentrated the fire of two batteries of 77 m.m. guns upon the Wadi near Tel el Saba, but we were able to get the horses away before many casualties had occurred among them. Owing to rain having fallen a few days before there was an abundance of surface water available, so that we were able to water the horses and replenish water bottles. While watering in the Wadi several enemy planes bombed us, but failed to do any damage. The regiment then moved to Point 960, and bivouacked, having previously despatched a squadron to Beersheba to get in touch with the 1st Regiment. This squadron returned at 10 p.m. During the day our transport, which had been left at Point 1300, were heavily bombed by enemy planes, the casualties being four other ranks killed and five wounded, 10 horses killed and seven wounded.

The regiment remained in bivouac on 1st November; parties were sent out to collect tibben, which was found in large quantities. Quantities of war material were also found. The surface pools having been used up, it now became necessary to water the horses at Beersheba; here all of the wells had been destroyed by the enemy, with the exception of one, and thus the horses of all units had to be watered at the one place, which meant great congestion at the watering area day and night. This presented a splendid target for enemy planes, which were particularly active during these operations, and did a great deal of bombing. Machine guns and Hotchkiss rifles were used against them, and had the effect of keeping them at a high altitude, and occasionally brought one down. On November 6 the regiment joined the brigade, and moved to Kh.-El-Muweileh, from where we moved forwards about four miles, and took over outpost positions held by Berks. Regiment, and held same until next day, when we moved towards Tel-El-Sharia, whilst the enemy kept up shellfire, and long-range machine gun fire. Lieut. Bean, with a troop of B Squadron, remained at this point to guide up our transport wagons, which were following closely in rear of the advancing column. Then moving quickly across the undulating open ground E.N.E. of Sharia, on the railway station at Kh.-Um-Ameidat. Ameidat was captured with little resistance, about 400 prisoners being taken. Ameidat was a main dump. About a million shells and cases of ammunition, motor ambulances, stores, and feed, etc., much hospital furniture and stores were captured. The regiment then moved up to support 1st Regiment, which was attacking Tel-El-Nejila, about four miles N.E. This was captured without opposition, and the regiment withdrew on the vicinity of Ameidat, where all three squadrons were used on the outpost line covering to the east. The position now was that the enemy were still holding Gaza, 16 miles due west; we had driven their flank in, and come up between Hebron and Gaza, thus practically splitting them in half. Our object was to encircle Gaza, and force northwards and capture any enemy as we went, not forgetting our right flank towards the difficult country west of Hebron.

At an early hour on the 8th, C Squadron preceded the Regiment to Wadi-El-Muleiha, where developing operations to increase the water supply were commenced. This development consisted of sinking holes near soakage pools, thus drawing cleaner water through the gravel below. Whilst half of the troops were on this work, troops from A, B, and C Squadrons had gone N.N.E., patrolling and reconnoitring, and capturing 72 prisoners for the day. Orders were received to rejoin the Brigade, who had moved W.N.W. towards Jemame. C Squadron and R.H.Q. left, and arrived at Jemame, followed by A and B Squadrons at half-hour intervals. A Squadron was bombed by our own planes S.E. of Jemame, four other ranks being wounded and three horses killed. Immediately on arrival at B.H.Q. it was found that the 2nd A.L.H. Regiment was held up at Jemame by a strong enemy rearguard. C Squadron at once relieved A Squadron of 2nd Regiment, which was holding a position on the S.E. slope of the Jemame Hills, and as soon as the relief was completed, C Squadron pushed on rapidly round the southern flank of the hill, and at the same time B Squadron delivered a vigorous frontal attack, and swept up over the position. The rapid movement of C Squadron threatened the enemy's right flank and rear, and the combined movement caused the enemy to evacuate a position that he had held in a very determined manner the whole day. C Squadron continued their rapid movement well in the rear of the enemy's position, and captured many prisoners, while B Squadron, in the rapid dismounted movement, secured material, which the enemy was unable to move in his forced retirement. These Squadrons then joined the outpost line, connecting with the 2nd Brigade on our right and the 10th Regiment on our left astride the Buirer road. Nothing occurred during the night. Large fires were seen North-North-West, where the enemy were burning dumps. . At early morning on the 9th the Brigade moved forward, with the 3rd Regiment as advance guard, passing many wagons and several guns and ammunition wagons, arriving at Buirer without opposition, and then pushing on rapidly towards El-Huleikat, two miles north, from where B Squadron pushed rapidly through to Hemame, while C Squadron moved into Mejdel, capturing six Officers and 100 other ranks, and stores. Watering here, the Brigade moved towards Beit-Duras, four miles north-east. Enemy cavalry opened fire from sand hills on left flank guard of the brigade, and the C.O. swung B Squadron away to the left, to occupy high ground, and make all clear on that flank. Sergeant Kelly, acting as advance guard, rode rapidly out with two sections extended, and made the high ground, but the enemy had disappeared in the dusk. B Squadron rejoined the brigade, and formed a portion of the outpost line at Beit-Duras. Lieutenant Tongs with his troop remained at Mejdel, to guard wells and flour mills, and captured stores and prisoners. Captures for the day: Six officers, 160 other ranks, 26 wagons (gun and ammunition).

On the morning of the 10th, we left Beit-Duras, and moved towards Esdud across undulating plains. The enemy was holding strongly high ground across Wadi-Mejina, covering Esdud. The C.O. receiving orders to reconnoitre, and, if possible, occupy the ridge to secure Esdud and allow the Brigade to move to Jisr Esdud, to the water in the Wadi, orders were given to the O.C. B Squadron, Major E. C. Derrington, to move forward, and, if possible, gain the ridge. The Regiment at this time was distributed in open formation on a plain just S.E. of Esdud. Wadi-Mejina in front, close under a ridge occupied by the enemy. B Squadron sent forward two troops under Captain T. Kenyon, who advanced rapidly towards what proved to be the centre of the enemy's position. When the scouts had crossed the Wadi and were advancing towards the enemy's position, they opened heavy machine gun and rifle fire on the troops, who galloped forward and gained cover in the Wadi-Mejena, from where Hotchkiss guns were pushed forward along a bend in the Wadi, and engaged enemy M.G. positions. It was then realised that the positions were strongly held, and Inverness Battery came into action and shelled the enemy. The enemy's guns responded and shelled our troops, who were in the open. Throughout the day the regiment was subjected to shell fire, which had little effect, though there was no cover; the Regiment disposed in open order, we having by now fully realised that, unless troops are grouped together in large masses, shell fire is not deadly. The steadiness of our troops that day under shell fire was remarkable, as they were subject to continuous direct fire from the enemy all day, without cover of any kind. The C.O. having received orders to report on the strength and extent of the enemy's position, sent forward one troop to a point nearest Esdud, on the end of the ridge, and close to the Wadi-Mejina. This troop, under the direction of the C.O., galloped straight for the Wadi, enemy M.G.'s opening heavy cross fire as the troop advanced. The Wadi was gained, where the troop dismounted with the loss of two horses killed. They rushed quickly forward, and gained a valuable, though small, position within 100 yards of the enemy's strong redoubt. A second troop was now pushed forward in support. This troop was also subjected to machine gun fire as they advanced, but galloping horses in extended order are difficult to hit, and this troop also reached the Wadi with small loss. These troops withstood several attempts by the enemy to dislodge them, and were able to hold on to their positions throughout the day. At 5.15 p.m. the 157th Infantry Brigade moved up towards the enemy's position in readiness for an early night attack. The two troops withdrew at dusk, and rejoined their squadrons, which were then watering at Esdud from an ancient well, where the usual Egyptian endless bucket system was employed. After watering, the Regiment took up an outpost line commanding the left flank of the Infantry 157th Brigade, out upon the Esdud Plain, across N.W. to Jisr Esdud, the bridge over the Wadi-Mejina, two miles north of Esdud, and remained in this position during the night, and were relieved and withdrawn a few hundred yards in the rear of the line at early morning on 11th. The casualties on 10th were six other ranks wounded, six horses killed, and nine wounded. Watering this day was a long job, each Squadron moving at half-hourly intervals back south-east to New Kustineh, a Jewish Colony. Water was abundant from a very deep well, pumped up by an engine.

On the 12th November, the infantry commenced an advance on the enemy's positions towards Burka, four miles N.E. of Esdud. It was a fine sight, and the first that Light Horse troops had seen of Infantry moving steadily forward in waves in open order, followed by M.G. packs and pack mules carrying ammunition. Guns on both sides were firing, and enemy shrapnel was chiefly bursting over the steadily advancing Infantry. The Regiment moved due west to Sidret el Haruriyeh on the beach. The swim and wash for men and horses was greatly appreciated. The Brigade moved out on 13th towards Yebnah, about 12 miles N.N.E. of Esdud, across the Nahr Sukereih, or River Sukereir, where C Squadron had been sent to make a crossing by cutting down the steep banks at a shallow spot in its course about one mile north of Jisr Esdud (Bridge of Esdud). The Brigade bivouacked close to Yebnah at 6 p.m., having made about 18 miles (across heavy sandhills part of the way) in five hours. The waggons and transport column arrived at 6.30 p.m. followed by our ration convoy.

On 14th we moved towards Ramleh, nine miles N.E., to a winery 1000 yards north of Ras Deiran. Whilst at this place O/C B Squadron reported three columns moving towards him from Ramleh. The O.C. Inverness Battery immediately brought his guns into action upon the columns, which deployed, one column swinging away towards our left flank. The enemy were making a strong attempt to block our rapid advance on Ramleh, and north towards Jaffa patrols were sent forward to test the positions, and shortly after, heavy fighting commenced on our left at Ayun Kara, where the New Zealanders struck the enemy in strength; from our position with glasses we could distinctly view the charge, and counter-charge of New Zealanders, and after heavy fighting they threw the enemy back. At dusk an outpost line was taken up from the New Zealanders on the left through an almond orchard around the winery, extending south-east around Ras Deiran. The ensuing night was quiet. Casualties for the day, one other rank killed and three wounded.

On 15th the Brigade moved quickly on to Ramleh, passing through Ludd, where the 1st and 2nd Regiments were holding a line. The Regiment bivouacked for the night in an olive grove at the north end of Ludd. At noon on 16th the Brigade moved towards Safiriyeh, on the Jaffa main road, about four miles from Ludd, an outpost line being held here during the night, our right flank being in touch with Yeomanry Division at Sheik Mohammed Esselari on the flat plain between Ludd and Jaffa, our left flank being in touch with the New Zealand Brigade near Beit Deijaa. The next few days were spent in patrolling country to the north and in holding outpost lines at night. Quantities of tibben were obtained from various villages, where men were also able to buy bread, etc., which was much appreciated; about this time rain commenced to fall, which added very much to the discomfort of the men, especially when on outpost duty. On 21st November the Brigade moved back to Yebnah, camping there for the night, and moving next day to Sideret el Haririyeh, where we remained till 27th. On 27th the Brigade moved to a new camp site at Ayun Kara, as reserves to the 54th Infantry Division, who were then holding the line. On 5th December the Regiment moved to camp on to higher ground, in anticipation of wet weather. A few days later the old camp site was under water. On the 17th the Regiment went into the front line at Bald Hill, near Mulebbis, taking over from the 5th R.S.F. Owing to enemy artillery fire it was impossible to keep the horses near the front line, so they were sent back to our camp at Richon, one man being detailed to look after each four horses. The enemy were holding the dominating position of Bald Hill, about 900 yards in front of us, which was well protected by wire entanglements. From Bald Hill they had a communication trench running down to a strong forward post opposite A Squadron, who were in a rather exposed position on the forward slope, and to the left of Hill 265, which was our main position. The 11th London Battalion was on our right and the first Regiment on our left. The trenches were held by a few men on observation during the day, and during the night each Squadron post was manned by three troops and one Machine Gun Section. The enemy shelled our position on and off all day, but, owing to the soft nature of the ground, did little damage.

On the morning of 21st the Brigadier viewed the enemy's position with the C/O. of the Regiment from Hill 265, and a consultation was held with regard to the operations which were to take place on the following morning. The London Regiment on our right was to attack Bald Hill; our Regiment was to advance at the same time, and make good the left flank of the hill until dawn, when a general advance of three Brigades of Infantry towards Mulebbis was to commence. At midnight B Squadron moved to the trench of the Londoners, from where they were to start. All the batteries on our sector opened up a heavy bombardment of the enemy's position, which was almost immediately replied to by several enemy batteries. Shortly afterwards B Squadron moved forward, passing through an intense barrage, and reaching their objective, were reinforced by C Squadron, and proceeded to dig in about 100 yards from the enemy's trenches, which work was proceeded with all night. They were subject to heavy artillery fire till about one hour before dawn, but owing to the soft, sandy nature of the ground localising the effect, our casualties were very light, Lieutenant M'Bride and one man being killed, and Major Derrington, with 10 other ranks, wounded. Just before dawn a patrol was pushed forward, and reporting Bald Hill clear of the enemy, the Regiment moved forward. The communication trench from the enemy's forward position to Bald Hill was literally filled with dead Turks, our Artillery having evidently enfiladed the trench as the enemy attempted to withdraw. On 23rd we withdrew and returned to the camp near Richon. The last few days spent in the trenches were rendered very unpleasant by continuous heavy rain, which filled trenches and dug-outs.

The rain continued for about a week, and a very wet Christmas was spent. On 26th the Brigade moved to Esdud, across the Yebnah Plain, which had become almost impassable owing to the rain, and some very amusing incidents (though unpleasant for those concerned) occurred, owing to horses becoming bogged or falling in the mud, or when crossing wadis which were in flood. Men riding donkeys had in several instances to dismount and lift their mounts out of a bog. The wagons also had great difficulty in crossing the plain. The Brigade bivouacked on the sandhills north of Jisr Esdud. New Year's Day was an uneventful one; some Y.M.C.A. gifts arrived, and were distributed among members of the Regiment. On 8th January the Official Photographer took moving pictures of the Brigade mounted. On 12th the Brigade moved to a new camp site near Dieran. Heavy rain set in soon after the trek started, and continued all day. The Transport, with baggage, was held up by flood waters in a wadi near Yebnah, and did not arrive at the new camp till next day, a very cold and miserable night being spent by all ranks in consequence. On 18th the Brigade again moved to a new camp situate south of Richon, and for the next few weeks time was devoted to training and sports. Hotchkiss gun classes were held also classes for junior officers and N.C.O.'s. It was decided to hold a Divisional Sports Meeting, the competitors being winners of Brigade and Regimental events. The Regimental and Brigade Sports Meetings were first held. The prize money was subscribed by Officers of the Division, and everything was in readiness for the Divisional Meeting, which, however, it was found impossible to hold, owing to impending operations. The Regimental Sports Meeting was held on 10th February; 66 entries were received in the other ranks jumping event, of which 60 completed the course, and 18 had to jump off for places. There were 10 entries in the Officers' Hunters, the C/O. getting first place on his own horse. The Lloyd Lindsay Competition was an excellent event, some very fine horsemanship being shown by several of the competitors. A great deal of rain fell while we were in this camp, but it was an excellent wet weather one, being on a slope and the ground of a sandy nature. The horses did very well while here, as some good grazing was obtainable in the vicinity of the camp. The health of the men also was remarkably good, due largely, no doubt, to plenty of fruit being available. Another thing much appreciated by all ranks was a hot bath, which was obtainable in Richon at certain times.

On 16th February the Brigade moved out to take part in operations against Jericho, and after five days trekking over very mountainous country arrived at El-Muntar, near the Dead Sea. Here the enemy commenced shelling the column from Nebi-Musa, towards which we were advancing. The New Zealand Brigade had moved ahead of our Brigade in the early morning, and were now down amongst the wadis, moving into position to try and force through to Nebi-Musa. Our Brigade moved down to support them. The enemy were holding extremely strong positions, with machine guns, covering the only track possible to advance over, and thus held the New Zealand Brigade up. Our Brigade was ordered to move east, and try and work round and attack Nebi-Musa from the rear. We moved along the Wadi-Kumran towards the Dead Sea, and then north along a goat track. The whole of the Brigade was in single file. We finally formed up in the Wadi-Jofet-Zeban at dark, and remained here until 3.15 a.m., when C Squadron commenced to advance, leading their horses in single file. Just at dawn we made the north-west top corner of the Dead Sea, after two hours, moving over precipitous goat tracks. B Squadron moved up the main road toward Nebi-Musa from Jericho, whilst C Squadron moved direct across the hills, and arriving at the Monastery, found that it had been evacuated during the night by the enemy. A Squadron moved along the Jordan Valley towards Jericho. Lieutenant Kelly, with his troop, entered the town without resistance, capturing 23 prisoners. This troop was the first of our force to enter Jericho. The Turks shelled the town, and caused one casualty. A Squadron then proceeded to the River Jordan on reconnaissance, and found the enemy holding the high ground on the west bank, covering the Ghoraniyeh Bridge. After some days of outpost duty the regiment returned to El-Khudr for two days, during which time parties were sent to Jerusalem under an officer for sight-seeing. At 8 a.m. on the 25th we left El-Khudr, and marched to El-Bureij, arriving there at 5.30 p.m., and bivouacked for the night. On the 26th we moved off at 8 a.m., and marched to our old camp site at Richon, arriving thre at 4 p.m. This operation was very severe on the horses, as we had been travelling over extremely bad country continuously for a week; several of them died, and a large number had to be evacuated. On the 5th March we again moved out towards Jerusalem, by the main Jaffa-Jerasulem road. On the 7th the main road was left, and we proceeded over a rough track towards Beitunia, where we bivouacked for the night, and on the 8th moved up to Beitin, close behind the front line, as supports to the Infantry, who were to make an advance that night. The Infantry gained their objective, and we were not needed, and on the 13th we moved back to Bethlehem, during a heavy rain storm. For the next few days heavy rain continued to fall, and this, combined with extreme cold, made things very unpleasant for us all. On the 16th A Squadron proceeded to the Jordan Valley for duty with the Bridging Train, who were engaged in bridging the River Jordan, a most difficult operation, owing to the river being in flood. The enemy occupied the eastern bank, which was covered with dense scrub, and offered great facilities for sniping, which they made good use of. On the 20th the Regiment moved with the Brigade to Talat-Ed-Dumm, arriving there at 1.45 a.m. on the 21st., where we bivouacked for the remainder of the night. Nebi-Musa was reached at 9 p.m. on the 21st. On the 22nd we remained in readiness to cross the River Jordan as soon as the bridge was completed.

On March 23rd we moved off, and crossed over the pontoon bridge at Hajla, and formed up with the Brigade on the eastern bank of the river. We moved to Square 127, where this Regiment took over the outpost line, and was responsible for the protection of the Brigade. On 25th we moved off, our object being to reach Es-Salt by the track running from Unm Esk Shert over the Mountains of Moab. As we moved up the Valley we came under shell fire from the western bank of the Jordan, near Um-Es-Shert, but soon after we were enveloped in a thick mist, which effectually screened us from the enemy's view. As we neared the track one Squadron proceeded north-east into the hills, the remainder of the Regiment striking the track before commencing the ascent. The mist had made the track, which was very precipitous and stony, slippery, and it was only negotiable by leading the horses in single file, a very slow and tiring process, each man being heavily laden with ammunition, rations, etc. At the junction of Nos. 6 and 7 Roads we were joined by Infantry. The heights overlooking Es-Salt were reached without opposition. A patrol was sent into the town, outposts were put out, and the Regiment bivouacked for the night, which was misty and extremely cold. A good deal of rifle fire was heard in the town, but it was found that the inhabitants were firing in the air as a welcome to us. This night was the coldest experienced by the Regiment since the Gallipoli snow. On 27th the enemy was observed reconnoitreing our positions, his object evidently being to recapture Es-Salt, and thus break our communications with the force operating against Amman. One Squadron was sent to the Circassian village of Suweileh, where there was trouble impending between the Circassians and the Christians from the village of El-Fuheis. On the early morning of the 29th, the enemy made a half-hearted attack on our positions, but withdrew after throwing a few bombs and firing a few shots. At daybreak they were seen to be building stone sangars along the line held by them. Infantry now took over our line, and we were made responsible for the right flank, it evidently being the enemy's intention to work round to cut the road by which we had come. It being evident that the enemy intended to attack, all units now occupied the line during the night. On 30th a Turkish officer was captured, and gave the information that they had intended to attack the previous night, but that their bombing parties had got lost, and the attack would take place to-night. At 1.30 a.m. on 31st the Regiment moved about a mile down No. 6 Road, and, dismounting, moved up to within 800 yards of an enemy post, covering his right flank, one troop, pushing forward, got to within 200 yards of the post without being seen, with another troop following in support. Hotchkiss guns were placed in positions to give covering fire, and the two troops advanced quietly towards the enemy post. They were not seen until they were within a few yards of the post, which they completely surprised. The enemy retired in confusion, without firing a shot, leaving three machine guns, which were all ready for action and covering the ground we had advanced over. The two troops immediately opened fire on the retreating enemy, killing one officer and 13 other ranks, and wounding several others. The reserve troops were then quickly brought forward, and the enemy line crumpled up without offering any resistance, thus clearing up the situation on this flank. On reaching a high ridge overlooking the Jordan Valley, three hundred enemy cavalry were seen moving down the Nablus Road, and fire from several Hotchkiss guns was brought to bear upon them, causing many casualties, the remainder galloping away in disorder. This minor operation clearly proved the immense value of surprise in the attack, as here not more than 20 men, locating the enemy's flank, which they surprised and attacked, and then, moving quickly forward, stampeded his whole line for at least a mile, without sustaining a single casualty. On the night of 1st April the force withdrew to the bridgehead defences. On the 11th heavy machine gun and rifle fire was heard, and shortly afterwards a report was received that the enemy was attacking the bridgehead defences, and that our Regiment must be in readiness to move at short notice. The enemy attack had developed on a front of 2000 yards along the Wadi-Nimrin and in front of the sector held by the 2nd Regiment, which was approximately the centre of the defensive line. The attack was checked at the outset with machine-gun fire, heavy casualties being inflicted. The enemy did not press the attack with determination, though he brought heavy artillery and machine gun fire on our advanced posts. The regiment moved out through the left of our line, with the object of making a reconnaissance against the enemy's right flank. We had not gone far before we came under heavy artillery, machine gun, and rifle fire, from the enemy concealed in the thick scrub, and considerable casualties occurred among our horses. Twelve Turkish prisoners were captured. Our casualties were one killed and 10 wounded, 15 horses killed and 17 wounded. On 14th we relieved the 5th L.H. Regiment in the line, one Squadron of Hyderabad Lancers, and one Company of Alawa Infantry being attached to the Regiment to supplement its strength. A few Lancers were taken out each day with the patrols, and they showed great coolness under fire. Information was received that the C.O., Lieut.-Col. G. J. Bell, D.S.O., had been awarded the C.M.G., and on 17th that Lieuts. R. K. Kidman and C. A. Bennetto had both been awarded the M.C.

for work in the recent operations at Es-Salt. On the 19th the Regiment moved out to the left sector of the line, with the object of demonstrating towards the high ground about Wadi-Abu-Tarra, and, if possible, to seize Hill 127, with a view of obtaining information and observation of the enemy in the vicinity of No. 6 road. We were heavily shelled upon leaving the defensive line, and on approaching our objective it was seen to be held by the enemy. The two guns of 302nd R.H.A., which accompanied us, immediately opened up on the position, two troops at the same time advancing, occupied the low hills facing same, and also opened up with their Hotchkiss guns, with the result that the hill was occupied by us, the enemy retiring to high hills in the rear, which we found to command our objective. A message was received from Brigade that the enemy were being reinforced on our left flank, and ordering us not to press the attack further, and we withdrew. Up to April 29 our outpost duty was continuous. Then a move was made. Our objective was Es-Salt, via No. 7 Road (this being the second time we had climbed this track), and at 7 p.m. we caught up with the 5th Mounted Brigade, who had bivouacked about 1½ miles west of Es-Salt.

At 3 a.m. on 2nd we were ready to move with the Brigade, which had been ordered to cover Nos. 6 and 7 Roads from the north. Owing to the very dense fog and the precipitous nature of the country to be traversed, we were unable to move till 4 a.m. The Regiment was ordered to cover the left flank of 3rd Brigade, which was being attacked by the enemy. Two Squadrons were ordered to protect No. 7 Road from the North, and also to cover the right flank of the 4th Brigade, which was in difficulties, the enemy having got round its left flank to the rear, forcing them to withdraw and abandon their guns. The position at this stage was critical, as the enemy still held Shunet-Nimron and El-Haud, thus denying us the only road accessible to wheeled traffic, rations having to be transported on pack animals over a very precipitous and rough track. The 4th Brigade had been forced to withdraw, leaving Es-Salt open to attack from the north and north-west, and the enemy were also attacking along the Amman Road. During the night the enemy attacked the 2nd Brigade at Kefr-Hudr, on our right, but were repulsed. A good deal of enemy movement was observed on our front during the day. Rations by this time had run out, and the iron ration had been made to last 48 hours. During the day a few biscuits arrived, amounting to about two per man. Luckily water was available from a cistern close to our line, and the horses had good grazing from crops in the vicinity. At about 6 p.m. orders were received that the whole force would withdraw during the night, and the 3rd. Regiment would act as rearguard. All pack horses that could be spared were despatched to the Valley, and everything in readiness for a quick move. The withdrawal was likely to prove a difficult operation, as our only road was a rough, precipitous track, along which it was only possible to proceed in single file, and which was under enemy shell fire. There were three Brigades to withdraw, and the enemy was in close touch with us from the east, north, and north-west. At 2.20 a.m. the led horses were sent back to the foot of the high ground held by us, one man leading two horses, the remainder being left with Hotchkiss guns to hold the line until the rest of the force had withdrawn. At 3.30 the last of the 3rd Brigade had moved through us, and our right flank was thrown back on to high ground. At 4.20 a.m. two Squadrons were withdrawn and sent to take up a line covering No. 7 Road from the north, as the enemy were endeavouring to push in and cut the road. By this time the enemy had evidently appreciated the situation, and commenced to press us, but was kept in check by our machine gun fire, and also from Machine Guns which had been placed in position on high ground in rear of our forward line. At 5.15 orders were received that all the force had withdrawn, and that we were to do so as quickly as possible. One Squadron took up a position on high ground, and covered the retirement of the remainder. One machine gun covered the retirement of this Squadron. The enemy, quickly occupying the position, opened up heavy machine gun fire, and auto-rifle fire, but did not cause any casualties. The enemy also shelled No. 6 Road for some distance, but without effect. Later several enemy planes bombed and machine gunned the column while proceeding along a narrow defile, but this Regiment did not suffer any casualties other than a few horses. The Regiment emerged from the hill into the Valley at 9 a.m., and proceeded to Umm-Esh-Shert, coming under shell fire from El-Haud and Shunet-Nimrin en route. and we moved back on to the plain, where those who were lucky enough to have any rations left had breakfast. We remained in readiness all day, and at 6 p.m. moved out with the Brigade towards the foothills, to cover the withdrawal of the 4th Brigade, the Anzac Division having been ordered to proceed to the western bank of the river. At 1.30 a.m. on 5th, all troops having passed through, we moved, via Ghoraniyeh Bridge, to camping area, 1½ miles east of Jericho, and went into bivouac. The dust while in this camp was very bad, as the enormous amount of traffic consequent upon the recent operations had cut up the surface very much, and this, combined with the intense heat, made it very unpleasant. On 7th May a hostile squadron of planes bombed and machine gunned the Division, who were scattered over the area in the vicinity of Jericho. The Regiment suffered small casualties. On 12th, 67 cases of gift stores were received and distributed among members of the Regiment. These were appreciated even more than usual, in view of the fact that we had been on mobile rations for some time. On 16th we moved with the Brigade to a new camp, situated about two miles south of Solomon's Pools. This camp was nominally a rest camp, but a great deal of work had to be done, as it was a new camp and water had to to be developed, roads made, etc. While here all ranks underwent a course of instruction in the use of Turkish machine guns. Parties under an officer were given leave to Jerusalem and Bethlehem for purposes of sight-seeing. Weekly parties also proceeded to Egypt on seven days' leave. On 6th June the Regiment moved with the Brigade to the positions covering the Wadi-Auja, which were to be taken over by our Brigade. The Regiment on 18th took over, the horses being sent back (one man to four horses) to a camp about three miles from the line, Major C. Mills (S.I.C.) being in command of the camp. The enemy was holding the high and dominating ground north, and could shell our communications and horse camp with good results from their commanding heights, where they were also entrenching and erecting numerous sangars. Each of our positions was entrenched, and formed practically a redoubt, with provisions, water, ammunition, and bombs to hold out for some time. Much heavy work was done, blasting out the solid rock for trenches, and machine and Hotchkiss gun positions. Wire entanglements were erected over wide areas, the men chiefly working at night, both to keep out of view and to avoid the heat. The trenches were manned at night, and day observation posts, with glasses and telescopes, watched and reported every movement of the enemy. This was tiring work, as the heat was intense, and made observation difficult. The men not on duty in the trenches used either to sleep or go down to the Auja and enjoy a wash. Rations were brought up to the line by camels each night, as our line of communication was under enemy observation by day. The enemy daily shelled our positions, but did very little damage. The men on duty with the

Lent by Aust. War Museum

Light Horse in Palestine

horses were changed over with men in the trenches frequently, as those with the horses had a hard time, each man having four horses to look after, and the heat and dust were very bad. Each night several hours were spent in improving the trenches (which were in a very crude state when taken over by us), and also in wiring the whole line. Malaria was at this stage very bad. During the month of June, 48 men were evacuated sick, most of them suffering from this fever. The Adjutant (Lieut. Hean) was also evacuated, wounded as a result of an enemy explosive nose cap.

The following is a report of the enemy movement observed from our observation post on July 2nd:—"Two camels and one mounted man moved along road from hospital in U 15. At 7 a.m. 2 mounted men and 4 packs going south along foothills, entered Wadi-Rishen. At 7.20 a.m. 4 packs went north from Wadi-Mahmud along foothills to U20, then east towards Umm-Esh-Shert. At 7.30 a.m. 2 mounted men went north from W. Mahmud. At 7.45 a.m. did likewise. At 8.15 a.m. motor car from Hospital went N.E. along Roman road. At 1.30 p.m. 6 packs, going south from U20, entered Wadi-Mahmud. At 2.45 p.m. 1 camel, 1 horse, 1 mounted man, going south along foothills, entered W. Bakh. Al 3.50 white flag waved on what appears to be a dump near Wadi-El-Hau-mr, on bearing 70deg. from Abu-Tullul. Enemy artillery quiet throughout the day. Our Artillery fired 40 H.E. 4.B. on R360 and T17C, and ranged 1500 yards in front of 'Zoo' and 'Zeiss' posts."

Similar reports were sent back daily through Brigade to Division, where they were compared with the whole Divisional Area reports, and, together with information derived from other sources, especially from deserters, gave our Staff Officers an excellent idea of dispositions and intentions of the enemy. On the 13th July more movement than usual was noted on our front, and enemy artillery was more active. On 14th July, O.C. A Squadron holding "Vale," "View," and "Vaux" Posts reported to the C.O. that movements of an apparently large body of troops could be heard in front of both "Vale" and "View" Posts, at a distance of about 1000 yards. The C.O. immediately got into touch with C/301, C/303, and 11th Mountain Batteries, and arranged for a barrage to be opened on reported enemy. The matter was then reported to B.H.Q. At 2.15 a.m. the batteries opened fire, and this compelled the enemy to deploy, and "View" Post reported movement towards "Vaux." The enemy now opened up an intense bombardment of our front line, and also the back area. At 3.15 a.m. the C.O. moved his headquarters forward to a position, already prepared, on Abu-Tullul (left). At 3.30 a.m. the enemy strongly attacked "Vale" Post, which was held by 20 men, under Lieut. MacDonald. The attacking force was over a thousand strong, and Lieut. MacDonald was unable to check them, and retired when the enemy was only a few yards from him to No. 1 Post, on Abu-Tullul (left). The enemy pushed forward between "Vale" and "View" Posts, and occupied a post on Abu-Tullul (left). A portion of them also advanced up the Wadi behind "View" Post. This latter party were caught by machine gun fire from the right of "View" Post, and, after suffering heavy casualties, the remainder of this force surrendered. By this time the Reserve Squadron had occupied the second line on Abu-Tullul (left), one Squadron of the Reserve Regiment was occupying Abu-Tullul (right). It was now daylight, and the enemy who had broken through "Vale" Post were in a tight corner, as all our other posts were intact, and they were now subject to a heavy fire from every direction, and, when counter-attacked by a Squadron of the Reserve Regiment, were unable to withdraw through the opening where they had broken through, owing to it being very flat country, which was absolutely swept from either flank by machine gun fire. Meanwhile a furious and determined attack was made by the enemy against "View" and "Vaux" Posts, which were defended most gallantly. The steadfastness of the garrison and the manner in which they withstood furious onslaughts from an enemy far superior in numbers, at the same time enduring a heavy bombardment from the enemy's artillery, was most commendable. Our batteries co-operated in the defence of these posts in a splendid manner. At 6 a.m. the whole of our line had been re-established and the enemy's attack completely broken. Enemy concentration in front of "Vaux" Post was broken by the accurate fire of our batteries, and by 7.30 the enemy was everywhere withdrawing. The force attacking "Vale" Post proved to be Germans, and of these, 10 Officers and 348 Other Ranks were taken prisoners, in addition to 7 Officers and 60 Other Ranks, Turks. The brunt of the attack fell on "View" Post (Lieutenant Treloar) and "Vaux" Post (2nd-Lieut. Foster, A.C.). Both of these officers and Major A. Dick were subsequently decorated for their work in this attack. Throughout the battle communications were maintained with Brigade and between R.H.Q. and all posts by telephone, owing to the skill and courage of Sig. L/Cpl. H. W. Botten, who was subsequently decorated for his excellent work. He was in charge of the Regimental Signallers. Our casualties were Lieut. W. C. Kelly and 11 Other Ranks killed, and Lieut. L. S. Trensman and 9 Other Ranks wounded. The enemy continued to shell our positions intermittently all day. On 15th they also shelled our back area very heavily all day. On the early morning of 16th the camp of the 1st L.H. Regiment, situated near Wadi-Auja, was very heavily shelled, and later in the day our horse camp also suffered, casualties being 1 Other Rank and 3 horses killed, and 3 Other Ranks wounded. At 10 p.m. the 10th Regiment relieved us in the line, and we moved to Talaat-Ed-Dumm the same night, arriving there at 7 a.m. on 17th. The following congratulatory messages were received by the G.O.C. Anzac Division with reference to the battle on 14th July:—

From the C.I.C.: "Please convey the C.I.C.'s heartfelt congratulations to the Australians and New Zealanders who took part in yesterday's operations."

From the High Commissioner for Egypt: "Heartiest congratulations to you and all officers and men of your Corps who have been engaged in the most successful operations on your front."

From the G.O.C. Desert Corps: "Heartiest congratulations to yourself and your Division, and especially to General Cox, on to-day's operations, and gallantry displayed by all ranks."

On the 19th the Regiment moved with the Brigade, and on the 26th arrived at a new camp site at Wadi-Hanien, near Richon. This camp proved a very pleasant one, after the heat and dust of the Jordan Valley. Watermelons, grapes, tomatoes, etc., were obtainable, and very much appreciated by all ranks. One squadron at a time proceeded to the beach for two days, where swimming races were held and an enjoyable time spent.

The Regiment left this camp on 17th August, and marched through Jerusalem and Jericho, and took over support duties and camp from the 8th L.H. Regiment. This camp was situated in the vicinity of El-Madhbeh, south of Abu-Tulluh, really the reserve area, or horse camping area of our previous six weeks in the Auja line. The ground about the camp was terribly cut up and dusty; one when walking sank to the boot tops in powdered dust, and the daily wind made the dust unpleasant. The men and horses going to and from water came back coated in sweat and dust, for the heat was stifling. Nightly patrols went forward, filling a gap in the line on the plain between the foothills and the Jewish Battalion on the Wadi-Mellahah, and also our patrols moved out in front of the B.W.I., who were holding the

Abu-Tullul defences. This camp was the most trying of all, being dirty, very hot, and malaria was still rife, also debility and dysentery. The general breaking-up of men who had spent a long time in the Jordan Valley was very noticeable. Casualties for August were 2 Officers, 84 Other Ranks evacuated sick. On 5th September the Regiment was relieved by the Auckland Mounted Rifles, and proceeded to a new camp site situate near Wadi-Nueamieh. During the next few days the enemy shelled in the vicinity of our camp with a long-range gun from Shunet-Nimrin, a distance of about 8 miles, and as we were in full view of the enemy on east side of the Jordan, we moved camp on 10th September further up the Wadi-Nueamieh. Here parties were put on building dummy horses, with bamboos and blankets, to deceive the enemy airmen, our object being to make the enemy believe we were concentrating on this front. Another method we adopted was to march down towards Ghoraniveh Bridgehead just before dusk, the dust made by us being quite visible to the enemy, and after dark we would return to camp. It was apparent to all from the preparations being made that an attack on the enemy was to be made very soon, and speculation was rife as to the part we were to play in the operations. On 18th September heavy artillery fire was heard on the left, and we knew that we had commenced the attack. On 19th all spare gear was placed in a dump, clothing and necessaries to be carried being cut down to a minimum, and the Regiment was prepared to move at shortest possible notice, and on 21st we moved up to our old camp at El-Madhbeh.

On 22nd September the Regiment moved from El-Madhbeh, as advance guard to the Brigade, at 9.45 a.m., and marched via Abu-Tullul left to Kh-Fusail. We received orders to operate on the right of the 2nd B.W.I. Battalion, and, if possible, to reach the bridge at Mafid-Jozeleh, about four miles north of Umm-Esh-Shert. We found the enemy holding the line on the high ground on the west bank of the River Jordan, and as we approached we came under heavy machine gun fire. It was impossible to advance towards the bridge, owing to the precipitous nature of the country, and the enemy commanding the only road with machine guns. Touch was gained with the B.W.I. Battalion on our left by Officer's patrol, and we remained in contact with the enemy. Orders were received to remain in touch with the enemy, and reach the bridge as early as possible, and report whether it was passable for the Brigade. On 23rd the Regiment moved forward, and advance patrols reported having reached a small wooden bridge, of which a number of planks had been removed, but with the possibility of collecting these, the bridge might be made passable for animals. All the piles of this bridge were found to be mined and connected with a battery on the east bank of the river. Contact wires were cut, and the bridge crossed by dismounted patrols, and repairs were proceeded with. Two pontoon bridges situate north and south of the pile bridge had been totally destroyed. Insufficient planks being obtainable, it was reported to Brigade that the bridge could not be made safe, and orders were received to withdraw and rejoin the Brigade at X. During the morning's operations 1 Officer and 19 Other Ranks of the enemy were captured, and 4 killed. We rejoined the Brigade, and proceeded to Umm-Esh-Shert, where the river was forded. The Brigade moved off for Es-Salt by the No. 6 Road, the Regiment acting as Advance Guard, this being the third time the Regiment had climbed this precipitous track over the moutains of Moab to Es-Salt. Es-Salt was reached, without opposition, and it was found that we had been preceded there by the N.Z.M.R. Brigade, which had advanced via the Damieh-Es-Salt Road. On the 24th we moved through Es-Salt to Es-Sirra, situate on the Es-Salt-Amman Road, where we bivouacked for the night. The road from Es-Salt was for many miles strewn with enemy dead, dead animals, and war material, apparently the result of aerial attacks. On the 25th we moved with the Brigade towards Amman. The Regiment halted 3½ miles west of Amman, when orders were received to operate between N.Z.M.R. Brigade and 1st Regiment in the attack on Amman, which was then developing. The Regiment took up a position on the left of the Wellington Mounted Rifles, and shortly afterwards the enemy commenced to surrender. We moved on to Amman Station. The O.C. was instructed by G.O.C. Force to hold an outpost line towards the north and north-east, and to be responsible for the protection of Amman from that direction until the arrival of B.H.Q. Quantities of war material, including grain and Railway Rolling Stock, had been abandoned by the enemy at the Railway Station, also a complete Wireless set, which was found on a hill 300 yards east of the Station. On the 26th a report was received from Brigade that a force of Turks had been reported by our Air Service in position on the bank of Wadi Hammon, and C Squadron was despatched to reconnoitre in this direction and gain touch with the enemy. They reported that the enemy were holding a line on the South bank of the Wadi Hammon, and were commanding the Railway Line and road to Zirka; A Squadron was thereupon despatched to co-operate with C Squadron. A Squadron of the 1st Regiment, which had been ordered to make a reconnaissance of the road in Wadi Hammon reported that the road was held by the enemy, and C/O 3rd Regiment received instructions that this Squadron would operate under his command. A movement to envelope the enemy's right was attempted, but was checked on account of darkness, and an outpost line was held during the night. Throughout the night the enemy exchanged shots with our outpost line. B Squadron reached Zerka without opposition, but their despatch riders en route to Regimental Headquarters found the Wadi Zerka occupied by the enemy near Wadi Hammon, and they returned to their Squadron with the information. Later Cpl. Marchant, with 3 men, was sent to endeavour to get through to Ammon with a despatch, and under cover of darkness he succeeded in galloping through the enemy's lines, one of the horses being shot and its rider narrowly escaping capture. B Squadron, making a wide detour to the east, succeeded in evading the enemy, and reached Amman at 1 a.m. on the 27th. They reported good water in the Wadi Zerka from the junction of the Wadis Amman and Hammon to Zerka, the road passable for all wheeled traffic. Zerka was occupied by Circassians, who appeared to be greatly in fear of the Arabs, who were surrounding the village in a threatening manner. On the road from Amman to Zerka there were 20 abandoned motor lorries, two motor repair workshops, three motor cars, 1 4.2 field piece, and a quantity of miscellaneous war material.

At 4 a.m. on 27th orders were received that the Brigade would move to Wadi Hammon at 8 a.m., and the Regiment was ordered to operate against the enemy and clear the country, so as to ensure safe movement of the Brigade along the railway line. The C/O ordered the Squadron of 1st Regiment (Major Harris) to move forward and occupy the high ground immediately opposite and East of the junction of Wadis Amman and Hammon, with the intention of blocking the railway and road at that point, and so prevent the enemy's withdrawal towards Zerka. At 4.45 the 3rd Regiment moved towards the enemy's right flank, with the object of enveloping that flank and driving the enemy towards the Squadron of 1st Regiment. A Squadron moved rapidly north towards Wadi Hammon; it at once came under heavy machine gun fire from the centre of the enemy's position, but succeeded in turning their flank and moved down to the Wadi Hammon. C Squadron moved towards the enemy's right centre, and he commenced to withdraw, but was caught by A Squadron on his right flank, and without serious opposition began to surrender. The enemy on the north bank of the Wadi Hammon attempted to withdraw, but was caught by machine gun fire from one of our planes, and they also surrendered to our troops. Throughout this operation the co-operation between our aircraft (one machine) and our mounted troops was excellent. The machine early indicated the position of the enemy's line, and later, when they began to withdraw, he successfully hampered their retirement, and was largely responsible for the success of the operation, which resulted in the capture of the whole enemy force in the Wadi Hammon, totalling 13 Officers and 440 Other Ranks, with 3 Machine Guns, 1 Automatic Rifle, and 28 Pack Animals. At 7 o'clock it was reported to Brigade that the ground was clear as far as the North bank of the Wadi Hammon. The Regiment concentrated at the junction of Wadis Hammon and Amman, and rejoined the Brigade. At 9.30 the Regiment was ordered to move towards Zerka, along the railway line. A detachment of 2 troops was despatched to Zerka to garrison the village and protect the Circassian inhabitants from the Arabs. The remainder of the Regiment went into camp in the Wadi Zerka, 2½ miles south of Zerka; 75 sick and wounded Turks were found at Zerka, and on 28th were despatched to Amman by Cacholet Camels. One 4.2 field gun was found in the Wadi Zerka, having been abandoned by the enemy. A number of prisoners gave themselves up to our troops while we were in this area, apparently being very much afraid of the Arabs. The total number collected was 3 Officers and 116 Other Ranks, 3 of the latter being Germans, who had been stripped by the Arabs of all their clothing excepting shirts. On 2nd October the Regiment received orders to proceed to Ziza, situated on the railway about 20 miles South of Amman, and relieve the Canterbury Mounted Rifle Regiment, who were guarding prisoners and captured war material; 73 wagons from the Divisional train accompanied the Regiment for the purpose of bringing back sick and wounded prisoners and war material. On the 4th the loading of the prisoners and war material on to the wagons was commenced, and wagons despatched for Amman with an escort. The following is an approximate list of the prisoners and material loaded on the wagons:—

    29 Machine Guns.
    30 Machine Gun Tripods.
    2 Automatic Rifles and Tripods.
    1 Wireless Plant.
    4 Field Guns and Limbers.
    3 Mountain Guns.
    14 Machine Gun Barrels.
    450 Rifles.
    A quantity of Machine Gun and S.A. Ammunition.
    502 Sick and Wounded Prisoners.

There was still a quantity of war material and enemy rolling stock and railway engines left at the station. The latter were out of repair, but a party of Engineers were working on them, and on 4th they had completed the repairs. Our transport was engaged in carting water for the engines from a big catchment tank situated about 1½ miles away. Orders were received on 5th for the Regiment to withdraw to Kissir, leaving 1 Squadron to guard the remaining stores, etc., and to draw water for the engines. During the march to Ziza a number of men were suffering from malaria fever, a large number of whom, being unable to ride, completed the journey in transport wagons. Each day more and more became affected, and on 5th October

18 Cars from Headquarters Anzac Mounted Division proceeded to Ziza and brought back 50 of the worst cases. During the next week over 200 members of the Regiment were evacuated suffering from Malaria, included in these being 15 officers, amongst whom were the C.O. and S.I.C. Most of these had to be transported in G.S. wagons to the Field Ambulance at Amman, as other units of the Division were suffering in a similar manner, and the Ambulance Transport could not cope with the work. The Regiment's strength was at one period down to as low as 150. The Squadron left at Ziza was also suffering very badly, and it became apparent that unless they were able to rejoin the Regiment within a day or two, they would not have a sufficient number of men to bring the horses back. They were being detained there pending the arrival of a Railway Engine from Amman (the repairs to the engines at Ziza having proved unsuccessful). The engine had made several unsuccessful attempts to reach Ziza, and finally the C.O. decided to send down a party from Kissir with transport horses and endeavor to haul the rolling stock containing the balance of the war materials towards Kissir, and thus enable A Squadron to return. On the 8th Lieut. Kelly proceeded to Ziza with a party and 12 transport horses, the idea being to haul the loaded trucks as far as Leban station, where the material would be loaded on to G.S. wagons from the Divisional train. The party left Ziza, and succeeded in bringing the trucks to Leban. The wagons were loaded, and the party bivouacked at Leban for the night. A Squadron rejoined the Regiment at Kissir. Lieut. Kelly's party returned with the wagons the next morning, leaving a guard over the trucks at Leban pending the arrival of the engine. On 11th October the Regiment left Kissir en route for Am Hemar, situate on the main road about half way between Es-Salt and Amman. The Regiment on the move presented a somewhat uncommon sight, as, owing to our very low strength, each officer and man was leading three to four spare horses. The evacuations were now decreasing, and on 15th a very welcome batch of 40 reinforcements was received. The 22nd was the 4th anniversary of the Regiment's embarkation from Australia, and the remaining members of the original Regiment (24 all told, 8 of whom were officers) were called together, and a photograph taken. On 27th a rifle match was arranged between teams from a company of Indian Infantry, 2nd Regiment, and 3rd Regiment, the three Squadron teams from this Regiment winning the 1st, 2nd, and 3rd prizes. On 28th the official hoisting of the Hedjaz Flag took place at Amman. On 30th a composite Regiment, consisting of one Squadron of 2nd Regiment and two Squadrons of this Regiment, in command of Lieut.-Col. Bourne of 2nd Regiment, paraded mounted for inspection by Gaafa Pasha (C. in C. of the Hedjaz Army), who was accompanied by Major-General Chaytor and Staff. Gaffa Pasha, after inspecting the Regiment, addressed the officers, and on behalf of the King of the Hedjaz, thanked us for the part we had played in freeing his country from the hands of the Turk. During the month of October 14 Officers and 321 Other Ranks were evacuated to hospital sick, practically all of whom were suffering from malaria; 20 of these subsequently died.

On 2nd November the Regiment set out for Jerusalem. While at Jerusalem the Brigadier informed the acting C.O. of the Regiment that we (the Regiment) would be proceeding to Gallipoli very shortly after our arrival at Richon. On 6th we marched to Latron, and on 7th arrived at Richon, and went into camp on our old area. The C.O., Lieut.-Col. G. J. Bell, was awaiting us here, he having been wired for, in view of the possibility of the Regiment going to Gallipoli. This trip did not eventuate owing to the fact that the Regiment was so much below strength, and the 7th Regiment was sent instead. On 11th news was received from the Brigade that an armistice with Germany had been signed, and for hours afterwards there was much cheering, and verey lights were fired from all units camped in the area in celebration of the event. During the nights of 13/14 a severe thunder storm, with very heavy rain, occurred, most of the tents in our area being blown down, and during an extraordinarily loud clap of thunder, a tent in C Squadron lines was struck by lightning, the pole being splintered, and three of the occupants were badly burnt, and also suffered considerably from shock. On 30th information was received that Lieut.-Col. Bell, C.M.G., D.S.O., had been mentioned in General Allenby's main despatch of 3/4/18. On 3rd the Regiment paraded, and the C.O. explained fully the proposed Educational Scheme. On 4th our Brigade Sports took place, the following prizes being won by members of this Regiment:—First in best turned out G.S. Limber and V.C. Race; Second in Other Ranks' Hunters; Third in Officers' Hunters. The Regiment on the 18th marched through Wadi Hanein, thence across and alongside the railway towards Yebnah. This track was very boggy, and cut up by the wagons and heavy traffic, the ground being heavy, black, sticky mud, but the horses, pulling well, got through; several creeks and drains full of muddy slush had to be crossed, which meant water up to the horses' bellies. The mud through parts of Yebnah was very bad. Finally the Regiment arrived near Sukereir, and camped on the edge of the sandhills. Leaving camp next day, we marched to Mejdel, where we bivouacked. Difficulty was again experienced owing to the wet and boggy nature of the country, the transport horses especially having a bad time, floundering up to their bellies in the bog and wagons sinking to the axles. On the morning of 20th we again moved off, and marched to Gaza, camping in the vicinity of Chaytor's Hill, overlooking Gaza, and the following morning trekked to Belah. The following day the trek was completed, the Division arriving at the new camp site at Rafa, in the vicinity of the old battlefield, the whole Division being camped together in close formation, there being now no need for precautions against aerial attacks. On Christmas Day (the fifth that the Regiment had spent abroad) each member of the Regiment received a parcel from the Australian Comforts Fund. Oranges, vegetables, and eggs were purchased for the men out of the Regimental funds. Early in January the Educational Scheme commenced, lectures on the following subjects being delivered:—"Prevention of Disease," "Veterinary Science," "First Aid," etc., and the following classes formed:—"Bookkeeping," "English," "History," "Arithmetic," "French," "Geography," "Blacksmithing," "Motor Cycling," etc. Practically every member of the Regiment attended one or more of these classes. Four mornings per week were devoted to Educational Classes and two mornings to training, each afternoon being wholly devoted to sports. A Divisional Australian Rules Football Competition was inaugurated, comprising eight teams. The competition was ultimately won by A Squadron, B and C Squadrons being second and third respectively. Everything possible was done to keep the men interested and amused during this trying period of awaiting Demobilisation. Race Meetings were held frequently by different Brigades and Regiments. A club was opened near the Divisional Area by Miss McPhillamy, where the men could get meals and play cards, etc. This lady's untiring energy in providing for the amusement of the men was much appreciated. On 8th January the following wire was received from Australian Headquarters, and made known to all ranks:—

"London advises shipping accommodation capable 1st Brigade available this month, AAA. Anticipate whole Brigade will have embarked before end month. AAA. Cannot advise date yet."

This was very cheering news, and was received with joy by all ranks. Preparations were at once made for handing in to Ordnance of saddlery and equipment, all of which, excepting that required for camp use, was thoroughly cleaned and handed in, everyone working with a will, the men taking a delight in the polishing of steel work, etc. Training and Educational Classes were carried out as usual during the month. During the latter end of February the weather was very disagreeable, being windy and dusty. On 1st March a Regimental Australian Rules Football Team proceeded to Cairo to play a match with the 9th Regiment, who were the premier Regimental team of the Australian Division. Our team subsequently defeated the 9th Regiment by 38 points. We were given to understand that we would be embarking about 21st March, but a few days later, owing to trouble arising in Egypt with the Egyptians, all demobilisation was stopped, and on 22nd inst. orders were received that the remainder of the 1st L.H. Brigade would proceed to Kantara as soon as train arrangements could be made, there to be re-equipped and form part of the Mobile Column for duty in quelling the Egyptian disturbance.

On 24th we marched to Rafa station, where we entrained, and arrived at Kantara. Upon disentraining the Regiment marched to the Ordnance Depot, and each man there drew a rifle, bayonet, bandolier, and belt. After the equipment had been drawn, the Regiment marched to the Empire Club, where Mrs. Chisholm had very kindly arranged a free lunch for the men. After lunch we marched to our camping area on the West bank of the Canal, about two miles south of the Railway Station. For the next few days the work of re-equipping was proceeded with, but hope was not altogether lost of us ultimately not being required for duty, and of an early embarkation. Many boats passed through the Canal loaded with troops returning to Australia. All hope of an early embarkation was put an end to on 7th of April, when orders were received that the Regiment would proceed to Cairo for duty the next day. On arrival at Caliub A and B Squadrons detrained, the former proceeding to the Barrage, and the latter remaining at Caliub for duty. Regimental Headquarters and C Squadron proceeded to Cairo. The duties of the Regiment consisted of guards over bridges, patrols, inlying picquets, etc., which we continued to do till 8th May, when the Barrage and Caliub forces were relieved, and rejoined the Regiment at Ghezira. Nothing sensational happened during our period of duty, though on 21st April trouble was expected at the Barrage, and the force there was supplemented by one troop of C Squadron. On 9th May the Regiment entrained at Cairo with the Brigade Details en route to Kantara, to await embarkation.

The Regiment embarked on the *H.T. Orari* at Kantara on May 16, together with the remainder of 1st A.L.H. Brigade, comprising 1st Machine Gun Squadron, 1st Field Ambulance, 1st Signal Troop, and Brigade Headquarters Staff, Lieut.-Colonel G. J. Bell being O.C. Troops. After a successful voyage A and B Squadrons disembarked at Port Adelaide on June 27, and C Squadron at Melbourne on June 30, and after delay, owing to seamen's strike and quarantine at Portsea, on account of influenza epidemic on the mainland, finally disembarked at Devonport, Tasmania, on July 28, 1919.

DETAILS OF CASUALTIES.

Gallipoli	1	16	—	15	1	5	3	109	23	446
Wadi Natrun	—	—	—	—	—	—	—	—	2	96
Upper Egypt	—	—	—	—	—	—	—	—	2	80
Sinai	—	34	—	9	—	2	11	122	8	420
Palestine	3	20	—	7	—	23	9	89	32	1378
Total	4	70	—	31	1	30	23	420	67	2420

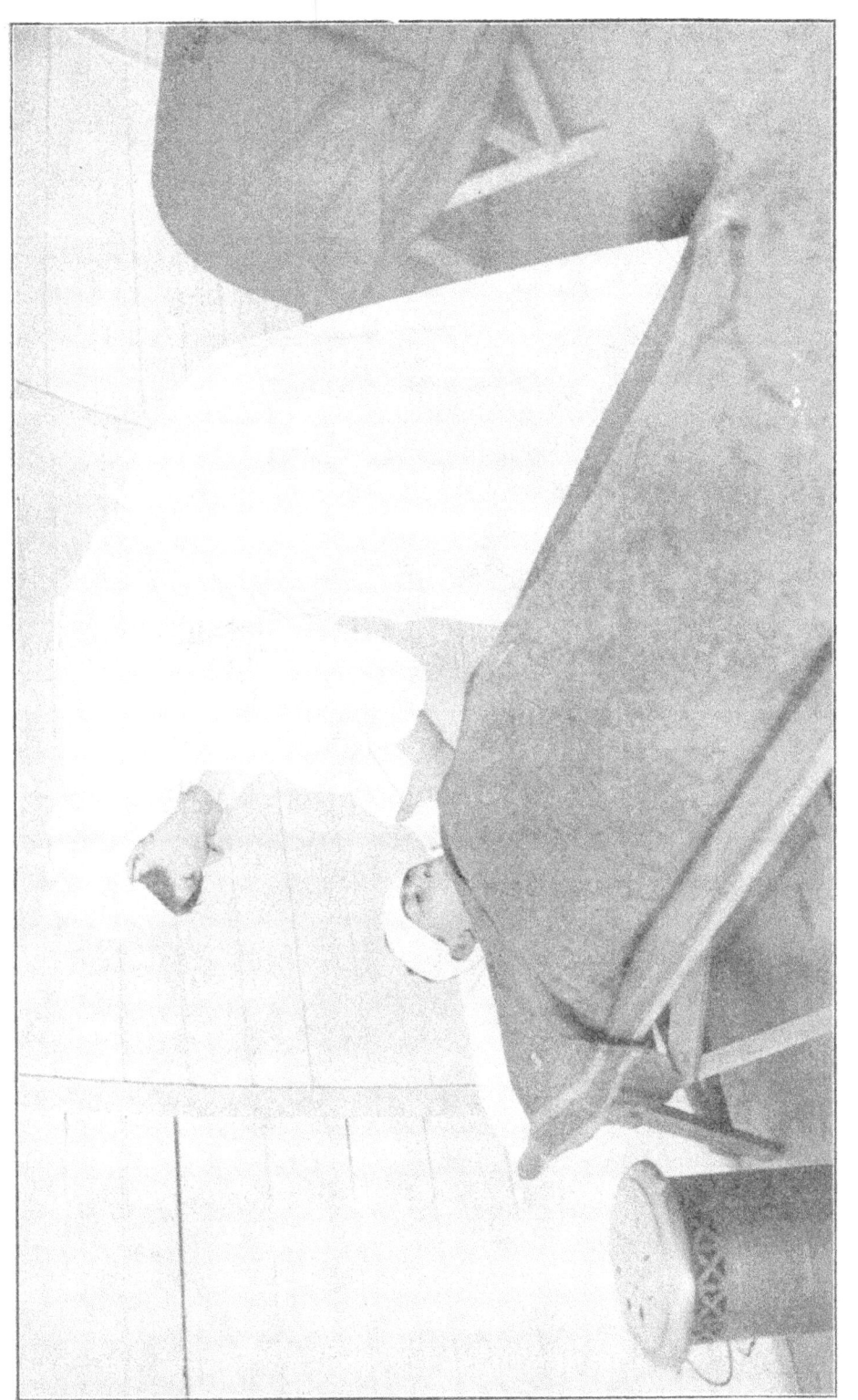

At the Casualty Clearing Station

Lent by Aust. War Museum

CHAPTER VII.

THE AUSTRALIAN ARMY MEDICAL CORPS.

MEDICAL ORGANISATION.—The War Zone.—Field Ambulance.—Clearing Stations.—Heroic Stretcher Bearers.—Lines of Communication.—Base.

TASMANIAN SECTIONS.—The Bearers.—Winter in France.—The Difficulties of Salvage.—Regimental Medical Officers.—3rd. Field Ambulance.—No. 1 Australian Casualty Clearing Station.—Anzac Cove.—France and Belgium.—7th Field Ambulance G. Section.—The Nurses.

In writing the medical section of this volume, the work naturally falls under two main headings, i.e., the nature and extent of the effort overseas with the A.I.F., and, secondly, that accomplished in the State itself.

For a full understanding of the former, before considering the separate records of Tasmanian Units, a brief account may be given of the nature and scope of A.M.C. duties with the troops, of the difficulties met with, and how, in most instances, they were overcome.

Tasmania contributed medical units in whole or part that served on Gallipoli, the War Zone beyond the Suez Canal, and in France, during the whole time the A.I.F. were there, i.e., April, 1916, to the termination of hostilities.

No Tasmanian Medical Units were attached to the Australian Light Horse for the campaign in Sinai and Palestine, or to the forces in Mesopotamia, Salonika, and German East Africa. It may be safely conjectured, however, that in almost every theatre of war Tasmania was represented by either medical officers, nurses, or men enlisted in medical units.

The general idea in the following description is to show the working of the medical service in an army, such as any one of the five British Armies under the command of the Commander-in-Chief in France. The general arrangement was the same in all theatres of the war, with modifications according to the nature and difficulty of the terrain to be fought over.

In any army during hostilities are certain recognised areas:—
1. The war zone proper.
2. Line of Communications (L of C).
3. Base.

and each of these areas, with its own medical organisation, will be considered in detail.

This corresponds to the area in which the actual fighting takes place. The fighting troops being grouped into Divisions, each Division comprising three Brigades, and in each Brigade (until our last four months of war) four Battalions of Infantry and subsidiary troops, such as Engineers, etc.

The medical services of a Division are under the control of the A.D.M.S. (Assistant Director Medical Service), who is attached to its staff. He is responsible, through his medical units, for the treatment and evacuation of all wounded and sick from his divisional area to the L. of C.; also for the sanitation and medical services proper of his area.

Three Field Ambulances are attached to the Division, and one usually is "grouped" with each Brigade. Their function is in quiet times to collect all sick and casualties from Battalions, hold a certain proportion for treatment, and evacuate the remainder to the Casualty Clearing Stations.

The Ambulance itself is divided into three sections. Each section containing three medical officers is self-contained, one-half its function being that of a small Field Dressing Station, the other the bearing of casualties out of the line to this station.

In an action, as a rule, all three Tent Subdivisions combine to form one Dressing Station, and all the bearers (112) work in relays, bearing the wounded from the line.

For actions on such a large scale as those in France, sometimes seven or eight hundred bearers are working under the command of the Ambulance Commander, who at his dressing stations may have ten or twelve medical officers working in two or more surgical dressing rooms.

At the Dressing Station essential operations only are done. The ideal arrived at was to dress and resuscitate all cases, and send them on by car in fair condition to the Casualty Clearing Station, where the great proportion of the surgical work was carried out. Every Battalion and the large units of the Division carry their own medical officer. The Regimental Medical Officer is attached to the Regimental Headquarters, and treats all sick and wounded of his Unit, and attends to its sanitation. His role being really an advisory one to the Battalion Commander and he is actually under the control of the A.D.M.S., who commands all the medical services of the Division.

When the Regiment goes to the attack, the R.M. Officer who has the Regimental Stretcher-bearers under his control forms a Regimental Aid Post in the rear of the Unit in a deserted dug-out, or any sheltered spot he can find, and gets to work.

A man wounded in the firing line is dressed rapidly and remarkably efficiently by the Regimental Stretcher-bearers (if he has not already roughly dressed his wound himself, with his first field dressing, which is carried by all ranks).

If unable to walk, he is placed on a stretcher, and two (if four are not available) Regimental Stretcher-bearers carry him to the Regimental Aid Post, where, if necessary, his case is further attended to.

From the Regimental Aid Post the Ambulance is responsible for his evacuation. All lightly wounded cases making their way out to the Advanced Dressing Station on foot in their own time.

The severe cases are slowly carried on the shoulders of four Ambulance bearers (if no prisoners of war are available for the duty) towards the rear to a Relay Post (usually about 400 yards), where a fresh squad of bearers take over the carry.

From relay to relay they are taken by the bearers as far as the Motor Loading Post, which is the nearest place to the line to which Ford Ambulances can be taken. After loading into the Ford (exceptionally into Horse Ambulance Wagons, which are very slow and clumsy), they are run to the Dressing Station, Advanced or Main.

At the Main Dressing Station, after being passed through the books and records, and being carefully examined, re-dressed if necessary, or treated for shock or exhaustion, they are sent by large motor ambulances to the Casualty Clearing Station.

At the Casualty Clearing Station a large staff of medical officers, with nurses and expert staffs, do the operative work proper, and hold the cases until fit for evacuation along the line of communication by hospital train.

The Casualty Clearing Station will be considered in the next section, but before passing to that, another of the Divisional medical units—the Sanitary Section—must be mentioned. This consists of one medical officer and about seven non-commissioned officers and men. Their function is to travel constantly, advising and helping units as to their sanitation, and building sanitary necessities to supply Divisional units. One Sanitary Section is attached to each Division, and works under the A.D.M.S. The Artillery in the Divisional Area have one medical officer to each Brigade of Artillery. He has his own stretcher-bearers, who carry his wounded to the nearest Ambulance bearers.

During the war, in the opinion also of almost all combatants, the work of the stretcher-bearers, both Regimental and Ambulance, has been heroic and beyond praise. The Australian wounded under all circumstances have been carried out by the stretcher-bearers at once, no matter how concentrated the enemy fire may have been. To carry a wounded man on the shoulder through intense shell fire, at a slow plod, not even to be able to duck or find shelter, requires one of the highest degrees of courage. "I have never heard," says an officer, "of a stretcher-bearer refusing the call or shirking his job, and their greatest reward was the gratitude and high esteem in which their mates held them."

In France, the line of communication practically commenced at railhead. The Casualty Clearing Station was either sited by railhead or in a position to which a loop line of railway could be run. At the commencement of the war, one Casualty Clearing Station was attached to each Division, and moved with the Division, evacuating through its wards all sick and wounded. In France, when the war of positions began, the Casualty Clearing Stations came to be collected, two, three, and four together, at a convenient railhead. To this group came by motor ambulance all the sick and wounded collected by the ambulances of the Divisions of their area.

Originally capable of dealing with only a few cases, each Casualty Clearing Station came to be able to expand to hold many hundreds. By degrees, wooden huts took the place of the tents, and the Casualty Clearing Station became a stationary unit, in effect a well-equipped Hospital, complete to X-rays and everything for up-to-date surgery.

"Operating teams," i.e., staffs of expert surgeons and nurses, were moved from group to group, where their services were most needed, and stayed until wanted elsewhere.

The rule of the Casualty Clearing Station was to keep all cases until they were fit to undertake the journey by hospital train down the line of communication to the base. The hospital train lay at the railway siding adjoining the Casualty Clearing Station, the train being fitted up purely for the transport of wounded. It carried a staff of one or two medical officers, nurses and orderlies, with a well-fitted operating theatre, in which urgent cases could be treated.

The journey to the Base by train, which during the Somme battles in 1916 may have taken up to 60 hours, later in the war took only from 8 to 12 hours. On arrival, the cases were moved by car to the various Stationary and General Hospitals, where, when sufficiently recovered, they were either drafted to the Convalescent Camp for return to the line, or by hospital ship across the Channel to England.

The line of communication medical units were, therefore, in France, the Casualty Clearing Station and Hospital Trains, with own details; Stationary Hospital; and Sanitary Squads.

The Hospital bases for the Armies in France were the Coastal Ports at Boulougne, Le Havre, etc. These were really advanced bases, as the great

English Hospitals were wholly or partially adapted for holding casualties, and might be considered the base proper.

At these towns various Stationary and General Hospitals had been established early in the war, and never having been moved, gradually, like the Casualty Clearing Stations, erected permanent wooden wards and theatres, and were capable of undertaking any surgical work required. In these units all cases that would be likely to recover sufficiently were treated until ready for return to their duties. Other cases requiring protracted treatment, or invaliding from the Army, when sufficiently recovered, were, as stated, sent to England.

It is safe to say that in almost every type of unit mentioned in this description, Tasmanians, either as medical officers, nurses, or trained and capable non-commissioned officers and orderlies, have taken their part. So having considered the functions of the medical units as a whole, the work done by those of Tasmania will be dealt with in as much detail as can be managed without the full official records.

There is an idea among a section of the people that the work of the Army Medical Corps is free from risk, and that any man not physically fit for combatant work is well suited for the Army Medical Corps; but the Bearer needs as stout a heart as any man in the Division, and, more than that, an iron frame.

The work of the Bearers on Gallipoli was arduous and continuous. No vehicles were available at all at Anzac, and the "carry" for the first months was entirely by hand. As there was no reserve of Bearers, and the casualties in the Army Medical Corps had been very heavy, every case to be carried was taken by two men only. This in the hot sun, and with the flies, was a very heavy burden. Add to this the fact that almost all the Bearers had gastric troubles, and were much weakened by them, and it will be realised how hard the physical work was. Later, in France, every case was carried on the shoulders of four men, with far less physical work for the Bearers.

In addition to the climate, in almost every part of Anzac the Bearers were under indirect rifle and machine gun fire, and occasionally direct. There was also a good deal of shrapnel encountered. Later, when saps were dug, the carry was safer, but with extremely hard toil for the Bearers. Also wheels were provided for the stretchers, but were never popular. The famous Murphy, of the 3rd Field Ambulance, used captured donkeys on which he used to bring out his wounded for some weeks, until he was himself killed in Shrapnel Valley.

In the August fighting the burden of the Bearers was too much for them, and in most cases they worked until they dropped from exhaustion. It was blazing midsummer, water was scarce, and on the left of Anzac the carry down Chailak Dere, Australia Gully, and Argyldere to the Beach was very rough and long. There was no reserve of Bearers to draw upon, and it meant each party of Bearers carrying on until exhausted, a brief rest, and then on again. In spite of all these difficulties, the work was done, but at the cost of much delay in the evacuation, and untold exhaustion and toil of the Bearers.

The dressers at the aid posts did their work also under very severe conditions. It was next to impossible to site an aid post or dressing station at Anzac that was not exposed to risk from bullet and shrapnel. The heat and continuous demand on their strength during the periods of fighting made a good physique for the dresser essential. When the line was quiet, their duty was the feeding and care of perhaps 20-40 or more cases of sickness, from

Regimental Aid Post

Lent by Aust. War Museum

dysentery to paratyphoid, which called for a man whose resistance to infection was of a high order.

In France, of course, conditions varied. The dysentery, Eastern sun, and flies were absent, but in other ways the Bearer's life was probably as hard as on Gallipoli. The one great advantage was, however, better food and rest in safe and fair billets between actions.

The action at Fromelles was the first in France on a large scale. From 6 p.m. of July 19th, to 12 noon of July 20th, 1916, every Bearer of the Division was toiling on a narrow front to get his wounded out. At first they were carried down the same saps as supplies and reinforcements were coming up; later the carry was overland to the Aid Posts and Dressing Stations, the congestion of traffic in the saps being such as to make it almost impossible to carry the stretchers out. After our men had been brought back to our own trenches, a very large number of wounded lay in no man's land. All the forenoon of July 20th the Germans allowed our Bearers to work in front of the wire, and bring their wounded in.

At Pozieres and Mouquet Farm (1916) the principal difficulties of the Bearers were—(1) the tremendous number of wounded, (2) the heat, and (3) the heavy shell fire along the saps and communication trenches. There was no chance of drawing on the Infantry for help in carrying, but eventually the work was done and wounded got out.

As winter set in at the Somme, the medical problems became harder. Speed in getting the wounded back to the Dressing Stations is such a very important factor in saving life, and every minute's delay means extra shock and collapse to the wounded man. The winter of 1916-1917 was the coldest France had had for 30 years, and this cold cost us many lives among the wounded. The Bearers could only move at the slowest pace in the mud, which was for weeks almost frozen and knee deep. Add to this the rain and sleet and the difficulty of keeping the patients' blankets dry and the problem of getting the wounded out to the Dressing Stations rapidly and in a dry and warm condition was almost an insuperable one. The devotion and care shown by all ranks to the wounded went some way towards overcoming the difficulties, but the wastage was terrible.

Trench Feet (a modified Frost Bite) also detracted from the strength of the Bearers, or added to their difficulties.

Whenever possible, light tramways and horse-drawn sledges were used to get the wounded out, but the great proportion of the work fell on the shoulders of the Bearers. Casualties by enemy shell fire among them during the winter, however, were not heavy; otherwise, they would never have been equal to the demands made upon them.

The fighting during the advance to the Hindenburg Line did not present any marked features. At Bullecourt, however, the Army Medical Corps shared with the other troops the disadvantage of attacking a very strongly entrenched position over practically open ground.

The Aid Posts had little or no shelter, and the squads of bearers resting in holes in the embankments and carrying over open country had many casualties, and there was much wastage from shell fire. Such was this that when the various Divisions were relieved, their Bearers did not move out with them, but remained to carry the wounded of other Divisions.

In the open country we used our Horse Ambulance Wagons for the first time in France to collect the wounded directly from the Bearers, who carried them to a collecting post in the middle of a field within view of the enemy's defences.

Perhaps the hardest trials of the Bearers was in the great Flanders offensive of late 1917. Working on a narrow front, and with a constant searching of the rear by enemy gun fire, the Ford cars could not be pushed far up to help the evacuation. In consequence at times a distance of 6000-7500 yards had to be covered by the Bearers in bringing back the wounded. This, of course, was divided into "carriers," each about 400-600 yards in length.

Casualties among the medical personnel were very heavy both from shell fire and from "gas." Again the Bearers of each Division were used during the attacks of other Divisions of the Corps. In consequence they obtained very little rest between the different phases of the attack. The carrying at night was very difficult and heavy, with a danger of their losing their way between relay stations.

In consequence of these causes, and the very large number of casualties among the Bearers, companies of Infantry were attached to the ambulances, and did great work in evacuating the wounded. In October, when the winter set in, conditions towards Passchendaele were about as bad as at the Somme during the winter of 1916. The evacuation was, therefore, more and more tedious and difficult as operations went on, with always very heavy casualties from shell fire and gas. "Personally," writes an officer, "I have never seen more exhaustion or greater courage among the Bearers than during these weeks in front of Ypres."

In 1918 the Bearers had a much better time. After August 10th the fighting was practically a moving battle over clean, open country, with, comparatively speaking, light casualties. In these actions Ford and other ambulance cars were pushed forward at times as far as the Regimental Aid Posts, and the dressing stations well up towards the fighting area. In this way the Bearers had far less carrying to do. In addition about all the fighting took place in warm summer, or fine autumn weather, which lessened the work that had to be done.

These instances of Bearers' work will give some idea of the demands made on the courage and strength of the Army Medical Corps personnel, and make it plain that from the Stretcher Bearer has been demanded as much in the way of bravery and endurance as from any man on the Front.

Having thus briefly considered the working of the Medical Services in the Field, it remains to take the work of the Units in some detail.

In succession will be considered—

(1) At various periods Tasmania supplied medical officers for the 12th, 26th, 52nd, and 40th Battalions.

The first R.M.O. to the 12th Battalion was Captain V. R. Rattan, Captain Carter (New Norfolk) was later appointed to the position, and did excellent work with the Unit on Gallipoli, particularly during the Lone Pine fighting. The sanitation and cleanliness of the trenches occupied by the 12th Battalion on the Peninsula was splendid, and largely due to his work.

For almost all the Battalion's service in France, Major W. Johnston, D.S.O., M.C., was R.M.O. He was decorated twice for his great work under fire.

With the 26th Battalion as R.M.O. was Captain Dunn, who remained with them through the Gallipoli campaign and eighteen months in France.

Captain G. B. Bailey was killed in action as Regimental Surgeon to the 52nd Battalion. He had been mentioned in despatches for his work as Bearer Captain in the 7th and 13th Field Ambulance. A brother officer of the same unit writes: "I know personally the value of the great work he had done during 1915-1916, and the advance up to the Hindenburg Line. It was before the latter he met his death; a shell killed him instantly. His death was a very great loss to his Brigade, and to the profession to which he belonged."

Captain J. Sprent also acted for a time as R.M.O to this Battalion.

Captain W. I. Clark left Tasmania with the 40th Battalion, and remained R.M.O. to the Regiment until 1918. He was decorated for his work at Messines in 1917.

(2) 3rd Field Ambulance.—This sub-section of two officers and 30 N.C.O.'s left Tasmania under the command of Major H. N. Butler by H.M.A.T. *Geelong* in October, 1914, to join the convoy forming at Albany, Western Australia. Major Butler, who was also senior medical officer to the ship, had with him Captain H. Ingram.

The men, a very fine body, with the 36 Bearers and one officer from West Australia, formed the complete C Section of the 3rd Field Ambulance.

(3) No. 1 Australian Casualty Clearing Station.—It was clearly seen by the time of the departure of the 1st Australian Division that extension of hospital service would be necessary. Tasmania's share was to provide the 1st Australian Clearing Hospital, and the P.M.O. of the State (Lieutenant-Colonel Giblin), placing his services at the disposal of the Defence department, went into camp at Claremont to raise and train the unit.

As already stated the conception of a Casualty Clearing Station at that time was of a mobile field hospital, able to move always with its division. Theory said its position would really be that of an operating centre at railhead, from which the wounded would be evacuated down the line of communication. How different its real functions were to be, experience soon showed. The complement of such a unit was laid down at 8 officers and about 80 N.C.O.'s and men. There was no difficulty in finding the men, and very soon the full number of picked men were in training.

The question of officers was more difficult. With the O.C. were Captains Campbell and Atkins, Lieutenant E. T. Boddam as Quarter Master, and at an early date Captain Mattei (of Melbourne) as sanitary officer. The remaining officers were appointed from Melbourne, and joined the unit on the *Kyarra* on embarkation.

Training proceeded uneventfully, and early in December the C.S.S. moved by ship to Melbourne, there to embark on the *Kyarra* with other Hospital Units for Egypt. The voyage was without incident, but the ship was a very crowded one. On disembarkation the Unit moved to Cairo.

During January, when an attack on the Suez Canal was immanent, the C.C.S. moved to Port Said. By late February the Casualty Clearing Station was under order to move, and after the journey to Alexandria, took ship to Lemnos. The stay of some 5-7 weeks was varied by practising disembarkation and route marches over the island, to keep all ranks fit.

The most epic chapter of the unit's history is, however, its work at Anzac Cove landing, with the 1st Division, early in the day, which was commenced in the open on the foreshore of what came to be known as "Anzac Cove." Only those who have seen the congestion of wounded during heavy fighting can understand the work that had to be done. In the circumstances, no hospital proper could be fitted up. The casualties were treated, as far as possible, and sent in returning boats to the ships. All work was done under direct and indirect rifle and machine gun fire, with constant shrapnel from the Turk 75in. (Beachy Bill and his kind) searching the Beach and its approaches. However, by the splendid efforts of all ranks, the work was done, and as conditions settled, sand-bag shelter was given to the dressing-rooms and to the "dug-outs' for themselves, excavated by the personnel.

From April 25th to October the Casualty Clearing Station remained at the Cove. Until August 6th all sick and wounded men from the Australian and New Zealand Divisions, who had to be sent away, passed through its dressing-rooms, and were recorded in its books.

Lieutenant-Colonel Giblin, after two attacks of illness, was invalided from Anzac, as were Captains Atkins, Campbell, and O'Brien. Major Richards, after much ill-health, died on a hospital ship off Anzac. An original officer of the Casualty Clearing Station, he had done magnificent work, and although urged to give up, remained at his duty until almost his death. Lieutenant-Colonel Gordon took over command for the hot and fly-infested months of the summer and autumn, only giving in to his illness just before the evacuation.

Captain Bóddam also did splendid work the whole time the Casualty Clearing Station was on Gallipoli. In October the unit was given enlarged tent accommodation, and moved, in preparation for the coming winter, to a site under Walker's Ridge. It was hoped to hold there 3-400 cases, in the event of rough weather delaying the evacuation of wounded and sick from the Peninsula.

Meetings of the Anzac Medical Association were held here, and Sir Victor Horsley also lectured on his way to Mesopotamia.

Shortly before the evacuation Major Campbell, on his return, took over the command and held it temporarily until Lieutenant-Colorel Newland arrived. Much pluck and self-sacrifice was shown at this time by the men, who volunteered to be left behind with the wounded, but as it turned out all got away safely when the Australians evacuated their positions at Anzac.

After a brief stay at Lemnos, the unit moved again to Egypt, and with the First Division moved to Serapeum, on the canal. From here in early April they landed in France, and moved by rail to Rouen, where the journey was broken for several days. First Anzac Corps being concentrated at Hazebrouck and the Casualty Clearing Station was sent to Estaires, and set to work to clean up a school there and installed their dressing rooms. From April, 1916, to about middle 1917, they remained at this village, although for a great part of the time no Australian troops were near them.

In 1916 Major Campbell, who had been second in command and Adjutant, left the unit for depot work in England. Lieutenant-Colonel Newlands, who had done excellent work, left on November 11th, 1916, and his place was taken by Lieutenant-Colonel J. A. Dick.

The routine of the Casualty Clearing Station during the winter was very simple—the sector of the line (the C.C.S. was less than three miles from the front line trenches) was one of the quietest in France, and the village was never molested by bombs or shell fire during their stay. Two main dressing rooms were fitted up and an operating theatre. Ordinarily, all cases after treatment were kept in the wards until fit to be evacuated by the hospital train from La Gorgue, one mile distant. Wards were also established for mild cases of sickness, who, after treatment, were returned to their units. The work of the dressers, and, in fact, of all ranks, impressed visitors as being very fine.

Events in March, 1917, all pointed to the great British offensive taking place in Flanders. No. 1 Australian Casualty Clearing Station was, therefore, removed to another school building—this time in Bailleul. There their stay was short owing to the bombing of the town at night and high-velocity gun-fire during the day. The next move was to a field at Outersteen, about two miles south-west of Bailleul, where a tented field hospital was formed, with hutments for the operating theatre and most important work. All through the weeks of heavy fighting at Ypres, the work was hard and continuous, but as ever the unit was more than equal to the demands made on it, and the high reputation it enjoyed was maintained.

Through the winter of 1917-1918 a quiet time was their lot, but in view of the coming German offensive, No. 1 and No. 2 Australian Casualty Clearing Stations were withdrawn to a position towards Hondigham and later when their army advanced they moved forward into Belgium—their movements after the Armistice are of lesser interest, and therefore not chronicled here.

In February, 1915, Tasmania was called on to provide for the 2nd Australian Divisions, two companies of the 26th Battalion and a section of Field Ambulance. Under instructions of the then P.M.O., Capt. W. L. Crowther went into camp at Claremont to raise and train the latter, which, at that date, was to be "C" Section of the 5th Field Ambulance. In a week the necessary men had commenced training, and Captain G. B. Bailey had come into camp. Captain H. V. Brownell, 14 days later, enlisted, and was attached to the section until transferred to "B" Section, then forming at Adelaide. Training took the form of company drill and stretcher excursions for the bearers, and instruction at the Hobart General Hospital for the Tent Subdivision.

In April the designation of the section was changed from the 5th to the 7th Field Ambulance, and the unit was ordered to Brisbane to join the 7th Brigade. Before the move took place, Major T. G. Ross arrived, and assumed command of the section. On May 1st, leaving the horses and waggons behind, the section moved with all its equipment by boat to Sydney on the *Ulimaroa*. The journey, via Sydney, to Brisbane was without incident.

After some weeks' training with the nucleus of the 7th Brigade, the Ambulance moved by sections overseas, and by August, 1915, were in camp with the brigade at Abbasieh, near Cairo, and commenced intensive training in the Egyptian mid-summer. On September 3rd the Ambulance entrained at Palais-de-Kouber for Alexandria. The unit, less a few details, were all accommodated on the *Knight Templar,* and on the next day she sailed, via Crete, for Lemnos. After five days in Mudros Harbour, the men were transhipped to the *Osmanieh,* and ferried to Anzac, landing at 6 a.m. of September 13th. A rain, luckily, prevented any casualties while disembarking, and the following day "C" Section took over from a New Zealand Field Ambulance, the dressing station on the extreme left of our position at Chailak Dere, under Hill 71.

No heavy fighting took place during the month that followed before the evacuation, but owing to the heat and disease there were many casuatlies to the Ambulance, and at the evacuation of Gallipoli, when it accompanied its Brigade, its numbers were very much reduced.

After a short stay at Lemnos, the Ambulance crossed to Alexandria, and moved with the Brigade to Tel-el-Kebir, for rest and reconstruction. On 2nd February, 1916, the Brigade moved to the eastern side of Suez Canal, and the Ambulance accompanied it, marching through Ismalieh and across the Canal by pontoon bridge. It appeared that the threatened Turkish attack on the Canal was about to come off; nothing, however materialised.

"C" Section, from February 4-23, were the advanced dressing station beyond railhead, in the desert, where, beyond sick and occasional cases of Cerebro Spinal Meningitis, there was little to do. On the latter date it was withdrawn, and transferred to Tel-el-Kebir, where, after combining with a section of the 3rd, the whole unit became the 13th Field Ambulance of the Fourth Australian Division.

With the Fourth Australian Division under command of Lieutenant-Colonel J. B. St. Vincent Welch, they crossed to France, and took part with the Brigade in the great assault at Mouquet Farm. Some Tasmanian bearers, in their zeal to maintain touch with the Brigade Battalions, were made prisoners of war, and were not released until many months later.

Captain Sprent was awarded the Military Cross for his work in the Somme, fighting with his Ambulance Bearers. All through the bitter winter of 1916-1917, the Ambulance took its share of the cold and exposure, followed up the German retreat to the Hindenburg Line in March, 1917.

At the April Bullecourt Battle they took their share, and then moving north of Flanders, were engaged at the Battle of Messines. After a few weeks' rest came the intensive fighting of Ypres and before Paschendale, and on the conclusion of that, the hurried march south to Peronne, when the German counter-attack at Cambrai looked so dangerous. The winter of 1917-1918 brought a quiet time in this sector, but when Von Ludendorff opened his great offensive of March, 1918, the Ambulance followed its Brigade into action once again, and did particularly good work behind Dernancourt. For this engagement the 13th ran the main dressing station at Vadencourt, the bearers working forward with those of the 4th and 12th Field Ambulance.

In front of Villers Brettoneux and the Battle of Hamel (July 4th), the bearers were again in action, and, as always, more than carried out all that was asked of them.

August 8th, 1918, marked the opening of our great offensive, and from that date, as did all the Australian Ambulances, they followed their Brigade in phase after phase (each with its heavy fighting) of the great 100 days. After their Division had fought its way to the outposts of the great German defence line of the canal at Bellicourt, they went with it, back towards Abbeville for rest.

When the Armistice was signed on November 11th, the 4th were with the 1st Division, moving up once again for the assault.

In writing of the work done by this section, it must be understood that, except on Gallipoli (where the 4th Field Ambulance were from the landing), the Ambulances of the 4th Division saw, perhaps, more service than those of any other Australian Division.

In all these actions the bearers were engaged, and their work was characterised by the same devotion to the wounded of their Division, and disregard of risk to themselves in getting those wounded out at once. The high standard of work of the Tent Sub-division also deserved special recognition, and was most favourably commented on by the successive commanding officers of the Ambulance;

To sum up.

In the short description of the medical services contributed by Tasmania, there has been no attempt made to mention officers, N.C.O's., or men for bravery or meritorious work, nor to compile a list of decorations conferred on the units. It would be invidious to do so, in view of the fine work done by the great majority, who had not the good fortune to receive these recognitions.

No account of Medical work in War time can pretend to be complete which does not include a record of the Organisation and the work of the Nursing Staff. A very considerable number of Sisters and Nurses went from Tasmania to every theatre of war, and the men who know most about it, that is to say the Medical Officers and the wounded, find no praise too great for them. Every effort has been made to obtain some sort of connected account of the work of the Tasmanian Nurses, but unfortunately, without success. The truth seems to be that those who did the work were kept so hard at it, and toiled under such trying conditions, that they emerged with a very vague-idea of anything beyond personal experiences. The work of Tasmanian Nurses was at least as worthy of full record as the work of any of the fighting men, and it is much to be regretted that this brief note is all that is possible.

CHAPTER VIII.

PRISONERS IN GERMANY.

Behind the German Front.—Miserable Experiences.—Life in the Camps.—The Notorious Neimeyers.—Attempts to Escape.—The Holyminden Tunnel.—Hospital Experiences.—Huddled Together in Huts.—Christmas on the Baltic.—Life at Wistenburg.—The Armistice Period.

The history of Tasmanians in the war would not be complete without some account of the experiences of those who in the close and desperate struggles of attack and counter attack had the misfortune to fall into the hands of the enemy. The chance of being taken prisoner during operations conducted over a soft, rain-sodden country, such as that of the Somme or Passchendaele in winter time, when the battlefields were covered with a sticky blanket of mud, when whole areas in the lower levels had been converted into black and treacherous lakes of mud, quaking with the thud of bursting shell, and when men had to crawl laboriously about like flies on a fly paper, was an ever-present contingency. The positions of the opposing outposts were often involved to a degree, gaps in the line were frequent until gains were properly consolidated, and in these circumstances isolated posts often found themselves pinned down to an oasis in a sea of mud, the Bosche apparently all round them, compelled to fight him off or be swamped and over-run. In the latter event those who were wounded were generally the most fortunate. They were carried back on their comrades' shoulders to be treated, in the later years of the war, with a certain amount of humanity by the German. The other unfortunates were forced to plod back through the mud, their dismal destination a German prison camp, with all the horrors and miseries of which they had read, making the journey ten times as laborious and painful as it would have seemed had their faces been turned in the other direction. Terrifically long distances they had often to cover during the first few days on the worst and scantiest of rations. We can imagine many such a string of newly-captured men struggling painfully along, perhaps after a week of exhaustion and lack of sleep in the trenches, the butt of the rough jokes of the guards, spied upon, interrogated, often treated brutally, hungry, cold, and unutterably heart-sick and weary, but keeping a stiff upper lip and a steady eye through it all. One Australian officer taken at Bullecourt still has an old bent walking stick given him in compassion by a kindly German soldier as he was staggering along after being on the road almost continuously for 30 hours. Once in Germany the officers and non-commissioned officers were sent to camps, and the soldiers were distributed among different parts of the country to work. The men generally had a most miserable time during the first six months. As a rule they were kept hard at work in the forward areas, a great part of the time under fire. They were stripped of their military issue clothes, and the warm woollen material was replaced by threadbare rags and their boots by wooden clogs. They were housed in bare, cheerless, and leaky huts, shockingly fed, subject to harsh treatment of every description, and everything possible was done to break their spirit and render them amenable to German discipline. Many of these unfortunate fellows died during the first months of their captivity, while hundreds of others were admitted to hospital, some of them never to wholly recover from their treatment. The writer remembers seeing two Australians who had just completed six months behind the German front. They were reduced to skeletons, and were braving a severe winter clothed in ragged German military trousers, thin cotton singlets, an overcoat, cotton socks, and wooden clogs. They had not yet received any parcels from the Red Cross, and did not even have a hair brush between them.

It can be seen from these authentic cases that, even after the war had been in progress for three years, many British prisoners were brutally treated. What our military prisoners must have suffered in the first twelve months of the war, when feeling against Great Britain and the Dominions was so frightfully intense, is too awful to think about.

Life as a prisoner in Germany varied according to the camp or hospital in which the prisoner was confined, and the conditions obtaining there in turn depended upon the character of the officer in charge of the command in which it was situated, and of the camp commandant himself. The Neimeyers—two twin brothers who spoke English with a strong American twang—were notorious, and several of our Tasmanian officers had the misfortune to see all too much of these typically Hunnish officials. Captain J. H. Honeysett, 47th Battalion, who was captured at Bullecourt in April, 1917, when the Australians, supported only by tanks, attacked the Hindenburg line, during his term of 20 months as a kriegsgefangenen, saw as much of Germany as most officers who spent the whole term of the war within the German barbed wire. He was in six camps altogether, and he made three attempts to escape. Once he and another officer got clear away, but after travelling 125 miles, were re-taken in an exhausted condition through lack of food.

Captain Honeysett tells some terrible stories of German brutality towards the prisoners.

"I have seen," he says, "three men, Britishers, bayoneted in cold blood by Hun sentries. I myself have been brutally punched and pummelled with the butts of rifles for absolutely no offence whatever. I have been confined as long as three months in a cell six feet by eight, deprived of tobacco, reading, and writing materials, the only things that made life at all bearable in the camps."

The first attempt to escape was from Strohen lager. Captain Honeysett noticed the sentries bringing in a man from somewhere outside the barbed wire enclosures. He learned that it was the practice to take men outside to be examined by the officers. An idea flashed through his mind, and, rushing into his hut, he dragged from under the floor an English soldier's greatcoat, which he donned, and, managing to convince the sentries that he was the next man to go out to be examined, he was escorted out through the barbed wire. Once out into the open, he had the best chance in the world of getting away, as the Germans are hopeless sprinters, and the frontier was not very far distant. However, luck was against him. He got a flying start; the first three shots fired by the guard missed him, but the fourth hit him in the thigh, and brought him down. He rolled into a ditch, thinking that he might be able to get away in the gathering dusk. He heard the guard go plunging past, but, beginning to feel the effects of the wound in his leg, he called out to one of them. The man came and promptly "put the boot into him" as he lay helpless on the ground. The rest followed, and one of them did his best to twist the captive's head off. Then they noticed he was wounded, and desisted. He was taken back to a closely guarded hospital, and that ended that little episode.

The second time he essayed escape was when he was incarcerated in the Holzminden camp. He was one of a party who commenced digging operations with the idea of burrowing under the surrounding wall, but when he saw how long this would take, he and another British officer decided to make a bold dash for it. They scaled the wall, cut the wire, and got clear away. For 125 miles they tramped through Germany in the bitterest of weather, hiding by day and travelling by night. They took some biscuits with them, but these soon gave out, and they existed on turnips and mangel wurzels taken from the fields. In a very weak and shaky condition they at last decided that it was absolutely necessary to go into a village, and get some food. They were standing looking into a window, when they were accosted by a couple of gendarmes. At first Captain Honeysett said they were German munition makers going to another village, but when the man asked for his papers, he was floored. They were too weak to make a "get away," surrendered, and were taken back badly frost-bitten.

Neimeyer was furious. He threatened them with all sorts of dire penalties, and charged them with espionage. This they denied, and they were sent away to another camp.

This was at Clausthal, in the Hartz Mountains, strangely enough the very place associated with the legend that tells of the original Father Santa Claus. The guard was quartered at what was before the war the fashionable resort of Hanover, at the foot of the mountains. It was typical of the Germans that this hotel had no baths whatever. The prisoners were allowed a shower, and it was remarkable to see the way in which the German sentries gathered round and watched the morning ablutions of their charges with all the interest that is usually attached to the antics of lunatics.

It was at this camp that the unprovoked assault, previously mentioned, was made on the captain. He was being brought down to headquarters, and was ordered to run. He refused, and was instantly levelled to the ground with a blow from a German officer's fist. He was then attacked with the butts of the sentries' rifles.

It was here also that the most elaborate and the most ill-fated attempt of all was made to escape. It was noticeable, the captain said, that the camps in which the treatment of the prisoners was the worst attempts to get away were most frequent. It was the rough time that he received in the first place that induced him to make his first try, and the treatment he received was never ameliorated after that. In a corner of a large room near to the wall of the prison a party of nine, sworn to the most careful secrecy, lifted some of the floor boards, and, with the aid of a couple of table knives and precious little else, started to dig their way to liberty. Surely no goal was more hardly earned. For six solid weeks they burrowed and burrowed. The soil was fairly peaty, and did not oppose much resistance. But it was hard work, just the same. In another corner was a dilapidated piano, which one of the party played while the others were working. When there was the slightest danger he played "The Campbells are Comin' "; when the coast was clear he switched on to "Onward, Christian Soldiers." A rope was also strung through the tunnel for the purpose of giving signals. The greatest secrecy had to be observed. The place was full of Neimeyer's spies, and dictaphones and such devices were employed. It was dangerous for the prisoners to discuss their plans amongst themselves, and so the project was strictly confined to the chosen nine. Everything went well. The secret was well kept, and two or three more days would have seen them through. Then the fates gave the unkindest cut of all. Captain Honeysett was down in the tunnel, when he received a message to come to the surface at once. He did so, and had scarcely replaced the boards, when in marched the guard with picks and shovels and candles. The fact was that at Holzminden some of the prisoners had got away by the tunnel that was being constructed when the captain was removed. Neimeyer, anxious to run absolutely no risk of a similar thing happening to him, had decided to search his premises thoroughly. They were raked from end to end. The tunnel was laid bare, and the game was up. Neimeyer did his best to find out who were responsible, but with no success.

Afterwards a commission was sent down to investigate, and from one of the members of this commission the captain secured a couple of photos of the tunnel as the Germans found it. These he is preserving amongst some highly interesting mementoes of his sojourn in the land of the Kaiser.

It was while he was at Clausthal that he was bitten by a watchdog. He was going out of his room one night, when one of the sentries came towards him, urging his dog to attack. The animal sprang, and before the captain had time to get away he was severely bitten in the leg. He was laid up in consequence.

In most instances, except in cases where men were terribly smashed about, prisoners who were wounded were more fortunate than their unwounded comrades. They made the journey into Germany in ambulances or hospital trains, and the food was quite passable. Those in the camps practically starved until their parcels began to arrive from England. One of our Tasmanian officers who spent five months in hospital with wounds found that conditions there, like conditions in the camps, varied in different commands. At the clearing hospital in Belgium, where he was first treated, the Germans were skilful, cruel, and clean. In the German hospital on the Baltic Sea, where he was sent next, they were most kind and considerate, but appallingly dirty, and they used paper bandages entirely. Wounded prisoners of war in this lazarett were nursed by German infantrymen on home service, most of whom had practically no knowledge of Red Cross work, and in the men's huts Britishers, Frenchmen, Italians, Indians, Serbians, Russians, and Senegalese were bundled together indiscriminately. Some of these men were in a most loathsome state with disease, and yet our British soldiers and merchant seamen were forced to lie for months side by side with them, their beds almost touching, whilst the atmosphere in the cold winter months was generally foetid to the last degree. However, the Germans who were running the hospital certainly did the best they could, and conditions in the hut which was set apart for wounded officers were very much better, because there were fewer of them, and the officer class in Germany, whether alien or not, is privileged.

An incident occurred at Christmas time in this hospital at Lubeck which showed that all Germans were not whole-hearted subscribers to the policy of unreasoning hatred of England, and that was when the commandant of the camp, with his wife and three daughters, visited all the huts of the prisoners of war, both officers and men on Christmas Eve, and the old lady made a presentation of a small Christmas gift—a cardboard box containing such things as pencils, writing paper, chocolate, honey, and apples—to each man, while the girls sang a Christmas carol. They certainly succeeded in making us feel home-sick.

The absence of all news, except what was contained in the German newspapers and a Germanised edition of the "Gazette des Ardennes," was very trying. After the great German victories against the Italians in November, 1917, the Germans went about boasting of the "German shoulder," which once applied, pushed all before it. "Your turn next," they would say.

The Tasmanian officer mentioned above, after five months at Lubeck, was sent to the prison lager at Furstenberg, in Mecklenburg-Strelitz, a camp which was generally acknowledged to be the best camp in Germany. It was most perishingly cold in the winter time, but during spring and summer life there was quite passable. The prisoners had made tennis courts themselves, and were allowed to buy tennis racquets and balls—at exhorbitant prices—or to get them from England. They were also allowed to play cricket and football, and to go for walks and swims, all, of course, on parole. There were many attempts at escape, but as the camp was north of Berlin, it was an almost hopeless task to get away. One Englishman, however, was out for six weeks, and actually got to the Dutch frontier. He had no more than 200 yards to go, and then took the wrong turning in the dark, and blundered into a German picket.

Everyone was much concerned during the last great German offensive, and the Germans were correspondingly jubilant. When the tide turned, however, events marched quickly. The Bulgarian collapse found the Germans almost incredulous, Turkey's capitulation left them dazed, and the press then ceased to blink the facts, and there came the great revulsion of feeling which led to the revolution and the Emperor's abdication. During the armistice period the British prisoners did much as they liked. The sentries were still posted round the camps, but they made few attempts to prohibit the men getting out, and long excursions were made round the countrysides, together with skating expeditions. One mercantile marine officer from Furstenberg even went so far as to go down to the town one night, and harangue the Soldiers' and Workmen's Council for not having already made arrangements to repatriate all the prisoners.

As a fair sample of the German lack of humor may be instanced the fact that when orders did come for the British officers to leave Furstenberg for Denmark, the German interpreter saw them off at the train, and distributed signed photographs of himself and his wife, with the inscription "In remembrance of your captivity in Germany."

No record of the life of prisoners of war in Germany would be complete without a grateful acknowledgment of the splendid efforts of the Australian Red Cross Society, prisoners of war section. The parcels they sent were excellent, and they promptly executed all requests sent to them by prisoners from Germany. Their attentions to the needs of the prisoners alone made life worth living; without their parcels it is impossible to say whether the men would have lived or died. They were the link between the captives and the home folk, and the knowledge of their devotion and interest brightened many a weary hour of exile.

CHAPTER IX.

THE CIVILIAN EFFORT.

THE RED CROSS.—The First Efforts.—Work Circles.—A Wonder of Organisation.—Shipments of Goods.—Care of the Wounded.—The V.A.D.'s.—The Hostels.—Information Bureau.—The Men's Part.

BATTALION FUNDS.—The A.I.F. Lounge.—Tobacco Fund.—Mayor's Patriotic Fund.—Disabled Soldiers' Fund.

THE O.A.S. FUND.—"Diggers'" Appreciation.—Comforts for the Trenches.—The Tasmanian Fund.—Other Comforts Funds.—Public Support.—The Northern Branch.

BELGIAN RELIEF.—The Tasmanian Contribution.—Clothing for Children.

SERBIAN RELIEF.—French Red Cross.

Y.M.C.A. FIELD SERVICE.—Work in Tasmania.—Camp Life.—Finding the Money.

THE AGENT-GENERAL.

REPATRIATION.

In the days when war was carried on wholly by professional soldiers, or, in the earlier times, largely by mercenaries, the man in the ranks had a value only in so far as he was effective for the work of fighting. The army provided absolutely necessary food or clothing, while men were in the field, and care of some sort was given to the wounded, especially those for whom there was reason for hope of recovery and subsequent fitness. But the bulk of the civilian population at home recognised no special obligation in the matter. The soldier was lauded for victory and blamed for defeat, but it was his business to fight and to take his chances. The more modern ideas of community obligation to those who are fighting the battles of civil life were, however, extended to those who fight the battles of the nation on stricken fields, and the growing sense of such obligation was immensely strengthened in this war by the fact that so great a proportion of the manhood of the nation went out cheerfully and voluntarily to risk everything. And so there sprang into being huge organisations intended to supplement the work of the military organisations, and, by voluntary effort, to alleviate the condition of our soldiers in sickness and in health.

In England, before the war, there was a skeleton Red Cross organisation; in Tasmania there was nothing. Everyone knew vaguely that some day we might be at war, but no one understood what it would mean. But so soon as war was declared, in August 1914, an Australian branch of the British Red Cross Society was formed, and, as part of the organisation, a Tasmanian Division in two sections. It was evident that the most convenient method of working would be to divide the work into a committee in Hobart for the south, and one in Launceston for the north. This method was adopted; each section had its own executive and its own officers. The sign of unity was the election of Lady Ellison Macartney, wife of the then Governor, as President of the Tasmanian Division. Later she was followed by Lady Newdegate, wife of the succeeding Governor. The joint secretaries, who held their positions throughout, were Mrs. A. C. Parker for the south, and Miss A. C. Miller for the north. To each of these ladies the distinction of Officer of the British Empire was given by His Majesty the King in recognition of their good work.

In the beginning, while there were plenty of women eager to help, there was a certain amount of vagueness as to what was needed, and much misunderstanding of method; so that, while the goal was clear enough, the path was so tangled that willing workers stumbled, and effort excellent in its intention was wasted. With the vague notion that Red Cross work had to do with nursing the wounded, special ambulance classes were started, where women of all ages learned bandaging and other mysteries. Then the word was given that shirts, pyjamas, and woollen socks were needed, and at once women with abundant enthusiasm, but strictly limited skill, made wonderful shirts, paradoxical pyjamas, and tragical socks. The crisis in patriotic enthusiasm brought to recognition certain lacks which had before been unnoticed. The discovery was made that a large proportion of women, especially the younger ones, had a very elementary, or no knowledge of knitting; that the sewing of a great number was crude, and that comparatively few had any knowledge of the cutting out of garments. And so it happened that in the first weeks there was much waste of labour, and a certain—perhaps even considerable—waste of material.

These things are the better worth recording because they accentuate the wonder of the organisation which so speedily reduced all to order, and brought system, method, and discipline to bear upon a chaotic medley of wandering endeavor. Individual effort was agglomorated into collective effort. The first great advance was the establishment of work circles, at which gatherings the most important personage was not the woman of wealth or social position, but the woman who had skill in the devising and making of the clothes which were required. Professional cutters were employed— many gave their services—and women gave one another the benefit of their knowledge and experience. 'There was between all these women the one bond, which became stronger as time went on and more and more men went to the war. Love of country and love of the men who fought had the effect of bringing womenkind on a common plane, when the only rivalry was in well-doing. Anxiety, fear, and—only too often—tears were solvents which destroyed what would have once been considered indestructible barriers. The unexpected capacity for organisation shown by women was a great wonder, but perhaps the greater marvel was their readiness to submit to discipline, making frank confession of ignorance or ineptitude, showing an eagerness to learn, and putting themselves under the guidance of those who had technical knowledge. In the beginning most of the women provided the material for their own work, with some extra for those who had capacity, but little money. To a certain extent this continued to the end, especially in regard to wool for knitting. But as the demand became greater the financial strain became too severe for many willing workers, and the various circles raised funds by direct collection and by fairs for the purchase of material. The movement spread throughout the country, and in every centre of population at least one came into being. In all 190 work circles and country branches were formed, 110 (44 work circles and 66 country branches) in Southern and 80 in Northern Tasmania. All these were under the general direction and supervision of the two central work sub-committees in Hobart and Launceston.

But the provision of clothing and other comforts, left eventually in the hands of the work circles, and to individual workers, was only a preliminary stage. The Red Cross Society undertook to supply comforts to the men on transports, going and coming, and for those in hospitals. It was necessary to sort out the goods, pack them, settle their destination, and arrange for their carriage. These arrangements in themselves required a complicated and effective organisation, and here again women with the smallest experience to help them did wonders. The goods were sent to Hobart and Launceston; most heterogenous collections of goods, and women worked long hours of day and night getting everything in order. The space for storage, and for sorting and packing, was limited, and it was necessary to use both vigilance and expedition to prevent congestion as fresh consignments arrived. How hard these women worked perhaps few of them realised until the strain was relaxed, and they had time to be tired. None of them had what the soldiers call "cushy jobs;" they had to keep up, whatever the cost to themselves. As the war went on, from one year to another, the numbers, both in work circles and in the central organisations who took on the sombre garb of mourning for their dead, became greater, but they worked the harder to provide for others what they could no longer give to their own.

An idea of the magnitude of the work can be gathered from a summarised account of the results, as shown by the actual shipments abroad.

From Hobart there were despatched: —

1914-15—176 cases containing 30,425 articles.

1915-16—635 cases, 37 bales, containing 35,941 articles.

1916-17—483 cases and 36 packages, containing 32,284 articles.
(In the last three months shipments had to be curtailed owing to lack of shipping space.)

1917-18—690 cases, containing 15,880 articles of clothing and 23,770 tins of preserved fruit and jam.

1918-19—1145 cases of foodstuffs, 40 cases of clothing.

From Launceston the shipments were:—

1914-15 ..	179 bales;	47 cases.
1915-16 ..	257 ,,	294 ,,
1916-17 ..	270 ,,	598 ,,
1917-18 ..	104 ,,	45 ,,
1918-19	84 ,,	— ,,
Total	894 ,,	984 ,,

The official records of the Society set the total value—material only— of goods sent at:—Hobart, £22,416; Launceston, £26,891; total, £49,307.

While the outward flow of able-bodied men was in full strength, a return stream began to come in of sick and wounded, and at once the Red Cross Society expanded its organisation to meet the fresh demands. The Defence Department established a base hospital in Launceston, and a convalescent hospital at Glenorchy, and both these at once came within the scope of Red Cross activities. Supplies of clothing and of delicacies were kept up, and the means of recreation and amusement were provided. It was found necessary to send some of the men who had come to Hobart to the General Hospital, as Roseneath, at Glenorchy, was not equipped as a hospital proper, and later the Defence Department built a base hospital near the Barracks-

These automatically came into the range of Red Cross work, and the Society was equal to the need.

A special feature was the work of the Voluntary Aid Detachment, made up of girls who gave their services at the hospitals. They placed themselves under discipline and in most cheerful fashion took on heavy menial work in order to relieve the nurses, and thus help the patients. They received a certain amount of practical training, which added to their usefulness, and throughout they won the hearty admiration of all who had opportunities of knowing their work. There was nothing picturesque; it was simple drudgery undertaken cheerfully and willingly because that was a way of helping the soldiers.

At an early stage after the men, invalided home, began to return, the need was felt for some kind of an abiding place where they might spend their spare time, get good meals at moderate prices, and obtain temporary lodging. There were a good many men, not ill enough to stay in hospital, but not well enough to settle down to work, and for lack of something better too great a proportion of them drifted to hotels and public-houses, to their manifest detriment. The Red Cross Society, after some discussion, decided that the making of provision for these men came properly within the sphere of work. Accordingly hostels were established; one at Hobart and one in Launceston. They were comfortably furnished, means of recreation were provided, and returned men were able to get meals and occasional beds—that is to say, they were not taken in as lodgers but were accommodated temporarily. Here again the Aids did hard and most useful work, going on for long hours, and carrying out the whole scheme. This work was very useful, and represented a very considerable money value, and a corresponding saving of funds.

Transport, too, was an important consideration. Men returning from the war had to be met at wharves or railway stations and taken to hospitals or hostels, or to their own homes. For this purpose owners of motor cars offered their services, and on all occasions the committees responsible for the reception of returning men were able to command all necessary means of transport.

The wives and sisters and other relatives of absent soldiers were frequently greatly troubled by their failure to receive regular and sufficient information about those men at the front in whom their anxieties particularly centred. Mails were irregular, cablegrams uncertain, and official records frequently defective, or very much in arrears. To meet this need a special branch of the Red Cross Society was established by the legal profession.

The Red Cross Bureau conducted by the legal profession for the purpose of obtaining for the relatives information as to sick, wounded, or missing soldiers, has done useful work, some idea of which will be gleaned from the following figures, covering the period October, 1915 (when the bureau was established) to July 31, 1919:

Inquiries	7,107
Inquiries by letter	1,430
Letters posted	7,965
Cables sent	2,773
Cables received	2,113
Reports received	4,000

The expense of maintaining the bureau was borne partly by subscriptions from the legal profession and partly by a subsidy from the Red Cross.

While the greater and more onerous part of the Red Cross work fell on the women, men also helped very materially. Some of them acted on committees; Mr. R. Nettlefold was honorary treasurer throughout, and others did excellent work in organising special collections. At an early stage work was found for those with some mechanical aptitude in a moderate, or considerable experience in the use of carpentering tools. They made crutches, walking sticks, deck chairs, and other articles which would be useful or helpful to the wounded. Some who did this kind of work were amateurs, others were craftsmen who used their spare time in this way. They made packing cases, and men with special experience helped to pack them.

The Australian "digger" will ever cherish the fondest memories of the organisations at home wnich, by providing regular supplies of comforts, sought to cheer him up and brighten his lot in the trenches, in camp, or on board a troopship. Each State in the Commonwealth had its fund for the purpose, but as these funds were originally inaugurated independently, without any central administration for the whole of the Commonwealth, each bore a different title. In Tasmania, for instance, the fund was known as the On Active Service Fund; in Victoria, the Lady Mayoress's Patriotic Fund; in New South Wales, the Citizen's War Crest Fund; in South Australia, the League of Loyal Women; in West Australia, the Victoria League; and in Queensland, the Patriotic Fund. All had the same object in view—the provision of comforts, in the shape of supplementary supplies of clothing, foodstuffs, tobacco, etc., to the men of the A.I.F., and in 1916, in view of the need for some systematic and organised co-ordination of the efforts of the various States, especially in the despatch of comforts abroad, and their distribution amongst the troops by the Commissioners and their assistants with the troops, all the State organisations were linked up under the title of the Australian Comforts Fund, with headquarters in Sydney. Each State then became a division of the A.C.F., with the right, if it desired to do so, of retaining its old name. Tasmania did retain its name, and to Tasmanians at home it has always been and still is the O.A.S. Fund. To the "digger" on active service, however, it was always known as the "Comforts Fund," after the name of the central organisation for all Australia, through which the comforts were distributed.

The Twelfth Battalion Comforts Fund was in existence for two years, and did excellent work, which was much appreciated by the men of that unit. The fund was incorporated at a meeting held in the Town Hall in June, 1917. Mrs. Macleod was president. The 12th Battalion shop, where wool was given out to be knitted into socks, and subscriptions were received, was at the City Hall. £640 17s. 6d. collected by subscriptions and fair; £354 9s. 1d. of this was spent on wool, and the remainder on tobacco, milk, biscuits, tinned fruit, etc., sent to the battalion in France.

The 40th Battalion Comforts Fund was established on June 1st, 1916, prior to the departure of the Battalion. A large meeting was held in one of the rooms at the Town Hall, with Mrs. J. E. C. Lord, the wife of the officer commanding the Battalion, in the chair. A general committee was formed of all those in attendance. This committee met once a month, or oftener, as required, and did a tremendous amount of work, to the extent even on sundry occasions of nailing up and stencilling cases of goods. One of the first acts of the committee was to circularise the next of kin of each member of the battalion in an effort to enlist their sympathy and help. This was accorded liberally, and a further outcome was the establishment of branches at Launceston, Devonport, Mathinna, and Cressy. The committee at once got to work with the collection of funds, and the making of articles of clothing, etc., for transmission to the troops abroad. For some considerable time an average of from five to seven cases went away about every six weeks. Christmas, 1916, saw despatched a special box to every man, and also plum puddings. Special cases of goods were also sent for 1917 Christmas, whilst in addition cash remittances were made for the purchase of comforts abroad, amounting to £200.

The battalion being a Tasmanian one, contributions in cash or kind were received from all over the State, some of which were regular remittances.

The Australian Mining Corps was organised by Professor David, C.M.G., of Sydney University, and he accompanied it to the front as geological adviser. When the unit reached France, the Australian infantry divisions were in Egypt, after the evacuation of Gallipoli, so the Australian Comforts Fund was not then operating in Europe. Friends and relations of the New South Wales members of the corps then established Australian Mining Corps Comforts Fund in Sydney, and promptly forwarded a good supply of comforts to the miners, this being the first appearance of Australian comforts for Australian troops in France. At the request of the Sydney committee, Mrs. Allan McIntyre, undertook to establish a Tasmanian branch of the A.M.C.C.F. branches being formed in the capitals of all the other States. The first meeting of the local branch was held in the Masonic Hall on March 29, 1916. A committee of five was formed, with power to add. Mrs. A. McIntyre was elected president, and Mrs. H. J. Spencer hon. secretary. Thanks to the City Council, a depot was obtained free of charge at the City Hall. In Hobart a number of excellent workers kept up a good supply of knitted and flannel clothing. In Launceston Mrs. W. H. Twelvetrees organised a work circle for the fund, and sent regularly parcels of beautifully-knitted garments to the Hobart depot. From Queenstown Miss Job's work circle forwarded many cases of clothing, the material for which was purchased with money donated in the Lyell district. It should be gratifying to all these workers to know that all the shipments (with the exception of one lost in the Ballarat) reached the Mining Corps, and were most gratefully acknowledged by the adjutant of the corps. In addition to clothing, the shipments included a good supply of food and smoking material. The fund was not as large as ordinary battalion funds, because the latter catered for a whole unit, whereas the Tasmanian branch of the A.M.C.C.F. was formed for the purpose of supplying comforts for the Tasmanian quota of a unit only. There were so many demands on the generosity of the public that the members of the committee were not out for all they could get, but felt constrained to collect just enough money to maintain a reasonable supply of comforts for the Tasmanian quota.

What the Red Cross was to the soldier in hospital, the Comforts Fund was to the soldier in the line and out of it. The Red Cross, by reason of its international character and constitution, is limited in its war activities to the requirements of sick and wounded soldiers, and is unable to do anything for the fighting men who are fit and well. It was for the sake of these men, many thousands of miles from home, and very differently situated from the British "Tommy," who was able to get all sorts of comforts from his relatives not far away, that the O.A.S. Fund in Tasmania came into existence. That it did the work it set out to do, and did it well, none will deny, and the soldiers who have participated in its bounty are the first to sing its praises. This expression of appreciation from a soldier at the front is typical of the general feeling of the A.I.F. for the noble bands of workers who steadily sent along their reinforcements of comforts right through the war:—"Things have been very rough for us over here at times, but when the comforts come along they put heart into us because we know that, although we are thousands of miles away from our native country, the people at home appreciate what we are doing and are always thinking of us."

The A.C.F. always had the reputation of following the troops right up to the firing-line, with its coffee stalls and other comforts for the men, and many a soldier has blessed the gallant distributors risking their lives as much as any combatant, for a hot cup of coffee or cocoa served when a fierce battle was at its height. Some of these distributors not only risked, but gave, their lives in this noble work, as at Bapaume in 1916, when the Australians captured the town. A coffee stall was established near the Town Hall, and as the Comforts Fund men, following close on the heels of the victorious Australians, picked their way through the ruins, they were greeted with shouts of "Good old Comforts Fund, your'e never far behind." A German mine, timed to explode a few days later, blew the stall and seven distributors to pieces. These distributors were heroes, and when General Birdwood officially paid the highest homage to these brave men, "faithful unot death," he was expressing the feelings of the whole A.I.F.

Tasmania's On Active Service Fund, which has done its full share in this great work on behalf of the Australian soldier, was formed in August, 1915, and crowded into its four years' existence a record which will bear comparison with any other patriotic organisation of the war period. In its officers and workers, the O.A.S. was very fortunate, and the general public have little idea of the vast amount of time and energy they devoted voluntarily and continuously for the benefit of the boys fighting for King and Empire. Not a penny piece was spent in salaries. It was all a labour of love, freely and willingly performed. The late Mrs. W. M. Williams, wife of Alderman Williams, then Mayor of Hobart, was the first president, and was followed in the office by the two succeeding Mayoresses—Mrs. Macleod and Mrs. J. E. C. Lord. At the beginning of 1918 Mrs. Macleod was again elected president, and continued in that capacity to the end.

Mrs. G. H. Bailey, to whose initiative the inception of the fund was largely due, was hon. secretary throughout, and discharged the duties in a most able and self-sacrificing manner.

During the first year of the existence of the O.A.S. formed in Hobart, it confined its activities to the south, as there was another similar organisation at Launceston known as the Trench Comfort Fund, which shipped its goods through the Lady Mayoress's Patriotic Fund in Melbourne. Towards the end of 1916 the two organisations were amalgamated under the title of the O.A.S., a step which proved thoroughly justified, and made for the increasing success of the work. Many country branches were started, and gave generous help in gifts, both of money and clothing. Three other smaller comfort funds were also worked in conjunction with the O.A.S.—the 12th Battalion, 40th Battalion, and Mining Corps.

The public supported the O.A.S. in most generous fashion, as is evidenced by the following figures of the amounts raised:—

12 months ended August 31, 1916	£2,960
13 months ended September 30, 1917	7,734
15 months ended December 31, 1918	16,706
1919—To September 18	5,093
Grand Total	£32,493

Special appeals always met with a gratifying response. One in December, 1917, realised £6882, and another in November, 1918, produced £6139. The regular monthly button day was also a useful source of income. The collectors stuck to their posts in all sorts of weather, and cheerfully persuaded citizens to part with their coin for a good cause. On the expenditure side regular remittances, chiefly at the rate of £600 a month, were sent to the A.C.F. Commissioner in London to be expended there by him for the benefit of the men. The local administration expenses were remarkably low.

In addition to its monetary remittances, the O.A.S. also despatched large quantities of clothing, and comforts of all kinds, for the men at the front. One band of workers, under Miss Power, met regularly at the City Hall depot to make shirts, of which 4,970 were shipped abroad up to the end of 1918. As for socks, the women of Tasmania plied their knitting needles to some purpose, and 21,612 pairs were sent away. The total value of the shipments was £14,394. Special efforts were always made to send extra cheer for the boys on Christmas Day, principally in the form of billy-cans filled with all sorts of good things. How much gifts of this kind were appreciated by the soldiers was shown by the many grateful letters of thanks received from soldiers by those who contributed billies. Every reinforcement that left Tasmanian shores was supplied by the O.A.S. with a gramophone and records, a book for each man, games, and dried fruit. Many letters were received from officers in command saying what a help these gifts had been in relieving the monotony of the long voyage.

What subsequently developed into the northern branch of the O.A.S. originated in an effort to supply sand bags for war purposes. This was in the first year of the war, and a body called the Northern Tasmanian Patriotic Supply Committee was formed for the purpose of organising the collection of these sand bags and their despatch to the seat of hostilities. No fewer than 22,000 bags were given or made and sent away, at a cost of only £38/9/2. Then efforts were directed to the provision of sheepskin vests for winter wear for the soldiers, and 1250 of these were supplied at a total cost of £429/1/. The name of the organisation was then changed to the Trench Comforts Fund, and soon afterwards it became known as the Northern branch of the O.A.S., and worked in conjunction with the Tasmanian headquarters of this fund in Hobart.

Since operations were started in August, 1915, the sum of £19,273/16/6 was raised, and all of this, with the exception of £3089/6/6 cash remaining in hand to June 30th, 1919, and the amount spent in expenses, was sent away or donated for war purposes, including goods to December 31st, 1918, valued at £10,820/15/1 .

Like most other Northern Tasmanian patriotic funds, the O.A.S. branch had zealous and capable officers at its head, who, with the committee, worked strenuously in the good cause.

The plight of brave little Belgium, over-run by the hordes of German militarism in their mad, but futile, rush for vital Channel ports in the early days of the war, aroused the sympathy of people throughout the whole world. That sympathy was intensified, and gave rise to great indignation, when it became known how atrociously the Germans were treating the Belgian civilian population in the occupied territory, and movements were set on foot throughout the British Empire, and in many Allied and neutral countries as well, with the object of helping the Belgians in a practical manner in their unhappy lot. Tasmanians admired Belgium for her refusal to bow the knee to Germany's demands in the first instance, and sympathised with her in her time of trial and sorrow, just as much as the people of any other friendly country, and in any record of Tasmania's war effort a prominent place must be assigned to the Belgian relief work. Generous and whole-hearted as was the response of the public to each and every call on their pockets, in no case did the appeal go quicker to their hearts than in the case of Belgium.

In Southern Tasmania the movement to help the Belgian people originated at a public meeting called by the Mayor of the day (Alderman W. M.

THE CIVILIAN EFFORT.

Williams) at the Town Hall, and attended by the then Premier (Hon. J. Earle) and many prominent public men. The suggestion to inaugurate a fund for the relief of the Belgians met with ready acceptance, for it was felt that it was the least that could be done "as some acknowledgment of the deep debt of gratitude which the British Empire owes to that nation for its gallant resistance to the German invasion," to quote from a resolution passed at the meeting.

In April, 1915, a large gathering took place, representing the various religious bodies in the city and suburbs, at which it was decided that it was desirable to have a house-to-house collection. The city was then allotted into districts, and official books were issued to authorised collectors only. As a result of this organisation a very large amount of money was raised by weekly and monthly contributions, extending over a period of two years, for it was not until May, 1917, that it was decided to cease collecting for the fund. Several very big "Days" were run in aid of the fund; in fact, the first patriotic "Day" on a big scale in Hobart was Belgian Flag Day, held in Franklin Square in November, 1915, with the good net result of £1493.

Altogether Southern Tasmania raised the highly satisfactory total of £27,909 for the fund, as follows:—

	£	s.	d.
1914	2,131	7	1
1915	19,394	18	3
1916	5,149	3	6
1917	1,159	9	11
1918	74	16	2
1919	0	4	0
Total	£27,909	18	11

The 1919 total includes a sum of £819 raised in response to a special appeal on behalf of the Belgian children.

All the administrative work in connection with the fund was voluntary, and the expenses were very small. The fund was wound up in January, 1918, and the committee then decided to transport the remaining balance of £1,969 to the Agent-General for distribution as he thought fit.

Another splendid work for the benefit of the Belgians was that of the Belgian clothing supplies, under the direction of Mrs. L. E. Hubbard, assisted by friends. Material was purchased for the first two consignments, valued by an expert shop assistant at over £1,500. As a result of publicity in the press the public then began to manifest an interest in the scheme, and gifts of clothing poured in from all parts of Tasmania. In the beginning of 1915 a small committee was formed, and the work went on with unabated vigour. Generous public support was forthcoming, and with the money subscribed, material, wool, etc., were purchased and made up into thousands of small garments. Blankets, furs, and comforts of all kinds were given. Children offered tops, gave up their prizes, and helped in every possible way, and each Christmas complete outfits of clothes were supplemented by presents for some thousands of children. All the money received was subscribed voluntarily, without any appeal being made, and without any button day or street collection.

Of the Serbian Fund there is little to be said, except that it was subscribed, for the most part privately, by citizens who, on reading of the terrible sufferings of the Serbians, were anxious to help in their relief. The fund was administered by the same committee as for the Belgian Relief Fund, with Mr. Chester Lord as hon. secretary. Five hundred and seventy pounds was raised.

The efforts of members of the Red Cross were mostly centered, as was to be expected, on the alleviation of the sufferings of our own men, but there was still room in the hearts of the people for something more where that was needed, and in addition to the fund raised for the suffering Belgians, a special effort was made to raise money for the support of the French Red Cross Society; not, perhaps, so much for the actual benefit which this comparatively small amount could give, as in token of the respect and admiration for a gallant Ally. Intense admiration for the magnificent spirit displayed and great sacrifices made by the French nation during a terrible ordeal was felt by Tasmanians throughout the war, and no less a sum than £11,304 was collected in the State for the French Red Cross Fund.

The Tasmanian branch had its inception at a meeting held in the Masonic Hall, Hobart, on June 4, 1915, presided over by the late Hon. W. H. Burgess, Consular Agent for France, who, up to the time of his death, took a keen and practical interest in the work. Mrs. J. G. Edwards was the first president, and continued in that capacity until 1918, when she resigned, owing to absence from the State, and was succeeded by Mrs. W. H. Burgess. Mr. A. J. Kennedy remained hon. secretary till the work was concluded.

Generally speaking, the policy of the committee was to ship goods to France instead of sending money. When the branch was formed a depot was established at the City Hall, and the members immediately got to work preparing clothing and other useful articles for despatch to Paris for use in the French Red Cross hospitals, and by the following August four cases were shipped away. After this regular shipments of goods were made as far as the exigencies of the shipping situation permitted, and when the shipping shortage became acute a large number of parcels were sent by post. The clothing sent to France makes quite a formidable list, and must represent many thousands of hours of steady, painstaking labour on the part of the women workers. Here are a few of the bigger figures extracted from the list, and they by no means represent the full extent of the gifts:—1240 blankets, 2572 sheets, 1941 pillow cases, 498 pairs of pyjamas, 11,886 towels, 5381 handkerchiefs, 6059 pairs socks, 1020 flannel day shirts, 15,670 assorted bandages. The branch also despatched a large quantity of comforts of all kinds to the French hospitals, including cigarettes (of which 22,950 packets were sent), tobacco, pipes, lollies, biscuits, fruits, confectionery, chocolate, jelly crystals, custard powders, chewing gum, evaporated apples, etc. That these gifts were highly appreciated by the French soldiers, especially when they had been sent so many thousands of miles across the seas, was frequently shown in charmingly-worded letters received by the Tasmanian branch and its workers. This is a typical sample from a lieutenant in the 10th Regiment:—"Dear Mademoiselle,—Just a few words to thank the friends of our beautiful France. Your address reached me at the same time as the flannel shirt you forwarded. The shirt will warm my body, but your kindness warms my heart, so that it is from a sense of pleasure and not from duty that I send you my thanks. Tasmania must be a very beautiful country, and, though I am in Champagne this evening, not many yards from the Boches, my thoughts fly there to the far distance."

Many acknowledgments were received from official sources, and Matron Dorothy E. Duffy, a Tasmanian nurse in the service of the French military authorities, to whom special parcels were sent for distribution in her hospital, also sent letters saying how much the French appreciated their contents. In the course of one letter she wrote:—"They (the soldiers) have all been so interested in Tasmania, so I showed them on the map just where it was. They are delighted with what has been done for them in Australia. . . . Please let everyone who helps know how appreciated their gifts are not only the gifts themselves, but the long, long way they come, and the loving thoughts and wishes that send them here to us."

The generosity of the public in subscribing to the French Red Cross was maintained throughout. The yearly amounts raised were as follows:—

1915-16	£2,101
1916-17	4,994
1917-18	2,875
1918-19	1,334
	£11,304

Of the several "days" promoted on behalf of the fund, Verdun Day, in 1917, was the most successful, the amount raised being £3263. The administration of the French Red Cross Fund was entirely voluntary.

During the visit of the French Mission to Tasmania in 1918, several members of the local branch had the pleasure and honor of meeting the veteran General Pau, who was president of the French Red Cross Society. Before leaving Australia, General Pau wrote to the president expressing appreciation of the work Tasmania had done for his country during the war, and also forwarded an autographed photograph of himself and a French flag autographed by the members of the French Mission.

The aim of the Australian Y.M.C.A. throughout the war was to promote the social welfare of the soldier, and to provide him with huts and other rendezvous, where, beneath the sign of the Red Triangle, he was enabled temporarily to put aside military duties, profitably spend his leisure hours, and receive such entertainment as would relieve his mind from the stress of war. The work of the Y.M.C.A. was stated in a short sentence before Bullecourt, when, after listening with his battalion to a Red Triangle entertainment, a colonel shook the hand of a Y.M.C.A. representative, and said, "You have prevented my men from thinking of to-morrow's battle." Every soldier who has been beneath the roof of a Red Triangle hut, who has sat in its chairs, who has used its writing-paper, attended its cinema shows, concerts, or lectures, and who found something pleasant for his soul in the "home from home" atmosphere, has received some benefit from the Australian Y.M.C.A. This service was free.

The field service work of the Tasmanian Y.M.C.A.'s commenced in 1913, when a field secretary with a tent and equipment was placed in the military camp at Ross. A similar service was rendered at the Perth camp in April, 1914. With the outbreak of war, and the opening of the Claremont camp, the field service committee of the Hobart association arranged for a large marquee to be placed in the camp, containing writing material, games, and reading material, permission also being granted by the Camp Commandant for concert parties to visit the camp weekly. It very soon became apparent that more suitable and permanent accommodation would have to be provided, and very little time was lost in erecting a hall 54ft. x 30ft., almost in the centre of the camp. This was opened in May, 1915. Mr. E. G. Cliffin, who had recently arrived from New Zealand, where he had an opportunity of doing field service work, was placed in charge as a resident secretary in the camp, and remained there until October, when he left for Egypt as Tasmania's first Y.M.C.A. representative abroad. During the first eight months after this hut was opened, the attendance totalled over 94,000, the letters written on Y.M.C.A. paper over 73,000, the attendance at concerts and entertainmens over 24,000, and at religious meetings 11,400. The building also was for many weeks used as a post office, the Y.M.C.A. secretary being the unofficial postmaster. In one month alone 18,000 stamps were sold.

Early in 1916 it was found that the work had outgrown the original building, and the association's honorary architects were asked to design a building about 97 x 35, to serve a three-fold purpose: first, accommodation for the holding of religious services by the chaplains; second, a portion set aside as a writing-room; third, a room set apart for the use of officers. This building was opened on April 5, 1916, and meant releasing the first hut for games and concerts.

The committee's work was: Organisation of a series of weekly concerts at Claremont camp and the transport arrangements connected therewith; the opening and supervision of two well-furnished A.I.F. club-rooms in the Hobart Y.M.C.A. building; the direction of a much-appreciated coffee stall from which went free guard and hospital suppers at one of the Claremont buildings; the provision of light refreshments from time to time at the Hobart building for soldiers and sailors on leave. One of the most important developments in the work at this time was within the walls of the Hobart building. Soldiers on leave from Claremont, men of the naval reserve, men from the garrisons, at the forts, returned soldiers, all responded in large numbers to the invitation to use the rooms. At different times, however, a careful count was taken, and it seems beyond doubt that at least 25,000 visits were paid to the building the last year by military and naval ratings. Two rooms, correspondence and reading room and a billiard-room, were reserved for the A.I.F. only.

In July, 1917, the Central Committee were approached by the camp officers and informed that for the future portion of the camp would be reserved for men returning from active service who were in a convalescent state, and were asked if they would provide accommodation for their recreation. The association's architects were again called upon to submit plans for a third building, and on September 5 what was known as the "Rest Hut" was opened. This was a weather-board building, and, as was appropriate for a home of this nature, the furnishings were comfortable.

Early in 1917 the attention of the Field Service Committee was drawn to the need of suitable accommodation for men from the camp spending their week-end leave in the city. It was pointed out that a number of them came from distant parts of the island, and often had difficulty in obtaining good lodgings. With the help of the ladies' committee a number of stretcher beds were obtained and placed on Saturday nights in the gymnasium in the Murray-street building. This soon became very popular, and the committee found it necessary to rent the building known as the Commercial Travellers' Club, in Collins-street, and use the whole of the top floor for dormitory purposes. Every inch of this floor was utilised, and even with the additional accommodation the demand was often in excess of the supply, but they never had occasion to turn a man away.

In addition to the above work, a small hut was placed in Claremont for the exclusive use of the chaplains, and a room was also furnished at the Anglesea Barracks for the use of members of the permanent guard.

The success of the work was only made possible by the generosity of the public in subscribing the necessary funds for not only the work in the State, but also Tasmania's quota for the work abroad and on transports. The receipts from all sources for field service work for the five war years were:—

	£	s.	d.
1915	27	9	1
1916	1,156	12	2
1917	8,635	10	11
1918	7,523	14	3
1919	6,342	18	2
Total	£23,686	4	7

One of the most popular of the home institutions for the benefit of our soldiers and sailors during the war was the A.I.F. Lounge in Hobart. The idea of establishing the lounge originated with Mrs. Rupert Shoobridge, in order to provide a place to which the soldiers could resort for rest, recreation, and refreshment when on leave in the city from Claremont Camp. Associated with Mrs. Shoobridge in the beginning was Miss Sorell, and the successful inauguration of the lounge in February, 1917, when it was formally opened by the then Governor, Sir William Ellison-Macartney, was in rooms in Elizabeth street, largely due to the enterprise and energy of these two ladies. Although named the A.I.F. Lounge, the institution was not confined exclusively to A.I.F. men. Sailors, home service men, and returned men, in fact, all who were doing their "bit" in connection with the forces, were welcomed there. Full use was made of the lounge from its very inception, and the men always spoke in highly appreciative terms of the way in which they were catered for. Within a month of the opening the work outgrew the accommodation in Elizabeth street, and new premises were obtained and opened at the old Commercial Travellers' Club in Collins street in June, 1917, and the additional accommodation enabled the committee to extend the scope of their operations by providing dinners, in addition to teas and light refreshments. Hot meals were served at nominal charges, and a good dinner could be obtained for 9d. Reading, writing, and billiard rooms were attractive features, and hot baths were available. When the lounge was first opened it was conducted entirely by a committee of ladies, the members of which were so enthusiastic in their good work that they paid the rent out of their own pockets for the first five months. The furniture was lent by members of the committee and other friends. In addition there was a host of voluntary lady workers, who took duty in turns at the lounge and rendered excellent service. a great many of whom, like the V.A.D.'s, had to work hard for their living, or in their own homes, but, nevertheless, found time to devote to the comfort of the men who were fighting for them. The lounge was open every day, Sundays included, and there was always a matron in charge. A smoother-running institution could scarcely have been found, and the ladies associated with it speak in the highest terms of the courtesy and good behaviour of the men who visited the lounge. The total revenue was £2670, about £900 of which represented receipts from meals, and the rest donations. When the lounge was closed, consequent on the cessation of hostilities and the breaking up of Claremont, there remained a balance in hand of £679; £100 of this was sent to St. Dunstan's Hospital for the Blind in England, and the remainder to the Returned Sailors and Soldiers' League.

If there was one comfort which the majority of the British soldiers appreciated above all others while in the fighting line, it was a smoke. The timely arrival of a packet of cigarettes cheered up many a man when he was feeling rather dumpy. Small wonder, then, that he has a warm corner in his heart for the Overseas Club Tobacco Fund, which looked after him admirably in the matter of smokes, and distributed several million shilling parcels of tobacco and cigarettes in the fighting line. The Hobart branch did its full share in raising money for this worthy object, and can boast a fine record. By means of lectures, smoke socials, and other enetrtainments, and also collections, the branch raised no less than £2682; £1000 of this was transmitted to the headquarters in London, through the Overseas Club Southern Cross Tobacco Fund, which had its headquarters in Melbourne.

The Mayor's Patriotic Fund was first inaugurated in Tasmania by the Mayor of Hobart (then Alderman R. J. Meagher) publicly calling on all those interested in the promotion of a fund to relieve distress directly consequent upon the war to meet at the Town Hall, Hobart, on August 15th,

1914. Many prominent citizens answered this call, and Mr. Chester Lord was that day appointed hon. secretary to the fund. By the 24th of the month £26,76 had been collected for the fund, and by September 19th £5333.

Below are the names of those who have been chairmen of the committee while holding the position of Mayor of Hobart. Each in his turn devoted a large portion of his time to the work, and has taken the greatest personal interest in dealing with the different cases as they arose:—

R. J. Meagher	1914
W. M. Williams	1915
L. H. Macleod	1916
R. D. Lord	1917
J. G. Shield	1918-19

In December, 1916, Mr. Chester Lord resigned his position as hon. secretary, after two and a half years of hard and valuable work, and Mr. H. G. Finlaison was appointed secretary.

The fund was established to provide for the dependents of soldiers of the A.I.F. and sailors of the Royal Australian Navy in cases of sickness, accident, or death; also to assist and relieve any persons whatsoever in distress directly consequent upon the war. Since 1914 the fund assisted many hundreds of soldiers' families. The amount of money collected for this fund up to September 17th, 1919, was £13,377, the figures for each year being:—

The amount of money collected for this fund up to September 17, 1919, was £13,377, the figures for each year being:—

1914	£8709	6	3
1915	3003	1	1
1916	432	18	8
1917	489	7	9
1918	568	8	1
1919	174	1	11

The amount disbursed during the same period was £12,124. Before making payments to applicants from the fund, careful inquiry was made into every case. The usual procedure was first to seek information (by telephone where possible, so as to save time) from the military and pension office authorities as to existing allotments, separation allowances, pensions, etc. Reports from the clergy, police authorities, and the different charitable societies were also sought to discover whether applicants were worthy of assistance. Every endeavor was made to grant relief quickly. Meetings of the committee were usually held weekly to deal with applications for assistance and other matters. A representative of the Returned Sailors' and Soldiers' League had a seat on the committee.

The Disabled Tasmanian Soldiers' Fund was inaugurated on October 15, 1915, at a meeting of interested citizens, called by the Mayor (then Alderman W. M. Williams), to consider the question of appointing a committee of management to administer funds placed in his hands for the relief of disabled Tasmanian soldiers. The fund had been started at the request of the associated breweries of Tasmania, which had handed sums of money to the Mayors of Hobart and Launceston for this purpose. An executive committee was at this meeting appointed to deal with the funds in the hands of the Mayor and for future collections. As in the case of the Mayor's Patriotic Fund, the Returned Sailors' and Soldiers' League was represented on the committee. Successive Mayors were chairman of the committee and took a keen interest in the work. Mr. W. A. Brain (town clerk) was appointed the first honorary secretary on March 15, 1916, which position, though a very busy man, he held until January 11, 1917, when, on account of the ever-increasing calls upon his time, due to the more frequent return of disabled soldiers, he was obliged to tender his resignation, but was still retained upon the committee. In this case also Mr. H. G. Finlaison was appointed hon. secretary.

The Disabled Soldiers' Fund was created for the assistance of returned wounded or disabled Tasmanian soldiers and sailors, and to help any Tasmanian soldier or sailor of the Royal Australian Navy in distress directly consequent upon the war. Since its inception it helped a large number of returned soldiers and sailors. Discretionary power was given to the Mayor, with the hon. secretary, to deal with applications for small sums of money, such payments being ratified at the next meeting of the executive committee. The amount of money collected for this fund up to September 17, was £5713. The yearly amounts raised were:—

1915 (from July)	£3086	5 10
1916	1210	16 9
1917	496	2 2
1918	288	0 11
1919	631	14 9

The expenditure for the same period was £3381. The first large donation granted by the fund was £250 to the Returned Soldiers' Association; £100 was also cabled to Egypt for Christmas, 1915, to Tasmanian troops. Some 3050 returned soldiers and sailors received help.

The total collections in Tasmania for all patriotic purposes were as follows:—

SOUTHERN FUNDS	£	s.	d.
Belgian Relief Fund	27,909	14	11
Belgian Children Fund	860	13	10
Serbian Relief Fund	569	9	5
Mayor's Patriotic Fund	13,203	11	10
Disabled Tasmanian Soldiers' Fund	5,286	0	8
Red Cross Funds	59,937	14	4
Ditto, value of goods to January 1919	21,870	13	8
French Red Cross Fund	11,150	6	1
Navy Day, 1917 (closed)	3,256	7	7
Mrs. Hubbard (estimated value of goods sent to Belgium)	9,220	0	0
Overseas Club Tobacco Fund (to Jan. 31)	1,682	12	10
Southern Cross ditto, ditto (closed)	1,000	0	6
Returned Sailors' and Soldiers' Imperial League of Australia Building Fund	6,095	8	7
Y.M.C.A. Field Service Fund	9,386	18	3
O.A.S. Fund	18,658	13	8
Ditto goods (six months ending 31/12/18)	3,000	0	0
Returned Wounded and Invalided Soldiers' Fund (sporting bodies)	630	9	5
Purple Cross	1,044	11	11
A.I.F. Lounge	2,650	19	1
40th Battalion Comforts Fund	1,179	13	11
12th Battalion Comforts Fund	618	9	10
Australian Mining Corps Comfort Fund	520	14	4
	£202,883	14	9

NORTHERN FUNDS

	£ s. d.
Mayor's Patriotic Fund	9,824 14 5
Mayor's Wounded Soldiers' Fund	1,513 13 7
Belgian Relief Fund	29,836 19 1
Belgian Children's Fund	1,111 6 11
Belgian Red Cross and Emergency Fund	413 11 3

Red Cross Funds—

	£ s. d.
Cash	20,192 10 10
Goods	21,153 1 4
Australia Day	11,624 12 10
French Red Cross	4,418 13 11
Special Appeal	3,920 5 11
House Badge Drive	1,581 3 3
Our Day Fund	3,640 0 0

Y.M.C.A.—

	£ s. d.		
Claremont Field Service	200 0 0		
General Field Service	2,697 2 11		
Soldiers' Club	1,244 17 4		
		4,142 0 3	

O.A.S. Fund—

	£ s. d.		
Cash	13,803 14 11		
Special Appeal	1,877 9 3		
Goods	6,369 19 6		
		22,051 3 8	

	£ s. d.
Blue Cross	229 6 5
Purple Cross	835 9 3
Tobacco Fund	638 9 0
Serbian Fund	567 8 8
Motor Ambulance	1,027 0 0
Band Instruments	375 14 6
Plum Pudding Fund	192 3 2
Naval Gifts	388 16 0
Our Sailors' Day Fund	2,875 6 6
Star and Garter House	129 11 2
Anzac Memorial Hostel	3,868 1 5
Anzac Buffet	449 8 11
Royal Australian Navy Day	702 5 8
40th Battalion Comforts Fund	196 17 8

Verdun Day—

	£ s. d.	
1917	537 15 3	
1918	202 13 8	
		740 8 11

France Day—

	£ s. d.	
1917	208 14 1	
1918	357 17 6	
		566 11 7

	£ s. d.
	£149,206 16 2
Southern total	202,883 14 9
Grand total	£352,090 10 11

Among the many men and women who, in one way or another, did friendly office for the Tasmanian Diggers, the late Sir John McCall, K.C.M.G., holds a high place. He was Agent-General for Tasmania during the whole period of the war, and his office in London was a recognised centre for Tasmanians on leave. He made no distinctions; the mere fact that a soldier was a Tasmanian was sufficient. He gave them generous hospitality, and was ever ready to aid them with advice as to the best way of getting what they wanted. Relatives in Tasmania frequently asked him to obtain news for them of soldiers, and such requests were to him commands, to which he responded by doing whatever was possible. One of the trials of the soldiers on short leave in London was the difficulty of obtaining remittances from home in time to be of any use. The cables were congested with business, and messages frequently took three weeks to reach their destination. Sir John McCall was able to get official messages through more quickly, and by his agency remittances of money were received, which made all the difference to the soldiers holidays. Hundreds of people in the State felt, when he died, that they had lost a friend to whom they owed very deep obligations, and their regret still lives that they will not be able to meet him and express something of their gratitude.

REPATRIATION.

In April, 1918, the Repatriation Department succeeded the State War Council in the direction of repatriation activities.

The War Council had already laid the foundations, and the new department found ready to its hands a mass of information, carefully compiled and tabulated, which proved most useful to the officials in the early stages of their work.

The staff of the War Council was transferred to the department, and additional assistance engaged, Lieutenant-Colonel J. F. Humphris being appointed Deputy Comptroller.

The accommodation available at the Barracks proved to be too limited for the extended scope of the work, and a suite of offices was leased on the third floor of the A.M.P. Buildings, in Elizabeth street. It was soon demonstrated, however, that these premises would not be satisfactory as a permanent location, and, in the latter half of 1919, the erection of offices capable of accommodating the rapidly expanding staff was undertaken.

The site selected was the vacant block of public land adjoining Anglesea Barracks, and in November, 1919, the new buildings were occupied. Thus in the short space of eighteen months the department changed its location twice.

The Repatriation Act passed in 1917 was the preliminary measure towards the great work of repatriation. It provided the foundation on which to build the superstructure. The Act did not define the scope of repatriation, but it gave power for the framing of regulations and the creation of certain bodies to administer the Act and regulations.

Thus there came into existence a central Commissoin, a State Board in each State, and numerous committees, all giving their services in a voluntary capacity. These voluntary workers were assisted by a highly organised paid staff, charged with administration of the Act and regulations, and the conduct of the business in a manner suitable to the requirements of a large public department.

Regulations have been issued from time to time defining the powers of the various bodies and setting the range, scope, and benefits provided for persons eligible under the Act.

Repatriation on the scale contemplated by the Act was an entirely new thing, and in framing the regulations there were no precedents to which one might look for guidance. As a natural consequence the regulations have been subject to constant revision, alterations, and extension. With the passage of time many problems arose, and the experience gained in dealing with these has been made use of in perfecting the machinery of administration, extending the range of benefits, and in generally making the department a fit instrument to discharge the obligations the country owes to the gallant men who ranged themselves on the side of liberty and freedom during the late titanic struggle.

The activities of the department now range over a wide field, but may be classified under a few main headings as follows:—

> Provision of employment for unemployed soldiers and a sustenance allowance whilst unemployed (subject to certain conditions and limitations).
> Care of totally and permanently incapacitated soldiers.
> Medical treatment for war disabilities.
> Living allowances for incapacitated soldiers, widows, and orphans of soldiers, and parents of deceased soldiers.
> Education of war orphans.
> Assistance to soldiers to enter business.
> Gifts of tools of trade.
> Loans of furniture.
> Transportation of soldiers to place of employment.
> Sustenance to land settlers.
> Vocational training of disabled men and those who enlisted under the age of twenty years.
> Many minor benefits.

Turning now to the work which has been accomplished in this State.

When the War Council dissolved in April, 1918, the war was still raging, recruiting was active, and the end of the struggle was not in sight. From eight to ten thousand men from this State were still abroad. There were, however, upwards of two thousand men who had returned and been discharged. Many of these had received assistance from the War Council, but there were still numbers who desired the assistance of the new department. Steps were taken immediately to create the organisation necessary to carry out the policy laid down.

The State Board had already been formed, with Mr. F. Lindsay Gunn as chairman, and held its first meeting on April 16th, 1918.

In the first two years of its existence the board dealt with 3090 applications and granted loans to the value of £26,080, besides dealing with a mass of general business incidental to the discharge of their duties.

At the beginning of 1920 an amending Bill was passed by the Federal Parliament, substituting a board of three, who were to receive fees. Mr. F. L. Gunn, C.B.E., was the appointed chairman; Mr. C. L. Pringle deputy chairman, and Mr. D. M'Rae representative of the soldiers.

In order that men residing outside the metropolitan area might have at hand a ready means of obtaining assistance, local committees were formed in each municipal area. The organisation of these committees was a task of considerable magnitude. The chairman of the State Board made a complete tour of the Island, interviewing prominent citizens in every locality, enlisting their sympathy and assistance, and explaining the powers and functions intended to be exercised by the committee. Mr. Gunn spent some months in this work, giving his services in an entirely voluntary capacity. His efforts resulted in the formation of an excellent committee in each municipality. The standard of membership was high, many of the most prominent residents coming forward to aid in this national duty.

The committees were entrusted with extensive powers, and were in a position to deal with the majority of applications without reference to the State office. Thus a local committee might grant tools of trade, furniture, medical attention, transportation, sustenance allowance, and a number of other benefits. These forms of assistance covered the general run of applications, and the soldier found that the local committee was a ready medium by means of which his immediate needs might receive attention.

The total membership of local committees was approximately six hundred, and the committees collectively performed a vast amount of work. As an illustration, it may be stated that forty per cent. of the money expended in the first two years in this State on repatriation was being disbursed by the local committees. Each committee also kept a register of applicants for employment, and many a soldier was found suitable employment through the medium of his local committee.

In busy centres the labour devolving on the secretaries was very heavy. The gentlemen who had undertaken this task were usually busy men, and had necessarily to devote all their leisure time to keeping the records of the committees up to date. The digger owes a deep debt of gratitude to the men who have so disinterestedly given many a weary hour to the discharge of this self-imposed task.

The cessation of hostilities in October, 1918, rendered possible the early return of the men still abroad. It was anticipated that many of the men would be applicants for employment, and steps were taken to create an employment bureau to deal with this phase of the work. In some quarters it was feared that the rapid discharge of thousands of men would cause a glut in the labour market, and the spectacle of many hundreds of discharged soldiers roaming about in search of employment was looked forward to with some apprehension. However, nothing untoward happened, and the returning troops were absorbed into the civil community without any noticeable dislocation of industrial conditions.

High-water mark in the number of applicants was reached towards the end of 1919, when there were over 1000 men on the books of the department seeking employment. This number has been gradually reduced, until at time of writing there are fewer than 500 men out of work.

Early in the year 1919, the Federal Government set aside a sum of £500,000 for the employment of discharged soldiers. This sum was distributed among the local governing bodies throughout Australia, Tasmania's share being £20,000. This grant was of material assistance in tiding over a period of stress and provided work throughout the State, thus avoiding any accumulation of unemployed in the principal centres of population.

Since its inception the employment section of the department has had a busy time in exploiting all possible avenues of employment. Employers of all classes of labor have given constant support and have ever shown a ready disposition to aid the department in its efforts to re-establish the soldier in a suitable civil avocation. Those industries which employ considerable labour have been especially considerate to the soldier, giving him preference in employment, and bearing with him when he showed that his war experiences had somewhat disturbed his inclination for a civil avocation.

During the first two years of its operations the department received 6865 applications for employment, and found work for 3499. A large number did not follow up their applications, which consequently lapsed. Many of these found employment for themselves. This result could not have been attained without the support of the community generally, and it speaks volumes for the industrial stability of the State that practically the whole of the discharged soldiers have been received once more into civil life without any measure of relief work of any magnitude being necessary. This is the more remarkable when it is remembered that the industrial life of the State was much disturbed by strikes, the influenza epidemic, the shortage of shipping, and the lack of supplies of many necessary commodities.

In October, 1918, regulations were gazetted which provided for the payment of living allowances to incapacitated soldiers, the widows and orphans of soldiers, and the parents of soldiers whose circumstances were such as to render an allowance necessary for their reasonable comfort, provided that dependence on the soldier prior to his enlistment was established. Steps were immediately taken to obtain the necessary information regarding the dependents of soldiers in this State, and living allowances were granted to all widows and orphans, and also to a number of parents of deceased soldiers. This allowance has proved a great boon to the recipients, enabling those members of the community who had lost their breadwinners to live in reasonable comfort. It was found that the number of widows in this State totalled 214, and orphans under sixteen years of age, 457. In all, 420 living allowances have been issued.

Provision has also been made for the education of children arriving at the age of sixteen years, whereby these orphans may receive further assistance which will make it possible for them to obtain an education in advance of what would have been possible without this additional assistance. The circumstances of the widows and children are kept under review, and where it is necessary for the proper upbringing of the children, the department steps in and makes the required arrangements. It has been found that in practically every instance the orphans in this State are being reared under conditions suitable to their circumstances to remove a child from the control of its relatives or guardians. Suitable provision has been made in cases where both the father and mother are deceased, the child being placed with responsible persons, who receive an adequate allowance for the child's maintenance.

One prominent feature of the work of the department is that connected with the vocational training of disabled soldiers, or of those who enlisted under the age of twenty years. An organisation has been created consisting of a vocational training committee, with Mr. R. J. Meagher as chairman, and numerous industrial committees, covering the various trades. An agreement was entered into with the State Government to place at the disposal of the department all technical training facilities. The State also undertakes the management of the training classes, the department reimbursing the State for all expenditure in connection with training. Considerable difficulties were encountered at the outset, owing to their being no extensive technical schools in operation in this State, and it became necessary to purchase buildings, plant and material, and to engage instructors to carry out the training. A property was acquired at the corner of Harrington and Melville streets, containing a floor area of 30,000 square feet. A vast amount of work was necessary to put the building in a fit state for the reception of the classes. Most of the work was performed by the students, and at the present time the school is a very complete and up-to-date establishment, the machinery installed being second to none in the State. Trade classes have been commenced covering all the principal trades, and the number of students now undergoing tuition is approximately 300, while there is still a large number on the waiting list.

After being given a course of training in the technical schools, students who have attained a sufficient degree of efficiency are placed out in private establishments on a percentage basis, that is to say, the employer pays a proportion of the standard wage, the department contributing the balance. The industrial efficiency of the trainees is assessed at periodical intervals, and an adjustment made as to the proportion of wages to be paid by the employer. Thus a progressive scale of payments is provided, which eventually eliminates the departmental proportion as the student reaches full efficiency. In the case of indentured apprentices, departmental assistance is forthcoming to make up to the trainee the wage he would have been receiving had his indentures not been interrupted by his war service.

The number of applicants for vocational training during the first two years of the department's operations was 1951. Many of these have completed their course of training, and are now earning full wages.

A complete system of after-discharge medical treatment has been instituted. Men in the metropolitan area may apply direct to the departmental medical officer for treatment for war disabilities. Medical officers have been appointed in every area in the State, and any man suffering from a war disability may apply to the medical officer of the area in which he resides, and receive treatment free of expense. If his disability is of a nature which prevents him following his occupation, he is granted a living allowance during the period of his incapacitation. The medical officers have been awarded a liberal scale of fees, and the arrangements that have been made have proved very satisfactory. Not only may disabled men consult medical officers of the department without charge, but all medicines, dressings, and similar requisites, are supplied at the expense of the department. Provision has been made also for the supply and renewal of artificial limbs and other surgical appliances. Soldiers with injured feet, necessitating the wearing of special boots, are kept supplied with these necessary articles at departmental expense, and many other medical benefits are also available.

The future care of mental cases, tuberculars, neurasthenics, and shell-shocks is receiving consideration, and arrangements are now in hand adequately to provide for the interests of all these types of war-worn soldiers.

If the first two years of the department's operations may be taken as a reliable guide, it is evident that in the not far distant future the great majority of the returned soldiers will be firmly re-established in the civil community, whilst those whose disabilities prevent them from taking a full share in the industrial life of the community will be comfortably provided for by pensions, medical treatment, and homes and hostels, where they may spend the remainder of their days in ease.

Another important feature of the work of repatriation was the provision of homes for soldiers. A special department was created to manage this, and had power to spend up to £700 in building or buying a house for any soldier with dependents. Already a large number of houses have been purchased or built in all parts of the State, and the work is still going on. The soldier makes payments in the nature of rent, which cover interest and gradually repayment of capital.

Provision was made also for soldiers to acquire farms on much the same terms, except in regard to the limitation of cost. This was done by arrangement with the State Government, which, through the Department of Lands, buys properties after valuation, and allows soldiers to acquire them, advancing, when necessary, money for the purchase of implements and stock. For the first two years the soldier pays nothing, and is free from municipal rates. After that, payment of interest and repayment of capital begin.

THE TASMANIA R.S.S.I.L.A.

It was at a picnic held on February 26th, 1916, at Montagu Bay, where the proposal was first mooted to form a Returned Soldiers' Association, and it is to the standing credit of a few energetic pioneers that the movement was then successfully inaugurated.

The first meeting was held in the committee room, Hobart Town Hall, on March 1st, 1916. It was presided over by the Mayor of Hobart, Mr. Shield, and was held for the purpose of forming an association to be called "The Returned Soldiers' Association of Tasmania." About 50 returned soldiers were in attendance.

The following motions were carried:—(1) "That the headquarters be established in Hobart"; (2) "That all returned soldiers and the Mayors of Hobart and Launceston be appointed vice-presidents." Sergeant H. Neilson was appointed secretary.

The Rules and Regulations obtaining in the R.S.L., Victoria, subject to amendment and alteration, were adopted, and it was left with the committee to select a design for a badge.

The affiliation of the Returned Soldiers' Association with the Australian Imperial League took place on the 7th August, 1916, under the chairmanship of Mr. R Phillips, when Mr. D. McRae was appointed treasurer and Mr. W. Cameron secretary.

In 1918 Lieutenant-Colonel D. P. Young was elected president, the position he holds in 1920.

Until securing other accommodation in the City Hall building, the league held its meetings in the Town Hall and the Masonic Hall, and (thanks to the kindness of Mr. Robert Nettlefold, O.B.E.) in The Dugout, Macquarie street, but in the year 1918, having secured an option over the present club building in Murray street from the board of directors of the Y.M.C.A., the president called a special general meeting on August 12th, 1918, to consider the question of purchasing it. The meeting appointed a sub-committee to consult the trustees, and with power to act for the league. The result was the purchase of the building for £5500, the floor coverings being presented by the Y.M.C.A.

A campaign for funds was immediately instituted, and when, on December 7th, 1918, the building was officially opened by His Excellency the Governor (Sir Francis Newdigate), the committee had the satisfaction of knowing that they had seen the branch in these fine quarters free of debt.

Especial mention must be made of the work of the various ladies' committees in connection with the fair and stalls, as well as of the furnishings committees.

Mr. George Fisher, who had held the position of secretary since the affiliation of the R.S.A. with the R.S.S.I.L.A., resigned the position after nearly two years of energetic and successful work, a record of appreciation of his services being placed upon the minutes. On May 22nd the committee decided to call for applications for the position of secretary and assistant secretary, G. Foster and L. Collis being appointed as the result of a ballot on June 7th, 1918.

The total number of members dealt with in Hobart during the year 1918 was 926 and 1731 for the whole State, as against 395 and 670 respectively in 1917, while the total number of sub-branches was 14.

During the following year, 1919, the total number of members dealt with in Hobart was no less than 2588, and for the whole of the State, 4460, as against 926 and 1731 respectively for 1918. The finances of the league were on a sound footing, the income from all sources being £7554.

For the purpose of entering the political arena, Mr. George Foster, the then secretary, who had held that position with marked success from June

7th, 1918, tendered his resignation, and received the thanks of the State branch for the able and energetic manner in which he had carried out his duties.

In November, 1919, Major F. E. Forrest, M.C., was appointed. No less than 43 branches of the league are now in existence throughout Tasmania, with a membership totalling nearly 7000 members.

With the assistance of a competent staff under Mr. Forrest's regime, a monthly newspaper, "The Tassie Digger," has been put on a sound business footing; the club billiard room and canteen have proved a sound financial proposition; a trading store, handling 1600 yards of Commonwealth tweed monthly, has been brought into existence, and a company formed under the name of "The Diggers' Co-operative Stores Ltd.," with a registered capital of £15,000, and these are only the forerunners of additional ventures to be floated for the benefit of returned soldiers in particular, and Tasmanians as a whole.

In the beginning the Returned Soldiers' Association, as it was then called, had no very definite object, except to keep in existence the ties of comradeship which had been formed during the war. A little later it began to assume in a general kind of way charge of the interests of returned soldiers, and in particular redress of grievances. At the present day the aims and objects of the league are—

To perpetuate the close and kindly ties of friendship created by mutual service in the great war and the recollections associated with that experience, to maintain a proper standard of dignity and honour among all returned sailors and soldiers, and to set an example of public spirit and noble-hearted endeavor.

To preserve the memory and records of those who suffered and died for the nation, to erect monuments to their valor, to provide them with suitable burial places, and to establish in their honour an annual commemoration day.

To provide for the sick, wounded, and needy among those who have served, and their dependents, including pensions, medical attention, homes, and suitable employment.

To inculcate loyalty to Australia and the Empire, and to secure patriotic service in interests of both.

To guard the good name and preserve the interests and standing of returned sailors and soldiers.

To induce members as citizens to serve Australia with that spirit of self-sacrifice and loyalty with which as sailors and soldiers they served Australia and the Empire, and to maintain an association non-sectarian and non-partisan in relation to party politics and industrial disputes.

To establish, maintain, furnish, and equip clubs, club-rooms, information bureau, libraries, literary, social, educational, and benevolent institutions for the benefit and advancement of members.

To establish branches and sub-branches throughout Tasmania.

To acquire by all lawful means real and personal property, and to apply both capital and income thereof, and the proceeds of the sale or mortgage thereof, or towards all or any of the objects herein specified.

To mortgage, charge, lease, dispose of, exchange, and otherwise deal with any property of or held by the league in any manner authorised by law.

To pay out of the funds of league all expenses incidental to the formation and management of the league, or carrying out any of its objects, including the payment of salaries to persons employed.

To do all such other lawful acts and things as are incidental or conducive to the attainment of the above objects.

APPENDIX

District Enlistments

THE ADDRESS GIVEN BY A SOLDIER ON ENTERING CAMP IS SHOWN IN OFFICIAL RECORDS AS HIS PLACE OF ENLISTMENT, AND IT IS FROM THESE FIGURES THAT THE NUMBERS FOR EACH TOWN ARE COMPILED.

Town.	Pop.	Enls.	Deceased.
ABBOTSHAM	266	9	3
ADVENTURE	150	2	—
ALONNAH	58	4	1
ALBERTON	128	2	—
ANDOVER	53	3	1
ANTILL PONDS	59	5	1
APSLEY	128	6	1
AUSTIN'S FERRY	61	17	2
AVOCA	213	19	5
BACK RIVER	173	1	—
BADEN	98	2	—
BAGDAD	407	27	4
BALFOUR	248	3	—
BANGOR	128	11	3
BARNES BAY	—	1	—
BARRINGTON	669	38	5
BEACONSFIELD	2618	124	14
BELLERIVE	918	75	13
BEAUTY POINT	121	5	2
BERRIEDALE	121	15	2
BEULAH	444	10	2
BICHENO	50	4	—
BIRCHES' BAY	88	6	1
BISHOPSBOURNE	299	1	—
BOTHWELL	755	79	14
BOAT HARBOUR	281	19	8
BLACK BRUSH	120	2	—
BLACK RIVER	125	6	3
BLACK SUGAR LOAF	131	8	—
BLACKWOOD	193	4	—
BLESSINGTON	236	10	1
BRANXHOLM	628	30	3
BREADALBANE	144	7	3
BREAM CREEK	123	8	1
BRIDGENORTH	136	14	1
BRIDGEWATER	410	34	6
BRIDPORT	63	3	—

Town.	Pop.	Enls.	Deceased.
BRIGHTON JUNCTION	54	28	10
BRACKNELL	226	12	4
BROADMARSH	181	12	3
BRUNI	289	36	9
BUCKLAND	166	7	1
BURNIE	2927	272	57
BUSHY PARK	575	3	1
CALDER	177	3	—
CAMBRIDGE	403	8	4
CAMPANIA	251	14	5
CAMPBELL TOWN	859	76	5
CARLTON	92	4	1
CARNARVON	140	5	2
CARRICK	263	15	2
CASTLE FORBES BAY	148	3	2
CASTRA	543	11	1
CAVESIDE	196	8	1
CAPE BARREN ISLAND	170	15	1
CHUDLEIGH	262	15	5
CHANNEL	—	8	2
CLAREMONT	208	61	18
CLARENDON	20	2	—
CLEVELAND	171	14	·5
COLLINS' VALE	264	19	4
COLEBROOK	384	42	6
COPPINGTON	126	11	1
CORNWALL	234	9	2
CONARA	78	8	—
CRADOC	160	3	1
CRESSY	615	30	6
CROTTY	80	1	1
CULLENSWOOD	83	2	—
CUPRONA	151	4	—
DEDDINGTON	86	1	—
DEEP BAY	60	5	2
DEEP CREEK ROAD	91	1	—
DELORAINE	1811	156	34
DERBY	1126	74	7
DERWENT PARK	255	12	1
DEVIOT	57	4	1
DEVONPORT	3620	329	56
DON	407	10	2
DOVER	520	18	4
DROMEDARY	156	21	2
DUNDAS	399	12	7
DULVERTON	113	7	1
DUNALLEY	107	12	3
DUNORLAN	230	11	1
DYSART	53	11	3
EAGLEHAWK NECK	96	6	1
EASTWOOD	15	1	1
EASTERN MARSH	62	11	2
ELDERSLIE	79	11	—
ELIZABETH TOWN	189	8	3

DISTRICT ENLISTMENTS.

Town.	Pop.	Enls.	Deceased.
ELLENDALE	201	25	8
ELLIOTT	195	6	1
ESPERANCE	190	18	1
EVANDALE	932	51	13
EXETER	134	15	3
EXTON	293	16	2
EPPING	11	2	1
FALMOUTH	62	2	—
FENTONBURY	221	5	2
FERN TREE	62	6	—
FINGAL	416	30	3
FLOWERDALE	514	18	7
FLINDERS ISLAND	170	25	6
FLOWERPOT	88	3	1
FORCETT	219	6	4
FORREST	684	40	5
FORRESTER	59	5	2
FORTH	260	26	1
FRANKFORD	272	13	1
FRANKLIN	1169	61	12
FRANKLIN VILLAGE	58	3	—
GARDNERS BAY	180	7	—
GARDEN ISLAND CREEK	58	5	—
GAWLER	365	11	3
GEEVESTON	1093	44	7
GEORGE TOWN	272	17	5
GLADSTONE	341	22	2
GLENORCHY	1209	90	11
GLAZIERS BAY	52	1	1
GLENFERN	172	1	—
GLENGARRY	301	10	1
GLEN HUON	209	17	2
GLENLUSK	76	9	1
GLENORA	403	4	1
GOLCONDA	76	5	1
GORDON	158	5	—
GORMANSTON	782	60	6
GOULD'S COUNTRY	212	8	1
GRETNA	375	19	4
GROVE	61	8	1
GUILDFORD JUNCTION	95	3	1
GUIMONS PLAINS	183	5	4
GUNNS PLAINS	83	6	1
HADSPEN	96	9	1
HAGLEY	426	14	4
HAMILTON	337	21	5
HARFORD	397	10	4
HASTINGS	378	11	2
HENRIETTA	129	2	—
HOBART	29,836	2672	408
HOLWELL	84	2	—
HOPETOWN	94	1	1
HUON (UPPER)	245	3	—
HUONVILLE	413	61	15

Town.	Pop.	Enls.	Deceased.
HYTHE	378	4	1
IRISHTOWN	411	29	5
IDA BAY	—	2	1
JACKY'S MARSH	61	1	—
JERICHO	187	17	4
KANOWNA	126	5	1
KAROOLA	195	9	—
KELLEVIE	221	7	—
KELSO	52	2	1
KEMPTON	374	23	4
KENTISH	593	25	3
KETTERING	225	11	3
KIMBERLEY	333	28	4
KINDRED	393	14	4
KING'S MEADOWS	204	4	—
KINGSTON	539	34	3
KINGBOROUGH	68	2	1
KOONYA	167	4	—
KING ISLAND	1000	63	8
LAPOINYA	53	2	—
LA GUNTA	15	1	—
LADYS BAY	56	2	—
LATROBE	1355	110	23
LAUNCESTON	20,937	1653	247
LEBRINA	20	11	6
LEFROY	398	37	10
LEITH	115	8	1
LEMANA JUNCTION	57	9	1
LEVENDALE	1363	9	2
LIETTINNA	55	7	1
LIFFEY	258	2	1
LILYDALE	729	52	12
LINDA VALLEY	767	16	3
LINDISFARNE	632	59	9
LISLE	384	6	2
LLEWELLYN	14	1	—
LONGFORD	1674	99	15
LONGLEY	288	24	4
LOTTAH	322	20	4
LOVETT	1489	98	20
LUNAWANNA	69	8	3
LUPOINA	—	1	—
LYELL	248	13	3
LYNCHFORD	128	1	—
LYMINGTON	58	2	1
MACQUARIE PLAINS	324	35	7
MAGNET	388	11	—
MATHINNA	620	36	7
MANGALORE	106	12	3
MANGANA	204	11	3
MARGATE	298	7	—
MAYFIELD	30	1	—
MARIA ISLAND	12	1	—
MEANDER	160	16	2

DISTRICT ENLISTMENTS.

Town.	Pop.	Enls.	Deceased.
MELROSE	176	6	1
MELTON MOWBRAY	129	11	3
MENGHA	151	9	2
MERSEY LEA	31	1	—
MIDDLETON	174	19	—
MOINA	81	2	—
MOLE CREEK	422	26	9
MOLESWORTH	317	9	—
MONTAGUE	236	10	1
MOONAH	1074	77	8
MOORE PLAINS	151	1	1
MOORINGA	294	5	1
MORIARTY	191	8	1
MOUNTAIN RIVER	147	1	—
MONTUMANA	16	1	—
MOOGARA	31	1	—
MOLTENA	26	1	1
MOOR LEA	62	7	1
MOORINA	60	8	2
MONTANA	23	2	1
MOWBRAY	143	3	2
MYALLA	105	14	5
MYRTLE BANKS	57	7	1
MUDDY CREEK	—	3	—
MOUNT BALFOUR	64	2	—
MOUNT BISCHOFF	56	2	—
MOUNT CAMERON	188	4	2
MOUNT DIRECTION	40	7	1
MOUNT CAMERON SOUTH	53	5	—
MOUNT HICKS	355	8	1
MOUNT NICHOLAS	155	14	4
MOUNT SEYMOUR	86	13	2
NATONE	75	9	2
NABOWLA	83	18	5
NEWNHAM	132	5	—
NEW NORFOLK	2041	159	23
NEWSTEAD	147	2	—
NEW TOWN	3382	173	35
NEEDLES	41	4	—
NIETTA	22	3	2
NICHOLLS RIVULET	177	3	1
NILE	186	9	3
NOOK	252	7	2
NORTHDOWN	202	8	1
NUBEENA	196	22	4
NUGENT	211	3	—
NUTTAL	62	1	—
NORTH MOTTON	446	37	10
OAKS	122	3	1
OAKWOOD	93	5	1
OATLANDS	739	51	12
OLD BEACH	158	11	1
OLDINNA	86	1	—
OONAH	69	2	—

Town.	Pop.	Enls.	Deceased.
ORFORD	64	7	1
OSTERLY	86	4	—
OUSE	363	18	5
OYSTER COVE	125	8	—
PALOONA	69	2	1
PARADISE	165	8	2
PARATTAH	271	15	3
PARKHAM	228	12	3
PATEENA	168	1	—
PATERSONIA	179	5	2
PELHAM	106	3	—
PENGUIN	1124	107	26
PENQUITE	87	1	—
PERTH	614	26	10
PENNA	10	1	—
PELVERATA	31	2	—
PIONEER	656	8	5
PIPER'S RIVER	165	9	1
PLENTY	290	18	1
PONTVILLE	310	10	—
PORTLAND	—	2	—
PREMAYDENA	84	9	1
PRESTON	307	19	4
PYENGANA	252	12	3
QUAMBY'S BROOK	129	1	1
QUEENSTOWN	3659	300	55
RAILTON	446	35	6
RAMENA	140	6	1
RANELAGH	641	42	12
RAVENSWOOD	78	2	—
RECHERCHE	198	7	3
REEDY MARSH	71	2	1
RENISON BELL	106	7	1
RHYNDASTON	146	7	1
RIANA	922	20	2
RICHMOND	539	32	9
RIVERSDALE	12	1	—
RIDGELEY	364	17	6
RIDGEWAY	86	4	2
RISDON	111	4	1
ROCKY CAPE	284	7	1
ROKEBY	145	8	2
ROSEBERRY	352	13	1
ROSEVALE	78	5	—
ROSEVEARS	154	10	3
ROSS	585	45	10
RUNNYMEDE	73	7	1
RINGAROOMA	—	64	11
ST. HELEN'S	485	36	11
ST. LEONARDS	425	32	2
ST. MARY'S	673	48	17
ST. PATRICK'S RIVER	164	12	—
SALT WATER RIVER	53	2	1
SANDFLY	298	19	3

DISTRICT ENLISTMENTS.

Town.	Pop.	Enls.	Deceased.
SANDFORD	145	6	2
SANDHILL	332	5	2
SASSAFRAS	534	20	1
SCAMANDER	113	1	—
SCOTTSDALE	1659	139	29
SEYMOUR	27	3	—
SHEFFIELD	1076	116	24
SHIPWRIGHTS POINT	68	1	—
SIDMOUTH	140	18	5
SISTERS' CREEK	257	8	1
SMITHTON	612	72	13
SNUG	113	4	—
SNAKE PLAINS	37	5	—
SOMERSET	332	38	10
SORELL	416	42	11
SOUTH ARM	89	1	—
SOUTHPORT	177	9	2
SPRING BAY	331	6	?
SPALFORD	59	1	1
SPRENT	253	34	7
SPREYTON	272	18	3
SPRINGFIELD	513	28	3
STANLEY	613	50	8
STAVERTON	161	4	—
STOODLEY	344	2	—
STOWPORT	667	20	4
STRAHAN	839	45	9
STRATHBLANE	83	7	2
STRICKLAND	71	1	1
STONOR	10	3	—
SULPHUR CREEK	169	7	2
SWANSEA	278	33	9
SUMMERLEAS	71	1	—
SWANPORT	50	5	—
SURGES BAY	43	1	1
TANGANAH	—	1	—
TAMAR	208	50	9
TARANA	152	18	2
TAROONA	155	4	—
TEA TREE	253	9	1
THIRLSTANE	126	9	4
TRIABUNNA	238	15	4
TROWUTTA	93	5	2
TULLAH	417	24	5
TULLOCHGORUM	56	1	—
TUNBRIDGE	266	13	3
TUNNACK	348	9	1
TUNNEL	157	8	1
TURNER'S MARSH	270	16	4
TYENNA	115	10	2
ULVERSTONE	2005	243	55
UNDERWOOD	184	8	—
UXBRIDGE	311	8	2
VICTORIA VALLEY	60	2	1

Town.	Pop.	Enls.	Deceased.
WARATAH	1639	100	23
WATTLE HILL	151	1	—
WELDBOROUGH	308	11	2
WESLEY VALE	327	22	6
WESTERN CREEK	123	1	—
WESTBURY	1074	98	24
WHITEFOORD	89	8	—
WHITEFOORD HILLS	151	2	—
WHITE HILLS	135	6	
WHITEMORE	79	5	—
WHYTE RIVER	88	5	—
WILLIAMSFORD	157	2	—
WILMOT	448	27	11
WINKLEIGH	192	9	1
WOODBRIDGE	250	19	4
WOODFORD	—	1	—
WIMMALEAH	58	4	—
WOODSDALE	184	7	1
WOODBURY	74	7	1
WYENNA	51	2	2
WYNYARD	1281	162	26
YOLLA	217	10	1
YORK PLAINS	156	19	3
YOUNG TOWN	106	5	—
ZEEHAN	3951	172	24
Total of men embarked		12,907	
Total of men who were killed in action or died of other causes, including 278 Tasmanians who enlisted in other districts		2,432	

DECORATIONS.

Victoria Cross	11
C.B.	4
C.M.G.	7
M.B.E.	7
O.B.E.	3
D.S.O.	30
D.S.O., with Bar	4
D.F.C.	4
M.C.	100
M.C., with Bar	3
R.R.C., second class	3
D.C.M.	63
D.C.M., with Bar	2
Medaille Militaire	1
Medaille D'Honneur	1
M.M.	359
M.M., with Bar	14
M.S.M.	33
Legion d'Honneur, Croix de Chevalier	3
Croix de Guerre	30
Order de Leopold	1
Cross of Karageorge	1
Bronze Medal for Military Valor	4

Tasmania's
Muster Roll
1914-1918

Nurses

NAME.	REMARKS.	RANK ON DISCHARGE. ENLISTED. SERVICE.
ACRES, L., S.-Nurse, 1 A.G.H.		30/ 6/17 S.-Nurse
ADAMS, D. M., S.-Nurse A.A.N.S.		12/ 9/16 3y 1m, S.-N.
BAILEY, H. J., S.-Nurse A.A.N.S.		18/ 5/17 1y 7m, S.-N.
BAUDINET, D., S.-Nurse A.A.N.S.		15/ 6/15
BERESFORD, R. E., S.-N., A.A.N.S.		29/ 5/17 1y 10m, S.-N.
BLACKETT, A. M., S.-Nurse 2 A.G.H		5/11/15
BONNILY, C., S.-Nurse A.A.N.S.		13/ 6/15 4y 3m, Sister
BURBURY, M. G., Sister A.A.N.S.	3 A.G.H.	14/ 5/15 4y 8m, Sister
BURKE, E. I		
CAMERON, A. C., S.-Nurse A.A.N.S.	M.I.D.	
CAMERON, M. L., Sister 3 A.G.H.		29/11/14 4y 4m, Sister
CARPENTER, C. A., Sister, 2 A.G.H.	3 A.G.H.	20/11/14 4y 6m, Sister
CHAPMAN, J., P.-Nurse A.M.C.N.		15/12/15 3m, Prob.-N.
CHERRY, P. E., Sister A.A.N.S.		18/ 5/17 2y, Sister
COTTON, K. M., S.-Nurse A.A.N.S.		9/11/17
CURTAIN, H. H., S.-Nurse A.A.N.S.		1/ 7/15 9m, S.-N.
CURTAIN, L. M.		
CURTAIN, M. K., S.-Nurse-A.A.N.S.		5/ 5/15 2y 5m, S.-N.
DEACON, C., Sister, A.A.N.S.	M.M.	13/11/14 4y 4m, Sister
DOYLE, A. I., Sister A.A.N.S.		3/ 8/15
DUNPHY, S. T., S.-Nurse, A.A.N.S.		7/11/17
EDWARDS, I. Y. M., S.-N. A.A.N.S.		18/ 5/17
FALKLAND, B. M. B., S.-N. A.A.N.S.		12/ 9/17 1y 8m, S.-N.
FARRINGDON, G., P.-N. A.M.C.N.		15/12/15 4m, A.M.C.N.
FAULKNER, L. E.		
FOLDER, M., S.-Nurse A.A.N.S.		31/ 5/17
FORMAN, K., S.-Nurse		1/ 7/15
FREEMAN, M., Sister, A.A.N.S.		
GALLOWAY, E.		27/ 8/15
GEDDES, M. B., S.-Nurse		
GIBSON, E. M., Sister A.A.N.S.		20/11/14 2y 5m, Sister
GRAF, J. D., S.-Nurse A.A.N.S.		9/ 7/18 1y 4m, S.-N.
GRAF, M. E., S.-Nurse A.A.N.S.		9/ 7/18 1y 4m, S.-N.
GRANT, A. M., S.-Nurse A.A.N.S.		18/12/16 2y 8m, S.-N.
GRUBB, L., S.-Nurse A.A.N.S.		18/ 5/17 2y 2m, S.-N.
HALL, A.	R.R.C.	
HARRIS, L. G., S.-Nurse A.A.N.S.		31/ 5/17
HEEREY, K. M., S.-Nurse A.A.N.S.		19/12/16 2y 3m, S.-N.
HOLMES, A., S.-Nurse		5/ 5/15
HOOD, I., 1 A.G.H.		
HORNSEY, R. M., S.-Nurse, A.A.N.S.		13/12/17 1y 4m, Sister
HUTT, E. V., Sister, A.A.N.S.	R.R.C., 2nd Class.	5/ 5/15 4y 7m, Sister
ILES, A. I., S.-Nurse A.A.N.S.		
JENKINS, V. G., Sister A.A.N.S.		12/ 6/15 4y 1m, Sister
JOLIFFE, B. E.		
KELLY, B., S. Nurse A.A.N.S.		10/11/17 1y 8m, S.-N.
KINDALDIE, V., Masseuse 1 A.G.H.		
KING, A. G., Sister A.A.N.S.		8/ 8/14 3y 4m, Sister
LADE, Z., S.-Nurse A.A.N.S.		12/ 9/16 3y 1m, S.-N.
LANE, N., S.-Nurse A.A.N.S.		6/ 7/18
LAWRENCE, H. R., Sister 1 A.G.H.		21/ 8/15 3y 7m, Sister
LORD, E. I., S.-Nurse A.A.N.S.		5/11/15 Sister
LYNE, L. H., Sister A.H.S.C.D.		1/ 7/15 4y 2m, Sister
MAHONEY, M. A, S.-N, 14 A.G.H.		Sister
MOORE, E., Sister 1 A.G.H.		Sister
MOREY, E. R., S.-Nurse A A.N.S.		
MOSEY, E., S.-Nurse A.A.N.S.	R.R.C. 2nd Class.	
MACAULAY, M. C., S.-N. A.A.N.S.		27/ 8/15 3y 10m, S.-N.
MACDOUGAL, A. A., S.-N. A.A.N.S.		31/ 5/17
M'GUINNESS, I., S.-N. A.A.N.S.		10/11/17 1y 8m, S.-N.
M'KENDRICK, M. D., S.-N. A.A.N.S.		18/ 5/17 2y 2m, S.-N.
M'KENDRICK, R. M., S.-N. A.A.N.S.		
M'KILLOP, M., Sister A.A.N.S.		13/11/14 3y 6m. Sister
NEWITT, G. A., A.A.N.S.		
NICHOLSON, K., Sister, 1 A.G.H.		20/ 4/15 1y, Sister
O'NEILL, A.A.N.S.		
PITMAN, L. M.		
PRIESTLY, A. B.		
RADCLIFFE, H. C., Mas., A.A.N.S.		21/ 8/15 3y 8m, Msuse.
RADCLIFFE, J., Sister A.A.N.S.	M.I.D	11/ 8/14 4y 9m, Sister
SALE, E. H., S.-Nurse A.A.N.S.		9/ 7/18 2y, S.-N.
SKIDMORE, J. G., S.-Nurse A.A.N.S.		19/12/16
SKINNER, R. W. Sister A.A.N.S.		9/ 7/18
STEPHENS, M. E., S.-N. A.A.N.S.		9/11/17
TAYLOR, R. S., Sister A.A.N.S.		16/ 7/15 4y 3m, Sister
TERRY, O. I, S.-Nurse A.A.N.S.		31/ 5/17
THOMPSON, M. E. L., Sister A.A.N.S		17/ 6/15 4y 6m, Sister

NAME.	REMARKS.	RANK ON DISCHARGE. ENLISTED. SERVICE.
TOAN, E. M., S.-Nurse A.A.N.S.		12/ 7/15 2y 2m, S.-N.
TREBILCO, G , Sister A.A.N S.		3/ 1/18 1y 11m, Sister
TUCKER, B. M., Sister A.A.N.S.		19/12/16
TUCKER, E.	R.R.C. 2nd Class.	
WALKER, J. B., S.-Nurse A.A.N.S.		15/ 6/15 3y 11m, Sister
WATSON, L., S.-Nurse A.A.N.S.		31/ 5/17 2y 7m, Sister
WELLARD, E. L., S.-Nurse A.A.N.S.		19/12/16
WHITFELD, L., S.-Nurse A.A.N.S.		7/11/17
WILLIAMS, S. E , S.-Nurse A.A.N.S.		13/12/17
WOODS, H. V., S.-Nurse A.A.N.S.		
YATES, B. F., Masseuse 3 A.A.H.		
YEAMAN, E. W.		

# Officers, N.C.O's. and Men

Reference ✤ { Killed in Action / Died of Wounds / Died on Service }

NAME.	REMARKS.	ENLISTED, SERVICE, RANK ON DISCHARGE.
ABBLITT, H. G., Pte. 12 Bn.	W., 4 D.A.C.	5/ 8/15 3y 8m, Dvr.
ABBLITT, J. W., Spr. 3 Tun. Co.	W.	19/ 1/16 3y 8m, Spr.
ABBOTT, C. N., Pte. 40 Bn.		26/ 5/16.
ABBOTT, D. W., Pte. 3 G.S. Rfts.		12/ 7/18 7m, Pte.
ABBOTT, H. D., Pte. 2 A.G.H.		12/10/14 2y 7m, Pte.
ABBOTT, H., Pte. 12 Bn.	W., 52 B., 51 Bn.	7/10/15 3y 10m, Pte.
ABBOTT, H. B. T., Pte. 26 Bn.		29/ 5/15 1y 2m, Pte.
ABBOTT, N. R., Pte. 26 Bn.	3 W. ✤ 10/8/18.	18/ 8/15 Pte. ✤
ABBOTT, P. De M., Pte. A.C.H.	M.S.M., M.I.D., A.C.H.Q.	3/12/14 4y 7m, S.Q.M.S.
ABEL, A. E., Pte. 15 Bn.	✤ 9/5/15/.	30/ 9/14 Pte. ✤
ABEL, C. A., Pte. 26 Bn.	W., A.C.H.Q.	19/ 6/15 4y 6m, Pte.
ABEL, G. W., Spr. 8 Fd. Co.	W., 15 Fd. Co.	17/ 1/16 3y 8m, Spr.
ABEY, C., Dvr. 4 Co. A.S.C.	M.C., 3 A.S.C.	17/ 8/14 4y 7 m., Capt.
ABREY, L., Pte. 12 Bn.	W., 52 Bn., 13 Fd. Amb., 3 A.G.H.	26/ 8/14 4y 5m, Pte.
ABSOLOM, D. L. C., Pte. 40 Bn.	W. ✤ 13/10/19.	29/ 5/16 Cpl. ✤
ACHESON, T. H., Sgt. 6 F.Art.	3 D.A.C.	31/12/15 3y 10m, Cpl.
ACKLIN, B. H., Spr., 3 Mners.	3 Tunnellers.	11/11/15 3y 7m, Spr.
ACKROYD, C. E., Pte. 40 Bn.	2W. ✤ 8/10/17.	29/ 2/16 Pte. ✤
ACKROYD, F., Pte. 12 Bn.	W., 40 Bn.	15/11/16 2y 4m, Pte.
ACKROYD, J. E., Pte. 40 Bn.	W., M.M.	1/ 3/16 1y 11m, L.-Cpl.
ADAIR, T. C., Pte. 1 A.G.H.		4/ 6/15 2y, L.-Cpl.
ADAMS, A. A., Pte. 40 Bn.	W., 15 Bn.	28/ 2/16 1y 8m, Pte.
ADAMS, A. J., Pte. A.M.C.	66 Bn.	8/ 3/16 1y 9m, Pte.
ADAMS, A. F., Pte. 40 Bn.	W., M.M. ✤ 7/12/18.	12/ 1/15 Sgt. ✤
ADAMS, A. J., Pte. 12 Bn.	M. ✤ 25-28/4/15.	29/ 8/14 Pte. ✤
ADAMS, B. H., Pte. 12 Bn.	✤ 25/7/16.	21/ 1/15 Pte. ✤
ADAMS, C. E., Pte. 26 Bn.	M. ✤ 5/11/16.	26/ 6/15 Pte. ✤
ADAMS, C. J., Pte. 12 Bn.	2W.	25/ 8/14 4y, Pte.
ADAMS, D. D., Gnr. 6 F.A.B.		25/ 9/15 4y 1m, Sgt.
ADAMS, E. B., Gnr. 8 F.A.B.	W., 15 F.A.B., 7 F.A.B.	11/ 8/16 1y 11m, Gnr.
ADAMS, R., 2 Lt., 12 Bn.	✤ 6/5/17.	10/ 1/16 2 Lt. ✤
ADAMS, E. V., Pte. 12 Bn.	✤ 29/7/16.	15/ 7/15 Pte. ✤
ADAMS, H., Pte. 15 Bn.	✤ 9/8/16.	10/ 6/15 Pte. ✤
ADAMS, H. L., Pte. 26 Bn.	W.	15/ 6/15 3y 10m, Cpl.
ADAMS, J. B. P., Pte. 40 Bn.		22/ 1/16 2y 2m, Pte
ADAMS, J. H. C., Pte. Corps Sig.		16/ 2/15 4y 3m, Pte.
ADAMS, J. R., Tpr. 3 L.H.		2/ 9/16 2y 5m, Tpr.
ADAMS, L. W., Gnr. 6 F.A.B.	W., 108 Bty., 23 How. Bde.	10/ 1/16
ADAMS, P. A., Pte. 26 Bn.	✤ 24/5/16.	26/ 2/15 Pte. ✤
ADAMS, S. R., L.-Sgt. 40 Bn.		17/ 1/16 2y 3m, Lt.
ADAMS, T. A., Gnr. 5 F.A.B.	W., 2 D.A.C., 15 Bty.	7/10/15 4y.
ADDISON, S. W., 2 Lt. A.F.C.	O.B.E., M.I.D., 44 Sqn. 69 Sqn. A.F.C.	10/ 7/16 2y 11m, Major.
ADDISON, B. W. Pte. 12 Bn.	✤ 3-5/9/16.	24/ 6/15 Sgt. ✤
ADDISON, P. H., Tpr. 3 L.H.		18/ 4/17 2y 6m, Tpr.
AGNEW, J., Pte. 4 M.G. Co.		26/ 6/16
AGNEW, L. L., Pte., 1 A.C.H.	M.C., 4 Bn.	30/ 6/15 1y 4m, Lt.
AGNEW, I. C. F., Gnr. 18 Fd. Bty	P.O.W., 68 F. Sqn. A.F.C.	13/ 9/15 4y 1m, Lt.
AHEARNE, C. M., Pte. 12 Bn.	W., 24 How. Bde., 10 F.A.B.	17/ 9/14 4y 4m, Dvr.
AHEARNE, F. C., Pte. 12 Bn.	W., 52 Bn.	2/12/15 1y 2m, Pte.
AHERNE, H. E., Pte. 12 Bn.	W., 52 Bn.	15/ 7/15 2y 4m, Cpl.
AHEARN, R. P., Pte. 15 Bn.	✤ 23/9/17.	4/ 1/15 Pte. ✤
AHEARNE, R. C., Dvr. 9 Fd. Bty.		26/ 8/14 4y 5m, Gnr.
AHERNE, W., Pte. 12 Bn.		9/ 9/14 4y 5m, Pte.
AIKIN, C. L., Pte. 12 Bn.	W.	23/ 7/15 3y 10m, Pte.
AIKEN, J. H., Dvr. 6 F.A.Bde.	M.M., 2 D.A.C., 4 F.A.B., 6 F.A.B. 17 Bty	22/ 9/15 3y 3m, Fitter.
AIKEN, M. T., Pte. A.M.C.	9 F. Amb.	24/ 2/16 3y 8m, Pte.
AINSWORTHY, H R., Pte. 12 Bn.	1 Div. Sig Co.	20/ 1/15 4y 4m, Sgt.
AINSWORTH, L., Dvr. 9 Fd. Bty.		22/ 8/14 4y 8m, Lt.
AIREY, E. M., Pte. 40 Bn.	2W.	4/ 4/16 3y 5m, C.S.M.
AIREY, H. E., Gnr. 6 F.A.B.	3 D.A.C., 30 Fd. Bty.	29/ 2/16 3y 8m, Dvr.
AIREY, J H., Gnr. 6 F.A.B	W., 23 How. Bty.	11/ 1/16 3y 5m, Gnr.
AIREY, R J., Pte. 40 Bn.	W.	26/ 8/16 1y 1m, L.-Cpl.
AIREY, T. T., Pte. 40 Bn.	W.	6/12/16 3y, Pte.
AIREY, W. J., Pte. 12 Bn.	✤ 5-8/5/17.	8/ 8/16 Pte. ✤
AIREY, W. R. R. T., Pte. 12 Bn.	✤ 19-22/8/16.	22/ 7/15 Pte. ✤
AITKEN, V., Pte. 12 Bn.	40 Bn.	7/ 2/18 1y 8m, Pte.
AJAR, J., M.W. Munitions.		
ALBURY, A. A., Pte. 26 Bn.	12 Bn. ✤ 19-22/8/16.	18/ 8/15 Pte. ✤

222 TASMANIA'S WAR RECORD, 1914-1918

NAME.	REMARKS.	RANK ON DISCHARGE. ENLISTED. SERVICE.
ALBURY, T. W., Spr. 6 Fd. Co.	69 Bn., 6 F. Co. ✤ 9/4/18.	1/ 9/15 Spr. ✤
ALCOCK, H., Pte. 12 Bn.	✤ 6-10/4/17.	26/ 6/16 Pte. ✤
ALCOCK, R. T., Tpr. 3 L.H.		24/ 8/15 4y 1m, Cpl.
ALEXANDER, A., Dvr. Fd. Bty.		2/ 2/15 4y 6m, Dvr.
ALEXANDER, B. D., Sgt. 3 L.H.	✤ 9/8/16.	2/ 9/15 Sgt. ✤
ALEXANDER, B., Pte. 40 Bn.	W.	9/ 2/16 2y 3m, Pte.
ALEXANDER, C., Pte. 40 Bn.	W.	9/ 2/16 2y 8m, Pte.
ALEXANDER, D. D., Pte. 12 Bn.	40 Bn.	18/ 9/14 3y 10m, Lt.
ALEXANDER, E. A., Pte. 15 Bn.	W., 47 Bn.	3/ 8/15 2y, Pte.
ALEXANDER, E., Pte. 40 Bn.	W.	9/ 2/16 2y 9m, Pte.
ALEXANDER, E., Pte. Tul Co.		7/ 8/16.
ALEXANDER, F. B., Pte. 15 Bn.	W., 4 Fd. Amb.,	12/ 8/15
ALEXANDER, H., Pte. 15 Bn.	M.M.	24/ 9/14 3y 11m, Pte.
ALEXANDER, J., Cpl. 15 Bn.	40 Bn.	8/ 1/15 4y 4m, Cpl.
ALEXANDER, L., Pte. 3 A.G.H.		31/ 7/16 2y 5m, Pte.
ALEXANDER, L. E., Gnr. D.A.C.		8/ 9/15
ALEXANDER, M. R., Pte. 40 Bn.	W.	16/ 5/16 2y 10m, Pte.
ALEXANDER, R. V., Cpl. 12 Bn.		26/ 7/15 4y 4m, Pte.
ALEXANDER, T. E., Pte. 12 Bn.		24/ 8/15
ALEXANDER, W., Pte. 12 Bn.	W., 69 Bn., 12 Bn.	29/ 8/14
ALEXANDER, W. H., Pte. 12 Bn.	2W.	12/ 7/16 3y 2m, Pte.
ALFORD, B. W., Gnr. 3 F.A.B.	W., 103 How. Bty.	15/ 9/15 3y 11m, Cpl.
ALFORD, S. J., Pte. 40 Bn.	3W.	9/ 5/16 3y, Pte.
ALLFORD, M. R., Pte. 40 Bn.		7/ 3/16 3y 3m, Pte.
ALLAN, F. J., Gnr. D.A.C.		3/ 9/15
ALLAN, F. L., Pte. 26 Bn.	2W., 69 Bn., 26 Bn.	2/ 4/15 4y. 7m. Pte.
ALLAN, H. J.		
ALLAN, H. L., Pte. 1 G.S.R.	112 How. Bty.	4/ 3/18 1y 7m, Gnr.
ALLAN, W. J., Pte. 15 Bn.		30/ 6/15 3y 10m, Pte.
ALLANBY, J. R., Pte. 40 Bn.	W., 51 Bn.	2/ 2/16 3y 7m, Pte.
ALLEN, B. A., Pte. Wireless.		1/ 2/18 10m, Pte.
ALLEN, C. T., Pte. A.M.C.	8 Fd. Amb.	5/ 1/16 3y 1m, Pte.
ALLEN, Ch. Alb., Spr. 8 Fd. Co.	14 Fd. Co.	25/ 1/16 3y 8m, 2 Cpl.
ALLEN, Ch. Art., Dvr. 3 F.A.B.		28/12/14 2y 8m, Dvr.
ALLEN, C W., Pte. 40 Bn.		1/12/16 1y 6m, Pte.
ALLEN, C. J., Pte. 12 Bn.		26/ 7/15 4y 1m, Sgt.
ALLEN, D. H., Pte. 12 Bn.	2W., 52 Bn., M.M. ✤ 26/4/18.	20/ 8/14 Sgt. ✤
ALLEN, E. R., Pte. 40 Bn.		30/ 3/16 1y 8m, Pte.
ALLEN, Edwin, Pte. 40 Bn.	✤ 28/7/17.	22/ 2/16 Pte. ✤
ALLEN, G. F., Tpr. 3 L.H.		16/ 4/17 7m, Tpr.
ALLEN, H., Dvr. Art.	C de G. (Belgian).	1/12/14 4y 5m, Dvr.
ALLEN, H. O., Pte. 4 M.G. Co.	15 Bn.	16/ 3/17 2y. 7m. Pte.
ALLEN, James, Pte 12 Bn.	52 Bn., 51 Bn.	1/8/15 4y, Cpl.
ALLEN, James, Pte. 26 Bn.	2W.	16/ 8/15 2y 10m, Pte.
ALLEN, Leslie, Pte. 12 Bn.	✤ 3-5/9/16.	17/11/15 Pte. ✤
ALLEN, L. R., Spr. Wireless U.	4 D.S.C.	2/11/17 1y 11m, Spr.
ALLEN, L. O., Spr. 5 Miners.	Tunn. Co.	7/ 3/16 1y 2m, Spr.
ALLEN, Paul, Pte. 40 Bn.	✤ 3/4/17.	1/ 3/16 Pte. ✤
ALLEN, R. S., Pte. 26 Bn.	12 Bn. ✤ 23/7/16.	11/8/15 Pte. ✤
ALLEN, Robert, Gnr. 1 F.A.B.	W., 9th Bty., 3 F.A.B.	14/ 9/14 2y 1m, Gnr.
ALLEN, Wesley, Pte. 40 Bn.		17/10/16 2y 6m, L.-Cpl.
ALLEN, William, Cpl. 3 L.H.		18/ 8/14
ALLEN, W. A., Sgt. 26 Bn.	W., 52 Bn.	20/ 9/15 3y 8m, Pte.
ALLENDER, L. T., Pte. 26 Bn.		11/ 8/15 1y, Pte.
ALLESTER, E. M., Capt. A.C.C.H.	1 A.G.H.	4/ 8/15
ALLEY, H. C., M.W.		
ALMOND, A. A., Pte. 12 Bn.	52 Bn	3/ 1/16 1y 8m, Pte.
ALMOND, Alg. Ather., Cpl. 12 Bn	3W.	20/ 8/14 3y 5m, Sgt.
ALMOND, Ash. Arn., Tptr 3 F.A.B	2W.	26/ 8/14 4y 6m, Bdr.
ALSTON, E. C., Pte. 12 Bn.		12/ 9/14 1y 8m, Cpl.
AMER, H G., Pte. 40 Bn.	W.	28/ 9/16 2y 6m, Pte.
AMIGUET, A. G., Pte. 40 Bn		21/ 1/16 3y 2m, Pte.
AMIGUET, F. A., Pte. 12 Bn.	2W.	30/ 8/16
AMOS, M., Pte. 12 Bn.	W. ✤ 1/5/18.	6/ 9/16 Pte. ✤
AMOS, R. McG., Pte. A.F.C.	69 F. Sqn., 3 Sqn. A.F.C.	18/10/16 2y 9m, 1 A.M.
ANDERSON, A. E., Pte. 40 Bn.		17/10/16 1y 8m, Pte.
ANDERSON, A. A., Pte. 1 A.G.H.		31/ 5/15 2y 11m, Pte.
ANDERSON, A., P. 40 Bn	W.	23/ 5/16
ANDERSON, A. F. S., Pte 4 M.G. Co		4/ 8/16 1y 5m, Pte.
ANDERSON, A. C., Cpl. 3 G.S.R.		3/ 6/18
ANDERSON, A. F. T. 1 G.S.A.MD.		9/ 5/18 1y 3m, Tpr.
ANDERSON, A. H., Cpl. 12 B.		2/ 4/16
ANDERSON, A. D., Pte. 40 Bn.	W., 69 Bn., 40 Bn.	18/ 2/16 3y. 4m. Pte.
ANDERSON, A., Pte. 40 Bn.	W.	8/ 3/16 1y 9m, Pte.
ANDERSON, A. L., Pte. 12 Bn.	✤ 25-29/4/15.	24/ 8/14 Pte. ✤
ANDERSON, A. G., Pte. 40 Bn.	3W.	1/ 4/16 3y 8m, Pte.
ANDERSON, B., Pte. 26 Bn.	52 Bn. ✤ 3-4/9/16.	20/ 7/15 Pte. ✤
ANDERSON, B. J. R., Pte. 26 Bn.	52 Bn. ✤ 4/9/16.	16/ 8/15 Pte. ✤
ANDERSON, E., Pte. 12 Bn.	2W., 52 Bn., 51 Bn.	6/10/14 4y 5m, Pte.
ANDERSON, F., Pte. 12 Bn.	W.	8/ 8/16
ANDERSON, F., Pte. T.M.B.		
ANDERSON, F. W., Pte. 26 Bn.	12 Bn ✤ 23/7/16.	1/ 8/15 Pte. ✤
ANDERSON, A. C., Lt. 26 Bn.	M.I.D.	24/ 8/15 2y 10m, Capt.
ANDERSON, K. H., Lt. 15 Bn.	✤ 14/6/15.	Lt. ✤
ANDERSON, Geo., Pte. 12 Bn.	✤ 5-8/5/17.	13/ 7/15 Pte. ✤

TASMANIA'S MUSTER ROLL.

NAME.	REMARKS.	RANK ON DISCHARGE. ENLISTED. SERVICE.
ANDERSON, George, Pte. 15 Bn.	5 Fd. Bky.	23/ 9/14 5y. Pte.
ANDERSON, G. A., Pte. Tnl. Co.		9/ 3/17
ANDERSON, G. H., Sig. 12 Bn.	4 Pn. Bn., 5 Pnr. Bn.	13/ 7/15 4y 5m, Lt.
ANDERSON, G. U., Cpl. 26 Bn.	3W.	16/ 6/15 Sgt.
ANDERSON, H. E., Pte. 26 Bn.	3W., 4 M.G. Co., 26 Bn.	3/ 3/15 4y 5m, Pte.
ANDERSON, J., Tpr. 3 L.H.		24/ 7/15 1y 7m, Tpr.
ANDERSON, J. A., Pte. 12 Bn.	W., 52 Bn., 51 Bn.	13/ 7/15 3y 11m, Pte.
ANDERSON, J. H., Pte. 40 Bn.	W., 51 Bn.	7/10/15 2y 5m, Pte.
ANDERSON, J., Pte. 12 B.	W.	6/10/15 4y, Pte.
ANDERSON, J. I., Sgt. 3 Fd. Amb.	2 M.I.D., 13 Fd. Amb.	20/ 8/14 4y 10m, Capt.
ANDERSON, J. H., Gnr. Fd. Art.		4/12/15
ANDERSON, L. J., Pte. 40 Bn.		5/ 2/16 3y 2m, Pte.
ANDERSON, O. R., Pte. 40 Bn.	W.	29/ 3/16
ANDERSON, P., Pte. 12 Bn.	W., 40 Bn.	23/10/16 2y 8m, Pte.
ANDERSON, R. R., Gnr. 6 F.A.B.	106 Bty. A.F.A.	31/ 1/16 3y 9m, Dvr.
ANDERSON, S. E., Pte. 40 Bn.		21/ 7/17
ANDERSON, S. H., Pte. 12 Bn.	W.	27/10/15 2y 2m, Pte.
ANDERSON, Thomas, Pte. 12 Bn.	W., M.M., 52 Bn., 51 Bn.	18/ 1/16 3y 9m, L.-Cpl.
ANDERSON, V. R., Pte. 12 B. (SALVADO, Victor)	W. (Assumed name. Correct one, Victor Salvado.)	26/ 8/14 3y 3m, Cpl.
ANDERSON, W., Pte. 40 Bn.	10 L.T.M. Bty., 40 Bn.	10/ 7/16 2y 7m, Pte.
ANDERSON, W. H., Spr. 3 Miners.	W., 3 Tnl. Co.	24/ 9/15 3y 11m, Spr.
ANDERSON, W., Pte. 26 Bn.		20/ 9/15
ALLIE, A. V., Tpr. 3 L.H.		21/ 8/17 1y 3m, Tpr.
ALLISON, A. F. W., Pte. Rmts.		5/10/15 1y 2m, Tpr.
ALLISON, F. T., L.-Cpl. 1 G.S.R.		15/10/17 1y 4m, Pte.
ALLISON, F. V., Cpl. 12 Bn.	✣ 29/5/15.	19/ 8/14 Cpl. ✣
ALLISON, H., Pte. 26 Bn.	2W.	17/ 3/15 4y 5m, Pte.
ALLISON, N. W., Pte. Fd. Amb.	W., 12 Bn., 3 Fd. Co., M.M. ✣ 3/2/18.	18/ 8/14 Spr. ✣
ALLISON, S. P., Pte. 12 Bn.	2W.	2/ 5/16 3y 1m, Pte.
ALLISON, V. H., Spr. 3 Fd. Co.	W.	20/ 8/14 4y 8m, 2 Cpl.
ALLOM, O. B., Pte. 15 Bn.	✣ 7/8/15.	23/ 9/14 Pte. ✣
ALLSEBROOK, G., Pte. 1 A.C.H.	✣ 20/6/15.	21/ 9/14 Pte. ✣
ALLWOOD, G. H., Gnr. 8 F.A.B.	8 B.A.C., 31 Bty.	22/10/15 4y, Dvr.
ALLWRIGHT, R. C., Tpr., 3 L.H.		9/ 7/15 4y 4m, Tpr.
ALLWRIGHT, S. H. L., L.-Cpl. 40 Bn.	M.I.D.	3/ 4/16 2y 8m, Lt.
ALLWRIGHT, S. T., Pte. 15 Bn.		21/ 9/14 3y 3m, L.-Cpl.
ANDREW, B. J., Lt. 12 Bn.		1/ 7/15 3y 11m, Tl Maj.
ANDREWS, A. R., Pte. 12 Bn.	✣ 25/7/16.	22/ 9/15 Pte. ✣
ANDREWS, B. D., Gnr. 6 F.A.B.	W.	20/ 8/15 2y 10m, Gnr.
ANDREWS, C. J., Pte. 12 Bn.	✣ 6-10/4/17.	18/ 4/16 Pte. ✣
ANDREWS, E. C., Pte. 12 Bn.	69 Bn., 12 Bn.	18/ 4/16 3y 5m, Pte.
ANDREWS, H., Pte. 12 Bn.	2 W., 57 Bn., 58 Bn.	9/ 9/15 2y 5m, Pte.
ANDREWS, J. C., Gnr. Fd. Art.		17/ 3/16
ANDREW, H. C., 1 A.M. A.F.C.	3 Sqn. A.F.C.	11/ 9/16 2y 11m, 1 A.M.
ANDREWS, H., Pte. 12 Bn.		27/11/17 1y 11m, Pte.
ANDREW, J., Pte. 26 Bn.		15/ 7/15
ANDREWS, J. P., Gnr. Fd. Art.		22/ 3/17
ANDREWS, P. F., Cpl. 11 F.A.B.	W., 43 Fd. Bty.	27/ 9/15 3y 7m, Cpl.
ANDREWS, R. H., Pte. 15 Bn.	W., P.O.W.	28/ 1/15 4y 5m, Pte.
ANDREWS, S., Pte. 15 Bn		10/ 6/15 3y, Pte.
ANDREWS, S. J. P., Pte. 40 Bn.	3W.	7/10/16 2y 5m, Pte.
ANDREWS, S. E., Dvr. 3 D.A.C.		1/ 2/16
ANDREWS, T. H., Pte. 40 Bn.	12 Bn.	5/10/16 2y 11m, Pte.
ANDREWS, W., Pte. 26 Bn.	2W., 12 Bn.	4/ 9/15 4y, Pte.
ANDREWS, W. J. T., Pte. 26 Bn.	✣ 5/8/16.	3/ 8/15 Pte. ✣
ANDERTON, A. E., Tptr. 3 F.C.		19/ 8/14 7m, Pte.
ANDREE, G. M., Pte. 26 Bn.		17/ 8/15 11m, Pte.
ANDREWARTHA, T., Spr 6 F.C.	31 Bn.	31/ 8/15 3y 11m, Spr.
ANDREWARTHA, W. H., Cpl 15 Bn	47 Bn. ✣ 5/3/16.	23/10/16
ANGUS, J., Spr. Tnl.	13 Fd. Co.	13/ 8/15 Sgt. ✣
ANNEAR, D., Pte. 3 Cyclists.		17/ 4/16
ANSELL, A. C., Pte. 12 Bn.	W.	18/10/16 Pte. ✣
ANSELL, C. N., Pte. 4 M.G. Co.	✣ 23/4/18.	13/ 2/17
ANSTIE, J. F., Pte. 3 L.H.	O.S.	6/ 6/17
ANTHONY, R S., Pte. 12 Bn.	W.	19/10/15 2y 9m, Gnr.
APPLEBEE, G. H., Pte. 12 Bn.		15/ 6/16 1y 9m, Pte.
APPLEBY, A. W. F., Dvr. 26 Bn.	24 How. Bde. 10 F.A.B., 4 Div Arty. 37 B, W.	13/ 4/15
APPLEBY, A. H., 2 Lt. 12 Bn.	✣ 6/5/17.	18/ 8/15 3y 9m, Pte.
APPELBEE, L. J., Pte. 15 Bn.	W., 47 Bn., 4 Pnr. Bn.	19/ 5/15 Capt. ✣
APPLEBY, R., Pte. 12 Bn.	✣ 6-10/4/17.	8/12/15 Pte. ✣
APPLEBY, R. J., Pte. 12 Bn.	2 W.	23/10/16
APPLEBY, W. W., Pte. 40 Bn.	✣ 4/12/16.	29/ 2/16 Pte. ✣
APPELDORFF, W. G., Tpr. 3 L.H.		12/11/17 1y 10m, Tpr.
APPLEYARD, W. E., Gr. 3 F.A.B.		16/ 9/14 4y 5m, Dvr.
APTED, E. E., Pte. 1 G.S.R.	46 Fd. Bty.	17/ 1/18 1y 9m, Gnr.
APTHORPE, A. E., Dvr. M.T.		22/ 9/16 2y 6m, M. Dr.
ARAM, C., Pte. 12 Bn.	24 How. Bde., 11 F.A.B.	2/12/15 3y 4m, Gnr.
ARCHBOLD, H. A., Sgt. 12 Bn.	2W., 51 Bn.	25/ 1/15 3y 8m, C.S.M.?
ARCHER, A., Pte. 40th Bn.	W.	22/ 5/16 1y 8m, Pte.
ARCHER, A. G., Sgt. 15 Bn.	2W., P.O.W.	1/10/14 4y 10m, Sgt.
ARCHER, A. J., Pte. 12 Bn.		29/ 6/17

TASMANIA'S WAR RECORD, 1914-1918

NAME.	REMARKS.	RANK ON DISCHARGE. ENLISTED, SERVICE.
ARCHER, B. J., Pte. 12 Bn.		9/ 9/15 2y 4m, Pte.
ARCHER, C. L., 2 A.M. A.F.C.	W.	4/ 4/18 1y 4m, 2 A.M.
ARCHER, E. N., Tpr. 3 L.H.		7/ 1/18 1y 7m, Tpr.
ARCHER, F. S., Pte. 40 Bn.	15 Bn., P.O.W.	28/ 3/16 3y 2m, Pte.
ARCHER, F., Pte. 15 Bn.	47 Bn. ✠10/8/16.	31/ 8/15 Pte. ✠
ARCHER, F., Pte. 12 Bn.	W., 3 M.G. Co.	22/ 8/14 5y, Lt.
ARCHER, G. R. D., Pte. 12 Bn.	✠ 6-10/4/17.	31/8/16 Pte. ✠
ARCHER, H. R., Pte. 12 Bn.	W.	2/ 9/16 1y 11m, Pte.
ARCHER, J. E., Gnr. 6 F.A.B.	109 Bty., 23 How. Bde. 7 F.A.B.	8/ 9/15 4y, Dvr.
ARCHER, J. N., Tpr. 3 L.H.		7/ 9/17 1y 11m, Tpr.
ARCHER, B. F., Pte. 26 Bn.	4 M.G. Co.	19/ 7/15 4y 1m, L.-Cpl.
ARCHLE, B. D., Pte. 40 Bn.	✠ 7/6/17.	16/ 5/16 Pte. ✠
ARMSON, G., Chaplain (4th class), 12 Inf. Bde. H.Q.		4/ 4/16 2y 10m, Ch. 3 class
ARKLEY, W. J., Pte. 2 G.S.R.	R.B.A.A.	19/ 4/18 1y 4m, Gnr.
ARMITAGE, H. A., Pte. 12 Bn.	W., M.M., 52 Bn., 15 Bn.	15/ 7/15 4y 1m, Sgt.
ARMITAGE, R. M., Cpl. 3 Fd. Amb.	13 Fd. Amb., 47 Bn. ✠ 11/4/17.	20/ 8/14 2 Lt. ✠
ARMITAGE, V. R., Cpl. 12 Bn.	2W., 26 Bn., 12 Bn.	29/ 7/15 4y 1m, Pte.
ARMSTRONG, C. H., Pte. 40 Bn.	W., Railway Unit, 49 Bn.	27/ 4/16 1y 11m, Pte.
ARMSTRONG, C., Pte. 15 Bn.		25/ 9/14 4y 5m, Sgt.
ARMSTRONG, D., Pte. 12 Bn.	52 Bn. ✠ 4/9/16.	15/ 7/15 Pte. ✠
ARMSTRONG, E. J., Pte. 40 Bn.	W., 49 Bn. ✠ 25/4/18.	3/ 5/16 Pte. ✠
ARMSTRONG, F., Pte. 26 Bn.	✠ 6/8/15.	23/ 2/15 Pte. ✠
ARMSTRONG, G., Spr. Tnl. Co.	W.	13/ 3/17
ARMSTRONG, G. A., Pte. 12 Bn.	2 W.	1/ 9/16
ARMSTRONG, H., Pte. 26 Bn.	✠ 5/8/16.	2/ 4/15 Pte. ✠
ARMSTRONG, J. F., Cpl. 12 Bn.	✠ 5-8/5/17.	31/ 8/16 Cpl. ✠
ARMSTRONG, J. S., Pte. 3 G.S.R.	12 Bn.	20/ 5/18 1y 1m, Pte.
ARMSTRONG, L. R., Pte. 12 Bn.	2W., 52 Bn., 49 Bn.	1/ 8/15 4y 2m, Lt.
ARMSTRONG, M. W., Spr. 5 Min.	W., 2 Tnl. Co., 5 Tnl. Co.	11/ 1/16 3y 2m, Spr.
ARMSTRONG, P. L., Pte. 12 Bn.		1/ 8/15 1y, Pte.
ARMSTRONG, R., Pte. 40 Bn.		7/ 3/16 3y 6m, Pte.
ARMSTRONG, S. B., Pte. 26 Bn.	W.	14/ 9/15 2y 6m, Pte.
ARMSTRONG, S. R., Pte. 40 Bn.	W. ✠ 1/9/18.	8/ 2/16 Pte. ✠
ARMSTRONG, T. L., Tpr. 5 G.S.R.	3 L.H. Regt.	13/ 6/18 1y 2m, Tpr.
ARMSTRONG, W. P., Tpr. 3 L.H.		17/ 8/14 4y 8m, S.S.M.
ARNOL, C. S., Pte. 12 Bn.	W.	11/ 9/16 2y 6m, Pte.
ARNOL, C. B., Pte. 40 Bn.		2/10/16 1y 5m, L.-Sgt.
ARNOL, G. M., Pte. 40 Bn.	2W. ✠ 12/4/18.	30/ 3/16 Cpl. ✠
ARNOL, M., Pte. 12 Bn.	40 Bn.	25/ 2/18 1y 9m, Pte.
ARNOLD, A. H., Pte. 12 Bn.		16/ 6/16 2y 6m, Pte.
ARNOLD, C. C. H., Pte. 26 Bn.	3W., 12 Bn.	10/8/15 4y 1m, Pte.
ARNOLD, D. R., Spr. Miners.	W.	19 2/16
ARNOLD, E. A., Pte. 12 Bn.	2 W.	1/ 5/16 2y 1m, Pte.
ARNOLD, J. T., Cpl. 40 Bn.	W.	2/ 3/16 8m, Cpl.
ARNOLD, J. M., Sgt. 7 Fd. Amb.	3 Fd. Amb.	16/ 3/15 4y 4m, Dvr.
ARNOLD, R. J., Pte. 15 Bn.	M., P.O.W.	18/ 2/15 4y 6m, Pte.
ARNOL, T. G., Tpr. 3 L.H.		28/ 3/17 2y 3m, Tpr.
ARNOLD, W. L., Pte. 12 Bn.	✠ 8/4/17.	26/ 6/15 Pte. ✠
ARNOTT, J. A., Pte. 15 Bn.	✠ 4/7/15.	24/11/14 Pte. ✠
ARNOTT, L. J. H., Pte. 40 Bn.	2 A.G.H. ✠ 31/8/18.	17/ 2/16 Pte. ✠
ARTHUR, G., Tpr. 3 L.H.		7/ 9/17 2y 2m, Tpr.
ARTHUR, F. A. R., Pte. A.A.M.C.	4 D.A. Sub. Park, 1 M.T. Co., 6 M.T. Co.	3/11/15 3y 11m, L.-Cpl.
ARTHUR, H. L., Dvr. B.A.C.	W., M.M.	17/10/14 Dvr.
ARTHUR, L. J. T., Pte. 12 Bn.	✠ 23/7/16.	1/ 7/15 Pte. ✠
ARTIS, C. G., Pte. 40 Bn.	W.	25/ 2/16 3y 3m, Pte.
ASHTON, E. W., Pte. 26 Bn.	12 Bn. ✠ 23/7/16.	1/ 9/15 Pte. ✠
ASHTON, H. J., Pte. 4 M.G. Co.	W., 12 Bn.	5/ 2/17 2y 1m, Pte.
ASHWOOD, J., Spr. Miners.	W., 3 Tnl.	25/11/15 3y 3m, Spr.
ASKEY, C. B. S., Pte. 12 Bn.		9/10/15 4y, Pte.
ASLEY, A. H., Pte. 3 G.S.R.	12 Bn.	13/ 7/18 11m, Pte.
ASLEY, C. S., Pte. 12 Bn.	W., 40 Bn.	26/ 6/17 1y 10m, Pte.
ASLEY, C. S., Pte. Remounts.		5/10/15 8m, Pte.
ASPINALL, P. W., 2 Lt. 12 Bn.		16/ 1/15 3y 3m, Lt.
ASTLEY, J. W., Gnr. A.F.A.	W., 2 D.A.C.	28/ 2/16 2y 4m, Dvr.
ASPINALL, L. J., W.O. 1 A.C.H.		1/10/14 4y 6m, Capt.
ATHERTON, J., Pte. 1 A.C.C.H.		27/ 7/15 1y 1m, Pte.
ATHERTON, J. C., Pte. 12 Bn.	W.	29/ 8/14 2y 5m, Pte.
ATHERTON, S. A., Pte. 12 Bn.	W.	5/ 8/15 2y 11m, Cpl.
ATKINS, A. S., Sgt. 40 Bn.	✠ 4/10/17.	9/ 6/16 Sgt. ✠
ATKINS, C. N., Capt. A.M.C.		7/10/14 1y 6m, Capt.
ATKINS, F. J., Pte. 15 Bn.		28/ 7/15 1y 1m, Pte.
ATKINS, G. E., Pte. 12 Bn.	✠ 19-22/8/16.	30/ 8/15 Pte. ✠
ATKINS, N. J., Pte. 1 G.S.R.	4 D.A.C.	14/ 3/18 1y 7m, Gnr.
ATKINS, R. T., Pte. 40 Bn.	5 M.G. Bn.	28/ 9/18 3y, Pte.
ATKINS, R. W., Pte. 12 Bn.		18/ 5/16 2y 11m, Pte.
ATKINS, V. R., Pte. 26 Bn.	12 Bn.	4/ 8/15 2y 11m, Pte.
ATKINS, W. J., Pte. 12 Bn.	W. ✠ 24/7/16.	2/ 9/14 Sgt. ✠
ATKINSON, A. J., Pte. 12 Bn.	W.	13/ 1/15 3y 3m, Lt.
ATKINSON, B. H. A., Pte. 12 Bn.	W., 4 Pnrs.	12/12/14 4y 10m, Pte.
ATKINSON, B. G., Gnr. 25 F.A.B.	3 F.A.B.	17/10/16 2y 11m, Dvr.
ATKINSON, F. W., Cpl. Art.	3 D.A.C.	27/ 3/16 2y 1m, Gnr.

TASMANIA'S MUSTER ROLL.

NAME.	REMARKS.	RANK ON DISCHARGE. ENLISTED, SERVICE.
ATKINSON, G. R., Dvr. 3 Fd. Co.	13 F.C.E.	26/ 7/15 4y, Dvr.
ATKINSON, L., Pte. 15 Bn.		24/ 9/14 1y 5m, Pte.
ATKINSON, R., Tpr. 3 L.H.	W., Art.	21/ 8/14 4y 6m, Gnr.
ATKINSON, R. L. A. B., Spr. 8 Eng	16 Engs., 1 Army Troop Co. Engrs.	11/ 8/15 4y, Dvr.
ATKINSON, T. C., Pte. 15 Bn.	✠ 10/5/15.	19/ 9/14 Pte. ✠
ATKINSON, P. O., Pte 40 Bn.		4/ 6/16 3y 6m, Pte.
ATKINSON, W., Dvr. 3 F.A.B.	9 Bty.	16/12/14 2y 9m, Dvr.
ATTFIELD, A., Pte. 40 Bn.		11/11/14 1y 11m, Pte.
ATLEY, C. W., Dvr. 4 A.S.C.		17/ 8/14 4y 5m, Dvr.
ATWELL, F. H., Pte. 12 Bn.	✠26/7/16.	28/ 5/15 Pte. ✠
ATWELL, R., Pte. 40 Bn.	✠ 17/2/17.	16/5/16 Pte. ✠
ATWELL, T. W., Pte. 12 Bn.	W.	30/11/14 1y 11m, Pte.
AUDLEY, A. N., Gnr. 3 F.A.B.	W., 4 Div. Arty.	26/ 8/14 4y 10m, Lt.
AULICH, G. L., Spr. Miners.	2 Tnl. Co.	7/ 3/16
AULICH, W. F., Cpl. 12 Bn.	2 W.	19/ 8/15 2y 9m, Pte.
AUSTIN, A. A., Pte. 3 G.|S.R.		6/ 8/18 1y 4m, Pte.
AUSTIN, E. T., Pte. 40 Bn.	W.	2/ 5/16 2y 11m, L.-Cpl.
AUSTIN, H. W., Spr., 3 Fd. Co.	W. M.M., 3 A.L.T., M.B.	15/ 6/15 4y 7m, Lt.
AUSTIN, J. H., Gnr. D.A.C.	W.	15/ 9/15 3y 9m, Dvr.
AUSTIN, J. W., Pte. 40 Bn.	W. ✠ 13/10/17.	16/ 3/16 Pte. ✠
AUSTIN, N., Pte. 3 G.S.R.		16/ 5/18 1y, Pte.
AUSTIN, T., Pte. 40 Bn.	W. ✠ 28/11/17.	16/ 3/16 Pte. ✠
AUSTIN, T. A., Pte. 12 Bn.		2/11/15 1y 7m, Pte.
AUSTIN, W. J., Pte. 12 Bn.		2/12/15
AVERY, A., Pte. 26 Bn.	2 W.	20/ 7/15 3y 9m, Pte.
AVERY, D. R., Pte. 15 Bn.	W.	27/ 7/15 4y 1m, Sgt.
AVERY, E. A., Pte. 15 Bn.	W., 47 Bn.	27/ 8/15 1y 7m, Pte.
AVERY, J. W., Pte. 40 Bn.		3/10/16 1y 3m, Pte
AXTON, A., Pte. 26 Bn.	✠ 5/8/16.	15/ 6/15 Pte. ✠
AXTON, L., Dvr. 3 F.A.B.		26/ 8/14 4y 5m, Dvr.
AXTON, L. C., Gnr. 3 F.A.B.		15/ 6/15 4y 2m, Dvr.
AYERS, W. B., Pte. 15 Bn	✠ 9/5/15.	22/ 9/14 Pte. ✠
AYLETT, C., Pte. 12 Bn.	W.	19/ 8/14, 5y 2m, Pte.
AYLETT, C., Pte. 3 G.S.R.	12 Bn.	2/ 2/18 1y 9m, Pte.
AYLETT, L., Pte. 40 Bn.	12 Bn.	17/ 9/16 3y, Pte.
AYERS, F. J., Pte. 12 Bn.	W.	21/ 5/17 2y 4m, Pte.
AYRES, G. W., Pte. 12 Bn.	40 Bn.	23/10/16 3y, Pte.
AYRES, R., Pte. 12 Bn.		14/10/16
AYTON, T., Pte. 26 Bn.		28/ 7/15
BACKHOUSE, J. V., Pte. 12 Bn.	W.	3/ 5/16 1y 11m, Pte.
BACKHOUSE, T. J., Pte. 1 A.C.C.S		24/11/14 4y 9m, Pte.
BACON, D., Pte. 12 Bn.		28/ 8/14 1y 9m, Pte.
BACON, J. H., Pte. 40 Bn.	2 W.	2/ 3/16 3y, Pte.
BACON, J. H., Mun. Worker.		
BACON, R. C., Gnr. 6 F.A.B.	W. 5 F.A.B.	3/11/15 2y 7m, Gnr.
BADCOCK, A. H., Pte. 12 Bn.	2W., 40 Bn.	19/10/16 2y 10m, Pte.
BADCOCK, E. E., Tpr. 3 L.H.	1 L.H., M.G. Sqdn.	26/ 7/15 4y 2m, L.-Cpl.
BADCOCK, L. M., Pte. 12 Bn.	W., 40 Bn.	4/ 4/16 3y 4m, L.-Cpl.
BADCOCK, P. C., Pte. 12 Bn.	W.	7/ 9/15 4y, Pte.
BADCOCK, R., Pte. 26 Bn.	W., P.O.W.	17/ 6/15 3y 5m, Pte.
BADCOCK, W., Pte. 12 Bn.	✠ 25/2/17.	2/ 5/16 Pte. ✠
BADKIN, J. J., Pte. 26 Bn.	2W., 15 Bn., 26 Bn.	15/6/15 2y 11m, Cpl.
BADKIN, S., Pte. 40 Bn.	3W.	12/4/16 1y 8m, Pte.
BAGULEY, B., Pte. A.M.C.	8 Fd. Amb.	19/ 9/16
BAILEY, A. B., Dvr. A.S.C.		27/ 8/14 1y 2m. Dvr.
BAILEY, A. E., Pte. 12 Bn.	W., 52 Bn. ✠ 7/6/17.	7/ 8/15 Pte. ✠
BAILEY, C. D., Gnr. 3 F.A.B.	M.M., 103 How. Bty.	10/ 8/15 4y 3m, Gnr.
BAILEY, D., Pte. 2 G.S.R.	12 Bn.	4/ 4/18 1y 9m, Pte.
BAILEY, E. S., Gnr. 6 F.A.B.	15 Bty.	7/10/15 3y 11m, Dvr.
BAILEY, F. L., Pte. 40 Bn.	2W.	15/ 3/16 1y 11m, Pte.
BAILEY, G. B., Capt. 7 F. Amb.	13 Fd. Amb. ✠ 27/3/17.	Capt. ✠
BAILEY, G. W., Pte. 40 Bn.	W.	2/ 3/16 3y 5m, Cpl.
BAILEY, H. E., Pte. 7 F. Amb.		Pte.
BAILEY, T. J., Pte. 26 Bn.	✠ 6/11/15.	5/ 4/15 Pte. ✠
BAILEY, J., Pte. 12 Bn.	3W. ✠ 28/8/18.	7/ 8/15 Pte. ✠
BAILEY, J. A. A., Tpr. 3 L.H.	✠ 14/6/15.	19/ 8/14 Tpr. ✠
BAILEY, L. C., Gnr. 10 F.A.B.	5 F.A.B.	7/10/15 4y, S.-Smith.
BAILEY, L. C. G. C., Tpr. Remts	10 F.A.B.	13/10/15 3y 10m, Dvr.
BAILEY, O., Pte. 12 Bn.		6/10/16 3y 2m, Pte.
BAILEY, P. T., Gnr. Fd Art.	1 D.A.C.	10/ 4/17 2y 6m, Gnr.
BAILEY, R. St. C., Pte. 12 Bn.	W., 10 Bn., 12 Bn.	30/10/16 2y 6m, Pte.
BAILEY, R. B., Tpr. 3 L.H.	W., 2 D.A.C.	4/12/14 4y 4m, Cpl.
BAILEY, S. J., Pte. 12 Bn.		21/ 9/15 2y 3m, L.-Cpl.
BAILEY, T. J., L.-Cpl. 40 Bn.		28/ 3/17 2y, L.-Cpl.
BAILEY, T. A., Tpr. 3 L.H.	1 Dble. Sqdn.	13/ 7/15 4y 3m, Sgt.
BAILEY, W., Pte. 12 Bn.	W.	15/ 6/16 1y 7m, Pte.
BAILEY, W T., Pte. 40 Bn.	43 Bn., 12 Bn.	9/10/16 3y 1m, Pte.
BAILY, V. R., Pte. 12 Bn.	W.	19/ 8/15 2y4m, Pte.
BAILY, W. J., Gnr. Art.	1 D.A.C., 1 H.Q. Fd. Arty.	29/ 3/17 2y 6m, Gnr.
BAILLIE, R. B., Pte. 12 Bn.	W., 47 Bn.	30/11/14 2y 4m, L.-Cpl.
BAILLIE, W., Pte. 12 Bn.	2W., M.M., 51 Bn.	9/ 8/15 3y 8m, Pte.
BAIN, A. L., Sgt. 12 Bn.	✠ 3-5/9/16.	1/ 8/15 Sgt. ✠

O

TASMANIA'S WAR RECORD, 1914-1918.

NAME.	REMARKS.	RANK ON DISCHARGE. ENLISTED, SERVICE.
BAIN, C. R., Gnr. D.A.C.	M.I.D., 22 How. Bde., 2 D.A.C., 6 F.A.B.	3/ 9/15 3y 11m, Sgt.
BAINES, F. G., Pte. 26 Bn.	✠ 13/9/16.	10/ 3/15 Cpl. ✠
BAKES, G. F., Pte. 40 Bn.		3/10/16 10m, Pte.
BAKES, W. F., Pte. 12 Bn.		28/10/16 1y 2m., Pte.
BAKES, H. R., Pte. 3 G.S.R.	12 Bn. ✠ 24/1/19.	21/6/18 Pte. ✠
BAKER, A. W., Tpr. 3 L.H.		3/ 1/15 4y 10m, Tpr.
BAKER, A. W., Pte. 40 Bn.		18/ 5/16 3y 3m, Pte.
BAKER, A. J., Pte. 12 Bn.	M.M.	20/12/15 3y 10m, Cpl.
BAKER, A. H. B., Cpl. 40 Bn.	W. ✠ 13/10/17.	13/ 3/16 Sgt. ✠
BAKER, B. H., Pte. 40 Bn.	15 Bn. ✠ 4/7/18.	1/ 3/16 Pte. ✠
BAKER, C. V., Pte. 26 Bn.	12 Bn. ✠ 23/7/16.	3/ 8/15 Cpl. ✠
BAKER, C. T., Pte. 12 Bn.	W., 40 Bn.	5/ 4/16 2y, L.-Cpl.
BAKER, C. H., Pte. 12 Bn.	2W., 52 Bn.	19/ 1/16 2y, Pte.
BAKER, C. S., Gnr. 3 F.A.B.	8 Bty.	1/ 9/15 4y, Cpl.
BAKER, E. F., Mun. Worker.		
BAKER, F. J., Pte. 12 Bn.	2W.	1/ 6/16 3y 3m, Pte.
BAKER, G., Pte. 26 Bn.	W. ✠ 14/4/18.	21/5/15 L.Cpl. ✠
BAKER, George, Pte. 12 Bn.	P.O.W.	1/ 6/16 2y 11m, Pte.
BAKER, G. A., Pte. 15 Bn.	✠ 11/4/17.	12/ 8/15 L.-Cpl. ✠
BAKER, G. L., Pte. 12 Bn.	W.	26/10/16 3y, Pte.
BAKER, H. C., Tpr. 3 L.H.		3/ 4/17 2y 4m, Tpr.
BAKER, H. E., Pte. 12 Bn.	W.	1/ 6/16 1y 10m, Pte.
BAKER, H. S., W.O. 1 A.G.H.	D.S.O., M.I.D., 4 Fd. Amb., 13 Bn.	26/ 2/15 4y 3m, Lt.
BAKER, H. T., Pte. 12 Bn.		14/12/15
BAKER, J., Pte. 12 Bn.	2W.	13/ 6/16 2y 11m, Pte.
BAKER, K. T., Dvr. 3 F.A.B.	8 Bty., 3 F.A.B.	1/ 8/15 4y, Dvr.
BAKER, N. R., Pte. 12 Bn.		21/12/15
BAKER, Nat. Robert, Pte. 40 Bn.	Vet. Hos., 40 Bn.	4/10/16 2y 9m, Pte.
BAKER, P. H., Pte. 40 Bn.		22/ 5/17 2y 4m., Pte.
BAKER, R. J., Spr. 3 F.C.E.	6 F.C.E.	3/ 8/15 4y, Spr.
BAKER, R., Pte. 12 Bn.	W.	6/ 6/16 3y 3m, Pte.
BAKER, T. J., Dvr. A.F.A.	8 Bty., 3 F.A.B.	11/ 2/15 4y 4m, Dvr.
BAKER, T. V., Pte. 15 Bn.	✠ 8/8/15.	29/ 9/14 Pte. ✠
BAKER, V. R., Pte. 15 Bn.		20/ 6/15
BAKER, W. R., Pte. 26 Bn.	2 D.H.Q., 13 Fd. Amb.	22/ 9/15 4y 1m, Dvr.
BAKER, V., P. 12 Bn.	W., 40 Bn.	5/ 4/16 2y 8m, Pte.
BAKER, W. E., Pte. 1 A.G.H.		10/ 6/15 Lt.
BAKER, W., Spr. Miners.		31/ 1/17
BALAAM, A. J., Pte. 4 M.G. Co.	6 M.G. C., 24 M.G. Co. ✠ 1/10/17.	10/ 8/16 Pte. ✠
BALD, J. J., Pte. 12 Bn.	✠ 19-22/8/16.	19/ 9/14 Cpl. ✠
BALD, W. R., Pte. 26 Bn.	2W.	20/ 5/15 3y 11m, Cpl.
BALDOCK, C. W., Pte. 12 Bn.	1 Fd. Bty.	3/ 1/16 3y 9m, Pte.
BALDOCK, A. H., Pte. 12 Bn.	70 Bn., 12 Bn.	3/ 1/16 3y 3m, Pte.
BALDOCK, A. E., Pte. 12 Bn.		21/11/16
BALDOCK, E., Pte. 12 Bn.	3 M.G. Co. ✠ 4/10/17.	4/ 9/15 Pte. ✠
BALDOCK, H., Pte. 40 Bn.	W.	30/ 5/16 1y 8m, Pte.
BALDOCK, W. J., Pte. 12 Bn.	W. ✠ 23/8/18.	13/10/16 Pte. ✠
BALDWIN, A. T., Pte. 40 Bn.	W.	27/ 4/16 3y 6m, Cpl.
BALDWIN, C. W., C.S.M. 40 Bn.	2W.	8/10/15 3y 2m, Lt.
BALDWIN, G. T., Pte. 40 Bn.		8/11/16 3y 1m, Pte.
BALDWIN, W. H., Gnr. 10 F.A.B.	14 F.A.B., 10 F.A.B. ✠ 11/8/18.	10/ 1/16 Dvr. ✠
BALFE, B. O., Spr. 3 Fd. Co.		19/ 8/14
BALGUE, R. E., Spr. 1 Tunl. Co.		30/ 3/16 3y 7m, Spr.
BALL, A., Cpl. 26 Bn.	W.	30/ 4/15 1y 6m, Sgt.
BALL, C. H., L.-Cpl. 40 Bn.		11/12/16 2y 6m, L.Cpl.
BALL, G. F., Pte. Dental Corps.	2W.	21/ 3/16 Pte.
BALL, V. Charles, Pte. 12 Bn.	2W.	8/ 6/16 2y 10m, Pte.
BALLANTYNE, R., T./S.-Ck. 40 Bn.	M.S.M.	11/10/15 4y 2m, Sgt Ck.
BALLANTYNE, S. H. Cpl. 15 Bn.	47 Bn., 24 How. Bde., 24 F.A.B.	28/ 7/15 2y 1m, Cpl S.S.
BALMAN, W., Pte. 12 Bn.		12/ 8/15
BALMER, H. A., Pte. 12 Bn.	3W.	15/ 7/15 3y 9m, Pte.
BALMER, W. H., Tpr. 3 L.H.		20/ 8/14 Tpr.
BALMFORTH, J. T., Pte. 40 Bn.	2W.	7/ 6/16 1y 10m, Pte.
BAMBLETT, R. T., Gnr. Art.	W.	1/ 5/16 Gnr.
BANBROOK, A. G., Gnr. 3 F.A.B.		27/ 8/18 Sgt.
BANFIELD, E. H., Pte. 40 Bn.	W.	17/10/16 1y 9m, Pte.
BANFIELD, G. A. T., Gnr. 8 F.A.B.	1 D.A.C.	7/12/15 3y 11m, Gnr.
BANFIELD, G. R., Pte. 12 Bn.	52 Bn. ✠ 4/9/16.	15/ 9/15 Pte. ✠
BANFIELD, H. C., Pte. 26 Bn.	✠ 29/7/16.	18/ 3/15 Pte. ✠
BANFIELD, S. J., Pte. 15 Bn.	W., 17 Bn.	1/ 9/15 3y 2m, Cpl.
BANKS, A., Pte. 40 Bn.	W.	9/10/16 1y 5m, Pte.
BANKS, D., Spr. 5 Miners.	1 Tnl. Co.	24/ 2/16 3y 7m, Spr.
BANKS, G., Pte. Tnl. Co.	Light Railway Unit.	23/ 8/16 1y 5m, Pte.
BANKS, J., Pte. 12 Bn.	52 Bn.	7/12/14 4y 5m, Cpl.
BANKS, R. B., Pte. 12 Bn.	W.	27/ 8/14 4y, Sgt.
BANNISTER, A. H., Pte. 40 Bn.	2W., 15 Bn., 40 Bn.	14/ 3/16 3y, Pte.
BANNISTER, C. R., Pte. A.S.C.		22/10/17 11m, Pte.
BANNISTER, E. V., Pte. 40 Bn.		9/11/16 3y 2m, Pte.
BANNISTER, G. W. J., Pte. 12 Bn.	2W., A.W. Section.	15/ 7/15 3y 10m, Pte.
BANNISTER, H. C., Pte. 12 Bn.	✠ 23/4/18/.	10/10/16 Pte. ✠
BANNISTER, S., Pte. 12 Bn.	2W., 40 Bn.	13/ 7/15 2y 9m, Pte.
BANNISTER, W. G., Pte. 12 Bn.		23/10/16 1y 3m, Pte.

NAME.	REMARKS.	RANK ON DISCHARGE. ENLISTED. SERVICE.
BANNISTER, V. H., M.W.		Mun. Worker.
BANNISTER, W. T., Pte. 40 Bn.	✠ 3/1/17.	14/ 2/16 Pte. ✠
BANNON, E., Pte. 12 Bn.	✠ 1/4/17. 51 Bn. Enlisted as E. Benson.	13/ 2/15 Pte.
BANTICK, A. W., Pte. 40 Bn.	W.	29/ 9/16 1y 2m, Pte.
BANTICK, E. A., Pte. 12 Bn.		4/ 9/14 4y 6m, Pte.
BANTICK, G. H., Pte. 12 Bn.	✠ 4/6/18.	17/10/17 Pte. ✠
BANTICK, L. D., Spr. Wireless		4/ 1/17 2y 5m, Spr.
BANTOFT, G. F. A., Pte. 10 F.Amb.		8/ 5/16
BANTOFT, R. G., Pte. 40 Bn.		5/10/16
BAPTIE, W. A., Tpr. 3 L. Horse	F.A.B.	22/ 2/15 3y 6m, Tpr.
BARBER, G., Pte. 12 Bn.	4 Div. Field Bakery.	7/ 8/15 4y, Pte.
BARBER, H., Pte. 40 Bn.		10/10/16 2y 5m, L.Cpl.
BARBER, R. W., Pte. 40 Bn.	W.	23/ 3/16 2y, Sgt.
BARBER, R., Pte. 40 Bn.	W.	10/10/16 2y 5m, L.Cpl.
BARCLAY, D. J., Tpr. 3 L. Horse.	✠ 4-5/8/16.	4/12/14 Tpr. ✠
BARCLAY, H. L., Lieut. 40 Bn.	69 Bn.	2/12/15 2y 11m, Lieut.
BARDEN, A. R., Pte. 12 Bn.	W.	11/10/16 3y, Pte.
BARDEN, W. J., Pte. 40 Bn.	✠ 30/4/17.	26/ 2/16 Pte. ✠
BARDENHAGEN, R. L., Pte. 12 Bn.	W.	21/ 8/16 3y 2m, Pte.
BARFOOT, L., Pte. 12 Bn.	✠ 18/9/18.	28/10/17 Pte. ✠
BARFOOT, R. L., Pte. 40 Bn.	W.	25/ 5/16 Pte.
BARING, C. A., Cpl. 12 Bn.	52 Bn. ✠ 4/9/16.	23/10/15 Sgt. ✠
BARKER, C. V., Spr. 3 Miners.	3 Tunn. Co. ✠ 28/11/16.	14/ 9/15 Spr. ✠
BARKER, E. G., Pte. 7 F. Amb.	2 W. M.M.	17/ 3/15 2y 9m, L.-Cpl.
BARKER, F. G., Pte. 12 Bn.	W.	2/ 5/17 Pte.
BARKER, F. T., Gnr. 3 F.A.B.	W. M.M. 10 F.A.B.	15/ 6/15 3y 10m, Gnr.
BARKER, G. A., Pte. 15 Bn.		12/ 8/15 L.-Sgt.
BARKER, G. H., L.-Sgt. 12 Bn.	W.	20/ 8/14
BARKER, J. R., Pte. 40 Bn.	✠ 31/8/18.	17/10/16 Pte ✠
BARKER, O. A., Pte. 12 Bn.	52 Bn. ✠ 11/4/17.	23/10/15 Pte. ✠
BARKER, O. J., Pte. 12 Bn.	W.	1/ 6/16 2y 1m, Pte.
BARKER, R. W., Cpl. 40 Bn.	W.	23/ 3/16 2y, Sgt.
BARKER, R. D., Pte. 12 Bn.		2/10/16 2y, Pte.
BARKER, S. J., Pte. 12 Bn.		11/10/16 2y 9m, Pte.
BARKWORTH, H. A., Pte. 12 Bn.	W. P.O.W.	29/ 8/16 2y 10m, Pte.
BARLING, A. C., Sgt. 40 Bn.	W.	29/ 3/16 3y 6m, Sgt.
BARLING, R. F., Dvr. 3 F.A.B.	W. 8 F.A.B.	17/10/16 2y 7m, Dvr.
BARLOW, War Worker.		War Worker.
BARLOW, B. W., Tpr. 3 L. Horse.		3/ 7/15 2y 7m, Tpr.
BARNARD, A. V., Sgt. 12 Bn.	52 Bn., 11 F.A.B., ✠ 22/10/17.	31/ 8/14 W.O.
BARNARD, C. C., Cpl. 8 F.A.B.	30 Bty. ✠ 3/8/17.	5/11/15 Sgt. ✠
BARNARD, E. R., Pte. 12 Bn.	W.	24/ 8/15 4y 3m, Sgt.
BARNARD, E. G., Sgt. 12 Bn.	✠ 6-10/4/17.	29/ 5/16 Sgt. ✠
BARNARD, G. R. E., L.-Cpl. 40 Bn.	W.	1/ 2/16 1y 10m, L.-Cpl
BARNARD, T. H., Pte. Rmt. Sec.		30/ 9/15 Pte.
BARNARD, W., Dvr. 40 Bn.		31/ 3/16 3y 6m, Dvr.
BARNARD, W. H., Pte. 12 Bn.	✠ 21/1/18. Re-enlisted with 15 Bn.	22/ 8/14 Pte. ✠
BARNES, A. L., Tpr. 1 G.S., A.M.D		11/ 4/18 1y 4m, Tpr.
BARNES, A. W., Gnr. 6 F.A.B.	✠ 31/7/16.	2/10/15 Gnr. ✠
BARNES, C., Pte. 40 Bn.		3/10/16 2y 7m, Pte.
BARNES, C. A., Pte. 15th Bn.	P.O.W. ✠ 14/6/19.	13/ 8/15 Pte. ✠
BARNES, C. W., Pte. 12 Bn.	2 W.	25/ 8/15 3y 9m, Pte.
BARNES, D., Pte. 40 Bn.	W.	30/ 9/16 2y 11m, Pte.
BARNES, E., Pte. 3 A.G.H.		7/ 2/16 3y 10m, Pte.
BARNES, E. J., Pte. 40 Bn.	2 W. 49 Bn.	27/ 4/16 3y 6m, Pte.
BARNES, F. S., Cpl. 7 F.A.B.		26/ 1/16
BARNES, G. J., Pte. 1 G.S.R.		21/ 1/18
BARNES, G W., Pte. 4 M.G. Co.		10/ 8/16 2y 7m, Pte.
BARNES, J. A., Pte. 40 Bn.		23/ 2/17 1y 8m, Pte.
BARNES, L. H., Pte. 12 Bn.		14/ 4/17 Pte.
BARNES, R. H., Pte. 12 Bn.	W.	14/12/14 4y 5m, Pte.
BARNES, T. V., Pte. Wireless.	Flying Corps.	16/10/16 2y 9m, Pte.
BARNES, W., Pte. 15 Bn.	✠ May-June, 1915.	18/ 9/14 Pte. ✠
BARNES, W. A., Pte. 26 Bn.		14/ 4/15 2y 2m, Pte.
BARNES, W. J., Pte. 26 Bn.	2 W.	14/ 4/15 4y, Sgt.
BARREN, C. W., Pte. A.F.C.		15/ 1/18 1y 6m, 2-A.M.
BARRENGER, A. H., Pte 12 Bn	✠ 14/4/17.	21/ 6/16 Pte. ✠
BARRETT, A. W., Pte. 3 G.S.R.		8/ 8/18 8m, Pte.
BARRETT, E. C., Pte. 40 Bn.		Pte.
BARRETT, E. A., Pte. 40 Bn.	W.	13/10/16 2y 10m, L.Cpl.
BARRETT, F. J., Gnr. 8 F.A.B.	M.M. 108 How. Bty.	16/11/15 3y 11m, Dvr.
BARRETT, F. H., Pte. Remount.		13/10/15 Pte.
BARRETT, F. P. H., Sgt. 1 A.C.H.	2 W. M.M.	4/10/14 4y 3m, Sgt.
BARRETT, G., Pte. 12 Bn.	2 W.	3/ 1/16 3y 1m, Pte.
BARRETT, H., Pte. 12 Bn.	W. 52 Bn., 69 Bn., 52 Bn.	31/ 1/15 4y 5m, Pte.
BARRETT, M. W., Pte. 40 Bn.	W.	26/ 6/16 2y 1m, Pte.
BARRETT, R. H., Gnr. 6 F.A.B.	W.	4/ 9/15 1y 11m, Gnr.
BARRETT, S. D., Pte. 12 Bn.	W. 40 Bn.	12/ 4/16 3y 5m, Pte.
BARRETT, S. J., Pte. 40 Bn.	M.M. ✠ 12/10/17.	31/ 5/16 Sgt. ✠
BARRETT, T. P., Tpr. 3 L. Horse.		27/ 3/17 Tpr.
BARRIE, R., Pte. 26 Bn.	D.C.M., 29 Bn. 49 Bn.	9/ 4/15 4y 7m, Pte.
BARROW, A. F., War Worker.		Munition Worker
BARROW, C., Gnr. D.A.C.		23/ 2/15 2y 3m, Gnr.

TASMANIA'S WAR RECORD, 1914-1918.

NAME.	REMARKS.	RANK ON DISCHARGE. ENLISTED. — SERVICE.
BARROW, J. A., Pte. 40 Bn.	2 W.	1/ 3/16 1y 11m, Pte.
BARROWS, A., Pte. 12 Bn.	W. 52 Bn., Vet. Hos., 52 Bn.	6/ 1/16 2y 9m, Pte.
BARRY, B. T., Pte. 15 Bn.	2 W 24 How., 10 F.A.B.	19/ 4/15 4y 5m, Dvr.
BARRY, F. C., Pte. 40 Bn.		16/10/16 Pte.
BARRY, P. C., Pte. 12 Bn.	2 W.	12/10/16 Pte.
BARTLES, C., Pte. 40 Bn.	W.	27/ 6/16 3y 3m, Pte.
BARTELS, G. P., Pte. 12 Bn.	W.	24/ 8/15 4y, L.-Cpl.
BARTELS, R. G. J., Pte. 12 Bn.		24/ 8/15 2y 8m, L.-Cpl.
BARTLE, V. N., Pte. 26 Bn.	2 W. 15 Bn., 3 Comd. Depot.	15/ 5/15 4y 1m, C.S.M.
BARTLETT, G., Dvr. 6 F.A.B.	2 D.A.C.	28/ 9/15 3y 7m, Dvr.
BARTLETT, J T., Pte. 40 Bn.	2 W., 26 Bn.	23/ 5/16 2y 10m, Pte.
BARTLETT, S. R., Pte. 40 Bn.	2 W., 69 Bn., 40 Bn.	1/ 3/16 3y, L.-Cpl.
BARTLEY, A. G., Dvr. 4 A.S.C.	✠ 4/9/15.	8/ 9/14 Dvr. ✠
BARTLEY, T. W., Pte. 1 A.G.H.	1 D.A.C., 3 F.A.B. Discharged 20/10/19.	Dvr.
BARTOLO, F., Pte. 26 Bn.	2 W. ✠ 9/8/18.	26/ 2/15 Pte. ✠
BARTON, A. G., Pte. 13 A.S.C.	W., 87 Bn.	4/12/14 4y 3m, Cpl.
BARTON, F. W., Pte. 40 Bn.	W.	20/ 3/16 2y 5m, Pte.
BARTON, L. T., Pte. 40 Bn.		20/ 3/16 4y 4m, Pte.
BARTON, R., Pte. 12 Bn.	✠ 22/9/17.	23/ 5/16 Pte. ✠
BARTUSH, C. A., Pte. Tun. Co.	✠ 1 A.G.H. Enlisted as Craig, C.	5/ 9/16
BARWICK, A. T., Pte. 40 Bn.	W.	17/ 4/16 3y 7m, L.-Cpl.
BARWICK, A. A., Sgt. 1 Bn.		24/ 8/14 4y 7m, Sgt.
BARWICK, A. J., Cpl. 40 Bn.		16/ 5/16
BARWICK, C. J., Sgt. 12 Bn.		1/ 3/17 2y 9m, Sgt.
BARWICK, E. V., Pte. 15 Bn.	12 Bn.	12/ 2/15 2y 1m, Pte.
BARWICK, E. J. C., Pte. 12 Bn.	2 W.	23/ 8/15 3y 8m, Pte.
BARWICK, J. T. L., Pte. 12 Bn.	M.M.	24/5/15/ 3y 4m, C.S.M.
BARWICK, J. T., Pte 15 Bn.	W.	29/ 9/14 4y 4m, Gnr.
BARWICK, L., Pte. 40 Bn.	2 W., 49 Bn.	16/ 4/16 3y, Pte.
BARWICK, N. S., Cpl. 12 Bn.	W. ✠8/10/17.	8/ 7/16 Cpl. ✠
BARWICK, R. J., Pte. 40 Bn.	2 W.	7/ 2/16 3y 6m, Pte.
BARWICK, R. J. E., Pte. 12 Bn.	41 Bty. A.F.A.	23/ 8/15 4y 2m, Dvr.
BARWICK, R. E., Pte. 40 Bn.	3 Dvl. Tun.	13/ 3/16 3y 7m, Pte.
BARWICK, W., Pte. 12 Bn.	2 W. M.M. ✠ 18/1/19.	4/ 9/16 Pte. ✠
BARNETT, A. J., Fr.-Sgt. 3 F.A.B.		26/ 8/14 Fr. Sgt.
BARNETT, E. C., Pte. 2 G.S.R.		5/ 6/18 11m, Pte.
BARNETT, G., Pte. 12 Bn.	2 W.	3/ 6/15 3y 2m, Pte.
BARNETT, H. S., Aviation.		
BARNETT, J. C., Pte. 12 Bn.		12/12/14 4y 4m, Pte.
BARNETT, O. L., Gnr. 24 F.A.B.	3 F.A.B., 103 How. Bty.	27/ 9/16 3y 1m, Gnr.
BARNETT, L. W., R.Q.M.S., 40 Bn.	M.C., M.I.D.	26/ 1/15 4y 5m, Lieut.
BARNETT, W. H., Pte. 12 Bn.	52 Bn., 6 M.T. Co.	13/ 7/15 3y 11m, Dvr.
BARNETT, T. G., Pte. 40 Bn.		31/ 5/16 1y 7m, Cpl.
BARNETT, W. J., Pte. 26 Bn.	52 Bn., 12 Bn. ✠ 6/10/17.	28/ 5/15 Pte. ✠
BASHFIELD, A. J., Pte. 3 Fd. Amb.	2 Fld. Amb.	9/ 6/15 4y 5m, Cpl.
BASHFIELD, H. D., Tpr. 3 L.H.	✠ 24/4/17.	24/ 7/15 Tpr. ✠
BASS, C. S., Pte. 15 Bn.		15/12/14 1y 8m, Pte.
BASS, J., Cpl. 12 Bn.		24/ 8/14 Capt.
BASS, S., Pte. 2 G.S.R.	12 Bn.	13/ 5/18 1y 6m, Pte.
BASSETT, A., Pte. 12 Bn.	W., 52 Bn.	21/ 7/15 3y 9m, Pte.
BASSETT, C., Pte. 40 Bn.		5/ 4/16 2y 8m, Pte.
BASSETT, E., Pte. 12 Bn.		30/ 7/15 1y 2m, Pte.
BASSETT, E. W., Pte. 40 Bn.	W.	2/ 4/16 3y 6m, Pte.
BASSETT, H. E., Pte. 12 Bn.	3 W., 52 Bn.	13/ 1/16
BATCHELOR, A. S., Pte. 3 G.S.R.	12 Bn.	26/ 6/18 1y 3m, Pte.
BATCHELOR, A. W., Cpl. 26 Bn.	✠ 13/11/16.	20/ 7/15 Sgt. ✠
BATCHELOR, C. G., Pte. 12 Bn.		17/ 8/14 2y 1m, Pte.
BATCHELOR, H. H. T., Pte. 12 Bn.		8/ 1/16 3y 10m, Pte.
BATCHELOR, J. A., Pte. 40 Bn.		30/ 8/17 2y 3m, Pte.
BATCHELOR, V. A. C., Gnr. Arty.	25 How. Bde. ✠ 4/10/17.	2/ 2/16 Gnr. ✠
BATCHELOR, W. M. C., Gnr. Arty.		2/10/16 2y 11m, Gnr. Pte.
BATE, Bernard, Pte. 12 Bn.	M.I.D.	11/ 1/15 Cpl. ✠
BATES, Charley, Pte. 12 Bn.	W., 52 Bn. ✠ 28/6/17.	5/ 7/16 3y 3m, Pte.
BATES, H., Pte. 40 Bn.	W.	11/ 2/16 1y 9m, Gnr.
BATH, E., Gnr. 14 F.A.B.		24/ 4/15 3y 3m, Pte.
BATH. L. H., Pte. 26 Bn.	2 W.	13/11/15 Spr. ✠
BATSON, W. H., Spr. 3 Miners.	3 Tunn Coy. ✠ 29/11/16.	24/10/16 2y 11m, Gnr.
BATT, W. P., Gnr. Art.	15 F.A.B., 1 D.A.C., 3 Bty. A.F.A.	3/ 2/16 1y 10m, Pte.
BATTEN, E. K., Pte. 40 Bn.	W., 12 Bn.	21 8/14 Lieut.
BATTEN, H. H., Pte. 3 L.H.		12/12/17
BATTEN, J. F., Pte. 46 Bn.		17/ 7/16 3y, Pte.
BAUCHOP, J. H., Pte. 12 Bn.		12/ 8/15 4y 1m, Sgt.
BAULD, S. G., Sgt 12 Bn.	W., 52 Bn., 15 Bn.	18/ 2/17 2y 1m, Gnr.
BAUER, G. W., Gnr. Art.	W.	1/ 3/15
BAWN, G. A. I., Pte. 26 Bn.	P.O.W.	13/ 1/15 Pte. ✠
BAXTER, W. L., Pte. 12 Bn.	✠ 3-5/9/16.	18/11/15 2y 3m, Sgt.
BAYES, W. A., Spr. 3 Miners' Bn.	W., 1 Miners.	12/10/16 2y 11m, Gnr.
BAYLES, A. J., Gnr. Arty.	1 D.A.C.	27/10/16
BAYLES, H. J., Gnr. Arty.		4/ 9/16 11m, Pte.
BAYLES, T. L., Pte. 12 Bn.		14/ 3/18 1y 4m, Pte.
BAYLES, W. H., Gnr. 3 F.A.B.		1/ 7/15 4y 1m, Dvr.
BAYLEY, C., Pte. 1 G.S.R.	40 Bn.	29/ 3/16 3y 5m, L.-Cpl.
BAYLIS, C. E., Pte. 40 Bn.	W.	

TASMANIA'S MUSTER ROLL. 229

NAME.	REMARKS.	RANK ON DISCHARGE. ENLISTED, SERVICE.
BAYLIS, G. P., Pte. 12 Bn.	51 Bn., 52 Bn. ✤ 10/7/18.	8/ 7/15 Pte. ✤
BAYLY, H. V., Gnr. Arty.	120 How. Bty.	6/ 3/16 3y 4m, Bdr.
BAYLEY, J. B., Gnr. 3 F.A.B.		24/ 8/14 3y, Bdr.
BEACH, A., Pte. A.M.C.	1 A.D.H., 4th Fld. Amb.	8/ 3/16
BEACH, G., Pte. 40 Bn.	✤ 7/6/17.	5/ 5/16 Pte. ✤
BEADLE, G., Pte. 15 Bn.		3/ 8/15 1y 10m, Pte.
BEALE, P. H., Pte. 12 Bn.		5/ 6/17 1y 2m, Pte.
BEAMISH, T. J., Pte. 40 Bn.	3 W.	18/ 5/16 3y 5m, Pte.
BEAMS, J. R., Pte. 15 Bn.	W., 47 Bn., 15 Bn.	26/ 8/15 3y 6m, Pte.
BEAN, A. W., Cpl. 3 L.H.		26/ 8/14 5y 2m, Lieut.
BEAN, G. M., A.M., Wireless.		19/ 2/18 10m, A.M.
BEAN, L. C., Dvr. 8 F.C.E.	W., 15 F.C.E.	1/ 4/16 3y 6m, L.-Cpl.
BEAN, N. V., Pte. 12 Bn.	4 Dvl. Cyc. Bn.	21/1015 4y, Pte.
BEARD, A. E., Gnr. 3 F.A.B.	W.	18/ 1/15 4y 7m, Sgt.
BEARD, D., Tpr. 3 L.H.		11/10/15 3y 11m, Dvr.
BEARD, E. F., Pte. 15 Bn.	✤ 26/5/15.	18/ 9/14 Pte. ✤
BEARD, J. H., Pte. 12 Bn.	A.O.C.	8/ 4/15 3y 5m, Pte.
BEARD, N. T., Pte. 40 Bn.	W. M.I.D.	15/ 5/17 2y 1m, Pte.
BEARD, N. E., Pte. 12 Bn.	✤ 6-10/4/17.	28/ 9/15 Pte. ✤
BEARD, S. C. A., Dvr. 3 F.A.B.		25/ 1/15 4y 3m, Gnr.
BEARD, T. J., Pte. 12 Bn.	✤ 15/4/17.	4/ 4/16 Pte. ✤
BEARD, W. G., Gnr. 6 F.A.B.	26 How. Bty., 106 How. Bty.	25/10/15 4y, Sgt.
BEARDS, N., Munition Worker.		
BEARUP, Harry, Pte. 12 Bn.	✤ 14/9/17.	8/ 1/15 Lieut. ✤
BEARUP, Hugh, Dvr. 4 F.A.B.	W., 2 D.A.C., 4th F.A.B	2/ 8/15 4y, Dvr.
BEASELEY, A. R., Pte. 12 Bn.		4/ 8/15
BEASLEY, C., Pte. Remounts.		29/ 9/15 9m, Pte.
BEASLEY, James Syd., Pte. 12 Bn.		25/10/15 3y 11m, Pte.
BEASLEY, Joseph S., Dvr. 3 F.A.B.	W.	26/ 8/14
BEATON, C. M., Pte. 40 Bn.	✤ 5/10/17.	16/ 2/16 L.-Cpl. ✤
BEATTIE, J. C. A., Pte. 40 Bn.	W.	10/10/16 2y 11m, Pte.
BEATTIE, John, Pte. 26 Bn.		2/ 8/15 1y 5m, Pte.
BEATTIE, L. W., Pte. Tun. Co.		23/10/16 6m, Pte.
BEATTIE, W. S., Pte. 26 Bn.	12 Bn., 52 Bn.	7/ 9/15 2y 2m, Pte.
BEAUCHAMP, R. E. P., Dvr. 40 Bn.		3/ 2/16
BEAUMONT, A. B., Pte. 12 Bn.	52 Bn. ✤ 17/1/17.	21/ 2/15 Pte. ✤
BEAUMONT, E. J., Dvr. 3 F.A.B.	✤ 25/4/15.	6/10/14 Dvr. ✤
BEAUMONT, F., Mun. Worker.		
BEAUMONT, Henry, Spr. Tnl. Co.	2 Tunn. Coy. ✤ 20/2/19.	9/11/16 Spr. ✤
BEAUMONT, James, Pte. 15 Bn.	W., 5 Bn. Discharged 11/10/18.	Pte.
BEAUMONT, W., Pte. 15 Bn.	M.I.D.	30/ 8/16 1y 5m, Pte.
BEAZLEY, C., Pte. 12 Bn.		
BELL, A. C., Pte. 12 Bn.		
BELL, A. J., Pte. 26 Bn.	D.C.M.	
BELL, A. S., Pte. 12 Bn.	✤ 14/1/16.	20/ 6/16.
BELL, Arthur, 15 Bn.		27/ 7/15, Pte. ✤
BELL, B. J., Pte. 26 Bn.		26/10/16 3y, Pte.
BELL, C. G., Pte. 12 Bn.		15/ 9/15.
BELL, C. V., Pte. Mob. Vet. Cps.	M.M.	
BELL, C. W., Pte. 40 Bn.		
BELL, G. W., Pte 40 Bn.		
BELL, J. R., Pte 12 Bn.	Prov. Cps., A.F.C., M.I.D.	27/ 3/18
BELL, Joseph, Gnr. Arty.		8/ 1/15 4y 6m, Lt.
BELL, R. T., Pte 15 Bn.	✤ 2/8/15.	20/ 5/15 Pte. ✤
BELL, Robert. Spr. 8 Fd. Co.	W., 12 Bn.	1/10/15 4y 3m, Spr.
BELL, Robert, Tpr. 3 L.H.	1 D.A.C.	19/ 8/14 5y 3m, Gnr.
BELL, W. J., Dvr. 13 Fd. Co.		13/ 1/16 3y 8m, Dvr.
BELL, W. H., Pte 12 Bn	1 Pnrs.	18/ 8/15
BECK, A. K., Sgt., 3 Fd. Co.	2 W., 16 F.C.E. ✤ 5/6/18.	17/ 9/14 Sgt. ✤
BECK, H. T., Pte. 12 Bn.	52 Bn.	8/ 7/15 4y 4m, Pte.
BECKETT, D., Sgt., 1 A.G.H.	M.I.D	17/ 9/14 4y 1m, W.O.
BECKETT, J. D., Gnr. 3 F.A.B.		1/ 8/15 4y 1m, Bdr.
BECKETT, John. Pte., 26 Bn.	2 W., M.M., 1 Pnrs.	28/ 7/15
BECKETT, F. J., Gnr. F.A.B.	3 D.A.C.	21/12/15 3y 9m, Gnr.
BECKETT, L. E, Dvr. 3 F.A.B.	W.	1/12/14 3y 10m, Gnr.
BEDELPH, Thos., Pte 12 Bn.	W., 3 M.G. Co.	7/12/14 2y 11m, L.-Cpl
BEDFORD, W. J., Pte. Remount.		20/ 9/15 9m, Pte.
BEECH, G. W., Pte. 40 Bn.	M.M. with Bar.	15/ 1/15 4y 5m, Sgt.
BEECH, S. T., Pte 40 Bn.	3 W.	6/ 6/16 3y, Pte.
BEECHEY, W. A., Pte 40 Bn.	W.	25/ 9/16 2y 8m, Pte.
BEECROFT, W. R., Dvr. 12 Bn.	2 W.	8/11/16 1y 7m, Pte.
BELBIN, A. G., Pte. 12 Bn.	67 A.F.C.	18/ 8/14 4y 4m, 1 A.M.
BELBIN, B W., Pte. 12 Bn.	2 W., M.M.	30/ 8/15 4y 2m, Pte.
BELBIN, F., Pte. 12 Bn.	W., 52 Bn.	21/ 1/16
BELBIN, H. E., Gnr. Arty.	40 Bn. ✤ 29/5/18.	18/10/16 Pte. ✤
BELBIN, L. J., Pte. 12 Bn.	W., 25 F.A.B., 11 F.A.B.	18/10/16 2y 11m, Gnr.
BELBIN, P. W., Pte. 40 Bn.	40 Bn.	24/10/16 3y, Pte.
BELBIN W. H., Spr. 3 Fd. Co.	W.	17/ 5/16 1y 9m, Pte.
BELL, G. J., 2nd-Lt., 3 L.H.	4 Aus C. Bn. 3 Anz C. Bn. D.S.O., C.M.G	14/ 8/15 3y 11m, Spr.
BELLCHAMBERS, B G., Pte Egrs.		27/ 8/14 5y 1m, Lt-Col.
BELLCHAMBERS, F. R., Pte. 4 M.G. Co.	2 M.G. Co., 3 M G Co. ✤ 29/9/18.	10/10/16 Pte. ✤
BELLCHAMBERS, H. R., Cpl. 12 Bn	52 Bn. ✤7/7/16.	1/11/15 Cpl. ✤
BELLETTE, A. A., Gnr. 6 F.A.B.	6 Army B.A.C.	25/10/15 4y, Sgt.

NAME.	REMARKS.	RANK ON DISCHARGE. ENLISTED. SERVICE.
BELLETTE, A. S., Pte. 40 Bn.	2 W.	1/ 3/16 3y 6m, L.-Cpl.
BELLETTE, H. A., Pte. 7 F. Amb.		
BELLETTE, N., Pte. 26 Bn.		
BELLETTE, S. J. C., Pte. Wireless.	3 D.S.C.	29/10/17 1y 10m, Dvr.
BELLINGER, A. F., Pte. 12 Bn.	M.M. with Bar.	20/ 8/14 4y 7m, Sgt.
BELLINGER, C. C., Pte. 40 Bn.	3 W., 10 M.G. Bn., 3 M.G. Bn.	4/ 4/16 3y 5m, Pte.
BELLINGER, H., Pt. 4 M.G. Co.	M.M., 44 Bn.	19/ 4/16 3y 6m, Pte.
BELLINGER, H. V., Spr. 3 Miners	Tunnellers	15/ 1/16 3y 6m, Spr.
BELLINGER, Percy, Pte. 40 Bn.	✠7/6/17.	4/ 4/16 Pte. ✠
BELLINGER, W. I. V., Pte. 15 Bn.	2 W., M.M., 4 Pnrs.	8/ 1/15 4y 7m, C.S.M.
BELSTEAD, A., Pte. 15 Bn.		3/10/14 2y 11m, Pte.
BELSTEAD, L. F., Pte. A.M.C. Rfts.	2 W., 20 Bn.	15/14/15 4y, L.-Cpl.
BELTON, P., Gnr. 6 F.A.B.	3 D.A.C.	3/ 3/16 3y 7m, Gnr.
BENDER, A. T. H., Pte. 40 Bn.	✠ 30/3/18.	2/ 3/16 Sgt. ✠
BENDER, C. S. G., Pte 26 Bn.	2 W., 52 Bn., 49 Bn.	8/ 5/15
BENDER, F. T., Pte. 4 M.G. Co.	12 Bn.	3/ 1/17 2y, Pte.
BENEFIELD, H. E., Pte. 12 Bn.	W. ✠ 11/8/18.	22/ 9/15 Pte. ✠
BENGER, J. D., Pte. 12 Bn.	52 Bn. ✠ 29/8/17.	24/ 5/15 Pte. ✠
BENJAFIELD, E., Gnr. Arty.	1 D.A.C.	23/11/16 3y 1m, Gnr.
BENJAFIELD, E. W., Gnr. 3 F.A.B.	120 How. Bty. ✠ 14/4/17	3/ 4/16 Gnr. ✠
BENJAMIN, A. V., Pte. 12 Bn.	W.	18/10/17 1y 6m, Pte.
BENN, F. W., Dvr. 8 Fd. Co.		16/ 3/16 3y, Dvr.
BENNETTO, A. F., Dvr. D.A.C.		7/10/15 3y 10m, Dvr.
BENNETTO, C. A., 3 L.H.	M.C.	20/ 8/14 5y 3m, Lt.
BENNETTO, H J., Pte. 26 Bn.		Pte.
BENNETTO, O. E. L., Gnr. F.A.B.	120 How. Bty., 14 F.A.B.	15/ 2/16 3y 8m, Dvr.
BENNEWORTH, C., Pte. Remounts.		28/ 9/15 4y 2m, Shoe S.
BENNIE, R., Gnr. Arty.		18/ 9/154y, Dvr.
BENNIE,	✠ At Claremont.	✠
BENSON, E., Pte. 12 Bn.	✠	✠
BENSON, J. E., Pte. 12 Bn.	W. ✠ 3/9/15.	3/12/14 L.-Cpl. ✠
BENSON, T., Tpr. 3 L.H.		20/ 1/17
BENSTEAD, C. E., Pte. 12 Bn.		5/11/15 1y 9m, Pte.
BENT, J. G., Pte. 26 Bn.	W., 12 Bn.	11/ 8/15 2y, Sgt.
BENTLEY, E., Pte. 1 G.S.R.	12 F.A.B.	22/12/17 2y, Gnr.
BENTLEY, J. A., Pte. 40 Bn.	67 Bn., L.T.M.B.	25/ 9/16
BENTLEY, J. C., Pte. 12 Bn.	✠ 19/4/17.	9 5/16 Pte. ✠
BENTLEY, J. E., Pte. 12 Bn.		Pte.
BENTLEY, T. W., Pte. 12 Bn.	W.	29/11/17 1y 7m.
BENNETT, A. E., Gnr. 6 F.A.B.	2 D.A.C., 6 F.A.B. ✠ 24/10/18.	14/ 9/15 Gnr. ✠
BENNETT, A. C., Gnr. 6 F.A.B.		13/ 9/15 4y, Saddler
BENNETT, A. T., Pte. 4 M.G. Co.		21/ 3/17
BENNETT, C. J., Tpr. 3 L.H.	W.	23/ 8/142y 7m, Tpr.
BENNETT, C. L., Pte. 12 Bn.		27/ 3/16 1y 5m, Pte.
BENNETT, C. P., Spr. 8 Fd. Co.	5 Fd. Co. Engrs	6/ 1/16. 1y 4m. Pte.
BENNETT, C. D., Pte. 40 Bn.	W.	31/10/16 Pte. 1y 9m.
BENNETT, C. J., Gnr. Fd. Arty.		7/ 4/15
BENNETT, D. J., Pte. 40 Bn.	15 Bn.	21/ 3/16 3y 4m, Pte.
BENNETT, E. H., Pte. 40 Bn.	10 M.G. Co.	2/ 3/16 3y 6m, Dvr.
BENNETT, E. L., Pte. 12 Bn.		8/12/15 1y 6m, Pte.
BENNETT, F. J., Gnr. 6 F.A.B.	13 F.A.B.	2/ 8/15 3y 8m, Gnr.
BENNETT, F. R., Cpl. 40 Bn.	✠ 4/11/18.	17/10/16 Cpl. ✠
BENNETT, G. M., Pte. 40 Bn.	3 W., 49 Bn. ✠ 11/11/19 (at No. 11 A.G.H. Launceston.)	24/ 4/16 Pte. ✠
BENNETT, G. T., Pte. 12 Bn.	24 How. Bty., 4 D.A.C.	12/ 1/15 4y 5m, Gnr.
BENNETT, H. J., Pte. 12 Bn.	W.	21/ 8/16.
BENNETT, H. G., Gnr. 3 F.A.B.	21 How. Bty. ✠ 8/8/16.	1/ 8/15 Gnr. ✠
BENNETT, J., Gnr. 6 F.A.B.	W.	16/ 9/15 4y 1m, Sgt.
BENNETT, J. E., Pte. 1st G.S.R.		22/ 1/18
BENNETTS, J. T., Pte. 4 M.G. Co.	W., 11 M.G. Bn.	29/ 9/16 2y 9m, Pte.
BENNETT, J. W., Pte. 12 Bn.	✠ 25/1/17.	25/ 9/16 Pte. ✠
BENNETT, John Wm., Pte. Rlwy.		8/ 1/17 2y 8m. Spr.
BENNETT, J., Pte. 12 Bn.		4/ 7/16 2y 4m. Pte.
BENNETT, L. A., Spr. Tnl. Co.	W.	31/10/16 2y 6m. Spr.
BENNETT, L., Gnr. 3 F.A.B.		30/ 8/14 4y 7m, Gnr.
BENNETT, L. L., Gnr. 6 F.A.B.	23 How. Bde., 6 F.A.B.	17/ 1/16 3y 3m, Gnr.
BENNETT, U. R. P., Pte. 40 Bn.	3 D.A.C.	1/ 2/16 3y 8m, Dvr.
BENNETT, R., Pte. 40 Bn.	W.	29/ 2/16. 2y, Pte.
BENNETT, R. H., Gnr. F.A. Rfts.	5 F.A.B. ✠ 22/9/18.	24/ 5/17 Gnr. ✠
BENNETT, R. J., Pte. 40 Bn.	W.	3/10/16 2y, Pte.
BENNETT, G. T., Pte. 12 Bn.		12/ 1/15 4y 5m, Pte.
BENNETT, T., Pte. Tnl. Co.		24/ 2/17 5m, Pte.
BENNETT, T. E., Pte. 12 Bn.	W., M.M., 9 Bn., 52 Bn., 49 Bn.	19/ 1/16
BENNETT, W. A., Pte. 12 Bn.	W., 4 Dvl. Arty., 24 F.A.B.	26/10/15 3y 8m, Pte.
BENNETT, W., Pte. 12 Bn.	✠ 16/8/15.	25/ 1/15 Pte. ✠
BERECHREE, B. S., Spr. 5 Miners	2 Tunnelling Co.	23/ 2/16 3y 8m, Spr.
BERECHREE, L. E., Pte. 26 Bn.	12 Bn. ✠ 19-22/8/16.	21/ 7/15 Pte. ✠
BERESFORD, A. G., Pte. 12 Bn.	W.	28/12/15 1y 7m, Pte.
BERESFORD, C. H., —— M.W.		M.W.
BERESFORD, C., Spr. Miners.		15/12/15 1y 8m, Spr.
BERGAN, T. G., Pte. 12 Bn.		26/ 8/14 2y, Pte.
BERNAL, A., Pte. Tnl Co.		18/10/16
BERRY, A. W., Pte. Tnl. Co.		20/10/17
BERRY, E. C., Pte. 4 M.G. Bn.	W., 41 M.G. Bn.	17/ 1/17 2y 3m, Pte.
BERRY, G. A., Pte. 40 Bn.	✠ 6/10/17.	10/11/16 Pte. ✠
BERRY, H. C., L.-Sgt. 12 Bn.		23/ 8/15 3y 9m, L.-Sgt.
BERRY, I. T., Pte. Tnl Co.		10/ 7/17

TASMANIA'S MUSTER ROLL. 231

NAME.	REMARKS.	RANK ON DISCHARGE. ENLISTED, SERVICE.
BERRY, J. J., Pte. 40 Bn.	W.	14/ 3/16 1y 11m, Pte.
BERRY, J. J., Pte. 12 Bn.	W.	23/ 7/15
BERRY, L. P., Pte. 12 Bn.	40 Bn.	21/ 5/17 1y 10m, Pte.
BERRY, M. J., Dvr. 15 Bn.	41 Bty. F.A.B.	1/ 8/15 3y 11m, Dvr.
BERRY, S. J. G., Pte. 12. Bn		15/ 7/15
BERRY, T. H., Pte. 12 Bn.		22/11/17 1y 11m, Pte.
BERRY, W., Cpl. 5 M.G. Co		15/11/15 1y 9m, Cpl.
BERRY, W. A. J., Pte. 15 Bn.		27/10/14 2y 5m, Pte.
BERRYMAN, C., Pte. 40 Bn.	W.	2/ 4/16 2y 3m, Pte.
BERRYMAN, E. W., Pte. 2 G.S.R.	25 Fd. Bty.	16/ 5/18 1y 4m, Gnr.
BERTRAM, A., Sgt. 40 Bn.	W.	9/ 2/16 3y 2m, Lt.
BERWICK, D., Gnr. 6 F.A.B.	2 W., 110 How. Bty., 10 F.A.B.	11/ 1/16 3y 10m, Bmb
BERWICK, S. F., Pte. 12 Bn.		12/10/15 2y 1m, Pte.
BERWICK, W., Pte. 4 M.G. Bn.		8/ 1/17 10m, Pte.
BESIER, E. F., Pte. 15 Bn.	✣ 11/7/17.	7/ 9/15 Pte. ✣
BESIER, H. H., Pte. 3 L.H.	W.	18/ 8/14 4y 6m, Sgt.
BESSELL, C., Pte. 12 Bn.		9/12/14 3y 3m, Pte.
BESSELL, C. A., S.S.-Mkr., 40 Bn.		1/12/15
BESSELL, C. E., Pte. 40 Bn.	✣ 5/10/17.	21/ 3/16 Pte. ✣
BESSELL, E. H., Pte. 40 Bn.	15 Bn.	21/ 3/16 1y 10m, Pte.
BESSELL, H. L., Pte. 40 Bn.	2 W.	21/ 3/16 3y 6m, Sgt.
BESSELL, L. J., Pte. 3 G.S.R.		6/ 8/18 1y 3m, Pte.
BESSELL, V.	✣ 25/1/18.	✣
BESSELL, W. G., Pte. 12 Bn.	W.	15/10/14 3y 11m, Pte.
BEST, A., Pte. 15 Bn.	W., 12 Bn. ✣ 14/3/18.	3/ 8/15 Pte. ✣
BEST, A. G J., Pte 12 Bn.	2 W.	2/ 5/16
BEST, C., Pte. 12 Bn.	W.	4/11/16 2y 11m, Pte.
BEST, F. W., Gnr. Art.	4 D.A.C.	7/ 2/16 3y 7m, Gnr.
BEST, G. W., Pte. Aviation.	71 S., A.F.C., 3 S. A.F.C. ✣ 12/4/18.	12/10/16 Lt. ✣
BEST, G. M., Pte. 26 Bn.		11/ 3/15 1y 7m, Pte.
BEST, J. R., Pte. 40 Bn.		30/ 9/16. 1y 4m. Pte.
BEST, T. H., Pte. 40 Bn.	2 W.	30/ 9/16 2y 7m, Pte.
BESTER, A. H., Pte. 26 Bn.		11/ 6/15 7y 7m, Pte.
BESWICK, B., Pte. 40 Bn.	W., D.C.M., M.M.	4/ 4/16 3y 7m, Pte.
BESWICK, D. V., Pte. 40 Bn.	W.	21/ 6/16 3y 3m, Pte.
BESWICK, J. L., Pte. 26 Bn.	✣ 18/11/15.	9/ 5/15 Pte. ✣
BESWICK, L., Pte. 40 Bn.		11/ 7/16 1y 10m, Pte.
BESWICK, M. E., Pte. 40 Bn.	W., 15 Bn., 40 Bn. ✣ 28/3/18.	21/ 3/16 L.-Cpl. ✣
BETHEL, W. M., Pte. 15 Bn.	✣ 7/8/16.	14/10/15 Pte. ✣
BETHUNE, F. P., Lt. 12 Bn.	W., M.C., 3 M.G. Co.	30/ 6/15 4y 1m, Capt.
BETTS, A. E., Pte. 12 Bn.	✣ 19-22/8/16.	5/ 1/15 Pte. ✣
BETTS, B. H., Gnr. 6 F.A.B.	W., 2 D.A.C., 6 F.A.B.	12/ 8/15 4y 2m, Bdr.
BETTS, C. R., Pte. 12 Bn.		17/ 8/14 2y, Pte.
BETT, H. D., Pte. 26 Bn.	1 A.G.H.	11/ 5/15 2y 8m, Pte.
BETTS, R. L., Pte. 12 Bn.	W.	19/ 8/14 4y 6m, Pte.
BETTS, W. F. J., Pte. 26 Bn.	W ✣ 28/4/17.	7/ 9/15 Pte. ✣
BEVEN, C. M., Pte. 12 Bn.		1/ 5/16 3y 6m. Pte
BEVEN, J. E., Pte. 40 Bn.	W.	31/10/16 2y 6m. Pte.
BEVAN, T. G., Pte. 3 L.H.	.	21/ 8/14
BEVAN, W. J.., Tpr. Rmts.		8/11/15 3y 6m. Tpr.
BEVEN, W. F., Pte. 40 Bn	W.	31/10/16 1y 7m, Pte.
BEVERIDGE, F., Pte. 40 Bn.		12/12/16 1y 8m, Pte.
BEVERIDGE, J., Pte. 40 Bn.		23/ 5/16 1y 3m, Ptc.
BEVERIDGE, S. H., Pte. 12 Bn.	W.	11/10/16 2y 6m, Pte.
BIBBY, E. B., Dvr. 26 Bn.		30/ 4/15 3y 1m, L.-Cpl.
BIBBY, L. H., Pte. Pte. 12 n.	52 Bn., 51 Bn.	19/ 7/15
BICKERTON, H., Pte. 12 Bn.	✣ 8/10/17.	14/ 9/16 Pte. ✣
BICKHAM, C. H., Pte. 40 Bn.	✣ 12/10/17.	30/ 3/16 Cpl. ✣
BICKHAM, C. W. G., Pte. 40 Bn.	✣ 7/6/17.	30/ 3/16 Pte. ✣
BIDDEL, P. J., Pte. 12 Bn.	W.	20/10/16 2y 2m, Pte.
BIDDULPH, B. W., L.-Cpl. 26 Bn.	W.	8/ 4/15 4y 4m, L.-Cpl.
BIDELPH, D. T., Cpl. Railway.		8/ 1/17 2y 6m, Cpl.
BIDGOOD, H. G., Pte. 26 Bn.	✣ 9/11/15.	23/ 4/15 Pte. ✣
BIDULPH, F., Spr. Miners.	✣17/7/16.	18/11/15 Spr. ✣
BIGGS, E. E., L.-Cpl. 40 Bn.	W. A.I.F. Hq	30/ 3/16 3y 2m, Cpl.
BIGGS, L. W., Pte 40 Bn.		25/ 2/16 3y 9m, Pte.
BIGGS, R. A., Pte. 40 Bn.		27/ 2/16
BIGNELL, J. M., Spr 8 Fd. Co.	W., C de G. (Belg.).	17/ 1/16 3y 9m, Cpl.
BIGNELL, N. F., Pte. 1 A.G.H.		10/ 6/15 4y 2m, T.-Sgt.
BILLETT, R G., Pte. 40 Bn.	2 W., 43 Bn. 12 Bn	26/ 9/16 3y, L.-Cpl.
BILLING, E. J., Sgt. 26 Bn.	2 W.	1/ 9/15 3y 7m, Sgt.
BILLING, E. W., Sgt. 40 Bn.	W., M.M., D.C.M.	9/ 3/16 3y 3m, Sgt.
BILLING, S. C., Pte 40 Bn.	2 W.	20/ 6/16 2y 8m, Pte.
BILLINGHURST, C. A., Dvr F.C E.	2 F.C.E.	31/ 1/16 3y 8m, Dvr.
BILLINGHURST, D., Pte. 40 Bn	15 Bn.	14/ 2/16 2y 5m, Pte.
BILLINGHURST, G., Pte. 40 Bn.	✣ 12/10/17.	30/9/16 Pte. ✣
BILSTON, A. S., Gnr. F.A. Rfts.	W., 4 D.A.C.	4/ 9/15
BILSON, C., Spr. Tunl Co.	1 Tunl. Co.	Spr.
BILSON, G. R., Pte 40 Bn.		18/ 8/17 2y 1m, Pte.
BINGHAM, E. C., Pte. Remts.		7/10/15 1y 2m, Tpr.
BINGHAM, O. E. H., Sgt 3 L.H.	✣ 4-6/8/16	19/ 8/14 Sgt. ✣
BINGHAM, T. E., Pte. 3 L.H.	W., 6 F A B	19/ 8/14 4y 5m, Bmbdr.
BINGLEY, F., Pte. 12 Bn		4/ 5/16 2y, Pte.
BINGLEY, T J., Pte. A C H.	14 M.G. Co.	18/9/14 4y 3m, Pte.
BINNS, E., Pte. A.S.C	4 Dvr. Trn., 7 A A S.C.	24/ 2/15 4y 8m, Pte.
BINNS, J. H., Pte. 12 Bn.	M.M.	12/10/15
BINNS, L. J., Pte. 40 Bn.	W.	8/11/16 2y 10m, Pte.

TASMANIA'S WAR RECORD, 1914-1918.

NAME.	REMARKS.	RANK ON ENLISTED.	DISCHARGE. SERVICE.
BINNS, W. J., Pte. 3 G.S.R.	12 Bn.	2/ 8/18	1y 2m, Pte.
BIRCH, L., Pte. 15 Bn.		5/ 1/15	1y 9m, Pte.
BIRCH, W., Spr. Miners.		12/11/15	2y 5m, Spr.
BIRCHALL, N. S., Pte. 40 Bn.	W., 49 Bn. ✚ 12/10/17.	29/ 3/16	Pte. ✚
BIRD, A. F. W., Pte. 12 Bn.		2/ 5/16	3y 6m, L.-Cpl.
BIRD, C. F., Pte. 2 G.S.R	A.C. Hqs.	22/ 5/18	1y 4m, Pte.
BIRD, E., Pte. A.M.C.	15 Fd. Amb.	9/11/16	2y 11m, Pte.
BIRD, G. H., Pte. 40 Bn.		20/10/16	2y 11m, Pte
BIRD, H. O., Pte. 12 Bn.		7/ 8/16	3y 1m, Pte.
BIRD, H. E., Pte. 2 G.S.R.		24/ 1/18	1y 11m, Pte.
BIRD, J C., Gnr. F.A.B	2 W.	12/10/16	2y 11m, Gnr.
BIRKETT, L J., Sgt. 12 Bn.	✚ 5-8/5/17.	20/ 8/14	Sgt. ✚
BIRNIE, F. R., Pte. 26 Bn.	W., 12 Bn. ✚ 16/1/17.	27/ 7/15	L.-Cpl. ✚
BIRNIE, R. G., Pte. 26 Bn.	2 W., 12 Bn.	27/ 7/15	2y 10m, Pte.
BISDEE, G. S., Capt. 40 Bn.		1/12/15	Capt.
BISHOP, C. W. T., Pte. 12 Bn	W.	23/11/16	1y 6m, Pte.
BISHOP, F. A., Pte. 1 G.S.R.	16 A.D.U.S.	23/11/17	1y 11m, Pte.
BISHOP, H E., Pte. 12 Bn.	W.	2/11/16	2y 10m, Pte.
BISHOP, J. M., Gnr. Arty.		4/ 8/16	Pte. ✚
BISHOP, O. G., Pte. 12 Bn.	✚ 5-8/5/17.	6/10/15	4y 1m, Dvr.
BISHOP, W. C., Dvr. A.M.C.	14 A.G.H., 1 L.H. Fd. Amb.	5/ 7/15	3y 4m, Sgt.
BISHTON, D G., Sgt. 12 Bn.	W., M.S.M	12/ 9/15	4y, Pte.
BISHTON, L. H., Pte. 12 Bn.	W., P.O.W.	16/12/16	2y 10m, Pte.
BJORKLUND, G. A., Pte. 40 Bn.	W., 23 A.A.S.C.	12/ 3/17	2y 8m, Gnr.
BLACK, A. H., Sgt. 40 Bn.	W. ✚ 13/10/17.	17/ 3/16	Sgt. ✚
BLACK, A. D., Spr. 4 Mtn. Co.		18/11/15	1y 6m, Spr.
BLACK, C. H., Pte. 15 Bn.		6/11/14	
BLACK,H. O., Pte. 12 Bn.		2/11/16	2y 5m, Pte.
BLACK, L. L. G., Pte. T.M.B.		18/10/16	
BLACK, W. M., Pte. R.U.		19/10/15	3y 3m, Pte.
BLACKABY, I. H., Pte. 12 Bn.	W.	8/ 1/18	1y 3m, Pte.
BLACKBERRY, R. J., Gun. 9 Bty.		18/ 8/14	5y, Sgt.
BLACKBURN, H. S. H., Cpl. R.U.		10/ 1/17	
BLACKETT, H., Pte. 12 Bn.	✚ 10/6/15.	28/ 8/14	Pte. ✚
BLACKHALL, A. J. Gnr. 6 F.A.B.		20/10/16	3y 2m, Dvr.
BLACKHALL, D. E., Pte. 3 Cycling	Pte. Cycl. 24 M.G. Co. ✚ 17/10/17.	11/ 3/16,	Pte. ✚
BLACKLER, E. E., M.W., Munitions	War Worker.		
BLACKLOW, A. J., Pte. 12 Bn.		7 12 14	4y 4m, Dvr.
BLACKLOW, E., L.-Cpl. 15 Bn.	W.	22/10/14	4y 2m, C.S.M
BLACKLOW, F., Pte. 15 Bn.	W.	11/ 1/15	4y 5m, Cpl.
BLACKLOW, M. W., Cpl. 12 Bn.	G. Rfts. ✚11/8/18.	23/ 8/15	Lt. ✚
BLACKLOW, N. F., Pte. 12 Bn.	✚ 15/4/17.	23/ 5/16	Pte. ✚
BLACKLOW, S. E., Pte. 12 Bn.		17/ 8/14	3m. Pte.
BLACKLOW, Wm. E., Pte. 12 Bn.	51 Bn. ✚8/10/19.	2/ 8/18	Pte. ✚
BLACKMAN, G. C. A., C.-F., 3 L.H.		19/ 8/14	1y 9m, Cpl.
BLACKMORE, A. R., Pte. 12 Bn.	3W. ✚2/11/18.	1/ 5/16	Pte. ✚
BLACKMORE, H., Pte. 15 Bn.	W., 47 Bn. ✚12/4/17.	15/ 6/15	Pte. ✚
BLACKWELL, E., Pte. 12 Bn.		27/ 7/15	
BLACKWELL, H. A., Pte. 15 Bn.	1 A.L.R. Unit.	21/ 4/14	4y 5m, Cpl.
BLACKWELL, W. L., Pte. A.M.C.	3 Fd. Amb. Aust. M.G. Co.	12/12/16	2y 10m, Dvr.
BLACKWOOD, A. W. H., P. 26 Bn.	✚ 19/5/16.	12/ 7/15	Pte. ✚
BLACKWOOD, G., Pte. 12 Bn.	3 L.T.M.B. ✚ 24/7/18.	29/ 5/15	Cpl. ✚
BLACKWOOD, H. W., Pte. 15 Bn.	W.	16/ 7/19	Sgt.
BLACKWOOD, J. F., Spr. Tun. Co.		17/ 5/16	3y 4m, Spr.
BLACKWOOD, T. K., Gnr. F.A.B.	W.	12/10/14	4y 4m, Gnr.
BLACKWOOD, D. B., C.-Chap. 4 AD	M.I.D.	16/10/15	
BLAIR, B. S., Gnr. F.A.B.	W.	15/10/14	4y 1m, Bdr.
BLAIR, B. L., Spr. F. Co.	W.	15/ 7/15	3y 10m, Cpl.
BLAIR, G. W., Gnr. F.A.		17/ 7/15	10m, Gnr.
BLAKE, A. C., Pte. 15 Bn.	✚ 8/8/16.	13/ 8/15	Pte. ✚
BLAKE, A. C., Pte. 12 Bn.	✚ 7/9/15.	28/ 8/14	Pte ✚
BLAKE, C. I., Pte. 12 Bn.	3W.	5/ 1/15	4y 5m, Pte.
BLAKE, C. W., Pte. 40 Bn.	2W.	12/ 5/16	3y 1m, Cpl.
BLAKE, C., Pte. M.G. Bn.		11/ 8/16	2y 10m, Pte.
BLAKE, C., Gnr. F.A.	3 Sig. Co.	5/10/16	
BLAKE, E. S., Pte. 12 Bn.	✚ 10/6/15.	20/ 8/14	Pte. ✚
BLAKE, F., Pte. Pt. A.G.H.C.D.	47 Bn., 49 Bn.	10/ 6/15	
BLAKE, G., Pte. 40 Bn.		28/ 9/16	3y, Dvr.
BLAKE, H. G., Pte. 12 Bn.	✚ 23/7/16.	22/ 8/14	Pte. ✚
BLAKE, K. N., Pte. 12 Bn.	W. M.G. Details	1/ 6/16	3y, Pte.
BLAKE, L. W., Pte. 40 Bn.		23/ 2/16	3y 3m, L.-Cpl
BLAKE, R. A., Pte. 40 Bn.	4W.	31/10/16	2y 11m, Pte.
BLAKE, T. C., Pte. A.S.C.		17/ 4/16	3y 5m, Pte.
BLAKE, W. T., Pte. 40 Bn.	2W.	9/ 2/16	2y 2m, Cpl.
BLAKNEY, C., Cpl. 12 Bn.	2W., 52 Bn.	17/ 8/14	3y 11m, Capt.
BLAKNEY, C. A., Gnr. 1 F.A.B.	2W.	26/ 8/14	4y 6m, Cpl.
BLANCH, C. H., Pte. 40 Bn.	W.	30/ 6/16	1y 11m, Pte.
BLANCH, J., Pte. 40 Bn.	W.	10/ 2/17	2y 1m, Pte.
BLANEY, J., Pte. 26 Bn.	Aust. Cps., H.T.M.B.	1/ 5/15	4y, Gnr.
BLANEY, R., Pte. 40 Bn.		17/10/16	
BLANEY, W., Spr. Miners	3 Tnl. Co.	26/10/15	3y 11m, Cpl.
BLAUBAUM, O., Cpl. Art.	Dental Co.	2/ 9/15	2y 9m, Lt.
BLAZELEY, H. W., Pte. 12 Bn.	W.	5/ 10/16	1y 7m, Pte.
BLIGH, F. W., Pte 40 Bn.	W.	19/ 6/16	2y 1m, Pte.
BLIGHT, J., Sgt. Pt. G.S.R.		23/11/16	3y 1m, Sgt.
BLINDELL, A. T., Dvr. A.S.C.		1/ 9/14	8m, Dvr.

TASMANIA'S MUSTER ROLL.

NAME.	REMARKS.	RANK ON DISCHARGE. ENLISTED, SERVICE.
BLINDELL, A. W. T., Pte. 40 Bn.		9/ 3/16
BLINDELL, C. G., Gnr. F.A.B.		16/ 5/16 3y 5m, Dvr.
BLINDELL, K. A., Dvr. 8 F.A.B.		3/10/16 3y, Dvr.
BLIZZARD, D. N., Spr. 4 Miners	3 Tunn. Co.	18/ 1/16 3y 10m, Spr.
BLIZZARD, E. L., Pte. 40 Bn.	✠ 5/10/17.	13/ 7/16 Pte. ✠
BLIZZARD, J. L., Pte. 40 Bn.	✠ 5/10/17.	9/ 2/18 Pte. ✠
BLONG, G. A., Pte. 12 Bn.		22/ 8/14 3y, Pte.
BLONG, R. E. B., Pte. Aviation		6/ 9/16 2y 10m, 2 A.M.
BLOOM, C. D., Pte. 40 Bn.		19/10/16 2y 6m, Pte.
BLOOM, J., Pte. T.M.B.	W.	19/10/16
BLOOMFIELD, A. R., Pte. 26 Bn.	W., 7 M.G. Co.	16/ 9/15 3y 11m, Pte.
BLOOMFIELD, F., Pte. 12 Bn.	2W.	20/12/15 3y 4m, Pte.
BLOXHAM, B., Pte. Cyclists	W., 10 F. Co. Engrs.	4/ 4/16
BLUCK, E. N., Spr. 8 F.C.E.	12 F.C.E., 2 A.M.T. Co.	30/12/15 3y 10m, MTD
BLUMER, H. E., Tpr. 3 L.H (Enlisted under assumed name STANLEY, H.)		18/10/16 Pte.
BLUNDELL, W. L., Sgt. 12 Bn.		26/ 8/15
BLUNDSTONE, E L., Dvr. A.M.C.	3 Fd. Amb.	16/10/16 3y, Dvr.
BLYTH, E. F., Gnr. Art.	23 How. Bde. Am. Col. ✠ 2/2/17.	1/10/15 Sgt. ✠
BLYTH, G. H., Dvr. A.S.C.	Aust. M.T. Div. Trn.	15/10/17 1y 9m, Dvr.
BLYTH, G. J. E., Pte. 12 Bn.	52 Bn. ✠ 4/9/16.	25/ 8/15 Pte. ✠
BLYTH, H. N., Tpr. 3 L.H.		21/ 9/14 2y, Tpr.
BLYTHE, M. S., Tpr. 3 L.H.	✠ 23/12/16.	29/ 1/15 Tpr. ✠
BLYTH, M. C., Pte. 26 Bn.	✠ 20/6/16.	31/ 7/15 Pte. ✠
BLYTH, K. C., Gnr. 8 F.A.B.	W.	18/11/15 4y, Bdr.
BLYTH, W. O., Pte. 12 Bn.	A. Ord. C.	12/ 9/14 4y 6m, Am.S.
BOA, J., Pte. 7 F. Amb.		9/ 3/15
BOAG, A. S., Gnr. 6 F.A.B		23/ 8/15 2y 1m, Bdr.
BOAG, H. L. G., Cpl. 15 Bn.		10/ 6/15 3y 1m, L.-Sgt.
BOARD, H., Pte. 26 Bn.	W., P.O.W.	25/ 6/15 2y 9m, Pte.
BOARD, M. A., Pte. 40 Bn.	2W.	7/ 8/17 1y 7m, Pte.
BOARDMAN, R., Pte. 26 Bn.	✠ 31/7/16.	19/ 7/15 Pte. ✠
BOCK, H. S., Pte. 12 Bn.		27/ 4/17 2y 7m, Pte.
BOCK, S. H, Pte. 40 Bn.		29/ 2/16 3y 6m, Pte.
BODDAM, E. T., Lieut. 1 A.C.H.	M.C., 2 Div. H.Q.	2/10/14 Capt.
BODEN, A. J., Pte. 26 Bn.	52 Bn. ✠10/6/17.	19/ 7/15 Pte. ✠
BODEN, H., Sgt 40 Bn., 15 Bn.	3W., M.C., C. De G. (Belgian), ✠ 29/9/18.	28/ 6/16 2-Lt. ✠
BODEN, R. S., Pte. 12 Bn.		16/ 6/16 2y 10m, Pte.
BODEN, M., Gnr. 21 Bty.		6/10/15 1y 9m, Gnr.
BODEN, S., Pte. 12 Bn.		6/ 1/15 4y 7m.
BOER, J., Pte. 40 Bn.	M.M.	27/ 9/16
BOLCH, A. R., Spr. Miners	W.	12/10/15 3y 6m, Spr.
BOLCH, A. A., Pte. 12 Bn.		16/10/17 2y 2m, Pte.
BOLCH, W. J., Pte. 12 Bn.	52 Bn. ✠ 4/9/16.	12/10/15 Pte. ✠
BOLTER, R., Pte. 12 Bn.	14 Bn.	14/10/16 2y 11m, Pte.
BOLTON, H., Tpr. 3 L.H.		5/ 6/15 4y 5m, Tpr.
BOLTON, J. L., Pte. 40 Bn.	W.	15/ 3/16 3y 6m, Pte.
BOLTON, L. J., Pte. 15 Bn.	2W., M.G. Bn.	2/ 1/15 4y 9m, L.-Cpl.
BOLTON, M. T., Pte. 12 Bn.	W.	8/ 1/16 4y, Cpl.
BOLTON, M. J., Pte. 26 Bn.	3W.	31/ 7/15 3y 9m, Pte.
BOLTON, R., Pte. 40 Bn.	✠ 18/10/16.	12/ 6/16 Pte. ✠
BOMFORD, C. E. R., Spr. 5 Miners		8/ 1/16 3y 8m, Spr.
BOND, C. J., Pte. 7 F. Amb.	M.M.	14/ 4/15 4y 2m, Pte.
BOND, F. J., Pte. 12 Bn.	W. ✠ between 6-10/4/17.	30/11/15 Pte. ✠
BOND, G., Capt. 26 Bn.	M.C.	21/ 8/16 1y 6m, Capt.
BOND, H., Pte. 8 Bn.		4/ 1/15 4y 5m, Pte.
BOND, H., Pte. 12 Bn.		21/ 8/16 2y 6m, Pte.
BOND, H. G., Pte. 26 Bn.		29/ 3/15 4y 6m, L.-Cpl.
BOND, R., Pte. 26 Bn.	W. ✠ 27/3/17.	18/ 6/15 Pte. ✠
BOND, W., Pte. 12 Bn.	✠ between 23-26/7/16.	18/ 6/15 Pte. ✠
BONE, J. J. C., Pte. 40 Bn.		30/ 9/16 3y 3m, Pte.
BONE, S. H., Spr. Tnl Co.		9/ 8/16
BONE, V. A., Tpr. L.H.	M.M.	18/ 1/15 4y 6m, L.-Cpl.
BONES, C. O., Pte. 12 Bn.	W., 1 Div., Trn.	27/ 2/17 2y 8m, Pte.
BONES, L., Pte. 12 Bn.	W., 1 Div., Trn.	23/ 5/16 4y 5m, Dvr.
BONHOTE, P., Pte. 12 Bn.	D.C.M., MM., 52 Bn. ✠ 24/4/18.	19/10/15 C.S.M. ✠
BONIWELL, H. B., Gnr. 31 F. Bty.		3/ 2/16 3y 11m, Gnr.
BONIWELL, R. O., Spr. 8 F. Co.		9/ 3/16
BONNER, A., Pte. 12 Bn.		11/ 1/16 1y 11m, Pte.
BONNER, C. A., Pte. 40 Bn.	W., 49 Bn.	14/ 3/16 3y 6m, Pte.
BONNER, E. R., Pte. Railways		30/10/17 2y 1m, Pte.
BONNER, J. E., Pte. 12 Bn.		30/10/17
BONNER, T., Pte. 12 Bn.	W.	16/10/16 1y 11m, Pte.
BONNER, W. J., Dvr. 9 F. Bty.	W.	27/ 8/14 4y 5m, Sgt.
BONNEY, R. S., Pte. 40 Bn.		13/ 3/16 3y 4m, Sgt.
BONNILLY, J., Pte. 12 Bn.	52 Bn. ✠ 20/4/18.	3/ 8/15 Lt. ✠
BONSER, A. A., Pte. 26 Bn.	W., 69 Bn., 26 Bn. ✠ 5/11/18.	15/ 6/15 Pte. ✠
BONSER, A., Pte. 40 Bn.	2W. ✠ 28/3/18.	24/ 7/16 Pte. ✠
BOON, A. B., Pte. A.M.C.	3 A.G.H.	30/ 1/17 2y 9m, Pte.
BOON, A., Pte 4 M.G. Co.	W., 5 M.C. Co.	29/ 7/16 3y 2m, Pte.
BOON, C. L, Pte A.F.C.	-	27/11/17 1y 8m, 2 A.M.
BOON, E, Pte 12 Bn.		9/10/16 2y 11m, Pte.
BOON, E. E, Tpr. 3 G.S.R.		4/ 4/18 1y 4m, Tpr.
BOON, E. J., Gnr. F.A.	7 D.A.C.	3/ 7/16 3y 2m, Dvr.

TASMANIA'S WAR RECORD, 1914-1918.

NAME.	REMARKS.	RANK ON DISCHARGE. ENLISTED. SERVICE.
BOON, H. E., Pte. 12 Bn.		20/ 8/14 4y 5m, A.-Sgt.
BOON, H. E. G., Gnr. 3 F.A.B.		17/ 9/15 3y 11m, Gnr.
BOON, H. E., Pte. A.M.C.	14 F.A.B.	17/ 5/16 3y 5m, Pte.
BOON, H J. G., Pte. 3 G.S.R.	12 Bn. ✼ 8/2/19.	6/ 6/18 Pte. ✼
BOON, H. W. J., Pte. 12 Bn.		20/ 4/17 11m, Pte.
BOON, M., Pte. 15 Bn.		14/ 9/15 1y 1m, Pte.
BOOTE, C. V., Pte. 40 Bn.		3/ 4/16 2y 11m, Pte.
BOOTE, C. E., L.-Cpl. 3 G.S.R.	W.	13/ 6/18 1y 6m, Pte.
BOOTH, E. J., Cpl. 29 Fd. Bty.	W.	6/10/15 3y 6m, Sgt.
BOOTH, G., Pte. 12 Bn.	W. ✼ 17/9/17.	5/ 8/15 Pte. ✼
BOOTH, H. L., Pte. 40 Bn.		21/ 9/16 3y 3m, L.-Cpl.
BOOTH, L. K., Pte. 12 Bn.	W.	1/ 8/17 Pte.
BOOTH, R. E., Pte. 12 Bn.		29/ 8/14
BOOTH, W. C., Cpl. 12 Bn.		5/ 8/15
BOGTON, J. T., Pte. 14 F.A.B.	3 Fld. Bakery.	2/11/15 3y 10m, Dvr.
BOREHAM, H. N., Pte. 40 Bn.	2W.	21/ 7/17 1y 8m, Pte.
BOYES, J. W., Capt. Remounts		14/10/15 1y 2m. Capt.
BOYLE, N. S., Lt. 26 Bn.		11/ 3/15
BOSSWARD, W. E., Pte. 1 A.G.H.	W., 13 F.A.B., 51 Bn.	9/ 6/15 3y 10m, Pte.
BOSWOOD, W. M., Gnr. F.A.B.	W., 23 How. Bde., 6 F.A.B.	16/ 9/15 3y 7m, Gnr.
BOSWORTH, L., Pte. 40 Bn.		13/ 9/16 3y 3m.
BOSWORTH, L., Tpr. 3 L.H.	W.	23/ 8/15 4y 1m, Tpr.
BOTTCHER, O. C., Gnr. 3 F.A.B.		6/ 9/15 4y, Gnr.
BOTTLE, F. J., Pte. 40 Bn.	2W., 2 A.G.H., 40 Bn.	19/ 2/16 3y 10m, Pte.
BOTTREILL, F. R., Pte. 40 Bn.	W.	7/ 2/17 2y 1m, Pte.
BOUCHER, A., Cpl. 5 F.Amb.		8/ 9/14 4y 5m, Cpl.
BOUCHER, C. H., Pte. 40 Bn.	3W., 49 Bn.	3/ 5/16 3y 11m, Cpl.
BOUCHER, J. H., Pte. 40 Bn.	W., 49 Bn.	7/ 6/16 1y 4m, Pte.
BOULTBEE, L. F., Cpl. 12 Bn.	W.	26/ 6/15 2y 6m, Pte.
BOUNDS, J. C., Pte. 26 Bn.	✼ 5/8/16.	15/ 6/15 Pte. ✼
BOUNDS, L. G., Pte. 12 Bn.		29/ 7/15
BOUNDS, W. C., Pte. 12 Bn.		22/10/17
BOURKE, A. C., Tpr. 3 L.H.		16/ 1/15 1y 6m, Tpr.
BOURKE, A. J., Dvr. 10 Fd. Co.		25/ 7/17 Dvr.
BOURKE, C. J., Spr. 40 Bn.	W., M.S.M.	16/ 5/16 3y 3m, Spr.
BOURKE, C. H., Pte. 12 Bn.	W., M.M., 52 Bn.	6/ 1/16 2y 3m, Pte.
BOURKE, E., Pte. 12 Bn.	W.	23/ 9/15 4y, Pte.
BOURKE, E. G., Pte. 40 Bn.	51 Bn. ✼ 16/11/16.	23/ 2/16 Pte. ✼
BOURKE, F. H., Tpr. L.H.		29/12/14 4y 3m, Tpr.
BOURKE, F. M., Pte. 40 Bn.	2W.	21/ 2/16 2y 5m, Pte.
BOURKE, F., Pte. 12 Bn.		5/ 8/18 11m, Pte.
BOURKE, J. H., Gnr. F.A.	10 Fd. Co. Engrs.	15/12/16 2y 11m, Dvr.
BOURKE, J. T., Pte. 40 Bn.	✼ 5/10/17.	10/ 8/16 Pte. ✼
BOURKE, J. J., Pte. 40 Bn.		23/ 8/17 2y 1m, Pte.
BOURKE, M. J., Pte. 12 Bn.		13/ 8/18 10m, Pte.
BOURKE, M. E., Pte. 12 Bn.	61 Bn., 69 Bn., 12 Bn.	30/ 4/16 3y, Pte.
BOURKE, R. H., Pte 26 Bn.	7 A.L.T.M.B.	4/ 3/15 4y 9m, RQMS
BOURNE, B. W., Cpl. 3 F.A.B.	4 Div. Artl.	27/ 8/14 4y 7m, Lt.
BOUTCHARD, H. Q., Pte. 6 F. Co.	W.	5/ 8/15 4y 1m, Pte.
BOWATER, W. E. Pte. 15 Bn.	45 Bn.	1/ 7/15 4y 5m, Pte.
BOWDEN, A. C., Spr. 3 Fd. Co.	Vet. Hosp., 3 Fd. Co. Engrs.	2/10/14 4y 3m, Spr.
BOWDEN, F., Spr. Tnl. Co.		24/11/16 6m, Spr.
BOWDEN, G. F., Pte. 12 Bn.	W.	25/ 4/17 2y 4m, Pte.
BOWDEN, G. R., Spr., 3 Fd. Cd.	✼ 23/7/15.	5/10/14 Spr. ✼
BOWDEN, H. L., Spr. 3 Fd. Co.		3/10/14 2y 1m, Spr.
BOWDEN, N. H., Sgt. 12 Bn.		31/12/14 2m, Sgt.
BOWDEN, R. J., Spr. 6 Fd. Co.	4 Div. Engrs.	24/ 7/15 4y 1m, Spr.
BOWDEN, T., Pte. 12 Bn.	✼ 20/4/18.	13/ 5/16 Pte. ✼
BOWDEN, W. R., Pte. 40 Bn.	3W., 15 Bn., 40 Bn.	21/ 2/16 3y 8m, L.-Cpl.
BOWEN, A. G., Pte. 26 Bn.		3/ 5/15
BOWEN, C. J., Pte. 40 Bn.	W. ✼ 13/10/17.	12/ 7/16 Pte. ✼
BOWEN, P. J. Gnr. 3 F.A.B.	24 Bty. A.F.A. ✼ 14/11/16.	26/ 8/14 Cpl. ✼
BOWERS, A. E., Cpl. 12 Bn.	W.	17/ 2/17 2y 8m, L.-Cpl.
BOWER, B. G., Gnr. F.A.B.	3 L.H.	1/11/15 3y 9m, Dvr.
BOWERMAN, G., Pte. 15 Bn.	✼ 14/6/15.	2/ 1/15 Pte. ✼
BOWERMAN, J. P., Pte. 26 Bn.	✼ 1/8/16.	30/ 8/15 Pte. ✼
BOWERMAN, J., Pte. 40 Bn.		3/10/16 1y 1m, Pte.
BOWIE, J., Pte. 15 Bn.	4 M.G. Bn.	21/ 5/15 4y 3m, Sgt.
BOWLAND, A. W., Pte. 26 Bn.	1 Anzac Hqrs. ✼ 18/3/17.	20/ 7/15 Pte. ✼
BOWLES, C., Pte. 15 Bn.		4/11/14
BOWLEY, E., Pte. 12 Bn.	W., 40 Bn.	5/10/16 2y 7m, Pte.
BOWLEY, L. E., Pte. 12 Bn.	W., 40 Bn.	22/10/16 2y 1m
BOWLING, H., Pte. 15 Bn.		26/ 9/14 11m, Pte.
BOWMAN, D. T., Pte. 4 M.G. Co.		21/ 7/16
BOWMAN, J. W., Pte. 40 Bn.	W.	29/ 3/17 2y 6m, Pte.
BOWMAN, V., Pte. 12 Bn.	W. ✼ 9/8/15.	20/ 8/14 Pte. ✼
BOWRING, A., Pte. 15 Bn.	✼ 4/7/18.	15/ 6/15 Pte. ✼
BOWRING, J. F. P., Sgt. 40 Bn.	✼ 7/6/17.	13/ 3/16 Sgt. ✼
BOWRING, H. T., Pte. 40 Bn.	W.	3/10/16 3y, Pte.
BOWRING, R., Pte 12 Bn.	W.	8/12/15
BOX, R H., Cpl. 12 Bn.	3W., M.M.	8/10/15 4y, Sgt.
BOYD, A. H., Pte. 3 L.H.		19/ 8/14 1y 6m, Pte.
BOYD, J. H., Pte. 40 Bn.	W., 15 Bn.	26/ 6/16 3y 4m, L.-Cpl.
BOYD, M., Pte. 1 G.S.R.	39 Bn.	14/ 3/18 1y 7m, Pte.
BOYD, T., Pte. 26 Bn.	W.	18/ 5/15 2y 5m, Pte.
BOYER, C., Dvr. 3 F.A.B.	W.	19/ 1/15 4y 7m, Cpl.

TASMANIA'S MUSTER ROLL. 235

NAME.	REMARKS.	RANK ON DISCHARGE. ENLISTED, SERVICE,
BOYER, R. D., Pte. 26 Bn.	2W., 12 Bn.	28/ 7/15 3y 9m, Pte.
BOYER, W., Tpr. 3 L.H.	W., 2 L.H.	25/ 8/14 4y 5m
BOYER, W. J., Pte. 12 Bn.	2W. ✠ 10/1/18.	2/ 5/16 Pte. ✠
BOYES, E., Cpl. 40 Bn.	M.C.	20/ 3/16 3y, Lt.
BOYES, A. A., Spr. 8 Fd. Cd.	W., 11 Fd. Co. Engrs.	26/ 1/16 3y 8m, Spr.
BOYES, J., Sgt. 9 Bty.	1 A.C.A.P., 13 F.A.B.	16/12/14 2y 6m, Sgt.
BOYLES, C. W., Pte. 15 Bn.		27/ 7/15
BOYLES, H. J., Spr. 8 Fd. Co.	14 Fd. Co.	1/ 2/16 3y 7m, Spr.
BOYS, G. H. Pte. 1 G.S.R.	40 Bn.	23/ 1/18 1y 9m, Pte.
BOYS, J. H., Pte. 26 Bn.		22/ 4/15 4y 4m, L.-Cpl.
BOYS, S. D., Pte. 4 M.G. Co.		30/ 9/16
BOZEN, W., Gnr. 4 D.A.C.		19/ 4/17 2y 6m. Gnr.
BRACEY, S. C., Pte. 1 G.S.R.	40 Bn.	16/ 7/17
BRACKEN, H. J., L.-Cpl. 12 Bn.	W.	19/ 9/14 4y 6m, L.-Cpl.
BRACKEN, W., Pte. 2 A.G.H.	13 Fd. Amb.	16/ 9/15 4y, Pte.
BRADBURY, J., Spr. Tnl. Co.		20/10/16 1y 6m, Spr.
BRADBURY, V. R., Chap., Chap. Dp.	W.	1/ 1/16 3y 11m, Chap.
BRADD, G. B., Pte. 12 Bn.	W., 26 Bn., 2 Fd. Bakery.	2/ 8/15 4y 1m, Pte.
BRADFORD, E. W., Pte. 12 Bn.	2W.	13/ 6/16 2y 1m, Pte.
BRADFORD, G., Pte. 40 Bn.		5/10/16 1y 1m, Pte.
BRADFORD, J. P., Sgt. 40 Bn.		15/ 1/16
BRADFORD, S., Pte. 40 Bn.	10 Bde., 1 A.G.H., 1 A.C.C.S.	22/ 9/16 3y, Pte.
BRADFORD, W. J., Pte. 12 Bn.		28/ 6/16
BRADLEY, A., Pte. 4 M.G. Co.	2W., 15 Bn., 2nd M.G. Bn.	17/11/16 1y 3m, Pte.
BRADLEY, D. L., Pte. 26th Bn.		16/ 4/17 1y 11m, Pte.
BRADLEY, E. J., Pte. 12 Bn.	M.S.M., M.I.D.	20/ 7/15 4y 2m, Pte.
BRADLEY, H., Pte. 3 G.S. Rfts.		25/ 8/14 4y 7m, Sgt.
BRADLEY, J. K., Pte. 12 Bn.	✠ 25-28/4/1915	20/ 8/14 Pte. ✠
BRADLEY, J. T., Pte. 40 Bn.	M.M., 10 Fd. Amb., 40 Bn.	24/ 2/16 3y 8m, Cpl.
BRADLEY, J., Tpr. 3 L.H.		26/ 3/17 0y 4m, Tpr.
BRADLEY, T. W., Pte. 4 M.G. Co.	W., 21 Bn., 2 M.G. Co.	5/ 1/17 2y 2m, Pte.
BRADLEY, W., Pte. 12 Bn.		2/ 9/17 2y 1m, Pte.
BRADMORE, E. H., Pte. 40 Bn.	✠ 30/1/17	3/ 2/16 Pte. ✠
BRADMORE, L. N. G., Pte. 12 Bn.	5 M.G. Co., 8 M.G. Co.	7/11/16 2y 7m, Pte.
BRADSHAW, A. L., Pte. 12 Bn.	M.M., 4 Div. Cyc., 4 Sig. Co.	1/11/15 3y 10m, L-Cpl.
BRADSHAW, G., Pte. 12 Bn.	39 Bn.	1/12/17 1y 6m
BRADSHAW, G. C., Gnr. 9th Bty.	2W., 24 Bty., 21 F.A. Bde.	26/ 8/14 3y 7m, Sgt.
BRADSHAW, R. E, Pte. A.M.C.	4 Fd. Amb.	2/10/16 3y 1m, Pte.
BRADSHAW, R., Pte. 12 Bn.	52 Bn.	31/ 8/14 4y 6m, Cpl.
BRADY, C. B., Gnr. Art.		2/12/16
BRADY, W., Pte. 12 Bn.	✠ 19-22/8/16.	1/ 2/15 Pte. ✠
BRAID, J., Pte 40 Bn.	W.	21/ 1/16 3y 8m, Sgt.
BRAIDFORD, W. W., Pte. 26 Bn.	W. ✠ 20/7/16.	1/ 4/15 Pte. ✠
BRAIN, B., Spr. 6 Fd. Co.	W. 4 Divl. Eng. ✠ 18/9/16.	4/ 8/15 Spr. ✠
BRAIN, C. E., Cpl. 3 F.A.B.	2W. 10 F.A.B.	20/ 8/14
BRAIN, C. E., Pte. 12 Bn.	2 Tunn. Co.	10/ 2/15 4y 5m, Pte.
BRAIN, E. L., Spr. Mnrs. Rfts.		24/ 8/17 2y 2m, Spr.
BRAIN, G. W., Gnr. Art.		21/ 5/17 2y 7m, Gnr.
BRAIN, H. H., Gnr. 18 Bty.	W. 17 Bty., 6 F.A.B.	23/ 8/15 3y 8m, Sgt.
BRAKEY, A. C., Pte., 12 Bn.	23 Bn. ✠ 7/11/17.	28/ 9/16 Pte. ✠
BRAMICH, A. B., Pte. 15 Bn.	47 Bn. ✠ 12/10/17.	4/ 8/15 Cpl. ✠
BRAMICH, A.W., Pte. 26 Bn.	12 Bn. ✠23/7/16.	14/ 8/15 Pte. ✠
BRAMICH, C. A., Pte 12 Bn.	W. 47 Bn.	16/ 6/16 1y 6m, Pte.
BRAMICH, C. A., Pte. 40 Bn.	W. ✠ 6/11/8.	22/ 5/16 2y 6m, L.-Cpl.
BRAMICH, C., Pte. 3 G.S.R.	12 Bn.	13/ 8/18 1y 3m, Pte.
BRAMICH, C. W., Pte. 40 Bn.	2W.	22/ 5/16 2y 7m, Pte.
BRAMICH, C. W., Pte. 40 Bn.	✠ 13/10/17.	10/10/16 Pte. ✠
BRAMICH, C. S, Pte. 12 Bn.	W.	20/ 7/16 3y, Pte.
BRAMICH, E. H., Pte. 40 Bn.	W. 26 Bn.	31/ 8/14 3y 6m, Pte.
BRAMICH, G. H., Tpr. 3 L.H.		16/ 6/16
BRAMICH, H. L, Pte. 40 Bn.		10/10/16 2y 11m, Pte.
BRAMICH, H. W, Pte. 40 Bn.		20/ 7/16 3y 1m, Pte.
BRAMICH, H. C., Pte. 3 G.S.R.		13/ 8/18 0y 11m, Pte.
BRAMICH, K. T., Pte. 13 Bn.	12 Bn., 47 Bn. ✠ 26/6/15.	19/ 8/17 Pte. ✠
BRAMICH, L. R., Pte. 12 Bn.	✠ 7/10/17.	16/10/16 Pte. ✠
BRAMICH, L. W., Dvr. 8 Fd. Co.	1 Sig. Co.	4/ 8/15 4y 1m, Dvr.
BRAMICH, L. F. J., Pte. 40 Bn.		30/ 8/16 1y 11m, Pte.
BRAMICH, L, Pte. 12 Bn.	✠ 15/3/18.	2/11/16 Pte. ✠
BRAMICH, S., Pte. 15 Bn.	✠ 28/9/17/.	26/ 8/15 L-Cpl. ✠
BRAMICH, W, Pte. 14 Bn.		24/11/15 1y 2m, Pte.
BRAMICH, W., Pte. 12 Bn.		30/11/15
BRAMICH, W. M R., Pte. 12 Bn.	W.	13/10/16 2y 5m, Pte.
BRAMMALL, F. J., Tpr. 3 L.H.	4 D.A.C. ✠ 30/9/18	20/ 7/15 Dvr. ✠
BRAMMER, J., Pte. 12 Bn.		8/ 4/16
BRAMPTON, T. T., Spr. 5 M.Cy.	1 Tun. Co.	27/ 3/16 2y 1m, Spr.
BRAMPTON, W. A., Spr. 5 M.Cy.	1 Tun. Co.	27/ 3/16 2y 5m, Spr.
BRANCH, C E. Gnr. 6 F.A.B.	1 D.A.C., 3 F.A.B., 1 A. Div. Trn.	10/ 1/16 3y 9m, S S Cpl.
BRANCH. C. Pte. 12 Bn.	W.	26/11/14 1y 8m, Pte.
BRANDON, H. H. B., Pte. 12 Bn.		1/11/16 1y 9m, Pte.
BRANDUM, J. J., Pte. 12 Bn.	2W. 52 Bn.	17/ 1/16 2y, Pte.
BRANLEY, J. M, Pte. 12 Bn.	W. 52 Bn. ✠ 16/10/17.	27/ 1/16 Pte. ✠
BRANLEY, W. A., Pte. 26 Bn.		21/ 9/15 1y 4m, Pte.
BRANSDEN, E J., Pte. 40 Bn.	2W.	11/ 3/16 2y 9m, Pte.
BRANSDEN, M. E. W., Tpr. 3 L.H.		21/ 8/14 5y 1m, Tpr.
BRANSGROVE, S., Pte. Wrlss. C.		1/ 2/18 0y 10m, Pte.
BRATTLE, E H., Spr. 6 Fd. Co.	Mech. Transport.	14/ 8/15

TASMANIA'S WAR RECORD, 1914-1918.

NAME.	REMARKS.	RANK ON DISCHARGE. ENLISTED. SERVICE.
BRAY, G. R., Gnr. F.A.B.	4 Div. Amm., Sub. Park.	10/ 9/15 3y 11m, Pte.
BRAY, W., Tpr. 4 G.S.R.		24/ 6/18 1y, Tpr.
BRAY, W. J., Pte. 12 Bn.	W.	9/ 5/16 3y 5m, Pte.
BRAZZILL, C., Cpl. 4 A.S.C.		28/11/14 4y 5m, Cpl.
BREADEN, W. C., Spr. 3 M. Co.		18/11/15 2y 2m, Spr.
BREEDON, W. H., Pte. 54 Bn.		11/ 9/15 3y 7m, Pte.
BREEN, C. W., Pte. 40 Bn.		28/ 3/16 1y 6m, Pte.
BREEN, J. A., Pte. 40 Bn.	69 Bn., 40 Bn. ✠ 29/9/18.	11/ 4/16 Pte. ✠
BRENNAN, D., Spr. 3 M. Co.	2W. 3 Tun. Co.	4/11/15 3y 10m
BRENNAN, J., Spr. 3 Miners		6/11/15
BRENNAN, J., Pte. 20 Bn.	W.	15/ 9/15 1y 9m, Pte.
BRENNAN, P., Pte. 15 Bn.	W.	17/ 9/14 1y 8m, Pte.
BRERETON, D. A. P., Pte. 40 Bn.	10 Fd. Amb.	10/ 4/16 3y 7m, Pte.
BRESNEHAN, J. B., Pte. 12 Bn.	1 Pnrs.	21/ 7/15 4y 3m, Pte.
BRESNEHAN, L., Pte. 40 Bn.	W.	1/ 5/16 1y 8m
BRESNEHAN, M. E., Pte. 40 Bn.	2W. ✠ 29/9/18.	3/ 3/16 Pte. ✠
BRETNELL, H., Pte. 12 Bn.		7/ 2/15
BRETT, A. G., Pte. 40 Bn.	2W.	28/ 2/16 3y 1m, Pte.
BRETT, C. W., Pte. 12 Bn.		3/11/15
BRETT, J. M., Dvr. 5 G S.R.		8/ 7/18 1y 2m, Dvr.
BREWARD, A. L., Pte. 12 Bn.	2 Bn., 5 Bn.	8/11/15 4y, Cpl.
BREWARD, G., Pte. 40 Bn.	W. ✠ 12/10/17.	1/ 3/16 Pte. ✠
BREWARD, H. A., Pte. 40 Bn.		20/ 3/16 3y 2m, Pte.
BREWARD, W., Pte. 26 Bn.	W. ✠ 5/8/16.	25/ 6/15 Pte. ✠
BREWER, E. M., Pte. 40 Bn.	✠ 7/6/17.	25/ 9/16 Pte. ✠
BREWER, H. J., Pte. Railways	W. 14 Bn.	26/ 4/17 2y 5m, Pte.
BREWER, P. R H., Pte. 12 Bn.	2W. M.M., 13 M.G. Co.	6/ 8/15 4y, Sgt.
BRICKNELL, J. G., Tpr. 2 G.S.R.	3 L.H.	13/ 5/18 1y 3m, Tpr.
BRICKNELL, J. W., Pte. 40 Bn.		7/10/16 1y 8m, Pte.
BRIDGER, G. H., Cpl. 12 Bn.		11/ 1/15 4y 1m, Cpl.
BRIDGES, N. C., Pte. 15 Bn.	.W.	10/ 6/15 1y 11m, Pte.
BRILL, E. W., Tpr. Railways		29/ 9/15 1y 3m, Tpr.
BRILL, L. W., Pte. 12 Bn.	M.M.	20/ 8/14
BRILLIANT, J. D., Pte. 12 Bn.	M.M. 40 Bn.	13/10/16 2y 9m, Sgt.
BRIMBLE, R. F., Tpr. 3 L.H.		20/ 7/15 4y ⁕ m, L.-Cpl.
BRIMBLE, R. J., Pte. R. Sec.		11/10/15 0y 9m, Pte.
BRIMFIELD, F, Pte. 12 Bn.	W.	17/ 5/16 3y 6m, Pte.
BRIMFIELD, J., Pte. 40 Bn.		4/10/16 1y, Pte.
BRINDLEY, W. L., Spr. Tnl. Co.	W.	19/ 4/16
BRISCOE, F. G, Pte. 12 Bn.	1 Pioneer Bn.	10/ 2/15 4y 6m, Sgt.
BRISCOE, J. M., Pte. 12 Bn.	W. 52 Bn. ✠ 19/10/17.	16/ 1/15 Pte. ✠
BRISCOE, J. B., Pte. 12 Bn.	2W.	26/ 4/17 2y 6m, Pte.
BRITCLIFFE, L R R., Pte. AM.C.	3 A.G.H.	3/ 5/17 2y 6m, Pte.
BRITCLIFFE, W. E., Tpr. 3 L.H.		3/ 5/17 2y 7m, Pte.
BRITTAIN, A., Gnr. 2 G.S.R.	4 F.A.B.	27/ 3/17 1y 10m, Gnr.
BRITTEN, A. O., Tpr. 3 L.H.	8 L.H. ✠13/11/18.	30/ 3/17 Tpr. ✠
BRITTON, A. J., Spr. Miners	2 Tunn. Co.	12/ 1/16 3y 9m, Spr.
BRITTON, C. A., Pte. 15 Bn.	W. M.M., 47 Bn.	8/ 9/15 3y 3m, L.-Cpl.
BRITTON, V D., Pte A.M.C.	9 Fd Amb	2/ 9/16 3y 1m, Pte.
BRIGGS, A. H., Tpr. 2 R. Sec.		5/10/15 3y, Tpr.
BRIGGS, C., Pte. 12 Bn.	✠ 30/7/18.	19/10/16 Pte. ✠
BRIGGS, C. H., Gnr. 9 Fd. Bty.	4 Div. Art., 24 and 10 F.A.B.	26/ 8/14 4y, Sgt.
BRIGGS, C. J., Pte. 12 Bn.	✠ 19-22/8/16.	31/ 8/15/ Pte. ✠
BRIGGS, E. C., Pte. 12 Bn.		8/ 6/16 Lieut.
BRIGGS, E. G, Gnr. 9 Bty		27/ 8/14 4y 6m, Gnr.
BRIGGS, E. L., Pte. 4 M.G. Co.	40 Bn ✠ 28/3/18.	8/ 1/17 Pte. ✠
BRIGGS, F. I., Pte. A.A.S.C.		3/10/15 3y 8m, Pte.
BRIGGS, F. R., Spr. 12 Bn.	14 F.A.B., 5 Sig Co.	24/ 5/15 4y 3m, Spr.
BRIGGS, G. C., Pte. 15 Bn.		2/ 9/15
BRIGGS, G. A., Pte. 12 Bn.	✠ 28/4/15.	19/ 8/14 Cpl. ✠
BRIGGS, H., Pte. 12 Bn.		5/ 1/16 3y 11m, Pte.
BRIGGS H. B, Pte. 12 Bn.	✠ 8/5/18.	16/10/16 Pte. ✠
BRIGGS, H. W., Pte 40 Bn.		29/11/16
BRIGGS, J. E., Pte. 12 Bn.	W:	28/ 3/17 2y, Pte.
BRIGGS, L. J., Pte. 26 Bn.	4W.	3/ 4/15 4y 5m, Sgt.
BRIGGS, T H., Gnr. 8 Bty	2W. D.C.M, 17 Bty.	28/ 9/15 3y 11m, W.O,
BRIGGS, T. W., Pte. 12 Bn.	2W.	16/10/15 2y 6m, Pte.
BRIGGS, V. H., Pte. 12 Bn.		19/ 1/15 1y 7m, Pte.
BROAD, D. A., Pte. 40 Bn.	✠ 10/6/17.	16/ 5/16 Pte. ✠
BROAD, T. M., Pte. 40 Bn.	4 M.G. Co.	2/10/16 1y 10m, Pte.
BROADBY, L W., Pte. 40 Bn.	W.	2/10/16 2y 6m, Pte.
BROADBY, S R., Pte. 12 Bn.	5 F.A.B., 104 How. Bty.	9/ 7/17 2y 3m, Gnr.
BROADHURST, W., Pte. 12 Bn.	2W., 40 Bn.	20/ 6/16 L.-Cpl.
BROCKEN, J., Pte. 15 Bn.	W., 47 Bn. ✠ 2/5/18.	27/ 7/15 Pte. ✠
BROCK., F. D, Pte. 40 Bn.	M M.	1/11/16 2y 7m, Pte.
BROCK. F. W., Pte. 40 Bn.	W.	1/11/16 2y 10m, Pte.
BROCKETT, E. W., Pte. 12 Bn.	C de G. (Belgian).	26/ 8/14 4y 5m, Pte.
BROCKETT, K. L., Dvr. 9 Bty.		26/ 8/14 4y 6m, S.-Sgt.
BROCKMAN, E. A., Pte. 15 Bn.	2W.	15/ 1/15 2y 5m, Pte.
BRODIE. H. J., Spr. 3 Fd. Co.		23/ 2/15 1y 4m, Spr.
BRODIE, P A. R., Pte 4 M.G. Co.	15 M.G. Co.	18/ 9/16 1y 7m, Pte.
BRODIE. T., Pte. 15 Bn.	3W, 24 How. B., 24, 10 F.A Bs.	17/ 5/15 4y, Gnr.
BRODRIBB. W. J. C., Pte 40 Bn.	67 Bn., 17 Fd. Amb.	2/10/16 1y 11m, Cpl.
BROMFIELD, A., Pte. 12 Bn.	52 Bn., 4 Pioneer Bn	2/ 8/18 1y, Pte
BROMFIELD, B, Pte. 12 Bn.	52 Bn., 51 Bn.	3/ 8/15 4y 2m, Dvr.
BROMFIELD, C, Pte 15 Bn.	47 Bn., 4 Pnr. Bn.	4/ 8/15 3y 11m. Pte.

TASMANIA'S MUSTER ROLL. 237

NAME.	REMARKS.	RANK ON ENLISTED.	DISCHARGE. SERVICE.
BRAMICH, A. W., Pte. 26 Bn.	12 Bn. ✤ 23/7/16.	14/ 8/14	Pte. ✤
BROOKE, C. V., Pte. 12 Bn.	P.O.W. ✤ 4/5/15.	20/ 8/14	Pte. ✤
BROOKE, S., Pte. 12 Bn.		6/ 8/15	
BROOKER, L. G., Pte. 12 Bn.	2W., 40 Bn.	29/11/16	2y 11m, Pte.
BROOKS, A., Pte. 12 Bn.	2W., 52 Bn., 13 M.G. Co.	4/11/15	2y 5m, Pte.
BROOKS, A. A., Sgt. 3 Miners	W., D.C.M., 15 Fd. Co.	1/ 9/15	3y 8m, Sgt.
BROOKS, A. A., Spr. 5 Miners	2 Tun. Co.	7/ 3/16	3y 3m, Spr.
BROOKS, A. E., Pte. 12 Bn.	W., 40 Bn.	20/10/16	2y 6m, Pte.
BROOKS, A., Pte. 40 Bn.		1/ 2/16	3y 11m, Pte.
BROOKS, C. H., Pte. 15 Bn.	47 Bn., 4 Pnrs.	25/ 8/15	4y, Dvr.
BROOKS, C., Pte. 1 A.C H.	13 Fd. Amb.	12/ 9/14	4y 4m, Pte.
BROOKS, E. A., Dvr. 109 How. Bty.	27 Bty.	6/ 1/16	3y 3m, Dvr.
BROOKS, E. A., Pte. 15 Bn.	2W.	12/ 1/15	4y 5m, Pte.
BROOKS, H. E., Pte. 12 Bn.	M.M.	25/ 8/15	4y 3m Sgt.
BROOKS, J. B., Pte. 40th Bn.		7/10/16	2y 11m, Pte.
BROOKS, J., Pte. 12 Bn.	W., 40 Bn.	8/ 6/17	2y 3m, Pte.
BROOKS, J. F., Pte. 15 Bn.		22/ 9/14	1y 11m, Sgt.
BROOKS, L. J., Pte. 12 Bn.	✤ 19-22/8/16.	24/ 8/15	Pte. ✤
BROOKS, M., Pte. 15 Bn.		12/ 8/15	2y 6m, Pte.
BROOKS, R. M., Pte. 12 Bn.	52 Bn., 51 Bn., P.O.W. ✤ 3/8/15.	11/11/18	Pte. ✤
BROOKS, R. G., Gnr. 107 How. Bty.	2W.	11/ 1/16	3y 2m
BROOKS, V. A., Pte. 15 Bn.	1 D.A.C., 4 D.A.C.	11/ 8/15	4y, Dvr.
BROOKS, W. C. D., Pte. 26 Bn.		7/ 9/15	3y 11m, Pte.
BROOKS, W., Pte. 26 Bn.		3/ 5/15	1y 3m, Pte.
BROOKS, W. H., Pte. 12 Bn.	49 Bn.	23/ 7/15	2y 3m, Pte.
BROOKS, W. J., Pte. 12 Bn.		3/ 5/16	3y 5m, Pte.
BROOMBY, A. R., Gnr. Arty.		5/ 2/18	1y 8m, Gnr.
BROOMBY, H. S., Dvr. F. Art.	3 D.A.C.	15/ 2/16	3y 7m, Dvr.
BROOMBY, T. W., Gnr. 3 D.A.C.		1/11/16	1y 8m, Gnr.
BROOMHALL, A. W., Pte. 26 Bn.	W., 12 Bn.	10/ 8/15	4y, Pte.
BROOMHALL, G. A., Pte. 12 Bn.	2W.	24/ 8/15	4y 1m, Cpl.
BROOMHALL, J. A., Pte. 12 Bn.	W.	21/ 8/16	3y 2m, Dvr.
BROOMHALL, R., Pte. 40 Bn.	15 Bn.	28/ 3/16	Pte.
BROOMHALL, R. C., Pte. 12 Bn.	2W.	14/10/15	3y 1m, Pte.
BROOMHALL, T. H., Pte. 12 Bn.	2 M.G. Co.	27/ 4/17	2y 8m, Pte.
BROOMHALL, T. H., Pte. 12 Bn.	110 How. Bty.	10/ 8/15	1y 1m, Gnr.
BROOMHALL, W., Pte. 26 Bn.	2W., 12 Bn.	11/ 8/15	3y 11m, Pte.
BROOMHEAD, E. T., Pte. 26 Bn.	W., 69 Bn., 26 Bn.	7/ 9/15	3y 3m, Pte.
BROPHET, G. R., Pte. 12 Bn.	1 Pioneer Bn. ✤ 29/9/17.	19/ 8/15	Pte. ✤
BROTHERTON, C., Sgt. Far. 3 L.H.		19/ 8/14	2y 6m, Sgt. F.
BROUGH, E. A., Pte. A.M.C.	6 Fd. Amb.	10/10/16	3y 1m, Pte.
BROUGH, G., Pte. 12 Bn.	W., M.M., 52 Bn.	29/10/15	Pte.
BROUGHTON, T. A., Gnr. 3 L.H.		8/ 7/15	4y 1m, Gnr.
BROWNELL, H. P., Capt. 7 Fd. Am.	M.I.D., D.S.O., 27 Bn.	21/ 3/15	Major
BROWNELL, R. J., Gnr., 9 Bty.		12/ 9/14	2y 6m, Sgt.
BROWNELL, L., 2nd Lt. 12 Bn.	27 Bn. ✤ 3/10/17.	3/ 9/15	Lieut. ✤
BROWNING, J. M., Pte. 12 Bn.		12/ 6/16	1y 3m, Pte.
BROXAM, A. L., Tpr. 3 L.H.	1 Anzac Cyc. Bn.	4/ 8/15	1y 5m, Pte.
BROXAM, F. E., Pte. 26 Bn.	W., M.M.	5/ 3/15	4y 2m, Pte.
BROWN, A. R., Bdr., 3 F.A.B.	W., D.F.C., A.F.C.	26/ 8/14	4y 7m, Capt.
BROWN, A., Pte. 12 Bn.		9/11/17	1y 5m, Pte.
BROWNE, A., Pte. A.M.C.		19/ 9/17	
BROWN, A., Pte. 12 Bn.	W.	5/ 9/16	1y 7m, Pte.
BROWN, A. E., Pte. 40 Bn.	W.	30/ 5/16	2y 11m, Pte.
BROWN, A. J., Pte. 12 Bn.	W., 1 Div. Sig. Co.	9/ 2/15	4y 1b, Cpl.
BROWN, A. G., Pte. 40 Bn.	W.	16/ 3/16	2y 6m, Pte.
BROWN, A. B., Gnr. 22 F.A.B.	2W., 5 F.A.B.	20/ 9/15	2y 11m, Gnr.
BROWN, A. J., Pte. 40 Bn.	W.	30/ 9/16	2y 5m, Pte.
BROWN, A. P., Pte. 40 Bn.	M.C.	16/ 2/16	3y 6m, Lieut.
BROWN, A. H., Pte. 12 Bn.		4/ 1/18	1y 8m, Pte.
BROWN, A. E., Pte. 40 Bn.	W. ✤ 4/10/17.	5/ 4/16	L.-Cpl. ✤
BROWN, C. B., Spr. 2 Fd. Co.		20/12/17	1y 8m, Spr.
BROWN, C. R., Pte. 40 Bn.	62 Bn.	13/ 9/15	3y 6m, Pte.
BROWN, C. R., Pte. 12 Bn.		10/ 7/15	4y 6m, Pte.
BROWN, C. E., Pte. 12 Bn.		24/ 6/16	1y 6m, Pte.
BROWN, C., Pte. 4 M.G. Co.	2W.	12/ 9/16	2y 8m, Pte.
BROWN, C. G., Pte. 12 Bn.	W.	19/ 2/15	3y 10m, Pte.
BROWNE, C. G., Gnr. 6 F.A.B.	13 A.F.A. Bde. ✤ 28/12/16.	3/ 9/15	2nd-Lt. ✤
BROWN, D. A., Pte. A.M.C.	1 A.G.H.	25/ 6/17	2y 3m, Pte.
BROWN, D., Pte. 15 Bn.	✤ 9/8/15.	9/ 1/15	L.-Cpl. ✤
BROWN, E., Pte. 12 Bn.		15/ 5/16	1y 6m, Pte.
BROWN, E. J., Pte. 26 Bn.	W. ✤ 6/3/17.	19/ 8/15	Pte. ✤
BROWNE, E. J., Gnr. 3 F.A.B.	1 D.A.C., 2 F.A.B.	9/ 2/15	4y 6m, Dvr.
BROWN, E. M., Gnr. 6 F.A.B.	23 How. Bde. ✤ 26/9/17.	11/ 1/16	Gnr. ✤
BROWN, F. B., Bdr. 42 Bty.		5/ 7/15	4y 1m, Bdr.
BROWN, F. C., Gnr. Art.		2/10/16	
BROWN, F., Pte. 26 Bn.	W.	2/ 7/15	4y 2m, Pte.
BROWN, F. H., Gnr. 9 Fd. Bty.	W.	26/ 8/14	1y 9m, Bdr.
BROWN, F. J., Pte. 3rd Cyc.	W., 4 D. Sig Co.	10/ 4/16	3y 6m, Spr.
BROWN, F. W., Pte. 40 Bn.		6/12/16	3y 1m, Pte.
BROWN, G., Pte. 15 Bn.	✤ 13/8/15.	19/11/14	Pte. ✤
BROWN, G. E., Dvr. 40 Bn.		15/11/16	3y 2m, Pte.
BROWN, G. E., Pte. 12 Bn.		6/10/16	3y 1m, Pte.
BROWN, G. K., Sgt. 3 Fd. Amb.		28/ 8/14	2y 6m, S.Sgt.
BROWN, H. G., Pte. 12th Bn.	51 Bn.	5/ 8/15	4y, L.-Cpl.
BROWN, H. G., Pte. 12 Bn. (Correct name ROSEVEAR, H. G.)	M.M.	5/12/16	1y 10m, Pte.

238   TASMANIA'S WAR RECORD, 1914-1918.

NAME.	REMARKS.	RANK ON DISCHARGE. ENLISTED, SERVICE.
BROWN, H. W., Pte. 12 Bn.	49 Bn., 42 Bn.	31/ 8/14 4y 10m, Sgt.
BROWN, H., Pte. 15 Bn.	4W. ✤ 8/8/18.	21/ 5/15 Pte. ✤
BROWN, H. B., Pte., 15 Bn.	✤ 2/5/15.	23/ 9/14 Pte. ✤
BROWN, H. G., Pte. 12 Bn.	2W., 52 Bn.	25/ 1/16 1y 8m, Pte.
BROWN, H. J., Pte. 12 Bn.	✤ 19-22/8/16.	16/11/15 Pte. ✤
BROWN, J. E., Pte. 26 Bn.		13/ 4/15
BROWN, J. R., M.W.		
BROWN, J., Pte. 40 Bn.	10 L.T.M.B.	11/ 7/16 3y 3m, L.-Cpl.
BROWN, J., Pte. 12 Bn.	60 Bn.	12/10/15 3y 9m, Pte.
BROWN, J. C. W., Pte. 12 Bn.	W. ✤ 30/5/18.	8/10/16 Pte. ✤
BROWN, J. G., Pte. 4 M.G. Co.	15 M.G. Co.	28/10/16 2y 7m, Pte.
BROWN, J. H., Pte. 12 Bn.	W.	5/ 9/16, 2y 2m, Pte.
BROWN, J. H., Tpr. 3 L.H.	W., 2 D.A.C.	14/ 9/15 4y 2m, Gnr.
BROWN, J. H., Pte. 40 Bn.		26/ 9/16 3y 1m, Pte.
BROWN, J. N., Gnr. 9 Bty.	How. Bty.	26/ 8/14 2y 5m, Gnr.
BROWN, J. R., Pte. 12 Bn.	2W., 52 Bn.	17/ 1/16 2y 5m, Sgt.
BROWN, J. T. A., Pte. 26 Bn.	✤ 6-10/4/17 12 Bn.	2/ 9/15 Pte. ✤
BROWN, J., Pte. 12 Bn.	W.	29/11/16 2y 5m, Pte.
BROWN, L. F., Pte. 2d Bn.	✤ 23/7/16.	11/ 8/15 Pte. ✤
BROWN, L. G., Dvr. 17 Bty.	5 F.A.B.	24/ 8/15 4y, Dvr.
BROWNE, L. E., Pte. 12 Bn.	W.	3/12/17 1y 7m, Pte.
BROWN, L. J., Pte. 40 Bn.	W.	21/ 3/16 2y 3m, Pte.
BROWN, L. N., Pte. 40 Bn.		13/ 7/16 2y 9m, Pte.
BROWN, M. B. N., Pte. 40 Bn.	✤ 11/6/17.	27/ 6/16 Pte. ✤
BROWN, M., Pte. 12 Bn.	✤ 27/2/17.	14/ 1/15 Sgt. ✤
BROWN, M. G., Pte. 1 A.C.H.		16/ 8/15 2y 1m, Pte.
BROWNE, N. R., Pte. 12 Bn.	2W.	10/ 9/14 3y 3m, Cpl.
BROWN, N. W., Pte. 12 Bn.	W., 52 Bn.	30/ 8/15 3y Pte.
BROWN, O., Pte. 15 Bn.	✤ 23/5/15.	2/11/14 Pte. ✤
BROWN, O. W., Pte. 40 Bn.	2W.	15/ 5/16 3y 3m, Pte.
BROWN, O., Pte. 12 Bn.	A. Prov. Cps.	2/11/15 4y, 2nd-Cpl.
BROWN, P., Tpr. R. Sec.		28/ 9/15 1y 2m, Tpr.
BROWN, P., Pte. 12 Bn.	40 Bn.	10/ 8/16 1y 10m, Pte.
BROWNE, R. H. K., Pte. 1 A.G.H.		5/ 6/15
BROWN, R. J., Sgt., 40 Bn.		21/ 7/16 3y Sgt.
BROWNE, R. J., Tpr. 3 L.H.		27/11/17 2y, Tpr.
BROWN, R. D., Pte. 12 Bn.	2W.	4/ 7/15 2y 8m, Pte.
BROWN, R., Pte. 12 Bn.	3 M.G. Co.	30/ 8/15 3y 7m, Pte.
BROWNE, R., Gnr. 6 F.A.B.	7 F.A.B.	6/11/15 3y 11m, Gnr.
BROWN, R. E., Pte. 26 Bn.	✤ 5/8/16.	2/10/15 Pte. ✤
BROWN, R. J., Pte. 26 Bn.	3W.	16/ 7/15 3y 9m, Pte.
BROWN, S. S., Pte. 40 Bn.		3/10/16 2y 9m, Pte.
BROWN, S., Pte. 4 M.G. Co.	W., 22 M.G. Co.	20/ 6/16 2y 7m, Sgt.
BROWN, S. I., Pte. 40 Bn.		21/ 3/16 3y 5m, Pte.
BROWN, T., Pte. 15 Bn.	W.	8/12/14 2y 5m, Pte.
BROWN, T. A., Pte. 40 Bn.		9/ 7/17 1y 9m, Pte.
BROWN, W. N., Dvr. 17 Bty.	W.	4/ 9/15 3y 9m, Dvr.
BROWN, W. A., Pte. 40 Bn.	2W.	28/ 3/16 3y 5m, Pte.
BROWN, W. D., Pte. 40 Bn.	26 Bn.	27/ 4/16 2y 10m, Sgt.
BROWN, W. H. F., C.S.M. 12 Bn.		1/ 3/17 3y 7m, Sgt.
BRUCE, W., Pte. 40 Bn.	A.V.C., 5 M.V.S.	15/ 3/16 3 y 7m, Pte.
BRUCE, W., Pte. 15 Bn.	✤ 8/8/15.	8/12/14 Pte. ✤
BRUFORD, A. T. B., Pte. 26th Bn.	W. ✤ 26/3/17.	5/ 7/15 Cpl. ✤
BRUFORD, H. R. B., Sgt. 26 Bn.	W., M.M., 69 Bn., 26 Bn.	5/ 7/15 3y 3m, Lieut.
BRUMBY, A. D., Sgt. 26 Bn.	✤ 29/7/16.	24/ 6/15 Sgt. ✤
BRUMBY, E. J., Pte. 1 G.S.R.	4 D.A.C.	14/ 3/18 1y 5m, Pte.
BRUNDLE, R., Pte. A.M.C.	1 Fd. Amb.	16/10/16 3y. L.-Cpl.
BRUNT, 1, Pte. 12 Bn.		24/ 7/15
BRUNTON, R. S., Spr. 8 Fd. Co. E.	12 Fd. Co.	25/ 9/15 4y 3m, Pte.
BRUNTON, T. T., Pte. 12 Bn.	W., 52 Bn., 49 Bn.	11/ 1/15 4y 6m, Pte.
BRYAN, A., Pte. 40 Bn.	2W.	2/ 2/16 3y 8m, Pte.
BRYAN, C. A., Pte. 40 Bn.	3W.	10/ 5/16 3y 4m, Pte.
BRYAN, C. L. K., Pte. 12 Bn.	46 Bn. ✤ 3/10/16.	7/10/15 Pte. ✤
BRYAN, D., Pte. 12 Bn.	8 Bn. ✤ 6-10/4/17.	26/ 8/15 Pte. ✤
BRYAN, F., Pte. 12 Bn.	W., 3 M.G. Bn., 40 Bn.	25/10/16 2y 9m, Pte.
BRYAN, F. J., Pte. 40 Bn.		21/11/16 2y 4m, Pte.
BRYAN, L., Pte. 26 Bn.	W.	8/ 5/15 4y 3m, Dvr.
BRYANT, A. R., Spr. 3 F.C.E.	12 Fd. Co.	20/ 9/15 2y 10m, Dvr.
BRYANT, A. W., Pte. 3 G.S.R.	12 Bn.	20/ 6/18 1y 4m, Pte.
BRYANT, F. E., Gnr. 6 F.A.B.	✤ 12/11/16.	1/ 9/15 Gnr. ✤
BRYANT, J. T., B.S.M. 12 Bn.		23/ 8/14 3y 5m, Lieut.
BRYANT, P. J., Tpr. 1 Rem. Sec.		6/10/15 4y 1m, Tpr.
BRYANT, T. H. L., Pte. 12 Bn.		27/ 1/15 2y 7m, Pte.
BRYCE, D. H., Pte. 2 G.S.R.		21/ 5/18 9m, Pte.
BRYCE, R., Sgt. 1 A.C.H.	W., M.I.D.	16/ 9/14 1y 10m, Sgt.
BRYCE, T., Tpr., 3 G.S.R.	3 L.H	19/ 3/18 1y 5m, Tpr.
BRYDON, W., Pte. A.M.C.	2 A.C.C.S.	1/ 5/16 3y 4m, Pte.
BUCHANAN, A. C., Pte. A.M.C.	W. 14 Fd. Amb.	30/ 9/16 2y 10m, Pte.
BUCHANAN, A. W., Pte. 12 Bn.	52 Bn., 51 Bn.	25/ 1/15 4y 3m, Dvr.
BUCHANAN, A. R., Pte. 12 Bn.	W.	9/ 8/17 2y 2m, Pte.
BUCHANAN, V. H., Pte. 40 Bn.	3W., 15 Bn., 40 Bn.	17/ 3/16
BUCIRDE, A. H., Gnr. 3 F.A.B.	2W.	12/ 1/15 4y 4m, Cpl.
BUCK, A. L., Pte. 26 Bn.	✤ 25/8/16.	7/ 7/15 Pte. ✤
BUCK, C., Pte. 12 Bn.	W. ✤ 6-10/4/17.	21/ 6/16 L.-Cpl. ✤
BUCK, F. J., Pte. 40 Bn.	W.	8/11/16 2y 4m, Pte.
BUCKLEY, G. H., Pte. 7 Fd. Amb.		17/ 3/15

TASMANIA'S MUSTER ROLL. 239

NAME.	REMARKS.	RANK ON DISCHARGE. ENLISTED, SERVICE,
BUCKLEY, G. D., Pte. 26 Bn.	2W.	24/ 6/15 3y 11m, Sgt.
BUCKLEY, J., Pte. 15 Bn.	W., 47 Bn.	27/ 8/15 3y 3m, Pte.
BUCKLEY, T. L., Pte. 12 Bn.		24/ 2/16
BUCKNELL, W., Pte. 40 Bn.		28/11/16 1y 5m, Pte.
BUCKNEY, A. J., Pte. 26 Bn.	3W., 15, 52, 40 Bns.	12/ 9/15
BUCKNEY, W. H., Sgt. 12 Bn.	M.M., 52 Bn., 4 Sig. Co.	6/ 7/15 4y 1m, Spr.
BUCKPITT, G. K., Pte. 12 Bn.	✠ 5/6/15.	17/ 8/14 Pte. ✠
BUCKPITT, S. H., Pte. 40 Bn.	W., 51 Bn.	21/ 2/16 2y 9m, Pte.
BUCKPITT, W. S., Spr. 8 Fd. Co.	T., 12 Fd. Co.	15/ 3/16 3y 7m, Spr.
BUDD, H. R., Pte. 12 Bn.	W. ✠ 16/3/18.	6/12/15 Pte. ✠
BUDGEON, J. A., Pte. 12 Bn.	W., 52 Bn., 49 Bn.	7/10/15
BUGG, B. C., Pte. 12 Bn.	✠ 19-20/8/16.	16/12/15 Pte. ✠
BUGG, J., Pte. 12 Bn.		18/ 5/16
BUGG, M. E., Pte. 3 G.S.R.	12 Bn.	9/ 7/18 1y, Pte
BUGG, P., Pte. 12 Bn.	W., 1 Pnrs., 4 Pnrs.	26/ 8/15 2y 4m, Cpl.
BUGG, P. K., Pte 12 Bn.		10/ 7/16 1y 11m, Pte.
BUGG, R. P., Pte. 12 Bn.	W., M.M.	16/12/15 2y 5m, Pte.
BULL, N. C. H., Pte. 1 A.G.H.	2W., 13 Fd. Amb.	1/10/15
BULLER, A. W. E., Gnr. A.F.A.		26/ 1/16
BULLOCH, C. J. G., Pte. 3 Fd. Amb.		12/ 1/15 2y 4m, Pte.
BULLOCH, W. T., Pte. 12 Bn.	W., 52 Bn., 51 Bn.	8/11/15 4y, Pte.
BULMER, B. J, Pte. 40 Bn.	W.	19/ 9/16 2y 7m, Pte.
BUMBLE, R. J., Pte. Remounts		11/10/15
BUMFORD, C. G., Dvr. 24 F.A.B.		23/10/16 3y 2m, Dvr.
BUMFORD, H. Gnr. 25 F.A.B.	1 D.A.C.	5/19/16 2y 11m, Dvr.
BUMFORD, L. J., Pte. 12 Bn.	✠ 19-22/8/16.	7/ 9/15 Pte. ✠
BUNTON, E. K., Pte. 3 Cyc. Bn.	59 Bn	4/ 4/16 4y 6m, Pte.
BUNTON, L. G, Pte., 26 Bn.		Pte.
BUNTON, S. K, Pte. 12 Bn.	60 Bn.	24/ 7/15 4y 4m, Sgt.
BUNYAN, J. C, Spr., 3 Miners	W., 3 Tnlrs	11/ 9/15 3y 7m, Spr.
BURBURY, A. C., Sgt. 3 L.H.	W. ✠ 30/4/19.	26/ 8/14 Sgt.
BURBURY, N. McK, Pte. 1 G.S.R.	16 A.D.M.S.	26/ 2/18 1y 10m, Pte.
BURBURY, T. J. G., Gnr. 6 F.A.B.		14/10/15 3y 11m, Dvr.
BURCH, E. G, Pte. 26 Bn.		24/ 8/15
BURDON, L, Spr., 8 Fd. Co.		18/ 1/16 3y 5m, Spr.
BURFORD, H. W., Pte. 12 Bn.		6/ 7/16 3y 2m, Pte.
BURGE, A., Sgt. 3 L. Horse.	W. ✠30/4/19.	26/ /8/14 Sgt. ✠
BURGE, A., Gnr. F. Art.		14/ 7/15. 4y 7m. L.-Cpl.
BURGE, D., Pte. 26 Bn.		23/ 4/17.
BURGE, E. C., Pte. 12 Bn.		30/ 8/16.
BURGE, F., Pte. 12 Bn.	W.	20/ 9/15. 4y 1m L.-Cpl.
BURGE, F., Gnr. 6 F.A.B.	W. 3 L.R. Co.	10/ 3/15. 4y 5m. Pte.
BURGE, H. J., Pte. 4 M.G. Co.		26/ 6/16.
BURGE, J., Spr. 3 Tnl. Co.		4/12/15 Spr. 3y 7m.
BURGE, N. J. H., Spr. Tnl. Co.	8 Bn.	30/ 8/16. 3y 1m. Pte.
BURGE, S. G., Pte. 12 Bn.	52 Bn. ✠ 3-5/8/16.	22/ 5/15. Cpl. ✠
BURGESS, A. M., Pte. 40 Bn.		24/ 6/16. 3y 6m. Pte.
BURGESS, C. P., Pte. 40 Bn.		10/ 3/16. 3y 5m. Pte.
BURGESS, C., Pte. 40 Bn.	W.	16/10/16 2y. Pte.
BURGESS, C. C., Pte. 12 Bn.	✠ 29/1/18.	30 1/15. Pte. ✠
BURGESS, C. J., Gnr. 3 F.A.B.		30/12/14. 4y 4m. Gnr.
BURGESS, D. M., Pte. 26 Bn.		16/ 8/15. 1y. Pte.
BURGESS, E. B., Pte. 12 Bn.	✠ 5-8/5/17.	18/ 6/16. Pte. ✠
BURGESS, E., Pte. 12 Bn.	✠ 8/2/17.	22/ 8/16. Pte. ✠
BURGESS, F., Pte. 12 Bn.	✠ 19-22/8/16.	16/10/15. Pte. ✠
BURGESS, F., Gnr. 15 F.A.B.	3 D.A.C.	13/10/16. 3y 1m. Dvr.
BURGESS, F. C., 2nd-Lt., 40 Bn.		1/ 5/16. Lieut. 1y 7m.
BURGESS, H. C., Pte. 40 Bn.	✠ 8/5/18.	20/ 7/17. Pte. ✠
BURGESS, J., Pte. 12 Bn.	W., 40 Bn.	20/10/16. 3y. Pte.
BURGESS, L., Pte. 12 Bn.	2W., A. Prov. Corps, 51 Bn., 12 Bn.	18/ 5/15. 3y 11m. Pte.
BURGESS, L. C. G., Gnr. 13 F.A.B.		7/ 1/16. 3y 8m. Gnr.
BURGESS, R. L., 12 Bn.	W. ✠ 30/518.	4/ 5/16. Pte. ✠
BURGESS, S., Pte. 12 Bn.	3W. 52 Bn.	25/ 1/16. 3y 2m. Pte.
BURGESS, S. C., Dvr. 15 F.A.B.	3 F.A.B., 3 D.A.C.	13/10/16. 2y 11m. Dvr.
BURGESS, T., Pte. 40 Bn.	M.M. and Bar, 12 Bn.	610/16. 3y. Cpl.
BURGESS, T. O., Tpr. 3 L.H.	8 F.A.B.	29/ 5/17
BURGESS, V. D., Gnr. 24 F.A.B.		28 9/16. 2y 6m. Bdr.
BURGESS, W. L. H., Maj. 3 F.A.B.	W., C.B., C.M.G., D.S.O., L'd Honneur, Croix de Officier, D.S.M. of America, 4M.I.D., 4 Dv. Art.	18/ 8/14. 5y 3m. Brig.-Gen.
BURGOYNE, J., 6 F.A.B.		21/ 9/15.
BURING, A. G. A., Pte. 40 Bn.		6/ 1/17 2y 3m. Cpl.
BURK, W.L., Pte. 40 Bn.	40 Bn.	7 3/16, 3y 7m, Sgt.
BURKE, C. E., Pte. 26Bn.	W.	6/ 9/15. 2y 5m. Pte.
BURKE, F. R., Pte. Tnl. Co.		24 2/17.
BURKE, F. R. J., Pte. 40 Bn.	W.	28 /9/16 2y 8m, Pte.
BURKE, G. F., Spr. Tnl. Co. Rfts.	3 Tnl Co.	27/10/16 3y, Spr.
BURKE, H. R., Gnr. 15 F.A.B.	W., 2 D.A.C..	3/10/16/ 2y 11m, Dvr.
BURKE, J. J., Gnr. 6 A.F.A.		1/ 8/15.
BURKE, J. L., Pte. 3 G.S.R.		1/ 8/18 2y 7m, Pte.
BURKE, J. T., Sgt. 1 A.C.H.		16/ 9/14 4y 9m, Sgt.
BURKE, R. C., Gnr. Art.	W., 12 Army Bde., A.F.A. ✠ 1/3/19.	10/ 4/17. Gnr. ✠
BURKE, R.R., Cpl. 40 Bn.		10/10/16/ 2y 7m, Cpl.
BURKE, T., Pte 12 Bn.	W.	7/ 16 4y 1m, Pte.
BURKE, W. H., Pte. 26 Bn.	2W.	20/ 7/15/, 3y 1m, Pte.
BURKERY, M., Spr. 3 Min.	3 Tnl. Co.	5/11/15 3y 8 m Spr.

NAME.	REMARKS.	RANK ON DISCHARGE. ENLISTED. SERVICE.
BURKETT, J. Pte. 15 Bn.		27/ 7/15 2y 9m, Pte.
BURLING, F. T. Pte. 26 Bn.	W.	29/ 7/15 3y3m, Pte.
BURLING, J. L., Cpl. 3 G.S.R.		20/ 6/18.
BURN, A. F., Pte. 15 Bn.	W., 47 Bn. ✱ 7/6/17.	5/ 2/15, Pte. ✱
BURN, H. F., Tpr. 3 L.H.	10 F.A.B.	19/ 8/15 4y, S. Smith.
BURN, W. T., Pte. 40 Bn.	M.M.	21/ 2/16 3y 7m, Lt.
BURNABY, T., Lt. 26 Bn.	12 Bn.	10/ 5/15 2y 7m, Lt.
BURNETT, T. H., Pte. 12 Bn.	40 Bn.	20/10/16 3y, Pte.
BURNEY, B., Pte. 12 Bn.	40 Bn. ✱ 22/4/18.	10/12/16, Pte. ✱
BURNIE, R. M., Pte. 26 Bn.	W.	2/10/15 3y 7m, Pte.
BURNLEY, B. Tpr. 3 L.H.	M.M., 4 D.A.C.	5/ 6/15 3y 11m, Gnr.
BURNSIDE, A., Pte. 15 Bn.		21 /5/15 1y 4 m, Pte.
BURR, C. E., Pte. 40 Bn.	51 Bn. ✱ 10/10/17.	17/ 2/16, Pte. ✱
BURR, L., Spr. 3 Min.	W., 3 Tnl. Co.	2/ 9/15 3y 11m, Spr.
BURR, W. J., Spr. 3 F. Co.	13 Fd. Co.	15/ 6/15 3y 11m, Spr.
BURR, W. C., Pte. 12 Bn.	W., M.M.	19/10/15 4y 3m, Pte.
BURRELL, B. F. S., Pte. 26 Bn.	2W.	19/ 2/15 3y 5m, Pte.
BURRIDGE, A. R., Pte. 12 Bn.		8/12/17 1y 10m, Pte.
BURRILL, H. A., Tpr. 3 L.H.	✱ between August 4 and 6, 1916.	3/ 7/15, Tpr. ✱
BURRILL, H B. C., Pte. 26 Bn.		17/ 6/15 1y 9m, Pte.
BURRILL, R. C., Cp. 26 Bn.	W., D.C.M., 12 Bn.	3/ 8/15 3y 4m, Sgt.
BURRISS, A., Pte. 26 Bn.	W., 2 Pnrs	8/ 4/15 3y 3m, Pte.
BURRIS, C. W., Spr., 3 Miners.	W.	10/11/15 2y 8m, Spr.
BURRISS, W., Cp. 3 F.A.B.	M.M., 4 Div. Arty.	26/ 8/14 4y 5m, Sgt.
BURROWS, H., Pte. 40 Bn.	2W.	27/ 9/16 2y, Pte.
BURROWS, J. R., Pte. 40 Bn.	W.	29/ 5/16 1y 7m, Pte.
BURROWS. L. W., Gnr. Art.	107 How. Bty.	21/ 5/17 2y 6m, Gnr.
BURROWS, R. L., Pte. 15 Btn.	4 Pnr. Bn., 47 Bn.	26/ 8/15 3y 8m, Pte.
BURROWS, W. E, Pte. 12 Bn.	2W. 69 Bn. 12 Bn. ✱ 11/8/18.	28/ 8/14, Pte. ✱
BURROWS, W. J., Pte. 26 Bn.	✱ 26/3/17.	27/ 9/15, Pte. ✱
BURRY, E. H., Cpl. 3 F.A.B.		26/ 8/14.
BURSLEM, C. H., Pte. 15 Bn.	✱ 8/8/16.	9/ 9/14, L'Cpl. ✱
BURT, A., Pte. 1 G.S.R.	40 Bn.	14/ 2/18 1y 9m, Pte.
BURT, W. Pte. 40 Bn.	2W. ✱ 15/6/17.	17/ 5/16, Pte. ✱
BURT, W. H., Pte. 12 Bn.		10/ 8/16 1y 7m, Pte.
BURTON, A. E., Pte. 12 Bn.	W., A.P.C.	18/ 9/14 3y 8m, Pte.
BURTON, F. M., Spr. 8 Fd. Co.	15 Fd. Co.	17/ 1/16 3y 8m, Spr.
BURTON, H. J., Pte. 15 Bn.	W.	30/ 6/15 3y 6m, Sgt.
BURTON, J. H., Spr. 8 Fd. Co.	14 Fd. Co.	1/ 2/16 3y, Spr.
BURTON, J., Pte. 40 Bn.		26/ 4/17.
BURTON, S., Pte. A.M.C.		18/10/16 2y 11m. Pte.
BURTON, T. A., Spr. 8 F.C.E.	14 Fd. Co. ✱ 13/10/17.	1/ 2/16, Spr. ✱
BURTON, T. A. Pte. 12 Bn		14/12/14.
BURTON, W., Pte. 40 Bn.	✱ 29/9/18.	6/ 2/17, Pte. ✱
BURNS, A., Pte. 1 G.S.R.		26/ 2.18.
BURNS, F. G., Sgt. 5 Miners	M.C., 2 Tnl. Co.	18/ 2/16 3y 7m, Lt.
BURNS, H. L., Pte. 4 M.G. Co	1 M.G. Co., 2 M.G. Co.	25/11/16 2y 10m, Pte.
BURNS, J. A., Pte. 40 Bn.	W., 3 Sig. Co.	5/ 2/16 3y 7m, Spr.
BURNS, J. W. E., Pte. 40 Bn.	W., 49 Bn. ✱ 22/4/18.	31/ 3/16, Pte. ✱
BURNS, J., Pte. 26 Bn	46 Bn.	12/ 5/15 2y 7m, Pte.
BURNS, J. D., Pte. 26 Bn.		12/ 5/15.
BURNS, L., Pte. 40 Bn.		18/ 9/16.
BURNS, R. A., Pte. 12 Bn.	W.	24/10/16 2y 6m, Pte.
BURNS, W. E., Pte. 1 G.S.R.	12 Bn.	28/ 1/18 1y 7m, Pte.
BURNS, W. J., Pte. 12 Bn.	Eng. Sig. Details.	16/ 6/16.
BUSH, C., Pte. 40 Bn.		13/ 5/16 2y, Pte.
BUSH, E. C., Pte. 26 Bn.		8/ 3/15 1y 4m, Pte.
BUSH, J. W. V., Pte. 12 Bn.	✱ 10/5/18.	26/10/16, Pte. ✱
BUSHBY, A. T., Pte. 26 Bn.	12 Bn., 47 Bn.	4/ 8/15 1y 9m, Pte.
BUSHBY, C., Pte. 7 F. Amb.		25/ 2/15.
BUSHBY, J., Gnr. 6 F.A.B.	2W., 23 How. Bde., 7 F.A.B.	10/ 1/16 2y 10m. Gnr.
BUTCHER, M. G., Tpr. 3 L.H.		20/ 8/14 1y 11m. Tpr.
BUTCHER, T. W., Gnr. 6 F.A.B	5 F.A.B.	2/10/15 3y 10m, Gnr.
BUTLER. E. L. A., 2nd-Lt., 12 Bn	✱ 23/8/16.	2/ 8/15 2nd-Lt. ✱
BUTT, C. H., Tpr. 3 L.H.		8/ 7/15 4y2m, Tpr.
BUTT, G. H., Tpr. 3 L.H.	W.	8/ 7/15 3y 9m, Tpr.
BUTLER. H. N., Maj. 3 F. Amb.	D.S.O.	22/ 8/14. 2y 11m. Lt.-Col.
BUTTERS, A. K., Gnr. 6 F.A.B.	W. 120 How. Bde.	19/ 1/16 3y 8m, Gnr.
BUTLER, L. T., 2nd-Lt. 12 Bn.		17/ 7/15.
BUTTERS, R. A., Pte. 12 Bn.		20/ 5/15.
BUTTERS, E. T., Gnr. 6 F.A.B.	120 How. Bty., 14 F.A.B.	19/ 1/16 3y 8m, Gnr.
BUTTERS, F. N., Pte. A.S.C.		8/10/17 1y 8m, Dvr.
BUTTERS, H. C., Gnr. 36 H.A.G.	✱ 10/7/17.	1/ 5/16, Gnr. ✱
BUTTERWORTH, C. H., Pte. 12 Bn	3W.	29/ 8/14 3y 2m, Pte.
BUTTERWORTH, Co'N. Pte. 12 Bn.	W., 40 Bn.	12/ 4/16 1y 9m. Pte.
BUTTERWORTH, C. J., Pte. 12 Bn	✱ 30/5/18.	11/10/16, Pte. ✱
BUTTERWORTH, D., Pte. 26 Bn.		20/ 7/15 1y 9m, Pte.
BUTTERWORTH, D., Pte. Rly.	1 A.L.R.O. Co.	23/10/17 2y 1m, 2nd-Cpl
BUTTERWORTH, F., Pte. 26 Bn.	W.	21/ 7/15. 4y 3m. Pte.
BUTTERWORTH, H. R. W., Pte. 3	W.	12/ 9/14 1y 8m, Tpr.
BUTTERWORTH, J. S., Pte. 12 Bn	W., 52 Bn.	2/ 8/15.
BUTTERWORTH, M. L., Pte. 4 M.G. Co.	2W., 11 M.G. Co., 3 M.G. Bn.	13/ 9/16 3y, Pte.
BUTTERWORTH, E. R., Pte 12 Bn	✱ 14/3/18	13/10/16, Pte. ✱
BUTTERWORTH, W. E., Pte. 12 Bn.	W.	11/10/16 2y 9m, Pte.
BUTTON, D. V., Pte. 15 Bn.	2W.	7/ 9/15 4y 1m, Sgt.

TASMANIA'S MUSTER ROLL.

NAME.	REMARKS.	RANK ON DISCHARGE. ENLISTED, SERVICE.
BUTTON, E. R., Pte. A.A.H.	3 A.G.H., 8 Fd. Amb.	1/11/15 3y 11m, Pte.
BUTTON, E. J., Pte. 40 Bn.	10 Fd. Amb.	7/ 3/16 3y 7m, Pte.
BUTTON, E. G., Gnr. Art.	4 M.T. Co.	27/ 3/18 1y 8m, Pte.
BUTTON, H. J., Pte. 40 Bn.		7/ 3/16 3y 7m, Dvr.
BUTTON, J., Pte. 40 Bn.	✠ 13/10/17.	7/ 3/16, Cpl. ✠
BUTTON, J. J., Pte. 26 Bn.	2 Pioneer Bn. ✠ 16/8/18.	12/ 6/15, Cpl. ✠
BUTTON, M., Dvr. 6 F.A.B.	W.	13/ 8/15 3y8m, Bdr.
BUTWELL, A., Pte. 26 Bn.	2W., 6 Bn.	3/ 8/15 3y 9m, Pte.
BUXTON, J. C., Pte. 40 Bn.	15 Bn ✠ 20/12/16.	19/ 4/16, Pte. ✠
BUXTON, R. J., Pte. 12 Bn.	✠ 1/11/17.	10/10/16, Pte. ✠
BUTLER, A. S., Pte. 26 Bn.	W. M.M., 12 Bn.	10/ 8/15 2y 4m, L'Cpl.
BUTLER, A. E., Pte. 12 Bn.	W. ✠ between May 5 and 8, 1917.	23/ 7/15, Pte. ✠
BUTLER, A. A., Pte. 12 Bn.	52 Bn., 28 Bn.	30/12/15 2y 4m, Pte.
BUTLER, A. A., Gnr., Arty.	W., 4 D.A.C.	6/12/16 2y 7m, Gnr.
BUTLER, B. R., Cpl. 3 G.S.R.		1/ 7/18.
BUTLER, B. N., Pte. 12 Bn.	✠ 18/9/18.	28/12/14, 2nd.-Lt. ✠
BUTLER, C. H., Sgt. 12 Bn.	52 Bn. ✠ 4/9/16.	22/ 7/15, Sgt. ✠
BUTLER, C. M., Tpr. 3 L.H.		20/ 8/14 2y 2m, Tpr.
BUTLER, C. A., Pte. 12 Bn.	✠ 26/7/17.	13/ 6/16, Pte. ✠
BUTLER, E., Pte. 12 Bn.	2W., M.M.	13/ 6/16 3y 1m, L'Cpl.
BUTLER, F., Pte. 12 Bn.		14/10/15 2y, Pte.
BUTLER, G. B., Pte. 12 Bn.	52 Bn. ✠ 10/8/16.	17/ 8/14, Sgt. ✠
BUTLER, H. B., Pte. 26 Bn.	1 A.L. Rly. Unit.	21/ 7/15 4y 2m, Spr.
BUTLER, H., Pte. 40 Bn.		23/ 2/16 3y, Pte.
BUTLER, H. E., Tpr. 3 L.H.	W., ✠ 12/1/17.	1/12/14, Tpr. ✠
BUTLER, H. J., Pte. 12 Bn.	W., 52 Bn., 49 Bn.	23/ 7/15. 3y 9m, Cpl.
BUTLER, H. L.-Cpl. 12 Bn.	52 Bn. ✠ 4/9/16.	17/ 8/15, Cpl. ✠
BUTLER, J., Pte. 12 Bn.		24/ 5/15 1y 5m, Pte.
BUTLER, J. M. T., Pte. A.F.C.		18/ 4/18 8m, Pte.
BUTLER, J. P., Pte. Tun. Co.	2W.	23/10/16.
BUTLER, J. C., Pte. 1 G.S.R.	40 Bn.	6/11/17 2y 2m, Cpl.
BUTLER, M. L., Pte. 12 Bn.	52 Bn.	22/ 7/15 2y 2m, Cpl.
BUTLER, R., Dvr., 4 A.S.C.		14/ 9/14.
BUTLER, S., Pte. 40 Bn.	2W., 49 Bn. ✠ 12/10/17.	3/ 5/15, Pte. ✠
BUTLER, T. J., Pte. 12 Bn.	W.	10/ 5/16 3y 7m, Pte.
BUTLER, W. A., Pte. 26 Bn.	12 Bn. ✠ between Augus 19 and 22, 1916.	11/ 8/15, Pte. ✠
BUTLER, W. J., Pte. 40 Bn.	W.	23/ 2/16 2y 1m, Pte.
BYE, A. W., Pte. 12 Bn.	✠ 28/5/18.	15/ 7/15, Pte. ✠
BYE, A. E., Pte. 40 Bn.	2W.	29/ 6/16 3y 2m, Pte.
BYE, A. J., Pte. 40 Bn.	2W., 69 Bn., 40 Bn.	15/ 3/16 3y 6m, Pte.
BYE, W. C., Pte. 40 Bn.	W., 69 Bn., 16 Fd. Amb., 40 Bn.	10/ 3/16 1y 6m, Pte.
BYERS, H., Gnr. 36 H.A.G.		7/ 6/15 4y, Gnr.
BYERS, P. E., Gnr. 17 Sge. Bat.	✠ 28/3/18.	28/12/17 1y 10m, Gnr.
BYERS, T. E., Pte. 40 Bn.	W.	1/11/16, Pte. ✠
BYERS, W., Pte. 40 Bn.	12 Bn.	1/11/16 2y 10m, Cpl.
BYGRAVES, E. G., Pte. 2 G.S.R.	W., Medaille Militaire, M.I.D.	1/11/17 1y 11m, Pte.
BYNON, H. L., Pte. 40 Bn.	12 Bn.	16/11/15 3y 8m, Pte.
BYNON, R. B., Pte. 3 G.S.R.	W., 2 D.A.C.	27/ 3/18 1y, Pte.
BYRNE, E. K., Gnr. 6 F.A.B.	4 A.B.G.R.G.C.	16/11/15 2y 9m, Gnr.
BYRNE, J., Pte. 12 Bn.		21/11/16 3y, Gnr.
BYRNE, V. A., Spr. 5 Miners.	✠ 8/8/15.	28/ 2/16 10m, Spr.
BYRON, J., Pte. 15 Bn.	W.	22/ 9/14, Pte. ✠
CABALZAR, R., Pte. 15 Bn.	W., 10 F.A.B.	11/ 8/15 4y, Cpl.
CACKETT, C., Pte. 12 Bn.		23/ 9/14, Pte. 5y 4m.
CADGER, N. A. H., Dvr. 3 A.F.A.	4 Dvl. Arty.	18/ 8/14, Pte. 4y 5m.
CADLE, L. W., Pte. A.A.M.C.	14 Fd. Amb.	17/ 8/15, Dvr. 4y.
CADMAN, C E., Pte. 12 Bn.	✠ 21/12/16.	25/11/16, Pte. 2y 2m.
CAHILL, A. R., Pte. 40 Bn.	✠ 13/10/17.	19/12/14, Pte. ✠
CAHILL, B. D., Spr. 3 Miners.		15/ 5/16, Pte. ✠
CAHILL, G., Spr. 5 Miners.	3 Tunn. Co. W	18/11/15, Spr. 2y 8m.
CAHILL, L. J., Pte. 26 Bn.	Re-enlisted 12 Bn.	7/ 3/16, Spr. 3y 7m.
CAHILL, M., Pte. 12 Bn.		23/ 4/15, Pte. 4y 8m.
CAHILL, T. P., Pte. 2 G.S.R.		25/ 7/15, Pte. 4y.
CAHILL, W., Tpr. 3 L.H.		23/ 5/18.
CAINE, J. E., Pte. 12 Bn.	W.	7/ 9/15, Tpr. 1y 10m.
CAIRNDUFF, A. G., Pte. A.A.M.C.		26/ 7/15, Pte. 4y.
CAIRNDUFF, R. E., L.-Sgt. 40 Bn.	W.	20/ 9/15.
CAIRNDUFF, T., Pte. 12 Bn.	W.	12/ 8/15, L.-Sgt. 2y 6m.
CAIRNS, F. R., Pte. 12 Bn.	52 Bn.	28/ 8/14.
CAIRNS, J. R., Pte. 12 Bn.		18/10/15, Pte. 2y 4m.
CAIRNS, J. A., Pte. 12 Bn.	✠ 7/4/18.	24/ 8/15.
CAIRNS J. W. R., Pte. 40 Bn.		22/ 8/14, Pte. ✠
CAIRNS, J. W., Pte. 40 Bn.		16/10/16.
CAIRNS, R., Pte. 40 Bn.		12/ 6/16.
CAIRNS, V. R., Pte. 12 Bn.	52 Bn.	28/ 9/16.
CAIRNS, W., Pte. 15 Bn.	W 14 Inf. Bde. H.Q.	29/ 5/15.
CALDER, H. W., L.-Cpl. 40 Bn.	W.	20/ 9/14.
CALDER, M. E., Sgt. 40 Bn.	W.	10/ 3/16, L.-Sgt. 3y 6m.
CALLAGHAN, R. G., Pte. 12 Bn.		15/ 3/16, C.S.M. 3y 8m.
CALLAGHAN, V. H., Tpr. 3 L.H.		6/10/16, Pte. 3y 2m.
CALLOW, C. R., Tpr. 3 L.H.		30/10/17, Tpr. 1y 10m.
CALLOW, R. A. R., Pte. 12 Bn.	W.	13/ 7/15, Tpr. 4y 2m.
CALVERT, H. E., Pte. 12 Bn.	✠ 22/12/17.	30/ 8/16, Pte. 2y 4m.
CAMM, H. E., Pte. 12 Bn.	✠ 8/8/15.	5/ 7/16, Pte. ✠
CAMM, R. A., L.-Cpl. 3 L.H.	2 W. 4 Anzac Camel Btn.	20/ 5/15, Pte. ✠
		18/ 8/14, 2nd Lieut. 4y 8m.

P

TASMANIA'S WAR RECORD, 1914-1918.

NAME.	REMARKS.	RANK ON DISCHARGE. ENLISTED. SERVICE.
CAMPBELL, A. W., Pte. 15 Bn.		22/ 6/15 1y 2m, Pte.
CAMPBELL, A. S., Lieut. Dental Cps.		
CAMPBELL, A. R., Pte. 26 Bn.	W. 6 Dvl. A.M.C. 26 Bty.	20/ 4/15. Pte. 3y 3m.
CAMPBELL, A., Pte. 12 Bn.	* 25-28/4/1915.	20/ 8/14. Pte. *
CAMPBELL, A. J., Gnr., 6 F.A.B.	W., 26 How. Bde., 3 D.A.C.	19/ 1/16. Bdr. 3y 3m.
CAMPBELL, A., Pte. 12 Bn.	* 28/7/15.	2/ 9/14. Pte. *
CAMPBELL, A. A., Spr. 3 F.C.E.	W.	20/ 8/14. Spr. 4y.
CAMPBELL, C., Tpr. 4 G.S.R.	3 L.H.	12/ 4/18. Tpr. 1y 5m.
CAMPBELL, D., Pte. 15 Bn.		1/12/14. Pte. 1y 7m.
CAMPBELL, E. J., Pte. 12 Bn.	* 3-5/9/16.	11/ 8/15. Pte. *
CAMPBELL, F., Pte. 26 Bn.	Sig. Dtls.	24/ 3/15
CAMPBELL, F. F., Sgt. 15 Bn.	47 Bn. * 7/6/17.	30/ 6/15. 2nd Lieut. *
CAMPBELL, G. S., Pte. 12 Bn.	52 Bn. * 7/6/17.	11/ 1/16. Pte. *
CAMPBELL, J., Pte. 1 A.G.H.	2 F. Amb. * 5/5/17.	21/ 5/15. Pte. *
CAMPBELL, J., Pte. 26 Bn.	* 5/8/16.	27/ 4/15. Pte. *
CAMPBELL, J. D., Pte. 26 Bn.		4/ 8/15.
CAMPBELL, J., Pte. 4 M.G. Co.		12/ 2/17.
CAMPBELL, K. M., Pte. 26 Bn.	12 Bn.	3/ 9/15.
CAMPBELL, L., Pte. 2 G.S.R.	2 F.A.B.	28/11/17. 1y 11m. Gnr.
CAMPBELL, L. J. Pte. 12 Bn.	W. 52 Bn.	11/ 8/15. 2y 3m. Pte.
CAMPBELL, M. M'K., Pte. 12 Bn.	W.	30/10/16. 2y 7m. Pte.
CAMPBELL, N. L. Pte. 1 G.S.R.	1 M.G. Co.	14/ 3/18. 1y 5m. Pte.
CAMPBELL, P. J., Pte. 4 G.S.R.	37 Coy. A.S.C.	13/ 4/18. 1y 5m. Pte.
CAMPBELL, R. D. Capt. 1 A.C.H.	D.S.O. C. De G. (French). 2 A.G.H., 3 A.C.C.S.	12/11/14. 3y 9m. Lt.-Col.
CAMPBELL, R. H., Pte. 12 Bn.	4 Pnrs. 4 M.G. Bn.	9/10/15. 3y 11m. L. Cpl.
CAMPBELL, S. R., Pte. 12 Bn.		7/11/17. 3y. Pte.
CAMPBELL, T., Pte. 12 Bn.	24 How. Bde. 3 A.S.C.	3/ 8/15. 4y. Dvr.
CAMPBELL, T., Pte. 40 Bn.	W.	1/11/16. 2y 8m. Pte.
CAMPBELL, W. A., Pte. 4 M.G. Co.		11/ 8/16.
CAMPBELL, W. M'G., Pte. 26 Bn.	W.	22/ 4/15. 3y 5m. Pte.
CAMPBELL, W. W., Sgt. 12 Bn.	* 19-22/8/16.	10/ 8/15. Sgt. *
CAMERON, C. W. Pte. 12 Bn.	W.	30/ 6/15. 2y 9m. Pte.
CAMERON, D. R. L. Pte. 12 Bn.		29/ 5/16. 2y. Pte.
CAMERON, D. H., Dvr. 3 F.A.B.	1 D.A.C.	16/ 6/15. 4y 2m. Dvr.
CAMERON, D. J. St. Sgt. 12 Bn.	1 A.A.H., A.M.C. Dtls.	22/ 8/14. 4y 5m. St. Sgt.
CAMERON, E. J., Pte. 26 Bn.	47 Bn.	9/ 3/15.
CAMERON, J., Pte. 12 Bn.		5/ 5/16. 2y 5m. Pte.
CAMERON, J. A. Pte. 12 Bn.		12/11/16. 2y 10m. Pte.
CAMERON, J. R. Pte. 12 Bn.	* 25-28/4/15.	26/ 8/14. Pte. *
CAMERON, P. C., Pte. 12 Bn.	W. * 22/7/18.	31/ 8/14. Pte. *
CAMERON, P. T. Pte. 12 Bn.		17/12/15.
CAMERON, R. N. Pte. 12 Bn.		25/10/17.
CAMERON, W. Spr. 3 F.C.E.	W.	12/ 9/14. 2y 1m. Spr.
CAMERON, W. T. Gnr. 6 A.F.A.	26 Bn., re-enlisted 12 Bn.	24/ 9/15. 3y 8m. 2 Lieut.
CANN, H. H., Pte. 15 Bn.	47 Bn. * 6/8/16.	Pte. *
CANE, C. H. Lieut. 40 Bn.		
CANNING, T. J. Spr. 3 Miners.	1 Mining Coy.	12/11/15. 1y 10m. Spr.
CANNELL, G. H. Spr. 3 F.C.E.		1/ 5/17. 2y 5m. Spr.
CANNON, G. D.		
CANNON, H. J. Pte. 3 Cyclists.		13/ 3/16.
CANNON, J. D. Spr. 8 F.C.	W. 15 F.C.E.	7/ 1/16. 3y 5m. Spr.
CANNAN, J. J. Sapper, 8 F.C.	15 F.C. * 12/12/16.	7/ 1/16. Spr. *
CANTLON, M. H. Pte. 4 M.G. Co.	14 Bn. 39 Bn.	25/11/16.
CANTRELL, C. Pte. 40 Bn.		23/ 8/17. 11m. Pte.
CANTRELL, C., Pte. 40 Bn.		30/ 4/17. 2y 6m. Pte.
CANTWELL, C. E. Pte. 12 Bn.	W.	16/ 9/15. 2y 6m. Pte.
CANTWELL, D., Pte. 12 Bn.	2 W. 52 Bn.	23/11/15. 3y 11m. Sgt.
CAPSTICK, V. Spr. 3 F.C.	* 22/7/16.	2/10/14. Spr. *
CARELESS, C. Pte. 12 Bn.		4/ 9/16. 3y. Pte.
CARELESS, H. E. Pte. 12 Bn.	2 W. 57 Bn.	9/ 2/15. 4y 7m. Pte.
CAREY, E. R. Pte. 15 Bn.	W.	13/ 8/15. 2y 3m. Pte.
CAREY, G. E. Pte. 12 Bn.		22/ 8/16. 1y 9m. Pte.
CAREY, J. G. Pte. 15 Bn.		16/ 1/15. 1y 7m. Pte.
CAREY, J. P. Pte. 40 Bn.	2 W.	4/10/16.
CAREY, M. L., Gnr. F. Art.	Z 3 A.M.T.M.B. * 16/9/17.	21/ 7/15. Dvr. *
CAREY, N. S. Pte. 40 Bn.	W. * 28/3/18.	7/ 4/16. Sgt. *
CAREY, W. P. Pte. 40 Bn.		8/11/16. 3y 1m. Pte.
CARGILL, T. Pte. 12 Bn.	2 W. 24 How. Bde. 1 F.A.B	7/12/15. 2y 7m. Gnr.
GARLAND, L. T., Pte. 12 Bn.	* 10/6/15.	28/ 8/14. Pte. *
CARLILE, G. S. Pte. 40 Bn.		26/ 7/16.
CARLILE, W. Pte. 40 Bn.	2 W.	26/ 3/16. 3y 6m. Pte.
CARLSEN, A. Pte. 15 Bn.	* 8/8/15.	9/12/14. Pte. *
CARLSON, A. J. Pte. 26 Bn.	W. 12 Bn	11/ 8/15. 3y 10m. Pte.
CARLSON, D. Pte. 12 Bn.	* 24/3/15.	6/ 9/14. Pte. *
CARLSSON, A. F. Pte. 7 F. Amb.	W.	10/ 4/15. 2y 3m. Pte.
CARMICHAEL, H. A. Pte. 12 Bn.		1/10/17. 1y 2m. Pte.
CARN, S. J. Pte. 40 Bn.	* 5/2/17.	3/10/16. Pte. *
CARN, T. J. Pte. 12 Bn.	W. 1 Pnrs	19/ 8/15. 3y 11m. Pte.
CARNES, G. M. Snr. 3 Miners.	3 Tnlrs	7/ 9/15. 3y 8m. Spr.
CARNES, W. J. Pte. 12 Bn.		19/ 1/16.
CARO, M. Pte. 12 Bn.		4/ 7/16. 2y 11m. Pte.
CARPENTER, W. T. Pte. 40 Bn.	W.	13/10/16. 2y 6m. Pte.
CARR, D. Spr. 3 Tun. Coy.		1/11/16. 3y 1m. Spr.
CARR, F. W. Pte. 40 Bn.	W.	14/ 3/16. 2y 2m. Pte.

TASMANIA'S MUSTER ROLL. 243

NAME.	REMARKS.	RANK ON DISCHARGE. ENLISTED. SERVICE.
CARR, J. Pte. 12 Bn.	W.	25/ 6/16. 3y 1m. Pte.
CARR, T. J. Gnr. 3 F.A.B.	102 How. Bty.	14/ 9/15 1y 8m, Bdr.
CARR, W. H., Pte. 12 Bn.	52 Bn. ✣ 7/7/16.	4/10/15. Pte. ✣
CARR, W. H. Pte. 12 Bn.	W.	22/ 6/16. 2y 8m. Pte.
CARRICK, H. N. Pte. 26 Bn.	2 W.	6/ 9/15. 3y 8m. Pte.
CARRICK, J. W. Pte. 12 Bn.	4 Dvl. Cyc. Bn.	2/12/15. 3y 9m. Pte.
CARRICK, S. R. Pte. 12 Bn.	✣ 10/5/18.	9/ 2/15. Pte. ✣
CARRINGTON, B. Q. Pte. 26 Bn.	52 Bn. ✣ 5/4/18.	27/ 2/15. Pte. ✣
CARRINGTON, F. D. Pte. 12 Bn.	W. ✣ 25/4/15.	28/ 8/14. Pte. ✣
CARROLL, A. V. Pte. 26 Bn.	W. 12 Bn.	19/ 8/15. 2y 3m. Pte.
CARROLL, A. H. Gnr. 3 F.A.B.	103 How. Bty.	27/ 7/15. Dvr.
CARROLL, D. F. Pte. 12 Bn.	24 How. Bde. 24 F.A.D. 4 Div. Arty.	2/11/15. 3y 10m. Bdr.
CARROLL, F. M. Pte. 12 Bn.	W. 52 Bn.	20/ 8/14. Lieut.
CARROLL, H. M. Pte. 26 Bn.	✣ 19-22/8/16.	7/ 8/15. Pte. ✣
CARROLL, H. M. Tpr. 3 L.H.	39 Bn.	26/ 7/15.
CARROLL, L. Pte. 40 Bn.	M.M.	15/11/15.
CARROLL, R. T. Pte. 12 Bn.	52 Bn. ✣ 4/9/16.	9/10/15. Pte. ✣
CARROLL, T. R. Pte. 12 Bn.	52 Bn. ✣ 4/9/16.	29/ 9/15. Pte. ✣
CARRUTHERS, G. Pte. 40 Bn.		10/10/16. Pte. ✣
CARRUTHERS, W. W. F. Pte. 1 A.G.H.C.D.	✣ 28/3/18.	29/ 5/15. 8m. Pte.
CARTER, A. C. Pte. 40 Bn.	15 Bn. 40 Bn.	13/ 3/16. 3y 5m. Pte.
CARTER, A. J. Gnr. 13 F.A.B.		27/ 3/16. 2y 3m. Gnr.
CARTER, C. W. Pte. 40 Bn.	12 Bn.	14/ 3/16. 2y 5m. Pte.
CARTER, G. A. Pte. 12 Bn.	W.	20/ 7/16. 3y 1m. Pte.
CARTER, G. T. Pte. 12 Bn.		22/ 7/15. 4y 1m. Pte.
CARTER, H. J. Dvr. 1 Remount.		29/ 9/15. 4y 2m. Dvr.
CARTER, H. J. Spr. 8 F.C.	4 Fd. Co.	15/ 1/16. 3y 5m. Pte.
CARTER, J. M. S. Pte. 40 Bn.	✣ 8/6/17.	23/ 5/16. Pte. ✣
CARTER, J. E. Cpl. 12 Bn.	W. 52 Bn. ✣ 3-4/9/16.	22/ 7/15. Cpl. ✣
CARTER, L. L. Pte. 15 Bn.	M.M. 47 Bn.	16/11/14. 4y 8m. Lieut.
CARTER, R. H. Pte. 15 Bn.	W. 4 Pnrs.	21/ 1/15. 3y 2m. Pte.
CARTER, W. J. Dvr. 7 Fd Amb.	13 Fd. Amb.	16/ 3/15. 4y 4m. Sgt.
CARTER, W. R. Pte. 12 Bn.	2W.	21/ 8/14. 3y 2m. Pte.
CARTLEDGE, A. Pte. 12 Bn.	4 Pnrs. ✣ 6/7/18.	6/12/15. Pte.
CARTLEDGE, G. G. Pte. 12 Bn.		20/ 6/16. 3y 6m. Pte.
CARTLEDGE, G. Pte. 15 Bn.		3/ 8/15.
CARTLEDGE, G. Ptel 40 Bn.		7/12/16. 1y 3m. Pte.
CARTLEDGE, H. Pte. Miners.	39 Bn	8/12/15. 2y. L. Cpl.
CARTLEDGE, J. S. Pte. 40 Bn Bty.		23/ 9/15. 2y 11m. Pte.
CARTLEDGE, R. C. B.Q.M.S. 3 F.A.B.	W.	26/ 8/14. 4y 5m. B.Q.M.S.
CARTLEDGE, R. G. Pte. 40 Bn.		17/ 5/16. 3y 6m. Pte.
CARTLEDGE, S. F. Pte. 12 Bn.	3 F.A.B.	9/ 7/17. 2y 3m. Gnr.
CARTLEDGE, W. Pte. 12 Bn.	2W. 6 Bty. A.F.A.	4/ 4/16. 3y 5m. Gnr.
CARTY, C. E. Pte. 26 Bn.	W. 12 Bn.	28/ 7/15. 2y 11m. Pte.
CASAS, J. E. Pte. 12 Bn.		5/ 9/16.
CASBOURNE, E. E. Pte. 40 Bn.	✣ 5/5/17	3/ 2/16. Pte. ✣
CASE, J. S. Gnr. 6 F.A.B.	8 F.A.B. 3 D.S.C.	24/ 1/16. 3y 9m. Spr.
CASEY, A. Pte. 2f Bn.	W.	8/ 7/15. 4y 4m. rte.
CASEY, E. W. Pte. 40 Bn.	✣ 4/10/17.	10/11/16. Pte. ✣
CASEY, H. C. Pte. 12 Bn.		29/ 8/14. 4y 8m. Pte.
CASEY, J. L. Pte. 12 Bn.		27/11/17. 1y 11m. Pte.
CASEY, P. Pte. 2 G.S.R.	12 Bn.	6/ 5/18.1y 4m. Pte.
CASEY, W. Pte. 12 Bn.	W.	13/ 9/15.
CASEY, W. H. Pte. 12 Bn.		22/ 7/15.
CASHION, A. Pte. 12 Bn.	2W. 52 Bn.	13/ 1/16. 2y 11m. Pte.
CASHION, A. Pte. 12 Bn.	W. 52 Bn.	13/11/15. 2y 4m. Pte.
CASHION, F. B. Pte. 12 Bn.	52 Bn. ✣ 6-10/4/17.	13/ 1/16. Pte. ✣
CASHION, J. C. Pte. 26 Bn.	W. 12 Bn.	2/ 3/15. 4y 7m. Pte.
CASHION, J. V. A. Cpl. Rly Unit.	3 A.L.R.O. Coy.	19/ 9/16. 2y 9m. Pte.
CASHION, P. Pte. 40 Bn.	W. 12 Bn.	22/11/17. 2y. Cpl.
CASHMAN, C. P. Gnr. Arty.	5 D.A.C.	28/ 5/17. 2y 5m. Dvr.
CASHMAN, F. A. Spr. 3 Miners.	1 Tunn. Coy.	18/11/15. 3y 10m. Spr.
CASSIDY, E. J. Pte. 12 Bn.	M.M.	26/ 8/14. 4y 4m. L.-Cpl.
CASSIDY, H. J. Pte. 12 Bn.	M S.M M.I.D.	26/ 8/14. 4y 9m. R.Q.M.S.
CASSIDY, H. J. Gnr. 6 F.A.B.	W.. 5 F.A B.	12/10/15. 4y. Gnr.
CASSIDY, J. Pte. 26 Bn.		4/ 8/15.
CASTLE, A. Pte. 40 Bn.		26/10/16. 1y 3m. Pte.
CASTLE, E. Pte. 40 Bn.	M.M.	1/ 3/16. 3y 5m. L.-Cpl.
CASTLE, G. E. Pte. 40 Bn.	15 Bn.	1/ 3/16. 3y 5m. Pte.
CASTLES, R. M. Pte. 40 Bn.		25/10/16. 3y 2m. Pte.
CATCHPOLE, A. H. Pte. 12 Bn.	3 M.G. Coy.	18/ 8/14. 3y 5m. Pte.
CATO, A. B. Gnr. 6 Fd. Arty. B.	25 F A B., 120 How. Bty., 10 B.A.B. ✣ 20/9/17.	17/ 1/16. Gnr. ✣
CATO, E. S Gnr. Fd. Arty.		31/ 1/16. 2y 5m. Gnr.
CATO, H. G. Pte. 12 Bn.	W. ✣ 18/9/18.	31/ 1/16. Pte. ✣
CAULFIELD, H E. Pte. 40 Bn.	W. ✣ 5/10/17.	3/10/16. Pte. ✣
CAULFIELD, J. Gnr. 6 F.A.B.		17/11/15. 3y 11m. Dvr.
CAULFIELD, J. Pte. 12 Bn.	2W.	28/ 8/16. Pte. 3y.
CAVANAGH, P. C. Gnr. Fd. Arty.		4/10/15. 11m. Sgt.
CAVILLE, T. W. Pte. 26 Bn.	W. ✣	21/ 9/15. Pte. ✣
CAWLEY, J. A. Pte. 12 Bn.	40 Bn.	6/ 9/15. 2y 3m. Pte.
CAWTHEN, J. A. Pte. 40 Bn.	✣ 7/6/17.	2/12/15. Pte. ✣
CEARNS, C. C. Gnr. 3 F.A.B.	24 F.A.B. ✣ 21/8/16.	26/ 8/14. Cpl. ✣

TASMANIA'S WAR RECORD, 1914-1918.

NAME.	REMARKS.	RANK ON DISCHARGE. ENLISTED, SERVICE.
CECIL, H. M. S. Spr. Tunn. Rfts.	1 Tunn. Coy.	19/ 2/17. 2y 8m. Spr.
CHADWICK, A. V. Cpl. 12 Bn.		30/ 9/16. 3y. Lieut.
CHADWICK, H. W. Pte. 40 Bn.	2W.	7/10/16. 2y 7m. Pte.
CHADWICK, W. J. Pte. 4 M.G. Co.	15 Bn. 32 Bn.	3/ 1/17.
CHAFFEY, B. L. Pte. 15 Bn.	47 Bn., 47 Pnr. Bn.	31/ 8/15. 4y. Pte.
CHAFFEY, C. C. Gnr. 6 F.A.B.	W.	24/ 8/15 3y 9m. Cpl.
CHAFFEY, G. W. Pte. 26 Bn.	W.	15/ 4/15. 2y 6m. Cpl.
CHAFFEY, H. W. Pte. 40 Bn.	W.	17/ 4/16. 3y 5m. Pte.
CHALK, E. T. Pte. 15 Bn.		19/ 7/15. 4y. L. Cpl.
CHALK, R. G. Pte. 40 Bn.	✠ 13/5/17.	28/ 4/16. Cpl. ✠
CHALLEN, W. A. Cpl. 12 Bn.	✠ 19-22/8/16.	25/ 8/15. Cpl. ✠
CHALLIS, A. H. Pte. 26 Bn.	3W.	24/ 8/15. 4y. Pte.
CHALLIS, W. A. Pte. 40 Bn.	51 Bn. ✠ 24/4/18.	2/ 3/16. Pte. ✠
CHALMERS, C. E. A. Sgt. 12 Bn.	52 Btn. ✠ 7/6/17.	23/ 8/15. 2 Lieut. ✠
CHALMERS, G. J. S. Dvr. 12 F.A.B.	4 D.A.C.	2/ 2/16. 3y 7m. Dvr.
CHALMERS, L. E., Spr. 6 Fd. Coy.	5 Fd. Amb. ✠ 25/9/17.	10/ 8/15. Cpl. ✠
CHALMERS, R. H. Dvr. 3 F.A.B.	1 D.A.C. 3 B.A.C.	23/ 9/14. 4y 5m. Dvr.
CHAMBERLAIN, A. W. Pte. 12 Bn	48 Bn. 12 M.G. Co.	6/ 1/15. 4y 5m. Pte.
CHAMBERLAIN, D. T. Pte. 1 G.S.R.	111 How. Bty.	9/ 3/18. 1y 7m. Gnr.
CHAMBERLAIN, H. Pte. 40 Bn.	✠ 30/3/18	4/ 4/16. Lieut. ✠
CHAMBERLAIN, J. H. Pte. 12 Bn.	W.	5/10/17. 1y 8m. Pte.
CHAMBERS, C. Pte. 40 Bn.	W. ✠ 30/3/18.	12/ 9/16. Pte. ✠
CHAMBERS, F. J. Gnr. 3 F.A.B.	V./1A.H.T.M.B.	21/ 8/14. 3y 3m. Gnr.
CHAMBERS, H. Pte. 26 Bn.	W.	12/ 4/15. 4y. Pte.
CHAMBERS, J. A. Pte. 12 Bn.	W.	12/ 1/15. 4y 9m. Pte.
CHAMBERS, L. T. G. Sgt. 12 Bn.	W. 69 Bn. 12 Bn. ✠ 3/11/17.	23/ 8/14. Sgt. ✠
CHAMBERS, V. E. Spr. 8 F.C.	W. 3 Fd. Co.	1/ 3/16. 3y 8m. Spr.
CHAMLEY, B. Pte. 40 Bn.	✠ 3/8/17.	9/ 6/16. Pte. ✠
CHAMBERS, F. J. Gnr. 3 F.A.B.	A.M.C.	26/ 8/14. 3y 3m. Pte.
CHAMLEY, L. Pte. 40 Bn.	W.	9/ 6/16. 1y 8m. Pte.
CHAMLEY, R. R. Pte. 26 Bn.	✠ 22/9/15.	10/ 5/15. Pte. ✠
CHAMP, J. Pte. 12 Bn.		23/ 8/14. 10m. Pte.
CHAMPION, C. S. Pte. 12 Bn.		16/10/16.
CHANCE, J. S. Pte. 12 Bn.	52 Bn. P.O.W.	9/ 8/15.
CHANCE, T. W. Pte. 12 Bn.	13 Inf. Bde., M.G. Coy., 52 Bn. ✠ 19/1/17.	11/ 1/15. Pte. ✠
CHANCELLOR, C. Spr. 8 Fd. Co.	12 Fd. Co.	4/12/15. 3y 9m. Dvr.
CHANDLER, C. P. G. Dvr. 3 F.A.B.	3 Dvl. Arty.	26/ 8/14. 4y 7m. Dvr.
CHANDLER, O. Pte. 3 G.S.R.	12 Bn.	26/ 8/18. 1y 1m. Pte.
CHANDLER, W. A. Pte. 14 M.G. Co.		12/ 1/15. 3y 7m. Pte.
CHANNING, J. A. Nav. and Lab.		
CHAPLAIN, C. Spr. 3 Miners.	3 A.T.C.	24/11/15. 3y 11m. Spr.
CHAPLIN, G. Pte. 12 Bn.	W. 52 Bn. 51 Bn.	11/ 1/16. 3y 8m. Pte.
CHAPLAIN, A. Pte. Wireless Sqdn.	A.F.C.	2/11/16. 2y 4m. 2 A.M.
CHAPLIN, T. Pte. 40 Bn.	2 W. A.C. Sig. Coy.	7/12/16. 2y 4m. Pte.
CHAPMAN, A. F. X. Gnr. 6 F.A.B.	M.M.	14/ 9/15.
CHAPMAN, D. S. Pte. 12 Bn.	W.	9/11/15.
CHAPMAN, F. A., Pte. 12 Bn.	✠ 10/10/16.	25/ 8/15. Pte. ✠
CHAPMAN, G. R., Gnr. 36 F.A.B.		25/ 2/18. Gnr. 1y 4m.
CHAPMAN, G. W., Gnr. 3 F.A.B.	102 How. Bat.	8/ 8/15. Gnr. 4y.
CHAPMAN, H. W. Pte., 40 Bn.	✠ 18/2/17.	2/ 3/16. Pte ✠
CHAPMAN, J. Pte. 15 Bn.	✠ 26/5/15.	22/ 9/14. Pte. ✠
CHAPMAN, K. V., Gnr. F. Art.	55 Bty.	6/ 3/16. 3y 10m. Lt.
CHAPMAN, R. V., Pte. 7 F. Amb.	A.F.C.	15/ 3/15. 2A.M. 4y 7m.
CHAPMAN, W., Pte., 12 Bn.	12 Bde. M.G. Co. ✠ 8/8/16.	4/ 8/15. Pte. ✠
CHAPPELL, P. C., Spr. 3 Fd. Co.	✠ 23/7/16.	4/ 8/15. Spr. ✠
CHARLES, C. F., Pte. 3 G.S.R.	39 Bn.	14/ 2/17. L-Cpl. 2y 10m
CHARLES, F. J., Pte. 12 Bn.	✠ 26/2/17.	1/ 6/16. ✠
CHARLES, H. F., Pte. 12 Bn.		13/10/16. Pte. 3y 2m.
CHARLESTON, E., Pte. 40 Bn.	✠ 13/1/17.	30/11/15. Pte. ✠
CHARLESTON, J. A., Pte. 40 Bn.	2 W.	7/ 4/16. 3y 3m.
CHARLESTON, J. J., Pte. 40 Bn.		8/ 8/16. Pte. 1y 4m.
CHARLESTON, L. L., Pte. 40 Bn.	W.	12/ 7/16. Pte. 2y 8m.
CHARLESWORTH, A. J., Pte. 26 Bn.	W.	17/ 6/15 Pte. 3y.
CHARLESWORTH, C. W., Pte. 12 Bn.	52 Bn. ✠ 4/9/16.	27/ 1/16 Pte. ✠
CHARLESWORTH, G. A., Pte. 40 Bn.	2 W. M.M.	13/ 3/16. Sgt. 3y 2m.
CHARLESWORTH, M. L., Pte. 26 Bn	2 W.	17/ 6/15. Cpl. 2y 10m.
CHARLTON, C. H., Pte. 12 Bn.	W.	11/ 6/17. Pte. 1y 4m.
CHATTERS, A. E., Pte. 12 Bn.		5/ 7/15. Pte. 8m.
CHATTERS, A. E., Pte. 1 G.S.R.	2 A. Fd. Butchery.	12/12/17
CHATTERS, H., Pte. 40 Bn.		20/ 8/17. Pte. 11m.
CHATTERS, E. J. Tpr. 1 Rmt.		13/10/15. Tpr. 4y 1m.
CHATTERTON, J. R., Tpr. 3 L.H.		16/ 7/17. Dvr. 2y 1m.
CHATWIN, A., Pte. 12 Bn.	W.	2/ 9/16. Pte. 1y 4m.
CHATWIN, A., Pte. 12 Bn.	W. 52 Bn. 51 Bn.	26/ 1/15. Dvr. 4y 7m.
CHATWIN, C., Pte. 12 Bn:	52 Bn.	1/ 8/15. Pte. 2y 7m.
CHATWIN, C. H., Pte. 12 Bn.	W. 52 Bn.	1/ 8/15. Pte. 1y 11m.
CHATWIN, D. Pte. 40 Bn.	51 Bn.	22/ 2/16. Pte. 2y 6m.
CHATWIN, A. R., Pte. 26 Bn.	47 Bn. 6 M.T. Co.	1/ 5/15. Pte. 4y 4m.
CHATWIN, W. R., Pte. 15 Bn.	✠ 31/12/16.	12/ 8/15 Pte. ✠
CHAWNER, L. E., Pte. 12 Bn.	2 W. 1 M. G. Bn.	15/ 7/15 Pte. 4y 1m

TASMANIA'S MUSTER ROLL. 245

NAME.	REMARKS.	RANK ON DISCHARGE. ENLISTED. SERVICE.
CHAWNER, R. C., Pte. 12 Bn.	W.	30/ 8/14. Pte. 2y 3m.
CHEEK, R. L., Pte. 3 G.S.R.	12 Bn.	5/ 8/18. Pte. 1y 3m.
CHEEK, W. M., Cpl. 12 Bn.	4 M.G. Co. ✢ 27/7/16.	19/ 8/15. Cpl. ✢
CHEESE, A. R., Pte. 26 Bn.	A.A. Postal Cps.	8/ 3/15. L.-Sgt. 4y 7m.
CHEESEMAN, C., Gnr. 36 H.A.G.	1 Siege Bt	22/ 4/18. Gnr. 1y 5m.
CHEESEMAN, H. T., Pte. 12 Bn.	W.	28/ 8/14. Cpl. 3y.
CHENERY, A., Gnr. F. Art.		20/ 6/16.
CHENHALL, T. R., Pte. 3 G.S.R.		30/ 7/18. Pte. 1y 5m.
CHEPMELL, C. H. D., Gr. F. Art.	3 F.A.B.	30/ 4/17. Gnr. 1y 11m.
CHERRY, P. H., Qms. 26 Bn.	3 W. V.C. M.C. ✢ 27/3/17.	5/ 3/15. Cpt. ✢
CHERRY, W. A., Pte. 12 Bn.	✢ 7/10/17.	22/ 8/14. Sgt. ✢
CHESSELL, R., Pte. 40 Bn.	✢ 2/4/17.	31/ 1/16. Pte. ✢
CHESTER, J. R., S/Sgt. A.A.D.C.		1/ 1/16. St.-Sg. 3y 5m.
CHICK, C. A., Gnr. F. Art.	W. 7 F.A.B.	28/ 9/16. Dvr. 3y.
CHICK, C. W., Pte. 40 Bn.	2 W. ✢ 28/3/18.	25/ 5/16. Pte. ✢
CHICK, C. H., Dvr. 8 F. Co.	15 Fd. Co.	11/ 1/16. Dvr. 3y 8m.
CHICK, P. C., Pte. 12 Bn.	2 W.	16/ 9/14. Pte. 4y 4m.
CHIDGEY, L. A., Gnr. 6 F.A.B.		7/ 9/15. Gnr. 1y 4m.
CHILCOTT, A., Cpl. Rly.		6/ 1/17. Cpl. 2y 8m.
CHILCOTT, C. D., Cpl. Rly.		10/ 1/17. Cpl. 2y 2m.
CHILCOTT, C. T., Pte. 40 Bn.		10/ 6/16. Pte. 3y 6m.
CHILCOTT, D. T., Pte. 12 Bn.	W.	1/ 2/15. Pte. 1y 8m.
CHILCOTT, G. A., Pte. 12 Bn.	52 Bn.. 4 D.H.Q.	6/ 3/16. Pte. 3y 4m.
CHILCOTT, J., Pte. 40 Bn.		30/ 9/16. Pte 1y 3m.
CHILCOTT, L. D., Pte. 40 Bn.	2 W.	26/ 4/16. Pte. 3y 7m.
CHILCOTT, R., Pte. 12 Bn.		6/ 9/16. Pte 1y 3m.
CHILCOTT, T., Pte. 12 Bn.		8/10/16. Pte. 3y 1m.
CHILCOTT, T., Pte. 12 Bn.		31/12/15.
CHILCOTT, V. J., Pte. 26 Bn.	W. 12 Bn. ✢ 18/10/17	10/ 8/15. Pte. ✢
CHILCOTT, W. P., Pte. 26 Bn.	W.	7/ 5/15.
CHILDS, A. W., Pte. 40 Bn.	W.	3/ 7/16. Pte. 2y 1m.
CHILDS, H. H., Pte. 40 Bn.	W.	1/10/16. Pte. 1y 7m.
CHILDS, T. N., Pte. 15 Bn.	W., 5 F. Bky.	19/ 9/14 Pte. 5y.
CHISHOLM, C. R., Pte. 40 Bn.	W. ✢ 12/10/17.	30/ 9/16. Pte. ✢
CHISHOLM, J. D. W., Cpt. 40 Bn.	W. M.I.D.	7/ 3/16. Capt. 3y 7m.
CHITTEM, H. R., Pte. 26 Bn.	W. 12 Bn.	9/ 8/15. Pte. 2y 10m.
CHIVERS, A. J., Pte. 4 M.G. Co.	6 M.G.C., 3 M.G. Bn.	11/10/16. Pte. 2y.
CHIVERS, R., Pte. 12 Bn.		20/ 8/14. Sgt. 4y 4m.
CHIVERS, R. R., Pte. 12 Bn.	52 Bn. 49 Bn.	12/11/15. Pte. 3y 10m.
CHIVERS, V. N., Pte. 12 Bn.	W. 40 Bn.	7/ 4/16. Cpl. 3y 4m.
CHIVERS, W., Pte. 1 G.S.R.	A.B. Depot.	10/12/17. Pte 1y 11m.
CHOPPING, R. E., Pte. 12 Bn.	✢ 29/1/16.	1/ 6/15. Pte. ✢
CHORLEY, T. O., Spr. 5 Min.	W. 2 Tun. Co.	4/ 3/16. Spr. 2y 7m.
CHRISTENSEN, C. H., Pte. 40 Bn.	✢ 26/12/16.	17/ 6/16. Pte. ✢
CHRISTIAN. R. T., Pte. 4 M.G. Co.	P.G.W.	29/ 6/16.
CHRISTIAN, W. R., Pte. 12 Bn.	✢ 30/8/18.	30/10/17. Pte. ✢
CHRISTIE, A. V., Tpr. 3 L.H.		12/ 7/15. Tpr. 4y 5m.
CHRISTIE, T. J. E. E., Pte. 26 Bn.	2 W. M.G. Co.	10/ 5/15. Pte. 3y 2m.
CHRISTIE, J. E., Pte. 1 A.G.A.	W.	19/ 9/14. Pte. 4y 6m.
CHRISTIE, R. J. H., Pte. 26 Bn.	✢ 29/7/16.	10/ 5/15. Pte. ✢
CHRISTMAS, J. F., Pte. 26 Bn.	7 M.G. Co. ✢ 13/8/16.	25/ 3/15. Pte. ✢
CHRISTMAS, T. R., Dvr 3 F.A.B.		26/ 8/14 Dvr. 4y 5m.
CHRISTOPHERS, C., Pte. 12 Bn.		12/ 5/16. Pte. 2y 9m.
CHUGG, C., Pte 12 Bn.		10/ 4/16. Pte. 3y 1m.
CHUGG, C. W., Pte. 40 Bn.	49 Bn.	4/ 4/16. Pte. 3y 6m.
CHUGG, H. W., Pte. 26 Bn.	✢ 5/11/16.	6/ 7/15. Pte. ✢
CHUGG, R. R., Tpr. 3 L.H.	4 D.A.C., 4 M.T.M.B.	3/ 8/15. Bdr. 4y.
CHURCH, F. C., Pte. 26 Bn.	W. M.M. ✢ 29/7/16.	8/ 6/15. Pte. ✢
CHURCHER, E. D., Pte. 40 Bn.		2/ 3/16. C.Q.M.S. 3y 5m.
CHURCHER, E. H., Pte. 12 Bn.	M.M. 52 Bn., 51 Bn.	7/ 9/15. Lt. 4y 2m.
CHURCHER, R. E., Pte. 26 Bn.	2 W. 52 Bn. ✢ 4/4/18.	31/ 3/15. Sgt. ✢
CHURCHILL, C., Pte. 12 Bn.	W.	29/ 5/16. Pte. 3y 6m.
CLAMPETT, F. P., Pte. 40 Bn.	12 Bn.	15/ 8/16.
CLARE, G. W. B., Gnr. 3 F.A.B.	W. M.M.	20/ 8/14. Lt.4y 9m.
CLARIDGE, A. G., Pte. 12 Bn.	W.	26/ 8/16. Pte. 1y 9m.
CLARIDGE, E. G., Pte.	W. 49 Bn.	29/ 3/16. Pte. 3y 7m.
CLARIDGE, C. F., Pte. 12 Bn.	W.	22/ 6/16.
CLARKSON, L. C. G., Pte. 15 Bn.	✢ 16/8/17.	29/ 7/15. Pte. ✢
CLAW, R. A. J., Pte. 26 Bn.		19/ 7/15.
CLAXTON, F. J., Spr. 3 Miners	3 Tun. Co.	25/11/15. Spr. 2y 3m.
CLAY, E. R., Pte. 12 Bn.		13/ 7/15. Pte. 4y 1m.
CLAYTON, A B., Pte. 12 Bn.	2 W.	13/ 9/15. 2y 3m.
CLAYTON, C., Pte. 40 Bn.	✢ 7/6/17.	2/ 3/16. Pte. ✢
CLAYTON, C. E., Pte. 12 Bn.	2 W.	22/ 8/14. L.'Cpl. 4y 7m
CLAYTON, E. C., Pte. 12 Bn.	52 Bn. ✢ 12/4/17.	3/ 8/15. Pte. ✢
CLAYTON, F. G., Pte. 40 Bn.	W.	21/ 3/16. Pte. 3y 5m.
CLAYTON, H. E., Pte. 4 M.G. Co.	12 Bn.	9/ 1/17. Pte. 2y 4m.
CLAYTON, H., Pte. 12 Bn.	W. 52 Bn., 51 Bn.	28/ 7/15. Pte. 4y 1m.
CLAYTON, J. C. N., Cpl. G S.R.	R.B.A.A.	1/12/17. Gnr. 1y 10m.
CLAYTON, L., Pte. 12 Bn.	40 Bn.	16/ 5/16 Sgt. 3y 4m.
CLAYTON, N. J., Pte. 12 Bn.		6/ 8/15. Pte. 2y 4m.
CLAYTON, W., Spr. 8 Fd. Co.		6/10/15. Dvr. 2y 8m.
CLAYTON, W. A., Pte. 12 Bn.	✢ 12/4/17	8/ 1/16. Pte. ✢
CLAYTON, W. J., (Correct name WILTSHIRE, W. H.)		

NAME.	REMARKS.	RANK ON ENLISTED. DISCHARGE. SERVICE.
CLARK, A. E., Pte. 12 Bn.	W.	27/ 9/15. Pte. 2y 7m.
CLARK, A. E., Pte. 40 Bn.	2 W.	16/ 8/16. Pte. 3y 1m.
CLARK, A. J., Pte. 40 Bn.	W. 12 Bn.	18/ 2/16. Pte. 2y 6m.
CLARK, A., Pte. 40 Bn.	✤ 7/6/17.	21/ 9/16. Pte. ✤
CLARK, A., Pte. 12 Bn.	W.	11/10/15. Pte. 4y 1m.
CLARK, A. H., Pte. 12 Bn.	W.	2/ 5/17.
CLARK, A. J., Pte. 4 A.S.C.	M.I.D.	2/ 8/15. Cpl. 3y 8m.
CLARK, A., Pte. 15 Bn.		11/12/14. Pte. 1y 5m.
CLARK, A., Pte. 40 Bn.	W. ✤7/7/17.	2/10/16 Pte. ✤
CLARKE, A. B., Pte. 12 Bn.		31/10/16 3y, Pte.
CLARKE, A. D., Tpr. 3 L.H.		24/ 1/17 2y 7m, Dvr.
CLARK, A. V. A., M.W.		
CLARK, B., Dvr. 8 Fd. Co.	W., 15 Fd. Co., 13 Fd. Co.	20/10/15 4y 1m, Dvr.
CLARKE, B. G., Pte. 40 Bn.	W. ✤ 28/3/18.	21/ 3/16 Sgt. ✤
CLARK, C. A., Pte. 3 G.S.R.	1 D.A.C.	8/ 7/18 1y 4m, Gnr.
CLARK, C. R., Pte. 26 Bn.	W. ✤ 9/8/18.	12/ 4/15 Sgt. ✤
CLARK, C., Pte. 12 Bn.	✤ 25th-28th April, 1915.	24/ 8/14 Pte. ✤
CLARKE, C. E., Pte. 12 Bn.	40 Bn. ✤ 19/12/16.	4/ 4/16 Pte. ✤
CLARK, C. H., Pte. 26 Bn.	7 L.T.M.B.	17/ 5/15 4y 3m, Pte.
CLARKE, C. H., Spr. 3 Miners.	1 Miners Bn.	8/10/15 1y 8m, Spr.
CLARK, C. V., Pte. 40 Bn.	W.	19/ 7/16 1y 8m, Pte.
CLARKE, C. E., Pte. 12 Bn.	W.	11/ 1/15 4y 3m, Pte.
CLARK, C. K., Pte. 12 Bn.	5 Bn. ✤3/3/17.	28/ 1/15 L.-Cpl. ✤
CLARK, C., Pte. 40 Bn.	✤ 29/3/18.	10/ 5/16 Cpl. ✤
CLARK, C. I., Pte. 7 Fd. Amb.	5 Fd. Co., A.C.H.Q.	25/ 2/15 4y 6m, Cpl.
CLARK, C. H., Pte. 12 Bn.	52 Bn. ✤ 7/6/17.	6/10/15 Pte. ✤
CLARK, C. J., Pte. 12 Bn.	M.M.	Pte.
CLARKE, W. M., Dvr. 6 F.A.B.		28/ 9/15
CLARKE, E. A., Pte. 40 Bn.	3 W.	3/ 4/16
CLARK, E. A. S., Spr. 8 Fd. Co.	12 Fd. Co.	15/11/15 3y 9m, Spr.
CLARKE, E. W., Spr. 3 Miners.	3 Tunn Co.	23/10/15 3y 10m., Spr.
CLARK, E. A., L.-Cpl. 40 Bn.		11/12/16 3y 1m, L.-Cpl.
CLARK, E. H., Pte. 12 Bn.		22/ 5/16 1y 11m, Pte.
CLARKE, F. G., Pte. 12 Bn.	W. ✤ 9/8/15.	21/ 8/14 Pte. ✤
CLARK, F. E., Pte. 12 Bn.		14/ 4/16 1y 9m, Pte.
CLARK, F. M., Pte. 40 Bn.		30/ 9/16 3y 2m, L.-Cpl.
CLARK, F. G., Pte. 15 Bn.	47 Bn. ✤ 8/8/16.	31/ 8/15 Pte. ✤
CLARK, G., Pte. 40 Bn.	2 W.	16 /2/16 3y 3m, Pte.
CLARK, G., Pte. 12 Bn.	3 W., 52 Bn.	29/ 9/15 2y 9m, Pte.
CLARKE, G. H., Gnr. 3 F.A.B.	W.	29/ 1/15 4y 3m, Gnr.
CLARK, G. C. L., Pte. 12 Bn.	M.C.	2/ 2/16 3y 3m, Lt.
CLARK, H. J., Pte. 12 Bn.	✤ 25/8/18.	24/ 8/15 Cpl. ✤
CLARK, H. D. F., Pte. 40 Bn.	12 Bn., 1 D. Salv. Co., Cps. H. Qrs.	24/ 2/16 3y 8m, Pte.
CLARK, H. R., Gnr. 6 F.A.B.	W., 106 How. Bty.	12/10/15 4y 1m, Cpl.
CLARKE, J., Pte. 12 Bn.	W. ✤ 30/3/19.	24/ 8/15 Pte. ✤
CLARK, J., Pte. 26 Bn.	✤ 18/12/15.	16/ 4/15 Pte. ✤
CLARK, J. A. N., Pte. 12 Bn.	W. ✤ 23/7/16.	22/ 8/14 Sgt. ✤
CLARK, J. H., Gnr. 6 F.A.B.	A.G.B.D., 6 F.A.B.	3/11/15 3y 11m, Gnr.
CLARKE, J. J. R., Sgt Fd. Art. Rfts	119 How. Bty.	9/11/16 2y 9m, Gnr.
CLARKE, J., Gnr. Siege Bde.	3 W.	7/ 6/15 4y 2m, Bomb.
CLARK, J., Pte. 4 M.G. Co.	W.	30/ 9/16 3y, Pte.
CLARKE, J. J., Tpr. 3 L. Horse.	✤ 15/8/15.	20/ 8/14 Tpr. ✤
CLARK, J. C., Tpr. 1 G.S.R	3 L.H.R.	26/ 4/18 1y 1m, Tpr.
CLARK, J. E., Pte. 4 M.G. Co.		4/ /8/16 2y 7m, L.-Cpl.
CLARK, J. P., Major 40 Bn.	D.S.O. 44 Bn.	7/ 3/16 Lt.-Col.
CLARK, K. C., Pte. 12 Bn.		29/ 1/15
CLARK, L. A., Pte. 40 Bn.		31/10/16 3y 2m, Pte.
CLARK, L. F., Lt.-Col. 12 Bn.	✤ 5/5/15.	17/ 8/14 Lt.-Col. ✤
CLARKE, L. E., Pte. 15 Bn.	2 W., 24 How. Bde., 10 F.A.B.	21/ 9/14 3y 4m, Pte.
CLARKE, L. C., Pte. 12 Bn.	✤ 23/8/18.	15/11/16 Pte. ✤
CLARKE, M. J.., Lieut. 26 Bn.	69 Bn.	21/ 5/15 2y 6m, Lt.
CLARK, M. A., Pte. 12 Bn.	W., 40 Bn.	24/10/16 2y 11m, Pte.
CLARK, N. A., Pte. 26 Bn.	2 W.	5/ 2/15 3y 10m, Pte.
CLARK, N. C., Pte. 12 Bn.		20/ 8/14 10m, Pte.
CLARK, N. C., Pte. 40 Bn.	W.	11/ 2/17 2y 7m, Pte.
CLARK, N. F., Pte. 3 G.S. Rfts.		8/ 7/18
CLARKE, P. C., Pte. 12 Bn.	✤ 24/7/16.	31/ 8/14 Pte. ✤
CLARK, R. T., Pte. 15 Bn.	2 W., M.M.	31/ 8/15 3y 10m, Pte.
CLARKE, R., Pte. 12 Bn.	W.	29/ 8/14 4y 5m, Sgt.
CLARK, R. W., Pte. 12 Bn.		7/ 9/15
CLARKE, R. J., Gnr. 6 F.A.B.	✤8/8/18.	3/ 8/15 Cpl. ✤
CLARK, R. T., Pte. 12 Bn.	W.	5/ 9/16 2y 6m. Pte.
CLARK, R. J., Sgt. 7 Fd. Amb.	M.M. 13 Fd. Amb	W.O.
CLARKE, S. J., Pte. 12 Bn.	3 W. M.M.	27/ 5/15 4y 3m, Cpl.
CLARKE, S. G., Tmptr. 3 L.H.	12 Bn.	19/ 8/14 4y 5m, Pte.
CLARKE, S. J., Pte. 12 Bn.	W., 40 Bn.	23/10/16 2y 11m, L.-Cpl.
CLARKE, T. L., Pte. 26 Bn.	✤ 20/4/16.	14/ 4/15 Pte. ✤
CLARKE, T. A., Pte. 12 Bn.	W., A. Cps., Hd. Qrs.	31/10/16 2y 11m, Pte.
CLARKE, T. L., Pte. 26 Bn.	W.	21/ 9/15 4y, Pte
CLARKE, T. R., Gnr. Fd. Arty.	3 F.A.B.	20/ 4/17 2y 1m, Gnr.
CLARK, V. A., Pte. Signallers.	3 L H. Tnl. Rgt.	31/ 5/17 2y 5m, Tpr.
CLARKE, W. J., Pte. 40 Bn.	3 W. ✤ 4/10/17.	9/ 5/16 Cpl ✤
CLARK, W. J., Tpr. 3 L.H.	W.	19/ 7/15 2y 4m, Tpr.
CLARK, W. J., Pte. 26 Bn.		14/ 4/15 3y 1m, Pte.
CLARK, W. J., Capt. 40 Bn.	M.C. 10 Fd. Amb	1/ 3/16 3y 7m, Maj.
CLARK, W. C., Pte. 40 Bn.		28/ 3/16 1y 5m, Pte.

TASMANIA'S MUSTER ROLL.

NAME.	REMARKS.	RANK ON DISCHARGE. ENLISTED. SERVICE.
CLARK, T. W., Pte. 40 Bn.		1/11/16 2y 10m, Pte.
CLARK, W., Pte. 26 Bn.		19/ 7/15 Pte.
CLARK, W. A., Pte. 12 Bn.	✠ 8/5/16.	24/ 8/15 Pte. ✠
CLARKE, W. E., Pte. 15 Bn.	✠ 9/8/15.	14/12/14 Pte. ✠
CLARKE, W. E. W., Pte. 12 Bn.	Miners' Corps. ✠ 14/9/18.	25/ 8/15 Pte. ✠
CLARKE, W. E., Pte. 3 G.S. Rfts.	12 Bn.	1/ 8/18 1y 3m, Pte.
CLARK, W. G, Pte. 40 Bn.		31/10/16 3y 1m, Dvr.
CLARK, W. H., Pte. 4 M.G. Co.	W., 2 Dvl. Trn., 4 M.G. Bn.	14/ 6/15 4y 4in, Pte.
CLARK, W. J., Pte. 26 Bn.	✠ 19/11/15.	6/ 4/15 Pte. ✠
CLARKE, W. L., Spr. 3 Fd. Co.		25/ 8/14
CLARK, W. P., Pte. 1 A.C.H.		16/ 9/14 4y 4m, Pte.
CLARKE, W. W., Pte. 4 M.G. Co.		2/ 4/17 2y 8m, Pte.
CLEAR, C. L., Pte. 12 Bn.	W. 52 Bn.	11/ 2/15 3y, Pte.
CLEARY, D'E., Pte. 2 G.S.R.	40 Bn.	11/ 2/18 1y 10m, Pte.
CLEARY, E. V., Pte. 15 Bn.	✠ 7/8/15.	10/2/15 Pte. ✠
CLEARY, J. H., Spr. 3 Fd. Co.	✠ 22/7/16.	24/ 8/15 Spr. ✠
CLEARY, S. G., Spr. 3 Fd. Co.		10/12/14
CLEARY, W. F., Spr. 3 Fd. Co.	M.M.	26/ 7/15 3y 3m, Spr.
CLEAVER, A. E., Pte.		1/ 3/15
CLEAVER, A. E., Pte. 15 Bn.	W. P.O.W.	2/ 7/15 4y 4m, Pte.
CLEAVER, E., Spr. Tunn. Co.		26/ 4/16 2y 9m, Spr.
CLEAVER, F. B., Pte. 12 Bn.	W., 52 Bn.	11/ 8/15 2y 10m, Pte.
CLEAVER, G., Pte. 26 Bn.	✠ 28/7/16.	16/ 3/15 Pte. ✠
CLEAVER, G., Pte 12 Bn.		27/ 9/16 1y 4m, Pte.
CLEAVER, J. H., Gnr. Fd. Arty.		10/10/16 3y 2m, Gnr.
CLEAVER, J. H., Spr. Tunn. Co.		6/10/17
CLEAVER, L., Pte. 40 Bn.	3 W.	17/10/16 2y 6m, Pte.
CLEAVER, L., Pte. 40 Bn.	3 Dvl. T.M. Bty., 1/3 A.M.T.M.B. ✠ 10/2/18	15/ 2/16 Pte. ✠
CLEAVER, L. E., Cpl., Fd. Arty.		3/11/16 3y 1m, Gnr.
CLEAVER, W, Pte. 40 Bn.	6 A.M.T.M.B.	11/ 3/16 3y 8m. Bdr.
CLEGG, J., Tpr. 3 L. Horse.		23/ 8/14 4y 7m, Pte.
CLELAND, G. P., Pte. 12 Bn.		7/ 8/15 3y 1m, Pte.
CLEMENTS, C. E., Pte. 40 Bn.	2 W.	29/ 2/16 2y 3m, Cpl.
CLEMENTS, J. J., Spr. 8 Fd. Co.	W., 5 Fd. Co.	5/ 1/16 3y 9m, Spr.
CLEMENTS, P. E. R., Pte. 40 Bn.		24/ 8/17 2y 4m, Pte.
CLEMENTS, R. C., Pte. 15 Bn.		17/ 9/14 1y 3m, Pte.
CLEMENTS, R., Pte. 15 Bn.	5 M.G. Co. ✠ 8/8/16.	5/ 2/15 L.-Cpl. ✠
CLEMENTS, R. H., Pte. 26 Bn.	W. ✠ 20/9/17.	15/ 6/15 Pte. ✠
CLEMENTS, R. W., Pte. 12 Bn.	W. ✠ 11/8/15.	20/ 8/14 Pte ✠
CLEMENTS, W. C., Pte. 40 Bn.	W.	29/ 2/16 3y 7m. L.-Cpl.
CLEMENTS, W. H., Spr 3 Fd. Co.		7/ 9/15 3y 8m. Spr.
CLEMONS, A. J., Pte. 40 Bn.	✠ 6/2/17.	25/ 5/16 L.-Cpl. ✠
CLENNETT, A. J., Gnr. 3 F.A.B.	M.M. 4 Dvl. Arty., 10 F.A.B.	23/ 9/14 4y 8m. Sgt.
CLENNETT, H. G., Pte. 26 Bn.	✠ 5/8/16.	27/ 7/15 Pte ✠
CLENNETT, J. H., Gnr 3 F.A.B.	2 W. M.M.	12/ 9/14
CLERKE, A. G., Pte. 40 Bn.	✠ 3/1/17.	17/ 4/16 Sgt. ✠
CLERKE, A. H., Sgt. 1 A.G H.		9/ 6/15 Lt.
CLERKE, J. M., Sec. Lieut, 3 L.H.R.	W.	21/ 8/14 5y 1m, Mjr.
CLIFF, C. L., Spr. 8 Fd. Co.	12 Fd. Co.	14/12/15 3y 10m, L.-Cpl.
CLIFFORD, J., Pte. 12 Bn.		2/ 6/15 2y, Pte.
CLIFFORD, S. C., Pte. 40 Bn.	W.	2/ 6/15 2y 5m, Pte
CLIFFORD, T G., Pte. 40 Bn.		2/ 2/16 3y 1m, Cpl.
CLIFFORD, W. J., Pte. 12 Bn.	2 W., 52 Bn. ✠ 25/9/17.	15/ 1/16 Pte. ✠
CLIFTON, G. G., Pte. 12 Bn.		21/ 8/16 3y 2m, Pte.
CLIFTON, L. D., Pte. 40 Bn.	W. ✠ 10/2/18.	13/ 3/16 Pte. ✠
CLINGELEFFER, A. B., Pte. 26 Bn.	2 W.	8/ 6/15 2y 8m. Pte.
CLINGLEFFER, R H., Pte 26 Bn.	3 W.	29/ 7/15 4y 1m. L.-Sgt.
CLOSE, C. J., Pte. 26 Bn.	2 W., 12 Bn.	29/ 9/15 4y, Pte.
CLOSE, P. V., Pte. 12 Bn.	W., 51 Bn.	3/4/16 3y 4m, Pte
CLOUGH, H., Pte. 12 Bn	52 Bn.	12/ 7/15 2y 7m., Pte.
COAD, E. H., Pte. 12 Bn.	✠ between 6th-9th August, 1915.	11/ 1/15 Cpl. ✠
COAD, H. J., Spr. Tunn. Co.		26/ 4/16 2y 1m. Spr.
COATS, C. H., Pte 40 Bn		3/ 3/16 2y 8m. CQMS
COATES, D., Pte. 12 Bn.	W., 52 Bn	6/10/15 1y 10m, Pte
COATES, E. T., Dvr. 40 Bn		15/ 3/16 1y 10m. Dvr.
COATES, G. R., Pte. 26 Bn.	2 Pnr. Bn.	14/ 5/15 3y 11m. Sgt.
COBBETT, A. L., Pte. 40 Bn.	15 Bn. ✠ 4/7/18.	1/ 2/16 Pte ✠
COBBETT, C. A., Gnr. 6 F.A.B.	3 W., 25 Bty A.F.A.	11/ 1/16 3y 9m, Sgt.
COBBETT, W. J., Sgt. 15 Bn.	2 W., C. de G., 47 Bn.	20/ 7/15 3y 2m. CSM
COBERN, C. M., Pte. 40 Bn	✠ 12/10/17.	28/ 3/16 Pte. ✠
COCHRANE, A. F., Pte. 12 Bn.	2 W., 23 How. Bde., 4 D.A.C.	
COCHRANE, H. W. G, Gnr. 6 F.A.B.	W.	6/ 8/15
COCK, J. A., Pte. 40 Bn.		15/ 5/16 3y 4m. Pte
COCK, W., Pte. 40 Bn.		29/ 3/16 3y 6m. Pte.
COCKER, A. H., Pte. 12 Bn.		14/12/14 4y 6m. Pte
COCKER, A. T., Pte. 40 Bn.	W.	25/ 7/17 1y 8m. Pte.
COCKER, H. F., Pte. 40 Bn.	W., 69 Bn., 12 Bn.	9/11/16 2y 11m. Pte.
COCKER, L. M., Pte. 40 Bn.	69 Bn., 12 Bn.	9/11/16 2y 5m. Pte
COCKERILL, C. W., Tpr. 3 L Horse	2 D.A.C. ✠ 12/8/16	25/ 8/15 Dvr. ✠
COCKERILL, J. M., Pte. 40 Bn.	49 Bn.	20/ 4/16
COCKS, A. R., Gnr 8 F.A.B.	W., 108 How. Bty.	1/11/15 3y 11m, Gnr.
COCKSHUTT, C., Pte. 3 G.S.R.		28/ 5/18
COCKSHUTT, W., Pte. 4 M G. Co.	W. M M. 15 Bn., 42 Bn.	4/12/16 2y 3m, Pte.
CODY, L. W. P. H., Pte. 12 Bn.	24 How. Bde.	7/12/15
COE, A. V., Pte. 40 Bn.		11/ 6/18 Pte.

TASMANIA'S WAR RECORD, 1914-1918.

NAME.	REMARKS.	RANK ON DISCHARGE. ENLISTED. SERVICE.
COE, H., Pte. 12 Bn.	W., 1 Pnrs.	9/ 6/15 2y 2m, Pte.
COETZEE, J. W., Pte. 26 Bn.		31/ 3/15 1y 5m, Pte.
COFFEE, W. J., Pte. 12 Bn.	✠ 25/4/18.	30/ 9/16 Pte.
COFFIN, C. H., Pte. 26 Bn.	12 Bn. ✠ 25/7/16.	10/ 8/15 Pte. ✠
COGHLAN, H. H. L., Dvr. 3 F.A.B.		19/ 7/15 4y 1m, Dvr.
COGHLAN, J., Pte. 40 Bn.	2 W.	28/ 9/16 1y 9m, Pte.
COGHLAN, M., Pte. 40 Bn.	W. ✠ 7/7/17.	28/ 9/16 Pte. ✠
COGHLAN, R. H., Dvr. 3 F.A.B.	102 How. Bty.	20/ 7/15 4y 1m, Dvr.
COGHLAN, W. B., Pte. 4 M.G. Co.		30/ 6/16 1y 6m, Pte.
COLBECK, F., Pte. 40 Bn.		5/ 4/16 3y 4m, Pte.
COLBECK, R. A., Pte. 4 M.G. Co.	15 Bn., 3 M.G. Bn.	
COLBOURN, F. B., Dvr. 4 A.S.C.	A.F.C.	17/ 8/14 4y 7m, Cpl.
COULBOURN, R. J., Pte. 7 Fd. Amb	13 Fd. Amb., 4 A.S.C., 1 Dvl. Tun.	15/ 2/15 4y 6m, Dvr.
COLBY, W. P., Tpr. 3 L.H.		20/ 8/14
COLE, A. H., Pte. 40 Bn.	W.	11/10/16 2y 11m, Pte.
COLE, A. V., Pte. 15 Bn.	W., 12 Bn., 69 Bn.	11/ 6/15 2y 5m, Pte.
COLE, A. J., Pte. 40 Bn.	W., A.A. Post. Cps.	3/11/15 3y 11m, L.-Cpl.
COLE, C. J., Pte. 12 Bn.	W.	12/ 1/16 3y 8m, Pte.
COLE, C. J., Pte. 12 Bn.		Cpl.
COLE, G. H., Pte. 12 Bn.		25/ 8/15 4y, Pte
COLE, H., Pte. 40 Bn.	W.	22/5/16 3y 5m, Cpl.
COLE, J., Pte. 12 Bn.	W.	1/ 6/15 3y 11m, Pte.
COLE, J., Pte. 40 Bn.		15/ 8/16 2y 2m, Pte.
COLE, L. H., Gnr. Fd. Arty.		6/10/16 2y 10m. Gnr.
COLE, L. N. M., Pte. 40 Bn.		13/10/15 4y 3m, Pte.
COLE, Q., Pte. 12 Bn.	2 W., 40 Bn.	3/ 4/16 3y 6m, Pte.
COLE, R. W., Pte. A.A.M.C.	6 Fd. Amb.	6/10/16 3y, Pte.
COLE, S. J. E., Pte. 40 Bn.		11/10/16 3y 2m, Pte.
COLE, S. R., Cpl. 15 Bn.	Re-enlisted 40 Bn. ✠ 13/9/18.	30/10/14 Sgt. ✠
COLE, W. R., Pte. 4 M.G. Co.	✠ 18/10/17	4/ 7/16 Pte. ✠
COLE, W. E., Pte. 40 Bn.		16/10/16 1y, Pte.
COLE, W. G., Pte. 40 Bn.	W.	28/ 9/16 2y 8m, Pte.
COLEMAN, C. H., Sgt. 12 Bn.		13/ 3/17 2y 3m, CSM
COLEMAN, E. A., Pte. A.S.C.		21/ 2/18 1y 1m, Dvr.
COLEMAN, H. E., Tpr. 3 L.H.	W., A.A.S.C., 35 Co. Dvl. Train.	22/ 8/17 2y 2m, Dvr.
COLEMAN, H. D., Gnr. 6 F.A.B.	106 How. Bty.	19/10/15 4y, Sgt.
COLEMAN, L. J., Pte. 12 Bn.		2/ 8/15
COLEMAN, M. H., Gnr. 6 F.A.B.	3 D.A.C.	10/ 2/16 3y 4m, Dvr.
COLES, D. H., Tpr. 3 L. Horse.	4 D.A.C., 10 F.A.B. ✠ 20/10/17.	1/ 9/14 Cpl. ✠
COLES, F. E., Pte. 3 G.S.R.	12 Bn.	21/ 6/18 1v 5m. Pte.
COLGAN, W. J., Pte. 12 Bn.		17/ 8/15 2y 2m, Pte.
COLGRAVE, R. G., Pte. 12 Bn.	P.O.W. ✠ 19/1/18.	1/ 5/16 Pte ✠
COLGRAVE, T. A., Pte. 26 Bn.		10/ 4/15 1y 7m, Pte.
COLGRAVE, W., Pte. 26 Bn.	W. ✠ 8/8/18.	24/ 4/15 Sg'. ✠
COLHOUN, J. C., Pte. 40 Bn.		6/ 1/16 4y. Dvr
COLHOUN, V., Pte. 12 Bn.	W., 52 Bn. ✠ 24/4/18.	8/ 1/16 Pte. ✠
COLK, G., Pte. 12 Bn.	✠ 23/4/18.	25/10/16 Pte ✠
COLK, L., Pte. 12 Bn.	W.	27/ 4/16 2y 1m, Pte.
COLLEDGE, A. E., Pte. 15 Bn.	W., 47 Bn.	28/ 7/15 1y 8m, Sgt.
COLLETT, A., Pte. 40 Bn.	26 Bn.	9/ 4/16 1y 10m, Pte.
COLLETT, L. R., Pte 12 Bn.		20/10/15
COLLIDGE, G., Pte. 12 Bn.		20/ 4/17 1y 2m. Pte.
COLLIER, C. G.		10/11/17
COLLIER, J. D. A., Sgt. 15 Bn.	47 Bn. P.O.W.	23/ 7/15 4y 5m, Lt.
COLLIDGE, P. T., Pte. 40 Bn.		30/ 5/16 1y, Pte.
COLLING, G. W., Pte. 40 Bn.	W.	30/ 5/16 Pte.
COLLINGS, A. E., Pte. Tnlrs.		20/10/16
COLLINGS, E D, Pte. 40 Bn.	W. MM. ✠ 28/3/18.	14/12/15 Pte. ✠
COLLINGS, J., Pte. 12 Bn.	3 Fd. Cd	5/ 9/14 4y 5m, Spr.
COLLINGS, L. C., Dvr. 26 Bn.	✠ 1/5/18.	9/ 3/15 Dvr. ✠
COLLINGS, P. F., Pte 12 Bn.	W.	29/ 8/16 2y 7m. Pte.
COLLINSON, F., Pte. 15 Bn.	47 Bn., 15 Bn.	28/ 7/15 4y 4m, Pte.
COLLINS, C. R., Lieut. 40 Bn.	47 Bn	24/ 5/16 Capt.
COLLIS, A. E., Pte. 12 Bn.	✠ 21/9/17.	19/ 9/16 P.e
COLLIS, A J., Pte. 40 Bn.		8/ 8/15 4y 5m, Cpl.
COLLIS, B. C., Pte. A.A.M.C.	3 A.G.H.	30/ 3/17 2y 6m, Pte.
COLLIS, C. W., Pte. 40 Bn.		30/ 8/15 3y 8m. Pte.
COLLIS, C. J., Gnr. Fd. Arty. Rfts.	1 D.A.C.	7/ 12/16 2y 9m. Dvr.
COLLIS, E. B., M.W.		
COLLIS, E. G., Pte. 12 Bn.	3 F.A.B	15/ 2/15 4y 8m. Cpl.
COLLIS, E. T., Pte. 3 Cyc. Co.	W. 4 Dvl. M.G. Co., 1 M.G. Co.	18/ 4/16 3y 3m. Pte
COLLIS, F. J., Pte. 12 Bn.	W. ✠ 24/3/18.	1/10/16 Pte. ✠
COLLIS, G. A., Pte. 3 Fd. Amb.	2 A.S.H.	19/ 8/15 1y 2m, Pte
COLLIS, H. C., Pte. 12 Bn.	W.	19/ 8/14 1y 9m, Pte
COLLIS, H. E., 2/A.M. A.F.C.		1/ 3/18 1y 4m, 2-A.M.
COLLIS, L. G., Pte. 12 Bn.	W.	15/ 9/14 1y 7m, Pte.
COLLIS, T. W., Pte. 4 M.G. Co.		21/10/16 2y 5m, Pte.
COLLIS, W. H., Pte. 3 L.H.	6 M. V. Section.	19/ 8/14 4y 6m, Pte.
COLMAN, W., Pte. 1 G.S.R.	5 M.G. Bn.	25/ 2/18 1y 8m, Pte.
COLSON, N. B., Pte. 26 Bn.	W.	18/ 5/15 3y 11m, Pte.
COLTHEART, S. J., Pte. 15 Bn.	2 W.	23/ 9/14 2y 5m, Pte.
COLUMBINE, A. G., Pte. 12 Bn.	W. 52 Bn., 4 Dvl. M.G. Co.	27/ 8/14 4y 6m, L.-Cpl.
COLUMBINE, C. M., Pte. 40 Bn.	3 W.	20/ 5/16 2y 3m. Sgt.
COLUMBINE, J. A., Pte. 40 Bn.	5 M.G. Co.	28/ 9/16 2y 8m. Pte.
COLVIN, A. M., Pte. M.G.	4 M.G. Bn., 2 M.G. Bn.	12/ 6/17 2y 2m. Pte.
COLLINS, A. J. A., Pte. 3 G.S.R	12 Bn.	5/ 8/18 10m. Pte.

TASMANIA'S MUSTER ROLL.   249

NAME.	REMARKS.	RANK ON DISCHARGE. ENLISTED. SERVICE.
COLLINS, A. C., Pte. 26 Bn.	40 Bn. ✤ 24/7/18	Pte. ✤
COLLINS, A. V. Pte. 15 Bn.	W., 24 How. Bde., 10 F.A.B.	9/ 9/15 3y 11m. Dvr.
COLLINS, C. J., Gnr., 3 F.A.B.	4 Dvl. Arty. 5 M.T. Co.	19/ 5/15 Dvr.
COLLINS, F., Pte. Rly.		26/ 2/18 1y 9m. Pte.
COLLINS, G., Pte. 15 Bn.	W., 24 How. Bde., 10 F.A.B.	18/ 5/15 4y 3m. Dvr.
COLLINS, G. H., Pte. 12 Bn.	W.	27/10/16
COLLINS, G. J., Pte. 26 Bn.	W., 52 Bn. ✤ 18/4/17.	30/ 7/15 Pte. ✤
COLLINS, G. R., Gnr. 3 F.A.B.	W., 5 D.H.Q., 111 How. Bty.	21/ 8/14 4y 11m. Lt.
COLLINS, G., Pte. 12 Bn.		28/ 8/14 1y 7m. Pte.
COLLINS, H. A. T., Pte. 12 Bn.	52 Bn.	5/ 7/15 1y 3m. Pte.
COLLINS, H. J., Spr. Miners		7/ 2/16
COLLINS, H. R., Pte. 26 Bn.		3/ 6/15 4y 2m. L.-Cpl.
COLLINS, J., Pte. 12 Bn.	26 Bn., 49 Bn.	20/ 8/15 4y 2m. Pte.
COLLINS, J., Pte. 12 Bn.	✤ 3/1/18.	25/ 8/15 L.-Cpl.
COLLINS, L. V., Pte. 12 Bn.	52 Bn. ✤ 4/9/16.	Pte. ✤
COLLINS, M. H., Spr. 6 Fd. Co.	✤ 11/6/17.	L.-Cpl. ✤
COLLINS, P. J., Pte. 7 Fd. Amb.		10/ 2/15 3y 11m. L.-Cpl.
COLLINS, P. A., Dvr. 4 A.S.C.		17/ 8/14 1y 10m. Dvr.
COLLINS, R. J., Pte. 26 Bn.	W., P.O.W.	19/ 7/15
COLLINS, R., Pte. 26 Bn.	W. ✤ 24/6/17.	15/ 6/15 Pte. ✤
(Correct name RICE, R. J.)		
COLLINS, R. W., Pte. 40 Bn.	W. ✤ 12/10/17.	28/ 9/16 Pte. ✤
COLLINS, R. R., Pte. 3 G.S.R.	12 Bn.	13/ 3/17 2y 8m. Pte.
COLLINS, S. F., Pte. 15 Bn.	W.	12/ 8/15 2y 7m. Pte.
COLLINS, V. A., Tpr. 3 L.H.	6 F.A.B.	28/ 7/15 4y. Dvr.
COLLINS, V. G., Pte. 40 Bn.	2W.	1/ 3/16 3y 6m. Pte.
COLLINS, V. P., C.S.M. 12 Bn.	✤ 30/10/17.	5/ 4/16 C.S.M. ✤
COLLINS, W., Pte. 26 Bn.	12 Bn.	13/ 8/15 1y 11m. Pte.
COLLINS, W. E., M.W.		
COMBES, A. K. Y., Pte. 12 Bn.	W. ✤ 18/9/18.	4/ 9/16 Pte. ✤
COMMANE, A. J., Pte. 26 Bn.	W.	14/ 9/15 Pte.
COMMANE, M. H., Pte. 26 Bn.	✤ 5/11/16	20/ 9/15 Pte. ✤
COMPLIN, F. J., Spr. Tnlrs.	3 Tun. Co.	5/ 4/17 2y 2m. L.-Cpl.
COMPTON, C. J., Pte. 3 L.H.		20/ 8/14 1y 10m. Dvr.
COMPTON, C. S., Spr. 8 Fd. Co.	13 Fd. Co.	25/ 2/16 2y 7m. Spr.
COMPTON, E. P., Pte. 12 Bn.		4/ 7/16 2y. Pte.
CONACHER, C. G., Pte. 1 A.C.H.		12/ 9/14 4y 4m. Pte.
CONACHER, K. J., Pte. 40 Bn.		10/ 3/16 3y 4m. Pte.
CONACHER, P. R., Pte. 15 Bn.	47 Bn., 48 Bn.	27/ 7/15 2y 1m. Pte.
CONLAN, B., Pte. 15 Bn.	W.	26/10/14 2y 1m. Pte.
CONLEY, C. J., Pte. 15 Bn.	2W., 47 Bn.	25/ 9/14 4y 4m. Pte.
CONLEY, E. A., Pte. 12 Bn.	2 D. Sig. Co.	25/10/16 3y 1m. Spr.
CONLEY, G. E., Pte. 12 Bn.	2W., M.M., 1 Prn. Bn.	11/ 8/15 3y 11m. Sgt.
CONLEY, L. L., Pte. 40 Bn.	W.	1/ 3/16 3y 2m. Pte.
CONLAN, W. A., Pte. 26 Bn.	W.	19/ 7/15 2y 4m. Pte.
CONNEL, J., Dvr. 3 F.A.B.		30/11/14 4y 9m. Dvr.
CONNELL, M., Dvr 3 F.A.B.		31/ 8/14 5y. Dvr.
CONNELL, O. E., Pte. 12 Bn.	52 Bn. ✤ 24/4/18.	Sgt. ✤
CONNEL, T., Pte. 12 Bn.	W. ✤ 8/8/15.	Pte. ✤
CONNELL, W. A., Cpl. 12 Bn.	D.C.M., 2 M.I.D. ✤ 28/12/17.	Capt. ✤
CONNELLY, L. H., Pte. 40 Bn.		27/ 7/16 3y 5m. L.-Cpl.
CONNOLLY, E. A., Spr. 6 F.C.E.	2W., 13 Fd. Co.	16/ 8/15 4y. Spr.
CONNOLLY, G. G., Bugler 12 Bn.		20/ 8/14 2y 2m. Bglr.
CONNOLLY, H. H., Pte. 40 Bn.		23/ 4/17 2y. Pte.
CONNOLLY, J. B., Pte. Rly.	4 B.G.R.O. Co.	26/ 2/17 2y 7m. Cpl.
CONNOR, J. V., Pte. 15 Bn.	2W., 24 How. Bde., 10 F.A.B.	23/ 9/14 4y 4m. Dvr.
CONNOR, M., Spr. 8 Fd. Co.	11 Fd. Co.	20/ 4/16
CONNOR, J. A., Pte. 12 Bn.	3 M.G. Co. ✤ 19/10/17.	3/12/14 Pte ✤
CONNORS, C. W., Pte. 40 Bn.	2W., M.M.	15/ 9/16 2y 7m. Pte.
CONNORS, C. P., Tpr. 3 L.H.		6/ 7/15 4y 5m. Tpr.
CONNORS, D. J., Pte. 40 Bn.	2W., 15 Bn., 10 M.G. Co.	27/ 3/16 3y 9m. Pte.
CONNORS, J. J., Pte. 40 Bn.		11/10/16 1y 4m. Pte.
CONNORS, M. L., Pte. 12 Bn.	W., 40 Bn.	8/ 4/16 3y 4m. Pte.
CONNORS, L. J., Spr. 8 Fd. Co.		29/10/15 1y 10m. Spr.
CONRAD, C. J., Dvr. 40 Bn.	12 Bn.	17/ 2/16 2y 5m. Dvr.
CONRADES, C. A., Pte. 40 Bn.	W.	28/ 3/16 1y 9m. Pte.
CONRADES, F., Pte. 15 Bn.	24 How. Bde.	12/ 8/15 1y 5m. Gnr.
CONROY, A. J., Pte. 12 Bn.	A.M.C. Dtls., 13 Fd Amb	27/10/16 3y. Pte.
CONROY, W P., Pte. 4 M.G. Co.		27/10/16
CONTENCIN, F. W., Pte. 12 Bn.	W., 52 Bn.	9/12/14 3y 8m. Cpl.
CONTENCIN, S. A. T., Cpl. 12 Bn.		2/11/16 2y 11m. L.-Cpl.
CONTENCIN, T. L., Pte. 40 Bn.	52 Bn., 4 Vety Ser	21/ 7/16 2y 11m. Pte.
CONWAY, A., Pte. 12 Bn.		29/ 8/14
CONWAY, L. H., Pte. 40 Bn.		20/ 3/17 1y 3m. Pte.
CONWAY, W J., Sig. 12 Bn.	✤ 25/7/16.	10/ 6/15 Sig. ✤
COOPER, A. A. H., Pte. A.S.C.		8/12/17 1y 10m. Dvr.
COOPER, A. H., Pte. 12 Bn.	W., 40 Bn.	14/11/16 2y 7m. Pte.
COOPER, A. V., Spr. 6 Fd. Co.	W.	28/ 8/15 2y 3m. Pte.
COOPER, A. V., M.W.		
COOPER, A. T., Q.M.S. 12 Bn.		21/ 2/17 2y 3m. Sgt.
COOPER, B. F., Pte. 12 Bn.		2/12/15 2y. Pte.
COOPER, C. H., Pte. 12 Bn.	48th Bn., 49 Bn.	14/ 9/15 3y 11m. Cpl.
COOPER, C. J., Pte. 12 Bn.	W., 40 Bn.	12/ 4/16 3y. L.-Cpl.
COOPER, C. T., Pte. 40 Bn.	W.	25/ 7/16 3y. Pte.
COOPER, D. B., Pte. 12 Bn.	✤ 30/5/18.	10/10/16 Pte. ✤
COOPER, D., Pte. 12 Bn.	2W., 52 Bn.	29/ 9/15 3y 7m. Pte.

250   TASMANIA'S WAR RECORD, 1914-1918.

NAME.	REMARKS.	RANK ON DISCHARGE. ENLISTED. SERVICE.
COOPER, E. J., Pte. 26 Bn.	W., 12 Bn. ✠ 6/10/17.	19/ 8/15 Pte. ✠
COOPER, E. G., Pte. 12 Bn.		30/ 8/14 4y 1m, Pte.
COOPER, F. G., Spr. 3 Miners		18/11/15
COOPER, F. J., Pte. 12 Bn.	W., 47Bn.	24/ 8/15 3y 7m, Pte.
COOPER, F. N., Pte. 1 A.C.H.	6 Fd. Amb.	15/ 9/14 4y 4m, Pte.
COOPER, G. E., Tpr. Remts.		30/ 9/15 4y 2m, Tpr.
COOPER, H., Pte. 26 Bn.	W.	12/ 6/15 4y 3m, Pte.
COOPER, H., Pte. 12 Bn.	40 Bn.	10/12/16 2y 5m, Pte.
COOPER, H., Pte. 12 Bn.	4 D. Salv. Co., 52 Bn.	29/ 8/16 1y 10m, L.-Cpl.
COOPER, J., Pte. 40 Bn.	49 Bn.	28/ 3/16 3y 7m, Dvr.
COOPER, J., Sgt. 12 Bn.	2 W., M.M.	31/ 8/14 4y 5m, W.O.
COOPER, L., Pte. 4 M.G. Co.	3 L.H.	9/ 1/17 1y 3m, Tpr.
COOPER, L. F., Pte. 12 Bn.	✠ 24/7/18.	28/10/16 Pte. ✠
COOPER, L. V., Pte. 12 Bn.	2W.	21/ 2/16 3y 7m, Pte.
COOPER, M. C., Gnr. Siege Arty.		7/ 6/15
COOPER, N. A., Pte. 12 Bn.		7/10/15 2y 4m, L.-Cpl.
COOPER, P. N., Pte. 12 Bn.		5/ 6/17 1y 2m, Pte.
COOPER, R., Pte. 12 Bn.	4 M.G. Co. ✠ 27/11/18.	8/ 2/16 Dvr. ✠
COOPER, R., Pte. 12 Bn.		9/ 3/17
COOPER, R. W. A., Pte. 26 Bn.	W., 2 Pnrs., 15 Amb. F.D.	12/ 4/15 4y 5m, Pte.
COOPER, S. F., Pte. 40 Bn.	✠ 26/5/18.	9/ 9/17 Pte. ✠
COOPER, T., Pte. 12 Bn.		28/ 5/15
COOPER, V. M., L.-Cpl. 40 Bn.	3 Dvl. Trn.	28/ 2/16 3y 8m, Dvr.
COOPER, W. J., Pte. 12 Bn.	W., 1 Pnr. Bn.	21/12/14
COOPER, W. V., Pte. 12 Bn.		26/ 6/16 3y 4m, Pte.
COOPER, W., Pte. 3 M.G. Bn.	49 Bn.	11/10/16 2y 10m, Pte.
COOPER, W. M., Pte. 26 Bn.		27/ 3/15 4y 5m, L.-Cpl.
COOPER, W. R., Pte. 40 Bn.	✠ 12/12/17.	2/10/16 Cpl. ✠
COODY, H. A., Dvr. 8 Fd. Co.		31/ 1/16
COOGAN, R. F., Cpl. 12 Bn.	W., 52 Bn.	28/10/15 3y 9m, Cpl.
COOLEY, A. E., Pte. 15 Bn.	W.	16/ 8/15 1y 10m, Pte.
COOLEY, A. V., Pte. 12 Bn.		19/ 8/14
COOLEY, C. H. T., Pte. 12 Bn.	A.M.C., 1 A.G.H.	30/ 4/17 2y 6m, Pte.
COOLEY, E. T., Pte. A.A.M.C.	1 A.G.H.	1/ 3/16 3y 4m, Pte.
COOLEY, F. J., Pte. 15 Bn.	✠ 7/8/15.	9/ 2/15 Pte. ✠
COOLEY, H., Pte. 15 Bn.		9/ 2/15 2y 2m, Pte.
COOLEY, K. R., Gnr. 6 F.A.B.	2W., 11 F.A.B.	14/ 2/16 3y 3m, Dvr.
COOLEY, L. H., Spr. 3 Fd Co.		22/ 9/15
COOLEY, R. C., Sgt. A.A.P.C.		2/ 3/15 4y 9m, Sgt.
COOLEY, T. P., Pte. 12 Bn.	W.	25/ 9/15 2y 1m, Pte.
COOLS, L., Gnr. F.A.		16/ 4/17
COOMBE, A. C., Pte. 15 Bn.	W., 47 Bn.	4/ 9/15 1v 7m, Cpl.
COOMBE, B. R., Pte. 15 Bn.	47 Bn., 12 M G. Co	20/ 9/14 4v 5m, Sgt.
COOMBE, C. A., Tpr. 1 Remts.		15/10/15 4y 1m, Tpr.
COOMBE, C. G., Pte. 12 Bn.		21/ 8/14 2y 4m, Pte.
COOMBE, M., Pte. 40 Bn.	✠ 4/10/17.	16/ 5/16 Pte ✠
COOMBE, V. D., Sgt. 15 Bn.	✠ 29/9/15.	20/ 9/14 Sgt. ✠
COOMBES, R., Pte. 12 Bn.		19/ 1/15 3y 2m, Pte.
COOMBS, E. W., Pte. 12 Bn.		29/ 8/14 2y 1m, Pte.
COOTES, G. F. J., Pte. M.T.		28/ 5/18
COOK, A. J., Pte. 40 Bn.		10/10/16 2y 7m, Pte.
COOK, A. C., Gnr. F.A.	W., 3 F.A.B.	20/10/16 2y 5m, Gnr.
COOKE, A. C. G., Pte. 12 Bn.		27/ 7/15 3y 11m, Pte.
COOK, A. E., Tpr. 3 L.H.	W., M.M.	25/ 8/14 4y 5m, Sgt.
COOKE, A. G., Pte. A.A.M.C.	8 Fd. Amb.	15/10/15 4y 2m, Pte.
COOK, C., Pte. 12 Bn.	52 Bn. ✠ 6/9/16.	9/ 9/15 Pte. ✠
COOK, C. H. R., Pte. 40 Bn.		1/ 8/16
COOK, C. E. V., Pte. 26 Bn.		11/ 6/15
COOK, C. W., Spr. Tnlrs.	3 Tun. Co.	27/10/16 2y 11m, Spr.
COOK, E. A., Pte. 40 Bn.	4W., M.M.	31/ 7/16 2y 10m, Sgt.
COOKE, E. H., Spr. 4 Miners	5 Tun. Co.	1/ 3/16 3y 6m, Spr.
COOK, F. M., Gnr. 3 F.A.B.	T.M. Bty. ✠ 21/7/17	15/ 9/15 Gnr. ✠
COOK, F. H., Pte. 26 Bn.	✠ 1/12/15.	5/ 5/15 Pte. ✠
COOK, G P., Spr. Tnlrs		26/ 4/16 2y 3m, Spr.
COOK, H. G., L.-Sgt. 26 Bn.	W.	29/ 3/15 2y 3m, Sgt.
COOK, J., Pte. 12 Bn.	Commission in West Surrey Rgt.	3/ 9/15 1y 4m,
COOK, J. C., Cpl. 3 L.H.		27/ 8/14 4y 4m, Cpl.
COOK, J. M., Cpl. 12 Bn.	✠ 25/1/17.	10/ 7/16 Cpl. ✠
COOK, J. W., Pte 15 Bn.	✠ 8/8/15.	18/ 9/14 Pte. ✠
COOK, N. J., Pte. 40 Bn.	W.	13/ 3/16 2y, Pte.
COOK, P., Dvr. 10 A.S.C.		8/ 9/14 1y 8m, Dvr.
COOKE, R. R., Pte. 26 Bn.	✠ 3/3/17.	12/ 4/15 Pte. ✠
COOK, T. A., Pte. 40 Bn.	W.	11/10/16 3y 1m, Cpl.
COOKE, W. A., Dvr. D.A.C.		13/ 9/15 3y 11m, Dvr
COOKE, W. C., Gnr. 6 F.A.B.	1 D.A.C., 114 How. Bty.	11/ 1/16 2v 7m, Gnr.
COOPER, A. D., Sec.-Lt. 12 Bn.		5/ 4/16 3y, Lt.
COPCUTT, A. A., Pte. 40 Bn.	W.	29/ 2/16 1v 8m, Pte.
COPCUTT, R. A., Pte. 2 G.S.R.	3 F.A.B.	16/ 4/18 1v 5m, Gnr.
COPCUTT, W. G., Pte. 26 Bn.	M.M. ✠ 26/7/16	28/ 7/15 Pte. ✠
COPE, R. H., Pte. 26 Bn.		14/ 4/15 11m, Pte
COPPLEMAN, F., Pte. 3 G.S.B.	3 A.B.R.C.	26/ 8/18 1v 2m, Pte.
COPPLEMAN, H. C. J., Pte. 40 Bn.	2W.	20/ 6/16 1v 10m, Pte.
COPPLESTONE, C. S., Gnr. 6 FAB	W.	17/ 9/15 3v 11m, Gnr.
CORBETT, L. Gnr. 3 A.F.A.	W., 2 F.A. ✠ 14/3/18.	Gnr. ✠
CORBETT, L., Pte. 15 Bn.	47 Bn. ✠ 8/8/16.	3/ 7/15 Pte. ✠
CORBY, E. J., Pte. 15 Bn.	✠ 9/5/15.	12/12/14 Pte. ✠

TASMANIA'S MUSTER ROLL. 251

NAME.	REMARKS.	RANK ON DISCHARGE. ENLISTED, SERVICE.
CORBY, J. J., Pte. 12 Bn.	W.	23/ 8/14 1y 4m, Pte.
CORBY, M. J., Spr. 8 Fd. Co.	W. ✽ 27/10/17.	12/ 1/16 Spr. ✽
CORDELL, G. R., Pte. 15 Bn.	24 How. Bwe., 10 F.A.B.	18/ 6/15 4y, Sgt.
CORDWELL, A. A., Pte. 12 Bn.	36 H.A.G.	27/ 6/17 2y, Gnr.
CORDWELL, G. R. D., Pte. 12 Bn.		11/ 8/16 1y 2m, Pte.
CORFIELD, A., Gnr. F.A.	14 F.A.B.	6/ 5/16 3y 4m, Dvr.
CORKERY, D. F., Pte. 4 Miners	5 Tun., 3 Tun. ✽ 2/11/18.	13/ 2/16 L'Cpl. ✽
CORKERY, J. J., Pte. 40 Bn.	W., 10 M.G. Bn.	27/10/16 2y 5m, Pte.
CORKERY, W. J., Dvr. 3 A.F.A.	W. ✽ 18/9/18.	3/12/14 Dvr. ✽
CORKINDALE, M., Pte. 40 Bn.	2W., 12 Bn.	25/ 9/16 2y, Pte.
CORKISH, T., Pte. 12 Bn.		19/ 9/14
CORLETT, H. R., Pte. 40 Bn.		28/ 3/16 5m, Pte.
CORLETT, O. K., Pte. 12 Bn.	W., 52 Bn.	14/ 8/15 2y 6m, Pte.
CORMACK, G. B., Pte. 40 Bn.	3W.	6/ 6/16 2y 2m, Pte.
CORMICK, J. B., Spr. 3 F.C.E.		17/ 8/14 7m, Spr.
CORNELL, H. G., 2 A.M. A.F.C.	✽ 11/12/17.	6/10/16 2 Lt. ✽
CORNES, C. S., Pte. 40 Bn.	M.M.	10/ 9/15 3y 11m, Pte.
CORNEY, A. C., Pte. 40 Bn.		28/ 3/16 2y 3m, Pte.
CORNEY, W. J., Pte. 12 Bn.	✽ 19/22 August, 1916.	9/ 8/15 Pte. ✽
CORNISH, E. H., Pte. 40 Bn.	W.	18/ 3/16 1y 10m, Pte.
CORNISH, G. H., Pte. 12 Bn.		26/ 8/14
CORNWELL, L., Gnr. 3 F.A.B.	24 F.A.B., 12 F.A.B.	28/ 9/14
CORNWALL, R. H. C., Pte. 40 Bn.	✽ 4/2/17.	4/ 4/16 Pte. ✽
CORREA, L. J., Pte. 12 Bn.	28 Bn.	27/10/15 3y 6m, Pte.
CORREA, L. W., Pte. 12 Bn.		26/ 8/14 9m, Pte.
CORRIGAN, L. J., Tpr. 3 L.H.	2W. ✽ 24/10/18.	6/10/14 Pte. ✽
CORRIGAN, J. J., Sgt. 15 Bn.	2W., D.S.O. and Bar., 2 M.I.D.	19/ 9/14
COSGROVE, B. R., Pte. A.C.C.H.		28/12/14 4y 7m, Pte.
COSGROVE, J. N., Spr. 6 Fd. Co.	13 Fd. Co.	12/ 8/15 4y 2m, L.-Cpl.
COSGROVE, P. L., Pte. 12 Bn.	W., 40 Bn., 10 M.G. Co.	14/ 3/16 3y 5m, Pte.
COSKER, J., Pte. A.A.M.C.	1 Fd. Amb.	9/10/16 3y 1m, Dvr.
COSSOM, C. S., Pte. 40 Bn.	3 M.G. Bn.	26/ 9/16 3y, L.-Cpl.
COSSUM, E. C., Pte. 12 Bn.	W., 52 Bn., 51 Bn	7/ 3/15 4y 5m, Pte.
COSSOM, J. W., Pte. 12 Bn.	✽ 7/10/17	15/ 1/16 Pte. ✽
COSSOM, O. W., Pte. 12 Bn.	W.	17/ 9/14 1y 9m, Pte.
COSTAIN, C. M., Dvr. 3 F.A.B.	1 D.A.C., 3 F.A.B.	3/ 6/15 4y 3m, Dvr.
COSTAIN, W. C., Tpr. 3 L.H.	2 D.A.C.	19/ 1/15 2y 11m, Gnr.
COSTELLO, A. E., Pte 12 Bn.		10/ 3/15 10m, Pte.
COSTELLO, A. J., Pte. 12 Bn.	2W.	16/ 5/16 3y 5m, Pte.
COSTELLO, T. A., Pte. 2 G.S.R.		13/ 4/18 5m, Pte.
COSTELLO, T. E., Pte. 12 Bn.	✽ 5/8 May, 1917.	22/11/15 Pte. ✽
COTTAM, C. G., Spr. 8 Fd. Co.	6 Fd. Co.	1/ 2/16 3y 8m, Dvr.
COTTERILL, G. W., Pte. 40 Bn.	W.	11/10/16 2y 11m, Pte.
COTTERILL, L. C., Pte. 12 Bn.	W., M.M., 52 Bn., 51 Bn	12/ 7/15 4y 3m, L.-Cpl.
COTTERILL, W., Pte. 4 M.G. Co.		25/11/16
COTTON, A. G., Tpr. 3 L.H.	8 L.H.R.	22/10/17 1y 11m, Tpr.
COTTON, F. J. J., Pte. A.A.H.	5 Fd. Amb.	2/10/15
COTTON, F. E. W., Pte. 12 Bn.		26/ 8/15
COTTON, G. A., Pte. 26 Bn.		10/ 5/15 5m, Pte.
COTTON, H. K., Pte. 40 Bn.	W.	1/11/16 2y 10m, L-Cpl.
COTTON, J. H., Tpr. 3 L.H.		11/10/17
COTTON, R., Pte. 40 Bn.		26/ 7/16 3y 5m, Pte.
COTTON, R., Pte. 12 Bn.	4 D.A.C.	5/ 8/15 4y, Dvr.
COTTRELL, H. J., Pte. 12 Bn.	W., 52 Bn., 40 Bn.	5/10/15 3y 10m, Pte.
COULSON, H. A., Pte. 40 Bn.	W.	28/ 3/16 3y, Pte.
COULSON, H. F., M.W.		
COULSON, H. F., Pte. 15 Bn.		25/ 9/14 1y 8m, Pte.
COULSON, J., Gnr. F.A.	2 D.A.C.	4/10/16 2y 11m, Gnr.
COULSTON, J., Spr. Tnlrs.	2 Tun. Co.	29/10/16 2y 7m, Spr.
COULSON, T., Spr. 3 Miners	W., 3 Tun. Co.	17/11/15 3y 10m, 2 Cpl.
COUNSEL, B., Pte. 12 Bn.		27/ 5/15 2y 4m, Pte.
COUNSEL, L. W., Gnr. F.A.	3 D.A.C.	19/ 3/17 2y 7m, Gnr.
COUNSEL, M., Pte. 12 Bn.	2W.	27/ 4/16 3y 3m, Pte.
COUNSEL, W. J., Pte. 15 Bn.	3W, 4 Bde. M.G. Co. ✽ 11/4/17.	26/10/14 Sgt. ✽
COUPE, R. R. A., Gnr. 8 F.A.B.	A.A.P.C.	27/ 9/16 3y 1m, Gnr
COURT, H. A., Cpl. 12 Bn.		19/10/16
COURTNEY, R., Pte. 26 Bn.	W., 2 Prns. ✽ 29/7/19.	27/ 4/15 Cpl. ✽
COURTNEY, W., Pte. 12 Bn.	W.	13/10/16
COURTO, F. J., Pte. 40 Bn.	W.	30/ 9/16
COUSINS, J. W., Spr. Tnlrs.	W.	22/ 3/17
COUSINS, M. J., Pte. 12 Bn.	W.	19/10/16 2y 6m, Pte.
COUSENS, W. D., Pte. 26 Bn.	✽ 24/6/16.	29/ 4/15 Pte. ✽
COUSTON, J., Spr. Tun. Co.		29/10/16 2y 7m, Spr.
COVENTRY, E. O., Pte. 1 A.G.H.		1/10/15 4y 2m, Pte.
COWARD, F., Pte. 40 Bn.	W.	30/ 9/16 1y 5m, Pte.
COWARD, W. E., Pte. 12 Bn.	2W., 52 Bn	10/ 9/15 2y 1m, Pte.
COWBURN, N. E., Pte. 26 Bn.	W., 2 Pnr. Bn., A.A.V.C.	27/ 7/15 3y 9m, Pte.
COWDERY, A. D., Dvr., 3 A.F.A.		15/ 6/15 4y 7m, Dvr.
COWEN, A., Pte. 40 Bn.	W.	2/ 3/16 2y 7m, Pte.
COWEN, C. W., Pte. 40 Bn.	✽ 23/7/17	4/ 7/16 Pte. ✽
COWEN, E. J., Pte. 40 Bn.	2W.	16/ 3/16 3y 1m, Pte.
COWEN, G., Pte. 12 Bn.	✽ 28/12/16.	31/ 7/16 Pte. ✽
COWEN, H., Pte. 40 Bn.	W., 12 Bn.	2/ 3/16 2y 9m, Pte.
COWEN, S., Pte. 40 Bn.	W., 49 Bn.	23/ 5/16 1y 9m, Pte.
COWEN, T., Pte. 40 Bn.	W.	1/ 3/16 2y 8m, Pte.
COWEN, T., Pte. 40 Bn.	W	23/ 5/16 3y 3m, Pte.

252   TASMANIA'S WAR RECORD, 1914-1918.

NAME.	REMARKS.	RANK ON DISCHARGE. ENLISTED. SERVICE.
COWIE, W. J., Pte. A.M.C.	14 Fd. Amb.	16/ 2/16 3y 8m, Pte.
COWIE, W. H., Pte. 40 Bn.	W.	9/ 1/17 2y 2m, Pte.
COWLE, C. E., Pte. 12 Bn.	52 Bn., 4 M.G. Bn.	17/ 1/16 3y 8m, Dvr.
COWTAN, M. D., Pte. 1 A.C.H.	D.C.M. (Commission in R.A.M.C.)	2/10/14 1y 3m, Pte.
COX, A. F., Pte. 15 Bn.	24 How. Bde., 4 D.A.C.	1/ 7/15 3y 11m, Gnr.
COX, A. H., Gnr. 6 F.A.	W. ✣ 14/11/16.	17/ 8/15 Sgt. ✣
COX, C. H., Pte. 12 Bn.		21/10/16 2y 2m, Pte.
COX, C. T., Pte. 12 Bn.	✣ 23/4/18.	23/10/16 Pte. ✣
COX, C. V., Pte. A.F.C.	15 F.A.B., 1 F.A.B.	16/10/16 2y 11m, Gnr.
COX, C. W. A., Pte. 40 Bn.	✣ 12/10/17.	14/ 3/16 Sgt. ✣
COX, C. H., Pte. 40 Bn.	✣ 4/8/17.	22/ 3/16 Pte. ✣
COX, E. J., Pte. 12 Bn.	2W.	4/ 8/16 2y 8m, Pte.
COX, F. C. C., Pte. 26 Bn.		21/ 4/15 4y 4m, Sgt.
COX, F., Pte. 15 Bn.	✣ 13/5/15.	4/ 1/15 Pte. ✣
COX, F. J., Pte. 40 Bn.	2W., M.M., 51 Bn.	3/ 3/16 3y 6m, Pte.
COX, H. F., Pte. 26 Bn.	2 Dvl. T.M. Bty. ✣ 12/10/16.	22/ 6/15 Pte.
COX, H., Pte. 15 Bn.	47 Bn., 45 Bn.	18/ 8/15 4y 1m, S.-Sgt.
COX, H. J., Pte. 15 Bn.	✣ 29/5/15.	12/12/14 Pte. ✣
COX, J., Pte. 40 Bn.	M.M.	31/ 5/16 3y 7m, Pte.
COX, J., Pte. 12 Bn.	M.M.	3/ 8/16 3y 2m, Pte.
COX, J. S., Pte. 26 Bn.	✣ 5/11/16.	12/ 4/15 Pte. ✣
COX, M. E., Pte. 40 Bn.	2W.	20/ 3/16 3y, L.-Cpl.
COX, P. E., Pte. 12 Bn.	W.	27/10/16 3y, Pte.
COX, P. T., Pte. 40 Bn.	2W.	18/ 5/16 3y, Cpl.
COX, T. G., Pte. 12 Bn.	4 M.G. Bn.	27/ 7/15
COX, W., Pte. 40 Bn.		20/ 3/16 3y 5m, Pte.
COX, W. E., Lt. 6 F.A.B.	W., M.C., 11 F.A.B.	20/10/15 3y 10 m, Maj.
COXALL, C. C., Pte. 40 Bn.	✣ 7/6/17.	27/ 3/16 Pte. ✣
CRABTREE, S. H., Gnr. S. Art.		7/ 6/15 3y 5m, Sig.
CRABTREE, T. H., Pte. 40 Bn.	2W.	6/ 3/16 3y, Pte.
CRACKNELL, W. J., Spr. 3 Fd. Co	2 W., 13 F.C.E.	7/ 9/15 4y, L.-Cpl.
CRADOCK, W. H., Pte. 1 A.G.H.	6 Fd. Amb.	6/ 6/15 4y, Pte.
CRAGG, W. L., Pte. 12 Bn.	W. ✣ 1/6/16.	23/ 8/15 Pte. ✣
CRAIG, A. J., Cpl. 12 Bn.		26/ 8/14 3y 10m, Sgt.
CRAIG, F. N., Pte. 12 Bn.	M.M. ✣ 24/4/18	12/ 1/15 Pte. ✣
CRAIG, H. W., Pte. 4 M.G. Co.	2 A.M.G. Bn.	20/ 6/16 3y 3m, Pte.
CRAIG, H. de B., Pte. 26 Bn.		10/ 5/15 1y 5m, Pte.
CRAIG, H. de B., Tpr. 3 L.H.	1 M.G. Sqdn.	20/10/17 1y 8m, Tpr.
CRAIG, J. W., Pte. A.A.M.C.	14 Fd. Amb.	8/ 6/17 2y 4m, Pte.
CRAIG, L. H., Pte. 12 Bn.	Re-enlisted A.F.A.	15/ 1/15 3y 10m, Pte.
CRAGIE, J. C., Cpl. 40 Bn.		17/ 4/17 2y 7m, Pte.
CRAIGIE, B., Pte. 12 Bn.		20/ 8/14
CRAMP, C. R., Gnr. 6 F.A.B.		30/ 8/15, 4y 3m, Lt.
CRANE, E. K., Pte. 12 Bn.	11 Bn.	5/ 6/15 2y 1m, Pte.
CRANE, G. M., Pte. 12 Bn.	✣ 23/9/18	2/ 5/16 Pte. ✣
CRANE, J. F., Pte. 3 G.S.R.	12 Bn.	18/ 1/18 1y 5m, Pte.
CRANE, M. S., Tpr. 5 L.H.	3 L.H.	25/ 6/18 1y 3m, Tpr.
CRANE, W. J., Pte. 12 Bn.	W. ✣ 25-28/4/15.	20/ 8/14 Pte. ✣
CRANER, J., Tpr. 3 L.H.		3/ 2/17
CRANNY, P. W., Pte. 12 Bn.	W.	14/10/16 1y 5m, Pte
CRANSTON, A., Gnr. 6 F.A.B.	W., 2 D.A.C., 6 F.A.B.	29/ 9/15 4y 1m, Sgt.
CRANSTON, H. J., Gnr. 6 F.A.B.		20/ 9/15 4y 1m, Gnr.
CRANSWICK, J. S., Pte. 12 Bn.	40 Bn. ✣ 13/1/17.	24/ 8/14 2nd Lt. ✣
CRANSWICK, T. G., Cpl 40 Bn.	W., D.C.M., M.C., M.I.D.	7/ 2/16 Lieut.
CRANWELL, H. A. B., Cpl. 12 Bn.	W.	1/ 9/15 3y 2m, Sgt.
CRANWELL, H. A., M.W.		
CRAW, G. A., Dvr. 6 F.A.B.		17/ 9/15 3y 11m, Dvr.
CRAW, H. McD., Pte., 3 G.S.R.	12 Bn.	2/ 4/18 1y 7m, Pte.
CRAWFORD, H. J., Spr. 3 F.C.E.		29/ 8/14 4y 6m, 2nd-Cpl
CRAWFORD, A. E., Pte. 40 Bn.	12 Bn.	24/ 5/16 3y 4m, Pte.
CRAWFORD, A., Pte. 12 Bn.	W.	13/ 1/16 2y 5m, Pte.
CRAWFORD, C., Pte. 15 Bn.	47 Bn., 26 A.A.S.C.	31/ 8/16 4y 1m, Dvr.
CRAWFORD, D. A., Pte. A.S.C.	38 A.S.C.	8/ 3/18 1 y 7m, Dvr.
CRAWFORD, E. A., Spr. 3 Min.	M.M. ✣ 12/10/18.	28/10/15 Spr. ✣
CRAWFORD, E., Dvr., B.A.C.	3 A.F.A. ✣ 21/10/17.	17/10/14 Dvr. ✣
CRAWFORD, H., Gnr. 3 F.A.B.		26/ 8/14 3y 10m, Gnr.
CRAWFORD, H. G., Pte. 40 Bn.	12 Bn.	23/ 9/16 3y 1m, Pte.
CRAWFORD, H. S. W., Cpl. 12 Bn.	2W.	1/ 9/15 3y, Sgt.
CRAWFORD, J., Tpr. 3 L.H.		23/ 2/17 6y 8m, Tpr.
CRAWFORD, J. W., Pte 40 Bn.	W., 12 Bn.	12/ 9/16 3y 1m, Pte.
CRAWFORD, J. H., Pte. 40 Bn.	W.	2/ 3/16 2y 11m, Pte.
CRAWFORD, L. G., Pte. 40 Bn	2W.	24/ 2/16
CRAWFORD, M., Pte. 12 Bn.	W.	14/ 6/16 1y 9m, Lieut.
CRAWFORD, N., Dvr 3 A.F.A.	✣ 4/9/18.	26/ 8/14 Sgt. ✣
CRAWFORD, R. H., Pte. 12 Bn.	W., 52 Bn., 3 F.C.E.	13/ 7/15 4y, Dvr.
CRAWFORD, R. A., Pte. 15 Bn.	W., 3 A.F.A. ✣ 14/11/16.	2/ 7/15 Pte. ✣
CRAWFORD, R. W., L.-Cpl. 12 Bn.	2W.	17/ 8/ 14, 4y 7m, Sgt.
CRAWFORD, T. J., Cpl. 40 Bn.	2W.	13/ 1/16 3y 7m, Cpl.
CRAWFORD, W. C., Gnr. F.A.		1/ 3/17, 2y 7m, Dvr.
CRAWFORD, W. H., Dvr. 3 F.A.B.	W., 21 F.A.B., 2 F.A.B.	12/12/14 4y 6m, Dvr.
CRAWLEY, A. C., Pte. 12 Bn.	W.	23/10/16
CRAWRBY, W., Pte. 12 Bn.		15/ 6/16 1y 8m, Pte.
CREACH, A., Sgt., 1 A.C.H.		18/ 8/14 1y 9m, Sgt.
CREELY, J., Pte. 40 Bn.		17/ 7/17 1y, Pte.
CREIGHTON, J. G., Pte. 12 Bn.	52 Bn. ✣ 4/9/16.	4/10/15 Pte. ✣
CRESSINGTON, E., Pte. 40 Bn.	10 L.T.M.B., A.A.S.C.	10/ 7/16 2y 10m, Pte.

TASMANIA'S MUSTER ROLL. 253

NAME.	REMARKS.	RANK ON DISCHARGE. ENLISTED, SERVICE.
CRESSWELL, E., Pte. 12 Bn.	✠ 15/2/17.	13/10/16 Pte. ✠
CRESWELL, A. R., Pte. 12 Bn.	W.	9/ 2/15 4y 6m, Lieut.
CRESWELL, R., Pte. 40 Bn.	W. (M.M., Ship's Roll.)	20/ 7/16 3y 1m, Pte.
CRIDLAND, A., Gnr. 6 F.A.B.	23 How. Bde.	11/ 1/16 3y 8m, Dvr.
CRIPPS, A.V.H., Pte. 4 M.G. Co.		3/10/16
CRIPPS, F., Pte. M.G. Co.	15 Bn., 2 M.G. Co.	4/ 6/17 2y 3m, Pte.
CRIPPS, H. J., Pte. 4 M.G. Co.		27/10/16.
CRISP, A. L., Gnr. F.A.	7 F.A.B.	21/ 5/17 2y 1m, Gnr.
CRISP, A. E., Sgt.-Maj. 26 Bn.		21/ 4/15 1y 2m, S.-Maj.
CRISP, A. E., C.S.M. 2 G.S.R.		22/ 3/18
CRISP, A. P., Lt. 3 F.A.B.	D.S.O., C. de G. (French), 3 M.I.D.	14/ 8/14 4y 11m, Major
CRISP, A. T., Pte. 26 Bn.	12 Bn., Dental Services.	26/ 7/15 3y 11m, Pte.
CRISP, C. L., Gnr. 6 F.A.B.	23 How. Bde., 7 F.A.B.	3/ 2/16 3y 8m, Cpl.
CRISP, E. G., 12 Bn.		6/ 8/15 Lieut.
CRISP, E. B., Pte. 1 G.S.R.		22/ 1/18 1y 11m, Pte.
CRISP, E. V., Sgt. 7 Fd. Amb.	13 Fd. Amb.	16/ 2/15 4y 7m, Sgt.
CROCKER, A., Pte. A.M.C.		5/ 3/17 2y 3m, Pte.
CROCKER, B. S., Pte. 40 Bn.		4/10/16 1y 5m, Pte.
CROCKER, A. C., Pte. 40 Bn.	W.	20/ 2/16 3y 7m, Pte.
CROCKETT, J. C., Pte. 26 Bn.	2W., 4 Fd. Co.	24/ 4/15
CROFT, A. J., Gnr. Siege A.		7/ 6/15 0y 10m, Gnr.
CROFT, C. L. T., Gnr. 3 F.A.B.	W.	14/ 6/15 3y, Lieut.
CROFT, E., Pte. 15 Bn.	W.	15/ 1/15 4y 4m, Pte.
CROFT, C. L. T., Gnr. 3 F.A.B.	W.	14/ 6/15 3y, Lieut.
CROFT, P. H., Gnr. F.A.		15/ 5/17
CROFT, S. F., Pte. 40 Bn.		14/ 8/17 2y 2m, Pte.
CROLE, F. C., Pte. 40 Bn.	✠ 8/5/17.	10/ 2/16 Sgt. ✠
CROLE, P. A. W., Pte. 26 Bn.	69 Bn.	9/ 5/15 2y 5m, Pte.
CROMPTON, J., Pte. 12 Bn.	W., 3 Fd. Co., 32 Bn. ✠ 29/7/18.	3/ 9/14 L.e.
CRONIN, D. F., Cpl. 26 Bn.	✠ 25/8/16.	26/ 7/15 Cpl. ✠
CRONIN, P. L., Spr. 3 Miners	W., 3 Tunn. Co.	14/ 9/15
CROOK, C. A., Pte. 12 Bn.		29/ 8/14 4y 7m, Cpl.
CROOK, J. F., Cpl. 26 Bn.	A.A. Pay Corps.	19/ 5/15 3y 3m, Sgt.
CROOKS, H. G., Pte. 26 Bn.	2W., 12 Bn.	12/ 8/15 3y, Cpl.
CROOKS, J. A., Dvr. A.F.A.		27/ 7/15
CROOKS, K. S., Pte. 12 Bn.	M.M., 51 Bn.	12/11/15 4y, Pte.
CROOKS, P. L., Dvr. 6 F.A.B.		5/ 8/15 4y, Dvr.
CROOK, W. H., Pte. 15 Bn.	W., 4 Pnrs.	12/ 8/15 3y, Pte.
CROSBY, A. W., Sgt. 26 Bn.	A.F.C.	29/ 4/15 4y 4m, Lieut.
CROSBY, G. V., Pte. 40 Bn.	✠ 10/9/18.	7/ 6/16 Pte. ✠
CROSBY, W. M. B., Tpr. 3 L.H.		20/ 8/14 0y 7m, Tpr.
CROSBY, W. T., Pte. 40 Bn.	W.	12/ 6/16 3y 2m, Lieut.
CROSS, A. G., Pte. 12 Bn.	W., 40 Bn.	11/ 4/16 1y 8m, Pte.
CROSS, A. C., Pte. 2 G.S.R.	R.B.A.A.	1/ 6/18 1y 3m, Gnr.
CROSS, D. O., Pte. 40 Bn.	✠ 31/1/17.	5/ 5/16 Pte. ✠
CROSS, F. C., Pte. 12 Bn.		19/ 4/17 0y 11m, Pte.
CROSS, H. A., Pte. AN and MEF		8/11/16 1y 3m, Pte.
CROSS, H. G., Pte. 12 Bn.	W.	27/10/15 2y 5m, Pte.
CROSS, H., Pte. 40 Bn.	2W.	18/ 7/16 2y 9m, Pte.
CROSS, J. W., Spr. 5 Miners	5 and 3 Tunn. Co.	23/ 2/16 3y 8m, Cpl.
CROSS, R., Pte. 26 Bn.	✠ 4/1/16.	16/ 7/15 Pte ✠
CROSS, R., Pte. 1 G.S.R.		19/ 3/18 1y 9m, Pte.
CROSS, S. R., Pte. 12 Bn.	Between April 25 and May 1, 1915.	19/ 9/14 Pte. ✠
CROSS, W. J., Pte. 1 G.S.R.		16/ 1/18 1y 11m, Pte.
CROSSING, C., Tpr. 3 L.H.		14/8/15 2y 5m, Tpr.
CROSSIN, C. J., Tpr. 3 L.H.	4 D.A.C.	30/ 8/16 1y, Pte.
CROSSIN, J., Pte. 12 Bn.		3/ 8/17 1y 10m, Pte.
CROSSWELL, A., Pte. 40 Bn.	3W.	28/ 9/16 3y, Pte.
CROSSWELL, W. J., Spr. 3 Mns.	4 and 1 Tunn. Co.	15/11/15 3y 9m, Spr.
CROTHERS, W. J., Pte. 12 Bn.	2W., M.M.	27/ 4/16 3y 1m, Pte.
CROTTY, M. J., Pte. 12 Bn.	A. Prov. Cps.	14/ 9/15
CROUCH, A., Pte. 12 Bn.	W.	21/ 8/14 2y 3m, Pte.
CROUCH, R. W., Pte. 40 Bn.		22/ 6/16
CROUCH, R., Pte. 40 Bn.	✠ 13/10/17.	21/ 6/16 Pte. ✠
CROW, J., M.W.		
CROW, J. L., Gnr. 13 F.A.B.	15 Bn., 25 Bn. ✠ 3-4/5/17.	3/ 2/16 Pte. ✠
CROWCROFT, W. R., Gnr. 6 F.A.B.	2 D.A.C., 6 B.A.C.	3/11/15 3y 11m, Gnr.
CROWDEN, G. B., Pte. 12 Bn.		16/11/16 3y 1m, L.-Cpl.
CROWDEN, H. A., Pte. A.A.H.	1 Fd. Amb.	13/ 1/16 2y 5m, Pte.
CROWDEN, L. L., Pte. 40 Bn.	✠ 7/6/17.	25/ 9/16 Pte. ✠
CROWE, E., Pte. 26 Bn.	W.	28/ 2/15 Pte.
CROWTHER, W. E. L. H., Capt., 7 F. Amb.	D.S.O., M.I.D., 5 Fd. Amb.	Lt.-Col. (no record).
CRUMPTON, W. H., Pte. 1 G.S.R.		28/ 1/18
CRUICKSHANK, A. la T., Capt. 40 Bn.		7/ 3/16 3y 9m, Capt.
CRUTCHLEY, G., Gnr. 24 F.A.B.	12 F.A.B.	4/10/16 2y 11m, Gnr.
CRYAN, J., Tpr. Rmts.		13/10/15 0y 6m, Tpr.
CUBITT, C. S. G., Pte. 15 Bn.	47 Bn. ✠ 6/8/16.	3/ 8/15 Pte. ✠
CUBITT, J. E. C., Pte. 26 Bn.	12 Bn. ✠ 23-25/7/16.	29/ 7/15 Pte. ✠
CUBITT, N., Pte. 12 Bn.	W., 51 Bn.	6/ 8/15 3y 10m, Pte.
CUDDY, A. R. W., Pte. 15 Bn.	24 H. Bde., 10 F.A.B.	2/ 7/15
CULL, E. L., Pte. 12 Bn.	✠ 24/7/16.	25/ 8/15 Pte. ✠
CULLEN, A. V., Pte. 12 Bn.	40 Bn.	4/10/17 2y 1m, Pte.
CULLEN, A. L., Pte. 1 A.G.H.C.D.		3/ 6/15 1y 9m, Pte.
CULLEN, A. R., Pte. 40 Bn.		23/ 5/16 3y 5m, Sgt.
CULLEN, E. S. R., Pte. A.M.C.	2 A.G.H.	12/ 9/16 2y 5m, Pte.

NAME.	REMARKS.	RANK ON ENLISTED.	DISCHARGE. SERVICE.
CULLEN, I. S., Pte. 40 Bn.	W.	20/10/16	2y 10m, Pte.
CULLEN, W., Pte. 15 Bn.	12 Bn.	27/10/14	5y 3m, Lieut.
CULLINAN, M., Pte. 12 Bn.	52 Bn., 51 Bn.	11/ 8/15	
CULLINAN, W. J., Pte. 40 Bn.	W.	10/ 7/16	2y, Pte.
CULTON, W. J., Lt. 40 Bn.	W. ✠ 12/2/17.	23/12/15	Lieut. ✠
CUMINE, G. F., Spr., 3 Fd. Co.	13 Fd. C.	17/ 8/14	
CUMMING, L., Pte. 12 Bn.		7/ 8/16	1y 9m, Pte.
CUMMING, M. L., Pte. 40 Bn.	W.	3/10/16	2y 6m, Pte.
CUMMING, W. G., Pte. 3 Fd. Amb.	13 Fd. Amb., 3 A.G.H.	21/ 8/15	4y 1m, Pte.
CUMMINS, F., Pte. 40 Bn.		29/ 6/16	1y 3m, Pte.
CUMMINGS, E. D., Pte. 15 Bn.	D.F.C.	27/10/14	4y 5m, Capt.
CUMMINGS, F. E., Tpr. 3 L.H.	3 Pnr. Bn.	31/ 5/16	1y 6m, Pte.
CUMMINGS, M. H., Cpl. 1 A.C.H.	M.M., 5 D. Supply Co., A.F.C.	21/10/14	4y 10m, 2nd-Lt
CUMMING, R. D., Pte. 12 Bn.	Anz. Prov. Cps.	15/12/15	3y 10m, Pte.
CUMMINGS, R. L., Pte. 3 Fd. Amb.	A.F.C. ✠28/8/18.	18/ 8/15	2nd-Lt. ✠
CUNNINGHAM, D., Pte. 12 Bn.	W., 52 Bn.	7/ 8/15	3y 5m, Pte.
CUNNINGHAM, D. J., Pte. 40 Bn.	W.	25/ 7/16	3y 3m, Cpl.
CUNNINGHAM, D. L., Pte. 40 Bn.		22/ 5/16	3y 2m, Pte.
CUNNINGHAM, F. J., Pte. 12 Bn.	3W., 40 Bn. ✠ 13/10/17.	3/ 4/16	Cpl. ✠
CUNNINGHAM, G., Pte. 26 Bn.	2W.	1/ 7/15	4y 1m, Pte.
CUNNINGHAM, G. E., Pte. 12 Bn.		8/ 6/17	
CUNNINGHAM, H., Pte. 26 Bn.	W., 7 L.T.M.B.	2/ 7/15	4y 1m, Pte.
CUNNINGHAM, J., Sgt. 40 Bn.		1/ 3/17	2y 9m, Sgt.
CUNNINGHAM, K. F., Pte. 1 G.S.R	55 Bn.	8/ 9/17	2y 2m, Pte.
CUNNINGHAM, L. W., Pte. 26 Bn.	3W.	22/ 6/15	
CUNNINGHAM, R., Pte. 12 Bn	W., 52 Bn., 51 Bn.	23/ 9/15	4y, Pte.
CUNNINGHAM, W., Pte. 12 Bn.	W.	21/ 8/14	4y 5m, Pte.
CUNLIFFE, L., Pte., 4 M.G. Co.		12/ 7/16	
CUPIT, A. E., Pte. 2 G.S.R.	23 G.S.R.	18/ 5/18	0y 8m, Pte.
CUPIT, D. W. F., Spr. 8 Fd. Co.	3 Fd. Co.	27/ 4/16	3y 4m, Spr.
CURBISHLEY, T., Gnr. 8 F.A.B.	W.	13/ 8/15.	
CURE, A. E., Pte. 40 Bn.	2W.	9/10/16	2y 11m, Pte.
CURE, E., Pte. 40 Bn.	W., 51 Bn.	17/ 3/16	3y 3m, Pte.
CURE, O., Pte. 40 Bn.	W.	17/10/16	2y 9m, Pte.
CURLE, E. J., Pte. 3 Fd. Amb.	13 Fd. Amb.	27/ 7/15	2y 9m, Pte.
CURLE, F. J., Pte. 3 Fd. Amb.	13 Fd. Amb., 1 A.G.H.	27/ 7/15	4y, Pte.
CURRAN, A., L.-Cpl. 40 Bn.	✠ 6/10/17.	7/ 2/16	T.-Sgt. ✠
CURRAN, C. C., Pte. 12 Bn.	52 Bn.	12/ 1/16	
CURRAN, J., Pte. 40 Bn.	3W.	4/ 5/16	2y 11m, Pte.
CURRAN, P., Pte. 12 Bn.	W.	16/ 6/16	3y 1m, Pte.
CURRAN, T. A., Pte. 12 Bn.	W., 4 A.A.S.C.	4/11/16	2y 11m, Pte.
CURRIE, A. E. W., Spr. 3 Fd. Co.	W. ✠ 20/9/17.	19/ 8/14	Spr. ✠
CURRIE, L. T., Pte. 12 Bn.		16/10/16	2y 6m, Pte.
CURRIER, C. G., Pte. 40 Bn.	2W.	13/ 3/16	
CURRIER, E. C., Pte. 12 Bn.	W., 52 Bn.	31/ 1/16	2y.
CURRIER, E. G., Pte. 1 G.S.R.		23/10/17	
CURRY, G., Pte. 12 Bn.	4 D. Sig. Co.	2/10/15	3y 10m, Spr.
CURTAIN, C. H., Pte. 12 Bn.	52 Bn., 13 Inf. Bde. H.Q.	3/ 7/15	
CURTAIN, J. D., Gnr. 6 F.A.B.	23 How. Bde., 3 D.A.S. Park.	30/11/15	3y 10m, Gnr.
CURTAIN, N. L., Tpr. 3 L.H.		30/ 8/15	4y 3m, Sgt.
CURTAIN, R., Pte. 40 Bn.		1/ 2/17	2y 8m, Pte.
CURWEN, W. G., Pte. 12 Bn.	W., M.S.M., 49 Bn.	20/ 8/14	4y 5m C.Q.M.S.
CURTIS, A. J., Pte. 12 Bn.	14 Bn.	7/10/15	3y 8m, Pte.
CURTIS, A. H., Pte. 40 Bn.	W.	5/ 4/16	3y 4m, Cpl.
CURTIS, B., Pte. 12 Bn.	2W., 52 Bn., 51 Bn.	11/11/15	3y 6m, Pte.
CURTIS, F. H., Gnr. A.F.A.		28/ 8/15	
CURTIS, F. L., Pte 3 G.S.R.	12 Bn.	11/ 6/18	1y 4m, Pte.
CURTIS, J. F., Cpl. 2 G.S.R.		23/ 2/18	
CURTIS, L. J., Pte. 12 Bn.		25/ 8/14	2y, Pte.
CURTIS, M., Pte. 12 Bn.	W.	22/ 8/14	1y 9m, Pte.
CURTIS, M. E, Pte. 12 Bn.	40 Bn. ✠24/8/18.	10/ 7/17	Pte. ✠
CURTIS, S. J., Tpr. 3 L.H.	4 D.A.C.	30/ 9/15	3y 9m, Dvr.
CURTIS, T. H., Pte. 12 Bn.	2W.	21/ 8/14	4y 6m, Pte.
CURTIS, T. H., Pte. 12 Bn.	✠ 6/10/17.	6/ 7/16	Pte. ✠
CUSICK, V., Pte. 40 Bn.		30/ 3/16	
CUTCLIFFE, W. N. C., Gnr. 6 F.A.B.	13 F.A.B.	17/ 1/16	3y 4m, Gnr.
CUTE, T. J., Pte. 4 M.G. Co.	5 M.G. Bn.	3/10/16	
CUTHBERTSON, A. J., Pte. 12 Bn.	W., 3 Fd. Co., 12 Bn.	12/ 1/15	4y 8m, Pte.
CUTHBERTSON, A. E., Spr. 3 Fd. Co	13 Fd. Co.	19/ 8/15	4y 1m, Spr.
CUTLER, F. W., Pte. 26 Bn.	W.	18/ 3/15	4y 5m, Pte.
CUTLER, H., Pte. 40 Bn.		15/ 4/16	0y 8m, Pte.
CUTTS, H. J., Cpl. 12 Bn.		3/ 8/15	Lieut.
DADD, E., Dvr., 3 F.A. Bde.		16/ 9/14	4y 5m, Dvr.
DADD, H., Spr. Miners	2 Tnlrs.	7/ 1/16	3y 9m, Spr.
DADSON, H. J., Spr. 8 Fd. Co.	✠ 4/10/16.	22/ 1/16	Spr. ✠
DADSON, J. E., Pte. 15 Bn.	8 Fd. Cd	11/ 8/15	3y 11m, Spr.
DADSON, J., L.-Cpl. 40 Bn.	✠ 4/10/17.	28/ 3/16	L.-Cpl. ✠
DADSON, L., 2nd-lt. 12 Bn.	M.C. and 2 Bars.	28/ 8/14	4y 6m, Lieut.
DADSON, P., L.-Cpl. 12 Bn.		2/11/17	1y 11m, L.-Cpl.
DAFT, E., Pte. Tnlrs.	5 Bn.	21/ 2/17	2y 6m. Pte.
DAFT, E. F., Sgt. 3 L.H.		8/ 6/15	4y 4m. Sgt.
DAKIN, E. T., Gnr. 3 F.A.		25/ 8/14	3y 4m, Gnr.
DALCO, C. S., Cpl. 40 Bn.	W ✠ 11/6/18.	20/ 7/16	Cpl. ✠
DALE, C. S. H., Pte. 26 Bn.	4W., 69 Bn., 26 Bn.	10/ 3/15	4y 3m, Pte.
DALE, C. F., Pte. Wireless		26/ 2/18	0y 10m, Pte.
DALE, E. A., Pte. 40 Bn.	W.	8/ 8/16	2y 7m, Pte.

TASMANIA'S MUSTER ROLL.

NAME.	REMARKS.	RANK ON DISCHARGE. ENLISTED. SERVICE.
DALE, G., Pte. 12 Bn.	2W., 52 Bn., 51 Bn.	4/12/14 4y, Pte.
DALE, G., Pte. 12 Bn.		Pte.
DALE, J. H., A.B.D., R.N.B.T.		31/ 3/15 2y 4m, A.B.D.
DALE, J., Pte. 26 Bn.	W.	13/ 5/15 2y 8m, Pte.
DALE, L. D., Pte. 12 Bn.	✸ 1/5/18.	9/10/16 Pte. ✸
DALE, R. H., Pte. 40 Bn.		20/10/16 1y 3m, Pte.
DALE, S., Gnr. 3 F.A.B.	2W., 2 F.A.B.	3/10/14 5y, Dvr.
DALE, S. E., Pte. 40 Bn.	2W., M.M.	5/ 5/16 3y 2m, L.-Cpl.
DALE, T. W., Pte. 40 Bn.	W.	7/ 3/16 3y 1m, Pte.
DALEY, E. W., Cpl. 1 A.C. Hos.		18/ 9/14 4y 4m, Cpl.
DALEY, James, Pte. 12 Bn.		28/ 8/14 0y 9m, Pte.
DALEY, J. E. J., Pte. 15 Bn.	✸ 13/8/15.	4/ 5/15 Pte. ✸
DALEY, L. F., Pte. 40 Bn.	✸ 14/4/17.	14/ 2/16 Pte. ✸
DALEY, P., Pte. 4 M.G. Co.		3/ 2/17
DALEY, R. R., S.-Smith, 3 F.A.B.		16/ 8/15 4y, S. Smith.
DALGLEISH, A., 26 Bn.		22/ 3/15 4y 6m, Lieut.
DALGLEISH, C. E., Pte. 26 Bn.	69 Bn., 26 Bn.	8/12/14 5y 1m, Dvr.
DALGLEISH, F., Cpl. 12 Bn.	W.	2/ 9/15 2y 4m, Cpl.
DALGLEISH, G., Cpl. 26 Bn.	✸ 21/8/16.	18/ 2/15 L.-Sgt. ✸
DALGREN, C. G., Pte. 40 Bn.	W., 26 Bn.	19/ 1/16 3y 4m, Pte.
DALGREN, E., Pte. 12 Bn.	W., 7 Bn.	19/ 1/16 2y 7m, Pte.
DALLAS, H. P., Pte. 40 Bn.		16/ 5/16 1y 8m, Pte.
DALTON, A. E., Dvr. 3 L.H.		25/11/14 4y 7m, Dvr.
DALTON, C. T., Pte. 40 Bn.	12 Bn.	8/ 3/16 1y 5m, Pte.
DALTON, G. E., Gnr. Fd. Art.		6/ 2/17
DALTON, H. H., Pte. 12 Bn.	W., D.C.M., 52 Bn.	12/12/14 4y 4m, Sgt.
D'ALTON, T. A. de L., Pte. 12 Bn.	2W. ✸ 18/9/18.	6/11/16 Pte. ✸
DALWOOD, H. B., Pte. 2 G.S.R.	11 F.A.B.	2/ 2/18 1y 7m, Gnr.
DALWOOD, V. O., Pte. 12 Bn.	W.	18/10/16 2y 3m, Pte.
DALY, G. I., Pte. 3 G.S.R.	12 Bn.	16 /7/18 0y 11m, Pte.
DALY, H. J., Dvr. 4 A.S.C.		18/ 8/14 4y 5m, Dvr.
DALY, J. A., Pte. 40 Bn.		29/ 6/16
DALY, J., Pte. 15 Bn.	2W., 24 F.A.B., 10 F.A.B.	18/ 8/15 4y, Dvr.
DALY, R. R., Gnr. Fd. Art.	W.	22/ 5/17
DALY, S. W., Dvr. 40 Bn.		29/ 2/16 3y 6m, Dvr.
DANCE, B. J., Pte. 12 Bn.	2W., 40 Bn. ✸ 26/5/19.	16/9/16 Pte. ✸
DANCE, J. E., Tpr. 3 L.H.		0/ 8/17 0y 5m, Tpr.
DAND, C., Pte. 12 Bn.		17/ 8/14 3y 10m, Sgt.
DANDY, C. J., Pte. 40 Bn.		10/ 7/17 2y 1m, Pte.
DANIELS, A. P., Pte. 12 Bn.		25/ 8/15 1y 6m, Pte.
DANIELS, A. H., Pte. 12 Bn.	2W., M.M., 26 Bn.	2/ 8/15 4y, L.-Cpl
DANIELS, J. H., Pte. 12 Bn.		10/ 9/16 2y 2m, Pte.
DANIELS, J. R., Gnr. 3 F.A.B.	M.M., 12 F.A.B.	6/10/14 4y 5m, Gnr.
DANIELS, O. H., Pte. 12 Bn.		13/ 3/16 0y 10m, Pte
DANIELS, R., Spr. 3rd Miners	3 Tnlrs. Co. ✸ 28/11/16.	13/ 2/16 Pte. ✸
DANIELS, R. H., Pte. 12 Bn.	✸ 2/4/15.	3/10/14 Pte. ✸
DANIELS, S. W., Dvr. 3 F.A.Bde.	21 F.A. Bde, 2 F.A.Bde.	16/ 8/15 4y 5m, Pte.
DANIELS, T. S., Sgt. 6 F.A.B.	D.C.M., 112 How. Bty.	11/ 1/16 3y 8m, Sgt.
DANN, G. M., Pte. 12 Bn.		4/10/15 0y 11m, Pte.
DANN, W. R., Gnr. 6 F.A.B.		30/11/15 3y 4m, Dvr.
DARBY, H., Pte. 40 Bn.	37 Bn.	7/ 5/17
DARBY, L., Pte. 12 Bn.	✸ 15/4/17.	9/ 5/16 Pte. ✸
DARCY, A., Pte. 40 Bn.	W., 3 M.G. Bn.	28/ 2/16 3y 9m, Pte.
DARCEY, D., Spr. Tnlrs. Co.		4/ 9/16 1y 7m, Spr.
DARCEY, M. C., Pte. 12 Bn.	W.	29/ 8/14 2y 5m, Pte.
DARCEY, R. H., Pte. 4 M.G. Co.	3 M.G. Bn., 23 M.G. Co.	23/ 1/17, 2y 9m, Pte.
DARE, H. N. C., Pte. 15 Bn.	W.	29/ 6/15 4y 2m, Pte.
DARE, H. W. F., Pte. 12 Bn.	W.	12/10/16 1y 7m, Pte.
DARE, J. E. E., Pte. 15 Bn.	1 Anzac Sal. Section.	9/ 6/15
DARE, S. J., Spr. 3 Miners	1 Tnlrs. Co.	4/ 4/16 3y 5m, Spr
DARKE, E., Pte. 12 Bn.	10 Bn.	2/11/16 2y 10m, Pte.
DARLING, G. J. F., Gnr. 14 F.A.B.	W.	25/10/16 2y 9m, Gnr.
DART, A. H., Pte. 40 Bn.		20/ 3/16 3y 5m, Pte.
DART, C. S., Pte. 12 Bn.	10 M.G. Co. ✸ 4/10/17.	11/ 4/16 Pte. ✸
DAVERN, C., Pte. 12 Bn.	W. ✸ 29/8/18.	29/10/16 Pte ✸
DAVEY, A. L. S., 12 Bn.	M.M., M.C.	5/ 8/15, 4y 2m, 2nd-Lt
DAVERN, J. F., Spr. Miners	W., 2 Tnlrs. Co.	7/ 3/16 3y 5m. Spr.
DAVERN, J. T., Pte. 12 Bn.	✸ 6-10/4/17	25/ 5/15 Pte. ✸
DAVERN, L. W., Dvr. 3 L.H.	3 D.A.C., 7 F.A.B.	9/ 9/15 4y, Dvr.
DAVERN, L., Pte. 26 Bn.	7 M.G. Co. ✸ 5/11/16.	7/ 5/15 Dvr. ✸
DAVEY, C., Lieut. 15 Bn.	W., M.B.E., M.I.D.	16/ 3/15 4y 6m, Lt.
DAVEY, R., Pte. 15 Bn.	4 Pnrs	3/ 5/15 4y 3m, Cpl.
DAVEY, F. L., 2nd-Lieut. 26 Bn.	✸ 7/6/17.	26/ 7/15 Capt. ✸
DAVIDSON, A., Gnr. F Art.	3 D.A.C.	23/11/15.
DAVIDSON, C. G., Pte. 12 Bn.	✸ 29/3/16.	31/12/14 Pte. ✸
DAVIDSON, D. C., St.-Sgt. Dental Corps		23/10/17 1y 8m, S. Sgt.
DAVIDSON, G., Pte. 15 Bn.	47 Bn., 48 Bn.	31/ 7/15 3y 9m, Pte.
DAVIDSON, G. E., Pte. 4 M.G. Co	W. ✸ 3/10/17.	14/ 7/16 Pte. ✸
DAVIDSON, H., Tpr. 3 L.H.		1/ 6/17 2y 2m, Tpr.
DAVIDSON, H. A., Pte. Wireless		3/12/17.
DAVIDSON, H. E., Gnr. 36 H.A.G.		5/ 6/15 4y 2m, Gnr.
DAVIDSON, H. J., Pte. 12 Bn.	W. ✸ 7/10/17	23/ 9/15 Pte. ✸
DAVIDSON, J. R., Pte. 15 Bn.	47 Bn. ✸ 4/8/16.	12/ 8/15 Pte. ✸
DAVIDSON, L. G., Pte. 12 Bn.	W.	17/12/14 3y 4m, L'Cpl.
DAVIDSON, T., Pte. 4 Bn.	3W., M.M.	21/ 3/16 3y 6m, Cpl.

TASMANIA'S WAR RECORD, 1914-1918.

NAME.	REMARKS.	RANK ON DISCHARGE. ENLISTED. SERVICE.
DAVIDSON, W., Gnr. 6 F.A.B.	W., 4 D.A.C., 8 M.T.M.B.	28/ 2/16 3y 3m, Gnr.
DAVIE, B. J. J. Gnr. 34 F.A.B.	112 How. Bty.	10/ 5/17 2y 4m, Gnr.
DAVIE, C., Pte. 40 Bn.	M.I.D.	24/ 3/16 3y 8m, Pte.
DAVIE, G. S., Pte. 12 Bn.	12 Bn.	30/ 5/16 1y 6m, Pte.
DAVIE, G. R., Pte. 40 Bn.	12 Bn. ✣ 6/10/17.	27/ 9/16 Pte. ✣
DAVIE, H., Dvr. 9 Fd. Bty.		31/ 8/14 Dvr.
DAVIE, M., Pte. 40 Bn.		27/ 9/16 11m, Pte.
DAVIE, P. H., Pte. 12 Bn.	1 Pioneer Bn.	24/ 8/15 3y 11m, Pte.
DAVIE, R. L., Pte. 12 Bn.	W., M.M., 13 M.G. Co.	6/ 8/15.
DAVIE, R., Pte. 12 Bn.	W., 28 Bn.	10/ 4/16 3y 6m, Pte.
DAVISON, E., Cpl. 2 F.A.B.		23/10/14.
DAWE, A. H., Pte. 12 Bn.		9/ 8/16 3y 1m, Pte.
DAW, E. D., Gnr. 1 G.S.R.	12 F.A.B.	17/ 1/18 1y 9m, Pte.
DAWES, C. C., Pte. 40 Bn.	10 F.A.B. ✣ 6/12/17.	1/ 3/16 Pte. ✣
DAWES, H. E., Pte. 15 Bn.	2W., 4 M.G. Co.	20/10/14 3y 2m, L'Cpl.
DAWKINS, E. E., Pte. 3 G.S.R.	12 Bn.	13/ 8/18 1y 2m, Pte.
DAWKINS, T. D. M., Dvr. 6 F.A.B.		4/ 8/15 4y, Dvr.
DAWSON, A, Pte. 12 Bn.	✣ 19/8/16.	30/ 1/15 Pte. ✣
DAWSON, F., Gnr. 4 F.A.B.	104 How. Bty.	20/11/15 3y 6m, Gnr.
DAWSON, G. A., M.W.		
DAWSON, G. A., Pte. 3 Fld. Amb.	13 Fd. Amb.	9/ 7/15 1y 3m, Pte.
DAWSON, H., Dvr. D.A.C.		6/ 9/15.
DAWSON, H. J., Pte. 26 Bn.	3W., 2 M.G. Bn.	24/ 4/15 4y 8m, Dvr.
DAWSON, J. McK., Pte. 15 Bn.	✣ 7/5/15.	15/12/14 Pte. ✣
DAWSON, J. W., Tpr. 3 L.H.	W. ✣ 9/1/17.	6/ 1/15 Tpr. ✣
DAWSON, P. W., Dvr. A.V.C. 2 V.S.		4/12/14 4y 11m, Cpl.
DAWSON, R. S., Pte. 40 Bn.	W.	15/ 3/16 3y 7m, Pte.
DAWSON, R. H. A., Pte. 40 Bn.	✣ 29/7/17.	14/ 3/16 Pte. ✣
DAWSON, S. A., Pte. 12 Bn.	B.D.H.Q.	9/11/15 3y 10m, Pte.
DAWSON, W. A., Spr. A. Cycle	W., A. Elec. and Mech. Mining Unit.	4/ 4/16 2y 3m, Spr.
DAWSON, W. J., Pte. 12 Bn.	3W.	23/12/14 4y 4m, Cpl.
DAWSON, W. O., Pte. 12 Bn.		28/10/16 2y 9m, Pte.
DAWSON, W. R., Pte. 12 Bn.	W.	3/ 9/17 1y 8m, Pte.
DAY, A., Pte. 1 G.S.R.		20/ 3/18.
DAY, A., Pte. 12 Bn.		22/ 8/16 1y 2m, Pte.
DAY, A. G, Pte. 26 Bn.	✣ 14/8/15	18/ 6/15 Pte. ✣
DAY, C. O. W., Pte. 1 G.S.R.		18/ 2/18.
DAVIS, A., M.W.		
DAVIS, A. W., Pte. 26 Bn.	12 Bn. ✣ 5/5/17.	11/ 8/15 Pte. ✣
DAVIS, A. W., Pte. 12 Bn.	51 Bn. ✣11/9/18.	5/10/15 Pte. ✣
DAVIS, A. H., Pte. 40 Bn.	57 Bn. ✣ 29/9/18.	18/ 2/16 Pte. ✣
DAVIS, A. I., 12 Bn.	6 F.A.B.	2/ 8/15 4y, Dvr.
DAVIS, A. H., Pte. 12 Bn.	W.	4/ 9/16 2y 10m, Pte.
DAVIS, A. Z., Pte. Miners	2W., 57 Bn.	21/ 2/16 2y 10m, Pte.
DAVIS, A. J., Pte. 15 Bn.		28/ 8/15.
DAVIS, A. C., Pte. 26 Bn.	2W., 41 Bn. ✣ 3/7/17	11/ 8/15 Pte. ✣
DAVIS, A. C., Pte. 12 Bn.		4/ 9/16.
DAVIS, A. H., Pte. 1 G.S.R.	4 D.A.C.	25/ 2/18 1y 8m, Gnr.
DAVIS, C. H., Tpr. 3 L.H.	12 Bn. ✣ 15/4/17.	18/ 8/14 Pte. ✣
DAVIS, C. W., Pte. 12 Bn.	W., 51 Bn.	1/ 8/15 4y, Pte
DAVIS, C. A., Pte. 12 Bn.		16/10/17.
DAVIS, C. C., Cpl. 26 Bn.	2W.	22/ 6/15 4y 6m, Cpl.
DAVIS, C. R., Pte. 4 M.G. Bn.		18/ 9/16 2y 6m, Pte.
DAVIS, D. M., Major 26 Bn.	W., Or. de Le'd. C. de G. (Belg.), Cmdr. Cycle Bn., 2 Entr. C., Bn., 22 Div. Cdr	18/ 6/15 Lt.-Col.
DAVIS, E. J., Pte. 12 Bn.	W., 52 Bn.	1/ 6/15 3y, Pte.
DAVIS, E. R., Pte. 1 G.S.R.		17/ 9/17 1y 4m, Pte.
DAVIS, E. J., Pte. 12 Bn.	✣ 10/6/15.	8/ 9/14 Pte. ✣
DAVIS, E. T., Pte. 40 Bn.	W.	20/10/16 2y 10m, Pte.
DAVIS, F. R., Pte. A.A.M.C.		24/10/16 3y 2m, Pte.
DAVIS, F. W., Pte. 26 Bn.	3W. ✣ 5/11/16.	15/ 4/15 Pte. ✣
DAVIS, F. D., Pte. 40 Bn.	W.	27/ 6/16 1y 8m, L'Cpl.
DAVIS, G. E. O., Pte. 12 Bn.	W. ✣ 23/8/18.	15/ 4/15 Pte ✣
DAVIS, G. P., Pte. 12 Bn.	W.	7/ 1/18 1y 10m, Pte.
DAVIS, J. G. R., Pte. 12 Bn.	2W., 52 Bn.	7/10/15 3y 6m, Pte.
DAVIS, G. D., Pte. 12 Bn.	52 Bn.	20/ 8/15 1y 5m, Pte.
DAVIS, H., Pte. 12 Bn.	✣ 6/12/16.	3/ 5/16 Pte. ✣
DAVIS, H. F., Pte. 40 Bn.	W., M.M.	29/ 9/16.
DAVIS, J. A., Pte. 12 Bn.	✣ 15/11/18	24/10/14 Cpl. ✣
DAVIS, James, Pte. 12 Bn.	69 Bn., 12 Bn.	25/ 1/15 Lt
DAVIS, L. T., Pte. 12 Bn.	W.	24/ 8/15 1y 10m, Pte.
DAVIS, K. H., Gnr. 9 Fd. Bty.	W., A.F.C.	5/ 2/15 4y 6m, 2nd Lt.
DAVIS, L. W., Pte. Railway.	W., 4 A.B.G.R.O.C.	10/ 1/17 2y 9m, 2nd Cpl.
DAVIS, N. B., Gnr. Fd. Arty.		21/ 5/17 2v 4m, Gnr.
DAVIS, P. D., A.-Sgt. 12 Bn.	✣ 2/5/17.	2/ 8/16 Sgt. ✣
DAVIS, Richard, Pte. 15 Bn.	✣ 9/5/15.	5/ 1/15 Pte. ✣
DAVIS R. A., Gnr. 8 F.A.B.		2/ 2/18 3- 2m, Sgt.
DAVIS, R. H., Pte. 1 A.C.H.		12/ 9/14 4y 4m, Pte.
DAVIS, J., Pte. 12 Bn.	52 Bn.	7/12/14 4y 9m, Pte.
DAVIS, R. V., Pte. 12 Bn.	W. ✣ 25/8/18.	3/ 5/16 Pte. ✣
DAVIS, R. J., Pte. 12 Bn.	✣ 11/1/18.	15/ 1/18 Pte ✣
DAVIS, S. P., Pte. 40 Bn	W., 15 Bn.	21/ 3/16 2y 3m, Pte.
DAVIS, Thos., Pte. 1 Tunnellers.		26/10/16.
DAVIS, W. H., Pte. A.A.M.C.		20/10/14.
DAVIS, W. A., Pte. 40 Bn.		29/ 6/17.

TASMANIA'S MUSTER ROLL. 257

NAME.	REMARKS.	RANK ON DISCHARGE. ENLISTED. SERVICE.
DAVIS, W. J., Pte. 12 Bn.	40 Bn. ✣ 23/10/18	3/ 4/16 Pte. ✣
DAVIS, W. S., Pte. 12 Bn.		18/ 8/14.
DAVIS, W. O., Pte. 40 Dn.		4/10/16 3y, Pte.
DAVIS, W. W., Pte. 12 Bn.	✣ 7/5/15.	29/ 8/14 Pte. ✣
DAVIES, A. A., Pte. 3 L.H.	2 W.	24/ 8/14 4y 6m, Sgt.
DAVIES, A. J., Pte. 4 M.G. Co.		27/11/16.
DAVIES, C. W., Pte. 12 Bn.	A. Emp. Co.	31/ 8/15 3y 2m, Pte.
DAVIES, C. G., Pte. 12 Bn.	52 Bn. ✣ 4/9/16.	25/ 8/15 Pte. ✣
DAVIES, D., Dvr. 13 F.A.B.	8 F.A.B.	11/ 2/16 3y 8m, Dvr.
DAVIES, D. L., Pte. 12 Bn.	2 A.G.H.	10/10/16 3y 3m, Pte.
DAVIES, D. W., Pte. 12 Bn.		1/ 7/15 10m, Pte.
DAVIES, E. J., Pte. 40 Bn.		2/10/16.
DAVIES, E. H., Dvr. Engrs.		20/ 9/14 4y 4m, Cpl.
DAVIES, G. W., Tpr. 3 L.H.	4 L.H.	11/ 4/17 2y 1m, Tpr.
DAVIES, G. G., Bdr. 3 F.A.B.	3 G.S.R.	26/ 8/14 4y 7m, Bdr.
DAVIES, H., Pte. 12 Bn.	W.	17/ 2/17 2y 9m, Pte.
DAVIES, H. C., Lt., 15 Bn.	W.	19/10/14 2y 2m, Capt.
DAVIES, H. T., Pte. 40 Bn.	✣ 9/6/18.	17/10/16 Pte. ✣
DAVIES, H. O., Tpr. 3 L.H.	13 Fd. Co.	18/10/15 4y 1m, Cpl.
DAVIES, J. H., Pte. 15 Bn.	2 W.	12/ 8/15 3y 8m, Cpl.
DAVIES, J., Pte. 12 Bn.	40 Bn.	15/ 6/16 2y 4m, Pte.
DAVIES, J. E., Pte. 3 L.H.		23/ 8/14 7m, Pte.
DAVIES, J. M'L., Pte. 40 Bn.	✣ 3/1/17.	8/ 2/16 Pte. ✣
DAVIES, J. W., Cpl. 7 Fd. Amb	13 Fd. Amb.	29/ 1/15 4y 7m, Cpl.
DAVIES, L., Pte. 1 A.C.H.		17/ 9/14 4y 4m, Pte.
DAVIES, R. H. T., Pte. 4 M.G Co	5 Dvl. M.G. Co. ✣ 8/10/19.	10/10/16 Pte. ✣
DAVIES, R. M. J., Gnr. 6 Fd. Arty.	3 D.A.C.	14/ 3/16 3y 7m, Dvr.
DAVIES, W., Pte. 12 Bn.	3 W., 51 Bn., 12 Bn.	20/ 1/15 2y 11m, Pte.
DEACON, A. S., Pte. 15 Bn.	W., 10 F.A.B.	17/ 8/15 3y 8m, Dvr.
DEACON, C. W., Pte. 12 Bn.		28/ 8/16 1y 2m, Pte.
DEACON, F. R., Pte. 15 Bn.	W.	3/10/14 2y 4m, Pte.
DEACON, J. D., Pte. 15 Bn.	✣ 15/9/15.	20/ 5/15 Pte. ✣
DEACON, J. H., Pte. 15 Bn.	4 W., 46 Bn.	19/ 9/14 4y 11m, Pte.
DEAKIN, P., Pte. 26 Bn.	✣ 28/8/16.	16/ 6/15 Pte ✣
DEAKIN, R. H., Pte. 26 Bn.	2 W.	19/ 7/15 3y 10m, Pte.
DEAN, A. E., Spr. 8 Fd. Co. Engrs	D.C.M.	9/12/15.
DEAN, E. E., Pte. 41 Bn.		10/10/16 2y 9m, Pte.
DEAN, H. C., Pte. 2 G.S.R.		13/ 5/18 1y 6m, Gnr.
DEAN, H. E., Cpl. 12 Bn.	2 W., M.I.D.	23/ 8/15 Sgt.
DEAN, J., Pte. 2 G.S.R.	A.G.B.D. Staff.	13/ 5/18 1y 4m, Pte.
DEAN, T. E., Pte. 12 Bn.		21/ 3/16 1y 5m, Pte.
DEAN, W. H. G., Pte. 15 Bn.	W., M.M. and Bar, 11 F.A.B.	18/ 8/15 3y 8m, Sgt.
DEBNAM, F. A., Gnr. Fd. Arty.		17/ 1/17 1y 6m, Gnr.
DE BOMFORD, E., Pte. 2 A.F. Sqdn	3 Sqdn., A.F.C.	18/ 8/16 3y 4m, Sgt.
DE BOMFORD, F. M., Gnr. Fd. Arty	W., 3 D.A.C.	10/ 2/16 3y 10m, Cpl.
DEEGAN, A. T., Pte. Sigs	2 Sig. Sqdn.	31/ 5/17 2y 6m, Spr.
DEEGAN, M. J., Cpl. 8 Fd. Arty.	4 D.A.C.	10/ 2/16 3y 7m, Cpl.
DEEGAN, S. E., Cpl. 1 A.G.H.	G.H.Q. (Records Section).	1/10/15 3y 11m, S. Sgt.
DEEGAN, T. M., Gnr. 3 F.A.B.		27/ 9/14 Gnr.
DE JERSEY, L. H., Pte. 26 Bn.	W.	3/ 6/15 1y 11m, Pte.
DE JERSEY, M. L., Pte. 1 A.C.H.	5 D.A. Sub. Park.	7/11/14 4y 3m, Cpl.
DE LA BERE, R. St. J., Pte. 12 Bn.		23/ 6/16 1y 4m, Pte.
DELANEY, B. C., Pte. 4 M.G. Co.	11 M.G. Co.	22/ 8/16 3y 1m, Pte.
DELANEY, J. L., Spr. 6 Fd. Co.		1/ 9/15 3y 11m, Spr.
DELANEY, P. O., Dvr. 12 F.A.B.	46 Bty.	17/10/16 2y 5m, Gnr.
DELANEY, T. C., Tpr. 3 L.H.		30/ 8/15 1v, Tpr.
DELANEY, W. G., Pte. 12 Bn.	W., Adm. H.Q.	27/ 8/14 5y 3m, S. Sgt.
DELANEY, W. E., Pte. 40 Bn.	W.	13/ 3/16 1y 11m, Cpl.
DELANTY, J. P., Pte. 40 Bn.		18/10/16 2y 11m, Pte.
DELL, E., Pte. 40 Bn.	A.A.V.C.	23/ 2/16 3y 6m, S'smith
DELL, G. C., Pte. 40 Bn.		4/ 5/16.
DELL, H. J., Sgt. 40 Bn.	W.	20/ 3/16 2y 3m, 2nd Lt.
DELL, R. R., Pte. 26 Bn.	W., M.M., 9 Bn.	14/ 9/15 4y 3m, Lt.
DELPHIN, D., Spr. 3 A.T.C.		2/ 7/17 1y 8m, Spr.
DELPHIN, G. J., Pte. 12 Bn.		20/10/16 3y, Pte.
DELPHIN, K. W., Pte. 26 Bn.	✣ 4/8/16.	1/ 7/15 Pte. ✣
D'EMDEN, F., Pte. A.S.C.	M.I.D., 4 Dvl. Trn.	2/ 8/15 4y, Sgt.
D'EMDEN, M. R., Pte. 4 A.S.C.	14 A.A.S.C.	10/ 6/15 4y 5m, Cpl.
D'EMDEN, T., Dvr. 4 A.S.C.		14/ 7/15 11m, Dvr.
DE MEY, F. F., Gnr. 3 A.F.A.		18/ 7/15.
DENHOLM, D. A., Pte. 40 Bn.		9/10/16 1y, Pte.
DENHOLM, F. J., Pte. 12 Bn.	W. ✣ 12/1/18.	16/ 4/16 Pte. ✣
DENHOLM, H. G., Spr. 8 Fd Co.	15 Fd. Co.	17/ 1/16 3y 6m, Spr.
DENHOLM, H. J., Gnr. 6 A.F.A.	6 A.B.A.C.	20/ 3/17 2y 6m, Dvr.
DENHOLM, R. B., Tpr. 1 G.S.R.	3 L.H.R.	2/ 4/18 1y 4m, Tpr.
DENMEN, D., Dvr. 6 Fd. Arty.		28/ 7/15 2y 6m, Dvr.
DENMEN, F. M., Gnr. 3 L.H.	W., 2 HTMB.	18/ 8/15 4y, Gnr.
DENMEN, J., Pte. 12 Bn.	W., 1 Pnr. Bn.	18/ 8/15 3y 11m, Pte.
DENMEN, J. C., Pte. 12 Bn.		21/ 3/16 1y 5m, Pte.
DENMEN, W. H., Pte. 40 Bn.	3 W.	24/ 2/16 2y 9m, Pte.
DENNE, V. E., Pte. 12 Bn.	2 W., M.M., 52 Bn. ✣ 26/5/18.	20/ 8/14 Lt. ✣
DENNISON, A. A., Pte. 12 Bn.		21/ 3/16 3y 2m, Pte.
DENNISON, D. J., Pte. 12 Bn.	W.	12/ 4/16 1y 11m, Pte.
DENNISON, J. S., Pte. 12 Bn.		28/ 7/16 2y 9m Pte.
DENNISON, F. H., Pte. 40 Bn.	2 W., 10 M.G. Co.	18/ 7/16 3y 3m, Pte.
DENNY, C. F., L.-Cpl. 26 Bn.	2 W.	28/ 7/15 3y 5m, L'Cpl.

Q

258   TASMANIA'S WAR RECORD, 1914-1918.

NAME.	REMARKS.	RANK ON DISCHARGE. ENLISTED. SERVICE.
DENNY, R. F., Pte. 12 Bn.		28/ 8/16 1y 3m, Pte.
DENNY, W., Pte. 12 Bn.	W.	13/ 2/15 2y 9m, Pte.
DENT, C. L., Pte. 12 Bn.	W.	28/ 4/16 1y 8m, Pte.
DENT, C. E., Pte. 12 Bn.	M.M., 40 BN.	20/10/16 2y 10m, Pte.
DENT, L. J., Pte. 40 Bn.	W. ✣ 13/10/17.	1/ 7/16 Pte. ✣
DENT, R., Pte. 15 Bn.	2 W., M.M. and Bar.	10/12/14 4y 4m, Sgt.
DENTITH, C. H., Pte. 4 M.G. Co.		31/ 7/16 3y 2m, Pte.
DENTITH, V. G., Pte. 40 Bn.	W., 49 Bn.	3/ 4/16 2y, Pte.
DENNIS, A. R., Pte. 15 Bn.	A. Rec. Sec., G.H.Q.	21/ 5/15 4y 6m, S. Sgt.
DENNIS, A. J., Pte. 12 Bn.	1 Pnrs. Bn.	18/ 8/15 3y 8m, Pte.
DENNIS, A. B. C., Pte. 12 Bn.	W., 52 Bn. ✣ 4/9/16.	20/ 8/14 Pte. ✣
DENNIS, C. E., Pte. 40 Bn.	W.	30/ 3/17 2y 10m, Pte.
DENNIS, D. G., Pte. 12 Bn.	✣ 23/8/18.	3/11/17 Pte. ✣
DENNIS, D., Pte. 12 Bn.	W., 3 Fd. Co. Engrs.	9/12/14 4y 6m, Spr.
DENNIS, F., Pte. 12 Bn.	W.	8/ 8/16 2y 7m, Pte.
DENNIS, G., Pte. 40 Bn.		3/ 3/16 3y 6m, Pte.
DENNIS, H., Pte. 12 Bn.	W., 40 Bn.	25/ 1/16 3y 2m, Pte.
DENNIS, H. R., Pte. 12 Bn.		19/ 8/14 1y 6m, L'Cpl.
DENNIS, J. W., Pte. Fd. Arty.	12 F.A.B.	9/ 2/16.
DENNIS, L. C., Pte. 40 Bn.	W. ✣ 28/3/18.	4/ 3/16 Pte. ✣
DENNIS, M. W., Pte. 40 Bn.	W.	7/ 3/16 1y 9m, Pte.
DENNIS, R. G., Pte. 12 Bn.	✣ 10/6/15.	21/ 8/14 Pte. ✣
DENNIS, R. H., Pte. 12 Bn.	52 Bn., D.C.M. ✣ 26/4/18.	20/ 8/14 C.S.M. ✣
DENNIS, V W., Sgt. 40 Bn.	W.	7/ 3/16 2y 6m, Sgt.
DERBYSHIRE, F. A., Gnr. 13 F.A.B.		1/ 5/17 2y 3m, Gnr.
DERRICK, H. alias J. J., Tpr. 3 L.H.	37 Bn.	7/ 9/15 2y 6m, Pte.
DERRICK, J. S., Pte. 12 Bn.	3 W., 40 Bn.	28/ 3/16 3y 1m, Pte.
DERRICK, J. W., Pte. 12 Bn.	52 Bn. ✣ 8/6/17.	29/12/15 Pte. ✣
DERRICK, W. J., Pte. 12 Bn.	W., 40 Bn.	18/11/16 2y 10m, Pte.
DESMOND, J., Pte. 4 M.G. Co.		30/11/16.
DE SOZA, R. J., Pte. 3 G.S. Rfts.		10/ 6/18 7m. Pte.
DETTMAN, P., Pte. 12 Bn.		12/ 4/17 1y 5m, Pte.
DEVEREAUX, A. P., Pte. Remts.	10 L.H.	6/10/15 1y 2m, Tpr.
DEVEREAUX, G. F., Pte. 4 M.G. Co	W., 21 M.G. Co.	4/ 8/16.
DEVEREAUX, J. C., Pte. 4 M.G. Co.	W.	4/ 8/16 3y 1m, Pte.
DEVEREAUX, W. O., Gnr 36 H.A.G.	2 W., M.M., 2 Siege Bty.	7/ 6/15 4y 4m, Sgt.
DEVERELL, H., Pte. 26 Bn.	2W.	22/ 6/15 3y 5m, L. Sgt.
DEVINE, J., Pte Cycling.		5/ 4/16.
DEVINE, R. L., Pte. 26 Bn.	40 Bn. ✣ 12/10/17.	28/ 7/15. Pte. ✣
DEVINE, W. H., Pte. 12 Bn.	40 Bn.	21/ 5/17 2y 4m. Pte. ✣
DEVINE, W. K., Pte. 12 Bn.	10 F.A.B.	24/ 8/14 4y 5m. Dvr.
DEVINE, W. V., Pte. 12 Bn.		23/10/16 1y 3m. Pte.
DEVLIN, P. H., Pte. 4 A.S.C.	16 A.S.C.	18/ 8/14 2y 11m. Pte.
DEVLIN, S. K., L.-Cpl 26 Bn.	2 W.	26/ 6/15.
DEVLYN, J. A., Pte. 26 Bn.	W.	4/ 3/15 4y 4m. Pte.
DEVLYN, L. H., Dvr. 3 Fd. Arty.	W.	28/ 8/14 4y 9m. Dvr.
DEVONPORT, J. E., Pte. 12 Bn.		28/ 3/17 2y. Pte.
DEWARS, A., Gnr. Fd. Arty.		11/12/16.
DEWHURST, G. T., Spr. 4 Mnrs.	T.E.E.M. Unit.	24/11/15 3y 11m. Cpl.
DICK, A. S., Pte. 40 Bn.	W.	22/ 9/16 3y, Pte.
DICK, A. G., Pte. 12 Bn.	W., 52 Bn.	19/ 1/16 3y 4m. Pte.
DICK, A. T., Dvr. 3 L.H.	4 D.A.C. 10 F.A.B.	9/ 9/15 3y 7m. Dvr.
DICK, D, Pte. 4 M.G. Co.	2 M.G. Bn.	2/ 4/17 2y 7m. Pte.
DICK, F. J., Pte. 12 Bn.	W.	11/ 1/16 2y 2m. Pte.
DICK, H. B., Pte. 12 Bn.	W., M.M., 52 Bn. ✣ 24/4/18.	11/ 1/16. L.Cpl. ✣
DICK, J. G., Pte. 12 Bn.	1 A.S.C.	9/10/16 2y 11m. Pte.
DICK, L., Pte. 2 G.S.R.	R.B.A.A.	6/ 6/18 1y 5m. Gnr.
DICK, R. W., Pte. 3 L.H.	2 W., 42 Bn.	21/ 3/15 4y 1m. Pte.
DICKENS, C. M., Tpr. 3 L.H.	4 D.A.C., 10 F.A.B. ✣ 20/9/17.	15/ 9/15. Dvr. ✣
DICKENSON, A. G. J., Pte. 40 Bn	W.	16/ 6/16 3y 6m. Pte.
DICKENSON, C. C., Pte. 12 Bn.	2 W.	7/ 9/16 3y 1m. Pte.
DICKENSON, C. J., Pte. 12 Bn.		26/ 8/14 4y 8m. Cpl.
DICKENSON, Frank, Cpl. 3 L.H.	4 D.A.C.	18/ 8/14 4y 6m. Lieut.
DICKENSON, I. L., Pte. 3 L.H.		21/ 8/14 2y 8m. Cpl.
DICKENSON, J. M., Pte. 12 Bn.		17/ 8/14 1y 9m. Pte.
DICKENSON, P., Pte. 40 Bn.	✣ 9/5/18.	9/ 7/17. Pte. ✣
DICKENSON, W. J., Pte. 12 Bn.		8/ 6/16 2y 8m. Pte.
DICKER, D., Pte. 40 Bn.	Vet. Hosp.	13/ 9/16 1y 11m. Tpr.
DICKER, H. B., Dvr. 2 L.H.		19/ 8/14 4y 6m. Dvr.
DICKSON, C. J. A., Pte. 12 Bn.		12/ 6/17 1y 4m. Pte.
DICKSON, C. G., Pte. 1 A.C.H.	W.	12/ 9/14 3y 8m. Pte.
DICKSON, R. St. C., Gnr. 3 L.H.	2 W., 10 F.A.B.	20/ 8/14 4y 6m. Gnr.
DICKSON, W. G., Pte. 40 Bn.	✣ 29/9/18.	22/ 6/16. Pte. ✣
DIGNEY, A. M., Spr. 8 Fd. Co.	1 Fd. Co.	4/ 1/16 3y 9m, Spr.
DIGNEY, A. W., Saddler. Res. Pk.		2/ 9/14.
DIGNEY, S. C., Pte. 26 Bn.		15/ 4/15 4y 7m. Pte.
DILGER, A. W., Pte. 12 Bn.	3 W., M.M., 69 Bn. ✣ 31/5/18.	9/ 7/15. L.Cpl. ✣
DILGER, A. A. C., Pte. 12 Bn.	3 W.	29/ 5/16 2y 2m. Pte.
DILGER, C. F., Spr. Tnlrs.	37 Bn. ✣ 12/10/17.	6/ 4/16. Spr. ✣
DILGER, H. C., Pte. 40 Bn.	✣ 31/1/17.	10/ 3/16. Pte. ✣
DILLON, J., Pte. 40 Bn.	51 Bn. ✣ 4/5/18.	17/ 2/16. Pte. ✣
DILLON, J. E., Pte. 12 Bn.		10/12/14 4y 3m. Pte.
DILLON, F. S., Pte. 26 Bn.		28/ 4/15.
DILLON, P., Pte. 12 Bn.	W., 52 Bn., 4 Dvl. Salv. Co.	3/ 8/15 4y. Pte.
DILLON, T. B., Pte. 26 Bn.	W.	26/ 4/15 1y 11m Sgt.
DILLON, T., Tpr. Remnt. Unit.		4/10/15 4y 1m. Tpr.

TASMANIA'S MUSTER ROLL. 259

NAME.	REMARKS.	RANK ON DISCHARGE. ENLISTED, SERVICE.
DILLON, T. H., Pte. 40 Bn.	3 Dvl. H.Q.	3/ 4/17 2y 6m. Pte.
DINEEN, A. C., Pte. A.M.C.	57 Bn.	8/10/15 1y 7m. Pte.
DINEEN, A., L.-Cpl. 12 Bn.	✣ 28/5/18.	26/ 7/16 ✣
DINGLE, C. T. R., Pte. 1? Bn.	40 Bn.	25/ 8/15 3y 7m. Pte.
DINGLE, D. R. W., Dvr. 3 L.H.	A.S.C. Motor Transport.	18/ 8/15 4y. Dvr.
DINHAM, W., Gnr. 15 Bn.	W., 11 F.A.B.	17/ 8/15 4y. Gnr.
DIPROSE, A. W., Cpl. 12 Bn.	3 W., M.M., 57 Bn.	11/ 8/15 3y. Cpl.
DIPROSE, A. E., Pte. 3 L.H.	1 L.H.B. M.G.S.	18/ 8/14 4y 6m. Pte.
DIPROSE, D. A., Pte. 15 Bn.	47 Bn. ✣ 7/8/16.	29/ 6/15. Cpl. ✣
DIPROSE, L. R., Pte. 3 L.H.	A.P.C.	29/ 1/15 4y 8m. Pte.
DIPROSE, O. W. C., Gnr. 3 FA.B.		19/ 3/17 2y 6m. Gnr.
DIPROSE, Roy, Pte. 26 Bn.	W.	27/ 7/15 1y 8m. Pte.
DIPROSE, R. T., Pte. 12 Bn.		11/ 8/15 7m. Pte.
DIXON, C. E., Gnr. 6 F.A.B.	W., 13 F.A.B.	23/ 2/16 3y 8m. Gnr.
DIXON, F., Pte. 12 Bn.	✣ 18/9/18.	13/ 2/17. Pte. ✣
DIXON, G. M., Pte. 12 Bn.	W.	12/ 9/14 2y 2m. Pte.
DIXON, J. N. M'G., Spr. Tnlrs.		12/ 4/16 2y 4m. Spr.
DIXON, J. A., Pte. 15 Bn.	47 Bn.	18/ 6/15 2y 1m. Pte.
DIXON, L. G., Pte. 1 G.S.R.		10/ 1/18.
DOAK, A., Pte. 26 Bn.	2 W. ✣ 9/8/19.	28/ 7/15 Pte. ✣
DOBIE, E. J., A.-Cpl. 3 G.S.R.		1/ 7/18.
DOBSON, A. G., Pte. Remounts.		29/ 9/15 3y 10m. Pte.
DOBSON, C. A., Pte. 26 Bn.	5 W., 12 Bn.	2/ 9/15 4y 2m. Pte.
DOBSON, C. T., Pte. 12 Bn.	1 D. Sal. Coy.	21/ 7/15 4y 2m. Pte.
DOBSON, F. A., Spr. A.F.C.	5 Signal Coy.	19/10/16 3y. Spr.
DOBSON, H. E., Dvr. 13 F.A.B.	3 F.A.B.	1/11/15 3y 9m. Dvr.
DOBSON, H. W., Pte. 40 Bn.	✣ 7/6/17.	21/ 6/16. Pte. ✣
DOBSON, J., Pte. 26 Bn.		4/ 8/15 4y 1m. Pte.
DOBSON, L. A., Pte. 40 Bn.		30/12/15 1y 4m. Pte.
DOBSON, M. W., Pte. 26 Bn.	W. ✣ 29/8/18.	14/ 4/15 Cpl. ✣
DOBSON, P. W., Lt. S. Arty. Bde.	M.C 2 S. Bty.	21/ 5/15 4y 4m. Capt.
DOBSON, S. P., Dvr. 3 F.A.B.		15/ 9/14 3y 1m. Dvr.
DOBSON, S. J., Tpr. 3 L.H.	4 Pnr. Bn. ✣ 8/8/18.	26/ 1/15. Pte. ✣
DOBSON, S. W. H., Pte. A.M.C.	13 Fd. Amb.	11/ 4/16 2y 3m. Pte.
DOBSON, S. W., Cpl. 12 Bn.	2W.	28/ 8/14 3y 11m. Lieut.
DOCKING, F. L., Pte. 12 Bn.		28/ 8/14 1y 4m. Pte.
DOCKING F., Pte. A.M.C	5 Field Amb.	15/ 4/16 1y 8m. Pte.
DOCKING, G. S., Pte. 12 Bn.	3W.	13/ 6/16 2y 5m. Pte.
DOCKRELL, J. H., Gnr. Fd. Arty.		20/ 1/17.
DODD, C., Pte. 12 Bn.	✣ 6/10/17.	22/ 8/16 Pte. ✣
DODD, J., Pte. 12 Bn.		23/10/14 4y 3m. Pte.
DODD, J. C., Pte. 12 Bn.		16/ 9/14 1y 5m. Pte.
DODDRIDGE, F. P., Pte. 12 Bn.	W., 13 I.B.H.Q.	1/12/15 3y 9m. Pte.
DODDRIDGE, W.G.J., Dvr. 3 Fd.Co	8 and 15 Fd. Co. ✣ 27/10/17.	2/ 9/15. Dvr. ✣
DODERY, G. C., M.T. Dvr. 8 F.A.B	W. 6 M.T. Co.	12/10/15 3y 11m. M.T.D.
DODGE, C., Gnr. S. Arty. Bde.		7/ 6/15.
DOERING, E. L., Pte. 12 Bn	52 Bn.	1/12/15 1y 7m Pte.
DOGGETT, J., Cpl. 15 Bn.	W. 42 Bn., 15 Bn.	29/ 1/15. 5y 2m. Sgt.
DOHERTY, J., Pte. 12th Bn.	40 Bn.	19/ 1/16 3y 7m. Pte.
DOHERTY, T. C., Pte. 12th Bn.	M.M.	4/10/16 2y 11m. Cpl.
DOHERTY, W. A., Pte. 12th Bn.	W.	4/10/16 2y 11m. Pte.
DOHERTY, W. H., Spr. Tnlrs.	1 Tn. Coy.	24/ 4/16.
DOHERTY, W. J., Dvr. 3rd F.A.B.	2 D.A.C.	21/ 7/15.
DOLA, H., Spr. 3rd F. Coy. Eng.	W.	16/ 9/14 4y 5m. Spr.
DOLAN, J. S., Pte. 26th Bn.	2 Pnr. Bn.	19/ 2/15 2y 3m. Pte.
DOLBEY, E. F., Pte. 12th Bn.		21/ 8/16 3y 2m. Pte.
DOLE, J., Pte. 1 A.C.H.	A.F.C.	7/ 9/15.
DOLLERY, E. M., Pte. 12th Bn.	2W. M.M.	3/ 6/16 2y 10m. Lieut.
DOLLIVER, A., Pte. 40th Bn.	W.	28/ 9/16 3y 1m. Dvr.
DOLTING, L., Pte. 12th Bn.	W. 52 Bn. ✣ 25/9/17.	15/ 1/16. Pte. ✣
DOLTING, W. J., Pte. 12th Bn.	W. 40 Bn.	18/ 3/16 3y 5m. Pte.
DOMENEY, E. T., Pte. 12th Bn.	2W. M.M.	30/11/14 3y 8m. L.-Cpl.
DOMENEY, W. S. E., Pte. 15th Bn.	3W. M.M.	18/ 1/15 4y 4m. Capt.
DOMENEY, O. T., Pte. 40th Bn.	✣ 7/6/17.	6/10/16. Pte. ✣
DONACHER, E. C., Pte. 12th Bn.	52 Bn., A.A. Prov. Corps.	18/ 6/15 3y 11m. Pte.
DONAGHY, J., Spr. 3rd F. Coy. Eng.	W. 14 F. Co.	4/ 1/16 3y 7m. Spr.
DONAHOO, J. A., Pte. 26th Bn.	2W.	22/ 2/15 4y 4m. Pte.
DONALD, C., Pte. 40th Bn.	W.	7/10/16 2y 4m. Pte.
DONALD, H. F., Pte. 15th Bn.	W. ✣ 7/8/15.	14/ 9/14 Sgt. ✣
DONALD, L. C., Pte. 40th Bn.	W.	4/ 4/16 2y 11m. Pte.
DONALD, R. H., Pte. 40th Bn.	W.	4/ 4/16 2y 7m. Pte.
DONALD, T. W., Pte. R U.		4/10/15 1y 2m. Tpr.
DONALDSON, F., Pte. 12th Bn.	✣ 25/7/16.	30/11/14. Pte. ✣
DONALDSON, H. R., Sgt. 40th Bn.	W.	8/12/15 3y 9m. Sgt.
DONNELLAN, A., Pte. 12th Bn		22/11/16 2y 5m. Pte.
DONNELLAN, P. J., Pte. 12th Bn.	W. 52 Bn.	3/ 9/14 3y 3m. Sgt.
DONNELLAN, T. J., Pte. 12th Bn.		30/10/16.
DONNELLY, P. T, Pte. 4th M.G. Co.	15 M.G. Co., 11 M G. Co. ✣ 2/4/19.	4/10/16. Pte. ✣
DONNELLY, M. T., Pte. 12th Bn.		
DONNELLY, T. L., Gnr. 3 F.A. Bde. (alias WESTLAKE, J.)	W. 1 F.A.B.	12/ 8/15 3y 8m. Gnr.
DONNELLY, J. H., M.W.		15/ 4/19. M.W.

260　　　　　TASMANIA'S WAR RECORD, 1914-1918.

NAME.	REMARKS.	RANK ON DISCHARGE. ENLISTED. SERVICE.
DONOGHUE, D., Pte. 12th Bn.	✠ 6-10/4/17.	4/ 5/16. Pte. ✠
DONOGHUE, L. W., M.T. Dvr. 3 F.A.B.	2 Siege B.A.C.	6/10/15 3y 11m. Dvr.
DONOGHUE, T. E., Pte. 40 Bn.	2 W.	24/ 2/16. Cpl.
DONOHUE, J., Pte. A.M.C.		27/ 3/16.
DONOHOE, P., Pte. 40 Bn.	2W.,	30/10/16 1y 11m. Pte.
DONOHOE, W. H., Pte. 15 Bn.	✠ June, 1915.	29/ 9/14. Pte. ✠
DONOVAN, A. G., Dvr. 40 Bn.	1 A.M.G. Bn.	16/10/16 2y 11m. Dvr.
DONOVAN, E., Dvr. 1 A.G.H.	W., 8 Fld. Amb.	1/ 6/15 4y. Dvr.
DONOHOE, F., Pte. 40 Bn.		20/11/16 3y. Pte.
DONOVAN, G., Tpr. 3 L.H.		24/10/16 1y 10m. Tpr.
DONOVAN, J. E., Tpr., 3 L.H.		21/ 8/17 2y 4m. Tpr.
DONOVAN, P. W., Pte. 15 Bn.	W., 4 M.G. Bn.	10/ 2/15 4y 8m. Cpl.
DONOVAN, T. F., Pte. 1 A.G.H.	W., 5 Fld. Amb.	8/ 6/15 1y 9m. Pte.
DONOVAN, V., Pte. 3 L.H.	M.M.	17/ 8/14 4y 6m. Cpl.
DOODY, J., Pte. 26 Bn.	2W., 12 Bn. ✠ 6/10/17.	11/ 8/15. Pte. ✠
DOOLEY, B. R., Pte. 12 Bn.	W., 52 Bn. ✠ 8/6/17.	12/ 1/15. Sgt. ✠
DOOLEY, T. C., Pte. A.M.C.	9 Fld. Amb.	4/ 9/16 3y 1m. Pte.
DOOLING, W. J., L.Cpl. 26 Bn.	W.	14/ 5/15 3y 3m. L.-Cpl.
DORAN, A. J. A., Pte. 3 L.H.		3/ 6/17 2y 2m, Tpr.
DORAN, J. A., Dvr. 3 A.A. Mech. T. Coy.	5 A.M.T. Co.	18/ 9/16 3y 2m. Cpl.
DORAN, S., Dvr. 3 D.A.C.	1 D.A.C., 3 F.A.B.	8/12/14 4y 6m. Dvr.
DORAN, W. J., Pte. 12 Bn.	2W., 51 Bn.	15/ 2/15 4y 6m. Sgt.
DORKINS. A. J., Sgt. 12 Bn.		2/ 7/16.
DORNAUF, L., Pte. 12 Bn.	W., 52 Bn.	25/ 8/15 2y 11m. Pte.
DORUM, H. W., L.-Cpl. 40 Bn.	2W	22/ 8/16 2y 8m. L.-Cpl.
DOUCETT, J., Pte. 12 Bn.		5/10/16.
DOUGHERTY, A., Pte. 15 Bn.		18/ 9/14 2y 2m. Pte.
DOUGHARTY, D. H., Pte. A.A.H.	2 Fd. Amb.	11/11/15 4y 1m| Pte.
DOUGHARTY, F. G., Pte. 12 Bn.	✠ 23/4/18.	23/ 6/16. Pte. ✠
DOUGHERTY, J., Pte. Remnts.	8 M. Vet. Sec.	2/10/15 3y 10m. Tpr.
DOUGLASS, A., 2-Lt., 15 Bn.	21 Bn., 67 Bn.	28/ 9/14 3y 9m. 2 Lieut.
DOUGLAS, A. E., Gnr. 3 L.H.	W., 10 Bty. F.A.B.	13/ 8/15 3y 8m. Gnr.
DOUGLAS, A. H., Pte. 12 Bn.	W.	26/11/14 2y 10m. Pte.
DOUGLAS, A. H., Pte. 26 Bn.	12 Bn.	10/ 8/15 4y Pte.
DOUGLAS, A. J., Sgt. 40 Bn.		21/10/16.
DOUGLAS, C. A., Pte. 12 Bn.	W., M.M., 10 F.A.B.	17/ 7/15 4y 2m. Cpl.
DOUGLAS, C. K., Pte. 12 Bn.	✠ 15/3/18.	8/ 1/16. Pte. ✠
DOUGLAS, C. B., Pte. 7 F. Amb.	W., M.M.	18/ 3/15 3y 6m. Pte.
DOUGLAS, C. B., Pte. 12 Bn.	2W., M.M., 51 Bn.	28/ 7/15.
DOUGLAS, G., Pte. 12 Bn.	2W., 52 Bn., 15 Bn.	17/ 1/16 3y 8m. Pte.
DOUGLAS, G. F., Spr. 3 F. Coy.		29/ 8/14 4y 6m. Spr.
DOUGLAS, H. P., Pte. 12 Bn.	W., Aus. Record Sec.	31/ 8/14 2y 8m. Pte.
DOUGLAS, J., Pte. 40 Bn.	W.	18/ 7/17 1y 11m. Pte.
DOUGLAS, J. M., Pte. 26 Bn.	✠ 14/11/16.	22/ 9/15. Pte. ✠
DOUGLASS, R., Pte. 40 Bn.	W. 10 Fld. Amb.	6/ 3/16 1y 6m. Pte.
DOUGLAS, R. C., Pte. 3 L.H.		16/ 1/17 2y 3m, Tpr.
DOUGLASS, W. K., Chaplain, 2 Inf. Bde.	M.C.	1/ 7/15 3y 11m. Chapn.
DOUGLAS, W. S., Pte. 1 G.S.R.		28/ 1/18.
DOVE, B. J. P., Pte. 2 G.S.R.		30/11/17 1y 4m. Gnr.
DOVE, B. S., Pte. 40 Bn.	✠ 9/4/18.	12/10/16. Pte. ✠
DOVE, H. J. V. P., Pte. 40 Bn.	✠ 11/6/17.	31/10/16. Pte. ✠
DOVE, V. C., Pte. 12 Bn.	W.	3/ 5/16 3y 4m. Pte.
DOWDING, A. D., Gnr. F.Art.	11 F.A.B.	14/ 5/17 1y 10m. Gnr.
DOWDING, R. A., Gnr. F.Art.	W., 11 F.A.B.	22/ 5/17 2y 2m. Gnr.
DOWELL. G. T., Cpl. 3 L.H.		20/ 8/14 Gnr.
DOWIE, V. A., Pte. 40 Bn.	W.	21/ 3/16 2y 9m. Pte.
DOWLING, A., Cpl. 12 Bn.	W., 52 Bn., 13 A.L.T M.B.	15/ 7/15 4y 2m Cpl.
DOWLING, E. A., Pte. 15 Bn.	✠ 8/8/15.	21/ 5/15. Pte. ✠
DOWLING, G. G., Gnr. F.Art.	W., 101 How. Bty.	29/12/16 2y 9m. Gnr.
DOWLING, H. J., Pte. 12 Bn.	2W.	11/ 4/16 3y 6m. Pte.
DOWLIN. J. T., Pte. 26 Bn.		5/ 6/15.
DOWN. E., Pte. 40 Bn.	15 Bn.	18/ 3/16 3y 6m. Pte.
DOWN, F., Pte. 40 Bn.	5W.	15/ 4/16 3y 6m. Pte.
DOWNER, L., Pte. 12 Bn.		2/ 8/16.
DOWN, S., Tpr. 3 L.H.	4 Camel Regt., 14 L.H.	6/10/15 4y 1m. Cpl.
DOWNIE, A., Pte. 12 Bn.	2W., 52 Bn., 49 Bn.	6/10/15 3y 10m| Pte.
DOWNIE, A. A. W., 2 Lt. 40 Bn.	W.	1/ 5/16 3y 3m. Lieut.
DOWNIE, A. J., Pte. 26 Bn.	W.	27/ 7/15 4y 3m. Sgt.
DOWNIE, A., Gnr. Arty.		9/ 4/18.
DOWNIE, C. T., Pte. 1 A.C.H.	W., 40 Bn.	27/ 4/15 4y. Cpl.
DOWNIE, D. N. H., Cpl. 3 Fd. Co.	✠ June, 1915.	20/ 8/14. Cpl. ✠
DOWNIE, H. J., Pte. 12 Bn.	2W.	20/11/16 2y 5m. Pte.
DOWNIE, K. G., Gnr. 14 F.A.B.	114 How. Bty.	20/10/16 3y 1m. Dvr.
DOWNIE, V., Cpl. Miners.		15/ 2/16.
DOWNS, H. A., L.Cpl. 40 Bn.		10/ 3/16 3y 7m. L.Cpl.
DOWNWARD, B. H., Spr. 8 F. Co.		11/10/15 1y 10m. Spr.
DOYLE, C. B., Pte. 40 Bn.	W.	4/ 1/16 2y 6m. Pte.
DOYLE, Jack, Pte. 26 Bn.	2W., 12 Bn.	3/ 3/15.
DOYLE, J. E., Pte. 12 Bn.	✠ 2/3/16.	22/ 7/15. Pte. ✠
DOYLE, T., Pte. 40 Bn.		2/ 3/16 3y 4m. Pte.
DRAKE. A. T., Pte. 40 Bn.		15/11/15 3y 4m. Pte.
DRAKE, C. L., Gnr. 3 F.A.B.		27/ 8/14 4y 5m. Gnr.

TASMANIA'S MUSTER ROLL. 261

NAME.	REMARKS.	RANK ON DISCHARGE. ENLISTED. SERVICE.
DRAKE, C. S., Pte. 12 Bn.		26/11/15 10m. Pte.
DRAKE, C., Pte. A.M.C.	2 Fd. Amb.	2/ 3/16 3y 8m. Pte.
DRAKE, C. V., Gnr. 1 F.A. Bd.	W.	31/10/16 2y 10m. Gnr.
DRAKE, C. J., Sgt. 16 Bn.		7/10/15 3y 11m. Sgt.
DRAKE, J. L., W.O. A.S.C.		18/ 8/14 4y 6m. W.O.
DRAKE, K. G., Pte. 3 G.S.	12 Bn. ✢ 29/1/19.	24/ 8/18. Pte. ✢
DRAKE, L. A., Pte. 12 Bn.	✢ 5/9/16.	4/12/15. Pte. ✢
DRAKE, M. W., Pte. 7 Fd. Amb.	13 Fd. Amb.	8/ 3/15 4y 4m. Pte.
DRAKE, G. H., Pte. 12 Bn.	W.	30/10/17 1y 9m. Pte.
DRAKE, P. E., Pte. A.M.C.	13 Fld. Amb.	13/ 4/16 3y 6m. Pte.
DRAKE, R. H., Gnr. Sg. Art. Bd.	✢ 4/10/17.	7/ 6/15. Gnr. ✢
DRAKE, T. P., R.Q.M.S. 3 L.H.		26/ 8/14 2y 5m. RQMS.
DRAKE, W. W., Pte. 40 Bn.		9/ 3/16.
DRANSFIELD, F., Pte. 2 G.S.R.	12 Bn.	2/ 5/18 1y 4m Pte.
DRANSFIELD, P., Pte. 40 Bn.	2W.	8/ 8/15 3y 9m. Pte.
DRAPER, S. G., Pte. Rly. Unit.		12/ 1/17 2y 8m. Pte.
DRESSER, R. A., Gnr. 12 Bn.	W., 3 F.A.B.	10/ 5/17 2y 1m. Gnr.
DREW, D. G., Pte. A.M.C. Rfts.	✢ 15/10/17.	22/ 8/16. Pte. ✢
DREW, J., Sgt. 40 Bn.		16/ 8/14 5y 5m. S.Sgt.
DREW, P. P., Pte. 40 Bn.	W.	4/10/16 2y 6m. Pte.
DREW, C. Roy, Dvr. 12 Bn.	W., 4 Divl. Arty., 10 F.A.B.	25/11/15 2y 11m. Gnr.
DREW, W. G., Sgt. 15 Bn.	M.M., 47 Bn. ✢ 25/1/17.	7/ 8/15. 2 Lieut. ✢
DREW, W. J., Pte. 12 Bn.		11/ 5/15 2y 1m.
DREWITT, F. J., Pte. A.M.C.	16 F. Amb.	21/ 8/16 3y 2m. Pte.
DREWITT, F. W., Pte. A.M.C.		14/ 9/15 1y. Pte.
DREWITT, R. C., Pte. A.M.C.	2 A.G.H.	5/10/16 4y. Pte.
DREWITT, W. H., Spr. Rly.		16/10/17 1y 11m. Spr.
DRISCOLL, C. R., Pte. A.A.M.C.		9/10/16.
DRISCOLL, D. W. H., Pte. 15 Bn.	2W.	21/ 9/14 1y 9m. Cpl.
DRISCOLL, E., Pte. 26 Bn.	2W., 12 Bn., 3 M.G. Co.	9/ 8/15 3y 11m Cpl.
DRISCOLL, H. R., Gnr. 13 F.A.B.	104 How. Bty.	15/12/15 3y 9m. Gnr.
DRISCOLL, J., Pte. 2 AD. Sal. Cp.		1/ 4/15 4y 4m. Pte.
DRISCOLL, K., Pte. 12 Bn.	2W., M.M. ✢ 14/11/17.	11/12/14. Pte. ✢
DRISCOLL, P. A., Gnr. Fd. Art.	W., 6 F.A.B.	13/ 4/17 2y 8m. Gnr.
DRIVER, F. W., Pte. 12 Bn.	W., 1 Pnr. Bn.	22/10/14 4y 4m. Pte.
DRIVER, W. D., Pte. 15 Bn.		4/ 1/15 1y 8m. Pte.
DRIVER, W. C., Pte. 12 Bn.	W.	11/ 6/17 1y 9m. Pte.
DROUGH, J. M'F., Spr. 3 Fd. Co.	W., 7 Fd. Co.	22/ 9/15 2y 3m. Spr.
DRYSDALE, R. M., Pte. 5 L.H.		10/11/14 1y 6m. Tpr.
DUCE, W. R., L. Sgt. 40 Bn.	W.	26/ 6/16 3y 4m. L.Sgt.
DUCKWORTH, B. W., Pte. 12 Bn.	2W., 2 A.A.H.	23/ 7/15 4y 7m. Pte.
DUCKWORTH, H. E., Pte. 12 Bn.	13 L.T.M. Bty.	10/ 8/15.
DUCKWORTH, J. H., Pte. 12 Bn.	W. ✢ 23/7/16.	20/ 8/14. Pte. ✢
DUDGEON, R., Spr. 3 Tnlrs.		26/10/16 2y 8m. Spr.
DUDMAN, J. W., Tpr. 3 L.H.	W., 19 Bty., 22 F.A.B. (Re-enlisted Artillery, 25/2/18)	16/ 6/15 4y 5m. Gnr.
DUFF, F., Pte. 1 A.C.H.	1 A.C.C.S.	4/ 8/15 4y 1m. Pte.
DUFF, S. J., Pte. 15 Bn.	✢ 7/8/15.	20/ 5/15. Pte. ✢
DUFFY, A. T., Pte. A.M.C.		30/10/15.
DUFFY, C. M., Pte. 26 Bn.	W.	25/ 2/15 3y 9m. Pte.
DUFFY, E. P., Pte. 12 Bn.	11 Fld. Arty. Bde.	6/12/15 3y 9m. Dvr.
DUFFY, H. A., Spr. 3 Fd. Co.	12 Bn.	17/ 8/14 1y 9m. Spr.
DUFFY, H. W., Pte. 12 Bn.	✢ 22/11/16.	18/11/15. Pte. ✢
DUFFY, J. H., Pte. 40 Bn.	W. ✢ 9/4/18.	16/ 1/16. Pte. ✢
DUFFY, J. R., Spr. 8 Fd. Co.	12 F.C.E.	2/12/15 2y 4m. Spr.
DUFFY, K., Pte. 40 Bn.	W.	1/ 2/16 2y 3m. Pte.
DUFFY, G. C., Pte. 26 Bn.	✢ 5/8/16.	7/ 9/15. Pte. ✢
DUFFY, R. T., Pte. 40 Bn.	✢ 16/4/17.	14/ 2/16. Pte. ✢
DUGGAN, A., Pte. 26 Bn.	W.	20/ 7/15 2y 3m. Pte.
DUGGAN, B. L., Pte. 12 Bn.	7 Fld. Amb.	9/ 9/15.
DUGGAN, E. G., Pte. 12 Bn.		19/10/16 3y. Pte.
DUGGAN, F. L., Pte. 40 Bn.	W.	12/ 7/16 3y 3m. Pte.
DUGGAN, H., Pte. 4 M.G. Co.	3 M.G. Coy.	18/11/16 1y 10m. Pte.
DUGGAN, J. J., Pte. 12 Bn.	13 L.T.M.B.	17/ 9/15 4y. Pte.
DUGGAN, J., Pte. 40 Bn.		15/ 2/17.
DUGGAN, J. F., Pte. 12 Bn.	W., M.M.	5/11/16.
DUGGAN, L. M., Pte. 40 Bn.	W.	4/ 5/16 3y. Pte.
DUGGAN, P. M., Pte. 40 Bn.	✢ 12/8/18.	24/ 2/16. Pte. ✢
DUGGAN, T., Pte. 12 Bn.	2W., 40 Bn.	22/ 5/17 2y. Pte.
DUGGAN, T. J., Pte. 15 Bn.	M.M., 47 Bn. ✢ 12/10/17.	30/ 8/15. Sgt. ✢
DUGGAN, W. P., Pte. 1 A.C.H.	W., 12 Bn.	16/ 9/14.
DUGMORE, W., Pte. 15 Bn.	W.	11/ 8/15 3y 3m. Pte.
DUKE, H., Pte. 40 Bn.	W.	5/ 9/17 7m. Pte.
DUKE, N. A., Gnr. 9 Fd. Bty., 3 F.A.B.		26/ 8/14 4y 7m. Gnr.
DUMARESQ, H. J., Capt. 40 Bn.	W.M.C.	1/ 5/16 2y 7m. Capt.
DUMBLETON, A. V., Pte A.A.M.C.	8 Fld. Amb.	25/10/16 3y 1m. Pte.
DUNBABIN, J. M., Pte. 2 G.S. Rfs.	12 Bn.	17/ 6/18 1y 4m. Pte.
DUNBABIN, W., Pte. 12 Bn.	47 Bn., 45 Bn.	30/10/16 2y 9m. Pte.
DUNCAN, H. E., Pte. 40 Bn.		15/ 4/17 2y 5m. Pte.
DUNCAN, H., Sgt. 12 Bn.	2W., 52 Bn.	3/11/15 3y 6m. Sgt.
DUNCAN, J., Pte. 40 Bn.		10/ 7/16 3y 4m. Pte.
DUNCAN, P., M.W.		
DUNCOMBE, A. H., Pte. 12 Bn	W., 4 M.G. Coy.	6/ 1/15 4y 5m. Sgt.

NAME.	REMARKS.	RANK ON DISCHARGE. ENLISTED. SERVICE.
DUNGEY, E. R., Tpr. 3 L.H.	Arty. Dtls.	5/ 6/17.
DUNHAM, J., Pte. 12 Bn.		3/11/16 2y 6m. Pte.
DUNHAM, R. H., Tpr. 3 L.H.	W., 12 Bn. ✸ 16/7/18.	21/ 8/14 Tpr. ✸
DUNHAM, T., Sgt. 12 Bn.	3W., 52 Bn.	10/ 9/14 3y 10m. Sgt.
DUNIAM, R. M., Dvr. 12 Bn.		1/ 5/16 3y 4m. Dvr.
DUNKIN, M. A., Pte. 12 Bn.	W., 52 Bn., 51 Bn.	10/ 1/15 4y 10m. C.Q. M.S.
DUNKLEY, C. G., Pte. 12 Bn.	W.	10/ 6/16 3y 3m. Pte.
DUNLOP, M. J., Pte. 40 Bn.		16/ 2/16 1y 4m. Pte.
DUNN, C., Gnr. 15 F.A.B.	3 F.A.B.	9/10/16 2y 11m. Gnr.
DUNN, C. J., Pte. 12 Bn.	40 Bn.	20/10/16 2y 10m. Pte.
DUNN, E., Spr. 5 Tnlrs.	2 Tnlrs. ✸ 29/12/18.	31/ 3/16 Spr. ✸
DUNN, G. H., Dvr. 2 F.A.B.		11/10/16 2y 8m. Dvr.
DUNN, I., Pte. 40 Bn.	W.	20/12/16 2y 3m. Pte.
DUNN, M. E., Dvr. 3 F.A.B.		25/ 6/15 1y 11m. Dvr.
DUNN, P., Spr. Miners.	3 Tnlrs. ✸ 31/10/18.	10/11/15. Spr. ✸
DUNNE, P. E., Sr. 26 Bn.		23/ 3/15.
DUNN, T. H., Pte. 15 Bn.	47 Bn. ✸ 5/4/18.	31/ 8/15. Pte. ✸
DUNN, W., Pte. 40 Bn.	✸W., 12 Bn.	25/ 9/16 2y 7m. Pte.
DUNPHY, C. J., Pte. 26 Bn.	2W., 12 Bn.	27/ 7/15 4y 2m. Pte.
DUNPHY, L. J. R., Tpr. 3 L.H.		27/ 3/17 2y 4m. Tpr.
DUNSTAN, G. H., Pte. 12 Bn.	✸ 17/4/18.	21/10/16. Pte. ✸
DUNSTAN, H. W., Tpr. 3 L.H.		21/ 8/17 2y. Tpr.
DUNSTAN, J. A., Pte. 15 Bn.	W., 47 Bn.	31/ 8/15 1y 9m. Pte.
DURAND, F. H., Spr. M. Coy. No. 3.		24/ 9/15 1y 4m. Sgt.
DURKIN, J., Pte. 12 Bn.	W.	2/11/16 2y 11m. Pte.
DURRANT, T. H., Cpl. Rly. Unit.		9/ 1/17 2y 8m. Cpl.
DUTHOIT, G. J., Sgt. 1 A.C.H.		22/ 9/14 2y. Sgt.
DUTTON, A. L., Pte. 2 G.S.R.		5/ 6/18 5m. Pte.
DUTTON, C. F., Pte. 2 G.S.R.	13 F.A.B.	16/ 5/18 1y 6m. Gnr.
DUTTON, R. S., Pte. A.A.M.C. Gen. Rfts.	14 Fld. Amb.	16/ 7/17 2y 4m. Pte.
DWYER, D. P., Pte. 40 Bn.		23/ 2/16.
DWYER, E. J., Spr. 1 Tnlrs.		26/10/17 1y 1m. Spr.
DWYER, H. J., Pte. 12 Bn.	W., 40 Bn.	28/ 1/16.
DWYER, H. L., Pte. 4 A.F.A.	58 Bn., 10 M.G. Coy.	19/10/15 3y 11m. Pte.
DWYER, J., Pte. 1 G.S.R.	40 Bn.	7/ 6/17 2y 6m. Pte.
DWYER, J. J., Pte. 15 Bn.	W., V.C.	4/ 2/15 3y 10m. Lt.
DWYER, J. M., Spr. Wireless	3 D. Sig. Coy.	2/ 1/18 1y 4m. Spr.
DWYER, M.M., Pte. 40 Bn.		15/ 4/17 1y 1m. Pte.
DWYER, P. J., Cpl. 3 G.S.R.		1/ 7/18.
DWYER, T. V., Pte. 26 Bn.	M.M., 4 M.G. Coy.	26/ 2/15 4y 6m. Cpl.
DWYER, W. J., Gnr. D.A.C.	M.M., 10 F.A.B. ✸ 21/10/18.	7/10/15. Gnr. ✸
DYER, F. B., Pte. 40 Bn.	2W.	13/11/16 2y 11m. Pte.
DYMOND, T. W., L.Cpl. 40 Bn.		23/ 3/16 3y. L.Cpl.
DYNAN, D., Pte. 12 Bn.		15/ 3/16 3y 10m. Pte.
DYOTT, J., Pte. 12 Bn.		6/ 5/18 2y 2m. Pte.
DYSON, R. G., Gnr. Arty.		11/ 8/15.
DYSON, V. C., Pte. 40 Bn.	✸ 5/10/17.	8/11/16. Pte. ✸
EADES, R. H., Spr. 3 F.C.E.		24/ 8/15
EADIE, J. A., Pte. 40 Bn.	2W.	18/10/16
EADY, A. J., Pte. 15 Bn.	3W., 7 Training Bn., 26 Bn. ✸ 22/11/17	19/ 9/16 Cpl. ✸
EADY, J. S. B., Pte. 40 Bn.		11/ 1/17 1y 5m, Pte.
EADY, W. J., Pte. 26 Bn.	4W.	30/ 3/15 4y 2m, Pte.
EAGLING, A., Pte. 12 Bn.	✸ 5/7/16.	29/ 7/15 Pte. ✸
EALES, A. J., Gnr. 25 Fd. Art.		9/10/16
EAMES, W. J., Pte. 2 G.S.R.	A.D.M.H.Q.	29/4/18 1y 5m, Pte.
EAST, D. R., Pte. 3 G.S.R.	12 Bn	22/ 7/18 1y 5m, Pte.
EAST, S. J., Pte. 26 Bn.		24/ 6/15 1y 7m. Pte.
EASTERBROOK, G. S., Pte. 15 Bn	12 L.T.M. Bty.	17/ 8/15
EASTLEY, W. A., Pte. 12 Bn.	W.	13/10/16 1y 10m, Pte.
EASTMAN, D. G., A.-Cpl. 12 Bn.	W.	18/10/16 3y 1m, L.-Cpl.
EASTMAN, H. C., Gnr. 3 Fd. Art.	B.A.C., 3 F.A.B.	15/12/14 4y 7m, T.-B.SM
EASTMAN, J. C., Pte. 12 Bn.	W.	8/ 4/16 3y 3m, Pte.
EASTMAN, L. A., Pte. 40 Bn.	W.	16/ 7/17 2y 3m, Pte.
EASTOE, A. G., Pte. 15 Bn.	W., 47 Bn.	31/ 8/15 2y 4m, Pte.
EASTOE, C. C., Pte. Aviation.		24/10/16
EASTOE, H. W., Pte. 1 A.G.H.		23/ 9/14
EASTON, G. J., Pte. 40 Bn.	2W.	31/ 3/16 3y, L.-Cpl.
EATON, A. H., Pte. 1 G.S.R.	24 A.D.U.S.	30/ 1/18 1y 9m, Pte.
EATON, E., Pte. 26 Bn.	12 Bn	11/ 8/15 1y 5m, Pte.
EATON, J., A.-Cpl. 12 Bn.		28/ 6/16 1y 8m, Pte.
EBDON, F. H., Gnr. Fd. Art.		15/ 3/17 2y 9m, Gnr.
EBELL, E. B., Gnr. 2 G.S.R.	41 F.A.B.	20/5/18
EBERHARDT, W., Pte. 40 Bn.		31/ 3/16 3y 6m, Pte.
ECCLES, A., Pte. 3 Fd. Amb.	✸ 25/4/15	17/ 8/14 Pte. ✸
EDDIE, G. McK., Gnr. 6 F.A.B.		17/ 9/15 3y 11m, 2 Lt.
EDDINGTON, C. R., Gnr. Fd. Art.		31/ 1/16 3y 8m, Lt.
EDDINGTON, F. H., Pte. 1 A.G.H.		8/ 9/14 4y 4m, Pte.
EDDINGTON, G. O'C., Sgt. Fd Art.	1 D.A.C., 13 D.A.C. ✸ 30/9/17.	25/ 8/16 Sgt. ✸
EDDINGTON, H. R., Pte. 12th Bn.	1 Pnrs. ✸ 19/8/16.	21/ 8/15 Pte. ✸
EDDINGTON, O. F., Pte. 12 Bn.	✸ 15/4/17.	16/ 5/16 Pte. ✸
EDDY, A., Sig. C Sqn., 3 L.H.		28/ 8/14 2y 2m, Pte.
EDDY, S. E., Gnr. Fd Art Rfts		27/ 9/16
EDE, C. P., Sgt. 12 Bn.	2W.	26/ 8/14 3y 1m, Sgt.

TASMANIA'S MUSTER ROLL. 263

NAME.	REMARKS.	RANK ON DISCHARGE. ENLISTED. SERVICE.
EDE, H., Pte. A.A.M.C.	W., 15 Fd. Amb.	9/12/16 2y 5m, Pte.
EDGECOCK, A., Pte. 15 Bn.	4 Pnr Bn., 69 Bn., 52nd Bn. ✲ 14/9/18	11/ 1/15 Pte. ✲
EDGECOCK, T. A., Cpl. 15 Bn.		23/10/16 1y 1m, A.-Cpl.
EDGECOMBE, R. L. G., Pte. 3 L.H.		23/ 8/14 2y 2m, Tpr.
EDGELL, D. B., Pte. 40 Bn.	2W., 1 M.G.B.	14/ 3/16 3y 6m, Pte.
EDGELL, H. C., Pte. 12 Bn.	2W., M.M.	5/ 9/14 4y 7m, 2 Lt.
EDGERTON, A., Pte. 40 Bn.	3W.	7/ 6/16 2y 8m, Pte.
EDMUNDS, R. C., Sgt. 26 Bn.	2 Pnrs. ✲ 5/7/16	2/ 3/15 Sgt. ✲
EELES, E. C., Pte. 12 Bn.	2W.	15/10/16 2y 6m, Pte.
EELES, E., Pte. 40 Bn.	✲ 28/3/18.	9/ 3/16 L.-Cpl. ✲
EGAN, S. A., Pte. 15 Bn.	✲ 9/8/16.	14/ 5/15 Pte. ✲
EIDE, A., Pte. 2 G.S.R.	40 Bn.	8/ 4/18 1y 6m, Pte.
EDWARDS, A., Pte. 12 Bn.	✲ 12/8/15.	21/ 8/14 Pte. ✲
EDWARDS, A. R., Gnr. Fd. Art.		28/ 5/17
EDWARDS, A. H., Pte. 26 Bn.	W., 4 F.A.B.	19/ 2/15 4y 4m, Gnr.
EDWARDS, A. J., Pte. 3 G.S.R.		21/ 6/18
EDWARDS, A. R., Gnr. 13 Fd. Art	12 Fd. Art. ✲ 21/3/18.	9/ 8/15 Gnr. ✲
EDWARDS, B. W., Pte. 40 Bn.	W.	3/ 4/16 3y 5m, Pte.
EDWARDS, B., Pte. 3 L.H.	13 F.A.B.	10/ 8/15 4y 1m, Dvr.
EDWARDS, B., Pte. 12 Bn.		20/ 7/15 9m, Pte.
EDWARDS, B. G., Pte. 40 Bn.	W ✲ 12/4/18.	22/ 3/16 L.-Cpl. ✲
EDWARDS, C. W., Gnr. 5 F.A.B.	112 How. Bty.	16/ 8/15 4y, Sgt.
EDWARDS, E. A., Cpl. 12 Bn.	M.M.	17/ 9/14
EDWARDS, E. E., Pte. 15 Bn.	2W., 47 Bn., 10 F.A.B.	11/11/14 4y 2m, Sgt.
EDWARDS, F. E., Pte. 26 Bn.	2W.	16/ 2/15 4y 2m, Pte.
EDWARDS, G. J., Spr. 8 F. Co Eng		15/ 1/16 2y, Spr.
EDWARDS, H. V., Pte. Rly Unit.	2 A.L.R.O. Co.	25/ 4/17 2y 5m, C.Q.M.S
EDWARDS, H., Pte. 26 Bn.	✲ 25/8/16.	30/ 4/15 Pte. ✲
EDWARDS, H. F., Pte. 15 Bn.	✲ 8/8/16.	17/ 9/14 Sgt. ✲
EDWARDS, J. C., Gnr. 6 F.A.B.	5 F.A.B.	28/ 9/15 4y, Sgt.
EDWARDS, J. A., Pte. 15 Bn.		8/ 1/15 11m, Pte.
EDWARDS, J. W., Pte. 26 Bn.	W., M.I.D.	15/ 6/15 4y 2m C.Q.M.S.
EDWARDS, N. J. H., Pte 1 G.S.R.	40 Bn.	25/ 3/18 1y 8m, Pte.
EDWARDS, O., Pte. 7 Fd. Amb.		24/ 2/15 4y 3m, Pte.
EDWARDS, O. H., Pte. 40 Bn.		16/10/16 2y 11m, Pte.
EDWARDS, R., Gnr. 3 F. Art.	✲ 6/10/17.	26/ 8/14 Cpl. ✲
EDWARDS, R. W., Pte. 40 Bn.	W.	12/10/15 3y 5m, Pte.
EDWARDS, R. E., Pte. 26 Bn.		19/ 7/15 4y 1m, Pte.
EDWARDS, S. J., Pte. 40 Bn.	W.	12/10/15
EDWARDS, S. H., Pte. 12 Bn.		4/12/17, 1y 10m, Pte.
EDWARDS, T., Spr. 8 F.C.E.		1/ 2/16 3y 7m, Spr.
EDWARDS, T. E., Pte. 40 Bn.	✲ 19/2/18.	1/10/16 Pte. ✲
EDWARDS, T. J., Pte. 12 Bn.	14 Bn. ✲ 11/4/17.	25/ 8/15 Pte. ✲
EDWARDS, T. J., Pte. Fd Art		30/ 5/17
EDWARDS, W., Pte. 12 Bn.	W., 52 Bn., 51 Bn.	17/ 1/16 3y 8m, Pte.
EDWARDS, W. H., Pte. 33 Bn.		18/12/15 3y 4m, Pte.
ELEY, F., Pte. 40 Bn.		23/ 9/15 3y 11m, L.-Cpl
ELEY, G. F., Dvr. 17 Bty 6 F. Art.	✲ 2/11/16.	27/ 9/15 Dvr. ✲
ELFICK, G. J., Pte. 3 L.H.		22/ 8/14 2y 2m, Pte.
ELLEN, G. T., Pte. 40 Bn.	W.	20/ 3/16 2y 4m, Pte.
ELLERTON, C., Gnr. Fd. Art.		14/ 1/16
ELLERTON, C. A., Pte. 12 Bn.		3/12/17 10m, Pte.
ELLINGS, E. T., Pte. 40 Bn.	W.	20/ 6/16 3y 2m, Pte.
ELLINS, G. E., Pte. 12 Bn.	W.	21/ 8/14 1y 11m, Pte.
ELLICTT, A. J., Pte. 4 M.G.C.		11/ 9/16 3y, Dvr.
ELLIOTT, A. T., Pte. 12 Bn.	3W., 52 Bn., 40 Bn.	13/ 1/16 3y 5m, Dvr.
ELLIOTT, B., Pte 15 Bn	W. 6 Bn.	7/ 8/15 4y 1m, Pte.
ELLIOTT. C. H., Capt. 12 Bn.	3W., C.M.G., D S.O. and Bar, Legion d'Honneur (Croix de Chevalier), 2 M I D.	24/ 8/14 5y, Lt.-Col.
ELLIOTT, D., Pte. 12 Bn.	✲ 23/7/16.	2/ 6/15 Pte. ✲
ELLIOTT, F. G., Gnr. 3 A.F.A.	4 Div. Art.	19/ 1/15 4y 3m, Gnr.
ELLIOTT, F. T., Pte. 26 Bn.		27/ 7/15,4y 1m, Pte.
ELLIOTT, H. P., Pte. 40 Bn.	W. MM	20/ 3/16 2y L.-Sgt.
ELLIOTT. I. R., S.-Sgt. A.A.M.C.		13/ 8/17, 1y 8m, S.-Sgt.
ELLIOTT, J. W., Gnr. 9 Bty. F.A.	D.C.M.	11/ 1/15 4y 8m, Cpl.
ELLIOTT, P. F., Pte A.A.M.C.	8 Fd Amb.	3/10/16 3y, Pte.
ELLIOTT, R., Pte. 40 Bn.		23/10/16 2y 7m, Pte.
ELLIOTT, W. H., Pte. 12 Bn.	W.	13/ 1/16 3y 9m, Dvr.
ELLICTT, W. H., Pte. 15 Bn.	P.O.W.	12/ 2/15 4y 9m, Pte.
ELLIS, A. T., Pte. 26 Bn.	✲ 21/9/17.	13/ 5/15 2 Lt. ✲
ELLIS, A. C. M., Pte. 12 Bn.	W., 40 Bn.	25/ 9/16 2y 6m, Pte.
ELLIS, A. R., Dvr. B.A.C.		9/10/14 1y 8m, Gnr.
ELLIS, B. D., S.-Sgt. 12 Bn.	✲ 16/6/15.	1/ 9/15 S.-Sgt. ✲
ELLIS, C. G., Tpr. 4 G.S.R.	3 L.H.	3/ 3/18 1y 4m, Tpr.
ELLIS, C. H., Pte. 1 G.S.R.	43 Bty.	10/ 4/17 2y 6m, Gnr.
ELLIS, C., Pte. 40 Bn.	W.	29/ 3/16 1y 9m, Pte.
ELLIS, C. R., Dvr. 26 Bn.	W., 12 Bn. 12 F.A.B.	11/8/15 4y, Dvr.
ELLIS, E. B., Gnr. Fd. Art	W., 5 Div. Fld. and M.T.M. Bty.	9/ 2/16 3y 6m, Dvr.
ELLIS, F. G., Munition Worker.	War Worker.	
ELLIS, G., Pte. 40 Bn.		19/10/16
ELLIS, H. W., Pte. 40 Bn.	2W	17/ 7/16 2y 1m, Pte.
ELLIS, J. R., 2 Lt. 3 F.A.B.	4 Div Art.	18/ 8/14 3y 8m, Major.
ELLIS, N. M., Pte. A.M.C. Rfts.	4 Fd Amb.	17/ 4/16 3y 7m, L.-Cpl
ELLIS, R. N., Pte. 40 Bn.		11/ 9/16
ELLIS, W. R., Pte. 3 Cyc. Corps.	4 D.M.G. Co. 1 M.G. Co.	4/ 4/16 2y 4m, Pte.
ELLIS, W. T., Pte. 15 Bn	2W.	25/ 9/14 3y 6m, Lt.

NAME.	REMARKS.	RANK ON DISCHARGE. ENLISTED. SERVICE.
ELLISON, H., Pte. 26 Bn.		23/ 5/15 4y 4m, Pte.
ELLISTON, C. W., Tpr. 3 L.H.	10 F.A.B., 11 F.A.B.	15/ 9/15 4y 2m, Cpl.
ELLISTON, V. G., Cpl. 3 L.H.	2W., 10 F.A.B.	14/ 9/15 3y 11m, Lt.
ELLSTON, H. E., Pte. 12 Bn.		5/ 2/15 4y 9m, Q.M.S. and Hon. Lieut.
ELLSTON, H. R., Pte. 12 Bn.	✣ 6-10/4/17.	24/ 5/16 Pte. ✣
ELMER, C. J., Pte. 12 Bn.		20/ 8/15
ELMER, W., Pte. 40 Bn.	-	7/ 8/16 3y 6m, Pte.
ELMES, F. W., Pte. 26 Bn.		17/ 5/15
ELMORE, A., Pte. 4 M.G.C.		26/ 2/17
ELMORE, F., Pte. 26 Bn.	P.O.W. ✣ 21/8/16.	5/ 5/15 Pte. ✣
ELMS, A. H. E., Tpr. 3 L.H.		7/11/17 1y 8m, Tpr.
ELPHINSTONE, E. C., Pte. 12 Bn	40 Bn.	21/10/16 2y 10m, Pte.
ELPHINSTONE, C., Pte. 26 Bn.	12 Bn. ✣ 23/7/16.	16/ 8/15 Pte. ✣
ELPHINSTONE, H. W., Pte 26 Bn.	12 Bn., 69 and 12 Bns.	16/ 8/15 4y, Pte.
ELPHINSTONE, L. W., Pte. 12 Bn.	2W., 52 Bn., 13 L.T.M.B ✣ 25/9/17.	5/11/15 Pte. ✣
ELPHINSTONE, M.M, Dvr 6 F.A.B.		28/ 7/15 4y 3m, Gnr.
ELPHINSTONE, W., Dvr. 6 F.A.B.	W., 2 D.A.C., 6 F.A.B.	16/ 8/15 4y 3m, Bdr.
ELSON, A. J., Pte. 12 Bn.	W., 52 Bn. ✣ 19/10/17.	9/11/15 L.-Cpl. ✣
ELSON, J. T., Pte. 4 M.G.C.		30/10/16
ELSON, W. R., Pte. 12 Bn.	2W	4/ 8/16 2y 7m, Pte
ELTHAM, W. K., Gnr. 3 Fd. Art.	2W., 1 F.A.B. ✣ 31/12/16.	26/ 8/14 Lt. ✣
EMANUEL, J. C., Gnr. 3 F.A.B.	W., 2 F.A.B.	22/ 9/14 5y, Gnr.
EMBLING, S. H. A., A.-Sgt. 12 Bn.		29/ 6/15
EMERIE, A. J., Pte. 40 Bn.		18/ 8/16
EMERY, A. J., Pte. 4 M.G. Co.		19/ 3/17
EMERY, H. L., Pte] 12 Bn.	W., 2 M.G.B., 4 M.G.B.	30/ 8/16 1y 6m, Pte.
EMERY, H. W., Pte. 12 Bn.		30/10/16 1y 6m, Pte.
EMERY, V. J., Dvr. 40 Bn.	W.	1/ 2/16 3y 6m, Dvr.
EMMERTON, D. S., Pte. 26 Bn.	✣ 28/7/16.	8/ 6/15 Pte. ✣
EMMERTON, W. J., Pte. 12 Bn.	W., 40 Bn. P.O.W.	2/ 4/16 3y 2m, Pte.
EMMETT, A. S. H., Cpl. 26 Bn.		3/ 3/15 4y 10m, Lt.
EMMETT, R. R., Cpl. 26 Bn.	2W	3/ 3/15 4y 1m, Cpl.
EMMS, A. A., Pte. 40 Bn.	W.	17/10/16 3y 1m, Pte.
EMMS, H. J., Sgt. 40 Bn.	W.	22/ 7/16 3y 2m, Sgt.
EMMS, L. J., Gnr. 18 Bty 6 F.A.B		5/ 8/15 2y 5m, Gnr.
EMMS, S. E., Sgt. 7 Fd. Amb.	W., M.M., M.S.M., 3 Fd. Amb.	5/ 2/15 4y 9m, Q.M.
EMSLEY, F. V., Tpr. 3 L.H.	4 L.H.R.	23/ 4/17 2y 6m, Tpr
ENGLAND, R. W., Pte. 40 Bn.	W., A.A. Pay Corps.	8/11/16 2y 11m, Pte
ENMAN, P., Pte. 26 Bn.	W. ✣ 26/3/17	27/ 9/15Pte ✣
ENNISS, A. J., Pte. 40 Bn.	1 A.D.H.	17/ 3/16 2y 5m, Pte.
ENNISS, F. P., Pte. 15 Bn.	2W., 47 and 45 Bns	3/ 9/15 3y 11m, Pte.
ENNISS, H. J., Pte. 40 Bn.	W.	17/ 3/16 3y 7m, Pte.
ENNOR, S. J., Dvr. 9 Bty F.A.		26/ 9/14 1y 9m, Dvr.
ENRIGHT, W. J., Pte. 4 M.G.C.	14 Bn. ✣ 26/9/17.	1/ 8/16 Pte. ✣
ENSLOW, E., Pte. 15 Bn.	24 How. Bde., 10 F.A.B.	14/ 9/15 3y 11m,S.S Cpl
ENSLOW, H. E., Dvr. 26 Bn.	W., 38 Bty., 10 F.A.B.	13/ 8/15 2y 5m, Dvr.
EPPINGSTALL, G. R. R., Pte 26 Bn	✣ 5/10/17	23/ 7/15 L.-Sgt. ✣
EPPINGSTONE, H. D., Pte. 26 Bn.		27/ 9/15 4y 1m, Pte.
ERICSON, A., Spr. F.C.E. Rfts		7/ 8/17
ERICSON, A., Pte. 15 Bn.		18/ 5/15 1y 2m, Pte.
ERSKINE, W. C., Cpl. 6 F.A.B.	C. de G. (Belgium).	1/11/15 3y 11m. B.S.M.
ESCOTT, A. R., Dvr. 17 Bty F. Art	W. ✣ 8/8/18.	19/ 8/15 Dvr ✣
ESCOTT, W. L., Gnr. 6 A.F.A.	105 Bty	24/ 8/15 4y, Gnr.
ESPIE, J. H. K., Pte. 40 Bn.	W.	1/ 8/17 1y 7m, Pte.
ESSEN, A. R., Pte. 12 Bn.	W., 52 Bn.	6/10/15 2y 7m, Pte.
ESSEN, E. S., Spr. 5 Miners' Co.	2 Tun. Co.	24/ 2/16 1y 10m, Spr.
ETCHELL, E' J. H., Pte. 15 Bn.	W.	2/ 7/15 4y 1m, Cpl.
ETCHELL, H., Gnr. F.A.	W.	4/ 4/17 1y 11m, Gnr.
ETCHELLS, W. H., Pte 3 Cyc. Corp		5/ 3/16
EUSTACE, H. A., Pte. 15 Bn.	✣ 23/9/15.	17/ 9/14 Pte ✣
EUSTACE, J. M., Pte, 15 Bn.	3W., M.M. and Bar.	25/ 9/14 3y 3m, Pte.
EVANS, A. A., 2 Lt. D.A.C.	D.S.O., M.C., 2 M.I.D.	25/ 8/14 Major
EVANS, A. J., Pte. 12 Bn.	3 F.A.B	17/ 4/16 2y 8m, Pte.
EVANS, A. E., Pte. 12 Bn.	M.G. Details.	20/ 6/17 2y 2m, Pte.
EVANS, A. G., Pte. 12 Bn.	✣ 19-12/8/16.	11/ 2/15 Pte. ✣
EVANS, A. J. E., Pte. 40 Bn.	✣ 4/10/17.	4/ 4/16 Pte. ✣
EVANS, A. M., Tpr. 3 L.H.		14/ 6/17 2y 2m, Tpr.
EVANS, C. C., Pte. 3 L.H.		17/ 3/15 3y, L.-Cpl.
EVANS, E. E. E., Gnr. 9 Bty3 F.A.	W., F.A.B.	26/ 8/14 4y 6m, Gnr.
EVANS, E. J., Pte. 15 Bn.	W., 4 M.G.B.	14/ 8/15 3y 10m, Pte.
EVANS, E. J., Tpr Rmt. Sec.		14/10/15 1y 2m, Tpr.
EVANS, E. H., Gnr. 6 F.A.B.	23 How Bde.	10/ 1/16 3y 9m, Dvr.
EVANS, A. E. S., Pte. 12 Bn.	W., 40 Bn.	31/ 7/16 3y 1m, Pte
EVANS, F. E., A.-Cpl. 4 M.G.C.		31/ 8/16 3y 4m, A.-Cpl.
EVANS, F. H., Pte. 15 Bn.	W. ✣ 7/8/15	20/10/14 Pte ✣
EVANS, F. R., Spr. 3 F.C.E.	✣ 8/6/15.	19/ 8/14 Spr. ✣
EVANS, G. R., Pte. 12 Bn.	✣ 23/4/15.	23/11/14 Pte. ✣
EVANS, H. R., Dvr. 8 F.C.E.		25/ 2/16
EVANS, H. R., Cpl. 9 Bty. 3 F.A.		26/ 8/14 3y 2m, Lt.
EVANS, H., Pte. 40 Bn.	3W., M.M.	9/12/15
EVANS, H., Pte. 12 Bn.	✣ 25-28/4/15.	28/ 8/14 Pte. ✣
EVANS, H., Pte. 12 Bn.		9/ 7/15 1y 1m, Pte
EVANS, H. H., Pte 40 Bn.		9/11/15 2y, Pte.
EVANS, J. D., Gnr 6 F.A.D.A.C.	2W., 106 Bty., 6 F.A.B.	12/ 8/15 4y, Gnr.
EVANS, J. W., Spr Miners' Co.		7/ 9/15 2y 10m, Spr.
EVANS, J. L., Pte A.S.C.		30/ 8/15 4y 1m, Sgt.

TASMANIA'S MUSTER ROLL. 265

NAME.	REMARKS.	BANK ON DISCHARGE. ENLISTED. SERVICE.
EVANS, J. W., Pte. 12 Bn.		10/ 2/16
EVANS, J. G., Pte. 12 Bn.	W., 5 Bn., 39 Bn. ✠ 7/6/17.	7/10/15 Pte. ✠
EVANS, J., Pte. 12 Bn.	40 Bn.	15/ 3/16 1y 4m, Pte.
EVANS, L. L., Pte. 12 Bn.	W., 1 Pnr Bn.	19/ 8/15 3y 11m, Pte.
EVANS, N. H., Pte. 12 Bn.	52 Bn. ✠ 4/9/16	5/ 8/15 Pte. ✠
EVANS, N. I., Spr. 6 F.C.E.	W. ✠ 15/5/18	30/ 8/15 Spr. ✠
EVANS, O. A., Dvr. Mec. Mec. Trp.	6 M.T. Co.	29/ 8/16 3y 1m, Dvr.
EVANS, T. A., Pte. 12 Bn. A.M.C.	W., M.M., 3 Fd. Amb.	20/ 8/14 3y 7m, Cpl
EVANS, V. A., Gnr. A.F.A.	2W	12/10/15 3y 6m, Gnr.
EVANS, W. G., Pte. 12 Bn.	2W	14/ 8/16 2y 9m.
EVANS, W. H., Pte. 26 Bn.	Inf. Details.	17/ 5/15 3y 11m, Pte.
EVANS, W. H. Pte. 40 Bn.	W.	25/ 7/16 1y 11m, Pte.
EVENS, A., A.-C.S.M. 1 G.S.R.	40 Bn.	23/ 4/17 2y 6m, Sgt.
EVERARD, P. J., Sgt. 12 Bn.	W., 3 Echelon Corps.	3/ 7/15 4y 2m, Cpl. E.R.S/S.
EVERETT, J. C., Pte. 12 Bn.		23/ 6/16 2y 6m, Pte.
EVERETT, P. T., Pte. 12 Bn.	W.	20/ 8/14 3y 5m, L.-Cpl
EVERETT, W. C. F., Pte. 12 Bn.	52 Bn., 3 Fd. Co Engrs	13/ 7/15 3y 10m, Pte
EVERTON, D. S., Pte. 26 Bn.		8/ 6/15
EVES, J., Tpr. 3 L.H.		26/ 8/15 3y 8m, Tpr.
EWART, H. H., Pte. 40 Bn.		26/ 1/16
EWART, V. W. H., Pte. 12 Bn.	52nd Bn	28/ 5/15 2y 1m, Pte.
EWING, A. C., Pte. A.M.C. Rfts.		14/10/15
EWINGTON, G. S., Tpr. 3 L.H.		19/ 8/14 4y 5m, Tpr.
EWINGTON, H., Pte. 26 Bn.		18/ 5/15 1y 3m, Tpr.
EWINGTON, J. W. G., Tpr. G.S.R.	3 L.H.	15/ 5/18 1y, Tpr
EXCELL, P. R., Pte. 26 Bn.	12 Bn.	9/ 8/15 4y 1m, Pte.
EYLES, A. E., Spr. 8 F.C.E.	13 Fd. Co Engrs	19/11/15 1y 11m, Spr.
EYLES, A. S., Pte. 26 Bn.	✠ 29/7/16.	13/ 4/15 Pte. ✠
EYRES, W., Pte. 3 G.S.R.	12 Bn.	16/ 7/18 1y, Pte.
FACY, E. R., Sgt. 12 Bn.	2W	15/ 7/15 4y 2m, Lt.
FAGAN, J. A., Pte. 12 Bn.		26/ 8/14
FAGAN, T. E., Pte. 12 Bn.	M.M. 51 Bty. ✠ 9/6/17.	11/ 3/16 Pte. ✠
FAGERSTROM, A., Pte. 12 Bn.		31/ 1/19 Pte.
FAGG, H. W., Pte. 40 Bn.	W.	24/ 6/16 2y, Pte.
FAGG, R. T., Pte. 12 Bn.	W.	16/ 9/14 1y 10m, Pte.
FAGGART, O. D., Pte. 15 Bn.		4/ 8/15
FAHEY, F. M., Pte. 12 Bn.	W.	17/10/16 3y 2m, Pte.
FAHEY, J., Pte. 40 Bn.	✠ 13/10/17.	22/ 2/16 Pte. ✠
FAHEY, Joseph, Pte. 15 Bn.	W.	11/ 2/15 4y 4m, Pte.
FAHEY, M. J., Pte. 1 G.S.R.		17/ 6/18
FAHEY, R., Pte. 40 Bn.	2W, 7 A.S.C.	22/ 2/16 3y 8m, Pte.
FAHEY, V., Pte. 4 Pnrs.	2W	22/ 1/15 3y, Pte.
FAHEY, W. J., Pte. 12 Bn.		7/ 5/17 2y 5m, R.-Sgt.
FAIR, L. B., Pte. 12 Bn.		7/ 1/15 4y 5m, Pte.
FAIRBROTHER, F. J., Pte. 12 Bn.	52 Bn., P.O.W.	13/ 7/15 4y 4m, Sgt.
FAIRMAN, G. E., Pte. 15 Bn.	2 A.A.H.	20/ 9/14 Pte.
FAIRTHORNE, F. F., Gnr. 3 F.A.B.	M.I.D.	26/ 8/14 4y 8m, Capt.
FALCK-PAUL, R. E., N. N., Pte. 12 Bn.	2W., 1 M.G. Bn. ✠ 25/9/18.	10/ 7/15 Pte. ✠
FALCONER, G. H., Pte. 12 Bn.	24 How. Bde. ✠ 28/1/17.	12/ 9/14 Dvr. ✠
FANNON, C., Pte. 26 Bn.	✠ 26/1/19.	15/ 4/15 Pte. ✠
FARGIE, C., Pte. 12 Bn.	W., Anzac Prov. Cps.	2/12/15 Pte.
FARLEY, B., Pte. A.M.C. Rfts.	A.G.B.D.	5/12/17 y 11m, Pte.
FARLEY, V. J., Cpl. 3 L.H.		20/ 9/14 4y 6m, Cpl.
FARLEY, W. R. E., Pte. Tnlrs.		1/ 8/17 6m, Pte.
FARMER, B. S. C., Dvr. 11 Co. A.S.C.		19/ 8/14 2y 9m, Dvr.
FARMER, C. G., Sec.-Lieut. 4 A.S.C.	M.C. 2 M.I.D.	17/ 8/14 4y 7m, Mjr.
FARMER, J. L., Dvr. 3 A.S.C.		31/ 8/14 Dvr.
FARNELL, A. F., Pte. 12 Bn.	3W.	15/ 9/14 L.-Cpl. ✠
FARNELL, A. E., Pte. 12 Bn.	51 Bn.	25/11/15 4y 1m, Pte.
FARNFIELD, F., Pte. 40 Bn.		17/10/16 2y 4m, Pte.
FARNHAM, A. G., Tpr. 3 L.H.		12/11/17 Pte.
FARNHAM, C., Pte. 12 Bn.	W., 52 Bn.	13/ 9/15 1y 10m, Pte.
FARNHAM, L., Pte. 15 Bn.	✠ 23/5/15.	29/ 9/14 Pte. ✠
FARNHAN, V., Pte. 4 M.G. Co.	2 M.G. Co. ✠ 3/9/18.	9/ 9/16 Pte. ✠
FARNINGTON, W. J., Pte. 2 G.S.R.		7/ 6/18
FARQUHAR, A. J., Gnr. 2 D.A.C.		6/11/16 2y 8m, Gnr.
FARRELL, A., Pte. 12 Bn.		20/ 8/14
FARRELL, F., Pte. 12 Bn.	W. ✠ 28/12/15.	21/ 8/14 Pte. ✠
FARREL, J. M., Pte 12 Bn.	W., 52 Bn. ✠ 16/10/17.	21/ 9/15 Pte. ✠
FARRELL, J. P., Gnr. 25 F.A.B.	3 F.A.B. ✠ 28/5/18.	22/ 6/16 Dvr. ✠
FARRELL, R. T., Pte. 12 Bn.	✠ 18/9/18.	30/10/17 L.-Cpl. ✠
FARRELL, R., Pte. 40 Bn.		10/ 9/17 1y 8m, Pte.
FARRELL, R. H., Pte. 26 Bn.	✠ 31/8/16.	12/ 5/15 Sgt. ✠
FARRELL, W. A., Pte. 12 Bn.	W., 52 Bn., 51 Bn.	21/ 8/14 4y 5m, W.O.
FARRELLY, J. A., Pte. 40 Bn.	W., 49 Bn. ✠ 23/7/17.	14/ 3/16 Pte. ✠
FARRELLY, P. P., Pte. 7 Fd. Amb.	13 Fd. Amb.	31/ 1/15 4y 11m, Pte.
FARRER, T., Gnr. 3 F.A. Bde.		13/ 9/15 4y 2m, Gnr.
FARROW, G. H., Spr. 3 F.C.E.		21/ 8/14 1y 8m, Spr.
FAULDS, J., Pte. 12 Bn.		2/11/16 2y 3m, Pte.
FAULKNER, E. W., Pte. 40 Bn.	W.	18/ 5/16 1y 6m, Pte.
FAULKNER, H. S., Dvr. 3 F.A.B.	W., 2 Fd. Arty. Bde.	6/ 9/15 2y 11m, Dvr.
FAULKNER, S., Pte. 40 Bn.	26 Bn.	28/ 3/16 3y 6m, Pte.
FAULKINER, W., Pte. 4 M.G.C.		4/ 9/16 3y 2m, Pte.

NAME.	REMARKS.	RANK ON DISCHARGE. ENLISTED. SERVICE.
FAWCETT, C. H., Sec.-Lt. 40 Bn.	65 Bn., 63 Bn.	10/ 1/16 Lieut.
FAWKNER, J., Pte. 12 Bn.		20/11/17
FAY, A. H., Pte. 12 Bn.	W. ✠ 19-22/8/16.	29/ 9/14 Pte. ✠
FAZACKERLEY, A. J. T., Pte. 3 F.A.B.		9/ 8/15 4y 2m, Pte.
FAZACKERLEY, E. A., Pte. 12 Bn	W., 4 Pioneers.	7/12/15 3y 11m, Cpl.
FAZACKERLEY, J. T., Pte 40 Bn.	W.	4/ 5/16 1y 9m, L.-Cpl.
FAZACKERLEY, N. C., Pte. 40 Bn.	W.	26/ 9/17 1y 7m, Pte.
FAZACKERLEY, N. F., Pte. 3 G.S.R.	12 Bn.	18/ 7/18 1y 3m, Pte.
FEATHERSTONE, A. C. O., Pte. 12 Bn.		20/11/17 1y 7m, Pte.
FEATHERSTONE, P., Pte. 12 Bn.	52 Bn.	10/ 1/16
FEATONBY, G., Pte. 12 Bn.	2W., 4 D.A.C.	5/ 8/15 3y 8m, Pte.
FEATONBY, L., Pte. 40 Bn.	2W	15/ 3/16 3y 6m, Cpl.
FEBEY, A. G., Pte. 40 Bn.	✠ 16/2/18.	27/ 3/17 Pte. ✠
FEBEY, D., Pte. 15 Bn.	W., 45 Bn.	14/ 9/15 Pte.
FEBEY, F. J., Pte. 15 Bn.		14/ 9/15 4y, Pte.
FEBEY, H. W., Pte. 15 Bn.		16/9/14 2y 10m, Pte.
FEBEY, Herbert Walter, Pte. 12 Bn	W.	23/ 6/16 1y 11m, Pte.
FEBEY, W. E., Pte. 12 Bn.	W., 52 Bn.	13/ 1/16 1y 9m, Cpl.
FELMINGHAM, C., Pte. 12 Bn.		18/ 8/15 1y, Pte.
FELTHAM, A. A. S., Pte. 40 Bn.		2/ 3/16 3y 3m, Pte.
FELTHAM, W. J. E., Pte. 12 Bn.	P.O.W.	23/ 8/16 2y 11m, Pte.
FENNER, C. F., Pte. 40 Bn.	✠ 14/1/17.	2/10/16 Pte. ✠
FENNER, G. A. E., Pte. 12 Bn.	W.	6/11/16 2y 8m, Dvr.
FENNER, J. F., Dvr. 12 Bn.		2/ 6/15 4y 1m, Dvr.
FENTON, A. H., Pte. 15 Bn.	M.I.D.	29/ 9/14 4y 5m, Sec.-Lt.
FENTON, A. W., Pte. 15 Bn.	W., 4 Pioneers.	14/ 9/14 5y, Pte.
FENTON, C. J., Pte. 40 Bn.		6/ 8/17 1y 7m, Pte.
FENTON, G. A., Pte. 26 Bn.		23/ 2/15 2y 9m, Pte.
FENTON, R., Pte. 4 M.G. Co.	15 M.G. Co.	4/10/16 Pte
FERGUSON, A. D., Tpr. 3 L.H.		28/ 8/14 Tpr.
FERGUSON, A. H., Gnr. Arty.	W., 42 Bn.	13/ 4/16 2y 2m, Gnr.
FERGUSON, C. E. H., Lieut. 40 Bn	W., M.C., 3 D.S.C.	1/ 3/16 3y 6m, Capt.
FERGUSON, D. B., Pte. 15 Bn.	W.	Pte.
FERGUSON, I. J., Pte. 40 Bn.	W.	10/ 3/16 2y 4m, Pte.
FERGUSON, J., Pte. 12 Bn.	2W.	5/ 1/15 2y 6m, Pte.
FERGUSON, J. S., Pte. 40 Bn.	W.	30/ 5/17 Pte.
FERGUSON, John, Dvr. 13 F.A.B.		1/11/15 3y 8m, Dvr.
FERGUSON, John, L.-Cpl. 40 Bn.	✠ 30/1/17.	24/ 3/16 L.-Cpl. ✠
FERGUSON, L. G., Pte. 26 Bn.	4 M.G. Co., 29 A.F.C.	18/ 5/15 4y 8m, Dvr.
FERGUSON, M. C., Pte. 40 Bn.	W., 12 Bn.	1/ 7/16 Pte.
FERGUSON, O. B., Pte. 40 Bn.		10/10/16 2y 1m, Pte.
FERGUSON, R., Pte. 40 Bn.	2W.	4/ 4/16 2y 2m, Sgt.
FERGUSON, R. H., Gnr. 108 Bty. A.F.A.	M.M. 23 How. Bde.	4/ 1/16 2y 6m, Gnr.
FERGUSON, S. H., Tpr. 3 L.H.	5 D.A.C.	13/10/15 3y 11m, Dvr.
FERGUSSON, T., Pte. 14 F. Amb.		21/ 2/16 3y 10m, Dvr.
FERGUSON, W. J., Spr. 3 Mnrs.	1 M. Co.	18/11/15 2y 3m, Spr.
FERGUSON, W. T., Tpr. 3 L.H.	W., 14 F. A.	14/ 9/15 Gnr.
FERGUSSON, E. R., Pte. A.M.C.	14 Fd. Amb.	1/11/16 3y, Dvr.
FERRALL, A. B., Gnr. 3 F.A.		26/ 8/14 4y 6m, Gnr.
FERRALL, E., Pte. 40 Bn.	W., A.I.F. Hdq.	18/ 7/16 2y 9m, Pte.
FERRALL, H. W., Pte. 26 Bn.	W., 4 Pioneers.	7/ 8/15 3y 2m, Pte
FERRALL, N. W., Pte. 40 Bn.		27/ 4/18 3y 5m, Pte.
FERRAR, F. M., Pte. 26 Bn.	W.	27/ 7/15 4y 1m, Pte.
FERRAR, M. E., Tpr. 3 L.H.	W. ✠ 25/8/19.	8/12/14 v 1m, Tpr.
FERRAR, T. M., Gnr. 11 F.A.B.	W.	23/ 2/16 3y 2m, Dvr.
FERRIS, W. C., Gnr. 2 D. Trn.		28/ 1/16 3y 3m, Gnr.
FETHERS, N. D., Lieut., 12 Bn.	14 Bn.	24/ 8/14 3y 1m, Major
FESENEYER, L., Gnr. 3 F.A.B.	3W.	25/ 8/15 Gnr.
FIDLER, C. W., Spr. 6 Fd. Co.		14/ 2/17 2y 6m, Spr.
FIDLER, P. A., Pte. 40 Bn.		6/10/16 3y 2m, Pte.
FIDLER, J. R., Cpl. 6 Fd. Co.	4W. M.C.	11/ 8/15
FIELD, A. S., Cpl. 12 Bn.	52 Bn. ✠ 2/4/17.	4/ 8/15 Cpl. ✠
FIELD, Chas., Pte. 40 Bn.		8/10/16 1y 7m, Pte.
FIELD, J., Spr. Tnlrs.	W.	25/10/16 2y 10m, Spr.
FIELD, L. McR., Tpr. 3 L.H.	3 Camel Corps. ✠ 19/4/17.	20/ 8/14 Sgt. ✠
FIELDING, A. W., Pte. 12 Bn.		10/ 2/16 4y. Pte.
FIELDING, C. J., Pte. 12 Bn.	W.	31/ 7/16 2y, Pte.
FIELDING, L. J., Gnr. 2 D.A.C.	W., 104 How. Bty.	9/ 9/15 3y 11m, Gnr.
FIELDING, W. A., Pte. 26 Bn.	W., 4 F.A.B.	2/10/15 3y 3m, Dvr.
FIELDS, T., Pte. 12 Bn.	W.	3/ 3/17 2y 1m, Pte.
FIGG. H. R., Pte. 26 Bn.		13/ 3/15 7m, Pte.
FINDLAY, W. K., Lieut. 40 Bn.	M.C.	10/10/16 3y 2m, Capt.
FIGGIS, C. T., Pte. 26 Bn.	✠ 20/6/16.	13/ 3/15 Pte ✠
FILBEE, J. S., Pte. 12 Bn.	W., 52 Bn.	26/ 7/15 3y 2m, Pte.
FINCH, C. A., Spr. 2 Sig. Co.	✠ 20/9/17.	17/ 8/15 Spr. ✠
FINCH, C. R., Pte. 12 Bn.	✠ 19-22/8/16	9/ 2/15 Pte. ✠
FINCH, F., Spr. 1 F.S.E.		18/11/16 2y 5m, Sgt.
FINCH, W. D., Pte. Remount		1/10/15 8m, Pte.
FINCH, W. H., Gnr. A.F. Rfts.		4/ 2/15 Dvr.
FINDLAY, N. A. M., Cpl. 40 Bn.	W.	14/ 3/16 1y 7m, Sgt.
FINDLAY, W., Gnr. Arty.	110 How. Bty.	25/ 5/17 2y 7m, Gnr.
FINLAY, G. A., Gnr. 12 F.A. Bde.	W. M.M. 120 How. Bty.	7/ 3/16 3y 6m, Gnr.
FINLAY, J. H., Pte. 26 Bn.	1 Pioneers.	4/ 8/15 3y 11m, Pte.

TASMANIA'S MUSTER ROLL.

NAME.	REMARKS.	RANK ON DISCHARGE. ENLISTED. SERVICE.
FINLAYSON, F. V., Tpr. 3 L.H.	W., 1 Signal Troop.	13/ 5/15 4y 3m, Sgn.
FINLAYSON, J. M., Pte. 26 Bn.	12 Bn. ✽ 6-10/4/17.	5/ 5/15 Pte. ✽
FINLAYSON, W., Pte. 40 Bn.	Vet. Hospital.	24/10/16 2y 9m, Pte.
FINN, G. F. L., Tpr. 3 L.H.	15 Bn. ✽	25/ 5/15 Pte. ✽
FINN, J. T., Pte. 12 Bn.		5/ 4/16 Pte.
FINN, T. J., Gnr. 13 F.A. Bde.		10/ 3/17 2y 4m, Gnr.
FINNEY, R. T., Pte. 40 Bn.		8/ 6/15 3y 4m, Pte.
FIRTH, D. M. C., Pte. 12 Bn.	W.	23/10/16 2y 11m, Pte.
FISH, W. J., Pte. 26 Bn.	W.	13/ 9/15 4y, Pte.
FISHER, A. E., Pte. 12 Bn.	W.	17/10/15 1y 3m, Pte.
FISHER, A. K. C., Pte. 2 G.S.R.	12 Bn	10/ 5/18 Sgt.
FISHER, A. H., Pte. 12 Bn.	W. ✽ 7/8/15.	20/ 8/14 Pte. ✽
FISHER, E., L.-Cpl. 6 Fd. Co.		30/ 8/15
FISHER, F. C. D., Pte. 40 Bn.	W.	2/10/16 1y 10m, Pte.
FISHER, G. C., Cpl. 1 A.C.H.		16/ 9/14 1y 11m, Pte.
FISHER, G. G., Pte. 4 M.G.C.		23/ 6/16 2y 2m, Pte.
FISHER, H. G., Sgt. Cook, 40 Bn.	2 Comd. Depot.	15/ 9/15 2y 11m, S.-Ck.
FISHER, J. C., Pte. 26 Bn.	✽ 7/10/15.	18/ 6/15 Pte. ✽
FISHER, J. A., Pte. 40 Bn.	✽ 13/10/17.	20/ 9/16 Pte. ✽
FISHER, J. F., Pte. 26 Bn.	12 Bn	28/ 8/15 2y 6m, Sgt.
FISHER, L. J., Dvr. 3 F.A.B.		16/12/14 4y 5m, Dvr.
FISHER, L. G., Pte. 15 Bn.	3W., 47 Bn., 15 Bn.	26/ 3/15 3y 8m. Pte.
FISHER, M. M., Spr. Miners	W., 2 Tun. Co.	23/ 2/16 3y 8m, Spr.
FISHER, P. T., Spr. 6 Fd. Co.		2/ 9/15
FISHER, R. C., Pte. 12 Bn.	52 Bn.	6/ 7/15 2y 4m, Pte.
FISHER, T. M., Pte. 26 Bn.	2W.	16/ 3/15
FISHER, W. N., Sgt. 12 Bn.		20/ 8/14 4y 7m, C.S.M.
FISHER, W. R., Pte. 26 Bn.	1 A.C.C.S.	6/ 4/15 4y 4m, Pte.
FIST, A. G., Pte. 40 Bn.	12 Bn.	27/ 9/16 3y, Dvr.
FITCH, B., Pte. 12 Bn.	2W.	16/ 8/16 3y 1m, Dvr.
FITCH, H. P., Pte. 12 Bn.		1/ 6/16 3y 3m, Dvr.
FITCH, J. G. A., Pte. 4 M.G.C.	23 M.G.C.	27/ 9/15 3y 11m, Pte.
FITZALLEN, A. J., Cpl. Post. Unt.		21/10/15 R.-Sgt.
FITZALLEN, C. A., Pte. 40 Bn.	2W.	4/ 8/16 2y 10m, Pte.
FITZALLEN, J. C., Dvr. 4 Fd. Co.		13/ 1/16 2y 5m, Dvr.
FITZGERALD, A. C., S.-Sgt. A.A.M.C.		8/ 8/17 4y 7m, S.-Sgt.
FITZGERALD, E. S., Pte. Fd. Amb.		15/12/14 1y 5m, Pte.
FITZGERALD, E., Pte. 15 Bn.		6/12/14 1y 6m, Pte.
FITZGERALD, F. G., Gnr. 23 How. Bde.		26/ 2/16 1y 9m, Gnr.
FITZGERALD, G., Gnr. 6 F.A. Bd.	2 D.A.C., 16 Bty.	6/10/15 4y 2m, Gnr.
FITZGERALD, F. E., Pte. 12 Bn.	✽ 18/9/18.	2/11/15 Pte. ✽
FITZGERALD, J. C., Pte. 40 Bn.	W.	2/10/16 1y 9m, Pte.
FITZGERALD, L. E., Pte. 40 Bn.		2/ 3/16 3y 6m, Pte.
FITZGERALD, T., Gnr. Arty.		28/ 1/18
FITZGIBBONS, J. A., S.-Sgt 12 Bn.	W.	17/ 8/14 1y 7m, S.-Sgt.
FITZMAURICE, C. B., Pte. 12 Bn.	40 Bn.	21/10/16 2y 8m, Pte.
FITZMAURICE, C. C., Pte. 4 M.G	W., 40 Bn.	21/ 6/16
FITZMAURICE, H. A., Tpr. 3 L.H.		10/ 7/17 1y 10m, Tpr.
FITZMAURICE, H. J., Pte. 12 Bn.	✽ 24/12/16.	30/ 4/16 Pte. ✽
FITZMAURICE, Luke, Pte. 12 Bn.	2W.	7/10/16 3y 1m, Pte.
FITZMAURICE, M. P., Sgt. 36 H.A.G.		7/ 6/15 4y 2m, R.S.M.
FITZMAURICE, R. W., Pte. 12 Bn.	W., 40 Bn.	11/ 1/17 2y 8m, Pte.
FITZPATRICK, A. J., Pte. 12 Bn.		7/ 7/17 3y 2m, Pte.
FITZPATRICK, A. J., Pte. Remt.		16/ 9/15 9m, Pte.
FITZPATRICK, C., Pte. 12 Bn.	W., 51 Bn.	1/ 8/15 4y, Pte.
FITZPATRICK, J. E., Pte. 12 Bn.		1/ 8/15 4y, Pte.
FITZPATRICK, H. A., M.W.		M.W
FITZPATRICK, M. M., Gnr. S. Bty.		4/ 6/15 3y 6m, Gnr.
FITZPATRICK, M. J., Gnr. Arty.	W., 3 D.A.C.	21/ 1/16 3y 8m, Dvr.
FITZPATRICK, V., Pte. 12 Bn.	Anzac Prov. Corps.	7/ 9/16 E.R. 2nd Cpl.
FLAKEMORE, S. J., Pte. 12 Bn.		2/ 5/16 3y 2m, Pte.
FLANAGAN, J. E., Pte. 40 Bn.	3W.	5/10/16 2y 11m, Pte.
FLANAGAN, J. P., Gnr. Arty.		5/10/16 2y 6m, Gnr.
FLANAGAN, Jn. Ed., Gnr. 8 F.A.B.	✽ 24/4/18.	5/10/16 Gnr. ✽
FLANAGAN, W. J., Gnr. 1 D.A.C.		7/12/16 2y 6m, Dvr.
FLANAGIN, A. L., Pte. A.A.M.C.	11 Fd. Amb.	2/ 3/17 2y 8m, Pte.
FLANNERY, J. A., Pte. 12 Bn.		23/10/17 2y, Pte.
FLANDERS, W. E., Pte. Cmp. Un.	✽ 18/10/16.	14/10/16 Pte. ✽
FLEMING, A. C. M., Pte. 40 Bn.	51 Bn. ✽ 17/11/17.	8/ 2/16 Pte. ✽
FLEMING, A., Spr. 2 Tunn. Co.		31/10/16 3y 1m, Spr.
FLEMING, Arthur, Pte. 12 Bn.	✽ 6/10/17.	23/ 5/16 Pte. ✽
FLEMING, A. V., 15 Bn.	2W., 6 Bn.	10/12/14 4y 10m, Pte.
FLEMING, C. T., Pte. 40 Bn.	2W	18/ 3/16 3y 7m, L.-Sgt.
FLEMING, C. C., Pte. Remounts	3 M. Vet. Sec., Vet. Hosp. ✽ 11/11/18.	28/ 9/15 Pte. ✽
FLEMING, E. R., Pte. 12 Bn.	W., ✽ 25/4/15.	20/ 8/14 Pte. ✽
FLEMING, H. D., Pte. 1 G.S.R.	40 Bn.	26/ 2/18 1y 8m, Pte.
FLEMING, H., Pte. 12 Bn.	W.	7/ 8/15 2y 6m, Pte.
FLEMING, J. C., Pte. 26 Bn.		
FLEMING, J. G., W.O. Rly. Unit	D.C.M., 2 A.L.R.C.	16/10/17 2y, Lieut.
FLEMING, Jn., Pte. 40 Bn.	✽ 2/4/17.	23/ 2/16 Pte. ✽
FLEMING, P. J., Sgt 26. Bn.	M.I.D. P.O.W.	5/ 8/15 3y 10m, Sgt.
FLEMING, R., Dvr 9 Bty.		26/ 8/14 4y 6m, Dvr.
FLETCHER, C. E. J., Gnr. 4 Fd. Amb	W.	7/ 8/15 4y 1m, Dvr.
FLETCHER, F. A., Pte. 40 Bn.		7/ 6/16 2y 10m, Sgt.

NAME.	REMARKS.	RANK ON DISCHARGE. ENLISTED. SERVICE.
FLETCHER, F. V., Tpr. 3 L.H.		17/ 9/17 1y 11m, Tpr.
FLETCHER, G. H., Pte. 26 Bn.	✱ 29/7/16.	27/ 2/15 Pte. ✱
FLETCHER, G. J., Spr. F.C. Eng.		20/ 8/14 1y 9m, S.-Mjr.
FLETCHER, H. J. V., Pte. 15 Bn.		29/11/16
FLETCHER, I. M., Pte. 1 G.S.R.	A.G.B. Depot.	7/ 1/18 1y 9m, Pte.
FLETCHER, J. W., Pte. 12 Bn.	W.	19/ 6/15 1y 7m, Pte.
FLETCHER, L. W., Gnr. F.A. Rfts		22/11/16 3y, Gnr.
FLETCHER, M. C., Pe. 12 Bn.	✱ 19-22/8/16.	15/ 9/15 Pte. ✱
FLETCHER, R. W., Cpl. 12 Bn.	M.C.	8/12/14 4y 4m, Lieut.
FLETCHER, R. T., Pte. 2 G.S.R.	A.G.B. Depot.	15/ 3/18 1y 6m, Pte.
FLETCHER, W. E., Pte. 40 Bn.	W., 1 M.G. Co.	13/ 3/16
FLETCHER, W. H., Pte. 40 Bn.		6/12/16 2y 2m, Pte.
FLEXMORE, A. Y., Gnr. A.F.A. R.	120 How. Bty., 12 Fd. Bty. ✱ 18/9/17.	3/ 4/16 Gnr. ✱
FLIGHT, F. R., Gnr. 3 D.A.C.		5/ 1/17 2y 8m, Gnr.
FLIGHT, J. E., Spr. Eng. Rmts.		5/ 1/16 2y 10m, Dvr.
FLIGHT, W., Pte. 15 Bn.		5/ 1/15 1y 8m, Pte.
FLINT, A., Pte. 40 Bn.		3/10/16 3y 2m, Pte.
FLINT, A. A., Pte. 12 Bn.	2W., M.M.	4/ 5/16 2y 11m, L.-Cpl.
FLINT, F. W., Pte. 12 Bn.	W., 3 L.T.M.B.	15/ 7/15 4y, Pte.
FLINT, H. W., Pte. 40 Bn.	17 Fd. Amb.	19/ 9/16 1y 9m, Pte.
FLINT, L. C., Pte. 12 Bn.	W.	1/ 6/16 3y 6m, Pte.
FLINTON, J. P., Pte. 15 Bn	12 Bn., 24 How. Bty., 4 D.A.C., 10 F.A. Arty. Bde.	19/ 9/14
FLOOD, C. T., Pte. 40 Bn.	2W., M.M.	9/ 2/16 3y 8m, C.S.M.
FLOOD, C. W. T., Pte. 12 Bn.	W.	1/12/14 4y 4m, Pte.
FLOOD, D., Pte. 15 Bn.	3W., A.C.A.P.	9/ 2/15 3y 6m, Pte.
FLOOD, E., Pte. A.A.M.C.	W., 9 Fd. Amb.	9/10/16 3y, Pte.
FLOOD, H. C., Pte. 40 Bn.	✱ 28/9/16.	2/ 3/16 Pte. ✱
FLOOD, R. C., Pte. 40 Bn.	✱ 13/10/17.	2/ 3/16 Cpl. ✱
FLOOD, W., Pte. 12 Bn.		29/ 9/16 8m, Pte.
FLOOD, W. W., Tpr. 3 L.H.	✱ 18/8/18.	5/12/16 Tpr. ✱
FLOWERS, W. G., Pte. 12 Bn.	4 Sal. Coy.	10/ 2/15 Pte.
FLOWERS, W. J., Tpr. 3 L.H.	12 Bn.	17/ 9/14 3y 3m, Pte.
FLOYD, J. S., Pte. 12 Bn.	10 F.A. Bde.	15/ 9/15 3y 11m, Dvr
FLOYD, R., Pte. 12 Bn.	4 M.G. Coy.	22/ 7/15 4y 1m, Cpl.
FLOYD, R., Gnr. 9 Bty.		26/ 8/14 7m, Gnr.
FLUKES, E. C., Pte. 40 Bn.	✱ 10/6/17.	19/ 9/16 Pte. ✱
FLYNN, D. J., Pte. 40 Bn.	W.	1/10/16 2v 11m. Pte.
FOGARTY, A. H., Pte. 12 Bn.	✱ 7/10/17.	15/ 9/15 Pte. ✱
FOGARTY, A. E., Pte. 12 Bn.	W.	2/ 5/17 2y 3m, Pte.
FOGARTY, C. F., Pte. 12 Bn.	✱ 19-22/8/16.	7/ 9/15 Pte. ✱
FOGARTY, D. H., Pte. 26 Bn.	W.	11/ 4/15 2y 6m, Pte.
FOGARTY, J. P., Tpr. 3 L.H.		4/ 2/15 2y 8m, Tpr.
FOGARTY, R. H., Pte. 1 A.G.H.	13 Fd. Amb.	4/ 6/15 4y 1m, Pte.
FOGARTY, T. E., Pte. 12 Bn.		11/ 8/15 9m, Pte.
FOLEY, D. E., Gnr. A.F.A.	A.M.	26/ 4/17 2y 6m, Gnr.
FOLEY, A. L., Pte. 12 Bn.		4/12/17
FOLEY, E., Pte.	✱ 20/11/15.	Pte. ✱
FOLEY, J. E., Sgt. Remount		8/10/15 1y 2m, Sgt.
FOLEY, J. H., Dvr. 6 Bty.		1/12/16 Dvr.
FOLEY, L. S., Pte. 26 Bn.	12 Bn.	29/ 8/15 4y 4m, Cpl.
FOLEY, S. J., Pte. Remount	40 Bn.	3/10/15
FOLKS, T. J., Sgt. 6 Fd. Co.	16 Fd. Co. Eng., 6 Fd. Co.	11/10/15 Sgt.
FOOKS, E. V., Pte. 40 Bn.	10 Inf. B. Hdqrs.	4/ 4/16 3y 1m, Pte.
FOOKS, R. M., Pte. 12 Bn.		12/ 8/14
FOON, A. E., Pte. 26 Bn.		19/ 6/15 1y 3m. Pte.
FOOT, A. C., Pte. Remount.		29/ 9/15 9m, Pte. ✱
FOOT, H. H., Pte. 15 Bn.	W., 24 How. Bde., 10 F.A.B. ✱ 14/6/18.	4/ 8/15 Pte. ✱
FORBES, A. T., Pte. 12 Bn.	W.	22/ 6/15 4y 1m, Pte.
FORBES, C. A., Pte. 40 Bn.		4/ 4/16 1y 11m, Pte.
FORBES, H. J., Pte. 12 Bn.		13/ 7/16 3y 2m, Pte.
FORBES, P., Pte. 40 Bn.	3W.	4/ 4/16 3y 5m, Pte.
FORBES, W. A., Pte. 12 Bn.	49 Bn.	4/11/14 4y 6m, Pte.
FORDHAM, G. Z., Sgt. 40 Bn.	W.	8/12/15 3y 3m, Sgt.
FORDHAM, P. H., Spr. Miners.	3 Tunn. Coy.	17/ 8/17 2y 1m, Spr.
FORDHAM, T. W., Cpl. 12 Bn.	W., M.M., 4 Command Depot.	3/ 8/15 3y 7m, A.-Sgt.
FORDHAM, W. H., Spr. Miners	M.I.D., 3 Tunn. Coy.	22/11/15 3y 8m, S.-Sgt.
FOREMAN, C. B., Pte. 12 Bn.	✱ 6-10/4/17.	3/12/15 Pte. ✱
FOREMAN, F. W., Pte. 26 Bn.	W., 12 Bn.	23/ 8/15 4y, L.-Cpl.
FORREST, A. E. B., Spr. 3 Fd. Co	W.	21/ 8/14 1y 3m, Spr.
FORREST, F. E., S.M. 9 Bty.	M.C., 4 Divl. Arty.	26/ 8/14 4y, Major.
FOREST, F. C., Pte. 40 Bn.		14/ 3/16 1y 11m, Pte.
FORSLUND, A. J., Pte. 26 Bn.	2 Sig. Coy. Engrs. ✱ 21/9/17.	5/ 5/15 Spr. ✱
FORSLUND, A. H., Pte. 12 Bn.	2W. ✱ 2/5/18.	4/ 9/16 Pte. ✱
FORSLUND, F., Pte. 40 Bn.	3 Sig. Coy.	5/ 2/16 3y 7m, Spr.
FORSTER, C. W., Pte. 12 Bn.	✱ 23/9/18.	14/ 1/18 Pte. ✱
FORSTER, J. C., Pte. 26 Bn.	2W.	18/ 5/15 4y 3m, Cpl.
FORSYTH, L. M., Sgt. Miners.	W.	13/11/15 C.Q.M.S.
FORSYTH, T., Dvr 10 A.S.C.		15/ 9/14 4y 5m, Sgt.
FORSYTH, W. F., S.M. 4 A.S.C.	M.S.M. 18 A.S.C. 24 A.D.U.S.	7/ 9/14 4y 5m, W.O.
FORSYTHE, W. J., Pte. 3 S. A.F.C		30/ 8/16 3v, 2nd-A.M.
FORWARD, A. H., Pte. 12 Bn.		5/ 3/16 1y 8m, Pte.
FORWARD, R. C., Dvr. 12 Bn.	69 Bn.	14/ 7/15 4y, Dvr.
FORWARD, W. H., Pte. 12 Bn.	W.	16/ 7/15 4y, Dvr.
FORD, A. E., Pte. 3 G.S.R.	12 Bn.	19/ 8/18 1y, Pte.
FORD, A. L., Pte. 12 Bn.	W., 52 Bn. ✱ 3-4/9/16.	24/ 1/16 Pte. ✱
FORD, A. D., Pte. 15 Bn.	47 Bn.	28/ 5/15 1y 2m Pte.

TASMANIA'S MUSTER ROLL.

NAME.	REMARKS.	RANK ON DISCHARGE. ENLISTED, SERVICE.
FORD, A. Ed., Spr. Miners	W., 2 Tunn. Coy.	1/ 3/16 3y 6m. Spr.
FORD, B. L., Pte. 26 Bn.		20/ 6/16 2y 10m, Pte.
FORD, C. R., Pte. 40 Bn.		1/ 3/16 L.-Cpl. ✠
FORD, E. E., L.-Cpl. 40 Bn.	✠ 3/1/17.	15/12/14 4y 4m. Pte.
FORD, G., Pte. 3 Fd. Amb.	W.	20/ 1/16 3y 8m, Dvr.
FORD, H. W., Gnr. 23 How. Bde.		11/ 8/15 Pte. ✠
FORD, J. T., Pte. 15 Bn.	12 Bn. ✠ 13/9/17.	12/ 8/15 Sgt.
FORD, L. W., Pte. 12 Bn.	W. ✠ 15/4/17	1/ 5/16 3y 4m. Pte.
FORD, P. E., Pte. 12 Bn		18/10/16 11m, Spr.
FORD, P. H., Spr. Tun. Co.		6/ 1/15 3y 7m. Pte.
FORD, T. E., Pte. 12 Bn.	W.. 1 Poineer Bn.	3/ 7/18 1y 1m. Pte.
FORD, T. M., Pte. 3 G.S.R.	12 Bn.	3/12/17
FORD, V. T., Pte. 1 G.S.R		8/ 6/17 1y 2m. Pte.
FORD, W. J., Pte. 40 Bn.		12/ 6/16 Pte.
FOUNTAIN, R. S., Pte. 12 Bn.	P.O.W.	20/ 9/15 3y 10m, A-Bdr
FOSTER, A., Gnr. 6 F.A.B.		20/ 8/14 5y. 2nd-Lt.
FOSTER, A. C., Tpr. 3 L.H.	2W., M.C.	19/10/16 2y 8m, S.-Sgt.
FOSTER, B., Pte. 26 Bn.	A.A.O.C.	9/10/16 2y 11m. Pte.
FOSTER, C. H., Pte. 12 Bn.	40 Bn.	26/ 7/15 4y 3m, L.Cpl.
FOSTER, F. O., Tpr. 3 L.H.		11/ 9/17 1y 4m. Pte.
FOSTER, F. J., Pte. 12 Bn.		27/ 2/18 1y 6m, Lieut.
FOSTER, F. H., Sec.-Lt.	4 Divl. Engrs.	1/11/16 2y 11m. Fitter
FOSTER, F. H., Gnr.		31/ 8/14 2y 3m, Sgt.
FOSTER, G., Tpr. 3 L.H.		4/ 5/15 1y. Major.
FOSTER, H., Major 26 Bn.		7/11/16 2y 11m. Pte.
FOSTER, H. J., Pte. 12 Bn.	12 Bn.	24/ 7/18 1y 4m. Pte.
FOSTER, H. H., Pte. 3 G.S.R.	W., M.C.	22/ 2/16 3y 5m. Capt.
FOSTER, H. L., Lieut. 40 Bn.	W.	1/ 8/15 .
FOSTER, L. G., Pte. 12 Bn.	3W., M.I.D. ✠ 23/8/18.	28/ 8/14 Major ✠
FOSTER, J. A., Sec.-Lt. 12 Bn.		18/ 6/17 2y 3m. Tpr.
FOSTER, M. W., Tpr. 3 L.H.	W.	11/ 8/15 2y 8m, Pte.
FOSTER, O. R. H., Pte. 15 Bn.		12/ 3/17 Pte.
FOSTER, R., Pte. A.M.C.	✠ 9/10/17	2/ 5/16 Pte. ✠
FOSTER, T. G., Pte. 12 Bn.		16/ 4/16 3y 5m, Pte.
FOWLER, A. G., Pte. 40 Bn.	✠ 6/10/17.	26/ 1/16 Pte. ✠
FOWLER, A. G. W., Pte. 40 Bn.	47 Bn.	17/ 8/15 3y 8m, Cpl.
FOWLER, G. H., Pte. 15 Bn.		25/ 6/17 2y 2m. Gnr.
FOWLER, L., Gnr. 36 H.A.G.	W. ✠ 13/10/17.	14/ 3/16 Pte. ✠
FOWLER, P. L., Pte. 40 Bn.	W.	22/ 1/17 2y 7m, Pte.
FOX, A. J. E., Pte. 40 Bn.	W.	28/ 3/16 2y. Pte.
FOX, A. R., Pte. 12 Bn.		27/ 9/16 2y 3m, Pte.
FOX, A. J., Pte. 10 Fd. Amb.		13/ 4/16 2y 1m. Pte.
FOX, C. F., Pte. 40 Bn.	W., 15 Bn.	26/ 1/15 4y 0m. Pte.
FOX, E., Pte. 40 Bn.	W.	24/ 8/15 L.-Cpl.
FOX, E. J. L., Tpr. 3 L.H.	2W., M.M., Anzac Police.	13/ 9/14 4y 6m, L-Cpl.
FOX, F. R., Pte. 12 Bn.	W., M.M.	3/ 5/16 3y 5m, Pte.
FOX, J., Pte. 12 Bn.		9/ 4/18
FOX, John, Pte. 2 G.S.R.	✠ 29/10/16.	12/10/15 Pte. ✠
FOX, L. V., Pte. 12 Bn.	4 G.S.R.	4/10/17
FOX, R. E., Pte. 1 G.S.R.	W. ✠ 20/9/18.	7/ 8/16 Pte.
FOX, T. J., Pte. 12 Bn.	W.	21/ 3/16 3y 7m, Dvr.
FOX, W. F., Pte. 40 Bn.	W.	29/10/15 3y 6m, Pte.
FRA, F. A. L., Pte. Pstl Cpr.	W., 4 M.G. Coy.	29/ 1/15 4y 10m, Pte.
FRA, A., Pte. 15 Bn.	W.	22/ 8/14 1y 7m, Pte.
FRA, C. A. F., Pte. 12 Bn.		8/ 3/15 1y 5m, Pte.
FRAHM, W. A., Pte. 7 Fd. Amb.	⁘ D.S. Coy.	14/ 4/15 4y 3m, L-Cpl.
FRAKE, G., Pte. 26 Bn.	5⁻ Bn.	21/ 3/16 3y 6m, Cpl.
FRANCIS, C. G., Pte. 12 Bn.	✠ 28/11/16.	21/ 1/16 Spr. ✠
FRANCIS, H. F., Spr. 3 Tnlrs.	P.O.W.	17/ 7/15 Pte.
FRANCIS, P. S., Pte. 15 Bn.	M.M.	15/ 5/16 2y 9m. Cpl.
FRANCOMBE, D. C., Pte. 40 Bn.	W.	13/ 3/16 2y 4m, Pte.
FRANCOMBE, E. E., Pte. 40 Bn.		2/ 6/15 2y, Spr.
FRANCOMBE, G., Pte. 1 A.H.		1/ 9/14 4y 9m, Pte.
FRANCOMBE, Q. L., Pte. 1 A.G.H.		19/ 9/14 Pte. ✠
FRANCOMBE, V. E., Pte. 15 Bn.	✠ 31/5/15.	21/12/17 1y 10m, Pte.
FRANKLIN, G. J., Pte. 12 Bn.	W.	6/ 6/17 2y 5m. Pte.
FRANKLIN, G. C., Pte. 1 G.S.R.	40 Bn.	15/12/17 1y 9m. Pte.
FRANKLIN, G. C. H., Pte. 12 Bn.	W.	5/ 4/16 3y 4m. Pte.
FRANKLIN, J. R., Pte. 40 Bn.	2W.	5/ 7/15 Pte. ✠
FRANKS, E. J., Pte. 12 Bn.	✠ 19-22/8/16.	12/ 6/18 1y 2m, Pte.
FRANKS, J., Pte. 3 G.S.R.	12 Bn.	4/ 9/15 4y. Lieut.
FRANKS, L., Pte. 15 Bn.	W., M.M., D.C.M., 48 Bn., 47 Bn.	26/ 6/15 3y 5m, L-Cpl.
FRANKS, R., Pte. 26 Bn.	W., 40 Bn.	2/ 4/18 1y 6m, Dvr.
FRASER, A., Gnr. 11 F.A.B.	W.	31/ 7/16 3y 2m, Pte.
FRASER, A. W., Pte. 4 M.G. Co.	W., 15 Bn.	24/ 8/15 Pte. ✠
FRASER, C. A., Pte. 12 Bn.	✠ 23-26/7/16.	3/ 8/15 3y 8m, Pte.
FRASER, F. J., Pte. 26 Bn.	W., 12 Bn.	11/ 9/17 2y 3m. Pte.
FRASER, G., Pte. 40 Bn.		4/ 8/15 2y 5m. Pte.
FRASER, G. A., Pte. 12 Bn.	2W.	20/ 9/14 Spr. ✠
FRASER, H. V. R., Cpl. 12 Bn.	✠ 10/6/15.	29/11/15 3y 7m. Spr.
FRASER, J. L., Spr. Engrs.		15/ 2/15 2y 7m, Spr.
FRASER, N. G., Pte. 12 Bn.	W.	18/11/15 4y, Spr.
FRASER, W. A., Spr. 3 Mnrs.	A.E.M.M. and B. Coy.	9/10/16 Pte. ✠
FREE, W. T., Pte. 40 Bn.	✠ 17/4/17.	26/ 2/15 1y 11m, Gnr.
FREELAND, J. D., Gnr. 9 Bty.		25/ 6/15 4y 2m, Pte.
FREEMAN, A. F., Pte. 26 Bn.		8/10/15 1y 7m, Pte.
FREEMAN, A. L., Pte. 12 Bn.	A. Police.	

NAME.	REMARKS.	RANK ON DISCHARGE. ENLISTED, SERVICE.
FREEMAN, B., Gnr. 113 H. Bty.		3d/ 8/16 2y 8m, Pte.
FREEMAN, E. W., Pte. 40 Bn.	W.	19/ 6/16 3y 3m Pte.
FREEMAN, F. L., Pte. 12 Bn.	W.	12/ 4/16 1y 9m, Pte.
FREEMAN, G. J. E., Pte. 12 Bn.	W., 52 Bn., 51 Bn.	2/ 8/15 4y, Cpl.
FREEMAN, I. J., Pte. 7 Fd Amb	M.M., 13 Fd. Amb.	22/ 2/15 4y 3m, Pte.
FREEMAN, L. G., Pte. 4 M.G. Co	P.O.W.	7/ 8/16 Pte.
FREEMAN, L. J., Dvr. 6 F.A.B.	W.	15/ 9/15 2y 3m, Dvr.
FREEMAN, M. V., Pte. 12 Bn.	52 Bn. ✽ 28/3/17.	13/ 7/15 Pte. ✽
FREEMAN, R. W., Gnr. Arty.	2 D.A.C., 2 D.Hqtrs.	24/10/16 2y 10m, L-Cpl.
FREEMAN, T. D., Pte. 1 A.C.H.		20/11/14 1y 11m, Pte.
FREEMAN, W. H., Pte. 12 Bn.	4 Sal. Coy.	15/ 7/15 4y 1m, Pte.
FREEMAN, W. G., Spr. 3 Fd. Co.		13/11/15
FREEMAN, W. H. D., Pte. 15 Bn.		29/ 9/14 1y 4m, Pte.
FREER, J. R., Pte. 26 Bn.	W., 52 Bn. ✽ 9/6/17.	26/ 3/15 Pte. ✽
FREESTONE, J. A., 40 Bn.	4W.	19/ 2/16 3y 6m, Cpl.
FREESTONE, T., Pte. 40 Bn.	W., 26 Bn.	17/ 4/16 2y 11m. Pte.
FREIBOTH, A. W., Gnr. 5 F.A.B.	W.	11/10/15 Gnr.
FRENCH, A. D., Pte. 40 Bn.	2W., M.M., 49 Bn.	17/ 4/16 3y. L.-Cpl.
FRENCH, A. C., Spr. 3 L.H.R.	D.C.M., 18 Camel Cps.	1/ 8/16 4y 4m, R.S.M.
FRENCH, B. M., Tpr., 3 L.H.		16/ 9/14 2y, Tpr.
FRENCH, B., Whlr. 4 A.S.C.	W., 18 A.S.C.	14/ 9/14 W.S.S.
FRENCH, C. C., Pte. 12 Bn.	W. 58 Bn.	4/ 9/15 2y 11m, Pte.
FRENCH, E. B., Pte. 40 Bn.	W.	2/ 2/16 1y 11m, Pte.
FRENCH, G. R., Pte. 12 Bn.	✽ 23-25/7/16.	21/ 7/15 Pte. ✽
FRENCH, G. S., Pte. A.A.M.C.	3 L.H.R.	3/ 4/18 1y 4m, Tpr.
FRENCH, H. D., L.-Sgt. 15 Bn.		12/ 1/15 1y 6m, L.-Sgt.
FRENCH, H. L. W., Pte. 12 Bn.		10/12/17 Pte.
FRENCH, H. R., Pte. 3 L.H.R.		24/ 8/14 4y 6m, Spr.
FRENCH, J., Pte. 40 Bn.		28/ 1/16 Pte.
FRENCH, K. R., Gnr. Arty.	4 D.A.C.	14/10/16 2y 11m, Dvr.
FRENCH, L. E., Pte. 12 Bn.	M.M., 58 Bn., 57 Bn.	2/ 9/15 4y 2m. Lieut.
FRENCH, R. R., Gnr. 3 F. Arty.	✽ 4/9/18.	20/11/16 Gnr. ✽
FRENCH, R. W., Gnr. 2 F.A.B.		16/ 2/16 3y 7m, Gnr.
FRENCH, S., Dvr. 12 Bn.	5 Div. Train.	15/ 7/15 4y 1m, Dvr.
FRENCH, V. V., Pte. 12 Bn.	21 Bn., P.O.W.	23/ 9/15 Pte.
FRENCH, V. A., Pte. 12 Bn.	W. ✽ 25-28/4/15.	20/ 8/14 Pte. ✽
FRENCH, W. B., Pte. 40 Bn.	2W.	3/ 2/16 2y 2m, Pte.
FRENCH, W., Tpr. 3 L.H.	✽ 1/6/16.	14/ 9/15 Tpr. ✽
FRENCH, W. V., Tpr. 3 L.H.	M.M., 2 D.A.S.P.	15/10/15 4y 2m, M.T.D
FRESHNEY, C. E., Pte. 15 Bn.	2W., M.M., 10 F.A.B.	13/ 8/15 3y 9m, Dvr.
FRESHNEY, C. T., Pte. 40 Bn.		8/ 8/17 2y 4m, Pte.
FRENEY, J. T., Gnr. 36 H.A.G.		28/10/17 1y, Gnr.
FRIER, J. Y., Spr. 6 Fd. Co.	26 Bn. ✽ 28/5/18.	24/ 8/15 Pte. ✽
FRIGERIO, J. M., Pte. 1 A.C.H.	2 Fd. Amb.	19/ 9/14
FRITZELL, A. C., Pte. 1 G.S.R.	4 D.A.C.	12/ 2/18 1y 8m, Dvr.
FRIMLEY, B., Pte. 26 Bn.	47 Bn. ✽ 7/8/16.	10/ 8/15 Pte. ✽
FRIMLEY, C. P., Pte. 26 Bn.	12 Bn.	10/ 8/15 3y 8m, Pte.
FRIMLEY, H., Pte. 40 Bn.	W.	10/ 2/16 3y 1m, Pte.
FRITH, A. W., Dvr. D.A.C.	6 F.A. Bde. ✽ 13/8/18.	28/ 8/15 Cpl. ✽
FRITH, R., V.O. Cpl. T.M. Bty.	23 Bn. ✽ 19/8/18.	30/10/16 Pte. ✽
FRITH, W. E., Gnr. 6 F.A. Bde.		17/ 1/16 3y 9m, Bdr.
FRITZELL, A. C., Gnr. 1 G.S.R.		12/ 2/18 1y 8m, G.r.
FROST, F. V., Pte. 40 Bn.	W.	5/ 7/16 1y 6m, Pte.
FROST, H. C., Pte. 26 Bn.	2W. ✽ 30/8/18.	24/ 9/15 Pte. ✽
FROST, J. H., Pte. 40 Bn.	23 M.G. Coy.	18/10/16 3y 1m, Pte.
FROST, W. J., Pte. 12 Bn.	W.	12/10/15 4y 1m, Pte.
FROST, W., C.Q.S., 1 G.S.R.		21/ 2/17 2y 2m, C.Q.M.S
FROST, W., Sig. 15 Bn.		24/11/14 1y 7m, Sgnr.
FROST, W. J., Pte. 12 Bn.		29/ 8/14 1y, Pte.
FRY, A. L., Pte. T.M. Bty.	40 Bn.	3/ 1/17 1y 10m, Pte.
FRY, E. L., Pte. 12 Bn.	52 Bn.	20/ 9/14 5y 1m, Pte.
FRY, E. S. G., Gnr. F.A. Ref.	5 F.A.B.	18/ 4/17 2y 9m, Gnr.
FRY, G. H., Pte. 12 Bn.		27/ 4/16 3y, Pte.
FRY, G. L., Pte. 12 Bn.		20/ 8/14
FRY, L., Pte. 12 Bn.	2W., 51 Bn.	2/12/14 4y 10m, Pte.
FRY, S. P., Pte. 12 Bn.	W.	26/ 2/16 2v 5m, Pte.
FULLBROOK, G. H., Pte. 40 Bn.	2W.	1/ 8/16 3y 3m, Sgt.
FULLER, W. E., Spr. 8 F.C.E.	W.	1/ 2/16 3y 6m, W.O.
FULLERTON, D. J., Pte. 12 Bn.	2W., 4 M.G. Bn.	6/ 8/15 4y, Pte.
FULLWOOD, A., Pte. 12 Bn.	✽ 23-25/7/16.	25/ 8/14 4y 10m, Lieut.
FULTON, A. D., Dvr. 3 F.A. B.		26/ 8/14 4y 6m, Bdr.
FULTON, A. J., Pte. 12 Bn.	40 Bn.	18/11/16 Pte.
FULTON, G. W., Sgt. 12 Bn.	M.S.M., 4 Div. A. Hdqtrs.	27/ 7/15 3y 11m, W.O.
FULTON, G. W., Pte. 40 Bn.	W.	3/10/16 2y 11m, Pte.
FULTON, J., Pte. 12 Bn.		31/ 8/14
FULTON, J. L., Pte. 1 G.S.R.		21/ 1/18 1y 9m, Pte.
FULTON, W. H., Pte. 12 Bn.	✽ 7/8/15.	25/11 14 Pte. ✽
FURLONG, C. G. H. de L., Pte. 4 M.G. Co.		13/12/16 2y 7m, Pte.
FURMAGE, L. S., Pte. 40 Bn.		5/ 6/17 2y 2m, Pte.
FURMAGE, T. G. R., Pte. 12 Bn.	✽ 10/3/18.	15/ 5/16 Pte. ✽
FYSH, H. F., Pte. 1 A.C.G.		21/ 2/15 1y 8m, Pte.
FYSH, Hy. F., Dvr. 3 F.A.B.	21 F.A.B.	25/ 9/14 3y 3m, Gnr.
FYSH, H., Tpr. 3 L.H.R.	D.F.C.T., 1 M.G. Sqn., A.F.C.	25/ 8/14 Pte.
FYSH, P. O., 2nd Lt. M.T. Co.	A.F.C.	22/ 1/18 1y 7m, 2nd-Lt
GAMMON, G. C., Spr. 3 Fd. Co.	Motor Transport.	9/ 8/15 3y 11m, Sgt.
GANDY, G. T., 2nd. Lt, 12 Bn.	W., M.C., 69 Bn., 12 Bn.	21/10/15 Lieut.

TASMANIA'S MUSTER ROLL.

NAME.	REMARKS.	RANK ON DISCHARGE. ENLISTED, SERVICE.
GANDY, W. A., M.W.	War Worker.	
GANNON, P. A., Pte. Tnlrs.		2/ 3/16
GANNON, W., Spr. 4 Miners.	A.E.M., M. and B. Co.	16/ 3/16 3y 7m, Spr.
GARCIE, T. G., Pte. 12 Bn.		14/11/16 2y 4m, Pte.
GARD, J. H., Capt. 40 Bn.	✳ 31/7/18.	22/ 4/16 Capt. ✳
GARDAM, A. C., Pte. 12 Bn.		25/ 5/16 1y 7m, Pte.
GARDAM, B., Pte. 12 Bn.		16/10/16.
GARDAM, V. R., Pte. 12 Bn.	W.	21/10/16 2y 6m, Dvr.
GARDHAM, H. L., Pte. 15 Bn.	W.	29/ 7/15 3y 10m, Pte.
GARDNER, A., Pte. 40 Bn.		29/11/16 2y 8m, Pte.
GARDNER, G. R., Pte. 3 L.H.		12/ 9/14 4y 11m, Lieut.
GARDINER, H. G., Pte. 26 Bn.	W. ✳ 5/10/17.	5/ 5/15 Pte. ✳
GARDINER, J. W., Pte. 40 Bn.	M.M., A.L.B.G.R.O. Co.	26/ 9/16 3y, Spr.
GARDINER, J. J. R., Pte. 12 Bn.	W. ✳ 24/4/15.	31/ 7/16 Pte. ✳
GARDINER, R. A., Pte. Wireless.	Cav. Div. Sig. Sqn.	26/ 9/16 2y 9m, Spr.
GARDNER, H. W., Pte. 12 Bn.	✳ 5-10/4/17.	2/ 5/16 Pte. ✳
GARDNER, J. T., Pte. 40 Bn.		15/ 7/16.
GARDNER, P., Pte. 12 Bn.	2 W., 40 Bn.	7/ 4/16 2y 11m, Pte.
GARDNER, R. E., Pte. 26 Bn.	3 L.H.	12/ 3/15 4y 6m, Cpl.
GARITY, M. H., Pte. 40 Bn.		2/ 2/16 1y 9m, Pte.
GARITY, T. C., Gnr. 15 Fd. Arty.	3 D.A.C.	11/10/16 2y 11m, Dvr.
GARLAND, A. C., Pte. 40 Bn.		6/ 3/16 3y 7m, Dvr.
GARLAND, E. J., Pte. A.M.C.	W.	14/ 2/16 2y 1m, Pte.
GARLAND, G. V., Pte. 12 Bn.	2W., 1 Pnrs.	8/ 7/15.
GARLAND, G. M., Pte. 12 Bn.	W.	22/11/17 1y 3m, Pte.
GARLAND, J. A., Pte. 4 M.G.C.		9/10/16.
GARLAND, J. A., Pte. 1 G.S.R.	101 How. Bty.	11/ 2/18 1y 3m, Dvr.
GARLAND, J. H., Pte. 40 Bn.	W., 49 Bn.	18/ 4/16 3y 5m, Pte.
GARLAND, S. J., Pte. 12 Bn.	✳ 24/10/15.	8/ 7/15 Pte. ✳
GARLAND, T. J., Pte. 4 M.G. Co.		9/10/16 7m, Pte.
GABY, P. F., Sgt. 40 Bn.		4/11/15 2y, Sgt.
GADD, C. H., Sig. 12 Bn.		22/ 7/15.
GADD, L. V., Pte. 26 Bn.	W. ✳ 5/11/16.	27/ 9/15 Pte. ✳
GADD, T. L., Pte. 5 G.S.R.	1 D.A.C.	19/ 8/18 1y 2m, Pte.
GADD, W. M., Pte. 12 Bn.	✳ 15/4/17.	16/11/15 Pte. ✳
GADSBURY, E. J., Pte. 12 Bn.	W. ✳ 22/7/17.	1/ 5/16 Pte. ✳
GADSDEN, E. G., Pte. 12 Bn.	W., 4 M.G. Co. ✳ 16/8/17.	14/ 4/15 L.-Cpl. ✳
GAFFNEY, J. B., Pte. 12 Bn.	W., 26 Bn., 12 Bn.	19/ 7/15.
GAFFNEY, J. H., Pte. 12 Bn.	M.M., 3 L.T.M. Bty.	2/12/15 3y 5m, L.-Cpl.
GAGE, H. C., Pte. Remounts.	Mobile Vet. Cps.	8/10/15 2y, Pte.
GALE, A. J., Pte. 12 Bn.	40 Bn. ✳ 28/3/18.	17/ 4/17 Pte. ✳
GALE, A. M., Pte. 26 Bn.		11/ 6/15 3y 9m, Pte.
GALE, F. L., Pte. 40 Bn.	✳ 30/8/18.	8/ 2/16 Pte. ✳
GALE, F. G., Pte. 15 Bn.	3W., M.I.D.	19/ 9/14 3y 3m, Sgt.
GALE, L. T., Pte. 40 Bn.	W.	8/ 2/16 2y 1m, Pte.
GALE, W. G., Pte. 40 Bn.	D.C.M.	8/ 2/16 3y 7m, Pte.
GALL, A. J., Lt. Dental Dtls.	1 A.D.H.	1/ 2/16 3y 7m, Capt.
GALL, S. D., Pte. 40 Bn.		14/ 3/16 1y 8m, Pte.
GALLAGHER, B., Gnr. Arty.		14/ 8/17 1y 1m, Gnr.
GALLAHAR, C., Gnr. 6 A.F.A.		25/10/15.
GALLAHER, H., Pte. 40 Bn.	15 Bn., 40 Bn.	10/ 3/16.
GALLAHER, M. V., Tpr. 3 L.H.	W.	8/ 9/15 3y 7m, Gnr.
GALLAHER, P., Pte. 12 Bn.		16/10/16 3y 1m, Pte.
GALLAHER, T. M. P., Pte. 12 Bn	2W., 52 Bn. ✳ 6/12/16.	7/12/15 Pte. ✳
GALLAHER, V. M., Pte. 26 Bn.	3W.	20/ 4/15 4y, Sgt.
GALLAHER, W. C., Pte. 26 Bn.		17/ 3/15 11m, Pte.
GALLOWAY, A. O., Pte. 40 Bn.		1/ 5/16 3y 8m, Pte.
GALLOWAY, J., Pte. 40 Bn.	✳ 14/1/17.	1/ 5/16 Cpl. ✳
GALLOWAY, W. F., Pte. 2 G.S.R.		3/ 6/18.
GALLPEN, R. E., Pte. 2 A.G.H.		3/ 8/15 2y 3m, Pte.
GAME, P. O., Pte. 40 Bn.		26/10/16 2y 1m, Pte.
GAME, S. J., Cpl. 40 Bn.	✳ 7/6/17.	26/ 1/16 Sgt. ✳
GARLICK, D., Pte. 40 Bn.		1/ 8/17 1y 7m, Pte.
GARLICK, E. G., Pte. 12 Bn.	W.	2/ 2/16 2y 10m, Pte.
GARLICK, G. C., Pte. 40 Bn.	✳ 19/3/17.	21/ 2/16 Pte. ✳
GARLICK, L. R., Pte. 40 Bn.	2W.	21/ 2/16 3y 7m, Pte.
GARLICK, L., Pte. 12 Bn.	52 Bn. ✳ 7/6/17.	4/ 8/15 Pte. ✳
GARLICK, W. W., Pte. 40 Bn.	W., 51 Bn.	27/ 1/16 3y 8m, Pte.
GARNER, S. G., Pte. 2 G.S.R.		7/ 6/18 1y 6m, Pte.
GARRARD, G., Pte. 4 M.G. Co.		2/ 9/16 3y, Pte.
GARRARD, W. L., Spr. 12 Bn.		19/ 8/14.
GARRETT, B. B., Pte. A.A.M.C.		2 2/17.
GARRETT, M. R., Pte. 15 Bn.	W. P.O.W	24/10/14 4y 8m, Sgt.
GARRETT, R. R., Pte. 40 Bn.	2W.	24/ 2/16 3y 7m, Pte.
GARRETT, T., Pte. 26 Bn.		21/ 7/15 4y 1m, Pte.
GARROD, H. C., Dvr. 9 Fd. Bty.		31/ 8/14 4y 6m, L.-Cpl.
GARROD, L. G., Pte. 12 Bn.	103 How. Bty.	20/11/16 2y 10m, Dvr.
GARROD, W. G., Dvr. 9 Fd. Bty.		27/ 8/14 4y 6m, Gnr.
GARROD, W. L., Sgt. 12 Bn.		19/ 8/14.
GARTH, J. L. G., Pte. 40 Bn.	W.	4/ 1/16 2y 11m, Pte.
GARVIN, F. J., Pte. 40 Bn.		1/ 5/16 3y 3m, L.-Cpl.
GARWOOD, G. H., Pte. 12 Bn.	W.	29/ 1/15 3y 6m, Pte.
GARWOOD, L. M., Spr. 8 Fd. Co.	12 Fd. Co.	5/10/15 2y 10m, Spr.
GARWOOD, T. W., Pte. 12 Bn.	2W.	18/12/14.
GARWOOD, V., Pte. 26 Bn.	2W., A.L.R.O. Co.	27/ 7/15 4y 4m, Spr.
GARWOOD, W. G., L.-Cpl. 12 Bn.	2W.	24/ 8/15 4y, Cpl.

NAME.	REMARKS.	RANK ON DISCHARGE. ENLISTED. SERVICE.
GATEHOUSE, H. G., Spr. Miners.		24/11/15 3y 3m, Spr.
GATEHOUSE, H. G., Pte. 12 Bn.	W.	16/10/16 2y 11m, Pte.
GATENBY, J. J., Sgt. 40 Bn.	2W.	7/ 3/16 2y, Lieut.
GATENBY, L. F., Tpr. 3 L.H.	40 Bn. ✢ 14/1/17.	20/ 8/14 Sgt. ✢
GATES, E. W., Gnr. 6 F.A.B.		16/10/15 1y 3m, Bdr.
GATES, H. J., Pte. 26 Bn.	✢ 6/8/16.	14/ 8/15 Pte. ✢
GATES, H. J., Pte. 12 Bn.	W.	24/ 7/15 3y 11m, Pte.
GATES, S. J., Tpr. 3 L.H.		4/ 3/17 2y 6m, Tpr.
GATTY, C. G., Pte. Rly.		5/ 1/18 3m, Pte.
GATTY, L. F., Pte. 40 Bn.	W.	14/ 3/16 3y 5m, Pte.
GAUNT, F. A., Bdr. 9 Fd. Bty.		27/ 8/14 4y 5m, Lieut.
GAWNE, J., Pte. A.A.M.C.		6/ 5/17
GAYLE, B. G., Pte. 12 Bn.	W.	10/ 8/15 1y 10m, L.-Cpl.
GAYLE, R. G.		
GEALE, E. G., Pte. 3 L.H.	5 Div. Arty.	10/ 8/15 1y 7m, Gnr.
GEALE, F. F., Pte. 40 Bn.	51 Bn. ✢ 13/9/17.	2/ 2/16 Pte. ✢
GEALE, J. W., Pte. 12 Bn.	✢ 15/10/16.	11/ 1/16 Pte. ✢
GEAR, M., Pte. 12 Bn.		10/ 4/16 9m, Pte.
GEARD, A. S. J., Gnr. Arty.	103 How. Bty.	17/ 1/17 2y 10m, Gnr.
GEARD, E. S., Pte. 12 Bn	✢ 8/4/17.	4/ 4/16 Pte. ✢
GEARD, V. A., R.Q.M.S., 12 Bn.		21/ 5/17 2y 1m, R.Q.M.S.
GEARD, V., Pte. 8 Bn.	M.M.	11/ 8/14 4y 8m, Pte.
GEARD. W. S., Spr. Miners.	2 Tnl. Co.	12/11/15 1y 9m, Spr.
GEARING, W. J., Pte. 12 Bn.	2W., 52 Bn.	19 /7/15.
GEARRING, J., Pte. 40 Bn.	2W., 15 Bn.	15/ 3/16.
GEARY, A. E., Pte. 12 Bn.	W., 51 Bn.	25/ 8/14.
GEE, H., Pte. 40 Bn.	W.	7/10/16 1y 4m, Pte.
GEE, R. S., Lt. 3 F.A.B.	2W., D.S.O., M.I.D.	18/ 8/14 4y 8m, Mjr.
GEEVES, C., Pte. 40 Bn.		5/ 6/17 1y 5m, Pte.
GEEVES, F., Pte. 2 G.S.R.	40 Bn.	14/ 5/17 2y 5m, Pte.
GEEVES, A. J., Spr. 1 A.C.H.		20/10/14.
GEEVES, L. H., Pte. 12 Bn.	✢ 4/4/16.	21/ 1/15 Spr. ✢
GEEVES, R. C., Pte. 26 Bn.		18/ 5/15 4y 5m, Pte.
GEEVES, W. C., L.-Cpl. 12 Bn.	W.	22/ 7/15 3y 9m, Cpl.
GELLIBRAND, J., Capt. 1 D.H.Q.	2W., D.S.O., Bar, C.B., Legion d'Honneur. Croix de Guerre, Amer., D.S.M., K.C.B., 5 M.I.D., 2 D.H.Q., 12 Bn., 6 Inf. Bde., 12 Inf. Bde., 3 Division.	20/ 8/14 5y, Mjr-Gen.
GELLIE, H. G., Pte. 26 Bn.		2nd Lieut.
GELLIE, H. W., Pte. 15 Bn.		10/12/14 1y 8m, Cpl.
GELLIE, H. P., Gnr. 3 F.A.B.	W.	30/ 3/15 3y 1m, Fitter.
GELLIE, M., Pte. 26 Bn.	✢ 5/8/16.	18/ 3/15 Pte. ✢
GEMMELL, J. W., Gnr. Arty.		30/11/16.
GENDERS, H. C., L.-Cpl. 40 Bn.	W.	15/ 3/16 3y 4m, L.-Cpl.
GEORGE, E. A., Pte. 40 Bn.	W.	23/ 6/16 2y 3m, L.-Cpl.
GEORGE, H. E., Pte. 12 Bn.	W., M.M.	19/ 8/14 4y 6m, Sgt.
GEORGE, J. H., Pte. 40 Bn.		16/ 3/18.
GEORGE, O. W., Pte. 12 Bn.	2W.	13/ 1/16 3y 3m, Pte.
GERKE, R. O., Tpr. 2 G.S.R.		30/ 4/18 1y 4m, Tpr.
GERKE, W. L., Tpr. 2 G.S.R.		30/ 4/18 1y 5m, Tpr.
GERLACH, C. A. F., Pte. 40 Bn.		9/10/16 2y 11m, Pte.
GERRAND, E., Pte. 26 Bn.		6/ 5/15 1y 5m, Pte.
GHANANBURGH, C. W., Pte 1 G.S.R		24/ 1/18.
GHERKIE, F. G., Pte. 12 Bn.		Pte.
GIBB, R. F., Pte. 12 Bn.		31/ 8/14.
GIBBENS, E. E., Pte. 12 Bn.	W.	2/10/17 2y, Pte.
GIBBONS, A. J., Pte. 15 Bn.		21/11/14 Cpl.
GIBBONS, F. J., Pte. 26 Bn.	✢ 29/7/16.	21/ 7/15 L.-Cpl. ✢
GIBBONS, G. J., Pte. 12 Bn.		20/ 9/14.
GIBBONS, G. J. A., Pte. 12 Bn.	5W.	28/ 7/15 3y 9m, Pte.
GIBBONS, T., Gnr. Arty.		12/10/16.
GIBBONS, T. W., N. and Labourers.		
GIBBONS, W. A., Pte. 3 G.S.R.	12 Bn.	6/ 8/18 1y 3m, Pte.
GIBBONS, W., Pte. 15 Bn.	4 Pnr. Bn ✢ 5/8/16.	27/ 7/15 Pte. ✢
GIBBS, G. H., Pte. 12 Bn.	✢ 23/6/15.	22/ 8/14 Pte. ✢
GIBBS, J., Pte. M.G. Co.		8/11/16 1y 2m, Pte.
GIBBS, J. F. L., Pte. 12 Bn.		14/ 4/15 1y 2m, L.-Cpl.
GIBLIN, L. F., Capt. 40 Bn.	2W., D.S.O., M.C., M.I.D.	1/ 3/16 3y 7m, Mjr.
GIBLIN, W. W., Lt.-Col. 1 A.C.H.	C.B., M.I.D.	3/10/14 2y 6m, Col.
GIBSON, P., Lt. 15 Bn.	✢ 8/8/15.	24/ 5/15 Lieut. ✢
GIBSON, S. G., Capt. A.A.M.C.	2W., M.C., 1 A.G.H., 56 Bn.	9/ 5/19 3y 4m, Capt.
GIBSON, A. W., Pte. 15 Bn.	45 Bn.	18/ 6/15.
GIBSON, A., Gnr. Fd. Arty.	23 How., 109 Bty.	20/ 1/16 3y 8m, Dvr.
GIBSON, A. G., Pte. 12 Bn.	✢ 10/6/15.	27/ 8/14 Pte. ✢
GIBSON, C., Cpl. 4 A.S.C.		4/12/14 3y 2m, Cpl.
GIBSON, E. M., Gnr. Arty.	9 Bty.	11/ 4/17 2y 7m, Gnr.
GIBSON, G. A., Pte. 3 G.S.R.		5/ 1/18 1y 2m, Pte.
GIBSON, G. W., Spr. 26 Bn.	W. 12 Bn.	9/ 4/15 4y 9m, Lieut.
GIBSON, J. B., Tpr. 3 L.H.	A.O.C.	9/ 4/15 4y 4m, Pte.
GIBSON, J. R., Gnr. Arty.	W.	11/ 5/16 3y 3m, Gnr.
GIBSON, M. G., Gnr. 36 H.A.G.		22/12/17.
GIBSON, P. G., Pte. 40 Bn.	✢ 5/10/17.	30/ 9/16 Pte. ✢
GIBSON, W. E., Pte. 12 Bn.	W.	5/ 4/16 3y 2m, Pte.
GIBSON, W. H., Pte. 2 G.S.R.		28/11/17 1y 10m, Pte.
GIBSON, W. J., Pte. 15 Bn.	2W., 12 Bn.	27/ 7/15 3y 9m, Dvr.
GIBSON, W. R., Pte. 12 Bn.		18/ 8/15 1y 2m, Pte.

TASMANIA'S MUSTER ROLL. 273

NAME.	REMARKS.	RANK ON DISCHARGE. ENLISTED, SERVICE.
GIFFORD, J. F., Pte. 12 Bn.		8/12/14 3y 4m, Pte.
GILBERT, A. E., Tpr. 3 L.H.		16/ 4/17 2y 3m, Tpr.
GILBERT, E. A., Pte. 12 Bn.	2W.	13/ 7/15 3y 10m, Pte.
GILBERT, F. B., Pte. 26 Bn.	W.	15/ 4/15 4y 4m, Pte.
GILBERT, G. J., Gnr. Arty.		9/ 5/17.
GILBERT, G. R., Pte. 15 Bn.	✣ 21/2/17.	20/11/14 Sgt. ✣
GILBERT, H. R., Pte. 12 Bn.	W.	29/ 8/14 4y 5m, Pte.
GILBERT, J., Pte. 3 G.S.R.		8/ 4/18 1y 5m, Pte.
GILBERT, K. N., Pte. 12 Bn.	✣ 6/12/16.	14/ 9/15 Pte. ✣
GILBERT, R. E., Gnr. Arty.	W.	15/ 3/16.
GILBERT, R. E., Pte. 40 Bn.	✣ 31/1/17.	4/ 5/16 Pte. ✣
GILBERT, W. E., Pte. 12 Bn.	W. ✣ 19-22/8/16.	9/ 8/15 Pte. ✣
GILES, A., Pte. 40 Bn.		5/ 6/16 2y 1m, Pte.
GILHAM, C. H. R., Pte. 12 Bn.	W., 5z Bn. ✣ 3-4/9/16.	9/ 9/15 Pte. ✣
GILHAM, C. R., Pte. 12 Bn.		30/10/16.
GILHAM, L. P. V. C., Cpl. 26 Bn.		30/ 4/15 1y 9m, Cpl.
GILHOGLEY, T., Spr. Miners.	W., 2 Tnl. Co.	4/10/15 3y 6m.
GILL, A. R., Gnr. 18 Fd. Bty.	17 Bty., 6 Bde.	4/ 8/15 4y, Bdr.
GILL, A. B., Pte. 4 M.G. Co.	W., 12 Bn.	15/12/17 1y 10m, Pte.
GILL, B., Pte. 3 Fd. Amb.	W., 2 Fd. Amb.	18/ 3/17. Pte.
GILL, C., Pte. 40 Bn.		31/ 7/16 2y 9m, Pte.
GILL, F., Tpr. 3 L.H.		11/12/17 1y 10m, Tpr.
GILL, L. A., Spr. 8 Fd. Co.	6 Fd. Co.	6/ 3/15 4y 9m, Spr.
GILL, L. A., L.-Cpl. 26 Bn.	3W.	27/ 7/15 3y 10m, Cpl.
GILL, P. H., Pte. 12 Bn.		27/ 7/15 2y 10m, Pte.
GILL, R. A., Pte. 40 Bn.		31/ 7/16 2y 8m, Pte.
GILL, T. H., Pte. 40 Bn.	W.	22/ 3/16 3y 7m, Pte.
GILL, V. N., Pte. A.F.C.	2 Sqn. A.F.C.	27/10/16 2y 9m, Cpl.
GILL, W., Pte. 12 Bn.	W.	23/ 8/15 2y 6m, Pte.
GILL, W. K., Pte. 12 Bn.	4W.	20/ 8/14 4y 6m, Lieut.
GILLAM, A. J., Pte. 40 Bn.	W.	21/ 5/16 3y 6m, Pte.
GILLAM, A. A., Pte. 26 Bn.	2W	24/ 3/15 2y 2m, Pte.
GILLAM, H., L.-Sgt. 40 Bn.	W. D.C.M., C. de G. (Belg.)	8/ 3/16 3y 5m, W.O.
GILLAM, J. T., Pte. Tnlrs.	2 Tnl. Co.	23/10/16 3y 1m, Spr.
GILLAM, R. S., Gnr. Arty.		15/ 9/15.
GILLAM, S. R., Pte. 12 Bn.	2W., M.M.	28/ 4/16 Pte.
GILLAM, W. A., Pte. 12 Bn.	✣ 23/6/15.	20/ 8/14 Pte. ✣
GILLARD, H., Pte. 12 Bn.	W.	20/ 8/14 4y 9m, Pte.
GILLARD, H. V., Gnr. 13 F.A.B.		20/ 2/17 2y 9m, Gnr.
GILLARD, S. J., Pte. 15 Bn.		22/ 6/15 Pte.
GILLESPIE, C. J., Pte. 12 Bn.	W.	28/ 7/15 4y. Pte.
GILLESPIE, C. L., Pte. Tnlrs.	W.	13/10/16 2y 2m, Pte.
GILLESPIE, J., Pte Tnlrs.		12/10/16 2y 3m, Spr.
GILLESPIE, J. C., Gnr. Arty.		14/12/16 2y 10m, Dvr.
GILLETT, R. O, R. J., Pte, Wireless		25/ 8/16 2y 10m, Pte.
GILLETT, W. L. J., Gnr. 18 Fd. Bty.	W.	17/ 9/15 3y 6m, Gnr.
GILLEY, L. A., Spr. 8 Fd. Co.	W. Army T. Co. Engr.	20/ 1/16 3y 8m Spr.
GILLIES, J., Pte. 12 Bn.	✣ 25-28/4/15.	26/ 8/14 Pte. ✣
GILLIE, T., Pte. 40 Bn.		30/10/16 2y 11m, Pte.
GILLIGAN, F. H., Pte. 26 Bn.		14/ 6/15 3y 10m, Cpl.
GILLIGAN, J., Pte. 15 Bn.		18/ 9/14 2y 4m, Pte.
GILLIGAN, J. D., Pte. 12 Bn.		1/ 8/16 3y 2m, Pte.
GILLON, P. H., Pte. A.S.C.	35 Co. M.D. Train.	1/11/17 2y, Pte.
GILYOTT, W. N., Gnr. 9 Fd Bty.	W.	27/ 5/14 3y 11m. Gnr.
GITTINS, G., Pte. 12 Bn.	W., 51 Bn.	5/10/15 3y 11m, Pte.
GITTUS, C., Pte. 12 Bn.	✣ 5-8/5/17.	28/ 9/16 Pte. ✣
GITTUS, K. J., Pte. 40 Bn.	✣ 2/4/17.	21/ 2/16 Pte. ✣
GITTUS, L. A., Pte. 12 Bn.	✣ 3/11/19.	28/ 9/16 Pte. ✣
GITTUS, W. H. A., Pte. 12 Bn.		8/11/15 4y 3m, Pte.
GLADMAN, C., Pte. 12 Bn.		23/11/16 2y 11m, Pte.
GLANN, H. W., Pte. 26 Bn.		14/11/17 6m, Pte.
GLANVILLE, H. T., Tpr. 3 L.H.		9/11/17 1y 9m, Tpr.
GLASGOW, C., Pte. 12 Bn.	✣ 25-28/4/15.	27/ 2/15.
GLASKIN, J. S., Pte. 1 G.S.R.		25/ 8/14 Pte.
GLASS, W. J., Pte. 2 G.S.R.	12 Bn.	13/ 4/18 1y 9m, Pte.
GLASSER, H., Pte. 40 Bn.	W.	10/ 2/16 3y 3m, Pte.
GLEADOW, G. D., Pte. A.A.M.C.	1 Fd. Amb.	1/ 5/16 3y 5m, Pte.
GLEADLOW, J. R., Dvr. 3 F.A.B.		1/ 5/16 2y 9m, Dvr.
GLEESON, A., Pte. 3 G.S.R.	12 Bn.	1/ 7/18 1y 3m, Pte.
GLEESON, C. O., Tpr. 3 L.H.		12/ 9/14 4y 5m, Tpr.
GLEESON, D., Pte. 40 Bn.	2W.	21/ 3/16 3y 6m, Pte.
GLEESON, F., Pte. A.A.M.C.		2/ 5/17 2y 4m, Pte.
GLEESON, J., Pte. 12 Bn.		24/ 1/14 2y 5m, Pte.
GLEESON, M. N., Pte. 12 Bn.	2W.	27/ 7/15 3y 10m, Pte.
GLEESON, P. J. S., Tpr. L.H.		6/ 1/15
GLENDINNING, C., Pte. 15 Bn.	4 D.H.Q.	Pte.
GLENN, W., Pte. 12 Bn.		21/ 9/14 5y 4m, Pte.
GLENNON, W. R., Pte. 12 Bn.	✣ 6-10/4/17.	28/ 8/16 L.-Cpl. ✣
GLOVER, A., Pte. 12 Bn.		13/ 4/16 3y 7m, Pte.
GLOVER, A. P., Pte. 15 Bn.	W. ✣ 9/8/15.	1/10/14 Pte. ✣
GLOVER, C. E., Pte. 40 Bn.	W.	30/ 7/17 2y, Pte.
GLOVER, C. E., St.-Sgt., A.A.D.C.		18/ 1/16 3y 10m, S.-Sgt.
GLOVER, C. V., Pte., 12 Bn.	10 F.A.B.	21/ 7/15
GLOVER, G. F., Pte. 12 Bn.	2W. ✣ 25/8/18.	28/ 9/15 Pte. ✣
GLOVER, G. H., Pte. 12 Bn.	W.	12/ 7/15 1y 10m, Pte.

R

NAME.	REMARKS.	RANK ON DISCHARGE. ENLISTED. SERVICE.
GLOVER, H. V., Pte. 40 Bn.	2W.	10/ 3/16 3y 6m, Pte.
GLOVER, H. T., Cpl. 40 Bn.	W.	17/10/16 2y 7m, L.-Cpl.
GLOVER, J., Pte. 12 Bn.	✠ 5-8/5/17.	13/ 5/16 Pte. ✠
GLOVER, R. J., Pte. 12 Bn.	.W.	6/ 7/15 2y 7m, Pte.
GLOVER, R. C., Pte. 12 Bn.	W., 52Bn. ✠ 8/12/16.	28/ 7/15 Pte. ✠
GLOVER, R. W., Pte. 12 Bn.		28/ 6/15 4y 2m, Pte.
GLOVER, S. W., Pte. 40 Bn.	.W.	7/ 6/16 1y 8m, Sgt.
GLOVER, V. T., Pte. 12 Bn.		14/ 7/15 11m, Pte.
GLOVER, V. T., Tpr. 3 L.H.		2/ 1/18 1y 1m, Spr.
GLOVER, W. H., Pte. 12 Bn.	M.M.	28/ 8/16 3y 1m, Pte.
GLOZIER, M. R., Pte. 12 Bn.	W.	20/ 8/15 4y 1m, Sec. Lt.
GODDARD, G. R., Dvr. Art.	W., 3 D.A.C.	9/10/16 2y 11m, Dvr.
GODDARD, H. V., Sgnr. 12 Bn.	W., 10 F.A.B.	3/ 7/15 3y 4m, Sgnr.
GODFREY, A. R., Pte. 12 Bn.	✠ 6-10/4/17.	11/ 2/15 Pte. ✠
GODWIN, A. E., Pte. 12 Bn.	W.	7/ 8/15 4y, Pte.
GOLDING, H. F., Gnr. Art.		17/ 1/16
GOLDSMITH, C. M., Cpl. 40 Bn.	✠ 28/3/18.	24/10/16 Pte. ✠
GOLDSMITH, H. G., Spr. Wireless		2/ 7/15 3y 5m, Spr.
GOLDSMITH, H. V., Cpl. 4 A.S.C.		20/ 8/14 4y 5m, Sgt.
GOLDSMITH, H. G., Spr. Engrs.		2/ 7/15
GOLDSMITH, H. T., Pte. 12 Bn.	48 Bn ✠ 12/8/16.	25/ 5/15 Spr. ✠
GOLDSTRAW, W. A., Pte. 26 Bn.	✠ 5/8/16.	10/ 3/15 Pte. ✠
GOLDWORTHY, C. T., Pte. 12 Bn.	W., 40 Bn., 3 Dvl. Engrs.	24/10/16 3y 1m, 2 Cpl.
GONINON, E. F., Spr. Tunn.		29/ 3/16
GONINON, F., Pte. 40 Bn.		14/ 3/16 3y 6m, Pte.
GONINON, J. T., Pte. 40 Bn.		23/ 6/16 1y 2m, Pte.
GONINON, J. H. J., Gnr. Art.	2 D.A.C.	27/ 9/15 4y 1m, Gnr.
GONINON, R. B., Gnr. 3 G.S.R.	1 D.A.C.	18/ 1/18 1y 9m, Gnr.
GONINON, W., Pte. 15 Bn.	M.C.	24/11/14 4y 7m, Lt.
GOOCH, A. L., Dvr. Arty.	6 F.A.B.	3/ 8/15 4y 1m, Dvr.
GOOD, C. B., Pte. 12 Bn.		17/12/14 1y 11m, Pte.
GOOD, F. H., Pte. 7 Fd. Amb.	13 Fd. Amb. ✠8/6/17.	3/ 2/15 Pte. ✠
GOOD, F. W., Pte. A.M.C.		6/10/15
GOOD, J. A., Sec.-Lt. 15 Bn.	W.	28/ 9/14 1y 10m, Capt.
GOODE, G. N. M., Spr. 3 Fd. Co. E.	3 L.H. Bde. H.Q., 47 Bn. ✠ 12/6/17.	23/ 8/14 Lt. ✠
GOOD, T. L., Pte. 12 Bn.	W., 1 Aust. M.T. Co.	15/11/16 2y 11m, Pte.
GOOD, W. W., Pte. 12 Bn.		9/12/15 3y 9m, Pte.
GOODALL, A., Tpr. 3 L.H.	✠ 13/1/16.	19/ 8/14 Tpr. ✠
GOODEY, J. R., Pte. 26 Bn.	W.	27/ 9/15 3y 6m, Pte.
GOODING V. A., Pte. A.S.C.	38 Co. A.M.D.T.	16/10/17 2y, Tpr.
GOODLUCK, W., Pte. 26 Bn.		28/ 6/15 1y 2m, Pte.
GOODMAN, J., Tpr. Remount.		30/ 9/15 3y 7m, Tpr.
GOODMAN, M. C., Gnr. Arty.	W.	15/ 2/16 2y 2m, Gnr.
GOODWIN, A. J., Cpl. 12 Bn.	W.	19/ 8/14 3y 9m, Cpl.
GOODWIN, E. F. L., Pte. 26 Bn.	M.M.	30/ 9/15 4y 5m, Pte.
GOODWIN, G. H., M.W.		
GOODWIN, H. G., Pte. 40 Bn.	W. ✠ 12/8/18.	23/ 3/16 Dvr. ✠
GOODWIN, J. J. H., Gnr. 18 Fd. Bty.	W.	20/ 9/15 2y 5m, Gnr.
GOODY, H. A., Dvr. 8 Fd. Co.	12 Fd. Co. E.	31/ 1/16
GOODY, W. J., Pte. 40 Bn.	W. ✠ 3/10/17.	31/ 1/16 L.-Cpl. ✠
GOODYER, A. H., Pte. 26 Bn.		1/ 4/15 1y 6m, Pte.
GOODYER, B., Pte. 15 Bn.		12/ 7/15 1y 2m, Pte.
GOODYER, H. E., Pte. 12 Bn.	W.	23/ 7/15 3y 10m, Pte.
GOODYER, R. J., Pte. 40 Bn.		28/ 3/16 3y 7m, Lt.
GOOLD, A. R., Pte. 40 Bn.	W.	21/ 3/16 3y 6m, L.-Cpl.
GOOLD, F. L., Pte. 40 Bn.	W.	13/ 7/17 2y 2m, Pte.
GORDON, C., Pte. 40 Bn.		4/11/16 2y 4m, Pte.
GORDON, C. A., Pte. 1 A.C.H.		14/ 9/14 4y 4m, T.-Cpl.
GORDON, E., Pte. 40 Bn.	W.	20/ 7/16 3y 1m, Pte.
GORDON, E., Chaplain	Re-enlisted 22/3/17.	16/ 7/16 1y 3m, Capt.
GORDON, E. P., Pte. 12 Bn.		20/ 7/15
GORDON, F., Pte. 40 Bn.	W., 12 Bn.	2/ 3/16 3y 8m, Pte.
GORDON, G. L., Bdr. 36 H.A.G.		1/ 1/16 3y 7m, Bdr.
GORDON, J. E., Pte. 40 Bn.	W.	15/ 8/16 1y 1m, Pte.
GORDON, J. H., Pte. 26 Bn.	W.	9/ 8/15 4y, Pte.
GORDON, L. C., L.-Sgt. 15 Bn.	✠ 15/6/15.	5/10/14 L.-Sgt. ✠
GORDON, O. L. D., Gnr. Arty.	W., 15 F.A.B.	8/ 6/15 2y 3m, Gnr.
GORDON, R., Pte. 40 Bn.	W., 26 Bn.	23/ 5/16 3y 1m, Pte.
GORE, A. M., Tpr. G.S.R.		6/ 8/18 1y 1m, Tpr.
GORE, H. E., Cpl. 3 G.S.R.		26/ 6/18
GORE, R. J., Tpr. 7 G.S.R.		6/ 8/18 1y, Tpr.
GOREY, V. W. L., Pte. 12 Bn.	W., 52 Bn.	29/ 7/15 2y 8m, Pte.
GORHAM, H. S., Pte. 12 Bn.		14/ 8/15 4y 3m, L.-Cpl.
GORMAN, T. E., Pte. 12 Bn.	✠ 24/6/15.	2/ 9/14 Pte. ✠
GORRINGE, E. L. J., Pte. 15 Bn.	W.	3/ 8/15 Pte.
GORRINGE, G. A., Pte. 40 Bn.	✠ 15/10/17.	12/10/15 Pte. ✠
GOSS, A., Pte. 12 Bn.	3W., 52 Bn.	9/ 8/15 4y 1m, Pte.
GOSS, A. R., Pte. 40 Bn.	3W., 69 Bn., 40 Bn. ✠ 30/8/18.	4/ 4/16 Pte. ✠
GOSS, A. J., Pte. 12 Bn.	2W.	6/ 9/15 3y 1m, Pte.
GOSS, A. J., Pte. 40 Bn.	W.	20/ 6/16 3y 3m, Pte.
GOSS, A., Pte. 40 Bn.	W., 15 Bn., 40 Bn. ✠ 8/10/17.	20/3/16 Pte. ✠
GOSS, A. R., Pte. 12 Bn.	M.M.	6/ 9/16 3y 1m, Pte.
GOSS, A. C., Pte. A.S.C.		14/ 2/18 1y 6m, Pte.
GOSS, A. E., Pte. 12 Bn.		6/12/17 2y, Pte.
GOSS, C. S., Pte. 15 Bn.	M.C.	26/ 9/14 4y 4m, Capt.
GOSS, D. B., Pte. 12 Bn.		8/ 9/14 1y 9m, Pte.

TASMANIA'S MUSTER ROLL. 275

NAME.	REMARKS.	RANK ON DISCHARGE. ENLISTED. SERVICE.
GOSS, F. J., Pte. 26 Bn.	W., 40 Bn.	17/ 3/15 4y 5m, Sgt.
GOSS, F., Pte. 12 Bn.	W.	25/ 8/15 2y 4m, Pte.
GOSS, F., Gnr. Arty.		14/ 3/17 2y 4m, Gnr.
GOSS, G., Pte. 12 Bn.		30/ 8/16
GOSS, H. A., Pte. 12 Bn.	5 F.A. Bde.	21/ 6/17 2y 3m, Gnr.
GOSS, H. H., Pte. 40 Bn.	W.	9/ 3/16 3y 1m, Pt.
GOSS, L. G., Pte. 12 Bn.		25/ 8/15 2y, Pte.
GOSS, R. C., Gnr. Arty.		24/ 1/16
GOSS, R. G., Pte. 3 G.S.R.	12 Bn.	20/ 6/18 1y, Pte.
GOSS, S., Pte. 26 Bn.	2W., A.A.S.C.	18/ 5/15 3y 11m, Pte.
GOSS, W. N., Pte. 12 Bn.	W., 24 H. Bde., 10 F.A.B., 110 H. Bty. ✣ 18/4/18.	1/11/15 Gnr. ✣
GOSSAGE, R., Pte. 40 Bn.	W. ✣ 2/12/18.	10/ 1/17 Pte. ✣
GOUGH, H. E. St. J., Dvr. 3 F. Amb.	M.M.	20/ 8/14 5y, Lieut.
GOUGH, W. J., Pte. 40 Bn.	P.O.W., 15 Bn.	20/ 3/16 3y 2m, Pte.
GOULD, A. D., Pte. 12 Bn.	52 Bn. ✣13/8/16.	1/ 9/15 Pte. ✣
GOULD, A., Spr. 3 Fd. Co.	2W.	19/ 8/14 2y 2m, Spr.
GOULD, A. W., Pte. A.A.H.	6 Fd. Amb.	28/10/15 4y, Pte.
GOULD, B., Pte. 12 Bn.	✣ 10/6/15.	16/ 9/14 Pte. ✣
GOULD, D. W., Pte. 40 Bn.	W.	10/11/16 2y 10m, Pte.
GOULD, E. E., Pte. 26 Bn.	✣ 12/6/16.	14/ 8/15 Pte. ✣
GOULD, G. D., Major 26 Bn.	✣ 8/6/15.	Major ✣
GOULD, G., Artificer 4 M.T. Co.		10/ 9/14 4y 11m, Artl.
GOULD, G. F., C.Q.M.S. 26 Bn.		2/ 2/15
GOULD, T. E., Gnr. 6 F.A.B.	W., M.M.	17/ 9/15 4y 2m, Cpl.
GOULD, T. H., Pte. 1 A.C.H.		23/ 9/14 4y 4m, Sgt.
GOULLEE, F. C., Cpl. 12 Bn.	W., 28 Bn. ✣ 11/6/18.	26/ 9/15 Lt. ✣
GOULSTON, B. H., Tpr. 3 L.H.		19/ 8/14 4y 6m, T.-Sgt.
GOULSTON, C. F., Pte. 1 G.S.R.	50 Fd. Bty.	18/ 2/18 1y 8m, Gnr.
GOULSTON, V, S., Pte. 12 Bn.	W.	9/ 2/16 2y 4m, Pte.
GOULTER, H. L., L.-Cpl. 40 Bn.		28/ 2/16 3y 7m, Bdr.
GOURLAY, G. R., Pte. 40 Bn.	W.	30/10/16 2y 6m, Pte.
GOURLAY, W. J. Pte. 40 Bn.	3 W., M.M.	15/ 2/16 3y 5m, Sgt.
GOW, W. E., Pte. 3 Fd. Amb.		28/ 8/14 2y 1m, Pte.
GOWANS, A., Pte. 12 Bn.	2W.	4/ 4/16 3y 4m, Cpl.
GOWANS, A. T., Gnr. 30 Fd. Bty.	M.M.	1/11/15 3y 11m, Sgt.
GOWANS, J. C., Pte. 12 Bn.		8/ 7/15 4y 1m, Pte.
GOWER, B., Pte. 40 Bn.	✣ 28/3/17.	17/10/16 Pte. ✣
GOWER, C. W., Pte. 12 Bn.		12/ 5/17 1y 10m, Pte.
GOWER, J. D., Pte. 26 Bn.	✣ 31/7/16.	10/ 8/15 Pte. ✣
GOWER, L. J., Pte. 12 Bn.	W.	24/11/16 3y 1m, Pte.
GOYEN, H. K., Gnr. Arty.	M.S.M., 5 D.A.C.	6/ 1/15 4y 11m, 2 Lt.
GOYNE, T. A., Pte. 12 Bn.	1 M.G. Bn.	14/10/16 3y, Pte.
GRABE, E., Pte. 12 Bn.		13/10/16
GRACE, C. A., Pte. 12 Bn.		13/ 7/15 3y 10m, Pte.
GRACE, E. A., Spr. 8 Fd. Co.		8/12/15 3y 8m, L.-Cpl.
GRACE, M. F., Pte. 26 Bn.	2 W., 12 Bn.	14/ 8/15
GRACIE, W. H., Dvr. 3 L.H.		17/ 2/15 3y 7m, Dvr.
GRAF, H. M., Tpr. 3 L.H.		18/ 8/14 4y 6m, Sgt.
GRAY, H., Pte. 12 Bn.	W.	13/10/16 2y 11m, Pte.
GRAHAM, A. E., Pte. 12 Bn.	W.	11/ 8/15 3y 8m, Pte.
GRAHAM, A. J., Pte. 7 Fd. Amb.	W., M.M.	6/ 2/15 4y 4m, Pte.
GRAHAM, A. V., Tpr. 3 L.H.		24/11/14
GRAHAM, E. W., Pte. 12 Bn.		11/ 8/15 4y, Pte.
GRAHAM, F. C. M., Dvr. Arty.	2 Siege B.A.C.	18/10/15
GRAHAM, F. H., Pte. 12 Bn.	✣ 9/4/17.	2/ 5/16 Pte. ✣
GRAHAM, G. G., Pte. 40 Bn.		14/ 3/16 1y 3m, Pte.
GRAHAM, L. J., Pte. 12 Bn.	W.	3/ 5/16 2y 11m, Pte.
GRAHAM, L. W., Pte. 1 G.S.R.		17/ 9/17
GRAHAM, R. D., Pte. 40 Bn.	✣ 30/10/17.	8/11/16 Pte. ✣
GRAHAM, W. A., Spr. 8 Fd. Co.	W.	17/ 1/16 3y 3m, Spr.
GRAHAM, W. S. J., Pte. 12 Bn.		19/ 5/16
GRAINGER, C. V., Spr. Miners.		29/ 2/16 3y 5m, Spr.
GRAINGER, F., Dvr. 4 A.S.C.		14/ 9/14
GRAINGER, G., Pte. 12 Bn.	W., 52 Bn.	10/ 8/15 3y 2m, Pte.
GRAINGER, H., Tpr. 3 L.H.	3 F.A.B.	26/ 5/17 2y 5m, Dvr.
GRAINGER, J., Pte. 12 Bn.		5/ 9/14 2m, Pte.
GRAIGER, L. H., Pte. 40 Bn.		27/ 6/16
GRAINGER, R. C., Pte. 2 A.V.S.		22/11/14 1y, Pte.
GRAINGER, R. C., Tpr. 3 L.H.	4 L.H.	8/ 5/17 2y 5m, Tpr.
GRAINGER, T. H., Tpr. 3 L.H.	4 D.A.C.	8/ 5/17 2y 1m, Dvr.
GRANFIELD, G. A., Pte. 12 Bn.	57 Bn. ✣ 25/9/17.	25/ 8/15 Pte. ✣
GRANGER, F. H., Pte. 40 Bn.	✣ 1/4/17.	30/ 3/16 Pte. ✣
GRANT, A., Pte. 12 Bn.	52 Bn.	31/10/15
GRANT, A. J., Tpr. Remounts.		28/ 9/15 4y 2m, Tpr.
GRANT, G. D., Pte. 40 Bn.		9/ 1/17 1y 9m, Pte.
GRANT, J. W., Pte. 40 Bn.	W.	30/10/16 2y 10m, Pte.
GRANT, L. G., Pte. 26 Bn.	✣ 29/7/16.	23/ 3/15 Pte. ✣
GRANT, R. J., Pte. 15 Bn.	W., M.M. ✣ 5/7/18.	11/12/14 Pte. ✣
GRANT, R., Pte. 12 Bn.		11/ 6/17 1y 10m, Pte.
GRATTAN, J. P., Tpr. 3 L.H.		12/ 8/15 4y 1m, Tpr.
GRAVER, A. A., Pte. 12 Bn.	1 M.G. Bn. ✣ 17/4/18.	1/12/14 Spr. ✣
GRAVES, A., Pte. 12 Bn.	2W., 40 Bn.	7/ 4/16 2y 3m, Pte.
GRAVES, A. M., Cpl. 40 Bn.	W., 3 M.G. Bn.	3/10/16 3y, Pte.
GRAVES, C. F., Sgt. 12 Bn.		10/12/14 1y 1m, Sgt.
GRAVES, G. P., Pte. 12 Bn.	52 Bn. ✣ 4/9/16.	3/ 8/15 Pte. ✣

NAME.	REMARKS.	RANK ON DISCHARGE. ENLISTED. SERVICE.
GRAVES, J., Pte. Remounts.		15/ 9/15 9m, Pte.
GRAY, A. E., Pte. 40 Bn.	2W.	30/ 9/16 3y 1m, Pte.
GRAY, C. E., Pte. 12 Bn.	W.	16/ 6/17 2y, Pte.
GRAY, C. C., Gnr. Arty.	111 Bty.	26/ 2/18 1y 8m, Gnr.
GRAY, C. W. T., Pte. 12 Bn.	✠ 15/4/17.	17/ 7/16 Pte. ✠
GRAY, C. F., Pte. 12 Bn.		5/ 10/16 3y 1m, Pte.
GRAY, F., Dvr. 7 Fd. Amb.		25/ 2/15 4y 3m, Dvr.
GRAY, F. O., Pte. 3 Fd. Amb.		10/ 5/16 2y 11m, Pte.
GRAY, F. T., Pte. 26 Bn.	W.	15/ 5/15 4y 3m, Pte.
GRAY, H. C., Gnr. 14 F.A.B.	114 How. Bty.	15/11/16 3y, Gnr.
GRAY, O. H., Pte. R.A.M.C.	W., 17 Fd. Amb., 3 Fd. Amb. ✠ 24/8/18.	30/12/14 Pte. ✠
GRAY, T. E., A.A.M.C.	✠ 19/6/16.	
GRAY, V. J., Pte. 12 Bn.	✠ 10/4/17.	5/ 7/16 Pte. ✠
GRAY, W., Pte. 15 Bn.		20/ 1/15 2y 3m, Pte.
GRAY, W. H., Lt. 26 Bn.	3W.	5/ 6/15 2y 3m, Capt.
GREATBATCH, L. G., Pte. 1 G.S.R.		28/ 2/18
GREATBATCH, N., Pte. 12 Bn.	✠ 18/9/18.	16/11/16 Pte. ✠
GREAVES, W. T., Pte. 12 Bn.	2W.	15/12/15 2y 10m, Pte.
GREEN, A., Sec. Lt. 12 Bn.	2W.	21/ 8/14 3y 6m, Lt.
GREEN, F. C., Lt. 40 Bn.	M.C.	3/ 9/15 4y 1m, Capt.
GREENLAND, H. J., Pte. 12 Bn.	W., 3 Fd. Co.	29/ 8/14 5y 1m, L.-Cpl.
GREENLAND, P. W., Pte. 40 Bn.	✠ 17/7/18.	3/10/16 Pte. ✠
GREENLAW, R. M., Gnr. Arty.	25 H. Bde., 51 Bn., 52 Bn., 51 Bn., ✠ 11/6/18.	15/ 2/16 Gnr. ✠
GREENOUGH, L. H., L.-Sgt. 40 Bn	✠ 16/12/16.	15/ 9/15 Sgt. ✠
GRENWOOD, T., Pte. 3 G.S.R.	12 Bn.	6/ 8/18 1y 2m, Pte.
GREGG, A. C., Pte. 40 Bn.	W.	28/ 8/16 2y 7m, Pte.
GREGG, J. S., Pte. 40 Bn.		30/ 9/16 1y 10m, Pte.
GREGORY, G. W., Gnr. Arty.		12/10/18 11m, Gnr.
GREGORY, H. P., Pte. 40 Bn.	2W.	18/ 4/16 3y 5m, Pte.
GREGORY, J., Pte. 26 Bn.	W.	24/ 9/15 2y 5m, Pte.
GRESHNER, B., Spr. 8 Fd. Co.	2W. 14 Fd. Co.	24/ 1/16 3y 9m, Spr.
GREY, A. R., Pte. 40 Bn.	W.	17/10/16 2y 6m, L.-Cpl.
GREY, C. T., Pte. 40 Bn.	W.	17/10/16 2y 4m, Pte.
GREY, J. G., Spr. Miners.	1 Tunn. Co.	6/ 3/16 2y 6m, Spr.
GREY, S. W., Pte. 12 Bn.	W. ✠17/4/18.	31/ 5/16 Pte. ✠
GREY, W. N., Pte. 40 Bn.	W., D.C.M.	29/ 3/16 3y, Sgt.
GREEN, A., Spr. Tunn.		4/ 8/17 1y 5m, Spr.
GREEN, A. F., Pte. 26 Bn.		2/ 8/15 Lt.
GREEN, A. G., Pte.		24/ 2/16 3y 7m, Pte.
GREEN, A. B., Pte. 1 A.C.H.		14/ 9/14 4y 4m, Pte.
GREENE, B. V. C., Pte. A.S.C.		1/ 12/17 6m, Pte.
GREEN, C. M., Pte. 15 Bn.	Vet. Hospital.	17/ 7/18 9m, Pte.
GREEN, C. R., Pte. 40 Bn.	2W.	30/ 3/16
GREEN, C., Pte. 26 Bn.	12 Bn. ✠ 8/6/17.	13/ 8/15 Pte. ✠
GREEN, D. H., Pte. 40 Bn.	W.	2/11/16 1y 11m, Pte.
GREEN, E. C., Spr. Miners.	3 Tunn. ✠ 5/6/17.	18/11/15 Spr. ✠
GREEN, E., Pte. 40 Bn.	W., 69 Bn., 40 Bn.	7/ 3/16
GREEN, E. H., Pte. 12 Bn.	W.	10/ 8/15 4y, Sgt.
GREEN, F. W., Cpl. 12 Bn.	W.	23/ 7/15 3y 1m, Cpl.
GREEN, G. A., Pte. 12 Bn.	W.	31/ 8/15 4y 1m, Pte.
GREEN, G. L., Pte. 26 Bn.		13/ 9/15
GREEN, G. W., Bty. S.M. 9 Fd. Bty.		26/ 8/14 4y 9m, B.S.M.
GREEN, G. W., Pte. 12 Bn.	W.	20/ 8/14 4y 5m, L.-Cpl.
GREEN, H., Pte. 2 G.S.R.	24 D.U.S.	15/ 4/18 1y 6m, Pte.
GREEN, H. G., Pte. 26 Bn.	✠ 5/11/16.	3/ 9/15 Pte. ✠
GREENE, H. C., Pte. 12 Bn.	✠ 8/1/18.	2/ 9/16 Pte. ✠
GREEN, H., Gnr. Arty.	W., L.T.M. Bty.	17/ 8/15 2y 10m, Gnr.
GREEN, H. B., Cpl. 12 Bn.		19/ 1/15 4y 11m, L.-Cpl.
GREEN, J. H., Pte. 12 Bn.	W. ✠7/10/17.	24/ 8/15 Pte. ✠
GREEN, J., Gnr. 12 F.A.B.	W., M.M.	10/ 1/16 1y 11m, Gnr.
GREEN, L. W. F. F., Gnr. Arty.	2 F.A. Bde.	6/11/16 2y 10m, Dvr.
GREEN, L. M. J., Pte. 3 Cyc. Corps.	W., 12 Bn.	5/ 4/16 3y 5m, Pte.
GREEN, L. T., Gnr., Arty.	111 How. Bty.	3/ 2/16
GREEN, L. H. W., Gnr. Arty.	31 Bty.	3/12/16 2y 9m, Gnr.
GREEN, M. L., Gnr. Arty.	W., 23 How. Bde.	3/ 2/16
GREEN, R. W., Pte. 40 Bn.		23/ 2/16 3y 11m, Pte.
GREENE, S. H., Pte. 3 G.S.R.	12 Bn.	16/ 7/18 1y 3m, Pte.
GREEN, S. G. J., Spr. 8 Fd. Co.		18/11/15 1y 7m, Spr.
GREEN, S. J., Pte. 19 Bn.		8/ 7/16
GREEN, T. F., Gnr. Arty.	3 F.A.B.	8/ 2/17 2y 8m, Dvr.
GREEN, W., Pte. 12 Bn.		25/ 1/16
GRINDLEY, A. C., Pte. 26 Bn.	✠ 5/8/16.	22/ 9/15 ✠
GRIEVE, T., Pte. 26 Bn.	2 Div. Tnlrs.	9/ 3/15
GRIFFEN, D. J., Tpr. 3 L.H.	2W.	24/ 8/15 2y 5m, Tpr.
GRIFFIN, J. N., S.M., 3 L.H.	M.C.	18/ 8/14 5y 1m, Lt.
GRIFFITHS, A. J., Pte. 12 Bn.		20/ 8/14
GRIFFITHS, C., Pte. 12 Bn.	W.	19/ 4/16
GRIFFITHS, C. V., Gnr. 36 H.A.G.		24/ 6/18 1m, Gnr.
GRIFFITHS, D. E., Tpr. 3 L.H.	W., 13 F.A.B. ✠ 23/1/19.	6/ 8/15 Dvr. ✠
GRIFFTHS, E. R., Pte. 12 Bn.	W.	9/10/16 2y 6m, Pte.
GRIFFITHS, E. A., Gnr. 3 Arty.		20/ 7/15 2y 3m, Gnr.
GRIFFITHS, F. G., Pte. 26 Bn.	✠ 28/7/16.	8/ 9/15 Pte. ✠
GRIFFITHS, G. G., Gnr. Arty.	6 F.A.B.	2/10/16 2y 11m. Dvr.
GRIFFITHS, G. C., Pte. 12 Bn.	W.	30/10/15 3y 10m, Cpl.
GRIFFITHS, H., Pte. 12 Bn.	✠ 3/11/17.	20/ 1/15 Pte. ✠

TASMANIA'S MUSTER ROLL. 277

NAME.	REMARKS.	RANK ON DISCHARGE. ENLISTED, SERVICE.
GRIFFITHS, J. H., Dvr. 3 L.H.		23/ 8/15 2y 10m. Dvr.
GRIFFITHS, J., Pte. 12 Bn.		27/ 4/17. 2y 5m. Pte.
GRIFFITHS, J. K., Gnr. Arty.	12 F.A.B., 1 D.A.C.	2/10/16, 2y 11m. Dvr.
GRIFFITHS, L. J., Pte. 12 Bn.	✠ 24/4/18.	10/ 9/15 Pte. ✠
GRIFFITHS, M., Pte. 12 Bn.	W.	26/10/16, 3y. Pte.
GRIFFITHS, R. A., Pte. 40 Bn.	✠ 27/7/18.	3/ 2/17. Pte. ✠
GRIFFITHS, R. S., Pte. 15 Bn.	W.	28/ 1/15. 2y 3m. Pte.
GRIFFITHS, T. A., Pte. 1 G.S.R.		4/ 3/18, 1y 9m. Pte.
GRIFFITHS, W., Tpr. 3 L.H.		7/ 7/15 4y 1m.
GRIFFITHS, W. E., Dvr. 1 R.A.N.B.T.		31/ 5/15 2y 2m, Dvr.
GRIGGS, A. J.,		8/ 6/15 3y 6m. Pte.
GRIGGS, R., Pte. 3 G.S.R.	13 Fld. Amb.	12/ 8/18.
GRIGGS, S., Spr. Tunlrs.		12/ 2/17.
GRIGGS, W. E., Pte. 12 Bn.	W.	4/ 9/16 1y 11m. Pte.
GRILLS, N. E., Pte. 12 Bn.		18/ 8/15 4y 1m. Pte.
GRILLS, P., Pte. Anzac L.R.		17/ 9/14 3y 8m. Spr.
GRIMES, J. M., Pte. 12 Bn.	52 Bn.	28/ 7/15 1y 10m. Pte.
GRIMMOND, H. L., Pte. 40 Bn.		20/ 3/16 3y 6m. 2 Lt.
GRIMMOND, J. T., Pte. 40 Bn.	W.	20/ 3/16 3y 5m. Pte.
GRIMSEY, G. S., Pte. 40 Bn.	W.	6/ 3/16 3y 6m. Pte.
GROOM, A. G., Pte. 12 Bn.		21/ 8/15 2y Pte.
GROOM, B. J. G., Pte. Wireless.		6/ 8/17 1y 11m. 2 AM
GROOM, C. J., Pte. 12 Bn.	2W. ✠ 5-8/5/17.	7/ 9/15. Pte. ✠
GROOM, E. C., Pte. 12 Bn.	W. ✠ 7/5/17.	1/ 9/15. Pte. ✠
GROOM, R. E. D., Sgt. 40 Bn.		22/ 2/16 3y 2m. Lt.
GROOMBRIDGE, E. J., Pte. 12 Bn.		23/10/16 3y. Pte.
GROSE, W. C., Pte. 26 Bn.	3W.	27/ 3/15 4y 1m. Pte.
GROVES, C. J. S., Pte. 40 Bn.	W.	28/ 6/16 2y 1m. Pte.
GROVES, E., Pte. Tunlrs.		12/ 2/17.
GROVES, F. W., Sgt. 40 Bn.		6/ 3/16 3y 6m. Sgt.
GROVES, K., Pte. 1 G.S.R.	1 D.A.C.	27/ 2/18 1y 5m. Dvr.
GROVES, P., Pte. 40 Bn.	4W.	12/ 1/16 3y 5m. Pte.
GROVE, P. C. H., Pte. 12 Bn.	W. 52 Bn. ✠ 13/10/16.	30/ 9/15. Pte. ✠
GROVES, T., Pte. 12 Bn.	W.	12/ 2/16 3y 2m. Pte.
GRUBB, A. W., Signr. 7 Fld. Amb.		15/ 2/15 4y 3m. Signr.
GRUBB, F. R., Pte. 26 Bn.	12 Bn. ✠ 25/7/16.	3/ 8/15. Pte. ✠
GRUBB, H. B., Tpr. 3 L.H.	W.	7/ 7/15 4y 6m. L.-Cpl.
GRUBB, J. C., Pte. 12 Bn.		31/10/16.
GRUBB, W. E. K., Pte. 26 Bn.	40 Bn. ✠ 28/3/18.	11/ 5/15. Lt. ✠
GRUBY, A., Pte. 12 Bn.	✠ 5-8/5/17.	27/ 8/15. Pte. ✠
GRUEBER, A. G., Pte. 1 A.G.H.		9/ 8/15 4y 1m. L. Cpl.
GRUNDY, E., Pte. 40 Bn.	W.	21/ 3/16 3y 7m. Pte.
GRUNDY, F. H., Pte. 26 Bn.	W.	11/ 3/15 4y 5m. Pte.
GRUNDY, F., Pte. 12 Bn.	2 Fld Bakery.	31/ 5/16 3y 4m. Pte.
GRUNDY, H. T., Pte. 40 Bn.	✠ 3/1/17.	3/ 4/16. Pte. ✠
GRUNDY, J. W., Pte. 40 Bn.	✠ 3/1/17.	3/ 4/16. Pte. ✠
GRUNDY, T. C., Pte. 40 Bn.	W. ✠ 13/11/18.	3/ 4/16. Pte. ✠
GUERIN, J. J., Pte. Rmts.		8/10/15 Pte.
GUERIN, P. C., L.-Cpl., 12 Bn.		11/ 9/16 1y 10m. L. Cp.
GUERIN, P. C., Pte. 15 Bn.		19/12/14 Pte.
GUEST, C. V., Cpl. 1 A.G.H.		18/ 9/14 4y 4m. Sgt.
GUEST, F., Dvr. 6 F.A., 17 Bty.		14/ 9/15 3y 8m. Dvr.
GUEST, J. J., Pte. 40 Bn.	W.	30/10/16 2y 4m. Pte.
GUEST, J. T., Pte. 15 Bn.	2W.	27/ 8/15 4y 1m. Pte.
GULLIDGE, H. G., Pte. 12 Bn.	W.	5/ 9/14 4y 4m. Pet.
GULLS, P., Pte. 12 Bn.		17/ 9/14.
GUNN, C. K., Gnr. Arty.	W. 14 F.A.B.	4/10/16.
GUNN, G. F., Pte. 12 Bn.	✠ 3-5/9/16.	1/ 7/18. Pte. ✠
GUNN, R. M'G., Pte. A.A.M.C.	W.	20/ 8/14 3y 11m. Pte.
GUNN, V. W. T., Pte. 12 Bn.	W.	1/ 6/15 3y 11m. Pte.
GUNTER, F., Tpr. 3 L.H.		2/ 9/15 3y 7m. Gnr.
GUNTER, P. D., Pte. 3 L.H.		2/ 9/15.
GUNTON, H., Pte. 26 Bn.	W.	29/ 6/15 4y 1m. Pte.
GUNTON, L. G., Pte. 12 Bn.	W.	29/ 5/16 1y 7m. Pte.
GUNTON, T., Pte. 40 Bn.	2W.	15/ 3/16 8m. Pte.
GURNEY, G. A., Major, Transport.		29/ 7/16. Major.
GURR, A. E., Pte. 12 Bn.	W. ✠ 25-28/4/15.	19/ 8/14. Pte. ✠
GURR, C. H., Pte. 40 Bn.	W.	14/ 3/16 1y 10m. Pte.
GURR, E. P., Pte. 1 G.S.R.		27/ 2/18 1y 3m. Pte.
GURR, G. R., Pte. 40 Bn.	✠ 15/4/17.	14/ 3/16. Pte. ✠
GURR, H. A., Gnr. Arty.	2 F.A. ✠ 11/10/17.	7/12/16. Gnr. ✠
GURR, J. A., Pte. 12 Bn.	✠ 24/11/15.	7/ 9/15. Pte. ✠
GUTHRIE, A., Pte. 12 Bn.		20/ 8/14 3y 9m. L.Cpl.
GUTHRIE, N. R., Pte. 15 Bn.	W. ✠ 29/5/15.	7/12/14. Pte. ✠
GUTTERIDGE, L. Y., Dvr. 3 F.A.	✠ 4/2/17.	15/ 9/14. Gnr. ✠
GUY, F., Spr. 8 Fd. Co.		28/ 2/16 3y. 8m. Spr.
GUY, W. G., Pte. A.A.M.C.		26/ 2/17.
GWILLAM, C., Gnr. Arty.	12 F.A.B.	19/ 9/16.
HAAS, C. J., Pte. 12 Bn.	2W. A.I.F. Depot. H.Q.	11/ 4/16 3y 6m. Pte.
HAAS, T. J., Pte. 40 Bn.	✠ 13/12/16.	3/ 3/16. Pte. ✠
HAAS, W., Spr. Tunlrs.		17/ 1/17.
HABERLE, A. H., Pte. 12 Bn.	✠ 3/11/17.	22/ 8/16. Pte. ✠
HABERLE, C., Pte. 12 Bn.	✠ 3/8/16	22/ 8/14. Pte. ✠
HACK, A. E., Pte. 26 Bn.	2W. D.C.M.	23/ 6/15 4y 2m. Sgt.
HACK, F. J., Pte. 26 Bn.		15/ 6/15 4y 2m. Pte.

NAME.	REMARKS.	RANK ON DISCHARGE. ENLISTED. SERVICE.
HACK, H. A., Pte. 12 Bn.	✣ 19-22/8/16.	25/10/15. Pte. ✣
HACK, R., Pte. 26 Bn.	2W.	15/ 6/15 4y 2m. Cpl.
HADFIELD, L. A|, Pte. 40 Bn.		31/ 3/16 1y 10m. Pte.
HADFIELD, W. J., Tpr. 3 L.H.R.		28/ 8/15 10m. Tpr.
HADFIELD, W. R., Gnr. 3 F.A. Bd.	103 How. Bty.	27/ 8/14 4y 9m. Gnr.
HADLEY, E. G., Pte. 12 Bn.	4 Sal. Coy.	18/ 8/14 4y 6m. Pte.
HAIDON, W. C., Gnr. F.A. Rfts.		13/10/15.
HAIG, H., Pte. 40 Bn.	W.	9/ 9/16 2y 6m. Pte.
HAIG, J., Pte. 12 Bn.	40 Bn.	20/11/16 1y 9m. P.e.
HAIGH, E. A., A/Sgt. 12 Bn.	2 A.F.C.	11/ 9/16 2y 11m. 2 A.M.
HAIGH, J. E., Pte. 40 Bn.		27/ 7/16 3y. Pte.
HAINES, A. S. C., Pte. 26 Bn.	✣ 26/3/17.	21/ 7/15. Pte. ✣
HAINES, H. F. C., Pte. 26 Bn.	W.	21/ 4/15 2y 8m. Pte.
HAINES, L., Pte. 12 Bn.	✣ 15/4/17.	5/ 8/15. Pte. ✣
HAINES, S., Pte. 12 Bn.		5/ 2/17 2y 8m. Pte.
HAINSWORTH, J. T., Gnr. Arty.	120 How. Bty. 114 How. Bty.	13/ 8/15 4y 1m. Gnr.
HALE, E. G., Pte. 7 Fd. Amb.	✣ 25/10/15.	17/ 2/15. Pte. ✣
HALES, A. A., Pte. 12 Bn.		16/10/16 2y 11m. Pte.
HALES, C. H., Gnr. Arty. Rfts.	6 A.M.T.M.B.	27/ 1/16 3y 8m. Bdr.
HALES, N. C., Gnr. 3 F.A.B.		9/ 1/17 2y 6m. Gnr.
HALES, R. A., Pte. 12 Bn.	W., 52 Bn. ✣ 14/8/16.	4/ 1/16. Pte. ✣
HALES, R. C., Pte. 12 Bn.		26/10/15 3y 11m. Pte.
HALES, W. M., Pte. 1 G.S.R.	40 Bn.	15/10/17 2y 1m. Pte.
HALEY, A. A., Gnr. 15 F.A.B.	W. ✣ 25/12/18.	7/11/16. Pte. ✣
HALEY, J., Pte. 12 Bn.	69 Bn.	27/ 4/16 1y 8m. Pte.
HALEY, V. A. J., Cpl. 40 Bn.	1 D. Hqrs. M.S.M.	23/ 3/17 2y 7m. SQMS.
HALFACRE, H., Spr. Miners.		10/ 9/17.
HALLAM, A. T. H., Gnr. Arty.	2W. 4 F.A.B.	24/ 2/16.
HALLAM, C. W., Pte. 2 A.G.H.		16/ 7/17 2y. 3m. Pte.
HALLAM, E. S. W., Gnr. D.A.C.	106 How Bty.	6/ 9/15 3y 9m. Gnr.
HALLAM, J., Pte. 12 Bn.	3W. 52 Bn.	19/ 8/14 5y 1m. Pte.
HALLAM, J. L., Gnr. Arty.	3 D.A.C. 8 F.A.B.	6/ 2/17 2y 8m. Gnr.
HALLAM, P. W., Pte. 12 Bn.	2W. 52 Bn.	19/ 8/14 3y 11m. Pte.
HALLETT, H. L., Pte. 15 Bn.		9/ 6/15 4y 4m. Pte.
HALLEY, J., Pte. Tnlrs.	4 Anzac Cml. Bn.	16/10/16 2y 11m. Dvr
HALTON, C. J. L., Pte. A.A.M.C.		23/ 2/17.
HALTON, W. A., Pte. 12 Bn.	✣ 6-10/4/17.	1/ 9/16. Pte. ✣
HAMENCE, W. W., Tpr. 3 L.H.R.		22/ 6/15 1y 7m. Tpr.
HAMER, C. E. G., Pte. 40 Bn.		25/ 9/16 3y. Pte.
HAMER, J. C. E., Pte. 4 M.G. Co.	W. 5 M.G. Coy.	20/ 9/16 3y 2m. Pte.
HAMILTON, C. T., Pte. 40 Bn.	✣ 7/10/17.	11/10/16. Pte. ✣
HAMILTON, J., Pte. 12 Bn.	3W.	7/ 9/15 3y 7m. Pte.
HAMILTON, F. L., Gnr. 3 F.A.B.	2W. 4 D.A.C. 24 F.A.B. 37 Bty.	19/10/14 4y 3m. Gnr.
HAMILTON, R. F., Pte. 12 Bn.	✣ 7/10/17.	11/ 4/15. Pte. ✣
HAMILTON, T., Pte. 12 Bn.	M.M. ✣ 6/10/17.	7/ 9/15. Cpl. ✣
HAMMERSLEY, W. H., Pte. 26 Bn	2W. M.M and Bar. 12 Bn.	28/ 7/15. Cpl.
HAMMOND, J. O., Gnr. Siege Bd.	36 H.A.G.	1/ 7/15 4y 3m. Gnr.
HAMMOND, L. J., Dvr. 3 F.C.E.		24/ 9/14 2y 1m. Dvr.
HAMMOND, M., Tpr. 3 L.H.R.	4 L.H.R.	8/ 6/17 2y 3m. Tpr.
HAMMOND, R. E., Pte. 15 Bn.		30/12/14 Cpl.
HAMMOND, W. J., Pte. 12 Bn.	A.A. Post Cps.	30/12/14 3y 7m. Pte.
HAMMOND, W. A., Pte. 12 Bn.	✣ 6/5/17.	27/ 8/15 Pte. ✣
HAMPTON, D. A., Pte. 1 G.S.R.	A.A.M.C.	6/ 9/17 2y 2m. Pte.
HAMPTON, E. J., Pte. 12 Bn.	W.	20/ 3/14 4y 9m. W.O.
HAMPTON, G. A., Pte. 12 Bn.	4 A.S.C. 4 Dvl. Trn.	17/ 1/16 3y 10m. Dvr
HAMPTON, R. P., Pte. 12 Bn.		26/10/16 1y 11m. Pte.
HALL, A. M., Gnr. 36 H.A.G.		26/ 8/16 2y 9m. Gnr.
HALL, A. J., Pte. 40 Bn.	W.	1/11/16 2y 3m. Pte.
HALL, A. W., Pte. 12 Bn.		8/12/14 1y 9m. Pte.
HALL, A., Pte. 26 Bn.	W.	19/ 2/15 4y 1m. Dvr.
HALL, A. J., Pte. 40 Bn.		26/ 9/16 11m. Pte.
HALL, A., Pte. 26 Bn.	W. ✣ 5/11/16:	Pte. ✣
HALL, A., Pte. 12 Bn.	4W. 51 Bn.	21/ 1/16. Pte.
HALL, A. A. C., Pte. A.A.M.C.	A.A. Post Cps.	6/ 8/17 2y 3m. Pte.
HALL, B. F., Pte. 12 Bn.	W. 52 Bn.	5/ 8/15.
HALL, C. E., Pte. 40 Bn.	W.	16/ 3/16 3y 3m. L. Cpl.
HALL, C., Gnr. Arty.	W.	12/10/15 3y 2m. Gnr.
HALL, C. H. C., Pte. 26 Bn.		4/ 5/15 4y 3m. Cpl.
HALL, C. J., Tpr. 3 L.H.R.		26/ 7/17.
HALL, CLIFFORD, Pte. 3 Fd. Am.	13 Fd. Amb. ✣ 21/10/17.	2/ 9/15. Pte. ✣
HALL, E. A., Pte. 12 Bn.	W. 52 Bn. ✣ 18/10/17.	16/ 9/14. Sgt. ✣
HALL, E. V., Pte. 40 Bn.	✣ 13/2/17.	18/ 3/16. Pte. ✣
HALL, E. W., Pte. 12 Bn.	W. ✣ 22/2/17.	12/11/15. Pte. ✣
HALL, F. G., Pte. 40 Bn.	W. ✣ 13/10/17.	28/ 3/16. Pte. ✣
HALL, G. L., Pte. 1 A.C.C.S.		21/ 7/15 4y 1m. Pte.
HALL, G. A., Pte. 12 Bn.	2W. 11 M.G. Coy.	2/10/16 3y. Pte.
HALL, G. O. J., Pte. 15 Bn.	2W. 47 Bn.	13/ 8/15 3y 2m. Pte.
HALL, G. R., Pte. 12 Bn.	W.	10/ 5/16 2y 7m. Pte.
HALL, H., Pte. 26 Bn.	W. ✣ 2/9/18.	25/ 4/15. Pte. ✣
HALL, HY., Pte. R Sec.		18/10/15 1y 2m. Tpr.
HALL, H., Pte. 12 Bn.	40 Bn.	22/ 7/15.
HALL, H. J. W., Pte. 3 G.S.R.	12 Bn. ✣ 3/2/19.	3/ 7/18. Pte. ✣
HALL, JOHN, Pte. 12 Bn.	2W., 51 Bn.	12/ 4/16 2y 2m. Pte.
HALL, JOHN, Pte. 40 Bn.	✣ 13/10/17.	26/ 9/16. Pte. ✣
HALL, J. J., Pte. 12 Bn.	W. 40 Bn.	22/ 8/16 2y 2m. Pte.
HALL, JOHN J., Pte. 40 Bn.		29/ 2/16 3y 6m. Pte.

TASMANIA'S MUSTER ROLL.

NAME.	REMARKS.	RANK ON DISCHARGE. ENLISTED, SERVICE.
HALL, J. Mc., Cpl. 3 L.H.R.		20/ 8/14 11m. Cpl.
HALL, J. T., Pte. 12 Bn.	W. 23 D.V.S.	14/11/16 2y 8m. Pte.
HALL, J. T., Pte. 12 Bn.	W. ✤ 6/10/17.	26/10/15. Pte. ✤
HALL, K. C., Pte. 40 Bn.	✤ 12/10/17.	14/ 3/16. Cpl. ✤
HALL, L. G., Pte. 12 Bn.	5 F.A. Bde.	26/ 7/17 1y 11m. Pte.
HALL, N. J. A., L.Cpl. 12 Bn.	52 Bn. ✤ 14/8/16.	11/ 2/15. L. Cpl. ✤
HALL, R. F. F., Spr. Wireless.	A. Sig. Coy.	13/ 8/17 2y 2m. Spr.
HALL, R., Pte. 12 Bn.	W. 52 Bn.	12/10/15 2y 5m. Pte.
HALL, R. H., Pte. 12 Bn.	W. 40 Bn.	19/10/16 2y 6m. Pte.
HALL, S. J., Pte. 15 Bn.	W., M.M., 47 Bn.	31/ 8/15 3y 2m, Pte.
HALL, T. B., Pte. 4 M.G. Co.	W. 26 Bn.	19/ 3/19. Pte.
HALL, T. G., Pte. 40 Bn.		13/ 2/16 3y 1m. Pte.
HALL, U. R., Pte. 12 Bn.	W. 42 Bn.	23/ 2/16 3y. 8m. Pte.
HALL, W., Pte. 26 Bn.	3W.	15/ 4/15 4y. Cpl.
HALL, W. C., Pte. 12 Bn.	W. 52 Bn.	4/ 1/16 3y 3m. Pte.
HALL, W. E., Pte. 40 Bn.	2W.	25/ 9/16 2y 11m. Pte.
HANCOCK, A. J., Pte. 40 Bn.	3 Div Hqrs.	10/ 3/16 3y 8m. Pte.
HANCOCK, E. R., Spr. Miners.	W. 5 Tnlrs. Coy., 3 Tnlrs. Coy.	1/ 3/16 3y 5m. Spr.
HANCOCK, P. H., Pte. 26 Bn.	✤ 27/4/18.	23/ 4/15. Pte. ✤
HANCOCK, R., Pte. 40 Bn.		29/ 5/16.
HANCOCK, T. W., Gnr. 6 F.A.B.		21/ 9/15 3y 10m, Gnr.
HANCOX, J., Pte. 12 Bn.	✤ About June, 1915.	18/ 8/14 Pte. ✤
HAND, F. C., 40 Bn.	6 F.A. Bde.	Dvr.
HAND, R. V., Gnr. 6 F.A.B.		Gnr.
HANDLEY, D. T., Gnr. F. Arty.	W. 4 D.A.C.	23/11/16 Dvr.
HANEY, J. F., Pte. 12 Bn.	W. 52 Bn.	2/ 8/15 Pte. ✤
HANIGAN, C. H., L. Cpl. 15 Bn.	✤ 31/5/15.	4/11/14 .-Cpl. ✤
HANIGAN, C., Pte. 40 Bn.	W.	29/ 3/16 3y 2m, Pte.
HANIGAN, E. L., Pte. 40 Bn.	2W.	9/10/16 2y 5m, Pte.
HANIGAN, J. P. Gnr.		Gnr. 5/4/19
HANIGAN, P. J., Pte. 40 Bn.	W. 3 Dvl. Hqds.	5/10/16 3y, Pte.
HANKIN, R., Pte. 12 Bn.	W.	26/ 8/16 1y 4m, Pte.
HANKS, F. H., Pte. 40 Bn.	10 L T.M.B.	28/ 2/16
HANLON, A., Pte. 3 G.S.R.	12 Bn.	8/ 7/18 1y 3m, Pte.
HANLON, E., M.W.		M.W.
HANLON, H., Pte. 12 Bn.	9 Bn.	20/ 8/14 4y 5m, Pte.
HANLON, P. B., Pte. 40 Bn, 12Bn.	12 Bn.	18/ 2/16 3y 5m, Pte.
HANNAM, H. G., Pte. Rly.	35 Rly Coy.	24/ 4/17 2y 5m, 2 Cpl.
HANNAN, B. E., Gnr. 4 D.A.C.	W.	14/ 2/16
HANNAN, J., Pte. 15 Fd. Amb.		7/ 2/17 2y 7m, Pte.
HANNAN, J. K., Pte. 12 Bn.	W.	5/11/17 1y 5m, Pte.
HANNAH, T., Gnr. Arty.	108 How. Bty., 6 F.A.B.	10/ 1/16 3y 8m, Gnr.
HANNAM, V., Pte. 26 Bn.		19/ 5/15 1y 4m, Pte.
HANNGN, J., Pte. 2 G.S.R.		9/ 4/18 1y 4m, Pte.
HANSEN, F. J., Cpl. 12 Bn.		15/ 7/15 2y 11m, Pte.
HANSEN, H., Pte. 40 Bn.	W. A.I.F., Hqrs.	27/ 5/16
HANSEN, N., Pte. 12 Bn.	W.	26/10/15 4y 1m, Pte.
HANSEN, R. B., Pte. 26 Bn.		9/12/15
HANSLOW, G. A., Pte. 40 Bn.		14/ 2/16 2y 1m, Pte.
HANSLOW, T. S. R., Cpl. 12 Bn.	W., M.M., 4 Div. Sig. Coy.	28/ 7/15 4y 3m, 2 Cpl.
HANSON, A. E., Pte. 12 Bn.		17/ 3/16 1y 4m, Pte.
HANSON, C. M., Pte. 12 Bn.		24/ 7/16 2y 9m, Pte.
HANSON, E. H., Spr. 3 Fd. Co.		4/ 8/15 3y 11m, Spr.
HANSON, T. G., Pte. 12 Bn.	2W. 51 Bn.	3/ 8/16 3y 10m, Pte.
HANSON, W., Pte. 12 Bn.	2W. M.M., 52 Bn.	5/ 815 3y 3m, Sgt.
HANSON, W. T., Pte. 12 Bn.	W.	20/ 8/14 4y 7m, Pte.
HANSSON, O. H., Pte. 40 Bn.	W.	28/ 3/16 3y, Cpl.
HANTON, F. S., Cpl. 12 Bn.	W. 14 Bn.	16/10/16
HARBOTTLE, F., Capt. 6 F.A.B.	D.S.O., M.I.D.	27/ 9/15 2y 6m, Mjr.
HARDIDGE, A., Gnr. Arty.	57 Bn., 38 Bn.	24/ 2/17
HARDING, A. J., Pte. 40 Bn.	2W.	1/ 4/16 3y, L.-Cpl.
HARDING, A. G., Pte. 12 Bn.	W.	31/ 5/16 1y 7m, Pte.
HARDING, C., Pte. 3 Cyc. C.	1 M.G Coy.	Pte. 3/12/19
HARDING, C. S., Tpr. 3 L.H.R.	14 F.A.B.	11/ 8/15 3y 6m, Gnr.
HARDING, E., Pte. A.F.C.		8/10/16
HARDING, E. F., Pte. 26 Bn.	W. 12 Bn.	16/ 8/15 1y 11m, Pte.
HARDING, G. C., Pte. 12 Bn.	12 Fld. Amb.	2/ 4/17 2y 6m, Pte
HARDING, G. E., Pte. 15 Bn.	✤ 8/8/15.	17/ 9/14 Pte. ✤
HARDING, H., Pte. 12 Bn.		3/ 9/14
HARDING, H. T., Pte. 26 Bn.	2W.	23/ 4/15 4y 10m, Pte.
HARDING, L. J., Pte. 12 Bn.	✤ 3-5/9/16.	14/ 5/15 Pte. ✤
HARDING, T. S., Pte. 12 Bn.	W. 52 Bn., 51 Bn.	4/ 8/15 4y, L.-Cpl.
HARDING, W. H., Pte. 40 Bn.		11/10/16 1y 1m, Pte.
HARDIE, R., Gnr. B.A.C.		14/ 9/14 1y 10m, Gnr.
HARDMAN, B., Pte. 4 M.G.C.	40 Bn. ✤ 3/2/18.	8/ 1/17 Pte. ✤
HARDMAN, E, Pte. 12 Bn.	✤ 25/2/17.	27/ 4/16 Pte. ✤
HARDMAN, H., Pte. 12 Bn.		20/ 8/14 4y 4m. Pte.
HARDMAN, R., Pte. 15 Bn.	✤ 10/5/15.	8/12/14 Pte. ✤
HARDSTAFF, A. E., Pte. 1 G.S.R.	2 A.A.S.C.	2/ 3/18 1y 8m, Far.
HARDSTAFF, C. H., Pte. 15 Bn.	4 Pnr.	5/ 8/15 2y 8m, Cpl.
HARDSTAFF, N. J., Pte. 12 Bn.	W. 40 Bn.	3/ 4/16 2y 8m, Pte.
HARDWICK, G., Pte. 12 Bn.	W.	27/ 4/16 1y 8m, Pte.
HARDWICK, W. I., Pte. 12 Bn.	2W. 40 Bn.	4/ 4/16 2y 5m, Pte.
HARDY, A. W., Dvr. 4 A.S.C.		17/ 5/14 4y 6m, L.-Cpl.
HARDY, A., Pte. 12 Bn.	W. 2 Cyc. Cy.	1/ 4/16 3y 3m, Pte.
HARDY, A. E. R., Pte. M.T.	6 A.M.T.C.	16/11/17 1y 11m, Dvr.

280   TASMANIA'S WAR RECORD, 1914-1918.

NAME.	REMARKS.	RANK ON DISCHARGE. ENLISTED. SERVICE.
HARDY, C. M., Pte. 26 Bn.	2 Pnrs. ✣ 21/10/17.	24/ 6/15 2y 4m, Pte.
HARDY, C. R., Tpr. 3 L.H.R.		9/ 7/15 4y 2m, L.-Cpl
HARDY, E., Spr. 3 Fd. Co.	✣ 5/6/18.	21/ 8/14 Cpl. ✣
HARDY, E., Pte. 12 Bn.	2W. 49 Bn.	28/ 7/15 3y 11m, Pte.
HARDY, H. H., Pte. 40 Bn.	14 Bn.	1/ 9/16 2y 10m, Pte.
HARDY, I. St. C. E., Gnr. 14 FAB.	✣ 25/8/18.	26/ 1/17 Gnr. ✣
HARDY, J. A., Pte. 12 Bn.	1 F.A.B.	19/11/15 3y 9m, Gnr.
HARDY, J. C., Pte. 12 Bn.	W. 52 Bn. 31 Bn. ✣ 10/4/18.	16/10/15 Pte. ✣
HARDY, J., Pte. 4 M.G.C.		26/ 6/16 1y 9m, Pte.
HARDY, P. A., Pte. 12 Bn.	W. 52 Bn.	
HARE, C., Pte. 12 Bn.	W.	1/ 9/14 1y 9m, Sgt.
HARE, H. J., Pte 15 Bn.	W., D.C.M., Bronze Medal, 47 Bn.	26/ 7/15 4y 3m, W.O.
HARGRAVES, C. H., Sgt. 6 F.A.B.	✣ 15/8/16.	14/ 9/15 Sgt. ✣
HARINGTON, G. H., Tpr. 3 L.H.R.		1/ 3/17 2y 5m, Tpr.
HARINGTON, K., Tpr. 3 L.H.R.		20/ 2/17 2y 6m, Tpr.
HARKNESS, W. K., Pte. 12 Bn.		4/11/16 2y 4m, Pte.
HARLEY, L. P., Gnr. 120 How. By.		27/ 4/16 1y 11m, Dvr.
HARMAN, A., Pte. 40 Bn.	W.	27/10/16 2y 1m, Pte.
HARMAN, A. T., Pte. 13 Bn.	✣ 16/10/17.	7/ 9/15 Pte. ✣
HARMAN, E. C., Pte. Wireless.		30/11/16
HARMAN, G., Pte. 12 Bn.		9/ 7/15 4y 3m, Pte.
HARMAN, H. F., Pte. 12 Bn.	W. 52 Bn.	3/11/15 1y 6m, Pte.
HARMAN, S. A. J. L. Cpl. 26 Bn.	W.	25/ 2/15 2y 6m, Cpl.
HARMAN, L. H., Dvr. 8 Fd. Co.	W., 14 Engrs. ✣ 13/10/17.	31/ 1/16 Dvr. ✣
HARMER, F. A., Pte. 12 Bn.	W.	3/ 8/15 4y, Pte.
HARPER, A. T., Pte. 15 Bn.	W.	4/10/14 2y 5m, Pte.
HARPER, C., Pte. 26 Bn.	W. 36 Bn. ✣ 13/9/18.	22/ 6/15 Sgt.
HARPER, D. J., Pte. 15 Bn.	✣ 26/5/15.	3/10/14 Pte. ✣
HARPER, D. L., Pte. A.S.C.	27 Co. A.S.C.	14/ 3/16 3y 7m, Pte.
HARPER, E., Pte. 40 Bn.	✣ 13/10/17.	3/ 1/17 Pte. ✣
HARPER, G., Pte. 26 Bn.	✣24/5/18.	13/ 3/15 Pte. ✣
HARPER, H. L., Sgt. A.S.C. 27 Co.	27 Coy.	17/ 2/16 3y 8m, Cpl.
HARPER, H. A., Pte. 40 Bn.	W.	25/ 9/16 1y 5m, Pte.
HARPER, J. W., Pte. 4 M.G. Bn.		9/ 9/16 3y 7m, Pte.
HARPER, J. A., 12 Bn.	W. 15 Bn.	19/ 1/16 3y 8m, Pte.
HARPER, J. R., Pte. 40 Bn.	W.	6/ 4/16 1y 7m, Pte.
HARPER, J. S., Pte. 5 G.S.B.	3 L.H.R.	28/ 6/18 11m, Tpr.
HARPER, R. B., Pte. 40 Bn.	✣ 12/2/17.	24/ 1/16 Pte ✣
HARPER, R. H., Pte. 12 Bn.	W. M.M. 52 Bn. 49 Bn.	19/ 1/16 3y 3m, Pte.
HARPER, S. B., Pte. A.A.M.C.	15 Fd. Amb.	6/10/16 2y 5m, Pte.
HARPER, T., Pte. 26 Bn.		11/ 3/15
HARREX, A. E., Gnr. Arty.	23 How. Bde., 6 B.A.C	9/12/15 3y 9m, Dvr.
HARREX, C. L., Pte. 12 Bn.	W.	23/10/16 2y 5m, Pte.
HARREX, P. C., Pte. 12 Bn.	52 Bn., 4 M.G. Coy.	25/ 1/16 1y 7m, Dvr.
HARRINGTON, A. D., Pte. 12 Bn.	W.	22/ 8/14 1y 2m, Pte.
HARRINGTON, G. P., Pte. 40 Bn.	Re-enlisted 40 Bn., 19 Bn., 45 Bn.	11/ 3/16 Pte.
HARRINGTON, J., Cpl. Rly.	4 A.B.G.R.O.C.	28/ 9/16 2y 11m, L.-Cpl.
HARRINGTON, N., Pte. 12 Bn.	W.	24/ 8/14 2y 3m, Pte.
HARRIS, C. G., Lieut. A.A.D.C.		28/10/17 1y 11m, Capt.
HARRIS, R. B., Pte. 12 Bn.	W.	10/ 1/15 4y 5m, L.-Cpl.
HARRIS, R. J. P., Pte. 40 Bn.		22/ 2/17 2y 3m, Pte.
HARRIS, H. G., Lieut. 2 G.S.B.		1/ 7/18 Lieut.
HARROWFIELD, N., Pte. 12 Bn.		23/12/14
HARROWFIELD, R. H., 2 Lt. 12 Bn	W. ✣ 16/5/17.	17/ 1/16 Lieut. ✣
HARRY, V. C., Pte. 15 Bn.		5/ 1/15
HART, E. A., L Cpl. 12 Bn.	52 Bn. ✣ 8/10/16.	19/ 8/15 L.-Cpl. ✣
HART, E. S., Tpr. 3 L.H.R.		20/ 8/14 4y 6m, Sgt.
HART, J. A., Pte. 12 Bn.	1 Sal. Coy.	21/ 8/14 Pte.
HART, L. R., Lieut. 40 Bn.		7/ 3/16 1y 4m, Lieut.
HART, M. N., Tpr. 3 L.H.R.		1/12/14 2y, Pte
HART, O. R., Gnr. 9 Bty.	W. 3 L.T.M.B.	7/ 8/14 4y 7m, Gnr.
HART, R. G., Pte. 7 Bn.	W.	16/ 5/16
HART, R. J., Cpl. 3 L.H.	Re-enlisted A.F.C	24/ 8/14 4y 11m, Sgt.
HART, R. J., Pte. 40 Bn.	W., M.M.	27/ 2/16 3y 6m, Pte.
HART, T., Spr. 3 Fd. Amb.	13 Fd. Amb.	24/ 8/14 3y 9m, Sgt.
HART, W., Pte. 12 Bn.	2W., 51 Bn.	19/ 8/15 3y 1m, Pte.
HARTLEY, B., Pte. 40 Bn.		18/ 2/16
HARTILL, G., Pte. Wireless		28/ 1/18 11m, Pte.
HARNETT, A. L., Pte. 12 Bn.		3/ 5/16 2y 10m, Sgnr.
HARTNETT, A. J., Pte. 15 Bn.	4 Pnrs.	11/ 1/15 4y 3m, L.-Cpl.
HARTNEY, R., Gnr. Siege Arty.	A.A.O.C.	7/ 6/15 4y 1m, Gnr.
HARVEY, A. A., Pte. 40 Bn.	✣ 17/1/17.	14/ 3/16 Pte. ✣
HARVEY, A. K., Pte. 15 Bn.	2W. ✣ 3/9/16.	22/ 9/14 Pte. ✣
HARVEY, C. J. W., Gnr. 3 F.A.B.	W. 3 Fd. Co.	15/10/14 4y 4m, Dvr.
HARVEY, D. H., Pte. A.F.C.		1/ 2/18 1y 1m, 2 A.M.
HARVEY, E. T., Tpr. 3 L.H.R.	2 F.A. Bde.	21/ 7/15 4y 1m, Dvr.
HARVEY, F., Gnr. 10 F.A.B.	4 D.A.C.	21/ 2/16 3y 8m, Gnr.
HARVEY, H., Dvr. 3 F.A.B.		26/ 8/14 4y 5m, Bdr.
HARVEY, H. E., Pte. 12 Bn.	W., M.M.	6/12/15 3y 4m, Pte.
HARVEY, J. F., Dvr. 3 F.A.B.	W.	18/ 9/14 3y 10m, Dvr
HARVEY, J., Tpr. 3 L.H.R.	4 D.A.C.	1/ 8/15 2y 2m, Dvr.
HARVEY, J. B., Pte. 40 Bn.	✣ 29/9/18	30/ 9/16 Pte. ✣
HARVEY, J. W., Pte. 40 Bn.	W.	10/ 3/16 3y 1m, Pte.
HARVEY, J. J., Pte. 12 Bn.	W	30/ 5/17 2y 3m, Pte.
HARVEY, J. S., Pte. 12 Bn.		1/ 6/16 3y 6m, Pte.
HARVEY, L. W., Pte. 40 Bn.	✣ 7/6/17.	21/ 2/16 Pte. ✣

TASMANIA'S MUSTER ROLL.

NAME.	REMARKS.	RANK ON DISCHARGE. ENLISTED. SERVICE.
HARVEY, M. S., Pte. 12 Bn.	W. 51 Bn.	17/ 7/15 4y 3m, Pte.
HARVEY, N. G., Tpr. 3 L.H.R.		18/ 8/15 4y 1m, Sgt.
HARVEY, P. A., Tpr. 3 L.H.R.	W.	20/ 8/14 4y 1m, Tpr.
HARVEY, R. C., Pte. A.A.M.C.	3 A.G.H.	22/ 3/17 2y 7m, Pte.
HARVEY, R. C., Pte. 12 Bn.	W.	1/10/17 1y 5m, Pte.
HARVEY, R. M'F., Pte. 12 Bn.	W.	15/ 9/15 2y 8m, Pte.
HARVEY, R. P., Pte. 12 Bn.	2W	29/ 8/14 2y 9m, Pte.
HARVEY, S., Pte. 12 Bn.		2/ 9/14 2y 10m, Pte.
HARVEY, V. J., Pte. 40 Bn.	2W.	21/ 2/16 3y 6m, Pte.
HARVEY, W. B., Gnr. 6 F.A.B.	2W.	27/ 9/16 2y 9m, Gnr.
HARVEY, W. J., Pte. 15 Bn.	10 F.A. Bde.	8/ 6/15 4y 2m, Dvr.
HARWOOD, C. J., Pte. 12 Bn.	W.	18/ 6/17 Pte.
HARWOOD, G. E., Pte. 26 Bn.	W. 12 Bn.	11/ 8/15 1y 5m, Pte.
HARWOOD, T. W., Pte. 40 Bn.		3/10/16 1y, Pte.
HARRIS, A. A., Pte. 4 M.G. Coy.	✠ 27/7/17.	11/ 4/16 Pte ✠
HARRIS, A. E., Pte. 40 Bn.	W.	25/ 9/16 2y 9m, Pte.
HARRIS, A. G., Pte. 12 Bn.	W.	16/ 6/16 2y 11m, Pte.
HARRIS, A. G., Pte. 26 Bn.	W.	13/ 4/15 1y 7m, Pte.
HARRIS, A., Pte. 1 A.C.H.		15/ 9/15 1y 1m, Pte.
HARRIS, A. E. O., Pte. 40 Bn.		6/ 6/16 1y 2m, Pte.
HARRIS, A. J., Cpl. 40 Bn.	W. ✠ 9/4/18.	13/ 9/16 Pte. ✠
HARRIS, A. E., Spr. 3 Fd. Co.	M.T. Coy.	22/ 7/15 4y 6m, Cpl.
HARRIS, B. E., Pte. 40 Bn.	W.	27/ 6/16 3y 3m, Pte.
HARRIS, C. G., Spr. 1 Tnlrs.		23/ 3/16
HARRIS, C. M., Pte. 12 Bn.		4/ 1/16 2y 8m, Pte.
HARRIS, C. N., Pte. 40 Bn.		13/ 2/17 2y 3m, Pte.
HARRIS, E. E. G., Pte. 12 Bn.	14 Bn.	12/10/16 2y 1m, Pte.
HARRIS, E. A., Pte. 12 Bn.	2W. 52 Bn.	27/ 1/16 3y 1m, Pte.
HARRIS, E. F., Cpl. 12 Bn.	52 Bn.	9/ 8/15 4y, Lieut.
HARRIS, E. G., Gnr. 3 F.A.B	W.	27/ 8/14 4y 6m, Sgt.
HARRIS, E. V., Gnr. D.A.C.	22 How. Bde.	1/ 9/15 3y, Bdr.
HARRIS, F. W., Pte. 40 Bn.	2W., M.M.	26/ 9/16 2y 9m, L.-Cpl.
HARRIS, G., Pte. 12 Bn.	✠ 6-10/4/17.	21/ 8/15 Pte. ✠
HARRIS, G. A., Bdr. 3 F.A.B.	21 F.A. Bde.	26/ 8/14 4y 2m, Sgt.
HARRIS, G. H. J., Sgnr. 12 Bn.	Signrs.	14/11/14
HARRIS, G. D., Pte. 40 Bn.		27/ 8/17 1y 7m, L.-Cpl.
HARRIS, H. N., Pte. 40 Bn	4 M.G.B. ✠ 9/9/18.	17/10/16 Pte ✠
HARRIS, H. J., Pte. 40 Bn	✠ 7/6/17.	27/ 9/16 Pte. ✠
HARRIS, I. E. V., Pte. 12 Bn.	4W.	2/ 5/16 3y 4m, Pte.
HARRIS, J. W., Pte. 12 Bn.	15 Fd. Amb.	21/ 8/16 1y 10m, Pte.
HARRIS, J., Pte. 12 Bn.	2 A.A.M.T. Coy.	16/ 8/16 2y 6m, Pte.
HARRIS, L. E., Pte. 26 Bn.	M.M.	2/ 3/15
HARRIS, L. B., Pte. 1 A.G.H.	8 Fld Amb.	20/ 6/15 4y 5m, Pte.
HARRIS, R. L., Pte. 12 Bn.	✠ 15/4/17	29/ 5/16 Pte. ✠
HARRIS, R. B., Pte. 26 Bn.	W.	22/ 6/15 4y 2m, Pte.
HARRIS, T. T., Pte 12 Bn.	40 Bn.	19/ 2/16 3y 8m, Dvr.
HARRIS, T. W. F., Pte. 40 Bn.		11/ 9/16 3y, Sgt.
HARRIS, W. C., Pte. 12 Bn.	2W., 4 M.G. Bn.	11/11/15 3y 9m, Pte.
HARRIS, W., Pte. 12 Bn.	26 Bn.	25/ 8/15 4y, Pte.
HARRIS, W. A., Pte. 12 Bn.	✠ 19-20/9/17.	9/10/16 Pte. ✠
HARRIS, W. H., Pte 40 Bn.	4 M.G. Co. ✠ 17/2/18.	17/10/16 Pte. ✠
HARRIS, W. H., Pte. 12 Bn.	✠ 8/10/17.	16/ 6/16 Pte. ✠
HARRIS, W. J., Pte. A.A.M.C.	3 Fd. Amb.	14/ 8/17 2y 2m, Pte
HARRISON, A., Pte. 12 Bn.	✠ 23/7/16.	24/ 8/15 Pte. ✠
HARRISON, C. J., Pte. 40 Bn.		17/10/16 1y 6m, Pte.
HARRISON, C. Gnr. 6 F.A.B.		4/10/15 3y 10m, Gnr.
HARRISON, C., Pte. 12 Bn.		29/12/14 1y 8m, Pte.
HARRISON, C.-V., Pte. 12 Bn.	W. ✠ 23/7/16.	19/ 8/14 .-Cpl. ✠
HARRISON, C. W., Pte. 2 G.S.R.	12 Bn.	29/ 4/18 1y 3m, Pte.
HARRISON, E., Pte. 26 Bn.	✠ 29/7/16	28/ 9/15 Pte. ✠
HARRISON, E. W., Sgn. 15 Bn.	47 Bn.	23/ 4/15 4y 7m, 2 Lt.
HARRISON, G. A., Pte. 12 Bn.		6/ 7/17 1y 5m, Pte.
HARRISON, H. A., Pte. 40 Bn.	68 A.F.C., 40 Bn.	17/ 2/16 3v 5m, Pte.
HARRISON, H. C., L.-Cpl. 12 Bn.	✠ 25/4/15.	19/ 8/14 L.-Cpl. ✠
HARRISON, H. A., Dvr. 7 F. Amb.	13 Fd. Amb.	22/ 2/15 4y 2m, Dvr.
HARRISON, J., Pte. 12 Bn.	✠ 1/11/17.	21/ 3/16 Pte ✠
HARRISON, J. C., Pte. Wireless	A.F.C.	25/ 8/17 1y 9m. 2 A.M.
HARRISON, J. T., Cpl. 15 Bn.		25/ 9/14 2y 3m, Sgt.
HARRISON, J. W., Pte. 26 Bn.	12 Bn. ✠ 23/7/16.	19/ 8/15 Pte. ✠
HARRISON, J. W., Spr. 2 Tnlrs.		3/ 6/16 1y 9m, Spr.
HARRISON, M., Pte. 15 Bn.	W., 47 Bn. ✠ 5/4/18.	28/ 8/15 Pte. ✠
HARRISON, N. M., Pte 15 Bn.	✠ 16/10/15.	6/10/14 Pte. ✠
HARRISON, P. H., Cpl. 26 Bn.	W. ✠ 5/11/16.	21/ 7/15 Cpl. ✠
HARRISON, R. W., Pte. 12 Bn.	✠ 6-10/4/17.	16/ 1/15 Pte. ✠
HARRISON, R. W., Tpr. 3 L.H.R.	W.	23/ 9/14 1y 11m, L.Cpl
HARRISON, V., Pte. 15 Bn.	W., 4 T.M. By. ✠ 11/4/17.	13/ 8/15 Pte. ✠
HARRISON, W. A., Pte. 37 Bn.		21/ 1/16 2y 9m, Pte.
HARRISON, W. H., Pte. 26 Bn.	W.	21/ 7/15 1y 11m, Pte.
HASKING, A. G., Pte. 40 Bn.		26/ 8/15
HASLAM, A. N., Pte. 12 Bn.		27/10/15
HASLAM, T. W., Lt. 12 Bn.	M.B.E., 3 M.I.D.	16/ 5/15
HASLAM, T., 2 A.M. A.F.C.		8/12/16 2y 10m, 2 A.M
HASLAM, W. T., Spr. Engrs.	9 Co.	21/ 3/16 2y 2m, Spr.
HASSETT, F., Pte 12 Bn.	52 Bn., 13 T.M.B.	30/12/15 1y 10m, Pte.
HASSETT, J. H., Spr. 5 Mnrs.	5 Tnl. Co.	29/ 3/16 1y 3m, Spr.
HASTIE, A., Pte 40 Bn.	✠ 13/10/17.	31/ 3/16 Sgt. ✠
HASTIE, H. W., Pte. 40 Bn	W.	14/ 3/16 2y 3m, Pte.

282   TASMANIA'S WAR RECORD, 1914-1918.

NAME.	REMARKS.	RANK ON DISCHARGE. ENLISTED. SERVICE.
HASWELL, E. C., Pte. 1 A.C.H.		19/11/14
HATHAWAY, A. R., Pte. 3 G.S.R.		22/ 8/18 9m. Pte.
HATHAWAY, W. J., Pte. 40 Bn.	W. ✣ 13/10/17.	3/ 3/16 Pte. ✣
HATTON, J. Spr. 5 M. Co.	2 Tun. Co.	30/ 3/16 3y 7m. Spr.
HATTON, M. J. V., Pte. 4 M.G. Co.	6 M.G. Co.	30/11/18 11m. Pte.
HAWKER, A. F., Pte. 12 Bn.		7/10/16 Pte.
HAWKER, C. R. P., Lt. 40 Bn.	W.	14/ 3/16 2y 11m. Lt.
HAWES, H., Pte. 40 Bn.		16/10/16 2y 11m. Pte.
HAWKE, E. D., Pte. Rally.		1/ 3/18 2m. Pte.
HAWKER, A. F., Pte. 12 Bn.		7/10/16 2y 11m. Pte.
HAWKER, S. C. G., Pte. A.A.M.C.		15/12/17 1y 1m. Pte.
HAWKES, H. A., Pte. 12 Bn.	✣ 24/4/18.	27/ 4/17 Pte. ✣
HAWKESFORD, B., Pte. 12 Bn.	W., M.M. 52 Bn.	31/ 5/15 4y. Pte.
HAWKESFORD, H., Pte. A.S.C.	✣ 24/10/18.	17/ 1/16 Pte. ✣
HAWKESFORD, W. G., Pte. A.M.C.		2/ 3/16 2y 11m. L.-Cpl
HAWKESFORD, W. C., Pte. 12 Bn.	M.M., 51 Bn., 27 A.A.S.C.	14/ 7/15 4y 1m. Dvr.
HAWKEY, J. R., Pte. 12 Bn.		8/11/16
HAWKINS, A., Pte. 40 Bn.		2/ 3/16 2y 4m. L.-Cpl
HAWKINS, F., Pte 2 G.S.R.	12 Bn	10/ 6/18 1y 4m. Pte.
HAWKINS, H. N., Pte. 12 Bn.	W., 51 Bn.	11/ 1/16 3y 6m. Pte.
HAWKINS, L., Pte. 12 Bn.	✣ 25-28/4/15.	21/ 8/14 Pte. ✣
HAWKINS, R. G., Pte. 40 Bn.	W., 51 Bn., 9 Fd. Amb.	23/ 3/16 3y 7m. Pte.
HAWKINS, W. C., Pte. 26 Bn.	✣ 28/7/16.	1/ 4/15 Pte. ✣
HAWLEY, S., Mjr. 12 Bn	W.	19/ 8/14 2y 3m. Lt-Col.
HAWORTH, H., Tpr. 3 L.H.R.		4/ 9/15 4y 1m. L.-Cpl
HAY, A. S. L., Pte. 40 Bn.		2/10/16 2y 11m. Cpl.
HAY, B., Pte. 12 Bn.	✣ 4/2/19.	9/ 5/17 Pte. ✣
HAY, C. L., Pte. 40 Bn	2W.	29/ 2/16 2y 3m. Pte.
HAY, E., Pte. 26 Bn.	W.	18/ 5/15 4y 4m. Lt.
HAY, H., Dvr. 3 F.A.B.	W.	26/ 8/14 5y 3m. Dvr.
HAY, H. J., Pte. 12 Bn.	W.	15/11/17 1y 4m. Pte.
HAY, J., Pte. 12 Bn.	3W., 52 Bn., 42 Bn.	9/ 8/15 3y 8m. Pte.
HAY, L. P., Gnr. 3 F.A.B.	W., 1 A.F.C., 9 Bty.	5/ 3/15 4y 2m. Gnr.
HAY, M. A.		Spr.
HAY, N., Pte. 12 Bn.	W.	8/ 8/17 1y 10m. Pte.
HAY, P. O., Pte. 26 Bn.	W., M.M., 12 Bn.	8/ 9/15 4y 1m. Sgt.
HAY, T. D., Pte. 1 G.S.R.	40 Bn.	14/ 1/18 1y 9m. Pte.
HAY, W. G., Pte. 12 Bn.	W.	31/ 8/15 2y 3m. Pte.
HAYDEN, A. V., Pte. 15 Bn.	4 M.G. Co.	24/ 9/14 5y 3m. Dvr.
HAYDEN, B. G., Pte. 1 G.S.R.	11 M.G. Co.	14/ 2/18 1y 8m. Pte.
HAYDON, L. C., Pte. 15 Bn.	W., 47 Bn.	6/ 8/15 2y 10m. Pte.
HAYES, A. D., Pte. 12 Bn.	W., 69 Bn., A.M.C. Dtls., 12 Bn.	4/10/15 3y 6m. Pte.
HAYES, A. E., Pte. 12 Bn.	40 Bn.	24/10/16 2y 10m. L.-Cpl
HAYES, C. L. J., Cpl. 3 Fd. Amb.	M.M.	24/ 8/14
HAYES, C. O. J. C., Pte. 26 Bn.	W., 52 Bn., P.O.W.	3/ 9/15
HAYES, E. H. R., Pte. 40 Bn.	W. ✣ 12/2/17.	5/ 5/16 Pte. ✣
HAYES, F. G., Pte. 12 Bn.	W., 52 Bn.	9/ 9/15 1y 8m. Pte.
HAYES, H. H., Pte. 12 Bn.	✣ 13/6/15.	15/12/14 Pte. ✣
HAYES, J., Pte. 40 Bn.		27/ 8/17
HAYES, John, Pte. 1 A.C.H.		3/12/14
HAYES, L., Pte. 12 Bn.	W.	25/10/16 2y 4m. Pte.
HAYES, J. C., Pte. 37 Bn.	3W.	4/ 2/15 4y 2m. Pte.
HAYES, O. R., Spr. Miners.	2 Tun. Co.	24/ 1/16 3y 10m. Spr.
HAYES, R. W., Pte. 12 Bn.	W.	7/ 4/16 2y 1m. Pte.
HAYES, T. T., Pte. 12 Bn.	W., re-enlisted 40 Bn. ✣ 28/3/18.	28/ 1/15 Pte. ✣
HAYES, W. M., Pte. 2 G.S.R.	40 Bn.	17/ 4/18 11m. Pte.
HAYGARTH, A. W., F.-Sgt. 6 Fd. Co	M.I.D.	28/ 8/15 4y 5m. F.-Sgt
HAYNES, A. E., Pte. 2 G.S.R.	12 Bn. ✣ 23/10/18.	30/10/16 Pte. ✣
HAYNES, W. F., Pte. 12 Bn.	? ? ? ? . ?	18/ 5/15 Pte. ✣
HAYS, E. R. F., Pte. 12 Bn.	2 Sig. Sqn.	13/10/15 4y. Pte.
HAYS, W. H., Gnr. F.A.B.	2 Bty.	24/10/16 2y 11m. Dvr.
HAYTER, B., Pte. 40 Bn.	W., 26 Bn.	25/ 4/16 2y 3m. Pte.
HAYTER, R. C. St. J., Tpr. 3 L.H.	8 L.H.	1/ 9/15 1y 2m. Tpr.
HAYWARD, A. N., Pte. 1 G.S.R.	3 Div. H.Q.T.	9/ 3/18 1y 7m. Pte.
HAYWARD, C. H., Pte. 26 Bn.	12 Bn. ✣ 23-25/7/16.	29/ 7/15 Pte. ✣
HAYWARD, E. J., Pte. 4 M.G. Co.	3 M.G. Bn. ✣ 19/9/18.	26/10/16 Cpl. ✣
HAYWOOD, G., Pte. 12 Bn.	52 Bn., 51 Bn.	14/ 7/15 4y 1m. Cpl.
HAYWOOD, G. H., Gnr. Arty.	54 Seige Bty.	2/ 2/15 4v 3m. Gnr.
HAYWOOD, W., Pte. 12 Bn.		12/10/16 2v 9m. Pte.
HAZELL, F. A., Pte. 40 Bn.	✣ 30/9/17.	24/ 8/16 Pte. ✣
HAZLEWOOD, G. E., Pte. T.M. By.	40 Bn.	17/10/16
HAZLEWOOD, W. F., Pte. 15 Bn.	14 Bn.	22/ 9/14 3y 2m. Pte.
HEADLAM, A. V., Gnr. 12 F.A.B.		6/4/16 3y 5m. Gnr.
HEADLAM, E. S., Tpr. 3 L.H.	Imp. Camel Cps., 67 Sqd. A.F.C.	12/ 4/15 4y 2m. Lt.
HEADLAM, F. E., Gnr. 8 F.A.B.	W.	2/ 2/16 3y 8m. Gnr
HEADLAM, G. K., Pte. 12 Bn.	2W., 14 Fd. Amb.	17/12/14
HEADLY, A. St. C., Pte. 12 Bn.	W., 52 Bn. ✣ 2/2/17.	2/ 8/15 L.-Cpl. ✣
HEALD, H. G., Pte. 26 Bn.	3W.	27/ 7/15 3y 10m. Pte.
HEALD, J. F., Pte. 26 Bn.	W. ✣ 29/8/18.	25/ 9/15 L.-Cpl. ✣
HEALEY, D., Gnr. Arty.	17 Bty.	23/ 9/15 3y 9m. Bdr.
HEALEY, J., Pte. A.A.M.C.		30/10/16 2y 11m. Pte.
HEALEY, J. M., Pte. 40 Bn.	2W.	21/ 9/16 2y 7m. Pte.
HEALEY, N. D., Pte. 1 A.G.H.	3 F.A.B.	5/ 6/15
HEALY, L., Pte. 40 Bn.	W., 49 Bn.	29/ 3/16
HEALEY, R. D., Dvr. 23 How. Bty.		Dvr.
HEAN, A., Tpr. 3 L.H.	3W.	21/ 8/14
HEAN, C. A., Pte. A.M.C.	2 A.G.H.	6/ 9/16 3y 2m. Pte.

TASMANIA'S MUSTER ROLL. 283

NAME.	REMARKS.	RANK ON DISCHARGE. ENLISTED. SERVICE.
HEAN, C. T., Pte. 40 Bn.	3W.	2/10/16 2y 9m, Pte.
HEAN, K. D., Pte. 26 Bn.	✸ 20/6/16.	16/ 8/15 Pte. ✸
HEARNE, E., M.W.		
HEARPS, A. J., Sgt. 12 Bn.	W. ✸ 22/8/16.	20/ 8/14 2 Lt. ✸
HEARPS, C. C., Pte. 26 Bn.	W.	23/ 2/15 2y 5m, Pte.
HEARPS, G. C., Pte. 12 Bn.	W., 52 Bn.	4/ 8/15 3y 3m, Pte.
HEARPS, C., Pte. 40 Bn.	M.M.	7/ 3/16 3y 7m, Dvr.
HEARPS, W. N., Spr. 6 Fd. Co.	10 F.A.B.	10/ 4/16 3y 5m, Bdr.
HEATH, C. L., Gnr. 13 F.A.B.	W., 2 D.A.C.	12/11/15 3y 11m, Dvr.
HEATH, E. H., Gnr. 6 F.A.B.		11/ 1/17 2y 10m, Gnr.
HEATH, T. J., Pte. 26 Bn.	W., 12 Bn.	3/ 8/15 4y, Pte.
HEATH, W. J., Pte. 12 Bn.	5 M.T.M. Bty.	10/ 4/16 2y 6m, Pte.
HEATHCOTE, A. H., Pte. 12 Bn.	W.	2/ 5/16 2y 6m, Pte.
HEATHCOTE, G. T., Pte. 26 Bn.	W. ✸ 9/8/18.	10/ 4/15 Sgt. ✸
HEATHCOTE, J. P., Tpr. 3 L.H.R.		21/ 8/14 4y 6m, Cpl.
HEATHCOTE, W. J., Pte. 12 Bn.	2W., 1 M.G. Bn.	2/ 5/16 3y 4m, Pte.
HEATHER, F., Gnr. Arty.	1 D.A.C.	17/10/16 3y. Dvr.
HEATHERBELL, G. G., Pte. 12 Bn.	W.	29/ 6/16
HEATHERBELL, P. E., Pte. 12 Bn.	W. ✸ 5/10/17.	29/ 6/16 Pte. ✸
HEATHERBELL, W. E. Pte. 12 Bn.	3W.	8/ 4/16 2y 11m, Pte.
HEATHORNE, J. H., Pte. 12 Bn.		28/ 4/16 2y 2m, Pte.
HEATLEY, C. J., Dvr. 10 A.S.C.	Anzac T.C. and D.H.Q.	11/ 9/14 4y 4m, Dvr.
HEATON, G. F., Pte. 12 Bn.	W. ✸ 10/4/17.	19/ 8/15 1y 8m. ✸
HEAVEN, R., Pte. 12 Bn.	W.	4/ 8/15
HEAVER, J., Pte. 12 Bn.		10/ 7/17
HEAWOOD, E. O., Pte. 15 Bn.	2W. ✸ 8/8/16.	16/ 9/14 Pte. ✸
HEAWOOD, J. C., Pte. 12 Bn.	W. ✸ 19/5/15.	16/ 9/14 Pte. ✸
HEAWOOD, W. J. J., Pte. 12 Bn.	3W., 51 Bn.	26/11/14 3y 9m, Spr.
HEAZLEWOOD, C. E., Pte. 12 Bn.	W.	2/ 5/16 3y 4m, Pte.
HEAZLEWOOD, G. E., Pte. T.M. By	40 Bn.	17/10/16 2y 3m, Pte.
HEAZLEWOOD, W. G., Pte. 40 Bn.	✸ 31/8/18.	3/ 2/17 Pte. ✸
HECKRATH, C. A., Pte. 26 Bn.	✸ 14/11/16.	19/ 3/15 L.-Cpl. ✸
HEDBURG, D. E., Cpl. 15 Bn.	2 A.A.M.T.C.	18/ 8/15 3y 11m. Sgt.
HEDDLE, B. C., Pte. 15 Bn.	Vet. Hos.	28/ 8/15
HEDGE, B., Pte. 12 Bn.	W.	14/ 5/17 1y 11m, Pte.
HEDGE, E., Pte. 40 Bn.	W.	25/ 9/16 3y, Pte.
HEDINGTON, J., Gnr. Arty.	W., 3 F.A.B.	13/ 5/16 3y 4m, Gnr.
HEENEY, W. J., Pte. 40 Bn.	3W.	6/ 9/16 3y, Pte.
HEEREY, L. D., Gnr. Arty.	4 D.S. Co.	12/10/16 3y 1m, Spr.
HEFFERON, H., Pte. 12 Bn.	W.	6/12/14 3y 7m, Cpl.
HEFFERNAN, T. G., Gnr. 14 F.A.B.	✸ 1/10/17.	27/10/15 Gnr. ✸
HEFFERNAN, W. A., Pte. 12 Bn.		11/ 7/16 2y 9m, Pte.
HEFFORD, J., Gnr. 6 F.A.B.	27 Bty.	25/ 1/16 3y 8m, Gnr.
HEFFORD, W. P., Pte. 12 Bn.		2/ 5/16 1y 5m, Pte.
HEHIR, H. E., Pte. 12 Bn.	P.O.W.	29/ 7/16 3y 1m, Pte.
HEHIR, W. J., Pte. 15 Bn.	W., 47 Bn. ✸ 13/8/16	20/ 7/15 Pte. ✸
HELLESSEY, S. J., Gnr. 9 Bty.	1 D.A.C.	1/ 9/14 4y 5m, Gnr.
HELLEWELL, J. H., Spr. 3 Fd. Co.	2W., M.M.	4/ 8/15 3y 11m, Spr.
HEMPHILL, C., Pte. 1 A.C.H.	1 Div. M.T. Co.	28/ 9/15 3v 8m, Dvr.
HEMPHILL, J., Pte. 15 Bn.		3/ 8/15 1v 5m, Pte.
HEMPSEED, R. W., Tpr. 2 G.S.R.	3 L.H.	19/ 3/18 1v 5m, Tpr.
HENDERSON, A., Pte. 15 Bn.	W., 10 F.A.B.	9/12/14 4v 4m, Gnr.
HENDERSON, A. G., Pte. 12 Bn.	✸ 7/10/17.	30/11/14 Pte. ✸
HENDERSON, C., Cpl. 12 Bn.	W., 52 Bn.	4/ 8/15 1v 6m, Pte.
HENDERSON, D. S., Capt. A.A.M.C		20/ 7/17 1y. Capt.
HENDERSON, F. F., Pte. 3 G.S.R.	3 L.H.R. (enlisted under name Fleming)	6/ 4/18
HENDERSON, J. A., Pte. 12 Bn.	1 Pnrs. ✸ 20/12/16.	19/ 8/15 Pte. ✸
HENDERSON, J., Pte. 15 Bn.	✸ 9/8/16.	12/ 8, 15 Pte. ✸
HENDERSON, J. G., Dvr. 1 A. Wire		30/ 3/16 2y 2m, Dvr.
HENDERSON, J. S., Pte. 12 Bn.		3/ 9/16 3y 1m, Pte.
HENDERSON, Q. J., Gnr. Arty.	W., 51 Bty.	16/ 8/15 4y 2m, Gnr.
HENDERSON, R., Pte. 40 Bn.	W., 49 Bn. ✸ 8/3/17.	29/ 3/16 Pte. ✸
HENDERSON, R. A., Pte. 26 Bn.		19/ 5/15 1v 3m, Pte.
HENDERSON, W., Pte. 12 Bn.	✸ 1/5/18.	18/ 5/17 Pte. ✸
HENLEY, C. V., Pte. 12 Bn.	W. ✸ 19-22/8/16.	20/ 1/15 Pte. ✸
HENLEY, G. H., Pte. 40 Bn.	2W.	23/ 5/16 2y 11m, Sgt.
HENRI, L., Pte. 40 Bn.	W.	5/12/16 2v 10m, Pte.
HENRICKS, A. O., Pte. 12 Bn.	W., 51 Bn.	12/ 7/15 4v 2m, Pte.
HENRY, C. W., Pte. 1 G.S.R.	14 F.A.B.	13/ 2/18 1v 10m, Gnr.
HENRY, C. D. M'A., Gnr. 9 Fd. By		17/ 6/15 4y 2m, S.-Cpl.
HENRY, D. S., Gnr. 6 F.A.B.		24/ 8/15 4y 3m, Gnr.
HENRY, H. L., Pte. 40 Bn.	✸ 4/10/17.	16/10/16 L.-Cpl. ✸
HENRY, N., Pte. 15 Bn.		3/10/14 4m, Pte.
HENRY, V. A., Pte. 12 Bn.		27/11/16 2y 11m, Pte.
HENRY, W. C., Spr. 8 Fd. Co.		30/ 3/16 Spr.
HENRY, W. G., Pte. 12 Bn.	1 Div. Train.	19/10/16 3y, Pte.
HENRY, W. Y., Tpr. 3 L.H.R.		30/11/14 4y 10m, S.Q.M.S
HENRY, W. L., Pte. 26 Bn.	W., M.M., C. de G. ✸ 3/10/18.	13/ 5/15 C.S.M. ✸
HENSBY, G. A., Pte. 12 Bn.	W., 1 Div. Sig. Co.	17/ 9/14 3y 11m, Spr.
HENSBY, R., Pte. 12 Bn.	W., 3 Fd. Co.	20/ 8/14 1y 10m, Spr.
HENSHAW, F. T., L.-Cpl. 12 Bn.	W.	17/ 9/14 4y 1m, L.-Cpl.
HENSHAW, R., Pte. 12 Bn.	✸ 24/3/16.	22/12/14 Pte. ✸
HENWOOD, F., Pte. 3 G.S.R.	12 Bn	17/ 6/18 1y. Pte.
HEPBURN, C. L., Pte. 40 Bn.		6/12/16 3y. Pte.
HEPBURN, H. J., Pte. 4 M.G. Co.	2 M.G. Bn.	12/ 4/17 2y 7m, Pte.
HEPBURN, W B., Pte. 2 G.S.R.	3 L.H.R.	10/ 4/18 1y 4m. Tpr.
HEPWORTH, H., Pte. 26 Bn.	2W., 69 Bn., 26 Bn.	23/ 2/15 4v 1m, Pte.

284   TASMANIA'S WAR RECORD, 1914-1918.

NAME.	REMARKS.	RANK ON DISCHARGE. ENLISTED. SERVICE.
HEPWORTH, L. R., Pte. Remnts.		19/10/15 4y 1m, Pte.
HERBERT, D. A., Spr. 2 Tnlrs.	W.	27/ 3/16
HERBERT, F., Col.-Sgt. 12 Bn.	W., 52 Bn.	21/ 8/14 3y 5m, Lt.
HERBERT, G. C., Pte. 2 G.S.R.	12 Bn.	4/ 4/18 1y 6m, Pte.
HERBERT, H. C., Pte. 26 Bn.	W., 1 Pnr. Bn.	9/ 8/15 3y 11m, Pte.
HERBERT, R. D. V., Pte. 3 Fd. Amb.	4 Aux. Hosp.	16/ 2/15 1y 11m, Cpl.
HERBERT, W. R., Pte. 26 Bn.	P.O.W. ✠ 2/8/16.	19/ 7/15 Pte. ✠
HERIGHTY, J., Cpl. Rly.		19/ 1/17.
HERIOT, A., Pte. 40 Bn.	W.	2/10/16 1y 5m, Pte.
HERITAGE, A. A., 2nd. Lt. 12 Bn.	2W., M.C.	27/ 7/15 2y 7m, Lt.
HERITAGE, R. B., Spr. 6 Fd Co.	2 Pnr. Bn.	20/10/15 Pte.
HERN, J., Pte. 40 Bn.		1/ 3/16 3y 2m, Pte
HERON, F. J., Pte. 40 Bn.	P.O.W.	20/ 3/16 3y 1m, L.-Cpl.
HERON, G., Gnr. 8 F.A.B.	31 Bty.	14/10/15 3y 10m, Dvr.
HERON, G. H., Pte. 12 Bn.	12 M.G. Co. ✠ 12/10/17.	17/ 1/16 Pte. ✠
HERON, R. H., Pte. 12 Bn.	3W., 69 Bn., 12 Bn.	23/11/15 3y 5m, Pte.
HERON, W. F., Pte. 15 Bn.		17/ 9/14 .
HERRON, A. T., Pte. 40 Bn.		6/ 8/17 1y 9m, Pte.
HERRON, E. G., Pte. 26 Bn.	✠ 19/10/18.	23/ 3/15 Dvr. ✠
HERRON, H. T., Cpl. 12 Bn.		10/10/16.
HERTEL, S., Pte. 12 Bn.		25/11/16 1y 10m, Pte.
HERVEY, H., Pte. 12 Bn.	W., 40 Bn.	22/11/16.
HETHERINGTON, V., Pte. 40 Bn.	✠ 14/6/17.	15/ 5/16 Pte. ✠
HEWITT, A. J., Gnr. Arty.	6 Bty.	27/10/16 2y 11m, Gnr.
HEWITT, A. R., Tpr. 3 L.H.R.		16/ 4/17 1y 5m, Tpr.
HEWITT, B. J., Dvr. 3 F.A.B.	✠ 9/11/16.	17/ 8/15 Dvr. ✠
HEWITT, C., Pte. 1 A.G.H.		13/ 5/15 1y 1m, Pte.
HEWITT, E., Pte. 12 Bn.	W.	26/ 5/15 2y, Pte.
HEWITT, J., Gnr. 10 F.A.B.	2W.	25/ 1/15 4y 3m, Gnr.
HEWETT, C. B., Pte. 26 Bn.		22/ 4/15 4y 4m, Pte.
HEY, C. D., Pte. 40 Bn.		16/10/16 2y 9m, L.-Cpl.
HEY, G. H., Pte. 12 Bn.	3W.	29/ 8/14 2y 6m, Pte.
HEYWARD, H. G. R., Dvr. M.T.		27/ 9/16.
HEYWARD, R. W., Pte. Wireless.		4/ 4/18 8m, Pte.
HIBBARD, F. C., Gnr. Arty.	3 D.A.C.	16/ 5/16 2y 2m, Dvr.
HIBBARD, K. F., Sgt. 12 Bn.	W.	7/12/16.
HICKEY, J. D., Pte. A.A.M.C.	2 A.G.H.	25/ 9/16 3y 3m, Pte.
HICKEY, J. D., Pte. 40 Bn.	2W.	27/ 3/16 3y 4m, Spr.
HICKEY, J. R., Sgt. 26 Bn.	M.S.M., 12 Bn.	10/ 8/15 4y 2m, R.S.M.
HICKMAN, C. A., Pte. Remounts.	.	30/ 9/15 4y, Pte.
HICKMAN, C. D., Pte. 12 Bn.	✠ 20/9/17.	5/ 7/16 Pte. ✠
HICKMAN, E. H., Pte. 40 Bn.		6/ 3/16 1y 11m, Pte.
HICKMAN, F. N., Pte. 12 Bn.	3 B.H.Q.	1/ 6/16 3y 3m, Pte.
HICKMAN, H., Pte. 26 Bn.		23/ 3/15 1y 5m, Dvr.
HICKMAN, H. D. G., Pte. 3 Fd. Amb.	W.	8/ 6/15 3y 11m, Pte.
HICKMAN, K. M., Cpl. Arty.	5 M.T.M.B.	27/ 1/16 3y 6m, Sgt.
HICKMAN, P. G., Pte. 40 Bn.	W., 51 Bn.	22/ 2/16 3y 10m, Pte.
HICKMAN, V. V., Pte. 40 Bn.		27/ 8/17 1y 9m, Cpl.
HICKS, E. J., Pte. 40 Bn.	2W., M.M.	3/10/16 2y 11m, L.-Cpl.
HICKS, E. T., Pte. A.A.M.C.	W., 9 Fd. Amb.	5/10/16 3y, Pte.
HICKSON, A. V., Pte. 12 Bn.	W.	6/ 6/16 2y 10m, Pte.
HIGGINS, A. M., Pte. 12 Bn.	W., 10 F.A.B.	9/ 9/15 2y 11m, Dvr.
HIGGINS, J., Pte. 12 Bn.	W.	12/10/14 1y 9m, Pte.
HIGGINS, L. J., L.-Sgt. 26 Bn.	✠ 14/11/16.	20/ 2/15 Sgt. ✠
HIGGINS, N. A., Pte. 12 Bn.	W.	19/10/15 2y 9m, Pte.
HIGGINS, R. R., Bdr. 3 F.A.B.	✠ 1/8/15.	26/ 8/14 Bdr. ✠
HIGGINS, R., Pte 12 Bn.	W.	29/ 4/16 4y 4m, Pte.
HIGGINS, S., Pte. 40 Bn.	13 L.T.M.B.	3/ 4/16 2y 11m, Pte.
HIGGINS, S. R. R., Gnr. Arty.	113 How. Bty.	4/ 1/16 3y 5m, Pte.
HIGGINS, T., Pte. 12 Bn.	W., 49 Bn.	16/ 9/15 3y 6m, Pte.
HIGGINS, W., Pte. 40 Bn.	✠ 28/3/18.	28/11/16 Pte ✠
HIGGINS, W., Pte. 26 Bn.	1 Camel Bn.	20/ 7/15 3y 9m, L.-Cpl.
HIGGINS, W. L., Pte. 12. Bn.	M.M.	20/ 8/14 4y 5m, Cpl.
HIGGS, A. S., Pte. 12 Bn.		29/12/15 3y 4m, Pte.
HIGGS, F. T., Pte. 26 Bn.	W., 2 M.G. Co.	13/ 9/15.
HIGGS, P. W., Pte. 40 Bn.		8/ 8/16 3y 2m, Sgt.
HILDER, A. R., Pte. 15 Bn.	45 Bn.	12/ 8/15 3y 8m, Dvr.
HILDER, A. A. H., Pte. 15 Bn.	47 Bn.	21/ 5/15 3y 4m, Pte.
HILDER, B. R., Pte. 15 Bn.	W., ✠ 8/8/15.	6/ 5/15 Pte. ✠
HILDER, E. G., Pte. 12 Bn.		30/ 4/16 3y 5m, Pte
HILDER, T. R., Pte. 12 Bn.	M.M., 10 F.A.B.	19/10/15 3y 10m, Gnr.
HILDITCH, J., L.-Cpl. 15 Bn.	60 Bn.	14/ 9/15 2y 9m, L.-Cpl.
HILLAN, O., Pte 12 Bn.	3W., 4 M.G. Bn.	10/ 2/15 4y 6m, Pte.
HILLIARD, F., Pte. 40 Bn.		7/ 3/16 3y 10m, Pte.
HILLIER, H., Pte. 40 Bn.		11/10/16 2y 6m, Pte.
HILLIER, L., Pte. 15 Bn.	W.	12/ 1/15 Pte.
HILLIER, W. G., Pte. 40 Bn.	W.	11/10/16 2y 6m, Pte.
HILMER, E., Pte. 40 Bn.	M.M.	22/ 3/16 Cpl.
HINCHCLIFFE, S., Pte. 12 Bn	✠ 15/4/17.	14/ 8/16 Pte.
HINCHCLIFFE, S. F., Pte. 12 Bn.	13 M.G. Co.	26/ 7/15 Pte. ✠
HINCHMORE, A., Pte. 15 Bn.	3W.	7/12/14 Pte.
HINCHMORE, R., Pte. 12 Bn.	✠ 19-22/8/16.	15/ 7/15 Pte. ✠
HIND, H., Pte. 40 Bn.		12/ 5/17 2y 5m, Pte.
HINDELL, J. F., Pte. D.A.C.		20/ 7/15 Pte
HINDLE, R., Pte. 1 A.C.H.		27/10/14 2y, Pte.
HINDS, D. J., Spr. 3 Tnlrs.		8/ 2/16 3y 7m, Srp.

NAME.	REMARKS.	RANK ON DISCHARGE. ENLISTED. SERVICE.
HINDS, F. H., Pte. 12 Bn.	1 M.G. Bn.	16/10/16 3y, L.-Cpl.
HINDS, H. J., Pte 4 M.G. Bn.	P.O.W.	1/ 8/16 2y 10m, Pte.
HINDS, J., Pte. 15 Bn.	✠ 7/8/15.	1/10/14 Pte.
HINDS, J. J., Pte. 3 Cyc. Co.	3 Engrs. Dtls.	7/ 4/16 3y 3m, Spr.
HINDS, J. R. C., Pte. 12 Bn.	40 Bn.	23/10/16.
HINDS, J. W., Tpr. 3 L.H.R.	W., 39 Bn.	17/ 6/15 3y 9m, Pte.
HINDS, L. G., Spr. 2 Tnlrs.	P.O.W.	17/ 3/16 3y 4m, Spr.
HINDS, W. A., Pte. 40 Bn.		3/10/16 2y 11m, Pte.
HINE, H. L., Pte. 1 A.G.H.	1 Fd. Amb. ✠ 6/11/17.	2/ 9/15 Pte. ✠
HINE, V. H., Pte. Wireless.		2/ 2/18 1y 1m, Spr.
HINES, W. J., Pte. 3 Fd. Amb.	W., 15 Bn.	20/ 8/14 Lt.
HINES, W. T., Tpr. 3 L.H.R.	Bde. H.Q.	7/12/14 Tpr.
HING, F. G., Pte. 12 Bn.	✠ 7/10/17.	26/ 8/16 Pte. ✠
HINGSTON, E. S., Pte. 40 Bn.	✠ 14/5/17.	1/ 4/16 Pte. ✠
HINMAN, A. G., 2nd. Lt., 15 Bn.	✠ 3/6/15.	Sec. Lieut. ✠
HINTON, V. H., Pte. 15 Bn.		14/ 1/15 1y 9m, Pte.
HINMAN, W. F., Lt., 26 Bn	M.C., 2 M.I.D.	22/ 5/15 4y 1m, Capt.
HINMAN, W. S., Pte. A.A.S.C.		10/10/17, 2y, Dvr.
HIORT, T., Pte. 12 Bn.	2W.	21/ 5/15 L.-Cpl.
HIRST, A. P., Tpr. 3 L.H.R.	✠ 22/6/16.	19/ 8/15 Tpr. ✠
HIRST, J H., Pte. Rly.	W., 40 Bn.	16/ 1/17 2y 8m, Pte.
HIRST, P. C., Pte. 15 Bn.	W., M.M.	21/ 9/14 4y 5m, Pte.
HITCHEN, E. J., Sgt. 26 Bn.	W.	13/ 2/15 Sgt.
HITCHENS, F., Tpr. 3 L.H.R.	14 Fd. Co.	20/ 7/15 4y 4m, Dvr
HITCHENS, J., Pte. 4 M.G. Co.		7/10/16.
HITCHENS, R., Dvr. 8 Fd Co.	18 Fd. Co. ✠ 26/10/18	19/10/15 Dvr. ✠
HITCHENS, W., Pte. Rly.		13/ 4/17 11m, Pte.
HITCHENS, W. E., Gnr. Arty.	4 D.A.C.	26/11/16 2y 7m, Dvr.
HITE, C. E., Pte. 26 Bn.	W., 12 Bn. ✠ 10/4/17.	10/ 8/15 Pte. ✠
HITE, E. W., Pte. 26 Bn.	1 Pnrs.	10/ 8/15 Dvr.
HITE, J., Pte. 40 Bn.	W., 12 Bn.	14/ 3/16 3y 9m, Pte.
HIXON, F. R., Pte. 12 Bn.		9/ 7/15.
HILL, A. C., Pte. 12 Bn.	A.I.F. H.Q. Enlisted as Walker, W.	18/11/16 2y 11m, Pte.
HILL, A., Pte 12 Bn.	✠ 2/5/17.	3/ 5/16 Pte. ✠
HILL, A. C., Pte. 12 Bn.	✠ 19-20/9/17.	28/ 8/16 Pte. ✠
HILL, A. L., Pte. 12 Bn.		22/ 8/16 2y 1m. Pte.
HILL, A. R., Pte. 40 Bn.	✠ 7/6/17.	15/ 3/16 Pte ✠
HILL, A. R., Pte. 4 M.G. Co.	W., 12 Bn.	30/ 1/17 2y 3m, Pte.
HILL, C E., Pte. 4 M.G. Co.		26/ 6/16.
HILL, C. E., Pte. 26 Bn.		15/ 2/15 1y 6m, Pte.
HILL, E. J., Pte. 40 Bn.	-	5/10/16 2y 6m, Pte.
HILL, E. J., Pte. 12 Bn.		3/ 7/15.
HILL, G., Pte. 40 Bn.	10 L.T.M.B.	20/ 9/16 2y 1m, Pte.
HILL, G. A., Pte. 15 Bn.		31/ 1/17 1y 2m, Pte.
HILL, G H., Gnr. 6 F.A.B.	2W.	28/ 8/15 4y 3m, Dvr.
HILL, G. H., Pte. 40 Bn.		2/10/16 2y 2m, Pte.
HILL, H. G. B., Gnr. 3 F.A.B.	2 F.A.B.	15/ 9/15 4y, Gnr.
HILLS, H. H., Pte. 12 Bn.	W., 52 Bn.	27/ 7/15 2y 7m, Pte.
HILL, L. R., Spr. Tnlrs.	1 Tnl. Co.	20/10/16 2y 11m, Spr.
HILL, L W., Pte. 12 Bn.	M.M.	8/ 5/16 3y 4m, Pte.
HILL, M. J. H., Pte. 3 G.S.R.	12 Bn.	12/ 7/18 10m, Pte
HILL, N. W., Spr. Miners.		18/ 1/16.
HILL, R. B., Pte. 12 Bn.	✠ 5/6/18.	17/11/16 Pte. ✠
HILL, R. M., Pte. 13 Fd Amb	3W.	27/ 4/16 2y 11m, Pte.
HILL, T., Pte. 26 Bn.	W., 51 Bn.	7/ 9/15 3y 11m. Pte.
HILL, V. W., Pte. 2 G.S.R.	7 F.A.B.	8/ 4/18 1y 6m, Gnr.
HILL, W. P., Pte. 12 Bn.	52 Bn. ✠ 12/4/17.	15/11/15 Sgt. ✠
HILL, W. C., Pte 12 Bn.	W.	21/ 8/14 1y 9m. Pte
HILLS, C., Pte. 15 Bn.	11 F.A.B.	4/ 8/15 4y, Dvr.
HILLS, C. J., Pte. 15 Bn.	M.M.	29/ 9/14 3y,11m C.Q.M.S
HILLS, F. W., Pte. 12 Bn.	2W., 52 Bn.	7/ 1/16 2y 6m, Pte.
HILLS, F. G., Pte. 40 Bn.	38 Bn	10/10/16
HILLS, G. H., Pte. 12 Bn.	51 Bn., 52 Bn.	7/ 1/16 3y 8m, Pte.
HILLS, G. T., Pte. 12 Bn.	2W., 40 Bn.	9/ 7/15 4y 1m, Pte.
HILLS, G. R., Pte. 26 Bn.	W.	2/ 3/15 2y 2m, Pte.
HILLS, H. A., Pte. 12 Bn.	W.	3/ 1/15 4y 2m, Pte.
HILLS, J. H., Pte. Rly.	W. 1 Rly. Co.	13/11/17 Pte
HILLS, J. N., Pte 15 Bn.	W., 47 Bn. ✠ 5/4/18.	30/12/14 C.S.M. ✠
HILLS, L. F., Pte. 40 Bn.	W. ✠ 12/10/17.	25/ 9/16 Pte. ✠
HILLS, P., Pte. 15 Bn.	14 A.S.C.	29/ 8/15 4y 1m, Dvr.
HILLS, R. T., Pte 12 Bn.	4W.	9/ 5/16 2y 11m, Pte.
HILLS, R. T., Dvr. 10 A.S.C.		10/ 5/15 5y 2m, Dvr.
HOBBS, L. E. J., Gnr. 1 D.A.C.	3 F.A.B. ✠ 11/1/18.	30/11/14 Dvr. ✠
HOBSON, A. P., Pte. 40 Bn.	W.	12/ 2/16 1y 8m, Pte
HOBSON, O., Pte. 26 Bn.	2W., M.M. ✠ 8/8/18.	27/ 3/15 Pte. ✠
HODGE, C. J., Pte. 40 Bn.	✠ 13/12/16.	2/ 2/16 Pte. ✠
HODGE, J. E., Pte. 15 Bn.	✠ 8/8/16.	12/ 8/15 Pte. ✠
HODGES, H. M., Gnr. 33 F.A.B.	4 D.A.C.	9/ 5/17 2y 7m. Gnr.
HODGES, J., Pte. 26 Bn.	✠ 29/7/16.	25/ 6/15 Pte. ✠
HODGETTS, A. A., Tpr. 3 L.H.R.	W.	18/ 1/17 2y 7m. Tpr.
HODGETTS, C., L.-Cpl. 40 Bn.		28/ 2/16 3y 6m, Cpl.
HODGETTS, H. L., Pte. 12 Bn.	40 Bn. ✠ 30/8/18.	18/10/16 Pte. ✠
HODGETTS, H. Gnr. 36 H.A.G.		7/ 6/15 4y 4m, Gnr.
HODGETTS, M., Pte 40 Bn.	15 Bn., P.O.W. ✠ 6/5/17.	20/ 3/16 Pte. ✠
HODGMAN, A. G., Pte. 12 Bn.	W. 52 Bn. ✠7/6/17.	13/ 9/15 Cpl. ✠

TASMANIA'S WAR RECORD, 1914-1918.

NAME.	REMARKS.	RANK ON DISCHARGE. ENLISTED. SERVICE.
HODGMAN, C. H., Gnr. Arty.	5 D.A.C.	21/ 2/17 2y 11m, Gnr.
HODGMAN, D. A., Pte. 26 Bn.	W. 15 Bn. ✸ 3/5/17.	16/ 3/15 Pte. ✸
HODGMAN, F. R., Sgt. 12 Bn.	W., 52 Bn.	13/ 9/15 1y 11m, L.-Cpl
HCDGMAN, H. H., Gnr. 10 F.A.B.		28/11/16 2y 8m, Gnr.
HODGSON, H. M., Gnr. 3 F.A.B.		17/ 8/15 4y 1m, Gnr.
HCDGSON, W. J., Pte. Rly.		29/ 1/17.
HODSON, L. S. B., Gnr. Arty.		13/ 3/17 Gnr.
HODSON, T. B., Pte 3 Fd. Amb.		21/ 6/15 4y 2m, Pte.
HODGSON, W. R., 2nd Lt., 12 Bn.		4/10/17
HODSKISS, J., Pte. 26 Bn.		24/6/15. Pte. 2y 1m.
HOGAN, A. W., Spr. 5 Miners.	W., 3 Tnl. Co.	11/. 3/16 2y 8m, Spr.
HOGAN, H. R., Dvr. D.A.C	10 F.A.B., H.Q., 3 F.A.B.	14/12/14 4y 6m, Dvr.
HOGAN, J., Pte. 2 G.S.R.	12 Bn.	5/ 4/18 1y 3m, Pte.
HOGAN, L. T. G., Pte. 7 Fd Amb.	13 F Amb.	15/ 2/15 3y 4m, Pte.
HOGARTH, C. W., Pte 26 Bn.	✸ 5/8/16.	2/ 3/15 Sgt. ✸
HOGG, D., Pte. 12 Bn.	3W., 52 Bn. Enlisted as M'Donald, D.	6/10/15 2y 4m, Pte.
HOGGETT, C. J., Pte. 40 Bn.	3 D.S. Co.	6/ 3/16 3y 5m, Pte.
HOGGETT, H. F., Pte. Wireless.		11/ 2/18 10m, Cpl.
HOGGETT, R. J., Pte. 1 A.G.H.	12 Bn.	12/ 8/15 3y 10m, Pte
HOLBROOK, S. P., Gnr. 10 F.A.B.	W.	16/10/16 2y 7m, Gnr.
HCLCOMBE, E. J., Dvr. 3 F.A.B.	4 Div. Arty. ✸ 20/5/18.	20/ 7/15 Dvr. ✸
HOLDEN, R. J., Pte. 40 Bn.	W.	12/ 9/17.
HOLDEN, R. S., Pte. 12 Bn.	52 Bn. ✸ 4/9/16.	16/ 7/15 Pte. ✸
HOLDEN, R. V. C., Pte 12 Bn.	2W., 52 Bn.	20/ 7/15 L.-Cpl.
HOLDEN, W. J., Pte. 12 Bn.	2W., 52 Bn., 51 Bn. ✸ 10/6/18.	23/ 7/15 Pte. ✸
HOLDER, F. W. B., Gnr. 6 F.A.B	6 F.A.B., 24 How. Bde. ✸ 17/8/18.	25/11/15 Gnr. ✸
HOLDER, G., Pte. —		30/10/16.
HOLDER, G. R., Pte. 12 Bn.	60 Bn. ✸ 25/7/18.	19/ 8/14 Pte. ✸
HOLDER, H. E., Dvr. 7 Fd. Amb.	W.	24/ 2/15 3y, Dvr.
HOLFORD, S. J., Pte. 40 Bn	W.	19/ 7/16 3y 2m, Pte.
HOLGATE, G. W. A., Pte. 26 Bn.	W., 12 Bn.	11/ 8/15 4y, Pte.
HCLLAND, A. E., Pte. 15 Bn.	47 Bn., 52 Bn. ✸ 13/10/17	31/ 8/15 Pte. ✸
HOLLAND, S. G., Pte. 4 M.G. Co.	2 M.G. Bn. ✸ 28/7/18.	17/ 4/17 Pte. ✸
HOLLAND, V. H. C., Pte. 12 Bn.		23/ 5/16 3y 7m, Pte
HOLLAND, V. H., Pte. 12 Bn.		5/ 9/14 6m, Pte.
HOLLICK, A. G., Tpr. 3 L.H.R.	✸ 6/9/15.	22/ 1/15 Tpr. ✸
HOLLIDAY, F. L., Pte. 26 Bn.	3W.	20/ 4/15 Pte. ✸
HOLLINGSWORTH A., Pte. 15 Bn.	4 Div. Sig. Co	8/ 1/15 4y 3m, L.-Cpl.
HOLLINGSWORTH, B. G., Pte 40 Bn.	✸ 16/6/17.	7/ 3/16 L.-Cpl. ✸
HOLLINGSWORTH, E. W. R., Gnr. Arty.	25 Bty.	5/12/16 1y 4m, Gnr.
HOLLINGSWORTH, F. J., Gnr. 6 F.A.B.		13/ 8/15 4y 2m Lt.
HOLLOW, J., Spr. Tnlrs.		3/ 6/16 1y 1m, Spr.
HOLLOWAY, A. J., Pte 2 G.S.R.	Vet. Hosp.	6/ 5/18 1y 5m, Pte.
HOLLOWAY, A. W., Pte. 15 Bn.	4 Pnrs.	30/ 6/15 1y 6m, Pte.
HOLLOWAY, G., Spr. Miners.	W., A.A.O.C.	10/11/15 2y 10m, Spr.
HOLLOWAY, H. F., Dvr. 3 F.A.B		17/ 3/15 3y 4m, Dvr.
HOLLOWAY, W., Pte. 26 Bn	12 Bn. ✸ 23-26/7/16.	11/ 8/15 Pte. ✸
HOLMAN, H. G., Pte. 12 Bn.		20/ 8/14 2y, Pte.
HOLMBERG, M., Pte. 12 Bn.	W., A.D. Engrs.	19/ 8/14 4y 6m, Dvr
HOLMES, A. W., Pte. 12 Bn.	✸ 14/3/17.	20/ 1/15 Pte. ✸
HOLMES, E. E., Dvr. 4 M.G Bn.	M.G. Bn.	11/ 9/14 4y 5m, Pte.
HOLMES, E. J., Pte. 40 Bn		11/10/16 2y 11m, L.-Cpl
HOLMES, H. J., Pte. 26 Bn.	2 Pioneers. ✸ 29/7/16.	30/4/15 Pte. ✸
HOLMES, J. J., Pte. 26 Bn.	A.F.C.	4/ 8/15 4y Sec. Lt
HOLMES, L. L., Pte. 26 Bn.	P.O.W. ✸ 13/7/16 in Germany.	25/ 6/15 Pte. ✸
HOLMES, L. W., Cpl. 12 Bn.	2W.	21/10/14 4y 4m Sgt.
HOLMES, L. A., S/Sgt. A.M.C.	4 L.H. Amb.	16/11/16 2y 10m S./Sgt
HOLMES, W. A., Pte. 26 Bn.		10/ 8/15 3y 8m. Dvr.
HOLMSTROM, A. H., Pte. 40 Bn.	W.	10/10/16 2y 11m. Pte.
HOLMSTROM, H. C., Spr. 8 Fd Co	15 Fd Co.	14/ 7/15 Spr.
HOLMYARD, C. E., Pte. 12 Bn.	27 A.S.C.	3/ 8/15 4y. Dvr.
HOLMYARD, G., Pte. 12 Bn.	✸ 14/11/15.	15/ 7/15 Pte. ✸
HOLMYARD, R., Pte. 26 Bn.	W. 69, 26 Bn. ✸ 8/8/18.	10/ 6/15 Cpl. ✸
HOLSTROM, H. C., Pte. 12 Bn.		26/10/14 8m. Pte.
HCLT, A. E., Gnr. 36 Arty.		23/ 4/17 2y 7m. Gnr
HOLT, H. J., Pte. 15 Bn.	4 A.F.A.B., H.Q.	20/ 5/15 4y 6m. Gnr.
HOLT, W. J., Chaplain		22/ 3/19 5m. Chaplain
HOLTUM, C. R., Pte. 12 Bn.	✸ 11/8/18.	10/ 2/15 L./Cpl. ✸
HOLYMAN, J W., Cpl. 12 Bn.	4W., M.C., M.I.D.	18/ 8/14 4y 11m. Cap.
HCLTUM, H. E., Pte. 12 Bn.	M.M. ✸ 22/9/18	21/ 8/14 Sgt. ✸
HOMAN, A. H., Pte. 26 Bn.	W. M.M.	6/ 9/15 3y 11m. Pte.
HOMAN, H. R., Spr. Miners.	W. 3 Tun. Co.	10/11/15 3y 9m. Spr
HOMAN, W., Tpr. 3 L.H.R.	W.	29/ 8/14 4y 6m. S.S.M.
HONEY, P., Pte. 40 Bn.	W. 23 Bn.	16/ 6/16 Pte.
HONEYSETT, J. H., 2 Lt., 40 Bn		25/10/15
HONEYSETT. L. R., Bdr. 1 A.C.H	15 Fd. Amb.	23/ 9/14 4y 6m. Pte.
HONNER, S. J., Pte. 40 Bn.	W.	30/ 9/16 1y 8m. Pte.
HONNOR, T., Pte. 12 Bn.	W. ✸ 21/9/17	20/ 1/16 Pte ✸
HOOD, H. M., Pte. 12 Bn.		10/ 1/18 1y 8m. Pte.
HOOD, V. B., Dvr. 7 F Amb.		1/ 3/15 1y 5m. Dvr.
HOODLESS, C. J., Pte. 26 Bn.	W. 9 Bn. ✸ 31/5/17.	20/ 6/15 Pte. ✸
HOOK, G. N., Pte. Den. Cps.	M.S.M.	8/ 7/15 4y. Pte.
HOOKWAY, C. N, Pte. 1 A.G.H.	✸ 20/9/17.	3/ 6/15 Pte. ✸

TASMANIA'S MUSTER ROLL.

NAME.	REMARKS.	RANK ON DISCHARGE. ENLISTED. SERVICE.
HOGLE, C. J., Pte. 40 Bn.	67 Bn. ✤ 13/10/17.	25/ 9/16 Pte. ✤
HOOPER, A. P., Pte. 15 Bn.	W. 47 Bn. ✤ 19/8/17.	1/ 9/15 Pte. ✤
HOOPER, E. W., Pte. 40 Bn.	W.	17/10/16 1y 9m. Pte.
HOOPER, H. C., Dvr. 3 F.A.B.	W. 4 Fd. Co.	4/ 9/15 1y 11m. Spr.
HOOPER, H. V., Dvr 3 Fd. Co.		17/ 8/14 4y 4m. Dvr.
HOOPER, T., Gnr. D.A.C.	104 How. Bat.	23/ 8/15 4y. Dvr.
HOOPER, T., Pte. 40 Bn.	W. 3 M.G. Bn.	9/10/16 3y. Pte.
HOPE, A. F., Tpr. 3 L.H.R.		27/ 8/14 4y 5m. Tpr.
HOPE, A. H., Tpr. 3 L.H.R.		5/12/14 4y 9m. Tpr.
HOPE, A. J., Pte. 12 Bn.	✤ 3/4/15.	1/12/14 Pte. ✤
HOPE, C., Pte. 12 Bn.	3W. 40 Bn.	2/ 9/14 4y 7m. Sgt.
HOPE, E. S., Pte. 15 Bn.	✤ 17/5/15.	18/ 9/14 Cpl. ✤
HOPE, K. B., Pte. 2 G.S.R.	37 Bty.	8/ 5/18 1y Gnr.
HOPE, P., Chaplain, 40 Bn.	1 A.D.B.D.	1/ 6/16 2y 1m. Chap.
HOPE, W., Pte. 40 Bn.	A.A.O.C.	9/10/16 2y 11m. Pte.
HOPKINS, D. H., Spr. 6 Fd Co.	W. 4 Fd. Co.	28/10/15 3y 6m. Spr.
HOPKINS, D. M., Pte. 4 M.G. Co.		7/11/16 1y 3m. Pte.
HOPKINS, N. L., Cpl. 7 F. Amb.	M.S.M. Ad. Hd. Qrs	16/ 2/15 4y 10m. W.O.
HOPWOOD, D. M., Tpr. 3 L.H.R.	W.	3/ 3/17 2y 5m. Tpr.
HOARE, H., Pte. 12 Bn.	2W.	12/ 1/15 3y 9m. Pte.
HORKINS, J, Pte. 12 Bn.	W.	4/ 2/15 2y 9m. Pte.
HORLER, T. J., Q.M.S. 40 Bn.	M.I.D.	13/11/15 3y 11m. Capt.
HORNE, A., Pte. 40 Bn.	W., 3 D. Hd. Qrs. Anzac Prov. Cps.	14/ 2/16 3y 6m. Cpl.
HORNE, A. J., Gnr. 14 F.A.B.		24/ 1/16 3y 3m. Gnr.
HORNE, C., Tpr. 3 L.H.R.		13/ 7/15 4y 2m. Tpr.
HORNE, C. D., Pte. 12 Bn.	W., M.C., C. de G. (France), 4 Pnrs.	7/ 8/15 3y 9m. Maj.
HORNE, E G., Pte. 40 Bn.		25/ 9/16 11m. Pte
HORNE, G. L., Sgt. 26 Bn.	W.	2/ 3/15 2y 9m. C.S.M.
HORNE, H. H., Pte. 40 Bn.	W. ✤ 22/4/18.	23/ 9/16 Pte. ✤
HORNE, J. W., Pte. 26 Bn.	W. 52 Bn. ✤ 3-4/9/16.	30/ 8/15 Pte. ✤
HORNE, J. A., Pte. 12 Bn.		28/ 8/14 2y 2m Pte.
HORNE, J. R., Tpr. 3 L.H.	4 Pioneers	21/ 8/14 4y 6m. Sec.LT
HORNE, R. J., Pte 12 Bn.		2/ 8/14 2y. Pte.
HORNE, T. H., Pte. 12 Bn.		10/ 7/16 1y 3m. Pte.
HORNE, W. J., Pte. 12 Bn.	W. 52 Bn. ✤ 24/4/18.	19/ 8/15 Pte ✤
HORNSBY, F. H., Tpr. 3 L.H.	W. 36 H.A.G.	13/ 9/15 4y 4m. Gnr.
HORNSBY, N. G., Gnr. 36 H.A. Gp.	W. 4 Siege Bde.	1/11/15 3y 11m. Gnr.
HORNSEY, J. T., Pte. 1 G.S.R.		5/ 3/18
HORNSEY, V. W., Pte. Tun.	4 L.H.	17/10/16 2y 11m. Tpr.
HORNSEY, W. A, Pte. 15 Bn.	2 W. 47 Bn.	30/ 8/15 2y 6m. Spr.
HORSBURGH, W. H, Spr. 3 Min.	3 Tun Co.	12/11/15 Spr.
HORSEY, H. N. J., Pte. 26 Bn.	W ✤ 9/9/18.	12/ 8/15 Pte ✤
HORSEY, S., Pte, 26 Bn.	2W. 12Bn.	12/ 8/15 4y. Pte.
HORSELY, J. T., Pte. 26 Bn.	✤ 22/7/15	20/ 2/15 Pte. ✤
HORTIN, A. F., Gnr. 6 F.A.B.		24/ 8/15 Dvr.
HORTIN, A. H., Pte. 12 Bn.	2W.	23/7/15 Pte
HORTIN, E C., Pte. 12 Bn.		15/ 9/15 2y 4m. Pte.
HORTIN, H. P., Pte. 15 Bn.	2W. 47 Bn.	26/ 9/14 2y 7m. Pte.
HORTLE, R. T., Pte. 12 Bn.	✤ 12/1/18.	28/10/16 Pte. ✤
HORTON. A. S., Gnr. 25 F.A.B.		13/10/16 1y 8m. Gnr.
HORTON, A. J., Spr. Miners.	3 Tun. Co.	9/10/15 3y 11m. Spr.
HORTON, E. S., Pte 12 Bn.		7/ 8/15
HORTON, F. E. J., Pte. 12 Bn.	10 F.A.B.	9/10/15 3y 10m. Dvr.
HORTON, F. N., Pte. 12 Bn.	W., M.M., 28 Bn. ✤ 29/7/18.	8/ 6/15 Pte. ✤
HORTON, H., Pte. Wireless		1/ 3/18 9m. Pte.
HORTON, H., Pte. 3 G.S.R.	12 Bn.	4/ 6/18 1y Pte.
HORTON, W., Pte. Remounts		21/ 9/15 3y 11m. Tpr.
HOSKING, A., Pte. 40 Bn.		27/ 9/16 2y 6m. Pte.
HOSKING, C. P., Pte 26 Bn.		18/ 2/15 4y 6m. Pte.
HOSKING, J. D., Spr. 4 Miners	2 Tun. Co.	14/ 3/16 3y 7m. Dvr.
HOSKING, J. J., Pte. 40 Bn.	2W.	16/10/16 2y 5m. Pte.
HOSKINS, F. J., Pte. 40 Bn.	2W. 51 Bn.	23/ 2/16 2y 6m. Pte.
HOSKINS. T. T., Sgt. 40 Bn.		1/ 2/15 4y 7m. Lieut.
HOUGH, H., Tpr 3 L.H.R.	11 F.A.B.	11/ 8/15 Dvr.
HOUGH, W., Tpr. 3 L.H.R.		27/ 7/17 2y 2m. Tpr.
HOUGHTON, S. R., Sec. Lt. 12 Bn.	2W. M.C., D.S.O., M.I.D.	25/ 8/14 5y 1m. Capt.
HOUGHTON, R. W., Pte. 12 Bn.	W. 10 F.A.B.	28/ 7/15 4y 2m. Gnr.
HOUGHTON, W. R., Pte. 26 Bn.	W. 7 M.G. Co.	1/ 5/15 3y 1m. Pte.
HOUNAM, E. T., Spr., 3 Cyc. Co.	11 Fd. Co.	6/ 4/16 3y 8m. Spr.
HOUNAM, R., Pte. 15 Bn.	47 Bn. ✤ 16/11/16.	11/ 9/15 Pte. ✤
HOUSE, A. E., Gnr. Art.	3 D.A.C.	15/ 3/16 3y 5m. Dvr.
HOUSE, F. A., Gnr. 3 F.A.B.		4/ 1/15
HOUSE, F. C., Pte. 12 Bn.		8/ 4/16 2y 11m. Pte
HOUSE, F. W., Pte. 3 G.S.R.		5/ 7/18
HOUSE, W. M., Pte. 4 M.G. Co.		16/10/16 2y 11m. Pte.
HOUSEGO, R., Pte. 12 Bn.	✤ 2/4/17.	11/ 4/16 Pte. ✤
HOUSTON, C. K., Pte. 12 Bn.	W.	2/ 5/16 2y 10m. Pte.
HOUSTON, S. E., Tpr. 3 L.H.R.		8/ 7/15 3y 11m. Dvr.
HOUSTON, W. J., Tpr 3 L.H.R.		8/ 7/15 3y 9m. Dvr.
HOW, C., Pte. 12 Bn.	51 Bn.	28/10/15 3y 10m. Pte.
HOW, D. R., Pte. 40 Bn.	W. 49 Bn. ✤ 24/4/18.	15/ 4/16 Pte. ✤
HOW, J. R., Pte. 26 Bn.	2W. 69 Bn., 26 Bn.	6/ 7/15 3y 9m. Pte
HOW, N., Pte. 15 Bn.		4/ 6/15 4y 5m. Pte.
HOW, R., Pte. 15 Bn.		4/ 6/15 4y 7m. Cpl.
HOW, S. J C., Pte. 12 Bn.	52 Bn. ✤ 8/6/17.	13/ 1/16 Pte. ✤

TASMANIA'S WAR RECORD, 1914-1918.

NAME.	REMARKS.	RANK ON DISCHARGE. ENLISTED. SERVICE.
HOW, W. H. G., Pte. 12 Bn.	W.	29/ 9/15 1y 8m. Pte.
HOW, W. J. H., Pte. 12 Bn.	3W. 51 Bn.	31/ 8/14 5y. Cpl.
HOWARD, A. W., Pte. 14 Fd. Amb.	W.	11/ 4/16 3y 6m. Pte.
HOWARD, A. Pte 3 G.S.R.		16/ 5/18 1y 1m. Pte.
HOWARD, A., Pte. 40 Bn.		29/ 3/16 1y 7m. Pte.
HOWARD, A. C., Pte. 40 Bn.	W.	1/11/16 2y 4m. Pte.
HOWARD, B., Pte. 40 Bn.		12/ 9/16 1y 10m. Pte.
HOWARD, C., Pte. 15 Bn.	2W. M.M.	28/ 1/15 4y 5m. Sgt.
HOWARD, C. A., Gnr. 6 F.A.B.	W.	10/ 8/15 Gnr.
HOWARD, G., Cpl. 12 Bn.	W. 10 F.A.B.	1/ 8/15 4y. Cpl.
HOWARD, C. R., Pte. 3 G.S.R.		22/ 7/18 1y 2m. Pte.
HOWARD, C. R., Pte. 3 L.H.		19/ 8/14 3y 1m. 2 Lt.
HOWARD, D. H., Pte. 26 Bn.	W. ✠ 20/10/17.	30/ 9/15 Pte. ✠
HOWARD, E. J., Tpr. 3 L.H.R.	✠ 4-6/8/16.	30/11/14 Tpr ✠
HOWARD, E., Pte. 12 Bn.	2W.	31/ 7/16 Pte.
HOWARD, E. S., Pte. 15 Bn.	W.	23/ 9/14 1y 9m. Pte.
HOWARD, H. H., Pte. 12 Bn.	W. 40 Bn.	4/ 9/16 3y. Cpl.
HOWARD, H. D., Pte. 12 Bn.	✠ 9/4/17.	4/ 8/16 Pte. ✠
HOWARD, J. S., Pte. 15 Bn.	2W. 47 Bn., 15 Bn.	27/ 7/15 4y 2m. Pte.
HOWARD, J. J., Pte. A.A.M.C.	2 A.G.H.	14/ 3/16 3y 7m. Pte.
HOWARD, R., Pte. 12 Bn.		2/12/15
HOWARD, S., Pte. 15 Bn.	40 Bty.	26/ 7/15 1y 8m. Dvr.
HOWARD, T., Pte. 26 Bn.	✠ 27/5/16.	21/ 9/15 Pte. ✠
HOWARD, V. M. M., Pte. 26 Bn.	12 Bn.	3/ 9/15 3y 10m. L./Cpl.
HOWAT, G. A., Pte. 26 Bn.	29 Bn.	14/ 4/15
HOWE, F. A., Pte. 40 Bn.	W.	3/ 2/16 Pte.
HOWE, F. C., Gnr. Art.		24/10/16
HOWE, G. H., S./Sgt. 68 Den. Cp.	76 Dental Corps	7/ 7/16 1y 3m. S. Sgt.
HOWE, H. G., Pte. 12 Bn.	2W. 52 Bn.	19/ 8/14 4y 6m. Sgt.
HOWE, J. R., Pte. 4 M.G. Co.	A.A.D.C.	23/10/16 3y. Pte.
HOWE, T. E. B., Pte. 12 Bn.	W.	26/10/14 1y 6m. L./Cpl.
HOWELL, A. J., Pte. 40 Bn.		27/ 6/16 3y 7m. Pte.
HOWELL, C. A., Pte. 3 G.S.R.	12 Bn.	9/ 8/18 1y 3m. Pte
HOWELL, D. R. S., Pte. 40 Bn.	2W. ✠ 22/4/18.	15/ 3/16 Pte. ✠
HOWELL, E. C., Pte. 40 Bn.	✠ 4/10/17.	14/ 2/16 Pte. ✠
HOWELL, E., Pte. 40 Bn.	W. 15 Bn., 40 Bn. ✠ 4/10/17.	21/ 2/16 Pte. ✠
HOWELL, H. H., Gnr. 5 F.A.B.	W.	20/ 9/15 4y. Sgt.
HOWELL, J., Pte. 26 Bn.	W.	16/ 3/15 4y 5m. Cpl.
HOWELL, J. P., Pte. 3 G.S.R.	12 Bn.	14/ 6/18 1y 4m. Pte.
HOWELL, L. H., Gnr. 3 F.A.B.		17/ 9/14 2y 2m. Gnr.
HOWELL, L. A., Pte. 40 Bn.	W. ✠ 29/8/18.	1/ 3/16 L./Cpl. ✠
HOWELL, L. E., Pte. 26 Bn.	2W. ✠ 4/10/17.	11/ 5/15 L./Cpl. ✠
HOWELL, C. E., Pte. 26 Bn.	W.	11/ 3/15 4y 4m. Pte.
HOWELL, S. S., Gnr 2 D.A.C.		13/10/15 3y 9m. Gnr
HOWELL, W., Pte. 12 Bn.	W. 1 Pnr. Bn. ✠ 23/10/17	25/ 8/15 Pte. ✠
HOWELLS, J. W., Gnr. 3 D.A.C.		11/10/16 3y. Gnr.
HOWELLS, W. J. V., Pte. 40 Bn.	4W.	30/ 3/16 2y 11m. Cpl.
HOWES, W., Chap. 40 Bn.	40 Bn.	Chaplain
HOWLETT, T. C., Gnr 3 F.A.B.	W.	2/10/16 Gnr.
HOY, M. A., Pte. 1 G.S.R.		25/ 9/17 1y 6m. Pte.
HOY, M. A., Spr. 1 Tun. Co.		16/ 5/16 1y 3m. Spr.
HUBBARD, E. L., Spr. Miners.	3 Tun. Co.	26/10/15 1y 4m Spr.
HUBBARD, R. A. G., Gnr. Art.	15 F.A.B.	9/11/16 1y 3m. Gnr.
HUBBARD, S. M., Pte. 12 Bn.	52 Bn. ✠ 7/9/16.	2/ 8/15 Pte. ✠
HUBBARD, V. J. R., Sgt. Miners	4 Pioneer Bn.	26/10/15 Sgt.
HUDSON, A. D., Pte. 40 Bn.	4W.	21/ 5/16 3y 4m. Cpl.
HUDSON, A. J. D., Gnr. 7 F.A.B.		7/ 1/16 3y 8m. Dvr.
HUDSON, A. E., Pte. 40 Bn.	W.	20/ 6/16 2y 9m. Pte.
HUDSON, A. J., Gnr. 8 F.A.B.	W.	6/ 2/15 3y 10m. Gnr.
HUDSON, C. H., Pte. 12 Bn.		10/ 6/15 3y 1m. Pte.
HUDSON, E. L., S.Sgt. A.A.M.C.		2/ 2/15 4y 6m. S./Sgt.
HUDSON, F., Dvr. 3 F. Amb.	✠ 25/4/15.	19/ 8/14 Pte. ✠
HUDSON, F. S. H., Pte 12 Bn.	W. 52 Bn.	10/ 1/16 2y 3m. Pte.
HUDSON, G. A., Pte. 26 Bn.		20/ 7/15 3y 1m. Pte.
HUDSON, G. A., Sig. 12 Bn.		24/11/14
HUDSON, G. H., Cpl 4 F. Bakery		8/12/14 4y 3m. S.Q.M.S.
HUDSON, K. L., A./M. A.F.C.	M.S.M. P.O.W.	30/ 3/15
HUDSON, L., Pte. 12 Bn.	W.	16/11/15 3y 5m. Pte
HUDSON, R. H., Pte. 40 Bn.	W.	4/ 9/17 2y 3m. Pte.
HUDSON, S., Pte. 12 Bn.		19/11/15 3y 11m. Pte.
HUDSON, S. E. W. J., Pte. 26 Bn.	2 W. 3 M.G.B.	28/ 7/15 4y 4m. Pte.
HUDSON, T. G., Pte. 12 Bn.	52 Bn. ✠ 4/9/16.	2/ 8/15 Sgt. ✠
HUDSON, W. T. J., Pte. 40 Bn.		9/10/16 1y 1m. Pte.
HUDSON, W. T., Pte. Rly.	2 A.L.R.O.U.	26/ 4/17 2y 8m. Cpl.
HUETT, D. J., Gnr Art.	W.	11/ 1/17 2y 2m. Gnr.
HUITFELDT, A. C., Cpl. 12 Bn.	W.	15/ 9/16
HULBERT, J. E., Pte A.F.C.		20/ 9/16 9m. Pte.
HULCOMBE, A. J., Gnr. Art.		5/10/15 3y 9m. Dvr.
HULCOMBE, V. C., Gnr. 6 F.A.B.	2 D.A.C.	5/10/15 3y 11m. Dvr.
HULL, H. A., Pte. 12 Bn.	2W.	30/10/16 2y 4m. Pte.
HULL, H. D., Pte. A.A.M.C.		12/12/17
HULL, W. D., Pte. 12 Bn.	W.	4/ 9/16 3y. Pte.
HUGHES, A. E., Gnr. Art.	1 Siege Bat.	19/ 5/17 2y 6m. Gnr.
HUGHES, A., Pte. 12 Bn.	2W. 3 Fd. Co.	26/8/14 3y 11m. Spr.
HUGHES, A. J., Spr. 8 Fd Co.	15 Fd. Co.	5/ 1/16 3y 10m. Spr.

TASMANIA'S MUSTER ROLL. 289

NAME.	REMARKS.	RANK ON DISCHARGE. ENLISTED. SERVICE.
HUGHES, C., Spr. Miners	W.	15/ 2/16 1y 6m. Spr.
HUGHES, C. V., Pte. 12 Bn.		26/ 1/16 3y 6m. Pte.
HUGHES, C. B., Tpr. 3 L.H.R.	1 Fd. Co.	30/11/17 1y 11m. Spr.
HUGHES, C. R., Gnr. 6 F.A.B.	W. 13 Fd. Co.	6/ 9/15 3y 11m. Spr.
HUGHES, D. J., L./Cpl. 3 L.H.R.		21/ 7/15 4y 3m. L./Cpl.
HUGHES, E. E., Bdr. 2 D.A.C.		18/ 1/15 3y 1m. Bdr.
HUGHES, F., Pte. 40 Bn.		21/ 3/16
HUGHES, H. H., Pte. 34 Bn.		1/ 7/17 1y 8m. Pte.
HUGHES, L. C., Pte 12 Bn.	52 Bn.	11/ 1/16 3y 3m. Pte.
HUGHES, R., Pte. 26 Bn.		30/ 8/15
HUGHES, S. L., Lt. 12 Bn.	W.	1/ 1/16 1y 2m. Capt.
HUGHES, W. E., Tpr. 3 L.H.R.		27/11/14 4y 9m. Tpr.
HUGHES, W. J., Pte. 1 A.C.H.		17/ 9/14 3y 7m. Pte.
HUGHES, W. R., Pte. 12 Bn.	W. 51 Bn.	10/ 2/15 4y 8m. Pte.
HUME, A. E. R. N., Gr. 55 S.By.	W.	4/ 6/15 2y 8m Gnr.
HUME, H. R., Gnr. Art.	2 D.A.C.	3/11/15 3y 9m. Dvr.
HUME, W. J., Sgt. 39 Bn.	M.M.	7/ 3/15 3y 5m. Sgt.
HUME, W. J., Pte. 40 Bn.	✠ 1/2/17	14/ 2/16 Pte. ✠
HUMES, C. W., Gnr. Art.	25 Bty.	12/ 1/16 3y 8m. Dvr.
HUMPHREY, E. A. A., Pte 3 GSB	12 Bn.	10/12/17 1y 11m. Pte.
HUMPHREY, N. J., Pte. 2 A.G.H.		4/10/15
HUMPHREY, N W., Pte. 12 Bn.	✠ 27/8/16	24/ 8/15 Pte. ✠
HUMPHREYS, T. H., Pte. 12 Bn.	W. M.M. 10 F.A.B.	18/ 5/15 4y 7m. Sgt.
HUMPHRIES, E. A., Pte. 26 Bn.	12 Bn.	8/ 5/15 4y 2m. Pte.
HUMPHRIES, G. M., Pte. 12 Bn.	W.	28/ 4/16 3y 7m. L./Cpl
HUNN, A. H., Pte. 15 Bn.	✠ 9/8/16.	29/ 9/14 Pte. ✠
HUNN, A. W., Tpr. 3 L.H.	W.	1/12/14
HUNN, A. W., Pte. 40 Bn.		1/ 3/16 3y 10m. Pte.
HUNN, W. N., Gnr. Arty.	W., 46 Bty.	2/12/15 3y 3m. Gnr.
HUNT, A. W., Pte. 26 Bn.		2/ 4/15
HUNT, A. B., Lieut. 12 Bn.	2W., 52 Bn.	24/ 8/15 4y 3m. Capt.
HUNT, A. H., Pte. 3 G.S.R.	12 Bn.	17/ 6/18 1y 6m. Pte.
HUNT, G. A., Pte. 15 Bn.	✠ 12/5/15.	26/10/14 Pte. ✠
HUNT, J., Pte. 12 Bn.		15/ 1/15 7m. Pte.
HUNT, R., Pte 40 Bn.	2W., 10 L.T.M.B.	15/ 4/16 2y 11m. Pte.
HUNT, T. E., Signr. 15 Bn.	4 Divl. Cyc. Co	24/10/16 1y 6m. Pte.
HUNT, W., Pte. 40 Bn.	W., 15 Bn.	3/10/14 4y 7m. Pte.
HUNT, W J., Pte. 12 Bn.	40 Bn.	6/11/16 2y 11m. Pte.
HUNT, W. J., Pte. 12 Bn.	W., 52 Bn.	4/11/15 1y 6m. Pte.
HUNTER, E. J. D., Cpl. Engrs.	4 Tunn. Co. 12 Bn.	6/11/15 2y 11m. Sgt.
HUNTER, E. F., Pte. 40 Bn.	W., M.M.	24/ 4/16 3y 4m. Pte.
HUNTER, J. H., Spr 8 Fd. Co.	13 Fd Co ✠ 18/4/18.	4/10/15 Spr. ✠
HUNTER, J., Pte. Fd Co.	1 Pnrs. ✠ 24/7/16.	19/ 9/14 Pte. ✠
HUNTER, M., Dvr. 6 F.A. Bde.	14 F.A.B. ✠ 27/7/17.	4/10/15 Dvr. ✠
HUNTER, S. M., Pte. 12 Bn.	W., 52 Bn. ✠ 5/11/16.	28/ 7/15 Pte. ✠
HUNTER, W R., Pte. 40 Bn.	26 Bn. ✠ 6/5/17.	3/ 5/16 Pte. ✠
HUNTINGDON, S. L., Pte. 4 M.G. Co.		24/ 1/17
HURBURG, C., Pte. 7 Fd. Amb.	13 Fd. Amb.	19/ 3/15 4y 3m. Sgt.
HURD, C. H., Tpr. 2 G.S.R	3 L.H	11/ 2/18 1y 6m. Tpr.
HURD, C. H., Pte. 40 Bn.		7/ 2/16 1y 3m. Pte.
HURD, E., Pte. 12 Bn.	W.	26/ 8/16 1y 5m. Pte.
HURD, H. P., Pte. 26 Bn		26/ 4/15
HURLEY, W. P., Pte. 26 Bn.	12 Bn., 1 Div. Engrs.	14/ 8/15 2y 4m. Spr.
HURN, J. J., Pte. 12 Bn.		18/12/14 3y 9m. Pte.
HURSEY, F L. S., Pte. 3 G.S.R.		20/ 4/18 11m. Pte.
HURST, J. A., Pte. 15 Bn.	W., 47 Bn.	8/ 6/15 2y, 2nd-Lieut.
HURST, R. H., Pte. 12 Bn.	40 Bn.	12/ 4/16 10m. Pte.
HURST, W. A., Pte. 12 Bn.	✠ 18/9/18.	17/12/17 Pte ✠
HUSBAND, A. E, Pte. 7 Fd Amb.	✠ 12/7/16.	25/ 3/15. Pte. ✠
HUSBAND, L., Pte. 4 M.G. Co.	12 Bn. ✠4/6/18.	6/ 3/17 Pte. ✠
HUTCHEON, F. W., Pte. 40 Bn.	W. ✠ 17/7/18.	18/10/16 Pte. ✠
HUTCHINS, C., Pte. 15 Bn.		2/ 1/15 2y 4m. Pte.
HUTCHINS, D., Pte. 40 Bn.		9/ 2/16 3y 2m. Pte.
HUTCHINS, L., Dvr. 1 D.A.C.	12 F.A.B.	16/ 9/14 3y 8m. Dvr.
HUTCHINS, W. F., Pte. 12 Bn.	W., 52 Bn.	11/ 1/16 1y 5m. Pte.
HUTCHINSON, A. J., Gnr. 6 F.A.B	13 F.A.B.	14/ 2/16 3y 8m. Dvr.
HUTCHINSON, A M., Pte. 40 Bn.	W.	18/ 4/16
HUTCHINSON, E. A., Pte. 40 Bn.	2W.	22/ 2/15 4y 8m. W.O.
HUTCHINSON, G. H., Pte. 12 Bn.	17 Fd. Co.	19/ 8/14 4y 5m. Dvr.
HUTCHINSON, H. G., Pte. 26 Bn.		28/ 7/15 1y 1m. Pte.
HUTCHINSON, H. H., Pte. 4 A.S.C.	2 M.T. Co.	28/ 9/14 4y 5m. Pte.
HUTCHISON, A. M., Pte. 40 Bn.	W.	18/ 4/16
HUTT, E. J., Pte. 12 Bn.		7/ 1/18 1y 3m. Pte.
HUTT, R. W., Pte. 3 G.S.R.	1 D.A.C.	31/ 7/18 1y 3m. Gnr.
HUTT, T. J., Pte. Remounts		9/ 3/18
HUTT, W., Tpr. 3 L.H.	✠ 13/6/15.	18/ 8/14 Tpr ✠
HUTTING, W., Pte. 12 Bn.		30/12/14 1y 8m. Pte.
HUTTLEY, W. J H., Gnr. Arty.		10/ 4/17 2y 6m. Gnr.
HUTTLEY, W. J., Tpr. 3 L.H.		2/10/17 10m. Tpr.
HUTTON, A. E., Pte. 12 Bn.		31/ 5/15 4y 3m. Pte.
HUTTON, A. A., Gnr. Arty.	W., 11 F.A.B.	23/ 3/17 2y 6m. Gnr.
HUTTON, H., Dvr 40 Bn.	3 M.G. Co.	16/10/16 2y 11m, Dvr.
HUTTON, K. J., Pte. 12 Bn.	2W. M.M. 1 M.G. Bn.	24/ 5/15 4y 2m. Cpl.
HUTTON, N. G., Spr Signlrs.	5 Signal Trp	31/ 5/17 2y 5m. Spr.
HUTTON, W., Pte. 12 Bn.	✠ 3/11/17.	10/10/16 Pte. ✠
HUTTON, W., Cpl. 1 A.C.H.		17/ 9/14

S

NAME.	REMARKS.	ENLISTED.	RANK ON DISCHARGE. SERVICE.
HUXLEY, A. R., Gnr. 36 H.A.G.		28/ 6/16	3y 4m, Gnr.
HUXLEY, C. H. A., Pte. 12 Bn.	W., 40 Bn. ✤ 8/6/17.	13/ 4/16	Pte. ✤
HUXLEY, C. D., Sgt. 12 Bn.	W., 52 Bn.	2/ 3/15	4y 1m, Cpl.
HUXLEY, E. W., Cpl. 12 Bn.	M.M.	18/ 8/15	4y 1m, Sgt.
HUXLEY, F. G., Pte. 26 Bn.	M.C.	24/ 4/15	3y 3m, Lieut.
HUXLEY, G. W., Pte. 12 Bn.	W.	18/ 8/14	1y 10m, Pte.
HUXLEY, R. G., Pte 12 Bn.	2W., M.I.D	25/11/15	3y 10m, Pte.
HUXTABLE, A. J., Gnr. Arty.	108 How. Bty.	4/ 1/16	3y 9m, Gnr.
HUXTABLE, A. S., Pte. 40 Bn.		27/ 9/17	2m, Pte.
HYATT, R. G., Pte. 12 Bn.	2W., 52 Bn.	25/ 5/15	2y 11m, L.-Cpl.
HYATT, S. G., Pte. 15 Bn.	W., Camel Cps., 15 Bn.	1/12/14	2y 6m, Cpl.
HYDE, C., Tpr. 3 L.H.	W.	20/ 8/14	4y 6m, Tpr.
HYDE, C. T. G., Pte. 12 Bn.	A.T.B.D.	8/ 4/16	3y 6m, Pte.
HYDE, W. H., Pte. 12 Bn.	52 Bn ✤ 7/7/16.	10/ 8/15	Pte. ✤
HYLAND, E., Pte 12 Bn.	52 Bn. ✤ 7/7/16.	10/ 8/15	Pte. ✤
HYLAND, G. F., Pte. 40 Bn.		15/ 3/16	7m, Pte.
HYLAND, H. J., Pte. 12 Bn.	40 Bn.	18/ 4/16	3y 6m. Pte.
HYLAND, L. W., Pte. 40 Bn.	2W. ✤ 16/12/17.	18/ 4/16	Pte. ✤
HYLAND, M. F., Pte 40 Bn.	✤ 12/10/17.	2/10/16	Pte. ✤
HYLAND, P., Pte. 15 Bn.	45 Bn.	2/10/14	4y 4m, Pte.
HYLAND, W. J., Pte. 4 M.G. Co.	6 M.G.	19/ 9/16	Cpl.
HYNDS, E., Pte. 40 Bn.	M.M.	9/10/16	2y 11m, Pte.
HYNDS, J., Pte 26 Bn.		26/ 7/15	4y 1m, Cpl.
HYNES, H. P., Tpr. 3 G.S.R.		1/ 5/18	1y 1m, Tpr.
HYNES, S., Pte. 40 Bn.		30/ 9/16	1y 1m, Pte.
HYNES, W. P., Gnr. 6 F.A.B.	W.	17/ 1/16	3y 11m, Dvr.
HYNSON, R. D., Pte. 12 Bn.		8/ 9/15	
HYTT, A. H., Pte. 12 Bn.	W., 3 A.I.B.D. Hqrs.	15/ 7/15	4y 1m, Pte.
IBBOTT, D. A., Tpr 3 L.H.		5/ 6/17	2y 2m, Tpr.
IBBOTT, F. S., Tpr. 3 L.H.	✤ 6/8/16.	12/ 5/15	Cpl. ✤
IBBOTT, G. J., Pte. 12 Bn.	2W., 46 Bn.	12/12/14	4y 6m, Pte.
IBBOTT, I. G., Pte. 2 M.G. Co.		30/ 9/14	4y 5m, Pte.
IBBOTT, J. G., Tpr. 3 L.H.	W., 4 T.M. Bty.	14/10/15	2y 9m, Gnr.
IBBOTT, M. A., Pte. 40 Bn.		9/11/16	
IBBOTT, V. G., Pte 26 Bn.	2W., M.C.	1/ 3/15	4y 5m, Sgt.
IBBOTT, W. G., Pte. 12 Bn.	✤ 26/12/16	7/ 8/16	Pte. ✤
IKIN, A. J., Tpr. Remounts		5/10/15	4y 1m, Tpr.
IKIN, A. E., Pte. 12 Bn.		13/12/15	1y 6m, Pte.
IKIN, A. L., Pte 40 Bn.	W.	21/ 3/16	1y 6m, Pte
IKIN, D. B., Gnr. 18 Bty.	105 How. Bty.	22/ 9/15	3y 11m, Lieut.
IKIN, H. C., Lieut. A.I.F. Canteens			
IKIN, H. W., Tpr. 3 L.H.	3 Army B.A.C.	5/ 6/17	2y 4m, Gnr.
IKIN, J., Pte. 12 Bn.	M.M.	23/ 9/15	3y 11m, Pte.
IKIN, J. R., Pte. A.F.C.		29/10/17	
IKIN, L. F., Pte. 2 G.S.R.		27/ 4/18	1y 2m, Pte.
ILES, B. J., Gnr. Arty		17/10/16	2y 5m, Gnr.
ILES, G. H., Pte. 15 Bn.	24 F.A.B., 10 F.A.B. ✤ 5/4/18.	12/ 8/15	Bdr. ✤
ILES, W. H., Pte. 3 G.S.R.		22/ 7/18	11m, Gnr.
ILLINGWORTH, O. J., Pte. 40 Bn.	W., H.Q.A.B. Depot.	17/10/16	3y 1m, Cpl.
ILLINGWORTH, P. E., Pte. 15 Bn.	M.M., 4 A.M.G. Bn.	27/ 7/15	4y 1m, Dvr.
ILLMAN, C. G., Spr. 4 Fd Co.		18/ 8/15	3y 9m, Dvr.
ILLSLOW, C., Pte. 12 Bn.	4 Divl. Arty. Dtls.	4/ 8/15	2y 10m, Gnr.
ILLSLOW, J., Pte. 40 Bn.	3 Sal. Co., 3 M.G. Bn.	31/ 3/16	3y 1m, Pte.
IMLACH, J., Pte. 40 Bn.	W., 3 Divl Hqrs.	25/10/15	3y 11m, L.-Cpl.
IMLACH, W. T., Tpr. 3 L.H.		7/ 8/15	10m, Tpr
INCHES, A. J., Pte. 12 Bn.	2W.	15/ 9/15	3y 8m, Pte.
INCHES, C. E. V., Pte. 1 A.G.H.	1 A.C.C.S.	10/ 5/15	4y 4m, Sgt.
INGALL, W. G., Spr. 1 Div. Sig. Co.		2/ 8/15	4y, Spr.
INGLEBY, W. T., Pte. 12 Bn.		15/11/15	3y 10m, Pte.
INGLES, G., Pte. 3 Cyc. Co.		13/ 3/16	3y 9m, Pte.
INGLES, R., Sgt. 12 Bn.		10/ 8/16	1y 11m, Pte.
INGLIS, H. L., Pte. 26 Bn		24/ 6/15	4y 2m, Dvr.
INGLIS, R., Pte Wireless	4 Bty	26/11/17	1y 10m, Gnr.
INGLIS, T. J., Gnr. B.A.C.	W., 8 F.A.B.	3/10/14	
INGLIS, W., Pte. A.S.C.		18/12/17	1y 10m, Pte.
INGLIS, W. J. T., Pte. 26 Bn.	2W., 7 M.G. Co.	24/ 6/15	2y 3m, Pte.
INGRAM, B., Capt., A.M.C.		18/ 8/14	3y 5m, Major.
INGRAM, G. F., Dvr. 3 A.F.A.		1/12/14	
INGRAM, J. H., Pte. 40 Bn.		17/11/16	
INMAN, J. S., Tpr. 3 L.H.		26/11/17	1y 9m, Tpr.
INMAN, C., Spr. 3 Tnlrs.		6/12/16	1y 8m, Spr.
INNES, A. G., Pte. 12 Bn.	W., 52 Bn. ✤ 20/10/17.	9/ 7/15	Pte. ✤
INNIS, R. V., Pte. A.F.C.		1/11/16	2y 8m, 2nd A.M.
INNES, C., Pte. 2 G.S.R.	1 D.A.C.	21/ 5/18	1y 4m, Gnr.
INNES, E. E., Pte Remounts		7/10/15	8m, Pte.
INNES, L. H., Pte. 26 Bn.		8/ 6/15	4y 3m, Pte.
INNIS, A. R., L.-Cpl. 40 Bn.	15 Bn.	21/ 3/16	
ION, C. H., Pte. 12 Bn	W., 51 Bn.	5/ 2/15	4y 3m, L.-Cpl.
ION, G. W., Pte. 12 Bn.	✤ 15/4/17.	16/ 5/16	Pte. ✤
ION, W. J., Pte. 40 Bn.	2W.	16/ 2/16	3y 1m Cpl.
IRELAND, N. L., Pte. 40 Bn		27/ 3/16	1y 10m, Pte.
IRVINE, G. R., Spr. 3 Fd. Co.	✤ 31/7/15	20/ 8/14	L.-Cpl. ✤
IRVINE, W. H., Tpr. Remounts		21/ 3/18	1y 7m, Tpr.
IRVING, H. L., Gnr. 9 Bty.	W.	20/ 7/15	4y 2m. Bdr.
IRVING, W., Pte. 15 Bn.	12 Bn. ✤ 6-10/4/17.	13/10/15	Pte. ✤
IRVING, W. H. L., Gnr. 24 F.A.B	4 D.A.C.	24/10/16	3y, Gnr.

NAME.	REMARKS.	RANK ON DISCHARGE. ENLISTED, SERVICE.
IRWIN, E. A., Gnr. 3 F.A.B.	2 F.A.B. ✣ 1/8/17.	28/ 7/15 Gnr. ✣
IRWIN, H. B., Dvr. 9 Bty.		19/ 8/14 2y 1m, Dvr.
IRWIN, J. H., Pte. 12 Bn.	4 Divl. Tunlrs.	2/ 8/15 4y. Pte.
IRWIN, W. H., Gnr. 29 Bty.	W., M.M.	12/10/16 3y, Gnr.
IRWIN, W. J., Cpl. Cyclists		4/ 4/16
ISAAC, H., Pte 26 Bn.	12 Bn.	12/ 8/15 3y 11m, Pte.
ISAACS, L. E., Pte. 40 Bn.		14/ 8/17 1y 8m. Cpl.
IVES, F. S., Pte. 4 M.G. Co.	2 M.G. Co. ✣ 26/3/18.	6/12/12 Pte. ✣
IVORY, A. J., Tpr. 23 L.H.		20/ 8/14 4y 2m, Tpr.
IVORY, B. J., Pte. 40 Bn.	W.	18/ 5/16 1y 8m, Pte.
IVORY, B., Pte. 12 Bn.	✣ 1/5/18.	26/ 3/17 Pte. ✣
IVORY, C. J., Pte. 12 Bn.	52 Bn., 51 Bn.	15/12/14 4y 11m, Lieut.
IZARD, A. E., Pte. 40 Bn.		7/ 4/16 3y 4m, L.-Cpl.
IZARD, G. E., Pte. 12 Bn.	W., 52 Bn. ✣ 25/8/17.	9/10/15 Pte. ✣
JACK, A. E., Pte. 40 Bn.	W.	12/ 4/16 2y 11m, Pte.
JACK, A. C., Dvr. 12 Bn.	2W.	23/ 8/14 3y 4m, Pte.
JACK, C. L., Pte 40 Bn.	W., 15 Fd. Amb.	8/11/16 3y, Pte.
JACK, C. T., Pte. 12 Bn.	✣ 24/7/16.	11/ 1/15 Pte. ✣
JACK, L. C., L.-Cpl. 3 Fd. Co.	2W.	28/ 7/15 2y 3m, L.-Cpl.
JACK, R. M., Pte 2 G.S.R.	24 A.D.U.S.	23/ 4/18 1y 5m, Pte.
JACK, W., Gnr. 6 F.A.B.	13 F.A.B.	15/ 2/16 3y 10m, Dvr.
JACKLIN, H., Pte. 26 Bn.		29/ 7/15
JACKMAN, T. J., Pte. 40 Bn.	15 Bn.	17/ 5/16 3y. 2m, Pte.
JACOBS, E R., Pte. 15 Bn.	W., 47 Bn., P.O.W.	27/ 7/15 4y 2m, Pte.
JACOBS, B. H., Pte. 26 Bn.	W.	22/ 2/15 3y 1m, Pte.
JACOBS, F. J., Pte. 2 G.S.R.	16 A.D.U.S.	1/ 5/18 1y 4m, Pte.
JACOBS, W., Sgt. 3 L.H.	3 L.H.M.G. Co.	20/ 8/14 4y 10m, Sgt.
JACOBS, W G., Pte. 40 Bn.	2W.	19/ 7/16 2y 8m, Pte.
JACOBSON, A. J., Pte. 12 Bn.	W., 52 Bn, 51 Bn.	18/ 1/16 3y 11m, Pte.
JACOBSON, A. E., Pte. 40 Bn.	W., 15 Bn.	21/ 2/16 2y 5m, Pte.
JACOBSON, A., Pte. 40 Bn.	2W., M.M.	20/ 3/16
JACOBSON, C. T., Pte. 15 Bn	✣ 14/1/17.	25/ 9/14 Pte. ✣
JACOBSON, L. G., Pte. 1 A.C.H		16/ 5/15
JACOBSON, M. A., Pte, A.M.D.		4/ 7/18
JACQUES, A., Pte. 12 Bn.	✣ 3-5/9/16.	15/ 9/15 Pte. ✣
JACQUES, A. H., Pte. 40 Bn.		18/ 7/17
JACQUES, A. H., Pte. 12 Bn.	3W.	18/ 7/16 2y 9m, Pte.
JACQUES, C., Pte. 12 Bn		22/12/14
JACQUES, G. C., Gnr. 3 F.A.B	103 How. Bty.	15/ 2/17 2y 7m, Gnr.
JACQUES, J. V., Pte. 12 Bn.		14/ 8/16 2y 8m, Pte.
JACQUES, V. A., Sgt 12 Bn.	✣ 31/7/18.	20/ 8/14 C.S.M. ✣
JAFFRAY. W., Pte. 40 Bn.	✣ 13/10/17.	16/ 6/16 Pte. ✣
JAGO, A., L.-Cpl. 40 Bn.	✣ 7/10/17.	2/10/16 L.-Cpl. ✣
JAGO, G. H., Pte. 40 Bn.	✣ 7/6/17.	4/ 4/16 Pte. ✣
JAGO. H., Pte 12 Bn.		13/12/14 1y 1m, Pte.
JAGO, L. F., Pte. 26 Bn.	W. ✣ 29/7/16.	27/ 7/15. Pte. ✣
JAGO, W. C. H., Pte. 26 Bn.	2W	27/ 7/15 4y 1m. Pte.
JACKSON, B., Pte. 40 Bn.	W., 51 Bn.	24/ 3/16 3y 6m. Cpl.
JACKSON, B. J., Pte. 40 Bn.	W., M.C.	5/10/15 3y 10m. Lieut.
JACKSON, C., Gnr. Arty.		8/12/15.
JACKSON, C. C., Pte. 40 Bn.	2W.	25/ 9/16 1y 9m. Pte.
JACKSON, C. H., Gnr. 6 F.A.B.	5 F.A.B.	24/ 8/15 4y 1m. Gnr.
JACKSON, E. E., 2nd Cpl. Miners	M.M., 3 Tnlrs. Co.	17/11/15 2y 8m. Cpl.
JACKSON, G. R., Pte. 40 Bn.	W., 51 Bn.	1/ 3/16 3y 4m. Pte.
JACKSON, H., Pte. 12 Bn.	2W., 40 Bn.	9/10/16 2y 6m. Pte.
JACKSON, H. R., Pte. A.A.O.C.		26/10/17 1y 9m. Pte.
JACKSON, H., Pte. 12 Bn.		30/ 5/16.
JACKSON, H. V., Spr. Miners	3 Tnlrs. Co.	17/11/15 4y. Spr.
JACKSON, J. E., Spr. 2nd Tnlrs.	P.O.W	29/ 3/17 2y 3m. Spr.
JACKSON, J. E., Sgnlr. 12 Bn.		18/ 8/14 2y, Signlr.
JACKSON, J., Pte. 12 Bn.		15/11/15
JACKSON, J. V., Pte. 40 Bn.		3/ 1/17 2y 6m. Pte.
JACKSON, L. W. S., Pte. 40 Bn.	✣ 11/9/16.	17/ 2/16. Pte. ✣
JACKSON, T. C., Pte. 26 Bn.	✣ 3/10/18.	26/ 7/15. Sgt. ✣
JACKSON, W. S., Sgt. 12 Bn.	W.	18/ 8/14 1y. 9m. Sgt.
JACKSON, W., Pte. 15 Bn.		28/ 7/15
JAKOBSEN, H. G., Spr. 8 Fd. Co.		20/11/17 4y. Spr.
JAMES, A. E., Pte. 4 M.G. Co.	12 Bn. ✣ 26/7/18.	8/11/16 Pte ✣
JAMES, A. F. P., Sgt. 26 Bn.		20/ 4/15.
JAMES, A. H., Cpl. 1 A.G.H.	3 Fd. Amb	9/ 6/15.
JAMES, A. T., Pte. 15 Bn.	47 Bn. ✣ 16/6/17.	12/ 6/15. Sgt. ✣
JAMES, A. E., Pte. 40 Bn.	2W.	7/ 3/16 3y 1m. Pte.
JAMES, C. A., Pte. Miners	2 Tnlr. Co., 2 A.M.T. Co.	22/11/15 3y 7m. Pte.
JAMES, E. W., Pte. 1 A.C.H.	1 A.A.C.S.	18/ 9/14 4y 11m Sgt.
JAMES, E. W. R., Pte. 12 Bn	40 Bn.	5/ 6/17 2y 4m. Pte.
JAMES, G. C., Tpr. 3 L.H.		14/ 9/15 4y 1m. Tpr.
JAMES, G. F., Pte. 12 Bn.		27/ 9/16 1y 6m Pte.
JAMES, G. H., Pte. 15 Bn.	3W., 47 Bn. ✣ 19/5/18.	15/ 7/15. Pte. ✣
JAMES, H., Gnr. 3 F.A.B.	2W., 2 D.A.C., 5 F.A.B.	5/ 9/14 3y 11m. Gnr.
JAMES, H. F., Pte. 40 Bn.		7/ 3/16 3y 5m. Pte.
JAMES, H., Pte. 40 Bn.	W.	28/ 8/17 1y 7m, Pte.
JAMES, H. G., Pte. 26 Bn.	12 Bn ✣ 3-5/9/16	3/ 8/15. Cpl ✣
JAMES, H. O., Pte. 40 Bn	✣ 14/10/17.	3/ 5/16 Cpl. ✣
JAMES, J. R., Pte. 12 Bn.		13/ 9/16 3y. L.Cpl.
JAMES, R. R., Gnr. 6 F.A.B.	25 How. Bde., 14 A.F.A. ✣ 24/4/18	11/ 1/16. Gnr. ✣
JAMES, S. T., Pte. 12 Bn.	2 Divl. Hdqtrs.	18/ 8/14. 4y 7m. Pte.

NAME.	REMARKS.	RANK ON DISCHARGE. ENLISTED. SERVICE.
JAMES, T. A., Dvr. 3 L.H.	58 Bn.	12/10/15 3y 11m. Dvr.
JAMES, W. A., Pte. 40 Bn.	A. Prov. Cps., 40 Bn.	29/ 5/16 3y 4m. Pte.
JAMES, W. L., Cpl. 26 Bn.	✠ 21/4/17.	20/ 4/15 Cpl. ✠
JAMESON, A., Pte. 40 Bn.	2W.	28/ 8/16 2y 7m. Pte.
JAMIESON, F. D., Pte. 1 G.S.R.		11/ 3/18.
JANSSON, A. L., Pte. 12 Bn.	W	7/ 9/16 1y 8m. Pte.
JARMAN, C. L., Pte. 12 Bn.	69 Bn., 12 Bn. ✠ 17/4/18.	25/ 9/14. Pte. ✠
JARMAN, C. W., Pte. 12 Bn.	W., 52 Bn.	7/10/15 1y 7m. Pte.
JARMAN, L. A., Pte. 12 Bn.	M.M., C. de G. (Belgian), 51 Bn.	8/ 1/15 4y 9m. Pte.
JARMAN, M. A., Pte. 12 Bn.	W., 52 Bn.	7/10/15 1y 4m. Pte.
JARMAN, S. L., Pte. 15 Bn.	W. 47 Bn., 46 Bn.	2/ 9/15 2y 11m. Pte.
JARMAN, W. G., Pte. 12 Bn.	W.	10/ 7/17 1y 8m Pte.
JARRITT, C. W., Pte. 40 Bn.		29/ 6/16 11m. Pte.
JARVEY, G. G., Pte. 12 Bn.		31/12/15 1y 9m. Pte.
JARVIS, A. E., Pte. 12 Bn.	W., 52 Bn.	30/ 7/15 2y 5m. Pte.
JARVIS, A. T., Spr., Tnlrs.	W., 1 Tnlr. Co.	27/10/16 3y 2m. Spr.
JARVIS, G. Pte. 12 Bn.	52 Bn., 4 M.G. Co ✠ 10/8/18.	15/ 7/15. Pte. ✠
JARVIS, H. T. Pte. 12 Bn.	52 Bn. ✠ 4/9/16.	12/12/14. Pte. ✠
JARVIS, C. H., Spr., 5 Miners	2W., 2 Tnlr. Co.	28/ 2/16 3y 9m. Spr.
JARVIS, R. G., Pte. 12 Bn.	✠ 25-28/4/15.	17/ 8/14. Pte ✠
JARVIS, R. W., Pte. 40 Bn.	W., M.M., A.I.B.D.	2/ 6/16 3y 4m. Pte.
JARVIS, T., Pte. 12 Bn.	✠ 25/4/15.	17/ 8/14. Pte. ✠
JAYNES, W. T., Pte. 15 Bn.	2W	11/ 8/15 3y 7m. Pte.
JEANES, H. S., Tpr. 3 L.H.		20/ 8/14 4y 6m. Tpr.
JEFFREY, A. E., Pte. 1 G.S.R.		4/ 2/18.
JEFFREY, C., Pte. 12 Bn.	14 Bn.	7/ 8/15 4y 4m. L.Cpl.
JEFFREY, D., Pte. 40 Bn.	W. ✠ 4/8/17.	26/ 8/16. Pte. ✠
JEFFREY, E., Pte. 12 Bn.	W., P.C.W. ✠ 8/9/16.	28/ 9/15 Pte. ✠
JEFFREY, G. W., Pte. 12 Bn.	W., 52 Bn. ✠ 24/4/18.	16/ 7/15. Pte. ✠
JEFFREY, J. A., Pte. 4 M.G. Co.		17/11/16 3y 1m. Pte.
JEFFREY, J., Pte. 12 Bn.	W., 52 Bn. ✠ 3/9/16.	15/ 7/15. Pte. ✠
JEFFREY, J. D., Pte. 40 Bn.	4W., D.C.M.	26/ 4/16 3y 6m. Cpl.
JEFFREY, J. B., Gnr. 120 How. Bty		6/12/19 Pte.
JEFFREY, R. G. C., Spr. Wireless	4 Sgnl Tp., 2 Sig. Squad.	27/ 9/16 3y 1m, Spr.
JEFFREY, T., Tpr. Remounts		25/ 9/16 3y 6m, Tpr.
JEFFREY, V. Y., Dvr. 6 F.A.B.	W., 3 D.A.C., 107 Bty. A.F.A.	14/ 2/16 3y 8m, Dvr.
JEFFREY, W., Pte. 12 Bn.	✠ 6/10/17.	4/ 8/16 Pte. ✠
JEFFREY, W. O., Sgt., Arty.	M.M., C. de G (France), 13 F.A.B ✠ 14/2/16.	14/ 2/16. Sgt. ✠
JEFFREY, W. R., Pte 26 Bn.	W., 52 Bn., 51 Bn.	24/ 3/15 4y 5m, Pte.
JEFFS, E. A., Pte. 40 Bn.	✠ 5/7/18.	21/ 8/17. Pte. ✠
JELLIE, S. N., Pte. 12 Bn.		2/ 8/15 4y. Cpl.
JENKINS, A. E., Pte. 12 Bn.	52 Bn., 51 Bn.	12/10/15 3y 10m. Pte.
JENKINS, A. E., Pte. 26 Bn.	3W.	26/ 4/15 4y 1m. Sgt.
JENKINS, A. B., Pte. 40 Bn.	2W.	18/ 3/16 1y 9m. Cpl.
JENKINS, E. C., Pte. 12 Bn.	W., 28 Bn.	29/ 3/16 2y 3m Pte.
JENKINS, E. H., Gnr. Arty.		29/ 1/17.
JENKINS, F. W., Pte. 40 Bn.	W.	7/ 6/16 3y. Pte.
JENKINS, H., Spr. Miners	3 Tun. Co.	27/10/15 3y 8m. Spr.
JENKINS, H. J., Pte. 12 Bn.	W.	3/11/14 3y 3m. Pte.
JENKINS, H. C., Pte. 26 Bn.	✠ 29/4/16	10/ 4/15. Pte. ✠
JENKINS, H., Pte. 40 Bn.	W.	8/ 2/17 2y 1m. Pte.
JENKINS, L. S., Pte. 12 Bn.	W.	28/ 9/16 3y 2m, Pte.
JENKINS, R. E., Pte. 12 Bn.	51 Bn.	11/ 4/16 3y 5m Pte.
JENKINS, R. J., Pte. 12 Bn.	52 Bn. ✠ 7/1/17.	7/ 8/15. Pte. ✠
JENKINS, W. R. S., Pte. 40 Bn.	2W.	7/ 5/17 1y 11m. Pte.
JENKINSON, C. H., Pte. 12 Bn.		6/12/15.
JENNER, C., Gnr. 12 Bn.	12 F.A.B.	2/ 8/15.
JENNINGS, E. J. S., Spr. 3 Fd. Co.	M.M., 3 Fd. Co.	23/ 8/15 4y 1m. Spr.
JENNINGS, E. J., Pte. 12 Bn.	A.F.C.	6/11/16 2y 5m. 2A.M.
JENNINGS, H. W. C., Pte. 12 Bn.	A.C. Hqtrs	20/ 8/15 4y 1m. Pte.
JENNINGS, W. O., L.-Sgt., 12 Bn.		13/ 3/17.
JENNESON, J. R., Cpl. 3 Fd. Co.	W., 1 A.L.R. Unit.	27/ 8/14 3y 8m. Lieut.
JENSEN, L. H., Pte. 40 Bn.	W.	24/ 7/16 3y. Pte.
JENSEN, N. H., Bdr. 6 F.A.B.		3/ 8/15 4y. Bdr.
JENTZSCH, E. P., Pte. 12 Bn.	2W	26/ 8/15 3y 8m. Pte.
JEPSON, C. J., Pte. 26 Bn.		6/ 9/15 1y 9m. Pte.
JERRETT, R., Sgt.-Mjr. 12 Bn.	✠ 5/5/15.	22/ 8/14. S.M. ✠
JESCHEK, F., Pte. 12 Bn.		18/ 7/16 1y 1m, Pte.
JESSOP, A. L., Dvr. 3 F.A.B.	101 How. Bty. ✠ 22/10/17.	11/ 3/15. Dvr ✠
JESSOP, G. W., Gnr., 12 Bn.	24 How. Bty., 24 F.A.B., 10 F.A.B.	2/ 8/15 4y. Gnr.
JESSUP, W. W., Pte. 40 Bn.	✠ 23/10/16.	10/ 3/16. Pte. ✠
JETSON, D., Pte. 12 Bn.	1 Pnrs. Bn.	8/ 7/15 3y 2m. L.Cpl.
JETSON, E. J., Pte. 15 Bn.	W. ✠ 9/8/15.	12/ 1/15. Pte. ✠
JETSON, P. J., Pte. 12 Bn.		27/10/15 1y 10m. Pte.
JETSON, W. T., Pte. 12 Bn.	W., 40 Bn.	20/ 3/16 2y. 4m. Pte.
JEWELL, F. W., Pte. 1 A.G.H.		3/ 6/15.
JEWKES, F. S., Pte. 12 Bn.	52 Bn. ✠ 28/3/17.	1/ 8/15 Sgt. ✠
JOHANSON, O. W., Pte. 12 Bn.	W., 52 Bn. ✠ 4/9/16.	3/ 8/15. Pte. ✠
JOHN, A. J., Pte. 26 Bn.	W., 65 Bn., 26 Bn.	12/ 5/15 4y 4m. Pte.
JOHN, F. J., Mun Worker.		M W.
JOHNS, C., Pte., Remounts.		28/ 9/15 1y 3m. Tpr.
JOHNS, C. H., Pte. 12 Bn.	✠ 19-22/8/16.	29/ 1/10. Pte. ✠
JOHNS, G. R., Dvr. 3 L.H.	4 Div. Amm Col.	26/11/14 4y 5m. Dvr.
JOHNS, J. E., Pte. 12 Bn.	M.M. ✠ 15/4/17.	30/ 5/16. Pte. ✠
JOHNS, R. R., Dvr. 3 Fd. Co.	15 Bn.	26/10/15 3y 11m. Dvr.
JOHNS, S. R., Pte. 12 Bn.	W.	30/ 5/16 2y 3m. Pte.

TASMANIA'S MUSTER ROLL. 293

NAME.	REMARKS	RANK ON DISCHARGE. ENLISTED. SERVICE.
JOHNS, T., Dvr. 13 F.A.B.	51 Bty. F.A.B.	6/10/15 3y 11m. Dvr.
JOHNS, W. H., Pte. A.A.M.C.		13/ 4/16.
JOLLY, J., Pte. 40 Bn.		22/ 1/17 1y 8m. Pte.
JOLLY, W. G., Gnr. 6 F.A.B.	M.C., 17 Bty., 6 F.A.B.	28/ 8/15 4y 3m. Lieut.
JOHNSON, A. E., Pte. 12 Bn.	✠25/8/18.	19/10/17. Pte. ✠
JOHNSON, A. J., Pte. 12 Bn.	40 Bn.	18/10/16 2y 11m. Pte.
JOHNSTONE, A. J., Pte. 40 Bn.		20/ 7/16 2y 4m. Pte.
JOHNSON, A. C., Pte. 3 G.S.R.		4/ 7/18.
JOHNSON, A. R., Sgt. 12 Bn.	52 Bn. ✠ 4/9/16.	25/ 8/14. Pte. ✠
JOHNSON, A. W., Pte. 2 G.S.R.		4/ 6/18.
JOHNSON, A. M., Pte. 12 Bn.	10 Bn., P.O.W.	6/11/16.
JOHNSON, A. S., Pte. 12 Bn.	✠ 29/5/15.	29/10/14. Pte. ✠
JOHNSON, A. N., Pte. 12 Bn.	✠ 25-28/4/15.	26/ 8/14. Pte. ✠
JOHNSON, A. A. C., Pte. 12 Bn.		20/ 8/14.
JOHNSON, A., Pte. 12 Bn.	✠ 2/5/18.	26/ 6/17. Pte. ✠
JOHNSON, A., Pte. 4 M.G. Co.	W., 5 M.G. Bn.	11/10/16.
JOHNSON, A. A., Pte. 26 Bn.		27/ 2/15 4y 6m. Pte.
JOHNSON, A. B., Pte. 26 Bn.	2W.	17/ 2/15 3y 10m. Pte.
JOHNSON, A. P., Pte. 40 Bn.	2W	14/ 3/16 2y 5m. Pte.
JOHNSON, A. W. L., Pte. 12 Bn.	W.	12/10/16.
JOHNSON, B. J., Gnr. 8 F.A.B.		12/10/15 4y 2m. Gnr.
JOHNSTONE, C. W., Pte. 3 M.G. Bn		13/ 2/17 2y 2m. Pte.
JOHNSON, C. A. G., Pte. 40 Bn.	W.	24/ 9/17.
JOHNSTON, C. C., Pte.		12/11/17 1y 11m. Pte.
JOHNSON, C. E., Gnr. 1 G.S.R.		7/ 2/18 1y 8m. Gnr.
JOHNSON, C. C., Pte. 12 Bn.	W.	9/ 2/15 2y 8m. Pte.
JOHNSON, C. A., Pte. 15 Bn.	✠ 14/7/15.	19/12/14. Pte ✠
JOHNSON, C. H., 2nd-Lt. 1 G.S.R.	12 Bn.	4/10/17 2y. Lieut.
JOHNSON, C. R., Pte. 40 Bn.	2W	27/ 3/16 3y 2m. L.Cpl.
JOHNSTON, D. H., Pte. 12 Bn.	2W., 4 M.G. Bn.	15/ 7/15.
JOHNSON, E. H., Pte. 12 Bn.	4 Purs, 3 M.G. Co.	22/ 8/14 4y 3m. Cpl.
JOHNSON, E. H., Pte. 15 Bn.		18/ 9/14.
JOHNSTONE, E. T., Pte. 15 Bn.		2/ 9/15.
JOHNSON, E., Gnr., 2 G.S. Rfts.	10 D.A.C.	5/ 6/18 1y 3m. Gnr.
JOHNSTON, E. M., Dvr. Arty.	17 Bty.	8/11/15 3y 11m. Dvr.
JOHNSTON, E. E., Pte. 40 Bn.		20/ 7/16 3y 3m. Pte.
JOHNSTON, E. E., Pte. 2 G.S.R.	12 Bn.	2/ 4/18 1y 5m Pte.
JOHNSON, E. H., Pte. 40 Bn.	W. 3 M.G. Bn., 10 M.G. Co.	1/ 5/17 2y 5m. Pte.
JOHNSTONE, E. J. E. H., Pte. 40 Bn	W.	8/11/15 2y 9m. Pte.
JOHNSON, E. M., Lieut., 26 Bn.	M.I.D., H.Q. Aust. Cps.	1/ 8/15 3y 9m. Capt.
JOHNSTON, E. R. J., Spr. Engrs.		30/ 4/17 2y 1m. Spr.
JOHNSON, F. E., Pte. Railway	4 Fd. Co.	13/12/16 2y 9m. 2 Cpl.
JOHNSON, G., Pte. 26 Bn.	2W.	2/ 3/15 2y 11m. Pte.
JOHNSTONE, G., Pte. 26 Bn.	65 Bn., 7 Bn.	19/ 4/15 3y 6m.
JOHNSON, G., Spr. Tnlrs.		18/10/16 1y 5m. Spr.
JOHNSON, G. A., Pte. 15 Bn.	✠ 31/5/15.	30/ 9/14. Pte. ✠
JOHNSTON, G. A., Pte. 3 L.H.		25/ 8/14 2y. Sig.
JOHNSON, G. A., Pte. 12 Bn.	✠ 15/4/17.	4/ 5/16. Pte. ✠
JOHNSTON, G. A., Pte. 26 Bn.	W.	10/ 5/15 2y 9m. Cpl.
JOHNSTON, G. A., Cpl. Miners	2W., 3 Tnlrs.	12/ 9/15 4y. Sgt
JOHNSON, H. H., Dvr. Miners	3 Tnlrs. Co.	4/ 4/16 3y 4m. Dvr.
JOHNSON, H., Pte. 40 Bn.	W.	28/ 9/16 3y 2m. Pte.
JOHNSTON, H. W., Pte. 40 Bn.		13/10/16 2y 11m. Pte.
JOHNSON, H. J., Pte. 40 Bn.	✠ 18/7/18.	1/ 5/17. Pte. ✠
JOHNSON, J., Pte. 12 Bn.	52 Bn., 27 Co. A.S.C.	8/12/14 4y 5m. Dvr.
JOHNSTONE, J. A., Gnr., Arty.	7 A.F.C.	6/ 3/16 2y 10m. 2 Lt.
JOHNSON, J. H., Pte. 12 Bn.		14/11/17 2y. Pte.
JOHNSEN, J., Pte. 4 M.G. Co.	1 M.G. Bn. ✠ 10/8/18.	28/10/16 Pte. ✠
JOHNSTON, J. A., Gnr. Arty.	10 F.A.B.	5/ 2/17 2y 1m. Gnr.
JOHNSTONE, J. P., Gnr. Arty.	W.	11/12/16 2y 5m. Gnr.
JOHNSTONE, J. C. R., Gnr. Arty.	2W., 5 Divl. Arty. Dtls., 15 Bn.	25/11/15.
JOHNSTON, K. B., Pte. 12 Bn.		8/ 1/15 2y 1m. Pte.
JOHNSON, L. J., Gnr., 12 Bn.	W., 52 Bn., 24 How. Btyl., 24 F.A.B	13/ 7/15 4y 1m. Gnr.
JOHNSON, L. V., Pte. 12 Bn.	2W., 46 Bn.	26/10/15 3y 9m. Pte.
JOHNSON, L. G., Tpr. 3 L.H.	2 D.A.C.	19/ 7/15 2y 3m. Gnr.
JOHNSON, L., Pte. 40 Bn.	✠ 30/8/18.	1/ 4/16. Pte. ✠
JOHNSON, M. L., Tpr. 3 L.H.		16/ 9/15 1y 7m
JOHNSTON, N. J., Sgt. 1 A.G.H.	16 Fd. Amb., 2 A.G.H.	23/ 6/15 4y 6m. S.Sgt.
JOHNSON, N. P., Pte. 12 Bn.	9 Bn.	6/10/16 3y 1m. L Cpl
JOHNSON, P., Pte. 26 Bn.		16/ 8/15 10m. Pte.
JOHNSON, R. F. L., Pte. 40 Bn.	W.	27/ 3/16 3y 9m. Pte.
JOHNSON, R. E., Pte. 34 Bn.		23/ 9/16 2y. Pte.
JOHNSON, R. H., Pte. 12 Bn.	52 Bn. ✠ 23/9/17.	3/12/14. Pte. ✠
JOHNSON, R. H., Pte. 26 Bn.		7/ 4/15 1y 3m. Pte
JOHNSON, R. E., Pte. 12 Bn.		21/10/16.
JOHNSON, R. G., Pte. 26 Bn.		11/ 5/15 2y 2m. Pte.
JOHNSON, R. B., Tpr. 3 L.H.		19/ 9/14 2y 6m. Tpr.
JOHNSTON, S. H., Pte. 26 Bn.	2W., M.M., 12 Bn.	16/ 8/15 4y 3m. Cpl.
JOHNSTON, S., Pte. A.A.M.C.	6 Fd. Amb.	4/10/16 3y. Pte. ~
JOHNSTONE, T. E., Pte. 3 G.S.R.	12 Bn.	1/ 7/18.
JOHNSTON, L., Sgt. 1 A.C.H.		15/ 9/14 4y 5m. Capt.
JOHNSON, V. D., Pte. 12 Bn.		29/ 8/14 4y 5m. Dvr.
JOHNSTON, V. M., Cpl. 26 Bn.	W.	19/ 2/15 4y 2m. Sgt.
JOHNSTON, V. A., Pte. 12 Bn.		13/10/16.
JOHNSTONE, W., Spr. Tnlrs.	3 Tnlrs Co.	13/ 4/17 2y 2m. Spr.
JOHNSON, W. C., Pte. 12 Bn.	3W., 40 Bn.	22/ 3/16 3y 5m.

294   TASMANIA'S WAR RECORD, 1914-1918.

NAME.	REMARKS.	RANK ON DISCHARGE. ENLISTED, SERVICE.
JOHNSON, W. E., Pte. 12 Bn.	W., M.M.	12/ 7/15 4y. Cpl.
JOHNSON, W. H., Dvr. 12 Bn.	24 How. Bty., 24 F.A.B.	19/ 7/15 4y. Cpl.
JOHNSON, W. J., Pte. 12 Bn.		18/ 7/16.
JONES, —., M.W.		
JONES, A. E., Pte. 12 Bn.	M.M ✤ 5-8/5/17.	26/10/15. L. Cpl. ✤
JONES, A. H., Pte. 12 Bn.	4 Pioneers	1/11/15 1y 8m. Spr.
JONES, A. J., Pte. 12 Bn.		23/ 7/17 2y 3m. Pte.
JONES, A. L., Pte. 1 A.C.H.	1 A.A.H.T., 11 Fld. Amb.	8/ 6/15 4y 2m. Cpl.
JONES, A., Pte. 12 Bn.		31/ 5/16 2y. 3m. Pte.
JONES, A A. Pte. 40 Bn.	✤ 7/6/17.	29/ 9/16. Pte. ✤
JONES, A. C. Pte. 12 Bn.	W3. Fd. Co. ✤ 22/8/17.	19/ 8/14. Spr. ✤
JONES, A. J. Pte. 40 Bn.	W. 2 A.A.H.	4/ 6/16 2y. L Cpl.
JONES, A. J. B. Pte. 1 Rmt.	8 M.V. Sec.	19/10/15 3y 6m. Tpr.
JONES, A. J. Pte. 12 Bn.	52 Bn. ✤ 4/9/16.	29/10/15. Pte. ✤
JONES, A. N. Pte. 3 G.S.R.	12 Bn.	4/ 3/18 1y 6m. Pte.
JONES, A. R., Pte. 40 Bn.		25/ 5/16 1y 11m. Pte.
JONES, A. Pte. 26 Bn.	W. M.G. Bn.	21/ 7/15 4y 3m. Pte.
JONES, A. F. Dvr. A.M.C.	7 Fld. Amb., 13 Fld. Amb.	9/ 3/15 4y 1m. Dvr.
JONES, A. C. Tpr. 3 L.H.		16/ 8/17 2y. Tpr.
JONES, A. H., Pte. 12 Bn.		21/10/15
JONES, A. H., Pte. 12 Bn.	W.	21/ 8/16 3y 2m. Cpl.
JONES, B. L. Pte. 12 Bn.		6/ 9/16 3y 1m. Pte.
JONES, B. S. Dvr. A.M.C.	7 Fld. Amb., 13 Fld. Amb.	9/ 3/15 4y 1m. Dvr.
JONES, B. J. H. Pte. 40 Bn.	2W.	2/10/16 1y 11m. Pte.
JONES, C. A., Bdr. Arty.	1 F.A.B 101 How Bty.	15/ 2/16 3y 8m. Bdr.
JONES, C. F., Pte. 12 Bn.		29/ 8/14 5y 1m. Pte.
JONES, C. H. Dvr. 12 Bn.		30/ 4/16 3y 5m. Dvr.
JONES, C. J. Dvr. 8 F.A.B.	31 Bty.	19/11/15 3y 9m. Dvr.
JONES, C. M. Pte. 12 Bn.	57 Bn. ✤ 10/12/16.	15/ 9/15. Pte. ✤
JONES, C. L. Pte. A.F.C.	15 F.A.B., 101 How. Bty. ✤ 16/10/17.	24/10/16. Pte. ✤
JONES, C. M. Pte. 12 Bn.	52 Bn. 51 Bn.	19/ 1/16 3y 8m. Pte.
JONES, D. E. C. Pte. 12 Bn.		2/ 5/17 2y 7m. Pte.
JONES, D. Pte. 12 Bn.	✤ 25/7/16	25/ 8/15. Pte. ✤
JONES, D. L. Gnr. 40 Bn.	A.S.C., 6 F.A.B., 101 How. Bty.	14/ 3/17 2y 7m. Gnr.
JONES, D. W. Pte. 12 Bn.	W. 40 Bn.	4/ 4/16 1y 8m. Pte.
JONES, D. J. Cpl. Railway.		25/ 4/17 2y. 5m Cpl.
JONES, D. A. Pte. 12 Bn.		31/10/16.
JONES, E. W. Dvr. 12 Bn.	M.M., 52 Bn., 27 A.S.C.	9/ 7/15 4y 1m. Dvr.
JONES, E. W. J. Spr. Tnlrs.		26/ 3/17.
JONES, E. C. Pte. 12 Bn.		29/ 5/17.
JONES, E. T. Pte. 12 Bn.		12/12/19. Pte.
JONES, E. K. Tpr. 3 L.H.	W.	2/ 2/15 4y 1m. Tpr.
JONES, E. S. Dvr. 40 Bn.	W.	21/ 3/16 3y 1m. Dvr.
JONES, E. J. Pte. 40 Bn.	W. 9 M.G.D.H.	10/11/16 2y 5m. Pte.
JONES, E. E. Pte. 3 L.H.	5 Div. Amm. Col., re-enlistd N. and MEF	19/ 8/14 3y. Lieut.
JONES, F. E. Pte. 12 Bn.	W.	30/ 4/16 1y 6m. Pte
JONES, F. P. Pte. 40 Bn.	3W.	19/ 4/16 3y 4m. Pte.
JONES, F. W. Spr. Railway.	15 Rly. Coy., 1 L.R.O. Coy.	16/10/17 2y. Spr.
JONES, F. B. K. Pte. 1 G.S.R.		12/ 2/18.
JONES, F. G. Pte. 40 Bn.	W.	2/11/16 2y 5m. Pte
JONES, G. Pte. 40 Bn.	-	10/ 8/17.
JONES, G. E. Pte. 40 Bn.	W.	9/10/16 3y 2m. Pte.
JONES, G. V. Tpr. 3 L.H.		15/ 2/17 2y. Tpr.
JONES, H., Pte. 3 Fld. Coy.	W.	19/ 8/14 4y 5m. Sgt.
JONES, H. M. Pte. 12 Bn.	2W., 52 Bn.	22/ 1/15 4y 7m. Pte.
JONES, H. P. Pte. 12 Bn.	2W.	21/ 3/16 3y 6m. Pte
JONES, H. R. Pte. 3 G.S.R.	12 Bn.	31/ 7/18 1y 2m. Pte.
JONES, H. H. Pte. 40 Bn.	W., A.A.M.C.	10/ 5/16 3y 5m. Pte.
JONES, H. P. Spr. Railway.	A.L.R.O Co.	3/11/17 1v 9m. Spr.
JONES, J. A. Dvr. Tnlrs.	13 L.H., 30 Bty., 8 Bde.	10/10/16 3y. Dvr.
JONES, J. A. E. Pte. 40 Bn.	W., 12 Bn.	7/ 6/16 3y 3m. Pte.
JONES, J. G. Pte. 12 Bn.	Anzac Police, 57 Bn.	7/12/15 3y 9m. Pte.
JONES, J. L. Pte. 12 Bn.	W., 52 Bn. ✤ 5/4/18.	30/ 7/15 L./Cpl.
JONES, J. A. Pte. 4 M.G. Co.	40 Bn.	3/ 7/16 3y 1m. L. Cpl.
JONES, J. A. Pte. 26 Bn.	✤ 29/7/16.	10/ 3/15. Pte. ✤
JONES, J. B. Pte. 12 Bn.	3W. ✤ 30/6/18.	28/ 2/16. Pte. ✤
JONES, J. J. Pte. Remount.		4/10/15 1y 2m. Tpr.
JONES, J. T. Pte. 12 Bn.		2/11/16 2y 11m. Pte.
JONES, J. W. Gnr. F. Arty.	25 F.A.B.	28/11/16 1y 11m. Gnr.
JONES, L. A. Pte. 12 Bn.	✤ 10/11/16.	30/12/15. Pte ✤
JONES, L. N., Pte. 12 Bn.	1 D.A. Dermatological Hos.	7/ 9/16 1y 2m. Pte.
JONES, L. R. Gnr. 3 F.A.B.	✤ 26/9/17.	26/ 8/14. Sgt. ✤
JONES, L. T. Pte. 26 Bn.	✤ 29/11/15.	11/ 3/15. Pte. ✤
JONES, M. G. Pte. 40 Bn.		11/10/16.
JONES, M. O. Pte. 26 Bn.	W., 12 Bn.	5/ 8/15 4v 1m. Pte.
JONES, M. L. Pte. 3 Fld. Amb.		1/11/14 1y 8m. Pte.
JONES, P. F. Pte. 1 A.C.H.		19/ 9/14 4y 5m. Pte.
JONES, P. C. Pte. 12 Bn.	W.	9/10/16 2y 5m. Pte
JONES, P. D. Pte. 12 Bn.		13/10/16 1v 4m. Pte.
JONES, P. F. L.Cpl. 3 L.H.		8/10/14 4y 3m. W.O.
JONES, P. L. Pte. 40 Bn.		9/10/16 3y 1m. Sgt.
JONES, R. G. Gnr. 26 Bn.	A. Cps , H.T.M.B.	8/ 7/15.
JONES, R. Pte. 26 Bn.	W.	6/ 7/15 4y 6m. Cpl.
JONES, R. R. Dvr 40 Bn.	W.	4/10/16 2y 11m. Dvr
JONES, R. K. L.Cpl. 12 Bn.		6/10/16 3y 2m. L. Cpl.
JONES, R. A. Pte. 12 Bn.	W.	20/ 7/16 2y 7m. Pte.

TASMANIA'S MUSTER ROLL.

NAME.	REMARKS.	RANK ON DISCHARGE. ENLISTED. SERVICE.
JONES, R. T. Dvr. 6 F.A.B.	A.M.C.	21/ 9/15 4y 1m. Dvr.
JONES, R. H. Pte. 12 Bn.		1/10/14.
JONES, T. S. Pte. 40 Bn.	2W., M.M.	7/ 4/16 2y 7m. Sgt.
JONES, T. Pte. 40 Bn.	✻ 1/2/17.	23/ 2/16. Pte. ✻
JONES, T. A. Pte. 12 Bn.	✻ 24/2/17.	16/ 8/16. Pte. ✻
JONES, T. O. Cpl. 12 Bn.	W.	26/ 7/15 3y 3m. Cpl.
JONES, T. O. Pte. 40 Bn.	2W.	9/ 3/16 2y 5m Pte.
JONES, T. R. Pte. 26 Bn.	W. ✻ 11/8/18.	27/ 9/15. Sgt. ✻
JONES, W. E. 2 A.M. Wireless.	Flying Corps.	5/12/16 2y 7m. 2 A.M.
JONES, W. H. Pte. 40 Bn.	W. ✻ 7/5/17.	21/ 3/16. Cpl. ✻
JONES, W. W. R. Tpr. 3 L. Horse	✻ 18/7/16.	19/ 8/14. Tpr. ✻
JONES, W., Pte. 12 Bn.	W.	25/10/16.
JONES, W., Pte. 12 Bn.		13/ 6/16 3y 3m. Pte.
JONES, W. A. Tpr. 4 M.G. Co.	3 L.H.	17/ 2/17 2y 6m. Tpr.
JONES, W. C. Pte. 12 Bn.	2W., 52 Bn.	7/ 8/15 4y 2m. Pte.
JONES, W. D., Pte. 12 Bn.	W.	1/ 9/16 1y 7m. Pte.
JONES W. G. Pte. 40 Bn.	W	21/ 3/17 2y 6m. Pte.
JONES, W. H. Pte. 40 Bn.	2W., 15 Bn., 40 Bn.	28/ 2/16.
JONES, W. J., Pte. 40 Bn.	A.S.C. Dtls., 40 Bn.	11/ 5/17 1y 10m. Pte.
JONES, W. R., Dvr. 6 F.A.B.	2W., How. Bde., 2 D.A.C., 2 Sig. Co. ✻ 7/6/19.	20/ 9/15. Dvr. ✻
JONES, W. T., Pte. 40 Bn.	✻ 12/7/17.	5/ 4/16. Pte. ✻
JONES, W. T. Gnr. 8 F.A.B.	3W.	21/ 6/16 3y 4m. Gnr.
JORDAN, A. E. Tpr. 3 L.H.		25/ 3/15.
JORDAN, A., Pte. 7 Fd. Amb.		6/ 8/15 11m Tpr.
JORDAN, A. B. Pte. 40 Bn.	3W.	9/10/16 2y 5m. Pte.
JORDAN, A. H. Pte. 12 Bn.	W., 52 Bn., 4 M.G.B.	11/ 1/16 3y 8m. Pte.
JORDAN, C., Spr. Tnlrs.	2 Tun. Coy.	15/ 3/17 2y. Spr.
JORDAN, C. C., Dvr. Arty.	13 F.A.B., 113 How. Bty	25/ 8/15 4y 2m. Dvr.
JORDAN, E. T., Pte. 40 Bn.	W.	14/ 3/16 3y 6m. Pte.
JORDAN, G. B., M.W.		
JORDAN, H. W, Pte. 40 Bn.	3 Div. Sig. Coy.	3/11/15 3y 10m. Spr.
JORDAN, J., Pte. Remount.		22/ 9/15 1y 7m. Tpr.
JORDAN, M. R., Pte. 3 G.S.R.	12 Bn	30/ 7/18 1y 3m. Pte.
JORDAN, R. L., Pte. 12 Bn.		6/ 1/16 3y 8m. Cpl.
JORDAN, T. C., Pte. 3 L.H.		18/ 8/15 2y 4m. Tpr.
JORDAN, T. F. Pte. 15 Bn.	W	10/ 9/14 3m. Pte.
JORDAN, W., Pte. 12 Bn.		28/ 8/14 1y 10m. Pte.
JORDAN, W. L., Pte. 12 Bn.		23/ 7/15 1y 1m. Pte.
JORY, A. W. Dvr. Arty.		4/ 8/15 3m. Dvr.
JORY, E., Pte. 20 Bn.		2/ 4/15 1y 2m. Pte.
JOSEPH, E. L., Pte. 3 Fld. Amb.		29/12/14 4y 4m Pte.
JOSEPH, E., Pte. 12 Bn.	3W.	9/ 1/15 4y 6m. Pte.
JOSEPH, L. T. Pte. 4 M.G. Co.	W., 12 Bn. ✻ 23/8/18.	18/ 1/17. Pte. ✻
JOSEPH, M. P. G. Pte. 12 Bn.	✻ 6/10/17.	5/ 4/16. Cpl. ✻
JOWETT, A. C., Gnr. Arty.	9 Bty. F.A.	16/ 1/17 2y 8m. Gnr.
JOWETT, P., Tpr. 1 G.S.A.M. Div.	3 L.H.	26/ 3/18 1y 5m. Tpr.
JOYCE, H. W., Gnr. Arty.		29/–9/15 9m. Gnr.
JOYCE, R. K., Gnr. Arty.	1 F.A.B.	28/11/16 3y. Gnr.
JOYCE, S. E., Sgt. 12 Bn.	W., 51 Bn.	27/ 4/16 2y 2m. Lieut
JOYCE, T. P., Pte. 40 Bn.		4/11/16 2y 3m. Pte.
JOYNER, K. V., Pte. A.F.C.		3/ 1/17 2y 2m. 2 A.M.
JUBB, C. C., Pte. 12 Bn.	2W	17/ 8/14 4y 7m. Cpl.
JUDD, C., Pte. 12 Bn.	W.	21/10/16.
JUDD, J., Lieut. 15 Bn.		9/ 6/15 1y 7m. Lieut.
JUFFS, G. A., Gnr. 36 H.A.G.		8/ 6/15.
JUKES, W. T., Pte. A.A.M.C.	7 Fld. Amb.	27/ 4/16.
JULIEN, E. W., Chapln, 1 Inf. Bde		5/ 5/16 1y 5m. Chapln
JUPP, A. T. F., Pte. 12 Bn.	✻ 1/1/17.	8/ 6/16. Pte. ✻
JUPP, E. A., Spr. Miners.	3 Tnlrs.	1/11/15 3y 9m L. Cpl.
JUPP, J., Pte. 40 Bn.		19/ 7/17 11m. Pte.
JUPP, V. J., Spr. Miners.		18/11/15 1y 4m. Spr.
JURY, H. J., Pte. 2 G.S.R.		1/ 5/18 10m. Pte.
KAINE, J. M., Pte. 12 Bn.	W	24/ 8/14 4y 6m. Pte.
KAINE, W., Pte. 12 Bn.	W.	21/ 5/15 4y 6m. Pte.
KANE, F. B., Pte. 40 Bn.	W.	15/ 3/16 3y Pte.
KAVANAGH, J., Pte. 40 Bn.		29/ 2/16 2y 1m. Pte.
KAY, R. R., Pte. 12 Bn.	W.	15/ 7/15 1y 11m. Pte
KAY, A. B., Pte. 26 Bn.	W., 17 Fld. Amb.	9/ 8/15 2y 4m. Pte.
KAYE, P. G. L., Pte. 40 Bn.		4/ 4/16.
KAYSER, J. A. W., Capt. 12 Bn.		
KEAL, F., Pte. 12 Bn.	1 Wireless Sec., A.C. Sig Coy.	13/10/16 2y 10m. Spr.
KEAN, A. E., Spr. 3 Fd. Co.	2W., 12 Bn., 40 Bn.	16/ 4/15 Gnr.
KEAN, C. A. Pte. 12 Bn.	W., 52 Bn., 51 Bn.	12/10/15 3y 10m. Pte.
KEAN, H. H., Pte. 12 Bn.	W., 40 Bn.	23/10/16 2y 8m. Pte
KEARNAN, J. A., Pte. 12 Bn.	3W., 52 Bn., 13 M.G. Co.	2/ 7/15 4y 1m. Sgt.
KEARNEY, G., Gnr. 3 G.S.R.	1 D.A.C.	29/ 7/18 1y 2m. Gnr.
KEARNEY, G. P., Pte. 40 Bn.	W. 5 M.G. Bn.	29/ 2/16 3y 5m Pte.
KEARNEY, G. J., Pte. 15 Bn.		28/ 8/15 1y. Pte.
KEARNEY, J. W., Pte. 26 Bn.	W., 12 Bn.	16/ 8/15 2y 9m. Pte.
KEARNEY, J., Tpr. 3 L.H.	W.	1/12/14 2y 3m. Tpr.
KEARNEY, R. E., Dvr. 4 A.S. Co.		17/ 3/14 4v 5m. Cpl.
KEARNEY, T. E., Pte. 12 Bn.	✻ 8/4/17.	7/12/14. Pte. ✻
KEARNS, E. O., Pte. 15 Bn.		11/ 5/15 4y 3m. Pte.
KEATING, F. W., Pte. 15 Bn.	46 Bn.	26/ 7/15 4y 1m. Sgt.
KEATING, K. C., Pte. 26 Bn.	2W., 69 Bn., 26 Bn.	4/ 3/15 4y. Pte.
KEATING, M., Pte. 26 Bn.		4/ 3/15 4y 8m. Pte.

296   TASMANIA'S WAR RECORD, 1914-1918.

NAME.	REMARKS.	RANK ON DISCHARGE. ENLISTED. SERVICE.
KEATING, R. V., Pte. 12 Bn.	W., 52, 15 Bn.	28/ 7/15 3y 10m. Pte.
KEATING, T., Pte. 26 Bn.	12 Bn., ✽ 15/4/17.	10/ 8/15 Pte. ✽
KEATING, W. J. M., Pte. 7 F.Am.	✽ 5/8/16.	7/ 4/15. L. Cpl. ✽
KEATS, J. E., Pte. 40 Bn.	2W.	10/ 5/16 2y 10m. Pte.
KEATS, W. V., Pte. 12 Bn.	52 Bn. ✽ 10/6/17.	8/ 9/14. Lieut. ✽
KEEAMI, W. N., Dvr., 3 F.A.B.		20/ 7/15 9m. Dvr.
KEEGAN, C., Tpr. 3 L.H.		4/11/16 2y 10m. Tpr.
KEEFE, J. R., Pte. 26 Bn.		25/ 6/15 1y 9m. Pte.
KEEFE, J. R., Pte. 26 Bn.		25/ 6/15 1y 2m. Pte.
KEEFE, R. F., Pte. 15 Bn.	W.	16/ 9/14 1y 6m. Pte.
KEELAN, J., Pte. 40 Bn.		9/ 8/16 1y 6m. Pte.
KEELEY, G. D., Pte. 40 Bn.	W., 15 Bn., 40 Bn.	4/ 2/16 2y 5m. Pte.
KEELEY, R. G., Pte. 12 Bn.		22/10/17 1y 3m. Pte.
KEELEY, S. V., Pte. 40 Bn.	3W., 12 Bn.	4/ 2/16 3y 1m Pte.
KEELING, W. L., Pte. 1 G.S.R.		15/ 1/18.
KEEN, A. R., Dvr. 8 L.H.	6 F.A. Bde.	17/ 3/18 1y 1m. Dvr.
KEEN, C. H., Sgt. 40 Bn.	W.	23/ 8/16.
KEEN, C. S., Pte. 12 Bn.	W. ✽ 5-8/5/17.	21/ 8/14 C.S.M. ✽
KEEN, E., Pte. 12 Bn.		11/ 8/16 1y 3m. Pte.
KEEN, J. J., L.Cpl. 12 Bn.		21/ 8/14. Lieut.
KEENAN, M. J., Pte. 12 Bn.	✽ 2/9/16.	29/ 6/15. Pte. ✽
KEENAN, V. H., 2 A.M. A.F.C.	71 SQN. A.F.C.	31/10/16 2y 10m. 2 AM
KEEP, W., Tpr. 3 L.H.		5/ 6/17 4m Tpr.
KELB, A. H., Pte. 26 Bn.	W. 1 Pnrs	30/ 8/15 3y 11m. Pte.
KELB, E. C., Pte. 12 Bn.	4 M.G. Bn.	14/ 3/16 3y 5m. Pte.
KELB, H. A., Pte. 12 Bn.		8/ 7/15 9m. Pte.
KELB, L. A., Pte. 26 Bn.	W.	10/ 7/15 2y 2m. Pte.
KELB, R. W., Pte. 12 Bn.		29/ 2/16 7m. Pte.
KELB, W., Pte. 40 Bn.	✽ 17/7/17.	30/ 3/16. Pte. ✽
KELSEY, L. G., Pte. 12 Bn.	W.	28/11/17.
KELLEHER, H. F., Pte. 40 Bn.		5/10/17 1y 10m. Pte.
KELLEHER, J. P., Pte. 12 Bn.	52 Bn. ✽ 28/11/16.	8/ 7/15 Pte. ✽
KELLEHER, J., Dvr. 12 Bn.	40 Bn	17/ 3/13 3y 5m. Dvr.
KELLEHER, O. W., Pte. 26 Bn.	W.	1/ 9/15 1y 8m. Pte.
KELLEHER, V. E., Dvr. Arty.	W., 23 How. Bde., 10 F.A. Bde.	10/10/16 3y 1m. Spr.
KELLEHER, W. A., Spr. Tnlrs.	W., 2 Tnlrs Co.	10/10/16 3y 1m Spr
KELTIE, D., Dvr. 15 Bn.		31/12/14 4y 4m. Dvr.
KELTY, G. E., Pte. 40 Bn.	✽ 7/6/17.	2/ 3/16. Pte. ✽
KELTY, M. W., Pte. 40 Bn.	2W. ✽ 28/3/18.	9/ 5/16 Pte. ✽
KELTY, W., Pte. 40 Bn.	2W., M.M.	13/ 4/16 2y 10m. Pte.
KELLY, A. J., Pte. 40 Bn.	2W.	2/10/16
KELLY, A., Pte. 26 Bn.	2W.	13/ 5/15 1y 8m. Pte.
KELLY, C. J., Tpr. 3 L.H.	2 F.A.B.	19/ 3/17 1y 2m. Tpr.
KELLY, C. J., Pte. 12 Bn.		10/ 8/15
KELLY, E. H., Pte. 26 Bn.	P.O.W.	20/ 7/15 3y 11m. L. Cpl.
KELLY, H. G., Cpl. 12 Bn.	2W.	24/ 9/14 3y 4m. Cpl.
KELLY, H. S. D., Pte. 26 Bn.	W.	6/ 3/15 4y 2m. Pte.
KELLY, H. J., Pte. 12 Bn.	W.	28/ 7/15 3y 5m. Pte
KELLY, J. F., Pte. 26 Bn.	12 Bn.	10/ 8/15 4y Pte.
KELLY, J., Pte. 2 Pnrs.		13/10/16 1y 11m. Pte.
KELLY, J. J., Pte. 4 M.G. Co		11/ 1/17.
KELLY, J. J., Tpr. 3 L.H.	D.A.C., 4 H.T.M. Bty. ✽ 6/5/17.	23/9/18. Gnr. ✽
KELLY, J., Pte. 40 Bn.	W.	7/ 3/16 3y 8m. Pte.
KELLY, J. W., L.Cpl. 40 Bn.	W.	9/ 2/16 2y 3m. L. Cpl.
KELLY, R. J., Pte. 4 M.G.C.		16/12/16 2y 7m. Pte.
KELLY, P. J., Spr. Tnlrs.	✽ 17/8/17.	27/ 1/16 Spr. ✽
KELLY, P. W., Spr Tnlrs.	3 Tunn. Coy.	10/10/16.
KELLY, T. G., Dvr. Engrs.	8 F.A.B.	21/11/16 1y 9m. Dvr.
KELLY, T. W., Pte. 40 Bn.	W., 15 Bn., 40 Bn.	15/ 4/16 1y 11m. Pte.
KELLY, W., Pte. 4 M.G.C.	W.	9/ 8/16 3y 2m. Pte.
KELLY, W. E. J., Pte. 40 Bn.	W.	30/ 9/16 1y 6m. Pte.
KELLY, W., Pte. 40 Bn.		8/ 3/17 1y 1m. Pte.
KELLY, W., Pte. 4 M.G. Co.	W.	2/10/16 1y 6m. Pte.
KELLY, W., Pte. 12 Bn.		19/ 8/14
KELLY, W. J., Pte. 12 Bn.	2W.	9/10/14 4y 10m. Pte.
KELLY, W. J., Pte. 12 Bn.	W.	23/10/14 1y 8m. L. Cpl.
KEMP, E. D. F., Lt. 5 Div. Arty.	14 F.A.B.	16/ 2/15 4y 3m. Capt.
KEMPTON, W. R., Pte. 12 Bn.	Re-enlisted 12 Bn., 52 Bn., 49 Bn.	20/ 8/14 4y 10m. Pte.
KENDALL, R. W. W.		13/10/14
KENDRICK, C., Gnr. 3 F.A.B.	W.	22/11/16 1y 5m. Pte.
KENDRICK, H. E., Pte. A.M.C.		15/ 4/19 M.W.
KENNEDY, A. N., M.W.		4/ 9/15 3y 11m, Sgt.
KENNEDY, C. J., Cpl. 15 Bn.		30/11/16 2y 10m. Spr.
KENNEDY, G. M., Spr. 3 Tunn.		20/ 8/14 1y 10m. Pte.
KENNEDY, J. C., Pte. 12 Bn.		3/ 9/15
KENNEDY, J. S., Pte. 26 Bn.		21/ 6/17 1y Pte.
KENNEDY, L. J., Pte. 12 Bn.		11/ 8/16 2y 8m. Spr.
KENNEDY, P., Spr., Tunlrs.	3 Tunn. Co.	20/ 1/16 1y 8m. Spr.
KENNEDY, P. T., Spr. Miners.	5 Tunn. Co.	6/10/14
KENNEDY, W. S., L.-Cpl. 15 Bn.	W.	22/ 8/14 4y 6m. Mjr.
KENNEDY, W., R.S.M., 12 Bn.	M.C., M.I.D., 52 Bn., 51 Bn.	28/ 7/15 Pte. ✽
KENNEY, A. A., Pte. 12 Bn.	4 Aus. Div. Provost Corps. ✽ 2/4/18	6/12/17
KENNY, C F., Pte. 2 G.S.R.		3/ 9/15
KENNY, E. D., Pte. 26 Bn		7/11/16 2y 8m, Spr.
KENNY, J. H., Spr. 3 Tunnlrs	W.	19/ 1/18 1y 9m, Dvr.
KENNY, T., Dvr. 1 G.S. Rfts.	1 D.A.C.	16/ 8/15 Pte. ✽
KENSHOLE, E. S., Pte. 26 Bn.	12 Bn. ✽ 24/7/16	

TASMANIA'S MUSTER ROLL. 297

NAME.	REMARKS.	RANK ON DISCHARGE. ENLISTED, SERVICE.
KENT, A. R., Gnr. Arty.		11/ 2/16
KENT, A. F., Pte. 26 Bn.	W.	21/ 7/15 3y 10m, Pte.
KENTON, T., Dvr., 12 Bn.		5/ 3/17 2y 7m, Dvr.
KENWORTHY, E. K., Pte. 4 M.G.C.	5 M.G. Bn.	31/ 8/16 2y 11m, Pte.
KENWORTHY, R. C., Pte. 15 Bn.		20/ 9/14
KEOGH, C., Pte. 12 Bn.	W.	22/ 4/15 2y 8m, Pte.
KEOGH, H., Pte. 12 Bn.	W.	29/ 8/14 2y 1m, Pte.
KEOGH, J. P., Pte. 26 Bn.	3W., 69 Bn., 26 Bn.	14/ 4/15 3y 11m, Pte.
KEOGH, L., Pte. 40 Bn.		17/10/16 2y 5m, Pte.
KEOGH, P. H., Pte. 26 Bn.		24/ 2/15 2y 8m, Pte.
KEOGH, R., Pte. 12 Bn.	W., 51 Bn.	12/ 1/16 3y 8m, Pte.
KEOGH, W. T., Pte. 12 Bn.	W.	31/12/14 1y 3m, Cpl.
KEOGH, W. T., Pte. 12 Bn.		31/12/14 1y 3m, Pte.
KEPPLER, A. E., Pte. 12 Bn.	W.	17/ 8/14 1y 7m, Pte.
KEPPLER, T. G., Pte. 15 Bn.		12/ 1/15
KERR, J., Pte. 12 Bn.		30/ 1/15 11m, Pte.
KERR, J., Dvr. Arty.	W.	3/ 9/15
KERR, J., Pte. 12 Bn.	52 Bn.	5/ 8/15 2y 4m, Pte.
KERR, R. G., Pte. 26 Bn.	✠ 29/11/15.	12/ 3/15 Pte. ✠
KERRISON, E. H., Cpl. 1 A.C. Hos.	W., 6 F.A.B.	12/ 9/14 3y 11m, Cpl.
KERRISON, E. A., Pte. 12 Bn.	2W., 52 Bn.	4/10/15 1y 8m, Pte.
KERRISON, F., Pte. 40 Bn.	W., 51 Bn. ✠ 20/10/17	19/ 2/16 Pte. ✠
KERRISON, G., Pte. 1 G.S.R.	40. Bn.	5/ 3/18 1y 7m, Pte.
KERRISON, J., Pte. 40 Bn.	W.	20/ 6/16 3y 4m, Lt.
KERRISON, M., Sgt. 40 Bn.	W.	20/ 6/16 3y 3m, Sgt.
KERRISON, V., Pte. 40 Bn.		24/ 9/17 5m, Pte.
KERSLAKE, B., Pte. 3 L.H.	✠ 5/8/16	10/ 9/14 Pte. ✠
KERSLAKE, C. H., Tpr. 26 Bn.	W.	9/ 7/15 3y 8m, Tpr.
KERSLAKE, D. V., Pte. 12 Bn.	W.	30/11/16 3y, Pte.
KERSLAKE, E. E., Pte. 12 Bn.		25/ 9/16 3y 1m, Pte.
KERSLAKE, R. H., Pte. 15 Bn.	M.M. ✠ 9/8/16.	12/ 8/15 Pte. ✠
KESTLE, L., Pte. 40 Bn.	2W.	2/ 2/16 2y 1m, Pte.
KETTLE, A., Pte. 40 Bn.	2W., 69 Bn., 40 Bn.	5/ 4/16 2y 11m, Pte.
KETTLE, L. J., Pte. 40 Bn.	2W.	19/ 9/16 3y, Pte.
KEYGAN, J. H., Spr. 8 Fd. Co.	W., 15 Fd. Co.	25/ 1/16 3y 8m, Spr.
KEYS, L. G., Sig. 12 Bn.		11/11/14
KEYS, P., Spr. Tunnlrs.	W., 1 Tunn. Co.	12/ 2/17
KEYWOOD, P., Pte. 26 Bn.	✠ 29/7/16.	17/ 4/15 Pte. ✠
KHAN, F. A., Tpr. Remounts		12/10/15 2y 10m, Tpr.
KIDD, J. A., Pte. 15 Bn.		12/ 1/15 1y 4m, Cpl.
KIDD, M. M'L., Pte. 12 Bn.	W., 52 Bn. ✠ 15/4/18.	19/ 1/16 Pte. ✠
KIDDLE, R., Pte. 12 Bn.	W., 40 Bn. ✠ 28/3/18.	21/ 3/16 L.-Cpl. ✠
KIELY, W. A., Pte. 4 M.G. Co.	2W., 58 Bn.	4/10/16
KIERNAN, H., Pte. 26 Bn.	2W.	6/ 5/15 3y 11m, Pte.
KIERNAN, L. J., Gnr. 38 H.A.G.		1/ 6/15 4y 2m, Gnr.
KILBURN, H. C., Pte. 12 Bn.	2W.	20/ 8/15 1y 9m, Pte.
KILBY, F. H., Pte. 12 Bn.		27/10/15
KILBY, L. K., Gnr. Arty.		29/ 2/16
KILBY, R. J., Dvr. 6 F.A.B.	Croix-de-Guerre.	5/ 5/15 4y 5m, Dvr.
KILLALEA, H., Pte. 3 L.H.	W., M.M.	12/ 9/14 3y 8m, L.-Cpl.
KILLALEA, R. J., Pte. 12 Bn.	W., 69 Bn., 12 Bn. ✠ 24/4/18.	8/ 9/14 Cpl. ✠
KILLALEA. T. M., Spr. 6 Fd. Co.	Kit Stores.	5/10/15 2y 7m, Spr.
KILMARTIN, B. M., Pte. 4 A.S.C.	A.A. Post. Cpl.	3/ 2/15 C.S.M.
KILMARTIN, J. T., Sgt. 3 F.A.B.		27/ 8/14 4y 7m, Sgt.
KILMARTIN, J. D., Gnr. 6 F.A.B.	✠ 1/1/17.	9/ 9/15 Gnr. ✠
KILPATRICK, B. W., C.S.M. 15 Bn.	3W., 45 Bn.	13/10/14
KILJATRICK, H. G., Pte. 40 Bn.		7/ 3/16 3y 7m, Pte.
KIMBERLEY, C. A., Pte. 12 Bn.	✠ 8/1/18.	3/10/16 Pte. ✠
KIMBERLEY, E. E. L., Pte. 26 Bn.	✠ —/6/16.	31/ 8/15 Pte. ✠
KIMBERLEY, J. F., Pte. 40 Bn.		24/ 4/17
KIMBERLEY, J. W., Pte. 15 Bn.	P.O.W.	6/ 6/15 4y 2m, L.-Cpl.
KIMBLEY, C., Cpl. 1 A.C.H.		25/ 9/14
KINCADE, H. V., Pte. 12 Bn.	✠ 4/9/16., 52 Bn.	1/11/15 Pte. ✠
KINGSLEY, J. T., Pte. 26 Bn.		14/ 4/15 8m, Pte.
KINGSLEY, T. L., Pte. 12 Bn.	3W.	20/ 8/14 5y 3m, Pte.
KINGSMILL, H. L., Pte. 4 M.G. Co.	2 M.G. Bn.	15/ 5/17 2y, Pte.
KINGSTON, A. R. N., Pte. 12 Bn.	W.	6/10/16 2y 11m, Pte.
KINGSTON, C. E., Pte. 12 Bn.	W. ✠ 11/8/18.	31/ 5/16 Pte. ✠
KINGSTON, C. F., Pte. 26 Bn.	2W.	22/ 2/15 3y, Pte.
KINGSTON, C. H., Pte. 1 G.S.R.	40 Bn.	28/ 2/18 1y 9m, Pte.
KINGSTON, D. W., Pte. 12 Bn.	69 Bn., 1 M.G. Bn.	15/ 3/16 3y 7m, Pte.
KINGSTON, G. E. H., Pte. 40 Bn.	2W.	26/ 1/16 3y 3m, Pte.
KINGSTON, H. I., Pte 26 Bn.	W.	22/ 2/15 3y 2m, Pte.
KINGSTON, K., Dvr. 26 Bn.		8/ 5/15 4y, Dvr.
KINGSTON, W. E. J., Pte. 12 Bn.	W.	13/10/16 1y 11m, Pte.
KING, A. B., Gnr. 5 F.A.B.	2W., 6 F.A.B.	29/ 2/16 3y 4m, Gnr.
KING, A E., Pte. 40 Bn.		16/ 4/17 1y 11m, Pte.
KING, A. J., Pte. Tunnlrs.		5/10/16
KING, B. G. C., Pte. 12 Bn.		12/10/16 1y 11m, Pte.
KING, C. G., Spr. 8 F.C.E.		19/ 4/16 1y 7m, Spr.
KING, C. A., Pte. A.A.M.C.	4 Fd Amb.	24/10/16 3y 1m, Pte.
KING, D. J., Pte. 12 Bn.	W. ✠ 1/5/18.	1/ 6/16 Pte. ✠
KING, E. A., Pte. A.A.M.C.		22/ 4/17
KING, E., Pte. 12 Bn.		13/10/16 2y 1m, Pte
KING, E. B., Pte. 12 Bn.		8/12/14

NAME.	REMARKS.	RANK ON DISCHARGE. ENLISTED. SERVICE.
KING, E. J., Gnr., 15 F.A.B.		19/10/16 3y 2m, Gnr.
KING, F., Pte. 15 Bn.	✶ 31/5/15.	16/ 9/14 Pte. ✶
KING, F. A. J., Pte. 12 Bn.	W.	6/11/16
KING, F. H., Gnr. 3 F.A.B.	21 F.A.B., 1 D.A.H.Q.	14/ 8/15 4y 4m, Gnr.
KING, G. J., Cpl. F.A.B.	3 G.S.R.	26/ 8/14 4y 9m, Cpl.
KING, H. J., Pte. 12 Bn.	✶ 28/7/18.	21/ 8/14 Pte. ✶
KING, J. O., Pte. 40 Bn.	49 Bn., 11 M.G. Co., 3 Bn.	26/ 4/16 3y 5m, Pte.
KING, J. R., Pte. 40 Bn.	W.	10/10/16 2y 5m, Pte.
KING, S. T., Gnr. Arty.	7 F.A.B.	26/ 2/17 2y 7m, Gnr.
KING, P. F. S., Dvr. Arty.	3 D.A.C.	28/ 8/16 3y 1m, Dvr.
KING, R., Pte. A.M.C.	W., 2 Fd. Amb.	23/ 2/16 3y 1m, Pte.
KING, B. I. L., A. Cps. Sch.	53 Bn.	17/ 8/15 3y 11m, L.-Cpl.
KING, S. C., Spr. 8 Fd. Co.	W., 7 Fd. Co.	15/ 1/16 3y 8m, Spr.
KING, W., Pte. 12 Bn.		4/ 8/16 3y 1m, Pte.
KIPPAX, K. M., Pte. 40 Bn.		13/10/16 3y 2m, Pte.
KIRBY, A. R., Pte.		7/12/14
KIRBY, B. J., Pte. 12 Bn.		21/ 1/15
KIRBY, C. A., Pte. 12 Bn.		21/ 8/14 2y 9m, Pte.
KIRBY, G. H., Pte. 15 Bn.	41 Bn	29/ 8/14 3y 10m, Pte.
KIRBY, J., Pte. 26 Bn.		9/ 5/15
KIRBY, K. R., Pte. 12 Bn.		3/ 5/16 3y 2m, Pte.
KIRBY, T., Pte 12 Bn.		1/12/15 1y 9m, Pte.
KIRBY, T. W., Gnr. 36 H.A.G.	A.F.C	24/10/16 2y 11m, 2-Lt.
KIRK, E., Pte. 12 Bn.	✶ 4/6/15	20/ 8/14 Pte. ✶
KIRFOOT, R. H., Pte. 40 Bn.		14/ 8/17 3y 9m, Pte.
KIRCALDY, R., Tpr. 3 L.H.		10/ 5/17 1y, Tpr.
KIRKCALDY, W. I. N., Pte. 40 Bn.		10/10/16 2y 11m, Pte.
KIRK, R., Bdr., D.A.C.		24/11/14 4y 5m, Gnr.
KIRKHAM, G. T., Pte. 4 M.G. Co.	W. 4 Dvl. H.Q.	15/ 3/17 2y 7m, Pte.
KIRKHAM, R. J., Spr. Miners.		18/ 1/16
KIRKLAND, R. W., Pte. 12 Bn.	W.	30/10/17
KIRKUP, F. E., Bdr., 3 L.H.	2W., T.M. Bty., 4 A.M.T.M. Bty.	29/ 9/15 3y 3m, Bdr.
KIRKWOOD, A., Tpr. 3 L.H.		24/ 8/15 4y 3m, Tpr.
KIRKWOOD, A., Pte. 26 Bn.		22/ 6/15 2y 3m, Pte.
KIRKWOOD, A. P., Tpr. 3 L.H.		2/11/17 1y 9m, Tpr.
KIRKWOOD, R. W., Pte. 12 Bn.	A.F.C.	5/ 5/15 4y 3m, Lt.
KIRKWOOD, S., Pte. 40 Bn.		7/11/16
KIRKWOOD, S. R., Tpr. 3 L.H.		30/10/17 5m, Tpr.
KIRWAN, R., Pte. 3 L.H.	1 Anzac H.Q.	22/ 1/15 3y 11m, Pte.
RITTO, D. O. L., Lt. 6 F.A.B.	4W., M.C., 11 F.A.B., M.I.D.	20/10/15 4y 1m, Mjr.
KLIMEEK, H. T., Dvr. 6 F.A.B.	W.	23/ 8/15 3y 11m, Dvr.
KLINE, D., Pte. Tunnlrs.	W.	7/ 3/16
KLINE, J. W., Pte. 12 Bn.	W.	5/ 6/15 2y 6m, Pte.
KLYE, G. L., Pte. A.A.M.C.	13 Fd. Amb., 3 Fd. Amb.	20/ 9/16 3y 1m, tPe.
KNAPP, A. L., Pte. 7 Fd. Amb.	W., 62 Bn. ✶ 3-4/9/16.	23/ 3/15 4y 5m, Pte.
KNOTT, J. B., Pte. 26 Bn.	✶ 24/8/18.	17/ 8/15 Pte. ✶
KNOWLES, F. D., Pte. 12 Bn.	4 Pioneer Bn.	22/ 8/14 Pte.
KNOWLES, H. C., Pte. 15 Bn.		12/ 1/15 4y 5m, Cpl.
KNOWLES, H. G., Tpr. 3 L.H.	2W.	9/ 1/17 2y 7m, Tpr.
KNOWLES, J. H., Pte. 12 Bn.	W., 7 Fd. Amb.	9/ 8/16 3y 3m, Pte.
KNOWLES, P. C., Pte. A.A.M.C.	15 Bn., 4 Sig. Co.	16/ 3/16
KNOWLES, T., Spr. 40 Bn.		20/ 3/16 3y 6m, Spr.
KNOWLES, T., Dvr. 26 Bn.		23/ 3/15 4y 5m, Dvr.
KNUBLEY, C., Cpl 1 A.C.H.		25/ 9/14 4y 4m, Cpl.
KNUCKEY, I. L., S.S. Remounts		4/10/15 3y 3m, S.-S.
KNIGHT, A., Pte. 40 Bn.		8/11/16 1y 9m, Pte.
KNIGHT, A., Pte. 12 Bn.		19/ 8/15
KNIGHT, A. G., Pte. 26 Bn.	W., 12 Bn. ✶ 5-8/5/17	17/ 8/15 Pte. ✶
KNIGHT, B., Pte 2 G.S.R.	40 Bn.	17/12/17 1y 9m, Pte.
KNIGHT, C., Spr. Tunnlrs.	W., 3 Tunn. Co.	6/12/16 1y 6m, Spr.
KNIGHT, C. E., Pte. 4 M.G. Co.	W.	3/ 7/16 3y 4m, Pte.
KNIGHT, C. I., Pte. 40 Bn.		20/ 3/16 3y, Pte.
KNIGHT, C. H., Pte 7 Fd. Amb.		2/ 3/15 4y 7m, Pte.
KNIGHT, H., Pte. 40 Bn.	2W	16/11/16 3y, Pte.
KNIGHT, H., M.W.		
KNIGHT, H. H., Pte. 40 Bn.	✶ 4/10/17.	20/10/16 Pte. ✶
KNIGHT, J., Pte. 12 Bn.	W., 52 Bn. ✶ 21/12/16.	20/ 1/16 Pte. ✶
KNIGHT, J. G. Gnr. 3 F.A.B.	W., 1 F.A.B., 21 F.A.B.	26/ 8/14 3y 10m, Lt.
KNIGHT, J. W., Pte. 40 Bn.	W.	8/11/16 1y 11m, Pte.
KNIGHT, L. T., Pte. 40 Bn.	2W.	4/10/16 2y 9m, Pte.
KNIGHT, W. G. E., Spr. 8 Fd. Co.		17/ 1/16 3y 8m, Spr.
KNIGHT, N., Pte. 40 Bn.		15/ 3/16
KNIGHT, R. D., Dvr. Arty.	23 How. Bde., 7 F.A.B.	20/ 1/16 3y 8m, Dvr.
KNIGHT, R. A., Pte. 3 Fd. Co.	W., 12 Fd. Co. Eng., 1 A.T.P.S. Co. Engrs	4/ 8/15 4y, L.-Cpl.
KNIGHT, T. G., Pte. 40 Bn.	W. ✶ 13/1/17.	24/ 2/16 Pte. ✶
KNIGHT, W. G. H., Spr. Miners		31/ 3/16
KNIGHT, W. J., Pte. 40 Bn.		28/ 4/16 3y 5m, Pte.
KNIGHTS, A. H., Pte. 2 G.S.R.		6/12/17
KNIGHTS, E. C., Pte. 3 L.H.	11 Co. Imp. Camel Cps.	17/ 8/14 4y 6m, Lt.
KNIGHTS, W. N., Pte. 12 Bn.	W., M.M., 52 Bn., 51 Bn.	16/ 8/15 4y, Sgt.
KNIGHTS, P. J. G., Pte. 40 Bn.		22/ 5/16 2y 8m, Pte.
KOGLIN, M., Pte. Tunnlrs.	59 Bn.	5/ 5/16 2y 3m, Pte.
KOGLIN, O. A., T Cpl. 6 Fd. Co.	A.A.O.C.	4/ 8/15 3y 9m, Cpl.
KOPPLEMAN, L. C. E., Pte. 15 Bn.		5/ 9/14 5m, Pte.
KOPPLEMAN, L., Pte. 12 Bn.	2W.	3/ 4/16 1y 8m, Pte.

TASMANIA'S MUSTER ROLL.

NAME.	REMARKS.	RANK ON DISCHARGE. ENLISTED, SERVICE.
KOPPLEMAN, W., Pte. 40 Bn.		1/ 3/16 3y 6m, Sgt.
KOLOSQUE, F. A., Sgt. 4 L.H.M.G.B.	D.C.M.	13/ 1/15 4y 7m, Sgt.
KRISTIANSEN, O., L.-Cpl. 12 Bn.		22/12/14 4y 3m, L.-Cpl.
KRUSHKA, H. M., Pte. 52 Bn.	2W., 3 G.S.R.	8/10/14 4y 7m, Pte.
KRUSHKA, O., Pte. 12 Bn.	W. ✠ 19/10/15.	29/ 8/14 Pte. ✠
KRUSHKA, W. H., Pte. 12 Bn.	✠ 8/6/17	1/ 9/15 Cpl. ✠
KUPSCH, F. W., Pte. 40 Bn.	2W.	11/ 8/16 3y 1m, Pte.
KUBANK, V. E., Pte. 40 Bn.	✠ 16/1/18.	18/ 9/17 Pte. ✠
KYME, D. G., S.-Sgt. A.C.H.	A.M.C	15/ 9/14 4y 7m, S.-Sgt.
LACEY, J. V., A.-Cpl. 40 Bn.	W., 1 M.G. Co.	28/ 9/16
LACEY, V., Pte 12 Bn.	W.	7/ 8/16 3y 1m, Pte.
LACK, C. E., Pte. 12 Bn.	14 Bn., P.O.W.	3/11/15 3y 7m, Pte.
LACK, H. R., Pte. 12 Bn.	W.	3/11/16 2y 4m, Pte.
LACK, J. A., Pte. 12 Bn.	W.	5/ 8/15 4y, Pte.
LADD, A. E., Spr. 3 Miners	3 Tunnlrs. ✠ 28/11/16.	1/ 8/15 Spr. ✠
LADE, C. A., Cpl. 12 Bn.	2W., M.M. 51 Bn.	31/ 8/15
LADE, C. H., Sgt. 3 L.H.	✠ 25/4/17.	21/ 8/14 Sgt. ✠
LADE, F. G., Pte. 40 Bn.	W.	3/ 3/16 2y 2m, Pte.
LADE, H. J. H., Pte. 12 Bn.	28 Bn.	16/ 8/15 4y, 2m, Pte.
LADE, R. W., Pte. 12 Bn.	52 and 51 Bn.	28/ 7/15 4y 1m, Pte.
LADELLE, J. H., Pte. 12 Bn.	W.	1/ 6/16 1y 6m, Pte.
LAHEY, L. A., Pte. 12 Bn.	1 Dvy. Trn.	3/ 1/18 1y 10m, Pte.
LAHEY, P., Pte. Tunnlrs.	W., 3 Tunnlrs.	15/ 3/16 3y 7m, Spr.
LAHEY, T. J., Pte. 15 Bn.	✠ 23/8/15.	26/11/14 Pte. ✠
LAIRD, F. G. H., Pte. Rly.	4 A.B.G.R.O.	13/ 2/17 2v 8m, Spr.
LAIRD, F. P., Pte. 12 Bn.		12/11/17 1y 11m, Pte.
LAIRD, J., Pte. 15 Bn.		23/ 1/15 4y 7m, Cpl.
LAIRD, W. H., Cpl. 12 Bn.		28/ 8/14 1y 8m, Cpl.
LAIRD, W. M., Pte. 12 Bn.	M.M., 52, 51 Bn.	19/ 1/16 3y 8m, Pte.
LAKE, W G., Pte. 7 C. Sec. A.M.C.	W., 13 Fd. Amb.	13/ 3/15 4y 3m, L.-Cpl.
LAKIN, F. L., 2nd-Lieut., 40 Bn.		26/ 4/16 3y 4m, Lieut.
LAKIN, N. E., Lieut. 40 Bn.		10/10/16 2y 11m, Lieut.
LAKIN, F. H., Gnr. Fd. Art.	7 Fd. Art. ✠ 23/10/18.	30/ 3/17 Gnr. ✠
LAKIN, S. K, Pte. 26 Bn.	W., 12 Bn.	1/ 9/15 3y 7m, Pte
LAMB, E. R., Pte. 12 Bn.		22/ 6/15 1y 3m, Pte.
LAMB, H., Pte. 9 Bn.		18/ 8/14 4y 7m, Pte.
LAMBERT, A. W. Pte. 4 M.G. Co.	11 M.G. Co.	9/11/16 2y 11m, Pte.
LAMBERT, C. W. W., Dvr. Arty.		1/ 5/17
LAMBERT, F. A., Pte. 3 G.S.R.	12 Bn.	31/ 7/18 1y 3m, Pte.
LAMBERT, H. L., Pte. 40 Bn.	W. ✠ 8/5/18.	12/ 6/16 Pte. ✠
LAMBERT, H., Pte. 40 Bn.	W., M.M.	27/ 9/16 3y, L.-Cpl.
LAMBERT, J. S., Pte. 12 Bn.	W.	9/ 2/16 3y 5m, Pte.
LAMBERT, R. G., Pte. 15 Bn.	W., 47 Bn. ✠ 8/8/16.	20/ 1/15 Cpl. ✠
LAMBERT, R. H., Pte. 15 Bn.	2W., A.A.M.C.	18/ 8/15 4y, L.-Cpl.
LAMBERT, T. F., Pte. Rly.		31/ 1/17 1y 6m, Pte.
LAMBERT, W. T., Pte. 15 Bn.		18/ 8/15 2y 10m, Pte.
LAMBERT, W., Pte. 1 A.G.H.	✠ 13/11/16.	31/ 5/15 Pte. ✠
LAMONT, A. J., Pte. 40 Bn.		28/ 7/17 2y 3m, Pte.
LAMP, C. A., Spr. 8 Fd. Co.	W., 9 Fd. Co.	28/ 1/16 3y 6m, Spr.
LAMPKIN, P. J., Cpl. 40 Bn.		20/ 3/16 1y 2m, Cpl.
LAMPREY, W. A., Pte. 12 Bn.	W., 40 Bn	19/10/16 2y 5m, Pte.
LAMPIERE, R., Pte. Tunnlrs.	W.	10/ 4/17
LANCASTER, A. A., Pte. 26 Bn.	2W.	17/ 6/15 4y 2m, Sgt.
LANCASTER, H. V. C., Cpl. D.A.C.		14/10/14 4y 4m, Cpl.
LANCASTER, L. O., Pte. 46 Bn.	✠ 7/6/17.	23/ 2/16 Pte. ✠
LANE, D. A., Capt. 12 Bn.	52 Bn.	26/ 8/14 5y 5m, Lt.-Col.
LANE, F. W., Lieut. 15 Bn.	W., 47 Bn. ✠ 28/3/18.	8/ 6/15 Lieut. ✠
LANE, A. B., Pte. 4 M.G. Bn.	W.	16/ 1/17 2y 5m, Pte.
LANE, B. V., Pte. 12 Bn.	✠ 17/5/17.	5/ 9/16 Pte. ✠
LANE, B. G., Pte. 40 Bn.	2W., M.M.	22/ 5/16 3v 4m, Pte.
LANE, H. A., Cpl. S-Smith 9 Fd. Bty	4 Div. Arty.	26/ 8/14 4y 4m, Far.-Sgt
LANE, N. F. S., Tpr. 3 L.H.	50 Bn. ✠ 8/6/17.	26/11/14 Pte. ✠
LANE, N. B., Pte. 12 Bn.		9/ 9/14
LANG, P. F., Pte. 12 Bn.		22/ 8/14
LANGDALE, G R., Gnr. 8 F.A.B.	31 Bty.	30/11/15 2y 11m, Gnr.
LANGDON, A. B., Pte. 15 Bn.	3W.	18/11/14 3y 2m, Sgt.
LANGDON, H. G., Dvr. 6 F.A.B.		11/ 8/15 4y 1m, Dvr.
LANGDON, N. A., Pte. 40 Bn		10/ 5/16 2y 1m, Pte.
LANGDON, S. W., Spr. 8 Fd Co.		18/11/15
LANGDON, W. R. C., Pte. 40 Bn.	W., 3 Div. M.T.M.B., 6 M.T.M.B.	12/ 4/16 3y 7m, Gnr.
LANGE, F. E., Pte. 12 Bn.	✠ 8/8/15	15/ 2/15 Pte. ✠
LANGE, T. A., Pte. A.A.M.C.	14 Fd. Amb.	15/10/15 3y 8m, Pte.
LANGFORD, A. J., Gnr. F.A.B.	3 F.A.B.	8/ 2/17 2y 3m, Gnr.
LANGFORD, J. H., Gnr. Fd. Arty.	23 How. Bde.	6/ 1/16 1y 1m, Gnr.
LANGLEY, A., Pte. L.T.M. Bty	49 Bn.	16/ 5/15 2y 9m, Pte.
LANGLEY, G. H., Spr. 8 Fd. Co	W., M.M.	8/ 1/16 3y 6m, Spr.
LANGLEY, T., Pte. 40 Bn.	2W.	24/ 7/16 3y 1m, Pte.
LANGMAID, A P., Dvr. 2 D.A.C.	6 F.A.B.	Dvr.
LANGRIDGE, C. C. R., Pte. 12 Bn.	W.	14/10/16 2y 6m, L.-Cpl.
LANGRIDGE, L. A., Pte. 12 Bn.		2/ 9/16 2y 8m, Pte.
LANHAM, T. S., Pte. 12 Bn.		29/ 8/14 3y 11m, Pte.
LANHAM, A. J., Spr. Tunnlrs.		3/ 6/16
LANIGAN, H. W., Spr. Miners		16/ 3/16 2y 7m, Spr. M.W.
LANSDELL, B. A. R., M.W.		4/ 8/17 1y 7m, Pte.
LANSDELL, C. E., Pte. 40 Bn.		3/ 3/16 Pte. ✠
LAPHAM, M, Pte 40 Bn	✠ 13/10/17.	4/ 4/16 3y 4m, Sgt.
LAPTHORNE, C. G., Pte. 40 Bn.	2W.	

NAME.	REMARKS.	RANK ON DISCHARGE. ENLISTED. SERVICE.
LAPTHORNE, R., Pte. 12 Bn.	2W., M.M.	12/ 9/14 4y 6m, Sgt.
LAPWORTH, L. A., Pte. 12 Bn.	W., 13 Fd. Amb.	27/ 7/15 4y 4m, Pte.
LARCOMBE, S. D., Pte. 40 Bn.	26 Bn. Employ Co.	30/ 3/16 3y 6m, Pte.
LAREDO, A. J., Pte. 40 Bn.	23 M.G. Co.	24/ 2/16 3y 5m, Pte.
LAREDO, F., Spr. Engrs.		23/ 8/15 3y 10m, Spr.
LARGAN, P., Gnr. F.A.B.	23 How. Bde., 109 Bty., D.A.C.	24/ 8/15 4y 1m, Gnr.
LARGE, R. J., Pte. 12 Bn.	W., 40 Bn.	18/10/16 2y 5m, Pte.
LARKIN, H., Gnr. Fd Arty.		26/10/16
LARKINS, E. W., Cpl. 1 A.G.H.	1 A.G.H., 12 Bn. ✠ 23/8/18.	9/ 6/15 Cpl. ✠
LARKINS, J., Pte. 2 G.S.R.		13/ 4/18 11m, Pte.
LARSEN, A. V., Pte. 40 Bn.	W., 12 Bn. ✠ 28/5/18.	1/ 2/16 Pte. ✠
LARSEN, S. J., Pte. 1 G.S.R.	40 Bn.	9/ 7/17 2v 3m, Pte.
LARTER, A. H., Pte 12 Bn.	52 and 51 Bn.	22/ 9/15 3y 11m, Pte.
LARTER, L. E., Gnr. F.A.B.	2 D.A.C., 2 D.A.P.	21/ 9/15 3y 8m, Dvr.
LASKEY, F. A., Dvr. 9 Fd. Bty.		19/ 8/14 7m, Dvr.
LAST, C., Pte. 12 Bn.	2W., 3 M.G. Co.	11/12/15 2y 11m, Pte.
LAST, E., Pte. 12 Bn	W., 51 Bn.	11/ 4/16 3y 5m, Pte.
LAST, J. A., Pte. 40 Bn.	W.	18/11/16 2y 4m, Pte.
LAST, J., Pte. 12 Bn.	✠ 7/8/15.	19/ 2/15 Pte. ✠
LATCHFORD, L. H., Gnr. 36 H.A.G.		1/ 9/17
LATHAM, A., Pte. 4 M.G. Co.		24/11/16 11m, Pte.
LATTA, D. M., Pte. 40 Bn.	W.	15/ 3/16 3y 5m, Lieut.
LATHAM, P. A., Pte. 12 Bn.		6/11/17 1y 11m, Pte.
LAUGHER, W., Dvr. 3 Fd. Amb.	13 Fd. Amb. ✠ 6/1/18.	19/ 8.14 Dvr. ✠
LAUGHTON, H. L., Cpl. 26 Bn.	W.	21/ 7/15 2y 8m, L.-Sgt.
LAUGHTON, S. T., Cpl. A.A.S.C.		31/ 8/14 2v 5m, Cpl.
LAURENCESON, E., Pte. 40 Bn.	A.S.C., Fd. Arty.	31/10/16 2v 5m, Gnr.
LAURIE, B., Pte. 15 Bn.	✠ 30/4/15.	21/12/14 Pte. ✠
LAURIE, W. J., Pte. 40 Bn.	2W.	13/ 4/16 3y 5m, C.Q.M.S.
LAVELL, A. E., Pte. 40 Bn.		28/ 4/17 1y, Pte.
LAVELL, C. J., Pte. 4 Fd. Amb.	1 Divl. Train	4/ 5/15 4y 5m, Pte.
LAVELL, E. A., Pte. 40 Bn.		12/10/16 2y 11m, Dvr.
LAW, E., 1 D.H.Q.		
LAWES, W. G., Pte. 40 Bn.	W.	26/ 2/16 2y 2m, Pte.
LAWLER, A., Cpl. 15 Bn.	11 M.G. Co.	8/ 1/15 4v 11m, Cpl
LAWLER, A. S., Pte. 13 G.S.R.		29/ 6/18
LAWLER, C., Pte 15 Bn.	3W., 69 Bn., 15 Bn.	21/ 9/14 4y 7m, L.-Cpl.
LAWLER, C. J., Pte. 12 Bn.		30/ 9/16 2y 10m, Pte.
LAWLER, G. H., Pte. 12 Bn.	W., 3 T.M.B.	20/8/14 3y 7m, Pte.
LAWLER, H. W., Pte. 40 Bn.	W.	14/ 3/16 2y 7m, Sgt.
LAWLER, H., Pte. 26 Bn	W.	7/ 4/15 3y 1m, Pte.
LAWLER, J. D., Pte. 12 Bn.	✠ 11/11/16.	30/10/15 Pte. ✠
LAWLER, O. M., Tpr. 3 L.H.	Camel Cps. ✠ 22/12/17.	17/ 8/14 Tpr. ✠
LAWLER, P. B., Gnr. F.A.B.	3 D.A.C., 6 F.A. Bde.	25/ 1/16 3y 8m, Gnr.
LAWLER, R. J., Pte. 15 Bn.	✠ 9/8/15.	11/11/14 Pte. ✠
LAWLER, S. H., Pte. 40 Bn.	2W.	5/ 3/16 3y 7m, Cpl.
LAWLER, W. P., Tpr. 3 L.H.		8/10/17 1y 10m, Tpr.
LAWRENCE, C. E., 2nd-Lt. 40 Bn.	M.I.D.	6/ 6/16 3y 4m, Lieut.
LAWRENCE, A., Sgt. 40 Bn.		8/ 1/16 3y 2m, Sgt.
LAWRENCE, J., Dvr. 8 Fd. Co.		20/ 4/16
LAWRENCE, V., Pte. 40 Bn.		21/ 9/15
LAWSON, A. V., Pte. 12 Bn.	1 Pnrs. ✠ 25/7/16.	13/ 7/15 Pte. ✠
LAWSON, E., Pte. 12 Bn.	✠ 23/7/16.	16/ 9/14 Pte. ✠
LAWSON, E. A., Gnr. F.A.B.	120 How. Bty., 112 H.B., 12 F.A.B.	Gnr.
LAWSON, G., Pte. 12 Bn.		6/11/16 2y 10m, Pte.
LAWSON, H., Gnr. 6 Fd. Arty.	W. ✠ 18/9/18.	17/ 8/15 Dvr. ✠
LAWSON, R. J., Sgt. Remounts	3 L.H.	16/ 9/15 4y 1m, S.Q.M.S.
LAY, C. C., Sgt. 15 Bn.		25/12/14 2y 11m, Sgt.
LAY, E. E., Pte. 4 M.G. Co.	W.	25/11/16 2y 8m, Pte.
LAY, F., Gnr. Arty.	W.	1/ 5/16
LAY, T. A., Sgt. 12 Bn.		31/ 8/14 5y 1m, Lieut.
LAYCOCK, A. N., Pte. 12 Bn.	2W., 52 Bn., 51 Bn.	7/ 8/15 4y Pte.
LAYCOCK, A., Pte. 1 A.C.H.		15/ 9/14 2v 1m, Pte.
LAYCOCK, F. G., Pte. 26 Bn.	W., 12 Bn., 1 Pnr. Bn.	2/ 8/15 3y 11m, Pte.
LAYCOCK, G. A., Pte. 2 G.S.R.		12/ 2/18 1y 8m, Pte.
LAYCOCK, G. S., Pte. 12 Bn.	W.	9/10/14 4y 5m, Pte.
LAYCOCK, H. G., Pte. A.A.M.C.	15 Fld. Amb.	16/ 1/17 2y 2m, Pte.
LAYCOCK, J. H., Pte. 12 Bn.		20/ 8/14 4y 5m, Dvr.
LAYCOCK, S. L., Pte. 15 Bn.	2W.	9/10/14 4y 5m, Pte.
LAYCOCK, W. G., Pte. 12 Bn.	✠ 16/10/15.	25/ 1/15 Pte. ✠
LAYH, W. O., Gnr. 9 Fd. Bty.	2W., 5 Bty.	14/ 9/15 3y 11m, Bdr.
LAZENBY, F. C., Spr. 8 Fd. Co.		9/ 2/16 9m, Spr.
LAZENBY, L. C., Pte. 26 Bn.	W., 12 Bn.	9/ 8/15 3y 4m, Pte.
LAZENBY, R. J. B., Pte. 4 M.G. Co.	15 M.G. Co., 5 M.G. Bn. ✠ 9/8/18.	9/10/16 Pte. ✠
LEAHY, G. Z., Pte. 26 Bn.		6/ 7/15
LEAHY, J., Gnr. 3 F.A.		27/ 8/14
LEAHY, J S., Pte. 26 Bn.	2W., 69, 26 Bn.	5/ 7/15 3y 10m, Pte.
LEAKE, F. R., Pte. A.F.C.	5 Sqd. A.F.C.	20/10/16 2y 10m, 1 A.M.
LEAMAN, A. C., Pte. 4 M.G. Co.	W.	31/10/16 2y 8m, Pte.
LEAMAN, A. W., Pte. 40 Bn.		3/10/16 1v 1m, Pte.
LEAMAN, F., Pte. 12 Bn.		6/ 1/16 3v 9m, Pte.
LEAMAN, W. E., Pte. 12 Bn.	W.	31/10/16 2v 11m, Pte.
LEAR, J. H., S.S.M. 3 L.H.		8/ 1/17
LEAROYD, R. E., Dvr. 6 F.A.B.		16/ 9/15 3y 10m, S.-Sgt
LEAROYD, W. C., Pte. 26 Bn.	A.A.P.C.	13/ 8/15 4y, Sgt.
LEARY, A. J., Spr. Tunnlrs.		1/ 8/16 2y 11m, Spr.
LEARY, A. H., Pte. 12 Bn.		16/12/15 3y 9m, Pte.

TASMANIA'S MUSTER ROLL. 301

NAME.	REMARKS.	RANK ON DISCHARGE. ENLISTED, SERVICE.
LEARY, C., Pte. 12 Bn.	✠ 9/8/15.	22/ 1/15 Pte. ✠
LEARY, C. A., Pte. 2 G.S.R.		3/ 3/18
LEARY, J. C., Pte. 1 G.S.R.		14/ 1/18
LEARY, J. C., Pte. 40 Bn.		23/ 9/16 2y 8m, Pte.
LEARY, L. E., Pte. 1 G.S.R.		14/ 1/18
LEARY, V. G., Gnr. 9 Fd. Bty.		22/ 8/14 4y 6m, Cpl.
LEATHAM, W. H., Tpr. 3 L.H.		30/11/17 1y 11m, Tpr.
LEE, A. E., Pte. 12 Bn.		6/ 9/16 3y 1m, Pte.
LEE, C. J., Pte. 12 Bn.	✠ 12/8/15.	20/ 8, 14 Sgt. ✠
LEE, C. L., Pte. A.A.M.C.	14 Fld. Amb.	18/10/16 3y, Pte.
LEE, D. S., Tpr. 3 L.H.	4 D.A.C., 25 H. Bde. 10 Fd.A. ✠ 20/9/17	13/ 3/15 Tpr. ✠
LEE, E. K., Pte. 12 Bn.	70 Bn., 12 Bn.	20/12, 15 3y 9m, Pte.
LEE, E. J., Tpr. 3 L.H.		19/10/16 2y 11m, Tpr.
LEE, E., Sgt. 26 Bn.	W.	15/ 5/15 1y 10m, Sgt.
LEE, E. A., Gnr. Arty.	2W.	5/ 1/16 2y 9m, Gnr.
LEE, E. H., Pte. 26 Bn.	2 Div. Sal. Co.	3/ 5/15 4y 8m, Pte.
LEE, F. C., Pte. 40 Bn.		8/10/15 4y, Cpl.
LEE, F. G., Pte. 15 Bn.		11/ 8/15 3y 6m, Pte.
LEE, F. J., Pte. 12 Bn.	W.	8/11/15 1y 4m, Pte.
LEE, G., Pte. 26 Bn.		15/ 5/15 1y, Pte.
LEE, H. R., Pte. 40 Bn.	W.	24/ 8/16 3y 2m, Pte.
LEE, H. G., Pte. 12 Bn.		7/ 7/16 1y 10m, Pte.
LEE, J. B., Pte. A.A.M.C.	15 Fd. Amb.	9/10/16
LEE, J. O., Pte. 12 Bn.	W.: 52 Bn ✠ 7/6/17.	8/11/15 Pte. ✠
LEE, L. A., Pte. 26 Bn.		3/ 8/15
LEE, L. D., Pte. 12 Bn.	✠ 5-8/5/17.	11/ 8/16 Pte.
LEE, M. R. T. V., Pte. 12 Bn.	40 Br	11/ 4/25 3y 4m, Dvr.
LEE, O. M., Sgt. 3 L.H	M.C. P.O.W.	20/ 8/14 4y 8m, 2nd Lt.
LEE, R. E., Pte. 40 Bn.	2W., 15 Bn., 69 Bn., 40 Bn.	7/ 3/16 3y 3m, Pte.
LEE, R. S., Pte. 12 Bn.	✠ 15/4/17.	16/12/14 Cpl. ✠
LEE, T. L., Spr. 3 Fd. Co.	✠ 22/7/16.	22/ 7/15 Spr. ✠
LEE, T. R., Pte. 12 Bn.	W.	11/12/16 2y 1m, Pte.
LEE, V. D., Pte. A.A.M.C.	15 Fld. Amb.	27/ 3/16 3y 2m, Pte.
LEE, W., Pte. 26 Bn.		1/ 5/15
LEE, W. J., Tpr. 3 L.H.	W., M.M.	5/ 1/15 4y 5m, Dvr.
LEECH, J. S., Pte. 12 Bn.	2W.	2/ 6/16
LEEDHAM, W. E., Pte. 26 Bn.		5/ 9/15
LEES, H., Pte. 12 Bn.	W.	21/ 8/14 2y, Pte.
LEES, J. B., Pte. 12 Bn.	✠ 8/8/18.	17/ 8/14 Pte. ✠
LEES, W. J., Pte. 26 Bn.		28/ 6/15 2y, L.-Cpl.
LE GRAND, B., Pte. 40 Bn.		21/12/16
LEHMANN, J., Pte. Fd. Bakery	4 Fld. Bakery.	7/12/14
LEHMAN, S. G., Gnr. 6 F.A.B.		Gnr.
LEIGH, W. H., Gnr. Arty.	1 D.A.C.	9/ 1/17
LEITCH, R. W., Pte. 40 Bn.	✠ 31/5/17.	29/ 2/16 Pte. ✠
LEITCH, W. D., Pte. 12 Bn.	2W. ✠ 4/5/19.	21/ 5/15 Cpl ✠
LELLO, T. H., Pte 12 Bn.	W., M.M.	13/11/15 2y 1m, Pte.
LEMIN, A. T., Pte. 12 Bn.	W., M.M., 60 Bn.	21/ 8/14
LENDERS, L. C. F., Pte. 15 Bn.		27/10/14 4y 9m, Pte.
LENNON, G., Pte. 12 Bn.	12 Bn	9/ 5/16 3y 4m, Pte.
LEO, J. F., Pte. 12 Bn.	✠ 11/11/16.	19/ 2/15 Pte.
LEO, J. B., Pte. 12 Bn.	✠ 8/8/15.	29/10/14 Pte. ✠
LEONARD, A. G., Pte. 12 Bn.	W. ✠ 3/5/18.	31/ 5/16 Pte. ✠
LEONARD, C. C., Pte. 40 Bn.	M.M.	11/ 3/16 3y 7m, Pte.
LEONARD, W., Pte. 12 Bn.	W., M.M., M.I.D.	21/ 8/16 3y 8m, L.-Cpl.
LEONARD, W. J., Pte. 3 M.G. Bn.		13/ 5/16 3y 2m, Pte.
LEPPARD, R. L Spr. 4 Miners (Correct name SHEPPARD)	A A. Prov. Cps.	29/10/15 4y 1m, Pte.
LESLIE, A. J., Pte. 26 Bn.	✠ 29/7/16	12/10/15 Pte. ✠
LESTER, A. G., 4 M.G. Co.		3/ 2/17
LESTER, A. C., Pte. 3 L.H.		12/ 9/14 1y 4m, Pte.
LESTER, E. W., Gnr. 3 F.A. Bde	2W.	3/ 8/15 3y 1m, Gnr.
LESTER, J. H., Pte. 12 Bn.		1/12/14
LESTER, L. G., Pte. 12 Bn.	17 Fd. Amb. 5 Fd. Amb.	28/ 9/16 3y 1m, Pte
LETCHER, J. A., Pte 12 Bn.	3 D. Sig. Co	31/ 5/16 4v 2m, Sgt.
LETCHER, T. W., M.W.		
LETHBORG, E. A., Gnr. F.A.B.	3 D.A.C.	11/10/16 2y 6m, Gnr.
LETHBORG, L. G., Gnr 3 F.A.B.	B.A.C., D.A.C.	21/10/15 3y 11m, Dvr.
LETHBORG, M. W., Pte. 40 Bn.	W., 12 Bn.	29/ 7/16 3y, Pte.
LETTE, R. K., Pte. 4 M.G. Co.	23 Bn.	5/ 2/17
LETTS, E., Pte. 15 Bn.		28/ 7/15
LEVERTON, S. C., Pte. 31 Bn.		14/ 4/15 4y, Pte.
LEVIS, J. W., Pte. 26 Bn.	✠ 29/7/15.	26/ 7/15 Pte. ✠
LEVY, F., Pte. 1 G.S.R.		23/11/17
LEVY, S. M., Cpl. Arty.		7/12/15 2y 11m, Gnr.
LEWIS, A. E., Dvr. 3 F.A.B.		16/ 8/15 4y 2m, Dvr.
LEWIS, A. H., Pte. 12 Bn.	✠ 17/10/15.	13/ 1/15 Pte. ✠
LEWIS, A. J., Pte. 3 Tunnlrs.		30/ 9/16
LEWIS, A. R., Spr. 3 Tunnlrs.		31/10/16 2y 11m, Spr.
LEWIS, E. St. L., Capt. 3 L.H.	W., 47 Bn.	19/ 8/14 4y 8m, Major
LEWIS, B. H., Pte. 12 Bn.	A Corps Work Party.	24/ 5/17 1y 10m, Pte.
LEWIS, C., Pte. 12 Bn.	W.	24/10/17 1y 5m, Pte.
LEWIS, C. O., Gnr. Sg. Art. Bde.	338 Siege Bty., 36 H.A.G.	7/ 6/15 3y. Gnr.
LEWIS, C. J., Pte. 40 Bn.		15/ 2/17 8m. Pte.
LEWIS, D., Pte. 12 Bn.		7/ 1/16 1y 11m. Pte.
LEWIS, E., Dvr. 7 Fld. Amb.	13 Fld. Amb.	15/ 2/15 4y 4m, Dvr.
LEWIS, F., Pte. 40 Bn.	2W. 12 Bn.	11/ 7/16 3y 3m. Pte.

NAME.	REMARKS.	RANK ON DISCHARGE. ENLISTED. SERVICE.
LEWIS, F. N., Pte. 12 Bn.	W.	23/ 8/15 2y 2m. Pte.
LEWIS, F. W., Spr. 40 Bn.	W. ✣ 31/1/17.	10/ 2/16. Spr. ✣
LEWIS, G. E., Pte. 26 Bn.		20/ 7/15 4y 1m. Cpl.
LEWIS, G. Y., Spr. 5 Tnlrs.	2 Tunn. Coy., P.O.W. ✣ 5/12/18.	29/ 3/16. Cpl. ✣
LEWIS, G. W., Dvr., 8 Fld. Coy.	2 Fd. Co.	20/ 4/16 3y 5m. Dvr.
LEWIS, G. C., Pte. 3 Tnlrs.		31/10/16 2y 11m. Spr.
LEWIS, H. A., Dvr. 3 F.A.B.		30/ 8/18 9m. Dvr.
LEWIS, H. G., Gnr. 7 Fd. Bty.		23/10/16 2y 9m. Gnr.
LEWIS, H. M., Pte. 26 Bn.	✣ 28/7/16.	27/ 7/15. Pte. ✣
LEWIS, H. L. Dvr. 8 Fd. Co.		12/ 3/17 1y 10m. Dvr.
LEWIS, J. H., Pte. 12 Bn.	M.M. ✣ 7/10/17.	4/ 9/16. Pte. ✣
LEWIS, J., Pte. 26 Bn.		10/ 8/15 1y. Pte.
LEWIS, J. F., Pte. 12 Bn.		1/ 6/15.
LEWIS, L. V., Pte. 12 Bn.	2W. M.M., 69, 12 Bn.	5/ 1/15 4y 4m. Pte.
LEWIS, L. W., Pte. 40 Bn.	2W.	12/ 6/16 3y 2m. L.Cpl.
LEWIS, L., Pte. 40 Bn.	✣ 5/10/17.	26/ 9/16. Pte. ✣
LEWIS, M. J., Pte. 4 M.G. Co.		4/ 7/16.
LEWIS, R. M., Pte. 12 Bn.	9 Bn.	28/ 9/16 2y 7m. Pte.
LEWIS, R. N., Pte. 40 Bn.	✣ 12/8/18.	28/ 9/16. Cpl. ✣
LEWIS, R. B., Spr. 8 Fd. Co.		27/ 4/16 2y 9m. Spr.
LEWIS, R. H., Gnr. Arty.	W., 6 F.A., 14 F.A. ✣ 9/8/18.	15/10/15. Gnr. ✣
LEWIS, R. L., Pte. 12 Bn.	W 4 M.G. Bn.	26/ 8/15 4y 3m. Pte.
LEWIS, V., Pte. 12 Bn.	51 Bn., 52 Bn.	8/12/14 4y 4m. L.Cpl.
LEWIS, W., Pte. 12 Bn.		11/ 2/15.
LEWIS, W., Pte. 40 Bn.	W.	7/ 1/16 2y 5m. L.Cpl.
LEWIS, W., Gnr. Arty.	15 F.A.B.	27/ 3/16 2y. Gnr.
LIDDALL, E. E., Pte. 40 Bn.	✣ 11/12/18.	22/ 2/16. L.-Cpl. ✣
LIGHTEN, A., Dvr. 3 Fd. Co.	8 Fd. Co. E., 15 Bn. ✣ 4/8/16.	6/ 9/15. Dvr. ✣
LILLICO, H. D., Pte. 40 Bn.		29/ 3/16 1y 10m. Dvr.
LIMBRICK, G. T., Pte. 26 Bn.	2W. ✣ 15/8/18.	17/ 5/15. Pte. ✣
LIMBRICK, G. T. A., Pte. 12 Bn.		26/10/14.
LIMBRICK, H. C. H., Pte 4 M.G.C.		31/ 7/16 3y 5m. Pte.
LINCEY, J. A., Pte. 40 Bn.	✣ 28/11/17.	24/ 5/16. Sgt. ✣
LINCOLN, C. A., Pte. 12 Bn.		19/ 8/14.
LINCOLN, J. T., Pte. 12 Bn.		1/ 6/15 1y 2m. Pte.
LINCOLN, W. R., Pte. 26 Bn.	✣ 19-22/8/16.	10/ 8/15 Pte. ✣
LINDERS, L. C. F., Pte. 15 Bn		27/10/14.
LINDLEY, D. R., Pte. 40 Bn.		30/ 7/17.
LINDLEY, J. R., Gnr. 3 F.A.B.	✣ 5/11/15.	9/ 3/15. Gnr. ✣
LINDLEY, T. M., Pte. 26 Bn.	M.M.	21/ 6/15 4y 2m. Pte.
LINDRIDGE, H., Pte. 12 Bn.	52 Bn.	24/ 1/16 4y. Pte.
LINDSAY, J., Tpr. 3 L.H.		6/ 2/17.
LINDSAY, R. V., Pte. 26 Bn.	W. 12 Bn., 69 Bn., 12 Bn. ✣ 23/4/18.	4/ 8/15. Pte. ✣
LINDSAY, W., Gnr. Fd. Arty.		27/ 8/15.
LINDSAY, W. A., Pte 40 Bn.	W.	21/ 2/16 1y 11m. Pte.
LINDUS, L. T., Lieut. 26 Bn.	✣ 29/7/16.	3/ 5/15 Lieut. ✣
LINES, E. W. L., Lieut. 12 Bn.		1/ 5/16
LINES, D. H. E., Capt. A.A.M.C.		15/ 7/15 8m, Lt.-Col.
LINES, W. R., Pte. 26 Bn.	12 Bn., 52 Bn., ✣ 13/3/17.	11/ 8/15. L.Cpl. ✣
LING, C. B., Pte. 26 Bn.	2W.	18/ 8/15 3y 10m. Pte.
LING, C. H., Pte. 40 Bn.	W.	15/ 3/16 3y 6m. Pte.
LING, C. R., Pte. 40 Bn.	W.	15/ 3/16 3y 6m. L.Cpl.
LING, H. J., Pte. 1 A.G.H.		3/ 6/15 2y 5m. Pte.
LING, L., Pte. 26 Bn.	✣ 14/11/16.	4/ 6/15. Pte. ✣
LING, W. G., Pte. 40 Bn.	2W.	15/ 3/16 3y 1m. Pte.
LING, W. J., Pte. 12 Bn.	W.	1/ 5/16 2y 4m. Pte.
LINNELL, E. J. A., Cpl. 26 Bn.		19/ 6/15 1y 2m. Cpl.
LINNELL, J. E., Cpl. 40 Bn.	W.	29/ 2/16 2y. Cpl.
LINTON, G. W., Pte. 3 Cyc. Cps.	1 Bn.	6/ 4/16 3y 1m. Pte.
LINTON, J., Pte. 26 Bn.		10/ 8/15.
LINTON, J. E., Pte. 15 Bn.	2W. 15 Bn.	12/ 8/15 3y 9m. Pte.
LINTON, P. J., Pte. 1 G.S.R.		4/ 3/18.
LINTON, P., Pte. 12 Bn.	W., 52 Bn.	23/ 7/15 2y. Pte.
LINTON, R. F., Pte. 12 Bn.	52 Bn., 69 Bn., 52 Bn. ✣ 24/4/13.	9/ 2/16. Pte. ✣
LINTON, S., Pte. 46 Bn.		3/10/16.
LINTON, T., Pte. 40 Bn.	51 Bn. ✣ 31/3/17.	29/ 2/16. Pte. ✣
LINTON, W. W., Pte. 12 Bn.	52 Bn. ✣ 31/3/17.	23/ 7/15. Pte. ✣
LIPSCOMBE, G., Pte. 26 Bn.	W. M.M. 7 A.L.T.M.B.	12/ 2/15 4y 9m. L.Cpl.
LIPSCOMBE, J. H. F., Bdr. DAC		8/10/14.
LIPSCOMBE, S. M., Gnr. Arty.		23/11/15 3m. Gnr.
LISBEY, A. R., Cpl. 40 Bn.	W.	6/12/15 2y 3m, Pte.
LISSON, V. T., Pte. 26 Bn.	W. ✣ 29/7/16.	23/ 8/15. Pte. ✣
LISTNER, C. L., Pte. 1 G.S.R.	113 How. Bty.	11/ 2/18 1y. 8m. Gnr.
LITTLE, A. R., Spr. 3 Mnrs.		18/11/15.
LITTLE, A., Pte. 40 Bn.	M.M., 15 Bn., 40 Bn., D. Sal Coy.	4/ 4/16 3y 3m, Pte.
LITTLE, C. A., Pte. 40 Bn.		11/10/16 1y 9m. Pte.
LITTLE, F., Pte. 12 Bn.	W.	19/ 5/16 2y 6m. Pte.
LITTLE, R. J., Dvr. Arty.		16/ 3/15.
LITTLE, W. D., A/Cpl. 12 Bn.	M.M.	2/ 5/16 3y 4m. Pte.
LITTLEJOHN, A. G., Pte. AAMC.	1 A.C.C.S.	21/ 9/15 4y 4m. Pte.
LITTLEJOHN, C. G., Tpr. 3 L.H.		7/ 8/15 1y 8m. Tpr.
LITTLEJOHN, P. W., Pte. 12 Bn.		10/ 5/16.
LITTLEJOHN, S. C., Pte. 12 Bn.	W. A.S.C.	26/10/16 2y 9m. Pte.
LITTLER, C. A., Lieut. 12 Bn.	D.S.O ✣ 3/9/16.	25/11/14 Capt. ✣
LITTLER, G. A., Pte. 6 M.G.C.		13/ 2/15 2y 2m. Pte.
LITTLER, J., Pte 12 Bn		27/11/16 2y 11m, Pte.
LITTLER, R. F., Pte. 12 Bn.	W.	20/ 8/14 1y 10m. L.Cpl.

TASMANIA'S MUSTER ROLL. 303

NAME.	REMARKS	RANK ON DISCHARGE. ENLISTED. SERVICE.
LIVINGSTONE, D., Pte. 12 Bn.		22/ 7/15 4y. Pte.
LIVINGSTONE, H. W. J., Pte. 40 Bn.	2W.	19/ 4/16 1y 10m. Pte.
LIVINGSTON, W. J., Cpl. 6 FAB.	23 H. Bde. 14 Fd. A. ✠ 4/10/17.	11/ 1/16. Cpl. ✠
LLEWELLIN, J. A., Pte. 26 Bn.		29/ 7/15 1y 4m. Pte.
LLEWELLYN, J. R., Pte. AAMC.	15 Fd. Amb.	16/10/16 3y. Pte.
LLEWELLYN, R., Spr. Tnlrs.	2 Tun. Coy.	7/ 9/16 1y 3m. Spr.
LLOYD, A. R., Cpl. 9 Bty. 3 FAB.	M.S.M.	29/ 8/14 5y 1m. Sgt.
LLOYD, C. G. H., Dvr. Arty.	13 F.A.B.	19/ 8/15.
LLOYD, N., Spr. Miners.	1 Tun. Coy.	19/ 4/16 2y 6m. Spr.
LLOYD, N., Spr. Tunlrs.		14/11/16. 11m. Spr.
LLOYD, R. C., Pte. 3 G.S.R.	12 Bn.	30/ 7/18 1y 3m. Pte.
LOANE, H. C., Pte. 40 Bn.	W. ✠ 30/8/18.	22/ 7/16. Pte. ✠
LOANE, R. J. D., Spr. 40 Bn.		23/ 3/16.
LOBBAN, G. M., Pte. 40 Bn.		21/ 8/16 1y 8m. Pte.
LOCKE, C. A., Pte. 40 Bn.	W.	21/ 2/16 3y 5m. Pte.
LOCKE, E., Pte. 40 Bn.		9/ 9/16.
LOCKE, F. J., Pte. 40 Bn.		3/ 7/16 2y 1m. Pte.
LOCKE, S. G., Pte. 12 Bn.	W. ✠ 20/9/17.	29/ 7/15 Pte. ✠
LOCKETT, M. J., Pte. 26 Bn	2W	7/ 9/15 3y 9m. Pte.
LOCKETT, R. C., Pte. 40 Bn.		7/10/16 1y 3m. Pte.
LOCKETT, T. N., Pte. 40 Bn.	W.	4/ 7/16 2y 9m. Pte.
LOCKHART, J., Pte. 40 Bn.	✠ 5/10/17.	26/ 5/16. Pte. ✠
LOCKHART, V., Pte. 40 Bn.	W.	17/ 7/17 1y 9m. Pte.
LOCKLEY, A., Tpr 1 G.S.R.		15/ 4/18 1y 4m. Tpr.
LOCKLEY, C. M., Pte. 15 Bn.		20/10/14 1y 11m. Pte.
LOCKLEY, H. T., Pte. 40 Bn.	✠ 5/10/17.	31/10/16. Pte. ✠
LOCKWOOD, A., Pte. 40 Bn.		7/ 5/17 2y 7m. Pte.
LOCKWOOD, C. F., Pte. 40 Bn.	M.M.	2/10/16 2y 11m, Pte.
LOCKWOOD, S. W., Cpl. 15 Bn.	D.C.M.	6/10/14 4y 9m. Sgt.
LOCKWOOD, W., Pte. 12 Bn.		22/ 5/15 2y 4m. Pte.
LOCKWOOD, W. G. Pte. 40 Bn.		11/ 1/17 2y 11m. Pte.
LODGE, A. L., Pte. 12 Bn.	24 H. Bde., 4 D. Arty., 4 D.H.M., M. Bty. ✠ 3/5/17.	8/11/15. Pte. ✠
LOFTUS, T. J., Pte. 12 Bn.	52 Bn.	8/10/15 2y 6m. Pte.
LOGAN, L. W., Pte. 12 Bn.		10/ 9/15 3y 10m. Pte.
LOGAN, T. M'N., Pte. 12 Bn.		25/ 6/17 2y 4m. Pte.
LOMASNEY, T. L., Gnr. Arty.	3 D.A.C.	6/10/16 2y 11m. Dvr.
LONDON, S. E. H., Pte. 12 Bn.	3 A.G.H.	9/12/14 4y 5m. Cpl.
LONERGAN, F. C., Pte. 40 Bn.	W., 69 Bn., 40 Bn.	29/ 5/16 3y 4m. Pte.
LONERGAN, J., Cpl 15 Bn.	W., M.M. and Bar.	5/ 1/15 4y 5m. Sgt.
LONERGAN, P. F., Pte. 12 Bn.	✠ 25-28/4/15.	27/ 8/14. Pte. ✠
LONERGAN, S., Pte. 12 Bn.		24/12/14.
LONERGAN, W. T., Dvr. D.A.C.	22 How. Bde. 106 How. Bty.	21/ 8/15 4y. Dvr.
LONG, A., Pte. 12 Bn.	2W. M.M. and Bar.	4/ 7/15 4y 1m. Pte.
LONG, A. L., Dvr. 8 Fd. Co.	W., 1 Army Training Coy.	25/ 1/16 3y 6m. Pte.
LONG, A. L., Pte. 1 A.G.H.	3 A.G.H., 2 Sqd. A.F.C.	31/ 5/15 4y 4m. Lieut.
LONG, C. J., Pte. 26 Bn.		3/ 5/15 4y 7m. Cpl.
LONG, G. A., Pte. 12 Bn.		31/ 8/15 4y 3m. Pte.
LONG, G. H., Pte. 12 Bn.	2W. ✠ 23/7/18.	31/ 7/16. Pte. ✠
LONG, C. J., Pte. 12 Bn.	2W.	8/ 7/15 2y 5m. Pte.
LONG, H. C., Cpl. 40 Bn.	W., D.C.M. ✠ 28/3/18.	26/ 1/16. Sgt. ✠
LONG, J. A., Pte. 26 Bn.	52 Bn.	1/ 5/15 1y 7m. Pte.
LONG, J. J., Pte. 3 L.H.	W., M.G. Sqd., 1 L.H., 3 Sqd. A.F.C.	25/ 8/14 4y 5m. 1 A.M.
LONG, J. J., Spr. Tunlrs.	W.	3/ 4/16 2y 1m. Spr.
LONG, L. E., Pte. 4 M.G.C.	W., 40 Bn.	30/10/16 3y 1m. Pte.
LONG, L. G., Cpl. 12 Bn.		23/ 2/15 1y 2m. Cpl.
LONG, L. H., Tpr. 3 L.H.	4 L.H.	26/ 4/17 2y 7m. Tpr.
LONG, L. W., Pte. 12 Bn.	W. 52 Bn. ✠ 16/10/17.	9/ 7/15. Pte. ✠
LONG, M. J., Pte. 3 Fd. Amb.		11/ 9/14.
LONG, R. G., Dvr. D.A.C.		5/ /6/15 3y 10m. Dvr.
LONG, T. P., Pte. 4 A.A.S.C.	W., 52 Bn., 50 Bn., 12 Bn.	19/ 8/14 4y 7m. Lieut.
LONG, W. H., Pte. 12 Bn.		10/12/14 2y 2m. Pte.
LONGLEY, F. R., Pte. 1 G.S.R.	6 F.A.B., 2 Bty.	22/ 1/18 1y 9m. Dvr.
LOONE, C. H., Pte. 40 Bn.		15/ 5/16.
LOONE, C. H., Pte. 12 Bn.	W.	18/ 7/16 3y 4m. Pte.
LOONE, S. P., Dvr. 3 Fd. Arty.		1/ 7/15.
LOPEZ, F. E., Pte. 12 Bn.	✠ 8/5/18.	16/10/16. Pte. ✠
LORD, J. E. C., Lt.-Col. 40 Bn.	C.M.G., D.S.O., C de G. (F.), 2 M.I.D.	10/ 2/16 3y 6m. Lt.-Col.
LORD, A. E., Pte. 26 Bn.	2W.	9/ 7/15 4y 1m. Pte.
LORD, A., Pte. 40 Bn.		4/10/16.
LORD, E F., Pte.		9/12/14 1y 3m. Pte.
LORD, H., Tpr. 3 L.H.		2/11/16 2y 9m. Tpr.
LORD, H. E., Pte. 12 Bn	3W 6. Bn 12 Bn. ✠ 25/8/18.	20/ 8/14. L.Cpl.
LORD, H., Pte. 40 Bn.	W. ✠ 1/7/17.	20/ 3/16 Pte. ✠
LORD, H. T., Pte. 12 Bn.		25/ 4/17 1y 2m. Pte.
LORD, J. F., Signr. 12 Bn.	2W. 69 Bn., 12 Bn.	13/ 7/15.
LORD, R. S., Pte. 15 Bn.	✠ 8/8/15.	27/10/14. Pte. ✠
LORD, W. C., Spr. 4 Fd. Co.	W.	21/ 8/14 3y 5m. Cpl.
LOVE, J., Capt. A.A.M.C.		28/ 5/18
LOVE, A. F., L./Cpl. 40 Bn.	W., M.S.M.	23/ 3/16.
LOVE, C. E., Pte 15 Bn.	47 Bn., ✠ 12/10/17.	13/ 8/15. Pte. ✠
LOVEDAY, J. F., Pte. 26 Bn.		10/ 5/15 1y. Pte.
LOVELESS, A. W., L./Cpl. 2 GSR		15/ 4/18.
LOVELESS, W. A., Pte. 40 Bn.	W.	13/10/16 2y 6m. Pte.
LOVELESS, W. J., Pte. 15 Bn.	W. (Enlisted as LOVELACE, W. J.)	9/10/14 4y 4m. Pte.
LOVELL, E., Pte. M.G. Sec.		8/ 2/16 1y 11m. Pte.

TASMANIA'S WAR RECORD, 1914-1918.

NAME.	REMARKS.	RANK ON DISCHARGE. ENLISTED. SERVICE.
LOVELL, H. E., Pte. Rmts.		30/ 9/15 4y 2m. Tpr.
LOVELL, W. H., Spr. Miners	W., 2 Tunn. Co.	1/ 3/16 3y 7m. Spr.
LOVERGRAVE, C. D., Pte. 12 Bn.		10/ 8/15.
LOVETT, A. J., Pte. 3 L.H.		20/ 8/14 1y 4m.
LOVETT, F. A., Pte. 12 Bn.	52 Bn.	23/10/15 3y 10m. Pte.
LOVETT, K. E., Pte. 2 G.S.R.		4/ 6/18 1y 3m. Pte.
LOVETT, L., Gnr. 9 Fd. Bty.	M.M.	26/ 8/14 4y 5m. Sgt.
LOVETT, L. F., Pte. 26 Bn.	W.	12/ 5/15 4y 3m. Sgt.
LOVETT, T. W., Pte. 40 Bn.		15/ 5/16 3y 4m. Lieut.
LOVETT, W. De F., Pte. 12 Bn.	✠ 3-5/9/16.	22/ 7/15. Pte. ✠
LOWE, A., Pte. A.A.M.C.		25/ 9/16.
LOWE, C., Pte. 12 Bn.	✠ 26/2/17.	15/ 3/16. Pte. ✠
LOWE, E. G., Pte. 26 Bn.	3W.	12/10/15 4y 1m. Pte.
LOWE, G. T., Cpl. 40 Bn.	W.	16/10/16 2y 10m. L.Cpl.
LOWE, H. W., Pte. 4 M.G. Co.		2/ 8/16.
LOWE, H. J., Pte. 15 Bn.	4 L.T.M.B. 15 Bn.	17/ 8/15 1y 11m. Pte.
LOWE, J. M., Tpr. 3 L.H.		31/10/17 1y 10m. Tpr.
LOWE, J. D., Pte. 40 Bn.	M.M.	26/ 1/17 2y 6m. Pte.
LOWE, J. W., Pte. 12 Bn.		5/ 9/16.
LOWE, L., Pte. 12 Bn.	✠ 25-28/4/15.	26/ 8/14. Pte. ✠
LOWE, R. S., Tpr. 3 L.H.		16/ 6/17 2y 2m. Tpr.
LOWE, R., Pte. 12 Bn.	2W. 52 Bn. 13 A.R.T.M.B	8/12/15 3y 8m. Pte.
LOWE, W. J., Pte. 40 Bn.	✠ 31/8/18.	5/ 2/17. Pte. ✠
LOWE, W., Spr. Miners.		15/10/15.
LOWE, W. J., Dvr. 1 D.A.C.		20/ 8/14 5y 2m. Dvr.
LOWE, W. V., Pte. 12 Bn.		11/ 2/15 6m. Pte.
LOWERY, D. A., Tpr. 3 L.H.	13 L.H. 17 Fd. Bty.	3/ 4/17 1y 3m. Gnr.
LOWERY, H. J., Pte. 2 G.S.R.	39 Fd. Bty.	8/ 4/18 1y 5m. Gnr.
LOWRIE, F. C. W., Pte. 7 F. Amb.		25/ 3/15.
LOWRY, J. J., Pte. 4 M.G. Co.	2 M.G. Co. ✠ 18/5/18	16/12/16. Pte. ✠
LOWRY, J., Pte. 40 Bn.	W.	23/11/16 2y 9m. Pte.
LOWTHER, C. St. G., Pte. 4 MGC.	W. 1 M.G. Co., 4 M.G.C.	10/11/16.
LUCAS, C. D., Lieut. 12 Bn.	✠ 24/7/16.	17/ 3/15 Lieut. ✠
LUCAS, A. K., Pte. 40 Bn.	✠ 8/11/17.	21/ 2/16 T/Cpl. ✠
LUCAS, A. C., Pte. 12 Bn.	2W., 52 Bn., 51 Bn.	31/ 8/14 4y 5m. Pte.
LUCAS, B. S., Sgt. 12 Bn.	W.	11/ 7/16 2y 1m. Pte.
LUCAS, C. A., Pte. 12 Bn.	W.	10/ /12/17 1y 3m. Pte.
LUCAS, C. E., Pte. 1 G.S.R.	3 F.A.B.	7/ 3/18 1y 7m. Gnr.
LUCAS, E. J. F., Pte. 40 Bn.		15/11/16 2y 10m. Pte.
LUCAS, E. T., Pte. 40 Bn.		13/10/16 1y 4m. Pte.
LUCAS, E. W. S., Pte. 12 Bn.	3W. Anzac Police. 12 Bn.	30/ 8/14
LUCAS, E. J., Pte. 26 Bn.		24/ 9/15 1y 8m. Pte.
LUCAS, E. O., Sgt. 12 Bn.		20/ 7/16 3y 3m. Cpl.
LUCAS, G. M., Gnr. D.A.C.	22 How. Bde. 106 How. Bde.	15/ 9/15 3y 11m. Gnr.
LUCAS, G. M., Pte. 12 Bn.		9/10/16 2y 3m. Pte.
LUCAS, H. P., Pte. 12 Bn.		11/10/16 3y Pte.
LUCAS, J. D., Gnr. Arty.	W., 9 Bty.	29/ 1/15 4y 7m. Cpl.
LUCAS, K. F., Pte. 3 G.S.R.	12 Bn.	24/ 6/18 1y 6m. Pte.
LUCAS, L. C., Sgt. 12 Bn.	52 Bn. ✠ 4/9/16.	16/ 9/15. Sgt. ✠
LUCAS, L. E., Pte. 12 Bn.		31/ 8/14.
LUCAS, R. E., Gnr. Arty.	8 F.A.B.	22/11/16 1y 9m. Gnr.
LUCAS, R. H., Pte. 1 A.G.H.		8/6/15.
LUCAS, R. J., Dvr. 10 F.A.B.	W. 38 Bty.	12/ 5/15 2y 9m. Dvr.
LUCAS, R. K., Cpl. 12 Bn.	✠ 19/1/19.	24/ 7/15 1y 5m. Cpl.
LUCAS, W. G., Pte. 12 Bn.	52 Bn.	22/ 7/15 2y 10m. Pte.
LUCAS, W. H., Pte. 12 Bn.	✠ 2/5/18.	6/11/16, Pte. ✠
LUCAS, J. H., Dvr. 6 F.A.B.	11 Bty. A.F.A.	15/ 9/16 3y 2m. Cpl.
LUCAS, M. A., Dvr. 9 Fd. Bty		31/ 8/14 3y 5m. Gnr.
LUCK, E S., Pte. 4 M.G. Co.	22 M.G.B. ✠ 21/4/17	11/ 7/16. Pte. ✠
LUCK, D. S., Pte. 26 Bn.	69 Bn. 26 Bn.	1/ 6/15 4y 2m. Pte.
LUCK, N. C., Dvr. 17 Fd. Bty.	W.	15/ 9/15 3y 9m. Dvr.
LUCKMAN, H., Pte. 26 Bn.		24/ 6/15 1y 2m. Pte.
LUCY, R. G., Gnr. Arty.	3 F.A.B.	5/12/14
LUDBEY, C., Pte. 12 Bn.	2W.	30/12/14 2y 3m. Pte.
LUDBY, H., Pte. 15 Bn.		22/ 9/14 3y 11m. Pte.
LUDBEY, K., Pte. 40 Bn.	W.	21/ 8/17 2y. Pte.
LUDBEY, R., Gnr. 6 F.A.B.	49 Bty. 13 F.A.B.	6/12/15 3y 10m. Gnr.
LUDBEY, W., Tpr. 3 L. Horse.	✠ 4-6/8/16.	23/ 8/14. L.Cpl. ✠
LUHRS, T., Pte. 12 Bn.		10/ 8/16. Pte.
LUKEHURST, W., Pte. 51 Bn.		12/ 7/15 4y 2m. Pte.
LUNDMARK, F. C., Spr. Tunlrs.	2 Tunlrs. Coy., re-enlisted.	13/ 5/15 2y 8m. Spr.
LUNMARK, F. C., Dvr. A.S.C		8/ 9/14.
LUNNEY, J. H., Pte. A.C.H.	W., M.M. 12 Fld. Amb.	14/12/14.
LUNSON, J., Pte. 12 Bn.		25/ 7/16 3y 3m. Pte.
LUNSON, L., Pte. 26 Bn.	3W., 2 M.G. Bn.	15/ 7/15 4y 1m. Pte.
LUNSON, R. J., Pte. 12 Bn.	W.	2/ 5/16 1y 7m. Pte.
LUNSON, R., Pte. 4 M.G. Co.	5 M.G. Bn., 22 M.G. Co.	24/ 7/16 3y. Pte.
LUTHOLD, E. N., Pte. 7 Fd. Amb.		27/ 2/15 2y 10m. Pte.
LUTTRELL, A. A., Pte. Rerfs.		30/ 9/15 9m. Pte.
LUTTRELL, C. F., Pte. 26 Bn.	M.M.	19/ 4/15 4y 4m. Pte.
LUTTRELL, C. E., Cpl. 26 Bn.	✠ 21/11/16.	25/ 3/15. Sgt. ✠
LUTTRELL, G. W., Pte. 15 Bn.	47 Bn.	18/ 8/15 4y. Lieut.
LUTTRELL, H. L., Pte. 12 Bn.	W.	25/10/16 3y. Pte.
LUTTRELL, T. G., Pte. 40 Bn.	2W.	24/ 7/17 1y 11m. Pte.
LUTTRELL, W., Pte. 40 Bn.	W.	19/ 7/17 2y. Pte.
LUTWYCHE, H., Pte. 4 M.G. Co.	11 M.G. Co.	16/ 9/16 3y 3m. Pte.

TASMANIA'S MUSTER ROLL. 305

NAME.	REMARKS.	RANK ON DISCHARGE. ENLISTED. SERVICE.
LYALL, A. G., Pte. 15 Bn.	P.O.W.	13/ 8/15 3y 10m. Pte.
LYALL, A. W., Pte. 1 Remts.		27/ 7/15 3y 6m. S. Sm.
LYALL, G. T., Dvr. Fd. Art.	21 H. Bde. ✤ 20/9/17.	27/ 7/15. Dvr. ✤
LYALL, H. H., Pte. 40 Bn.	W. 1 M.G. Coy.	4/ 7/16 2y 10m. Pte.
LYALL, J. C., Pte. 12 Bn.	A.O.C.	15/ 2/14 5y 2m. Pte.
LYALL, L. G., Pte. 2 G.S.R.	W. 4 G S R.	6/ 5/18 8m. Pte.
LYALL, W. C., Pte. 15 Bn.	W.	17/ 9/14 1y 4m. Pte.
LYDEN, A .Spr. 8 Fd. Co.	✤ 1/9/18	9/11/15. Dvr. ✤
LYDEN, C. J., Pte. 12 Bn.	W.	7/ 4/16 3y. Pte.
LYDEN, S., Pte. 12 Bn.	D.C.M.	25/11/15 3y 10m. Pte.
LYELL, L. G., Pte. 2 G.S.R.	4 G.S.R.	6/ 5/18 8m. Pte.
LYNCH, C. T., Chaplain, Transport Service		17/ 2/17 7m, Capt.-Chap 4th class.
LYNCH, C. C., Pte. 12 Bn	W. 52 Bn.	5/ 1/15.
LYNCH, F. J., Pte. 12 Bn	52 Bn.	5/ 1/15 3y 5m, Pte.
LYNCH, H., Pte. 12 Bn.	W. ✤ 25-28/4/15.	3/10/14. Pte. ✤
LYNCH, H. S., Pte. 26 Bn.		8/ 3/15 4y 7m. Pte.
LYNCH, J. E., Gnr. 8 F.A.B.	31 Bty.	5/ 1/16 3y 9m. Gnr.
LYNCH, L. C., Pte. 12 Bn.	10 F.A.B. ✤ 27/9/17.	22/ 8/14. Pte. ✤
LYNCH, M., Pte. 15 Bn.	3W.	4/ 1/15 4y 3m. Cpl.
LYNCH, M. W., Pte. 15 Bn.		30/ 6/15 3y 3m. Pte.
LYNCH, O. A., Pte. 40 Bn.		11/ 7/16 2y 4m. Pte.
LYNCH, P. A., Dvr. 15 Fd. Bty.		19/ 9/14 4y 6m. Gnr.
LYNCH, T., Pte. 12 Bn.		21/ 1/15 1y. Pte.
LYNCH, T. E., Pte. 26 Bn.	15 L.H.	Tpr.
LYND, J. W., Pte. 3 G.S.R.	12 Bn.	18/ 1/18 1y 10m. Pte.
LYNE, F. J., Pte. 12 Bn.	W. ✤ 6/10/17.	22/ 8/14 Lt. ✤
LYNE, C. H., O.R./S. 12 Bn.	W. ✤ 7/4/16.	22/ 8/14 Lt. ✤
LYNE, R. B., Pte. 40 Bn.	2W.	10/ 3/16 3y 7m, Spr.
LYON, R. W., Spr. 8 Engrs.		11/ 1/16 3y 8m. Spr.
LYON, T. J., Pte. 12 Bn.	24 How. Bde., 10 F.A.B., 112 H. Bty	8/10/15 3y 11m. Gnr.
LYONS, A., Tpr. 3 L. Horse.	✤ 15/9/15.	18/ 8/14. Dvr. ✤
LYONS, C. J., Cpl. 1 A.G.H.		14/ 9/14 3y 11m. Cpl.
LYONS, F., Pte. 21 Bn.		5/ 1/15 4y 5m. Pte.
LYONS, F. A., Pte. 1 G.S.R.		4/ 2/18 1y 8m. Pte.
LYONS, G. E., Gnr. Arty.	21 F.A.B.	17/ 5/16 1y 9m. Gnr.
LYONS, A. M., Pte. 12 Bn.	W.	26/11/16 2y 4m. Pte.
LYONS, J. L., Pte. 15 Bn.	W. 24 How. Bde. 11 F.A.B. 4 D.A.C.	23/ 9/14 4y 5m. Dvr.
LYONS, L. T., Pte. 12 Bn.		29/ 8/16 2y 1m. Pte.
LYONS, M. L., Pte. 26 Bn.		14/ 6/15 2y 2m. Pte.
LYONS, M., Spr., 3 Miners.	3 Tunnlrs. ✤ 28/11/16	7/ 8/15. Spr. ✤
LYONS, S. J. T., Pte. 26 Bn.		25/ 2/15 1y 9m. Pte.
LYONS, T., Spr. Miners.	5 Tnlrs, 2 Tnlrs.	3/ 4/16 3y 6m. Spr.
LYONS, T. H., Pte. 12 Bn.		19/ 8/14.
LYONS, W., Tpr. 3 L.H.	Provost Corps.	26/ 8/14 5y 4m. Tpr.
LYSTER, S. J., Pte. 15 Bn.		1/ 9/15.
MACE, C. T., Pte. 15. Bn.	W., 4 M.G. Co.	9/12/14 4y 3m, Pte.
MACE, C. W. A., Gnr. Arty.	W., 9 F.A.B., 8 Bty.	7/12/15 3y 9m, Dvr.
MACE, D R., Pte. 12 Bn	W.	5/10/15 4y. Pte.
MACE, W R., Dvr. 6 F.A.B.	W., 2 D.A.C., 6 F.A.B. ✤ 9/8/18	24/ 8/15 Dvr. ✤
MACDONALD, G., Pte. 12 Bn.		22/ 1/15 2y 11m. Pte.
MACFARLANE, C. W., Pte. 12 Bn	2W., M.M., C. de G. (Belgian).	16/10/16 2y 7m, L.-Cpl
MACFARLANE, W., Pte. 12 Bn.	W.	17/ 5/17
MACGARVEY, H. J., Bdr. 3 F.A.B.	3W.	12/ 1/15
MACHEN, A. J., Pte. 4 M.G. Co.	12 Bn.	4/10/16 3y, Pte.
MACHEN, J. C., Pte. 40 Bn.		4/ 3/13 3y, Pte.
MACHIN, R. F. C., Pte. 12 Bn.	A.F.C. ✤ 18/9/18.	16/ 6/14 Lt. ✤
MACHEN, V. L., Pte. 12 Bn.	5W.	17/11/14 4y 10m, L.-Cpl
MACHIN, W., Pte. 40 Bn.	51 Bn. ✤ 13/10/17.	15/ 3/16 Pte. ✤
MACKENZIE, D. M., Pte. 4 M.G. Co	10 M.G. Coy.	7/ 9/16.
MACKENZIE, R. S., Sgt. 40 Bn.		1/ 3/16 Lt.
MACKEY, A. C., Pte. 40 Bn.		8/11/15 2y 7m, Pte.
MACKEY, F. J., Pte. 40 Bn.	✤ 5/10/17.	30/10/16 Pte. ✤
MACKEY, J. T. M., Gnr. 3 F.A.B.	✤ 18/9/18.	26/ 7/15 Gnr. ✤
MACKEY, J., Pte. 40 Bn.	2W.	7/ 3/16 3y 5m, Pte.
MACKEY, J. K., Gnr. 18 Fd. Bty.	17 Bty., 4 Div. Supply Co., 17 Bty.	26/ 7/15 3y 2m, Gnr.
MACKEY, L. M. T., Pte. 12 Bn.	A.A.G.C.	22/11/17 1y 11m, Pte.
MACKERELL, W., Pte. 15 Bn.	59 Bn.	31/ 6/15 1y 9m. Pte.
MACKINNON, A. D., Lt. 40 Bn.	2W.	7/ 3/16 2y 3m, Capt
MACKRILL, C. E., Pte. 26 Bn.		24/ 8/15
MACLENNAN, A., Pte. 12 Bn.		4/12/15 2y, Pte.
MACLEOD, T. B., 3 L.H.		
MACMICHAEL, R., Pte. 12 Bn.	52 Bn. ✤ 28/3/17.	1/ 8/15. L. Sgt. ✤
MACMICHAEL, W. N., Pte. 12 Bn.	52 Bn., 51 Bn.	17/ 1/16 3y 9m. Pte.
MACNICOL, R. P. D., Gnr. 13 F.A.B.	2W.	14/ 2/16 2y 7m. Gnr.
MACPHERSON, D. A., Pte. 4 M.G.		7/ 6/16
MACRAE, A., Pte. 1 A.C.H.	2W., D.C.M., M.M., 1 F. Amb.	8/ 9/14 5y. Sgt.
MACROSTIC, D. H., Pte. 12 Bn.	3W.	23/ 7/15 3y 8m, Pte.
MADDEN, E., Gnr. 13 F.A.B.	49 Bty.	14/ 1/16 3y 8m, Gnr.
MADDEN, J., Pte. 40 Bn.		14/11/16 2y 10m, Pte.
MADDISON, G., Pte. 12 Bn.	2W.	3/ 4/16 Pte.
MADDISON, H. A., Pte. 15 Bn.	W., 47 Bn.	2/ 9/15 1y 9m, Pte.
MADDOCK, C. V., Cpl. Arty		31/ 8/16 3y 1m, Bdr.
MADDOCK, D. R., Pte. 26 Bn.	W., 7 M.G. Co.	26/ 7/15 2y 10m, Cpl.
MADDOCK, V. J., Pte. 12 Bn.	W., 52 Bn., 13 M.G. Co.	31/12/15 2y 3m, Cpl.
MADDOX, A., Pte 12 Bn.	3W.	9/ 8/15 3y 8m, Pte.

T

TASMANIA'S WAR RECORD, 1914-1918.

NAME.	REMARKS.	RANK ON DISCHARGE. ENLISTED. SERVICE.
MADDOX, C. A., Pte. 40 Bn.	W.	6/10/16 2y 4m, Pte.
MADDOX, G. J., Pte. 12 Bn.	52 Bn., 13 M.G. Co.	8/ 2/16 6y 6m, Pte.
MADDY, J.	(Enlisted as SHANNON, J.)	25/11/14 Spr.
MAGGS, A. W. J., Cpl. Miners.	Spr. 6 Fd. Co.	19/11/15 1y 2m, Cpl.
MAGRATH, T. H., Pte. 12 Bn.		12/ 1/15 3v 4m, Pte.
MAGUIRE, J. P., Pte. 12 Bn.		9/ 3/17 1y 10m, Pte.
MAGUIRE, J. P., Pte. 12 Bn	W.	2/ 5/17 2y 5m, Pte.
MAHAR, A. C., Pte. 3 Cyc Cps.	W.	4/ 4/16 3y 5m, Pte.
MAHERA, B. H., Pte. 12 Bn.	W., 40 Bn.	23/ 8/15 3y 11m, Pte.
MAHERA, E. A., Pte. 40 Bn.		8/ 7/19 Pte.
MAHERA, H. A., Pte. 40 Bn.		16/10/16 3y. Pte.
MAHERA, L. E., Pte. 12 Bn.	A.F.C.	21/ 7/15 4v 4m, 1 A.M.
MAHERA, M., Pte. 15 Bn.	W.	14/12/14 1y 6m, Pte.
MAHERA, P., Pte. 26 Bn.	W., 69 Bn., 12 Bn.	11/ 8/15 4y, Pte.
MAHERA, S., Pte. 26 Bn.	2W.	12/ 8/15 3y 7m, Pte.
MAHONEY, A. P., Pte. 12 Bn.	W.	17/12/17 1y 4m, Pte.
MAHONEY, C., Pte. 12 Bn.		21/ 7/15
MAHONEY, C. L., Pte. 2 A.G.H.	15 Fd. Amb.	1/10/15 3y 9m, Pte.
MAHONEY, D., Dvr. 3 L.H.		13/ 9/15 3y 10m, Dvr.
MAHONY, J. W., Pte. 2 G.S.R.	1 Bn.	8/ 4/18
MAHONY, J., Pte. 4 M.G. Co.		11/12/16 2y 9m, Pte.
MAHONEY, L. R., Pte. 5 D.M.G. Co.		24/ 7/16 3y 3m, Dvr.
MAHONEY, W., Pte. 15 Bn.	W., P.O.W., 4 M.G. Co., 15 Bn.	28/ 1/15 6m, Pte.
MAINE, C. W., Cpl. 15 Bn.	✠ 2/6/15.	22/ 9/14 Cpl. ✠
MAIN, T., Gnr. Arty.	W., 14 F.A.B. ✠ 1/9/18.	14/10/15 Gnr. ✠
MAINE, H. C., Pte. 15 Bn.		25/ 9/14 2y 5m, Pte.
MAINGAY, B. St. C., Pte. 40 Bn.	69 Bn., 40 Bn.	3/ 4/16 3y 4m, Pte.
MAINGAY, C. F. C., Pte. 12 Bn.	✠ 18/9/18.	6/ 7/16 Pte. ✠
MAINGAY, L. C., Pte. 40 Bn.	W.	3/ 4/16 1y 9m, Pte.
MAINWARING, C. G., Cpl. 2 G.S.R.	12 Bn.	4/ 4/18 1y 5m, Pte.
MAINWARING, G. A., Pte. 15 Bn.	W.	19/ 5/15 10m. Pte.
MAINWARING, G. J., Tpr. ? L.H.	W., 4 D.A.C.	4/ 8/15 2y 7m, Dvr.
MAINWARING, W. J., Pte. 12 Bn.	W., 52 Bn.	12/ 1/16 3y 3m, Cpl.
MAJOR, B., Pte. Arty.		5/ 2/17 2y 9m, Pte.
MAJOR, F. W. F., Gnr. 18 Bty.	2W., 17 Bty., 26 Bn., P.O.W.	19/ 9/15 3y 9m, Lt.
MALCOLM, A., Pte. 12 Bn.		19/10/16
MALE, C. J., Pte. 1 A.G.H.		2/ 9/15
MALLINSON, D. R., Pte. 12 Bn.	W.	7/ 9/14 1y 11m, Pte.
MALLOTT, J., Pte. 40 Bn	W., 69 Bn., 40 Bn.	29/ 5/16 3y 5m, Cpl.
MALONEY, W. B., Pte. 15 Bn.	4 Pioneers	10/ 2/15 4y 4m, Pte.
MALONEY, M., Pte. 26 Bn.		23/ 7/15
MANEY, A. E., Spr. Miners.		11/ 1/16 1y 11m, Spr.
MANEY, R. P., Spr. Miners.	14 Fd. Co.	15/ 9/15 4y, Spr.
MANION, A. J., Tpr. 3 L.H.	W.	7/12/14 2v 3m, Tpr.
MANION, H., Gnr. Arty.		10/ 1/16
MANION, M., L-Cpl. 26 Bn.	✠ 29/7/16	22/ 6/15 Cpl. ✠
MANION, P. F., Gnr. 9 Fd. Bty.	4 Div. Art. H.O., 4 D.A.C., D.A.H.Q.	17/ 8/15 4y, Gnr.
MANLEY, C. E., Cpl. 12 Bn.		3/ 4/16 2y 2m, Pte.
MANN, H. E., Tpr. 3 L.H.		25/ 6/15 4v 2m, Dvr.
MANN, L. D., Spr. Engrs	13 Fd. Co., 3 Fd. Co.	10/ 8/15 4y 1m, Dvr.
MANNING, D. R., Spr. Miners.		24/ 2/16 3y 8m, Spr.
MANNING, G. A., Spr. Tunlrs.		17/10/16 1y 4m.
MANNING, G. W., Pte. 12 Bn.	✠ 25-28/4/15	24/10/14 Pte. ✠
MANNING, J., Pte. 26 Bn.		19/ 6/15
MANNING, R., Pte. 12 Bn.		21/ 7/15 4y 1m, Pte.
MANNIG, R., Pte. 12 Bn.	W.	13/ 6/16 2y 3m, Pte.
MANNING, S. T., Pte. 12 Bn.	W.	23/ 9/13 2y 8m, Pte.
MANNING, W., Pte 26 Bn.		8/ 7/15 1y Pte.
MANNING, W. T., Pte. 26 Bn.	4W.	21/ 7/15 4y 4m, Cpl.
MANSELL, A. D., Pte. 12 Bn.	W.	25/ 1/15 3y 7m, Pte.
MANSELL, G. E., Pte. 12 Bn.	52 Bn.	23/ 3/16 3y 5m, Pte.
MANSELL, J. V., Pte. 12 Bn.	W.	14/12/15 2y 4m, Pte.
MANSELL, M., Pte. 40 Bn.	✠ 1/11/18.	6/12/16 Pte. ✠
MANSELL, T. E., Pte. 12 Bn.	52 Bn. ✠ 5/12/16.	25/ 1/16 Pte. ✠
MANSELL, W. H., Pte. 40 Bn.		1/ 1/17 2y 9m, Pte.
MANSER, A. V., Pte. 12 Bn.	W.	12/10/16 2y 5m, Pte.
MANSER, E., Pte. 12 Bn.	W.	30/ 5/16 1y 10m, Pte.
MANSER, F., Pte. 12 Bn.	3W., M.M.	7/10/14 4y 10m, Sgt.
MANSFIELD, A., Pte. 12 Bn.		4/ 2/16 2v 4m, Pte.
MANSFIELD, A. D., Pte. 15 Bn.	✠ June, 1915.	16/ 9/14 Pte. ✠
MANSFIELD, A. J., Pte. 40 Bn.	W., 12 Bn.	12/ 2/16 2y 4m, Pte.
MANSFIELD, E. W., Pte 4 M.G. Co.	W.	4/ 8/16 2y 2m, Dvr.
MANSFIELD, H. E., Pte. 12 Bn.	3W.	25/ 1/15 4y 5m, Sig.
MANSFIELD, H. C., M.G.S. 12 Bn.	W., 3 Inf. Bde., M.G. Co. ✠ 6/5/17.	19/ 8/14 L.-Cpl. ✠
MANSFIELD, H. L., S.-Sgt. Details	Dental Corps.	22/ 3/15
MANSFIELD, K. L., Gnr. Arty.		2/10/16 2y 11m, Gnr.
MANSFIELD, S., Pte 4 M.G. Co.	W.	4/ 8/15 2v 11m, Pte.
MANSFIELD, T., Pte. 12 Bn.	W.	13/10/15 3y 6m, T.-Cpl.
MANSFIELD, T. L., Gnr. Arty.		10/ 2/16
MANSFIELD, V., Pte. 4 M.G. Co.	11 M.G. Co	9/ 9/15 3y, Pte.
MANSFIELD, W., Dvr. 8 Fd. Engrs.		1/ 2/16 3y 7m, Dvr.
MANSON, C. F., Pte. 15 Bn.	W.	19/ 5/15 4v 3m, Cpl.
MANSON, J. A., Gnr. 9 Bty A.F.A.	W.	12/ 9/14 3y 3m, Bdr.
MANSON, A., Gnr. 9 Bty. F.A.		19/ 8/14 1y 10m, Gnr.
MANSON, R. H., Pte. 40 Bn.	W., 51 Bn.	7/ 2/16 1y 8m, Pte.
MANSON, T., Pte. 40 Bn.		16/10/16 2y 7m, Pte.
MANTACH, E. J. A., Cpl. 40 Bn.	✠ 12/10/17.	20/ 3/16 L.-Sgt. ✠

TASMANIA'S MUSTER ROLL. 307

NAME.	REMARKS.	RANK ON DISCHARGE. ENLISTED, SERVICE.
MANTERFIELD, A., Pte. 12 Bn.		10/12/17 1y 11m, Pte.
MANTERFIELD, S., Pte. A.A.M.C.	W., 9 Fd. Amb.	25/ 9/16 2y 6m, Pte.
MAPLEY, D. N., Pte. 1 A.C.H		4/ 8/15 4y 1m, Pte.
MARCHANT, A. E., Pte. 12 Bn.	52 Bn. ✻ 27/3/17.	7/ 10/15 Pte. ✻
MARCHANT, C. H., Pte. 26 Bn.		4/ 4/16 3y 6m, Dvr.
MARGETTS, I. S., Sec. Lt. 12 Bn.	M.I.D. ✻ 24/7/16.	22/8/14 Capt. ✻
MARGETTS, E. E., Pte 3 Fd Amb.		28/ 8/14 2y 1m, Pte.
MARGISON, A. J., Gnr. Fd. Arty.	W., 14 F.A.B., 112 How. Bty.	28/ 1/16 3y 8m, Gnr.
MARKBY, F. H., Gnr. 3 F.A.B.		5/10/14 4y 4m, Gnr.
MARKEY, H. M., Gnr. Hy. A. Group	4 A.M.T. Co.	25/ 2/15 1y 10m, Gnr.
MARKEY, J. L., Tpr. 1 Remt Sec.		1/10/15 4y Tpr.
MARKHAM, H. J., Pte. 12 Bn.	✻ 20/5/16.	8/ 7/15 Pte. ✻
MARKHAM, H., Pte. 15 Bn.	✻ 9/8/15.	19/10/14 Pte. ✻
MARK, E. L., Pte. 15 Bn.	W. ✻ 11/4/17.	14/10/14 Cpl. ✻
MARLEY, M., Gnr. A.F.A.	19 Bty. A.F.A.	30/ 4/17 2y 3m, Dvr.
MARNEY, R., Pte. 12 Bn.		1/ 7/16 1y 6m, Pte.
MARNEY, R., Pte. 12 Bn.		26/ 1/15 1y 3m, Pte.
MARNEY, T. H., Pte. 12 Bn.	✻ 3/11/17.	18/12/15 1y 11m, Pte.
MARQUIS, D. C., Pte. 12 Bn.	W., 40 Bn.	3/ 4/16 2y 11m, Pte.
MARR, F., Pte. 12 Bn.		28/10/15
MARRINER, L. W., Pte. 12 Bn.	W. ✻ 5-8/5/17.	20/ 8/14 A.-Sgt. ✻
MARRIOTT, F., Lt. 12 Bn.	W.	19/11/15 1y 10m, Lt.
MARRIOTT, D., Pte. 12 Bn.	✻ 7/6/17.	3/ 4/16 Pte. ✻
MARSDEN, A. L., Gnr. 6 F.A.B.	107 How Bty.	16/ 9/15
MARSDEN, H., Pte. 40 Bn.	W.	17/ 8/17
MARSDEN, L. W., Cpl. 40 Bn.	8 M.G. Co.	1/ 3/16 3y 5m, Cpl.
MARSDEN, T. G., Pte. 4 M.G. Co.		3/ 1/17 1y 6m, Pte.
MARSH, A. L., Pte. 1 A.C.H.	✻ 6/9/15.	24/11/14 Pte. ✻
MARSH, F. H., Pte. 40 Bn.	W., M.G. Details, 9 M.G. Co.	11/11/16 2y 10m, Pte.
MARSH, G., Pte. 40 Bn.	W., 15 Bn., 40 Bn.	16/ 3/16 3y 6m, Crl.
MARSH, H. J., Pte. 12 Bn.	W., M.M., 1 Pnr. Co.	20/11/14 4y 6m, Cpl.
MARSH, L., Pte. 12 Bn.	W.	2/ 5/16 3y 3m, Pte.
MARSH, R., 40 Bn.	Died in Hobart Hospital before embarking	
MARSHMAN, S. E., Pte. 12 Bn.	✻ 23/3/16.	27/ 7/15 Pte. ✻
MARSTON, E., Pte. 40 Bn.	W. ✻ 13/10/17.	30/ 9/16 Pte. ✻
MARSHALL, A. E., Dvr. Fd. Engrs.	8 Fd. Co., 16 Fd. Co., A.T.C. Engrs., A. Tun. Co	31/ 8/15 3y 11m. Spr.
MARSHALL, C. S., Tpr. C Sqd., 3 L.H.	A.A.S.C. Motor Transport	6/12/17 1y 10m. Dvr.
MARSHALL, D. B., Pte. M.G. Sec., 40 Bn.	2W.	13/ 3/16 3y 7m. Cpl.
MARSHALL, D. R., Pte. 12 Bn.	W.	7/ 2/15 1y 3m. Pte.
MARSHALL, E., Pte. 40 Bn.	✻ 30/9/17	30/ 9/16. Pte. ✻
MARSHALL, E. W., Pte. 12 Bn.	52 Bn. ✻ 19/10/17.	11/ 1/13 Pte. ✻
MARSHALL, E. A. B., Pte. 26 Bn.	2W. 12 Bn. ✻ 10/4/17.	10/ 8/15 Pte. ✻
MARSHALL, C. W., Sgt. 40 Bn.	W.	24/ 1/16. Lieut.
MARSHALL, H., Pte. 26 Bn.		17/ 6/15.
MARSHALL, A. M., Pte. 15 Bn.	P.O.W.	6/10/14 4y 8m. Lieut.
MARSHALL, J. G., Pte. 3 G.S.R.		3/ 6/13
MARSHALL, J. H., Pte. 26 Bn.	✻ 5/8/16.	6/ 5/15. Sgt. ✻
MARSHALL, W. S. J., Pte. 15 Bn.		18/10/15 4y 2m. Pte.
MARSHALL, K. P., Tpr 3 L.H.		9/12/14 4y 9m. Sgt.
MARSHALL, L. L., Gnr. F.A. Rfts.	13 F.A.B. ✻ 21/8/17.	23/ 2/16. Gnr. ✻
MARSHALL, L., Pte. 40 Bn.		7/ 6/16 3y 2m. Pte.
MARSHALL, N. G., Dvr. 3 F.A.B.	3 L.H Regt. Dtls.	12/10/14 4y 7m. L. Cpl.
MARSHALL, P. C., Pte. 4 M.G. Co	2W. M.M., 22 A.M.G. Coy.	17/ 7/16 3y. Pte.
MARSHALL, R. D., Pte. 12 Bn.	52 Bn. 3 LH.	17/ 1/16 3y 7m. Tpr.
MARSHALL, S. A. G., Pte. 40 Bn.	W. ✻ 13/10/17.	31/ 1/16. Pte. ✻
MARSHALL, T. J., Pte. 2 A.G.H.	W. 3 Fld. Amb. 12 Bn.	2/8/15 2y 8m. Pte.
MARSHALL, V. C., Pte. 26 Bn.	✻ 26/9/15.	22/ 4/15. Pte. ✻
MARSHALL, W. C., Pte. 40 Bn.	W.	7/ 4/15 5y 5m. Pte.
MARSHALL, W. F., Pte. 6 Bn.		14/11/17 2y Pte.
MARSHALL, W. E., Pte. 1 G.S.R.		12/ 2/18 1y 4m. Pte.
MARTIN, A. C., Pte. 12 Bn.	W.	29/ 8/14 Sgt.
MARTIN, A. J., Pte. 12 Bn.	W. 52 Bn. 51 Bn.	11/ 1/16 3y 4m. Dvr.
MARTIN, A. V., Pte. 40 Bn.	2W.	6/10/15 2y 6m. Pte.
MARTIN, C. E., Gnr. Fld. Art.	2 Div. H.Q., 17 Bty., 6 F.A.B.	14/ 1/17 2y 8m. Gnr.
MARTIN, C. L., Pte. Rly. Unit	16 L.R. Op. Sec.	30/ 4/17 1y 6m. Spr.
MARTIN, E. R., Pte. 15 Bn.	✻ 6/5/15.	17/ 9/14. Pte. ✻
MARTIN, E. Pte. 40 Bn.	✻ 1/4/18.	14/11/16. Pte. ✻
MARTIN, E. S., Pte. 12 Bn.	✻ 19/10/17.	27/ 5/15. Cpl. ✻
MARTIN, E. C. W., Gnr. Fld. At.	4W. 29 Bty., 8 F.A.B	5/ 1/15 3y 9m. Gnr.
MARTIN, E. C., Tpr. 3 L.H.		3/ 2/15 4y 1m. Dvr.
MARTIN, E. J., Pte. 40 Bn.		29/ 3/16 2y 3m. Pte.
MARTIN, G. W., Gnr. 18 Bty., 6 Bde.	2W.	6/8/15 4y 1m. 2 Lieut.
MARTIN, G. A., Pte. 15 Bn.	1 Pioneers. ✻ 8/8/15.	21/ 1/15. Pte. ✻
MARTIN, G. W., Pte. 12 Bn.	✻ 3/8/16.	24/ 8/15 Pte. ✻
MARTIN, H., Pte. 12 Bn.		14/11/15. 2y 5m. Pte.
MARTIN, L, Spr. 3 Fd. Co.	1 Div. Engrs. Dtls.	17/ 8/14 5y 1m. Spr.
MARTIN, H. P., Pte. 4 M.G. Co.		16/ 9/16.
MARTIN, J. B., Pte. 12 Bn.	W.	16/ 9/16 1y 5m. Pte.
MARTIN, J., Pte. 12 Bn.	✻ 24/8/18. 40 Bn.	10/10/16. Pte. ✻
MARTIN, J. R., Sap. Mnrs. 3 Co.	Tun. Coy Dtls	17/ 5/16 2y 2m. Spr.
MARTIN, J. H., Pte. 40 Bn.	✻ 30/8/18.	28/ 9/16. Pte. ✻
MARTIN, J. P., Pte. 12 Bn.	W.	21/ 3/17 2y 8m. Pte.
MARTIN, J., Pte. 4 M.G. Coy.	12 M.G Coy.	30/ 9/13.

NAME.	REMARKS.	RANK ON DISCHARGE. ENLISTED. SERVICE.
MARTIN, L., Spr., 3 Fd. Co.		17/ 8/14 4y 7m. Spr.
MARTIN, M. Z., Gnr. Fld. Arty.		18/ 1/16.
MARTYN, R. E., Gnr. 3 F.A.B.	24 How. Bde., 24 F.A.B., 10 Bty., 37 Bty.	14/ 9/15 3y 11m. Dvr.
MARTIN, R., Pte. 40 Bn.	W.	21/ 9/16 1y 2m. Pte.
MARTIN, S. C., Gnr. 6 F.A.B.	W.	28/ 8/15 4y. Cpl.
MARTIN, V. B., Pte. 12 Bn	52 Bn. ✣ 19/1/17.	13/ 1/16. Pte. ✣
MARTIN, W. J., Pte. 12 Bn.	W.	15/ 9/16.
MARTIN, W. P., Pte. 12 Bn.	✣ 6-10/4/17.	3/ 5/16. Pte. ✣
MARTIN, W. L., Pte. 12 Bn.	2W. M.C. and Bar, 3 M.G.C., 21 M.G.C.	22/ 8/14 4y 10m. Lieut.
MARTIN, W., Pte. 40 Bn.	W.	20/ 6/16 1y 11m. Pte.
MARTION, P., Spr. Tunlrs.		4/ 4/17
MARTYN, H., Pte. 40 Bn.		27/11/16 1y. Pte.
MARTYN, J. T., Pte. 40 Bn.		26/ 6/16 1y 8m. Pte.
MARVELL, C. R., Pte. 40 Bn.	✣ 22/6/17.	14/ 5/16. Pte. ✣
MARVELL, W. C., Pte. 40 Bn.	2W. ✣ 7/6/17.	14/ 5/16. Pte. ✣
MASON, A. W., Pte. 12 Bn.		3/ 1/18 11m. Pte.
MASON, C., Pte. A.F.A.	Div. Amm. Col. 4 Fld. Bky, 1 Fld. Bky.	29/ 1/15 4y 9m. Pte.
MASON, F. I., Pte. 12 Bn.	52 Bn., 24 How. Bde., 10 F.A.B.	5/ 7/15 3y 9m. Dvr.
MASON, G., Pte. 4 M.G. Coy.	15 M.G. Coy.	8/10/16 2y 1m. Pte.
MASON, G. B., Pte. 40 Bn.	✣ 6/10/17.	5/10/16. Pte. ✣
MASON, G. C., Pte. 12 Bn.	52 Bn.	26/ 5/15 2y 9m. Pte.
MASON, G. T., Pte. 12 Bn.	1 Pnr Coy., Aust. G.H.Q.	15/ 8/15 4y 1m. Pte.
MASON, I. S., Pte. 12 Bn	W. 40 Bn.	22/ 3/16 2y. Pte.
MASON, L. S., Pte. 40 Bn.		10/ 5/16 1y 5m. Pte.
MASON, R. E., Pte. 12 Bn.	52 Bn. ✣ 4/9/16.	9/ 7/15. Pte. ✣
MASON, R. L., Pte. 12 Bn.		20/10/14 7m. Pte.
MASON, R. L., Pte. 12 Bn.	W.	10/ 5/16 1y 7m. Pte.
MASON, R. J., Pte. 40 Bn.	3W.	9/ 3/16.
MASON, R. M'D., Pte. 12 Bn.		3/ 6/15 3y 6m. Pte.
MASON, R. C., Pte. 12 Bn.	40 Bn.	19/10/16 2y 11m. Pte.
MASON, R. St. C., Pte. 12 Bn.	✣ 19-20/9/17.	25/10/15. Pte. ✣
MASON, W. H., Pte. 12 Bn.		10/ 2/15 1y 5m. Pte.
MASON, W. H., Pte. 40 Bn.	2W., M.G. Dtls., 9 M.G. Co.	28/ 2/15 3y 8m. Pte.
MASON, W. D., Far. Cpl., 3 L.H.	W.	19/ 8/14 4y 1m. Sgt.
MASON, W. J., S. Sgt. 3 Fld Amb		25/ 8/14 2y 3m. S. Sgt.
MASSEY, H. E. M., Sec. Lt. 12 Bn.	52 Bn. ✣ 3/9/16.	22/ 8/14 Capt.
MASSEY, C. J., Sgt. Bglr., 12 Bn.		20/ 8/14 3y 5m. Cpl.
MASSEY, E. H., Gnr. Fld. Art.	W. 29 Bty., 8 Fld. Art.	26/ 9/15 4y Dvr.
MASSEY, E., Spr. 8 F.C. Engrs.	W., MT. Service, 1 Fld. Co. Engrs.	5/ 2/16 3y 7m. Spr.
MASSEY, W. E. G., Pte. 26 Bn.	W.	10/ 8/15 2y 7m. Pte.
MASTERMAN, K. C., Pte. 40 Bn.	P.G.W.	27/ 8/17.
MASTERS, E. G., Pte. 12 Bn.	✣ 25/7/18.	17/11/16. Pte. ✣
MASTERS, H. H., Pte. 40 Bn.	2W.	17/ 5/16 3y 8m. Pte.
MASTERS, J. A., Pte. 12 Bn.		21/ 6/17 2y 4m. Pte.
MASTERS, J. T., Pte. 40 Bn.	✣ 3/1/17.	17/ 5/16. Pte. ✣
MASTERTON, C., Pte. 15 Bn.	W.	4/ 9/15 4y 1m. CQMS.
MASTERTON, O. C., Pte. 12 Bn.	51 Bn., 52 Bn.	2/10/15 3y 10m. Pte.
MATHERS, A. P., Pte. 12 Bn.	W.	29/ 8/14 3y, Pte.
MATHERS, D. A., Pte. 15 Bn.	W.	20/ 5/15 3y 9m. Pte.
MATHERS, F., Gnr. Fld. Arty.	2W. 25 F.A.B., 1 D.A.C., 1 F.A.B.	18/10/15 2y 9m. Gnr.
MATHERS, H. C., Pte. 40 Bn.	3W.	22/ 2/16 3y 2m. Pte.
MATHERS, K., Pte. 26 Bn.	W. 9 Bn., 26 Bn.	29/ 4/15 5y 4m. Pte.
MATHER, S. E. J., Gnr. A.F.A.		23/ 9/15 4y 1m. Dvr.
MATHIESON, L., Pte. 12 Bn.	W. 52 Bn.	22/ 8/14 3y 1m. Pte.
MATHESON, M., Pte. 12 Bn	W. ✣ 6-10/4/17.	20/ 8/14. Sgt. ✣
MATHESON, N., Pte. 15 Bn	W. ✣ 29/5/15.	29/ 9/14 Pte. ✣
MATHESON, W. T., Pte. 15 Bn.	✣ 31/5/15.	24/ 9/14. Pte. ✣
MATHEWS, A. G., Pte. 26 Bn.		1/ 3/15 3y 1m. Dvr.
MATHEWS, B., Pte. 12 Bn.	3W. 52 Bn.	5/ 8/15.
MATHEWS, C., Pte. 4 M.G. Coy.	40 Bn. ✣ 26/10/18.	8/ 1/17. Pte. ✣
MATTHEWS, C. G., Pte. 3 G.S.R.	12 Bn. ✣ 29/1/19.	5/ 8/18. Pte. ✣
MATTHEWS, C W. V., Pte. 40 Bn.	2W.	4/10/16 3y 1m. Pte.
MATHEWS, E. J., Pte. M.G. Co.	W. 15 Bn., 4 M.G.B., 6 M.G. Bn.	28/ 8/17 1y 7m. Pte.
MATTHEWS, E. L., Pte. 12 Bn.	W. ✣ 22/2/17.	18/ 1/15. Pte. ✣
MATHEWS, H. H., Pte. 12 Bn.	52 Bn. ✣ 4/9/16.	5/10/15. Pte. ✣
MATTHEWS, J. F. L., Pte. 1 A.C.H.		29/11/14.
MATHEW, J. T., Gnr. 3 Fld. Art.	1 M.T. Coy.	10/ 3/15 4y 3m. Dvr.
MATHEWS, J. W., Pte. 12 Bn.	W. 52 Bn., 51 Bn.	7/ 1/15 4y 5m. Pte.
MATTHEWS, F. J., Pte. 12 Bn.		25/ 8/15 4y 3m Cpl.
MATTHEWS, L. O., Pte. 15 Bn.	4 M. Gun Coy.	23/ 9/14 4y 5m. Dvr.
MATTHEWS, L. V., Pte. 1 GSR		15/ 1/18.
MATTHEWS, L. C., Pte. 12 Bn.		8/11/15.
MATTHEWS, R. T., A.-Sgt. A.F.A.	2 D.A.C.	14/10/15 2y. Sgt.
MATHEWS, W. E., Pte. 12 Bn.	✣ 26/8/16.	5/ 1/16. Pte. ✣
MATTHEWS, W. I., Gnr. 2 G.S.R.	4 D.A.C.	11/ 6/18 1y 3m. Gnr.
MATHEWSON, W. C., Pte. 12 Bn.	2W.	9/ 6/15 3y 3m. Pte.
MATSON, F., Pte. A.S.C.	Aust. M.D.T.	29/ 8/17 2y 5m. Dvr.
MATSON, H. S., Pte. 40 Bn.	2W.	3/10/16 2y 11m. Pte.
MATTEI, C., Capt. 1 A.C.H.	5 D. San. Sctn., 1 San. Sctn.	17/ 9/14 5y 3m. Lt.-Col
MATZEN, A., Pte. 12 Bn.		1/ 6/16 1y 6m. Pte.
MATZEN, A. N., Pte. 12 Bn	✣ 6/10/17.	1/ 6/16. Pte. ✣
MAUMILL, J. H., Pte. 12 Bn.	W. 48 Bn., 47 Bn. P.O.W.	22/ 7/15.
MAUMILL, L. J., Gnr. 3 Fld. Art.	M.M. Aus. M.T.M. Bty.	11/ 8/15 3y 8m. Cpl.
MAUSER, A. V., Pte. 12 Bn.		12/10/16 2y 5m. Pte.
MAWBEY, N., Pte. A.A.M.C.		1/ 2/17 2y 5m. Pte.
MAWSEY, W. N., Pte. 7 Fld. Amb.	W.	15/ 3/15 4y 1m. Pte.
MAWER, L. K., Dvr. 111 How. By.		28/12/14 4y 8m. Dvr.

TASMANIA'S MUSTER ROLL. 309

NAME.	REMARKS.	RANK ON DISCHARGE. ENLISTED. SERVICE.
MAWER, P., Pte. 1 Cmd. Depot.	15 Bn.	16/11/14 4y 9m. Pte.
MAWER, S. J. H., Tpr.	W. 12 Bn.	20/ 8/14 3y 10m. Pte.
MAWER, W., Pte. 15 Bn.	23 Bn.	7/12/14. Pte.
MAWSON, P., Pte. 12 Bn.	✠ 11/8/18.	15/ 7/15. L. Cpl. ✠
MAXFIELD, C. E., Pte. 12 Bn.	✠ 10/8/15.	24/ 3/15. Pte. ✠
MAXFIELD, F. J., Pte. 40 Bn.	W.	16/ 5/16 2y. Pte.
MAXFIELD, J. P., Pte. 40 Bn.	2W.	9/ 3/16 2y 1m. Pte.
MAXFIELD, W. E., Pte. 40 Bn.	W.	17/10/16 1y 11m. Pte.
MAXFIELD, W. G., Pte. 40 Bn.	W.	16/ 5/16 2y 2m. Pte.
MAYHEAD, K. W., Gnr. 36 HAG.	W.	10/ 6/15 3y 2m. Gnr.
MAYNARD, C. W. L., Pte. 12 Bn.		14/12/15.
MAYNARD, E. L., Pte 15 Bn	✠ 8/8/15.	21/ 5/15. Pte. ✠
MAYNARD, F., Pte. 26 Bn.	✠ 13/8/16.	2/ 5/15. Pte. ✠
MAYNARD, J. H. P., Pte. 12 Bn.	W.	20/ 9/16 3y 1m. Pte.
MAYNARD, L. V., Pte. 12 Bn.		17/ 6/15 1y 10m. Pte.
MAYNARD, R. L., Pte. 12 Bn.	W.	21/ 7/15 3y 2m. Pte.
MAYNARD, W. S., Pte. 12 Bn.	✠ 6-10/4/17.	19/ 6/16. Pte. ✠
MAYNE, H., Pte. 40 Bn.		1/ 3/16 3y 5m. Pte.
MAYNE, L. A., Pte. 12 Bn.	52 Bn. ✠ 4/9/16.	4/ 8/15. Pte. ✠
MAYNE, R. H., Pte. 12 Bn.		31/10/16 3y. Pte.
MAYS, E. H., Gnr. 3 F.A.B.		15/9/15.
MAYSON, A., Pte. 12 Bn.	40 Bn.	15/ 2/17 2y 2m. Pte.
MAZEY, G. H. A., Pte. 12 Bn.	52 Bn. ✠ 4/9/16.	20/ 9/15. Pte. ✠
MAZEY, L. W., Pte. 40 Bn.	✠ 13/10/17.	3/10/16. Pte. ✠
MAZEY, R., Pte. 12 Bn.	W.	22/ 8/16 1y 11m. Pte.
MAXWELL, D. L., Pte. 26 Bn.	W., 12 Bn. ✠ 5-8/5/17.	14/ 8/15. Pte. ✠
MAXWELL, F. G., Pte. 4 M.G.C.	2 M.G. Bn.	13/ 2/17 2y 9m. Pte.
MAXWELL, G. S., Pte. 12 Bn.	28 Bn. ✠ 1/6/18.	3/ 1/16. Cpl. ✠
MAXWELL, D. S., Tpr. 3 L.H.	M.C., 51 Bn., 52 Bn., Div. H.Q.	19/ 8/14.
MAXWELL, J., Pte. 12 Bn.		4/11/16.
MAXWELL, J. A., Pte. 26 Bn.	✠ 10/9/16.	24/ 2/15 Pte. ✠
MAXWELL, T. J., Tpr. 3 L.H.		24/ 8/14 2y 3m. Tpr.
MAXWELL, W. J., Pte 12 Bn.	W.	10/ 1/15 1y 5m. Pte.
MEAD, A. E., Pte. 2 Wireless Sq.	L.M., W. Sec.	18/10/16 2y 8m. Pte.
MEAD, F. M., Cpl. 2 G.S.R.	A.A.P.C.	19/11/17 1y 11m. Pte.
MEAD, V. S., Tpr. 3 L.H.	3 A.M.C.S.	5/10/17 2y 1m. Tpr.
MEAD, W. H., Cpl. 40 Bn.	2W.	30/ 3/16 2y 8m. Cpl.
MEANY, T. J., Pte. 40 Bn.	W.	17/ 3/16 3y 6m. Pte.
MEARS, A. A., Pte. 12 Bn.	2W., M.M., 3 Inf. Bde. H.Q. ✠ 7/3/19.	19/ 8/14. Pte. ✠
MEARS, C. W., Pte. 12 Bn.	✠ 17/2/17.	25/10/15. Pte. ✠
MEARS, L. G., Gnr. Fld. Art.		12/12/14 4y 6m. Gnr.
MEDCRAFT, O. W., Pte. 12 Bn.	✠ 6-10/4/17.	18/ 9/16. Pte. ✠
MEDHURST, P. A., Gnr. 2 Bty.	W. M.M.	27/ 8/14 4y 6m. Bdr.
MEDHURST, T. W., Gnr. 6 F.A.B.	1 F.A.B.	15/11/15 4y. Gnr.
MEDHURST, V. G., Gnr. 3 F.A.B.	W. 4 Div. Arty., 37 Bty.	27/ 8/14 3y 6m. Cpl.
MEDWIN A. S., Pte. 12 Bn.	52 Bn. Fld. Butchery.	18/ 7/15 4y 5m. Cpl.
MEDWIN, P. R. E., Pte. 40 Bn.	✠ 1/10/18.	3/10/16. Pte. ✠
MEE, W. W., Gnr. 1 G.S.R.	112 How. Bty.	1/ 3/18 1y 8m. Gnr.
MEERS, A. F., Pte. 40 Bn.	2W.	15/ 2/16 2y 8m. Pte.
MEERS, A. P., Pte. A.A.M.C.	9 Fd. Amb.	14/11/16 2y 8m. Pte.
MEERS, J. H., Pte. 12 Bn.	W., M.M., 52, 51 Bn.	4/ 8/15 4y. Pte.
MEHEGAN, F., Pte. 40 Bn.		14/ 3/16 3y 10m. Pte.
MEIKLE, H., Pte. 12 Bn.		22/ 8/16 3y 4m. Pte.
MEIKLE, W. M., Pte. 12 Bn.		25/ 8/14 2y. Pte.
MENNIE, L. S., Pte 40 Bn.	W 15 Bn., 40 Bn.	5/ 3/16 2y 4m. Pte.
MENHITZ, W. F., Pte. 40 Bn.	W., 9 M.G. Co.	28/ 9/16 2y 2m. Pte.
MENZIE, F. B., Pte. 12 Bn.	✠ 7/9/17.	12/ 6/16 Pte. ✠
MENZIE, R., Pte. 12 Bn.	W.	6/10/16 4y Pte.
MENZIES, S. F., Pte. Rmt. Sec.		20/ 9/15 1y 3m. Pte.
MERCHANT, W. L., Pte. 1 A.C.H.		24/ 3/15
MERKULSKI, J. B., Dvr. 3 F.A.		14/ 6/15
MERRICK, J. S., Pte. 12 Bn.	W. 40 Bn.	15/ 5/17 2y 3m. Pte.
MERRICK, J. S., Pte. 15 Bn.		30/ 6/15 10m. Pte.
MERWIN, S. F., Dvr. 3 Fd. Amb.	W. ✠ June, 1915.	26/ 8/14 Dvr. ✠
MESSENER, M. A., Pte. 12 Bn.	W. ✠ 20/7/18.	19/ 6/16 Pte. ✠
MESSNER, O. C., Pte. 12 Bn.	W.	19/ 6/16 3y. Pte.
METCALF, L. J., Pte. 40 Bn.	W. ✠ 7/6/17.	15/ 5/16 Pte. ✠
METCALFE, W. E., Tpr. 3 L.H.	Art. Details, 2 D.A.C.	3/ 4/17
METSER, P., Spr 6 Fd. Art.	6 Engrs., 13 Fd. Co. Engrs.	11/ 8/15 2y 1m. Spr.
MEYER, B. R., Tpr. 3 L.H.		17/10/16 3y. Tpr.
MICHAEL, H. W., Pte. 12 Bn.	✠ 15/4/17.	4/ 8/16 Pte. ✠
MICHALL, W., Pte. R. Unit.	W., A.L.R.O.C.	24/ 1/17 1y 6m. Spr.
MIDDAP, H. J., Spr. 4 S.M.C.		14/ 1/16 2y 8m. Spr.
MIDDAP, J. K., Spr. 4 S.M.C.	5 Tun. Co., 2 Tun. Co.	10/ 2/16 3y 5m. Spr.
MIDSON, F. G., Pte. 12 Bn.	W. ✠ 6/10/17.	9/ 9/16 Pte. ✠
MIDSON, T., Gnr. 2 G.S.R.		3/ 6/18 1y 3m. Gnr.
MIDWOOD, E., Gnr. Fd. Art.	3 D.A.C.	14/ 2/16 1y. Gnr.
MIKKELSON, W., Pte. 40 Bn.	69 Bn., 40 Bn.	17/ 1/16 3y 2m. Lieut.
MILBOURNE, H L., Pte. 40 Bn.	2W. ✠ 28/3/18.	17/ 5/6 L./Cpl. ✠
MILBOURNE, J D., Pte. 15 Bn.	W. ✠ 3/5/15.	8/10/14 Pte. ✠
MILBOURNE, S., Pte. 40 Bn.	A.M.C. Details, 7 Fd. Amb.	18/11/16
MILES, A. C., Gnr. Fd. Art.	8 F.A.B., 29 Battery.	5/ 1/16 3y 8m. Dvr.
MILES, G., Pte 15 Bn.		12/12/14 Pte.
MILES, G., Pte. 12 Bn.	Aust. Employ Coy., 12 Bn.	11/10/15 2y 11m. Pte.
MILES, G., Pte 12 Bn.	✠ 16/2/17.	13/ 9/15 Pte. ✠
MILES, H. A., Pte 12 Bn.	A. Prov. Corps.	9/ 2/15 4y 9m. Pte.
MILES, K. G., Gnr. 3 F.A.B.	9 Bty.	11/ 8/15 3y 11m. Gnr.

310   TASMANIA'S WAR RECORD, 1914-1918.

NAME.	REMARKS.	RANK ON DISCHARGE. ENLISTED, SERVICE.
MILES, T. A., Pte. 12 Bn.	M.C., T.M. Bty.	27/ 8/14 Lieut.
MILES, F. F., Pte. 15 Bn.	W.	7/ 9/15 3y 11m. Pte.
MILLAR, R. M., Capt. A.A.P.C.		21/ 9/14 1y 11m. Capt.
MILLAR, A. G., Pte. 58 Bn., alias Millar, G. D.	W.	17/ 1/18 1y 2m. Pte.
MILLAR, D., Pte. 2 G.S.R.	13 F.A.B.	13/ 5/18
MILLAR, F. H., Pte. Wireless		6/11/16 2y 5m. Spr.
MILLAR, F. W., A./Sgt. F. Art.	29 Bty.	31/ 8/16 3y 2m. Bdr.
MILLAR, H. C. L., Dvr. 6 F.A.B.	A. Prov. Corps.	16/ 9/15 4y 2m. Dvr.
MILLAR, W. J., Pte. 12 Bn.		8/ 6/17 2y 4m. Pte.
MILLARD, J., Dvr. F.A.R.	3 F.A.B.	7/12/14
MILLEN, C. J., Pte. 15 Bn.	✣ 8/8/15.	24/ 9/14 Pte. ✣
MILLER, A. H., Pte. 40 Bn.	W.	11/ 8/15 3y 1m. W.Q.C.
MILLER, A. S., Spr. Tun. Co.	A.B.R. Co., A.G. Base Depot.	13/10/16 3y Pte.
MILLER, B., Gnr. Fd. Art.	W., 5 F.A.B., 15 Bty., 25 Bn.	28/10/15 3y 2m. Cpl.
MILLER, C. A. J., Pte. 40 Bn.	W.	30/ 9/16
MILLER, D., Pte. 12 Bn.	W.	31/ 5/16 2y 10m. Pte.
MILLER, F. R., Pte. 12 Bn.	W., M.M.	28/ 8/14 4y 7m. Sgt.
MILLER, F. R., Pte. 15 Bn.	2W.	16/12/14 4y 6m. Pte.
MILLER, G. E., Pte. 12 Bn.	52 Bn. ✣ 4/9/16.	12/ 1/15 Pte. ✣
MILLER, G. R., Gnr. Fd. Art.	W. A.I.F. Depot, Hdqrs.	17/ 1/16 3y 8m. Gnr.
MILLER, H. S., Spr. 6 F.A.B.	6 Engrs., 2 Rfts.	4/ 9/15 2y 6m. Spr.
MILLER, J., Pte. 26 Bn.	W.	2/ 9/15 3y 6m. Pte.
MILLER, J. T., Sgt. Fd. Art.	15 F.A.B., 2 Div L.T.M.B., 11 Bty.	14/ 2/16 3y 7m. Sgt.
MILLER, J. W., Pte. 12 Bn.	✣ 25-28/4/15.	19/10/14 Pte. ✣
MILLER, J., Pte. 26 Bn.	W. 4 Pnr. Bn.	20/ 3/15 4y, Pte.
MILLER, U. V., Pte. 4 M.G. Co.	12 Bn. ✣ 23/8/18.	10/ 2/17 Pte. ✣
MILLER, R., Pte. 15 Bn.	✣ 8/8/16.	29/ 6/15 Pte. ✣
MILLER, S., Pte. 12 Bn.		29/12/17.
MILLER, T., Tpr. 1 G.S.R., A.M.D.		30/ 4/18 1y 8m. Tpr.
MILLER, T. J., Pte. 40 Bn.		31/ 5/16 1y 11m. Pte.
MILLER, T. R., Sgt. 12 Bn.	W. M.C.	15/ 7/15 4y 3m. Lt.
MILLER, W. T., A./Sgt. 40 Bn.		18/10/16
MILLER, W., Pte. Tun. Coy.	2 Pioneers.	2/ 9/16 1y 5m. Pte.
MILLER, W., Tpr. 1 Rmt. Unit.		23/11/15 1y 1m. Tpr.
MILLER, W. C., Pte. 12 Bn.		23/10/16 3y 2m. Pte.
MILLER, W. C., Gnr. 3 F. Art.		27/ 8/14
MILLER, W. J., Pte. 40 Bn.		24/ 2/16
MILLER, W. J., Pte. 26 Bn.	2W.	12/ 5/15 3y 11m. Pte.
MILLER, W. J., Pte. 12 Bn.	W.	20/ 8/14 2y 5m. Pte.
MILLER, W. T., Gnr. 9 Bt., 3 F.A.	W. 4 Div. Art., 10 F.A.B.	27/ 8/14 4y 6m. Sgt.
MILLHOUSE, C., Pte. 12 Bn.	W. ✣ 6-10/4/17.	3/ 9/14 A./Sgt. ✣
MILLHOUSE, H., Pte. 15 Bn.	✣ 9/8/15.	30/ 9/14 Pte. ✣
MILLHOUSE, J., Pte. 2 G.S.R.	7 F.A.B.	16/ 5/13 1y 6m. Gnr.
MILLHOUSE, L. E. H., Pte. 12 Bn.		Pte.
MILLINGTON, A. E., Dvr. 3 F.A.B.		7/10/14 3y 5m. Gnr.
MILLINGTON, C. O., Pte. 2 G.S.R.	39 Bty.	20/ 2/18 1y 7m. Gnr.
MILLINGTON, C. A., Pte. 12 Bn.		24/10/15
MILLINGTON, J. E. G., A/Cpl. 12 Bn.	W.	3/ 7/16 1y 4m. A./Cpl.
MILLINGTON, J. H., Pte. 40 Bn.	✣ 30/1/17.	21/ 2/16 Pte. ✣
MILLINGTON, T., Pte. 26 Bn.		23/ 4/15 4y 7m. Pte.
MILLS, A. R., Sec. Lt. 40 Bn.	W.	8/ 3/16 3y 6m. Lt.
MILLS, C., Lt. 3 L.H.		20/ 8/14
MILLS, C. U. A., Pte. 12 Bn.		17/ 8/14 1y 10m. Pte.
MILLS, C. S., Pte. 26 Bn.	12 Bn., 1 Div. Hd. Qrs. ✣ 16/2/19.	28/ 7/15 L./Sgt. ✣
MILLS, C. M. Gnr. 18 Bty. F.A.	D.C.M., 17 Bty.	28/ 9/15 2y 11m. Sgt.
MILLS, E. A., Pte. 12 Bn.	W.	16/10/16 2y 6m. Pte.
MILLS, E. H., Pte. 12 Bn.	2W. ✣ 17/4/18.	8/12/14 Cpl. ✣
MILLS, E. N., Pte. C. Sqd. 3 L.H.	Re-enlisted M. Workers.	26/ 8/14 2y Tpr.
MILLS, G. A., Cpl. Postal Cps.		21/10/15 2y 5m. Sgt.
MILLS, H., Pte. 40 Bn.	2W.	28/ 7/16 3y 1m. Pte.
MILLS, J. R., Gnr. Siege Bde.		29/12/16 2y 8m. Gnr.
MILLS, K. D., Pte. 40 Bn.	49 Bn. ✣ 10/4/18.	20/ 4/16 Pte. ✣
MILLS, L. W., Gnr. 9 Bty. 3 F.A.B.	11 F.A.B., D.H.A.	21/ 7/15 4y 1m. Gnr.
MILLS, W. T., Pte. 15 Bn.		7/ 1/15 1y 7m. Pte.
MILNE, S. C., Pte. 40 Bn.		22/ 9/17 1y 6m. Pte.
MILNE, T., Pte. 40 Bn.	49 Bn.	26/ 4/16 3y 5m. Dvr.
MILNE, W. B., Pte. 26 Bn.	2W.	20/ 7/15
MILNER, C N., Gnr. F. Art.		15/ 9/15
MILNER, E., Sgt. 26 Bn.	2W.	21/ 2/15 4y 8m. Lt.
MINAHAN, W. T., Pte. 26 Bn.	W.	19/ 2/15 2y 9m. Pte.
MINCHIN, C. R., Gnr. Fd. Art.	M.M., 120 How. Bde., 13 F.A.B	15/ 3/16 3y 7m. Gnr.
MINCHIN, J. W., Pte. 2 A.F. Squa		11/ 4/16 3y 4m. 2-A.M.
MINTY, B., Pte. 4 M.G. Co.		15/11/16
MIRRLEES, W. McK., Pte. 40 Bn.	W.	3/ 2/16 3y 7m. Pte.
MITCHELL, A. C., L./Cpl. 12 Bn.	W. 52 Bn., 51 Bn.	4/ 1/16 3y 2m. S.S. M.
MITCHELL, A. F., Pte. 40 Bn.	✣ 14/2/17.	3/ 3/16 Pte. ✣
MITCHELL, C. J., Pte. 12 Bn.	2W.	20/ 8/14 4y 6m. Pte.
MITCHELL, C., Tpr. 3 L.H.		22/10/17 1y 5m. Tpr.
MITCHELL, C. E. S., Pte. A.A.H.	M.M.	5/10/15 4y. Lieut.
MITCHELL, C. C., A-Cpl. Rail.Unit.	4 A.G.B., R.O.C.	14/12/16 2y 8m. 2-Cpl.
MITCHELL, H. J., Pte. 40 Bn.	2W.	27/ 3/16 3y 8m. L.-Cpl.
MITCHELL, H. J., Pte. 40 Bn.	W.	3/ 3/16 3y 8m. Pte.
MITCHELL, J. A., Pte. 12 Bn.		28/ 6/15 4y 3m. L.-Sgt.
MITCHELL, J., Pte. 12 Bn.	✣ 25/7/16.	4/ 8/15 Pte. ✣
MITCHELL, R., Pte. 4 M.G. Co.	W.	16/ 9/16 2y 9m. Pte.

TASMANIA'S MUSTER ROLL. 311

NAME.	REMARKS.	RANK ON DISCHARGE. ENLISTED. SERVICE.
MITCHELL, R. G. M., Pte. 15 B	✠ 10/16/16.	13/ 9/15 Pte. ✠
MITCHELL, R. P., Gnr. Fd. Arty.	3 Bty., 3 Div. H. and T.M. Bty. 5 T.M.B.	7/11/16 3y 8m, Sgt.
MITCHELL, S. A., Pte. 12 Bn.	2W.	4/ 8/15 4y 3m, Pte.
MITCHELL, S. J. L., Pte. 12 Bn.	W.	21/ 1/16 1y 4m, Pte.
MITCHELL, T., Pte. 1 Tnl. Coy.		25/ 9/16 2y 6m, Pte.
MITCHELL, T. G., Pte. M.G. Co.	4 M.G. Bn., 23 M.G. Co.	23/ 6/17 2y 4m, Pte.
MITCHELL, T. J., Pte. M.G. Co.	2W, 12 Bn.	1/ 2/16.
MITCHELL, W. A., Pte. 40 Bn.	W., 69 Bn, 49 Bn.	30/ 8/15 4y 1m, Pte.
MITCHELL, W. C., Pte. 12 Bn.	?W., P.O.W.	1/ 7/15 4y 2m, Pte.
MITCHELSON, R., Pte. 40 Bn.		6/ 3/16 1y 1m, Pte.
MITTY, J. E., S.-Sgt. Dental Cps.	A.A. Dental Cps.	7/ 3/16 3y 6m, S.-Sgt.
MOAR, W. D., Pte. 12 Bn.	✠ 25-28/4/15	26/ 8/14 Pte. ✠
MOATE, W. J., Tpr. 3 L.H.		22/ 2/15 1y 6m, Tpr.
MOFFAT, A. J., Pte. Rem. Sec.		14/10/15 8m, Pte.
MOFFAT, K. McA., Pte. 2 G.S.R.		15/ 5/18.
MOGGRIDGE, L. E., Pte. 12 Bn.	W.	31/ 8/14 2y 2m, Pte.
MOIR, D. V., Spr. 13 F.C. Engrs.		10/ 8/15 4y, Spr.
MOIR, W. G., Spr. 12 Bn.	Aust. Cps. H.T.M.B., 3 A.B.A.C.	31/12/15 3y 7m, Cpl.
MOLAN, A. W., Pte. 3 G.S.R.		1/ 7/17 2y 2m, Pte.
MOLES, E., Pte. 15 Bn.	W., M.M.	20/ 3/14 4y 3m, Pte.
MOLES, G. A., Pte. 3 G.S.R.	12 Bn	1/ 8/18 1y 2m, Pte.
MOLES, H., Pte. 26 Bn.	3W.	10/ 5/15 4y 3m, Pte.
MOLES, I., Spr. Miners Rfts.	3 Tnl. Co. ✠ 27/12/16.	7/ 2/16 Gnr. ✠
MOLES, J., Pte. 12 Bn.	W., 52 Bn.	7/10/14 3y 9m, Pte.
MOLES, K., A.-Sgt. 12 Bn.	W. M.M.	5/ 7/16 2y, Pte.
MOLES, L, Pte. 12 Bn.	W., 51 Bn., 12 Bn., A.M.C.	18/ 3/16 3y 3m, Pte.
MOLLER, C. G., Pte. 3 G.S.R.		21/ 5/18.
MOLLINEAUX, E., Gnr. 6 A.F.A.	W., 106 How. Bty.	24/ 9/15 4y 1m, Cpl.
MOLLINEAUX, D., Dvr 23 How. Bde		14/ 1/16 3y 8m, Dvr.
MOLLINEAUX, B., Pte. 15 Bn.	W., 69 Bn., 15 Sig. Co., 4 Sig. Co.	7/12/14 4y 10m, Spr.
MOLLINEAUX, H. W., Spr. 8 Fd. Co. Engrs.	13 Fd. Co. Engrs.	17/ 4/16 3y, Spr.
MOLLISON, R. J., Pte. 12 Bn.	W., 40 Bn.	18/10/16 2y 7m, Pte.
MOLLISON, R., Gnr. Fd. Arty.	6 F.A.B., 16 Bty.	30/ 9/16 3y 1m, Gnr.
MOLLOY, H., Dvr. 3 F.A.B.	W.	19/ 7/15 3y 4m, Gnr.
MOLLOY, J. C., Sig. 12 Bn.	M.M., 52 Bn., 4 Div. Sig Co	27/ 2/15 4y 4m, Spr.
MOLLOY, L, Dvr. 9 Bty. 3 F.A.B.	2W., D.C.M.	27/ 8/14 4y 6m, Cpl.
MOLLOY, W., Pte. 40 Bn.	W., 43 Bn., 40 Bn.	29/ 5/15 3y 3m, Pte.
MOLLROSS, G. L., Pte. 40 Bn.	W.	31/ 1/16 3y 5m, Pte.
MOLLROSS, R. H., Pte. 40 Bn.		15/ 2/16 3y 2m, Pte.
MONAGHAN, J. W., Pte. 40 Bn.	W.	11/10/16 2y 10m, Cpl.
MONCREIFF, E. W., Q.M.S. 1 D.A.C.		1/ 2/16 5y 2m, C.Q.M.S
MONDON, C. A., Pte. 8 Bn.		1/11/16 1y 8m, Pte.
MONK, C. R., A.-Bdr. 3 D.A.C.		22/11/15 2y 8m, Dvr.
MONKS, E P., Spr. 3 Miners.		17/11/15 1y 5m, Spr.
MONKS, O. L., Pte. 12 Bn.	2W., M.M., 26 Bn., 12 Bn.	15/ 3/15 4y, Pte
MONKS, T. J., Cpl. Fd. Bakery.		3/12/14 4y 2m, Cpl.
MONKS, W. T., Pte. 40 Bn.	✠ 1/4/17	23/ 8/15 Pte. ✠
MONSON, C. A., Pte. 2 G.S.R.	40 Bn	12/11/19 Pte.
MONSEN, L. E., Pte. 12 Bn.		11/10/16 1y 3m, Pte.
MONTEATH, E. J., Pte. 26 Bn.	W.	9/ 8/15 4y, Pte.
MONTEATH, G. F., Pte. 4 M.G. Co	11 M.G. Co., 3 M.G. Co.	22/ 7/16 2y 5m, Pte.
MONTEITH, J. F., Pte. 4 M.G. Co.	W.	11/ 9/16 2y 7m, Pte.
MONTGOMERY, A., Pte. 12 Bn.	✠ 1/3/17.	8/ 7/15 Pte. ✠
MONTGOMERY, A. E., Pte. 12 Bn.	W.	5/ 8/15 2y 6m, Pte.
MONTGOMERY, A., Pte. 12 Bn.		22/ 8/14 Pte.
MONTGOMERY, J. F., Pte. 12 Bn.		12/12/14 1y 3m, Pte.
MONTGOMERY, M., Pte. 40 Bn.	✠ 27/1/17.	7/ 1/16 Pte. ✠
MONTGOMERY, R., L.-Sgt. 40 Bn.	69 Bn., 15 Bn.	1/ 7/16 2y 10m, C.Q.M.S.
MONTGOMERY, R., Pte. 15 Bn.	W.	7/10/14 1y 6m, Pte.
		17/ 9/14.
MONTGOMERY, T. W., Pte. 12 Bn.		28/10/14 Pte. ✠
MONTGOMERY, W. D., Pte. 15 Bn	✠ June, 1915	25/10/14 2y 11m, Spr.
MONTGOMERY, W. R., Spr. 3 Tnl. Co.		
MONTRESSOR, C. A., Pte. 40 Bn.	2W.	16/10/16 1y 2m, L.-Cpl.
MONTRESSOR, W. H., Pte. 12 Bn.		14/12/14 1y 9m, Pte.
MOODIE, A. R., Dvr. 6 Fd. Arty.	W.	17/ 8/15 4y 1m, Dvr.
MOODY, E. C., Pte. 12 Bn.	✠ 7/1/19.	2/ 5/16 Pte. ✠
MOODY, J., 12 Bn.		16/10/16.
MOODY, J., Spr. Tnlrs.	1 Tnl. Co. ✠ 13/2/19.	21/11/16 Spr. ✠
MOODY, W., Pte. 12 Bn.		2/ 5/16 3y 2m, Pte.
MOON, G. E. H., Pte. 26 Bn.	40 Bn.	17/ 8/15 4y, Lt.
MOORHOUSE, T., Pte. 3 G.S.R	12 Bn.	3/ 7/12 11m, Pte.
MOORE, H. M. B., Lt. 15 Bn.	W., D.S.O.	24/ 7/15 1y 11m, Capt.
MOORE, S., Lt. 40 Bn.	W.	1/ 5/16 1y 5m, Lt.
MOORE, T. C. B., Lt 12 Bn.	W.	1/ 7/15 1y 10m, Capt
MOORE, A C., Pte. 40 Bn.		18/ 4/17 1y 11m, Pte.
MOCRE, A. J., Gnr. Fld. Art.	W., 14 F.A.B.	10/ 1/16 3y 6m, Gnr.
MOCRE, A. R., P'e. Wireless		22/11/17
MOORE, A. R., P'e. 40 Bn.	51 Bn. ✠ 1/4/17.	14/ 3/16 Pte. ✠
MOORE, B. R., Pte. 15 Bn.	W., M.C., 47 Bn.	21/ 9/14 Lt.
MOORE, C. E. C., Gnr. 6 F.A.B.	W.	11/ 9/15 3y 7m, Cpl.
MOORE, C. E. G., Pte. 26 Bn.	✠ 19-22/8/16.	27/ 7/15 Pte. ✠
MOORE, E. P., Pte. 1 A.C.H.	1 A.C.C.S.	19/ 9/14 2y 9m, Sgt.
MOORE, F. B., Gnr. 18 Bty. 6 Bde.	17 Bty., 18 Bty.	30/ 8/15 3y 8m, Cpl.

NAME.	REMARKS.	RANK ON DISCHARGE. ENLISTED. SERVICE.
MOORE, C. E. B., Mtr. Dvr. Engrs.	5 Fld. Amb., 2 Divl. Supply, 2 A.M.T. Co.	30/ 8/15 4y 2m, M.T. Dvr
MOORE, F., Dvr. A.S.C.	32 Co A.S.C.	15/10/17
MOORE, F. J., Tpr. 3 L.H.		15/ 9/14 4y 5m, Tpr.
MOORE, F. W., Pte 12 Bn.	✠ 15/5/15.	24/ 8/14 Pte. ✠
MOORE—BRETTINGHAM, G. R., A/ Sgt. 40 Bn.		8/ 2/16 3y 5m, 2nd Lt.
MOORE, G. J., Pte. 40 Bn.	15 Bn.	2/ 2/16 1y 9m, Pte.
MOORE, H., Pte. 12 Bn.	✠ 25/8/18.	24/11/16 Pte. ✠
MOORE, H. J., Pte. 4 M.G. Co.	12 Bn., M.G. Bn	13/ 2/17 2y 4m, Pte.
MOORE, H. J., Pte. 1 G.S.R.		22/12/17 1y 6m, Pte.
MOORE, H. J., Pte. 4 M.G. Co.	W., 42 Bn.	17/11/16 2y 2m, Pte.
MOORE, J. L., Dvr.		27/ 8/14 1y 11m, Dvr.
MOORE, J. L., Pte. 3 Cyc.Coy.	2W M.M.	13/ 4/16 3y 1m, Dvr.
MOORE, K. F., Dvr. 3 Fld. Amb.		24/ 8/14 4y 5m, Dvr.
MOORE, L. T., Pte. 3 G.S.R.		10/ 7/18 1y 3m, Pte.
MOORE, L. J., Pte. 12 Bn.	M.G. Bn.	28/10/16 3y, Pte.
MOORE, M. E., Pte. 26 Bn.	3W.	6/ 5/15 4y 1m, Pte.
MOORE, P., Pte. 12 Bn.		28/ 8/16
MOORE, R. E., Gnr. Fld. Art.	2 D.A.C., 2 D.A.C. 5 F.A.B., 2 D.A.C.	19/ 2/16 3y 7m, Dvr.
MOORE, R. L., Cpl. 15 Bn.	2W., M.M. and Bar	24/ 9/14 Lieut.
MOORE, R. C. B., Gnr. Fld. Art.	M.M., 120 How. Bde., 17 Bty. A.F.A.	29/ 2/16 2y, Gnr.
MOORE, S. G., Pte. 12 Bn.		30/ 9/15 2y 10m, Pte.
MOORE, S. E., Pte. 40 Bn.	W.	18/ 4/17 2y 2m, Pte.
MOORE, T. R. J., Pte. 12 Bn.	Fld. Arty. Bde., 110 How. Bty.	9/10/15 3y 10m, Dvr.
MOORE, V. H., Pte. 12 Bn.	Anzac Police, 12 Bn.	15/ 9/15 4y, Pte.
MOORE, W. A., Pte. 15 Bn.		24/ 9/14 4y 4m, Pte.
MOORE, W. C., Pte. 12 Bn.	W.	8/ 2/15 1y 4m, Pte.
MORAN, C. E., Cpl. 40 Bn.		29/ 2/16
MORAN, C. F., Pte. 40 Bn.	✠ 7/6/17.	14/ 3/16 Pte. ✠
MORAN, C., Pte. 40 Bn.	2W., M.M.	2/ 3/16 3y 1m, Pte.
MORAN, D. J., Pte. 40 Bn.	✠ 12/10/17.	31/ 5/16 L.-Cpl. ✠
MORAN, M., Pte. 26 Bn.	4W.	13/ 5/15 3y 11m, Pte.
MORAN, W. H., Spr. 3 Miners.	D.C.M.	28/10/15
MOREY, H. A., Gnr. Fld. Arty.	25 F.A.B., 4 D.A.C., 5 F.A.B.	3/10/16 2y 5m, Gnr.
MOREY, H. H., Pte. 1 A.G.H.	M.M., 14 Fd. Amb. ✠ 1/9/18	8/ 6/15 L.-Cpl. ✠
MOREY, J., Gnr. Fld. Arty.	23 How. Bde., H.Q. 12 F.A.B., 8 F.A.B., 31 Bty.	29/12/15 3y 10m, Cpl.
MOREY, W. S., Pte. 12 Bn.	✠ 7/6/17.	7/ 2/16 Spr ✠
MORGAN, A. E., Lt. 15 Bn.		9/ 9/15
MORGAN, P. J., Lt. 3 F.A.B.	21 How. Bde. ✠ 4/4/17.	14/ 8/14 Major ✠
MORGAN, A. L., Pte. 12 Bn.	W., 4 Div. Arty., 10 F.A.B.	10/12/15 3y 8m, Gnr.
MORGAN, D., Pte. 15 Bn.	✠ 8/8/15.	22/ 4/15 Pte. ✠
MORGAN, D. O., Sgt. 1 A.G.H.		24/ 9/14 4y 4m, S.-Sgt.
MORGAN, F. L., Gnr. Fd Arty.		15/ 2/16 3y 3m, Dvr.
MORGAN, G., Dvr. 3 Fd. Arty.		31/ 5/15 1y 3m, Dvr.
MORGAN, G. W., Pte. 12 Bn	2W., 3 Bde. M.G. Co.	18/ 8/14 4y 5m, Pte.
MORGAN, H. J., Pte. 1 G.S.R.	40 Bn.	5/ 2/18 1y 10m, Pte.
MORGAN, H. A., Tpr. 3 L.H.	W., M.M.	29/ 8/14 5y, Tpr.
MORGAN, H. D., Gnr. 3 F.A.B.	2W.	15/12/14 2y 10m, Gnr.
MORGAN, J. H., Pte. 12 Bn.	W., 52 Bn.	19/ 1/16 1y 6m, Pte.
MORGAN, J., Pte. 12 Bn.		3/ 1/16
MORGAN, J. E., Pte. 4 M.G. Co	W., 10 F.A.B., 4 Div. Arty., 4 D.A.C, 52 Bn 5 Div. M.G. Co., 1 M.G. Co	28/ 7/16 3y 5m, Pte.
MORGAN, L. H., Pte. 40 Bn.	W.	18/ 9/17 1y 6m, Pte.
MORGAN, L. R., Spr. 3 Miners.		18/11/15 3y 9m, Spr.
MORGAN, M., L-Cpl. 40 Bn.	W.	21/ 8/17 1y 10m, L.-Cpl.
MORGAN, M., Pte. 12 Bn.	W	21/ 8/14 2y 5m, Pte.
MORGAN, P. H., Pte. 4 M.G. Co.		16/ 4/17.
MORGAN, R. T., Pte. 12 Bn.		1/ 6/15 4y 2m, Pte.
MORGAN, S. R., Tpr. 3 L.H.	4 D.A.C. ✠ 11/4/17.	20/ 7/15 Tpr. ✠
MORGAN, W., Pte. 40 Bn.	2W.	24/ 4/16 2y 6m, Pte.
MORGAN, W., Pte. 1 G.S.R.		24/ 1/18 1y 9m, Pte.
MORGAN, W. F., Pte. A.F.C.		18/10/16.
MORLEY, A. R. J., Pte. 12 Bn.		12/ 1/16 1y 10m, Pte.
MORLEY, E. W., Sig. 12 Bn.	W., Engrs.' Sig. Det. 4 Co. Engrs.	2/ 7/15 4y 6m, Sig.
MORLEY, G., Dvr. 9 Bty. 3 F.A.		27/ 8/14 4y 6m, Dvr.
MORLEY, H. D., Gnr. Fd. Arty.	2 F.A.B., 6 Bty.	2/10/16 2y 11m, Dvr.
MORLEY, J. W., Dvr. 4 Fd. Co.		1/ 9/15.
MORLEY, S. N., Sgt 9 Bty. 3 F.A.	W., 21 F.A.B., 5 Bty	27/ 8/14 3y 3m, Bdr.
MORLING, J. W., Pte. 15 Bn.	3W.	11/ 1/15 4y 5m, Pte.
MORLING, P. C., Spr. 4 Sec. Engrs.	W.	18/ 8/15
MORLING, W. G., Tpr. Remt. Sec.		19/10/15 1y 2m, Tpr.
MORONEY, L. A., C.S.M. 3 G.S.R.	12 Bn	28/ 3/18 1y 3m, Pte.
MORONEY, M., Pte. 15 Bn.	W., 25 Bn. ✠ 4/10/18.	14/12/14 Pte. ✠
MORRELL, J. E., Tpr. 7 G.S.R.	Anzac M'd. Div. ✠ 24/11/18.	20/ 7/18 Tpr. ✠
MORRIS, A. B., Pte. 40 Bn	✠ 18/7/18.	23/11/16 Pte. ✠
MORRIS, D., Pte. 26 Bn.	2W.	17/ 5/15 3y 11m, Sgt.
MORRIS, E. A., Tpr. 7 G.S.R.	3 L.H.	2/ 5/18 1y 5m, Tpr.
MORRIS, G., Pte. 40 Bn.	✠ 3/1/17	21/ 2/16 L.-Cpl. ✠
MORRIS, G. J., Pte. 26 Bn.	W. 52 Bn.	4/ 5/15 2y 4m, Pte
MORRIS, H. W., Pte. 12 Bn.	2W.	22/ 8/14.
MORRIS, J. W., Pte. 15 Bn.	W. 47 Bn. ✠ 28/3/18	4/ 8/15 Sgt. ✠
MORRIS, J W., Sgt. 12 Bn.	4W.	9/ 1/15 4y 11m, 2nd Lt.
MORRIS, J. A., Pte. 3 G.S.R	12 Bn.	6/ 8/18 1y 2m, Pte.
MORRIS, J. C., Pte. 26 Bn.	✠ 22/9/15.	22/ 4/15 Pte. ✠
MORRIS, J. C., Pte. 12 Bn	W. 52 Bn ✠ 3-4/9/16.	19/ 8/14 Sgt. ✠
MORRIS, O., Cpl. 15 Bn.	47 Bn.	27/ 7/15 2y 3m, C.Q.M.S
MORRIS, R., Dvr. 28 Bn.		4/ 5/15 4y 3m, Dvr.

TASMANIA'S MUSTER ROLL. 313

NAME.	REMARKS.	RANK ON ENLISTED.	DISCHARGE. SERVICE.
MORRIS, R. W., Pte. 26 Bn.	4W.	1/ 3/15	4y 1m, Cpl.
MORRIS, W. C., A.-Cpl. 40 Bn.		2/11/16	2y 5m, Pte.
MORRISBY, E. L., Gnr 6 F.A.B.	4 F.A.B., 6 F.A.B.	17/11/15	3y 10m, Gnr.
MORRISBY, E. A., Pte. 12 Bn.	W., A.M.C., 1 A.D.H.	7/ 1/16	2y 6m, Pte.
MORRISBY, J. G., Pte. 12 Bn.		31/10/17	2y 2m, Pte.
MORRISBY, J. V., Pte. 12 Bn.	A.A.S.C.	17/11/17	2y, Pte.
MORRISBY, P. F., Pte. 15 Bn.	✢ 8/5/15.	10/12/14	Pte. ✢
MORRISON, A. F., Pte. 40 Bn.		14/ 3/15	3y 8m, Pte.
MORRISON, A., Pte. 2 G.S.R.		18/ 4/18.	
MORRISON, D., Pte. 12 Bn.		28/10/15	4y, Pte.
MORRISON, E., Pte. 26 Bn.	2W.	17/ 6/15	1y 10m, Pte.
MORRISON, E. C., Pte. 12 Bn.	D.C.M. and Bar, 52 Bn.	8/ 7/15	3y 8m, Cpl.
MORRISON, H. H., Pte. 2 G.S.R.	A.B. Depot	18/ 4/18	1y 1m, Pte.
MORRISON, H., Cpl. 5 Fld. Amb.		9/ 6/15	4y 4m, Cpl.
MORRISON, J. C. L., Tpr. 3 L.H.	2W.	20/ 7/15	4y 4m, Sgt.
MORRISON, M. J., Sgt 5 Co. Miners	D.C.M.	18/11/15	2y, Sgt.
MORRISON, W. J., Pte. 40 Bn.		21/ 9/17	2y 2m, Pte.
MORRISON, W R., Pte. 12 Bn.	W., 57 Bn.	2/ 9/15	4y 2m, Pte.
MORSE, H. I., Tpr. 3 L.H.	12 Bn. ✢ 26/2/17	21/ 8/14	Tpr. ✢
MORSE, V., Pte. 1 A.G.H.	W.	2/ 6/15	3y 10m, Pte.
MORTIMER, A., Pte. 12 Bn.	W., 69 Br 12 Bn	13/ 7/15	4y 1m, Cpl.
MORTIMER, F., Tpr 3 L.H.		15/ 1/15	
MORTON, A. G., Pte. Remt. Sec.		30/ 9/15	
MORTON, G. S., Pte. 40 Bn.		10/ 3/16	3y 5m, Dvr.
MORTON, T. A., Dvr. Fld. Art.	40 Bn.	1/12/16	
MORTON, T. A., Gnr. F. Art.		2/12/16	2y 9m, Dvr.
MORTON, W., Pte. 15 Bn.		16/ 1/15	Pte.
MORTYN, G. McA., Tpr. 3 L.H.		14/ 6/15	4y 3m, S.S.M.
MORTYN, L. A. McA., Spr. 2 D.v. Sig.		17/ 8/15	4y 1m, Spr.
MORTYN, T. P. M., Pte. 40 Bn.		27/ 3/16	2y 3m, Pte.
MOSES, J. E., Pte. 40 Bn.		15/ 3/16	3y 9m, Pte.
MOSLEY, E. E., Pte. 12 Bn.		7/10/15	
MOSELEY, G. T Spr. 3 Mnr. Co.		13/11/15	2y 5m, Spr.
MOSS, J R., Pte. 12 Bn.	W. ✢ 19-20/9/17.	24/11/15	Pte. ✢
MOTT, R. W., Pte. 25 M.G. Coy.	W., 5 Div. M.G. Co., 12 Bn.	10/ 7/16	2y 9m, Pte.
MOTTON, W., Pte. 2 G.S.R.	12 Bn.	21/ 5/18	1y 5m, Pte.
MOULD, W. C., Pte. 12 Bn.	52 Bn., 51 Bn.	1/ 2/15	4y 3m, Pte.
MOULDEN E. L., Pte. C Sqd. 3 L.H.	W.	24/ 8/14	2y 9m, Pte. M.W.
MOULTON, L. E. R., M.W., Navvys			
MOUNTAIN, G. J., Pte. 12 Bn.		12/11/17	2y, Pte.
MOUNTNEY, Pte. 26 Bn.	W 12 Bn., 13 Fld. Amb.	26/ 3/15	4y 3m, Pte.
MOUSELEY, W. E., Pte. 1 G.S.R.	40 Bn.	1/ 2/18	1y 9m, Pte.
MOY, A. T., Gnr. Fld. Art.	3 D.A.C	16/ 2/16	3y 8m, Dvr.
MUCKRIDGE, G. F., Pte. 15 M.G. Co.	53 Bn.		Pte.
MUDGE, B., Pte. 40 Bn.	2W.	2/10/16	2y 7m, Pte.
MUDGE, W. L., Pte. 12 Bn.	40 Bn.	20/11/16	2y 8m, Pte.
MUIR, A R., Pte. 12 Bn.	2W.	24/ 8/14	4y 6m, L/Cpl.
MUIR, C. R., Pte. 26 Bn.	W., 52 Bn., 12 Bn., 40 Bn., 13 Bn	18/ 8/15	4y, L/Cpl.
MUIR, C. C., S/Sgt. A.A.D.C		30/ 7/18	1y 1m, S/Sgt.
MUIR, F. L., Pte. 1 A.C.H.		7/ 9/14	4y 4m, Pte.
MUIR, G. W., Sgt. 12 Bn.	2W.	26/ 4/15	4y 5m, Lt.
MUIR, J. N., Pte. 12 Bn.	52 Bn.	21/ 7/15	3y 2m, Pte.
MUIR, M., Pte. 26 Bn.	2W., M.M. 7 Bde., M.G. Co.	19/ 7/15	3y 10m, Cpl.
MUIR, S. F., Pte. 12 Bn.	3 M.G. Co. ✢ 18/6/16.	21/ 7/15	Pte. ✢
MUIR, W. McG., Pte. 1 G.S.R.	4 Bn.	3/ 3/17	2y 8m, Pte.
MULCAHY, E. L., Pte. 3 Fld. Amb.	2 Fld. Amb.	20/ 9/15	4y 1m, Dvr.
MULCAHY, F., Pte. 12 Bn.	2W., 51 Bn., 52 Bn.	8/ 9/15	4y L/Cpl.
MULLEN, L. M., Lt. 12 Bn.	2W., D.S.O., C. de G. (Belgian) ,2 M.I.D 9 Bn.	24/ 8/14	5y 1m, Lt-Col
MULLIGAN, A., Gnr. 6 F.A.B.	15 F.A.B., 14 F.A.B. ✢ 2/10/17.	5/ 1/16	Gnr ✢
MULLIGAN, H. T., Gnr Fld. Art.	15 F.A.B. 14 F.A.B., 114 How. Bty.	9/ 2/15	3y 7m, Sgt.
MULLIGAN, K. S., Pte. 12 Bn.	W.	8/10/15	1y 7m, Pte.
MULRENNAN, G., Pte. 12 Bn.	W	27/ 8/14	Pte.
MULRENNAN, J., Pte. 15 Bn.	4 Pioneers	11/ 2/15	3y 9m, Pte.
MUMFORD, T. W., Pte. 12 Bn.	✢ 15/4/19.	3/ 4/16	Pte. ✢
MUNDAY, A. B., Pte. 40 Bn.	M.G. Cc.	19/10/16	3y, Pte.
MUNDAY, W C., Tpr. 3 L.H.	L.H. Fld. Amb.	29/12/14	2y 9m, Dvr.
MUNDAY, A. W., Pte. 12 Bn.	W. ✢ 23/7/16.	20/ 8/14	Sgt. ✢
MUNRO, D. C., Pte. 40 Bn.	W.	4/ 4/16	3y 4m, Pte.
MUNRO, F. J., Pte. 12 Bn.	2W., 52 Bn.	2/ 8/15	2y 6m, Pte.
MUNRO, G. A., Pte. 12 Bn.		18/ 7/16	3y 2m, Pte.
MUNRO, M. C., Pte. 12 Bn.	W., Art. Details, 8 F.A.B.	24/ 4/17	2y, Gnr
MUNRO, T. H., Pte. 12 Bn.	M.M., 52 Bn. ✢ 17/10/17.	2/10/15	Pte. ✢
MUNTING, R. F., Pte. 15 Bn.	47 Bn. ✢ 3/9/16.	27/ 7/15	Pte. ✢
MURCHISON, M G., Gnr. Fd. Arty.	1 H.T.M. Bty.	1/ 6/15	4y 9m, Lt.
MURCUTT, W. C., Pte. 12 Bn.	12 Bn., 52 Bn., 69 Bn.	1/10/15	
MURDOCH, W., Sec. Lt. 56 Bn.	✢ 1/6/16.	3/ 5/15	Lt ✢
MURDOCH, A. G., Pte. Dntl. Cps.		9/ 6/15	4y 4m, Pte.
MURDOCH, J., Dvr. C Sqd. 3 L.H.		20/ 8/14	4y 6m, Cpl.
MURDOCH, R., Pte. 3 L.H.	1 B.A.C.	23/ 3/16	3y 5m, Dvr.
MURDOCH, W. J., Pte. A.A.M.C.		18/ 9/16	
MURFETT, H. G., Pte. 26 Bn.	2W.	28/ 7/15	3y 1m, Pte.
MURFETT, C. J., A A.M.C. Rfts.	3 A.G.H.	31/ 3/17	2y 8m, Pte.
MURFET, C. W., Pte. 40 Bn.	W., M.G. Dtls., 3 M.G. Btn.	7/11/16	
MURFET, L. J, Pte. 40 Bn.		1/10/16	2y 11m, Pte.
MURFETT, R. D., Pte. 26 Bn.	✢ 14/11/16.	2/10/15	Pte. ✢

NAME.	REMARKS.	RANK ON DISCHARGE. ENLISTED. SERVICE.
MURGATROYD, J. H., Pte. 12 Bn.	W.	1/ 6/16 2y 9m, Pte.
MURPHY, F. J., Tpr. 3 L.H.	W.	26/ 7/15 4y 3m, Tpr.
MURPHY, F., Pte. 40 Bn.	✣ 7/6/17.	20/ 3/16 Pte. ✣
MURPHY, H. S., Pte. 12 Bn.	W.	20/ 8/14 1y 10m, Cpl.
MURPHY, J. E., Dvr. 12 Bn.		20/ 8/14 3y 7m, Pte.
MURPHY, O., Pte. 2 G.S.R.	8 Bty., 3 F.A.B.	13/ 6/18 1y 4m. Gnr.
MURPHY, R. J., Pte. 15 Bn.	2W., 47 Bn.	27/ 8/15 2y 4m. Pte.
MURPHY, W. J., Pte. 40 Bn.	49 Bn., 2 A.G.H	28/11/16 2y 7m, Pte.
MURPHY, W., Pte. 3 G.S.R.		20/ 6/18 1y 1m, Dvr.
MURPHY, W. H., Pte. 26 Bn.		9/12/15
MURPHY, W. C., Pte. 12 Bn.	W.	24/11/16 2y 10m, Pte. Dvr.
MURRELL, L. G., Dvr. 3 F.A.B.		13/ 7/18 1y 1m, Tpr.
MURRELL, M. M., Tpr. 7 G.S.R.	9 Rfts. 3 F.A.B., 9 Bty.	22/ 8/16 Pte. ✣
MURRELL, S., Pte. 12 Bn.	2W. ✣ 23/8/18.	8/ 2/16 3y 8m. Gnr.
MURTAGH, C. T. R., Pte 12 Bn.	L.T.M. Bty., 40 Bn. 3 Div. H., M.T. Bde.	28/ 2/17
MURTAGH, W. R., Gnr. 3 F.A.B.		11/ 8/15 Pte. ✣
MURRAY, A. J., Pte 26 Bn.	✣ 19-22/8/16.	5/ 8/15
MURRAY, A. H. G., Sgt. 6 Fd. Co.	M.S.M., 4 Div. Engrs.	7/ 9/15 Pte ✣
MURRAY, D. N., Pte. 12 Bn.	✣ 19-22/8/16.	1/ 7/15 4y. L/Cpl.
MURRAY, D. G., Pte. 15 Bn.	4 Pnr. Bn.	6/11/16
MURRAY, E. S., Pte. Wireless		30/10/16 2y 7m, Pte.
MURRAY, F. Pte. 40 Bn.	W.	3/ 8/15 4y, Pte.
MURRAY, G. G., Pte. 26 Bn.	W.	10/11/15
MURRAY, G. R., Spr. Miners.		24/ 9/17 7m, Pte.
MURRAY, H. J., Pte. 40 Bn.		14/ 8/14 5y 4m
MURRAY, H. V., Dvr. A.S.C.	4 Div. Supply Co., 4 M.T. Co.	31/ 5/16 Pte. ✣
MURRAY, H. V., Pte. 12 Bn.	✣ 5-8/5/17.	2/ 9/15 3y 11m, L/Cpl.
MURRAY, J. T., Pte. 15 Bn.	47 Bn, 46 Bn.	6/12/16 2y 9m, Dvr.
MURRAY, J. B., Gnr. A.F.A. Bde.	W., 6 Bty.	8/ 6/15 1y 11m. Pte.
MURRAY, J. L., Pte. 26 Bn.		14/ 3/17 2y 6m. Dvr.
MURRAY, L. A., Gnr. Fd. Arty.	3 D.A.C.	23/ 7/15 Pte. ✣
MURRAY, L. V., Pte 12 Bn.	✣ 27/2/17	10/ 5/15 4y 10m. Pte.
MURRAY, L. W., Pte. 26 Bn.		11/ 8/15 4y 3m, L/Cpl.
MURRAY, U. T., Pte. 26 Bn.	4 Pnr. Bn.	10/11/15 2y 10m. Pte.
MURRAY, T. R., Pte. 4 Tnlrs. Co.		23/ 2/16
MURRAY, T., Pte. 40 Bn.	W.	20/ 8/14 4y 7m, Spr.
MURRAY, W. H., Spr. Engrs.	5 Div. Engrs.	19/ 9/14
MURRAY, W. H., Pte. 15 Bn.		17/11/16
MURRAY, W. H., Cpl. 40 Bn.		1/12/15
MUSCHAMP, E. G., Chap., Chaplains		22/ 5/16 Pte. ✣
MUSKETT, R. J., Pte. 12 Bn.	✣ 26/2/17.	20/ 8/14 2y 1m, Pte.
MYERS, H. J., Pte. 12 Bn.	W.	29/ 6/15 Pte. ✣
MYERS, T. C., Pte. 26 Bn.	✣ 25/8/16.	8/ 7/15 4y 2m, Pte.
MYLES, J., Pte. 23 Bn.		17/ 7/17 Gnr.
McALISTER, R. F., Gnr. Atry.		21/ 9/15 Cpl. ✣
McALISTER, T. W., Pte. 7 Fd. Amb.		25/11/15 2y 3m, Spr.
McALISTER, W. H., Gnr. 6 A.F.A.	22 How. Bde., 5 A.F.A. ✣ 29/9/18.	27/ 7/15 1y 5m, Pte.
McARDELL, O. L., Spr. Miners	Tunnlrs.	11/ 6/15 2y 8m, Pte.
McARTHUR, C., Pte. 15 Bn.	47 Bn.	1/ 4/16 2y, Pte.
McARTHUR, G. W., Pte. 15 Bn.	W.	20/10/16 Pte. ✣
McARTHUR, J., Pte. 40 Bn.	W.	17/ 2/15 4y 1m, Pte.
McARTHUR, J. B., Pte. 12 Bn.	W., 40 Bn. ✣ 3/8/18	25/ 9/14 4y 4m, Pte.
McARTHUR, R. A., Pte. 26 Bn.	2W.	25/10/16
McAULEY, L. G., Pte. 15 Bn.	W., M.G. Dtls.	17/ 5/18 1y 7m, Pte.
McAULIFFE, J. C., Spr. Tnlrs.		24/11/15 3y 10m. L/Cpl.
McAULIFFE, J., Pte. 2 G.S.R.		2/ 1/18 1y 9m, Pte.
McAULIFFE, W. E., Dvr. 3 Fd. Co.	W., 14 Fld Coy.	19/ 6/17 2y 2m. Pte.
McBAIN, H., Pte. 1 G.S.R.	40 Bn.	22/ 1/17 1y 5m. Pte.
McBAIN, J., Pte. 12 Bn.	40 Bn.	28/ 8/14 Pte. ✣
McBAIN, J., Pte. 40 Bn.		11/ 4/16
McBAIN, J. T., Pte. 12 Bn.	✣ 25-28/4/15.	10/10/16. Lieut. ✣
McBAIN, J. H., Pte. 12 Bn.		4/ 8/15
McBEAN, H. W., Lt. 40 Bn.	✣ 9/5/18.	25/ 7/15
McBEAN, D., Pte. 26 Bn.	W.	12/ 7/16
McBEAN, F. S., Pte 12 Bn.	W.	19/ 8/14 Pte. ✣
McBEAN, W. L., Pte. 40 Bn.		10/ 8/15 4y. Pte.
McCABE, H. F., 3 Fd Amb	✣ 14/3/15.	15/11/15 3y 5m, Pte.
McCAFFERTY, B. J., Pte. 26 Bn.	2W., 12 Bn.	7/11/15 2y 5m, Pte.
McCAFFERTY, J. T., Pte. 12 Bn.	W.	28/ 9/15 3y 8m, Pte.
McCAFFERTY, R. F., Pte. 12 Bn.	2W	31/10/16 2y 5m. Pte.
McCAFFERTY, P. R., Pte 26 Bn.	2W., M.M.	19/ 1/17 2y 9m. Spr.
McCALL, C. W., Pte. 12 Bn.	W.	22/11/15 4y, Sgt.
McCALLUM, C., Pte. Rly.	A B.G.R.O. Co.	9/10/15 3y 10m. Dvr.
McCALLUM, C. H., Gnr 8 F.A.B		7/ 8/15 2y 2m. Dvr.
McCALLUM, E., Pte 12 Bn.	4 Pioneers	20/11/16 2y 10m. Dvr.
McCALLUM, S., Dvr Art.	2W., 5 F.A.B.	19/ 7/16
McCAMBRIDGE, R. J., Dvr. Art.	W. 2 F.A.B.	18/ 2/15 4y 7m. Cpl.
McCANN, H., Pte. 4 M.G. Co.		19/ 4/15 2y 9m. Pte.
McCANN, R., Pte. 7 F. Amb.	W., D.C.M., 4 D. Sply. Col. 4 M.G.C	19/ 3/18 1y. Pte.
McCANN, W. J., Pte. 7 F. Amb.	W.	23/ 2/17 2y 1m. Pte.
McCARRON, F.A.F., Pte. 2 G.S.R.		24/ 4/16
McCARTHY, C. J., Pte. 40 Bn.	W.	10/ 7/15 4y 2m. Pte.
McCARTHY, G., Spr. 8 Fd. Co.	W. M.M. 52 Br.	31/ 1/16
McCARTHY, J., Pte. 12 Bn.	W.	
McCARTNEY, J. J., Pte. 40 Bn. (Correct Name, ALLEN, G. C.)		
McCARTON, W., Pte. 12 Bn.	W. 3 M.G Co. ✣ 20/9/17.	30/12/14 Pte. ✣

TASMANIA'S MUSTER ROLL. 315

NAME.	REMARKS.	RANK ON DISCHARGE. ENLISTED. SERVICE.
McCAULEY, E. N., Pte. 12 Bn.	W. 40 Bn.	17/ 4/17 2y 1m. Pte.
McCLELLAN, F. D., Pte. 15 M.G.C.	W. 21 M.G. Bn.	3/10/16 2y 10m. Pte.
McCLUTCHEY. M. G., Pte. 12 Bn.	W.	24/ 7/16 2y 3m. Pte.
McCLYMONT. R. A., Pte. 12 Bn.		1/ 6/16 1y 5m. Pte.
McCONNELL, D. J., Dvr. 40 Bn.	W.	16/ 5/16 3y 5m. Dvr.
McCONNELL, J. D. D., Pte. 26 Bn.	3W. 69 Bn., 26 Bn.	12/ 2/15 3y 11m. Pte.
McCONNELL, L. J., Pte. 15 Bn.	W.	26/11/14 4y 2m. Pte.
McCONNELL, T., Pte. 26 Bn.	2W.	9/ 9/15 3y 8m. Pte.
McCONNON, F. C., Pte. 12 Bn.	W.	27/10/16 2y 10m. Pte.
McCONNON, H. J., Gnr. Art.		15/12/15 3y 4m. W.O.
McCORMACK, F., Dvr. 12 Bn.		12/ 7/15 Dvr.
McCORMACK, F. A., Gnr. 3 F.A.B.	2W. 24 F.A.B., 38 Bn.	27/ 8/14 4y 8m. 2-Lt.
McCORMICK. A. N., Dvr. 12 F.A.B.	W. 12 F.A.B.	7/10/16 2y 7m. Dvr.
McCORMICK, G. J., Pte. 40 Bn.		14/11/16 2y 10m. Pte.
McCORMACK, L. J., Pte. 40 Bn.	W.	21/ 8/17 1y 7m. Pte.
McCOY, A. T., Pte. 1 G.S.R.		25/ 2/18 1y 10m. Pte.
McCOY, J., Pte. 40 Bn.	4W	15/ 5/16 3y 4m. Pte.
McCRACKAN, J., Pte. R.U.	A.I.F. Hd. Qrs. Cairo.	21/10/15 3y. Pte.
McCREA, J., Pte. R.U.		13/10/15 1y 2m. Tpr.
McCREDIE, T., Sec. Lt. 12 Bn.		4/10/17 2y. Lieut.
McCREDIE, G. A., Gnr. S. Art.	✣ 24/2/17.	4/ 6/15 Gnr. ✣
McCREAGAN, P., Pte. 12 Bn.	✣ 22/3/17.	13/10/16 Pte. ✣
McCREGAA, J., Pte. 12 Bn.	✣ Between 6 and 10 April, 1917.	30/ 8/16 Pte. ✣
McCRORY, L. J., Gnr. F. Art.	13 F.A.B.	24/ 2/16
McCRORY, R., Pte. 26 Bn.	12 Bn. ✣ 11/8/18.	11/ 8/15 Pte. ✣
McCRORY, V. A., Pte. 12 Bn.	W.	26/ 6/16 2y 2m. Pte.
McCROSSIN, T., Pte. 12 Bn.	W.	26/ 8/14 1y 6m. Pte.
McCUAIG, G. J. V., P.e. A.A.M.C.		1/10/17 2y 2m. Pte.
McCULLOCH, A., Pte. 12 Bn.	W.	10/ 9/15 4y 1m. Pte.
McCULLOCH, A. J. S., Pte. 12 Bn.	W. ✣ 23/7/16.	20/ 8/14 Cpl. ✣
McCULLOCH, J. B., Pte. 12 Bn.	M.M.	9/ 9/15
McCULLOCH, V. J., Gnr. F. Art.	W. 120 How. Bd., 4 F.A.B.	14/ 5/16 2y 7m. Gnr.
McCULLOCH, W., Pte. 12 Bn.		23/12/14 3y 1m. Pte.
McCULLUM, N.		
McOUTCHEON, J. H. R., Capt. A.A.M.C.		12/ 5/17 1y 10m. Capt.
McDERMOTT, A., Spr. Miners.	18 Tunnelers Co.	16/ 4/16 3y. Spr.
McDERMOTT, A., Spr. Miners.	3rd Tunnelers Co.	20/11/15 3y 10m. Spr.
McDERMOTT, A. J., Pte. 26 Bn.		15/ 4/15
McDERMOTT, C., Cpl. F. Art.	24 F.A.B., 11 F.A.B.	30/11/14 4y 5m. Cpl
McDERMOTT, F. J., Pte. 40 Bn.	✣3/2/17.	15/ 3/16 Pte. ✣
McDERMOTT, G., Pte. Tnrs.	2 Pnrs.	4/10/16 2y 4m. Pte.
McDERMOTT, P. J., Pte. 15 Bn.		12/ 8/15 3y 9m. Cpl.
McDERMOTT, R. W., Tpr. 3 L.H.		16/ 2/15 Tpr.
McDERMOTT, R. J., Pte. Miners	W 57 Bn.	27/ 3/16 3y 4m. Pte.
McDEVITT, C. W., Dvr. 1 Fd. Co.	W., M.I.D.	29/ 9/14 1y 9m. Dvr.
McDEVITT, H. E., Pte. 26 Bn.	2W.	7/ 7/15
McDEVITT, J. J., Tpr. 3 L.H.		26/10/16 3y, Tpr.
McDONALD, A. C., Pte. 12 Bn.	52 Bn.	26/ 7/15 2y 9m. Pte.
McDONALD, A. A., Pte. 9 Bn.	3W.	11/ 3/15 4y 5m. Pte.
McDONALD, A. P., Pte. 12 Bn.		14/ 4/15 4y. Pte.
McDONALD, D., Pte. 12 Bn. (Correct Name, HOGG, W.)		6/10/15 2y 4m. Pte.
McDONALD, D. C., Pte. 1 G.S.R.	40 Bn	16/10/17 2y. Pte.
McDONALD, F. N., Pte. 4 M.G. Co.	15 M G. Co. ✣ 16/10/17.	31/10/16 Pte. ✣
McDONALD, F., Pte. 40 Bn.		10/ 3/16 3y 8m. Cpl.
McDONALD, G. H. T., Pte. 40 Bn.	W	5/10/15 3y 8m. L/Cpl.
McDONALD, J. F., Pte. 15 Bn.	W. 69 Bn., 15 Bn.	8/ 1/15 4y 10m. Pte.
McDONALD, F., L/Cpl. 3 Fd. Co.	W. M.S.M.	17/ 8/14 4y 5m. C.S.M.
McDONALD, P. A., Pte. 12 Bn.	W. M.M. 52 Bn., 51 Bn.	4/10/15 3y 10m. Pte.
McDONALD, T. R., Tpr. 3 L.H.		13/12/17 1y 9m. Tpr.
McDONALD, W., Pte. 40 Bn.		18/ 5/16 1y 10m. Cpl.
McDONALD, W. B., Sgt. 26 Bn.	52 Bn., 49 Bn.	13/ 4/15
MacDONNELL, R. A., Pte. 12 Bn.	W. ✣19-22/8/16.	13/10/14 Pte. ✣
McDONOUGH, H., Pte. 12 Bn.	✣ 25/8/18.	29/ 4/16 Pte. ✣
McDONOUGH, P. T., Pte 12 Bn.		4/ 4/17
McDONOUGH, W., Pte. 12 Bn.	8 Bn.	1/12/14
McDOUGALL, A. B., Pte. 12 Bn.	52 Bn. ✣ 4/9/16.	11/ 1/16 Pte. ✣
McDOUGALL, F. J., Tpr. 3 L.H.		7/ 6/17 6m. Tpr.
McDOUGALL, F. R., Pte. 40 Bn.		1/11/16 3y 2m. Pte.
McDOUGALL, J. H. G., Pte. 40 Bn.	✣ 13/10/17.	25/11/16 Pte. ✣
McDOUGALL, R., Pte. 12 Bn.	✣ 26/7/16.	11/ 8/15 Pte. ✣
McDOUGALL, R. W., Pte. 12 Bn.	W., 52 Bn. ✣ 5/5/18.	21/10/15 Pte. ✣
McDOUGALL, S. R., Pte. 12 Bn.	V.C., M.M., 47 Bn., 48 Bn.	30/ 8/15 3y 4m. Sgt.
McDOUGALL, W. C., Pte. 40 Bn.	✣ 7/6/17.	29/ 2/16 Pte. ✣
McDOUGALL, W. J., Pte. 40 Bn.	3W.	1/11/16 2y 5m. Pte.
McDOWALL, J., Pte. 15 Bn.	W	11/12/14
McDOWALL, J. D., Pte. 40 Bn	W.	5/ 4/16 2y 1m. Pte.
McDUFF, H. R.		
McDUFF, H. R., Spr. 3 Fd. Co.		3/ 2/15 1y 2m. Cpl.
McELWEE, G. E., Pte. 40 Bn.	W. 9 M G. Co.	16/ 7/16 3y. Pte.
McELWEE, R. A. L., Lt. 12 Bn.	W	25/ 8/14 5y 4m. Capt.
McELWEE, W., Gnr. F. Art.	2W. 22 F.A.B, 5 F.A.B.	14/ 9/15 2y 8m. Gnr.
McENNULTY, H. J., Pte. 40 Bn.	W	21/ 9/16 2y Pte.
McEWAN, T., Pte. 15 Bn.		26/11/14 4y 11m. Pte.
McEWAN, W., Pte. 15 Bn.	M.I.D.	26/11/15
McEWAN, W. G. F., Pte. 18 Bn.		11/ 6/15 3y 11m. Pte.

NAME.	REMARKS.	RANK ON DISCHARGE. ENLISTED, SERVICE.
McFARLANE, H. S., Pte. 40 Bn.	2W.	17/ 3/16
McFARLANE, W., Pte. 12 Bn.	W.	17/ 5/17
McFARLIN, J. H., L/Cpl. 40 Bn.		12/ 1/16
McGARRY, W. T., Pte. 12 Bn.		24/ 8/15 1y 7m. Pte.
McGARVIE, P. D., Spr. 8 Fd. Co.	W. 1 Pioneers.	4/11/15
McGEE, C., Gnr. 12 Bn.	10 F.A.B.	17/ 9/15 3y 8m. Gnr.
McGEE, C. J., Gnr. Art.	4 A.M.T.M. Battery.	5/ 8/15 3y 1m. Gnr.
McGEE, J. T., Pte. 12 Bn.		30/12/14 3y 6m. Pte.
McGEE, L., L/Cpl. 40 Bn.	V.C. ✠ 13/10/17.	1/ 3/16 Sgt. ✠
McGEE, R., Pte. Rly.	4 B.G.R.C.	22/ 9/16 2y 11m. Cpl.
McGHEE, T. H., Gnr. A.F.A.		27/ 1/16
McGILVERY, J., Spr. Tun.		22/ 7/16 1y 9m. Spr.
McGINLEY, W., Pte. 12 Bn.	15 Bn. ✠ 11/4/17.	28/ 7/15 Pte. ✠
McGINLEY, W. H., Pte. 12 Bn.	✠ 8/10/17.	2/ 3/16 Pte. ✠
McGINTY, A. H., Pte. 12 Bn.		8/11/16 3y 1m. Pte.
McGINTY, E. F., Tpr. 3 L.H.		3/ 8/15
McGINTY, N. C., Pte. 12 Bn.		8/11/16
McGINTY, W., Pte. 12 Bn.	W	5/ 9/16 2y 11m. Pte.
McGIVERON, C. G., Pte. 40 Bn.	✠ 13/10/17.	23/ 5/16 Pte. ✠
McGIVERON, J. H. T., Pte. 26 Bn.	✠ 29/7/16.	17/ 3/15 Pte. ✠
McGIVERON, J. J., Pte. 12 Bn.	3W. 52 Bn.	12/ 1/15 3y 11m. L.-Cpl.
McGLADERY, W. H., Gnr. F. Art.	W. 102 How. Bty.	22/11/16 1y 11m. Gnr.
McGOUGH, W. H., Pte 40 Bn.		3/ 4/16 1y 11m. L.-Cpl.
McGOWAN, R. J., Spr. 8 Fd. Co.	M.C.	13/ 1/16 Lieut.
McGOWAN, S., Gnr. 6 A.F.A.	✠ 27/11/16.	17/ 8/15 Bdr. ✠
McGRATH, T., Dvr. 4 A.S.C.	29 A.S.C., 4 Div. Train. ✠ 18/3/18.	12/ 9/14 L./Cpl. ✠
McGREE, T. M., Pte. 40 Bn.	W. ✠ 30/4/19.	27/10/16 Pte. ✠
McGREGOR, J., Dvr 3 A.F.A.	W.	31/ 8/14 1y 10m. Dvr.
McGREGOR, J., Gnr. Art.		8/ 4/18
McGREGOR, J., Munitions		
McGREGOR, J., Dvr. 15 Bn.	24 How. Bde., 10 F.A.B.	3/ 2/15 4y 6m. Dvr.
McGUANE, G. A. B., Tpr.3.L.H.	W.	15/ 6/15 2y, Tpr.
McGUINNESS, A., Pte. 12 Bn.	W.	5/ 8/16 2y 11m. Pte.
McGUINNESS, A. E., Pte. 40 Bn.	4W.	30/ 9/16 2y 5m. L./Cpl.
McGUINNESS, A. E., Pte. 3 G.S.R.	12 Bn.	8/ 7/18 1y 1m. Pte.
McGUINNESS, C. W. R., Pte 26 Bn		17/ 9/15 4y. Cpl.
McGUINNESS, E., Pte. 3 L.H.	W. 15 Bn.	19/ 7/15 2y 11m. L./Cpl.
McGUINNESS, F. F., Pte. 40 Bn.	✠ 7/6/17.	1/ 4/15 Pte. ✠
McGUINNESS, F. H., Pte. 26 Bn.	2W.	4/ 3/15 4y 5m. Pte.
McGUINNESS, J. T., Gnr. 1 Tun.	W. 9 Bty. A.F.A.	13/ 9/16 2y 1m. Gnr.
McGUINNESS, O. J., Pte. 40 Bn.		14/ 2/16 1y 6m. Pte.
McGUINNESS, V. L., Pte. 26 Bn.	W. 12 Bn.	16/ 8/15 3y 4m, Pte.
McGUINNESS, W. A., Pte. 40 Bn.	2W.	6/ 3/16 3y 6m. Pte.
McGUIRE, A. H., Pte. 40 Bn.	✠ 29/11/17.	20/ 3/16 Pte. ✠
McGUIRE, E. G., Pte. 40 Bn.	W.	7/11/16 2y. Pte.
McGUIRE, H., Pte. 40 Bn.		26/ 4/17 1y 5m. Pte.
McGUIRE, J. R., Pte. 26 Bn.	3W	25/ 4/15 4y. Pte.
McGUIRE, P. F., Pte. 12 Bn.	2W. 52 Bn.	5/10/15 3y 5m. Pte.
McGUIRE, T., Pte. 12 Bn.	W., H.Q., A.B.D.	19/11/17 1y 11m. Pte.
McHENRY, T., Tpr. 3 L.H.		19/10/17
McHUGH, A. W., Pte. 12 Bn.	✠ Between 3 and 5 Sept., 1916.	8/ 7/15 Pte. ✠
McHUGH, A. J., Pte. 12 Bn.	4W.	26/ 8/14 4y 8m. Pte.
McHUGH, J., Pte. 40 Bn.		21/ 3/16
McHUGO, D. G., Gnr. Art.		7/10/16 3y, Gnr.
McHUGO, E., Pte. 26 Bn.	W.	17/ 6/15 1y 1m. Pte.
McHUGO, W. G., Pte. 40 Bn.	2W.	4/ 3/16 3y 2m. Pte.
McHUGO, W. H., Pte. 1 A.C.H.	W. M.M. 15 Bn. Pro. Cps.	21/ 9/14
McILDOWNEY, G E., Sgt. 12 Bn.		6/ 7/15
McILROY, W., Pte. A.A.M.C.	W. 3 F. Amb.	7/ 4/16 3y 2m Pte.
McINNES, S. A., Lt. 40 Bn	✠ 1/2/19.	12/ 8/15. Lieut. ✠
McINNES, P., Sgt. 12 Bn.	2W. 52 Bn.	20/ 8/14 4y 6m. Sgt.
McINNES, W., Pte. 12 Bn.	W	22/12/14
McINROY, H., Cpl. 40 Bn.	3W	17/ 2/16 3y 5m. Sgt.
McINTOSH, A. J., Gnr. Art.	2W. 8 F.A.B. 30 Bty.	2/ 9/15 2y 3m. Gnr.
McINTOSH, A. G., Pte. 26 Bn.		1/ 2/15 4y 6m. Pte.
McINTOSH, C., Pte. 40 Bn.	M.M.	27/ 3/16 3y 1m. Dvr.
McINTOSH, G. A., Spr. 8 Fd. Co	7 Fd. Co.	29/ 2/16 3y 4m. Spr.
McINTOSH, J., Pte. 12 Bn.	W.	5/ 9/15 3y 9m. Pte.
McINTOSH, J., Spr. Tun.	W. 1 Tun. Co.	31/10/16 3y 5m. Spr.
McINTOSH, W., Gnr. Art.	24 How. Bty. 4 F.A.B.	4/12/15 4y 4m. Gnr.
McINTOSH, W. D., Dvr. 4 A.S.C.		20/ 8/14 4y 6m. Dvr.
McINTYRE, G. L., Lt. 40 Bn.	M.C.	9/ 9/15 4y 4m. Capt.
McINTYRE, C. D., Pte. 1 A.C.H.		8/ 6/15
McINTYRE, E. G., Pte. 12 Bn.	2W. 52 Bn., 51 Bn.	9/ 9/15 3y 9m. Pte.
McINTYRE, M. B., Pte. 12 Bn.	3W. 52 Bn.	29/ 5/15 3y 11m. Pte.
McIVER, J. S., Gnr. 6 F.A.B.	W. 18 Bty., 17 Bty.	1/ 9/15 3y 11m. Gnr.
McIVOR, E. A., Pte. 40 Bn.		30/ 5/16 3y 4m. Pte.
McKAY, A. C., Spr. C.D. Sig. Sq	Wireless Unit.	7/ 9/16 2y 10m. Spr.
McKAY, D. T., Pte. 4 M.G.C.	W.	27/ 2/17
McKAY, F., Pte. 4 M.G. Co		26/10/16
McKAY, V. A., Pte. 3 G.S.R.	12 Bn.	24/ 6/18 1y 2m. Pte.
McKEE, N., Spr. Tun.	2W.	9/ 9/16
McKELLAR, C. A., Pte. 15 Bn.	M.G. Details. 16 Bn.	1/12/14 4y 6m. Pte.
McKELLAR, H. B., Pte. 26 Bn.	W.	19/ 5/15 2y 1m. Pte.
McKENDRICK, A. N., Pte. 26 Bn.	✠ 29/7/16	1/10/15 Pte. ✠
McKENDRICK, J. T., Pte. 12 Bn.	W. ✠ 11/8/15.	1/ 9/14 Pte. ✠
McKENDRICK, R. J. M., Pte. 15 Bt.	W.	7/ 1/15 4y 5m. C.S.M.

TASMANIA'S MUSTER ROLL. 317

NAME.	REMARKS.	RANK ON DISCHARGE. ENLISTED. SERVICE.
McKENNA, C., Pte. 12 Bn.		24/ 8/14 5y. S./Sgt.
McKENNA, E. A., Sgt. 26 Bn.	3W.	21/ 6/15 Lieut.
McKENNA, H.		
McKENNA, J. T., Pte. 40 Bn.	W	26/ 6/16 2y 9m. Pte.
McKENNA, L. J., Pte. 12 Bn.		18/12/17 1y 4m. Pte.
McKENNA, L. J., Pte. 4 M.G. Co.		4/ 2/17 5m. Pte.
McKENNA, S. P., Pte. 40 Bn.	W.	25/ 9/16 2y 6m. Pte.
McKENNA, W., Pte. 40 Bn.	W. ✠ 29/11/17.	17/10/16 Pte. ✠
McKENNA, W. W., Pte. 40 Bn.	W.	31/ 7/16 2y 8m. Pte.
McKENNY, T., Pte. 12 Bn.		9/ 5/16 1y 6m. Pte.
McKENZIE, A. A., Pte. 40 Bn.	W., 12 Bn.	2/10/16 2y 6m. Pte.
McKENZIE, A. J., Pte. 12 Bn.	W., 52 Bn.	5/ 8/15 2y 5m. Pte.
McKENZIE, A. H. W., Pte. 26 Bn.	W.	2/10/15 3y 6m. Pte.
McKENZIE, D. J., Pte. 40 Bn.		31/ 5/16 3y 4m. L. Cpl.
McKENZIE, D. W., Pte. 8 Fd. Co.	1 D.M.T. Co.	4/10/15 3y 10m. L Cpl
McKENZIE, G. A., Pte. 12 Bn.	W., M.M. and Bar.	1/12/14 2y 9m. Pte.
McKENZIE, J. G., Pte. 40 Bn.	W.	10/11/16 2y 5m. Pte.
McKENZIE, G. F., Spr 1 Div Engrs	D.C.M.	27/ 8/14 4y 5m. Spr.
McKENZIE, L., Pte. 40 Bn.	3W.	31/ 5/16 3y. Pte.
McKENZIE, M. S., Sgt. 1 A.C.H.	✠ 8/12/15.	17/11/14. Sgt. ✠
McKENZIE, M., Pte. 12 Bn.		15/ 6/16 3y 1m. Pte.
McKENZIE, R. G. W., Pte. 12 Bn.	✠ 8/4/17.	22/ 7/15. Pte. ✠
McKENZIE, R. H., Pte. 40 Bn.		18/ 8/16 3y 4m. Pte.
McKENZIE, R. S., Pte. 40 Bn.	✠ 4/10/17.	21/ 3/16. Pte. ✠
McKENZIE, W. G., B.S.M. 3 F.A.B.		27/ 8/14 4y 5m. B.S.M.
McKERROW, K. S., Pte 12 Bn	W.	24/ 8/15 3y 3m. L Cpl.
McKIBBEN, K., Pte. 40 Bn.	W., 12 Bn.	5/ 7/16 2y 10m. Pte.
McKILLOP, R. J., Dvr. 3 L.H.	4 F.A.B.	7/ 8/15 4y Dvr.
McKINLEY, D. J., Bdr. 36 H.A.G.		1/ 6/15.
McKINLAY, L. J., Gnr. Siege Bde.		29/12/16 2y 8m. Gnr.
McKINLEY, P. F., L.-Cpl. 40 Bn.	2W., M.M.	22/ 2/16.
McKINNELL, L., Dvr. 3 F.A.B.	W., 102 How. Bty.	15/ 6/15 4y 2m. Dvr.
McKINNON, J. J., Spr. Miners.	1 Tun. Coy.	1/ 7/19 Spr.
McKNIGHT, T. J., Pte. 26 Bn.		6/ 4/15.
McLAGAN, L S., Pte. 26 Bn.		22/ 3/15 4y 5m. Pte.
McLAGAN, L. F., Dvr. 3 F.A.B.	2 D.A.C., 5 F.A.B.	28/ 7/15 4y 2m. Dvr.
McLAGAN, T. R., Dvr. 6 F.A.B.	M.M.	23/ 8/15 4y. Dvr.
McLAREN, A. F., Pte. 12 Bn.	W., 3 L.T.M.B.	7/ 3/16 3y 6m. Pte.
McLAREN, A. D., Pte. 12 Bn.	52 Bn. ✠ 4/9/16.	13/10/15. Pte. ✠
McLAREN, H. H., Pte. 1 G.S.R.		29/ 1/18.
McLAREN, H. N., Gnr. Arty.	W., 11 F.A.B. ✠ 18/9/18.	30/ 9/16. Gnr. ✠
McLAREN, J. A., Spr. Tunnellers		19/ 8/15 1y. Spr.
McLAREN, P. A., Spc. 3 Fd. Co.	2W., 12 Fld. Coy. Engrs.	25/ 1/15 4y. Spr.
McLAREN, R. C., Pte. 12 Bn.		21/11/17 1y 11m. Pte.
McLEAN, D., Pte 4 A.S.C.		20/ 8/14.
McLEAN, W. J. A.		7/ 3/18.
McLENNAN, A., Pte. 12 Bn.	W.	25/ 8/14 4y 3m. Cpl.
McLENNAN, K., Spr. Tunlers.		5/10/17 2m. Spr.
McLEOD, D. M., Pte. 40 Bn.		29/ 3/16.
McLEOD, E. A., Pte. 12 Bn.		8/ 7/15.
McLEOD, C. J. D., Sgt. Arty	3 D.A.H.Q.	12/ 3/17 2y 4m. Sgt.
McLEOD, H. E., Pte. 12 Bn.	2W.	29/ 5/16 2y 11m. Pte.
McLEOD, H. N., Pte. 26 Bn.	12 Bn. ✠ 24/7/16.	10/ 8/15. Pte. ✠
McLEOD, J. A., Tpr. 3 L.H.		21/ 8/14 4y 6m. Sgt.
McLEOD, J. N., Pte. 40 Bn.	W.	12/ 5/16 3y 5m. Pte.
McLEOD, M., M.G.S.		20/ 8/14.
McLEOD, M. J., Spr. Miners.		2/10/17 1y 7m.
McLEOD, P., Pte. 26 Bn.	2W. 12 Bn.	10/ 8/15 3y 11m. L.Cpl.
McLEOD, S. D., Dvr. 4 A.S.C.	10 A.S.C. ✠ Aug., 1915.	9/ 9/14. Dvr. ✠
McLOUGHLIN, E. A., Pte. 40 Bn.	3W.	25/ 5/16 3y 2m. Pte.
McLOUGHLIN, T. H., Pte. 2 G.S.R.	A.H.Q., A.I.F.	22/ 4/18 1y 6m. Pte.
McLOUGHLIN, T. J., Pte. 12 Bn.		2/ 9/16.
McMANUS, C., Dvr. 12 Bn.	24 How. Bde., 3 D.A.C.	6/ 1/16 1y 9m. Dvr.
McMAHON, J. A., Pte. 40 Bn.	2W. ✠ 2/10/17.	26/ 9/16. Pte. ✠
McMASTER, H. R., Pte. 12 Bn.	W.	14/ 8/16 3y 1m. Pte.
McMASTER, J., Pte. 15 Bn.	W. 4 Fd. Bakery. ✠ 28/9/17.	28/ 1/15. Pte. ✠
McMICHAEL, L. W., Pte. 12 Bn.	✠ 28/11/15.	24/ 3/15 Signr. ✠
McMICHAEL, R. H., Pte. 4 Fd. Bky		4/11/14 4y 6m. Pte.
McMILLAN, S. S. S., Sec. Lt. 40 Bn.	W., M.C.	20/ 1/16 3y 8m. Lieut.
McMILLAN, A. R., Pte. 12 Bn.	✠ 19–22/8/16.	3/ 8/15. Pte. ✠
McMURRAY, P., L.-Cpl. 12 Bn.	52 Bn., 51 Bn.	18/ 1/16 3y 10m. Cpl.
McNAB, H. A. J., Pte. 26 Bn	W.	20/ 7/15 4y 2m. CQMS.
McNAB, W. D., Pte. 26 Bn.	2W., 69 Bn., 26 Bn.	15/ 6/15 4y 2m. C.S.M.
McNALLY, C. C., Pte. 12 Bn.	40 Bn.	13/ 6/17 2y 5m. Pte.
McNALLY, H. J., Pte 26 Bn.		6/ 7/15.
McNALLY, J., Sgt. 40 Bn.	✠ 28/3/18.	3/ 8/15 Sgt. ✠
McNALLY, P. H., Pte. 12 Bn.	52 Bn.	25/ 5/15 2y 8m. Pte.
McNAMARA, F. J., Lieut. 12 Bn.	52 Bn. ✠ 3/9/16.	19/ 9/15. Capt. ✠
McNAMARA, C. E., Pte. 12 Bn.		7/ 9/15 2y 1m. Pte.
McNAMARA, E. A., Pte 26 Bn	✠ 2/9/18.	25/ 5/15. Pte. ✠
McNAMARA, H., Pte 12 Bn.	2W.	12/ 6/16 3y 4m. Pte.
McNAMARA, J. T., Pte. 1 G.S.R.	40 Bn.	6/11/17 1y 11m. Pte.
McNAMARA, J. P., Pte. 12 Bn		8/ 9/15.
McNAMEE, R., Dvr. Arty.	4 D.A.C.	31/ 5/17 2y 4m. Dvr.
McNAMEE, W., Pte. 26 Bn.		22/ 4/15.
McNAUGHTON, M., Pte 4 M.G. Co.		15/ 8/16.
McNEICE, Q., A.B.D. 1 A.R.N.B.T.		3/ 4/15 2y 3m. A.B.D.

NAME.	REMARKS.	ENLISTED. SERVICE. RANK ON DISCHARGE.
McNIECE, W. L., Pte. 40 Bn.		31/ 1/16 3y 7m. Pte.
McNEICE, W. M., Pte. 12 Bn.	2W.	15/11/17 1y 8m, Pte.
McNEILL, A. D., Spr. 8 Fd. Co.	W., 1 Fd. Co. ✠ 26/3/18.	1/ 3/16. Spr. ✠
McNEIL, A G., Cpl. 12 Bn.		20/ 2/17 2y 5m. Cpl.
McNEILL, D. T., Pte. 15 Bn.	47 Bn. ✠ 31/8/16.	30/ 8/15. L. Cpl. ✠
McORMOND, T. R., Pte. 12 Bn.	W.	22/ 7/15 3y 9m. Pte.
McORMOND, W. G., Tpr. 3 L.H.		19/ 1/17 2y 7m. Tpr.
McPARTLIN, F. C., Gnr. 3 F.A.B.	2W.	31/ 8/14 4y 5m. Sgt...
McPARTLIN, T. P., Gnr. 3 A.F.A.	✠ 16/6/17.	4/ 8/15. Gnr. ✠
McPHEE, A. D., Pte. 6 Fd. Co.		31/ 8/15.
McPHEE, P. J., Pte. 40 Bn.	W.	23/ 2/16 2y 4m. Pte.
McPHERSON, H. A., Lt. 12 Bn.	M.I.D. ✠ 24/12/18.	28/ 8/14. Major. ✠
McPHERSON, B. T., Pte. 26 Bn.	12 Bn.	2/ 9/15 4y 1m. Cpl.
McPHERSON, C. D. J., Pte. 12 Bn.	W.	5/ 1/16 3y 6m, Pte.
McPHERSON, C. A., Pte. 12 Bn.	W.	20/10/16 2y 5m. Pte.
McPHERSON, H., Pte. 7 F. Amb.	13 Fld. Amb.	3/ 3/15 4y 3m. Cpl.
McPHERSON, J., Pte. 40 Bn.	W.	6/ 4/16 2y 6m. Pte.
McPHERSON, J. D., Pte. 12 Bn.	W. ✠ 6-10/4/17.	26/ 8/14. Pte. ✠
McPHERSON, P. T., Pte. 15 Bn.	4 D.H.Q. ✠ 11/2/19.	24/ 6/15. Pte. ✠
McPHERSON, W., Pte. 15 Bn.	✠ 17/5/15.	17/12/14. Pte. ✠
McPHILLIPS, H. G., Pte. 26 Bn.	3W.	15/ 5/15. Lieut.
McPHILLIPS, W. J., Pte. 40 Bn.	W.	20/ 2/17.
McQUALD, E. W., Cpl. 12 Bn.		17/ 8/14.
McQUARRIE, J. D., Pte. 12 Bn.		20/ 6/17 1y 3m. Pte.
McQUEEN, J., Pte. Remounts.		29/ 9/15 1y 3m. Tpr.
McQUEENEY, M. C., Pte. 1 G.S.R.	A.G.B.D.	23/ 1/18 1y 9m. Pte.
McQUESTION, J, Pte. 12 Bn.	W., 47 Bn.	1/ 9/15 1y 8m. Pte.
McQUESTION, P., Pte. 12 Bn.	52 Bn., 51 Bn.	28/ 7/15 3y 7m. Pte.
McQUITTY, J. McC., Pte. 40 Bn.		16/10/16.
McRAE, A, L.-Cpl. 12 Bn.	✠ 23/4/18.	20/ 1/15. L. Cpl. ✠
McRAE, D., Spr. 2 Fd. Co.	2 B.A.C.	18/ 8/14 2y 5m. Spr.
McRAE, H., Gnr. 15 F.A.B.		11/10/16 2y 10m. Dvr.
McROBERTS, W, Cpl. 12 Bn.	W., M.M., 52 Bn.	24/ 8/14 4y 4m. Sgt.
McSHANE, E. P. J., Spr. 40 Bn.	A.C.S.C.	1/10/16 2y 11m. Spr.
McSKIMMING, G. L., Pte. 3 F.A.B.	A.A.O.C.	27/ 8/14 4y 1m. Pte.
McSORLEY, J. P., Spr. 8 Fd Co	2W., M.M., 7 Fd. Co.	4/ 5/16 3y 5m. L. Cpl.
McTIGHE, D P., Pte. 15 Bn.	2W., 47 Bn.	13/ 8/15 2y 6m. Pte.
McTYE. T. M., Pte. 15 Bn.	2W., D.C.M., 12 M.G. Co.	30/ 8/15 3y 4m. L. Cpl.
McVAN, A., Pte. 40 Bn.	3W. ✠ 31/8/18.	8/ 2/16. ✠
McVILLEY, C. C., Dvr. 12 Bn.	24 How. Bde., 11 F.A.B.	7/ 9/15 3y 8m. Dvr.
McVILLY, A. F., C.S.M. 26 Bn.	W., re-enlisted.	23/ 2/15 4y. Lieut.
McVILLY, C. L., Lt. 40 Bn	2W., M.C., M.I.D.,	19/ 7/15 3y 11m. Capt.
McVILLY, O. R. S., Spr. Railway	2 Rly. Co., 2 L.R.O.C.	
McWELLS, K. A., Pte. 3 L.H.	W., 4 A. Sub. Park.	23/ 8/14 3y 7m. Dvr.
McWILLIAMS, D. L., 2 A.M. A.F.C.		19/10/17 1y 9m. 2 A.M.
McWILLIAM, W. G., Spr. Tunlers.	W., 3 Tun. Co.	9/ 8/16 3y. Spr.
NADEN, N. C., Cpl. 40 Bn.	✠ 9/5/18.	1/ 8/16 Cpl. ✠
NAILER, H. H., Pte. 12 Bn.	W. ✠ 12/8/18.	12/ 7/15 Pte. ✠
NAILER, L. J., Gnr. Arty.	W., 2 D.A.C., A. Prov. Cps.	6/10/15 4y, Gnr.
NAIRN, K. C., Gnr. Arty.	2W. 120 How. Bty., 5 Sig. Coy.	6/ 3/16 2y 6m, Spr.
NANCE, C., Pte. 40 Bn.	W.	27/ 6/16 1y 7m, Pte.
NANGLE, J. G., Gnr. Arty.	2W.	11/11/15
NANKIVILLE, S. J., Pte. 12 Bn.	W.	14/11/17 1y 11m, Pte.
NAS, B. W., Pte. 40 Bn.	3W., 15 Bn., 40 Bn.	14/ 3/16 3y 1m, Cpl.
NASH, C. H. Pte. 12 Bn.	W.	2/ 8/15 3y 8m, L.-Cpl
NASH, C. E., Whlr., 4 T.R. Park.	5 Dvl. Trn. Coy.	16/ 9/14 4y 5m, Pte.
NASH, E. T., Pte. 40 Bn.	4W.	15/ 3/16 3y 1m, Pte.
NASH, G., Tpr. 3 L.H.		2/5/17 2y 3m, Tpr.
NASH, G., Pte. 12 Bn.	✠ 3-5/9/16.	15/ 9/14 L.-Cpl. ✠
NATHAN, B. V., Gnr. 9 Bty.	21 F.A.B.	20/ 8/14 4y 3m, Sgt.
NATHAN, M., Pte. T.M. Bty.	24 Bn. ✠ 23/5/18.	1/ 3/17 Pte. ✠
NATION, C., Pte. 12 Bn.	W., 40 Bn.	23/10/16 2y 4m, Pte.
NATION, T., Pte. 12 Bn.		6/ 9/15 4y 4m, Pte.
NATTEY, F. C. S., Pte. 1 G.S.R.	5 M.G. Bn.	20/ 2/18 1y 9m, Pte.
NAYLOR, E. B., Pte. 12 Bn.	52 Bn. ✠ 16/7/17.	26/ 5/15 Pte. ✠
NAYLOR, F. A., Pte. 40 Bn.	✠ 28/3/18.	31/10/16 Pte. ✠
NAYLOR, H. U., Pte. 12 Bn.	3 Fd. Co.	19/ 8/14 4y 5m, Spr.
NAYLOR, I. J., Pte. 12 Bn.	W.	25/ 8/14 2y 2m, Pte.
NAYLOR, T. M., Pte. 12 Bn.	W., 69 Bn., 52 Bn	25/ 8/14 4y 5m, Pte.
NAYLOR, U. B., Cpl. 12 Bn.	52 Bn. ✠ 16/10/17.	25/ 8/14 C.S.M. ✠
NEAL, A. H., Pte. 40 Bn.		17/ 5/16 2y 9m, Pte.
NEAL, J. S., Pte. 7 Fd. Amb.		23/ 3/15
NEASEY, A. J., Spr. Miners.		10/ 9/15 2y 6m, Spr.
NEASEY, J. E., Pte. 12 Bn.	W., M.M.	9/ 6/16 3y 3m, Pte.
NEAVES, F. J., Pte. 4 M.G. Co.	22 M.G. Co. ✠ 7/10/17.	18/ 9/16 L.-Cpl. ✠
NEELY, J. A., Tpr. 3 L.H		22/10/17 1y 10m, Tpr.
NEEDHAM, F. W., Mun. Worker		
NEIGHBOUR, J., Gnr. 8 F.A.B.		28/ 7/15
NEIGHBOUR, R., Pte. 15 Bn.	W., P.O.W.	1/ 6/15 4y, Pte.
NEIL, A., Sgt Arty.	5 D.A.C.	20/ 4/18 1y 7m, Gnr.
NEIL, E., Pte. 40 Bn.	W.	4/ 3/16 3y 6m, Pte.
NEIL, J., Pte. 4 A.S.C.		7/ 1/16 1y 6m, Pte.
NEILSON, F. O., Pte. 12 Bn.	52 Bn.	29/ 8/14 2y 3m, Pte.
NEILSON, H. D., Pte. 12 Bn.		17/10/16 2y 6m, Pte.
NEILSON, J. V., Munition Worker		
NEILSON, J. W., Pte. 40 Bn.	2W.	17/10/16 2y 6m, Pte.
NELSON, G., Dvr. 9 Fd. Bty.	W., 4 Div. Arty.	31/ 8/14 3y 7m, Bdr.

NAME.	REMARKS.	RANK ON DISCHARGE. ENLISTED. SERVICE.
NELSON, G. E., Pte. 15 Bn.	✠ 31/5/15.	24/ 9/14 Pte. ✠
NELSON, J. G., Pte. 12 Bn.	11 F.A.B	9/11/15 3y 9m, Dvr.
NELSON, J. T., Pte. 12 Bn.	52 Bn. ✠ 4/9/16.	14/ 9/15 Pte. ✠
NELSON, J. J., Pte. 40 Bn.	W.	7/ 4/16 1y 9m, Pte.
NELSON, S. J., Tpr. 3 L.H.	✠ 24/10/18.	19/ 8/14 Dvr. ✠
NETTLEFOLD, J., Pte. 12 Bn.		30/10/16 2y 11m, Pte.
NEUTEBOOM, P., Pte. 40 Bn.	✠ 29/7/18	29/ 8/17 Pte. ✠
NEVILLE, J. H., Pte. 12 Bn.	52 Bn., 51 Bn.	5/ 8/15 4y Pte.
NEVIN, A. R., Lt. 15 Bn.	4 L.T.M.B. ✠ 23/9/16.	15/ 9/15 Lt. ✠
NEW, D. J., Pte. 40 Bn.	2W., M.M.	9/10/16 2y 6m, Pte.
NEW, R. W., Pte 2 GS.R.	50 Bty.	22/ 2/18 1y 7m, Gnr.
NEWBOLD, F. K., Pte. 12 Bn.	✠ 19-22/8/16.	22/12/14 Pte. ✠
NEWBON, P., Tpr. 3 L.H.		31/ 8/15 4y, Cpl.
NEWBON, W., Tpr. 3 L.H.		20/ 8/14 2y 3m, Tpr.
NEWBURY, W. T., Pte. 12 Bn.		14/10/16 3y, Pte.
NEWCOMBE, A. J., Pte. 40 Bn.		9/10/16 3y 2m, Pte.
NEWELL, A. T., Pte. 12 Bn.	2 Tun. Co.	8/10/17 2y, Spr.
NEWETT, C. L., Tpr. 3 L.H.	M.M., 11 F.A.B.	15/ 7/15 4y 4m, Dvr.
NEWITT, E T., Pte. 26 Bn.	2W.	17/ 2/15 4y 4m, Pte.
NEWITT, F. R., Pte. 12 Bn.	✠ 10/6/17.	2/ 8/15 Pte. ✠
NEWITT, J., Pte. 12 Bn.	W., 26 Bn.	13/ 4/15 3y 9m, Pte.
NEWETT, J. H., Pte. 12 Bn.	2W., 52 Bn., 51 Bn.	6/ 8/15 4y, Pte.
NEWITT, S. D. P., Pte. 12 Bn.	W.	29/ 4/16 1y 8m, Pte.
NEWITT, R. D., Pte. 12 Bn.	2W., M.C,	21/ 8/14 4y 2m, Lt.
NEWLAND, H., Pte. 12 Bn.		6/ 7/16 3y 2m, Pte.
NEWLAND, J. E., Q.M.S. 12 Bn	3W., V.C., M.I.D.	17/ 8/14 3y 9m, Capt.
NEWMAN, A. H., Pte. 40 Bn.	W.	3/ 9/17 2y 1m, Pte.
NEWMAN, A., Pte. 12 Bn,	W., 52 Bn.	15/11/15 2y 1m, Pte.
NEWMAN, A. J., Gnr. Arty.	1 D.A.C	5/ 3/17 2y 8m, Gnr.
NEWMAN, A., M.G.S. 12 Bn.	W., 3 L.T.M.B. ✠ 25/7/16.	30/ 8/14 M.G.S. ✠
NEWMAN, C. R., Pte. 3 G.S.R.	12 Bn.	17/ 5/18 1y 2m, Pte.
NEWMAN, C., Dvr. A.A.M.C.		Dvr.
NEWMAN, E., Pte. 12 Bn.	W., 10 F.A.B.	7/ 9/15 2y 6m, Gnr.
NEWMAN, E. W., Pte. 15 Bn.	✠ 23/5/15	19/ 9/14 Pte. ✠
NEWMAN, G. E., Pte. 1 G.S.R.	40 Bn.	17/11/17
NEWMAN, H., Pte. 40 Bn.	2W. ✠ 25/8/18.	21/ 1/16 Pte. ✠
NEWMAN, H. W., Pte. 12 Bn.	W.	7/11/16 2y 6m, Pte.
NEWMAN, R. C., Pte 40 Bn.		7/11/16 1y 10m, Pte.
NEWMAN, R. T., Pte. 12 Bn.	✠ 15/4/17.	12/ 8/16 Pte. ✠
NEWMAN, S., Pte. 2 G.S.R.	16 A.D.U.S.	7/ 1/18 1y 9m, Pte.
NEWNHAM, C. A., Pte. 40 Bn.		23/10/16
NEWPORT, N. J., Pte. 12 Bn.	22 M G. Bn.	14/12/15 3y 9m, Pte.
NEWPORT W., Dvr. 3 F.A.B.	W., M M.	21/ 8/15 3y 2m, Gnr.
NEWTON, A., J., Pte. 12 Bn.	2W.	1/ 5/16 3y 4m, Dvr.
NEWTON, A. E., Pte. 12 Bn.	M.S.M., M.I.D. A.I.F.H.Q.	8/ 1/15 4y 7m, W.O.
NEWTON, C. R., Dvr. 3 A.F.A.	4 Div Arty, 3 A.F.A. Bde ✠ 10/9/18	22/ 7/15 Dvr. ✠
NEWTON, L. M., Cpl. 12 Bn.	Croix de Guerre	24/ 8/14 4y 7m, Lt.
NEWTON, T. J., Pte. 12 Bn.	M.I.D., 1 Div. Traffic Control	1/ 6/15 4y 1m, Cpl.
NEWTON, V. G., Dvr. 8 Fd. Co.		3/ 5/16
NIBBS, C. L., Pte. 40 Bn.	W. ✠ 12/10/17.	4/ 4/16 Pte. ✠
NIBBS, L. R., Pte. 40 Bn.	49 Bn.	17/ 4/16 3y 6m, L.-Cpl.
NIBBS, T., Gnr. 9 Fd. Bty.	W., M.M., 6 Bty.	4/ 9/15 4y, Sgt.
NIBBS, T. H., Pte. 12 Bn.	W., 51 Bn.	11/ 1/16 3y 6m, Pte.
NIBBS, W. F. D., Pte, 40 Bn	W.	4/ 3/16 2y 11m, Pte.
NIBBS, W. J., Pte. 15 Bn.	✠ 26/5/15.	19/ 9/14 Pte. ✠
NICHOLAS, T. D., Sgt. 12 Bn.		19/ 6/16 3y 3m, Lt.
NICHOLAS, H. C., Tpr. 3 L.H.	✠ 4-6/8/16.	26/ 8/14 L.-Cpl. ✠
NICHOLAS, N., Pte. 40 Bn.	2W., 69 Bn., 40 Bn.	14/ 2/16 2y 5m, Pte.
NICHOLAS, P. D., Pte. 12 Bn.	M.G. Co. ✠ 25/7/16.	2/9/14 Capt. ✠
NICHOLL, G. J., Pte. A.A.M.C.	7 F.A.B.	9/10/16
NICHOLSON, A. D., Gnr. Arty.		4/ 1/17 2y 2m,, Gnr.
NICHOLSON, E. P. W., Pte 12 Bn	2W., 52 Bn. ✠ 26/9/17	7/10/15 Pte. ✠
NICHOLSON, F G., Pte. 12 Bn.	✠ 11/12/16.	25/11/14 L.-Cpl. ✠
NICHOLSON, G. R., Pte. 12 Bn.	2W.	30/ 5/16 3y 4m, Pte.
NICHOLSON, J., Gnr. Arty.	1 D.A.C.	8/11/16 2y 10m, Dvr.
NICHOLSON, P., Pte 12 Bn.	4 Co. A.S.C.	27/10/16 2y 11m, Pte.
NICHOLSON, R., Pte. 12 Bn.		12/ 6/16 1y 7m, Pte.
NICHOLSON, R. N., Tpr. 3 L.H.	1 L H. Training Regt.	29/11/17
NICKEL, A. A., Pte. 15 Bn,	M M., 8 Bn.	25/ 9/14 4y 9m, C.S.M
NICHOLLS, A. E., Pte. 15 Bn.	4 M.G. Bn	17/ 8/15 4y, Sgt.
NICHOLS, A. Pte. 12 Bn.	W., 47 Bn. ✠ 1/11/17.	16/ 9/15 Pte. ✠
NICHOLS, A. L., Pte. 12 Bn.	2W.	20/ 8/14 4y 5m, L.-Cpl.
NICHOLS, A. D., Pte. 12 Bn.	W. 1 Pnrs.	17/ 2/16 3y 7m, Gnr.
NICHOLS, D R., Gnr. Arty.	10 F A B.	17/ 2/16 3y 7m, Gnr.
NICHOLLS, E., Dvr. 6 Fd. Co.	14 Fd. Co.	2/10/15 3y 11m, Dvr.
NICHOLLS, E. J., Pte. 12 Bn.	W., M.M.	19/ 8/14 5y 2m, Lt.
NICHOLLS, E. F., Pte. 12 Bn.	1 Div. Sig. Co.	9/ 2/15 4y 5m, Sgt.
NICHOLS, E. A., Spr. Tnlrs.	1 Tun. Co.	5/ 4/16
NICHOLS, E. A. Gnr. Arty.	W. 13 F.A.B.	27/ 1/16 2y 7m, Gnr.
NICHOLS, E. G., Pte. 40 Bn.		7/ 3/16 3y 7m. Dvr.
NICHOLS, G. A., Pte. 12 Bn.	10 F.A.B.	10/ 8/15 3y 8m. Dvr.
NICHOLS, G. V., Pte. A.A.M.C.	1 Fd. Amb.	24/ 2/16 3y 9m. Pte.
NICHOLS, H. G., Pte. 3 G.S.R.	12 Bn.	10/ 5/18 1y 7m. Pte.
NICHOLLS, H. G., Pte. 12 Bn.		2/ 6/16 3y 4m. Pte.
NICHOLS, H. J., Tpr. 3 L.H.		20/ 8/14 4y 6m. SQMS
NICHOLS, H., Pte. 15 Bn.	W. 10 F.A.B., 37 Bn.	18/ 9/14 4y 6m. Dvr.
NICHOLS, H. L., Gnr. Rfts.	110 Bty.	28/11/16 2y 9m. Gnr.

NAME.	REMARKS.	RANK ON ENLISTED, DISCHARGE. SERVICE.
NICHOLS, J. T., Tpr. 3 L.H.		20/ 8/14 2y 2m. Tpr.
NICHOLS, J. G., Tpr. 3 L.H.	1st Bty.	28/ 8/15 2y Gnr.
NICHOLS, J. J., Pte. 40 Bn.		30/ 9/16
NICHOLS, J., Gnr. Art.	1D.A.C.	2/11/15 3y 10m. Dvr.
NICHOLS, M. R., Pte. 26 Bn.	W. 69 Bn., 26 Bn.	19/ 4/15 4y 5m. Pte.
NICHOLS, N. J., Cpl. 7 Fd. Amb.	W.	9/ 2/15
NICHOLS, R. V., Pte. 40 Bn.	28 A.A.S.C.	8/11/16 2y 8m. Pte.
NICHOLS, R. J., Pte. 3 G.S.R.	12 Bn.	30/ 7/18 Pte.
NICHOLS, R. H., Pte. Rly.	4 Rly Co.	20/ 9/17
NICHOLS, T. J., Pte. 12 Bn.		13/11/15 3y 10m. Sgt.
NICHOLLS, T., Pte. 12 Bn.	W. 49 Bn.	4/ 4/16 3y 4m. Pte.
NICHOLS, T., Pte. 1 A.G.H.		16/ 9/14 2y 3m. Pte.
NICHOLS, V. A., Gnr. Art.	W. 112 How. Bty.	13/ 9/15 4y. Gnr.
NICHOLS, W., L/Cpl. 40 Bn.		21/ 2/16 Lieut.
NICHOLS, W. H., Dvr. 3 F.A.B.	W.	20/ 9/15 4y. Gnr.
NICHOLS, W., Pte 12 Bn.	W.	19/ 7/16
NICHOL, A. F., Munition Worker		
NEILSON, H. R., Pte. A.S.C.	2W. 12 Bn.	19/ 8/14 4y 8m. L-Cpl.
NEILSON, M. T. A., Pte. 12 Bn.	T.M.B.	25/ 8/15 2y 9m. Pte.
NIELSON, P., Pte. 4 M.G. Co.		21/ 7/16
NIELSON, P. V., Pte. 12 Bn.	W. M.M.	20/ 8/14 4y 5m. Pte.
NIGHTINGALE, G. A., Pte. 26 Bn.	12 Bn. ✠ 11/12/16	20/ 3/15 Pte. ✠
NILLSON, E. B., Pte. 12 Bn.	W.	11/ 8/15 1y 9m. Pte.
NILLSEN, O. N., Spr. 6 Fd. Co.	8 Fd. Co., 16 Fd. Co., 6 Fd. Co.	11/ 8/15 3y 8m. Spr.
NILSEN, J. H., Gnr. 8 A.F.A.	W. 13 A.F.A. Bde. ✠ 10/8/18	2/ 2/16 Gnr. ✠
NISBET, R. R., Pte. 12 Bn.	W.	1/11/16 2y 5m. Pte.
NISI, H., Dvr. D.A.C.	W. 4 F.A.B.	12/ 8/15 4y 1m. Gnr.
NISI, W., Pte. 52 Bn.	W.	10/ 8/15 2y 6m. Pte.
NOBES, G. C., Pte. 15 Bn.	✠ 21/12/16	14/ 9/15 L-Cpl. ✠
NOBES, K., Gnr. Art.	27 Fd. Bty.	10/10/16 3y 1m. Gnr.
NOBES, M. C., Pte. 3 Fd. Amb.	W. 6 Fd. Amb.	9/ 6/15 4y 2m. Pte.
NOBLE, C. E. L., Dvr. 3 F.A.B.	103 How. Bde.	31/ 8/15 4y 2m. Dvr.
NOBLE, L. A., Pte. 15 Bn.	W. 12 L.T.M.B.	31/ 8/15 3y 8m. Cpl.
NOLAN, H. G. B., Tpr. L.H.	W.	18/10/15 1y 11m. Tpr.
NOLAN, J., Spr. Rly.	2 L.O. Rly. Co.	23/ 4/17 2y 5m. Spr.
NOLAN, J., Pte. 12 Bn.		23/ 4/17
NOLAN, T. W., Pte. 2 G.S.R.	6 A.M.T. Co.	23/ 3/18 1y 8m. Pte.
NOLAN, W., Pte. 15 Bn.	4 Pioneers.	3/ 2/15 4y 2m. Pte.
NOLAN, W. H., Pte. 12 Bn.	W. M.M. 40 Bn.	22/ 5/15
NORBURN, J. B., Sgt. 12 Bn.	W.	14/ 7/15 3y. Sgt.
NORBURY, F., Pte. 12 Bn.		29/ 8/14 4y 5m. Dvr.
NORDQUIST, F. A., Pte. 40 Bn.		28/11/16
NORMAN, A., Pte. 40 Bn.		19/ 3/17 2y 5m. Pte.
NORMAN, E., Pte. 15 Bn.		25/11/14 1y 10m. Pte.
NORMAN, J., Pte. 12 Bn.	Anzac Police	16/11/15 10m Pte.
NORMAN, M., Pte. 40 Bn.	3W.	23/11/16 2y 10m. Pte.
NORMAN, G. H. L., Gnr. Art.	3 A.F.A. Bde. ✠ 20/10/18.	1/ 3/17 Gnr. ✠
NORMAN, W. J., Pte. 40 Bn.		4/ 2/18 1y 2m. Pte.
NORTHCOTT, J., Lt. 12 Bn.		24/ 8/14 2y 1m, Capt.
NORQUAY, J. C., Spr. S. Sig. Ser.	1 Sig. Co.	21/ 3/17 2y 6m. Dvr.
NORQUAY, W. J., Pte. 40 Bn.	✠ 13/10/17.	29/ 5/16 Cpl. ✠
NORRIS, A. J., Pte. 12 Bn.		28/ 8/16 3y 4m. Pte.
NORRIS, A. A., Pte. 26 Bn.	4 Fd. Co.	4/ 5/15 1y 3m. Spr.
NORRIS, F. G., Tpr. 3 L.H.	4 L.H.	20/ 1/17 2y 8m. Tpr.
NORRIS, J., Pte. 40 Bn.		8/ 2/16 3y 2m. Pte.
NORRIS, R. R., Pte. 12 Bn.	W.	8/ 6/16 3y 5m. Pte.
NORRIS, R., Tpr. 3 L.H.	4 L.H.	13/ 4/17 2y 5m. Tpr.
NORRIS, R. A., Pte. 12 Bn.		5/12/17
NORRIS, T., Pte. 12 Bn.	W.	19/ 5/16 3y 4m. Pte.
NORRIS, T. H., Pte. 40 Bn.		25/ 8/16 1y 4m. Pte.
NORRIS, W. J., L/Cpl. 12 Bn.	52 Bn. ✠ 29/3/17.	15/ 7/15 Cpl. ✠
NORTH, E. N., Tpr. 3 L.H.		22/10/17 1y 9m. Tpr.
NOTHROP, E., Pte. 12 Bn.		4/ 4/16 3y 8m Pte.
NOTHROP, P., Pte. 12 Bn.	51 Bn.	4/ 4/16 3y 4m. Pte.
NORTHROP, P. D., Cpl. 12 Bn.	✠ 15/1/16.	4/ 8/15 Cpl. ✠
NORTON, C. C., Pte. 12 Bn.		15/ 1/18 1y 9m. Pte.
NORTON, H. O., Pte. 40 Bn.	W.	28/ 9/16 2y 10m. Pte.
NORTON, S., Pte. 12 Bn.		1/ 5/16 2y Pte.
NORTON, S. R. J. J., Pte 1 A.G.H.		4/ 6/15 8m. Pte.
NORTON, W. H., Pte. 13 Fd. Amb.		7/12/14 4y 5m. Dvr.
NUGENT, J. W., Pte. 12 Bn.	13 M.G. Co.	3/ 8/15 4y. Dvr.
NUNN, E. A., Pte. 40 Bn.		28/ 8/17 2y 2m. Pte.
NUNN, E. H., Pte. 40 Bn.	49 Bn.	26/ 4/16 3y 5m. Dvr.
NUNN, H., Spr. 3 Tunlrs.		16/10/16 10m. Spr.
NUNN, J. E., Pte. 2 G.S.R.	103 How. Bty.	7/ 5/18 1y 6m. Gnr.
NUNN, J. L. Pte. 12 Bn.	W. ✠ 16/3/18.	27/ 7/15 Pte. ✠
NUNN, J. E., Pte. 40 Bn.	3W.	7/ 6/16
NUNN, R. C., Pte. 40 Bn.		7/11/16 1y 10m. Pte.
NUTTING, J. R., Pte. Rly.	W.	10/ 1/17 2y 8m. Spr.
NUTTING, W. H., Pte. 26 Bn.	W. 1 Anzac Co.	1/ 5/15 4y 6m. Pte.
OAKDEN, J. R., Pte. 12 Bn.	W., 13 L.T.M. Bde., 52 Bn.	7/ 9/15 3y 7m, Pte.
OAKES, W. F. J., Pte. 12 Bn.		6/ 3/16.
OAKFORD, J. J., Spr. Tnlrs.	W.	4/ 9/16 3y, Spr.
OAKLEY, H., Pte. 26 Bn.	W.	20/ 7/15 3y 10m, Pte.
OAKLEY, H. J., Pte. 12 Bn.	W., 13 Fd. Co.	14/ 1/15 2y 6m, Pte.
OAKLEY, J. S., Pte. 12 Bn.	✠ 12 /4/17.	3/11/15 Pte. ✠

TASMANIA'S MUSTER ROLL. 321

NAME.	REMARKS.	RANK ON DISCHARGE. ENLISTED. SERVICE.
OAKLEY, J. W., Pte. 40 Bn.	W.	18/ 5/16 3y 5m, Pte.
OAKLEY, R., Pte. 40 Bn.	2W.	28/ 9/16 2y 5m, Pte.
OAKLEY, W. H., Pte. 12 Bn.	✤ 25-28/4/15.	29/ 8/14 Pte. ✤
OATES, A. T., Pte. 40 Bn.		19/ 7/16. ! /
OATES, C., Pte. 40 Bn.	2W., 51 Bn.	29/ 2/16 2y 3m, Pte.
OATES, D. R., Pte. 40 Bn.	2W., M.M.	19/ 7/16 3y 1m, Pte.
OATES, E. J., Pte. 12 Bn.		25/ 9/16 3y, Pte.
OATLEY, W. J., Pte. 12 Bn.	W.	3/ 9/14 2y, Pte.
ODDY, E. W., Gnr. Arty.	3 F.A.B., A.O.C.	6/10/14 4y 10m, Gnr.
OGILVIE, F. A., Gnr. Arty.	W., 23 How. Bde., 8 F.A.B.	11/ 1/16 3y 5m, Gnr.
OGILVIE, G. H., Pte. 1 G.S.R.		15/ 3/18 1y 9m, Pte.
OHLSON, O. E., Pte. 40 Bn.	W. ✤26/2/17.	3/ 3/16 Pte. ✤
OHLSON, T., Pte. 12 Bn.	52 Bn. ✤ 4/9/16.	17/ 1/16 Pte. ✤
OLDEN, A. G., Spr. Tnlrs.	2W., 2 Tnl. Co.	8/ 6/16 3y, Spr.
OLDHAM, N. F., M. Worker.		
OLDHAM, O. M'G., Pte. 15 Bn.	12 Bn., 10 F.A.B. ✤ 2/6/18.	3/ 8/15 Dvr. ✤
OLDHAM, T. F., Pte. 12 Bn.	✤ 16/4/17.	7/ 8/16 Pte. ✤
OLDHAM, W. C., Dvr. 4 M.G. Co.	W., 12 M.G. Co., 4 M.G. Co.	9/10/16 2y 11m, Dvr.
OLDING, C. A., Pte. 40 Bn.	2W.	31/ 1/16 3y 2m, Pte.
OLDING, J. S., Pte. 40 Bn.	W.	31/10/16 2y 9m, Pte.
OLDING, R. F., Pte. 12 Bn.	✤ 5-8/5/17.	4/ 9/16 Pte. ✤
OLIVER, A. J., Tpr. 3 L.H.		10/ 3/15 1y 10m, Tpr.
OLIVER, A., Pte. 12 Bn.	W., M.M., 49 Bn.	26/10/15 4y 1m, Pte.
OLIVER, E., Pte. 12 Bn.	W.	7/ 1/15 1y 9m, Pte.
OLIVER, F., Spr. 6 Fd. Co.	W., 12 Fd. Co., 8 Fd. Co.	6/ 1/16 4y, Dvr
OLIVER, H. M., Pte. 40 Bn.	3 A.A.H.	14/ 3/16 3y 8m, Pte.
OLIVER, J., Pte. 26 Bn.	W.	22/ 6/15 4y 2m, Pte.
OLIVER, J. W., Pte. 26 Bn.		1/ 5/15 1y 4m, Pte.
OLIVER, M. B., Pte. 12 Bn.	✤ 6/9/15.	30/11/14 Pte. ✤
OLIVER, M. H., Pte. 40 Bn.		31/10/16 3y 3m, Pte.
OLIVER, N. O., Pte. 40 Bn.	15 Bn. ✤ 11/4/17.	2/ 6/16 Pte. ✤
OLIVER, R. J., Tpr. 3 L.H.		13/10/15 4y 1m, Tpr.
OLIVER, R. M., Spr. Miners.	3 Tnl. Co.	16/ 8/18 1y, Spr.
OLIVER, W. S., Pte. 3 G.S.R.	12 Bn. ✤ 27/1/19.	24/ 6/18 Pte. ✤
OLSEN, A. W., Pte. 26 Bn.	2 Div. H.Q.	13/ 3/15 4y 7m, Pte.
OLSEN, C., Pte. 12 Bn.	2W.	31/ 5/15 4y 2m, Pte.
OLSEN, F. K., Pte. 12 Bn.		17/ 5/17.
OLLEY, E. H., Sgt. 26 Bn.	✤ 4/8/16.	1/ 4/15 2nd. Lt. ✤
ONIONS, A. C., Pte. 15 Bn.	M.M. ✤ 11/6/17.	5/12/14 Pte. ✤
ONIONS, E. I., Pte. 12 Bn.	52 Bn., 51 Bn.	2/ 8/15 3y 8m, Pte.
OLDMEADOW, H. R. J., Gnr. 6 F.A.B.	A.F.C.	13/ 9/15 4y 2m, 2nd Lt.
ORBELL, H. C., Lt. 12 Bn.	W.	20/ 9/14 2y 6m, Lt.
ORCHARD, A. A., Bdr. 3 F.A.B.	M.C., 4 Div. Arty., 10 F.A.B.	27/ 8/14 5y 1m, 2nd Lt.
ORCHARD, A. W., Sig. 12 Bn.	M.M., 52 Bn., 24 How. Bde. ✤ 15/7/17.	7/ 3/15 Gnr. ✤
ORCHARD, L. D., Cpl. 3 F.A.B.	W., 4 Div. Arty.	27/ 8/14 4y 5m, Cpl.
ORCHARD, W., Pte.		18/11/16.
ORCHARD, W. A., Pte. 40 Bn.	W., 10 M.G. Co. ✤ 11/4/18.	16/ 3/16 Pte. ✤
ORDERS, W., Pte. 12 Bn.		26/10/16 2y 9m, Pte.
ORME, R. H., 2-A.M. A.F.C.	4 A.F.C.	11/ 9/16 2y, 2nd A.M.
ORPWOOD, A. M., Pte. M.G. Rfts.	37 Bn.	12/ 8/17 1y 2m, Pte.
ORPWOOD, W. E., Pte. 12 Bn.	W., 52 Bn., 50 Bn.	9/11/15 3y 9m, Pte.
OSBORNE, A. E., Pte. 12 Bn.	2W.	5/ 4/16 2y 11m, Pte.
OSBORNE, G., Pte. 26 Bn.	12 Bn.	13/ 7/15.
OSBORNE, J. H., Pte. 40 Bn.		3/ 5/16.
OSBORNE, R., Pte. 40 Bn.		1/ 7/16 3y 2m, Pte.
OSBORNE, W. G., Gnr. Arty.	W., 5 D.A.C. 14 F.A.B.	9/10/16 2y 11m, Gnr.
OSMOND, A. E., Pte. 40 Bn.		4/ 9/17 1y 2m, Pte.
OSMOND, G., Dvr. 3 A.A.M.T.	W., 5 A.S. Park, A.M.T.S.	7/10/16 3y, Dvr.
OSWALD, B., Pte. 40 Bn.		15/ 9/16.
OSWIN, A., Spr. Miners.	2 Tnl. Co.	27/ 3/16 3y 7m, Spr.
OSWIN, G. L., Pte. 2 A.L.H.		15/11/15 1y 3m, Pte.
OVERALL, A. C. R., Pte. 12 Bn.	15 Bn.	7/12/15 3y 10m, Pte.
OWEN, A. E., Cpl. 26 Bn.	Re-enl. 12 Bn., A.I.F. H.Q.	12/ 5/15 3y 7m, Cpl.
OWEN, A. W., Pte. 26 Bn.	✤ 23/7/18.	27/ 9/16 Pte. ✤
OWEN, D., Pte. 26 Bn.		23/ 3/15.
OWEN, H. E. R., Pte. 12 Bn.	✤ 14/3/18.	11/10/16 Pte. ✤
OWEN, H. G., Gnr. Arty.	10 F.A.B., 39 Bty.	20/ 1/17 2y 7m, Gnr.
OWEN, J. W., Dvr. Arty.	3 D.A.C. Employ. Co., 3 D.A.C.	29/ 2/16 3y 1m, Gnr.
OWEN J. T., Pte. 26 Bn.	✤ 5/8/16.	19/ 2/15 Pte. ✤
OWEN, L. D., Tpr. 3 L.H.		9/11/17 1y 9m, Tpr.
OWEN, L. J., Pte. 15 Bn.	✤ 8/8/15.	21/ 5/15 Pte. ✤
OWEN, O. P., M.T. Dvr. 3 G.S.R.	A.M.T. Service.	29/ 7/18 1y 4m, Dvr.
OWEN, R. T., Pte. 12 Bn.	W.	30/ 7/15 2y 2m, Pte.
OWEN, R. V., Pte. 1 G.S.R.	40 Bn.	19/ 2/18 1y 1m, Pte.
OWEN, S. J., Pte. 40 Bn.		3/ 4/16 1y 11m, Pte.
OWERS, A. L., Pte. 12 Bn.	W.	21/ 5/17 2y, Pte.
OXLEY, C., Pte. 2 G.S.R.	1 Bn.	6/11/17 1y 10m, Pte.
OXLEY, E. A., Pte. 40 Bn.	W., 15 Bn., 40 Bn. ✤ 2/10/17.	18/ 3/16 Pte. ✤
O'BEIRNE, J. B., Pte. 40 Bn.	W.	7/ 6/16 1y 10m, Pte.
O'BRIEN, A., Pte. 4 M.G. Co.		7/11/16 Pte.
O'BRIEN, B. C. H., Pte. 40 Bn.	✤ 7/6/17.	26/ 2/16 Pte. ✤
O'BRIEN, B. A., Pte. 26 Bn.		18/ 3/15 4y 9m, Cpl.
O'BRIEN, B. J., Pte 15 Bn	W., M.M. ✤ 29/3/18.	6/ 9/15 Sgt. ✤
O'BRIEN, C. E., Pte. 12 Bn.	✤ 3-5/9/16.	22/ 7/15 Pte. ✤
O'BRIEN, E. H., Tpr. 3 L.H.		10/ 4/17 2y 6m, Tpr.

U

322 TASMANIA'S WAR RECORD, 1914-1918.

NAME.	REMARKS.	RANK ON DISCHARGE. ENLISTED. SERVICE.
O'BRIEN, E., Pte. 40 Bn.	W.	16/10/16 2y 6m, Pte.
O'BRIEN, G. G., Pte. 40 Bn.		12/10/16 2y 11m, Pte.
O'BRIEN, H., Pte. 40 Bn.	W. ✠ 10/4/17.	28/ 3/16 Pte. ✠
O'BRIEN, H. J., M. Worker.		
O'BRIEN, J. D., Pte. 2 G.S.R.	12 Bn.	17/ 6/18 1y 3m, Pte.
O'BRIEN, K. L., Tpr. 3 L.H.	5 D.A.C.	Tpr.
O'BRIEN, M. J., Pte. 40 Bn.		18/ 5/16 3y 4m, Pte.
O'BRIEN, M. M., Dvr. Arty.	2 D.A.C., 22 F.A.B., 4 F A.B.	7/11/15 3y 9m, Dvr.
O'BRIEN, P., Pte. 26 Bn.	W.	2/ 5/15 1y 1m, Pte.
O'BRIEN, R. B., Pte. 15 Bn.		13/ 8/15 3y 9m, Pte.
O'BRIEN, S. G., Pte. 40 Bn.	✠ 30/3/18.	5/ 3/16 Pte. ✠
O'BRIEN, W. J., Pte. 26 Bn.	✠ 29/7/16.	15/ 9/15 Pte. ✠
O'BRIEN, W., Dvr. 12 Bn.		24/ 5/15 2y 9m, Pte.
O'CALLAGHAN, I. J., Pte. 1 A.G.H.		1/ 6/15.
O'CONNOR, C., Pte. 12 Bn.	2W.	17/10/16 2y 6m, Pte.
O'CONNOR, F. R., Pte. 40 Bn.	2W.	15/ 3/16 2y, Pte.
O'CONNOR, M., Pte. 12 Bn.	W.	6/ 9/14 2y 9m, Pte.
O'CONNOR, P., Pte. 1 A.C.H.		20/ 7/15.
O'CONNOR, R., Pte. 12 Bn.		1/12/14.
O'CONNOR, R. R., Pte. 12 Bn.	✠ August, 1916.	27/ 1/15 Pte. ✠
O'CONNOR, W. N., Pte. 40 Bn.	2W., 49 Bn.	29/ 3/16 3y 9m, Pte.
O'CONNOR, W. S., Dvr. 7 Fd. Amb.	13 Fd. Amb.	14/ 4/15 4y 6m, Dvr.
O'DOHERTY, H. P., Pte. 26 Bn.	3W., 69 Bn., 26 Bn.	15/ 2/15 4y 3m, Pte.
O'DOHERTY, J. F., Pte. A.S.C.	A.D.T. ✠ 9/2/19.	6/12/17 Pte. ✠
O'DONNELL, J. F., Tpr. 3 L.H.	Re-enl. 20/11/16.	28/ 3/15 2y 2m, Tpr.
O'DONNELL, A., Pte. 40 Bn.	W., 12 Bn.	5/10/16 1y 11m, Pte.
O'DONNELL, D., Pte. 12 Bn.		17/11/16 2y 10m, Pte.
O'DONNELL, J., Gnr. F.A. Rfts.		11/ 1/16.
O'DONNELL, J., Pte. 12 Bn.	40 Bn. ✠ 5/10/17.	7/ 4/16 Pte. ✠
O'DONNELL, T., Tpr. 3 L.H.		3/ 2/17.
O'DWYER, J. H., 2nd Cpl. Miners.	W., 2 Pnr. Bn.	24/ 2/16.
O'GAREY, R. A., Pte. 40 Bn.	W.	8/ 2/16 2y 5m, Pte.
O'HALLARON, C. A., Pte. 26 Bn.	W.	4/ 8/15 2y, Pte.
O'HALLARON, J. W., Cpl. 12 Bn.	✠ 25/2/17.	29/ 9/15 Cpl. ✠
O'HALLARON, M. J., Pte. 12 Bn.	2W., 52 Bn.	15/ 7/15 4y 1m, Pte.
O'HARA, S., Gnr. 3 F.A.B.	2W., B.M.	27/ 8/14 3y 9m, 2nd Lt.
O'HALLORAN, V. E., Pte. 4 M.G. Co		17/10/16 10m, Pte.
O'KEEFE, A. H., Pte. 40 Bn.	2W.	17/10/16 2y 5m, Pte.
O'KEEFE, D. L., Pte. 4 M.G. Co.	W., 15 M.G. Co., 3 M.G. Co.	20/11/16 2y 5m, Pte.
O'KEEFE, J. F., Gnr. Arty.		14/ 3/17.
O'KEEFE, J. M., Pte. 12 Bn.	40 Bn.	18/10/16 2y 11m, Pte.
O'KEEFE, M., Tpr. 4 G.S.R.	3 L.H.	15/ 3/17 2y 5m, Tpr.
O'KEEFE, M., Pte. 12 Bn.	M.M.	3/ 8/15.
O'KEEFE, R., Pte. 40 Bn.		21/ 8/16 1y 10m, Pte.
O'KELLY, A. R., Pte. 3 L.H.	W.	20/ 8/14 Tpr.
O'LEARY, A., Pte. 12 Bn.	52 Bn., 51 Bn.	5/ 7/15 4y 1m, Pte.
O'LEARY, S., Pte. 2 Pnrs.	52 Bn.	24/ 2/17 2y 10m, Pte.
O'LEARY, W. J., Pte. 26 Bn.		13/ 4/15.
O'LOUGHLIN, J. J., Dvr. 12 Bn.		4/ 9/14 4y 4m, Dvr.
O'MALLEY, A., Pte. 12 Bn.	✠ 27/9/18.	6/ 9/16 Pte. ✠
O'MALLEY, C. A., Cpl. 12 Bn.	✠ 3-5/9/16.	19/ 8/14 Sgt. ✠
O'MALLEY, J., Pte. 12 Bn.		8/ 1/15 3y 3m, Pte.
O'MALLEY, J. E., Pte. 12 Bn.		18/ 8/16.
O'NEAL, A. Pte. 40 Bn.	W.	15/ 2/17.
O'NEIL, A. H. H., Pte. 12 Bn.	51 Bn.	17/ 8/14 4y 4m, L-Cpl.
O'NEAL, H. A., Pte. 12 Bn.	52 Bn.	4/ 1/16 1y 4m, Pte.
O'NEAL, J. T. A., Pte. 12 Bn.	W., 52 Bn. ✠ 26/1/17.	4/ 1/15 Cpl. ✠
O'NEILL, J. A., Pte. 12 Bn.	W., M.M. ✠ 25/11/19.	1/ 6/15 2nd Cpl. ✠
O'NEIL, J. R., Spr. 3 Fd. Co.	5 Fd. Co., 15 Fd. Co. ✠ 21/8/16.	7/ 9/15 Spr. ✠
O'NEILL, S. H., Pte. 12 Bn.	Enlisted as Smith, S.H. ✠ 23/8/18.	22/ 9/16 Pte. ✠
O'REILY, J. J., Pte. 12 Bn.	W.	16/ 7/15.
O'REILLY, M. E., Pte. 12 Bn.	W.	9/ 8/16 2y 9m, Pte.
O'REILLY, O., Pte. 40 Bn.		
O'REILLY, O. M. Worker.		1/ 7/16 1y 4m, Pte.
O'REILLY, T. G., Pte. 12 Bn.	69 Bn., 12 Bn.	12/ 1/15 3y 3m, Pte.
O'ROURKE, A. J., Pte. 40 Bn.		23/ 5/16 3y 6m, Cpl.
O'ROURKE, E. F., Pte. 12 Bn.	40 Bn. ✠ 4/10/17.	8/ 8/16 Pte. ✠
O'ROURKE, H., Pte. 2 G.S.R.		7/ 6/17.
O'ROURKE, J. D., Pte. 40 Bn.	✠ 5/4/17.	4/ 5/16 Pte. ✠
O'ROURKE, L. W., Pte. 26 Bn.	✠ 29/7/16.	9/ 4/15 Pte. ✠
O'ROURKE, P. J., Spr. Tnlrs.		5/ 5/16
O'ROURKE, T. G., Pte. 12 Bn.		17/10/16 2y 11m, Pte.
O'ROURKE, W., Spr. Tnlrs.		20/ 2/17 6m, Spr.
O'SHANNESSY, E., Pte. 40 Bn.	W. ✠ 5/10/17.	9/11/16 Pte. ✠
O'SHEA, H., Pte. 12 Bn.	3W., 69 Bn., 3 A.L.T.M. Bty.	22/ 8/14 4y 7m, Pte.
O'SHEA, J., Gnr. Arty.	3W.	12/12/14 4y 5m, Gnr.
O'SULLIVAN, J., Pte. 4 M.G. Co.		1/ 2/16.
O'TOOLE, C., Pte. 12 Bn.	W.	1/12/14 4y 7m, Pte.
O'TOOLE, C. J., Pte. 40 Bn.	W.	12/ 2/16 2y 7m, Pte.
O'TOOLE, H., Pte. 40 Bn.	W.	29/ 9/16 3y, Pte.
O'TOOLE, M. G., Pte. 12 Bn.	W., 51 Bn.	5/ 1/16 3y 8m, Cpl.
O'TOOLE, M. P., Spr. Miners.		11/11/15.
PACE, J. S., Spr. 3 Fd. Co.	15 Fd. Co. ✠ 10/4/18.	22/ 7/15 Spr. ✠
PACEY, A. L., Dvr. 26 Bn.	M.S.M., M.I.D.	20/ 4/15 4y 5m, Sgt.
PACEY, H. C., Pte. 26 Bn.	✠ 5/8/16.	4/ 5/15 Pte. ✠
PACKER, J. S., Gnr. F.A. Rfts.	1 D.A.C.	2/10/16 2y 6m, Dvr.

TASMANIA'S MUSTER ROLL. 323

NAME.	REMARKS.	RANK ON DISCHARGE. ENLISTED. SERVICE.
PACKER, S. S., Pte. 12 Bn.		20/ 8/14 3y 3m, L.-Cpl.
PADMAN, C. V., Pte. 1 G.S.R.	3 D.A.C.	1/ 3/18 1y 7m, Gnr.
PADMAN, F. W., Pte. 12 Bn.	40 Bn.	17/ 9/15 1y 11m, Pte.
PAGE, C. W., Pte. 40 Bn.	W.	2/10/16.
PAGE, D., Pte. 15 Bn.	2W.	6/ 9/15 3y 11m, Pte.
PAGE, F., Pte. 12 Bn.		16/11/14 7m, Pte.
PAGE, G. E., Pte. 1 A.G.H.	M.S.M., 1 A.G.H.	27/ 5/15 4y 6m, Sgt.
PAGE, G. R., Gnr. A.F.A.	✢ 7/8/16.	13/ 9/15 Gnr. ✢
PAGE, H. L. H., Pte. 12 Bn.	✢ 9/12/16.	3/11/15 Pte. ✢
PAGE, I., Dvr. 6 A.F.A.		13/ 9/15.
PAGE, J. L. J., Pte. 1 G.S.R.	40 Bn.	16/ 8/17 2y 2m, Pte.
PAGE, L. F., Cpl. 26 Bn.	✢ 13/11/16.	19/ 4/15 C.S.M. ✢
PAGE, O. A., Sgt. 12 Bn.	✢ 27/11/17.	7/ 8/16 Sgt. ✢
PAGE, P., Pte. 26 Bn.	2W., 69 Bn., 26 Bn.	29/ 9/15.
PAGE, R, Pte. 12 Bn.	✢ 1/11/17.	27/ 6/16 Pte. ✢
PAGE, R. M., Cpl. 6 Fd. Co.	W.	27/ 8/15 1y 10m, Spr.
PAGE, R. H. J., Pte. 1 G.S.R.		19/ 3/17.
PAGE, S. G., Pte. 40 Bn.	W.	2/10/16 2y 3m, Pte.
PAGE, V. J., Pte. 40 Bn.		2/11/16
PAINTON, G. C., Pte. 12 Bn.	3 M.G. Co. ✢ 23/7/16.	20/ 8/14 Sgt. ✢
PALFREYMAN, J. W., Pte. 12 Bn.	W. ✢ 25-28/4/15.	21/ 8/14 Pte. ✢
PALLISER, A. T., Pte. 12 Bn.	1 A.M.T. Co.	13/ 7/15 4y 3m, Dvr.
PALMER, A., Pte. 40 Bn.	W. ✢ 22/4/18.	13/ 5/16 Pte. ✢
PALMER, A. J. B. T., Pte. 12 Bn.	4 D.A.C.	17/11/15 3y 10m, Dvr.
PALMER, C. F., Pte. 15 Bn.	✢ 23/8/15.	1/10/14 Pte. ✢
PALMER, E., Pte. 40 Bn.	W.	1/11/16 2y 8m, Pte.
PALMER, E. S., L.-Cpl. 15 Bn.	W. ✢ 8/8/15.	30/ 9/14 L.-Cpl. ✢
PALMER, J. A., Pte. 26 Bn.	W.	21/ 4/15 4y 4m, Pte.
PALMER, J. H., Cpl. 12 Bn.	W., 1 M.G. Co.	26/ 9/16 2y 6m, Pte.
PALMER, J., Pte. 40 Bn.	W.	27/ 3/16 3y, Pte.
PALMER, J., Pte. 12 Bn.	W.	30/10/16 2y 6m, Pte.
PALMER, J. T., Pte. 12 Bn.		26/12/17.
PALMER, L., Pte. 40 Bn.	W.	1/11/16 1y 10m, Pte.
PALMER, L. R., Pte. 40 Bn.	2W.	3/ 4/16.
PALMER, P., Pte. 40 Bn.	2W.	27/ 3/16 2y 3m, L.-Sgt.
PALMER, R. A., Pte. 40 Bn.	W.	3/ 4/16 1y 7m, Pte.
PALMER, S. H., Pte. 40 Bn.	W., A.I.F. H.Q.	2/11/16 3y, Pte.
PAMPHLETT, J. T., Pte. 26 Bn.		28/ 8/15 1y 7m, Pte.
PAMPLIN, A. T., Pte. 15 Bn.	W.	9/ 2/15 4y 3m, Pte.
PAMPLIN, F. W., Gnr. 3 F.A.B.		26/ 7/15 3y 9m, Bdr.
PAMPLIN, O. H., Gnr. 112 H. Bty.		18/ 2/14 1y 8m, Gnr.
PANTON, B. M., Pte. 12 Bn.		21/ 8/14 1y 8m, Pte.
PANTON, E. J., Pte. 26 Bn.	2W., 69 Bn., 26 Bn.	17/ 5/15 3y 11m, Pte.
PAPWORTH, E., Pte. 26 Bn.	12 Bn.	16/ 8/15 4y, Pte.
PARDOE, D., Gnr. 9 Bty., 3 F.A.B.		12/ 4/15 4y 9m, Gnr.
PARISH, C. H., Pte. 40 Bn.	15 Bn.	20/ 3/16 3y 1m, Pte.
PARISH, E. R., Gnr. Arty.	16 Bty.	28/ 9/15 4y, Gnr.
PARISH, J. H., Pte. 40 Bn.	W.	27/ 9/16 1y 6m, Pte.
PARK, J. H., Pte. A.S.C.		22/10/17 2y, Pte.
PARKER, G. M., Capt 1 A.G.H.		16/ 7/15 2y, Capt.
PARKER, A. E., Pte. 15 Bn.	W., 47 Bn.	1/ 9/15 2y 7m, Pte.
PARKER, A. W., Pte. 12 Bn.	52 Bn. ✢ 4/9/16.	21/ 8/14 Sgt. ✢
PARKER, A. S. M., Pte. A.A.M.C.	W., 14 Fd. Amb.	15/ 3/16 3y 7m, Pte.
PARKER, A. W., Pte. 12 Bn.	✢ 11/2/15.	31/ 8/14 Pte. ✢
PARKER, A. G., Pte. 12 Bn.	✢ 15/4/17.	19/ 1/15 Pte. ✢
PARKER, B., Pte. 40 Bn.		13/ 6/17 2y 4m, Pte.
PARKER, C. T., Cpl. 12 Bn.	✢ 5-8/5/17.	28/ 4/16 Cpl. ✢
PARKER, D. W., M. Worker.		
PARKER, D. J., Pte. 3 G.S.R.	12 Bn.	25/ 6/18 1y 4m, Pte.
PARKER, E. H., Pte. 15 Bn.		13/ 8/15.
PARKER, G. T., Pte. 12 Bn.	W.	14/11/16 2y 5m, Pte.
PARKER, H., Pte. 40 Bn.	W., 26 Bn.	10/11/15 3y 10m, Pte.
PARKER, J. M., Pte 12 Bn.	W.	20/ 9/14 4y 7m, Pte.
PARKER, J. M., Gnr. Arty.	26 Bty.	24/10/16 3y, Gnr.
PARKER, J. H., Pte. 12 Bn.	✢ 19-22/8/16.	28/ 8/14 Pte. ✢
PARKER, J. M., Pte. 12 Bn.	W.	20/ 9/14 4y 7m, Pte.
PARKER, L. H., Pte., A.A.M.C.	9 Fd. Amb.	21/10/16 3y 1m, Pte.
PARKER, R., Tpr. 3 L.H.	5 D.A.C.	16/ 8/15 4y 1m, Dvr.
PARKER, R. Y., Pte. 15 Bn.	✢ —/7/15.	30/10/14 Pte. ✢
PARKER, W., Gnr. Arty.	112 How. Bty.	9/10/16 2y 11m, Fitter
PARKER, W. B., Pte. 12 Bn.		7/10/15 4y 3m, Pte.
PARKER, W. G., Pte. 15 Bn.	W. ✢ 9/4/18.	13/ 8/15 Pte. ✢
PARKES, A. L., Pte. 40 Bn.	4W. ✢ 5/2/19.	4/10/16 Pte. ✢
PARKES, D., Tpr. 3 L.H.		1/ 1/15.
PARKES, E., Pte. 7 Fd. Amb.		15/ 2/15.
PARKES, R. H., Gnr. 36 H.A.G.	W.	1/ 3/16 3y 6m, Gnr.
PARKIN, G. H., Gnr. Arty.	2W.	4/10/15 3y 6m, Gnr.
PARKINSON, W. T., Pte. 12 Bn.	M.M., 51 Bn.	27/10/15 3y 10m, L.-Cpl.
PARLATO, E. T., Gnr. Arty.	6 F.A.B.	16/ 4/17 2y 7m, Dvr.
PARMLEY, J., Dvr. 9 Fd. Bty.	W.	27/ 8/14 4y 7m, Dvr.
PARRINGTON, T W., Pte 1 A.G.H.		8/ 6/15.
PARRIS, J. J., Pte. Rly. Unit.	4 A.B.G.R.O.C.	8/ 1/17 2y 10m, B. smith.
PARRY, A. W., Gnr. 3 A.F.A.	✢ 11/5/15.	18/ 9/14 Gnr. ✢
PARRY, C. S., St.-Sgt. A.A.P.C.		21/ 9/14 4y 4m, Capt.
PARRY, F. C., Pte. 3 G.S.R.		24/ 6/18.

NAME.	REMARKS.	RANK ON DISCHARGE. ENLISTED. SERVICE.
PARRY, G. M., Dvr. 7 Fd. Amb.	12 Bn. ✽ 15/4/17.	25/ 2/15 Sgt. ✽
PARRY, J. S., Pte. 15 Bn.	47 Bn. ✽ 9/6/17.	1/ 6/15 Pte. ✽
PARRY, L. L., Pte. 12 Bn.	W., 40 Bn.	20/ 8/14 5y 4m, Lt. Spr.
PARRY, R. J., Spr. 1 Tnlrs.		
PARRY, R. O., Pte. 40 Bn.	W.	3/ 2/16 3y 6m, Sgt.
PARRY, W., Pte. 40 Bn. ¼	W.	22/ 9/17 1y 11m, Pte.
PARRY, W., Pte. 15 Bn.	2W., 48 Bn.	23/ 1/15 4y 7m, Lt.
PARSELL, G. H., Pte. 12 Bn.	M.C., 40 Bn.	18/10/16 2y 10m, Pte.
PARSELL, J. H., Pte. 26 Bn.	D.C.M., 4 M.G. Bn.	20/ 9/15 3y 11m, Cpl.
PARSEY, A. E., Pte. 12 Bn.		16/10/16 1y 10m, Pte.
PARSEY, F. T., Tpr. 3 L.H.		14/ 8/15 1y 1m, Tpr.
PARSEY, W. O., Gnr. Art.	4 D.A.C.	26/ 2/17 2y 8m, Dvr.
PARSISSONS, J. S. J., Dvr. 40 Bn.	W. ✽ 11/8/18.	23/ 2/16 Dvr. ✽
PARSONAGE, J., Pte. 40 Bn.	✽ 4/1/17.	28/ 3/16 Pte. ✽
PARSONS, A. E.		
PARSONS, A. J., Sgt. Rly. Unit.		22/ 1/17 2y 5m, C.S.M.
PARSONS, A. C., Pte. 2 A.G.H.	2 A.M.T.C.	23/ 8/15 3y 4m, Cpl.
PARSONS, A. J., Gnr. Arty.	W., 112 How. Bty.	28/ 1/16 3y 8m, Cpl.
PARSONS, A. J., Pte. 15 Bn.	W.	22/ 5/15 2y 5m, Pte.
PARSONS, C., Pte. 12 Bn.		3/ 1/18 1y 11m, Pte.
PARSONS, E., Gnr. Arty.	15 F.A.B.	23/ 2/16 2y 6m, Gnr.
PARSONS, E. F., Pte. 15 Bn.	3W., M.C., 45 Bn.	7/ 8/15 4y Lt.
PARSONS, F., Pte. 4 M.G. Co.	5 A.M.T. Co.	28/11/16 2y 11m, Pte.
PARSONS, F. C., Pte. 40 Bn.	✽9/5/17.	20/ 7/16 Pte. ✽
PARSONS, G. S., Sgt. 26 Bn.		2/ 3/15 1y 6m, Sgt.
PARSONS, J. H., Pte. 15 Bn.	2W.	7/ 8/15 3y 2m, Pte.
PARSONS, J. R. C., Spr. 3 Fd. Co.	W., 16 Fd. Co.	20/ 8/14 5y 3m, L.-Cpl.
PARSONS, N. H., Pte. 15 Bn.	W., P.O.W.	3/ 6/15 4y Pte.
PARSONS, R., Tpr. 3 L.H.	W.	8/ 1/15 3y 1m, L.-Cpl.
PARSONS, T. E., Pte. 12 Bn.	52 Bn. ✽ 11/1/17.	27/ 7/ 15 Pte. ✽
PARSONS, T. E., Pte. 12 Bn.		9/ 8/15
PARSONS, W., Spr. 5 Miners.	Aus. E.M.M.B. Co.	1/ 3/16 3y, Spr.
PARSONS, W. G. R., Gnr. Arty.	38 Bty.	13/ 1/16 3y, Dvr.
PARTRIDGE, A. H., Pte. 12 Bn.	W., 40 Bn.	10/ 8/16 1y 6m, Pte.
PARTRIDGE, A. C., Pte. 15 Bn.	W., 47 Bn.	27/ 7/15 1y 10m, Cpl.
PARTRIDGE, C. V., Pte. 26 Bn.	12 Bn. ✽ 19-22/8/16.	16/ 8/15 Pte. ✽
PARTRIDGE, L. T., Pte. 40 Bn.	W.	4/ 4/16 3y 7m, Sgt.
PARTRIDGE, W. J., Pte. 40 Bn.	W.	18/ 1/16 3y 3m, Pte.
PARTRIDGE, W. T., Pte. 40 Bn.	W.	28/ 9/16 1y 11m, Pte.
PATERSON, J., 1 A.M. A.F.C.		30/10/16 2y 10m, 1 A.M.
PATERSON, J. F., Pte. 12 Bn.	A.A. Postal Cps.	12/ 7/15 2y 2m, Pte.
PATIENCE, W. A., Spr. 3 Miners.	3 Tnlrs. Co.	12/10/15 3y 10m, Spr.
PATMAN, C. G., Pte. 40 Bn.		3/10/16
PATMAN, T. H., Pte. 3 G.S.R.		19/ 3/18
PATMAN, W. F., Cpl. B.A.C.	W., 103 How. Bty.	22/ 7/15 4y 4m, Cpl.
PATMORE, C. G., Pte. 4 M.G. Co.	1 M.G. Bn.	1/12/16
PATMORE, J., Pte. 15 Bn.	3W., 47 Bn.	17/ 7/15 3y 9m, Pte.
PATMORE, J. B., Pte. 12 Bn.	W.	14/ 9/14 4y 4m, L.-Cpl.
PATMORE, W. A., Pte. 12 Bn.	2W., 69 Bn., 12 Bn.	13/ 1/15 4y 5m, Pte.
PATON, W. C. W., Lt. 5 Fd. Co.	8 Fd. Co.	23/ 6/15 4y 2m, Lt.
PATON, D. M'M., Sgt. 26 Bn.	W. ✽ 29/10/17.	12/ 7/15 C.S.M. ✽
PATON, H. E., Cpl. 12 Bn.	✽ 29/5/18.	5/ 7/16 Cpl. ✽
PATON, N. H., Gnr. 6 F.A.B.	W.	19/ 8/15 4y 1m, Cpl.
PATON, W. R., Gnr. Arty.	W., 120 How. Bty.	3/ 4/16 3y, Bdr.
PATTEN, A. R., Pte. 15 Bn.	11 F.A.B.	14/ 5/15 4y 4m, Saddler
PATTEN, P. W., Dvr., 26 Bn.	W.	17/ 3/15 4y 4m, Dvr.
PATTERSON, G. H., Capt. 25 How. Bde.	107 How. Bty. ✽ 14/4/17.	1/ 4/16 Major ✽
PATTERSON, P. J., Lt. 12 Bn.	M.I.D. ✽ 25-28/4/15.	14/ 8/14 Lt. ✽
PATTERSON, W. J., Lt. A.A.D.C.		1/12/16.
PATTERSON, A., Pte. 40 Bn.	2W.	2/10/16 2y 6m, Pte.
PATTERSON, C. C., Gnr. Arty.	10 F.A.B. ✽ 16/4/17.	Cpl. ✽
PATTERSON, H. R., Pte. 12 Bn.	2 Pnrs. ✽ 22/12/17.	13/11/15 Pte. ✽
PATTERSON, P. J. K., Pte. 3 G.S.B		4/ 2/18 1y 1m, Pte.
PATTERSON, R., Pte. 12 Bn.	51 Bn.	Pte.
PATTERSON, R. H., Gnr. 25 How B		Gnr.
PATTERSON, S. D., Spr. 3 Fd. Co.	✽ 19/5/15.	12/10/14 Spr. ✽
PATTERSON, W., Pte. 12 Bn.		13/ 6/17
PATTERSON, W. C., Pte. 12 Bn.	✽ 3-5/9/16.	2/12/15 Pte. ✽
PATTON, J. A., Pte. 40 Bn.		18/ 8/15 4y, Pte.
PATULLO, G. S., Pte. 26 Bn.	W.	16/ 7/15 3y 9m, Pte.
PAUL, E. L., Pte. 40 Bn.	3W.	8/11/16 2y 10m, Pte.
PAUL, H. L., Pte. 12 Bn.	W., 69 Bn., 12 Bn.	4/11/14 4y 9m, L.-Cpl.
PAUL, M., Sgt. 12 Bn.	2W.	6/ 9/15 4y 1m, Pte.
PAULL, S. C., Pte. 4 M.G. Co.		9/11/15
PAUL, T. J., Pte. 12 Bn.	✽ 8/4/17.	12/10/16 Pte. ✽
PAUL, V. W., Pte. 3 L.H.	4 D.A.C.	18/ 1/15 3y, Dvr.
PAUL, W. J., Pte. 12 Bn.		5/ 7/16 3y 3m, Pte.
PAULY, W. H., Dvr. D.A.C.		3/ 8/15
PAYNE, C. A., Capt. A.A.M.C.		14/ 5/15 2y 3m, Capt.
PAYNE, L. H., Mjr. 40 Bn.	2W., D.S.O., M.I.D.	7/ 3/16 3y 4m, Major.
PAYNE, A., Pte. 3 G S.R.		1/ 8/18
PAYNE, A., Pte. 12 Bn.		8/10/15 1y 10m, Pte.
PAYNE, E. K., Pte. 12 Bn.	W., 52 Bn.	12/10/15 5m, Pte.
PAYNE, K. T., Cpl. 12 Bn.	2W.	28/ 7/15 4y 2m, Lt.
PAYNE, L., Spr. Tnlrs	1 Tnlrs. Co.	26/10/16 3y, Spr.
PAYNE, O. G., Pte. 26 Bn.	W.	23/ 9/15 2y 1m, Pte.

TASMANIA'S MUSTER ROLL.

NAME.	REMARKS.	RANK ON DISCHARGE. ENLISTED. SERVICE.
PAYNE, P. J., Pte. 40 Bn.	W., 12 Bn.	7/ 3/16 2y 2m. Pte.
PAYTEN, G. N., Pte. 1 A.C.H.		17/ 9/14
PEACE, H. C. C., Pte. 12 Bn.	4 D.A.C.	22/ 7/15 4y 6m. Gnr.
PEACOCK, J. E., Pte. 1 A.G.H.	12 F.A.B., 119 How. Bty. ✣ 23/6/18.	2/ 6/15 Pte. ✣
PEARCE, A. A., Pte. 40 Bn.	2W.	14/ 2/17 2y 9m, Pte.
PEARCE, A. H. A., Pte. 40 Bn.	✣ 7/1/17.	20/ 3/16 Pte. ✣
PEARCE, B., Cpl. 12 Bn.		22/ 8/14
PEARCE, B., Pte. 12 Bn.	W. ✣ 5-8/5/17.	2/ 9/16 Pte. ✣
PEARCE, C. E., Gnr. Arty.	✣ 12/11/16.	6/ 9/15 Gnr. ✣
PEARCE, E. J., Tpr. 3 L.H.	2W., 12 Bn.	8/ 1/15 3y 11m Cpl.
PEARCE, G. R., Pte. 12 Bn.	W., 10 F.A.B. ✣ 20/11/18.	18/11/15 Dvr. ✣
PEARCE, H. G., Pte. 26 Bn.	✣ 13/11/16.	21/ 7/15 Cpl. ✣
PEARCE, H. R., Pte. 12 Bn.		20/ 8/14
PEARCE, J., Pte. 15 Bn.	W.	23/ 9/14 1y 10m, Pte.
PEARCE, N., Gnr. 9 Bty.	W.	27/ 8/14 4y 4m, Gnr.
PEARCE, R. N., Pte. 26 Bn.	✣ 5/8/16.	1/ 4/15 Pte. ✣
PEARCE, R. H., Dvr. 40 Bn.	W.	21/ 2/16 3y 2m, Dvr.
PEARCE, V. W., Pte. Rmnts.		17/ 7/18 1y 2m, Pte.
PEARCE, V. R. H., Pte. 12 Bn.	W.	15/ 7/15 4y, Dvr.
PEARCE, W. C. B., Spr. 3 Fd. Co.		24/ 8/15 4y 1m, Spr.
PEARDON, P. K., Pte. Rmnts.	A.F.C.	22/ 9/15 3y 9m, Pte.
PEARL, S. K., Spr. 5 Fd. Co.		9/11/15 4y, Spr.
PEARN, E. A., Pte. A.A.M.C.	2W., 1 Fd. Amb.	17/ 5/16 3y 5m, Pte.
PEARN, H. E. L., Pte. A.A.M.C.	1 Fd. Amb.	17/ 5/16 3y 5m, Pte.
PEARSALL, A., Pte. 12 Bn.	✣ 6/10/17.	2/10/16 Pte. ✣
PEARSALL, E. D., Pte. 12 Bn.	52 Bn. ✣17/6/17.	10/ 1/16 Pte. ✣
PEARSALL, L. V., Pte. 1 G.S.R.	3 L.H.	29/ 4/18 1y 7m, Tpr.
PEARSALL, T. J., Pte. 1 A.C.H.	Postal Cps.	22/ 2/15 3y 5m, Pte.
PEARSON, A., Gnr. Arty.	53 Bty.	10/ 4/17 2y 6m, Dvr.
PEARSON, A. J., Pte. 12 Bn.		10/ 9/15 7m, Pte.
PEARSON, C. W., Pte. 15 Bn.		4/ 4/15 4y 5m, Pte.
PEARSON, F. W., Pte. 40 Bn.	2W.	9/ 5/16 3y 6m, Pte.
PEARSON, H. G., Pte. 12 Bn.	✣ 15/4/17.	24/10/14 Pte. ✣
PEARSON, J. G., Pte. A.A.M.C.	3 Fd. Amb. ✣ 25/8/18.	21/ 3/16 Pte. ✣
PEARSON, W. G., Pte. 12 Bn.		24/ 5/15 11m, Pte.
PEART, C. J., Spr. 5 M. Co.	A.E. and M.M.U.	23/ 2/16 3y 7m, Spr.
PEART, W. E., Pte. 12 Bn.	2W., 4 Pnrs. ✣ 13/11/16.	24/10/14 Cpl. ✣
PEARTON, A. J., Pte. 40 Bn.	W., 12 Bn.	3/ 2/16 3y 7m, Pte.
PEARTON, J. A., Cpl. 15 Bn.	47 Bn. P.O.W.	3/ 8/15 4y, Sgt.
PEASE, B. A., Pte. 12 Bn.		24/ 8/16 3y 4m, Pte.
PEASE, C. D., Pte. 12 Bn.	W.	7/11/16 2y 11m, Pte.
PEASE, E. A., Pte. 12 Bn.	W.	7/11/16 3y 2m, Pte.
PEASE, L., Tpr. 3 L.H.		16/ 5/17 2y 3m, Tpr.
PEASNELL, J. H., Pte. 12 Bn.	3 Fd. Co. ✣17/10/17.	17/ 9/14 Spr. ✣
PEATE, A. F., Pte. 12 Bn.	51 Bn., A.A.P.C.	5/ 4/16 3y 7m, Sgt.
PECK, C. L., Pte. 12 Bn.	W., 3 M.G. Co.	15/ 6/16 3y 3m, Pte.
PECK, C. S., Pte. 40 Bn.	✣ 28/10/18.	6/ 4/16 Pte. ✣
PECK, E. W., Pte. 12 Bn.	3 M.G. Co.	8/ 8/15 4y, Dvr.
PECK, G. A., Pte. 26 Bn.	W., 7 M.G. Co., 2 A.M.G.B.	1/ 8/15 4y, L.-Sgt.
PECK, H. S., Pte. 12 Bn.	W.	10/ 5/16 2y 6m, Pte.
PECK, J. N., Pte. 12 Bn.	A.A.M.C. ✣ 6-10/4/17.	18/11/15 Pte. ✣
PECK, J., Pte. 12 Bn.		6/12/14 1y 6m, Pte.
PECK, L. R., Pte. 40 Bn.	2W.	17/12/15 3y, Cpl.
PEDDER, A. W., Pte. 4 M.G. Co.	W., 1 M.G. Bn.	9/11/16 2y 11m, Pte.
PEDDER, B. J., Pte. 40 Bn.	W.	20/ 3/16 2y 5m, Pte.
PEDDER, F. E., Pte. 40 Bn.	40 Bn. ✣ 7/6/17.	3/ 4/10 Pte. ✣
PEDDER, J. H. A., Pte. A.A.M.C.	2W., 8 Fd. Amb.	22/ 3/16 3y. Pte.
PEDDLE, G., Pte. 40 Bn.	W., 40 Bn.	28/ 9/16 1y 4m, Pte.
PEDDLE, G., Pte. 40 Bn.	W. ✣ 13/10/17.	4/10/16 Pte. ✣
PEDLEY, H. L., Pte. 12 Bn.	2W., M.M.	8/12/15 3y 8m, L.-Cpl.
PEEBLES, A., Pte. 40 Bn.	W.	21/ 5/16 1y 6m. Pte.
PEEBLES, A. J., Pte. 26 Bn.	W., M.M.	22/ 7/15 4y 1m, Pte.
PEEBLES, A. H., Pte. 40 Bn.	✣ 28/3/18.	14/ 2/17 Pte. ✣
PEEBLES, D., Pte. 40 Bn.	W.	12/12/16 2y 3m, Pte.
PEEBLES, G., Pte. 40 Bn.	✣ 1/2/17.	19/ 2/16 Pte. ✣
PEIRCE, V. W., Pte. 12 Bn.	W.	2/ 9/16 2y 1m, Pte.
PEIRCE, L., Pte. 12 Bn.	40 Bn.	21/11/16 2y 10m, Pte.
PEET, C. J., Tpr. 3 L.H.	Arty Tng. Depot.	18/ 8/15 2y 8m, Dvr.
PEGLER, W., Pte. 40 Bn.	W. ✣ 4/10/17.	20/ 5/16 Pte. ✣
PELHAM, A., Pte. 12 Bn.	W., 52 Bn., Vet. Hos.	22/11/15 2y 11m, Pte.
PELHAM, F. H., Pte. 12 Bn.	2W. 69 Bn., 12 Bn. ✣ 25/8/18.	23/ 8/15 Pte. ✣
PELHAM, W., Pte. 4 M.G. Co.	W., 12 Bn.	1/ 8/16 3y, Pte.
PENDRY, J. A., Pte. 15 Bn.	✣ 8/9/16.	9/ 4/15 Pte. ✣
PENFOLD, W. J., Pte. 15 Bn.	4 Inf. Bde. H.Q.	19/ 9/14 4y 4m, Pte.
PENMAN, H. A., Dvr. 7 Fd. Amb.	13 Fd. Amb.	9/ 3/15 4y 10m. Dvr.
PENNEFATHER, C. F., Cpl. 3 L.H.		25/ 8/14 2y 5m, Sgt.
PENNEFETHER, E. T. B., Pte 12 Bn	22 Bn.	28/ 8/15 1y 11m. Pte.
PENNEYSTON, E., Spr. 5 Miners.	W., 2 Tnlrs. Co.	2/ 3/16 3y 6m, Spr.
PENNICOTT, C. A., Pte. 26 Bn.	2W., 12 Bn. ✣ 20/9/17.	13/ 8/15 Pte. ✣
PENNICOTT, L. G., Spr. 3 Miners.	51 Bn.	19/ 5/15 3v 3m, Pte.
PENNICOTT, R. G., Pte. 12 Bn.	Anzac Fro. Cps.	23/ 9/15 4v 2m, Sgt.
PENNINGTON, C. J., Pte. 12 Bn.	69 Br., 12 Bn.	13/ 1/15 4y 7m, L.-Cpl.
PENNINGTON, F., Pte. 40 Bn.		27/ 6/16 1y 5m, Pte.
PENNINGTON, D. H., Tpr. 3 L.H.	1 D.A.C.	31/ 8/15 5y 5m, Gnr.
PENNINGTON, W., Pte. 12 Bn.	W., 40 Bn.	13/ 4/16 3y 7m, Pte.
PENNINGTON, W., Pte. 40 Bn.		11/ 8/16 1y 4m, Pte.
PENNY, R., Pte. 26 Bn.		25/ 5/15

326   TASMANIA'S WAR RECORD, 1914-1918.

NAME.	REMARKS.	RANK ON DISCHARGE. ENLISTED, SERVICE.
PENNY, R. B., Pte. 40 Bn.		8/ 3/16 3y 5m, Lt.
PENNYCUICK, A. M., Pte. 12 Bn	✸ 6-10/4/17.	22/ 8/16 Pte. ✸
PENNYCUICK, J., Pte. 12 Bn.	W.	1/ 6/16 Pte. ✸
PENNYCUICK, R. J., Tpr. 3 L.H.	W. ✸ 8,10/17.	4/ 2/15 1y 11m, Tpr.
PEPPER, H. R., Tpr. 3 L.H.		8/10/17
PEPPIATT, W. J., Cpl. 12 Bn.		27/ 9/16 3y. Pte.
PERCEY, A. A., Pte. 15 Bn.		28/ 8/15 1y 1m, Pte.
PERCEY, A. R., Pte. 12 Bn.		2/10/16 1y 1m, Pte.
PERCEY, C. F., Pte. 26 Bn.		14/ 4/15 4y 9m, Pte.
PERCY, C., Pte. 15 Bn.	10 F.A.B.	6/ 8/15 4y 4m, Dvr.
PERGER, F., Pte. 12 Bn.	W.	3/ 4/16 3y 3m, Pte.
PERKINS, C. H., Lt. 12 Bn.	52 Bn., 1 Army Cyc. Bn.	1/ 4/15 4y 8m, Capt.
PERKINS, H. S., Chap. Chaplains.		20/ 1/17 1y 7m, Chap.
PERKINS, A., Pte. 1 G.S.R.		17/10/17
PERKINS, C. O., Pte. 26 Bn.		12/12/15
PERKINS, C. C., Gnr. Arty.	15 F.A.B.	19/ 1/16 2y 3m, Gnr.
PERKINS, T. J., Pte. A.M.C.C.	W., M.C., 4 Bn.	5/12/14 2 Lt.
PERKS, G. S., Spr. 4 Fd Co. Engrs.		20/ 8/14 1y 11m, Spr.
PERRIN, R. R., Pte. 12 Bn.	3 A.G.H.	22/11/16 3y 2m, Pte.
PERRY, C. D., Dvr. A.A.S.C.		30/11/14 4y 5m, L.-Cpl.
PERRY, C. H., Pte. 40 Bn.	W.	26/ 9/16 1y 10m, Pte.
PERRY, G. D., Pte. 12 Bn.		14/11/16
PERRY, G. H., Pte. 12 Bn.		28/10/15
PERRY, J. G., Pte. 40 Bn.	W. ✸ 12/10/17.	29/ 2/16 L.-Cpl. ✸
PERRY, R. A., Pte. 12 Bn.	W.	20/ 8/14 4y 7m, Pte.
PERRY, R. J., Pte. 12 Bn.		14/ 6/15
PERRY, T. E., Pte. 4 M.G. Co.	W., M.M.	18/ 9/16
PESCIO, L. A., Pte. 15 Bn.		22/ 9/14
PETER, C. C., Pte. 40 Bn.	2W., 15 Bn., 40 Bn.	12/ 4/16
PETER, E. A., Pte. 12 Bn.	W., 51 Bn., 52 Bn.	27/ 2/15
PETER, R. W., Wheeler 9 Fd. Bty.	M.M. and Bar.	27/ 8/14 4y 7m, Cpl.
PETERS, F. C., Pte. 3 Cyc. Co.	W., 12 Bn.	5/ 4/16 2y 2m, Pte.
PETERS, J., Pte. 12 Bn		28/11/17 2y 1m, Pte.
PETERS, J. R., Gnr. Arty.	2 M. Vet. Sec.	1/11/15 3y 11m, Pte.
PETERS, R. G., Pte. 2 G.S.R.	49 Bty.	17/ 6/18 1y 5m, Gnr.
PETERS, R. A. V., Tpr. 3 L.H.		8/ 7/15 4y 4m, Tpr.
PETERSEN, A. J., Pte. 40 Bn.	W.	16/ 3/16
PETERSON, J. R., Spr. 3 Miners.		20/11/15
PETERWOOD, A. G., Pte. 12 Bn.	W.	21/ 8/14 2y 5m, Pte.
PETRIE, C. D., Pte. 26 Bn.	W., 12 Bn.	10/ 8/15 2y 4m, Pte.
PETRIE, D. J., Pte. 40 Bn.	✸ 9/6/17.	28/ 3/16 Pte. ✸
PETTERD, A. G., Cpl. 12 Bn.	W., M.M.	10/ 7/16 3y 5m, Cpl.
PETTERD, H. A., Gnr. Arty.	109 How. Bty., 7 F.A.B. ✸ 22/10/18.	31/ 1/16 Gnr. ✸
PETTERSON, F. O., Gnr. 9 Fd Bty	✸ 14/11/16.	27/ 8/14 Cpl. ✸
PETTERSON, V. J., Pte. 12 Bn.	1 Pnr. Bn.	25/ 8/15 1y 9m, Pte.
PETTERWOOD, J. H., Tpr. 3 L.H.		22/ 7/15 4y 1m, Dvr.
PETTIT, J. T., Pte. 40 Bn.		14/ 3/16 2y 8m, Pte.
PFAN, W. J., Pte. 12 Bn.	✸ 25/8/18.	10/10/16 Pte. ✸
PHAROAH, H. W. C., Gnr. 6 F.A.B.	102 How. Bty. ✸ 16/8/17.	8/10/15 Gnr. ✸
PHEGAN, R. L., Pte. 12 Bn.		5/ 8/17 2y 4m, Pte.
PHELAN, W. D., Pte. A.A.M.C.		23/ 4/17
PHILLIPSON, T. F., Pte. 40 Bn.	W., 51 Bn.	8/ 2/16
PHILPOTT, J. V. G., Pte. 12 Bn.	W., 40 Bn. ✸ 24/8/18.	6/11/16 Pte. ✸
PHIPPS, A. E., Pte. 12 Bn.	W., 14 Bn. ✸ 28/9/17.	12/10/16 Pte. ✸
PHILLIPS, A., Pte. 15 Bn.	✸ 31/5/15.	19/11/14 Pte. ✸
PHILLIPS, A., Pte. 12 Bn.	2W.	17/ 1/15 4y 8m, Pte.
PHILLIPS, A. W., Pte. 26 Bn.		24/ 2/15 1y 7m, Pte.
PHILLIPS, A. C., Pte. 12 Bn.	8 Bn.	25/ 8/15 1y 6m, Pte.
PHILLIPS, F. J., Pte. 2 G.S.R.		21/ 9/17 1y 9m, Pte.
PHILLIPS, G. R. H., Pte. 12 Bn.	W., 52 Bn., 51 Bn.	2/ 8/16 3y 1m, Pte.
PHILLIPS, L. F., Pte. 12 Bn.		1/ 2/16 3y 7m, Sgt.
PHILLIPS, R., Dvr. 3 Fd. Amb.	6 Fd. Amb.	24/ 8/14 4y 8m, Dvr.
PHILLIPS, S. L., Pte. A.A.M.C.	W., M.M.	5/ 4/16 3y 6m, Pte.
PHILLIPS, V. A. R., Pte. 40 Bn.	3W.	15/ 3/16
PHILLIPS, V. H., Pte. 12 Bn.	W.	20/ 7/15 4y 4m, Pte.
PHILLIPS, W., Pte. 12 Bn.	2W.	7/10/16 2y 9m, Pte.
PHILLIPS, W., Pte. 12 Bn.	W.	11/ 1/15 4y 5m, Sgt.
PHILLIPS, W., Pte. 26 Bn.	W., 8 Fd. Co., 6 Fd. Co.	25/ 4/15 2y 1m, Pte.
PICKEN, G. M., Spr. Engrs.	W.	17/ 1/16 3y 8m, 2 Cpl.
PICKETT, A. W., Pte. 12 Bn.	23 Bn.	20/ 9/16 2y 8m, Pte.
PICKETT, G. V., Pte. 40 Bn.	W.	4/ 8/16 Pte.
PICKETT, F. W., Pte. 40 Bn.	W.	21/ 7/17 1y 8m, Pte.
PICKETT, H. W., Pte. 40 Bn.	2W.	1/11/16 1y 7m, Pte.
PICKETT, J. G., Pte. 12 Bn.	W. ✸ 7/8/15.	20/ 8/14 3y 4m, Pte.
PICKETT, J. V., Pte. 12 Bn.	23 How. Bty., 8 F.A.B. ✸ 12/2/19.	20/ 8/14 Sgt. ✸
PICKET, C. V., Gnr. 6 F.A.B.		28/ 1/16 Dvr. ✸
PERCE, A. R., Pte. 13 A.S.C.	W. ✸ 9/8/15.	2/12/14 1y 5m, Pte.
PIERCE, J., Pte. 15 Bn.	11 Fd. Amb.	10/11/14 Pte. ✸
PIERCE, S. R., Cpl. 40 Bn.	W., 15 Bn., P.O.W.	7/ 9/15
PIERSON, A. F., Pte 40 Bn.	10 F.A.B.	30/ 3/16 3y 2m, Pte.
PIESSE, C. G., Gnr Arty.	4 D.A.C., 8 M.T.M.B.	10/ 4/17 2y 2m, Gnr.
PIESSE, E. V., Gnr. Arty.	W., 4 D.A.C.	9/10/16 3y 1m, Sgt.
PIESSE, F. C., Gnr. Arty.	✸ 13/10/17.	2/ 4/17 2y 2m, Gnr.
PIESSE, J. S., Sgt. 40 Bn.	2W.	26/ 7/16 Pte. ✸
PIGGOTT, I. E., Pte. 12 Bn.	5 A.D.M.G.C.	21/ 6/16 3y 3m, Pte.
PIKE, A. C., Pte. 4 M.G. Co.	Aus. Cps. Trps. M.T. Co.	5/ 8/16 2y 8m, Pte.
PIKE, G. M., Dvr. 1 D.A.S.F.		31/ 5/16 3y 5m, L.-Cpl.

TASMANIA'S MUSTER ROLL.

NAME.	REMARKS.	RANK ON DISCHARGE. ENLISTED. SERVICE.
PIKE, J. H., Pte. 12 Bn.	69 Bn., 12 Bn.	24/ 8/15 3y 8m, Pte.
PIKE, L., Pte. 26 Bn.	✠ 27/9/15.	18/ 2/15 Pte. ✠
PILCHER, G., Pte. 12 Bn.	✠ 18/9/18.	16/10/16 Pte. ✠
PILGRIM, H. V., Gnr. Siege Bde.		22/ 2/17
PILKINGTON, J. T., Pte. 12 Bn.	W., M.M. 40 Bn.	24/10/16 2y 9m, Pte.
PILLING, L. J., Pte. 1 A.G.H.	W., 3 Fd. Amb. ✠ 23/8/16.	2/ 6/15 Pte. ✠
PINEL, A. E., Munitions.		
PINEL, P. J., Pte. 12 Bn.	47 Bn. ✠ 28/3/18.	28/10/16 Pte. ✠
PING, E. H., Pte. 12 Bn.	M.M.	6/ 6/17 1y 4m, Pte.
PINKARD, E. D. Pte. 40 Bn.		22/ 2/16 3y 8m C.Q.M.S.
PINKARD, F. J., Pte. 40 Bn.		14/ 2/16
PINKARD, W. W., Pte. 12 Bn.	W., 3 L.R.O.C.	6/ 8/15 4y, 2 Cpl.
PINKERTON, H. Pte. 4 A.S.C.		30/11/14 2y 5m, Pte.
PINKERTON, R. Pte. 12 Bn.	2W., 52 Bn. ✠ 24/4/18.	12/ 1/16 Pte. ✠
PINNER, A. W., Pte. 12 Bn.		7/11/17 10m, Pte.
PINNER, J. A. B., Pte. 12 Bn.		9/ 5/16 3y 4m, L.-Cpl.
PINNER, P., Pte. 12 Bn.	✠ 27/2/17.	9/ 5/16 Pte. ✠
PIPER, E., Pte. 12 Bn.	40 Bn. ✠ 25/8/18.	21/11/16 Pte. ✠
PITCHFORD, D. L., Pte. 12 Bn	W., M.M. 40 Bn.	4/ 4/16 1y 9m, Pte.
PITCHFORD, J. E., Pte. 15 Bn.	2W., 47 Bn.	11/ 1/15 4y 3m, Cpl.
PITCHFORD, S., Pte. 12 Bn.	W.	8/ 9/14 4y 5m, Cpl.
PITFIELD, L. A., Pte 12 Bn.	52 Bn.	31/12/15 1y 7m, Pte.
PITFIELD, L. C., 2 A.M. A.F.C.		30/ 1/17 2y 8m, 2 A.M.
PITHAM, D., Pte 3 G.S.R.	15 Bn.	15/ 6/18 1y 4m, Pte.
PITHAM, J. A., Pte. 40 Bn.	51 Bn. ✠ 10/6/17.	4/ 3/16 Pte. ✠
PITHAM, W. H., Pte. 26 Bn.		17/ 7/15 11m, Pte.
PITMAN, T. H., Pte. 40 Bn.	✠ 29/9/18.	4/ 9/17 Pte. ✠
PITSTOCK, T. H., Pte. 12 Bn.		3/ 2/15 2y 11m, Pte.
PITT, A., Pte. 26 Bn.	✠ 5/11/16.	29/ 4/15 Pte. ✠
PITT, A. A., Gnr. Arty.	2W., 4 Div. Arty., 103 How. Bty.	4/ 1/15 4y 5m, Sgt.
PITT, C. C., Pte. 15 Bn.	M.S.M., 48 Bn.	3/ 8/15 4y, C.Q.M.S.
PITT, E. W., Spr. Tnlrs.		27/ 4/16 3y 5m, Spr.
PITT, G. A., Dvr. 7 Fd. Amb.	13 Fd. Amb.	15/ 2/15 4y 6m, Dvr.
PITT, I., Pte. 40 Bn.	W.	27/ 3/17 2y 10m, Pte.
PITT, J. W., Pte. 40 Bn.		5/12/16 2y 11m, Pte.
PITT, K. S., Pte. 1 G.S.R.		16/ 2/18
PITT, P., Pte. 12 Bn.	W., 52 Bn. 51 Bn.	5/ 8/15 4y 2m, Pte.
PITT, W. E., Pte. 12 Bn.	W., 52 Bn. ✠ 8/6/17.	14/10/15 Pte. ✠
PLAISTER, E. R., Pte. 15 Bn.	10 F.A.B.	5/ 8/15
PLAISTER, L. J., Pte. 12 Bn.	✠ 19-22/8/16.	22/ 6/15 Pte. ✠
PLAYSTED, A., Sgt. 13 F.A.B.		6/12/15 4y 1m, Sgt.
PLAYSTED, E. H., Cpl. 40 Bn.		10/10/16 3y 2m, Cpl.
PLAYSTEAD, S. V., Sgt. 12 Bn.		3/ 5/17
PLEWMAN, A. E., Tpr. 3 L.H.		16/ 9/15 2y 7m, Tpr.
PLOUGHMAN, S. H., Pte. 26 Bn.		26/ 7/15
PLUMBRIDGE, T. W., Pte. 40 Bn.		23/ 5/16 1y 5m, Pte.
PLUMLEY, C. E., Pte. 15 Bn.	✠ 5/7/15.	29/12/14 Pte. ✠
PLUMMER, A. S., Pte. 12 Bn.	51 Bn. ✠ 14/10/17.	4/ 4/16 Pte. ✠
PLUMMER, B., Pte. 12 Bn.	40 Bn., 10 A.L.T.M.R.	20/10/16 2y 10m, Pte.
PLUMMER, C. H., Gnr. Arty.	53 Bty.	12/ 4/17 2y 7m, Dvr.
PLUMMER, C. F., Pte. 12 Bn.	10 F.A.B.	8/12/15 4y, Dvr.
PLUMMER, C. P. P., Spr. 3 Fd. Co.	1 Tnl Co.	18/ 8/14 5y 5m, Lt.
PLUMMER, E. F., Pte. 12 Bn.	W., 69 Bn., 12 Bn.	12/ 6/16 3y 6m, Pte.
PLUMMER, J. P., Pte. 12 Bn.	51 Bn.	4/ 4/16 3y 9m, Pte.
PLUMMER, J. W., Pte. 40 Bn.		30/ 3/16 3y 7m, Sgt.
PLUMMER, S. J., Pte. A.A.H.		4/10/15
PLUNKETT, A. W., Pte. 12 Bn.	2W.	3/ 5/16 3y 4m, Pte.
PLUNKETT, E. W. D., Pte. 40 Bn	✠ 7/6/17.	28/ 9/16 Pte. ✠
PLUNKETT, F. F., Pte. 26 Bn.	W. ✠ 29/7/16.	26/ 7/15 Pte. ✠
PLUNKETT, R. G., Pte. 12 Bn.	W.	3/ 5/16 2y 5m, Pte.
POCOCK, C. W., Pte. 6 Fd. Co.		18/ 3/15
POINTON, J. R. S., Gnr. 8 F.A.B.		1/10/15 3y 11m, Dvr.
POKE, E. E., Pte. Rmnts.	A.I.F. Canteen.	16/10/15 4y, Cpl.
POKE, F. T., Tpr. 3 L.H.	5 D.A.C. ✠ 15/8/18.	24/ 8/15 Tpr. ✠
POKE, H. J., Pte. 7 Fd. Amb.	13 Fd. Amb.	9/ 3/15 2y 5m, Pte.
POKE, W. J., Pte. 2 G.S.R.	A.B.D.C.	13/ 3/18 1y 8m, Gnr.
POLDEN, G. D., Pte. 15 Bn.		28/ 6/15
POLLARD, J. T., Pte. 4 M.G. Co.	W., 15 Bn., 4 M.G. Bn.	10/ 3/17 2y 1m, Pte.
POLLEY, F. J., Pte. 26 Bn.	W., 12 Bn.	31/ 8/15 4y, Pte.
POLLINGTON, L. V., Pte. 40 Bn.	W.	2/12/16 2y 9m, Pte.
PONSONBY, F. H., Tpr. 3 L.H.		19/ 9/14 4y 6m, Cpl.
PONSONBY, J. B., Pte. Wireless.		1/ 2/17 1y 9m, 2 A.M.
PONTING, C. J., Pte. 26 Bn.	12 Bn. ✠ 19-22/8/16.	30/ 7/15 Pte. ✠
PONTING, C. H., Pte. 12 Bn.	Anzac Provost Corps, 12 Bn.	1/12/15 3y 10m, Pte.
POOLE, A. H., Pte. 12 Bn.	✠ 22/5/18.	23/ 6/17 Pte. ✠
POOLE, C. V., Spr. 8 Fd. Co.	W.	11/ 1/16 3y 5m, Spr.
POOLE, G. A., Pte. 15 Bn.	✠ 12/5/15.	14/12/14 Pte. ✠
POOLE, T. F., Pte. 40 Bn.	W.	14/ 5/17 2y 1m, Pte.
POOLE, L. N., Sgt. 12 Bn.	W.	10/ 8/16 2y 8m, Pte.
POOLE, R. W., Pte. 26 Bn.	W., 12 Bn.	27/ 7/15 1y 6m, Pte.
POPE, J. F., Pte. Tnlrs.	4 Fd. Co., 4 A.M.T. Co.	30/ 9/16 3y 1m, Artficer
POPOWSKE, J. P., Pte. 40 Bn.	W.	17/10/16 2y 11m, Pte.
PORCH, L. R., Pte. 15 Bn.	W., Anzac Provost Corps.	17/ 8/15 4y 4m, Pte.
PORTEOUS, A. Y., Pte A.A.M.C.	2 A.A.H.	24/ 8/15 2y 2m, Pte.
PORTER, A. T., Pte. 12 Bn.	M.I.D., Anzac T.C. and D. Camp, 4 M.G.S	20/ 8/.4 4y 5m, S.S.M.
PORTER, A. B., Gnr. 2 Siege Bty.		27/ 8/17 2y 3m, Gnr.
PORTER, C. H., Sgt. 3 L.H.		16/ 8/14 2y 3m, Sgt.

NAME.	REMARKS.	RANK ON DISCHARGE. ENLISTED. SERVICE.
PORTER, D., Pte. 26 Bn.	W., 12 Bn.	16/ 8/15 2y 8m. Pte.
PORTER, E. H., Pte. 12 Bn.	W., 40 Bn.	13/ 4/16 1y 6m. Pte.
PORTER, G. 11., Pte. 40 Bn.	4W.	9/ 5/16 3y 4m. Pte.
PORTER, J. F., Pte. 12 Bn.	W.	1/ 9/15 4y 3m, L.-Cpl.
PORTER, N. J., Pte. 12 Bn.	✣ 7/8/15.	4/ 9/14 Pte. ✣
PORTER, R. W., Pte. 4 M.G. Co.	15 M.G. Co.	4/10/16 1y 6m. Pte.
PORTER, R. E., Pte. 40 Bn.		21/ 2/16 3y 4m, Pte.
PORTHOUSE, A. C., Tpr. 3 L.H.	W.	9/ 6/15 3y 11m, Dvr.
PORTHOUSE, J. W., Pte. 4 M.G. Co.		2/ 9/16 3y 1m, L.-Cpl.
PORTHOUS, T. H. F., Pte. 7 Fd Amb		11/ 3/15 3y 5m, Pte.
POTTER, G. P., Lt. 26 Bn.	12 Bn.	1/ 9/15 1y 8m, Lt.
POTTS, W. N., Pte. 12 Bn.	P.O.W.	11/ 8/15
POULSON, R., Pte. 12 Bn.	W.	8/ 9/14 1y 8m, Sgt.
POULTNEY, F., Pte. 12 Bn.	✣ 9/1/17.	22/ 8/14 S.-Sgt. ✣
POULTON, M. B., Pte. 2 G.S.R.		26/11/17
POVEY, J. A., Pte. 15 Bn.	W., 10 F.A.B.	3/ 8/15 3y 8m, Gnr.
POVEY, L. R., Pte. 26 Bn.	W.	26/ 6/15 2y 8m, l'te.
POWE, A. W., Spr. Tnlrs.		5/12/16 7m. Spr.
POWE, H. J., Pte. 40 Bn.		29/ 2/16 3y 6m, Pte.
POWELL, E. J., Pte. 26 Bn.	3W., M.M. ✣ 2/9/18.	20/ 6/15 C.S.M. ✣
POWELL, E. C., Pte. 26 Bn.	2 Remount Unit.	1/ 3/15 1y 3m, Tpr.
POWELL, E., Pte. 15 Bn.	W.	20/ 9/14 1v 10m, Pte.
POWELL, F., Pte. 12 Bn.		12/ 1/15 3y 2m, Pte.
POWELL, G. A., Pte. 12 Bn.	W., 52 Bn.	10/ 9/15 1y 9m, Pte.
POWELL, H. H., Gnr. Arty.	3 D.A.C., 6 F.A.B.	14/ 2/16 3y 5m, Dvr.
POWELL, J. J., Pte. 12 Bn.	W.	3/ 5/16 3y 4m. Pte.
POWELL, L., Dvr. 9 Fd. Bty.	11 F.A.B.	31/ 8/14 4y 5m, Gnr.
POWELL, N. R., Pte. 12 Bn.	A.A.P.C., 12 Bn., M.I.D.	29/ 7/15 4y 5m, Lt.
POWELL, R. G., Cpl. 26 Bn.	✣ 5/8/16.	12/ 2/15 Cpl. ✣
POWELL, S. J., Pte. 40 Bn.	✣ 8/10/17.	13/ 9/16 Pte. ✣
POWELL, T. W., Pte. 40 Bn.	W.	1/11/16 2y 5m, Pte.
POWELL, W. C., Pte. 12 Bn.		23/10/17 1y 5m, Pte.
POWELL, W. F., Pte. 15 Bn.	M.M., 48 Bn.	13/ 8/15 4y, Pte.
POWELL, W. H., Pte. 40 Bn.	W	5/ 4/17 2y, Pte.
POWER, D., Pte. 40 Bn.		14/ 8/17 2y 1m, Pte.
POWER, F. W., Pte. 26 Bn.	✣ 26/4/17.	25/ 4/15 Pte. ✣
POWER, W., Pte. 12 Bn.	3W., 69 Bn., 12 Bn.	23/10/14 4y 7m, Pte.
POWERS, W. C., Pte. 40 Bn.		7/ 3/16 3y 5m, Pte
POWLETT, H., Pte. 40 Bn.	2W.	19/ 8/16 3y, Pte.
POYNTON, J. F., Pte. 40 Bn.	2W.	30/ 9/16
PRATCHETT, F. W., Pte. 40 Bn.	✣ 28/3/18.	16/10/16 Pte. ✣
PRATT, A. C., Pte. 4 M.G. Co.	W., 14 Bn.	13/ 3/17 2y. Pte.
PRATT, A. W., Pte. 26 Bn.	W., 7 M.G. Co.	18/ 3/15
PREECE, J. T., Pte. 26 Bn.		8/ 4/15
PREECE, T. E., Pte 12 Bn.	2W.	6/11/16 2y 4m, Pte.
PREGNALL, J., Pte. 40 Bn.	W	12/ 3/17 2y 2m, Pte.
PREGNALL, J. C., Pte. 26 Bn.	2W., 12 Bn.	12/ 8/15 2y 7m, Pte.
PREGNELL, S. G., Pte. 40 Bn.	✣ 2/9/18	3/ 5/17 Pte. ✣
PREGNELL, I., Pte. 26 Bn.	3W.	6/ 5/15 4y, Pte.
PRENTICE, A., Sgt. 26 Bn.	W., M.M., 12 Bn.	21/ 4/15 4y 6m, Cpl.
PRERE, A. P., Pte. 12 Bn.		5/ 8/17 2y 3m, Pte.
PRESCOTT, A. C., Pte. A.A.M.C.	W., 8 Fld. Amb.	5/10/15 4y 1m. Pte.
PRESCOTT, W. G., Pte. 15 Bn.	W	3/10/14 4y 5m. Pte.
PRESTON, F. T., Spr. Engrs.		24 8/15 3y 9m, Cpl.
PRESTON, W. J., Pte. 12 Bn.		4/10/16 1y 1m, Pte.
PRESTON, W. P., Pte. 12 Bn.	W	16/ 3/16 2y 7m, Pte
PRETTY, B. B., Pte. 12 Bn.	P.O.W.	7/ 7/16
PRETTY, C., Pte. 15 Bn.		30/ 8/15 10m, Pte.
PRETTY, J., Pte. 12 Bn.	4 Divl. Cyclist Co., 1 Anzac Cyc. Bn.	27/ 8/15 4y 1m. Pte.
PRETTYMAN, E. R., Cpl. 40 Bn.	W.	20/12/15 3y 1m, Sgt.
PRETTYMAN, H., Pte. 26 Bn.	W	19/ 7/15 3y 7m, Pte.
PREWER, R. G., Pte. A.A.M.C.	W., 1 Fd. Amb.	17/ 5/16 3v 4m. Pte.
PREWER, W. H. P., Pte. 40 Bn.	2W.	16/10/16 2y 1m, Pte.
PRICE, A., Pte. 40 Bn.	✣ 7/6/17.	29/ 3/16 Pte. ✣
PRICE, A. V., Pte. 40 Bn.	W	1/ 2/16 2y 5m Pte.
PRICE, A. W., Pte. 40 Bn.	W.	1/ 9/15
PRICE, A. J., Pte. 3 G.S.R.	12 Bn.	15/ 4/18 1y. Pte.
PRICE, B. K., Pte. 3 Cyc. Cps.	W., 10 Fd. Co.	13/ 3/16 3y 5m. Spr.
PRICE, C. E., Pte. 15 Bn.	✣ 8/8/15.	5/ 2/15 Pte. ✣
PRICE, D. C., Pte. 12 Bn.	W	4/ 1/16 3y 9m. Pte.
PRICE, D. J., Pte. 12 Bn.	✣ 3/11/17.	5/ 9/16 Pte. ✣
PRICE, Ed. S., Spr. 8 Fd. Co.	15 Fd. Co. ✣ 20/8/16.	30/10/15 Cpl. ✣
PRICE, E. J. M., Tpr. 3 L.H.	2W., 32 Co. A.S.C.	29/ 1/15 4y 10m, Dvr.
PRICE, H., Pte. 1 G.S.R.	40 Bn.	6/11/17 1y 11m, Pte.
PRICE, H. E., Cpl. 12 Bn.	✣ 19-23/8/16.	27/ 8/15 Cpl. ✣
PRICE, J., Spr. 3 Miners		12/ 9/15
PRICE, J. A., Pte. 12 Bn.	51 Bn.	5/ 1/15 4y 5m, Pte.
PRICE, L., Pte. 26 Bn.	31 Bn.	19/ 7/15 2y 10m. Pte.
PRICE, L., Pte 26 Bn.	W., 3 Fd. Co.	19/ 7/15
PRICE, S. G., Spr. 3 Fd. Co	W	22/ 7/15 2y, Spr.
PRIDMORE, W. H. T., Sgt. 9 Fd. Bty		27/ 8/14 1v 11m, Sgt.
PRIEST, A. V., Pte. 12 Bn.	W., 40 Bn.	13/ 9/16 3y 3m, L.-Cpl.
PRIEST, C. J., Sdlr. 9 Fd. Bty.	W	27/ 8/14 4y 7m, Bdr.
PRIEST, C. T., Pte. 40 Bn.	3 M.G Bn.	8/11/16
PRIESTLEY, E. A., Gnr. Arty.	2 M. Vet. Sec.	25/10/15
PRINGLE, F. N., Gnr. Arty.	W., 37 Bty.	21/ 5/17 2y 3m. Gnr.
PRIOR, E. W., Pte. 12 Bn.	W., 3 M.G. Co.	18/ 8/14 4y 6m, Cpl.

TASMANIA'S MUSTER ROLL. 329

NAME.	REMARKS.	RANK ON DISCHARGE. ENLISTED, SERVICE.
PRIOR, S., Gnr. Arty.		16/10/16
PRISMALL, W. J., Pte. 40 Bn.	W.	7/ 8/17
PRITCHARD, A. P., Pte. 15 Bn.	47 Bn., 41 Bn.	5/ 8/15
PRITCHARD, F., Pte. 12 Bn.		2/12/15 9m, Pte.
PRITCHARD, H. M., Pte. 12 Bn.	52 Bn. ✣ 4/9/16,	27/ 1/16 Pte. ✣
PRITCHARD, J., Spr. 8 Fd. Co.		24/ 4/16
PRITCHARD, J. H. L., Pte. 15 Bn.		18/ 6/15 1y 6m, Pte.
PRITCHARD, J., Pte. 40 Bn.		3/ 4/16 2y 4m, Pte.
PRITCHARD, M., Pte. 12 Bn.	W., 40 Bn.	3/ 5/17 1y 10m, Pte.
PRITCHARD, P. N., Tpr. 3 L.H.	Anzac Provost Cps. ✣ 16/8/18.	22/ 1/15 Pte. ✣
PROCTOR, C. O., Pte. 1 A.G.H.		9/ 6/15 1y 1m, Pte.
PROCTOR, R. O., Gnr. 9 Fd. Bty.		27/ 8/14 4y 5m, Gnr.
PROCTOR, S. J., Tpr. Remounts.		12/10/15 1y 2m, Tpr.
PROCTOR, S. J., Tpr. 3 L.H.	A.A.M.C.	8/ 1/17 2y 8m, Dvr.
PROCTOR, W. E., Pte. 12 Bn.	24 Bn. ✣ 4/10/17.	15/ 9/15 Pte. ✣
PROPSTING, A. C., Clerk, 1 W.H.Q. A.F.C.		26/ 1/16 3y 6m, Clerk
PROPSTING, F., Cpl. 40 Bn.		5/ 1/16 3y 7m, Cpl.
PROPSTING, S. W., Pte. 12 Bn.	A.F.C. Tng. Depot.	3/ 8/15
PROSS, C. W., Pte. 12 Bn.		25/ 8/15 4y, L.-Cpl.
PROSS, H. J., Pte. 12 Bn.	2W., 1 Pnrs.	25/ 8/15 3y 3m, Pte.
PROSS, W. C., Gnr. 9 Bty.	W.	17/ 8/14 1y 9m, Gnr.
PROUSE, A. H., Gnr. 18 Bty.	W., 17 Bty.	23/ 8/15 4y 3m, Gnr.
PROUSE, C. A., Pte. 15 Bn.	W.	13/ 8/15 3y 3m, Pte.
PROUSE, T. R., Dvr. 23 How. Bde.	8 F.A.B.	23/ 8/15 4y 2m, Dvr
PROUSE, W. H., Pte. 26 Bn.	W., 51 Bn., 4 M.G. Bn.	3/ 8/15 4y, Pte
PROUT, H. V., Pte. 40 Bn.	W.	16/10/16 1y 8m, Pte.
PRYOR, W. T., Pte. 15 Bn.	W., 47 Bn., 49 Bn.	31/ 8/15 4y, Pte.
PUCKERIDGE, W., Pte. 4 M.G. Co.		12/ 7/16
PUGH, C. V., Pte. 1 A.G.H.	14 Fld. Amb. ✣ 15/5/17.	9/ 6/15 Pte. ✣
PUGH, J., Pte. 40 Bn.	✣ 28/1/17.	1/ 3/16 Sgt. ✣
PUGH, V. L., Pte. 26 Bn.	W.	28/ 7/15 4y 1m, Pte.
PUGH, W. A., Pte. 40 Bn.		14/ 3/16 3y 5m, Pte.
PULFORD, A., Pte. 26 Bn.	52 Bn. ✣ 3-4/9/16.	12/ 8/15 Pte. ✣
PULFORD, C. L., Pte. 12 Bn.	W., Provost Cps., 12 Bn. ✣ 9/9/18.	20/ 8/14 L.-Cpl. ✣
PULFORD, G. R., Pte. 12 Bn.		3/12/14 4y 5m, Pte.
PULFORD, T., Pte. 12 Bn.		21/ 8/16
PULLEN, B. H., Pte. 12 Bn.	2 Fld. Amb.	7/12/14 2y 1m, Pte.
PULLEN, C. H., Cpl., 12 Bn.		27/ 9/16 3y 4m, Sgt.
PULLEN, C. C., Pte. 15 Bn.	4 D.A.C.	11/ 8/15 3y 11m, Dvr.
PULLEN, H. T., Pte. 15 Bn.	4 D.A.C.	11/ 3/15 4y, Dvr.
PULLEN, W. I., Pte. 12 Bn.		11/ 8/15
PUNSHON, H. J. D'R., Pte. 40 Bn.		22/ 2/17 2y 5m, Pte.
PURCELL, C. M., Pte. 40 Bn.	✣ 31/1/17.	17/ 5/16 Pte. ✣
PURCELL, E., Pte. 40 Bn.		17/ 5/16
PURCELL, J., Dvr. 6 F.A.B.		20/ 9/15 2y 5m, Dvr.
PURCELL, J., Pte. 12 Bn	W. ✣ 6-10/4/17.	29/ 5/16 Pte. ✣
PURCELL, P., Pte. 12 Bn.		27/ 7/15
PURCELL, W., Pte. 26 Bn.	W., A.O.C.	8/ 3/15
PURSELL, K., Pte. 40 Bn.	W., 15 Bn., 40 Bn.	1/ 3/16 2y 11m, Pte.
PURCHAS, F. W., Sgt. 1 G.S.R.	16 A.D.U.S.	7/ 5/17 2y 5m, Pte.
PURCIVALL, A. J., Pte. 12 Bn.	3W.	8/ 7/15 4y, L.-Cpl.
PURDON, A. G., Sgt. 26 Bn.	3W.	15/ 3/15 4y 3m, Sgt.
PURDON, R., Pte. 40 Bn.	12 Bn.	14/ 2/16 3y 9m, Pte.
PURDY, H. C., Pte. 26 Bn.		4/ 8/15 4y 1m, Pte
PURSELL, D., Pte. 12 Bn.	W., 40 Bn.	2/ 6/17 2y 5m, Pte.
PURSELL, R., Pte. 40 Bn.	W.	1/ 6/16 2y 1m, Pte.
PURTON, A. S., Pte. 12 Bn.	W.	18/ 9/15 2y 3m, Pte.
PURTON, A. H., Pte. 12 Bn.	4W., M.M.	21/ 3/14 4y 8m, Cpl.
PURTON, H. R., Pte. 15 Bn.	2W., 69 Bn., 15 Bn.	26/ 8/15 3y 8m, Pte.
PURTON, H. T., Pte. 2 G.S.R.	4 D.A.C.	10/ 4/18 1y 6m, Dvr.
PURTON, J. D. R., Pte. 12 Bn.	W. ✣ 11/1/19.	24/10/17 Pte. ✣
PURTON, R. S., Pte. 40 Bn.		4/ 4/16 1y 8m, Pte.
PURTON, L. C., Pte. 40 Bn.		21/ 5/16 3y 5m, Pte.
PURTON, W. H., Spr. 5 Tunnlrs	1 Tun. Co.	17/ 9/15 3y 6m, Spr.
PURTON, W. D. J., Pte. 12 Bn.		10/ 5/16 3y 2m, Pte.
PURVIS, J. S., Sgt. 40 Bn.		22/ 2/16 Lieut.
PYBUS, R. K., Lt. 3 F.A.B.	M.I.D., 4 Div. Arty. ✣ 15/4/17.	Major ✣
PYE, H., Pte. 12 Bn.	69 Bn., 52 Bn. ✣ 24/4/18.	28/ 5/15 Pte. ✣
PYE, P., Pte. 12 Bn.		8/11/16
PYKE, H. J., Pte. 12 Bn.	W	8/ 1/16 3y 4m, Pte.
PYKE, R. D., Pte. 12 Bn.	W.	17/10/16 3y. Pte.
PYKE, T. A., Pte. 40 Bn.	W.	30/ 3/16 3y 6m, Pte.
PYNE, J., Pte. 40 Bn.	7 Bn.	27/ 9/16
QUAMBY, H. L., Pte. 15 Bn.		9/ 2/15 1y 2m, Pte.
QUAMBY, J. T., Pte. 12 Bn.	W. ✣ 25-28/4/15.	31/ 8/14 Pte. ✣
QUAMBY, L., Pte. 12 Bn.		21/ 5/17
QUANTRELL, A. J., Gnr. Arty.	3 D.A.C.	10/ 2/16 2y 9m, Gnr.
QUANTRELL, L. M., Gnr. 6 F.A.B.		17/ 6/15 4y 2m, Gnr.
QUANTRILL, W. E., Pte. 12 Bn.	W., Postal Corps.	1/ 9/14 4y 6m, Sgt.
QUARRELL, A. G., Pte. 12 Bn.		6/ 7/16 1y 6m, Pte.
QUARRY, A. C., R.S.M. 1 D.A.C.	M.M., 3 D.A.C	15/ 5/16 3y 2m, R.S.M.
QUARRY, H. R., Pte. 4 M.G. Co.	W.	3/ 2/17
QUARRY, S. A., Dvr. Arty.	119 How. Bty.	15/ 3/16 3y 6m, Dvr.
QUAYLE, J., Pte. 2 G.S.R.	12 Bn.	28/ 5/18 1y 4m, Pte.
QUIGLEY, J. F., Dvr. 3 L.H.	W., 1 M.G. Sqdn	23/ 8/14 4y 6m, Dvr.
QUILLERAT, J. H., Pte. 3 G.S.R.	12 Bn	1/ 7/18 1y 4m, Pte.

330   TASMANIA'S WAR RECORD, 1914-1918.

NAME.	REMARKS.	RANK ON DISCHARGE. ENLISTED. SERVICE.
QUINN, A., Pte. 12 Bn.	W.	21/11/16 2y 1m, Pte.
QUINN, D. A., Pte. 26 Bn.	✷ 28/7/16.	14/ 4/15 Pte. ✷
QUINN, E., Pte. Arty.		28/ 5/17
QUINN, F. F., Pte. 40 Bn.		16/ 3/16
QUINN, G. H., Gnr. 40 Bn.	2W., L.T.M. Bty.	27/ 3/16 3y 1m, Gnr.
QUINN, H. R., Pte. 40 Bn.	✷ 30/3/18.	28/ 7/16 Pte. ✷
QUINN, J. L., Pte. 40 Bn.	W., 69 Bn., 40 Bn. ✷ 13/6/18.	7/ 2/16 Pte. ✷
QUINN, M., Pte. 12 Bn.	W., 52 Bn.	5/ 8/15 3y 9m, Pte.
QUINN, T. J., Gnr. 6 F.A.B.		27/ 3/15
QUINN, T., Pte. 12 Bn.	2 Pnrs. ✷ 18/4/19.	7/12/15 Pte. ✷
QUINN, W. M., Gnr. 3 F.A.	2W., 2 A.A.H.	27 /8/14
QUINTAL, R. E., Pte. 40 Bn.	✷ 5/10/17.	31/10/16 Pte. ✷
QUIRK, W. C., Spr. 7 Fd. Co.		21/ 1/16 3y 8m, Spr.
QUODRILL, W. L., Pte. 26 Bn.	W., P.O.W.	3/ 6/15 4y, Pte.
RADCLIFFE, R. E., Pte. 40 Bn.	W.	3/ 1/16 3y 9m.
RADFORD, A., Pte. 40 Bn.		10/10/16 1y 8m.
RADFORD, A., Pte. 40 Bn.		2/10/16 1y 10m.
RADFORD, A., Pte. 15 Bn.	✷ 12/5/15.	4/10/14 Pte. ✷
RADFORD, E., Pte. 26 Bn.		16/ 8/15 4y, Pte.
RADFORD, R. C., Pte. 40 Bn.	✷ 28/3/18.	11/10/16 Pte. ✷
RADFORD, S., Pte. 40 Bn.	W., 3 A.L.H.	28/ 9/16 3y, Pte.
RADFORD, W. J., Tpr. 3 G.S.R.		6/ 4/18 1y 5m, Pte.
RADIN, J. E., Pte. Rly. Unit.		23/ 4/17 2y 5m, Spr.
RADNELL, C. Tpr. 3 L.H.	1 L.H. Bde., M.G. Sqd. ✷ —/8/16	17/ 8/14 Pte. ✷
RAFFERTY, R. A., Sec. Lt. 12 Bn.	W., D.S.O., 2 M.I.D., 11 Bn	28/ 8/14 Lt.-Col.
RAFFERTY, T., Spr. 8 Fd. Co.		4/11/15
RAINBIRD, C. D. L., Pte. 12 Bn.	W.	14/ 8/16 2y 4m, Pte.
RAINBIRD, B., Pte. 4 M.G. Co.	28 Bn.	2/ 8/16 3y, Pte.
RAINBOW, O. D., Pte. 40 Bn.	W.	10/ 8/17 1y 7m, Pte.
RALPH, G. J. T., Tpr. 3 L.H.		6/ 1/15 2y 3m, Tpr.
RALPH, J. K, Gnr. Arty.	3 D.A.C.	15/ 2/16 1y 11m, Gnr.
RALPH, L. I., Pte. 12 Bn.	W.	20/ 8/14 4y 7m, Pte.
RALSTON, G. A., Pte. 26 Bn.	2W., 12 Bn.	11/ 8/15 4y 3m, Pte.
RAMSAY, L., Pte. 15 Bn	2W.	13/ 5/15 3y 11m, Pte.
RAMSAY, P. M., Gnr. 2 F.A.B.	2W., 22 F.A.B., 2 D.A.C., 3 Bty.	12/10/15 3y 11m, Gnr.
RAMSDALE, R. N., Dvr. 17 F.A.B.	W.	11/ 8/15 4y, Dvr.
RAMSKILL, L. G., Pte. 1 G.S.R		26/ 2/19
RAMSKILL, L. V., Spr. Tnlrs.	W., 2 A.T.C.	21/10/16 3y 1m, Spr.
RAND, L. G., Pte. A.A.M.C.		11/ 5/17 2y 7m, Pte.
RANDALL, E. A. H., Sec Lt D.A.C.	2W., D.S.O., 1 F.A.B.	25/ 8/14 5y 1m, Major
RANDALL, C R., Pte. 12 Bn.	W.	10/ 2/15 3y, Pte.
RANDALL, F. D., Spr. 3 Fd. Co.		24/ 8/15 4y 1m, L.-Cpl.
RANDALL, G. A., Spr. Engrs.	W.	11/ 1/16 3y 7m, Spr.
RANDALL, J., Pte. 40 Bn	2W., 51 Bn., 12 Bn.	3/ 3/16 2y, Pte.
RANKIN, J. W., Sgt. 15 Bn.	W.	12/ 7/15 2y 1m, Sgt.
RANSLEY, C. G., Pte. 12 Bn.		28/ 9/16 3y 1m, Pte.
RANSLEY, G. A., Pte. 26 Bn.	W., P.O.W. ✷ 28/11/17.	23/ 9/15 Pte. ✷
RANSLEY, V. S., Pte. 12 Bn.	W., 40 Bn.	19/10/16 2y 10m, Pte.
RANSOM, D., Sec. Lt., 12 Bn.	A.F.C.	26/ 7/15 2y 1m, Sec. Lt.
RANSOM, C. G., Sgt. 8 F.A.	M.M., 3 Div. B.A.C. ✷ 16/10/17.	21/10/15 Sgt. ✷
RANSOM, N., Pte. 12 Bn.	W., M.M.	31/ 8/14 5y 3m, Lt.
RAPLEY, A. H., Pte. 3 L.H.	Aus. Dpt. Store.	27/ 8/14 4y 5m, Pte.
RAPLEY, L. M., Pte. 40 Bn.	✷ 12/2/17.	23/ 2/16 Pte. ✷
RAPP, G. M., Sgt 3 G.S. Div.		16/11/17 1y 4m, Sgt.
RASMUSSEN, G. R., Pte. 40 Bn.	W.	26/ 9/16 3y, Pte.
RATCLIFFE, E. J., Pte 26 Bn.	W.	20/ 7/15 1y 10m, Pte.
RATCLIFFE, E. V., Pte. 12 Bn.	W. ✷ 24/7/16.	8/ 9/14 L.-Sgt. ✷
RATCLIFFE, J. T. D. L., Pte 4 M.G.	W., 5 M.G. Co.	20/ 7/16 1y 9m, Pte.
RATCLIFFE, P. A., Pte. 12 Bn.	2W. ✷ 11/8/18.	9/ 6/16 Pte. ✷
RATCLIFFE, R. J., Pte. 40 Bn.	2W.	25/ 3/16 3y 6m, Cpl.
RATCLIFFE, W. H., L.-Cpl. 2 G.S.R	12 Bn	24/ 5/17 2y 4m, Pte.
RATH, H., Pte. 4 M.G. Co.	3 MG Co., 9 M.G. Co.	4/ 1/17 2y 9m, Pte.
RATHBONE, H. R., Pte. 12 Bn.	✷ 10/10/15.	26/ 5/15 Pte. ✷
RATHBONE, P. R., Pte 12 Bn.	40 Bn. 14/4/18.	51 6/17 Pte. ✷
RATTEN, V. R., Capt. 12 Bn.		20/ 8/14 1y 7m, Capt.
RATTRAY, A. A., Pte. 12 Bn.	W.	5/ 7/17 2y 3m, Pte.
RATTRAY, J. S., Pte. 40 Bn.	M.C.	21/ 2/16 3y 6m, Lt.
RATTRAY, L. W., Pte. 12 Bn.	Re-enlisted 3 L.H.	6/ 1/15 4y 3m, Pte.
RATTLE, T. B.		
RATTLE, W. B., Pte. 40 Bn.	W.	9/11/16 2y, Pte.
RAVENOR, H., Pte. 15 Bn.	✷ 27/8/16.	5/ 1/15 Pte. ✷
RAWLEY, E. H. V., Pte. 12 Bn.		4/ 3/15
RAWSON, F., Pte. 40 Bn.	M.M. ✷ 5/10/17	12/ 2/16 Sgt. ✷
RAY, E., Pte. 40 Bn.	W., 51 Bn.	29/ 2/16 3y 7m, Pte.
RAY, F. L., Gnr. Arty.	108 How. Bty, 23 How. Bde, 108 How Bty.	14/10/15 3y 11m, Gnr.
RAY, F. C., Pte. 12 Bn.	W., 13 Fd. Co., A.D.U.S.	5/ 9/15 3y 11m, Spr.
RAY, H. K., Gnr. 9 Fd. Bty.		27/ 8/14 5m.
RAY, J. W., Pte. 4 M.G. Co.		22/ 6/16
RAY, K. G., Pte. 1 A.G.H	13 Fd. Co. ✷ 4/8/16.	9/ 6/15 Spr. ✷
RAY, L. W., Pte. 40 Bn.	W.	14/ 3/16 2y 2m, Pte.
RAY, S. L., Pte. 15 Bn.	W., 13 Fd. Co.	23/12/14 3y 10m, Pte.
RAY, W., Pte. 40 Bn.	W., 12 Bn.	23/ 9/16 2y 7m,
RAYCROFT, J., Pte. 12 Bn.	W.	28/ 5/17 1y 10m, Pte.
RAYMOND, C. E., Pte. 40 Bn.	W. ✷ 5/10/17.	3/10/16 Pte. ✷
RAYNER, E. G., Pte. 12 Bn.		18/ 7/16
RAYNER, E. R., Pte. 3 G.S.R.	12 Bn	13/ 6/18 1y 1m, Pte.

TASMANIA'S MUSTER ROLL. 331

NAME.	REMARKS.	RANK ON DISCHARGE. ENLISTED. SERVICE.
RAYNER, T., Gnr. Arty.	W.	11/ 5/17 1y 10m, Gnr.
RAYNOR, J. A., Pte. 40 Bn.	15 Bn., 40 Bn., 10 L.T.M.B., 40 Bn.	18/ 3/16 2y 11m, Pte.
READ, L. B., Pte. 12 Bn.	A.I.B.D.	29/ 9/16 3y 1m, Pte.
READER, A. E. C., Pte. 1 GS.R		13/ 2/18
READER, A. A., Pte 12 Bn.	W., M.M. ✸ 15/4/17	17/ 8/14 Pte. ✸
READING, A. H., Pte 12 Bn.	43 Bn.	15/ 7/15 4y, Dvr.
READING, A., Pte. 12 Bn.	✸ 13/10/17.	16/10/16 Pte. ✸
READING, J. J., Pte. 26 Bn.	W.	9/ 8/15 2y, Pte.
READING, L. J., Pte. 15 Bn.	✸ 9/5/15.	28/ 9/14 Pte. ✸
READING, P., Pte. 3 Fd. Co.	16 Fd. Co., 1 A.T. Co. Engrs.	23/ 8/14 4y 6m, L.-Cpl.
READMAN, G., Spr. Miners.	W., 3 Tun. Co.	1/ 3/16 2y 4m, Spr.
READY, M. M., Pte. 40 Bn.		17/10/16 1y 9m, Pte.
READY, T. P., Pte. 40 Bn.	W.	2/10/16 2y 7m, Pte.
REARDON, A H., Pte. 26 Bn.	✸ 5/8/16.	20/ 9/15 Pte. ✸
REARDON, B. J., Pte. 12 Bn.		7/ 6/16 1y 3m, Pte.
REARDON, E. V., Pte. 12 Bn.	M.M., 40 Bn.	20/11/16 2y 7m, L.-Sgt.
REARDON, J. J., Pte. 12 Bn.		24/ 8/15 1y 7m, Pte.
REARDON, L. H., Pte. 12 Bn.	✸ 19-22/8/16.	19/ 2/15 Pte. ✸
REARDON, L. C., Pte. 40 Bn.	2W.	2/10/16 2y 2m, Pte.
REARDON, R. L., Pte. 12 Bn	✸ 5/5/18.	30/ 8/16 Pte. ✸
REASON, J., Pte. 15 Bn.		12/ 8/15 4y, L.-Cpl.
RECORD, A. G., Pte. A.A.M.C.		3/ 5/16
RECTOR, F., Pte 40 Bn	2W.	3/ 5/16 3y 5m, Cpl.
REDMAN, A. J., Pte. 12 Bn.		22/ 8/16 1y 7m, Pte.
REDMAN, B. J., Pte. 12 Bn.	W.	23/11/16 2y 11m, Pte.
REDMAN, F. A., Pte. 1 A.G.H.	1 Aus. Aux. Hos.	2/ 6/15 3y 9m, Pte.
REDMAN, W., Pte. 12 Bn.	✸ 20/9/17.	22/ 8/16 Pte. ✸
REEMAN, E. E., Tpr. 3 L.H.	1 M.G. Co., 67 A.F.C.	20/ 8/14 4y 8m, 2 A.M.
REEMAN, R W., Tpr. 3 L.H.	M.G. Sqd., 67 Sqd. A.A.C., A.F.C.	30/10/16 2y 7m, 2 A.M.
REES, E., Pte. 12 Bn.	W.	2/ 9/15 4y 4m, L.-Cpl.
REES, R. C., Pte. 1 A.G.H.	1 Aus. Aux Hos	13/ 5/15 4y 5m, Sgt.
REEVE, D. C., Pte. A.A.M.C.	9 Fd Amb	24/ 4/17 2y 7m, Pte.
REEVE, L. H., Pte. 12 Bn	27 Bn. ✸ 23/6/16.	24/ 8/15 Pte. ✸
REEVE, R V., Pte. 12 Bn.	51 Bn.	11/ 4/16 3y 5m, Dvr.
REEVE, S. A., Pte. 26 Bn.	24 How. Bde., 10 F.A.B., 17 Bty., 41 Bty.	14/ 8/15 3y 8m, Bdr.
REEVES, A., Pte. 12 Bn.	7 Bn.	8/ 5/17
REEVES, G. J., Pte. 4 M.G. Co.	15 M.G. Co.	9/10/16 2y 6m, Pte.
REGGETT, W., Pte. A.A.M.C.		15/ 1/17
REARDON, J. T., Gnr Arty.	53 Bty., 14 F.A.B.	10/ 5/17 2y 5m, Dvr.
REARDON, C. A., Pte. 12 Bn.		2/ 9/15 4y 1m, Sgt.
REILLY, A. J., Pte. 26 Bn.	2 Div. Sig. Co., 2 Sig. Co., A.C. Sig. Co.	18/ 6/15 4y 2m, Spr.
REILLY, F. W., Pte. 40 Bn.	2W.	16/ 7/16 2y 4m, Pte.
REILLY, J. T., Pte. 12 Bn.	✸ 24/8/18	4/10/17 Pte. ✸
REINMUTH, E. H. W., Pte. Rmts.	2 M. Vet. Co. ✸ 7/9/18	22/ 9/15 Pte ✸
REINMUTH, H. C., Pte. 15 Bn.	W.	19/ 6/15 2y 8m, Pte.
REISZ, W. L., Dvr. Wireless		29/ 3/16 3y 3m, Dvr.
REID, A. J., Pte. A.A.M.C.		13/ 9/16 3y 3m, Pte.
REID, A., Pte. 12 Bn.	52 Bn., 51 Bn.	13/ 1/16 3y 9m, L.-Cpl.
REED, A. R., Spr. Miners.	5 Tun. Co., 3 Tun. Co.	1/ 3/16 2y 3m, Spr.
REID, A., Pte. 12 Bn.	W., 52 Bn. ✸ 25/11/16.	10/ 8/15 Pte. ✸
REED, A., Pte. 40 Bn.		22/11/16 1y 11m, Pte.
REID, C. F., Pte. 40 Bn.	2W.	16/ 3/16 3y 5m, Pte.
REED, C. T. H., Pte 12 Bn.		18/10/16 3y 2m, Pte.
REID, C. A., Pte. 26 Bn.		13/ 4/15 1y 7m, Pte.
REED, D. G., Pte. 12 Bn.	W., 52 Bn., 67 Bn., 12 Bn., 1 Pnr. Bn. 5 M.G. Co. ✸ 7/10/18.	26/ 6/15 Sgt. ✸
REID, E. V., Pte. 3 G.S.R.	12 Bn.	8/ 7/18 1y 3m.
REED, E. H., Pte. 12 Bn.	W. ✸ 23/4/18.	18/ 7/16 Pte. ✸
REED, F. S., Gnr. 18 Fd. Bty.		24/ 9/15 1y 6m, Gnr.
READ, H. R., Gnr. Arty.		14/ 4/16
REED, H., Pte. 40 Bn.	W.	1/ 9/15 3y 1m. Pte
REID, J. S., Pte. 26 Bn	✸ 29/7/16	7/ 8/15 Pte. ✸
REID, J. A., Pte. 3 Fd.Amb.	A.P.C.	24/ 8/14 4y 6m, Sgt.
REID, J., Pte. 12 Amb.		9/12/14 1y 6m, Pte.
READ, L. B., Pte. 12 Bn.		16/10/16 3y. Pte.
REID, L. J., Pte 26 Bn		10/ 8/15 4y 3m. Dvr.
REID, M. M., Gnr. 9 Fd. Bty.	2W.	27/ 8/14 4y 7m, Gnr.
REED, M. W., Pte. 12 Bn.	40 Bn.	18/10/16 2y 5m, Pte.
REED, P. E., Pte. 12 Bn.	✸ 6-10/4/17	7/ 9/15 Pte. ✸
REID, R., Pte. 12 Bn.	W.	3/ 8/15 4y, Dvr.
REID, R. H., Pte. 1 G.S.R.	17 Bty. 6 F.A.B.	19/12/17 2y 4m. Cpl.
REID, T., Pte. 26 Bn.	✸ 29/7/16	6/ 6/15 Pte. ✸
REID, W., Gnr. Arty.		17/ 1/17 2y 9m, Gnr.
REID, W., Pte. 40 Bn.	W.	17/10/16
REID, W. C., Pte. 40 Bn.		3/ 7/16 3y, Spr.
REID, W., Pte. 12 Bn.	52 Bn.	25/ 9/15 1y 11m, Pte.
REMINGTON, P. T., S.-Sgt. 1 A.G.H.	M.B.E., M.I.D.	29/ 9/14 4y 6m, Lt.
RENSHAW, T. S., Lt. 12 Bn.		Lt.
RENTOUL, J. B., Chaplain.		11/ 3/15 1y 10m. Chap.
REUBENICHT, R., Pte. 15 Bn.	✸ 31/5/15	24/11/14 Pte. ✸
REVELL, A. H., Pte. 26 Bn.	12 Bn. ✸ 23/7/16	11/ 8/15 Pte. ✸
REVILL, C. R., Pte. 15 Bn.	2W., 69 Bn.	9/ 9/15 3y 2m, Pte.
REVELL, J. P., Pte 15 Bn.	40 Bn., 49 Bn. ✸ 26/9/17	8/ 9/15 Pte. ✸
REVILL, L. E. R., Pte. 15 Bn.		12/ 9/14 1y 5m, Pte.
REVELL, R. L., Pte. 40 Bn.	3W., 3 M.G. Bn.	23/ 2/15 3y 8m, Pte.

NAME.	REMARKS.	RANK ON DISCHARGE. ENLISTED. SERVICE.
REVIE, J. S., Pte. 1 G.S.R.		17/12/17 1y 8m, Pte.
REX, A. R., Gnr. 3 F.A.B.	W.	19/ 8/14 3y 8m, Gnr.
REX, B. R., Tpr. 3 L.H.		27/ 3/17 11m, Gnr.
REX, P. H., Pte. 15 Bn.	✠ 31/5/15	27/10/14 Pte. ✠
REYNOLDS, B. A., Pte. 12 Bn.	✠ 8/10/19.	1/ 8/17 Pte. ✠
REYNOLDS, C. T., Pte. 40 Bn.	2W.	12/ 7/16.
REYNOLDS, D., Pte. 4 M.G. Co.	15 Bn.	15/ 2/17 2y 8m, Pte.
REYNOLDS, E. B., Gnr. Arty.		30/ 9/16 3y 1m, Dvr.
REYNOLDS, F. T. C., Pte. 12 Bn.	M.M.	30/10/16 3y, Pte.
REYNOLDS, H. J., Pte. 10 Bn.	52 Bn. ✠ 3/4/17.	25/ 8/14 Dvr. ✠
REYNOLDS, H. L., Pte. 12 Bn.	2W.	25/ 8/14 3y 9m, Cpl.
REYNOLDS, J., Spr. Miners.		12/11/15 5m, Spr.
REYNOLDS, M., Pte. 12 Bn.	A.T.M. Bty.	2/ 8/15 3y 4m, Gnr.
REYNOLDS, O. W., Pte. 7 Fd. Amb.	W., 14 Fd. Amb.	6/ 3/15.
REYNOLDS, R., Pte. 12 Bn.	W.	20/ 8/14 4y 7m, Pte.
REYNOLDS, R. R., Pte. 26 Bn.	✠ 3/8/16.	25/ 6/15 Pte. ✠
REYNOLDS, T. W., Tpr. 12 Bn.	3 L.H.	2/12/14 4y 9m, Cpl.
REYNOLDS, V. W., Pte. 12 Bn.		25/ 8/17 1y 7m, Pte.
REYNOLDS, W. H., 40 Bn.	W.	9/ 5/16 1y 8m, Pte.
REYNOLDS, W. H., Pte. 40 Bn.		4/ 7/16.
REYNOLDS, W. J., Pte. 12 Bn.		6/ 8/15 3y 7m, Pte.
REYNOLDS, W. R., Tpr. 3 L.H.		1/ 9/14 1y 11m, Tpr.
RHODES, A. J., Gnr. 3 F.A.B.	9 Bty.	7/ 8/15 11m, Gnr.
RHODES, J. E., Pte. 40 Bn.		18/ 3/16 3y 6m, Cpl.
RHODES, A. W., Pte. 40 Bn.	✠ 30/8/18.	15/ 4/16 Pte. ✠
RICE, B. W., Tpr. 3 L.H.		5/11/17 1y 8m, Tpr.
RICE, F. E. J., Pte. 12 Bn.		31/ 8/14 3m, Pte.
RICE, F., Pte. 40 Bn.		25/ 1/16 3y 7m, Pte.
RICH, A. J., Gnr. 9 Fd. Bty.	W.	27/ 8/14.
RICHARDS, R. H., Chaplain 12 Bn		8/ 9/14 4y 3m, Chap.
RICHARDS, A., Pte. 40 Bn.	2W.	9/11/16 2y 4m, Pte.
RICHARD, N. B., Pte. 12 Bn.		21/ 1/15 3y 3m, Dvr.
RICHARD, R. N. B., Pte. 12 Bn.	W.	19/ 8/14 1y 7m, Pte.
RICHARDS, A. H., Pte. 40 Bn.	W., M.M., 52 Bn., 49 Bn., 18/7/18.	11/ 4/16 Cpl. ✠
RICHARDS, A. R., Pte. 12 Bn.	2W. 52 Bn. 49 Bn.	4/11/15.
RICHARDS, C., Pte. 10 Bn.		28/ 9/16 2y 8m, Pte.
RICHARDS, C. E., Pte. Tnlrs.		21/10/16 3y, Spr.
RICHARDS, G. S., Pte. 3 Cyc. Co.		19/ 1/16 3y 10m, Pte.
RICHARDS, G. A., Pte. 40 Bn.	W.	9/11/16 2y 1m, Pte.
RICHARDS, G. F., Pte. 40 Bn.	W. ✠ 28/3/18.	15/ 3/16 L.-Cpl. ✠
RICHARDS, H. G., Pte. 15 Bn.		30/12/14 1y 4m, Pte.
RICHARDS, H. J., Pte. 12 Bn.		20/ 7/15 2y 10m, Pte.
RICHARDS, H. E., Spr. Miners.	3 Tnl. Co.	31/ 1/16.
RICHARDS, H. J., Pte. 40 Bn.	3 F.A.B., H.Q. 3 F.A.B.	12/ 1/16 3y 8m, L.-Cpl.
RICHARDS, J., Pte. 40 Bn.		4/ 7/16 1y 3m, Pte.
RICHARDS, K. E., Pte. 12 Bn.	24 How. Bde., 3 D.A.C.	28/10/15 3y 11m, Dvr.
RICHARDS, M. V., Spr. 8 Fd. Co.		10/ 1/16.
RICHARDS, S. G., Pte. Wireless.		23/ 1/18 11m, Pte.
RICHARDS, T., Pte. 12 Bn.		7/12/14 1y 6m, Pte.
RICHARDSON, A. E., Spr. Miners.	W.	15/ 9/15 4y, Cpl.
RICHARDSON, A. H., Pte. 12 Bn.	W., 52 Bn., 51 Bn.	4/ 8/15 4y 1m, Pte.
RICHARDSON, A. L., Gnr. Arty.		30/ 9/16.
RICHARDSON, A. C., Tpr. A.M.D.T.	3 L.H.	2/ 8/18 1y 1m, Tpr.
RICHARDSON, A. G., Pte. 1 G.S.R.	40 Bn.	18/ 1/15 1y 9m, Pte.
RICHARDSON, C. E., L-Cpl 12 Bn.	✠ 3-5/9/16.	15/ 7/15 L.-Cpl. ✠
RICHARDSON, C. G., Pte. 26 Bn.	W., 2 Bn. ✠ 26/3/17.	3/ 3/15 Pte. ✠
RICHARDSON, C. W., Pte. 40 Bn.	✠ 3/8/17.	6/10/16 Pte. ✠
RICHARDSON, C. A., Gnr. Arty.		12/ 2/17 2y 7m, Gnr.
RICHARDSON, E., Pte. 15 Bn.	W., M.M., Camel Cps. 14 L.H.	20/ 1/15.
RICHARDSON, E. I., Pte. 40 Bn.	✠ 10/11/18.	31/ 3/16 Pte. ✠
RICHARDSON, E. A., L.-Cpl. Engrs.	4 Div. Engrs., 14 Fd. Co.	22/ 7/15 4y, L.-Cpl.
RICHARDSON, E. W., Dvr. 3 F.A.B.		22/ 7/15 4y, Dvr.
RICHARDSON, G., Pte. 12 Bn.		30/10/15 3y 9m, Pte.
RICHARDSON, G. C., Pte. 40 Bn.	✠ 2/10/17.	14/10/16 Pte. ✠
RICHARDSON, I. M. R., Pte. 1 A.C. Dft.	✠ 9/4/19. A.F.C.	22/10/16 2nd A.Mec. ✠
RICHARDSON, L. D., Gnr. 30 Fd. Bty.	2W.	1/11/15 2y 6m, Pte.
RICHARDSON, M. W., Pte. 12 Bn.	✠ 23/8/18.	1/ 8/17 Pte. ✠
RICHARDSON, C. N., Sgt. 12 Bn.	4W., M.C.,	18/ 8/14 4y 5m, Capt.
RICHARDSON, P. D., Gnr. 14 F.A.B.		8/12/15 3y 11m, Gnr.
RICHARDSON, R. W., Pte. 40 Bn.	W.	27/ 5/16 3y 5m, L./Sgt.
RICHARDSON, U. J., Pte. 12 Bn.	52 Bn.	21/ 9/15 4y, Pte.
RICHARDSON, W., Pte. 4 M.G.Co.	W.	10/ 7/16 3y 2m, Pte.
RICHMOND, G. H., Pte. 12 Bn.	2W.	13/ 2/15
RICHMOND, J., Pte. 26 Bn.		19/ 6/15
RICHMOND, J., Pte. 26 Bn.	✠ 25/7/16.	21/ 7/15 1y 5m, Pte.
RICKETTS, A., Pte. 12 Bn.	2W., 49 Bn.	25/ 8/14 Pte. ✠
RICKETTS, A., Pte. 40 Bn.	W.	2/ 3/16 3y 1m, Pte.
RICKETTS, G. C., Pte. 12 Bn.		14/ 9/14 4y 1m, Pte.
RICKETTS, H. G., Gnr. F. Art.	12 F.A.B., 4 D.A.C., 11F.A.B.	28/12/15 3y 9m, Dvr.
RICKETTS, H. R., Pte. 26 Bn.	28 Bn.	Pte.
RICKETTS, L. B., Pte. 12 Bn.	40 Bn.	29/10/16 2y 11m, Pte.
RICKETTS, S. T., Pte. 26 Bn.	W.	15/ 8/15
RIDE, A. J., Pte. 1 A.G.H.	M.M., 4 F. Amb.	9/ 6/15 4y 5m, Sgt.
RIDE, H. T., Munitions		

NAME.	REMARKS.	RANK ON ENLISTED. DISCHARGE. SERVICE.
RIDER, G. E., Pte. 3 Fd. Amb.	13 Fd. Amb.	20/ 8/14 4y 5m. Dvr.
RIDER, L., Pte. 12 Bn.	4 Div. Tr. Depot, 13 Fd. Amb.	1/ 9/15 3y 11m. Pte.
RIDGE, A. V., Cpl 26 Bn.	✠ 21/11/15	20/ 4/15 Cpl. ✠
RIDGERS, J., Pte. 12 Bn.	51 Bn. ✠ 19/10/17	26/ 1/15 Pte. ✠
RIDGERS, W. H., Pte. 12 Bn.		30/ 5/17
RIDGWAY, J., Pte. 12 Bn.	W., Anzac Prov. Corps. ✠ 23/4/18.	4/12/14 Pte. ✠
RIELLY, J., Dvr. 3 F.A.B.	9 Bty.	3/12/14 4y 9m. Dvr.
RIGBY, A. J., Pte. 40 Bn.	✠ 2/4/17.	22/ 4/16 Pte. ✠
RIGBY, N. W., Pte. 12 Bn.	W., 1 Pnrs. ✠ 24/7/16	7/12/14 Pte. ✠
RIGBYE, P., Pte. 12 Bn.	✠ 25-28/4/15.	20/ 8/14 Pte. ✠
RIGBY, W. T., Pte. 15 Bn.	✠ 9/8/15	16/ 9/14 Pte. ✠
RIGGS, A. C., Pte 15 Bn.	✠ 9/8/16.	5/ 1/15 Pte. ✠
RIGGS, R W., Pte. 12 Bn.	40 Bn. ✠ 5-8/5/17.	5/ 7/16 Pte. ✠
RIGGS, W. J., Spr. Min. Cps.	2 Tun. Co.	11/ 3/16
RIGNEY, W. R., Pte. 12 Bn.	A.B.R.C.	14/12/17 1y 11m. Pte.
RILAT, L., Pte. 15 Bn.	P.O.W.	30/ 9/14 4y 8m. L./Cpl.
RILEY, A. J., Pte. 26 Bn.	3W., 26 Bn., 69 Bn.	18/ 2/15 4y 7m. Pte.
RILEY, A., Pte. 15 Bn.	W.	29/ 9/14 1y 8m. Pte.
RILEY, E. R., Pte. 12 Bn.		11/ 1/16 3y 6m. Pte.
RILEY, H. G., Pte. A.A.M.C.	W.	16/ 5/16 2y 11m. Pte.
RILEY, J. E., Gnr. 3 F.A.B.		30/11/14 4y 5m. Gnr.
RILEY, J. S., Pte. 26 Bn.		11/ 5/15 2y. Cpl.
RILEY, J. M., Pte. 40 Bn.		6/ 9/17 1y 7m. Pte.
RILEY, J. T., Sgt. 3 L.H.		20/ 8/14 4y 4m. 2 Lt.
RILEY, J., Pte. 26 Bn.	W.	6/ 5/15 1y 11m. Pte.
RILEY, J., Pte. 26 Bn.	2W. 69 Bn. ✠ 6/10/17.	19/ 6/15 Pte. ✠
RILEY, R. E., Pte. 26 Bn.	✠ 22/12/15.	18/ 2/15 Pte. ✠
RILEY, T., Pte. 40 Bn.	28 Bn.	19/ 9/16 3y 1m. Pte.
RILEY, T. H., Pte. 26 Bn.	✠ 29/7/16	16/ 3/15 Pte. ✠
RILEY, W. R., Pte. 15 Bn.	✠ 26/5/15	24/11/14 Pte. ✠
RIMON, N., Pte. 12 Bn.	W.	1/ 8/16 2y 7m. Pte.
RING, A. E., Spr. 3 Fd. Co.	15 Fd. Co., 29 A.S.C.	11/11/15 3y 11m. Whlr.
RING, N. E., Pte. 40 Bn.	2W.	19/ 9/16 3y.
RINGROSE, A. J., Pte. 40 Bn.	W.	3/ 5/16 2y 8m. Pte.
RIPPER, F. H., Pte. 12 Bn.	2W.	24/ 8/14 4y 11m. WO 2
RISBY, J., Gnr. 3 F.A.B.	W., D.A.C., 24 F.A.B., 37 Bty.	7/10/15 3y 9m. Cpl.
RISELEY, A. H. R., Dvr 6 F.A.B.		27/ 9/15 3y 11m. Dvr.
RISELEY, E. W., Spr. Tunnelers.		25/ 9/16 2y 8m. Spr.
RISELEY, G. H., Pte. 4 M.G. Co.	15 Bn., 4 M.G. Co.	17/ 4/17
RISELEY, J. C. E., Pte. 12 Bn.	W., 48 Bn. ✠ 13/4/17.	19/ 8/15 L./Cpl. ✠
RITCHIE, A. A., Pte. 26 Bn.		12/ 5/15 4y 7m. L./Cpl.
RITCHIE, D. C., Pte. 12 Bn.		18/ 1/18 1y 7m. Pte.
RITCHIE, H. P., Gnr. Art.	10 F.A.B., 39 Bty.	20/12/17 2y 7m., Sgt.
RITCHIE J. F., Pte. 26 Bn.	W., 21 Bn.	5/ 5/15 2y 7m. Pte.
RIVETT-CARNAC, C. W., Pte. 40 Bn.		13/ 9/15 3y 5m. Pte.
RIXON, M., Tpr. 3 L.H.	13 Bn., 4 Pnr. Bn.	17/ 8/14
ROACH, A. L., Pte. 12 Bn.		26/10/16
ROACH, C. B., Pte. 12 Bn.		8/12/15 3y 10m. Pte.
ROACH, C. A., Pte 12 Bn.	W., 40 Bn.	3/ 4/16 1y 9m. Pte.
ROACH, C. J., Pte. 40 Bn.	✠ 17/8/16	26 /2/16 Pte. ✠
ROACH, L. D., Pte. 26 Bn.	W., 12 Bn.	1/ 8/15 1y 6m. Pte.
ROACH, M. E., Pte. 40 Bn.	10 M.G. Co.	14/ 9/16 3y. Dvr.
ROACH, T. B., Munitions		
ROACH, W. W., Pte. 40 Bn.	2W., 2 M.G. Co.	5/ 2/16 3y 5m. Pte.
ROBEY, C. V. T., Sgt. 12 Bn.	52 Bty., 49 Bty.	11/ 8/15 4y. 2 Lt.
ROBINS, L. E., Dvr. D.A.C.		23/ 7/15 1y 7m. Tpr.
ROBINS, A. W., Pte. 12 Bn.	Anzac Police. ✠ 15/4/17.	28/ 8/15 Pte. ✠
ROBINS, H., Pte. 12 Bn.	W.	3/ 1/18
ROWBOTTOM, L. E., Dvr. D.A.C.	22 How. Bde., 104 How. Bde.	30/ 8/15 4y. Dvr.
ROWBOTTOM, P., Pte. 40 Bn.		5/ 9/16 3y 4m. Pte.
ROBSON, C. J., Gnr. 3 F.A. Bde.	24 How. Bde., 37 Bty., 10 F.A.B.	15/ 9/15 3y 11m. Pte.
ROBSON, E. T. Munitions		
ROBSON, T. K. McL., Pte. 15 Bn.	W. ✠ 9/5/15.	10/12/14 Pte. ✠
ROBERTS, A. A., Pte. 12 Bn.	W., 52 Bn., 51 Bn.	4/ 8/15 4y. Dvr.
ROBERTS, B. H., Tpr. 3 L.H.		20/ 8/14 2y 6m. Tpr.
ROBERTS, C. F., Pte. 26 Bn.	W., 51 Bn., 69 Bn., 26 Bn.	23/ 6/15 4y. Pte.
ROBERTS, D. E. A., Pte. 12 Bn.		10/ 2/16 11m. Pte.
ROBERTS, E. E., Pte. 12 Bn.	52 Bn. ✠ 6/10/17	16/10/15 Pte. ✠
ROBERTS, E. G., Pte. 12 Bn.	W.	20/ 8/14 2y 8m. Pte.
ROBERTS, E. M., Pte. Arty.	32 T.M. Bde.	28/ 5/17 2y 5m. Dvr.
ROBERTS, E., Pte. 12 Bn.	W., 52 Bn., 38 Bty., 10 F.A.B.	9/ 7/15 4y 1m. Gnr.
ROBERTS, E., Pte. 26 Bn.		19/ 7/15
ROBERTS, F., Spr. 8 Fd. Co.		20/12/15 1m. Spr.
ROBERTS, G. W., Munitions		
ROBERTS, G. S., Gnr. 3 F.A.B.	11 F.A.B.	9/ 6/15 4y 4m. Gnr.
ROBERTS, G. F., Spr. 8 Fd. Co.	7 Fd. Co.	1/ 4/16
ROBERTS, H. E., Pte. 12 Bn.	W.	3/ 4/16 3y 4m. Pte.
ROBERTS, H., Pte. 12 Bn.	W.	25/10/16 3y 1m. Pte.
ROBERTS, H., Pte. 26 Bn.	2W. ✠ 5/10/17	16/ 6/15 Pte. ✠
ROBERTS, H O., Gnr. 7 T.M.B.		15/ 2/15 2y 5m. Gnr.
ROBERTS, J., Pte. 12 Bn.	W.	12/ 7/15 4y 1m. Spr.
ROBERTS, J. H., Pte. 40 Bn.	W.	1/ 3/16 3y 2m. Cpl.
ROBERTS, L. H., Spr. 8 Fd. Co.	W.	13/ 9/15 3y 7m. Spr.
ROBERTS, L. J., Pte. 12 Bn.	W.	9/ 9/15 1y 6m. Pte.
ROBERTS, N. C. G., Pte. 1 A.C.H.	9 F. Amb. ✠ 29/9/18.	27/ 7/15 Dvr. ✠

NAME.	REMARKS.	ENLISTED. SERVICE. RANK ON DISCHARGE.
ROBERTS, C. Q., Pte. A.A.M.C.	3 A.G. Hos.	5/ 4/16 3y 6m. Pte.
ROBERTS, R., Pte. 26 Bn.	2W., 12 Bn.	30/ 8/15 3y 7m. Pte.
ROBERTS, R. G., 3 F.A.B.		23/10/14 1y 3m.
ROBERTS, R. H., Pte. 12 Bn.	2W., 52 Bn. ✠ 25/4/18.	8/11/15 Pte. ✠
ROBERTS, R. R., Pte. 12 Bn.	40 Bn., 10 M.G.C., 3 M.G.B. ✠ 29/9/18	21/ 7/16 Pte. ✠
ROBERTS, S. P., Pte. 12 Bn.		24/ 8/15.
ROBERTS, W., Pte. 2 G.S.R.		27/ 5/18
ROBERTS, W. E., Pte. 15 Bn.		17/ 9/14 4y 3m. Cpl.
ROBERTS, W. G., Pte. 12 Bn.		23/ 9/16 2y 7m. Pte.
ROBERTS, W. J., Pte. 12 Bn.	52 Bn., 49 Bn.	3/ 8/15 4y Pte.
ROBERTSON, A. G., Pte. 40 Bn.	✠ 8/6/17.	12/ 7/16 Pte. ✠
ROBERTSON, A. E., Dvr. 40 Bn.	2W.	20/10/16 2y 11m, L.-Cpl.
ROBERTSON, A. J., Spr. 3 Fd. Co.		30/ 8/15 3y 11m. Spr.
ROBERTSON, C., Pte. 40 Bn.	W.	2/ 3/16
ROBERTSON, E. T., Pte. 40 Bn.	✠ 5/10/17.	6/10/16 Pte. ✠
ROBERTSON, F. H., Pte. 26 Bn.	W.	19/ 2/15 Pte.
ROBERTSON, G. T., Sgt. 26 Bn.	✠ 29/7/16.	4/ 8/15 Sgt. ✠
ROBERTSON, H., Pte. 12 Bn.	✠ 6-10/4/17	4/ 6/15 Pte. ✠
ROBERTSON, J., Gnr. 26 Bn.	W., 2 D.A.C.	20/ 7/15 4y 1m. Gnr.
ROBERTSON, J. C., Dvr. 15 Bn.	2W., 10 F.A.B.	4/ 8/15
ROBERTSON, J. R., Munitions		
ROBERTSON, J., Pte. 12 Bn.	W., 16 Bn.	16/10/16 3y. Pte.
ROBERTSON, J. A., Dvr. 40 Bn.	M.M.	23/ 5/16 3y 1m. Dvr.
ROBERTSON, K. D., Gnr. Arty.		11/ [illegible]/16 10m, Gnr.
ROBERTSON, K. A., Pte. 12 Bn.		15/12/14 4y 10m, Pte.
ROBERTSON, L. E., Pte. 12 Bn.	W. ✠ 25/-28/4/15.	21/ 8/14 Pte. ✠
ROBERTSON, R. A., Dvr. 6 F.A.B.		19/ 8/15 3y 8m, Dvr.
ROBERTSON, S. J., Pte 2 G.S.R.	11 F.A.B.	7/ 6/18 1y 3m, Gnr.
ROBERTSON, W., Pte. 3 Fd. Amb.		20/ 8/14 1y 10m, Pte.
ROBERTSON, W. T., Pte. 12 Bn.	W.	17/12/15 3y 10m, Pte.
ROBINSON, A. J., Pte. 3 Fd. Amb.	M.M., 13 Fd. Amb.	28/ 8/14 5y 1m, L.-Cpl.
ROBINSON, A. P., Pte. Remounts.		20/ 9/15 1y 3m, Cpl.
ROBINSON, A. G., Pte. 12 Bn.	✠ 19-22/8/16.	23/ 9/15 Pte. ✠
ROBINSON, A. H., Pte. W'less.	4 Div. Sig.	5/ 9/17 1y 6m, Spr.
ROBINSON, B. W., Tpr. 3 L.H.		19/ 7/15 4y 2m R.S.M.
ROBINSON, C. H., Gnr. 3 F.A.B.	9 Bty.	10/ 8/15 4y 2m. 2-Lt.
ROBINSON, C. W., Pte. 1 A.C.H.		12/ 9/14 4y 4m. Pte.
ROBINSON, E. H., Gnr. 32 F.A.B.	2 D.A.C.	3/ 5/17 2y 7m, Gnr.
ROBINSON, E. A., Spr. Engrs.	W.	4/ 1/16 3y 8m, 2nd Cpl.
ROBINSON, F. E., Pte. A.F.C.	71 Sqd. A.F.C.	27/10/16 2y 10m, 2nd A. Mec.
ROBINSON, G. C., Pte. 4 M.G. Co.	25 M.G. Co. ✠ 27/10/17.	21/ 7/16 L-Cpl. ✠
ROBINSON, G. E., Tpr. 3 L.H.	Desert Mtd. Corps.	7/ 9/15 4y, Tpr.
ROBINSON, G. S., Pte. 4 M.G. Co.		17/ 1/17.
ROBINSON, H. H., Pte. 15 Bn.		17/ 8/15 4y 3m, Pte.
ROBINSON, J., Tpr. 3 L.H.	W., 1 M.G. Sqd.	6/ 1/15 3y 4m, Tpr.
ROBINSON, J., Pte. 12 Bn.	W., 48 Bn. ✠ 12/10/17.	22/ 8/14 Pte. ✠
ROBINSON, J. M., Tpr. 3 L.H.	5 D.A.C., 2 Cyc. Bn.	24/ 8/15 4y 2m, Pte.
ROBINSON, M. J., Pte. T.M. Bty.		12/10/16 2y 4m, Pte.
ROBINSON, J. H., S.S.M., 6 F.A.B	H.Q. 3 Army F.A.B.	2/10/15 3y 10m, W.O. 1
ROBINSON, O., Tpr. 3 L.H.	M.G. Squad, 1 L.H., 1 M.G. Co., 3 L.H.	19/ 8/14 4y 6m, Pte.
ROBINSON, R. T., Pte. 12 Bn.	W., 3 Fd. Amb.	22/ 5/15 4y 1m, Pte.
ROBINSON, R., Pte. 40 Bn.	15 Bn., 40 Bn.	21/ 3/16 1y 9m, Pte.
ROBINSON, R. C., Pte. 12 Bn.		31/12/14 3y 5m, Pte.
ROBINSON, S. G., Tpr. 3 L.H.	W., 4 L.H., 6 F.A.B.	12/ 4/17 1y 10m, Gnr.
ROBINSON, M. J., Tpr. 3 L.H.	2W., A. C. Cyc. Bn., 7/8 M.T.M.B.	24/ 8/15 4y 2m, Gnr.
ROBINSON, T., Pte. 12 Bn.	2W.	12/ 7/15 4y 1m, Pte.
ROBINSON, W. G., Pte. 3 Fd. Amb.	C. de G. (Belgian), 13 Fd. Amb.	19/ 8/14 4y 5m, Pte.
ROCHE, J., Pte. Remounts.		21/ 9/15 1y 3m, Pte.
ROCHE, W., Pte. 40 Bn.		25/ 4/16 3y 5m, Pte.
ROCHER, T. T., Spr. Miners.		23/10/15 1y 5m, Sgt.
ROCK, C. W. D., Lt. 40 Bn.		1/ 5/16
ROCK, A., Pte. 40 Bn.	2W.	27/ 9/16 2y. Pte.
ROCK, H. C., Pte. 15 Bn	✠ 8/8/16.	15/ 9/15 Pte. ✠
ROCKLIFF, A. A. A., Cpl. 12 Bn.		18/ 4/18 3y 5m, Cpl.
ROCKLIFF, A. W., Pte. 4 M.G. Co.	4 M.G. Co. ✠ 18/9/18.	9/12/16 Pte. ✠
ROCKLIFF, A. C. H., Pte. 12 Bn.	47 Bn. ✠ 5/4/18.	7/11/16 Pte. ✠
ROCKLIFF, C. B., Tpr. 3 L.H.		15/ 5/17 2y 6m. Dvr.
ROCKLIFF, E. Pte. 12 Bn.	W.	7/11/15 2y 3m, Pte.
ROCKLIFFE, F., Pte. 12 Bn.	4W.	24/ 8/15 4y, Pte.
ROCKLIFF, J. T., Gnr. Arty.		15/ 9/15 1y 6m, Gnr.
ROCKLIFF, V. H., Pte. 12 Bn.	W., M.M. ✠ 5-8/5/17.	17/ 4/16 Pte. ✠
ROCKLIFF, V. T., Pte. 12 Bn.	✠ 19-22/8/16.	22/ 7/15 Pte. ✠
ROCKLIFFE, W. R., Pte. 15 Bn.		5/ 1/15 2y 8m, Pte.
ROCKWELL, R. G. A., L.-Cpl. 10 Bn		19/ 8/14 4y 8m, L.-Cpl.
ROCKWELL, V. J., Pte. 4 M.G. Co.	15 Bn., 4 M.G. Co., 23 M.G. Co.	13/ 2/17 2y 8m, Pte.
RODD, H. C., Pte 40 Bn.		26/ 3/17 2y 10m, Pte.
RODEN, F. W. A., Pte. 12 Bn.		23/ 7/15 4y, Sgt.
RODEN, P. H., Pte. 15 Bn.	24 How. Bde., 10 How. Bde.	28/ 3/15 3y 4m, Gnr.
RODEN, W. J., Pte. 26 Bn.	2W. ✠ 11/8/18.	12/ 8/15 Pte. ✠
RODGER, R. H., Pte 12 Bn.	M.S.M., 52 Bn., Aus. Rec. G.H.Q.	8/ 7/18.
RODGERS, A., Pte. 12 Bn.	3W. ✠ 5-8/5/17.	28/ 8/14 Pte. ✠
RODGERS, E. J., Gnr. Arty.	4 D.A.H.Q.	18/ 2/15.
RODGERS, G. A. E., Pte. 12 Bn.	52 Bn., 51 Bn.	20/ 8/14 4y 7m, Pte.
RODGERS, J. A., Pte. 15 Bn.	✠ 9/8/15.	2/10/14 Pte. ✠
RODGERS, J., Pte. A.A.M.C.	8 Fd. Amb.	15/11/15 3y 8m, Pte.

TASMANIA'S MUSTER ROLL. 335

NAME.	REMARKS.	RANK ON ENLISTED.	DISCHARGE. SERVICE.
RODMAN, C. D., Pte. 40 Bn.		27/ 6/16	3y 3m, Pte.
RODWAY, S. F., Gnr. Arty.		27/11/16	2y 4m, Gnr.
ROE, E. G., Pte. 4 A.A.S.C.	2 Co. A.S.C., 1 Div. Train.	20/ 9/15	Pte. ✠
ROE, R. E G., Cpl. Arty.	W.	27/ 3/16	Pte. ✠
ROE, R. J., Dvr. 3 L.H.		9/10/16	3y 2m, Pte.
ROEBUCK, P. A., Cpl. 4 M.G. Co.		18/ 9/14	2y, Pte.
ROGERS, C. C., Pte. A.A.M.C.	M.M., 3 Fd. Amb.	9/10/16	3y 2m, Pte.
ROGERS, C. J., Pte. 40 Bn	2W.	28/ 9/15	3y 11m, Gnr.
ROGERS, E., Pte. 26 Bn.		9/10/16	Pte. ✠
ROGERS, E. S., Pte. 12 Bn.		14/ 2/16	3y 6m, Cpl.
ROGERS, H. A., Pte. A.A.M.C.	3 Fd. Amb.	31/ 8/15	4y, Pte.
ROGERS, H., Gnr. 6 F.A.B.	✠ 24/10/18.	11/ 8/15	Pte. ✠
ROGERS, J. L., Gnr. S. Arty Bde.	W.	2/ 3/16	3y 5m, Pte.
ROGERS, J. R., Pte. 40 Bn.	✠ 9/12/17.	19/ 3/17	2y 6m, Gnr.
ROGERS, J. T., Pte. 12 Bn.	52 Bn, 12 Bn.	20/ 8/14	Cpl. ✠
ROGERS, L., Pte. 40 Bn.	M.M.	8/ 3/16	Pte. ✠
ROGERS, W. J., Gnr. Arty.	13 Fd. Bty.	20/ 9/15	Dvr. ✠
ROOKE, C. K. T., Cpl. 12 Bn.	✠ 25/4/15.	24/11/16.	
ROLES, L. H., Pte. 40 Bn.	W., 12 Bn., ✠ 15/4/17.	28/ 2/16	1y 8m, Pte.
ROLES, W. J., Gnr. 6 F.A.B.	✠ 21/12/16.	12/ 1/15	4y 4m, Bdr.
ROLLINGS, C. L., Pte. 4 M.G. Co.	12 Bn.	28/ 2/16.	
ROLLINS, J. C., Pte. 40 Bn.	W.	26/ 2/16	3y 6m, Pte.
ROLLINS, J., Pte. 12 Bn.	2W., M.M.	30/ 4/15	4y 6m, Pte.
ROLLINS, L. V., Pte. 40 Bn.	2W.	19/ 1/15.	
ROLLINS, L. O., Pte. 12 Bn.	52 Bn. ✠ 2/4/17.	31/12/15	2y 8m, Pte.
ROLLINS, V. E., Pte. 40 Bn.	W. ✠ 5/10/17.	27/10/15	Gnr. ✠
ROLLS, A. C., Pte. 15 M.G. Co.		5/ 6/15.	
ROLLS, B., Pte. 1 A.G.H.		12/ 7/16	Pte. ✠
ROLLS, E. B., Pte. 4 M.G. Co.	W., 2 M.G. Bn.	16/ 9/15	4y, Pte.
ROLPH, R. S., Gnr. D.A.C.	22 How. Bde.	3/ 8/15	4y 1m, Sgt.
ROMETCH, A. S., Pte. 40 Bn.	✠ 13/10/17.	9/ 9/15.	
ROOM, W. H., Sec. Lt. 12 Bn.		28/ 8/14	3y, Capt.
ROONEY, A., Pte. 40 Bn.	2W., M.S.M.	20/ 8/14	4y 8m, Dvr.
ROONEY, P., Pte. 15 Bn.	W., M.M., 47 Bn., 45 Bn.	25/10/16	2y 5m, Pte.
ROOTES, J. H., Pte. 26 Bn.	W., 12 Bn. ✠ 15/4/17.	1/ 2/16	3y 8m, Pte.
ROOTES, W. A., Pte. 40 Bn.		26/11/14	1y 9m, Tpr.
ROOTES, W. H., Pte. 15 Bn.	✠ 26/5/15.	22/ 3/16	Pte. ✠
ROPER, O. J., Sec. Lt. 12 Bn.	W.	19/ 7/15	Sy Lt.
ROSCOW, J. R., Pte. 4 M.G. Co.	5 Div. M.G. Co.	25/ 2/16	2y 6m, Pte.
ROSE, F. A., Pte. 40 Bn.		22/ 9/14	Pte. ✠
ROSE, C. H., Gnr. Arty.		23/ 6/16	3y 3m, Pte.
ROSE, E., Pte. 12 Bn.	✠ 1/6/18.	1/ 2/16	3y 8m, Sgt.
ROSE, F., Pte. 40 Bn.	✠ 17/7/18.	12/ 1/17	3y 2m, Gnr,
ROSE, F., Tpr. 3 L.H.	W.	18/ 9/17	Pte. ✠
ROSE, G. W. P., Pte. 40 Bn.	W.	15/ 3/16	2y 10m, Pte.
ROSE, H., Pte. A.A.D.C.		31/ 3/16	3y 8m, Pte.
ROSE, H., Pte. 12 Bn.	W.	25/ 8/14	1y 10m, Pte.
ROSE, J., Pte. 3 G.S.R.		1/ 8/13	
ROSE, L. T., Cpl. 15 Bn.	W., P.O.W.	23/ 9/14	4y 9m, Sgt.
ROSENDELL, C. W., Pte. 12 Bn.	2W., M.M., C. de G.	16/ 8/15	4y 2m, Lieut.
ROSENDELL, G. C., Pte. 26 Bn.		16/ 8/15	3y 10m, Pte.
ROSENDELL, H. A., Pte. 26 Bn.	12 Bn. ✠ 6-10/4/17.	4/ 8/15	Pte. ✠
ROSENDELL, R. H., Tpr. 2 G.S. Rfts.	3 L.H.	29/ 4/18	1y 4m, Tpr.
ROSEVEAR, A. E., Pte. 26 Bn.	W.	20/ 7/15	Pte.
ROSEVEARS, C. H., Pte. 12 Bn.	✠ 13/5/18.	27/ 11/17	Pte. ✠
ROSEVEAR, K. G., Pte. 12 Bn.		23/ 7/15	1y, Pte.
ROSVEAR, W. H., Dvr. 9 Fd. Bty.		27/ 8/14	4y 5m, Dvr.
ROSS, T. G., Major 7 Fd. Amb.	D.S.O., M.I.D., 12 Fd. Amb.	1/ 5/15	2y 5m, Lt.-Col
ROSS, A. K. F, Tpr. 3 L.H.	Re-enlisted 3 L.H.	7/ 8/14	3y, Sgt.
ROSS, C. L. F., Pte. 15 Bn.	10 F.A.B.	20/ 5/15	4y 8m, Gnr.
ROSS, C. J., Pte. 12 Bn.		20/12/15	
ROSS, F. C., Pte. 12 Bn.	✠ 25/2/17.	6/ 4/16	Pte. ✠
ROSS, J., Pte. 4 M.G. Co.	W.	11/ 1/17	2y 2m, Pte.
ROSS, J., Pte. M.G. Rfts.		10/ 1/17	2y 2m, Pte.
ROSS, L., Pte. 12 Bn.	21 Bn.	23/ 8/15	Pte. ✠
ROSS, R., Pte. 12 Bn.	1 Pnrs. ✠ 15/5/16.	22/ 9/16	
ROSS, T. T., Gnr. F.A.B.	2W.	24/11/14	
ROSS, T.			
ROSS, W. D., Sgt. 26 Bn.	W. ✠ 29/7/16.	12/ 4/15	Sgt. ✠
ROSSINGTON, G. M., Pte. 40 Bn.	15 Bn. ✠ 11/4/17.	20/ 3/16	Pte. ✠
ROTHWELL, A. L., Gnr. Arty.		26/10/16	6m. Gnr.
ROUGH, G., Pte. 12 Bn.	Vet. Corps Dtls., A.S.C.	1/ 5/16	
ROUGHLEY, A. R., Pte. 40 Bn.	W.	25/ 2/17	2y 9m, Pte.
ROUGHLEY, C. W., Pte. 12 Bn.	W. ✠ 9/6/18.	18/ 7/16	Pte. ✠
ROUGHLEY, G. A., Pte. 40 Bn.	3W., 15 Bn., 40 Bn. ✠ 2/11/18.	29/ 3/16	Pte. ✠
ROUGHLEY, J. T., Pte. 40 Bn.	✠ 28/3/18.	7/11/16	Pte. ✠
ROUGHLEY, S. S., Pte. 2 G.S. Rfts.	W., 4 G.S. Rfts.	25/ 3/18	11m. Pte.
ROUND, A., Pte. 12 Bn.	W., 40 Bn.	19/10/16	2y 11m, Pte.
ROUSE, A. N., Pte. 26 Bn.		20/ 6/15	3y 10m, Pte
ROUSE, L. L., Pte. 26 Bn.		18/ 8/15	4y 1m, Pte.
ROUSE, S. A., Pte. 12 Bn.	W.	19/10/16	Pte. ✠
ROUT, F., Pte. 4 M.G. Co.	✠ 23/4/18.	2/ 4/17	
ROWBERRY, W. G., Pte. 40 Bn.	W.	13/ 3/16	2y, Pte.
ROWBOTTOM, R. A., Pte. 40 Bn.	2W.	4/10/15	2y 11m, Pte.
ROWBOTTOM, W. M., Pte. 12 Bn.	3 Imp. Cam. Corps.	8/ 1/15	3y, Pte.
ROWE, E. M, Lt. 3 G.S.R.		1/ 7/18	

NAME.	REMARKS.	RANK ON DISCHARGE. ENLISTED, SERVICE.
ROWE, C. C., Gnr. Arty.	W., 49 Bty.	18/10/16 3y, Gnr.
ROWE, F. H., Pte 40 Bn.		27/ 9/16 3y 3m, Pte.
ROWE, J. S., Gnr. 15 F.A.B.	Amm. Col. 3 Bde.	18/10, 16 3y, Dvr.
ROWE, J. R., Pte. 13 Bn.		30/11/15 1y 9m, Pte.
ROWE, L. A., Spr. 8 Fd. Co.	F.A.B. ✷ 16/8/18.	19/10/15 Gnr. ✷
ROWELL, A. W., Gnr. Arty.	3 F.A.B., 1 A.C.D.	16/ 5/16 2y 1m, Gnr.
ROWELL, C. E., Pte. 4 M.G. Co.	12 Bn. ✷ 23/8/18.	2/ 2/17 Pte. ✷
ROWLAND, D. O., Pte. 26 Bn.		1/ 9/15 1y, Pte.
ROWLAND, H., Pte. 4 M.G. Co.	2W.	14/11/16 2y 8m, Pte.
ROWLANDS, H. J., Pte. 1 Rmts.		20/ 9/15 4y 2m, Farrier
ROWLANDS, H. J., Tpr. 1 Rmts.		20/ 9/15 4y 2m, S/Smith
ROWLES, C., Pte. 15 Bn.		4/11/14 6m, Pte.
ROWLEY, J., Spr. 13 Fd. Co.	M.M.	2/11/15 3y 5m, L.-Cpl.
ROWLEY, R. L., Spr. 8 Fd. Co.		21/ 2/16 3y 10m, Cpl.
ROWSE, J. T., Pte. 12 Bn.	✷ 23/8/18.	23/ 7/15 Dvr. ✷
ROWSTHORN, W. G. W., Sgt. 12 Bn.	✷ 6-10/4/17.	13/ 9/15 Sgt. ✷
ROXBURGH, K. G., L.-Cpl. B.A.C.	W., 9 Fd. Bty.	8/10/14 5y, Lieut.
RUDD, A. R., Pte. 12 Bn.	51 Bn. ✷ 2/12/17.	9/ 7/15 Pte. ✷
RUDD, H. O., Pte. 12 Bn.		9/ 2/15 1y 4m, Pte.
RUDD, H. C., Pte. 40 Bn.	12 Bn.	4/ 5/15 4y 4m, Pte.
RUDD, S. V., Pte. 12 Bn.	W.	27/ 3/16 2y 2m, Pte.
RUDDOCK, W. C. G., Capt. 40 Bn.	2W.	23/ 2/16 3y 6m, Capt.
BUFFELS, C. V., Tpr. 3 L.H.	✷ 12/9/18.	9/ 1/17 Tpr. ✷
BUFFELS, E. C., Pte. 26 Bn.		10/ 8/15 2y 10m, Pte.
RUFFIN, C. R., Pte. 12 Bn.		9/10/14 3y 7m, Pte.
RULE, A. C., Pte. 12 Bn.		1/ 8/15
RULE, A. L., Pte. 40 Bn.	W.	4/ 7/16 3y 2m, Pte.
RULE, G. T., Gnr. 3 F.A.B.	W., 9 Bty.	1/ 8/15 4y 2m, Lieut.
RULE, J. C., Cpl. 12 Bn.	✷ 7/8/15.	1/ 2/15 Cpl. ✷
RULE, R. K., Spr. 8 Fd. Co.	2 Fd. Co.	25/ 2/16 3y 9m, Spr.
RUMNEY, E., Pte. 15 Bn.		11/ 1/15 4y 5m. Pte.
RUMNEY, H., Pte. 12 Bn.	✷ 8/8/15.	9/ 1/15 Pte. ✷
RUMNEY, H. J., A.-Bdr. 55 S. Bde.		1/ 9/15 2y 5m, Gnr.
RUNDLE, F. D., Gnr. 6 F.A.B.	15 Bty. ✷ 25/10/17.	1/10/15 Gnr. ✷
RUNDLE, G. J. G., Pte. 12 Bn.		22/ 8/14 3y 9m, Pte.
RUNDLE, L. C., Pte. 2 G.S. Rfts.	26 Fd. Bty.	23/ 5/18 1y 5m, Gnr.
RUSSELL, A., Dvr. 10 A.S.C.	6 Bn. ✷ 30/10/17.	12/ 9/14 Pte. ✷
RUSSELL, A. D., Tpr. 3 L.H.		4/ 8/17 2y, Tpr.
RUSSELL, C. E., Pte. 40 Bn.		31/ 3/16 3y 6m, Pte.
RUSSELL, C. F., Gnr. Arty.	2 D.A.C., 5 F.A.B., 14 F.A.B., 54 Bty.	4/ 9/15 4y, Gnr.
RUSSELL, E. W., Pte. 40 Bn.	W.	10/ 7/16 1y 11m, L.-Cpl.
RUSSELL, E. O., Gnr. 3 F.A. Bde.	2W.	12/ 1/15 3y 11m, Gnr.
RUSSELL, G. A., Pte. A.A.M.C.	9 Fd. Amb.	14/ 9/16 3y 2m, Pte.
RUSSELL, G. A., Pte. 26 Bn.	2W. ✷ 19-20/9/17.	31/ 8/15 Pte. ✷
RUSSELL, H. McD., Pte. 40 Bn.	W. ✷ 31/5/17.	17/ 4/16 Pte. ✷
RUSSELL, M. E., Pte. 40 Bn.	W.	17/10/16 2y 11m, Pte.
RUSSELL, M. T. Pte. 12 Bn.	2W., M.M.	29/ 8/14 4y 5m, C.S.M.
RUSSELL, P. H., Pte. M.G. Co.		3/ 7/16
RUSSELL, R. G., Sgt. 12 Bn.	✷ 8/8/15.	20/ 1/15 Sgt. ✷
RUSSELL, T., Pte. 12 Bn.	W.	20/ 8/14
RUSSELL, W., Pte. 12 Bn.		7/ 2/16 3y 7m, Pte.
RUSSELL, W., Pte. 12 Bn.		24/ 8/14 3y 11m, Pte.
RUSSELL, W., Pte. 40 Bn.		31/ 7/16 3y 5m, L.-Cpl.
RUSSELL, W., 15 Bn.	W. ✷ 20/8/15.	15/ 9/14 Cpl. ✷
RUSSELL, W. H., Pte. 26 Bn.	51 Bn. ✷ 28/3/17.	14/ 8/15 L.-Cpl. ✷
RUSSELL, W. T., Pte. 26 Bn.	2W., 12 Bn.	18/ 8/15
RUSDEN, W. T., Pte. 4 M.G. Co.	M.M., 5 M.G. Co.	29/ 7/16 2y 11m, Pte.
RUSH, F. R., Pte 15 Bn.	24 How. Bde., 4 D.A.C.	6/ 9/15 3y 11m, Dvr.
RUSHTON, A., Gnr. 1 G.S.R.	26 Bty.	24/ 2/18 1y 8m, Gnr.
RUSHTON, C. W., Pte. 12 Bn.	✷ 8/4/17.	23/ 8/15 Pte. ✷
RUSHTON, E. G., Pte. 40 Bn.	P.O.W.	7/ 3/16 3y 4m, Pte.
RUSSEN, C. C., Bugler 12 Bn.		27/ 8/14 2y 5m, Pte.
RUSSEN, R. O., Sgt. 13 A.A.S.C.		4/12/14 1y 6m, Sgt.
RUST, J., Gnr. Arty.	W., 23 How. Bde. 3 D.A.C.	30/ 8/15 4y 2m, Dvr.
RUST, T., Pte. 40 Bn.	✷ 29/12/16.	23/ 3/16 Pte. ✷
RUTHERFORD, E., Pte. 12 Bn.	W., 40 Bn.	17/10/16 3y, L.-Cpl.
RUTTER, A. L., Q.M.S. 26 Bn.		16/ 2/15 1y 9m, Q.M.S.
RUTTER, J. C., Pte. 40 Bn.	W.	4/ 2/16 3y 9m, Sgt.
RUTTER, W. L., Pte. 12 Bn.	✷ 19-23/8/16.	18/ 1/16 Pte. ✷
RYAN, A. E., Pte. 4 M.G. Co.	W., 5 Divl. M.G. Co.	31/ 5/16 3y 5m, Cpl.
RYAN, A., Pte. 12 Bn	2W.	13/ 4/16 3y 3m, Pte.
RYAN, C F., Pte. 12 Bn.	✷ 24/7/16.	27/ 7/15 Pte. ✷
RYAN, E. J., Gnr. Arty.	104 Bty.	22/ 5/16 3y 5m, Gnr.
RYAN, J. J., Pte. 40 Bn.	✷ 7/6/17.	16/ 9/16 Pte. ✷
RYAN, J., Pte. 1 A.C.H.	W. ✷ 2/4/19.	19/ 9/14 2y 1m. ✷
RYAN, J., Spr. Miners	W.	18/ 4/16 2y 8m, Spr.
RYAN, J., Gnr. 2 C.S. Rfts.	A.B.D.H.Q.	27/ 5/18 1y 7m, Gnr.
RYAN, J., Pte. 26 Bn.	W.	23/ 9/15
RYAN, P. G., Pte. 26 Bn.	✷ 4/16/6.	19/10/15 Pte. ✷
RYAN, M., Spr. 3 Miners		23/11/15
RYAN, P. J., Pte. 26 Bn.		20/ 5/15 10m, Pte.
RYAN, M. P., Pte. 40 Bn.	✷ 11/8/18.	8/ 2/16 Dvr. ✷
RYAN, P. J., Pte. 12 Bn.	W.	15/ 8/16 7m, Pte.
RYAN, P., Pte. 15 Bn.	4 L.T.M. Bty. ✷ 11/4/17.	8/ 6/15 Pte. ✷
RYAN, W. D., Pte. 15 Bn.	2 W., 10 F.A. Bde.,	19/ 9/14 4y 5m, Dvr.
RYDER, A. G. A., Pte. 4 M.G. Co.	2W., 10 F.A. Bde.	22/ 6/15 2y, Dvr.
RYDER, H. F., Pte. 26 Bn.	11 M.G. Co.	6/10/16 3y, Pte.

TASMANIA'S MUSTER ROLL.

NAME.	REMARKS.	RANK ON DISCHARGE. ENLISTED. SERVICE.
RYLETT, A. B., Pte. 2 G.S.R.		23/ 5/18
SADLER, B. T., Lieut. 40 Bn.	C de G. (Belgian).	18/ 3/16 3y 5m. Lieut.
SADDINGTON, J., Pte. 40 Bn.	MM. ✠ 21/2/18	4/ 4/16 Cpl. ✠
SAGGARS, A. W., Pte. 3 Fd. Amb.	4 Fd. Amb.	5/ 1/15 3y 1m. Pte.
SAGGARS, E. J., Spr. Wireless	18 A. Sig. Squad	18/ 5/15 3y 4m. Spr.
SAGGARS, E., Pte. 40 Bn.		21/12/17
SAINSBURY, A. W., Gnr. 13 F.A.B.	14 F.A.B.	Gnr.
SAINSBURY, C. J., Pte. 40 Bn.	W. 3 M.G. Co.	8/11/16 2y 9m. Pte.
SAINTY, H., Pte. 40 Bn.		26/ 9/16 10m. Pte.
SAINTY, J. T., Pte. 40 Bn.	2W.	25/ 6/16 2y 9m. Pte.
SALE, A. T., Pte. 12 Bn.	1 Div. Sal. Co. ✠ 3/7/18	1/ 6/15 Pte. ✠
SALE, R. H. M., Pte. 12 Bn.	W. ✠ 19-20/9/17	8/7/15 Pte. ✠
SALE, B. E., Pte. 3 Fd. Amb.	✠ 6/1/17	25/ 8/15 2y 10m. Pte.
SALES, H. T., Pte. 3 Fd. Amb.		25/ 8/15 Pte. ✠
SALES, J. C., Pte. 3 Fd. Amb.	6 Fd. Amb.	25/ 8/15 2y 7m. Pte.
SALES, W. K., Pte. A.A.M.C.		18/ 4/16 2y 3m. Pte.
SALES, G. A., L/Cpl. 3 L.H.		19/ 8/14 4y 5m. SQMS
SALISBURY, C. N., Cpl. 12 Bn.	✠ 10/7/16	13/ 7/15 Cpl. ✠
SALISBURY, J. C., Pte. 12 Bn.		19/ 9/16 2y 4m. Pte.
SALISBURY, J., M. Worker.		M.W.
SALMON, C. G., Pte. 40 Bn.	✠ 28/3/18.	6/ 3/16 Pte. ✠
SALTS, G., Pte. 12 Bn.	W.	22/ 8/14 2y 6m. S/Cook
SALTER, E. H., Pte. 12 Bn.	11 Bn.	25/ 5/15 3y 4m. Lieut.
SALTER, E. J., Pte. 3 G.S.R.	12 Bn.	29/ 5/18 1y 3m. Pte.
SALTER, G. M., 4 M.G. Co.		1/12/16 3m. Pte.
SALTER, J. H., Pte. 12 Bn.	4 D.A.C. 8 A.M.T.M. Bty.	27/ 4/16 3y 5m. Pte.
SALTER, O., Tpr. 3 L.H.	W.	24/ 9/15 3y 11m. Lieut.
SALTER, R. E., Pte. 40 Bn.	69 Bn. 26 Bn.	8/ 2/16 3y 6m. Pte.
SALTER, W. F., Pte. 26 Bn.		17/ 3/15 4y 5m. Pte.
SALTER, W. H., Pte. 4 M.G. Co.		28/ 9/16 9m. Pte.
SALTMARSH, E. W., Pte. 12 Bn.	2W. M.M.	30/ 7/15 4y 3m. Pte.
SALTMARSH, H. E., Pte. 40 Bn.	W. ✠ 5/10/17	12/ 9/16 Pte. ✠
SALTMARSH, L. R., Pte. 12 Bn.	2W. M.M.	4/ 9/15 4y 2m. Pte.
SALTMARSH, W., Pte. 12 Bn.		10/ 5/16 1y 3m. Pte.
SALVADO, V., Pte. 12 Bn.	W. (enlisted as Anderson, R. V., correct name SALVADO)	26/ 8/14 3y 3m. Cpl.
SAMPSON, B., Lieut., 15 Bn.	2W., D.S.O., M.I.D.	29/12/14 Major.
SAMPSON, C. E., Pte. 15 Bn.	2W.	21/ 9/14 4y 5m L-Cpl.
SAMPSON, C. C., Pte. 12 Bn.	W. 15 Bn.	8/ 7/15 4y 1m. Pte.
SAMPSON, S., Pte. 15 Bn.		16/ 9/14 Pte. ✠
SAMPSON, W. A., Pte. 15 Bn.	W. ✠ 14/5/15	25/10/16 Gnr. ✠
SAMPSON, W. H., Gnr. Art.	✠ 14/4/18.	7/ 3/16 3y 6m. Pte.
SAMPSON, W. K., Pte. 40 Bn.	2W. 51 Bn.	20/ 6/16 3y 3m. Pte.
SANDERS, M., Pte. 40 Bn.	W.	19/ 5/15
SANDERSON, G. A. Pte. 26 Bn.		4/ 1/16 Pte. ✠
SANDERSON, R., Pte. 12 Bn.	52 Bn. ✠ 1/1/17.	
SANDY, C., Pte. A.A.M.C.		24/ 8/14 9m. Sgt.
SANSOM, A. H., Sgt. 12 Bn.	1 F.A.B.	3/ 8/16 3y 1m. Gnr.
SANSOM, J. B., Gnr. 5 F.A.B.	1 F.A.B.	2/ 8/16 3y 1m. Gnr.
SANSOM, P. H. R., Gnr. Art.	13 F.A.B. 5 Bty.	8/12/15 3y 8m. Gnr.
SARGISON, R., Gnr. Art.	3 A.L.H.R.	2/ 1/15 4y 8m Tpr.
SARICH, M. F., Tpr. 3 F.A.B.	1 Div. Tun. A.S.C.	19/ 8/14 4y 7m. Pte.
SARKIES, D. K., Pte. 4 D.A.C.	W. 52 Bn.	4/ 1/16 1y 5m. Pte.
SAUNDERS, A., Pte. 12 Bn.	✠ 13/10/17	7/11/16 Pte. ✠
SAUNDERS, A. F., Pte. 40 Bn.	9 Bn.	9/ 3/15 1y 9m. Pte.
SAUNDERS, A., Pte. 26 Bn.	3 L.H.	17/ 7/18 1y 1m. Tpr.
SAUNDERS, A. V., Tpr. R.U.	3 Div. Train, 67 A.S.C.	28/ 2/16 2y. Dvr.
SAUNDERS, D. W., Dvr. 40 Bn.	10 F.A.B.	Gnr.
SAUNDERS, G. H. J., Pte. 15 Bn.	2W. 12 Bn.	19/ 8/14 5y 1m. Pte.
SAUNDERS, H. W., Pte. 15 Bn.	52 Bn. 15 L.T.M. Bty. ✠ 5/4/17	3/ 9/14 Pte. ✠
SAUNDERS, H., Pte. 12 Bn.	✠ 2/10/17	13/ 7/16 Pte. ✠
SAUNDERS, H. J. L., Pte. 40 Bn.	40 Bn. ✠ 8/2/18	20/10/16 Pte. ✠
SAUNDERS, L. J., Pte. 12 Bn.	12 Bn. ✠ 26/3/17	23/ 2/15 Pte. ✠
SAUNDERS, L. J., Pte. 26 Bn.	✠ 8/10/17	9/ 6/16 Pte. ✠
SAUNDERS, N. B. L., Pte. 12 Bn.	✠ 28/2/17	6/ 6/16 Pte. ✠
SAUNDERS, R. H., Pte. 26 Bn.	✠ 4/10/17	15/ 6/15 Pte. ✠
SAUNDERS, R. E. A., Pte. 40 Bn.	6 M.G. Bn., 42 M.G. Co. ✠ 5/10/18.	4/ 8/15 Cpl. ✠
SAUNDERS, R. J., Pte. 12 Bn.	2W.	15/ 2/15 4y 6m. Pte.
SAUNDERS, W. G., Pte. 26 Bn.	4 D.A.C.	14/ 3/18 1y 7m. Pte.
SAUNDERS, J. W., Pte. 1 G.S.R.	4 Div. D.U.S.	21/ 8/14 4y 7m. Cpl.
SAUNDERS, W. D., Pte. 12 Bn.		4/ 9/16 2y 3m. Pte.
SAUNDERS, W. A., Pte. 12 Bn.		14/12/16 Cpl. ✠
SAUNDERS, W. H., Pte. 12 Bn.	W., 52 Bn. ✠ 16/10/17.	24/ 4/17 2y 5m. Pte.
SAVAGE, R., Pte. 12 Bn.		5/ 8/15 1y 11m. Pte.
SAVILLO, J. W., Pte. 12 Bn.	W.	19/10/16 2y 11m. Pte.
SAWARD, A. G., Pte. 12 Bn.	W. 40 Bn.	19/10/16 2y 11m. Pte.
SAWARD, H. H., Pte. 12 Bn.	40 Bn.	19/10/16 2y 9m. Tpr.
SAWARD, J. H., Tpr. 3 L.H.	45 Bn.	2/ 9/15 3y 8m. Pte.
SAWARD, V. C. A., Pte. 15 Bn.	13 A.L.H.	4/ 9/15 4y 2m Tpr.
SAWFORD, J. J., Tpr. 3 L.H.	✠ 12/11/15	15/ 6/15 Pte. ✠
SAWFORD, P. C., Pte. 26 Bn.	10 A.A.S.C.	15/ 9/14 4y 8m Dvr.
SAWYER, A., Dvr. Reserve Park	✠ 27/5/15	26/ 8/14 Pte. ✠
SAYE, D., Pte. 12 Bn.	✠ 23/4/18.	8/ 1/17 Lieut. ✠
SAYER, W. S., Lieut. 12 Bn.	W. ✠ 25-28/4/15	24/ 8/14 Pte. ✠
SAYER, G. G., Pte. 12 Bn.	W. A.O.C.	24/ 8/14 4y 6m. Pte.
SAYER, H. H., Pte. 12 Bn.		

V

NAME.	REMARKS.	RANK ON DISCHARGE. ENLISTED. SERVICE.
SAYER, K. H. W., Pte. 40 Bn.		25/ 9/16 2y 8m. Pte.
SCAIFE, R., Pte. 4 M.G. Co.	W. 21 M.G. Co.	11/ 7/16
SCALES, A., Pte. 10 A.S.C.	4 Div. Train.	8/ 9/14 4y 4m. Pte.
SCALES, W. A., Pte. 40 Bn.		20/ 3/16 3y 6m, Pte
SCANLON, J., Pte. 26 Bn.		19/ 7/15 2y 10m, Pte.
SCANLON, J., Gnr. Arty.	12 F.A.B., 15 Bn.	3/ 2/16 1y 5m. Gnr.
SCANLON, M., Pte. 40 Bn.	2W.	28/ 7/16 3y 1m, Pte.
SCANLON, P., Pte. 4 M.G. Co.	12 Bn. ✠ 23/8/18.	13/ 2/17 Pte. ✠
SCARR, R. S., 2nd Lieut., 3 F.A.B.	M.C.	2/ 9/15 Capt.
SCHEER, H., Gnr. 6 F.A.B.	5 T.M. Bde. ✠ 20/7/17.	6/ 1/16 Gnr. ✠
SCHILL, A. F., Pte. 26 Bn.	12 Bn., 1 Pnrs.	10/ 8/15 2y 2m, Pte.
SCHOFIELD, A. S., Dvr. 3 F.A.B.	9 Bty.	26/ 7/15 4y 1m, SS Cpl
SCHOLES, C. E., Pte. 3 G.S.R.		21/ 8/17.
SCHOLES, H. W., Spr. Miners.	W., 3 Tnl. Co. ✠ 18/3/18.	26/ 9/15 Spr. ✠
SCHOTT, F., Pte. 3 G.S.R.		5/ 6/18.
SCHOTT, V. G., Pte. 1 G.S.R.	8 M.G. Co.	25/ 3/18 1y 8m, Pte.
SCHWARTKOPFF, E., Pte. 12 Bn.	W.	21/ 8/14 3y 5m, Pte.
SCOBLE, R. W., Pte. 12 Bn.	W. ✠ 2/9/16.	24/ 8/14 Pte. ✠
SCOLLICK, A. N., Gnr. Arty.	5 F.A.B. ✠ 20/4/17.	4/10/15 Gnr. ✠
SCOLYER, A. V., Pte. 15 Bn.	2W., 47 Bn.	31/ 8/15 1y 11m. Pte.
SCOLYER, B. L., Pte. 26 Bn.	✠ 5/8/16.	9/ 6/15 Pte. ✠
SCOLYER, F. H., Pte. 15 Bn.	W., 47 Bn., 42 Bn. ✠ 25/9/18.	31/ 8/15 Pte. ✠
SCOLYER, M. W., Pte. 40 Bn.	5W.	15/ 3/16 3y 1m, L.-Cpl.
SCOLYER, R., Pte. 26 Bn.	✠ 5/8/16.	20/ 1/15 Pte. ✠
SCOLYER, R. C., Pte. 40 Bn.	W.	15/ 3/16 3y 5m, Pte.
SCOTNEY, W. T., Pte. 12 Bn.	5 Div. Tun. Dtls., 2 Fd. Bky.	22/ 5/16 3y 6m, Pte.
SCOUGALL, C. F., Pte. 26 Bn.	12 Bn.	23/ 8/15 3y 4m, Pte.
SCOUGALL, T., Pte. 12 Bn.	52 Bn.	
SCULL, W., Pte. 40 Bn.	W. ✠ 14/7/18.	17/11/16 Pte. ✠
SCULLY, W. J., Pte. 40 Bn.	✠ 20/9/17.	26/ 9/16 Pte. ✠
SCURRAH, A. E., Pte. 1 A.C.H.	14 Fd. Amb. ✠ 21/3/18.	22/ 7/15 Bdr. ✠
SCURRAH, H. M., Gnr. Arty.		30/10/16 3y 2m, Gnr.
SCHULTZ, M. C., Pte. 40 Bn.		2/ 3/16 3y 7m, Sgt.
SCOTT, A. J., Spr. Rly. Unit.	1 Rly. Co.	13/10/17 1y 9m, Spr.
SCOTT, A., Pte. 1 A.C.H.	1 A.G.H.	15/ 9/14 4y 11m, Pte.
SCOTT, A. W., Pte. 12 Bn.	W., 52 Bn., Dental Corps.	5/ 8/15 3y 10m, S.-Sgt
SCOTT, C., Pte. 15 Bn.	W.	14/ 8/15 3y 8m, Sgt.
SCOTT, C., Dvr. 3 F.A.B.	102 How. Bty.	30/ 6/15 4y 2m, Sgt.
SCOTT, C. C., Pte. 12 Bn.	W., 8 A.D.N.S.	5/ 8/15.
SCOTT, Claude, Pte. 12 Bn.	D.C.M., 51 Bn.	30/11/14 5y, Lt.
SCOTT, C., Pte. 40 Bn.	2W.	30/ 9/16 3y 2m, Pte.
SCOTT, D. M., Dvr. 8 F.A.B.	108 How. Bty.	28/12/15 3y 10m, Dvr.
SCOTT, D., Pte. 15 Bn.	W. ✠ 11/4/17.	18/ 8/15 Pte. ✠
SCOTT, E. M., Pte. 26 Bn.	7 M.G. Co.	Pte.
SCOTT, E. R., Gnr. 2 F.A.B.	102 How. Bty.	27/11/16 3y, Gnr.
SCOTT, G., Pte. 12 Bn.	W.	31/ 5/16 1y 7m, Pte.
SCOTT—HOLLAND, E. S., Sgt. 40 Bn.		5/ 1/16.
SCOTT, H. T., Pte. 12 Bn.	✠ 25-28/4/15.	27/ 8/14 Pte. ✠
SCOTT, H. R., Pte. 12 Bn.	W.	26/11/14 1y 4m, Pte.
SCOTT, I. H., Tpr. 3 L.H.		30/ 8/17 2y, Tpr.
SCOTT, J., Pte. 40 Bn.		23/ 3/16 3y 5m, Dvr.
SCOTT, J. A., Pte. 40 Bn.		29/ 2/16 3y 6m, L.-Cpl.
SCOTT, J. H., Pte. 12 Bn.	40 Bn.	4/ 4/16 2y, Pte.
SCOTT, J. J., Dvr. 26 Bn.		18/ 2/15 4y 6m, Dvr.
SCOTT, J. K., Pte. 12 Bn.	2W.	8/ 1/15 3y 11m, Sgt.
SCOTT, J., Pte. 26 Bn.	3W.	3/ 1/15 4y 5m, Pte.
SCOTT, L. G., Pte. 12 Bn.	W. ✠ 6-10/4/17.	20/ 8/14 Sgt. ✠
SCOTT, L. T., Dvr. 6 A.F.A. Bde.		5/ 8/15 4y 5m, Lt.
SCOTT, N. R., Sgt. 12 Bn.	✠ 3-4/9/16.	4/ 6/15 Sgt. ✠
SCOTT, N. T., Pte. 1 A.C.H.		18/ 9/14 5y 1m, Pte.
SCOTT, P. E., Pte. 12 Bn.	2W.	4/ 7/16 3y 2m, Pte.
SCOTT, P. H., Pte. 1 A.G.H.	15 Fd. Amb.	3/ 6/15 4y 3m, Pte.
SCOTT, R. McG., Cpl. 12 Bn.		25/ 1/15 1y 10m, Cpl.
SCOTT, R. A., Pte. 26 Bn.	47 Bn. ✠ 30/1/17.	10/ 8/15 Pte. ✠
SCOTT, R., Pte. 15 Bn.	✠ 12/10/16.	22/ 6/15 Pte. ✠
SCOTT, S., Spr. 8 Fd. Co.	16 Fd. Co., 8 Fd. Co.	24/ 8/16.
SCOTT, V. G., Gnr. Arty.	3 Army Bde.	9/ 3/17 2y 7m, Gnr.
SCOTT, W. G., Pte. 40 Bn.		10/10/16 2y 11m, Pte.
SCOTT, W. H., Pte. 26 Bn.		17/ 3/15 4y 5m, Pte
SCOTT, W. P., Pte. Remounts.	Re-enlisted for munitions.	25/10/15 8m, Pte.
SCOTT, W. R., Pte. 26 Bn.	2W. ✠ 2/9/18.	4/ 6/15 Pte. ✠
SEABOURNE, W., Dvr. 14 Fd. Co.	W.	11/ 1/16 3y 3m, Dvr.
SEABROOK, A. L., Pte. 12 Bn.	1 Div. San. Sec.	15/ 7/16.
SEABROOK, C., Pte. 7 Fd. Amb.	3 A.G.H.	6/ 3/15 4y 5m, Pte.
SEABROOK, C. N., Gnr. 3 F.A.B.	24 How. Bty. ✠ 13/9/17.	9/ 6/15 Gnr. ✠
SEABROOK, E. C., Pte. 12 Bn.	52 Bn. ✠ 4/9/16.	25/ 5/15 Pte. ✠
SEABROOK, L., Pte. 3 Fd. Amb.	1 Pnrs.	21/12/14 3y 10m., Pte.
SEABROOK, R. H., Spr. 6 Fd. Co.		23/ 8/15 2y 8m, Spr.
SEABROOK, W. W., L.-Cpl. 3 Fd. Co.	W.	20/ 8/14 4y 5m, L.-Cpl.

TASMANIA'S MUSTER ROLL. 339

NAME.	REMARKS.	RANK ON DISCHARGE. ENLISTED. SERVICE.
SEAGER, A. E., Sgt. 40 Bn.	W., 52 Bn., 49 Bn.	14/ 3/16 3y 5m, Sgt.
SEARLE, E. G., Pte. 15 Bn.	4W., M.M.	22/ 9/14 4y 5m, C.S.M.
SEARLE, F. V., Pte. 12 Bn.	✠ 13/8/15.	25/ 8/14 Pte. ✠
SEARLE, R. V., Pte. 12 Bn.	52 Bn. ✠ 23/8/17.	25/ 8/14 Pte. ✠
SEARLE, W N., Cpl. 3 Miners		Sgt.
SEARSON, H. G., Pte. 26 Bn.		4/ 5/15 1y 1m, Pte.
SEARSON, J. L., Spr. Tnlrs.		6/ 6/17 1y 5m, Spr.
SEATON, C. C., Pte. 12 Bn.		8/ 1/15 3y 5m, Pte.
SEATON, J. W., Spr. Sig. Unit.	1 Sig. Engrs.	15/ 5/17 2y 3m, Spr.
SEEN, C. V. H. G., Spr. Miners.	W., 2 A.T.C.	8/11/15 3y 11m, Spr.
SEIDEL, B. F., Gnr. Arty.	14 F.A.B. ✠ 26/11/18.	1/11/16 Gnr. ✠
SELBY, J. R., Gnr. 6 F.A.B.	✠ 12/6/17.	13/10/15 Gnr. ✠
SELBY, N., Pte. 12 Bn.	W., 52 Bn.	2/ 9/15 2y 4m, Pte.
SELBY, F., Pte. 12 Bn.	✠ 11/8/18.	15/ 1/18 Pte. ✠
SELWYN, T., Sgt. 12 Bn.	W., 40 Bn.	24/ 8/14 4y 1m, Lt.
SELF, F., Pte. 12 Bn.	✠ 11/8/18.	15/ 1/18 Pte. ✠
SELF, H. J., Pte. 12 Bn.		Pte.
SELF, R. J., Pte. 26 Bn.	52 Bn., 51 Bn.	26/ 4/15 4y 4m, Pte.
SELLERS, F. A., Pte. 12 Bn.	52 Bn. ✠ 4/9/16.	8/ 1/16 Pte. ✠
SELLERS, G. I., Pte. A.A.M.C.		20/ 2/17 2y 9m, Pte.
SELLERS, H. T., Pte.: 40 Bn.	Re-enlisted 3 L.H. 21/4/17.	24/ 5/16 11m, Tpr.
SEMPLE, E. A., Pte. 12 Bn.	3W.	1/12/14 3y 4m, Pte.
SENIOR, F. W. B., Pte. 15 Bn.	P.O.W.	26/ 8/15 3y 11m, Pte.
SENIOR, J., Dvr. 40 Bn.		4/ 4/16 3y 4m, Dvr.
SENIOR, R. A. H. P., Pte. 4 A.S.C		25/ 2/16.
SEWARD, F., Pte. 12 Bn.	40 Bn.	11/ 6/17 1y 9m, Pte.
SEWELL, R. A., Gnr. 21 F.A.B.	10 F.A.B. ✠ 22/10/17.	28/10/16 Gnr. ✠
SEYMOUR, A. E., Pte. 12 Bn.		14/ 6/15 4y 4m, Pte.
SEYMOUR, A. J. J., Tpr. 3 L.H.		23/ 8/15 1y 9m, Tpr.
SEYMOUR, A. G., Pte. 12 Bn.	W.	21/ 2/15 3y 1m, Pte.
SEYMOUR, A., Dvr. 4 A.S.C.		14/ 9/14 4y 6m, Dvr.
SEYMOUR, C. H., Pte. 12 Bn.	3 L.T.M. Bty. ✠ 23/7/18.	9/ 2/15 Pte. ✠
SEYMOUR, C. E. Dvr. 3 F.A.B.	1 D.A.C.	16/ 8/15 4y, Dvr.
SEYMOUR, H. A., Cpl. 3 L.H.	✠ 12/8/15.	21/ 8/14 Cpl. ✠
SEYMOUR, H. J., Pte. 26 Bn.		19/ 4/15 1y 6m, Pte.
SEYMOUR, L. P., Pte. 12 Bn.		22/ 8/16 3y 2m, L.-Cpl.
SEYMOUR, R. J., Pte. 26 Bn.	2W., 12 Bn.	30/ 8/15 3y 8m, Pte.
SEYMOUR, T., Pte. 26 Bn.	12 Bn. ✠ 26/8/18.	29/ 8/15 Pte. ✠
SEYMOUR, T., Dvr. Res. Park.	W., 1 A.S.C.	8/ 9/14 3y 10m, Dvr.
SHACKCLOTH, F. H., Pte. 15 Bn.		3/10/14 4y 4m, L.-Cpl.
SHADBOLT, L. G., Spr. 8 Fd. Co.	12 Fd. Co., 7 Fd. Co.	4/11/15 3y 10m, Spr.
SHADWICK, E., Pte. 40 Bn.	✠ 1/2/17.	2/10/16 Pte. ✠
SHADWICK, F., Pte. 40 Bn.		10/ 3/16 3y 5m, Pte.
SHADWICK, O. S., Dvr. 12 Bn.		29/ 8/14.
SHADWICK, T. G., Pte. 3 L.H.	Aus. Cps. Cyc. Bn.	21/ 7/15 4y 1m, Pte.
SHALLESS, C. W., Pte. 40 Bn.	3W., M.M.	10/ 3/16 1y 1m, Cpl.
SHALLES, P. C., Gnr. 3 F.A.B.	2W., 10 F.A.B.	27/ 8/14 3y 11m, Sgt.
SHANNON, J. A., Tpr. 1 Rmts.		
SHARLAND, C. F., 2nd Lieut. 40 Bn.	✠ 12/10/17.	6/12/15 Lieut. ✠
SHARLAND, J. E. F., Gnr. Arty.	105 How Bty.	3/ 4/16 3y 3m, Gnr.
SHARMAN, C. A. V., Pte. 26 Bn.	2W., 7 M.G. Co., A.A.M.C.	11/ 3/15 3y 5m, Pte.
SHARMAN, N. J. R., Pte. 15 Bn.	✠ 8/8/15.	19/ 9/14 Pte. ✠
SHARMAN, S., Pte. 12 Bn.	W.	12/ 6/16 2y 9m, Pte.
SHARP, H., Tpr. 3 L.H.		12/10/17 2y, Tpr.
SHAW, A., Pte. 26 Bn.	40 Bn. ✠ 13/5/17.	23/ 2/15 Pte. ✠
SHAW, A. N., Pte. 12 Bn.	W.	29/ 8/14 2y 5m, Pte.
SHAW, B. J., Sgt. 15 Bn.	M.M. ✠ 8/8/18.	8/ 1/15 Lt. ✠
SHAW, B. V., Pte. 12 Bn.	W., 52 Bn.	29/ 7/15 2y 7m, Pte.
SHAW, C. J., Tpr. 3 L.H.		18/ 8/15 8m, Tpr.
SHAW, H., Pte. 15 Bn.	4 Div. L.T.M. Bty., 15 Bn.	6/10/14 3y 3m, Dvr.
SHAW, H., Pte. 12 Bn.		16/ 7/15.
SHAW, H. W., Tpr. 3 L.H.	4 DA.C., 110 How. Bty.	Gnr.
SHAW, J. A., Pte. 26 Bn.	✠ 5/8/16.	19/ 6/15 Pte. ✠
SHAW, J., Pte. 15 Bn.	W. ✠ 7/8/15.	28/ 9/14 Pte. ✠
SHAW, L. L., Pte. 40 Bn.		16/ 6/16 3y 6m, Pte.
SHAW, R., Spr. 3 Cyclists.	A.E.M.M.T.B. Co.	17/ 3/16 3y 6m, Spr.
SHAW, T., Spr. Miners.		13/ 4/16.
SHAW, W., Cpl. 12 Bn.		20/ 8/14 2y 2m, Cpl.
SHAW, W., Tpr. 3 L.H.		6/12/17.
SHAW, W. A., Tpr. 26 Bn.	3 Camel Btn., 15 A.L.H.	23/ 6/15 4y 5m, Tpr.
SHARP, A. V., Pte. 40 Bn.	W.	29/ 7/16 1y 5m, Pte.
SHARP, A. G., Wireless.		
SHARP, C. A., Gnr. Arty.	23 How. Bty.	5/ 1/16 2y 5m, Gnr.
SHARPE, C. F., Dvr. 3 Fd. Art.	2 F.A.B. ✠ 22/8/17	27/ 8/11 Cpl. ✠
SHARP, C. S., Pte. 40 Bn		3/ 1/17 3y. W.O.
SHARP, C. W., Gnr. 6 Fd. Art.		10/ 9/15
SHARP, D. T., Tpr. 3 L.H.		14/ 9/15
SHARP, F. H., Pte. 40 Bn.	W. ✠ 13/10/17	18/ 3/16 Cpl. ✠
SHARP, F. H., Pte. 12 Bn.		20/ 8/14 4y 5m, Cpl.
SHARP, H. G., Gnr. Arty.	2W., 14 F.A.B.	29/ 2/16 3y 8m, Gnr.
SHARP, J., Pte. 1 A.G.H.	3 Fd. Amb.	4/ 6/15 4y 2m, Pte.
SHARP, R. M., Pte. Wireless		26/ 2/18 10m, Pte.

TASMANIA'S WAR RECORD, 1914-1918.

NAME.	REMARKS.	RANK ON DISCHARGE. ENLISTED. SERVICE.
SHARP, R. R., Pte. 1 A.G.H.	3 Fd. Amb. ✹ 7/5/17	11/ 6/15 Pte. ✹
SHARP, R. H., Pte. 15 Bn.	W.	26/ 9/14 3y 10m, Pte.
SHARP, S. H., Pte. 1 A.C.H.	3 Fd. Amb.	14/ 1/15 3y 7m, Pte.
SHARP, S. H., Pte. Remounts.		9/ 9/15 1y 3m, Tpr.
SHARP, W. C., Spr. 3 Fd. Co.		22/ 8/14 4y 6m, Spr.
SHARP, W. J., Pte. 26 Bn.	15 Bn.	27/ 4/15 4y 8m, Pte.
SHEA, A. E., Pte. 40 Bn.	W.	27/ 3/17 2y 8m, Pte.
SHEA, G., Pte. 40 Bn.	W.	20/ 6/16 3y 3m, Pte.
SHEA, H., Pte. 26 Bn.	W. ✹ 26/3/17	10/ 5/15 Pte. ✹
SHEA, J. A., Pte. 12 Bn.	52 Bn. ✹ 4/9/16.	10/ 8/15 Pte. ✹
SHEA, L. G., Pte. 26 Bn.	W., 12 Bn., 4 A.A.S.C., 1 Div. Train	3/ 5/15 4y 5m, Pte.
SHEA, L. J., Gnr. 3 Fd. Art.		27/ 8/14
SHEA, T., Gnr. 36 H.A.G.		22/10/17
SHEA, V. R., Pte. 15 Bn	47 Bn., 15 Bn.	16/ 8/15 4y, Pte.
SHEA, W., Pte. 3 G.S.R.		20/ 5/18
SHEARGOLD, J. F., Pte. 15 Bn.	W., 7 Fd. Amb., 6 Fd. Amb.	24/ 9/14 3y 10m, Pte.
SHEARING, A., Spr. Tunlers	W., 2 A.T. Co.	24/10/16 3y 1m.
SHEARING, E. J., Pte. 12 Bn.	2W., 52 Bn., 15 Bn.	27/ 7/15, 4y 1m, Pte.
SHEARING, E. A., Pte. 3 L.H.	1 L.H.M.G. Co.	17/ 8/14 4y 6m, Pte.
SHEARING, M., Pte. 40 Bn.	W. ✹ 26/11/17	13/ 3/16 Cpl. ✹
SHEARING, H. H., Pte. 15 Bn.	✹ 9/5/15	24/ 9/14 Pte. ✹
SHEARING, J., Pte. 40 Bn.	69 Bn., 40 Bn.	22/ 3/15 3y 6m, Pte.
SHEARING, J. L., Spr. Miners.	W., M.M., 3 Tun. Co.	20/11/15 3y 11m, Spr.
SHEARING, T. E., Pte. 40 Bn.	W., A.A.M.C. ✹ 26/11/19.	30/3/16 Pte. ✹
SHEDDON, C. H., Chap., 4th class		17/ 5/15
SHEEAN, X., Dvr. 3 Fd. Co.		21/ 8/14
SHEEDY, D., Pte. 40 Bn.		26/ 8/16 2y 9m, Pte.
SHEEDY, W. W., Pte. 12 Bn.	W., M.M. ✹ 18/5/18	22/ 8/14 C.S.M. ✹
SHEEN, E. J., Gnr. Arty.	112 How. Bty.	11/ 4/17 2y 6m, Gnr.
SHEEN, E. W., Pte. 12 Bn.	✹ 13/11/16	6/12/15 Pte. ✹
SHEEN, P. C., Pte. 26 Bn.	2W.	28/ 9/15 1y 6m, Pte.
SHEEN, W. W., Pte. 26 Bn.	✹ 5/8/16	14/ 9/15 Pte. ✹
SHEGOG, J. W., Bdr. 3 F.A.B.	4 Div. Art.	27/ 8/14 4y 5m, Sgt.
SHEGOG, S. G., Pte. 12 Bn.	W.	26/10/15 3y 11m, Pte.
SHEGOG, S. H., Pte. 26 Bn.	12 Bn. ✹ 24/7/16	10/ 8/15 Pte. ✹
SHELLEY, E. M., Pte. 4 M.G. Co.		3/10/16 6m. Pte.
SHELTON, E., Pte. 26 Bn.	M.M.	16/ 5/15 4y 3m, Pte.
SHELTON, H. E., Pte. 12 Bn.	2W.	15/ 9/15 2y 6m, Pte.
SHELTON, L. C., Pte. 12 Bn.	W. ✹ 19-20/9/17	15/ 9/15 Pte. ✹
SHELTON, L. T., Pte. 26 Bn.	W., 12 Bn.	11/ 8/15 4y, Pte.
SHELTON, R. J., Pte. 26 Bn.	2W., 12 Bn. ✹ 23/9/18	11/ 8/15 Pte. ✹
SHELTON, W., Pte. 12 Bn.	W., 52 Bn., 40 Bn.	15/ 9/15 3y 11m, Cpl.
SHELTON, H. W., Pte. 15 Bn.	✹ 15/9/15	21/ 9/14 Pte. ✹
SHELVERTON, S., Pte. 12 Bn.	2W., M.M.	19/ 9/14 4y 5m, L.-Cpl
SHENNAN, C., Pte. 12 Bn.		16/ 1/15
SHENNAN, E. F., Pte. 12 Bn.	2W., 52 Bn.	25/ 3/15 2y 7m, L.-Cpl
SHEPHERD, A. E., Mun. Worker	✹ 6/12/18	M.W. ✹
SHEPHERD, A. C., Gnr. 25 F.A.B.	14 F.A.B. ✹ 24/10/17	14/10/16 Gnr. ✹
SHEPHERD, C. G., Dvr. 6 F.A.B.	17 Bty.	18/ 8/15 2y 10m, Sgt.
SHEPHERD, C. M., Spr 12 Bn	A Corps Sig. Co.	4/ 4/16 3y 5m, Spr.
SHEPHERD, E. V., Pte. 40 Bn.	✹ 2/1/17	3/ 4/16 Pte. ✹
SHEPHERD, F. L., Pte. 12 Bn.	51 Bn. ✹ 29/8/18	6/ 8/15 Pte. ✹
SHEPHERD, F. C., Pte. 40 Bn.	W.	5/ 4/16 2y 10m, L-Cpl
SHEPHARD, J. D., Pte. 40 Bn.	12 Bn. ✹ 15/4/17	1/ 3/16 Pte. ✹
SHEPHERD, J. S. R., Tpr. 3 L.H.		23/ 8/14 4y 5m, Tpr.
SHEPHERD, L N., Cpl. 12 Bn	W., 52 Bn. ✹ 8/8/16.	23/10/15 Cpl. ✹
SHEPHEARD, M., Pte. 12 Bn.	2W.	11/12/14 4y 6m, Cpl.
SHEPHEARD, M. E., Pte. 40 Bn.	✹ 3/10/17	17/ 5/16 Pte. ✹
SHEPHERD, W. J., Dvr. Fd Art.		26/ 8/15 4y, Dvr.
SHEPPARD, A., Bdr. 1 Siege Bty.	W.	7/ 6/15 4y 5m, Bdr.
SHEPPARD, F., Pte. 40 Bn.	51 Bn. ✹ 22/2/19	1/ 3/16 Pte. ✹
SHEPPERD, A. E., Pte. 3 G.S.R.	12 Bn. ✹ 9/1/19.	12/ 6/18 Pte. ✹
SHEPPERD, H. E., Dvr. 40 Bn.		21/ 2/16 3y 7m, Dvr.
SHEPPARD, T., Pte. 12 Bn.		12/ 6/16 3y 3m, Pte.
SHERIDAN, S., Pte. 15 Bn.	46 Bn.	17/ 8/14 3y 1m, Pte.
SHERIDAN, S., Sgt. 15 Bn.		7/ 9/14 3m, Sgt.
SHERLOCK, C. B., L.-Cpl. 1 A.C.H.	✹ 12/10/15	11/ 9/14 L.-Cpl. ✹
SHERWIN, R., Lieut. 12 Bn.	M.C. ✹ 8/4/17.	24/ 6/15 Lieut. ✹
SHERRAR, E. C., Pte. 1 A.C.H.		30/11/14
SHERRAR, R. O., Pte 1 A.C.H.		19/11/14
SHERRIN, A., Pte. 15 Bn	W., 4 Pnrs.	21/ 3/15 4y 5m, Pte.
SHERRIN, C. R., L.-Cpl. 40 Bn.	W.	16/ 3/16 1y 9m, L.-Sgt
SHERRIN, E. C., Pte. 40 Bn	✹ 6/5/17	15/ 3/16 L.-Cpl. ✹
SHERRIN, G., Pte. 40 Bn.	2W.	10/ 3/16 3y 5m, Pte.
SHERRIN, H. T., Pte. 40 Bn.		16/10/16 3y 1m, Pte.
SHERRIN, M., Gnr. 15 Bn.	24 F.A.B., 4 D.A.C.	18/ 9/14 4y 4m, Gnr
SHIELDS, A., L.-Cpl. 15 Bn.	47 Bn. ✹ 7/6/17	5/ 6/15 Sgt. ✹
SHIELDS, A. J., Pte. 15 Bn.	12 Bn. ✹ 30/7/16	2/ 7/15 Pte. ✹
SHIELDS, C., 15 Bn.		8/ 6/15
SHIELDS, G. A., Gnr. Camel Cps.		20/ 2/15 4y 9m, Gnr.
SHIELDS, L. J. P., Pte. 12 Bn.	✹ 23—26/7/16	31/ 5/15 Pte. ✹
SHIELDS, A. S., Pte. 26 Bn.		22/ 4/15
SHIELDS, T. J., Pte. 12 Bn.		8/12/14 1y 6m, Pte.
SHIMMINS, A. G., Pte. A.M.C.	15 Fd. Amb.	10/10/16 2y 11m, Pte.

TASMANIA'S MUSTER ROLL. 341

NAME.	REMARKS.	RANK ON DISCHARGE. ENLISTED. SERVICE.
SHIPLEY, J. C., Pte. 12 Bn.	2W., 40 Bn.	6/ 4/16 2y, Pte.
SHIPP, D., Pte. 15 Bn.		14/ 9/15 3y 11m, Pte.
SHIPP, J., Spr., 6 Fd. Co.	2W., 57 Bn.	20/ 8/15 3y 9m, Cpl.
SHIPP, L. R., Dvr. Arty.	13 F.A.B., 49 Bn.	10/ 2/16 3y 8m, Dvr.
SHIPP, S. R., Pte. 12 Bn.		18/10/16 2y 6m, Pte.
SHIPP, V. G., Pte. 2 G.S.R.		6/ 3/18
SHIPTON, A W., Pte. 12 Bn	W., 52 Bn. ✢ 11/6/17	25/ 1/16 Cpl. ✢
SHIREFF, J. W., Dvr. D.A.C.		20/ 7/15
SHIRES, A. A., Pte. 40 Bn.	✢ 1/9/18	14/10/16 Pte. ✢
SHIRES, J. C., Spr. 8 Fd. Co.		26/ 1/16
SHIRES, T. C., Pte. 40 Bn.	W.	18/ 5/16 1y 10m, Pte.
SHIRLEY, C., Pte 12 Bn.	3W., 69 Bn., 12 Bn.	2/ 8/15 3y 9m, Cpl.
SHONE, C. E., Tpr. L.H.		1/ 8/18 1y, Tpr.
SHOOBRIDGE, A. W., Pte. 12 Bn.	✢ 1/5/18	21/11/16 Pte. ✢
SHOOBRIDGE, E. J. R., Pte. 26 Bn.	12 Bn.	3/ 8/15 2y 5m, Pte.
SHOOBRIDGE, F. S. R., Pte. 3 Fd. Amb.	2W.	3/ 8/15 3y 9m, Pte.
SHOOBRIDGE, M. R., Spr. Engrs.		30/ 4/17
SHOOBRIDGE, M. G., Pte. A.A.M.C.	1 A.G.H.	10/10/16 2y 9m, Pte.
SHOOBRIDGE, R. O., Pte. 40 Bn.	W.	18/ 5/16 2y, Cpl.
SHOOTS, War Worker		
SHORE, J. F., Pte. 12 Bn.		31/ 8/14 5y 1m, Sgt.
SHORT, E., Pte. 12 Bn.	W., 52 Bn. ✢ 18/10/16.	13/ 7/15 Pte. ✢
SHREEVE, E., Pte. 4 M.G. Co.	23 M.G. Co., 3 M.G. Co.	8/ 9/16 3y, Pte.
SHREEVE, H., Pte. 12 Bn.	W., M.M.	30/ 8/16 2y 8m, Pte.
SHREEVE, H. G., Pte. 12 Bn.	52 Bn., 3 M.G. Bn.	12/ 1/16 3y 5m, Pte.
SHREEVES, W. J., Pte. 12 Bn.	W. ✢ 3/6/17	6/ 7/16 Pte. ✢
SIBLEY, F. H., Pte., 12 Bn.	W.	2/ 1/15 4y. 3m. L.-Cpl.
SIBLEY, H. H., Gnr., 3 F.A.B.		29/ 8/15 4y. Gnr.
SIBLEY, W. C., Tpr., 3 L.H.	✢ 22/12/18.	30/ 8/17 Tpr. ✢
SICE, A. B., Pte., 26 Bn.	W., 12 Bn.	16/ 8/15 3y. 9m. Sgt.
SICE, T. A., Pte., 26 Bn.	W., 12 Bn.	16/ 8/15 1y. 10m. Pte.
SIDWELL, K., Pte., 26 Bn.	A.A. Post. Cps.	24/ 6/15 4y. 2m. L.-Cpl.
SIGGINS, W. C., Pte., 12 Bn.	W.	2/ 5/16 1y. 7m. Pte.
SILVA, G. H., Pte., 12 Bn.	✢ 23/4/18.	17/10/16 Pte. ✢
SIMMONDS, F. E., Pte., 40 Bn.		28/ 7/16 1y. 8m. Pte.
SIMMONDS, A. E. Spr., & Miner	3 Tunnl. Co	15/ 9/15 3y. 9m. Spr.
SIMMONDS, N., Gnr., 10 F.A.B.		10/ 5/16 2y. 1m. Gnr.
SIMMONDS, P., Pte., 12 Bn.		15/ 2/15 1y. 6m. Pte.
SIMMONDS, W. J., Pte., 40 Bn.	69 Bn.	14/ 2/16 2y. Pte.
SIMMONDS, J. R. T., Pte., 12 B		18/12/14 2y. 6m. Pte.
SIMMONS, J. G., 2nd Lieut. 12 Bn.	W. ✢ 19/9/18.	18/ 5/16 Lieut. ✢
SIMMONS, G A., Pte., 4 M.G. Co	5 M.G. Co., 1 M.G. Co.	8/ 8/16 2y. 11m. Pte.
SIMMONS, G. L., Pte., 26 Bn.	W.	19/ 5/15 3y. 11m. Pte.
SIMMONS, H. J., Pte., 12 Bn.		15/ 7/15 8m. Pte.
SIMMONS, N. W., 2 A.M., A.F.		20/11/17
SIMON, H. F., Spr., 3 Miners,	3 Tunnl. Co.	25/ 9/15 2y. 7m. Sgt.
SIMPKINS, G. D., L.-Cpl., 40		26/ 9/16
SIMPSON, D. E., Spr., Tunnls.	2 Tunnl. Co.	6/ 4/17
SIMPSON, G., Gnr., 6 F.A.B.,	13 F.A.B.	24/11/15 1y. 9m. Gnr.
SIMPSON, L. S., Pte. 12 Bn.		23/11/17 1y. 8m. Pte.
SIMPSON, L. S., Pte., 12 Bn.		30/12/14
SIMPSON, P. C., Spr., Miners,	Tunnlrs.	12/11/15 2y. 9m. Pte.
SIMPSON, S., Spr., 3 Miners.		24/ 2/16
SIMPSON, S. J., Pte., 26 Bn.	W.	15/ 6/15 4y. 2m. Pte.
SIMPSON, T. W., Gnr., 13 F.A.	W.	3/2/16 2y. 5m. Gnr.
SIMS, A. R., Pte., 40 Bn.		17/ 4/16 3y. 5m. Cpl.
SIMS, C. C., Pte., 4 M.G. Co.	12 Bn., ✢ 18/9/18.	24/ 2/17 Pte. ✢
SIMS, C. B., Gnr., Arty.	11 F.A.B.	17/ 5/17 2y. 5m. Dvr.
SIMS, H. J., Pte., 12 Bn.	✢ 3/7/16.	10/ 8/15 Pte. ✢
SIMS, H. T., Pte., 12 Bn.	W.	6/10/15 3y. 7m. Pte.
SINCLAIR, E. H., Gnr., 3 F.A	W.	1/ 8/15 4y. 2m. Sgt.
SINCLAIR, G., Cpl., 6 F.A.B.	2W., 8 F.A.B	6/ 1/16 3y. 7m. Sgt.
SINCLAIR, L., Pte., 1 A.G.H.		8/ 6/15
SINCLAIR, R. R., Pte., 12 Bn.	✢ 14/10/16.	11/ 1/16 Pte. ✢
SINCLAIR, S. C., Pte., 1 A.G.H		14/ 6/15
SING, G., Pte., 15 Bn.		23/ 9/14 9m. Pte.
SING, G. B., Pte., 12 Bn.	52 Bn., ✢ 7/9/16.	8/ 7/15 Pte. ✢
SING, N., Pte., 26 Bn.	W. ✢ 3/10/18.	17/ 6/15 Pte. ✢
SINGLETON, A. W., Pte., 12 Bn.		18/ 8/14 3y. 4m. Pte.
SINGLETON, E. J., Dvr., 3 F.C.	W., A.F.C. Details.	1/11/14 5y. 1st A.M.
SINGLETON, R. J., Pte., 26 Bn	12 Bn., 1 Dvl. M.T. Co.	13/ 5/15
SINGLINE, G. T., Pte., 40 Bn.	2W., 2 A.M.G. Bn.	12/ 4/16 3y. 5m. Pte.
SINGLINE, K. K., Pte., 40 Bn.		28/ 2/16 3y. 5m. Pte.
SINGLINE, L., Pte., 40 Bn.	2W.	5/11/16 2y. 4m. Pte.
SINGLINE, W., Pte., 12 Bn.		29/11/17 2y. Pte.
SINNITT, L. G., Pte., 12 Bn.		28/ 9/16 3y. 4m. Pte.
SINNATT, H. C., Pte., 12 Bn.	W., 52 Bn., ✢ 11/6/17.	23/10/14 Pte. ✢
SINNOTT, G., Pte., 26 Bn.	W.	19/ 3/15 3y. 1m. Pte.
SIZER, V., Pte., 12 Bn.	✢ 23/4/18.	9/ 7/17 Pte., ✢
SKEGGS, A. E., Pte., 12 Bn	W., 52 Bn.	8/ 1/16 2y. 7m. Pte.
SKEGGS, H. G., Pte., 12 Bn.	W., 52 Bn.	26/ 1/16 1y. 9m. Pte.
SKEGGS, W. O., Pte., 40 Bn.		30/ 3/16.
SKEMP, L. C., Pte., 12 Bn.		26/10/15 11m. Pte.
SKEMP, L. C., Gnr., Arty.	W.	20/ 2/17 2y. 1m. Gnr.
SKIDMORE, W. J., Pte., 26 Bn.		16/ 2/15

NAME.	REMARKS.	RANK ON DISCHARGE. ENLISTED, SERVICE.
SKINNER, A. A., Pte., 12 Bn.		29/ 8/14 Sgt.
SKINNER, C. P., S.-Sgt., 12 Bn.	52 Bn., A.O.C.	26/10/14 4y. 4m. S.-Sgt.
SKIPWORTH, J., Pte., 12 Bn.		28/ 4/16 3y. 5m. L.-Cpl.
SKJOTTRUP, A. W., Pte., 40 Bn.	W.	2/ 4/17 2y. 2m. Pte.
SLADE, A., Spr., 8 Fd. Engrs.		11/ 1/16 2y. 4m. Spr.
SLADE, C., Pte., 12 Bn.	✠ 25/7/18.	28/10/16 Pte. ✠
SLADE, C., Pte., 12 Bn.	W., ✠ 6/10/17.	8/ 5/16 Pte. ✠
SLADE, E. G., Pte., 3 G.S.R.	12 Bn.	15/ 7/18 1y. Pte.
SLADE, G. A., Pte., 12 Bn.	24 How. Bde., 4 D.A.C.	26/ 7/15 4y. 1m. Dvr.
SLADE, L. R., Pte., 40 Bn.	✠ 26/5/18.	30/ 8/17 Pte. ✠
SLADE, R. J., Pte., 40 Bn.		9/ 2/16 3y. 4m. Pte.
SLATER, A. E., Pte., Wireless Cp		17/12/17
SLATER, H. E., Pte., 2 G.S.R.	16 A.D.U.S.	4/ 4/18 1y. 6m. Pte.
SLATER, H. C., Pte., 40 Bn.	W., 12 Bn.	2/ 2/16 3y. 8m. Dvr.
SLATER, H. A., Pte., 26 Bn.	12 Bn., ✠ 9/6/17.	4/ 8/15 Pte. ✠
SLATER, W. G., Gnr., 6 F.A.B.	W., 23 How. Bde.	13/10/15 2y. 7m. Dvr.
SLATTER, R. A., Pte., 15 Bn.	2W.	13/10/15 3y. 7m. L.-Cpl.
SLINGSBY, T. W., Gnr., 25 F.A.B.	2 D.A.C., 4 F.A.B.	29/ 9/16 3y. Dvr.
SLOANE, A. G., Pte., 26 Bn.	12 Bn., ✠ 25/7/16.	3/ 9/15 Pte. ✠
SLOANE, W. H., Pte., 12 Bn.	✠ 10/6/15.	19/ 8/14 Pte. ✠
SLY, R. E., 2 A.M., 4 Sqd., A.F.C		3/ 5/16 3y. 3m. 2 A.M.
SMALLBON, J., Pte., 12 Bn.	W., 40 Bn.	25/10/16 2y. 11m. Pte.
SMART, A. G., Pte., 12 Bn.	2W., 52 Bn.	28/ 7/15 3y. Pte.
SMART, B. F., Pte., 12 Bn.	2W., 40 Bn., ✠ 30/4/18.	4/ 4/16 L.-Sgt. ✠
SMART, F. A., Pte., 40 Bn.	W.	17/10/16 2y. 5m. Pte.
SMART, L. E., Pte., 26 Bn.	W., ✠ 14/11/16.	1/10/15 Pte. ✠
SMART, L. W., Pte., 40 Bn.	2W.	2/ 3/16 3y. Pte.
SMART, W. H., Pte., 12 Bn.		4/ 4/16 5y. Pte
SMEDLEY, H. R., Pte., 26 Bn.	✠ 14/11/16.	16/ 7/15 Pte. ✠
SMEDLEY, J. R., Tpr., 3 L.H.	4 L.H. Fd. Amb.	8/12/14 4y. 6m. Dvr.
SMELLIE, W., Capt. A.M.C.		11/ 9/16 1y 1m. Capt.
SMITHERN, V. A., Pte., 12 Bn.	M.M., 4 M.G. Bn.	8/11/15 3y. 9m. Dvr.
SMITHURST, F. G., Pte., 12 Bn.	W., 52 Bn., 51 Bn.	28/10/15 3y. 11m. Pte.
SMITHURST, J. W., Pte., 12 Bn.	W.	2/12/15 2y. 6m. Pte.
SMYTHE, A. E. E., Pte., 40 Bn.		6/ 3/16 11m. Pte.
SMYTHE, A. F., Gnr., 6 F.A.B.	K. Ammn. Park.	5/ 8/15 3y. 3m. Gnr.
SMYTHE, J. B., Pte., T.M. Bty.	24 Bn.	30/ 8/16
SMYTH, L. T., Pte., 7 Fd. Amb.		16/ 3/15 1y. 4m. Pte.
SMYTH, P. N., Pte., 40 Bn.	12 Bn.	4/ 3/16 3y. 5m. Pte.
SMYTH, R., Pte., 15 Bn.		15/ 1/15 6m. Pte.
SMYTHE, W., Gnr., 15 F.A.B.	13 F.A.B.	3/10/16 3y. 1m Gnr.
SMITH-HOSIER, Capt. A.M.C.		Capt.
SMITH, E. H., Capt. 12 Bn.	C.B., 11 Bn.	24/ 8/14 4y, Lt.-Col.
SMITH, R. H., Lieut. 40 Bn.	W.	1/ 5/16 3y 1m. Lieut.
SMITH, R. E., Capt. 26 Bn.	12 Bn.	1/ 5/15 2y 4m. Capt
SMITH, V. C., Lieut. 40 Bn.		1/ 5/16
SMITH, A., Pte., 26 Bn.	7 M.G. Co., ✠ 20/9/17.	17/ 6/15 Pte. ✠
SMITH, A. C. E., Gnr., 6 F.A.B.	W., 4 F.A.B., ✠ 18/9/18.	3/11/15 Gnr. ✠
SMITH, A. C., Spr., Tunl.lrs.	1 A. Tunnl. Co.	12/10/16 2y. 11m. Spr.
SMITH, A. E., Pte., 40 Bn.	15 Bn., ✠ 7/6/17.	23/ 3/16 Pte. ✠
SMITH, A. H., Pte., 12 Bn.	✠ 8/8/15.	27/ 8/14 Pte. ✠
SMITH, A. M., Pte., 15 Bn.	W.	6/10/14 1y. 8m. Pte.
SMITH, A. F., A.-Cpl., 12 Bn.		8/ 5/16
SMITH, A. V., Pte., 4 M.G. Co.	2 M.G. Co., 4 M.G. Bn.	22/11/16 3y. Pte.
SMITH, A. W., Pte., 12 Bn.	4 B.G.R.O. Co.	14/10/16 2y. 6m. Pte.
SMITH, A., Pte., 12 Bn.	W., 51 Bn	28/ 7/15
SMITH, A. E., Pte., 26 Bn.		26/ 7/15 4y. 1m. Pte.
SMITH, A. L., Pte., 40 Bn.	✠ 4/10/17.	9/10/16 Pte. ✠
SMITH, A. R., Pte., 12 Bn.	W.	18/ 7/16 2y. 4m. Pte.
SMITH, A. W., Gnr., 6 F.A.B.	14 F.A.B.	3/11/15 3y. 8m. Gnr.
SMITH, A. A., Pte., A.M.C.	11 Fd. Amb.	15/ 3/16 3y. 6m. Pte.
SMITH, A O., Pte., 4 M.G. Co.	3 M.G. Bn.	1/11/16 3y. Pte.
SMITH, A. B., Pte., 15 Bn.	47 Bn.	Lieut.
SMITH, A. C., Pte., 40 Bn.	✠ 15/8/18.	28/ 8/17 Pte. ✠
SMITH, A. E. F., Pte., 26 Bn.	W.	24/ 6/15 2y. 8m. Pte.
SMITH, A. H., Pte., 12 Bn	24 How. Bde., 10 F.A.B.	9/ 9/15 3y. 11m. Fitter
SMITH, A. J., Pte., 15 Bn.	✠ 1/5/15.	10/12/14 Pte. ✠
SMITH, A. P., Pte., 12 Bn.		1/ 6/16 3y. 5m. Pte.
SMITH, A. J., Gnr., 6 F.A.B.	2 D.A.C.	15/ 2/16 3y. 7m. Dvr.
SMITH, A. E., Pte., 26 Bn.	W., ✠ 19/12/19.	29/ 7/15 Pte. ✠
SMITH, A. J., Pte., 3 G.S.R.	12 Bn.	1/ 7/18 1y. 3m. Pte.
SMITH, B. L. W., Pte., 4 M.G. Co.	15 Bn., 4 M.G. Co.	12/ 2/17 2y. 7m. Pte.
SMITH, B. S., Pte., 12 Bn.		6/ 4/16 2y. 3m. Pte.
SMITH, B. T., Spr. 6 Fd. Co. En		24/ 8/15
SMITH, B. H., Pte., 40 Bn.	M.M., 51 Bn.	23/ 2/16 3y. 2m. Pte.
SMITH, B., Pte., 15 Bn.	W., 47 Bn., ✠ 28/3/18.	12/ 8/15 Pte. ✠
SMITH, B., Pte., 12 Bn.	52 Bn.	16/ 9/15 2y. 3m. Pte.
SMITH, C. A., Tpr., 2 Vet. Sec.	8 M.V.S., 2 A.V.C.	4/12/14 3y. 1m. Tpr.
SMITH, C. A., Pte., 26 Bn.	3W.	24/ 6/15 4y. 1m. Pte.
SMITH, C. A., Pte., 40 Bn.	✠ 9/4/17.	4/ 4/16 Pte. ✠
SMITH, C. E., Pte., 40 Bn.	W., ✠ 12/10/17.	28/ 2/16 L.-Cpl. ✠
SMITH, C. E., Pte., 12 Bn		10/ 7/16 1y. 8m. Pte.
SMITH, C. E., Pte., 12 Bn.	W., 52 Bn.	12/ 9/15 1y. 10m. Pte.
SMITH, C. E., Pte., 12 Bn. (Correct Name, Sladen, C. E.)	W., 52 Bn., ✠ 3-4/9/16.	4/ 6/15 Cpl. ✠
SMITH, C. G., 2 Cpl., 3 Fd. Co. En	13 Fd. Co., Engrs., ✠ 31/3/17.	23/ 8/14 Cpl. ✠
SMITH, C. R. A., Pte., 26 Bn.		19/ 2/15

TASMANIA'S MUSTER ROLL. 343

NAME.	REMARKS.	RANK ON DISCHARGE. ENLISTED. SERVICE.
SMITH, C. J R., Tpr., 3 L.H.	12 A.B. Ammn. Col.	10/ 9/15 4y. Dvr.
SMITH, C. P., Pte., 12 Bn.	1 D. Salv. Co.	18/ 8/14 5y. 2m. Pte.
SMITH, C. V., Gnr., Arty.		5/ 3/17 1y. 8m. Gnr.
SMITH, C. G. G., Dvr., 1 D.A.C.		19/ 7/15 4y. 2m. Dvr.
SMITH, C. H., Cpl., 3 F.A.B.	W., D.C.M. & Bar. 21 F.A.B.	27/ 8/14 3y. 7m. Sgt.
SMITH, C., Gnr., 8 F.A.B.	W., ✠ 14/5/18.	18/10/16 Gnr. ✠
SMITH, C. H., Pte., 26 Bn.	W., ✠ 20/9/17.	12/ 5/15 Cpl ✠
SMITH, C. R., Gnr., 6 F.A.B.	2W.	17/ 9/15 4y. 2m. Whlr.
SMITH, D., Pte., 12 Bn.	W.	7/ 8/15 3y. 2m. Pte.
SMITH, N. D., Gnr., 3 F.A.B.		17/ 8/15 2y. 10m. Gnr.
SMITH, E. T., Pte., 12 Bn.	✠ 25-28/4/15.	19/ 8/14 Pte. ✠
SMITH, E. W., Pte., 12 Bn.	40 Bn., Vet. Hosp.	11/ 4/16 3y. 4m. Pte.
SMITH, E., Pte., 40 Bn.	W., 51 Bn., ✠ 12/10/17.	5/ 2/16 Pte. ✠
SMITH, E A., Pte., 12 Bn.	2W., 69 Bn., 1 Pnr. Bn.	6/10/15 3y. 10m. Pte.
SMITH, E. C., Pte., 26 Bn.	2W., 26 Bn., 24 M.G. Co.	4/ 8/15 4y. Pte.
SMITH, E. C., Pte., A.S.C.	34 Co., A.S.C.	6/11/17 1y. 11m. Pte.
SMITH, E. R., Gnr., 6 F.A.B.	2 D.A.C.	24/ 2/16 3y. 8m. Dvr.
SMITH, E. R. C., Pte., 26 Bn.		1/ 5/15 3y. 1m. Pte.
SMITH, E. L., Gnr., 1 D.A.C.	17 Bty., ✠ 9/9/17.	8/ 6/15 Gnr. ✠
SMITH, F., Pte., 40 Bn.		22/ 2/16 3y. 6m. Pte.
SMITH, F. E., Tpr., 3 L.H.		20/ 8/14 3y. 10m. Tpr.
SMITH, F. S., Pte., 12 Bn.	52 Bn., 51 Bn.	19/ 1/16 3y. 9m. Pte.
SMITH, F. C., Pte., 12 Bn.	W.	4/ 5/16 1y. 11m. Pte.
SMITH, F. E., Pte., 12 Bn.	W., 52 Bn., 4 D.H.Q.	26/11/15 3y. 9m. Cpl.
SMITH, F. T. N., Pte., 12 Bn.	W., 52 Bn., 51 Bn.	30/11/15 3y. 10m. Pte.
SMITH, F.		
SMITH, F. J., Pte., 4 M.G. Co.	12 Bn.	31/ 7/16 3y. 1m. Pte.
SMITH, F. S., Pte., 12 Bn.	W.	6/10/15 3y. 11m. Pte.
SMITH, F. W., Pte., 26 Bn.	A.M.C.	22/ 4/15 3y. 7m. Pte.
SMITH, G., Pte., 40 Bn.	3W.	22/ 3/16 3y. 5m. Pte.
SMITH, G. D., Spr., 6 Fd. Co. Engrs	W., 16 Fd. Co. Engrs., 7 Fd. Co. Engrs.	30/ 8/15 3y. 7m. Spr.
SMITH, G. E., Gnr., D.A.C.	✠ 15/10/15.	8/12/14 Gnr. ✠
SMITH, G. H., Pte., 4 M.G. Co.	W., 12 M.G. Co.	24/11/16 2y. 11m. Pte.
SMITH, G. H., Pte., 12 Bn.	52 Bn.	25/ 5/15 3y. 3m. Pte.
SMITH, G. H., Pte., 12 Bn.	✠ 11/12/16.	19/ 9/14 L.-Cpl. ✠
SMITH, G. R. V., Pte., 12 Bn.	5 Pnr. Bn., ✠ 5/8/16.	25/ 8/15 Pte. ✠
SMITH, G. P., Pte., 12 Bn.	2W., 2 Pnr. Bn., 3 F.A.B.	28/ 9/15 3y. 11m. Gnr.
SMITH, G. T., Spr., Tunnls.	2 Tunnl. Co., ✠ 27/6/17.	18/ 4/16 Spr. ✠
SMITH, G. T. J., Pte., 40 Bn.	W.	3/ 3/16 1y. 9m. Pte.
SMITH, G. C., Fitter, Rly. Unit.		27/ 2/17
SMITH, G W., Pte., 40 Bn.	W.	29/ 3/16 3y. 6m. Pte.
SMITH, G. C., Pte., 12 Bn.	W., 40 Bn.	8/ 6/17 1y. 9m. Pte.
SMITH, G. K., Pte., 40 Bn.	2W.	23/ 5/16 3y. 4m. Pte.
SMITH, G. R., Gnr., 24 F.A.B.	W., 8 F.A.B.	24/10/16 2y. 5m. Gnr.
SMITH, G. H., Pte., 40 Bn.	W.	22/ 3/16 3y. 6m. Pte.
SMITH, H. C., Pte., 12 Bn.	✠	20/ 8/14 Pte. ✠
SMITH, H. E. E., Pte., 12 Bn.	3W., 52 Bn.	22/11/15
SMITH, H. F., Pte., 12 Bn.		19/ 8/14 2y. 5m. Pte.
SMITH, H. F.		
SMITH, H. I., Pte., 26 Bn.	4W.	12/ 4/15 4y. 1m. Pte.
SMITH, H. E., Pte., 12 Bn.	52 Bn., ✠ 4/9/16.	22/ 9/15 Pte. ✠
SMITH, H., Pte., 12 Bn.	Anz. Prov. Cps., ✠ 14/3/18.	4/ 1/15 Pte. ✠
SMITH, H. L., Pte., 40 Bn.		6/ 5/16 2y. 1m. Pte.
SMITH, H., Pte., 40 Bn.	28 Bn.	14/ 4/16 2y 11m L.-Cpl
SMITH, H. A. H., Pte., 40 Bn.	4W.	14/ 3/16 3y. 6m. Pte.
SMITH, H. C., Tpr., 1 Remt. Unit		3/11/15 1y. 1m. Spr.
SMITH, H. G., Pte., 12 Bn.		18/ 8/14
SMITH, H. G., Gnr., 8 F.A.B.	W.	21/ 1/16 3y. 2m. Dvr.
SMITH, H. G., Sgt., 12 Bn.	W., M.C., D.C.M.	26/10/14 4y. 4m. Lieut
SMITH, H. H., Pte., 12 Bn.	W., 1 M.G. Bn.	8/12/14 4y. 9m. Pte.
SMITH, H. J., Pte., 4 A.S.C.	1 Anzac L.R. Unit.	3/ 8/15 3y. 1m. C.S.M.
SMITH, H. J., Tpr., 3 L.H.	3 Anz. Camel Bn.	18/ 8/14 4y. 6m. Sgt.
SMITH, H. J., Pte., 40 Bn.	M.M. and Bar.	22/ 7/16 3y. Sgt.
SMITH, H. J., Pte., 12 Bn.	1 Camel Bn., 3 L.H.R.	1/ 8/15 4y. 1m. Tpr.
SMITH, H. N., Pte., 12 Bn.	W.	5/ 9/16 2y. 2m. Pte.
SMITH, H. R., Pte., 15 Bn.		26/ 8/15 3y. 9m. Pte.
SMITH, H. N. T., Pte., 12 Bn.	7 M.T.M.B.	16/11/15 3y. 11m. Gnr.
SMITH, H. R., Pte., 15 Bn.	W., P.O.W.	26/ 8/15 3y. 9m. Pte.
SMITH, H. G., Pte., 26Bn.	3W., 2 M.G. Bn.	20/ 4/15 3y. 7m. Pte.
SMITH, H. J., Pte., 40 Bn.	W., M.M.	8/ 3/16 3y. 1m. Pte.
SMITH, I. L., Pte., 12 Bn.	W., M.M., 52 Bn., 51 Bn.	13/11/15 3y. 9m. Pte.
SMITH, I. P., Pte., 1 A.G.H.	A.I.F. H.Q.	2/ 9/15 9m. Pte.
SMITH, J., Dvr., 3 A.A.M.T.	M.M., 2 D.S.C., 1 Dvl. M.T. Co.	18/ 9/16 3y 3m M.T. Dvr
SMITH, J., Tpr., 3 L.H.	1 Fld. Amb.	1/12/14 4y. 4m. Dvr.
SMITH, J. L., Pte., 4 A.S.C.		17/ 8/14 4y. 8m. Pte.
SMITH, J., Tpr., 3 L.H.	1 Fld. Amb.	1/12/14 4y. 4m. Dvr.
SMITH, J. H., Pte., 40 Bn.		25/ 5/16 3y. Pte.
SMITH, J., N. and Labourers.		
SMITH, J. C., Pte., 12 D.U.S.		30/ 4/18
SMITH, J. D., Pte., 12 Bn.	2W., 40 Bn.	8/ 4/16 2y. 11m. Pte.
SMITH, J. H., Pte., 12 Bn.	52 Bn., 51 Bn.	5/10/14 5y. Cpl.
SMITH, J. J., Pte., 40 Bn.	12 Bn.	24/ 7/16 1y. 10m. Pte.
SMITH, J. L. L., Spr., 3 F.C.E.		30/ 7/15
SMITH, J. W., Gnr., 25 F.A.B.	7 F.A.B.	14/10/16 2y. 3m. Dvr.
SMITH, J. E., Spr., 3 Miners.		31/ 3/16
SMITH, J. W., Pte., 12 Bn.	✠ 17/5/18.	4/10/17 Pte. ✠
SMITH, J., Sgt., 40 Bn.	W.	13/ 8/15 3y. 8m. W.O.

NAME.	REMARKS.	RANK ON DISCHARGE. ENLISTED. SERVICE.
SMITH, J., Pte., 12 Bn.		19/10/17
SMITH, J., Pte., 26 Bn.	2W.	5/ 6/15 4y. 2m. Pte.
SMITH, J. F., Pte., 40 Bn.	W.	24/ 1/16 2y. 4m. Pte.
SMITH, J. G., Pte., 12 Bn.	69 Bn., 3 L.T.M.B.	5/ 2/15 4y. 5m. L.-Cpl.
SMITH, J. H., Pte., 15 Bn.	W.	19/ 9/14 4y. 4m. Pte.
SMITH, J. J., Pte., 2 G.S.R.	4 G.S.R.	4/ 5/18 9m. Pte.
SMITH, J. J., Pte., 12 Bn.	52 Bn.	29/ 9/15 4y. 1m. Pte.
SMITH, J. P., Pte., 1 A.G.H.C.D.	W., 9 Fd. Amb.	4/ 6/15
SMITH, J. T. C., L.-Cpl., 12 Bn.		15/11/16 3y. 1m. L.-Cpl.
SMITH, J. V., Pte., 12 Bn.	40 Bn.	20/10/16 3y. 2m. Pte.
SMITH, K. L., Pte., 12 Bn.	52 Bn., ✠ 16/8/16.	19/10/15 Pte. ✠
SMITH, L. L., Pte., 40 Bn.	2W.	28/ 3/16 2y. 3m. Cpl.
SMITH, L. S., Pte., 3 G.S.R.	12 Bn.	5/ 7/18 1y. Pte.
SMITH, L. W., Pte., 12 Bn.		26/ 8/15 1y. 7m. Pte.
SMITH, L. J., Dvr., 3 F.A.B.		19/ 2/15 4y. 9m. Dvr.
SMITH, L. J., Pte., 12 Bn.	W., 1 Pnr. Bn.	19/ 8/15 3y. 11m. Sgt.
SMITH, L. J., Pte., 12 Bn.	2W.	1/ 6/16 2y. 11m. Pte.
SMITH, L. W., Pte., 4 M.G. Co.	1 M.G. Bn.	6/12/16 2y. 7m. Pte.
SMITH, M. C., Pte., 40 Bn.	3W.	2/ 5/16 3y. 2m. Pte.
SMITH, M. C., Pte., 40 Bn.		3/ 2/17 10m. Pte.
SMITH, M. J., Pte., T.M. Bty.	40 Bn.	14/ 2/17
SMITH, N. L., Pte., 12 Bn.	2W., 10 F.A.B.	1/ 8/15 3y. 10m. Dvr.
SMITH, P. J., Pte., 26 Bn.	W.	23/ 7/15 2y. Pte.
SMITH, P. H., Pte., 2 G.S.R.		23/ 3/18 1y. 9m. Pte.
SMITH, P., Pte., 40 Bn.	W., ✠ 28/3/18.	18/ 2/16 L.-Cpl. ✠
SMITH, P. J., Pte., 40 Bn.		5/10/16 1y. Pte.
SMITH, P. W., Pte., 12 Bn.		22/10/17 1y. 3m. Pte.
SMITH, P., Pte., 15 Bn.	✠ 8/8/15.	3/12/14 Pte. ✠
SMITH, R. E. J., Pte., 40 Bn.		23/ 2/16 3y. 6m. Pte.
SMITH, R., Pte., 12 Bn.		3/ 8/16 3y. 1m. Pte.
SMITH, R., Spr., 3 Miners.	W.	12/11/15 2y. 1m. Spr.
SMITH, R., Pte., 40 Bn.	3W., M.M.	4/ 4/16 3y. Pte.
SMITH, R. L., Spr., 8 Fd. Co.	14 Fd. Co. Engrs.	2/ 1/16 3y. 8m. Spr.
SMITH, R. J., Pte., 12 Bn.	A. Prov. Cps.	6/ 8/15 4y. 3m. Pte.
SMITH, S., Pte, 3 Fd. Amb.	13 Fd. Amb.	25/ 4/15 2y. 6m. Pte.
SMITH, S. J., Pte., 12 Bn.	2W., 52 Bn.	22/ 8/14 4y. 4m. Cpl.
SMITH, S. D., Pte., 12 Bn.	52 Bn., ✠ 4/9/16.	8/ 7/15 Pte. ✠
SMITH, S. J., Pte., 12 Bn.	W.	13/ 1/15 4y. 7m. Cpl.
SMITH, S. J., Pte., 15 Bn.	12 Bn.	31/ 8/15 1y. 9m. Pte.
SMITH, S. D., Pte., 3 G.S.R.	✠ 23/8/18.	31/ 7/18 11m. Pte. ✠
SMITH, S. H., Pte., 12 Bn.	A. Fd. Butchery.	22/ 8/16 Pte. ✠
SMITH, S. W., Pte., 2 G.S.R.		13/ 4/15 1y. 8m. Pte.
SMITH, S. H., Sgt., 40 Bn.	M.M.	29/12/15 2y. 6m. Lieut.
SMITH, S., Pte., 26 Bn.	✠ 28/4/15 and 2/5/15.	18/ 3/15
SMITH, T., Pte., 12 Bn.		20/ 8/14 Pte. ✠
SMITH, T. H. H., Pte., 15 Bn.	52 Bn. A.I.B.D.	9/11/14
SMITH, T. E., Pte., 12 Bn.	2 D.A.C.	28/ 7/15 4y. 4m. Pte.
SMITH, T. J., Tpr., 3 L.H.	2W., 12 Bn., 51 Bn.	3/ 8/15 1y. 6m. Gnr.
SMITH, T. J., Pte., 26 Bn.		3/ 8/15 4y. Pte.
SMITH, T. L., Pte., 40 Bn.		21/ 9/16
SMITH, T. P., Spr., 3 Miners.	1 Tunnl. Co.	7/ 9/15 2y. 6m. Spr.
SMITH, T. W., Spr., Tunnls.	40 Bn.	9/11/16 2y. 5m. Spr.
SMITH, T. J., Pte., 1 G.S.R.		21/ 6/17 1y. 11m. Pte.
SMITH, V., Pte., M.G. Rfts.		23/ 2/17
SMITH, V. W., Pte., 15 Bn.	W., A.L.R.O. Co.	28/ 8/15 4y. 3m. Spr.
SMITH, V. G., Sgt., 12 Bn.	M.M.	28/ 6/15
SMITH, V. J., Pte., 12 Bn.	4W.	2/ 9/16 2y. 8m. Pte.
SMITH, V. L., Pte., 4 M.G. Co.	15 Bn., 4 M.G. Bn.	27/11/16 2y. 5m. Pte.
SMITH, W. J., Sgt Dmr., 12 Bn.		28/ 8/14 1y 7m Sgt Dmr
SMITH, W. L., Pte., 12 Bn.		15/ 9/15 2y. 10m. Pte.
SMITH, W., Tpr., 3 L.H.	✠ 4-6/8/16.	26/ 7/15 Spr. ✠
SMITH, W., Pte., 12 Bn.	52 Bn.	11/ 1/15 4y. 7m. Pte.
SMITH, W. A., Pte., 12 Bn.		10/ 1/18
SMITH, W. A., Pte., 40 Bn.	M.M., 10 L.T.M.B.	10/ 1/16 3y. 2m. L.-Cpl.
SMITH, W. C., Dvr., 2 F.A.B.	1 D.A.C.	11/ 2/15
SMITH, W. E., Pte., 26 Bn.	Imp. Camel Cps., ✠ 12/4/18.	9/ 4/15 Pte. ✠
SMITH, W. H., Pte., 40 Bn.	2 Fd. Amb.	23/ 2/16 3y. 8m. Pte.
SMITH, W. H., Pte., 40 Bn.	✠ 5/10/17.	7/11/16 Pte. ✠
SMITH, W. H., Spr., Tunnl. Rfts	W.	9/10/16 2y. 11m. Spr.
SMITH, W. H., Spr., 5 Miners.	W., 3 Tunnl. Co.	23/ 2/16 3y. 8m. Spr.
SMITH, W. J. R., Pte., 1 G.S.R		15/ 6/17
SMITH, W. J., Spr., 8 Fd. Co. En	W., 15 Fd. Co. Engrs.	31/ 1/16 3y. 8m.
SMITH, W. J., Gnr., Arty.	7 F.A.B.	22/ 5/17 1y. 10m. Gnr.
SMITH, W. J., Spr., Tunnlrs.	W., 2 Tunnl. Co.	13/ 2/17 2y. 1m. Spr.
SMITH, W. M., Pte., 12 Bn.	W., 52 Bn., ✠ 27/3/17.	12/ 1/16 Pte. ✠
SMITH, W. E. H., Pte., 40 Bn.	2W.	21/ 9/16 2y. 7m. Pte.
SMITH, W. T., Pte., 40 Bn.	2W.	10/ 5/16 2y. 4m. Pte.
SMITH, W. C., Spr., 8 Fd Co. En	W., 6 Fd. Co. Engrs.	21/ 2/16 3y. 7m. L.-Cpl.
SNARE, G. M'K., Pte., 40 Bn.	2W.	15/ 3/16 2y. 8m. Pte.
SNOW, C. W., Pte., Tunnlrs.		25/ 6/17
SNOWDEN, R. E., Major 15 Bn.	47 Bn.	28/ 9/14 2y 1m. Lt.-Col.
SNOWDEN, R. C., Pte., 40 Bn.		24/ 8/16
SNOXALL, J. D., Pte., 26 Bn.	2W., M.M.	15/ 3/15 4y. 1m. Pte.
SODEN, A., Tpr., 3 L.H.		11/ 7/17 2y. 2m. Spr.
SODEN, R., Sgt., 3 L.H.		20/ 8/14 4y. 8m. Lieut.
SOLOMON, E. L., Gnr., 3 F.A.B	24 How. Bde., 10 F.A.B.	29/12/15 3y. 3m. Gnr.
SOLOMON, H. E., Gnr., Arty.		14/ 2/17

TASMANIA'S MUSTER ROLL.

NAME.	REMARKS.	RANK ON DISCHARGE. ENLISTED. SERVICE.
SOLOMON, H. F., Gnr., Arty.	W., 3 F.A.B.	15/ 4/17 2y. 6m. Gnr.
SOLOMON, L. E., Gnr., 13 F.A.B	✣ 16/10/17.	10/12/17 Gnr. ✣
SOLOMON, R. F., Pte., 12 Bn.		2/12/15 1y. 3m. Pte.
SOLOMON, T. H., Gnr., 3 F.A.B.	52 Bn.	30/ 8/15 1y. Gnr.
SOLOMON, W. A., Gnr., 6 F.A.B		25/ 8/15 3y. 2m.
SOMERFIELD, L. P., Pte., 12 Bn	W.	19/ 8/14 1y. 6m. Pte.
SOMERS, O. G., Cpl., 12 Bn.	✣ 13/8/18.	30/ 7/17 Cpl. ✣
SOMERVILLE, L., Pte., 12 Bn.		27/ 8/14 2y. 11m. Sgt.
SORARN, H. G., Pte., 12 Bn.	✣ 25/7/18.	15/ 8/15 Pte. ✣
SORELL, E. T., Gnr., 25 F.A.B.	W., A.F.A. Details, ✣ 24/11/17.	29/ 9/16 Gnr. ✣
SOUTHWOOD, J. H., Pte., 26 Bn	W., ✣ 29/7/16.	13/ 8/15 Pte. ✣
SOWBY, W., Pte., 12 Bn.	52 Bn. ✣ 19/4/18.	19/ 8/14 1y. Pte.
SPARKES, A. J., Gnr., 6 F.A.B	W., 2 D.A.C.	5/10/15 3y. 11m. Dvr.
SPARKES, A. F., Pte., 26 Bn.	W., 12 Bn., ✣ 2/11/17.	5/ 8/15 Pte. ✣
SPAULDING, B. J., Pte., 12 Bn.	W., 52 Bn., 10 F.A.B.	13/ 7/15 3y. 10m. Sgt.
SPAULDING, C. F., Pte., 12 Bn.	W.	26/10/16 4y. 1m. Pte.
SPAULDING, D. E., Pte., 40 Bn.	W.	21/ 9/16 2y. 8m. Sgt.
SPAULDING, G. T., Gnr., Arty.		26/ 4/17 1y. 11m. Pte.
SPAULDING, M., Pte., 12 Bn.	2W., 24th/10th F.A.B.	2/ 4/17 2y. 3m. Pte.
SPAULDING, R. L., Pte., 12 Bn.	52 Bn.	13/ 7/15 3y. 9m.
SPEED, C., Pte., 12 Bn.		1/12/14 8m. Pte.
SPEED, E. J., Pte., 40 Bn.		17/ 5/16 3y. 4m. Pte.
SPEED, G., Pte., 40 Bn.	2W., ✣ 17/4/18.	17/ 5/16 L.-Sgt. ✣
SPEIRS, A. E., Spr. 6 Fd Co Engrs	15 Fd. Co. Engrs.	18/ 9/15 3y. 11m. Dvr.
SPEERS, E. S., Pte., 12 Bn.	3W., 49 Bn.	25/11/15 4y. Pte.
SPELLMAN, J. J., Pte., 40 Bn.	✣ 29/9/18.	16/ 3/16 L.Sgt. ✣
SPENCER, T. A., Lt.-Col., 3 D.A.C.		23/ 3/16 1y 3m. Lt.-Col.
SPENCER, C. A., Tpr., 3 L.H.		27/ 8/14 2y. Tpr.
SPENCER, E. G., Pte., 12 Bn.	3W., 52 Bn., 42 Bn.	11/ 1/16 3y. 3m. Pte.
SPENCER, K., Pte., 12 Bn.	W., 5 Bn.	16/ 8/15 3y. 8m. Pte.
SPENCER, M. H., Pte., 12 Bn.		17/ 9/14 1y. 8m. Pte.
SPENCER, R. S., Pte., 12 Bn.	✣ 6-10/4/17.	5/ 7/15 Pte. ✣
SPENCER, T., Pte., 12 Bn.	2W.	17/ 9/14 4y. 9m. Pte.
SPERRING, H. O., Pte., 12 Bn.	Aus. Depot Stores.	20/ 8/14 4y. 7m. Pte.
SPICER, A. G., Tpr., 3 L.H.		27/ 8/15
SPICER, A. J., Tpr., 3 L.H.		27/ 8/15
SPICER, V. J., Pte., 12 Bn.	W., 52 Bn., 51 Bn.	27/ 8/15 4y. 1m. Dvr.
SPICER, W. E., Gnr., 6 F.A.B.	120 How. Bty.	2/ 2/15 Pte. ✣
SPILLANE, D. J., Pte., 15 Bn.	✣ 8/8/15.	3/10/16 2y. 7m. Pte.
SPILLANE, T. F., Pte., 40 Bn.	2W., 67 Bn.	23/ 2/16 3y. 2m. Pte.
SPINKS, C. L., Pte., 40 Bn.	2W., 15 Bn., 40 Bn.	8/ 6/15 1y. 11m. Pte
SPINKS, D. G., Pte., 26 Bn.	W.	19/ 1/16 3y. 10m. Spr.
SPINKS, E. J., Pte., 12 Bn.	3 A.L.R.F. Co.	4/ 1/16 Pte. ✣
SPINKS, G. H., Pte., 12 Bn.	2W., 52 Bn., ✣ 3-4/9/16.	6/ 4/16 2y. 11m. Pte.
SPINKS, H. W., Pte., 12 Bn.	2W., 40 Bn.	23/ 2/16 3y. 8m. Pte.
SPINKS, K., Pte., 40 Bn.	W.	24/10/16 4y. 6m. Pte.
SPINKS, T., Pte., 12 Bn.	W., 40 Bn.	3/ 7/17 1y. Pte.
SPLANE, M., Pte., 12 Bn.	✣ 20/9/18.	10/ 7/15 Pte. ✣
SPLANE, W. H., Pte., 12 Bn.		4/ 8/15 4y. 1m. Dvr.
SPOTSWOOD, C. D., Dvr. 6 F.A.B.	114 How. Bty.	14/ 2/16 3y. 4m. Cpl.
SPOTTSWOOD, D. M'L, Cpl., Arty		17/ 8/14 1y. 6m. Pte.
SPOTSWOOD, G. F., Pte., 4 A.S.C.	W., M.C.	29/ 8/14 4y. 10m. Capt
SPOTTSWOOD, H. E., Pte., 12 Bn.		1/12/14 2y. Pte.
SPOTSWOOD, L. J., Pte., 12 Bn.		24/ 8/15 1y. 4m. Pte.
SPOTSWOOD, M. C. D., Pte. 12 Bn		26/ 2/15
SPOWART, W., Pte., 26 Bn.	3W., ✣ 1/10/18.	26/ 3/16 Cpl. ✣
SPRADON, M. A., Pte., 40 Bn.	15 Fd. Amb.	8/ 3/16 3y. 7m. Pte.
SPRAY, F. A., Pte., A.M.C.	M.C.	23/ 7/15 2y 4m. Major.
SPRENT, J., Capt. A.M.C.		31/ 3/15 4y. 4m. Pte.
SPRENT, C. M., Pte., 7 Fd. Amb.		15/ 7/15 10m. Pte
SPRING, W. F., Pte., 12 Bn.	W., ✣ 5/10/17.	25/ 9/16 Pte. ✣
SPROULE, E. F., Pte., 40 Bn.	2W.	19/ 2/15 4y. 6m. Pte.
SPROULE, J. C., Pte., 26 Bn.	2W., 52 Bn., 51 Bn.	6/ 8/15 3y. Sgt.
SPROULE, R., Pte., 12 Bn.	2W., 52 Bn.	2/ 8/15 3y. 8m. Pte.
SPURLING, R. L., Pte., 12 Bn.		7/11/16 1y. 6m. Pte.
SPURR, T. H., Pte., 40 Bn.	M.M., 2 M.G. Co.	12/ 5/15
SQUIRE, A. W., Pte., 26 Bn.		24/ 4/17 2y. 5m. Cpl.
SQUIRES, D. N., Pte., 12 Bn.	W., ✣ 17/4/18.	8/ 1/15 Pte. ✣
SQUIRES, J.		4/ 9/17
SQUIRES, V. A., Pte., 12 Bn.	3W., 40 Bn., ✣ 10/9/18.	4/ 4/16 Pte. ✣
STACEY, A. J., Pte., 40 Bn.	✣ 28/4/16.	12/ 2/15 Pte. ✣
STACEY, E. J., Pte., 12 Bn.	3W.	12/ 2/15 4y. 5m. Pte.
STACEY, J. W., Pte., 26 Bn.	2W.	15/ 3/16 3y. Pte.
STACEY, R. E., Pte., 26 Bn.	46 Bty., A.F.A.	23/ 2/15 8m. Gnr.
STACEY, T. A., Pte., 40 Bn.		4/ 2/15 4y. 2m. Tpr.
STACKHOUSE, L. M., Cpl., 1 G.S.R.	12 Bn., ✣ 23/8/18.	7/ 9/15 Pte. ✣
STAGOLL, A. G., Tpr., 3 L.H.	38 Co., A.M.D.T.	3/12/17 1y. 10m. Dvr.
STAGOLL, W. W., Pte., 26 Bn.		30/ 8/16 3y. 1m. Dvr.
STAGG, H.R., Pte., A.S.C.	10 F.A.B.	28/ 7/15 4y. 2m. Pte.
STAGG, H. R., Pte., 4 M.G. Co.	2W., 52 Bn., 51 Bn.	20/ 4/16 1y. 6m. Tpr.
STAMFORD, C. F., Gnr., Arty.		20/ 8/14 Tpr. ✣
STANDAGE, C. A., Pte., 12 Bn.	✣ 8/8/15.	9/10/16 2y. 11m. Pte.
STAMFORD, O. C., Tpr., 8 L.H.	W.	12/ 1/16 3y. 9m. Dvr.
STANDJAN, A., Tpr., 3 L.H.	13 F.A.B., 5 D.A.C.	20/11/16
STANFIELD, D. S., Pte., 40 Bn.		4/11/14 Pte. ✣
STANFIELD, E. G., Gnr., 6 F.A.B.		
STANFORD, W T., Pte., 4 M.G Co		

NAME.	REMARKS.	RANK ON DISCHARGE. ENLISTED. SERVICE.
STANLEY, A. C., Pte., 15 Bn.	✠ 28/8/16.	2/10/15 1y. 2m. Tpr.
STANLEY, C. J., Tpr., Rem. Unit.		6/ 9/16
STANLEY, F. W., Pte., 12 Bn.	2W.	29/ 8/14
STANLEY, F. V., Pte., 12 Bn.		30/10/16 1y. 6m. Pte.
STANLEY, H. M., Pte., 12 Bn.		22/ 9/15
STANLEY, H. J., Pte., 1 Rem Unit		10/ 9/14 L.-Cpl. ✠
STANLEY, H. R. K., Pte., 12 Bn.	W., ✠ 6-10/4/17.	23/ 7/15
STANLEY, R. W., Cpl., 1 L.H.		26/10/15 4y. Gnr.
STANLEY, W. M., Gnr., 8 F.A.B.	3 D.A.C., 8 F.A.B.	7/ 9/15 4y. 1m. Dvr.
STANNARD, N. J., Tpr., 3 L.H.	W., 13 F.A.B.	2/10/16 Pte. ✠
STANSALL, C. W., Pte., 40 Bn.	W., ✠ 10/9/18.	8/ 7/15 16/7/19.
STANSFIELD, C. W., Pte., 12 Bn.	W., 3 L.T.M.B.	2/11/16 1y. 2m. Pte.
STANSFIELD, G. O., Pte., 40 Bn.		30/ 4/15 4y. 4m. Pte.
STANSFIELD, P., Pte., 26 Bn.	2W.	22/ 7/15 Pte. ✠
STANSFIELD, G. R., Pte., 12 Bn.	52 Bn., ✠ 4/9/16.	22/ 9/14 Cpl. ✠
STANTON, A. J., Pte., 15 Bn.	2W., 12 Bn., ✠ 18/4/18.	14/ 7/15 1y. 6m. Pte.
STANTON, E., Pte., 12 Bn.		6/ 9/16 2y. 11m. Pte.
STANTON, H. J., Pte., 40 Bn.	W.	15/11/16 2y. 8m. Pte.
STANTON, L. R., Pte., 12 Bn.	A.A.V.C.	15/11/16 2y. 8m. Pte.
STANTON, W. A., Pte., 40 Bn.	W.	20/ 9/16 2y. 7m. Pte.
STANTON, W. E., Pte., 40 Bn.	✠ 12/7/17	2/ 2/16 Pte. ✠
STANWIX, C. P., Gnr., 6 F.A.B.	W., 15 Bty., A.F.A.	8/10/15 3y. 7m. Gnr.
STAPLETON, F., Gnr., 8 F.A.B.	2W.	5/ 1/16 2y. 6m. Gnr.
STAPLETON, J. R., Dvr., 8 F.C.E.	3 Fd. Co. Engrs.	27/ 4/16 3y. 6m. Dvr.
STATTON, E. K., Pte., 12 Bn.	W.	22/ 8/14 2y. 6m. Pte.
STATTON, G., Pte., 7 Bn.		24/ 7/16 Pte.
STATTON, P. C., L.-Cpl., 40 Bn.	V.C., M.M.	29/ 2/16 3y. 11m. Cpl.
STEADWELL, M. A. J., Pte., 12 Bn	40 Bn., ✠ 16/6/18.	18/11/16 Pte. ✠
STEANE, J. B., Pte., 4 A.S.C.		17/ 8/14 3y. 4m. Pte.
STEARNES, A. G., Pte., 40 Bn.	49 Bn.	18/ 4/16 3y. 6m. Pte.
STEARNES, W., Pte., 12 Bn.		14/10/17 1y. 6m. Pte.
STEARNES, W. H., Pte., 15 Bn.	12 Bn., 1 Pnr. Bn., ✠ 25/8/18.	2/ 9/15 Pte. ✠
STEBBINGS, S. G. L., Pte., 40 Bn	W., M.C.	5/ 1/16 3y. 10m. Lieut.
STEBBINGS, S., Pte., 40 Bn.		6/ 6/17 1y. 9m. Pte.
STEELE, A. T., Tpr., 3 L.H.	22 F.A.B., 2 D.A.C.	18/12/14 4y. 4m. Gnr.
STEELE, E. H., Tpr., 3 L.H.		3/12/17
STEELE, F. W., Pte., 40 Bn.		25/ 5/16 3y. 5m. Lieut.
STEELE, G. M., Pte., 15 Bn.	W., ✠ 7/8/16.	30/ 9/14 L.-Cpl. ✠
STEELE, J., Bmdr., Sge. Art. Bde.	D.C.M., M.M., Croix de Guerre.	1/ 6/15
STEELE, N. P., Pte., 40 Bn.	✠ 28/3/18.	8/ 1/17 Pte. ✠
STEELE, P. W., Pte., Rem. Unit.		19/10/15 8m. Pte.
STEELE, R. A., Pte., 12 Bn.	40 Bn.	20/11/16 2y. 10m. Pte.
STEEL, R., Pte., A.S.C.	37 A.A.S.C.	29/ 9/17 2y. 1m. Pte.
STEEL, S. J., Pte., A.A.M.C.	15 Fd. Amb.	2/ 3/17 2y. 8m. L.-Cpl
STEER, A. B., Pte., A.A.M.C.		6/12/16
STEERS, W. R., Pte., 40 Bn.	W.	26/ 4/16 1y. 6m. Pte.
STEERS, H. R., Pte., 40 Bn.	W.	8/ 2/16
STEERS, T.		
STEERS, W. S., Pte., 26 Bn.	2W., 12 Bn.	10/ 8/15 2y. 4m. Pte.
STEIN, A. J., Pte., 15 Bn.	✠ 10/5/15.	6/10/14 Pte. ✠
STEIN, J., Pte., 12 Bn.	W., ✠ 19/9/18.	13/10/16 Pte. ✠
STENNINGS, H., Pte., 4 M.G. Co.	W., 21 Bn., 6 Bn.	21/11/16 2y. 9m. Pte.
STEPHENS, E. C., 2nd Lt. 1 G.S.R.	12 Bn.	9/10/16 3y 1m. Lieut.
STEPHENS, H. Z., Capt. A.A.M.C.		11/10/15 2y. Major.
STEPHENS, A. A., Pte., 26 Bn.	2W., 2 D.H.Q.	5/ 5/15 3y. 4m. L.-Cpl
STEPHENS, C. H., Pte., 40 Bn.		10/ 7/17 2y. Pte.
STEPHENS, E. S., Tpr., 3 L.H.	8 Bn.	6/10/15 3y. 7m. Cpl.
STEPHENS, E. T., Pte., 40 Bn.	2W.	7/ 3/16 3y. 5m. Cpl.
STEPHENS, E. W., Cpl., 40 Bn.	Croix de Guerre.	4/ 3/16 3y. 1m. C.S.M.
STEPHENS, F. H., Pte., 12 Bn.	2W., 52 Bn.	11/11/15 3y. 5m. Pte. ✠
STEPHENS, G. E. G., Pte., 26 Bn.	12 Bn., ✠ 19-22/8/16.	17/ 8/15 Pte. ✠
STEPHENS, H., Pte., 1 G.S.R.		4/ 3/18
(Correct Name Stanford. H.)		
STEPHENS, H. S., Pte., 40 Bn.	12 Bn., ✠ 25/8/18.	26/ 8/16 Pte. ✠
STEPHENS, H. J., Sgt., 40 Bn.		30/ 9/15 2y. 4m. Sgt.
STEPHENS, H. S., Pte., 26 Bn.	✠ 5/8/16.	27/ 4/15 Pte. ✠
STEPHENS, J. F., Cpl., 12 Bn.	3 M.G. Co., ✠ 25/4/18.	1/ 9/15 2nd Lieut. ✠
STEPHENS, L., Pte., 40 Bn.		3/10/16 3m. Pte.
STEPHENS, L. A., Pte., 40 Bn.	W.	12/10/16 2y. 5m. Pte.
STEPHENS, L. H., Gnr., Arty.	5 D.A.C.	18/12/16 2y. 4m. Gnr.
STEPHENS, M. J., Tpr., L.H.		29/ 1/18 1y. 2m. Tpr.
STEPHENS, M., Spr., 5 Tunnlrs.	2 Tunnlrs.	15/ 4/16 3y. 5ml Spr.
STEPHENS, R., Pte., 12 Bn.	2W.	2/ 5/16 3y. 4m. Pte.
STEPHENS, R., S.-Sgt., 12 Bn.	✠ 12/6/15.	21/ 8/14 S.-Sgt. ✠
STEPHENS, R. H., Pte., 12 Bn.	M.T. Service, A.F.C. Hqtrs.	14/ 7/16 2y. 8m. 2nd Lt
STEPHENS, R., Pte., 12 Bn.	40 Bn.	11/ 4/16 3y. 4m. Pte.
STEPHENS, R. D., Gnr., 6 F.A.B	W., 5 F.A.B.	8/10/15 2y. 3m. Gnr.
STEPHENS, T. B., Pte., 40 Bn.	W.	24/ 9/17 2y. 1m. Pte.
STEPHENS, W. G., Pte., 40 Bn.		4/ 7/16 3y. 1m. Pte.
STEVENS, W. H., Pte., 12 Bn.	✠ 25-28/4/15.	31/ 8/14 Pte. ✠
STEPHENS, W. H., Pte., 40 Bn.	✠ 7/1/17.	15/ 3/16 Pte. ✠
STEPHENSON, H. R., Pte., 26 Bn.		26/ 6/15 2y. 1m. Pte.
STEPHENSON, F., Pte., 15 Bn.	W., M.C.	7/ 8/15 3y. 8m. Lieut.
STEPHENSON, W. W., Pte., 26 Bn.		22/ 4/15 4y. 4m. Pte.
STEVENS, A. H. J., Pte., 12 Bn.	✠ 9/4/17.	7/ 8/16 Pte. ✠
STEVENS, E. W., Pte., 40 Bn.	2W., M.M., ✠ 28/3/18.	16/ 3/16 Cpl. ✠

TASMANIA'S MUSTER ROLL. 347

NAME.	REMARKS.	RANK ON DISCHARGE. ENLISTED, SERVICE.
STEVENS, E. W., Pte., 40 Bn.		4/ 3/16 3y. 1m. C.S.M.
STEVENS, F., Gnr., 5 D.A.C.		28/12/15
STEVENS, F. E., Spr., 3 Fd Co Eng		24/ 3/14 5y. 3m. Spr.
STEVENS, G. W., Pte., 1 A.C.H.	1 Fd. Amb.	17/ 9/14 4y. 5m. Pte.
STEVENS, H. V., Gnr., D.A.C	W., 22 How. Bde	20/ 8/15 3y. 8m. Gnr.
STEVENS, H. C., Pte., 12 Bn.	W., M.M.	27/ 4/16 3y. 5m. Dvr.
STEVENS, I. W., Pte., 12 Bn.	10 F.A.B.	1/ 8/15 4y. Cpl.
STEVENS, J. H. H., Pte., 40 Bn.		12/ 7/16 2y. 8m. Pte.
STEVENS, J. C., Gnr, 6 F.A.B.	4 F.A.B.	1/11/15 3y. 11m. Dvr.
STEVENS, L. D., Tpr., 3 L.H.	W., 1 Camel Bn.	21/ 8/14
STEVENS, R. A., Gnr., 6 F.A.B.	W., 8 F.A.B., 2 D.H. & M.T.M. Bde.	31/ 8/15 3y. 7m.
STEVENS, R. E., Pte., 26 Bn.	W., 12 Bn.	24/ 4/15 4y. Pte.
STEVENS, W. L., Tpr., 3 L.H.	150 How. Bty., ✠ 16/4/17.	9/ 3/15 Pte. ✠
STEVENSON, C., Pte., 15 Bn.		30/12/14 1y. 4m. Pte.
STEVENSON, L. D., Pte., 12 Bn.	✠ 23/4/18.	23/ 5/17 Pte. ✠
STEVENSON, L. M., Cpl., 40 Bn.	1 M.G. Co., ✠ 28/1/18.	16/ 5/16 Cpl. ✠
STEVENSON, R., Pte., 12 Bn.	W., 52 Bn., 51B.l.	28/ 1/16
STEVENSON, S. B., Pte., 12 Bn.	✠ 24/4/18.	7/11/16 Pte. ✠
STEWART, A. M., 2nd Lieut. 12 Bn.	52 Bn.	21/ 2/15 3y. Capt.
STEWART, A., Tpr., 3 L.H.	4 D.A.C.	19/10/15 3y. 11m. Sgt.
STEWART, A., Pte., 12 Bn.	2W.	24/10/16 2y. 1m. Pte.
STEWART, A. W., Pte., 26 Bn.	12 Bn., 2 A.A.H.	7/ 4/15 5y. 7m. Cpl.
STEWART, C. W., Gnr., 6 F.A.B.	6 B.A.C.	14/ 9/15 4y. Gnr.
STEWART, C. J., Pte., 40 Bn.	✠ 7/6/17.	21/ 3/16 Pte. ✠
STEWART, C. M., Pte., 40 Bn.	W.	1/12/15 3y. 5m. Pte.
STEWART, D. A., Pte., 12 Bn.	M.M., 52 Bn., 51 Bn.	25/ 8/15
STEWART, E. R., Pte., 12 Bn.	M.M.	29/ 1/15 4y. 3m. L.-Cpl.
STEWART, E. A., Gnr., 24 F.A.B.	5 F.A.B., 105 How. Bty.	13/10/15 2y. 11m. Dvr.
STEWART, E. A., Pte., 12 Bn.	W., 52 Bn., ✠ 23/9/17.	6/ 8/15 Pte. ✠
STEWART, E. J., Pte., 12 Bn.	3W., ✠ 6-10/4/17.	26/ 8/15 Pte. ✠
STEWART, F. G., Gnr., 6 F.A.B.	22 F.A.B., 5 F.A.B.	29/ 9/15 4y. Gnr.
STEWART, H. W., Tpr., 3 L.H.		27/ 2/15 4y. 10m. Tpr.
STEWART, H., Gnr., 6 F.A.B.	113 How. Bty.	23/11/15 3y. 10m. Dvr.
STEWART, J. J., Pte., 40 Bn.	1 A.V.H.	7/11/16 2y. 8m. Pte.
STEWART, J., Pte., 12 Bn.	✠ 9/8/15.	1/ 2/15 Pte. ✠
STEWART, J. F., Spr., 18 Fd Co En	2 Commd. Depot.	19/ 2/16
STEWART, J. H., Pte., 15 Bn.	W., M.M., 47 Bn.	25/ 8/15 3y. 10m. Sgt.
STEWART, R., Gnr., 6 F.A.B.		2/12/15
STEWART, R., Pte., 40 Bn.	51 Bn.	2/ 3/16 1y. 11m. Pte.
STEWART, R., Pte., 4 A.S.C.	1 Dvl. Train.	27/ 8/14 5y. Pte.
STEWART, W. L.-Cpl., 3 L.H.	M.M.	24/ 8/14 4y. 8m. Sgt.
STEWART, W., Spr., S Miners		18/11/15
STEWART, W. F., Dvr., D.A.C.	W., M.M., A.F.C.	17/ 9/15 Lieut.
STEWART, W. J., Pte., 12 Bn.	W.	12/ 8/15
STIEBEL, R., Gnr., 3 B.A.C.		14/ 3/17 2y. 9m. Pte.
STILES, A. R. S., Pte., 15 Bn.	W.	14/ 5/15 4y. Sgt.
STILLMAN, A., Pte., 26 Bn.		28/ 6/17 2y. 5m. Pte.
STINGEL, A. A., Pte., 12 Bn.	15 Dvl. Train.	8/12/14
STIPECK, A., Pte., 12 Bn.		20/ 5/15
STIRLING, H., Pte., 12 Bn.		24/ 2/17 2y. 9m. Pte.
STIRLING, J. H., Pte., 1 A.C.H	W., 2 Fd. Amb.	9/ 9/14 y. 1m. Pte.
STIRLING, R. F., Cpl., 40 Bn.	✠ 13/10/17.	26/ 6/16 L.-Cpl. ✠
STIRLING, J. W., Pte., 1 G.S.R. (Assumed Name, Steward, J W.)		29/ 1/18 1y. Pte.
STOCK, T. W., Pte., 40 Bn.		25/ 9/16 11m. Pte.
STOCKDALE, G. E., Pte., 40 Bn.	W.	29/ 7/16 2y. 9m. L.-Cpl.
STOCKOE, G. W., Pte, 2 L.T.M.B.		18/ 8/14 4y. Pte.
STOCKS, P. L., Tpr., 3 L.H.	12 A.B.A.C	2/ 8/15 3y. 4m. Dvr.
STOCKS, V. N., Pte., 12 Bn.		5/ 8/15 1y. 1m. Pte.
STOKES, A. G., Pte., 40 Bn.	2W.	5/10/16 2y 7m. Pte.
STOKES, J. E., Pte., 12 Bn.	2W., 47 Bn.	29/ 7/15
STOKES, J. J., Pte., 40 Bn.	✠ 3/7/17.	16/10/16 Pte. ✠
STOKES, T. A., Cpl., 12 Bn.	2W., Cyc. Bn., O.S. Tng Bde., 12 Bn	7/ 9/15 3y. 7m. Cpl.
STOKES, W. N., Gnr., 3 F.A.B.	10 F.A.B.	13/10/14 3y. Gnr.
STOKES, W. C., Gnr., Arty.		18/10/14
STOKES, W. F., Pte., 40 Bn.	W.	16/10/16 2y. 5m. Pte.
STOKES, W. J., Pte., 15 Bn.	2W.	8/ 6/15 4y. 4m. L.-Cpl.
STONE, A. H., Pte., 12 Bn.	W., M.I.D., 52 Bn.	4/ 8/15 3y. 8m Sgt
STONE, A. G., Pte., 4 M.G. Co.		27/10/14
STONE, G. F., Pte., 40 Bn.	W., A. Prov. Cps.	23/ 9/16 3y. 1m. Pte.
STONE, R. J., Pte., 40 Bn.	W.	23/ 2/16 2y. 1m. Pte.
STONE, T. W., Pte., 12 Bn.	52 Bn., 51 Bn.	28/ 7/15 Pte.
STONE, W. E., Pte., 12 Bn.	W.	19/ 8/14 1y. 9m. Pte.
STONEHOUSE, E. C., Spr., 5 Mnrs	2W., 2 Anzac Tunlrs.	1/ 3/16 3y. Cpl.
STONEHOUSE, P. W., Pte., 4 M.G.C	2 M.G. Bn.	29/ 7/16 3y. 3m. Cpl.
STOPS, A. F., Pte., 12 Bn.	40 Bn., 3 M.G. Bn.	20/12/16 2y. 3m. Pte.
STOPS, F. R., L.-Cpl., 40 Bn.	W	20/ 3/16 2y. 2m. L.-Cpl.
STORAY, A. F., Pte., 15 Bn.	✠ 20/9/15.	18/ 5/15 Pte. ✠
STORAY, F. L., Pte., 12 Bn.	51 Bn.	14/ 9/15 3y. 7m. Pte.
STORAY, P. J., Pte., 12 Bn.	✠ 29/4/17.	5/11/15 Pte. ✠
STORAY, C., Pte., 12 Bn.	✠ 13/9/15.	3/12/14 Pte. ✠
STOREY, J. O., Lieut. 26 Bn.	W.	22/ 5/15 2y Lt.
STOREY, G. A., Dvr., 6 F.A.B.	W., 2 D.A.C.	21/ 8/15 2y. 7m. Dvr.
STOREY, R. C., Cpl., 3 Fd Co Eng	W., 1 Pioneers	27/ 8/14 5y. 1m. Lieut.
STOTT, A. V., Pte., 12 Bn.	W.	9/ 5/16 2y. 11m. Pte.

NAME.	REMARKS.	RANK ON DISCHARGE. ENLISTED. SERVICE.
STOTT, A. A., Pte., 12 Bn.	2W., 40 Bn.	12/ 4/16 3y. 4m. Pte.
STOTT, C. E., Pte., 12 Bn.	W.	12/ 4/16 3y. 5m. Pte.
STOTT, E. H., Pte., 12 Bn.	W., 52Bn.	23/ 2/16 2y. 6m. Pte.
STOTT, H. V., Pte., 12 Bn.	2W., 40 Bn.	12/ 4/16 3y. Pte.
STOTT, L., Pte., 40 Bn.	✣ 13/10/17.	23/ 9/16 Pte. ✣
STOTT, P. S., Cpl., 15 Bn.	3W., D.C.M., 12 Bn.	29/ 9/14 5y. 3m. Lieut.
STOTT, R., Pte., 40 Bn.		23/ 9/16 3y. Pte.
STOTT, R., Pte., 4 M.G. Co.	15 Bn., 42 Bn.	5/ 2/17 2y. 3m. Pte.
STOTT, T. S., Sgt., 12 Bn.	✣	19/ 8/14 Sgt. ✣
STOUGHTON, C. B., Pte. A.M.D. Clerks.		5/ 8/18 6m. Pte.
STRACHAN, C., Sgt., 15 Bn.	W.	24/ 9/14 2y. Sgt.
STRANG, A., Pte., 12 Bn.	✣ 14/6/15.	20/ 8/14 Pte. ✣
STRANGE, J. J. W., Pte., 12 Bn.	W.	3/10/15 4y. 1m. Pte.
STRANGER, G. W., Gnr., 6 F.A.B.	A.F.C.	28/ 9/15 4y. 2m. Lieut.
STRATTON, J W. G., Pte., 26 Bn.	✣ 8/8/16.	15/ 9/15 Pte. ✣
STREET, A. J., Gnr., Arty.	4 D.A.C.	15/ 2/17 2y. 7m. Gnr.
STREET, A. J., Gnr., 6 F.A.B.	4 D.A.C., 10 F.A.B.	7/ 1/16 3y. 6m. Dvr.
STREET, C. W. T., Pte., 12 Bn.		20/ 8/14 1y. 10m. Pte.
STREET, L. A., Spr., 3 Miners.	D.C.M., 3 Tunnlrs.	10/11/15 3y. 7m. Sgt.
STREET, M. B., Pte., 26 Bn.	✣ 5/8/16.	4/ 5/15 Pte. ✣
STREET, W. L., Pte., 12 Bn.	W.	20/ 8/14 2y. 5m. Pte.
STREET, W., Spr., Miners' Co.	W., 3 Pnr. Bn.	10/ 2/16 2y. 6m. Spr.
STRETTON, R. W., Pte., 12 Bn.		18/ 1/15 4y. 3m. Sgt.
STRETTON, W. M. J., Gnr. 6 F.A.B.	W.	7/ 9/15 4y. 1m. Gnr.
STRICKLAND, L. V., Spr., 3 F.C.E.		5/10/15 4y. Spr.
STRIDE, R. V., Pte., 12 Bn.	12 Fd. Co. Engrs.	17/11/16 2y. 8m. Pte.
STRINGER, A. E., Pte., A.M.C.	2W.	15/ 3/16 2y. 8m. Pte.
STROCHNETTER, F., Pte., 12 Bn.	W.	25/10/16 Pte. ✣
STROCHNETTER, W. H., Pte. 15 Bn	✣ 18/9/18.	19/ 9/14 4y 4m C.Q.M.S
STRONACH, W., Pte., 15 Bn.	2W.	5/ 1/15 1y. 9m. Pte.
STRONG, T. H., Pte., 40Bn.		18/ 9/17 1y. 6m. Pte.
STUART, A. J., Pte., 40 Bn.		8/11/16 1y. 10m. Pte.
STUART, A. G., Pte., 12 Bn.		8/ 5/16 3y. 4m. Pte.
STUART, R., Pte., 26 Bn.	12 Bn.	17/ 8/15 4y. 1m. Pte.
STUART, R. S., Pte., 40 Bn.		14/ 3/16
STUART, W. A., Pte., 26 Bn.	12 Bn., ✣ 5/7/16.	5/ 7/15 Pte. ✣
STUART, W. G., Pte., 26 Bn.	✣ 31/5/16.	17/ 8/15 Pte. ✣
STUBBINGS, A. H., Pte., 12 Bn.	W., 2 G.S.R., 12 Bn.	27/ 8/14 5y. 2m. Sgt.
STUBBINGS, C. H., Col.-Sgt., 12 Bn	2W., M.C., 49 Bn.	21/ 8/14 Capt.
STUBBINGS, F. E., Pte., 1 A.C.H.	W., 40 Bn.	19/ 9/14 3y. 5m. L.-Cpl.
STUBBINGS, G. A., Pte., 12 Bn.	52 Bn.	8/ 7/15 4y. 1m. Pte.
STUBBINGS, O. G., Pte., 40 Bn.	9 Fd. Amb.	27/ 9/15 4y. 1m. Pte.
STUBBINGS, W. J., Pte., 12 Bn.	W., 51 Bn.	26/11/14 4y. 8m. Sgt.
STUBBS, A. J. H., Pte., 12 Bn.	W.	15/ 9/15 2y. 9m. Pte.
STUBBS, A B., Pte., 12 Bn.	✣ 2/9/17.	10/ 8/16 Pte. ✣
STUBBS, C. J. S., Gnr., Arty.	8 F.A.B.	1/12/16 2y. 10m. Gnr.
STUBBS, C. H., Pte., 40 Bn.	W.	18/ 4/16 1y. 1m. Pte.
STUBBS, D. L. O., Pte., 12 Bn.	52 Bn., ✣ 4/9/16.	20/ 9/15 Pte. ✣
STUBBS, G. J., Pte., 12 Bn.		14/ 7/16 3y. 2m. Pte.
STUBBS, G. J., Pte., 12 Bn.	W., 4 Pnr. Bn.	25/ 8/15 3y. 8m. Pte.
STUBBS, H. C., Pte., A.A.M.C.	A.F.C.	21/ 5/17
STUBBS, H. R., Pte., 26 Bn.		28/ 8/15 4y. 2m. Pte.
STUBBS, J. F., Pte., 12 Bn.		2/ 8/17 2y 2m. Pte.
STUBBS, L., Pte., 12 Bn.		25/ 8/15 1y. 9m. Pte
STUBBS, M. J., Pte., 12 Bn.	W.	7/ 7/16 2y. 8m. Cpl.
STUBBS, P. J., Pte., 40 Bn.		15/ 3/16 2y. 2m. Pte.
STUBBS, T. V., Gnr., 6 F.A.B.	M.I.D., 15 Bn.	5/ 1/16 3y. 8m. Pte.
STUDDERD, D. K. J., Gnr. 6 F.A.B.		17/ 9/15
STURGEON, R., Pte., 12 Bn.	W.	10/10/16 2y. 11m. Pte.
STURMAN, C. J., Pte., 40 Bn.		2/11/16 1y. 6m. Pte.
STURZAKER, A., Pte., 12 Bn.	52 Bn., 51 Bn.	3/ 8/15 4y. Cp.
STURZAKER, G. H., Cpl., 40 Bn.		10/ 2/16
STURZAKER, L., Pte., 12 Bn.	W.	18/10/16 2y. 11m. Pte.
STURZAKER, L., Pte., 40 Bn.	W.	30/ 3/16 2y. 8m. Pte.
STURZAKER, N., Pte., 12 Bn.	2W.	4/ 4/16 3y. 2m. Cpl.
STURZAKER, W., Pte., 12 Bn.	W.	4/10/16 3y. 2m. Pte.
STUTTERD, D. K. J., 2-Lt., A.F.C.		18/ 9/15
STYLES, L A., Tpr., 3 L H.		7/ 9/15 1y. 1m. Spr.
ST. LEGER, A. W., Lt. Spec. G.S.R.	40 Bn.	12/12/18
STYLES, L., Pte., 40 Bn.	12 Bn., 69 Bn., 40 Bn., ✣ 12/8/18	4/ 3/15 Pte. ✣
SUCKLING, J., Pte., 40 Bn.	✣ 5/10/17.	19/ 7/16 Pte. ✣
SUGDEN, G., Spr., Tunnlrs.	3 Tunnl. Co.	17/ 1/17 2y. 5m. Spr.
SUITOR, L. G., Dvr., 3 F.A.B.	W.	27/ 8/14 4y 6m Saddler
SULLIVAN, C., Tpr., 3 L H.		4/ 2/15 4y. 10m. Cpl.
SULLIVAN, D., Pte., 12 Bn.	M.M., ✣ 8/5/18.	18/11/15 Pte. ✣
SULLIVAN, E. F., Pte., 12Bn.	W., 24 F.A.B., 10 F.A.B.	3/ 7/15 4y. Gnr.
SULLIVAN, G. E., Spr., 3 Miners.		10/ 8/15 2v. 9m. Spr.
SULLIVAN, J. E., Pte., 40 Bn.	W.	31/10/16 2y. 11m. Pte.
SULLIVAN, J., Dvr., 6 F.A.B.	W.	2/ 8/15 3y. 9m. Dvr.
SULLIVAN, L. D., Pte., 40 Bn.	2W.	2/ 2/16 3y. 6m. Pte.
SULLIVAN, R. A., Spr., 5 Miners	5 Tunn. Co., 3 Tunn. Co.	29/ 2/16 3y. 6m. Spr.
SULLIVAN, S. J., Spr., 4 Miners	3 Tunn. Co., ✣ 20/2/17.	14/ 2/16 Spr. ✣
SULLIVAN, T. C., Pte., 40 Bn.		17/ 3/16
SULLIVAN, W. A., Spr., 6 F.C.E.	15 Fd. Co. Engrs.	25/ 9/15 4y. Spr.
SUMMERS, A. C., Pte., 2 G.S.R.		15/ 4/18

TASMANIA'S MUSTER ROLL.

NAME.	REMARKS.	ENLISTED.	RANK ON DISCHARGE. SERVICE.
SUMMERS, A. A., Pte., 12 Bn.	3 Fd. Co. Engrs., ✽ 16/1/18	3/11/14	L.-Cpl. ✽
SUMMERS, A. J., Pte., 3 G.S.R.	12 Bn.	5/ 7/18	1y. 3m. Pte.
SUMMERS, C. H., Pte., 40 Bn.		6/ 3/16	3y. 4m. Pte.
SUMMERS, F. N., Cpl., Rly. Unit	4 B.G.R.O. Co.	25/10/16	2y. 10m. Cpl.
SUMMERS, F., Pte., 12 Bn.	69 Bn.	25/ 8/15	
SUMMERS, H. C. T., Pte., 12 Bn.	W.	27/ 7/15	3y. 10m. Pte.
SUMMERS, R. C., Pte., 12 Bn.	W., 52 Bn., 13 L.T.M.B.	15/ 7/15	4y. 1m. Cpl.
SUMMERS, T. G., Pte., 12 Bn.	52 Bn., ✽ 4/9/16.	4/ 2/16	Pte. ✽
SUMMERS, T. J., Pte., 40 Bn.	2W.	7/ 3/16	3y. 4m. Pte.
SUMNER, C., Pte., 12 Bn.	52 Bn., ✽ 28/3/17.	11/10/15	Pte. ✽
SUMNER, J. H., Gnr., 13 F.A.B.		29/ 9/15	
SUMPTER, H., Pte., 40 Bn.	W.	17/ 5/16	
SUNDERLAND, D., Pte., 4 A.S.C.	3 A. Dvl. Train.	17/ 8/14	4y. 11m. S.-Sgt.
SUNDQUIST, C. H., Pte., 12 Bn.	40 Bn., ✽ 31/8/18.	28/10/15	Pte. ✽
SUTCHKOFF, S., Pte., 12 Bn.	47 Bn., P.O.W.	20/10/16	2y. 6m. Pte.
SUTCLIFFE, C. S., 2nd Lt. 40 Bn.		23/ 5/16	1y 11m. 2-Lt
SUTCLIFFE, C. E., Pte., 40 Bn.	49 Bn.	24/ 5/16	2y. 3m. Pte.
SUTCLIFFE, E. A., Tpr., 3 L.H.	2 F Sqd., Engrs.	2/ 1/18	1y. 9m. Dvr.
SUTCLIFFE, W. A., Pte., 40 Bn.	3W.	15/ 5/16	3y. 4m. Pte.
SUTER, S. I., Lieut. 40 Bn.	M.C.	20/ 1/16	Capt.
SUTTON, A. J., Pte., 40 Bn.	2W.	13/ 7/16	3y. 1m. Pte.
SUTTON, A. L., Pte., A.A.M.C.	13 Fd. Amb.	10/10/16	2y. 11m. Pte
SUTTON, A. E., Pte., 40 Bn.	W.	27/ 3/17	2y. Pte.
SUTTON, B., Pte., 12 Bn.	W., M.M.	26/ 8/14	4y. 5m. Pte.
SUTTON, E. H., Pte., 40 Bn.	✽ 5/10/17.	24/ 5/16	Pte. ✽
SUTTON, E., Pte., 12 Bn.		20/ 8/14	1y. 11m. Pte.
SUTTON, E., Pte., 12 Bn.		9/ 8/16	3y. 2m. Pte.
SUTTON, H. L. A., Gnr., 6 F.A.B.	W., M.I.D.	17/ 8/15	3y. 8m. Sgt.
SUTTON, H. W., Pte., 26 Bn.	W.	1/ 5/15	2y. Pte.
SUTTON, P. V. H., Pte., 12 Bn.	✽ 23/4/18.	10/12/14	Pte. ✽
SUTTON, R. V., Tpr., 3 L.H.	5 D.A.C.	21/ 7/15	
SUTTON, R. C., Pte., 12 Bn.		2/12/14	
SUTTON, W., Pte., 4 M.G.Co.	M.M., 4 Dvl. M.G. Co., 12 M.G Co	8/ 7/16	3y. 2m. Pte.
SUTTON, W., Pte., 26 Bn.	52 Bn.	18/ 5/15	2y. 6m. Pte.
SWAIN, C. R., Pte., 15 Bn.	26 Bn., ✽ 2/3/17.	3/ 8/15	Pte. ✽
SWAIN, R., Pte., 40 Bn.	✽ 8/1/17.	13/ 3/16	Pte. ✽
SWAIN, W. J., Pte., 26 Bn.	12 Bn., ✽ 23-26/7/16.	17/ 8/15	Pte. ✽
SWAN, A. G., Pte., 40 Bn.	12 Bn.	16/ 2/16	2y. 8m. Pte.
SWAN, A., Pte., 40 Bn.	W.	3/ 4/16	2y 3m. Pte.
SWAN, B., Pte., 1 G.S.R.	40 Bn.	4/ 2/18	1y. 9m. Pte.
SWAN, E. T., Gnr., Arty.	14 F.A.B.	22/ 9/16	3y. 1m. Gnr.
SWAN, R. C., Cpl., 12 Bn.	3 A.L.R.O. Co.	5/ 6/15	4y. 3m. Spr
SWAN, R. A., C.S.M. 40 Bn.	W.	29/ 8/16	2y. 10m. Lieut.
SWAN, W. J., Pte., 40 Bn.		1/ 2/16	2y. 5m. Pte.
SWAN, W. N., Pte., 40 Bn.	W.	16/ 2/16	3y. 3m. Pte.
SWEENEY, D., Pte., 26 Bn.	✽ 8/11/16.	15/ 5/15	Pte. ✽
SWEENEY, E. J., Pte., A.C.H.	W., 14 Fd. Amb.	5/12/14	4y. 7m. Pte.
SWEENEY, E. R., Tptr., 3 F.A.B.	✽ 11/8/18.	27/ 8/14	Dvr. ✽
SWEENEY, E. S., Pte., 40 Bn.	W.	11/ 4/16	3y. 1m. Pte.
SWEENEY, M., Spr., 8 F.C.E.	W., 7 Fd. Co. Engrs.	21/ 2/16	3y 4m Spr.
SWEENEY, N. D., Pte., 26 Bn.	12 Bn., ✽ 19-22/8/16.	2/ 9/15	Pte. ✽
SWEENEY, O. W., Pte., 40 Bn.	W., M.I.D.	27/ 4/16	3y. 6m. Cpl.
SWEENEY, S. F., Pte., 12 Bn.	W.	14/ 8/16	3y 1m Pte.
SWEENEY, W. F., Pte., A.A.M.C.	2 Fd. Amb.	1/11/17	Pte.
SWEET, A. C., Pte., 12 Bn.	2W.	14/ 4/16	3y. 5m. L.-Cpl.
SWEET, C. J., Pte., 12 Bn.	52 Bn., 1 A.A.H.	9/ 8/15	4y. 5m. L.-Cpl.
SWEET, W. T., Pte., 4 M.G. Co.		18/ 9/16	1y 3m Pte.
SWEETMAN, A., Pte., 12 Bn.	W., 52 Bn., ✽ 16/7/17.	1/ 8/15	Pte. ✽
SWEETMAN, R., Pte., 40 Bn.	W., 49 Bn.	3/ 5/16	2y. 5m. Pte.
SWIFTE, G. L., Pte., 12 Bn.		10/12/17	1y. 10m. Pte.
SWIFT, J. A., Sgt 12 Bn.	52 Bn., ✽ 3-4/9/16.	19/ 8/15	Sgt. ✽
SWIFT, J. H. W., Cpl., 12 Bn.	W., 52 Bn.	18/ 8/15	2y. 10m. Cpl.
SWIFT, L. R. W., Pte., 1 G.S.R.	A.A. Pay Cps.	28/ 8/17	2y. 3m. Pte.
SWIFT, T. W. W., Pte., 12 Bn.	✽ 25-28/4/15.	16/ 1/14	Pte. ✽
SWINDELLS, A. W., Pte., 7 Fd Aml	13 Fd. Amb.	24/ 3/15	4y. 3m. Pte.
SWINDELLS, R. O. C., Pte., 40 Bn	2W.	23/ 9/16	2y. 3m. Cpl.
SWINTON, B. W., Pte., 1 A.C.H.	W.	21/ 9/14	1y. 6m. Pte.
SWINTON, C. H., Pte., 40 Bn.		2/ 3/16	3y. 10m. Lieut.
SWINTON, D. L., Pte., 7 Fd Amb	14 Fd. Amb.	15/ 2/15	4v. 4m. Pte.
SWINTON, H. E., Pte., 4 M.G. Co.	11 Fd. Co. Engrs	3/ 7/16	Dvr.
SWINTON, H. Cpl., 40 Bn.	W.	2/ 3/16	2y. 3m. L.-Sgt.
SWINTON, N. G., Gnr., Siege Art		7/ 6/15	4y 6m. Gnr.
SWINTON, R. C., Dvr., 7 Fd. Amb	13 Fd. Amb.	25/ 2/15	4y. 4m. Dvr.
SYKES, R., Pte., 4 M.G. Co.	2 M.G. Co.	3/ 1/17	1y. 5m. Pte.
SYLVESTER, T. G., Pte., 40 Bn.	W.	1/ 2/16	2y. 2m. Pte.
SYMES, E., Pte., 40 Bn.	W.	14/10/16	2y. 11m. Pte.
SYMES, N. H., Pte., 1 A.C.H		25/11/14	
SYMES, O. R., Pte., 1 G.S.R.	12 G.S.R.	5/11/17	
SYMMONDS, V. J., Pte., 12 Bn.	W., 51 Bn.	12/ 9/15	3y. 11m. Pte.
SYMONDS, J., Pte., 26 Bn.	12 Bn.	10/ 8/15	2v. 5m. Pte.
SYMONS, A. W. J., Pte., 26 Bn.	✽ 20/1/16.	11/ 8/15	Pte. ✽
SYMONS, G. M., Pte., 12 Bn.	✽ 20/5/18.	23/10/16	Pte. ✽
SYNNOTT, W. T., Pte., 12 Bn.	2 A Div. Traffic Control.	16/11/15	4y Pte.
TABER, A. C., Pte., 40 Bn.	W. ✽ 4/10/17.	17/ 5/16	Pte. ✽
TAFFIN, C. M., Gnr. Arty.	36 H.A.G.	1/ 9/15	4y 2m. Gnr.
TAFFIN, V. R., Cpl. 6 F.A.P.	W.	1/ 9/15	3y 11m. Bdr.

350 TASMANIA'S WAR RECORD, 1914-1918.

NAME.	REMARKS.	RANK ON DISCHARGE. ENLISTED. SERVICE.
TAGGART, D. O., Pte. 15 Bn.	45 Bn., 26 A.A.S.C.	4/ 8/15 4y, Dvr.
TAIT, D. R. R., L.-Cpl. 6 Fd. Co.	W., re-enlisted as Munition Worker.	5/ 8/15 2y 4m, Cpl.
TAIT, L., Pte. 15 Bn.	✻	8/ 1/15 Pte. ✻
TAIT, P. G., Dvr. Arty.		3/11/15 3y 11m, Dvr.
TALBOT, A. E., Pte. 26 Bn.	✻ 29/7/16.	26/ 7/17 Pte. ✻
TALBOT, D., Pte. 12 Bn.	W., 40 Bn.	5/ 4/16 3y 4m, Pte.
TALBOT, G. F., Pte. 12 Bn.	✻ 13/4/17	19/ 8/14 W.O. ✻
TALBOT, R. Wm., Pte. 12 Bn.	52 Bn. ✻ 4/9/16.	29/ 5/15 Cpl. ✻
TALBOT, T. A., Pte. 26 Bn.	2W., 4 M.G. Co., 4 A.M.G.B.	19/ 7/15 4y 1m, Pte.
TAMLYN, C. P. H., Pte. 12 Bn.	3 Inf. Bde. Headquarters	28/ 6/15 4y 2m, Pte.
TAMLYN, J. A., Pte. 12 Bn.	W., 1 Div. Sal. Co., 12 Bn., 1 Sal. Co.	18/ 5/15 4y 3m, Pte.
TANG, E. O., Pte. 40 Bn.	W., M.M. ✻ 12/8/18.	21/ 7/16 Pte. ✻
TANNER, C., Spr. Wireless.	Cavalry D Sig. Sqn.	5/10/16 1y 5m, Spr.
TANNER, H. J., Pte. 26 Bn.	W., 12 Bn.	11/ 8/15 2y, Pte.
TANSLEY, R., Pte. 15 Bn.	12 Bn.	18/12/14 1y 4m, L.-Sgt
TAPNER, F., Pte. 40 Bn.	W.	30/ 3/16 3y 1m, Dvr.
TAPNER, W., Pte. 40 Bn.	W. ✻ 4/10/17.	30/ 3/16 Pte. ✻
TARGETT, A., Tpr. 3 L.H.	W.	18/ 1/15 4y 8m, Tpr.
TARGET, E. A., Sgt. 12 Bn.	51 Bn.	20/ 1/16 1y 10m, Sgt.
TARGETT, G. J., Far. Cpl. 3 L.H.		28/ 9/15 4y, Far. Cpl.
TARGETT, R. H., Pte. 40 Bn.	✻ 25/1/17.	20/ 3/16 Pte. ✻
TARR, R. H., Pte. 40 Bn.		15/ 3/16 1y 2m, Pte.
TARRANT, A. E., Pte 12 Bn.	13 M.G. Co. ✻ 25/9/17	11/ 8/15 Pte. ✻
TARRANT, A. E., Pte. 12 Bn.	✻ 11/11/15.	22/ 8/14 L.-Cpl. ✻
TATE, J., Pte. A.M.C.	8 Fd. Amb.	17/ 4/16 3y 5m, Pte.
TATE, J. A., Pte. 40 Bn.		27/ 3/16 1y 7m, Pte.
TATHAM, G. E., C.Q.M.S. 40 Bn.		24/ 2/16 1y 6m, C.Q.M.S
TAYLOR, A. E., Pte. 40 Bn.	W. ✻ 17/7/18.	10/11/16 Pte. ✻
TAYLOR, A. J. G., Pte. 15 Bn.	M.M., 47 Bn. ✻ 12/10/17.	31/ 8/15 Pte. ✻
TAYLOR, A. E., Pte. 26 Bn.	W.	15/ 9/15 2y 3m, Pte.
TAYLOR, A. E., Gnr. 4 M.G. Co	W., 15 M.G. Co., 11 M.G. Co	6/10/16 2y 11m, Gnr.
TAYLOR, A. A., Cpl. 40 Bn.	✻ 13/10/17	27/ 6/16 L.-Sgt. ✻
TAYLOR, A., Munition Worker.		
TAYLOR, A. J., Spr. Miners.	W., 5 Tun. Co., 2 Tun. Co.	23/ 3/16 3y 7m, Spr.
TAYLOR, A. J. W., Pte. 40 Bn.	✻ 17/7/17.	28/ 3/16 Pte. ✻
TAYLOR, B. L., Pte. 12 Bn.	✻ 10/5/15.	29/ 8/14 Pte. ✻
TAYLOR, C. H., Pte 26 Bn.	9 Fd. Co. Engrs.	29/ 9/15 2y 2m, Spr.
TAYLOR, D., Gnr. Arty.		9/ 3/17
TAYLOR, E. A., Pte. 40 Bn.	51 Bn., 12 Bn., 1 A.G.H.	8/ 3/16
TAYLOR, E. A., Pte. 26 Bn.		18/ 5/15
TAYLOR, E. A., Pte. 12 Bn.	W., 69 Bn., 12 Bn. ✻ 15/3/18.	9/12/15 Pte. ✻
TAYLOR, E. R., Gnr. Arty.	105 How. Bty.	2/10/15
TAYLOR, F. W., Pte. 12 Bn.	W.	6/ 2/15 3y 2m, Pte.
TAYLOR, F. H., Pte. 40 Bn.	W. ✻ 31/3/18.	24/ 2/16 2y 1m, Pte.
TAYLOR, G. C. R., Pte. 12 Bn.	W., 52 Bn.	28/10/15 3y 1m, Pte.
TAYLOR, G. H., Pte. 12 Bn.	✻ 27/2/17.	8/ 5/16 Pte. ✻
TAYLOR, G. L., Pte. A.M.C.	8 Fd. Amb.	19/10/16 3y 1m, Pte.
TAYLOR, G. W., Pte. 12 Bn.	W.	11/ 1/15 4y 4m, Pte.
TAYLOR, G., Pte. 15 Bn.	✻ 8/8/15.	30/12/14 Pte. ✻
TAYLOR, G., Pte. 3 G.S.R.	12 Bn.	27/ 5/18 1y 7m, Cpl.
TAYLOR, H. S., Cpl. A. Pos. Cps.		22/10/15 4y, Cpl.
TAYLOR, H., Pte. 1 G.S.R.		12/ 2/18
TAYLOR, H., Dvr. 8 Fd. Co. Engrs		24/ 9/15
TAYLOR, H. C., M.W., N. and L. Unit.		
TAYLOR, I. C. E., Pte. 12 Bn.	W., 3 L.T.M. Bty.	4/12/14 4y 4m, Pte.
TAYLOR, I. G., Pte. 12 Bn.	W.	17/ 1/16 3y 9m, Pte.
TAYLOR, J. W., Pte. 40 Bn.	49 Bn.	19/ 4/16 3y 8m, Pte.
TAYLOR, J. A., Pte. 12 Bn.		8/ 5/16 3y 5m, Pte.
TAYLOR, J., Pte. 12 Bn.		21/12/15
TAYLOR, J. R., Pte. 12 Bn.		2/ 9/14 5y 2m, Lt.
TAYLOR, J., Spr. 8 Fd. Co. Engrs.		13/ 1/16 4y, Spr.
TAYLOR, V. K. C., Cpl. 26 Bn.	W., 51 Bn., 12 Bn.	23/ 8/15 4y 2m, Sgt.
TAYLOR, L., Tpr. 1 Cam. Cps.		2/12/14 2y 1m, Tpr.
TAYLOR, L. T., Bdr. Arty.	W., 3 D.A.C.	21/ 1/16 3y 9m, Bdr.
TAYLOR, M., Pte. 12 Bn.	W., 1 Pnrs. Bn.	5/ 7/15 2y, Pte.
TAYLOR, W. K. H., Pte. 12 Bn.	W.	17/ 9/17 1y 6m, Pte.
TAYLOR, M. H., Gnr. Arty.	W., 4 F.A.B.	19/10/16 2y 11m, Gnr.
TAYLOR, O. N. W., Spr. Miners.	W., 3 A.T.C.	28/10/15 4y 1m, Spr.
TAYLOR, O., Pte. 3 G.S.R.		7/ 6/18
TAYLOR, R. A. I., Pte. 12 Bn.	W., 52 Bn. ✻ 5/4/18	11/11/15 Pte. ✻
TAYLOR, T., Pte 40 Bn.	3W.	19/ 9/16 2y 7m, Pte.
TAYLOR, V. E, Pte. 12 Bn.	1 A.G.H.	21/10/13 4y 2m, Pte.
TAYLOR, W. E., Tpr. 3 L.H.		21/11/17 1y 9m, Tpr.
TAYLOR, W., Dvr. 3 F.A.B.		27/ 8/14 4y 5m, Dvr.
TAYLOR, W. H., Spr. 5 Tun. Co.	A.E. and M.M.U.	22/ 2/16 3y 5m, Spr.
TAYLOR, W. S., Pte. 12 Bn.		26/ 8/15 4y, L.-Cpl.
TAYLOR, S. C., Cpl. 40 Bn.	M.S M.	2/ 7/15
TAYLOR, W. Y., Pte. 15 Bn.	✻ 22/8/16.	30/ 8/15 Pte. ✻
TEAKLE, F. A., Pte. 12 Bn.	M I D.	28/12/14 4y 11m, Capt.
TEDMAN, E. J., Pte. 1 A. Tunlrs.		2/ 9/16 2y 3m, Pte.
TEGG, C. S., Pte. 12 Bn.		24/ 8/14 4y 11m, Dvr.
TELFORD, R., Dvr. 3 F.A.B.	W.	27/ 8/14
TEMPLAR, P. C., Tpr. 3 L.H.	W., 1 F.A.B. ✻ 15/10/17.	6/ 3/15 Gnr. ✻

TASMANIA'S MUSTER ROLL. 351

NAME.	REMARKS.	ENLISTED.	RANK ON DISCHARGE. SERVICE.
TEMPLAR, R., Pte. 12 Bn.	W., 6 Bn.	12/10/16	2y 6m, Pte.
TEMPLAR, R. E., Pte. 15 Bn.	W., 47 Bn.	2/ 9/15	3y, Pte.
TEMPLE, C., Pte. 12 Bn.	52 Bn.	11/ 1/16	3y 2m, Pte.
TEMPLE, C. W., Pte. 15 Bn.	✠ 31/5/15.	29/10/14	Pte. ✠
TEMPLE, J. L., Spr. Tunlers.	1 Tun. Co.	26/10/16	3y-1m, Spr.
TEMPLER, R., Pte. 12 Bn.	6 Bn.	12/10/16	2y 6m, Pte.
TEMPLETON, C., Pte. 40 Bn.	2W.	3/10/16	2y 1m, Pte.
TEMPLETON, C., Cpl. 12 Bn.	2W., 52 Bn., 49 Bn.	11/12/14	4y 7m, Cpl.
TEMPLETON, L. J., Gnr 4 M.G. Co	W.	4/ 8/16	2y 8m, Gnr.
TENNANT, A. J., Pte. 12 Bn.		21/ 6/17	1y 7m, Pte.
TENNANT, J. M., Dvr. 3 L.H.	W., 4 L.H. Fd. Amb., A.M.C.	20/ 8/17	2y 2m, Dvr.
TENNANT, R. J., Pte. 12 Bn.		24/10/16	1y 11m, Pte.
TERRY, A. J., Dvr. Arty.	W., 6 F.A.B.	1/11/15	3y 11m, Dvr.
TERRY, E. C., Pte. 12 Bn.	✠ 14/8/15.	3/12/14	Pte. ✠
TERRY, E. E., Pte. 12 Bn.	W., M.M. ✠ 25/8/18.	9/ 8/15	Lt. ✠
TERRY, E. J., Pte. 3 Cyc. Co.		3/ 4/16	
TERRY, G. P., Pte. 12 Bn		1/10/17	2y, Pte.
TERRY, H., Pte. 40 Bn.	W.	8/11/16	2y 10m, Pte.
TERRY, K. R., Pte. 12 Bn.		26/ 8/15	1y 4m, Pte.
TERRY, K. J., Pte. 12 Bn.	W., 3 Inf. Bde. M.G. Co.	24/ 8/14	4y 6m, L.-Cpl.
TERRY, L. M., Pte. 26 Bn.	W., 31 Bn.	6/ 4/15	2y 6m, Pte.
TERRY, L. M., Pte 40 Bn	✠ 13/10/17.	3/ 7/16	Pte. ✠
TERRY, R. F., Gnr. Arty.	W., 13 F.A.B.	6/12/15	3y 9m, Gnr.
TERRY, T., Pte. 40 Bn	✠ 4/10/17.	8/11/16	Pte. ✠
TERRY, T., Pte. 12 Bn.	W.	24/ 8/15	
TERRY, W., Pte. 40 Bn.	2W.	10/10/16	2y 11m, Pte.
TERRY, W. G., Pte. 15 Bn.	W.	21/ 9/14	2y, Pte.
TEESDALE, J., Pte. 7 Fd. Amb.		14/ 4/15	
TESSIER, A. N., Gnr. 2 G.S.R.	14 F.A.B.	22/ 4/18	1y 6m, Gnr.
TEW, C. G. F., Tpr. 3 L.H.		30/ 4/17	2y 2m, Tpr.
TETLOW, R. A., Pte. 26 Bn.		27/ 8/15	
THEAKER, N., Pte. 7 Fd. Amb	W., 13 Fd. Amb. ✠ 26/10/18.	17/ 3/15	Sgt. ✠
THICKENS, W., Pte. 15 Bn.	✠ 8/8/15.	7/12/14	Pte. ✠
THIRKELL, G. L. A., 2-Lt., 3 F.C.E.		20/ 8/14	
THIRKELL, R. M. W., Lieut. 12 Bn.	W., M.B.E., M.I.D.	4/ 8/15	
THOLLAR, W. H., Pte. 12 Bn.	✠ 8/10/17.	28/ 3/16	Pte. ✠
THOMAS, A. G., Pte 3 G.S.R.	12 Bn.	3/ 7/15	4y 3m, Pte.
THOMAS, A. G., Pte. 12 Bn.		23/ 8/15	1y 2m, Pte.
THOMAS, A. P., Pte 2 G.S.R.	12 Bn.	14/ 6/18	1y 5m, Pte.
THOMAS, A. E., Pte. 12 Bn.	W., 40 Bn.	21/11/16	2y 1m, Pte.
THOMAS, A. G., Spr. Miners.	3 Tun. Co.	29/ 2/16	
THOMAS, A. J., Pte 12 Bn		22/ 9/14	
THOMAS, A. J. S., Gnr. Ar.y.	3 F.A.B.	1/11/16	2y 10m. Gnr.
THOMAS, A. J., Pte. 26 Bn.		7/ 8/15	
THOMAS, E. H., Pte. 12 Bn.	52 Bn.	13/ 7/15	
THOMAS, C., Gnr. Arty.		18/10/16	
THOMAS, F. R., Pte. 26 Bn.	W., O.S.T. Bde., 12 Bn.	6/ 8/15	3y 11m, Sgt.
THOMAS, E., Pte. 2 G.S.R.	✠ 23-25/7/16.	2/ 4/18	1y 5m, Pte.
THOMAS, G. H., Pte. 12 Bn.	2W., 52 Bn.	25/ 5/15	Pte. ✠
THOMAS, G. J., Pte. 12 Bn	A.M.C., 3 L.H.	11/ 1/16	1y 10m, Pte.
THOMAS, H. A. R., Tpr. 4 G.S.R.	✠ 4/6/16.	1/ 3/18	1y 5m, Tpr.
THOMAS, H., Pte. 12 Bn.	M.S.M.	10/12/14	Pte. ✠
THOMAS, H., Pte 15 Bn.	✠ 5-8/5/17.	7/ 9/15	4y 1m. S.S. Ck
THOMAS, H. E., Pte. 12 Bn.	52 Bn., 4 M.G. Co. ✠ 11/4/17.	26/10/15	Pte. ✠
THOMAS, H. W., Pte. 12 Bn.		30/12/15	Pte. ✠
THOMAS, J G., Pte. 12 Bn.		24/ 2/16	1y 9m, Pte.
THOMAS, J. L., Gnr. Arty.		12/ 3/17	1y 1m, Gnr.
THOMAS, J., Spr. Miners.		18/11/15	
THOMAS, J. McD., Gnr 6 F.A.B.		9/ 9/15	4y 3m, Dvr.
THOMAS, K., Pte. 40 Bn.	3W.	21/ 3/16	3y 2m, Pte.
THOMAS, L. R., Spr. Engr. Dtls.		16/ 1/17	2y 10m, Spr.
THOMAS, L. A., Pte. 12 Bn.	52 Bn. ✠ 24/4/18.	6/ 8/15	Cpl. ✠
THOMAS, M., Pte 1 A.C.H.		18/ 9/14	2y 2m, Pte.
THOMAS, N. L., 2 Cpl. Railway	A.B.G.R.O. Co.	11/ 1/17	2y 9m, Cpl.
THOMAS, N. H., Pte. 12 Bn.	W., 52 Bn., M G. Dtls., 5 M.G Bn.	22/ 6/15	4y 1m, Pte.
THOMAS, P. H., Pte. 1 A.C.H.		16/10/14	
THOMAS, T. N., Pte. 12 Bn.	P.O.W.	23/ 8/15	
THOMAS, V. S., Pte. 26 Bn.		13/ 3/15	2y, Pte.
THOMAS, D. W., Gnr 3 F.A.B.	4D.A.C., 111 How. Bty.	21/ 6/15	3y 4m, Gnr.
THOMLINSON, R. B., Pte. 26 Bn		11/ 5/15	
THOMPSON, P. C., 2-Lt. 12 Bn.		25/ 6/17	2y 3m, Major.
THOMPSON, C. G., Capt. A.A.M.C.	W.	10/10/16	1y 8m, Lieut.
THOMPSON, A. A., Pte. 40 Bn.	W.	18/ 4/16	2y 11m, Pte.
THOMPSON, A. R., Pte. 15 Bn.		31/ 8/15	1y, Pte.
THOMPSON, A .H. J., Gnr. 6 F.A.B.		14/ 9/15	2y 10m, Cpl.
THOMPSON, A., Spr. 8 Fd. Co. Engrs.	15 Fd. Co. Engrs.	31/ 1/16	3y 3m.
THOMPSON, B. H., Pte. 1 A.C.H.	W.	9/ 9/14	1y 7m. Pte.
THOMPSON, B. J, Gnr 12 Bn	Arty. Dtls., 2 D.A.C.	23/12/14	4y 6m. Gnr.
THOMPSON, C., R.Q.M.S. 40 Bn		24/ 2/17	2y 1m, R.Q.M.S
THOMPSON, C. R., Pte. 40 Bn		15/ 3/16	3y, Pte.
THOMPSON, C. R., Pte. 26 Bn		20/ 7/15	4y 6m, Pte.
THOMPSON, C. T., Cpl. 12 Bn.	W., 40 Bn.	25/ 8/14	
THOMPSON, C., Pte. 2 A.G.H.	M.M., 5 Fd. Amb.	1/10/15	4y, Pte.

352 TASMANIA'S WAR RECORD, 1914-1918.

NAME.	REMARKS.	RANK ON DISCHARGE. ENLISTED. SERVICE.
THOMPSON, C. G., Pte. 12 Bn.	W.	23/ 3/14 1y 9m, Pte.
THOMPSON, E. G., Wheeler Sgt. 3 F.A.B	M.C., C. de Guerre, M.I.D., A.O.C., 3 F.A.B.	27/ 8/14 4y 8m. W.O.
THOMPSON, E. G. G., Spr. Engrs.		8/11/16
THOMPSON, E. J., Gnr. 1 G.S.R.	6 F.A.B.	1/ 3/18 1y 7m, Gnr.
THOMPSON, E. J., Pte. 1 G.S.R.	Arty. Dtls., 40 Bn.	1/ 3/19 1y 7m, Pte.
THOMPSON, F., Pte. 12 Bn.		28/ 9/16
THOMPSON, F., Pte. 40 Bn.	15 Bn.	20/ 3/16
THOMPSON, G., Pte. 40 Bn.	2 M.V. Sec., 1 A.V. Evac. St.	15/ 3/16 3y 4m, S.-Sm.
THOMPSON, H. L., Pte. 12 Bn.	2W., 40 Bn. ✠16/11/18.	4/ 7/16 Pte. ✠
THOMPSON, J., Pte. 40 Bn.	W.	10/10/16
THOMPSON, J., Pte. 26 Bn.	W., 52 Bn.	20/ 9/15 2y 2m, Pte.
THOMPSON, J. P., Pte. 12 Bn.	1 Pnr. Bn.	27/ 5/15
THOMPSON, L. B., Bdr. 3 F.A.B	W., 4 F.A.B.	27/ 7/15 2y 7m, Bdr.
THOMPSON, L., Gnr. Arty.		19/ 1/19 2y 1m, Gnr.
THOMPSON, L. F., Gnr. D.A.C.	6 F.A.B., 106 How. Bty.	17/ 8/15 2y, Gnr.
THOMPSON, L., Spr. Tunnellers	3 Tunnelling Co.	4/ 1/17 2y 5m, Spr.
THOMPSON, M. E., Gnr. Arty.		29/ 9/15 2y 11m, Gnr.
THOMPSON, N., Pte. 12 Bn.	10 F.A.B. ✠ 6/11/18.	27/12/15 S.-Smith ✠
THOMPSON, N. H., Pte. 26 Bn.		10/ 5/15
THOMPSON, O. J., Gnr. Arty.		22/11/15
THOMPSON, R. O., Pte. 12 Bn.	W., 52 Bn.	17/ 1/16 1y 5m, Pte.
THOMPSON, R. C., Pte. 40 Bn.		26/ 4/16 3y 6m, Pte.
THOMPSON, R. O., Tpr. 3 L.H.	W.	17/ 6/15 1y 7m, Spr.
THOMPSON, R. R., Pte. 26 Bn.		16/ 4/15 1y 4m, Pte.
THOMPSON, T. W., Pte. 40 Bn.		16/10/16
THOMPSON, W. L., Pte. 40 Bn.	59 Bn. ✠ 15/1/17.	4/ 1/16 L.-Cpl. ✠
THOMPSON, W., Pte. 12 Bn.		21/ 8/14
THOMPSON, W., Pte. 12 Bn.		1/12/14 4y 3m, Pte.
THOMPSON, W., Pte. 40 Bn.	2 A.M.T. Bty.	27/ 2/17 2y 8m, Pte.
THOMPSON, W., Pte. 12 Bn.	2W., 10 F.A.B.	22/ 9/15 3y 8m, Gnr.
THOMPSON, W., Pte. 15 Bn	✠ 31/5/15.	1/11/14 Pte. ✠
THOMPSON, W. J., Pte. 12 Bn.		4/ 8/15 2y 9m, Pte.
THOMPSON, H. M. D., Cpl. 40 Bn.		23/ 3/16 2y 3m, Sgt.
THOMSON, A. F. R., 4 Divl. Arty.	12 F.A.B.	Major.
THOMSON, H. H., Pte. 1 A.D. Train		13/ 1/15 4y 7m, Pte.
THORNBURN, A. J., Gnr. Engrs.	.	5/ 1/16 3y 4m, Sgt.
THORNE, A. E., Pte. 26 Bn.	W., 1 Pnrs.	3/ 8/15 3y 11m, Pte.
THORNE, B. G., Spr. Tunlers.	W., 2 Tun. Co.	25/ 5/14 4y 11m. Spr.
THORNE, A. J., Pte. 12 Bn.	✠ 17/9/15	1/ 6/15 Pte. ✠
THORNE, C. B., Pte. 12 Bn.	W. ✠ 6/1/17.	26/ 8/14 Cpl. ✠
THORNE, C. A., Pte 26 Bn.		9/ 3/15 4y 4m, Pte.
THORNE, D. C., Dvr 26 Bn.		22/ 6/15 4y 4m, Dvr.
THORNE, G. F., Pte. 26 Bn.	✠ 29/7/16.	21/ 4/15 Pte. ✠
THORNE, H. W., Pte. 12 Bn.		31/ 8/16 1y 8m, Pte.
THORNE, H. N., Pte 12 Bn.	17 Fd. Amb., 4 Fd. Amb.	16/10/16 3y, Pte.
THORNE, H C, Pte. 26 Bn	✠ 27/6/18.	4/ 3/15 Pte. ✠
THORNE, J. E., Pte. 40 Bn.	W., 26 Bn.	18/ 4/16 3y, Pte.
THORNE, L. W., Pte. 40 Bn		26/ 2/17 2y 1m, Pte.
THORNE, R. D., Dvr. 12 Bn.	W., 3 G.S.R., 10 F.A.B.	2/12/14 4y 5m, Dvr.
THORNE, R. E., Pte. 40 Bn.	W.	21/ 2/16 3y 4m, Pte.
THORNE, W., Pte. Arty.		12/ 5/17
THORNTON, A. G., Cpl. 12 Bn.	3W.	28/ 8/15
THORNTON, C. W., Pte. 40 Bn.	W.	3/10/16 2y 11m, Pte.
THORNTON, J., Munition Worker		
THORNTON, M. J., Spr. 2 Tunlrs.	W.	16/ 3/16 1y 4m, Spr.
THORNTON, W. J., Gnr. 4 M.G. Co	15 Bn., 4 M.G. Co.	8/ 3/19 3m, Gnr.
THORPE, C. J., Dvr. 8 Fd. Co. Engrs.		2/ 3/16
THORPE, E. G., Pte. 26 Bn.	✠ 5/8/16	23/ 6/15 Pte. ✠
THORPE, G. W., Sgt. 12 Bn.		22/ 3/14 8m, Sgt.
THORPE, R. S., Cpl. 12 Bn.	52 Bn. ✠ 13/9/16.	20/ 8/15 Cpl. ✠
THORPE, T. R., Pte. 40 Bn		14/ 3/16 1y, Pte.
THORP, F., Tpr. 3 L.H.	3 L.H.	19/11/17 1y 10m, Tpr.
THOP, G. A., Sgt. 15 Bn.		16/ 9/14 5y 2m, Lt.
THORS, C. R., Pte. 26 Bn.	2W., 2 Pnrs.	24/ 6/15 3y 10m, Pte.
THOW, J. F., Pte. 40 Bn	W.	14/ 3/16 3y 4m, Pte.
THUMMLER, W. H., Gnr. Arty.	9 Bty. A.F.A.	12/10/16 2y 11m, Gnr.
THUNDER, P., Pte. 12 Bn.	40 Bn	20/ 9/16 2y 6m, Pte.
THURLEY, E. H., Pte. 15 Bn.		12/ 1/15 11m, Pte.
THURLEY, S., Pte. 12 Bn.		20/ 9/14
THURLEY, W. S., Sgt. 12 Bn.	.W.	1/ 9/14 3y 9m, Sgt.
THURLEY, W. L., Pte. 12 Bn.	2W., 52 Bn.	8/ 2/16 1y 9m, Pte.
THURLOW, W., Pte. 12 Bn.	2W.	1/ 8/15 3y 8m. L.-Cpl.
THURSTANS, A. C., 2-Lt., 40 Bn.	✠ 5/4/18.	2/ 5/16 2-Lieut. ✠
THURSTAN, B., Dvr. 3 L.H.	5 D.A.C.	31/ 8/15
THURSTON, C. G., L/Cpl. 3 Cyc. Co.	Engr. Dtls., 1 Cyc. Bn.	5/ 4/16
THYNNE, J. E., Pte. 12 Bn.		7/ 7/16 3y 2m, Pte.
TIDEY, C. R., Spr. 8 F.C.E.	W., 15 Fd. Co. Engrs.	28/ 4/16 3y 2m, Spr.
TIFFIN, C., Pte. 12 Bn.	W., 49 Bn. ✠ 19/5/19.	7/10/15 Pte. ✠
TIFOOT, A., Gnr. 3 F.A.B.		6/ 8/15
TILLACK, A. W., Pte 12 Bn.	W.	24/10/16 2y 6m, Pte.
TILLACK, K., Spr 3 F.C.E.	✠ 12/9/18.	8/ 8/17 Spr. ✠
TILLACK. L. C., Pte 26 Bn.	W. ✠ 3/10/18.	6/ 3/15 Pte. ✠

TASMANIA'S MUSTER ROLL.

NAME.	REMARKS.	RANK ON DISCHARGE. ENLISTED. SERVICE.
TILLEY, A. J., Pte. 12 Bn.	✠ 6–10/4/17.	24/ 8/14 Pte. ✠
TILLEY, E. B., Pte. 12 Bn	W., 52 Bn.	27/ 1/16 2y 10m.
TILLEY, L. W. M., Pte. 40 Bn.	W.	21/ 3/16 3y 4m, Pte.
TILLEY, L. J., Tpr. 3 L.H.		19/ 9/14 2y 2m.
TILYARD, H. C., Pte. 40 Bn.	W. ✠ 28/3/18.	2/10/16 Pte. ✠
TIMBS, H. R. J., Pte 7 Fd. Amb		20/ 4/15 9m, Pte.
TIMOTHY, C. B., Pte. 12 Bn.	2W., M.M.	20/ 8/14 4m, 7m, Sgt.
TIMOTHY, N. M., Pte. 12 Bn.	28 Bn.	25/ 6/15 3y 10m, Sgt.
TIMOTHY, W. J., Pte. 12 Bn.	✠ 7/5/17.	29/ 5/16 Pte. ✠
TIPPER, F. L., Spr. Miners.		24/ 2/16
TIPPETT, A. E. A., Pte 15 Bn.	✠ 31/5/15.	1/10/14 Sgt. ✠
TIPPETT, A. S., Pte. 40 Bn.	2W.	7/ 6/15 3y 5m, Pte.
TIPPET, M. L., Pte. 12 Bn.		19/ 8/14
TODD, G. B., Gnr. Arty.		21/ 1/15 Gnr. ✠
TODD, G. J., Tpr. 3 L.H.	24 F.A.B., 11 F.A.B. ✠ 24/4/18.	24/ 8/14 S.-Cook ✠
TODD, R. J., Pte. 7 Fd. Amb.	✠ 12/4/17.	8/ 3/15 4y 6m, S.-Sgt.
TODOROFF, J. M., Pte. 12 Bn.	4 D. Arty., 2 Div. H.Q.	16/ 9/14
TOFFT, W. H., Capt. No. 10 A.G.H.	W., 3 M.G. Co.	20/ 8/15 4y 6m, Major.
TOLE, C., Dvr. 7 Fd. Amb.	M.B.E.	9/ 2/15 Dvr. ✠
TOLE, W. C., Pte. 12 Bn.	13 Fd. Amb. ✠ 9/8/18.	14/ 1/16 3y 9m, Pte.
TOLLAND, C. J., Dvr. 3 F.A.B.	2W., 52 Bn., 1 A.G.H.	17/ 9/15 4y, Dvr.
TOLLAND, D. A., 2 A.M. Wireless	103 How. Bty.	12/10/16 2y 9m, 2 A.M.
TOLLARD, V. K., Dvr. Arty.	A.F.C.	7/ 9/16 2y 6m, Dvr.
TOLLAND, V. W., Gnr. 6 F.A.B.	15 F.A.B., 4 D.A.C.	17/ 9/15
TOLMAN, A. G., L.-Cpl. 3 L.H.	✠ 4–6/8/16.	19/ 9/14 Sgt. ✠
TOLMAN, G. H., Pte. 26 Bn.	15 M.G. Co.	27/ 9/18 1y 8m, Gnr.
TOLMAN, H. O., Pte. 40 Bn.	M.G. Dtls., 1 M.G. Co.	18/10/16 2y 11m, Gnr.
TOLMAN, M. E., Pte. 26 Bn.	W.	14/ 8/15 2y 5m, Pte.
TOLMAN, O. S., Pte. 26 Bn.	✠ 12/8/16.	21/ 7/15 Pte. ✠
TOLSON, G. H., Dvr. 5 Miners	A.C. Tps. M.T. Co. ✠ 17/11/18.	15/ 3/16 Dvr. ✠
TOLSON, T. E., Dvr. 40 Bn.		15/ 3/16 3y 5m, Dvr.
TOMES, R. B., Pte. 12 Bn.	W.	20/11/17
TOMLIN, W. J., Pte. 40 Bn.	W., 1 A.T.C.E.	3/10/16 2y 6m, Pte.
TOMPKINS, W., Spr. 3 F.C.E.		17/ 8/15 3y 7m, Cpl. M.W.
TONG, A., Munition Worker.		18/10/16 1y 8m, Pte.
TONG, R., Pte. 12 Bn.	12 Bn.	11/ 8/15 2y 4m, L.-Cpl.
TONGS, A. L., L.-Cpl. 26 Bn.	W.	19/ 8/14 5y 2m, Lt.
TONGS, C. J., Cpl. 3 L.H.		18/ 9/16 2y 11m, Pte
TONKS, C. R., Pte. 12 Bn.	26 Supply Depot.	3/ 8/15 4y Pte.
TONKS, C., Tpr. 3 L.H.	3W., 14 A.G.H., 32 Co. A.A.S.C.	3/ 8/15 4y 2m, Pte.
TONKS, T., Tpr. 3 L.H.	W., 4 Fd. Co. Engrs. 2 Div. Engrs	30/ 4/15 3y 9m, Pte.
TOOLEY, D. J., Pte. 26 Bn.	W, M.M.	28/ 8/14 4y 5m, Pte.
TOOLEY, W. R., Pte. 12 Bn.	✠ 12/2/17.	17/ 1/16 Spr. ✠
TOOMBS, W. G., Spr. Miners.	52 Bn.	22/ 8/14 2y 11m, Lt.
TOPE, W., Pte. 12 Bn.	✠	22/ 9/14 Pte.
TOOP, R. D., Pte. 15 Bn.		27/ 4/16 1y 5m, S.-Sgt.
TOPLIS, J. A., S.-Sgt. A.M.C.	52 Bn. ✠ 24/4/18.	27/ 8/14 Pte. ✠
TOPLIS, G. C., Pte. 12 Bn.	W. ✠ 6–10/4/17.	1/ 6/15 Pte. ✠
TORPHY, A. J., Pte 12 Bn.	W., 5 Tun. Co., 2 Tun. Co.	9/ 2/16
TORPY, R. F., Spr. Miners.		4/ 8/15
TOSBAGH, R. J. K., Dvr. Arty.	W.	10/ 4/16 2y, Pte.
TOTHAM, L. W., Pte. 12 Bn.	14 Fd. Amb.	3/ 5/15 3y 7m, Pte.
TOTHAM, R. E., Pte. 1 A.C.H.	3 Div. Train., H.Q. A.B.D.	21/ 2/16 3y 6m, Dvr.
TOTHAM, R., Dvr. 40 Bn.	W., ✠ 6–10/4/17	29/ 8/14 Pte. ✠
TOWERS, A., Pte. 12 Bn.	3W.	28/ 8/14 3y 7m, L.-Cpl.
TOWERS, A. J., Pte. 12 Bn.		21/10/14
TOWERS, W., Pte. 15 Bn.	13 Fd. Amb.	29/ 4/15 4y 9m, Pte.
TOWNLEY, C. H., Pte. 7 Fd. Amb.		30/ 5/16 3y 6m, Pte.
TOWNS, A. T., Pte. 12 Bn.	W. 52 Bn., 49 Bn.	27/ 7/15 4y 1m, L.-Cpl.
TOWNS, M. R., Pte. 12 Bn.		22/ 8/17 1y 7m, Pte.
TOWNSEND, C. B., Pte. 40 Bn.	M.M., 12 Bn. ✠ 8/10/17.	27/10/16 3y. Pte.
TOWNSEND, E. J., Pte. 12 Bn.	A.V.H.	10/ 8/15 Pte. ✠
TOWNSEND, F. F., Pte. 26 Bn.	✠ 24/8/18.	16/ 9/15 4y 4m, Tpr.
TOWNSEND, F. G., Tpr. 1 Rmnts.	✠ 19–20/9/17.	1/ 9/16 Pte. ✠
TOWNSEND, F. H. G., Pte. 40 Bn		19/ 8/14 Cpl. ✠
TOWNSEND, G. L., Pte. 12 Bn.		12/12/17 9m, Pte.
TOWNSEND, J. H., Pte. 12 Bn.		2/12/17
TOWNSEND, M., Pte. 3 G.S.R.	W.	1/ 6/16 2y 3m, Pte.
TOWNSEND, T., Pte. 40 Bn.	10 Bn.	8/11/16 3y 1m, Pte.
TOWNSEND, S. C., Pte. 12 Bn.	2W., 52 Bn.	6/10/15 2y 7m, Pte.
TOWNSEND, V. B. S., Pte. 12 Bn.	40 Bn.	22/11/15 3y 4m, Pte.
TOWNSEND, W. D., Pte. T.M. Bty.	✠ 27/2/17.	9/ 8/15 Pte.
TOWNSEND, W., Pte. 12 Bn.	1 A. Div. Train.	11/ 9/14 4y 5m, Dvr.
TOWNSEND, W. J., Pte. 4 A.S.C.	103 How. Bty.	18/ 2/18 1y 8m, Gnr.
TRACEY, L. A. S., Pte 1 G.S.R.	W. (assumed name O'Sullivan, T. J.)	31/12/15 1y 7m, Lt.
TRACEY, T. J., Dvr. 40 Bn.	2W., 15 Fd. Amb.	19/ 8/15 3y 11m, Pte.
TRAILL, H. W., Pte. A.M.C.	2W.	30/10/16 2y 10m, L.-Cpl
TRAPPES, M. B., Pte. 12 Bn.	W.	9/11/14 1y 9m, Pte.
TRAPPES, M. B., Pte. 15 Bn.	6 F.A.B., 6 B.A.C.	14/ 9/15 3y 11m, Dvr.
TRAVERS, C. A., Dvr. Arty.		19/ 7/15
TRAVERS, E. H., Tpr. 3 L.H.	12 Fd. Co. Engrs.	4/10/15 3y 11m, Spr.
TRAVERS, E. P., Spr. 3 Fd. Co Engrs.		7/ 7/15 4y 1m, Dvr.
TRAVERS, H. W., Dvr. 1 D.A.C.		30/ 9/15 1y 5m, Tpr.
TRAVERS, W. C., Pte. Railway.		26/10/15 3m, Spr.
TRAVIS, T. J. C., Spr. Miners.		

W

NAME.	REMARKS.	RANK ON DISCHARGE. ENLISTED. SERVICE.
TRAYNOR, M. J., Sgt. 40 Bn.	W.	1/ 3/17 1y 11m, Sgt.
TREBILCO, G. T., Pte. 12 Bn.	W.	18/ 8/14 1y 10m, Pte.
TREBILCO, S. D., Gnr. Arty.	24 How. Bde., 4 D.A.C.	9/ 2/16 3y 7m, Sgt.
TREBILCOCK, C. E., Pte. 4 M.G. Co.	3 M.G. Co. ✠ 27/3/18	10/10/16 Pte. ✠
TREBILCOCK, H. L., Pte. 26 Bn.	3W, 7 Bde. M.G. Co., 22 M.G. Co.	20/ 3/15 4y 1m, Pte.
TREBILCOCK, R. G., Pte. 4 M.G. Co.	15 M.G. Co., 11 M.G. Co.	10/10/16 2y 8m, Pte.
TREBILCOCK, W. N., Pte. 12 Bn.	3 M.G. Bn.	20/11/17 1y 10m, Pte.
TREGEAR, A. F., Pte. 40 Bn.	W.	21/ 3/16 2y 6m, L.-Cpl
TREGENNA, H. E., Pte. 40 Bn.	W., M. G. Dtls., 3 M.G. Bn.	18/10/16 2y 11m, Pte.
TREGENNA, P. A., Pte. 40 Bn.	W., M. G. Dtls., 3 M.G. Bn.	18/10/16 2y 9m, Pte.
TREGURTHA, C. E., Tpr. 3 L.H.		26/ 2/17 2y 1m, Tpr.
TRELOGGEN, G. C., Gnr. Arty.	17 Bty ✠ 28/10/17.	13/ 9/16 Gnr. ✠
TREMAYNE, W. J., Gnr. 3 F.A.B	2W., 103 How. Bty., 3 F.A.B.	13/10/14 4y 11m. Gnr.
TRESSIDER, S., Pte. 12 Bn.		29/ 1/15 1y 4m, Pte.
TRETHEWEY, E. C., Gnr. 6 F.A.B.	Arty. Dtls. ✠ 11/8/18.	17/ 9/15 Gnr. ✠
TRETHEWIE, H. R., Pte. 12 Bn.	✠ 5-8/5/17.	13/ 7/15 Pte. ✠
TRETHEWIE, H. R., Sgt. 40 Bn.	2W.	22/ 3/16 2y 6m, Lt.
TREWEEK, A. J., Pte. 12 Bn.		29/ 6/15 3y 4m, Pte.
TREWEEK, D. L., Pte. 40 Bn.	W., M.M.	1/ 3/16 3y 5m, Pte.
TREWEEK, F. C., Pte. 26 Bn.	2W., 12 Bn.	17/ 8/15
TREWEEK, P. J., Pte. 12 Bn.	W. ✠ 23/8/18.	24/11/15 Pte. ✠
TREZISE, J. A., Pte. 12 Bn.	52 Bn. ✠ 4/9/16.	18/ 1/16 Pte. ✠
TRIBOLET, J. W., Pte. 40 Bn.		26/ 7/16 3y 5m, Cpl.
TRIBOLET, L. N., 3 A.M. Wireless	4 Sqd. A.F.C.	27/12/17 1y 11m, 3 A.M
TRICKETT, R., Pte. 15 Bn.	✠ 8/8/15.	29/12/14 Pte. ✠
TRIFFITT, A. C., Pte. 40 Bn.	2W.	15/ 5/16 1y 5m, Pte.
TRIFFITT, A. Mc., L.-Cpl. 12 Bn.		24/ 8/16
TRIFFITT, A. J., Pte. 15 Bn.	W., 47 Bn., 15 Bn.	30/ 8/15 4y, Cpl.
TRIFFITT, A. M., Tpr. 3 L.H.	46 Bn.	4/ 9/15 3y 1m, Pte.
TRIFFITT, B. C., Dvr. D.A.C.		8/ 9/15
TRIFFITT, G. L., Dvr. 3 L.H.	A.T. Depot. 5 D.A.C.	26/ 7/15 4y 3m, Dvr.
TRIFFITT, L. G., Pte. 40 Bn.	W.	3/ 2/16 3y 7m, Pte.
TRIFFETT, G. T., Pte. 26 Bn.	2W., 15 Bn.	30/ 3/15 3y 1m, Pte.
TRIFFETT, B. L., Gnr. Arty.	W., 1 A. Siege Bty., 14 F.A.B.	4/10/15 3y 10m. Gnr.
TRIFFETT, V. E., Cpl. 40 Bn.	2 Div. H.Q. ✠ 3/10/18.	13/ 3/17 Cpl. ✠
TRIFFETT, W. A., Pte. 12 Bn.		2/11/16 1y 7m, Pte.
TRIGG, N. L., Pte. 12 Bn.		17/10/15
TRINDER, F. J., Spr. 8 Fd. Co. Engrs.	4 Fd. Co. Engrs.	18/ 4/16 3y 5m, Spr.
TRINDER, S. G., S.S.-Sgt. 4 A.S.C.		18/ 8/14 4y 6m, S.S.-Sgt
TRINGROVE, D. C., Pte. 12 Bn.		10/ 1/16 2y 4m, Pte.
TRINGROVE, G. A., Pte. 1 G.S.R.		22/ 2/18 1y 1m, Pte.
TRONERUD, E. C., Pte. 1 G.S.R.	12 Bn.	15/ 2/18 1y 10m, Pte.
TROON, B. A., Pte. 15 Bn.	47 Bn., 45 Bn.	27/ 7/15 4y 1m, Pte.
TROON, J. J., Pte. 15 Bn.	47 Bn.	9/ 8/15 2y, Pte.
TROTTER, D., Cpl. 40 Bn.	W.	15/10/15 2y 2m, S.-Sgt.
TROTTER, W., Pte. 40 Bn.		24/ 4/16
TRUDGIAN, L. J., Gnr. 6 F.A.B.	W.	7/ 9/15 4y 1m, Gnr.
TRUE, C. T., Pte. 26 Bn.	1 Anzac Entrench. Co. ✠ 29/7/16.	9/ 4/15 Pte. ✠
TRUE, G. H., M.G.S. 12 Bn.	✠ 15/4/17.	20/ 8/14 M.G.S. ✠
TRUEMAN, C. W., Pte. 12 Bn.		20/ 8/15 Pte. ✠
TRULL, W. A. D., Pte. 15 Bn.		2/ 7/15 3y 11m, L.-Cpl
TRUSCOTT, N. A., Pte. 12 Bn.		3/ 5/16 3y 11m, L.-Cpl
TUBB, A. L., Cpl. 2 G.S.R.	12 Bn. ✠ 25/10/18.	24/11/17 Cpl. ✠
TUBB, C. G., Cpl. 40 Bn.	✠ 8/12/16.	20/ 3/16 Cpl. ✠
TUCK, F. G., Sgt. 40 Bn.	✠ 31/1/17.	20/ 9/15 Sgt. ✠
TUCK, H. E., Pte. 12 Bn.	W.	5/10/17 1y 5m, Pte.
TUCKER, H. F., Pte. 26 Bn.	W., 2 Pnrs.	17/ 7/15 2y 8m, Pte.
TUCKER, W. F., Pte. 12 Bn.	W. ✠ 15/4/17.	2/ 5/16 Pte. ✠
TUCKWELL, T. L., Pte. 12 Bn.		8/ 1/18
TUDOR, E. H., Pte. 26 Bn.	12 Bn.	2/ 9/15
TUFFIN, A. J., Pte. 12 Bn.	52 Bn., 51 Bn.	11/ 1/16 3y 8m, Pte.
TUFFIN, F. R., Pte. A.M.C.	W., 2 A.G.H.	29/11/15 3y 10m, Pte.
TULLOCH, N. W., Lieut. 26 Bn.		3/ 5/15 1y 3m, Lieut.
TUMILTY, J., Pte. 26 Bn.	40 Bn., 26 Bn.	13/ 2/15 4y 5m, Pte.
TUNKS, C. S., Pte. 12 Bn.	52 Bn.	25/ 1/16 3y 5m, Pte.
TURMINE, H., Pte. 12 Bn.	M.M. ✠ 23/8/18.	2/ 7/17 Pte. ✠
TURNBULL, F. H., Pte. 26 Bn.	✠ 5/8/16.	12/ 3/15 Pte. ✠
TURNBULL, G. A., Pte. 40 Bn.	✠ 28/3/18.	5/ 7/16 S.-Sgt. ✠
TURNBULL, G. B., Pte. 12 Bn.		26/ 4/16
TURNBULL, J. G., Spr. Miners.	W., 3 Tun. Co.	10/10/15
TURNBULL, J. C., Pte. 40 Bn.	2W.	28/ 3/16 3y. Pte.
TURNBULL, S. G., Pte. 40 Bn.	2W.	28/ 3/16 3y 3m, L.-Cpl
TURNLEY, L. L., Cpl. 12 Bn.		24/10/16 3y 2m, Cpl.
TURVEY, H. W., Pte. 40 Bn.	3 Salvage Co.	1/ 3/16 3y 4m, Pte.
TUSON, J., Pte. 12 Bn.	52 Bn. ✠ 4/9/16.	4/ 2/16 Pte. ✠
TUTHILL, V. J., Pte. 40 Bn.	W., 12 Bn.	2/10/16
TUTT, A. E., Pte. 2 G.S.R.		12/ 5/17 1y 8m, Pte.
TUTT, I. W. G., Pte. 12 Bn.		23/12/15
TUTTLE, F., Pte. 4 M.G. Co.	W., 13 F A.B.	7/ 9/16 2y 7m, Cpl.
TUTTLE, F. A., Gnr. Arty.		20/11/15 3y 5m, Dvr.
TUTTLE, H. J., Pte. 12 Bn.	W.	3/ 9/17 1y 6m, Pte.
TUTTLE, H. T., Pte. 12 Bn.		8/12/15

TASMANIA'S MUSTER ROLL. 355

NAME.	REMARKS.	RANK ON DISCHARGE. ENLISTED, SERVICE.
TUTTLE, J. T., Pte. 12 Bn.	W.	4/10/16 2y 6m, Pte.
TUTTLE, K. McK., Pte. 12 Bn.	2W.	19/ 2/16 3y 2m, Pte.
TUTTLE, K. McK., Pte. 12 Bn.		8/12/14 2m, Pte.
TUTTLE, R., Pte. 12 Bn.		8/11/17 1y 11m, Pte.
TURNER, J. W., Lieut. 108 How Bty	3 Divl. Arty., 6 F.A.B.	27/ 4/16 3y 3m, Capt.
TURNER, A. V., Pte. 12 Bn.	W., D.C.M.	20/ 8/14 4y 7m, Cpl.
TURNER, A., Pte. 2 G.S.R.		17/ 5/18 1y 3m, Pte.
TURNER, A., Pte 12 Bn.		15/ 9/14 2m, Pte.
TURNER, A. D., Spr. Miners.	W., 5 Tun. Co. ✠ 21/1/17.	15/10/15 Spr. ✠
TURNER, A. E., Pte. 12 Bn.	W., A.I.F. Depot H.Q., 12 Bn.	21/ 8/14 4y 2m, Cpl.
TURNER, A., Pte. 40 Bn.		16/10/16 2y 11m, Pte.
TURNER, B. W., Cpl. 40 Bn.		17/ 1/16 3y 6m, Lt.
TURNER, B. M., Pte. 12 Bn.		16/10/16
TURNER, C. H., Pte. 40 Bn.		4/ 3/16 3y 5m, L.-Cpl.
TURNER, C. H., Gnr. 1 D.A.C.		7/ 9/15 2y 6m, Gnr.
TURNER, C. J., Pte. 40 Bn.	W.	31/10/16 2y 6m, Pte.
TURNER, D., Pte. 40 Bn.	W., 49 Bn., 4 M.G. Bn.	31/ 3/16 3y 6m, Pte.
TURNER, E. A., Pte. 12 Bn.		8/ 1/18 1y 10m, Pte.
TURNER, E. C., Pte. 15 Bn.	W., 40 Bn., M.M.	29/ 1/15 4y 10m, Pte.
TURNER, E. K., Pte. 15 Bn.		22/ 7/15 4y 6m, Pte.
TURNER, F. W., Pte. 12 Bn.	✠ 12/12/16.	12/ 4/16 Pte. ✠
TURNER, G. R., Gnr. Arty.	3 F.A.B., 5 Salvage Co.	26/ 2/16 3y 2m, Gnr.
TURNER, G. A., Pte. 12 Bn.		5/ 2/15 3m, Gnr.
TURNER, G. A., Tpr. 3 L.H.		29/ 3/15 4y 7m, Sgt.
TURNER, G. W., Pte. 12 Bn.	2W., M.M., D.C.M.	15/ 7/15 4y 4m, Lt.
TURNER, G. W., Pte. 15 Bn.	W., 1 A. Salvage Sec	11/ 8/15 4y, Pte.
TURNER, H., Pte. 12 Bn.	W, 1 Div. M.T. Co., A.C.T.M.T. Co.	3/12/14
TURNER, H., Pte. 40 Bn.	✠ 31/1/17.	3/ 2/16 Pte. ✠
TURNER, H. A. F., Spr. Miners.	1 Tun. Co.	11/ 9/17 2y 3m, Spr.
TURNER, H. E. V., Pte. 12 Bn.		7/ 8/16 2y 9m, Pte.
TURNER, J., Pte. 40 Bn.	2W.	28/ 4/16 2y 6m, Pte.
TURNER, J. C., Pte. 40 Bn.	W.	26/ 3/16 1y 11m. Pte.
TURNER, J. E., Pte. 12 Bn.	3W., 1 Pnr. Bn. ✠ 3/11/17.	9/10/14 Pte. ✠
TURNER, J. F., Pte. 3 G.S.R.	12 Bn.	10/ 7/18 1y 4m, Pte.
TURNER, J. H., Pte. 12 Bn.		10/ 5/16 3y 6m, Pte.
TURNER, J., Pte. 12 Bn.	✠ 8/1/18.	28/10/16 Pte. ✠
TURNER, J. N., Spr. 3 Tunlrs.	W.	20/10/16 2y 11m, L.-Cpl
TURNER, L. H., Pte. 12 Bn.	46 Bn. ✠ 11/4/17.	15/12/14 Pte. ✠
TURNER, L., Pte. 40 Bn.	3W.	4/ 3/16 3y, Pte.
TURNER, L. J., Pte. 15 Bn.		20/ 7/15
TURNER, L. A., Spr. 8 Fd. Co. Engrs.	✠ 27/10/17.	25/ 1/16 Spr. ✠
TURNER, N. J., Pte. 26 Bn.	2W.	3/ 5/15 2y, Pte.
TURNER, O. H., Pte. 15 Bn.		14/ 9/15 4y 1m, Pte.
TURNER, P. B., Gnr. 6 F.A.B.	17 Bty. ✠ 3/11/16.	20/ 7/15 Cpl. ✠
TURNER, R. T., Pte. 12 Bn.	21 Bn.	26/ 9/15 4y, Pte.
TURNER, R., Pte. 40 Bn.	W.	29/ 3/16 3y 6m, Cpl.
TURNER, S. C., Dvr. Arty.	W., M.M., 3 F.A.B.	1/12/14 4y 5m, Sgt.
TURNER, T. F. C., Spr. 8 Fd. Co. Engrs.	12 Bn.	27/ 9/15 3y 8m, Spr.
TURNER, V. G., Dvr. 3 L.H.	M.G. Sqd., 1 L.H. Bde., 1 M.G. Sec.	13/ 8/15 4y, Dvr.
TURNER, W. S., Pte. 12 Bn.		21/ 6/17 2y 4m, Pte.
TURNER, W. H., Spr. Railway.		15/10/15 8m, Tpr.
TURNER, W. H., L.-Cpl. 7 Fd. Am'l	13 Fd. Amb.	25/ 3/15
TURNER, W., Pte. 40 Bn.	W.	18/ 1/16
TURNER, W. J. L., Cpl. 15 Bn.	47 Bn. ✠ 5/4/18.	29/ 7/15 Sgt. ✠
TWINING, G. A. Pte. 1 G.S.R.	40 Bn.	27/ 2/18 1y 8m, Pte.
TWINING, F. A., Pte. 12 Bn.	✠ 23/9/17.	1/ 5/16 Pte. ✠
TYLER, C. P., Pte. 1 A.C.H.	W., 2 Fd. Amb.	29/ 9/14 5y 2m, Pte.
TYLER, E. A., Pte. 40 Bn.	W.	9/10/16 1y 9m, Pte.
TYLER, I., Pte. 26 Bn.	7 Fd. Co. Engrs.	9/ 7/15 3y 1m, Spr.
TYLER, J. B., Tpr. 3 L.H.		19/ 8/14
TYLER, J. N., Pte. 26 Bn.		25/ 1/15 1y 7m, Pte.
TYNAN, W. J. T., Dvr. Arty.	8 F.A.B., 108 How. Bty.	11/10/16 2y 11m, Dvr.
TYNAN, A. D., Sgt. 12 Bn.	M.C.	28/ 7/15 4y 3m, Lt.
TYRRELL, J. T., Capt. 26 Bn.	40 Bn. ✠ 10/1/17.	1/ 9/14 4y 11m Lt.-Cl.
TYRRELL, G. R., S.Q.M.S. 3 L.H.	2W.	19/ 8/14 2y 10m S.Q.M.S
TYSON, A., Gnr., 23 How. Bty.		15/ 5/16
TYSON, G. A., Pte. 40 Bn.	1 Railway Unit.	17/10/16 2y 8m, Pte.
TYSON, R. R., Pte. 12 Bn.		27/ 5/15 3y, Pte.
ULBRICH, G. H., Pte. 1 G.S.R.	40 Bn.	8/ 1/18 1y 11m, Pte.
ULETT, C. H., Pte. 40 Bn.		30/ 4/17 2y 9m, Pte.
UMFREVILLE, G. F., Pte. Railway		21/10/15 3y 4m, Cpl.
UNSWORTH, J. C., Pte. 12 Bn.		25/10/16 3y 1m, Pte.
UPCHURCH, A., Pte. 26 Bn.	52 Bn. ✠ 6-10/4/17.	18/ 8/15 Pte. ✠
UPCHURCH, C. E., Pte. 12 Bn.	M.M., 52 Bn. ✠ 16/7/17.	28/ 7/15 Pte. ✠
UPCHURCH, H. J., Gnr. Arty.	W., 14 F.A.B., 114 Bty.	10/10/16 3y, Gnr.
UPCHURCH, W. J. W., Pte. 40 Bn.	2W., 69 Bn., 40 Bn., M.I.D.	31/ 3/16 3y 4m, Cpl.
UPHAM, S., C.S.M. 26 Bn.	W.	24/ 2/15
UPSTON, G. J., Pte. 12 Bn.		26/ 4/16 3y 5m, Pte.
UPTON, A. J., Pte. 12 Bn.	W.	23/ 8/15 1y 10m, Pte.
UPTON, A. J., Pte. 12 Bn.		30/ 9/14 8m, Pte.
UPTON, G. H., Spr. 26 Bn.	4 Fd. Co. Engrs., 2 Div. Engrs.	10/ 5/15 2y 2m, Spr.
UREN, H. F., Cpl. 12 Bn.	3 Cyc. Bn. ✠ 9/4/17.	15/ 2/15 Lt. ✠
UREN, L. S., S.-Sgt. 12 Bn.	A.A.D.C.	S.-Sgt.
UTTERIDGE, A., Pte. 40 Bn.	✠ 26/2/17.	10/ 3/16 Pte. ✠

NAME.	REMARKS.	RANK ON DISCHARGE. ENLISTED. SERVICE.
UTTERIDGE, W., Pte. 12 Bn.	W., 4 Salvage Co., 52 Bn.	4/ 1/16 2y 10m. Pte.
VAIL, V. T., Cpl. 2 G.S.R.		22/ 4/18 1y 8m. L.-Cpl.
VALE, F. W., Spr. Miners.		11/ 4/16
VALENTINE, C. H., Pte. 40 Bn.		1/11/16 2y 9m. Sgt.
VALENTINE, E. R. W., Cpl. 12 Bn.	W., 4 D.A.C.	19/ 8/15 4y. Bdr.
VALENTINE, S. H., Pte. 15 Bn.	4W., 24 How. Bde., 8 T.M. Bty.	2/12/14 4y 4m. Pte.
VALLANCE, D., Gnr. Arty.	2 D.A.C.	12/10/16
VANDERVEKEN, E. J. M., Dvr. Arty.	24 How. Bde., 4 Div. H.Q.	16/11/15
VANDRIEL, W., Pte. 12 Bn.	3 L.T.M. Bty., 12 Bn ✠ 1/5/18.	10/ 5/16 Pte. ✠
VAUGHAN, A. E. G., Pte. 12 Bn.	✠ 25/8/18.	17/10/17 Pte. ✠
VAUGHAN, A. R., Pte. 40 Bn.	W., 49 Bn.	4/ 5/16 3y 2m. Pte.
VAUGHAN, B., Cpl. 12 Bn.	✠ 21/4/18.	21/ 9/15 Lt. ✠
VAUGHAN, E. P., L.-Cpl. 12 Bn.	W.	30/10/17
VAUGHAN, G., Pte. 12 Bn.	W., M.C. and Bar.	18/ 8/14 5y 3m. Lt.
VAUGHAN, J. B., Dvr. 3 F.A.B.		
VAUGHAN, J. C., Pte. 12 Bn.	D.C.M.	20/ 8/14
VAUGHAN, P., Spr. Railway.	3 Railway Co., 3 A.L.R.O. Co.	4/12/17 1y 9m. Spr.
VAUGHAN, W., Pte. 15 Bn.	✠ 12/10/16.	9/ 8/15 Sgt. ✠
VAUGHAN, W. M., Pte. 40 Bn.	2W.	27/ 3/16 3y 3m. Pte.
VAUTIN, A. C., Gnr. Arty.		27/ 9/15 2y 7m. Bdr.
VAUTIN, L. G., Pte. 2 G.S.R.	3W., 6 F.A.B., 17 Bty.	4/ 4/18 1y 8m. Pte. M.W.
VAUX, W. G., M.W., N. and L.		
VENN, A. R., Pte. 26 Bn.		29/ 6/15 1y 5m. Pte.
VENN, G. J., Pte. 2 Pnrs.		2/ 8/16 3y 2m. Pte.
VENN, J. H., Spr. 5 Miners.	2 Pnrs. ✠ 13/6/18.	27/ 1/16 Spr. ✠
VENN, M. R., Pte. 12 Bn.		12/12/17
VENN, M. S., Pte. 4 M.G. Co.	15 M.G. Co. ✠ 15/12/17.	18/10/16 Gnr. ✠
VENUS, H. G., Pte. 12 Bn.	✠ 25/6/16.	16/ 8/15 Sgt. ✠
VERNON, T. A., Spr. Miners.	2 Tun. Co. ✠ 29/9/18.	18/10/15 Spr. ✠
VERON, E., L.-Cpl. Railway.		16/ 9/15
VERRELL, R., Sig. 12 Bn.	52 Bn., 51 Bn.	25/ 5/15 4y 3m. Cpl.
VERREN, E. J., L.-Cpl. 40 Bn.	-	2/10/15 3y 2m. Cpl.
VERRIER, C. H., Sgt. 26 Bn.	2W.	26/ 4/15
VERTIGAN, A. C., Pte. 40 Bn.	W., M.G. Dtls., 1 M.G. Co.	17/10/16 2y 8m. Pte.
VERTIGAN, J. W., Pte. 15 Bn.	14 Bn. ✠ 9/8/15.	11/10/14 Sgt. ✠
VERTIGAN, O., Pte. 40 Bn.	✠ 16/1/17.	10/ 3/16 Pte. ✠
VINCE, E. W. R., Pte. 12 Bn.	1 Pnrs. ✠ 23/7/16.	18/ 8/15 Pte. ✠
VINCE, O. H., Pte. 40 Bn.	W.	25/ 2/16 2y 9m. Pte.
VINCE, W. L., Pte. 40 Bn.	W., M.M.	1/ 3/16 3y 3m. Pte.
VINCE, W. C., Pte. 40 Bn.	2W.	9/11/16 2y 7m. Pte.
VINCENT, T. H., Major, 4 Tun Co		1/3/16 1y 4m. Major.
VINCENT, E. L., Pte. 12 Bn.	2W.	7/ 9/16 3y. Pte.
VINCENT, F. A., Pte. 2 G.S.R.	✠ 11/10/18.	28/ 5/18 Pte. ✠
VINCENT, G. R., Tpr. 3 L.H.	W.	21/ 8/14 4y 2m. Cpl.
VINCENT, H. L., Pte. 12 Bn.	W., 52 Bn.	2/ 7/15 2y 7m. Pte.
VINCENT, J. D., Pte. 3 G.S.R.	12 Bn. ✠ 30/1/19	3/ 7/18 Pte. ✠
VINCENT, N. H., Gnr. Arty.	10 F.A.B.	16/ 4/17
VINEN, H., Pte. 15 Bn.	W.	2/11/14 2y. Pte.
VINEN, R., Pte. 12 Bn.	W.	1/ 5/16 1y 8m. Pte.
VINEY, A. R., Pte. 15 Bn.	3W., 12 M.G. Co.	23/ 9/14 5y. Pte.
VINEY, C. L., Pte. 40 Bn.	W., 12 Bn.	22/ 9/16 3y 1m. Pte.
VINEY, C. T., Pte. 12 Bn.	3W., 40 Bn.	14/ 3/16 2y 8m. Pte.
VINEY, D. D., Dvr. 6 F.A.B.	✠ 29/11/16.	13/ 9/15 Dvr. ✠
VINEY, F., Dvr. 3 L.H.	104 How. Bty.	18/ 8/15 4y. Dvr.
VINEY, J. G. L., Tpr. 3 L.H.	W.	2/ 8/15 1y 5m. Tpr.
VINEY, J. A., Tpr. 3 L.H.	W.	18/ 8/15 4y 1m. L.-Cpl.
VINEY, L. G., Pte. 40 Bn.		22/10/15 3y 10m. Pte.
VINEY, R. W., Pte. 12 Bn.	A. Sig. Sqd.	1/11/15 3y 5m. Spr.
VINEY, S., Tpr. 5 G.S.R.	37 Co. A.M.D. Train.	2/ 6/18 1y 3m. Tpr.
VINEY, V. L., Pte. 4 M.G. Co.	W., 2 M.G. Co., 1 M.G. Bn.	11/ 1/17 2y 6m. Pte.
VINEY, W. T., Pte. Railway		19/10/15 10m. Pte.
VINEY, W. T., Pte. 40 Bn.	3W.	3/10/16 3y 2m. Pte.
VIREUX, A. E., Pte. 12 Bn.	W.	16/ 6/16 3y 4m. Cpl.
VIREUX, J. L., Pte. 12 Bn.	✠ 10/6/15.	19/ 6/16 2y. Pte.
VISTARINI, H., Pte. 12 Bn.	✠ 30/5/15.	20/ 8/14 Pte. ✠
VIVIAN, G. A., Spr. 3 Fd. Co. Engrs.		23/ 8/14 Spr. ✠
VODDEN, W., Spr. Miners.	2W., 3 Tun. Co.	16/ 3/16 1y 5m. Spr.
VON BIBRA, C., Pte. 12 Bn.	✠ 6–10/4/17.	5/ 6/16 Pte. ✠
VON BIBRA, E. L., Pte. 15 Bn.	✠ 30/9/17.	20/ 5/15 Cpl. ✠
VON BIBRA, E E., Pte. 12 Bn.	4W., 15 L.H.T.M. Bty.	24/ 8/14 3y 6m. Capt.
VON SCHILL, W. A., Pte. 1 A.G.H.	10 Fd. Amb. ✠ 24/8/18.	17/ 8/15 Pte. ✠
VON STIEGLITZ, H. L., Gnr. Arty	8 F.A.B.	14/11/16 2y 11m. Dvr.
VON STIEGLITZ, H. W. A., Pte. 12 Bn.		28/ 8/14 2y 5m. Pte.
VOSS, B., Dvr. Arty.	2W.	15/ 5/16 2y 11m. Dvr.
VOSS, H M., Pte. 26 Bn.	W., 114 How. Bty.	21/ 6/15 3y 10m. Pte.
VOSS, O., Pte. 40 Bn.	W., 68 Sqd. A.F.C.	4/ 2/16 2y. Cpl.
VOSS, S. J., Pte. 40 Bn.	W.	6/12/16 2y 9m. Pte.
WADDINGTON, A., Pte. 12 Bn.		26/ 8/15 4y. Pte.
WADDINGTON, D. J., Pte. 12 Bn.	2W.	3/ 4/16 3y 5m. Pte.
WADDINGTON, W. T., Pte. 4 M.G. Co.		4/ 8/16
WADDLE, H. A. C., Pte. 12 Bn.	W., 4 A.M.T.M.B.	13/ 7/15 2y 7m. Gnr.
WADDLE, P. C. E., Pte. 12 Bn.		31/ 5/16 2y 11m. Pte.
WADE, A. B., Pte. 1º Bn.	W., 52 Bn.	14/ 9/15 2y 6m. Pte.

TASMANIA'S MUSTER ROLL.

NAME.	REMARKS.	RANK ON DISCHARGE. ENLISTED. SERVICE.
WADE, B. J. S., Pte. A.A.M.C.	10 Fd. Amb.	4/ 7/16 2y 9m. Pte.
WADE, F. H., Pte. 40 Bn.		2/ 3/16 1y 9m. Pte.
WADE, M. A., Pte. 12 Bn.	✠ 10/11/15.	4/ 8/15 Pte. ✠
WADE, T., Pte. 12 Bn.	8 M.T.M.B.	25/10/15 3y 6m. Gnr.
WADE, W. J., Pte. 15 Bn.	2W.	13/ 8/15 2y 7m. Pte.
WADLEY, T. W. J., Pte. 12 Bn.		26/10/16 2y 9m. Pte.
WADSLEY, L. L., Lieut. 15 Bn	52 Bn. ✠ 3/9/16.	18/11/14 Lieut. ✠
WAGNER, M. L., Pte. 26 Bn.	2W.	11/ 8/15 4y 1m. Cpl.
WAGNER, W. J., Pte. 12 Bn.	2W., M.I.D., T.M.B., 12 Bn.	1/ 6/15 4y 2m. Lieut.
WAGSTAFF, W. J., Pte. 12 Bn.	10 Bn.	2/11/16 2y 11m. Pte.
WAINWRIGHT, G. A., Pte. 40 Bn.		7/ 3/16 3y 5m. Pte.
WAINWRIGHT, H. W., Pte. 15 Bn	W., 47 Bn.	3/ 9/15 2y 4m. Sgt.
WAINWRIGHT, R. S., Pte. 4 M.G. Co.	1 M.G. Bn.	19/12/16 2y 10m. Pte.
WAKEFIELD, W. B., Pte. 40 Bn.	W. ✠ 7/11/18.	16/10/16 Pte. ✠
WAKEFIELD, W. R., Pte. 3 G.S.R.		25/ 6/18 9m. Pte.
WAKELING, D., Tpr., 3 L.H.	8 L.H.	16/ 4/17 2y 3m. Tpr.
WAKELING, F. J., Pte. 40 Bn.	W.	15/ 7/16 2y 11m. Pte.
WAKELING, M., Pte. 12 Bn.		11/10/15
WAKELING, W. T., Pte. 12 Bn.	Aust. Provost Corps.	16/11/15 4y. Cpl.
WALCH, M., Pte. 12 Bn.	W.	25/ 4/17 2y 6m. Pte.
WALCH, G., Gnr. 13 Arty.	✠ 25/10/17.	29/ 9/15 Gnr. ✠
WALCH, G. A., Gnr. Arty.	9 Bty., 3 F.A.B.	12/ 3/17 2y 10m. Gnr.
WALCH, J. H. B., Pte. 1 G.S.R.		2/ 4/17 2y 1m. Pte.
WALSH, E. C. Capt. Chap.		Capt. Chap.
WALSH, A. T., Pte. 12 Bn.	W.	21/ 9/14 4y 6m. Pte.
WALSH, F. T., Pte. 12 Bn.	✠ 22/7/15.	28/11/14 Pte. ✠
WALSH, J. V., Spr. 5 M.G. Co.	W., 2 Tun. Co.	17/ 3/16 3y 6m. Spr.
WALSH, J., Pte. 26 Bn.	Croix de Guerre, 12 Bn.	19/ 8/15 3y 10m. CAMS
WALSH, W., Pte. 15 Bn.		19/ 9/14
WALDON, E., Dvr., 40 Bn.		15/ 3/16 3y 7m. L.-Sgt.
WALDRON, J. P., Pte. 12 Bn.	✠ 15/4/17.	14/ 9/15 Pte. ✠
WALDUCK, R. G., Pte. 12 Bn.	2W., M.C.	5/ 6/15 3y 1m. Lieut.
WALES, D. T., Pte. 15 Bn.	✠ 8/8/16.	2/ 7/15 Pte. ✠
WALES, E., Gnr., 18 Bty. 6 F.A.B.	17 Bty. ✠ 10/6/17.	18/ 8/15 Sgt. ✠
WALFORD, J. W., Pte. 12 Bn.		21/ 8/14 2y. Pte.
WALKEM, J. B., Pte. A.F.C.		27/ 2/18 1y 5m. Pte.
WALKENDEN, A. W., Pte. 26 Bn	✠ 5/8/16.	22/ 6/15 Pte. ✠
WALKENDEN, J. B., Pte. 12 Bn.	W., 52 Bn.	27/ 7/15 2y 8m. Pte.
WALKLEY, A. G., Pte. 2 A.G.H.		
WALL, E., Spr., 3 M.G. Co.	3 Tunn. Co.	3/12/15 2y 7m. Spr.
WALL, J. G., Gnr. F.A. Rfts.		5/ 5/17
WALL, T. E., Gnr. F.A. Rfts.		5/ 5/17
WALLACE, C., Pte. 12 Bn.		9/ 9/15
WALLACE, G., Pte. 40 Bn.	W.	5/ 4/16 3y 4m. Pte.
WALLACE, G. A., Pte. 12 Bn.	W., 52 Bn.	13/ 1/16 2y 1m. Pte.
WALLACE, G. C., Pte. 12 Bn.	52 Bn.	7/10/15 2y 3m. Pte.
WALLACE, H., Pte. 26 Bn.	✠ 4/10/17.	31/ 3/15 Pte. ✠
WALLACE, R. A. T., Pte. 12 Bn.	2W., 40 Bn.	5/ 4/16 2y 11m. Pte.
WALLACE, S. E., Pte. 40 Bn.	W., 69 Bn., 40 Bn.	11/ 4/16 2y 8m. Pte.
WALLACE, T., Gnr., F.A. Rfts.	13 F.A.B.	10/ 9/15
WALLACE, V. H., Pte. Fld. Bky.		8/12/14
WALLACE, V. I., Pte. 12 Bn.		17/ 8/14
WALLACH, H., Pte 12 Bn.	W.	27/ 7/15 3y 4m. Cpl.
WALLEN, F. A., Pte. 26 Bn.	2 Bn. ✠ 24/7/16.	11/ 5/15 Pte. ✠
WALLER, F. J., Pte. 12 Bn.		15/12/16 3y. Pte.
WALLER, G. H., Pte. 40 Bn.		1/ 3/16 3y 5m. Sgt.
WALLER, S. M., Pte. 12 Bn.	40 Bn. ✠12/11/18.	30/10/16 Pte. ✠
WALLER, W., Tpr. 3 L.H.		7/11/17 2y. Tpr.
WALLER, W. R., Pte. 1 A.C.H.		25/11/14
WALLEY, J., Pte. 12 Bn.	W., 51 Bn.	14/ 9/15 4y 2m. L.-Cpl.
WALLS, W., Spr. 3 M. Coy.		11/11/15 1y 11m. Spr.
WALTER, S. W., Gnr., F.A. Rfts.	8 Bty.	10/11/15 3y 10m. Gnr.
WALTERS, B. W., Pte. 40 Bn.	W., 12 Bn.	8/ 3/16 3y 8m. Pte.
WALTERS, C., Pte. 12 Bn.	W.	19/10/16 2y 11m. Pte.
WALTERS, F. C., Pte. 12 Bn.	52 Bn. ✠4/9/16.	1/ 8/15 Pte. ✠
WALTERS, F. P., Gnr. Arty.	104 How. Bty.	31/10/15 4y 1m. Dvr.
WALTERS, H., Pte. 12 Bn.	W., 52 Bn.	1/ 8/15 1y 8m. Pte.
WALTERS, H. T., Pte. 26 Bn.		16/ 5/15
WALTERS, J. T., Pte. 40 Bn.	49 Bn.	3/ 5/16 3y 2m. Sgt.
WALTERS, J. W., Pte. 26 Bn.	W.	10/ 4/15 3y 2m. Pte.
WALTERS, L A., Gnr. Arty.	W., 6 F.A.B.	14/10/15 4y 2m. Gnr.
WALTERS, M. W. A., Pte. 12 Bn.	W.	26/10/17 2y. Pte.
WALTERS, W. T., Pte. 26 Bn.	✠ 6/8/16.	9/10/15 Pte. ✠
WALTON, E. T., Pte. 26 Bn.		18/ 3/15
WALTON, L. G., Gnr. Arty.	14 Bty.	2/11/16 2y 10m. Dvr.
WALTON, V. D., Pte. 1 A.C.H.	M.M., 15 Fd. Amb.	3/ 6/15 4y 1m. Pte.
WALKEDEN, A. W. Pte. 26 Bn.	✠ 5/8/16.	22/ 6/15 Pte. ✠
WALKER, A. E., Pte. 40 Bn.	W. ✠ 1/9/18.	22/ 2/16 Pte. ✠
WALKER, A. G., Pte. 40 Bn.	✠ 12/10/17.	22/ 3/16 Cpl. ✠
WALKER, A., Tpr. 3 L.H.	4 L.H.	5/ 6/17 1y 8m. Tpr.
WALKER, A. C., Pte. 12 Bn.		15/12/17
WALKER, A. G., Pte. 15 Bn.	W., P.O.W. ✠ 21/10/17.	4/ 9/15 Pte. ✠
WALKER, A. F., Pte. 40 Bn.		2/ 6/15 4y 4m. C.Q.M.S.
WALKER, B. R., Pte. A.A.M.C.	3 A.G.H.	5/ 4/17 2y 7m. Pte.
WALKER, C., Tpr. 3 L.H.	5 A.A.C.	6/ 9/15 4y. Dvr.
WALKER, E., Pte. 26 Bn.	✠ 23/9/18.	18/ 3/15 Cpl. ✠
WALKER, E. J., Pte. 12 Bn.	2W.	29/ 9/14 4y 7m. Pte.

TASMANIA'S WAR RECORD, 1914-1918.

NAME.	REMARKS.	RANK ON DISCHARGE. ENLISTED, SERVICE.
WALKER, E. G., Dvr. 6 F.A.B.		16/9/15
WALKER, G. H., Pte. 12 Bn.	2W.	16/ 9/14 4y 4m Pte.
WALKER, G. W., Pte. Tunnellers		16/10/16
WALKER, G. W., Pte. 12 Bn.	4 Divl. Arty.	2/11/15 4y 1m, Dvr.
WALKER, H. G., Pte. 40 Bn.	W.	17/10/16 2y, Pte.
WALKER, H. J., Pte. 12 Bn.		23/ 7/15 4y 1m, Pte.
WALKER, H. C., Pte. 7 Fld. Amb.	13 Fld. Amb.	9/ 3/15 4y 5m, Sgt.
WALKER, J. A., Pte. 26 Bn.		29/ 4/15 2y 4m, Pte.
WALKER, J. W., Pte. 12 Bn.	3W. 41 Bn.	2/8/15 4y 3m, L.-Cpl.
WALKER, L., Pte. 40 Bn.		26/ 9/16 2y 11m, Pte.
WALKER, L. J., Dvr. 40 Bn.		7/ 3/16 3y 9m, L.-Cpl.
WALKER, T. R., Tpr. 3 L.H.		28/ 9/17 2y 11m, Tpr.
WALKER, W. T., Pte. 40 Bn.	2W.	23/ 5/16 3y 3m, Cpl.
WALKER, W. C., Pte. 40 Bn.	3W.	3/ 4/16 2y 8m, Pte.
WALKER, W., Cpl. 40 Bn.		10/ 7/16 4y 6m, Sgt.
WALKER, W. G., Pte. 12 Bn.	W.	29/ 9/14 1y 9m, Pte.
WALKER, W. H., Pte. 12 Bn.	W.	21/ 8/14 1y 7m, Pte.
WALKER, W. P., Pte. 40 Bn.	W.	7/11/16 3y 4m, Pte.
WALKLEY, A. G., Pte. 2 A.G.H.	14 A.G.H.	1/ 9/15 4y 2m, L.-Cpl.
WARBURTON, C. G., Pte. 40 Bn.	W.	3/ 4/16 3y, Sgt.
WARD, A. T., Spr. 8 Fd. Co. Engrs	1 Pnr. Bn.	28/ 2/16 3y 1m, Spr.
WARD, C. H., Sgt. 9th Bty.	24 Bty.	27/ 8/14 3y 4m, B.S.M.
WARD, D. H. G., Gnr. Arty.	104 How. Bty.	15/ 5/16 3y 4m, Bdr.
WARD, F. H., Pte. 20 Bn. (Correct name, ROMETCH, F. R. S	✻ 31/12/16.	9/ 8/15 ✻
WARD, H. J., Pte. 12 Bn.	W., M.I.D. ✻ 11/8/15.	17/ 8/14 Pte. ✻
WARD, H. A., Tpr. 3 L.H.	✻	11/ 8/15 Tpr. ✻
WARD, J. H., Pte. 15 Bn.	✻ 6/8/18.	14/ 9/15 Pte.
WARD, J. K., Pte. 40 Bn.	W.	19/ 9/16 2y 1m, L.-Cpl.
WARD, J. T., Pte. 12 Bn.	●	17/ 9/14 1y 11m, Pte.
WARD, L. R., Pte. 12 Bn.	W.	10/ 9/15 2y 11m, Pte.
WARD, P. E., Gnr. Arty.	26 Bty.	9/10/16 3y, Gnr.
WARD, S. M., Pte. 12 Bn.		9/ 9/15 3y 11m, Pte.
WARD, V. A., Pte. Rly. Unit.	4 A.L.R.O.C.	13/12/16 2y 8m, L.-Cpl.
WARD, V. T., Gnr. Arty.	12 F.A.B.	25/ 9/14 4y 11m, Bdr.
WARD, W., Pte. Remount Sec.		23/ 9/15 9m, Pte.
WARDEN, L. W., Pte. 40 Bn.		20/10/16 2y 11m, Pte.
WARDLE, C. G., Spr. 3 M.G. Co.		18/11/15 1y 2m, Spr.
WARDLAW, A. L., Lieut. 12 Bn.	2W., M.I.D.	20/ 5/16
WARDROP, H., Pte. 4 M.G. Co.	W., 25 M.G. Co.	29/ 5/16 2y 10m. Pte.
WARE, A. H., Pte. 26 Bn.	✻ 7/7/16.	2/ 9/15 Pte. ✻
WARE, J. G. F., Pte. 15 Bn.	W., 4 M.G. Co. ✻ 12/4/17.	30/ 8/15 Pte. ✻
WARNE, E. W., Pte. 12 Bn.		7/ 8/16 1y 4m, Pte.
WARNE, J. T., Pte. 12 Bn.	W.	19/12/17 1y 5m, Pte.
WARNE, W. J., Pte. Tunnlrs. Rfts.	W.	20/ 6/17 1y 8m, Spr.
WARNER, C. H., Pte. 3 Fd. Amb.	3 A.G.H.	21/ 8/15 4y 4m, L.-Cpl.
WARNER, R. H., Sgt. 40 Bn.		16/10/16 2y 7m, Sgt.
WARREN, A., Pte. 12 Bn.	✻ 6-10/4/17.	2./ 8/18 Pte. ✻
WARREN, A. T., Pte. 4 M.G. Co.		20/ 2/17 1y 5m, Pte.
WARREN, C. W., Pte. 15 Bn.	W., M.M., 4 M.G. Bn.	12/ 8/15 4y 4m, L.-Cpl.
WARREN, D., Pte. T.M. Bty.	40 Bn.	14/12/16 2y 3m, Pte.
WARREN, D. W., Pte. 40 Bn.	16 Bn.	26/ 9/16 2y 11m, Pte.
WARREN, F., Pte. Tunnrs Cps.		24/ 2/17
WARREN, G. J., Pte. Rly. Unit	2 A.L.R.O.C.	28/ 5/18 1y 5m, Pte.
WARREN, H. E., Tpr. 3 L.H.	55 Bty.	13/ 9/15 4y 1m, Dvr.
WARREN, J. T., Pte. 15 Bn.	✻ 10/8/16.	30/ 8/15 Pte. ✻
WARREN, J. W., Pte. A.M.C.	3 A.G.H.	24/ 2/16 3y 8m, Ptr.
WARREN, R. G., Gnr. Arty.	17 Bty.	2/10/15 4y, Dvr.
WARREN, R. G., Pte. 12 Bn.		25/11/16 1y 7m, Pte.
WARREN, R., Pte. 12 Bn.	2W., 40 Bn.	24/10/16 2y 5m, Pte.
WARREN, S. R., Dvr. A.G.B.D.	10 M.G. Co.	14/ 5/17 2y 5m, Dvr.
WARREN, T. S., Pte. 40 Bn.	✻ 15/6/18.	25/ 1/17 Pte. ✻
WARREN, W. H., Pte. 40 Bn.		24/ 4/16 3y 7m, Pte.
WARREN, W. V. J., Pte. 26 Bn.		15/ 5/15 3y 4m, Pte.
WARREN, V. R., Pte. 15 Bn.	W.	7/10/15 4y 1m, Cpl.
WARRING, T. R., Pte. 40 Bn.		11/ 5/16 1y 1m, Pte.
WARRING, W. H., Pte. 40 Bn.	W.	30/ 3/16 3y 3m, Pte.
WARRINGTON, E. A., Dvr. 8 Fd. Co. Engrs.		13/ 1/16
WASHINGTON, A., Sgt. 40 Bn.	✻ 5/10/17.	3/ 8/15 ✻
WASHINGTON, H., Pte. 12 Bn.	W., 3 L.T.M. Bty.	20/ 8/14 4y, Cpl.
WATCHORN, A., Pte. 1 G.S.R.	40 Bn.	28/ 1/18 1y 10m, Pte.
WATERHOUSE, A. R., Capt. A.M.C.		11/ 1/17
WATERHOUSE, E. S., Tpr. 3 L.H.		11/ 7/17 1y 2m, Tpr.
WATERHOUSE, M. M., Tpr. 3 L.H.		28/ 8/14 5y 2m, Tpr.
WATERHOUSE, G. A., Gnr. Art.	A.F.C. Training Depot.	24/ 2/16 3y 5m, Lieut.
WATERHOUSE, P. M., Cpl. 3 L.H.		19/10/14 4y 6m, Sgt.
WATERS, A. J., Pte. 2 A.G.H.	3 A.G.H.	1/10/15 4y. Cpl
WATERS, G. R., Tpr. 3 L.H.	4 L.H.	1/ 3/17 2y 6m, Tpr.
WATERS, H. W., Pte. 12 Bn.		8/12/14 4y 6m, Pte.
WATERS, H., Pte. 12 Bn.	2W.	2/ 9/15 1y 9m, Pte.
WATERS, H. D., Cpl. 1 Rmnt. Unit		25/10/15 3y 10m, Cpl.
WATERS, J. E., Cpl. Rly. Unit.	M.M., 4 A.B.G.R.O.C.	5/ 1/17 2y 9m, Cpl.
WATERS, J., Pte. 40 Bn.	W., 15 Bn.	21/ 3/16 1y 7m, Pte.
WATERS, M. F., Pte. 1 A.C.H.	3 A.G.H.	2/ 8/■■ 4y, Pte.
WATERS, P., Pte. 15 Bn.	4 D.A.C.	25/ 9/■■ 4y 4m, Dvr.
WATKINS, A. C., Pte. 1 A.C.H.	M.S.M., Aust. Cps. Hqrs.	4/ 2/15 4y 4m, S.^

TASMANIA'S MUSTER ROLL. 359

NAME.	REMARKS.	RANK ON DISCHARGE. ENLISTED. SERVICE.
WATKINS, H. T., Pte. 40 Bn.		29/ 9/16 1y 9m, Pte.
WATKINS, L., Pte. 12 Bn.	26 Bn.	3/ 3/15 2y 10m, Pte.
WATKINS, T. J., Pte. 15 Bn.	W.	25/ 6/15 3y 6m, Sgt.
WATKINS, W. H., Pte. 40 Bn.		13/ 2/17 2y 1m, Pte.
WATKINSON, A. H., Pte. 12 Bn.	✣ 9/8/15.	15/ 1/15 Pte. ✣
WATLING, A., Pte. 15 Bn.	✣ 7/8/15.	30/10/14 Pte. ✣
WATLING, A., Pte. 15 Bn.	✣ 9/8/15.	30/ 9/14 Pte. ✣
WATLING, E., Pte. 15 Bn.	W.	1/ 6/15 2y Pte.
WATLING, R., Spr. Tunnellers	2 Tun. Co.	7/ 2/16 3y 6m, Spr.
WATSON, A. J., Pte. 1 Rmts.		30/ 9/15 1y 4m, Tpr.
WATSON, A. E., Pte. 12 Bn.	1 Pnr. Bn. ✣ 17/9/16.	5/ 1/15 1y 8m, Pte.
WATSON, F. H., Pte. 12 Bn.	W.	16/10/17 1y 5m, Pte.
WATSON, G., Pte. 40 Bn.	49 Bn. ✣ 24/11/16.	21/ 3/16 Pte. ✣
WATSON, G. B., Dvr., 18 Bty.	W.	22/ 9/15 3y 7m, Dvr.
WATSON, H. J., Gnr. Arty.	2W., 15 Bn. ✣ 5/10/17.	5/10/15 Gnr. ✣
WATSON, H., Pte. 2 G.S.R.	17 Bty.	23/ 3/18 1y 6m, Gnr.
WATSON, I., Cpl. 5 L.H.		7/ 4/16
WATSON, I., Pte. 40 Bn.	W., 51 Bn.	2/ 3/16 1y 11m, Pte.
WATSON, J., Pte. 40 Bn.	W., 26 Bn.	27/ 3/16 3y 1m, Pte.
WATSON, J. A., Pte. 26 Bn.		17/ 2/15 1y 6m, Pte.
WATSON, J. G., Pte. 26 Bn.		9/ 5/15
WATSON, J. E., Gnr. Arty.		17/ 1/16
WATSON, M. T., Pte. 1 A.G.H.	W., M.M., 1 Fd. Co. Engrs.	8/ 6/15 3y 11m, Spr.
WATSON, P., Pte. 26 Bn.	W.	2/ 3/15 4y 5m, Dvr.
WATSON, P., Pte. 12 Bn.		12/10/16
WATSON, T., Munition Worker		
WATSON, T. J., Pte. 12 Bn.		18/ 6/15 4y 6m, Pte.
WATSON, V. J., Pte. 40 Bn.		5/11/17 1y 11m, Pte.
WATSON, W. F., Pte. 12 Bn.	✣ 26/6/15.	21/ 8/14 Pte. ✣
WATSON, W., Pte. 40 Bn.	W.	12/ 5/16 1y 10m, Cpl.
WATSON, W. J. D., Pte. 40 Bn.	3 D.H.Q., 40 Bn.	28/10/16 2y 11m, Pte.
WATT, J. C., Pte. 12 Bn.		19/ 8/14
WATT, R. T., Pte. 12 Bn.	W., 5 Bn.	27/10/15 2y 8m, Pte.
WATTERS, W. H., Pte. 2 G.S.R.	13 Bty.	10/ 1/18 1y 11m, Gnr.
WATTS, B. J., Pte. 2 G.S.R.		1/ 5/18
WATTS, E., Pte. 4 M.G. Co.		16/11/16
WATTS, G. E. K., Pte. A.A.M.C.		9/10/17 2y 1m, Pte.
WATTS, G. H., Pte. 12 Bn.	M.M.	5/ 7/15 4y 2m, Cpl.
WATTS, E., Pte. 10 M.G. Co.	2W., 40 Bn.	15/11/16 2y 10m, Pte.
WAUGH, G. T., Dvr. D.A.C.		24/ 8/15 4y 2m, BQMS
WAUGH, J. G., Pte. 26 Bn.	2W.	4/ 3/15 2y 8m, Pte.
WAXMAN, R. H., Pte. 12 Bn.		20/ 8/14 4y 6m, Pte.
WAY, H. J., Pte. 12 Bn.	52 Bn., 51 Bn.	9/ 8/15 3y 8m, Pte.
WEAVER, G. V., Pte. 40 Bn.		4/ 4/16 3y, Pte.
WEAVERS, T. E., 2-Lt., 12 Bn.	W.	28/ 8/14 2y 8m, Capt.
WEAVERS, J. C. Spr. 3 Fd. Co.	✣ 22/7/15.	20/ 8/14 L.-Cpl. ✣
WEAVER, R. N. W., Tpr. 3 L.H.	✣ 4-6/8/16.	21/ 6/15 Tpr. ✣
WEAVING, H., Pte. 26 Bn.	12 Bn.	9/ 8/15 1y 10m, Pte.
WEAVING, H. J. F., Pte. 12 Bn.	W.	28/ 7/15 4y 1m, Pte.
WEBB, A. S., Lieut. 12 Bn.	2W.	2/ 9/15
WEBB, C. A., Pte. 12 Bn.	52 Bn., 51 Bn.	16/11/15 4y, Pte.
WEBB, C., Pte. 12 Bn.		17/11/15 3y 9m, Pte.
WEBB, C. A. E., Pte. 12 Bn.	✣ 20/9/15.	9/ 9/14 Pte. ✣
WEBB, E. C., Pte. 40 Bn.	1 A.D.H.	2/ 2/16 2y 1m, Pte.
WEBB, E. E., Pte. 40 Bn.	2W., 15 Bn.	21/ 3/16 3y 7m, Sgt.
WEBB, F. C., Pte. 40 Bn.	2W.	30/ 9/16 3y, Pte.
WEBB, F. W., Pte. 15 Bn.		28/ 7/15 11m, Pte.
WEBB, G. J., Gnr. D.A.C.		23/ 5/15 1y, Gnr.
WEBB, H. J., Pte. 40 Bn.	3W.	27/ 9/16
WEBB, H. R., Sgt. 5 Mining Co.	5 Tun. Co.	3/ 12/14 1y 4m, Sgt.
WEBB, H. G., Pte. 12 Bn.	W., 2 M.G. Bn.	9/10/16 2y 6m, Pte.
WEBB, J.		14/ 7/19
WEBB, J., Pte. 26 Bn.	W., 12 Bn., 1 Pnrs.	14/ 8/15 2y 8m, Pte.
WEBB, J., Pte. 2 G.S.R.		30/ 5/18 1y 2m, Pte.
WEBB, J. H. W., Pte. 40 Bn.	W.	5/ 5/16 1y 8m, Pte.
WEBB, J. L., Pte. 40 Bn.		13/ 3/17 3y 2m, Pte.
WEBB, L. G., Pte. 40 Bn.	W., 4 M.G. Bn.	22/ 4/15 5y 9m, Pte.
WEBB, R. W., Pte. 26 Bn.		6/ 2/16 3y 10m, Pte.
WEBB, T. H., Pte 40 Bn.	W.	14/10/16 3y, Pte.
WEBB, V. P., Gnr. Arty.	2 D.A.C.	1/11/15 3y 11m, Dvr.
WEBB, W., Pte. 12 Bn.		28/ 4/17 1y 8m, Pte.
WEBB, W. E., Pte. 40 Bn.	✣ 30/1/17.	8/ 2/16 Pte. ✣
WEBB, W. H., Pte. 40 Bn.	✣ 8/12/17.	3/10/16 Pte. ✣
WEBBER, F. L., Pte. 12 Bn.	52 Bn. ✣ 4/9/16.	28/ 7/15 Pte. ✣
WEBBER, G. J C., Pte. 12 Bn.	31 Bn.	19/ 1/16 2y 2m, Pte.
WEBBER, H. W., Gnr. Arty.	5 F.A.B.	26/10/16 2y 9m, Gnr.
WEBBER, T., Pte. 40 Bn.	W.	17/ 4/16 1y 9m, Pte.
WEBSDALE, E. G., Pte. 40 Bn.		28/11/16 3y 1m, Pte.
WEBSTER, A. A., Gnr. 18 Bty.	W., 17 Bty.	11/ 9/15 2y 6m, Gnr.
WEBSTER, A. D. T., Pte. 26 Bn.	2W.	26/ 5/15 4y 3m, Sgt.
WEBSTER, A. C., Spr. 5 Mining C	2 Tun. Cps.	30/ 3/16 3y 6m, Spr.
WEBSTER, A. F., Dvr. Arty.	W., 2 F.A.B.	7/ 1/15 3y 11m, Bdr.
WEBSTER, D. S., Pte. 40 Bn.		10/ 7/16 2y 1m, Pte.
WEBSTER, E. L., Pte. 40 Bn.	2W.	27/ 9/16 1y 1m, Pte.
WEBSTER, ▇., Pte. 12 Bn.	W., 52 Bn.	8/ 7/15 2y, Sgnlr.
WEBSTER, F. W., Cpl. 12 Bn.		20/ 6/17
WEBSTER, H. C., Pte. 40 Bn.	49 Bn.	30/ 3/16 3y 6m, Pte.

TASMANIA'S WAR RECORD, 1914-1918.

NAME.	REMARKS	RANK ON DISCHARGE. ENLISTED. SERVICE.
WEBSTER, J., Sgt. 12 Bn.	3W.	23/ 7/15 2y 8m, Sec. Lt
WEBSTER, J. L., Pte. A.M.C.	W., 6 Fd. Amb.	14/ 3/16 2y 7m, Pte.
WEBSTER, T. L., Tpr. 3 L.H.	✠ 15/6/15.	13/ 9/14 Tpr. ✠
WEBSTER, W l., Pte. A.M.C. Rfts.	✠ 30/9/19.	2/10/17 Pte. ✠
WEEDING, W., Pte. 12 Bn.	W.	18/ 7/16 2y 5m, Pte.
WEEDON, W., Pte. 4 M.G. Co.		1/ 8/16
WEEKS, E. B., Tpr. 3 L.H.	Arty. Details.	24/ 4/17 1y 11m, Gnr.
WEEKS, J. C., Pte. 15 Bn.	48 Bn.	16/ 7/15 4y 1m, Cpl.
WEEKS, L. E., Tpr. 3 L.H.	W.	20/ 8/14 4y 7m, Cpl.
WEEKS, M., Pte. 12 Bn.		5/ 9/16 3y 4m, Pte.
WEEKS, S. S., Pte. 40 Bn.	2W.	28/ 9/16 2y 7m, Pte.
WEEKS, T. L., Pte. 26 Bn.	W.	28/ 7/15 1y 8m, Pte.
WEIGHT, A. B., Pte. A.M.C.		14/ 3/16
WEILKY, H., Gnr. 18 Bty.	17 Bty.	27/7/15 4y 1m, Bdr.
WEIR, C. A., Pte. 12 Bn.	M.G. Dtls., 12 Bn. ✠ 17/8/18.	29/ 3/16 Pte. ✠
WELCH, P. M., Pte. 3 Cyc. Co.	7 Fd. Co. Engrs.	5/ 4/16 3y 8m, Spr.
WELDON, C., Pte. 40 Bn.	✠ 7/6/17.	22/ 3/16 Pte. ✠
WELLARD, C. V., Gnr. 17 Bty.		13/ 8/15 4y, Gnr.
WELLARD, L. W., Pte. 15 Bn.		16/ 6/15
WELLER, L., Pte. 12 Bn.	W., 52 Bn.	4/ 1/16 2y 11m, Cpl.
WELLER, M. D., Gnr. Arty.		21/ 3/17 1y 6m, Gnr.
WELLER, W. D., Pte. 12 Bn.		14/10/16 2y 11m, Pte.
WELLING, W. J., Sgt. 1 G.S.R.	✠ 24/7/16.	20/ 2/17 2y 7m, Sgt.
WELSH, E. R., Pte. 26 Bn.	2W.	18/ 8/15 Pte. ✠
WELSH, F. J., Gnr. 9 Bty.	W., 7 Fd. Amb.	16/ 9/15 3y 7m, Gnr.
WELSH, G., Pte. 3 G.S.R.	2W., M.M., 13 Fd. Amb.	6/10/14 4y 7m, Pte.
WELSH, J. T., Pte. 7 Fd. Amb.		12/ 3/15 4y 3m, L.-Cpl.
WELSH, P. S. 3 F.A.B.		27/ 8/14
WELSH, R. W., S/Smith 1 Rmt. Dpt.	26 Bty.	23/ 9/15 3y 11m, S/Smt
WELSH, W., Pte. 2 G.S.R.		16/ 5/18 1y 4m, Gnr.
LUCADO-WELLS, D. P., Lt. A.A.D.C	1 A.M.C. Bn.	24/12/17 1y 9m, H.-Capt.
WELLS, A. J., Pte. 4 M.G. Co.		4/12/16 2y 10m, Pte.
WELLS, A. W., Pte. 12 Bn.		2/ 9/16 2y 6m, Pte.
WELLS, A. W., Pte. 40 Bn.		17/10/16 1y 7m, Pte.
WELLS, A. B., Pte. 3 Fd. Amb.	6 Fd. Amb. ✠ 1/11/17.	25/ 8/15 Pte. ✠
WELLS, A. L. J., Gnr. 15 F.A.B.	W., 4 F.A.B.	24/10/16 3y, Gnr.
WELLS, C. F., Pte. 12 Bn.	✠ 7/8/15.	3/ 2/15 Pte. ✠
WELLS, C., Pte. 2 G.S.R.		22/ 4/18 11m, Pte. ✠
WELLS, G. H., Tpr. 3 L.H.	1 L.H., Fd. Amb.	23/ 8/17 1y 9m, Tpr.
WELLS, G. G. T., Pte. 12 Bn.		10/ 1/18 1y 6m, Pte.
WELLS, G. A., Pte. 40 Bn.	W.	16/10/16
WELLS, H. H. A., Pte. 4 M.G. Co.	W., 69 Bn., 12 Bn. ✠ 23/8/18.	10/ 8/16 3y 1m, Pte.
WELLS, H. E. C., Pte. 12 Bn.	✠ 30/3/18.	10/ 4/16 Pte. ✠
WELLS, J., Pte. 40 Bn.	40 Bn.	18/10/16 Pte. ✠
WELLS, J. B., Pte. 1 G.S.R.		25/ 3/18 1y 7m, Pte.
WELLS, J. L., Dvr. 8 Fd. Co. Engrs		23/ 8/15 4y 1m, Dvr.
WELLS, J. C., Pte. 40 Bn.		5/ 4/16 8m, Pte.
WELLS, L. F., Tpr. 3 L.H.		29/ 1/15 1y 9m, Tpr.
WELLS, M. V., 8 Fd. Co. Engrs.	14 Fd. Co. ngrs. ✠ 24/6/18.	25/ 1/16 Spr. ✠
WELLS, M. L., Gnr. Arty.		27/ 3/17 1y 8m, Gnr.
WELLS, M. U., Spr. 8 Fd. Co. Eng	14 Fd. Co. Engrs. ✠ 24/6/18	25/ 1/16 Spr. ✠
WELLS, P., Pte. 12 Bn.	W., 52 Bn.	3/ 2/16 2y 4m, Pte.
WELLS, R. P., Pte. 12 Bn.	W., 52 Bn., 51 Bn.	31/ 8/15 4y, Pte.
WELLS, R. J., Pte. 12 Bn.	52 Bn. ✠ 4/9/16.	5/ 8/15 Pte. ✠
WELLS, T., Pte. 12 Bn.	52 Bn., 49 Bn. ✠ 6/9/18.	16/10/15 Dvr. ✠
WELLS, V. E. O., Pte. 12 Bn.		31/10/16 2y 5m, Pte.
WELLS, V. K., Pte. 3 G.S.R.	12 Bn.	14/ 6/18 1y 4m, Pte.
WELLS, V. E., Pte. 12 Bn.	W.	3/ 5/16 1y 6m, Pte.
WELLS, W. H., Pte. 12 Bn.	2W., 69 Bn., 12 Bn.	8/ 2/15 4y 6m, Pte.
WELLS, W. A., Dvr. 3 F.A.B.	102 How. Bty.	4/15 4y 4m, Pte.
WELLS, W. J., Pte. 40 Bn.	3W.	5/ 5/16 2y 11m, Pte.
WELLS, W. A. D., Pte. 40 Bn.	W.	28/ 7/16 2y 1m, Pte.
WELLS, W. R., Pte. 40 Bn.	✠ 3/1/17.	29/ 2/16 Pte. ✠
WELLS, W. A., Pte 12 Bn.		2/ 9/16
WERTHEIMER, M. T., Gnr. 8 F.A.B	108 How. Bty.	5/ 1/16 3y 9m, Dvr.
WESCOMBE, A. J. D., M.W., Navvies and Laborers		M.W.
WESCOMBE, E. R. Pte. 12 Bn.	5 M.G. Bn.	12/10/16 2y 11m, Pte.
WESCOMBE, G. V., Pte. 12 Bn.	2 Cyc. Cps.	12/10/16 1y 1m, Pte.
WESLEY, W., Tpr. 3 L.H.		8/11/17 1y 6m, Tpr.
WEST, A. E., Pte. 15 Bn.	W., 110 How. Bty.	27/ 7/15 3y 4m, Pte.
WEST, B., Pte. 30 Bn.	2W.	2/ 3/16 3y 1m, Cpl.
WEST, C. B., Pte. 12 Bn.		17/ 4/17 2y 6m, Pte.
WEST, E. W., Pte. 15 Bn.	W. ✠ 7/6/17.	4/ 8/15 Pte. ✠
WEST, G., Gnr. Art.		15/ 2/16 3y 1m
WEST, P. J., Pte. 15 Bn.	W.	13/10/14 4y 4m, Pte.
WEST, R., Pte. 12 Bn.		9/10/16 1y 10m, Pte.
WESTBROOK, J., Spr. 8 Fd. Co. Eng		29/ 2/16 3y 3m, Dvr.
WESTBROOK, L. M., Spr. 3 F.C.E.	2W.	24/ 8/14 4y 7m, Cpl.
WESTBROOK, L. J., Pte. 40 Bn.	W.	28/ 3/16 1y 9m, Pte.
WESTBROOK, P., Dvr. 8 Fd. Co. Eng	3 Fd. Co. Engrs.	28/ 2/16 3y 8m, Dvr.
WESTBROOK, V. G., Pte. 40 Bn.	✠ 18/6/17.	15/ 3/16 Pte. ✠
WESTBURY, R. E., Pte. 12 Bn.	✠ 24/4/16.	4/ 2/16 Pte. ✠
WESTCOTT, A. R., Pte. 12 Bn.		7/12/15 2y 4m, Pte.
WESTCOTT, F. D., Pte. 40 Bn.	W.	20/ 3/16 2y 2m, Pte.
WESTCOTT, W. W., Pte. 26 Br	W. 12 Bn. ✠ 18/4/18.	17/ 8/15 L.-Cpl. ✠
WESTELL, J., Spr. Tunnellers Co.		31/ 3/17 1y 11m, Spr

TASMANIA'S MUSTER ROLL.

NAME.	REMARKS.	RANK ON DISCHARGE. ENLISTED. SERVICE.
WESTERGREEN, A. E., Spr. Miners		23/ 2/16 2y 7m, Spr.
WESTERMAN, B. T., Pte. 12 Bn.	W., 1 Anzac Sal. Sec.	27/ 1/16 3y 7m, L.-Cpl.
WESTERWAY, E., Gnr. Arty.	6 M.T.M.B. ✠ 29/9/18.	18/10/16 Gnr. ✠
WESTERWAY, N. W., Dvr. 6 F.C.E	15 Fd. Co. Engrs.	6/ 9/15 3y 7m, Dvr.
WESTERWAY, W. L., Spr. 8 F.C.E.	6 Fd. Co. Engrs.	29/ 2/16 3y 7m, Spr.
WESTLAKE, C. St. C., Dvr. 6 F.C.E	W. M.M.	24/ 8/15 3y 9m, Dvr.
WESTMORE, P. C., Pte. 2 G.S.R.	12 Bn.	30/ 4/18 1y 2m, Pte.
WESTON, E. D., Pte. 12 Bn.		24/ 8/15 .
WESTON, F., Pte. 1 G.S.R.		9/ 3/18
WESTON, V. E., L/Cpl. 12 Bn.		20/ 8/14
WESTWOOD, A. E., Pte. 1 A.C.H.	W.	29/ 9/14 4y 4m, Sgt.
WESTWOOD, J. W., Pte. 15 Bn.	3W., D.C.M., M.M.	31/ 8/15 4y 1m, Lieut.
WESTWOOD, R. E., Pte. 12 Bn.	4 D.A.C.	5/10/15 3y 11m, Dvr.
WESTWOOD, R. T., Pte. 40 Bn.	W.	15/ 3/16
WEYMOUTH, A. E., Pte. 3 Fd. Am	M.M., 13 Fd. Amb.	24/ 8/14 4y 6m, S/Sgt.
WEYMOUTH, G., Pte. 7 Fld. Amb.	13 Fd. Amb.	8/ 3/15 4y 3m, Pte.
WHARMBY, A., Pte. 26 Bn.	✠ 6/4/16	20/ 4/15 Pte. ✠
WHATLEY, W., Pte. 12 Bn.	W., 52 Bn.	7/ 9/15 1y 8m, Pte.
WHEAT, A., Pte. 40 Bn.	26 Bn.	20/ 1/16 3y 8m, Pte.
WHEAT, R., Pte. 12 Bn.	✠ 19-22/8/16.	24/ 8/15 Pte. ✠
WHEATLEY, A. V., Pte. 40 Bn.	✠ 11/2/17.	1/10/16 Pte. ✠
WHEATLEY, E. D. B., Pte. 40 Bn.	W., Vet. Hosp., 40 Bn.	1/ 6/16 3y 2m, Pte.
WHEATLEY, P. A., Pte. 15 Bn.	✠ 10/5/15.	21/ 9/14 Pte. ✠
WHEATON, J., Pte. 26 Bn.		2/ 2/15 1y 2m, Pte.
WHEELDON, M. J., Pte. 26 Bn.		27/ 7/15 2y 11m, Pte.
WHEELER, G., Pte. 12 Bn.	W., 52 Bn., 27 Co., A.A.S.C.	17/ 1/16 3y 9m, L.-Cpl.
WHEELER, H. J., Tpr. 3 L.H.		24/11/17 1y 9m, Tpr.
WHEELER, R., Pte. 12 Bn.	W., 52 Bn.	17/ 1/16 3y 8m, Pte.
WHEELTON, R. J., Pte. 2 G.S.R.	12 Bn.	19/ 3/18 1y 8m, Pte.
WHELAN, D., Pte. 12 Bn.	W.	29/8/14 2y 1m, Pte.
WHELAN, F. J., Spr. 6 Fd. C. Engrs		26/ 8/15 1y, Spr.
WHELAN, J., Pte. 40 Bn.		19/ 9/16 3y 2m, Cpl.
WHELAN, J. J., Pte. 40 Bn.		6/ 6/16
WHELAN, J. J., Pte. 15 Bn.		23/ 9/14 10m, Pte.
WHELAN, T. C., Pte. 26 Bn.		14/ 4/15 1y, L.-Cpl.
WHELAN, W. H., Pte. 26 Bn.	W. ✠ 16/12/17.	15/ 9/15 Pte. ✠
WHIFFEN, W. E., Pte. 12 Bn.	✠ 8/8/16.	4/ 8/15 Pte. ✠
WHILEY, W. T., Pte. 26 Bn.	7 L.T.M. Bty. ✠ 4/7/18.	21/ 7/15 Cpl. ✠
WISHART, A. G., Dvr. 3 F.A.B.	3 Fd. Co. Engrs.	5/10/14
WHISHAW, D., Pte. 7 Fd. Amb.	15 Fd. Amb.	27/ 3/15 4y 9m, L.-Cpl.
WHISHAW, R., Sgt. 7 Fd. Amb.	13 Fd. Amb.	27/ 3/15 1y 1m, Sgt.
WHITAKER, J. G., Spr. 3 F.C.E.	10 F.A.B.	4/ 8/15 3y 8m, W.O.
WHITAKER, M. H. O., Sgt. 40 Bn.	4W., M.C., M.I.D.	4/ 1/16 3y 8m, Lieut.
WHITCHURCH, D. C. A., D., 8 F.C.E.		31/ 1/16 3y 8m, Spr.
WHITCHURCH, F. E., Gnr. Arty.	5 F.A.B. ✠ 14/8/17.	1/10/15 Gnr. ✠
WHITCHURCH, G., Pte. 26 Bn.	2W.	17/ 6/15 2y 7m, Pte.
WHITCHURCH, J. V., Pte. 12 Bn.		25/10/16 1y 8m, Pte.
WHITCOMBE, J. F., Pte. 40 Bn.	2W., 69 Bn., 40 Bn.	21/ 4/16 2y 11m, Pte.
WHITCOMBE, W. E., Pte. 12 Bn.	52 Bn. ✠ 19/1/17.	10/ 1/16 Pte. ✠
WHITEHOUSE, F. J., Pte. 12 Bn.		25/10/16 1y 9m, Pte.
WHITEHOUSE, W. W., Pte. 12 Bn.		12/ 4/16 7m, Pte.
WHITEHOUSE, W. R., Pte. 2 A.G.H	14 A.G.H.	8/10/15 3y 10m, Pte.
WHITELAW, F. H., Pte. 40 Bn.		12/ 1/16
WHITELEY, W. H., Dvr. 9 Bty.	21 How. Bde.	15/ 7/15 3y 10m, Dvr.
WHITFELD, L. C., Lt.-Col. 2 Inf Bde H.Q.	D.S.O.	1/ 9/14 4y 11m, Lt.-Co.
WHITFIELD, D., Pte. 12 Bn.	2W., M.M.	24/ 2/16
WHITFIELD, G. P., Tpr. 3 L.H.	✠ 19/7/15.	9/ 4/15 Pte. ✠
WHITFORD, M. A., Spr. Tunn. Cps	Munition Workers.	18/ 5/16
WHITFORD, R. C., Dvr. 17 Bty.	W.	6/ 9/15 3y 2m, Dvr.
WHITHAM, J. L., Capt. 12 Bn.	C.M.G., D.S.O., M.I.D.	31/ 8/14
WHITING, D., Pte. 40 Bn.	2W.	28/ 3/16 1y 11m, Pte.
WHITING, F. C., Pte. 4 M.G. Co.	W., 24 Bn.	10/10/16 3y, Pte.
WHITING, H. T., Gnr. Arty.	29 F.A.B.	8/11/16 3y 1m, Gnr.
WHITING, J., Pte. Remount Sec.	4 Div. Arty. H.Q.	29/ 9/15 3y 11m, Dvr.
WHITING, J. S., Pte. 12 Bn.	P.O.W.	19/12/14 4y 8m, Pte.
WHITING, J. C., Pte. 15 Bn.	26 A.S.C.	27/ 5/15 4y 3m, Dvr.
WHITING, J. J., 15 Bn.	W., 47 Bn.	3/ 8/15 2y 8m, Sgt.
WHITING, S. M., Pte. 40 Bn.	4 A.M.T.	15/ 3/17 1y 8m, Pte.
WHITING, S. M., Dvr. 8 Fd. Co. Eng		8/ 2/16 1y 1m, Dvr.
WHITMORE, G. E., Pte. 12 Bn.		10/ 8/16 Pte.
WHITMORE, H. G., Pte. 12 Bn.	W., 52 Bn. ✠ 3/10/16.	4/ 8/16 Pte. ✠
WHITMORE, J. W., Pte. 12 Bn.	M.G. Co., 2 Bn.	13/ 4/16 3y 5m, Pte.
WHITMORE, W. L., Pte. 12 Bn.	D.C.M., 52 Bn., 51 Bn.	27/ 7/15 4y 1m, Cpl.
WHITNEY, A. J., Pte. 40 Bn.	M.S.M.	3/ 7/16 3y 3m, Sgt.
WHITNEY, A. C., Pte. 15 Bn.	✠ 18/6/15.	28/ 9/14 Pte. ✠
WHITNEY, J., Pte. 40 Bn.		7/ 8/15 3y 5m, Pte.
WHITNEY, T., Tpr. 3 L.H.	Anzac Troop Supply Column.	20/ 8/14 4y 5m, Tpr.
WHITPAINE, R., Gnr. 18 Bty.	W., 17 Bty.	5/ 8/15 3y 8m, Gnr.
WHITTAKER, W. L. C., Pte. T.M.B	W., 40 Bn.	27/10/16 2y 6m, Pte.
WHITTINGHAM, L. W., Pte. 40 Bn	✠ 14/5/17.	17/10/16 Pte. ✠
WHITTLE, B. H., Pte. 40 Bn.	3W.	17/ 3/16 3y 7m, Sec. Lt
WHITTLE, C. G., Pte. 12 Bn.	2W., M.M., 52 Bn.	4/ 8/15 2y 9m, Pte.
WHITTLE, C. P., Dvr. 7 Fd. Amb.	13 Fd. Amb.	12/ 2/15 3y 1m, Pte.
WHITTLE, E., Pte. Remount Sec.		28/ 9/15 9m, Pte.
WHITTLE, E. A., Pte. 12 Bn.	40 Bn. ✠ 31/8/18.	24/10/16 Pte. ✠
WHITTLE, E. L., Spr. Tunnellers	W., 1 G.T.C.	3/ 4/16 3y 5m, Spr.

NAME.	REMARKS.	RANK ON DISCHARGE. ENLISTED. SERVICE.
WHITTLE, G. H., Cpl. 3 G.S.R.	2W., 12 Bn.	17/ 8/14 4y 10m, Cpl.
WHITTLE, J. W., Cpl. 26 Bn.	3W., V.C., D.C.M., 12 Bn.	6/ 8/15 3y 4m, Sgt.
WHITTLE, M. J., Gnr. Arty.		26/10/16 2y 5m, Dvr.
WHITTLE, T. C., Pte. 12 Bn.	36 H.A.G.	14/ 7/15 4y 2m, Pte.
WHITTLE, W. A., Gnr. 6 F.A.B.	✠ 31/3/16.	31/ 7/15 Gnr. ✠
WHITTON, A. L., Spr. Tunnellers	2 D.A.C.	8/11/16 2y 11m, Gnr.
WHITTON, B. J., Gnr. Siege Art Bd		7/ 6/15
WHITTON, F. J. J., Spr. Tunnellers	W., 2 Pnr. Bn.	24/10/16 2y 10m, Spr.
WHITWORTH, J., Pte. 4 M.G. Co.	21 M.G. Co. ✠ 30/10/17.	3/ 7/16 Pte. ✠
WAYMAN, B. R., Pte. 15 Bn.	✠ 27/5/15.	29/11/14 Pte. ✠
WHYMAN, E. W., Pte. 12 Bn.		1/ 8/15 4y, Pte.
WHYMAN, L. P., Pte. 12 Bn.	40 Bn. ✠ 5/10/17.	11/ 3/16 Pte. ✠
WHITE, A. J., Navvies and Laborers		14/ 3/19
WHITE, B. D., Gnr. Arty.	30 Bty.	22/ 1/16 3y 9m, Gnr.
WHITE, B., L/Cpl. 2 G.S.R.		28/ 3/18
WHITE, C., Pte. 15 Bn.		21/12/14
WHITE, C., Pte. 12 Bn.	69 Bn., 12 Bn.	8/12/15 3y 9m, Pte.
WHITE, C. H., Pte. 15 Bn.	W.	19/ 9/14 2y 5m, Pte.
WHITE, C. P., Pte. 12 Bn.	52 Bn., 51 Bn.	1/12/15 4y 1m, Pte.
WHITE, C. W., Pte. 26 Bn.		23/ 3/15 4y 1m, CQMS
WHITE, C. W., Pte. 12 Bn.	52 Bn. ✠ 8/6/17.	11/ 1/16 Pte. ✠
WHITE, C. C., Pte. 12 Bn.	W., 52 Bn. ✠ 26/9/17	9/ 1/16 Pte. ✠
WHITE, C. A. W., Pte. 2 G.S.R.	17 Bty.	27/ 5/18 1y 6m, Gnr.
WHITE, D., Pte. 12 Bn.	W.	8/12/15
WHITE, E., Pte. 1 A.C.H.		15/ 9/14 1y 11m, Pte.
WHITE, E. J., Dvr. 3 Fd. Co. Engrs.		12/ 9/14 4y 5m, Dvr.
WHITE, E. J., Tpr. 3 L.H.	1 M.G.S.	9/ 6/15 4y 5m, Sgt.
WHITE, F. D. D., Pte. 40 Bn.		2/10/16 3y 2m, Pte.
WHITE, F. G., Pte. 12 Bn.		11/ 2/15 4y 10m, Pte.
WHITE, F. J., Pte. 40 Bn.	53 Bn., 40 Bn.	14/ 3/16 3y 5m, Cpl.
WHITE, F. W., Pte. 40 Bn.	W., 49 Bn.	6/ 4/16 3y 5m, Pte.
WHITE, G. D., Pte. 12 Bn.	52 Bn., 49 Bn.	29/11/15 3y 9m, Pte.
WHITE, G. H., Tpr. 3 L.H.		6/ 6/17
WHITE, H. L., Pte. A.A.M.C.	10 Fd. Amb.	16/10/16 3y, Pte.
WHITE, J. H., Pte. 1 A.C.H.	W., 15 Fd. Amb.	22/ 9/14 3y 9m, Pte.
WHITE, J. T., Cpl. 39 Bn.		10/ 4/16 1y 7m, Cpl.
WHITE, J. V., Pte. 3 L.H.	✠ 12/1/17.	9/ 4/15 Pte. ✠
WHYTE, D., Gnr. Arty.	18 Bty.	9/10/16 2y 9m, Dvr.
WHITE, J. J. H., Pte. 40 Bn.	2W.	19/ 6/16
WHITE, K. D., Gnr. 25 F.A.B.	10 F.A.B.	28/ 8/16
WHITE, L. L., Gnr. D.A.C.	W., 111 How. Bty.	7/ 1/15 4y 9m, Bdr.
WHITE, L. M., Gnr. Arty.	4 F.A.B.	9/10/16 2y 8m, Gnr.
WHITE, O. S., Gnr. 8 F.A.B.	29 Bty., 31 Bty.	2/11/15 3y 10m, Cpl.
WHITE, R. A., Pte. 12 Bn.	W., 69 Bn., 12 Bn.	14/ 7/15 4y 1m, Pte.
WHITE, R. J., Pte. 12 Bn.	W.	8/12/15 2y, Pte.
WHITE, R., Pte. 12 Bn.		14/ 9/16
WHITE, S. E., P.e. 40 Bn.		19/10/16 2y 6m, Pte.
WHITE, T., Pte. 12 Bn.	2W., 48 Bn., 12 Bn.	11/12/14 4y 5m, Pte.
WHITE, T. H., Tpr. 3 L.H.	1 L.H.M.G.S.	3/ 9/15 1y 7m, Tpr.
WHITE, W. W. W., Cpl. 5 M.G. Co.		20/ 9/15
WHITE, W. C., Pte. 4 M.G. Co.	W., 5 M.G.C.	4/ 7/16 3y, Pte.
WHITE, W. J., Pte. 15 Bn.		5/ 6/15
WHITELAW, F. H., Pte. 40 Bn.		12/ 1/16
WICKENS, R. G., Pte. 12 Bn.	52 Bn. ✠ 6-10/4/17.	20/ 8/14 L.-Cpl. ✠
WICKENS, T. E., Pte. 12 Bn.	1 Pnrs. Bn.	5/10/15 4y 2m, Pte.
WICKENS, V. J., Pte. 15 Bn.	✠ 8/8/15.	9/ 2/15 L.-Cpl. ✠
WICKHAM, A. H., Pte. 40 Bn.		2/ 2/16 3y 6m, Pte.
WICKHAM, E. J., Pte. 40 Bn.		28/ 3/16 3y, Pte.
WICKINS, L. G., Gnr. Arty.	3 F.A.B.	25/ 9/16 2y 10m, Gnr.
WICKINS, R. F., Spr. 3 F.C.E.	W.	6/ 9/15 3y 10m, 2-Cpl.
WICKS, A. L., Pte. 40 Bn.		30/10/16 2y 8m, Pte.
WICKS, E., Pte. 4 M.G. Co.		18/10/16
WICKS, J. S., Pte. 12 Bn.	W., P.O.W.	15/ 8/16 3y, Pte.
WIDDICOMBE, H. D., Pte. 40 Bn.		2/ 7/17 1y 11m, Pte.
WIDDIFIELD, C. C., Gnr. Sge. Bde.	36 H.A.G., 1 Siege Bde.	25/ 2/17 2y 7m, Gnr.
WIDOWSON, F., Pte. 12 Bn.		30/11/14 7m, L.-Cpl.
WIEDEMANN, E. A., Pte. 12 Bn.		23/11/15 2y 5m, Pte.
WIFFEN, W. E., Tpr. 3 L.H.		10/ 9/15
WIGG, D. G., Pte. 12 Bn.	14 Fd. Amb.	6/ 4/16 3y 5m, Pte.
WIGG, J. L., Tpr. 5 G.S.R.	7 G.S.R.	16/ 7/18 6m, Pte.
WIGGINS, A. W., Pte. A.M.C.	2W., 2 Fd. Amb.	11/ 4/16 3y, Pte.
WIGGINS, H. L., Pte. 26 Bn.	W., 12 Bn.	11/ 8/15 1y 11m, Pte.
WIGGINS, R. S., Pte. 12 Bn.	✠ 5/7/16.	23/ 3/16 Pte. ✠
WIGGINS, R., Pte. 12 Bn.	✠ 11/8/18.	16/10/16 Pte. ✠
WIGGINS, V. T., Pte. 40 Bn.	49 Bn. ✠ 20/11/16.	15/ 4/16 Pte. ✠
WIGGINS, W. T., Pte. 12 Bn.	M.M.	23/ 3/16
WIGMORE, H., Pte. 12 Bn.		8/ 5/16 1y 6m, Pte.
WIGGNALL, A. B. A., Pte. 26 Bn.		17/ 2/15 4y 2m, Pte.
WILBY, G., Pte. 40 Bn.	W., 26 Bn.	27/ 3/16 2y 4m, Pte.
WILCOX, R. J., Pte. 12 Bn.	W.	7/11/16 3y, Pte.
WILCOX, W., Pte. 40 Bn.	W. ✠ 5/10/17.	9/ 3/16 Pte. ✠
WILES, F. C., Pte. 15 Bn.		7/ 8/15 4v 3m, Pte.
WILKES, E. H., Pte. 3 G.S.R.	12 Bn. ✠ 12/2/19.	21/ 8/18 Pte. ✠
WILKES, H. B., Pte. 3 G.S.R.	12 Bn.	21/ 8/18 11m, Pte.
WILKES, W. G., Pte. 3 Cyc. Co.	4 Fd. Co. Engrs.	4/ 4/16 3y 5m, Spr.
WILKIE, C. E., Pte. 26 Bn.	D.C.M. ✠ 14/11/16.	15/ 6/15 C.S.M. ✠
WILKINS, G. H., Pte. 15 Bn.	M.C.	28/ 9/14 3y 10m, L.

TASMANIA'S MUSTER ROLL. 363

NAME.	REMARKS.	RANK ON DISCHARGE. ENLISTED, SERVICE.
WILKINS, L. W., Spr. 8 F.C.E.	2W.	28/ 1/16 3y 8m, Spr.
WILKINS, M. G., Pte. 4 A.S.C.	1 Div. Trn.	14/ 8/15 4y, L.-Cpl.
WILKINS, P. A., Cpl. 40 Bn.	✠ 3/1/17.	12/ 1/16 L.-Sgt. ✠
WILKINS, R., Pte. 4 M.G. Co.	15 M.G. Co. ✠ 1/11/17.	19/10/16 Pte. ✠
WILKINS, R. T., Pte. 40 Bn.		28/ 7/17 9m, Pte.
WILKINS, S. J. E., Pte. 12 Bn.	3 Fd. Amb.	13/7/15 3y 8m, Pte.
WILKINS, W., Pte. 12 Bn.		12/ 4/16 1y 11m, Pte.
WILKINSON, A., Gnr. Arty.	2 Dvl. Arty. H.Q.	5/10/15 4y, Gnr.
WILKINSON, C. A., Gnr. 18 Bty.	17 Bty.	13/ 8/15 4y 2m, Lieut.
WILKINSON, G. I., Pte. Wireless	Cavalry Divl. Sig. Sqd.	16/10/16 3y 1m, Cpl.
WILKINSON, J. B., Pte. 26 Bn.		28/ 6/15 4y 2m, Pte.
WILKINSON, R. C., Dvr. 10 A.S.C.		12/ 9/14
WILKINSON, T. C. B., Pte. 12 Bn.	W., M.M., 5th Bn.	2/ 8/15 3y 10m, L.-Cpl
WILKINSON, T. W., Sgt. Rmt. Sec.	4 Inf. Bde. ✠ 7/4/17.	24/10/15 W.O. ✠
WILKINSON, W. R., Gnr. Arty.	2W., 6 F.A.B.	17/ 7/16 3y 1m, Gnr.
WILL, G. R., Spr. 4 Fd. Co. Engrs.	Amm. Park	24/ 8/15 4y, Dvr.
WILL, J. H., Cpl. 12 Bn.	M.M.	18/ 8/14 3y 3m, Lieut.
WILLCOCK, C. C., Gnr. Arty.	7 F.A.B. ✠ 24/12/18.	24/ 4/17 Gnr. ✠
WILLEY, M. P., Pte. 26 Bn.	D.C.M.	4/ 5/15 4y 7m, Lieut.
WILLIAMSON, A. G., Pte. A.F.C.	1 Sqd.	7/10/16 2y 8m, 2-A.M.
WILLIAMSON, C. F., Pte. 12 Bn.	W., ✠ 23/3/18.	20/10/16 ✠
WILLIAMSON, C. I., Pte. 12 Bn.	W.	10/12/17 1y 4m. L-Cpl.
WILLIAMSON, E. H., Pte. 12 Bn.		20/ 8/14
WILLIAMSON, E. R., Pte. 4 M.G. C	W., 1 M.G. Co.	11/ 1/17 2y 2m, Pte.
WILLIAMSON, E. R., Pte. 26 Bn.		28/ 4/15 1y 2m, Pte.
WILLIAMSON, G. F., Pte. 12 Bn.	✠ 19-22/8/16.	23/11/15 Pte. ✠
WILLIAMSON, H. J., Pte. 12 Bn.	W., 52 Bn.	30/12/14 4y 8m, Sgt.
WILLIAMSON, S. F., Pte. 2 G.S.R.	12 Bn.	3/ 6/18 1y 4m, Pte.
WILLIAMSON, T., Pte. 12 Bn.	✠ 5-8/5/17.	8/ 2/15 Pte. ✠
WILLIE, G. A., Pte. 26 Bn.	✠ 5/8/16.	15/ 9/15 Pte. ✠
WILLIE, J., Pte. 12 Bn.		21/ 8/14
WILLIE, J., Pte. 26 Bn.		8/10/15
WILLIE, J. H., Pte. 12 Bn.		27/ 4/16 2y 1m, Pte.
WILLING, C. R., Pte. 12 Bn.	✠ 6-10/4/17.	6/ 8/15 ✠
WILLING, D., Pte. 1 G.S.R.	8 Bty.	7/ 3/18 1y 7m, Gnr.
WILLING, D. E., Gnr. Arty.	9 Bty.	20/ 9/16 3y 1m, Gnr.
WILLING, M., Tpr. 2 G.S.R.	2 Fd. Co. Engrs.	15/ 4/18 1y 5m. Spr.
WILLING, R., Dvr. 6 Fd. Co. Engrs.		29/ 7/15 4y 4m, Dvr.
WILLIS, M. R., Tpr. 3 L.H.	W.	25/11/14 4y 10m, S.S.M.
WILLIS, T. W., Pte. 12 Bn.	3W.	4/ 8/15 4y, Pte.
WILLIS, V., Pte. 12 Bn.	W.	26/ 8/14 3y 11m, Pte.
WILLIS, V. R., Pte. 12 Bn.	2W., 40 Bn.	5/ 4/16 3y 4m, Pte.
WILLISCROFT, H. F., Gnr. 6 F.A.B	15 F.A.B. ✠ 5/12/16.	19/10/15 Gnr. ✠
WILLISCROFT, V. G., Bglr. 12 Bn.		20/ 4/14 1y 9m, Bglr.
WILLISON, H. A., Gnr. 18 Bty.	W., A.F.C.	28/ 9/15 3y 11m, Lieut.
WILLITT, J., Spr. 8 Fd. Co. Engrs.	W.	5/ 1/16 3y 4m, Pte.
WILLMOTT, R., Dvr. 6 F.A.B.		10/ 9/15 3y 11m, Dvr.
WILLS, C. C., Pte. 1 G.S.R.		2/ 2/18
WILLS, W. H., Cpl. 12 Bn.	M.M.	19/ 8/15 4y, Cpl.
WILSHIRE, C. J., Pte. 26 Bn.	W., A.A.P.C.	1/ 3/15 4y 5m. Pte.
WILTSHIRE, C., Pte. 12 Bn.	W.	29/ 1/15 4y 3m, C.S.M.
WILTSHIRE, E. J.		
WILTSHIRE, W. H. H.	Enlisted as CLAYTON, W. J.	
WILLIAMS, F. M., 2-Lieut. 40 Bn.		16/ 7/17 2y 1m, Lieut.
WILLIAMS, A., Pte. 12 Bn.	W., 10 F.A.B., 38 Bty.	4/ 8/15 4y, Bdr.
WILLIAMS, A. B., Pte. 40 Bn.		18/ 4/16 2y 3m, Pte.
WILLIAMS, A. E., Pte. 12 Bn.	W.	27/10/16 2y 10m, Pte.
WILLIAMS, A. J., Pte. 7 Fld. Amb.	W.	24/ 2/15 1y 5m, Pte.
WILLIAMS, A., Pte. 1 G.S.R.	40 Bn.	6/ 3/18 1y 7m, Pte.
WILLIAMS, A., Pte. 40 Bn.	W.	28/ 9/16 2y 6m, Pte.
WILLIAMS, A. D., Pte. 12 Bn.	✠ 5-8/5/17.	9/ 9/16 Pte. ✠
WILLIAMS, A. G., Pte. 12 Bn.	✠ 21/5/15.	21/ 8/14 L.-Cpl. ✠
WILLIAMS, A. J., Pte. 12 Bn.		9/11/16 1y 6m, Pte.
WILLIAMS, A. L., Dvr. 40 Bn.		23/ 3/16 1y 1m, Dvr.
WILLIAMS, B. O., Pte. 12 Bn.		2/ 9/16
WILLIAMS, B. G., Pte. 4 M.G. Co.	15 Bn., 2 Bn. ✠ 30/10/17.	25/10/16 Pte. ✠
WILLIAMS, C. C., Tpr. Remt. Sec.		30/ 9/15 1y 4m, Tpr.
WILLIAMS, A., Pte. 40 Bn. (Correct name BASSETT, A. J.)		11/ 2/17
WILLIAMS, C. E., Pte. A.A.M.C.		7/ 8/16 1y 7m, Pte.
WILLIAMS, C. H. E., Pte. 15 Bn.	✠ 27/5/15.	26/ 9/14 Pte. ✠
WILLIAMS, C. G., Gnr. 6 F.A.B.	2 D.A.C., 6 F.A.B., B.A.C.	13/ 9/15 4y 1m, Dvr.
WILLIAMS, C. E., Pte. 15 Bn.		11/ 1/15
WILLIAMS, C. J., Pte. 12 Bn.	2W., 69 Bn., 12 Bn.	26/ 8/15 3y 8m, Pte.
WILLIAMS, C. T., Tpr. 3 L.H.		28/ 3/17 2y 2m. Tpr.
WILLIAMS, C. O., Pte. 15 Bn.	3W., M.M.	16/ 9/14 4y 6m, Sgt.
WILLIAMS, D. A., Gnr. 3 F.A.B.	110 How. Bty.	28/ 9/14 2y 9m, Gnr.
WILLIAMS, D. E., Pte. 12 Bn.	✠ 15/4/17.	7/ 8/16 Pte. ✠
WILLIAMS, D. E., Pte. 40 Bn.		25/ 7/16 3y 2m, Pte.
WILLIAMS, D. F., Spr. 8 F.C.E.	13 Fd. Co. Engrs., 4 Div. E.H.Q.	16/11/15 3y 7m, Dvr.
WILLIAMS, D. H., Pte. 12 Bn.		27/ 8/14
WILLIAMS, E. B., Spr. 5 Tun. Co.		24/ 9/15
WILLIAMS, E. O., Cpl. 15 Bn.	3W. M.C. 45 Bn.	26/ 9/14 4y 6m, Capt.
WILLIAMS, C. A., Pte. 15 Bn.	W.	5/12/14 3y 9m, Pte.
WILLIAMS, E. W., Dvr. 3 F.A.B.	9 Bty.	25/ 1/15-4y 4m, Dvr.
WILLIAMS, E. A., A/Cpl. 12 Bn.		1/ 2/18 3y 7m, Pte.
WILLIAMS, E. W., Pte. 12 Bn.	W. ✠ 20/9/17.	27/ 7/16 Pte. ✠

TASMANIA'S WAR RECORD, 1914-1918.

NAME.	REMARKS.	RANK ON DISCHARGE. ENLISTED. SERVICE.
WILLIAMS, T. A., Spr. 5 Pnrs.	2W., 1 Anzac Rly. Unit.	27/ 8/14 4y 8m, Spr.
WILLIAMS, F. H., L-Cpl. 12 Bn.	M.M. and Bar. 22 Bn.	8/12/14 3y 11m, L.-Cpl
WILLIAMS, F. J., Pte. 26 Bn.		22/ 4/15 1y 11m, Pte.
WILLIAMS, F. J., Pte. 40 Bn.	W.	6/ 2/17 1m, Pte.
WILLIAMS, G., Pte. 12 Bn.		12/11/15 2y 6m, Pte.
WILLIAMS, G. C., Tpr. 3 L.H.	✠ 8/6/15.	16/ 9/14 Pte. ✠
WILLIAMS, G. D., Pte. 40 Bn.	47 Bn. ✠ 2/5/18.	3/ 3/16 L.-Cpl. ✠
WILLIAMS, G. P., Spr. 4 M.G. Co.	2 Tun. Co.	24/-9/15 4y, Spr.
WILLIAMS, G. H., Pte. 12 Bn.	69 Bn., 12 Bn.	15/ 9/15 4y 2m, Pte.
WILLIAMS, G. T. C., Gnr. 3 F.A.B.	W., M.M. ✠ 26/10/17 B.A.C.	7/ 1/15 Gnr. ✠
WILLIAMS, G., Pte. 15 Bn.		29/10/14 4y 3m, Pte.
WILLIAMS, G., Pte. 40 Bn.	W.	4/ 4/16 3y 4m, Pte.
WILLIAMS, G., Pte. 12 Bn.		21/10/16 3y, Pte.
WILLIAMS, H., Pte. 12 Bn.		2/ 8/16 2y 7m, Pte.
WILLIAMS, H. J., Pte. 12 Bn.	W., 3 L.T.M.B., 12 Bn.	15/ 3/16 2y 8m, Pte.
WILLIAMS, H. J., Pte. 26 Bn.	W., 10 L.T.M.B., 40 Bn.	1/ 9/15 Pte. ✠
WILLIAMS, H., Pte. 12 Bn.	12 Bn. ✠ 19-22/8/16.	30/10/16 2y 4m, Pte.
WILLIAMS, H., Tpr. 3 L.H.		27/ 9/17
WILLIAMS, H. A., Pte. 40 Bn.		13/ 7/17 2y 5m, Pte.
WILLIAMS, H. D., Dvr. 3 A.F.A.		26/ 2/15 4y 5m, Dvr.
WILLIAMS, H. H., Spr. 3 F.C.E.	2W.	20/ 7/15 3y 10m, Spr.
WILLIAMS, H. J., Pte. 40 Bn.	W.	6/ 2/17 1y 11m, Pte.
WILLIAMS, H. R. T., Pte. 12 Bn.	✠ 2/7/18.	30/11/15 L.-Cpl. ✠
WILLIAMS, H. J., Pte. 40 Bn.	M.M., L.T.M.B.	5/ 9/17 1y 9m, Gnr.
WILLIAMS, H. M., Cpl. 15 B.a.		7/ 8/15 2y 10m, H.-Lt.
WILLIAMS, I. H., Pte. 4 M.G. Co.	W.	18/10/16
WILLIAMS, J. A., Pte. 40 Bn.	15 Bn.	15/ 3/16
WILLIAMS, J. B., Pte. 12 Bn.		6/ 9/15 2y 9m, Pte.
WILLIAMS, J. J., Pte. 40 Bn.	W.	9/11/16 2y 10m, Pte.
WILLIAMS, J. T., Pte. 12 Bn.	24 How. Bde., 10 F.A.B.	1/12/15 3y 8m, Gnr.
WILLIAMS, J., Pte. 12 Bn.		21/ 8/14 4y 7m, Pte.
WILLIAMS, J., Pte. 12 Bn.		19/10/16 2y 11m, Pte.
WILLIAMS, J., Pte. 12 Bn.	✠ 6/5/15.	20/ 8/14 Pte. ✠
WILLIAMS, J. A., Dvr. 3 F.A.B.	V/IA. T.M.B.	27/ 8/14 4y 6m, Gnr.
WILLIAMS, J. C. A., Pte. 40 Bn.		17/10/16 2y 6m, Pte.
WILLIAMS, J. C., Pte. 26 Bn.		1/ 9/15 3y 11m, Pte.
WILLIAMS, J. J., Pte. 40 Bn.	12 Bn., 69 Bn., 12 Bn.	16/ 2/16 3y 1m, Pte.
WILLIAMS, J. A., Tpr. 3 L.H.		20/ 8/14 5y 4m, Lieut.
WILLIAMS, J. H., Pte. 7 Fd. Amb.		25/ 2/15
WILLIAMS, J. R. A., Pte. 26 Bn.	W.	2/ 3/15 1y 7m, Pte.
WILLIAMS, J. W., Pte. 12 Bn.	W., 52 Bn., 12 Bn.	22/ 1/15 4y 9m, Pte.
WILLIAMS, K. C., Pte. 26 Bn.	4W.	11/ 8/15 3y 9m, Pte.
WILLIAMS, K. E., Pte. 12 Bn.	W., 40 Bn.	10/ 4/16 3y 5m, Sgt.
WILLIAMS, L., Pte. 12 Bn.	40 Bn.	6/ 2/17 2y 2m, Pte.
WILLIAMS, L., Gnr. 6 F.A.B.	113 How. Bty.	1/11/15 3y 2m, Dvr.
WILLIAMS, L. L., Pte. 1 A.G.H.C.D.	13 Fd. Amb., 7 Fd. Amb.	4/ 6/15 4y, Pte.
WILLIAMS, L. H., Dvr. D.A.C.	13 F.A.B.	20/ 9/15
WILLIAMS, O., Pte. 26 Bn.	W.	22/ 6/15 2y 9m, Pte.
WILLIAMS, O. M., Pte. 26 Bn.	W., 12 Bn.	10/ 8/15 3y 8m, Pte.
WILLIAMS, P. S. F., Pte. 40 Bn.	W. ✠ 1/12/17.	5/ 4/16 Pte. ✠
WILLIAMS, P. G., Pte. 4 M.G. Co.	2 M.G. Co., 15 Bn.	25/10/16 Pte. ✠
WILLIAMS, R., Pte. 40 Bn.		8/ 3/16
WILLIAMS, R., A/Sgt. 40 Bn.		8/ 3/16 3y, Cpl.
WILLIAMS, R., Pte. 12 Bn.	W., 52 Bn.	24/ 8/14 4y 2m, Sgt.
WILLIAMS, R., Pte. 12 Bn.	✠ 7/6/17.	2/12/14 Pte. ✠
WILLIAMS, R. C., Pte. 40 Bn.		24/ 2/16
WILLIAMS, R. V., Pte. 40 Bn.	.W.	10/10/16 1y 8m, Pte.
WILLIAMS, R. R., Dvr. 6 F.A.B.		1/ 9/15
WILLIAMS, R. G. J., Tpr. 3 L.H.		16/ 8/15
WILLIAMS, R., Tpr. 3 L.H.		6/ 8/15 Tpr. ✠
WILLIAMS, R. J., P e 7 Fd. Amb.	✠ 17/10/17.	24/ 2/15 4y 2m, Sec. Lt.
WILLIAMS, S. H., Pte. 40 Bn.	30 Bn.	22/11/16 2y 9m, Pte.
WILLIAMS, S. L., Pte. 15 Bn.	W.	20/ 5/15 Pte. ✠
WILLIAMS, T. A., Pte. 12 Bn.	✠ 7/8/15.	27/ 8/14 4y 8m, Pte.
WILLIAMS, T. C., Pte. A.A.M.C.	2W., 4 L.H., 5 Pnrs., 1 Rly. Unit.	19/ 2/16 3y 5m, Pte.
WILLIAMS, T. M., Pte. 40 Bn.	7 Sanitary Section.	1/ 3/16 1y 9m, Pte.
WILLIAMS, T. P., Pte. 12 Bn.	W., 26 Bn.	9/11/16 Pte. ✠
WILLIAMS, W., Pte. 12 Bn.	4 M.G. Co., 59 Bn., 14 Bn. ✠ 18/4/18.	12/ 2/17 2y 7m, Gnr.
WILLIAMS, W. J., Tpr., Remt. Sec.	3 F.A.B., 8 Bty.	9/10/15 3y 3m, Tpr.
WILLIAMS, W. A., Pte. 40 Bn.	2W. ✠ 5/10/17.	8/12/15 Pte. ✠
WILLIAMS, W. E. G., Pte. Rem. Sec.	4 Sqd., 1 Rmt. Sec.	22/ 9/15 4y 2m, S-Smth
WILLIAMS, W., Pte. 40 Bn.		12/ 1/16 3y 2m, Pte.
WILLIAMS, W., Spr. 3 Fd. Co. Engrs.		21/ 7/15 1y 10m, Spr.
WILLIAMS, W. A., Pte. 40 Bn.		17/10/16 3y 2m, Pte.
WILLIAMS, W. C., Spr. 4 Sec. M. Co	W., 2 Tun. Co.	2/ 3/16 3y 7m, Spr.
WILLIAMS, W. C., Pte. 4 M.G. Co.	8 M.G. Co.	1/ 9/16 3y 2m, Pte.
WILLIAMS, W. G., Pte. 12 Bn.	W.	28/ 9/16 3y 2m, Dvr.
WILLIAMS, W. H. H., Pte. 40 Bn.	W.	18/ 7/16 3y, Pte.
WILLIAMS, W. H., Pte. 12 Bn.	2W.	8/ 7/15 4y, Dvr.
WILLIAMS, W. J., Pte. 40 Bn.	W.	17/ 3/16 1y 11m, Sgt.
WILLIAMS, W. L., Pte. 40 Bn.	W.	15/ 3/16 3y 6m, Pte.
WILSON, C. P., 2-Lt. A.A. Post Cps	O.B.E.	21/10/15
WILSON, J. H., 2-Lieut. 15 Bn.	W., 47 Bn.	5/ 3/15 3y 5m, Capt.
WILSON, A., Gnr. F.A.B.	14 F.A.B., 13 F.A.B., 14 F.A.B.	3/11/15 3y 11m, Gnr.
WILSON, A. A., Tpr. 5 G.S.R.		1/ 6/18 1y 2m, Tpr.
WILSON, A. E., Pte. 4 M.G. Co.		31/10/16 1y, Pte.
WILSON, A. V. W., Pte. 12 Bn.	2W.	20/ 8/14 4y 7m, Cpl

TASMANIA'S MUSTER ROLL. 365

NAME.	REMARKS.	RANK ON DISCHARGE. ENLISTED. SERVICE.
WILSON, A., Pte. 26 Bn.		22/ 2/15 4y 7m, Pte.
WILSON, A. B., Pte. 1 G.S.R.	1 A.M.T.	17/ 5/17 2y 6m, Cpl.
WILSON, A. E., Pte. 40 Bn.	12 Bn. ✠ 23/4/18.	2/10/16 Pte. ✠
WILSON, C., Pte. 12 Bn.	✠ 23/4/18.	17/11/16 Pte. ✠
WILSON, C., Pte. 4 M.G. Co.	W., 11 M.G. Co., 10 Fd. Amb.	29/10/16 3y, Pte.
WILSON, C. E., Spr. 3 Engrs.		27/ 4/16 3y 8m, L.-Cpl.
WILSON, C., Pte. 40 Bn.	W.	25/ 7/16 3y 2m, Pte.
WILSON, C. M.W., Munitions		
WILSON, C. G., Dvr. 3 F.A.B.		31/10/16
WILSON, C., Pte. A.A.M.C.		19/12/17
WILLSON, E. R., Pte. 40 Bn.	W.	8/11/16 2y 10m, Pte.
WILSON, E. R., Pte. 12 Bn.	W., 40 Bn.	29/ 9/16 2y 7m, Pte.
WILSON, E. T., Spr. Tunnlrs.	1 Ent. Bn., 2 Tun. Co.	26/10/16
WILSON, E. G., Spr. 3 F.C.E.		17/ 8/15
WILSON, F. C., Pte. 12 Bn.	M.I.D., 52 Bn., 50 Bn.	19/ 8/14 4y 7m, Capt.
WILSON, F. H., Pte. 40 Bn.	✠ 7/6/17.	20/ 6/16 Pte. ✠
WILSON, F. J. C. W., Gnr. 9 Bty., 3 F.A.B.	W., 2 F.A.B., 102 How. Bty.	27/ 8/14 4y 6m, Gnr.
WILSON, G., Pte. 12 Bn.		20/ 9/15
WILSON, G., Pte. 40 Bn.		23/ 5/16
WILSON, L. G. H., Pte. 40 Bn.		3/ 2/16 2y 4m, Pte.
WILSON, G. R., Pte. 12 Bn.	W.	23/ 8/15 3y 6m, Pte.
WILSON, G. T., Pte. 40 Bn.	W., 49 Bn.	Pte.
WILSON, G. W., Pte. 12 Bn.	W. ✠ 11/1/18.	24/ 8/15 Pte. ✠
WILSON, H., Pte. 2 G.S.R.		5/ 6/18
WILSON, H., Pte. 12 Bn.		15/ 3/17
WILSON, H. E., Pte. 40 Bn.	2W.	28/ 9/16 1y 10m, Pte.
WILSON, H. V., Pte. 12 Bn.	W.	23/ 7/15 2y 1m, Pte.
WILSON, H. J., Pte. 26 Bn.	✠ 5/8/16.	11/ 6/15 Pte. ✠
WILSON, H. O., Pte. 12 Bn.		13/12/15
WILSON, J. R., Pte. 26 Bn.	W., P.O.W. 52 Bn.	11/ 8/15 3y 11m. Sgt.
WILSON, J., Dvr. 26 L.H.	12 F.A.B.	20/ 9/15
WILSON, J., Pte. 12 Bn.	2W.	31/ 8/15 4y 3m, Pte.
WILSON, J. E., Pte. 40 Bn.	2W.	3/ 7/16 3y 1m, Pte.
WILSON, J. H. A., Pte. 12 Bn.		2/12/14
WILSON, J. A., Pte. 26 Bn.	M.G. Dtls.	10/ 8/15 3y 4m, Pte.
WILSON, J. A., Pte. 12 Bn.	W., M.M.	29/ 5/15 4y 2m, Pte.
WILSON, J. M., Pte. 40 Bn.		23/ 2/16 2y, Sgt.
WILSON, J. R., Sgt. 40 Bn.	M.S.M.	19/ 1/16
WILSON, J. W. C., Dvr. 8 F.C.E.		29/10/15
WILSON, L. M., Pte. 26 Bn.	W.	26/ 2/15 3y 4m, Pte.
WILSON, L. C. P., Tpr. 4 G.S.R.		5/ 6/18 9m, Tpr.
WILSON, J.		
WILSON, L. J., Pte. 15 Bn.	✠	19/ 9/14 Pte. ✠
WILSON, N., Pte. 26 Bn.		27/ 2/15
WILSON, O., Pte. 26 Bn.		24/ 5/15
WILSON, R. A., Gnr. F.A.B.	15 F.A.B., 13 F.A.B.	30/11/15 3y 5m, Gnr.
WILSON, R. C. S., Pte. 40 Bn.	2W.	2/10/16 2y 6m. Pte.
WILSON, R. G., Gnr. F.A.B.	W., 12 F.A.B., 6 F.A.B.	2/10/16 2y 11m, Dvr.
WILSON, R. E., Spr. 6 F.C.E.		24/ 8/15
WILSON, R. K., Cpl. 40 Bn.	3W., Medaille Militaire. ✠ 12/10/17.	5/ 3/16 C.S.M. ✠
WILSON, S. M., Gnr. 39 Bn.		29/11/17 1y 5m, Pte.
WILSON, S., Pte. 40 Bn.	W.	16/ 5/16 1y 11m. Pte.
WILSON, T. H., Pte. No. 3 Cyc. Co.	14 M.G. Co., 11 M.G. Co.	24/ 8/15 3y 11m. L.-Cpl
WILSON, T. J., Pte. 12 Bn.	W. 4 Div. Art. ✠ 16/1/18 4 H.T.M.B.	2/11/15 Pte. ✠
WILSON, T. K., Tpr. 3 L.H.		2/ 1/18 1y 7m, Tpr.
WILSON, C. H. W., Pte. 40 Bn.	W., M.M., 12 Bn.	30/ 9/16 3y, Pte.
WILSON, T. U. W., Pte. 2 G.S.R.	12 Bn.	11/ 3/18 1y 3m, Pte.
WILSON, V. R., Pte. 40 Bn.		2/10/16 1y, Pte.
WILSON, W., Pte. 40 Bn.		2/10/16
WILSON, W., Pte. 15 Bn.		6/ 6/15 2y 4m, Pte.
WILSON, W. C., Pte. 12 Bn.		17/ 7/16 1y 8m, Pte.
WILSON, W., Pte. 15 Bn.	W.	10/ 6/15
WILSON, W., Pte. 40 Bn.		1/11/16 2y 10m. Pte.
WILSON, W., Pte. 12 Bn.		12/ 5/16 3y 4m, Pte.
WILSON, W. A., Pte. 12 Bn.	2W., 69 Bn., 12 Bn.	1/ 6/15 4y 1m, Pte.
WILSON, W. J., Pte. 15 Bn.	✠ 7/8/15.	26/ 1/15 Pte. ✠
WILSON, W. M., Pte. 4 M.G. Co.	W.	3/ 8/16 2y 9m, Pte.
WILLSON, C. J., Pte. 12 Bn.	69 Bn., 49 Bn.	27/ 7/15 4y 1m. Cpl.
WILLSON, R., A/Sgt., 7 G.S.R.	1 Sqd. A.F.C.	10/ 8/18 9m, 2-A.M.
WINBURN, F. G., Pte. 40 Bn.	W.	12/10/15 2y 11m. Pte.
WINBURN, H. S., Cpl. 40 Bn.	W. ✠ 13/10/17.	8/10/15 Sgt. ✠
WINBURN, W. P., Pte. 12 Bn.		8/ 9/14
WINCH, L., Pte. A.N. and M.E.F.		18/11/16
WINDRED, H. J., Pte. 12 Bn.		29/ 8/14 2y 2m, Pte.
WINDRIDGE, G., Pte. 12 Bn.	W.	22/ 8/14 4y 5m, Pte.
WINDSGR, A. R., Gnr. Fd. Arty.	15 Bty.	5/ 9/15 4y, Dvr.
WINDSOR, E. H. M., Gnr. 25 F.A.	1 F.A.B. ✠ 17/10/17.	11/10/16 Gnr. ✠
WINDSOR, L. D., Tpr. 3 L.H.		1/ 2/15 4y 7m, Cpl.
WINDSOR, P. G., Pte. 12 Bn.	W.	11/ 4/16 3y 5m, Pte.
WINDSOR, S. C., Spr. 6 F.C.E.	4 Div. Engrs., 13 Fd. Co. Engrs.	26/ 8/15 4y, Spr.
WING, A. J. J., Pte. 40 Bn.	✠ 13/10/17.	2/10/16 Pte. ✠
WING, G. J. A., Tpr. 3 L.H.	✠ 6/2/15.	19/ 8/14 Tpr. ✠
WING, R. W., Cpl. 3 L.H.		1/ 5/17 2y 3m, Cpl.
WING, R. A., Pte. 15 Bn.	Re-enlisted 40 Bn. 2/10/16.	5/12/14 2y 4m, Pte.
WING, R. G., Pte. 15 Bn.	✠ 9/8/16.	4/ 6/15 Pte. ✠
WINSLADE, W., Tpr. 3 L.H.		11/ 8/15 1y 5m, Pte.

NAME.	REMARKS.	RANK ON DISCHARGE. ENLISTED, SERVICE.
WINSPEAR, R., Pte. 12 Bn.	M.I.D.	29/ 7/15 4y 1m, L.-Cpl.
WINSPEAR, W. D., Gnr. A. Fd. Amb	24 F.A.B., 5 D.A.C.	16/10/16 2y 7m, Dvr.
WINSTANLEY, E. N., Spr. 8 F.C.E	A.F.C.	2-A.M.
WINTER, C. W., Pte. 12 Bn.	✻ 6-10/4/??	16/10/16 2y 7m, Dvr.
WINTER, F. B., Pte. 26 Bn.	W., V2/A.T.M. Bty.	12/ 3/15 4y 5m, Cpl.
WINTER, L. W., Pte. 12 Bn.	W.	10/ 8/16 1y 8m, Pte.
WINTER, P. E., Pte. 15 Bn.	W., 47 Bn. ✻ 6/8/16.	4/ 8/15 Pte. ✻
WINTERS, A. J., Pte. 15 Bn.		14/ 6/15
WINTERS, A. J. J., Pte. Remt. Sec.		12/10/15 8m, Pte.
WINTERS, E., Pte. 12 Bn.		19/ 9/14 1y 8m, Pte.
WINTERS, W. J., Pte. 12 Bn.	69 Bn., 12 Bn.	28/ 8/14 4y 6m, Pte.
WINTERSON, W., A/Cpl. 12 Bn.		10/10/16 3y, Pte.
WISE, C. N., Gnr. 18 Bty.	17 Bty., 2 D.A.C., F.A.B.	21/ 9/15 3y 11m, Dvr.
WISE, C. B., Pte. 15 Bn.	✻ 8/8/16.	5/10/15 Pte. ✻
WISE, F., Pte. A.A.S.C.	35 Co. A.M.D.T.	15/10/17 2y, Dvr.
WISE, H. A. C., Pte. 40 Bn.	W.	30/ 3/16 2y 1m, Pte.
WISE, H., Pte. 1 A.C.H.		20/ 9/15 3y 11m, Pte.
WISE, J. B., Gnr. 36 H.A.G.		28/10/18 2m, Gnr.
WISE, J. M., Pte. 12 Bn.	W.	28/11/16 2y 5m, Pte.
WISE, J. T. A., Gnr. Fd. Arty.	25 F.A.B., 5 Div. F.A. ✻ 18/5/17.	17/10/16 Gnr. ✻
WISE, L. C., Pte. 40 Bn.		25/ 7/16 2y 10m, Pte.
WISE, P. F., Tpr. Remt. Sec.		5/10/15 1y 6m, Tpr.
WISE, R., Pte. 12 Bn.		24/ 9/15 1y 8m, Pte.
WISE, R. A. G., Pte. 7 Fd. Amb.	✻ 3 L.H.	17/ 3/15 4y 5m, Tpr.
WISE, T. C., Pte. 26 Bn.		1/ 3/15 1y 10m, Pte.
WISEMAN, W. A., Pte. 26 Bn.		20/ 4/15 5y 6m, Pte.
WITHERS, A., Tpr. 3 L.H.	A.A.M.C., A.S. Hos.	19/ 4/17 2y 7m, Tpr.
WITCOMBE, H. G., Spr. 3 F.C.E.	M.C.	13/ 9/14
WITHERS, C. P., Tpr. 3 L.H.	4 L.H.	13/10/15 3y 8m. Tpr.
WITHERS, C. H. H., Pte. 12 Bn.		28/ 7/15
WITHERS, D., Pte. 40 Bn.		20/ 1/17 2y 3m, Pte.
WITT, H. S., Gnr. Arty.	W., 3 D.A.C., 8 F.A.B.	15/ 2/16 2y 7m, Gnr.
WITT, W., Pte. 12 Bn.	2W., 52 Bn.	14/ 9/15
WITTISON, W., Pte. 15 Bn.	W., 4 Pnr. Corps.	21/ 9/14 4y 4m, Cpl.
WITTON, C. R., Pte. A.A.M.C.	7 Fld. Amb.	28/ 4/17 2y 8m, Pte.
WITZERMAN, C. W., Pte. 12 Bn.	M.M.	29/12/14 4y 5m, Pte.
WITZERMAN, H. F. G., Pte. 12 Bn.		29/12/14 1y 5m, Pte.
WITZERMAN, L. J., Pte. A.A.S.C.		29/10/17 2y, Dvr.
WITZERMAN, R. H. J., Gnr. Arty.	W.	14/ 2/16 2y 4m, Dvr.
WOLFE, G., Cpl. 12 Bn.		26/ 6/15 4y 5m, Cpl.
WOLFE, L. J., Spr. Miners		12/11/15 2y 2m, Spr.
WOLFE, R. J., Pte. 40 Bn.		21/ 8/17 2y 1m, Pte.
WOOD, C. M. P., Pte. 26 Bn.		23/ 7/15 2y 7m, Pte.
WOOD, C. P., Pte. 40 Bn.		25/ 8/17 1y 8m, Pte.
WOOD, C. C., Pte. 40 Bn.	W.	14/ 3/16 1y 9m, Pte.
WOOD, C. V., Gnr. A.F.A.		18/ 1/15
WOOD, D., Pte. 3 G.S.R.		2/ 8/18 1y 2m, Pte.
WOOD, E. A., Pte. A.A.M.C.		18/10/16 2y 5m, Pte.
WOOD, H. E., Spr. 8 F.C.E.	12 Fd. Co. Engrs.	28/ 2/16 3y 6m, Spr.
WOOD, G. A., Pte. 40 Bn.	✻ 26/4/18.	1/ 8/16 Pte. ✻
WOOD, G. W., Gnr. 18 Bty. A.F.A.	M.G. Dtls., 6 F.A.B.	25/ 9/15 3y 10m, Sgt.
WOOD, H. J.		
WOOD, H. N. H., Pte. A.F.C.	4 A.F.C.	5/10/16 2y 9m, 2-A.M.
WOOD, H., Pte. 12 Bn.	W., M.M. 52 Bn. ✻ 25/9/17.	1/ 8/15 ✻
WOOD, H. P., Pte. 26 Bn.		6/ 5/15 2y 10m, Pte.
WOOD, J. R., Pte. 3 G.S.R.	12 Bn.	25/ 7/18 1y 3m, Pte.
WOOD, I., Pte. 40 Bn.		8/11/16 2y 10m, Pte.
WOOD, K. R. J. H., Pte. 40 Bn.	Dental Corps, 26 A.A.D.C.	8/11/16 2y 8m, Cpl.
WOOD, L. A., Pte. 12 Bn.		20/- 8/14 2y, Pte.
WOOD, L. A., Pte. 12 Bn.	W.	14/ 1/16 2y 8m, Pte.
WOOD, L. A., Cpl. 40 Bn.		3/ 2/16
WOOD, R. H., Gnr. 9 Bty. A.F.A.	W.	25/ 9/14 1y 8m, Gnr.
WOOD, T. J., Pte. 12 Bn.	W.	17/ 7/16 3y 4m, Pte.
WOOD, W. E., Pte. 40 Bn.		29/ 2/16 3y 1m, Pte.
WOODS, A. O., Lieut. 26 Bn.	W., M.C., M.I.D. ✻ 2/9/18.	31/ 4/15
WOODS, A. A., Pte. 15 Bn.	M.M., P.O.W.	19/ 9/14 4y 8m, Pte.
WOODS, A. W., Pte. 12 Bn.	W.	18/ 8/15 2y 3m, Pte.
WOODS, A. W., Pte. 40 Bn.		7/ 6/16 2y 6m, Pte.
WOODS, A. H., Pte. 26 Bn.	52 Bn.	20/ 7/15 2y, Pte.
WOODS, B. E., Pte. 40 Bn.	✻ 13/10/17.	4/ 3/16 Pte. ✻
WOODS, C., Tpr. 5 G.S.R.	38 Co. A.S.C.	19/ 6/18 1y 2m, Tpr.
WOODS, C. A. H., Cpl. 40 Bn.		7/ 2/17 1y, Pte.
WOODS, C. J., Pte. 26 Bn.	W.	18/ 8/15 3y 9m, Pte.
WOODS, C. J. W., Tpr. 3 L.H.		28/ 2/17 2y 6m, Tpr.
WOODS, C. J., Pte. A.C.H.		19/ 9/14 4y 7m, Dvr.
WOODS, E., Pte. 40 Bn.	W. ✻ 12/10/17.	2/ 2/16 Pte. ✻
WOODS, F. O., Pte. 26 Bn.	2W., 12 Bn. ✻ 5/6/18.	16/ 8/15 L/Cpl. ✻
WOODS, F W., Gnr. 18 Bty.	W., 17 Bty., 16 Bty.	11/ 8/15 2y 11m, Gnr.
WOODS, G. E., Gnr. Fd. Arty.	15 F.A.B.	4/10/16 Gnr.
WOODS, G. B., Gnr. D.A.C.	MM., 1 D.A.C.	27/ 7/15 4y 2m, Sec. Lt. ✻
WOODS, H. C.		
WOODS, J. R., Tpr. 1 Remt. Sec.		29/ 9/15
WOODS, L., Pte. 12 Bn.	✻ 18/2/17.	7/ 9/16 Pte. ✻
WOODS, R. T., Pte. 12 Bn.	W. ✻ 5-8/5/17.	2/12/15 Pte. ✻
WOODS, S. W., Pte. 40 Bn.	51 Bn. ✻ 16/10/17.	7/ 6/16 Pte. ✻
WOODS, S., Pte. 40 Bn.		11/11/16 1y, Pte.
WOODS, W., Pte. 12 Bn.		10/ 8/16 9m, Pte.

TASMANIA'S MUSTER ROLL.

NAME.	REMARKS.	RANK ON DISCHARGE. ENLISTED. SERVICE.
WOODS, W. B., Pte. 12 Bn.		9/10/16 2y 10m, Pte.
WOODARD, G. W., Spr. Tunnlrs.		3/ 1/17 2y 2m, Pte.
WOODARD (Jun.), G. W., Spr. Tun.	2 Pnr. Bn. ✤ 6/10/18.	3/ 1/17 Spr. ✤
WOODBERRY, C. W., Tpr. 3 L.H.		9/12/16 2y 8m, Tpr.
WOODBURY, E. M., Gnr. 3 F.A.B.	1 D.A.C.	17/ 6/15 4y 2m, Gnr.
WOODBURY, M., Pte. 12 Bn.	✤ 25–28/4/15.	17/ 9/14 Pte. ✤
WOODBERRY, V. A., Pte. 12 Bn.	W., 3 F.A.B., A.G.B.D. Staff. (Re-enlisted Arty. 7/3/17)	11/10/14 4y 5m, Gnr.
WOODGATE, A., Pte. 40 Bn.	W.	16/ 1/15 Lieut. ✤
WOODHOUSE, T. J., Lieut. 12 Bn.	✤ 9/8/15.	30/ 3/16 3y 2m, Pte.
WOODHOUSE, E. H., Pte. 2 G.S.R.		12/ 4/18 1y 8m, Pte.
WOODLAND, J. H., Pte. 12 Bn.	W.	14/10/16 3y 2m, Pte.
WOODLEIGH, C. A., Pte. 12 Bn.	52 Bn. ✤ 3–4/9/16.	28/7/15 Pte. ✤
WOODLEIGH, W., Spr. 8 F.C.E.	12 Fd. Co. Engrs.	11/11/15
WOODRUFF, A. W. J., Pte. 12 Bn.	1 M.G. Bn.	5/ 5/16 3y 5m, Pte.
WOODRUFF, H. B., Pte. 26 Bn.		3/ 5/15 Major ✤
WOODWARD, C. C. G., Pte. 12 Bn.	52 Bn. ✤ 4/9/16.	24/ 8/14 Sgt. ✤
WOODWARD, W. H. E., 2-A.M., A.F.C		2/10/19 2-A.M.
WOODWARD, W., Pte. 15 Bn.	✤ 11/5/15	23/10/14 L.-Cpl. ✤
WOODWARD, W., Pte. 40 Bn.	W. ✤ 31/8/18.	17/10/16 Pte. ✤
WOODWARD, W., Pte. 3 G.S.R.	12 Bn.	13/ 8/18 1y 2m, Pte.
WOODWORTH, A. E., Pte. 1 A.C.H.	1 San. Sec., Adm. H.Qrs.	19/ 9/14 5y 1m, Pte.
WOODWORTH, H. J., Pte. 12 Bn.		1/ 9/14 1y 9m, Pte.
WOOLCOCK, B. F., Pte. 40 Bn.	✤ 29/8/16.	4/ 3/16 Pte. ✤
WOOLRIDGE, W. J., Pte. 15 Bn.	✤ 10/4/15.	27/10/14 Pte. ✤
WOOLFORD, C., Pte. 12 Bn.		27/ 6/16 1y 1m, Pte.
WOOLFORD, J. C., Gnr., 6 F.A.B.	M.M., 7 F.A.B., 23 How. Bde.	13/ 1/16 3y 3m, Gnr.
WOOLLEY, A. C., Pte. 12 Bn.	✤ 8/10/17.	18/ 8/16 Pte. ✤
WOOLLEY, A. C. N., Spr. 8 F.C.E.	M.M.	17/ 1/16 3y 8m, L.-Cpl.
WOOLLEY, B. H., Gnr. 6 F.A.B.	W., 23 How. Bde.	26/ 1/16 3y 2m, Gnr.
WOOLLEY, C., Cpl. 12 Bn.	52 Bn. ✤ 4/9/16.	13/ 7/15 Cpl. ✤
WOOLLEY, E. C. M., Pte. 12 Bn.	✤ 29/5/15.	30/11/14 Pte. ✤
WOOLLEY, F. W., Pte. 40 Bn.	3W.	21/ 2/16 3y 6m, Pte.
WOOLLEY, G., Gnr. 23 How. Bde.		19/11/15 4y 2m, Gnr.
WOOLLEY, G. S., Pte. 26 Bn.	✤ 5/8/16.	30/ 3/15 Pte. ✤
WOOLLEY, H. V., Pte. 12 Bn.	W.	15/ 9/16 3y 1m. Pte.
WOOLLEY, H. E., M.W., Mun. Wkrs.		
WOOLLEY, J. N., Pte. 26 Bn.	W.	22/ 6/15 2y 9m, Pte.
WOOLLEY, J. C., L.-Cpl. 12 Bn.	2W.	15/ 7/15 3y 9m, Sgt.
WOOLLEY, J. P., Pte. 12 Bn.	1 Pioneers.	11/ 2/15 3y 9m, Pte.
WOOLLEY, J. P., Spr. 2 Tunnlrs.	W.	26/ 8/16 1y 3m, Spr.
WOOLLEY, K. H., Pte. 40 Bn.	W.	16/10/16 2y 2m, Pte.
WOOLLEY, R. W., Pte. 40 Bn.	W.	21/ 9/16 3y, Pte.
WOOLLEY, W. G. E., Pte. 40 Bn.	W., D.C.M. ✤ 21/2/18.	16/ 9/16 Sgt. ✤
WOOLEY, E. C., Gnr. 36 H.A.G.	2 A. Siege Bty.	22/ 4/18 1y 6m, Gnr.
WOOLMINGTON, A., Pte. 12 Bn.	52 Bn.	29/ 7/15 1y 10m, Cpl.
WOOLNOUGH, J. P., Pte. 26 Bn.	✤ 29/7/16.	10/ 8/15 Pte. ✤
WOOLNOUGH, W. W., Dvr. 9 Bty. 3 F.A.B.		27/ 8/14 4y 7m, Gnr.
WOOTTON, E. C., Pte. 12 Bn.	W., 40 Bn.	21/ 9/16 1y 8m, Pte.
WOOTTON, G. C., Pte. 12 Bn.		4/ 4/16
WORBEY, H. R., Pte. 40 Bn.		16/ 7/17 1y 7m, Pte.
WORDSWORTH, V. W., Spr. 5 Tnnlrs		4/ 4/16 2y 8m, Spr.
WORKER, H. H., Pte. 26 Bn.	12 Bn. ✤ 19–22/8/16.	31/ 8/15 Pte. ✤
WORKER, J. V., Pte. 26 Bn.		19/ 7/15 2y 11m, Pte.
WORKER, L. B., Pte. 26 Bn.	12 Bn., A.C.H.Q.	31/8/15 4y, Pte.
WORLADGE, A. I., Pte. 4 A.A.S.C.		17/ 8/14 4y 6m, Dvr.
WORLADGE, C. G., Pte. 1 A.C.H.		16/ 9/14 1y 10m, Pte.
WORLEY, W. H., Pte. 3 Fld. Amb.		15/ 3/15
WORNER, A. A., Sgt. 26 Bn.	✤ 29/7/16	15/ 6/15 Sgt. ✤
WORSLEY, E. K., Tpr. 3 L.H.	8 L.H.	2/ 8/15 4y 1m, Dvr.
WORSLEY, F. W., Tpr. 3 L.H.		2/ 4/17 2y, Tpr.
WORSLEY, T., Pte. 12 Bn.	✤ 11/7/15.	20 8/14 Pte. ✤
WORTHINGTON, D. E., Spr. 2 F.C.E.		31/10/16
WRAGG, C. C., Pte. 12 Bn.	W., 15 Bn., 40 Bn.	1/ 8/15 2y 1m, Pte.
WRAGG, T. H., Pte. 26 Bn.	W., 52 Bn.	11/9/15 Pte. ✤
WRANKMORE, W., Pte. 12 Bn.	W. ✤ 3/5/17.	21/10/15 1y 7m, Pte.
WRATHALL, R. J., Pte. 12 Bn.		2/12/14 8m, Pte.
WRATHALL, W., Spr. 5 Miners		10/ 4/16 Spr.
WRIGLEY, J. Z., Pte. 40 Bn.	W., 2 Tunn. Co., ✤ 7/8/18	15/ 4/16 Pte. ✤
WRIGHT, A., Gnr. 1 Aust. S. Bty.		7/ 6/15 4y, Gnr.
WRIGHT, A., Pte. 12 Bn.	✤ 3/11/17.	27/10/16 Pte. ✤
WRIGHT, A. D., Pte. 40 Bn.		19/ 7/16 1y 10m, Pte.
WRIGHT, B. R. A., Spr. 8 F.C.E.		4/ 1/16 1y 9m, Spr.
WRIGHT, C. F. S., 9 Bty. 3 A.F.A.	1 D.A.C.	25/ 8/14 4y 5m, Sgt.
WRIGHT, C. N., Cpl. 40 Bn.	✤ 5/10/17.	31/ 5/16 Cpl. ✤
WRIGHT, C. E., Pte. 12 Bn.	✤ 28/11/16.	15/ 7/15 Pte. ✤
WRIGHT, C. A., Pte. 12 Bn.	2W.	4/ 3/15 2y 10m, Pte.
WRIGHT, C. G., Pte. 40 Bn.	W.	5/ 2/16 3y 4m, Pte.
WRIGHT, E. S. K., Sadl'r. 3 L.H.		21/ 8/14 1y 1m, Sdler.
WRIGHT, E. L., Pte. 12 Bn.	52 Bn. ✤ 4/9/16.	11/ 1/16 Pte. ✤
WRIGHT, F. E. F., Pte. G.S.R.		10/ 6/17 1y 7m, Pte.
WRIGHT, G. C., Pte. 12 Bn.	W. ✤ 25/4/15.	21/ 8/14 Pte. ✤
WRIGHT, G. C. A., Pte. 40 Bn.	3W.	29/ 3/16 3y 5m, Cpl.
WRIGHT, G. S., Pte. 12 Bn.	40 Bn. ✤ 28/3/18.	20/11/16 Pte. ✤
WRIGHT, G. T., Pte. 40 Bn.		31/10/16 1y 11m, Pte.
WRIGHT, G. T., Pte. 26 Bn.	W.	15/ 7/15 2y 9m, Pte.

NAME.	REMARKS.	RANK ON DISCHARGE. ENLISTED. SERVICE.
WRIGHT, H. R., Pte. 12 Bn.	2W., D.C.M.	1/ 8/15 4y, Sgt.
WRIGHT, H., Gnr. 3 F.A.B.		16/ 9/15
WRIGHT, J., Cpl. 40 Bn.	12 Bn. ✠ 6/10/17.	2/ 5/16 Cpl. ✠
WRIGHT, L., Pte. 12 Bn.	40 Bn.	20/11/14 4y 10m, Pte.
WRIGHT, O., Pte. 2 G.S.R.	3 G.S.R.	19/ 3/18
WRIGHT, R. A., Pte. 40 Bn.	✠ 31/1/17.	20/ 3/16 Pte. ✠
WRIGHT, R. J., Pte. 15 Bn.		28/ 9/14 4y 5m, Cpl.
WRIGHT, R. C., Far.-Cpl. 9 Bty. 3 F.A.B.		27/ 8/14 4y 2m, Far-Cpl.
WRIGHT, R., Pte. 40 Bn.	W.	7/ 3/16 2y 11m, Pte.
WRIGHT, T., Pte. 26 Bn.	✠ 5/8/16.	2/ 9/15 Pte. ✠
WRIGHT, W. J., Pte. 40 Bn.	W.	13/10/16 2y 11m, Pte.
WRIGHT, W. L., Pte. 12 Bn.		23/10/16 2y 10m, Pte.
WRIGHT, W. A. H., Pte. 15 Bn.	47 Bn.	30/ 8/15
WRIGHT, W. E., Pte. 26 Bn.	4 M.G. Co. ✠ 17/10/17.	21/ 9/15 Cpl. ✠
WRIGHT, W. S., Pte. 40 Bn.		5/ 4/16 3y 6m, Dvr.
WRIGHT, W. W., Pte. 12 Bn.	2W.	25/ 8/15 3y 10m, Pte.
WURR, W., Pte. 2 G.S.R.	✠ 7/9/16.	19/ 4/17 2y 7m, Pte.
WYATT, B., Spr. Rly. Unit	A.A.M.C.	6/ 1/17 1y 1m, Pte.
WYATT, H. W., Cpl. 26 Bn.	4 Rly. Unit.	12/ 3/15 Lieut.
WYATT, L. H., Pte. 40 Bn.	✠ 9/6/17.	20/ 6/16 Pte. ✠
WYATT, G D., Pte. 12 Bn.	51 Bn.	7/ 8/15
WYLES, A. J., Pte. G.S.R.		26/. 4/17 2y 1m, Pte.
WYLES, J. H., Pte. 15 Bn.	W. ✠ 2/4/18.	25/ 9/14 Pte. ✠
WYLLIE, B. R., Pte. 4 M.G. Co.		11/ 9/16 3y, Pte.
WYLIE, J. A., Pte. 12 Bn.		19/ 9/14 1y 11m, Pte.
WYLIE, R. M., Pte. 15 Bn.	.	21/ 9/14 1y 11m, Pte.
WYLIE, R. M., Pte. 12 Bn.		19/ 9/16 Pte.
WYNWOOD, L. W., Pte. 4 M.G. Co.	W.	8/ 7/16 3y 2m, L.-Cpl.
YANNER, T. S., 12 Bn.	D.C.M.	
YATES, A. J., Pte. 12 Bn.	52 Bn. ✠ 6/4/18.	20/ 8/14 Sgt. ✠
YATES, A. W., Pte. 40 Bn.		29/ 3/16 3y 6m, Sgt.
YATES, C. C., Pte. 3 G.S.R.	12 Bn.	17/ 1/18 1y 9m, Pte.
YATES, J., Pte. 12 Bn.		22/ 8/14
YATES, R. G., Pte. 15 Bn.	2W., 47 Bn.	19/ 9/14 4y 3m, Cpl.
YAXLEY, A. G., Spr. 5 Tun. Co.		1/ 3/16
YAXLEY, E., Pte. 12 Bn.	2W., D.C.M.	28/ 1/15 2y 6m, L.-Cpl.
YAXLEY, J. K., Pte. 26 Bn.	✠ 28/7/16.	10/ 8/15 Pte. ✠
YAXLEY, L. L., Pte. 40 Bn.		27/ 4/16 1y 1m, Pte.
YAXLEY, P. Z., Gnr. 2 G.S.R.	8 Bty. F.A.B.	11/ 4/16 3y 5m, Gnr.
YEATES, A. E., M.W., Munitions		M.W.
YEOLAND, C. W., Pte. 12 Bn.	W.	14/ 6/16 2y 8m, Pte.
YORK, F. J., Gnr. F.A. Rfts.	13 F.A.B. ✠ 17/10/17.	11/ 2/16 Gnr. ✠
YORK, J. W., Pte. 40 Bn.	5 M.G. Bn. ✠ 9/4/18.	10/10/16 Pte. ✠
YORK, R. R., Tpr. 3 L.H.		19/ 6/15 1y 1m, Tpr.
YOST, R. L., 1-A.M., Aviation Cps.	71st Sqd. A.F.C.	20/10/16 1-A.M.
YOULL, W. H., Gnr. 6 F.A.B.	W.	24/ 7/15 4y 2m, Gnr.
YOUNG, D. P., Capt. Dvl. Trn.		15/ 8/14 2y 6m, Major.
YOUNG, A. H., Dvr. 40 Bn.		15/ 3/16 3y 9m Sgt.
YOUNG, A. M., Pte. 40 Bn.	W.	16/ 5/16 3y 2m, Cpl.
YOUNG, A. J. M., Pte. 12 Bn.	2W., 52 Bn., 42 Bn.	9/11/15 3y 5m, Pte.
YOUNG, A. L., Pte. 12 Bn.	52 Bn.	14/ 8/15
YOUNG, A. J., Dvr. F.A. Rfts.	3 F.A.B.	11/10/16 2y 10m, Dvr.
YOUNG, C., Pte. 40 Bn.	15 Bn. ✠ 11/4/17.	17/ 1/16 Pte. ✠
YOUNG, C. R., Pte. 40 Bn.	2W. ✠ 13/10/17.	2/10/16 Pte. ✠
YOUNG, D., Pte. 1 A.C.H.		17/ 9/14
YOUNG, E., Pte. 15 Bn.	✠ 8/8/15.	18/12/14 Pte. ✠
YOUNG, E. C., Gnr. F.A. Rfts.	13 F.A.B.	6/ 9/16 3y 1m, Gnr.
YOUNG, F. C. R., Pte. 26 Bn.	2W., 3rd Sqd. A.F.C.	27/ 7/15 4y 1m, F.-Sgt.
YOUNG, F. H., Pte. 40 Bn.		1/12/16 2y 10m, Pte.
YOUNG, G. S., Spr. 6 F.C.E.	✠ 17/9/17.	14/ 8/15 Pte. ✠
YOUNG, G. M., Pte. 40 Bn.	W., M.M.	13/11/15 3y 11m. Sgt.
YOUNG, H. E., Pte. 12 Bn.	3W.	24/ 8/15 2y 8m, Pte.
YOUNG, H. G., Pte. 40 Bn.	W.	15/ 4/17 2y 5m, Pte.
YOUNG, J. F., Pte. 12 Bn.	✠ 25/7/16.	23/ 7/15 Pte. ✠
YOUNG, J. F., Pte. 12 Bn.	52 Bn. ✠ 4/9/16.	5/ 8/15 Pte. ✠
YOUNG, J., Pte. 15 Bn.	✠ 9/8/16.	14/ 5/15 Pte. ✠
YOUNG, J. W., Pte. Dental Cps.	Army Dental Service.	9/ 7/15 4y 1m, S.-Sgt.
YOUNG, J. A., Pte. 40 Bn.	W. ✠ 4/10/17.	3/ 7/16 Pte. ✠
YOUNG, L. K., Pte. 12 Bn.	✠ 6-10/4/17.	22/ 8/16 Pte. ✠
YOUNG, M. S. G., L.-Cpl. 12 Bn.		17/10/16 1y, Pte.
YOUNG, M., Pte. 26 Bn.	✠ 10/12/15.	14/ 5/15 Pte. ✠
YOUNG, R. C., Pte. 40 Bn.	3W.	5/ 4/16 3y, L.-Cpl.
YOUNG, R. A., Pte. 1 A.G.C.	3 Fd. Amb.	28/ 7/15 4y 2m, Pte.
YOUNG, S. W. W., Dvr. 3 L.H.	W., 3 F.A.B.	4/ 8/15 4y 2m, Dvr.
YOUNG, S., Pte. Remounts		4/10/15 1y 2m, Tpr.
YOUNG, T. A., Pte. 12 Bn.		16/ 5/17 2y 6m, Pte.
YOUNG, T. C., M.W., Munitions		M.W.
YOUNG, T., Pte. 12 Bn.	✠ 6-10/4/17.	26/ 8/14 Sgt. ✠
YOUNG, W., Pte. 15 Bn.		28/ 8/15
YOUNG, W. W., Pte. 26 Bn.	W., M.M. ✠ 3/5/17.	26/ 7/15 Pte. ✠
YOUNG, W. A., Pte. 3 Fd. Amb.		24/ 8/14 4y 5m, Pte.
YOUNG, W. J., Gnr. 3 F.A.B.		6/ 8/15 Cpl.
YOUNG, W., Pte. 2 G.S.R.	1 D.A.C.	9/ 4/18
ZANKER, J. L., Gnr. F.A. Rfts.		16/ 2/17 2y 1m, Gnr.
ZANKER, R. Z., Gnr. F.A. Rfts.	1 D.A.C.	31/ /17 2y 6m. Gnr.
ZANTUCK, F., Pte. 12 Bn.	2W.	6/ 6/16 2y 10m, Pte.
ZEUSCHNER, F. W. H., Spr. 5 Miners	W., 2 Tun. Co.	24/ 2/16 3y 9m.

Tasmanians Enlisted in other States

NAME.	REMARKS.	ENLISTED, SERVICE RANK ON DISCHARGE.
ANDREWS, T., Pte. 21st N.Z. Forces	✠ 13/6/17.	19/ 1/17 Pte. ✠
BUTLER, A. L., Sgt. Gold Coast Rgt	W., 108 Tunl. Co. R.E.	1/ 3/15 4y 2m, Capt.
BROWNE, C. S.	M.C.	
BROWNE, A. S., Pte. 4 Bn.		21/ 8/14 Sgt.
BROWNE, H. S.		21/ 8/14
BATTEN, R. J. V., Pte. 7 Bn.	3 Fd. Co. Engrs.	
BALSTRUP, G. H., Pte. 17 Bn.	✠ 22/9/17.	13/ 6/16 Pte. ✠
BELSTEAD, B., Sister A.A.N.S.		—/5/15
BARLOW, F. C., Pte. 6 Bn.	✠ 8/5/15.	9/ 9/14 Pte. ✠
BARNES, W., Pte. 15 Bn.	✠ 14/6/15.	18/ 9/14 Pte. ✠
BINNS, P., 2nd-Lieut., 2 Bn.	✠ 13/8/18.	6/ 6/16 Lieut. ✠
CROCKETT, W. J.	✠ 4/8/16.	Sgt. ✠
CROCKETT, W. E.	✠ 23/7/16.	
CHOPPELL, P. C., Spr. 3 F.C.E.	✠ 23/7/16.	4/ 8/15 Spr. ✠
CLEARY, W. H., Cpl. 1 F.A.B.	M.M. ✠ 23/4/18.	24/ 8/14 Sgt. ✠
CHEVERTON, R., Gnr. 3 A.F.A.	✠ 9/11/15.	17/ 8/14 Gnr. ✠
CHEVERTON, R. T., Pte. Cyclists	5 Bn. ✠ 23/8/18.	—/ 1/17 Pte. ✠
COAD, L. J., Pte. 15 Bn.	✠ 7/12/16.	6/ 5/15 Pte. ✠
DARCY, M., Pte. 19 Bn.	36 Bn. ✠ 15/7/17.	4/ 3/16 Pte. ✠
DODERY, F. M., Sister, Queen Alexandra's Military Nursing Service Reserve	W., R.R.C.	1914
DRAKE, C. J., Pte. 16 Bn.		7/10/15 3y 11m, Sgt.
DUNKLEY, C. B., Pte. 22 Bn.	✠ 3/5/17.	3/ 5/16 Pte. ✠
DOWDE, D. R., Pte 22 Bn.	✠ 3/5/17.	6/ 3/16 Pte. ✠
DAVIS, H. S., Pte 1 Fd. Amb.	✠ 16/6/18.	1915 2-Lieut. ✠
DAVIS, L. S., 4 L.H.R.		18/ 8/14 Lieut.
EDWARDS, V. J., Pte. 21 Bn.		16/ 4/15 4y 3m, L.-Sgt.
EDWARDS, A. G., Pte. 26 Bn.	✠ 10/8/16.	26/ 4/15 Pte. ✠
ELLIOTT, I. R., S/Sgt. A.A.M.C.		13/ 8/17 1y 8m, S.-Sgt.
ENMAN, J. F., Pte. 24 Bn.	1 Pioneers	2/ 8/15 2y 9m, Pte.
EDDINGTON, W. H., Tpr. 2 L.H.		—/ 8/14 4y 10m, W.O.
EDDINGTON, W. J., Q.M., A.A.M.C.		18/ 9/14 4y 11m, Q.M. & Hon. Lieut.
FOLEY, J. G., Sgt. Gold Coast Bty.	M.C. and Bar, 2 M.I.D.	1/ 3/15 3y 10m, Capt.
FOX, W. A., Pte. 4 Bn.		26/11/15 3y 11m, Pte.
FAIR, R., Pte.		19/ 1/17 Pte. ✠
GARDINER, W. E., L.-Cpl. 15 A.L.H	✠ 4/10/17.	3/ 1/16 3y 6m, L.-Cpl.
GRACE, F., Pte. 3 Bn.		16/ 9/15 3y 10m, Pte.
GUEST, W., S/Smith. Imp. Army		10/ 6/15 3y 8m, S.-Smith
HALL, A.M., Sister, Brit. Red Cross Nursing Service.		—/11/14 4y 8m, Sister
HUTCHISON, A. J., Pte. 7 Bn.	✠ 25/4/15.	20/ 8/14 Pte. ✠
HILL, C. W., Bdr. 36 H.A.C.	✠ 27/4/17.	7/ 6/15 Bdr. ✠
HODGMAN, E. W., Pte. 35 Bn.	4 Divl. Sig. Co.	19/10/16 2y 11m. Cpl.
HIGGS, P. G., Pte. Wellington Inf. Rgt. N.Z		—/ 8/14 1y 6m, Pte.
JACKSON, R.N., Pte. 25 Bn.	✠ 28/7/16.	16/ 2/15 Pte. ✠
JONES, A. M., Pte. 8 L.H.	✠ 7/8/15.	21/10/14 L.-Cpl. ✠
KIRWAN, T., Sgt. A.S.C.	O.B.E. ✠ June, 1919.	1/ 3/15 Capt. ✠
KEENE, E. H. D., Pte. A.A.M.C.	1 A.C.C.S.	—/10/16 3y 4m, Pte.
KENNY, J. F., Pte. 4 Bn	W., 1 M G. Co.	5/11/15 3y 3m, Pte.
KENNY, J. R., Pte. 37 Bn		20/11/16 2y 10m, Pte.
KENNY, F. G., Pte. 23 Bn.	✠ 7/8/18.	2/ 8/17 Pte. ✠
LITTLECHILD, A. C., Pte. 60 Bn. (Enlisted as C. H. MORRIS)	M.M. ✠ 9/8/18	—/ 4/17 Pte. ✠
LOVETT, C. T., Tpr. N.Z. M.R.B.		24/ 8/14 4y 9m, S.S.M.
MILLAR, A. G., Pte. 58 Bn.	W.	17/ 1/15 1y 2m, Pte.
MORRIS, V. P., Pte. Otago Inf. Rg		17/12/15 3y, Pte.
MORRIS, R., Pte. 28 Bn.		4/ 5/15 4y 3m, Pte.
MORRIS, J. J., Pte. N.Z.E.F.	W.	21/ 8/14 3y 2m
McKENZIE, A. J, Pte. N.Z.B.E.F.	Imp. Army, Royal Navy	1/10/14 4y 8m, Lieut.
McLAREN, L. N., Dvr., 8 Bn.	✠ 23/8/18.	16/ 6/15 Dvr. ✠
NORMAN, K., Spr. 3 D S. Co. A Eng		16/11/16 2y 10m, Spr.
NICHOLLS, M., Pte. 30 Bn		29/ 8/15 3y, Pte.
O'BRIEN, E. A., Cpl. N.Z. Engrs		—/ 8/14 5y, Cpl.
O'BRIEN, J. L., Cpl. N.Z E F	W. ✠ 8/7/16.	—/10/14 Cpl. ✠
O'BRIEN, J. P., Pte. N.Z.E F.	2W.	—/ 5/16 2y 1m, Cpl.
O'BRIEN, L. J., Pte. N.Z. Rifle Bde		17/10/17 1y 11m, Pte.
PERKINS, H G., Pte. 13 Bn.	M.M., 13 Bn. ✠ 13/6/18.	3/ 5/15 Pte. ✠
PAYNE, L. A, Pte. 25 Bn.	✠ 29/7/16	4/ 6/15 Pte. ✠
PHILLIPS, L. H. R., Dvr. 3 F.A.B.		10/ 1/16 3y 3m, Gnr.
ROW, J. R., Pte. 1 Bn	✠ 11/8/18.	20/ 8/14 Sgt. ✠
ROUSE, C., Pte. N.Z.E F	M.M. ✠ 14/11/17.	12/ 8/14 Sgt. ✠
ROUSE, A. A., Pte. 57 Bn.		15/ 7/15 4y 3m, Dvr.
REYCRAFT, W., Cpl. 26 Bn.	48 Bn. ✠ 9/8/18.	25/ 8/15 Cpl. ✠

NAME.	REMARKS.	RANK ON DISCHARGE. ENLISTED. SERVICE.
RIDGE, L., Pte. 14 Bn.	✢ 11/4/17.	26/7/15 Sgt. ✢
ROWNTREE, E. F., Pte. 3 Bn.	D.F.C., A.F.C.	1/ 2/16 Lieut.
STUART, R. C. A., Gnr. N.Z.F.A.	✢ 8/8/15.	1914 Gnr. ✢
STUART, G. A., Rifleman, N.Z.F.A.		1916 3y, Rifleman
SELF, T. A., Pte. 22 Bn.		25/ 3/16
SMITH, J., Pte. Royal Marine Engrs.		12/ 4/18 6m. Pte.
SMITH, G. B., Pte. 27 Bn.		26/ 2/15 4y 3m, Pte.
SMITH, W. T. B., Pte. 19 Bn.		18/ 6/15 4y 1m, Cpl.
SMITH, C. O., Pte. 17 G.S.R.		29/ 8/18 4m, Pte.
SCOTT, S. J.		
SAVAGE, H., Pte. 2 L.H.F.A.		2/11/14 3y 7m, Pte.
SMITH, F., Pte. 8 Bn.		26/ 7/15
SHOGBRIDGE, C. M., Sister, Britis Red Cross Nursing Service		26/10/14 4y 3m, Sister.
TURNER, J. H. L., Spr., N.Z. Engrs. 3 Fd. Co.		—/ 7/15
TAYLOR, W. H., Pte. A.A.M.C.		13/ 7/15 3y 11m, Pte.
TOLE, F. E., St./Nurse. A.A.N.S.		—/ 1/15 3y 10m
TAYLOR, L. H. V., Pte. 1 Canterbur Regt., N.Z.E.F.		—10/14 4y 6m, Pte.
TURVEY, K., S/Nurse A.A.N.S.		9/ 6/17 2y, S.-Nurse
WALSH, R. E., 2nd-Lieut. 44 Bn.	✢ 8/6/17	12/ 2/16 Lieut. ✢
WHITFELD, R. E., Pte. 14 Fd. Amb		16/ 3/16 2y 11m, Pte.
WILLIAMS, J. J., Pte. 19 Bn.	40 Bn. ✢ 29/8/18.	7/10/16 Pte. ✢
WATSON, L., Pte. 35 Bn.		3/ 4/16 2y 1m, Pte.

ADDENDA

NAME	REMARKS	RANK ON DISCHARGE
EDDIE, M. H., Pte. 6 Fd. Amb.	A.F.C., ✢ 8/9/18	5/1/15 2 Lt. ✢
HARRISON, R. H., Lt., 12 Bn.	W. ✢ 16/5/17	18/1/16 Lt. ✢

www.ingramcontent.com/pod-product-compliance
Lightning Source LLC
Chambersburg PA
CBHW080633230426
43663CB00016B/2848